THE EU SUCCESSION REGULATION

The European Succession Regulation is a landmark in the field of EU private international law. It unifies the conflicts of laws, jurisdiction and recognition of foreign judgements, and of some other legal instruments in the field of succession and wills. This volume provides an article-by-article commentary on the individual provisions of the regulation, introduced by an overview of its general framework and underlying principles. As a reference tool for the regulation, this book is intended to promote a high standard of interpretation and application. With contributions from leading scholars in the field, it uses a comparative approach in its analysis to enrich the academic debate and highlight the problems likely to arise in the practical application of the regulation.

ALFONSO-LUIS CALVO CARAVACA studied law at the University of Murcia (LLM, Extraordinary Award, 1976) and at the University of Bologna (PhD, Vittorio Emanuele II Award, 1978). Since 1992 he has been Professor of Private International Law at the University Carlos III of Madrid. Formerly he was Professor of Private International law at the University Autónoma of Madrid and at the University of Murcia; visiting professor at UNESP in São Paulo (1993), at ITAM in Mexico, D.F. (2001), and at the School of Law of the University of Bologna (2012). Since 2009 he has been the co-director of *Cuadernos de Derecho Transnacional (CDT)*, published by the University Carlos III in Madrid. From 2005, he has been a permanent member of the General Codification Commission (Civil section) at the Spanish Ministry of Justice. From 1988, he has been a member of the *Hamburger Freunde des Max Planck Instituts für ausländisches und internationales Privatrecht*. From 2012, he has been a Fellow of the European Law Institute, and from 2015, a titular Member of the International Academy of Comparative Law (IACL).

He is author, co-author, editor or co-editor of approximately 300 publications in the fields of private international law, EU antitrust law, international commercial law, among which, in particular, *Derecho Internacional Privado*, vol. I (with J. Carrascosa González) and *Derecho Internacional Privado*, vol. II (with A.-L. Calvo Caravaca.), published in Granada, Editorial Comares, now at their 15th edition.

ANGELO DAVÌ is a Professor of Private International Law and of Public International Law on the Faculty of Law at the University of Rome "*La Sapienza*" and formerly a Professor at the Universities of Cagliari, Catania and Florence. He was a member of the Italian Delegation at the XVIth

Session of the Hague Conference of Private International Law in 1988, when the Succession and Wills Draft Convention was adopted, and he was invited in 2004 to present a report on the issue of applicable law at the conference held in Brussels for discussing the study "Conflict of Law of Succession in the European Union. Perspectives for a Harmonisation" made by the *Deutsches Notarinstitut*, upon request of the EU Commission, in view of the adoption of a EU regulation on matters of succession and wills. He is the author of several monographs and articles in legal journals in the areas of private international law, public international law and european law, as well as a comprehensive commentary of the EU Succession regulation together with Professor Alessandra Zanobetti, published in 2014. A lecturer at the Hague Academy of International Law, Davì taught a course entitled "*Le renvoi en droit international privé contemporain*", which was published in the Academy Collected Courses in 2012 (vol. 352) and awarded the prize for 2013 of the Italian Ministry of Culture, upon selection by the *Accademia Nazionale dei Lincei*. He is a member of the Italian Bar (Rome), admitted to practice before the Italian Supreme Court.

HEINZ-PETER MANSEL is the Director of the Institute for Private International and Comparative Law at the University of Cologne (Germany) and holds the Chair for Private Law, Private International Law, Comparative Law and Civil Procedure Law. He has held a guest professorship in Wuhan (China) and Berkeley (University of California) and has served as a legal expert for the Committee on Legal Affairs of the European Parliament (Successions and Wills, 2005). He has also been a lecturer at the Hague Academy of International Law (1998, 2008); president of the German Council of Private International Law (Scientific Council in connection with the German Ministry of Justice); and a member of the International Academy of Comparative Law, the *Società Italiana degli Studiosi del Diritto Civile* and the North Rhine-Westphalian Academy of Sciences, Humanities and the Arts. He is the managing editor of the journal *Praxis des Internationalen Privat- und Verfahrensrechts* (IPRax); his many publications are listed under www.ipr.uni-koeln.de.

THE EU SUCCESSION REGULATION

A Commentary

Edited by

ALFONSO-LUIS CALVO CARAVACA

Universidad Carlos III de Madrid

ANGELO DAVÌ

Università di Roma "La Sapienza"

HEINZ-PETER MANSEL

Universität zu Köln

CAMBRIDGE
UNIVERSITY PRESS

CAMBRIDGE
UNIVERSITY PRESS

University Printing House, Cambridge CB2 8BS, United Kingdom

One Liberty Plaza, 20th Floor, New York, NY 10006, USA

477 Williamstown Road, Port Melbourne, VIC 3207, Australia

4843/24, 2nd Floor, Ansari Road, Daryaganj, Delhi - 110002, India

79 Anson Road, #06-04/06, Singapore 079906

Cambridge University Press is part of the University of Cambridge.

It furthers the University's mission by disseminating knowledge in the pursuit of education, learning and research at the highest international levels of excellence.

www.cambridge.org
Information on this title: www.cambridge.org/9781107127302

First published 2016

A catalogue record for this publication is available from the British Library

Library of Congress Cataloging in Publication data
Names: Calvo Caravaca, Alfonso-Luis, editor. | Davì, Angelo, editor. | Mansel, Heinz-Peter, editor.
Title: The EU succession regulation : a commentary / edited by Alfonso-Luis Calvo Caravaca Universidad Carlos III de Madrid; Angelo Davì Universita di Roma "La Sapienza"; Heinz-Peter Mansel Universität zu Köln.
Description: Cambridge, United Kingdom : Cambridge University Press, 2016. | "This publication is co-funded by the Civil Justice Programme of the European Union." | "The book has its origin in the European Commission Research Project "The Europeanization of Private International Law of Successions" (JUST/2013/JCIV/AG/4000004710) led by Angelo Davì." |
Includes bibliographical references and index.
Identifiers: LCCN 2016026638 | ISBN 9781107127302
Subjects: LCSH: European Parliament. Regulation (EU) No 650/2012 of the European Parliament and of the Council of 4 July 2012 | Inheritance and succession – European Union countries. | Conflict of laws – Inheritance and succession – European Union countries. | LCGFT: Law commentaries.
Classification: LCC KJE1444.32012 .E93 2016 | DDC 346.2405/2–dc23
LC record available at https://lccn.loc.gov/2016026638

ISBN 978-1-107-12730-2 Hardback

CONTENTS

List of Contributors page x
Foreword and Acknowledgements xiii
List of Abbreviations xv

Introduction 1

CHAPTER I **Scope and Definitions** 71

Article 1 Scope 73

Article 2 Competence in Matters of Succession within the Member States 112

Article 3 Definitions 114

CHAPTER II **Jurisdiction** 125

Article 4 General Jurisdiction 127

Article 5 Choice-of-Court Agreement 149

Article 6 Declining of Jurisdiction in the Event of a Choice of Law 162

Article 7 Jurisdiction in the Event of a Choice of Law 171

Article 8 Closing of Own-Motion Proceedings in the Event of a Choice of Law 177

Article 9 Jurisdiction Based on Appearance 182

Article 10 Subsidiary Jurisdiction 186

Article 11 Forum necessitatis 199

Article 12 Limitation of Proceedings 209

Article 13 Acceptance or Waiver of the Succession, of a Legacy or of a Reserved Share 221

Article 14 Seising of a Court 234

Article 15 Examination as to Jurisdiction 240

Article 16 Examination as to Admissibility 245

Article 17 Lis pendens 251

Article 18 Related Actions 268

Article 19 Provisional, Including Protective, Measures 280

CHAPTER III **Applicable Law** 289

Article 20 Universal Application 291

Article 21 General Rule 298

Article 22 Choice of Law 323

Article 23 The Scope of the Applicable Law 351

Article 24 Dispositions of Property upon Death Other Than Agreements as to Succession 369

Article 25 Agreements as to Succession 380

Article 26 Substantive Validity of Dispositions of Property upon Death 394

Article 27 Formal Validity of Dispositions of Property upon Death Made in Writing 402

Article 28 Validity as to Form of a Declaration Concerning Acceptance or Waiver 412

Article 29 Special Rules on the Appointment and Powers of an Administrator of the Estate in Certain Situations 417

Article 30 Special Rules Imposing Restrictions Concerning or Affecting the Succession in Respect of Certain Assets 430

Article 31 Adaptation of Rights in rem 442

Article 32 Commorientes 452

Article 33 Estate without a Claimant 458

Article 34 Renvoi 469

Article 35 Public Policy (ordre public) 505

Articles 36–37–38 States with More Than One Legal System: Territorial Conflicts of Laws; States with More Than One Legal System: Inter-personal Conflicts of Laws; Non-application of This Regulation to Internal Conflicts of Laws 519

CHAPTER IV **Recognition, Enforceability and Enforcement of Decisions** 531

Article 39 Recognition 533

Articles 40–41 Grounds of Non-recognition; No Review as to the Substance 542

Article 42 Staying of Recognition Proceedings 561

Article 43 Enforceability 567

Articles 44–45 Determination of Domicile; Jurisdiction of Local Courts 574

Articles 46–47–48–49 Procedure; Non-production of the Attestation; Declaration of Enforceability; Notice of the Decision on the Application for a Declaration of Enforceability 578

Article 50 Appeal against the Decision on the Application for a Declaration of Enforceability 591

Articles 51–52 Procedure to Contest the Decision Given on Appeal; Refusal or Revocation of a Declaration of Enforceability 598

Article 53 Staying of Proceedings 604

Article 54 Provisional, Including Protective, Measures 608

Article 55 Partial Enforceability 612

Articles 56–57–58 Legal Aid; No Security, Bond or Deposit; No charge, Duty or Fee 615

CHAPTER V **Authentic Instruments and Court Settlements** 623

Article 59 Acceptance of Authentic Instruments 625

Article 60 Enforceability of Authentic Instruments 664

Article 61 Enforceability of Court Settlements 667

CHAPTER VI **European Certificate of Succession** 671

Article 62 Creation of a European Certificate of Succession 673

Article 63 Purpose of the Certificate 686

Article 64 Competence to Issue the Certificate 699

Article 65 Application for a Certificate 711

Article 66 Examination of the Application 723

Article 67 Issue of the Certificate 734

Article 68 Contents of the Certificate 744

Article 69 Effects of the Certificate 769

Article 70 Certified Copies of the Certificate 795

Article 71 Rectification, Modification or Withdrawal of the Certificate 805

Article 72 Redress Procedures 812

Article 73 Suspension of the Effects of the Certificate 819

CHAPTER VII **General and Final Provisions** 827

Article 74 Legalisation and Other Similar Formalities 829

Article 75 Relationship with Existing International Conventions 831

Article 76 Relationship with Council Regulation (EC) 1346/2000 836

Articles 77–78–79 Information Made Available to the Public; Information on Contact Details and Procedures; Establishment and Subsequent Amendment of the List Containing the Information Referred to in Article 3(2) 840

Articles 80–81–82 Establishment and Subsequent Amendment of the Attestations and Forms Referred to in Articles 46, 59, 60, 61, 65 and 67; Committee Procedure; Review 847

Article 83 Transitional Provisions 852
Article 84 Entry into Force 864

Bibliography 867
Index 903

CONTRIBUTORS

CHRISTINE BUDZIKIEWICZ Professor of Private Law, Private International Law, European Private Law and Comparative Law, University of Marburg

CELIA M. CAAMIÑA DOMÍNGUEZ Lecturer in Private International Law, University "Carlos III" of Madrid

ALFONSO-LUIS CALVO CARAVACA Professor of Private International Law, University "Carlos III" of Madrid

ERMANNO CALZOLAIO Professor of Comparative Private Law, Director of the Department of Law, University of Macerata

ESPERANZA CASTELLANOS RUIZ Associate Professor of Private International Law, University "Carlos III" of Madrid

GIANLUCA CONTALDI Professor of European Union Law and of Private International Law, University of Macerata; Member of the Italian Bar (Rome)

ELENA D'ALESSANDRO Associate Professor of Civil Procedure, University of Turin

ANGELO DAVÌ Professor of International Law and of Private International Law, University of Rome "La Sapienza"

LIVIA DI COLA Senior Researcher in Civil Procedure, University of Macerata

PASQUALINA FARINA Senior Researcher in Civil Procedure, University of Rome "La Sapienza"

PIETRO FRANZINA Associate Professor of International Law, University of Ferrara

CRISTINA GRIECO Ph.D. Candidate in International Law and European Union Law, University of Macerata and University of Cologne

BERNHARD KREẞE Privatdozent, LLM (Cologne/Paris), Maître en droit (Paris I – Panthéon-Sorbonne), FernUniversität Hagen, Rechtswissenschaftliche Fakultät

HEINZ-PETER MANSEL Professor of Private Law, Private International Law, Comparative Law and Civil Procedure; Director of the Institute for Private International and Comparative Law, University of Cologne

FABRIZIO MARONGIU BUONAIUTI, LLM (CANTAB.) Associate Professor of International Law, University of Macerata

JULIANA RODRÍGUEZ RODRIGO Associate Professor of Private International Law, University "Carlos III" of Madrid

LAURA VAGNI Associate Professor of Comparative Private Law, University of Macerata

MATTHIAS WELLER, MAG.RER.PUBL. Professor of Private Law, Civil Procedure and Private International Law, University of Wiesbaden

ALESSANDRA ZANOBETTI Professor of Private International Law, University of Bologna and LUISS University, Rome; former Deputy-Secretary General of UNIDROIT

SALVATORE ZIINO Associate Professor of Civil Procedure, University of Palermo; Member of the Italian Bar (Palermo).

This publication is co-funded by the Civil Justice Programme of the European Union.

FOREWORD AND ACKNOWLEDGEMENTS

As from 17 August 2015, all Courts and other authorities within the European Union Member States (with the exception of Denmark, Ireland and the United Kingdom) have to apply in matters of cross-border succession and wills the *Regulation (EU) No 650/2012 on jurisdiction, applicable law, recognition and enforcement of decisions and acceptance and enforcement of authentic instruments in matters of succession and on the creation of a European Certificate of Succession.*

With this Regulation, European Private International Law has erected a new corner stone of unification. The Regulation has broken with some national traditions in autonomous private international succession law, such as the nationality principle, which was central for a number of European legal systems, or the application of different succession laws for movables (*lex loci domicilii*) and immovables (*lex rei sitae*), as it was known in French – and English – inspired conflicts laws. The Regulation is a comprehensive codification of private international law of succession and wills, including jurisdiction, recognition and enforcement of judicial decisions and authentic acts, and the establishment of a European Certificate of Succession.

This article-by-article Commentary aims to provide help and advice for the application of the Regulation in legal practice, to secure a high standard in its autonomous interpretation and to enrich the scholarly discussion. It may be useful also for practitioners of third countries, or of Member States not bound by the Regulation, having to deal with a succession connected with one or more Member States which are bound by this instrument. The fact that the authors come from different Member countries and that most of them have an international background has prompted the adoption of a comparative and genuinely European approach in the analysis of the regulation.

The book's origins lie in the European Commission Research Project "The Europeanization of Private International Law of Successions" (JUST/2013/JCIV/AG/4000004710) led by Angelo Davì. As the editors, and on behalf of all the contributors to this volume, we are very grateful to the European Commission for the support it has granted to our work.

We express our deep appreciation to the scholars who willingly participated with their experience, knowledge, scholarship and thoughtful commitment in this project and in the Commentary. We would also gladly acknowledge that in the drafting of this book we benefitted from the help and advice of our colleagues Alessandra Zanobetti, Professor at the University of Bologna, and Fabrizio Marongiu Buonaiuti, Professor at the University of Macerata. We greatly appreciate their most valuable contribution.

Finally, we would like to convey our gratitude to Cambridge University Press for accepting the Commentary in their publishing programme and to their collaborators for their indispensable help.

May the book find its way in practice and scholarship and be a valuable assistance to its readers.

ABBREVIATIONS

AC	Appeal Cases (UK)
Actes et doc.	*Actes et documents*, Hague Conference on Private International Law
An esp der int priv	*Anuario español de derecho internacional privado*
AJCL	*American Journal of Comparative Law*
All ER	All England Law Reports
Ann Inst dr int	*Annuaire de l'Institut de droit international*
ATF	*Arrêts du Tribunal fédéral suisse*
BayObLGZ	*Sammlung der Entscheidungen des Bayerischen Obersten Landesgerichts in Zivilsachen*
BGB	*Bürgerliches Gesetzbuch* (Germany)
BGBl	*Bundesgesetzblatt*
BGHZ	*Sammlung der Entscheidungen des Bundesgerichtshofs in Zivilsachen*
Bull civ	*Bulletin des arrêts des chambres civiles de la Cour de cassation* (France)
BVerfG	*Bundesverfassungsgericht* (Germany)
BVerfGE	*Entscheidungen des Bundesverfassungsgerichts*
CdT	*Cuadernos de derecho transnacional*
CLJ	*Cambridge Law Journal*
CMLRep	*Common Market Law Reports*
CMLRev	*Common Market Law Review*
Dalloz	*Recueil Dalloz*
ECR	*European Court of Justice Reports*
ELRev	*European Law Review*
ER	*English Reports*
ERA	*Europäische Rechtsakademie* (Academy of European Law, Trier)
Eur Rev Priv Law	*European Review of Private Law*
EuZW	*Europäische Zeitschrift für Wirtschaftsrecht*
EWiR	*Entscheidungen zum Wirtschaftsrecht*
FamErbRÄG	*Familien- und Erbrechts-Änderungsgesetz* (Austria)
FamRZ	*Zeitschrift für das gesamte Familienrecht*

Foro it	*Il foro italiano*
Gaz pal	*Gazette du palais*
German LJ	*German Law Journal*
Giur it	*Giurisprudenza italiana*
Giust civ	*Giustizia civile*
Hague Recueil	*Recueil des cours de l'Académie de droit international de la Haye*
Harvard LR	*Harvard Law Review*
ICJ Reports	*Reports of the International Court of Justice*
ICLQ	*International and Comparative Law Quarterly*
IPRax	*Praxis des Internationalen Privat- und Verfahrensrechts*
IPRspr	*Die deutsche Rechtsprechung auf dem Gebiete des internationalen Privatrechts*
JCP	*Juris-classeur périodique (La semaine juridique)*
JDI	*Journal du droit international (Clunet)*
JPIL	*Journal of Private International Law*
KGE	*Sammlung der Entscheidungen des Kammergerichts*
LQR	*Law Quarterly Review*
LR	*Law Reports*
MLR	*Modern Law Review*
NILR	*Netherlands International Law Review*
NIPR	*Nederlands Internationaal Privaatrecht*
NJW	*Neue Juristische Wochenschrift*
N giur civ comm	*La nuova giurisprudenza civile commentata*
N l civ comm	*Le nuove leggi civili commentate*
OJ	*Official Journal of the European Union* (formerly: of the European Communities)
RabelsZ	*Rabels Zeitschrift für ausländisches und internationales Privatrecht*
Rev der not	*Revista de derecho notarial*
Rev dr priv	*Revista de derecho privado*
Rev crit dr int priv	*Revue critique de droit international privé*
Rev esp der int	*Revista española de derecho internacional*
Rev hell dr int	*Revue hellénique de droit international*
RGZ	*Sammlung der Entscheidungen des Reichsgerichts in Zivilsachen*
Riv dir int	*Rivista di diritto internazionale*
Riv dir int priv proc	*Rivista di diritto internazionale privato e processuale*
Riv dir proc	*Rivista di diritto processuale*
Riv not	*Rivista del Notariato*
Riv trim dir proc civ	*Rivista trimestrale di diritto e procedura civile*
RIW	*Recht der internationalen Wirtschaft*

RSuisseDIE	*Revue suisse de droit international et de droit européen*
S Ct	*Supreme Court/Supreme Court Reporter* (USA)
SZ	*Entscheidungen des österreichischen Obersten Gerichtshofes in Zivil- (und Justizverwaltungs-)sachen* (Austria)
TPR	*Tijdschrift voor privaatrecht*
Trust LI	*Trust Law International*
US	United States Supreme Court Reports
WPNotReg	*Weekblad voor Privaatrecht, Notariaat en Registratie*
YPIL	*Yearbook of Private International Law*
ZEuP	*Zeitschrift für europäisches Privatrecht*
ZEV	*Zeitschrift für Erbrecht und Vermögensnachfolge*
ZfRV	*Zeitschrift für Europarecht, internationales Privatrecht und Rechtsvergleichung*
ZVglRWiss	*Zeitschrift für vergleichende Rechtswissenschaft*

Introduction

ANGELO DAVÌ

Summary

I. PRELIMINARY REMARKS: THE DISPARITY BETWEEN NATIONAL LEGISLATIONS AND THE NEED FOR UNIFORM REGULATION ON EU LEVEL; THE PREVIOUS WORK OF THE HAGUE CONFERENCE ON PRIVATE INTERNATIONAL LAW *page* 1
II. THE ELABORATION OF THE ESR AND THE DECISIONS BY IRELAND AND THE UK NOT TO OPT IN 11
III. THE STRUCTURE AND GENERAL FEATURES OF THE ESR 18
IV. OBJECT AND SCOPE 22
V. THE KEY PRINCIPLES OF THE ESR 35
A. Unity of Succession 37
B. Unity of Jurisdiction and Applicable Law 45
C. Promotion of Certainty and Ease of Succession Planning 49
D. Spatial Continuity of the Legal Regime Applicable to the Succession. 61

I. Preliminary Remarks: Disparities between National Legislations and the Need for Uniform Regulation on EU Level; the Previous Work of the Hague Conference on Private International Law

1. Regulation (EU) no. 650/2012 of 4 July 2012 on international succession law (hereafter ESR = European Succession Regulation)[1] is one of the most important results hitherto achieved within the vast and ambitious programme for codifying private international law which the European Union has implemented since the Treaty of Amsterdam of 2 October 1997 (which has been in force since 1 May 1999) vested it with specific competence in the sector. The task taken on by the EU institutions was made particularly difficult in this case by the major complexity inherent within the area of succession, which lies at the confluence of various

[1] Regulation (EU) no. 650/2012 of the European Parliament and of the Council of 4 July 2012 on jurisdiction, applicable law, recognition and enforcement of decisions and acceptance and enforcement of authentic instruments in matters of succession and on the creation of a European Certificate of Succession, OJ 2012 no. L201, 27 July 2012, p. 107 *et seq.*

aspects and problems of family law, property law and the law of obligations, and where national legislation, including Member States legislation, is highly different both in terms of substantive law and private international law. Considered together, these elements of complexity contribute *inter alia* to explaining how the field of succession has been one in which the most renowned general problems relating to private international law, such as characterisation, *renvoi*, incidental questions and the adaptation of different rights or legal concepts, most frequently arise.[2]

2. In terms of substantive law, some of the main differences between the various national legislations concern the determination of the heirs and their respective shares both in the event of intestacy and testate succession. With regard to the latter, most legal systems contain provisions that protect the close members of the family of the deceased by granting them mandatory or forced heirship rights, thereby limiting the testator's freedom to dispose of his assets. In many of these systems the protection offered to the relatives of the deceased extends so far as to vest them with the right to claw back donations made whilst the deceased was still alive, or the value of such donations, not only from the recipients but at times also from persons to whom ownership of these assets was subsequently transferred, in order to safeguard the integrity of forced heirship shares. By contrast, other legal systems, in particular most common law systems, do not recognise any right to a reserved share and consequently grant the testator potentially unlimited freedom of action, even though some of them protect at least the essential needs of the members of the deceased's family through various instruments, including first and foremost the granting to the courts of a discretionary power to allocate income or other sums of money to them out of the estate (family provisions or family allowances). Further significant differences relate to agreements as to succession and reciprocal wills, which are

[2] On the high level of diversification within national regulations in this area and the resulting difficulties for achieving internationally uniform solutions, see, e.g., amongst the courses held concerning this issue at various times at the Hague Academy of international law, A. E. von Overbeck, 'Divers aspects de l'unification du droit international privé, spécialement en matière de successions', *Hague Recueil*, vol. 104 (1961), p. 555 *et seq.*; M. Ferid, 'Le rattachement autonome de la transmission successorale en droit international privé', *Hague Recueil*, vol. 142 (1974), p. 71 *et seq.*; Haopei Li, 'Some Recent Developments in the Conflict of Laws of Succession', *Hague Recueil*, vol. 224 (1990), p. 19 *et seq.*; A. Bonomi, 'Successions internationales: conflits de lois et de juridictions', *Hague Recueil*, vol. 350 (2010), p. 92 *et seq.*; see also A. Davì and A. Zanobetti, *Il nuovo diritto internazionale privato europeo delle successioni* (Torino, 2014), pp. 1–12.

broadly accepted under the legal systems which consider them as useful instruments for inheritance planning and prohibited, or permitted only to a limited extent, by other systems which, by contrast, see them as a dangerous source of conditioning on the testamentary freedom. Similar differences may be found regarding the admissibility of joint wills, that is wills drawn up in one single instrument by two or more persons without any bond of interdependence between the stipulations respectively made by them.

There are also considerable discrepancies in the regulation of the modalities of the transfer of ownership of the assets forming part of the estate to heirs or legatees. Also in this case the most important point of divergence concerns relations between civilian and common law systems. Within the first group of countries the heirs acquire assets directly (which may even be automatic, as under French law, or conditional upon acceptance, as under Italian law, or by a court order to that effect, such as the *Einantwortung* under Austrian law). By contrast, the second group requires the intermediation between the deceased and the heirs of a personal representative of the former, who is appointed by a court. This person is referred to as executor if designated by the deceased or as administrator if designated by the court itself. The personal representative acquires fiduciary ownership of the estate, attends (under the control of the court which appointed him or her) to the administration of those assets, and in particular to the payment of debts owed by the estate, including those due to the tax authorities, and to the payment of legacies, following which the residual estate is distributed among the heirs. Such discrepancies may easily give rise to complications in international successions, especially when it is necessary to apply a foreign law requiring the court seised to adopt measures or to exercise functions and powers that are difficult to reconcile with the procedural rules of the legal system of the forum, or are even entirely unknown to it.

3. As concerns private international law, the fundamental distinction between the different legal systems around the world consists in the well-known divide between systems that adopt the principle of unity of succession and those that follow the principle of scission, or the dualist principle. Under the former type of system, succession is regulated entirely by the personal law of the deceased, which is identified in some countries as his last national law and in other countries as the law of his last domicile or habitual residence. The latter system is based on the different treatment of succession to real estate, whereby each property is subject to the law of the country in which it is located, and succession to moveable property, which is subject uniformly to the personal law of the deceased.[3] Conflicts may naturally arise not only between legal systems falling respectively under one or the other of these two groups but also between legal systems from the same group, mainly due to the fact that they adopt connecting factors based on different personal characteristics (nationality, domicile, habitual residence). Other significant points of difference relate to the admissibility and scope of the testator's faculty to choose the law applicable to the succession (a right only granted under a few legal systems, usually subject to strict limits) as well as the admission of *renvoi* and, if so, the type of *renvoi* adopted. A similar disparity between positions may also be noted in relation to jurisdictional criteria. Some of these, such as the place at which the succession is opened, i.e. that of the last domicile or last habitual residence of the deceased, the place where the assets of the estate are situated, especially if real property is involved, and, in contentious proceedings, the domicile of the defendant, are used almost everywhere. Other criteria, such as for example the nationality of the deceased or of a party to the dispute, the forum chosen by the parties by common agreement and the *forum necessitatis*, are more rarely used. It should also be added that 'scissionist' countries almost always claim exclusive jurisdiction for their courts over succession relating to real estate situated in their respective territories.

4. The differences of legal regime described above have in the past resulted in a situation characterised by a serious lack of predictability and legal certainty both within the Union and in relations between Member States and other countries, creating a significant obstacle for inheritance planning within a transnational context. Before the ESR entered into force and became applicable, in cases involving successions related to two or more countries it was absolutely normal, both in Europe and elsewhere, for the courts of all or at least some of the countries in question to have jurisdiction to rule on these successions and to consider different laws to be applicable to them, leading to different results. Moreover, due to the absence of uniform jurisdictional criteria, but also for other reasons, it was non uncommon for decisions given in one of the countries concerned not to be recognised in the other countries, even when conflicting judgments had not been issued (or recognised) in these

[3] On the historical origins of these two different systems, see Haopei Li, 'Some Recent Developments', p. 22 *et seq.*; T. Brandi, *Das Haager Abkommen von 1989 über das auf die Erbfolge anzuwendende Recht* (Berlin, 1996), p. 149 *et seq.* Some Latin American countries (e.g. Mexico, Uruguay) apply the principle of territorial scission also in relation to the succession of moveable property.

countries.[4] This state of affairs and the difficulties that it entailed for European citizens, including in particular those who had exercised their freedom of movement within the space of the Union, explain why the creation of rules of private international law common to the Member States in matters of succession and wills was seen from the outset as a priority measure to be adopted as part of the broader project of the progressive construction of the 'area of freedom, security and justice without internal frontiers' which the institutions of the Union are required to create pursuant to article 3.2 TEU and articles 67 *et seq.* TFEU. In particular, the Summary of the Impact Assessment accompanying the proposal for the ESR presented by the Commission in 2009 defined the main objectives of the future regulation as follows: (i) 'To allow citizens to efficiently plan and to organise their succession in advance in a cross border context'; (ii) 'To increase the likelihood that the rights of potential heirs, persons formally or otherwise related to the deceased, private and public creditors etc. are respected in an efficient way'; (iii) 'To achieve a situation where parallel proceedings do not occur and where different substantive laws are not applied to the same international succession'; (iv) 'To ensure the recognition of rights, relevant acts and decisions regarding succession'.[5]

5. However, the international movement of persons and goods is not limited to the internal space of the EU but operates naturally across broader geographical areas in which the requirements of continuity and security within interpersonal legal relations obviously do not differ much from those existing within the European context. Attempts at

[4] For observations in this regard in some of the academic analyses published during the preparatory works for the ESR, see A. Davì, 'Riflessioni sul futuro diritto internazionale privato europeo delle successioni', *Riv dir int* (2005), pp. 299 *et seq.*, 303; A. Dutta, 'Succession and Wills in the Conflict of Laws on the Eve of Europeanization', *RabelsZ* (2009), p. 551 *et seq.*; E. Lein, 'A Further Step towards a European Code of Private International Law. The Commission Proposal for a Regulation on Succession', *YPIL* (2009), p. 109 *et seq.*, 111; Bonomi, 'Successions internationales', p. 92 *et seq.*

[5] See Commission Staff Working Document Accompanying the Proposal for a Regulation of the European Parliament and of the Council on Jurisdiction, Applicable Law, Recognition and Enforcement of Decisions and Authentic Instruments in Matters of Successions and on the Introduction of a European Certificate of Succession. Summary of the Impact Assessment, SEC(2009) 411 final, p. 5. In order to provide an assessment of the practical and economic importance of this area of law, based on the fact that around 4.5 million people die each year in the EU along with the reasonable estimate that around 10 per cent of the related successions involve international aspects, the Summary of the Impact Assessment, p. 4, estimated the total annual number of international successions at approximately 450,000, to which it allocated an average value of around 274,000 euros, and thus a global value of 123.3 billion euros.

multilateral codification of private international law in the area of succession have thus been made on various occasions in the past, including on a much wider scale. The principal role in this regard was performed since the outset by the Hague Conference on Private International Law, which had considered the scope for drawing up a draft convention in this area as early as the historic session of 1893 when it met for the first time, subsequently acting on this in 1904. This initial attempt, which remained unsuccessful due to the difficulties in reconciling the contrasting positions of the participant States, was followed over the subsequent decades by others, which also did not bear fruit.[6] In the immediate aftermath of the Second World War however, the Conference made a new political choice to avoid launching projects for conventions relating to entire sectors of private international law, such as succession and wills, on the grounds that projects of this type were regarded as excessively ambitious, instead preferring to concentrate its activity on specific questions internal to each sector which were considered to have a greater need for uniform regulation. This change in position had the positive effect of enabling the Convention of 5 October 1961 on the Conflicts of Laws Relating to the Form of Testamentary Dispositions to be adopted shortly afterwards, which may be regarded as an important achievement and has to date been adhered to by forty-two States, including seventeen Member States of the Union. Taking account of the international obligation taken on by these Member States to abide by the convention along with the need which nonetheless exists within the Union to establish a uniform conflict-of-laws regulation of the formal validity of dispositions of property upon death, the ESR includes a provision (article 27) which reiterates the essential content of the earlier instrument, thereby extending its scope to all Member States, along with a further provision (article 75.1) which states that the Member States that are parties to the convention may continue to apply it.[7]

[6] On the work of the Conference during the initial stage of its activity in this area, see von Overbeck, 'Divers aspects', p. 554 *et seq*.

[7] Since the Hague Convention only deals with the form of testamentary dispositions but not that of agreements as to succession, article 27 ESR extends the applicability of the conflict-of-laws rules that reproduce those contained in the convention also to the form of those agreements, thereby rendering the rules applicable to any kind of disposition of property upon death in all countries bound by the ESR, irrespective of whether or not they are parties to the convention. It is to be specified that only fourteen of the seventeen EU Member States that are parties to the Hague Convention are subject to the provisions of the ESR since, for the reasons illustrated in no. 12, Denmark, Ireland and the United Kingdom are not bound by the latter instrument.

6. A second though much less important result achieved by the Hague Conference during those years came with the Convention of 2 October 1973 Concerning the International Administration of the Estates of Deceased Persons. This convention entered into force in only three States in a rather fortuitous way, having reached the requisite minimum number of three ratifications only by virtue of the dissolution of Czechoslovakia into two separate States, and must now be regarded as having been superseded by the ESR.[8] With the aim of avoiding conflicts between two or more administrations competing over the same succession, the convention creates an international certificate which designates the person or persons authorised to administer it and indicates his or her powers. The limited success enjoyed by the convention is mainly due to the fact that it neglected to make any attempt at harmonising the conflict of laws rules applicable to successions in the contracting States, but rather limited itself to vesting exclusive competence to issue the certificate in the authorities of the State in which the deceased was last habitually resident and to providing that those authorities must make their assessments and take their decisions in this regard on the basis of the substantive law of the forum or, under certain conditions, the law of the State of which the deceased person was a citizen (article 3). It is thus easy to understand that participation in the convention was not very attractive for the States whose internal conflict of laws systems subjected the succession to a different law. The utility of this instrument is moreover lessened by the fact that it relates only to the moveable part of the succession (article 30). However, it is also true that the creation by the convention of an international certificate of this type may be regarded as a precursor for the choice made by the European legislator to introduce an analogous document into the ESR, the European Certificate of Succession, which nonetheless has a broader scope in that it relates to the whole of the succession and designates not only the persons entitled to administer it but also the heirs and their respective shares.[9]

[8] The convention had in actual fact only been ratified by Portugal and Czechoslovakia, though could nonetheless enter into force on 1 July 1993 after the two new States that arose out of the ashes of the latter, namely the Czech Republic and Slovakia, declared their intention to be bound by it. The convention is currently no longer applicable because the ESR, pursuant to its article 75.2, takes precedence over conventions concluded exclusively between two or more EU Member States and concerning matters governed by it. However, it would be theoretically possible for a country that is not a Member State of the EU to ratify or adhere to the convention, thereby rendering it applicable in its relations with the preceding three Member States as well as in reciprocal relations between them.

[9] In the proposals contained in the 'Étude de droit comparé sur les règles de conflits de juridictions et de conflits de lois relatives aux testaments et successions dans les États

7. Following the partial achievements mentioned above, the delegates of the Member States of the Conference, meeting at its fourteenth session held in 1980, concluded that the time was ripe for revitalising the project to draw up a general convention on conflict of laws for the entire area of succession and wills. In the wake of this decision, the question was placed on the agenda for the next session of the Conference held in 1984 and the text of the Hague Convention on the Law Applicable to Succession to the Estates of Deceased Persons was finally adopted at the sixteenth session in October 1988 (although the convention is officially dated 1 August 1989, the date on which the first signature was affixed). However, in contrast to the two previous instruments discussed, this convention never came into force as it was only ratified by the Netherlands and was only signed by Argentina, Luxembourg and Switzerland. The main reason for such modest result may be found in the major difficulty which emerged during the preparatory works of striking a satisfactory balance between the need to regulate efficiently the various aspects of this area of law and the need to achieve solutions capable of attracting consent from at least a majority of delegations in relation to problems concerning which their respective positions had been extremely different at the outset. This need made it necessary to accept on various issues what one distinguished commentator has defined as '*compromis imparfaits*'.[10] In effect, whilst general agreement on the adoption of the principle of unity of succession could be arrived at without major resistance on the part of delegations from countries with a 'scissionist' tradition, it proved to be much more laborious to reach a compromise between the opposite views of the representatives of the States that championed the criterion of a link to habitual residence (or domicile) and the States that endorsed the

membres de l'Union Européenne' prepared on behalf of the Commission by the Deutsches Notarinstitut in conjunction with Professors Dörner and Lagarde, which was published in the volume edited by the Deutsches Notarinstitut, *Conflict of Law of Succession in the European Union. Perspectives for a Harmonisation* (Würzburg, 2004), pp. 131 *et seq.*, in particular 145 (on this study see no. 9), the model used as the principal frame of reference for the future European certificate, which was already being planned at the time, is however explicitly mentioned not so much in the Hague Convention but rather in the 'lettre de vérification des testaments' contemplated under article 887 *et seq.* of the code of civil procedure of the Canadian province of Québec.

[10] P. Lagarde, 'La nouvelle Convention de La Haye sur la loi applicable aux successions', *Rev crit dr int priv* (1989), p. 252; for two further analyses of the convention see A. E. von Overbeck, 'La Convention du premier août 1989 sur la loi applicable aux successions pour cause de mort', *Annuaire suisse de droit international* (1989), p. 138 *et seq.*; Brandi, *Das Haager Abkommen.*

principle of nationality.[11] Furthermore, the lack of unanimous consensus concerning several important questions – such as the attribution to the testator of an albeit limited right to choose the law applicable to his succession, the admissibility of agreements as to succession and the acceptance of *renvoi* –required reservations to be formulated in relation to each of them (article 24). Finally, the unwillingness of the common law countries to relinquish the exclusive jurisdiction of their respective *lex fori* over the regulation of the transmission of inherited assets over which, as previously mentioned,[12] they provide for an administration procedure conducted by a personal representative of the deceased under the control of a specialist court (known as a probate or surrogate court) in order to provide greater guarantees to creditors and beneficiaries, resulted in a limitation of the scope of the convention solely to the allocation of the succession, whilst leaving contracting States free to extend it unilaterally to the administration and distribution of the estate (article 7).

8. The activity of the Hague Conference over the course of around a century offered a precedent of significant value for European lawmakers. They not only took over into the ESR almost verbatim the provisions contained in the most successful of the conventions adopted by the Conference, namely the 1961 Convention on the Conflicts of Laws Relating to the Form of Testamentary Dispositions,[13] but also borrowed the idea contained in the 1973 Convention on the International Administration of the Estates of Deceased Persons of creating a certificate of succession valid throughout all Member States, and in addition drew inspiration regarding many important points from the 1989 Convention on the Law Applicable to Succession to the Estates of Deceased Persons. As regards in particular the relationship between the ESR and the 1989 Convention, it is easy to note that the principal options adopted by them are very similar: acceptance of the principle of unity of succession; the granting of preference to the connecting factor of the last habitual

[11] The complex solution which was ultimately adopted involved the granting of prevalence to the law of the State in which the deceased at the time of his death was habitually resident if he had been resident there for a period of no less than five years immediately preceding his death, and otherwise to his national law (article 3), although in both cases subject to the addition of an exception clause. This solution has the not insignificant drawback of introducing uncertainty into inheritance planning, both due to the fact that it is obviously impossible to establish with certainty in advance whether the prescribed five-year residence period will be completed, and due to the presence of the two exception clauses.

[12] See no. 3. [13] On this point see no. 5.

residence of the deceased (albeit subject to an exception clause in both instruments); the granting to the testator of a limited ability to choose the law applicable to his succession; acceptance of *renvoi*. In addition, the solutions provided under each of the two instruments to certain specific questions, such as those relating to *commorientes*, estates without a claimant and the applicability of the special rules establishing a particular inheritance regime for certain real property or other classes of assets, are almost identical (articles 13, 15 and 16 of the convention; articles 30, 32, 33 ESR). However, the ESR represents the first attempt that met with success to induce a large number of States to give up the particularities of their national legislation in the area of conflict of laws relating to succession and to accept their replacement with rules common to all of them and of a comprehensive nature. The difficulties encountered for a number of years in achieving such a result, albeit within the geographically broader and politically distinct context of the Hague Conference on Private International Law, provide clear evidence of the importance of the success achieved by the Union institutions: this is all the more so the case as the ESR does not limit itself to introducing uniform conflict of laws rules throughout all states bound by it and creating the European Certificate of Succession, but also lays down common rules on jurisdiction, the mutual recognition and enforcement of decisions and mutual acceptance and enforcement of authentic instruments.[14]

[14] Prior to the adoption and entry into force of the ESR, various initiatives aimed at creating uniform multilateral legislation in the area of succession through international conventions had been adopted not only, as noted earlier, on the level of private international law but also on the level of substantive law. The latter form of initiative manifested itself in particular in the drafting within the Council of Europe of the Basel Convention of 16 May 1972 on the Establishment of a Scheme of Registration of Wills and, under the auspices of UNIDROIT, of the Washington Convention of 26 October 1973 Providing a Uniform Law on the Form of an International Will. Both conventions are currently in force, as each of them has been ratified by twelve different countries, some of which are EU Member States. Since their respective content is fully compatible with that of the ESR, they naturally remain applicable within the Member States of the EU that are parties to it, even after the entry into force of the ESR. However, none of them appears to have taken on much importance in practice. During the course of the adoption of the ESR, both the Council in its Hague Programme (cited in footnote 18) and the European Parliament in recommendation 12 annexed to its legislative resolution (cited in footnote 20) proposed the inclusion within the instrument of rules providing for the creation of an electronic European scheme or of a similar mechanism for the registration of wills enabling the search for and establishment of the content of last wills and testaments of European citizens and other Union residents to be simplified; however, the Commission preferred not to adopt the proposals made to this effect in order to prevent the projected instrument from becoming excessively complex.

II. The Process of Drafting the ESR and the Decision of Ireland and the UK Not to Opt-in

9. The inclusion of succession in the action programme to be implemented by the Union institutions in the area of private international law dates back to a time earlier even than the entry into force of the Treaty of Amsterdam (1 May 1999) which, as already mentioned,[15] for the first time vested the Union (at the time still European Community) with specific competence in this sector. In fact, the European Council of Cardiff, which was held on 15 and 16 June 1998, had called on the Council and the Commission to present an Action Plan at its meeting in Vienna on how best to implement the provisions of the Treaty of Amsterdam on an area of freedom, security and justice. That Action Plan, which was adopted by the Justice and Home Affairs Council on 3 December 1998 ('Vienna Action Plan') contemplated, alongside various other measures, an examination of the feasibility of drawing up a legal instrument concerning jurisdiction, applicable law, recognition and enforcement of judgments relating to succession.[16] The Commission then charged the Deutsches Notarinstitut with carrying out a comparative study on the subject, in cooperation with Professors Dörner and Lagarde acting as scientific coordinators. This study, which also contained specific suggestions concerning the general features of the future instrument, was discussed at an international workshop held in Brussels in 2004.[17] On the basis of this study, and at the express request made in the same year by the Council in the so-called Hague Programme,[18] the Commission published a green book in 2005 which invited the

[15] See no. 1.

[16] Action Plan of the Council and the Commission on how best to implement the provisions of the Treaty of Amsterdam on an area of freedom, security and justice – Text adopted by the Justice and Home Affairs Council of 3 December 1998, OJ 1999 no. C19, 23 January 1999, p. 10, para. 41(c). According to the Action Plan, the same possibility had to be examined also in relation to matrimonial property regimes, which were made the object of a recent regulation along with a further regulation concerning the property consequences of registered partnerships (respectively regulation no. 2016/1103 and no. 2016/1104). These two regulations will be applicable as of 29 January 2019 in the Member States participating to the enhanced cooperation (see footnote 45).

[17] Both the study and the proceedings of the workshop have been published in the volume edited by the Deutsches Notarinstitut *Conflict of Law of Succession in the European Union*, cited at footnote 9.

[18] The Hague Programme of the Council on strengthening freedom, security and justice in the European Union, OJ 2005 no. C53, 3 March 2005, p. 13: 'the Commission is invited to submit . . . a green paper on the conflict of laws in matters of succession, including the question of jurisdiction, mutual recognition and enforcement of decisions in this area,

submission of comments.[19] Most of the nearly sixty responses received from the Member State governments, entities and associations and private bodies viewed the initiative favourably. The European Parliament also displayed its interest by adopting a resolution in November 2006 in which it invited the Commission to present a proposal in this area. A list of twelve recommendations was annexed to this resolution, in which the Parliament indicated the solutions which, in its view, should have been given to the principal questions with which the projected instrument was to engage.[20] Consequently, the Commission, which had in the meantime created a group of experts charged with assisting it in preparing the proposal,[21] started work on this text. The work of the group of experts lasted for two years and the Commission presented its first proposal on 14 October 2009.[22] Following a first detailed examination by the Council in close informal contact with the European Parliament, during the course of which the proposal was subject to numerous changes,[23] the final text of the ESR was adopted on 4 July 2012.

10. As provided for under article 81(2)(c) TFEU with regard to measures of judicial cooperation in civil matters aimed at ensuring 'the compatibility of the rules applicable in the Member States concerning conflict of laws and of jurisdiction', the ESR was adopted in accordance with the ordinary legislative procedure, which requires a qualified majority within the Council and approval by the European Parliament. However, at the start of the preparatory works the question was raised over whether or not the different legislative procedure provided for at the time under article 67.5 of the EC Treaty (equivalent to the new article 81.3 TFEU, which replaced it following the entry into force of the Lisbon

a European certificate of inheritance and a mechanism allowing precise knowledge of the existence of last wills and testaments of residents of European Union'.

19 Green paper on successions and wills, COM(2005) 65 final of 1 March 2005.

20 European Parliament resolution with recommendations to the Commission on succession and wills of 16 November 2006, OJ 2006 no. C314E, 21 December 2006, p. 342 *et seq.*

21 OJ 2006 no C51, 1 March 2006, p. 3.

22 Proposal for a Regulation of the European Parliament and of the Council on jurisdiction, applicable law, recognition and enforcement of decisions and authentic instruments in matters of succession and the creation of a European Certificate of Succession, COM (2009) 154 final. Meanwhile, the importance of the planned regulation for the strengthening of the protection of individuals' rights in the legal space of the Union was also stressed by the European Council in the 2009 Stockholm Programme setting out the Union's priorities for the area of freedom, security and justice (The Stockholm Programme – An open and secure Europe serving and protecting citizens, OJ 2010 no. C115, 4 May 2010, p. 13, point 3.1.2).

23 In this respect see no. 14.

Treaty) should be followed, which required that, on an exceptional basis, the measures concerning areas involving 'aspects relating to family law' should be adopted by a unanimous vote within the Council preceded by a simple consultation of the European Parliament. In the explanatory memorandum accompanying its proposal, the Commission had indicated as a basis for the decision to use the ordinary legislative procedure (which was known at the time as the co-decision procedure) the argument that the law of succession should be deemed to be sufficiently distinct and autonomous from family law because its direct object was the definition of the rules for passing on an inheritance and not the regulation of legal relations between spouses, partners or relatives. Moreover, in the opinion of the Commission, since the provision requiring unanimity amounted to an exception from the general rule, it should be interpreted and applied narrowly.[24] The solidity of this position, which could perhaps raise some uncertainty if referred to article 67.5 of the EC treaty, the wording of which could be construed to include also measures that were only partially related to family law,[25] was however significantly reinforced by the fact that a few days after the Commission proposal was presented, the provision was superseded by article 81.1 TFEU, which entered into force on 1 December 2009, and which clearly limits the requirement for a unanimous vote within the Council to the adoption of 'measures concerning family law with cross-border implications'. Thus, it would not appear to be possible to call into question the legitimacy of the use of the ordinary procedure.

11. A different problem of legality which has been discussed results from the fact that, whilst the ESR refers to article 81.2 TFEU, and in particular to point (c) thereof, as its sole legislative basis,[26] it does not include solely rules concerning conflict of laws and jurisdiction but also contains a variety of provisions of substantive law, such as articles 31

[24] Proposal for a Regulation of the European Parliament and of the Council on jurisdiction, applicable law, recognition and enforcement of decisions and authentic instruments in matters of succession and the creation of a European Certificate of Succession, explanatory memorandum, COM(2009) 154 final, p. 3, point 3.1.

[25] A precedent along these lines which, among other things, could have been taken into consideration laid in the fact that Council Regulation (EC) no. 4/2009 of 18 December 2008 on jurisdiction, applicable law, recognition and enforcement of decisions and cooperation in matters relating to maintenance obligations (OJ 2009 no. L7, 10 January 2009, p. 1 *et seq.*) had been adopted according to the procedure requiring unanimity.

[26] The specific reference to point (c) is contained in recital 2 of ESR, but the reasons given by the regulation at the outset refer to article 81.2 as a whole as its legislative basis.

(adaptation of rights *in rem*), 32 (*commorientes*), 33 (estate without a claimant) and most of the provisions relating to the European Certificate of Succession. However, the presence of these rules within the instrument may be sufficiently justified by their ancillary status vis-à-vis its other parts and the fact that they are essential for the achievement of the objectives of judicial cooperation in civil matters having cross-border implications.[27] These objectives moreover consist in ensuring not only the compatibility between the rules applicable within the Member States to conflicts of laws and jurisdiction but also 'the mutual recognition and enforcement between Member States of judgments and of decisions in extrajudicial cases' as well as 'cooperation in the taking of evidence' and 'effective access to justice', as expressly provided under article 81(2)(a), (d) and (e) respectively. Also the European Council expressly recognised in the Hague Programme on strengthening freedom, security and justice in the European Union the possibility that the instruments adopted in this area may as well include uniform substantive rules 'as an accompanying measure' where they are necessary in order to realise the goals of judicial cooperation.[28]

12. The ESR is applicable in twenty-five Member States of the European Union, i.e. in the twenty-four of them that participated in its adoption and in the Republic of Croatia, which became the twenty-eighth Member State on 1 July 2013. On the other hand, the regulation does not apply to the other three Member States, namely Denmark, which, pursuant to articles 1 and 2 of protocol no. 22 on its position,[29] annexed to TEU and TFEU, does not take part in the adoption of proposed measures

[27] For a defence of the legitimacy of the inclusion of such provisions in the ESR, see Max Planck Institute for Comparative and International Private Law, 'Comments on the European Commission's Proposal for a Regulation of the European Parliament and of the Council on jurisdiction, applicable law, recognition and enforcement of decisions and authentic instruments in matters of succession and the creation of a European Certificate of Succession', *RabelsZ* (2010), p. 530; for similar positions see also H.-P. Mansel, 'Vereinheitlichung des internationalen Erbrechts in der Europäischen Gemeinschaft – Kompetenzfragen und Regelungsgrundsätze', in *Prof. Dr. Tuğrul Ansay'a Armağan* (Ankara, 2006), pp. 192–193; for an opposite view see, however, M. Buschbaum and M. Kohler, 'Vereinheitlichung des Erbkollisionsrechts in Europa, Zweiter Teil', *European Community Private Law Review* (2010), p. 166.

[28] The Hague Programme of the Council on strengthening freedom, security and justice in the European Union, approved by the European Council meeting in Brussels on 4 and 5 November 2004, p. 13, point 3.4.2: 'Rules of uniform substantive law should only be introduced as an accompanying measure, whenever necessary to effect mutual recognition of decisions or to improve judicial cooperation in civil matters'.

[29] OJ 2012 no. C326, 26 October 2012, p. 299 *et seq.*

pursuant to title V of part three of TFEU and is not subject to their application, and the United Kingdom and Ireland, which, pursuant to articles 1 to 4 of protocol no. 21 on their position in respect of the area of freedom, security and justice,[30] may decide in each particular case whether or not to participate (so-called right to opt-in).[31] Since the start of the preparatory work on the ESR, the UK and Ireland had been clear about their likely choice not to participate in its adoption due to their disagreement with certain aspects or implications of the Commission proposal which they considered to be important. However, negotiations aimed at persuading them to exercise their right to opt-in were pursued until the conclusion of the work. The main concerns of the United Kingdom and Ireland were twofold. The first related to their desire to be able to continue to subject in all cases to their respective *lex fori* rather than to foreign law the administration and distribution of the estate which, as mentioned above, they allocate to a personal representative of the deceased acting under the control of the court in order to provide more effective guarantees to the creditors and beneficiaries of the estate.[32] The second concern related to their desire to protect persons who have received a lifetime gift from the deceased and, if applicable, their possible assignees, as well as the beneficiaries of a trust that the deceased could have designated *inter vivos* against clawback claims which, under the legislation of a large number of continental countries, the relatives of the deceased who are entitled to a forced heirship share may invoke even several years later in the event that the estate, as established at the time the succession was opened, is insufficient to satisfy their rights.[33] It was possible to resolve the

[30] OJ 2012 no. C326, 26 October 2012, p. 295 *et seq.*

[31] More specifically, according to article 1 of the protocol, these two States shall not take part in the adoption of measures relating to the establishment of an area of freedom, security and justice but, pursuant to articles 3 and 4, they may notify the President of the Council, after a proposal or an initiative in the field has been presented to the Council, that they wish to take part in the adoption and the application of such proposed measure or may, at any time after its adoption, notify their intention to the Council and to the Commission that they wish to accept the measure in question.

[32] See no. 7, in particular regarding the role performed by these types of concern, which are generally shared by common law systems, during the preparatory works for the Hague Convention of 1989 on the Law Applicable to Succession to the Estates of Deceased Persons.

[33] On the contrast existing in this respect between common law systems and continental systems, see no. 2. For a full discussion of these and other concerns, which were already expressed by the UK government in its response to the green paper published by the Commission in 2005, see J. Harris, 'The Proposed EU Regulation on Succession and Wills: Prospects and Challenges', *Trust LI* (2008), p. 181 *et seq.*

first difficulty, at least partially, through the introduction into the ESR of article 29, which enables the courts of a Member State that have jurisdiction to rule on the succession to appoint an administrator in accordance with the *lex fori*, where that law so requires, even if the law governing the succession is a foreign law; the same article then goes on to delineate and coordinate the respective application of the two laws in question. On the other hand, the problem of clawback actions proved to be more thorny. The United Kingdom, along with most other common law countries, does not recognise mandatory inheritance rights and generally classifies clawback claims as a kind of challenge to the validity of donations, which are subject as such to the law governing the donations; according to the conflict of laws systems of these countries, this is the law of the location at which the assets donated are situated. Consequently, they are not inclined to accept that a donation that was valid at the time it was made may be subsequently annulled or revoked in accordance with a future *lex successionis* which could not even be identified with certainty at the time the donation was made.[34] On the other hand, the continental countries consider clawback actions as an area falling within the scope of the law governing the succession and are in turn equally ill inclined to give up the protection provided by this instrument for the rights of persons who, according to their own laws, are entitled to a reserved share. A compromise solution proposed during the preparatory work involved subjecting clawback claims to the 'hypothetical' *lex successionis*, that is to the law that would have hypothetically been applicable to the succession of the donor had he died at the time the donation was made. This solution would have maintained a certain level of protection for the close relatives of the deceased, whilst also enabling donees (and where appropriate their possible assignees) to avoid a serious situation of uncertainty as regards the fate of their gift.[35] Unfortunately, it did not attract the level of consensus

[34] This lack of predictability characterises both of the laws designated by the ESR which may regulate succession as alternatives, namely the law of the State in which the deceased had his or her habitual residence at the time of death (article 21) or the law of the State whose nationality the deceased possessed, if he or she had chosen it (in particular, even after the donation was made) by a declaration to that effect (article 22).

[35] See for a stance in favour of this solution A. Dutta, 'Succession and Wills in the Conflict of Laws on the Eve of Europeanisation', *RabelsZ* (2009), p. 583; E. Lein, 'A Further Step towards a European Code of Private International Law. The Commission Proposal for a Regulation on Succession', *YPIL* (2009), p. 134; a solution which is even more favourable to donees was that sponsored by the Max Planck Institute for Comparative and International Private Law, 'Comments', p. 629 *et seq.*, which suggested the inclusion in the ESR of a special provision subjecting clawback to the cumulative application both of the

necessary in order to be included in the ESR and, mainly due to their disagreement on this issue, the United Kingdom and Ireland confirmed their intention not to exercise their right to opt-in.

13. A consequence of the fact that the three aforesaid Member States (Denmark, Ireland and the United Kingdom) did not participate in the adoption of the ESR and are not bound by it is that, from the viewpoint of its application, they must be regarded as third States. The expression 'Member States' used by many provisions in the regulation must therefore be taken to refer to all Member States with the exception of the three States in question, and correspondingly the expression 'third States', which is also used at various points in the instrument, must be taken to include these States. In other words, Member States within the meaning of the ESR are only States that are bound by it and its rules on jurisdiction, the applicable law and the mutual recognition of decisions and authentic instruments in the area of succession, along with the rules on the European Certificate of Succession, are addressed exclusively to them. In particular, article 34 of the regulation, which contemplates the *renvoi* by the law of a third State to the law of a Member State or to the law of a different third State, must be interpreted on the same basis.[36] Such a conclusion may obviously be inferred without difficulty from protocols no. 21 and 22 regarding the respective positions of the three Member States concerned.[37] It may therefore be considered that the inclusion in the ESR of an article containing explicit clarification to this effect was not strictly necessary. Nevertheless, it would have probably been appropriate in order to avoid the emergency of uncertainty, all the more so because, prior to the adoption of the ESR, provisions of this type had been regularly included in instruments concerning judicial cooperation in civil matters that one or more of those three States was not required to apply,[38] and since a similar rule was also

hypothetical law governing the succession and that effectively applicable at the time of the donee's death; for an examination of the various possible solutions, see also Harris, 'The Proposed EU Regulation', p. 195 *et seq.*; Bonomi, *Successions internationales*, p. 274 *et seq.*

[36] See on this last point H. Dörner, 'EuErbVO: Die Verordnung zum Internationalen Erb- und Erbverfahrensrecht ist im Kraft!', *ZEV* (2012), p. 511, footnote 41; A. Davì and A. Zanobetti, 'Il nuovo diritto internazionale privato delle successioni nell'Unione europea', *CdT*, 5/2 (2013), p. 82; Davì and Zanobetti, *Il nuovo diritto internazionale privato europeo*, pp. 130–131; for a slightly more questioning view, see G. Khairallah, 'La détermination de la loi applicable à la succession', in G. Khairallah and M. Revillard (eds), *Droit européen des successions internationales* (Paris, 2013), p. 60.

[37] On these protocols see no. 12.

[38] See, e.g., article 1.4 of regulation (EC) no. 864/2007 on the law applicable to non-contractual obligations (Rome II), OJ 2007 no. L199, 31 July 2007, p. 40 *et seq.* ('For the

contained in the Commission proposal from 2009.[39] Its removal from the definitive text of the regulation appears to have inaugurated a new practice within this area, with which other regulations subsequently adopted have already complied.[40] Whilst it is true that the ESR does not fail to state in recitals 82 and 83 that Denmark, Ireland and the United Kingdom are not taking part in its adoption and therefore are not bound by it or subject to its application and that corresponding indications are also contained in the recitals of the following instruments, it is not however certain that such information is sufficient to prevent the emergence of doubts for readers and users of the instruments in question who are not particularly experienced in these matters.

III. Structure and General Features of the ESR

14. Complying largely with the indications contained in the Hague Programme of 2004,[41] the ESR engaged at the same time with the three principal aspects of the private international law of succession, namely jurisdiction, the applicable law and the recognition and enforcement of decisions, with the addition (also provided for under that programme) of the introduction and regulation of the European Certificate of Succession. The recognition and enforcement of decisions are supplemented by

purpose of this Regulation, "Member State" shall mean any Member State other than Denmark') and article 1.4 of regulation (EC) no .593/2008 on the law applicable to contractual obligations (Rome I), OJ 2008 no. L177, 4 July 2008, p. 6 *et seq.* ('In this Regulation, the term 'Member State' shall mean Member States to which this Regulation applies').

[39] The 2009 proposal of the Commission (on which see no. 9) contained an article 1.2 stating that '[i]n this Regulation "Member State" means all Member States with the exception of Denmark [the United Kingdom and Ireland]'.

[40] In particular, regulation (EU) no .1215/2012 of 12 December 2012 on jurisdiction and the recognition and enforcement of judgments in civil and commercial matters (recast), OJ 2012 no. L351, 20 December 2012, p. 1 *et seq.*, which replaced the previous regulation (EC) no. 44/2001 of 22 December 2000 on the same subject, OJ 2001 no. L12, 16 January 2001, p. 1 *et seq.*, removed the clarification that had been included in article 1.3 of the latter according to which '[i]n this Regulation the term "Member" shall mean Member States with the exception of Denmark'. The same approach appears to have been followed in relation to the replacement of regulation (EC) no. 1346/2000 of 29 May 2000 on insolvency proceedings, OJ 2000 no. L160, 30 June 2000, pp. 1 *et seq.* by the new regulation (EU) no. 2015/848 of 20 May 2015 on insolvency proceedings (recast), OJ 2015 no. L141, 5 June 2015, p. 19 *et seq.*: the former instrument was the only one relating to conflict of laws and jurisdiction adopted before the entry into force of the ESR that did not include an express clarification of the meaning of the concept of 'Member State', an omission which is confirmed by the second instrument.

[41] See footnote 18.

provisions concerning the acceptance and enforceability of authentic instruments and the enforceability of court settlements. Consequently, the regulation is divided into the following seven chapters: I (articles 1–3), Scope and Definitions; II (articles 4–19), Jurisdiction; III (articles 20–38), Applicable Law; IV (articles 39–58), Recognition, Enforceability and Enforcement of Decisions; V (articles 59–61), Authentic Instruments and Court Settlements; VI (articles 62–73), European Certificate of Succession; VII (articles 74–84), General and Final Provisions. On the other hand, as already mentioned,[42] the project of establishing a European scheme for the registration of wills, which had also been envisaged by the Hague Programme, was shelved. Being comprised of 84 articles and 83 recitals, the ESR was, at the time it was drafted, the most extensive instrument of private international law adopted until that time by the Union, although it has already lost this primacy following the recent enactment of regulation no. 2015/848 of 20 May 2015 on insolvency proceedings (recast).[43] Whilst the final text of the ESR reflects pretty faithfully in its general features the contents of the Commission proposal, it nevertheless makes various changes to the latter. The most significant include: the acceptance of *renvoi*, which had also been recommended by the European Parliament; the introduction of conflict rules dealing with the formal validity of dispositions of property upon death; the inclusion of an exception clause from the general conflict rule which subjects the succession to the law of the country in which the deceased was last habitually resident; the recognition of the possibility of an implicit *professio juris*; the addition of two recitals specifying the meaning of the concept of habitual residence; the extension to all dispositions of property upon death of the principle of the application to their respective admissibility and substantive validity of the 'hypothetical' *lex successionis*, which the proposal had by contrast limited to agreements as to succession; the creation of the *forum necessitatis*. Other provisions were also amended, including specifically those concerning jurisdiction, the acceptance of authentic instruments and the European Certificate of Succession.

15. Due to its structure and features previously outlined, the ESR must be included within a new generation of EU instruments on judicial cooperation in civil matters, which are distinguished by the fact that they

[42] On this point see footnote 14.

[43] In effect, especially because it includes new rules on the insolvency proceedings of groups of companies, this last instrument has a considerably greater breadth than the previous regulation no. 1346/2000 of 29 May 2000 concerning the same matter, and is comprised of 92 articles and 89 recitals.

bring together the regulation of all private international law aspects of the subject matter to which they apply within one single text. During the first stage of legislative action by the EU in the area, the rules on conflict of laws and on jurisdiction and the recognition and enforcement of decisions had by contrast been largely kept separate from one another and were contained in different instruments, in particular in the fields of contractual and non-contractual obligations along with divorce and legal separation.[44] The new tendency was inaugurated by regulation no. 4/2009 on jurisdiction, applicable law, recognition and enforcement of decisions and cooperation in matters relating to maintenance obligations, which was followed by the ESR; however, also the two regulations on matrimonial property regimes and the property consequences of registered partnerships adopted by the Council on 24 June 2016 follow the same pattern.[45] As is stressed in recital 8 of the ESR, the joint consideration of all of the said aspects enables the objectives of the instrument to be achieved with a level of efficiency and completeness which it would otherwise have been difficult to obtain.[46] In particular, the parallel appraisal and regulation of problems relating to jurisdiction and the determination of the applicable law significantly facilitated the

[44] In effect, within these areas, as is well known, conflicts of laws are dealt with by regulations nos. 593/2008 (Rome I), 864/2007 (Rome II) and 1259/2010 (Rome III), concerning respectively contractual and non-contractual obligations and divorce and legal separation, whilst jurisdiction and the recognition and enforcement of decisions had previously been addressed separately, with regard to contractual and non-contractual obligations by regulation no. 44/2001 (Brussels I), now replaced by regulation no. 1215/2012 (Brussels I-*bis*), and with regard to divorce and legal separation by regulation no. 1347/2000 (Brussels II), now replaced by regulation no. 2201/2003 (Brussels II-*bis*). The only instrument adopted during this initial stage that contained provisions applicable to the whole of those aspects was regulation no. 1346/2000 on insolvency proceedings, now replaced by regulation no. 2015/848. The exception may be explained by the objective difficulty in the area of insolvency of keeping issues of substantive law separate from procedural issues.

[45] Council regulation (EU) 2016/1103 of 24 June 2016 implementing enhanced cooperation in the area of jurisdiction, applicable law and the recognition and enforcement of decisions in matters of matrimonial property regimes; Council regulation (EU) 2016/1104 of 24 June 2016 implementing enhanced cooperation in the area of jurisdiction, applicable law and the recognition and enforcement of decisions in matters of the property consequences of registered partnerships. Both regulations will be applicable as of 29 January 2019 in the Member States participating to the enhanced cooperation, i.e. Belgium, Bulgaria, Cyprus, the Czech Republic, Germany, Greece, Spain, France, Croatia, Italy, Luxembourg, Malta, the Netherlands, Austria, Portugal, Slovenia, Finland and Sweden.

[46] Concerning these objectives see recital 7 of the ESR and the Summary of the Impact Assessment accompanying the 2009 Commission proposal, quoted in no. 4.

realisation of the broad coincidence between *forum* and *jus* which is one of the principal characteristics of the ESR and offers considerable practical benefits to private parties, courts and legal professionals.[47] In any case, it is certain that the adoption of common rules concerning only conflict of laws or only jurisdiction and the recognition of decisions would not have been sufficient in order to create the high level of coordination between the respective positions of the Member States legal systems at which it was directed. First and foremost, the problem of the law applicable to the succession may arise, in particular for individuals who wish to plan the inheritance of their assets, even prior to and separately from any legal proceedings and in situations in which it is not possible to predict with certainty which court may have jurisdiction in future. Secondly, the same problem may have to be addressed and resolved incidentally also in trials relating to non-succession issues, which thus do not fall within the scope of the provisions on jurisdiction and the recognition of decisions contained in the ESR, even though it cannot be excluded that such trials may however fall within the scope of other EU regulations providing for common jurisdictional criteria. It must also be borne in mind that, in view of the multiple links between the law of succession and various other sectors of substantive law, the unification of conflict of laws rules relating to the former cannot on its own guarantee that uniform solutions will be reached amongst the Member States in all cases. It is sufficient to recall the connections existing between the area of succession and matrimonial property regimes or the regulation of the property consequences of registered partnerships, or the decisive influence which differences in solutions to the underlying preliminary questions of family law, to which some Member States currently apply different conflict of laws rules, can have on the treatment of the estate. It follows that the introduction by the ESR of uniform rules which confer jurisdiction in the majority of cases on the courts of a single Member State provides a significant contribution to enhancing the predictability of the outcome to disputes and to restricting correspondingly the scope for *forum shopping*, despite the merely sectorial nature of the harmonisation of conflict of laws rules hitherto achieved.[48]

[47] On the principle of unity between jurisdiction and applicable law within the ESR see below, nos. 33–36.

[48] The breadth of the limitations described on the level of unification achieved to date in the area of conflict of laws will naturally be reduced when the two EU regulations concerning matrimonial property regimes and the property consequences of registered partnerships referred to, footnote 45, will be applicable (29 January 2019).

IV. Object and Scope

16. The object of the ESR is comprised of international successions, that is successions characterised by objective and/or subjective international elements. As an instrument in the area of private international law, it does not regulate questions of internal law and does not lay down provisions of substantive law, subject to the small number of exceptions referred to above.[49] Likewise, the jurisdictional provisions included within it relate solely to international jurisdiction and not also to local jurisdiction or internal competence, which continues to be regulated exclusively by the national legislation of the Member States, as is explicitly recognised by article 2 ('This Regulation shall not affect the competence of the authorities of the Member States to deal with matters of succession'). On the other hand, other instruments adopted in the area of judicial cooperation in civil matters, such as regulation no. 1215/2012 (Brussels I-*bis*), which follows its predecessor regulation no. 44/2001 (Brussels I) on this matter, and regulation no. 4/2009 relating to maintenance obligations deal in all or in most cases both with the issue of international jurisdiction and with that of internal venue. Also the choice made by the ESR not to interfere in the internal division of competence between the courts of the Member States is not however without exceptions. The first of these is provided for under article 5 which, with the aim of laying down a complete regulation for the choice-of-court agreements which it allows where the law applicable to the succession has been chosen by the testator, enables interested parties to agree that the courts or a *particular court* of the Member State whose law has been chosen are to have exclusive jurisdiction to rule on any matter concerning the succession in question. A second exception relates to local jurisdiction over declarations of enforceability in one Member State of decisions given in another Member State: such jurisdiction is conferred by article 45.2 – with the aim of ensuring that the applicant is able to obtain rapid and effective enforcement – by reference to the court of competent authority of the place of domicile of the party against whom enforcement is sought or to that of the place of enforcement.[50] As may easily be seen, also these two rules apply to situations with an international aspect.

[49] For a list of the main special rules included within the act which, whilst being substantive in nature, still relate to situations of an international nature, see no. 11.

[50] The applicability of the rule contained in article 45.2 is extended by articles 39.2, 60.1 and 61.1 respectively to disputes concerning the recognition of decisions, the enforceability of authentic instruments and the enforceability of court settlements.

17. In seeking to regulate the area of law comprising its object in as complete a manner as possible so as to leave little scope for the applicability of reciprocally divergent or contradictory national provisions of the Member States, the ESR adopts for the purposes of its application a broad definition of 'succession', indicating in article 3.1(a) that this concept 'covers all forms of transfer of assets, rights and obligations by reason of death, whether by way of a voluntary transfer under a disposition of property upon death or a transfer through intestate succession'. Recital 9 adds the further clarification that the scope of the instrument covers 'all civil-law aspects of succession'. The definition contained in the 2009 Commission proposal was by contrast narrower in that article 2(a) was limited to including within the concept of 'succession to the estate of deceased persons' adopted by it 'all forms of transfer of property as a result of death', thus leaving succession in respect of other situations or legal relations, including in particular the debts of the inheritance, outside of its scope. A distinction of this type was clearly more in keeping with the concept of succession endorsed in common law countries than with that prevailing in continental Europe, since in the former countries the succession is administered by a personal representative of the deceased who acquires fiduciary ownership of the estate, attends to the payment of the debts of the estate and transfers to each individual heir ownership only of the goods allocated to him or her, whilst in the latter countries each heir succeeds directly and personally to all legal relations of the deceased, including obligations, unless these are extinguished by the death of the obligor under the law applicable to them (*successio in universum jus*).[51] The only question relating to the civil law aspects of succession that the ESR does not regulate is, according to article 1.2(f), the formal validity of dispositions of property upon death made orally. This thus remains subject to the national conflict of laws provisions of the Member States or the provisions of the Hague Convention of 1961 on the Conflicts of Laws Relating to the Form of Testamentary Dispositions in the Member States that are parties to it. Similarly, the ESR does not deal either with tax liabilities or with other revenue or administrative matters, as these issues

[51] On this point see no. 2. Article 23.2(b) and (c) ESR expressly includes amongst the questions regulated by the law applicable to the succession according to the regulation 'the obligations which may be imposed' on beneficiaries 'by the deceased' and 'liability for the debts under the succession'. On the two definitions of succession adopted respectively by the proposal and the final text of the ESR see also G. Biagioni, 'L'ambito di applicazione del regolamento sulle successioni', in P. Franzina and A. Leandro (eds), *Il diritto internazionale privato europeo delle successioni* mortis causa (Milan, 2013), pp. 27–28.

cannot be classified under 'civil-law aspects of succession'. This exclusion is given explicit form by article 1.1 and is also specified in recital 10.

18. Although its aim is to lay down a private international law regulation which is essentially complete in the area of succession, the ESR however has no claim to apply within other areas of the civil law, as much as they may be closely related to the former area. It follows that it is necessary to trace an accurate dividing line between the categories of questions which, due to the fact that they may be classified as relating to succession, fall within the substantive scope of the instrument and those which, due to the fact that they are different in nature, are excluded from it (such as e.g. questions relating to matrimonial property regimes, the property consequences of registered partnerships, maintenance obligations, trusts and gifts, the nature of rights *in rem* and their recording in public registers).[52] The ESR responds to this need by following the same pattern as other EU private international law instruments according to a twin-track approach, i.e. both negatively through the provision of a list in article 1 stipulating the areas in which it does not apply, as well as positively by indicating in articles 23 and 26 the questions that are to be included within the scope of its provisions on the law governing the succession and, respectively, those concerning the law governing the substantive validity of dispositions of property upon death.[53] Although it seeks to be as complete as possible, the list provided in article 23 is not a closed list and may thus be supplemented through interpretation if necessary, and the same may perhaps be said in relation to the list laid down in article 26; however, some doubts may arise with regard to the latter from the fact that questions relating to the substantive validity of dispositions of property upon death are subject to special rules contained in articles 24 and 25, which depart from those normally applicable to the remaining aspects of the succession, to which accordingly all issues not expressly included in the former list should be allocated.[54]

[52] The importance of this delimitation is stressed in recital 11: 'This Regulation should not apply to areas of civil law other than succession. For reasons of clarity, a number of questions which could be seen as having a link with matters of succession should be explicitly excluded from the scope of this Regulation'.

[53] For the adoption of an analogous dual mode of delimitation see also articles 1 and 12 of regulation no. 593/2008 on the law applicable to contractual obligations (Rome I), articles 1 and 15 of regulation no. 864/2007 on the law applicable to non-contractual obligations (Rome II) and articles 1 and 7 of regulation no. 2015/848 on insolvency proceedings (recast).

[54] As noted by Biagioni, 'L'ambito di applicazione del regolamento', p. 27, although article 23 relates formally to the sole issue of the applicable law (amongst other things because it

A further contribution to delineating the substantive scope of the ESR may be provided by the provisions contained in article 3 which define the precise meaning of some of the principal legal terms used in the instrument. For example, the definition of 'agreement as to succession' provided in paragraph 1(b) of the article in question excludes from the scope of this notion any agreement to which the person or persons whose succession is at issue is not a party. Consequently, agreements in which one party disposes in favour of another party of the rights that may be vested in him under the future succession of a person who is not a party to the agreement do not fall within the scope of the ESR and must be classified as contracts, which are as such subject to the law ordinarily applicable to them under regulation no. 593/2008 (Rome I). All problems relating to the delineation of the scope of the ESR that may arise may naturally be subject to the interpretative jurisdiction of the Court of Justice of the EU.

19. On the other hand, the ESR avoids defining the international nature of succession, and in fact – in contrast to other EU private international law instruments – does not even contain any provisions that expressly limit, albeit in a generic way, its applicability to international cases.[55] An indication to that effect is provided only in recital 7 which states that one of the objectives of the instrument is to remove 'the obstacles to the free movement of persons who currently face difficulties in asserting their rights in the context of a succession having cross-border implications'. However, it is evident that an instrument such as the ESR, which was enacted on the legal basis of article 81 TFEU that empowers the EU institutions to adopt legislative measures aimed at developing 'judicial cooperation in civil matters having cross-border implications', can only concern situations with an international aspect, whilst it is equally certain

is included in chapter III of the ESR dedicated to that issue), in actual fact it contributes to delineating the scope of the regulation as a whole, and thus also in relation to issues of jurisdiction, recognition and enforcement of decisions, acceptance of authentic instruments and the European Certificate of Succession. The same may be asserted, *mutatis mutandis*, in respect of article 26.

[55] Contrary to the ESR, regulations no. 593/2008 on the law applicable to contractual obligations (Rome I), no. 864/2007 on the law applicable to non-contractual obligations (Rome II) and no. 1259/2010 implementing enhanced cooperation in the area of the law applicable to divorce and legal separation (Rome III) all specify in their respective articles 1.1 that they 'shall apply in situations involving a conflict of laws'. However, other instruments adopted in the area of judicial cooperation in civil matters, such as e.g. regulation no. 4/2009 on maintenance obligations, do not mention the international nature of the situations to be regulated as a necessary prerequisite for their applicability.

that, also from a more general point of view, the EU for the time being lacks the power to regulate internal successions. It may also be added that, whilst the inapplicability of the ESR to cases with no international element is not explicitly indicated, it may be inferred indirectly yet clearly from many of its provisions, or is assumed by those provisions as an implicit prerequisite. In particular, article 2, referred to previously,[56] confirms that the jurisdictional rules contained in the instrument govern only international jurisdiction and are not intended to regulate issues relating to internal competence. Moreover, the provisions of articles 17 and 18 concerning *lis pendens* and related actions both regard proceedings pending before the courts of different Member States. Likewise, the rules on the recognition and enforcement of decisions and those on the acceptance and enforceability of authentic instruments and the enforceability of court settlements by definition relate to questions concerning relations between Member States and are thus international in nature. According to article 62.1, also the European Certificate of Succession must be issued 'for use in another Member State'.[57] As regards the conflict of laws provisions contained in the instrument, their applicability solely to international cases may be inferred not only from their very function but also from article 38, which provides that '[a] Member State which comprises several territorial units each of which has its own rules of law in respect of succession shall not be required to apply this Regulation to conflicts of laws arising between such units only'.[58]

20. The reasons why the ESR is reticent concerning the need for the aforesaid prerequisite for its applicability probably lie in the difficulty encountered in defining the international nature of the succession and in the doubts that may arise concerning the very existence of this requirement in circumstances in which the regulation must nonetheless also be

[56] See no. 16.

[57] The fact that, according to article 62.3, the certificate produces its effects also in the Member State in which it was issued may be explained by the need to attribute this document the same effect throughout all Member States, and certainly does not exclude that it is conceived for being used in situations with an international aspect. Article 65.3(f) provides in this regard that the person applying for the certificate must specify its intended purpose in accordance with article 63, which in turn requires that it must be used 'in another Member State'.

[58] On the importance of this element for the purposes of excluding the applicability of the conflict-of-laws provisions of the ESR to purely internal situations, see A. Bonomi, 'Introduction', in A. Bonomi and P. Wautelet, *Le droit européen des successions. Commentaire du Règlement n° 650/2012 du 4 juillet 2012* (Bruxelles, 2013), p. 37; Biagioni, 'L'ambito di applicazione del regolamento', p. 52, footnote 81.

applied. As regards the former aspect, it must be borne in mind that a number of the most typical elements capable of establishing the international nature of the succession – such as the habitual residence of the deceased or his or her ownership of property in a given country, or the fact that he or she is a national of a certain State – are subject to vary over time. This means that a succession may be international at the time a will is drafted but may have lost that status at the time of the testator's death, or vice versa. A *professio juris* made in accordance with article 22 in favour of the national law of its author at the time it was drawn up, but which was no longer his national law at the time the succession was opened, must remain valid even if, due to the change intervened, the succession has become purely internal. Furthermore, article 22 permits the law of a future nationality to be chosen, that is the nationality of the testator at the time of death; the provision is thus applicable also to successions that, whilst not yet being international, could however become such at the time they are opened. With regard to the second aspect, it must not be forgotten that the place where the deceased was habitually resident at the time of death – which under article 21 is the main objective connecting factor adopted by the ESR – may be difficult to establish in some cases, as often occurs in relation to persons who divide their time between two or more countries, or who had moved their residence abroad for contingent reasons (for example, work, study or health), whilst maintaining close contact with the country of origin to which they planned to return. It is presumably due to these considerations that the European legislator, driven by the intention to ensure compliance with the objectives of the regulation in all the various circumstances that may arise, preferred to avoid limiting its application *ex ante* by providing an excessively rigid definition of the prerequisite of the international nature of the succession.[59]

21. As it has the purpose of regulating all private international law aspects relating to succession, the ESR deals with its object in a manner which seeks to be complete and exclusive, subject obviously to any limits

[59] It may also be added that certain special provisions of the regulation, such as articles 13 and 28, are applicable on the basis of international elements that are specifically related to them and do not necessarily extend to other aspects of the succession. Those articles stipulate respectively the courts having jurisdiction to receive the declarations of acceptance or waiver of the succession (or of a legacy or a reserved share) made by persons habitually resident in a country other than that in which the succession was opened and the law applicable to such declarations, also in situations in which, with regard to all other aspects, the succession does not have any international character: see in this regard Bonomi, 'Introduction', p. 37, text and footnote 47.

resulting from the fact that it may only establish reciprocal rights and obligations with regard to relations between the States that are bound by it and subject also to the requirement to comply with international conventions in force and a small number of other exceptions. In particular, the limitations of the former type imply that the parts of the instrument that impose obligations relating to the mutual recognition and enforcement of decisions, the acceptance of authentic instruments and the enforcement of these instruments and of court settlements (chapters IV and V) are only applicable within relations between the Member States as previously defined.[60] Also the European Certificate of Succession is intended to produce its effects solely in the Member States (articles 62.1 and 69.1). The recognition and enforcement of decisions or the effects and enforcement of other acts or documents originating from third States thus remain regulated in each Member State by internal law (or by the international conventions concluded by it), as is the case for all other EU private international law instruments.[61] As regards the relations between the ESR and international conventions, article 75.1 stipulates that the regulation shall not affect the application of international conventions to which Member States are party at the time of adoption of this act and which concern matters covered by it. However, paragraph 2 of the article provides that this rule is only to apply to the conventions to which one or more Member States along with at least one third State, towards which the participant Member States are obliged, are parties; on the other hand if a convention has been concluded exclusively between States falling in the former group, the regulation takes precedence over it. Similar provisions are found in most other EU regulations concerning conflicts of laws and/or jurisdiction.[62] Since most bilateral international

[60] On the concept of 'Member State' for the purposes of the application of the ESR see no. 13.

[61] In reality, nothing would stand in the way of the adoption by the EU Member States of common rules also on recognition and the enforcement of judicial decisions, and possibly of other legal acts, originating from third countries. Such a step would offer various benefits by introducing further simplification, enhancing legal certainty and rendering the legal regime governing the effects of judgments and other foreign acts within the European judicial area more uniform and complete. However, the EU has not yet decided to embark on this path. See for a brief analysis of the issue S. Carbone 'What about the Recognition of Third States' Foreign Judgments?', in F. Pocar, I. Viarengo and F. C. Villata (eds), *Recasting Bruxelles I* (Padova, 2012), p. 301 *et seq*.

[62] See, e.g., article 25 of regulation no. 593/2008 on the law applicable to contractual obligations (Rome I), article 28 of regulation no. 864/2007 on the law applicable to non-contractual obligations (Rome II), article 19 of regulation no. 1259/2010 implementing enhanced cooperation in the area of the law applicable to divorce and legal separation (Rome III) and article 69 of regulation no. 4/2009 on maintenance obligations.

agreements concluded by Member States with third States in the area of succession relate to the recognition and the mutual enforcement of decisions, the corresponding provisions of the ESR (which, as noted earlier, are only applicable *inter partes*) are not likely to interfere with the agreements in question; also for this reason, there will probably not be many opportunities for applying article 75.[63] In adopting the regulation the EU has now acquired exclusive competence in the area of the private international law of successions both internally and in relation to the conduct of external relations. Consequently, the negotiation and conclusion of any future international convention in this area may no longer be carried out by the Member States, but may be conducted solely by the EU institutions.[64]

22. In contrast to the part of the regulation concerning the recognition and enforcement of judicial decisions and the efficacy of other acts and documents,[65] the provisions laid down in chapter III (articles 20–38), which determine the law that is to govern the succession are applicable universally or *erga omnes*, as is explicitly stated by article 20 ('Any law specified by this Regulation shall be applied whether or not it is the law of a Member State'). In this regard the ESR follows the same pattern as the other EU private international law instruments.[66] Given its universal and thus unlimited character, the application of the conflict of laws rules contained in the instrument also occurs on an exclusive basis, in the sense that it precludes any scope for the parallel application of the corresponding national

[63] Concerning the relations between the ESR and multilateral conventions, see, with regard to the Hague Convention of 1961 on the Conflict of Laws Relating to the Form of Testamentary Dispositions, no. 5; concerning the Basel Convention of 1972 on the Establishment of a Scheme of Registration of Wills and the Washington Convention of 1973 Providing a Uniform Law on the Form of an International Will, see no. 8, footnote 14.

[64] See in this respect ECJ, opinion 1/03, *Competence of the Community to conclude the Lugano Convention on jurisdiction and the recognition and enforcement of judgments in civil and commercial matters* [2006] ECR I-1145, where the Court asserted in particular that the Community (now the Union) has exclusive competence to conclude an international agreement with one or more third countries when 'a specific analysis of the relationship between the agreement envisaged and the Community law in force' leads to establishing 'that the conclusion of such an agreement is capable of affecting the Community rules' (paragraph 124). See also articles 3.2 TEU and 216 TFEU.

[65] See the preceding paragraph.

[66] Rules identical or analogous to article 20 ESR are to be found, in particular, in article 2 of regulation no. 593/2008 on the law applicable to contractual obligations (Rome I), article 3 of regulation no. 864/2007 on the law applicable to non-contractual obligations (Rome II) and article 4 of regulation no. 1259/2010 implementing enhanced cooperation in the area of the law applicable to divorce and legal separation (Rome III).

provisions of the Member States. In this way it ensures that one of the main goals of the ESR is achieved to the fullest extent possible: the establishment in principle of a uniform regulation of international successions in the Union. The unlimited and exclusive nature of the application of the said rules are however subject to two small exceptions, alongside the limitations mentioned previously resulting from the need to comply with international conventions in force and the fact that the instrument does not regulate the formal validity of dispositions of property upon death made orally.[67] The first of these exceptions is laid down in article 29, which enables the courts of the Member States having jurisdiction to rule on the succession to apply in certain circumstances the provisions of their internal law on the appointment and powers of an administrator of the estate, if that law so requires, even when, according to the conflict of laws rules contained in the ESR, a foreign law should be applied in place of them; in this respect paragraph 3 of the article also enables the law of third States and the law of Member States other than the State of the forum to be treated differently. The second exception is contained in article 33, which deals with the problems that may arise in relation to estates without a claimant – that is estates for which there is no heir or legatee under a disposition of property upon death and no natural person is an heir by operation of law – solely in relation to assets located on the respective territories of the Member States, thus leaving the solution to the same problem for assets located on the territories of third States to the internal conflict of laws rules of the Member States.

23. Also the rules on jurisdiction contained in chapter II of the ESR (articles 4–19) have a scope that is in principle unlimited and exclusive, in the sense that they delineate the jurisdiction of the Member State courts both as regards relations with one another and also as regards relations with third States, so as not to leave room, subject to very few exceptions, for the application of the national laws of the Member States in this area. In other words, these rules apply equally to successions the international elements of which are all situated within the EU as well as those with connections also outside the EU. The objective pursued by this rule is that already seen in relation to the conflict of laws provisions of the instrument, namely that of achieving a codification in the sector that is as uniform and complete as possible so as to remove or reduce to a minimum the difficulties and intricacies that may be created by the continuing validity of a variety of national laws with diverging or

[67] On these two limitations, see nos. 17 and 21.

contradictory content. This tendency towards completeness reflects the approach followed by most new regulations of the EU in the area of private international law, such as regulation no. 4/2009 on maintenance obligations and the two recent regulations of 2016 implementing enhanced cooperation in the areas of matrimonial property regimes and the property consequences of registered partnerships.[68] Less recent instruments, starting from regulation no. 44/2001 on jurisdiction and the recognition and enforcement of judgments in civil and commercial matters and the 1968 Brussels Convention which preceded it by contrast limited the scope of the rules on jurisdiction contained in them in various ways. The project which had been devised to extend the scope of the jurisdictional provisions of regulation no. 44/2001, applicable in principle only when the defendant is domiciled in a Member State, to cases in which the defendant is domiciled elsewhere, was abandoned during work on its recast made through regulation no. 1215/2012, which maintained this limitation.[69]

24. An exception to the completeness and exclusive applicability of the rules on jurisdiction laid down by the ESR is contained in article 19, which permits the courts of a Member State to adopt provisional, including protective, measures as may be available under the law of that State even when, according to the jurisdictional criteria established by the act, jurisdiction to rule on the substance of the matter lies with the courts of another Member State. As is well known, the Court of Justice has however displayed in its interpretative case law a clear tendency to restrict considerably the scope and effects of the analogous provisions included

[68] See articles 3–8 of regulation no. 4/2009 and the respective articles 4–13 of regulations no. 2016/1103 and no. 2016/1104 (the latter are cited in footnote 45).

[69] Also regulation no. 2201/2003 concerning jurisdiction and the recognition and enforcement of judgments in matrimonial matters and the matters of parental responsibility (Brussels II-*bis*) allows in article 7, with respect to cases in which no court of a Member State has jurisdiction under its rules, the survival in matrimonial matters of a 'residual jurisdiction' to be determined by the domestic legislation of the Member States. A proposal presented by the Commission on 17 July 2006 (COM/2006/399 final) which provided, amongst other things, for the extension of the geographical scope of the jurisdictional provisions of the instrument was set aside. Similarly, regulation no. 1346/2000 on insolvency proceedings, article 3 of which conferred jurisdiction to open insolvency proceedings on the courts of the Member State within the territory of which the centre of the debtor's main interests was situated, did not exclude the possibility that, in cases in which it was situated in a third country, the courts of the Member States could establish jurisdiction on different grounds provided for by their respective internal laws, and the new regulation no. 2015/848 on insolvency proceedings (recast) did not affect this possibility.

in other EU instruments addressing the international jurisdiction of the Member States, and there is obviously no reason to doubt that the Court would confirm its position also in relation to the ESR.[70] A second exception appears to be necessary in relation to jurisdiction over disputes concerning the future succession of an individual, that is those that may arise before it is opened, such as example disputes concerning the validity of an agreement as to succession of or a lifetime renunciation of inheritance. The general jurisdictional criterion adopted by the ESR in article 4 is based on the habitual residence of the deceased at the time of death, and the implementation of the subsidiary jurisdictional criteria listed in article 10 also presupposes that it is possible to establish the country in which he was habitually resident at that time. In situations such as that referred to above, the jurisdictional provisions of the regulation cannot thus be applied. It follows that the only possible way of avoiding a denial of justice involves a conclusion that the instrument implicitly permits the Member States to apply their internal rules on jurisdiction within the area not covered by those contained in the regulation.[71] Decisions issued on the basis of the aforementioned national rules on jurisdiction will naturally have to apply the conflict of laws provisions of the ESR and will have to be recognised and enforced in the other Member States pursuant to chapter IV of the instrument.[72]

A further element of incompleteness of the legal regime established by the ESR in this area, which does not however concern the allocation of jurisdiction but the regulation of its actual exercise, lies in the fact that the provisions contained in articles 17 and 18 on *lis pendens* and related

[70] See ECJ, case 125/79, *Denilauler* v. *Couchet Frères* [1980] ECR 1553; case C-261/90, *Mario Reichert* v. *Dresdner Bank AG* [1992] ECR I-2149; case C-391/95, *Van Uden Maritime BV* v. *Deco-Line* [1998] ECR I-7091; case 99/96, *Mietz* v. *Intership Yachting Sneek BV* [1999] ECR I-2277; case 104/03, *St. Paul Diary Industries NV* v. *Unibel Exser BVBA* [2005] ECR I-3481.

[71] See on this point Davì and Zanobetti, 'Il nuovo diritto internazionale privato delle successioni', p. 113 *et seq*; Davì and Zanobetti, *Il nuovo diritto internazionale privato europeo*, p. 198. During the preparatory work for the ESR, in order to avoid the regulatory gap described, the Max Planck Institute for Comparative and International Private Law had suggested ('Comments', pp. 568, 570–571) the introduction into article 4 of a new paragraph formulated as follows: 'In matters relating to the future succession of a person, the courts where the person is habitually resident shall be competent'. However, this proposal was not accepted.

[72] The application of the provisions of the ESR on the recognition and mutual enforcement of decisions between the Member States is not subject to the condition that these decisions must have been adopted on the basis of the jurisdictional rules laid down by the instrument, as it is sufficient for that purpose that the decision concerned originate from a Member State and relate to succession.

actions are only applicable within relations between the Member States. Coordination with procedures pending before the courts of third States is thus left – in the same manner, as mentioned above, to the recognition and enforcement of the decisions issued by them[73] – to the domestic legislation of the Member States. The absence of any uniform European legislation on the subject is essentially the result of the logic of reciprocity according to which these problems have been addressed, along the lines of the Brussels Convention, by all EU private international law instruments adopted until the recent review of regulation no. 44/2001 on jurisdiction and the recognition and enforcement of judgments in civil and commercial matters (Brussels I) by the recast regulation no. 1215/2012 (Brussels I-*bis*), articles 33 and 34 of which for the first time lay down rules applicable in this area. The fact that the ESR was enacted before the process of drafting regulation no. 1215/2012 was completed is probably why it has not been possible to extend the progress achieved by the latter in this area to the former.

25. The scope of the ESR *ratione personae* is likewise unlimited, since it may also cover the successions of individuals who were not related to any Member State at the time of death by any personal connecting factors, such as in particular residence, domicile or citizenship. In order for it to be possible to actually deal with the succession in such cases before the courts of the Member States, it is however necessary that they have jurisdiction according to the rules laid down in the regulation. This requirement may be complied with in practice when the criteria of subsidiary jurisdiction laid down by article 10, paragraphs 1(b) and 2, are fulfilled, or when the prerequisites are met for the activation of the *forum necessitatis* provided for under article 11.

26. The temporal scope of the ESR is specified in articles 83 and 84. The latter provision, which follows the same pattern as the corresponding rules contained in most other EU instruments concerning judicial cooperation in civil matters, distinguishes between the date on which the instrument entered into force and the date on which its effects start to apply. Accordingly, in compliance with the general principle laid down in article 297.1 TFEU, the regulation entered into force on the twentieth day after its publication in the *Official Journal of the European Union*, i.e. on 16 August 2012, whilst its application started on 17 August 2015. The fundamental reason for stipulating such a long period of time between the two dates lies in the concern of ensuring that the Member

[73] See no. 21.

States are able to introduce into their respective legislation all amendments that might prove to be necessary, in particular to conform to the new European Certificate of Succession.[74] Having become applicable since 17 August 2015, the ESR governs all successions opened on or after that day. Thus, the validity and effectiveness of the dispositions of property upon death and of choices of law relating to these successions must be assessed on the basis of the law applicable according to its provisions, even though those acts may have been made prior to that time. This does not in any way amount to a retroactive application of the ESR, since successions opened prior to the date in question will continue to be regulated by the laws to which they were previously subject according to the domestic conflict of laws provisions of the Member States (or of the international conventions concluded by them, where applicable), even if a dispute relating to them were to arise at a later date. It is only a consequence of the applicability of the instrument to the full range of aspects relating to succession that it governs. However, the ESR has not failed to take due account of the fact that the change in the law applicable to succession in the Member States resulting from its provisions, combined with the obvious unpredictability of the time of death, could have had the effect of rendering uncertain and unverifiable the validity and effectiveness of legal acts and transactions carried out prior to that date but relating to a succession that was opened subsequently. Article 83 thus contains several transitional provisions aimed at eliminating this risk. In particular, paragraph 2 of the article acknowledges the formal and substantive validity of choices of law made prior to 17 August 2015 in relation to successions opened after that date (the only to which the ESR applies) if they meet the conditions laid down in chapter III of the instrument or if they are valid in accordance with the rules of private international law which were in force, at the time the choice was made, in the State in which the deceased had his habitual residence or in any of the States whose nationality he possessed. Paragraph 3 extends this rule to the formal and substantive admissibility and validity of dispositions of

[74] The date of entry into force of articles 77 and 78 concerning certain information which must be provided by the Member States was brought forward by article 84 to 16 November 2014 (the date of 16 January 2014, which had mistakenly been indicated in the original text of the regulation as published in the *Official Journal*, was subsequently rectified by a corrigendum which may be found in OJ 2013 no. L60, 2 March 2013, p. 140); similarly, the date of entry into force of articles 79, 80 and 81 concerning certain acts which must be carried out by the Commission, consisting mainly in the preparation of the forms intended to facilitate the operation of the ESR, was brought forward by the same article to 5 July 2012.

property upon death by supplementing the list of the States referred to above with the addition of the Member State (if different) of the authority dealing with the succession. The rules under examination are supplemented by paragraph 4 of the same article, which addresses the problem which may result from the fact that, even though a disposition of property upon death may be admissible and valid, it may however be deprived of effect by its contrast with the mandatory provisions of the *lex successionis* which grant forced heirship rights to certain close relatives of the deceased. The provision stipulates that, if a disposition of property upon death was made prior to the date in question in conformity with the requirements of the law that the deceased could have chosen in accordance with the ESR, that law shall be deemed to have been chosen as the law applicable to the succession. Since the law which the testator may choose under the terms of the regulation is that of the State or of one of the States of which he is a national, article 83 thus takes specific account of the fact that, before the instrument became applicable within the Member States, the national law of the deceased was that called upon to govern the succession under the majority of their respective conflict of laws systems.

V. The Key Principles of the ESR

27. The entire system of rules contained in the ESR on jurisdiction, the applicable law, the recognition and enforcement of decisions, the acceptance and execution of authentic instruments and the creation of the European Certificate of Succession has been constructed around four fundamental guiding principles: the unity of succession, or the monist principle; the unity between jurisdiction and applicable law, or the parallelism between *forum* and *jus*; the promotion of certainty and ease of succession planning; and the spatial continuity of the legal regime applicable to the succession. These principles share the common feature that they are all intended to achieve the principal objectives of the ESR as described in recital 7, that is removing the obstacles to free movement – and, more generally, ensuring adequate protection of the interests – of persons who, absent a uniform regulation common to the Member States, could encounter significant difficulties in effectively organising their succession in advance or in asserting their rights in relation to a succession with cross-border implications.[75] However, these principles

[75] The same objectives, considered from the viewpoint of their relationship with the principle of subsidiarity as set out in article 5 TEU, are reasserted by recital 80. For

are interrelated also in the sense that they mutually presuppose one another insofar as the possibility for each of them to achieve to the full the intended result is the product of their joint operation within the context of a single regulatory framework in which the combination of the almost automatic mutual recognition of decisions with the unification of jurisdictional criteria and the applicable conflict of laws rules has in practice given rise to a situation that is not very different from that existing within an individual State. For example, the operation of the principle of the unity of succession, which enables the many difficulties that may result from the subjection of the various assets comprising the estate to different laws and jurisdictions to be avoided,[76] is ensured within relations between the Member States by the fact that the principle in question is accepted by all of these States, which also recognise the decisions given on its basis in each of them and likewise apply to the succession the same conflict of laws rules. The implementation of the principle of the unity of succession is thus closely related to the spatial continuity of the legal regime introduced by the ESR. By contrast, as regards the assets comprising the estate that are situated in non-Member States and consequently fall under their exclusive material control, the effectiveness of the uniform solutions adopted on European level is not achievable without the consent of the States in question, which obviously cannot be obtained where they regulate succession differently and moreover refuse to recognise the jurisdiction of the courts of the EU Member States over those assets.[77] Similarly, the European Certificate of Succession – which is intended to facilitate and expedite the assertion

a more detailed formulation of these objectives, see also (earlier no. 4) the Summary of the Impact Assessment accompanying the proposal for the ESR presented by the Commission in 2009.

[76] See on these difficulties no. 30.

[77] The link between the creation by a more or less significant number of States of an internationally uniform private international law regime of the succession and the practical possibility of implementing the unitary principle at least within their mutual relations has been stressed by many authors: see, as regards the ESR, R. Hausmann, 'Community Instrument on International Successions and Wills', in C. Baruffi and R. Cafari Panico (eds), *Le nuove competenze comunitarie. Obbligazioni alimentari e successioni* (Padova, 2011), p. 158; P. Lagarde, 'Présentation du règlement sur les successions', in Khairallah and Revillard (eds), *Droit européen des successions*, pp. 7–8, 11; P. Franzina, 'Ragioni, valori e collocazione sistematica della disciplina internazionalprivatistica europea delle successioni *mortis causa*', in Franzina and Leandro (eds), *Il diritto internazionale privato europeo*, p. 9; with reference to the 1989 Hague Convention on the Law Applicable to Succession to the Estates of Deceased Persons, Davì, 'Riflessioni', pp. 312–313.

by heirs, legatees and the executors or administrators of an estate of their respective capacities and the exercise of their respective rights or powers of administration in a Member State other than that in which it was issued – is grounded on the unification of the conflict of laws rules realised by the ESR in this area, by virtue of which those rights and powers as determined by the issuing authority are identical throughout all Member States.[78] Therefore, the analysis of the key principles underpinning the ERS must constantly be carried out taking account of their mutual links.

A. *Unity of Succession*

28. The principle of unity of succession, or the monist principle, applies within the ESR both to jurisdiction and to the governing law. The meaning and value of this principle are at the same time spatial, or territorial, as well as functional. In the former sense, the principle implies that one single judicial authority has jurisdiction to rule on the succession and one single law is applicable to it, even when the assets comprising the estate are spread throughout different countries. In the latter sense it implies that the competence of the sole authority vested with jurisdiction and that of the sole applicable law cover all stages of the succession, and thus not only its opening and its devolution but also its administration, including the sale of assets and the payment of creditors, the transfer of ownership of the assets to the heirs and legatees and the sharing-out of the estate. In this way, the ESR seeks to avoid both the 'horizontal' and the 'vertical' splitting of the legal regime applicable to the succession. There are, though, a number of exceptions which are justified by the need to leave some space for the implementation of other principles or to satisfy different requirements.[79] The unitary connecting factor used by the ESR in order to give effect to this monist principle is the same with regard to the determination of jurisdiction and of the governing law, namely the last habitual residence of the deceased: articles 4 and 21 provide that the jurisdiction of the courts and respectively the application of the law of the country in which the residence in question was situated refer to 'the succession as a whole'. Article 22 grants the deceased the faculty of

[78] Conversely, the lack of harmonisation between the conflict of laws provisions of the contracting States was, as mentioned in no. 6, the main reason why the 1973 Hague Convention Concerning the International Administration of the Estates of Deceased Persons was substantially unsuccessful.

[79] On these exceptions see nos. 31 and 32.

subjecting his succession, by a declaration in the form of a disposition of property upon death, to the law of the State whose nationality he possesses, but also this faculty may only be exercised in respect of 'his succession as a whole'.[80]

29. The preference given by the ESR to the connecting factor of habitual residence, in spite of the fact that most domestic conflict of laws systems of Member States that also adopted the unitary principle by contrast provided for the application to the succession of the national law of the deceased, is due to considerations which are partly technical and partly political. As to the technical aspect, this choice is based on the assumption that the country of the last habitual residence of a person is normally that with which he and his succession are most closely linked, given that it usually includes the centre of his personal and economic life and often also the other objective and subjective elements of the succession, such as the assets comprising the estate, the heirs, the legatees and the creditors, the presence of whom facilitates the process of administration and liquidation. Whilst in some cases the deceased may have maintained closer links with the country of which he is a national or with a previous country of residence, the former scenario is statistically more frequent. The subjection of the succession to the law of the place of the last habitual residence of the deceased also offers the important practical benefit of ensuring, at least as a rule, the coincidence between the court with jurisdiction and the applicable law, since the criterion of habitual residence is used by articles 4 and 21 as an instrument for determining both issues. As regards the political aspect, there is no doubt that the use of the objective connecting factor of habitual residence rather than nationality, which was previously used in many Member States, is conducive to the objective of reinforcing and developing economic and social cohesion within the Union, as it favours the integration of European citizens who move from one Member State to another, as well as of third country immigrants, into the social and legal environment of the host State.[81] For this reason, the precedence afforded to the first

[80] Naturally, since the ESR only regulates succession from the viewpoint of private international law and not also substantive law, it does not provide for any limit of that type with regard to the possible scope of testamentary provisions or agreements as to succession.

[81] See on this last point, *inter alia*, Dutta, 'Succession and Wills', p. 565 *et seq*.; Davì and Zanobetti, 'Il nuovo diritto internazionale privato delle successioni', p. 30 *et seq*.; Davì and Zanobetti, *Il nuovo diritto internazionale privato europeo*, p. 44 *et seq*.; Franzina, 'Ragioni, valori e collocazione sistematica', p. 13 *et seq*.; also the Commission, in the explanatory memorandum annexed to the proposal for the ESR presented by it in 2009, justified (p. 6,

necessitatis introduced by article 11 with the aim of remedying situations involving a denial of justice may result, albeit exceptionally, in a fragmentation of jurisdiction as both the wording and the rationale of this provision do not appear to exclude the possibility of an exercise of jurisdiction limited to the succession of the assets that are situated in a non-Member State in which, due to extraordinary reasons, 'proceedings cannot reasonably be brought or conducted or would be impossible'.[90] A further split of the unity of the jurisdiction is finally admitted by article 12, which grants the seised court the discretionary power to decide, at the request of one of the parties, not to rule on the succession in relation to assets situated in a non-Member State where it may be expected that its decision in respect of those assets would for any reason not be recognised or enforced in the State in question. This renunciation of an exercise of jurisdiction which would be futile, given that it would result in a decision bound to remain a dead letter, fulfils a purpose of prevention of a conflict with the position of the legal system of the State in which the assets are situated, the viewpoint of which would in any case prevail.

32. The exceptions from the principle of the unity of the law applicable to the succession are more numerous. The most significant of these seek to render succession planning more certain and easier or perform a coordination function between legal systems. The former objective is pursued by articles 24 and 25, which subject the admissibility and substantive validity of testamentary dispositions and, respectively, of agreements as to succession (as well as, for the latter, their binding effects between the parties) to the so-called hypothetical succession law, that is the law which would have been applicable to the succession of the person or persons involved had they died on the day on which the testamentary dispositions were made or the agreements were concluded. The purpose of these provisions is to ensure stability in the organisation of the succession, avoiding the risk that a change in the habitual residence of the deceased that was not expected or was even unforeseeable at the time

principes de base du nouveau règlement européen sur les successions', *Rev crit dr int priv* (2013), p. 702; Bonomi, 'Introduction', pp. 42–43; A. Bonomi, 'Article 10', in A. Bonomi and P. Wautelet, *Le droit européen des successions. Commentaire du Règlement n° 650/2012 du 4 juillet 2012* (Bruxelles, 2013), p. 222; the latter author observes that a means for avoiding the occurrence of positive jurisdictional conflicts with the courts of non-Member States could have consisted in the subjection of the exercise of powers laid down by article 10 to the condition of the lack of jurisdiction or of inactivity by foreign courts, as is done by article 88 of the Swiss act on private international law.

90 See in this respect Lagarde, 'Les principes de base', p. 703.

the dispositions of property upon death in question were made might result in the applicability of a law which considers them to be inadmissible or invalid (or which, for agreements as to succession, regulates their effects in a different manner).[91] All of the remaining aspects of the succession, including the possible existence of forced heirship rights, are naturally to be governed by the law normally applicable to them according to the general rules contained in the ESR, subject to the further exceptions specified below. Article 27, which pursues the same aim of improving the certainty and ease of succession planning by reducing to a minimum the risks for the formal validity of dispositions of property upon death that may be caused by the considerable discrepancy between the prerequisites imposed upon the form of such dispositions under the national legislation of different States, sets out a catalogue of eight alternatively applicable laws, in accordance with any of which a testamentary disposition or an agreement as to succession may be validly drawn up. As mentioned above, this catalogue is borrowed by the Hague Convention of 1961 on the Conflicts of Laws Relating to the Form of Testamentary Dispositions, to which numerous Member States are parties.[92]

On the other hand, article 30 performs a function of coordination with the positions of conflict of laws systems of countries (be they Member or not) different from that whose law is designated to govern the succession by conferring priority over this law to the special rules of the State in which certain immovable property, enterprises or other particular categories of assets are situated which, 'for economic, family or social considerations, impose restrictions concerning or affecting the succession in respect of those assets', provided that, according to the law of the State concerned, the special rules in question 'are applicable irrespective of the law applicable to the succession'. One of the principal benefits created by the introduction of this limit to the principle of the unity of the law governing the succession is that it facilitates the

[91] As already indicated in no. 18, article 26 contains a list of the issues which are to be included within the notion of substantive validity of dispositions of property upon death. On the provisions contained in articles 24 and 25 see also nos. 41–43.

[92] On the relationship between the ESR and this convention, see more generally no. 5. It should be added that the applicability on an alternative basis of two different laws is provided for, with the same purpose of simplification, by article 28 as regards the form of declarations of acceptance or waiver of the succession, of a legacy or of a reserved share and the form of declarations designed to limit liability for the deceased's debts (the law ordinarily applicable to the succession pursuant to articles 21 and 22 or the law of the State in which the person making the declaration has his or her habitual residence).

recognition and enforcement of decisions in the State, Member or not, in which the assets are situated.[93] Another exception from the unitary principle which is accepted by the ESR in order to improve the coordination between the respective positions of the different legal systems concerned is that which may result from the admission, under the conditions laid down in article 34, of the partial *renvoi* or the multiple partial *renvois* which may be made, especially when immovable property is involved, by the law of a 'scissionist' State in relation to an estate comprised of assets situated in two or more States. In order to prevent this outcome, during the *travaux préparatoires* for the instrument several commentators had proposed that *renvoi* be excluded where it resulted in scission.[94] However, the wording of article 34 which was finally adopted does not contain any such limitation. It may be concluded that the objective of seeking coordination through *renvoi* was considered to be more important than the concern of avoiding the introduction in this way of a certain degree of scission within the European legal area. Further much narrower restrictions on the operation of the unitary principle may in addition result from the application of specific provisions intended to satisfy various needs or to achieve particular goals, such as article 29 (special rules on the appointment and powers of an administrator of the estate in certain situations), article 31 (adaptation of rights *in rem*), article 32 (*commorientes*) and article 33 (estate without a claimant). Also a merely partial incompatibility of the foreign law with the public policy of the forum State (article 35) may lead to a split in the unity of the rules applicable to the succession.

B. *Unity of Jurisdiction and Applicable Law*

33. In adopting the general connecting factor of the last habitual residence of the deceased as the principal criterion for determining both the court having jurisdiction to rule on the succession and the governing law (as provided for under articles 4 and 21.1 respectively), the ESR ensures that the competent court will apply the internal law of the forum in most cases. The achievement of this coincidence between

[93] A similar provision was contained in article 15 of the Hague Convention of 1989 on the Law Applicable to Succession to the Estates of Deceased Persons; on the relationship between article 30 and this latter see in greater detail footnote 133.

[94] See, for example, Dutta, 'Succession and Wills', p. 558 *et seq.*; A. Bonomi, 'Prime considerazioni sulla proposta di regolamento sulle successioni', *Riv dir int priv proc* (2010), p. 911.

jurisdiction and applicable law is underlined by recital 27[95] and is one of the main features of the instrument. Its purpose is to avoid the difficulties associated with the application of foreign law which, as is well known, in the field of succession are often greater than in other areas, especially as regards the regulation of the administration and liquidation of the estate, the modalities of the transfer of assets to the heirs or legatees and the conditions, formal requirements and effects of acceptance or waiver. In fact, these aspects share the common feature of a close interplay between substantive and procedural issues, which may at times make it extremely complex or even almost impossible to coordinate the respective application of the procedural law of the forum and of a foreign succession law, in particular since the latter not infrequently requires the competent court to adopt measures or to perform functions or exercise powers for which the law of the forum does not contain adequate provision or which are entirely unknown to it.[96] It is precisely in order to avoid such difficulties that, before the ESR came into force in the Member States, the national conflict of laws systems of some of them subjected the transmission and/or administration of the succession to the internal law of the forum, even where the remaining issues fell to be regulated by a foreign law.[97] However, this functional scission of the succession risked replacing the dissociation between the procedural law of the forum State and the substantive foreign law applicable to the merits of the case with a different dissociation between the law applicable to the transmission of the succession and the law applicable to its devolution, which was in its turn liable to give rise to problems of characterisation and adaptation that would not necessarily be less complex. Insofar as it can be kept free from exceptions,[98] the solution adopted by the ESR may thus be regarded as the best as it enables the activities relating to the administration and distribution of the estate to be simplified, expedited and rendered less cumbersome; further advantages that are worth mentioning consist in the elimination both of the difficulties associated with the establishment of the exact content of the foreign law and of the problems of

[95] 'The rules of this Regulation are devised so as to ensure that the authority dealing with succession will, in most situations, be applying its own law.'

[96] For two extensive analyses of all these problems see Ferid, 'Le rattachement autonome', p. 106 *et seq.*, and Bonomi, 'Successions internationales', p. 330 *et seq.*

[97] See, e.g. article 28.2 of the Austrian act on private international law, articles 10:149 and 10:150 of the Dutch civil code and article 15 of chapter 26 of the Finnish code of inheritance; see also article 92.2 of the Swiss act on private international law.

[98] See on these exceptions nos. 34–36.

compatibility with the *ordre public* of the State of the forum to which its application may at times give rise.

34. The coincidence in principle between *forum* and *jus* created by the ESR may obviously be disrupted by a *professio juris* by the testator in favour of his national law in accordance with article 22. However, taking account of the important practical benefits which its preservation insofar as possible may offer, the European legislator considered it appropriate to make available to the parties concerned an instrument for restoring the destroyed unity, provided that the law designated by the testator is the law of a Member State. In fact, in this case article 5 allows them to conclude an agreement conferring exclusive jurisdiction to rule on any succession matter on a court or the courts of that State.[99] Moreover, pursuant to articles 6(a) and 7(a), even in the absence of such a choice-of-court agreement, the courts of the Member State whose law was designated by the deceased shall have jurisdiction if a court of a different Member State, seised on the basis of one of the jurisdictional criteria laid down in articles 4 and 10, declines jurisdiction in their favour upon request by one of the parties, on the grounds that they are better placed to rule on the succession. Finally, article 9 adds that, where not all of the parties to the proceedings are also parties to the choice-of-court agreement, the court seised on the basis of the latter shall continue to exercise jurisdiction if the parties to the proceedings that are not parties to the agreement enter an appearance without contesting the jurisdiction of the court.

35. A further factor the intervention of which may negate the unity in principle between *forum* and *jus* under the regulation is the operation of the 'escape clause' or 'exception clause' contained in article 21.2, according to which '[w]here, by way of exception, it is clear from all the circumstances of the case that, at the time of death, the deceased was manifestly more closely connected with a State other than the State' in which the deceased had his or her last habitual residence, then 'the law applicable to the succession shall be the law of that other State'. The introduction of this provision into the ESR, which was not included in the 2009 Commission proposal, has been criticised by most commentators.[100] In effect, the clause

[99] Article 7(c) specifies that the jurisdiction of the courts of the Member State of the chosen law may be expressly accepted by the parties even after the proceedings have been initiated.

[100] See in particular H Dörner, 'EuErbVO: Die Verordnung zum Internationalen Erb- und Erbverfahrensrecht ist im Kraft!', *ZEV* (2012), pp. 510–511; F. M. Wilke, 'Das internationale Erbrecht nach der neuen EU-Erbrechtsverordnung', *RIW* (2012), p. 605;

under examination has several drawbacks given that, besides being prejudicial to the unity of principle between *forum* and *jus* intended by the regulation, it creates significant risks for legal certainty and the foreseeability of the applicable law, and consequently tends to favour the emergence of disputes between the parties involved; moreover, an investigation aimed at identifying the State with which the deceased was most closely connected, in particular in dubious or 'atypical' situations, must equally be carried out within the framework of the ordinary process for determining his last habitual residence;[101] it follows that, in most cases, the conduct of the same search a second time outside of that process would amount to pointless duplication. Moreover, the ESR itself does not fail to point out in recital 23 that '[i]n order to determine the habitual residence, the authority dealing with the succession should make an overall assessment of the circumstances of the life of the deceased during the years preceding his death and at the time of his death, taking account of all relevant factual elements' and that '(t)he habitual residence thus determined should reveal a close and stable connection with the State concerned'. It is likely that the inclusion of this clause in the regulation was born out of specific concerns, such as those of the Member States whose laws grant the close relatives of the deceased mandatory heirship rights, that the establishment of habitual residence abroad could be used by the testator in order to thwart these rights or the concern of certain northern European States that any of their nationals who spent the last few years of their lives in countries with a better climate could end up having the validity or effectiveness of their dispositions of property upon death called into question due to unexpected changes in the governing law. It may however be presumed that, given the disruptive effect that the operation of such a clause produces on the unity of jurisdiction and applicable law which the ESR seeks to achieve, the courts of the Member States will be reluctant to have recourse to it and will

Lagarde, 'Les principes de base', p. 701; F. Boulanger, 'Révolution juridique ou compromis en trompe-l'oeil? À propos du nouveau règlement européen sur les successions internationales', *JCP* (2012), p. 1122; Davì and Zanobetti, 'Il nuovo diritto internazionale privato delle successioni', p. 34 *et seq*; Davì and Zanobetti, *Il nuovo diritto internazionale privato europeo*, p. 51 *et seq*.

101 The principal situations involving doubts which may arise should include those in which the deceased lived between two or more countries or travelled from one country to another without settling permanently in any of them, those in which he resided for a period of time of some duration in a foreign country due to work or study reasons or to receive medical treatment, whilst however maintaining close and constant links with the State of origin, and those in which he moved to a new country shortly prior to death: see thereabout recitals 24 and 25 of the regulation.

rather prefer to address the problem of identifying the State with which the deceased was more closely connected as part of the interpretation of the concept of habitual residence, in such a way as to be able to determine the competent judicial authority and the applicable law as often as possible on the basis of the same criterion.

36. In addition to the effect which may be caused by the *professio juris* or the implementation of the 'escape clause' provided for under article 21.2, there are other elements which may undermine the parallelism between *forum* and *jus* established by the ESR. Since this parallelism stems from the use of the connecting factor of the law of the last habitual residence of the deceased in order to determine both jurisdiction and the applicable law, its termination may result either from the assumption of jurisdiction by Member States courts on the basis of other criteria, or from the subjection of certain aspects of the succession to different laws. The former scenario arises when the deceased had his last habitual residence in a third State, the law of which is thus that which will govern the succession, whilst the jurisdiction of a Member State court is founded on one of the subsidiary criteria listed in article 10, or when the conditions for recourse to *forum necessitatis* established under article 11 are met. However, in such cases it is still possible that the broken unity of *forum* and *jus* may be reconstituted by *renvoi* by the law of the foreign habitual residence to the law of the forum.[102] The latter scenario arises in the situations provided for under articles 24, 25, 27, 28 and 30 discussed earlier.[103]

C. *Promotion of Certainty and Ease of Succession Planning*

37. The creation of the most favourable conditions possible for promoting certainty and ease of succession planning in situations involving links with the laws of two or more countries is one of the core objectives of the ESR due to the significant contribution which it may provide to simplifying the lives of citizens in the European judicial area and removing the legal obstacles on the effective enjoyment of their basic freedoms

[102] Also the application of article 13, according to which the courts of the Member State of the habitual residence of any person who, under the law governing the succession, may make before a court a declaration of acceptance or waiver of the succession, of a legacy or of a reserved share or a declaration designed to limit the liability of the person concerned for the debts of the estate, shall have jurisdiction to receive such declarations, may give rise to a mismatch between *forum* and *jus*.

[103] See no. 32 and in particular, with regard to article 28, footnote 92.

of movement and establishment within the internal market. This functional link with the requirements of the internal market is repeatedly stressed in recitals 7, 37 and 80 of the regulation. The main instruments intended to achieve the said objectives consist in the granting to the testator of an albeit limited right to chose the law applicable to his succession, in subjecting the admissibility and substantive validity of dispositions of property upon death (and for agreements as to succession also their binding effects between the parties) to the 'hypothetical' succession law and in the adoption of a substantially favourable stance towards the possibility of recourse to agreements as to succession, in spite of the fact that they are prohibited under the national law of several Member States. Also the applicability on an alternative basis of the laws included in the copious list drafted in article 27 for the purposes of establishing the formal validity of dispositions of property upon death and the transitional provisions contained in article 83 aim to achieve the same purposes.[104]

38. The right granted to the testator by article 22 to choose the law of the State whose nationality he possesses as the law to govern his succession is basically intended to offset the possible inconveniences that may result from the exclusive and compulsory use of the connecting factor of the last habitual residence; at the same time, it is also a manifestation within the particular field of succession of the general trend towards liberalisation within European private international law. With regard to the former aspect it must be borne in mind that, although it might legitimately be assumed that the State of the last habitual residence of the deceased is ordinarily that with which the succession is most closely connected, the possibility that there may be stronger links with a different State in certain cases must not be ruled out entirely. This may occur in particular in relation to the succession of persons who frequently change residence between countries or who, whilst having transferred their residence to a foreign country for more or less contingent reasons, and even for a short period of time, have nonetheless maintained more significant relations with their country of origin, not only on a psychological and emotional level but also in material and financial terms. In situations of this type, the application of the national law may often be better suited to the expectations and requirements of the interested parties. Even more important is the practical benefit offered by the faculty to opt for the *lex patriae* of ensuring predictability and stability over time

[104] On these two articles see nos. 32 and 26 respectively.

of the law applicable to the succession, thus protecting its organisation in advance against the risks that may result from the difficulty that sometimes exists to establish the country of habitual residence of a person[105] or from a transfer of residence abroad that is unexpected or the duration of which cannot be determined *ex ante*. Within the context of a conflict of laws regime established by an instrument of uniform private international law, such as the ESR, which is binding upon a considerable number of States, the level of certainty and stability in the governing law which can be obtained through a *professio juris* is moreover enhanced by the guarantee that its efficacy will be recognised in all States in which the instrument applies.

Under the latter aspect, the testator's ability to choose between the respective laws of the State of which he or she is a national and of the State of habitual residence allows the testator to organise his or her succession on the basis of the system of rules with the substantive content that best meets his or her needs. The testator is thereby given the opportunity to reap the benefits which may result from differences in the national legislation of the Member States without the converse risk of encountering any obstacles to the preservation of his or her rights. The granting of this right of option to European citizens thus contributes appreciably to promoting their mobility and progressive social integration within a legal area that is larger than the territorial limits of a single country, gradually reducing their subjection to the dominion of State power and the importance of the ties linking them with any particular national society, since they are allowed to avoid on a significant scale the mandatory force of the laws of the different States with which they are more or less closely linked. In this way, the liberalising effect brought about by the role ascribed to party autonomy under the ESR not only protects the interests of individual citizens but also contributes to favouring the development of European integration.

39. The right to choose to subject the succession to the national law of the deceased is regulated by article 22 liberally, as the provision allows persons holding two or more nationalities to choose the law of one of them[106] and also allows the choice of the law of a nationality that is not

[105] As mentioned in no. 35, these risks are increased by the addition of an 'exception clause' made by article 21.2 of the ESR to the objective connecting factor of the deceased's last habitual residence.

[106] This solution is consistent with the settled case law of the European Court of Justice which, when the two or more nationalities held concurrently are all of Member States, maintains that any refusal to recognise the legal effects to which their possession may

held by the testator at the time it was chosen, provided that he or she holds it at the time of death. Yet, a partial choice of law which would render two or more laws applicable to the succession is not permitted, since such a possibility would contrast with the unitary principle which ESR attempts to preserve to the utmost.[107] On the other hand, European lawmakers' preference for the testator's autonomy has not been pushed so far as to permit a law other than his national law to be chosen, even though proposals to this effect were submitted from various quarters during the *travaux préparatoires* for the regulation. Particular emphasis was placed on the utility of recognising the possibility of choosing the law of the country of habitual residence at the time the choice was made.[108] However, this suggestion was not accepted, mainly due to the concern, which was made explicit in recital 38, of preventing the expectations of members of the testator's family to whom certain legal systems grant forced heirship rights from being frustrated by the designation of the law of the country of a merely temporary foreign residence acquired intentionally for that purpose.[109] These concerns were probably over-stated. Experience has shown that, in systems that allow such a choice, it is quite rare in practice for it to be exploited in order to evade the claims of relatives entitled to a compulsory share, so much so that such attempts may usually be made using less laborious and uncomfortable means than

give rise within the framework of the Union or the introduction of any order of preference between them will be inadmissible: see ECJ, case C-369/90, *Micheletti and others* v. *Delegación del Gobierno en Cantabria* [1992] ECR I-4239; case C-148/02, *Garcia Avello* v. *Belgian State* [2003] ECR I-11613; case C-168/08, *Laszlo Hadadi* v. *Csilla Marta Mesko* [2009] ECR I- 6871.

[107] On this point see also no. 28.

[108] The proposal to grant this right to the testator was made, *inter alia*, by the Deutsches Notarinstitut in the comparative study drawn up by it in cooperation with Professors Dörner and Lagarde on behalf of the Commission, cited in footnote 9 (see Deutsches Notarinstitut, *Conflict of Law of Succession*, p. 105), and by the Max Planck Institute for Comparative and International Private Law, 'Comments', p. 610 *et seq.*; the same right is already admitted under article 5 of the Hague Convention on the Law Applicable to Succession to the Estates of Deceased Persons, although article 24.1(c) and (d) of the convention permits the contracting States to make two different reservations in this regard.

[109] This risk was feared not only by the governments of certain Member States and their respective parliaments but also by the European Parliament which, in recommendation 8 annexed to its resolution with recommendations to the Commission on succession and wills of 16 November 2006, cited in footnote 20, had asked that the regulation to be adopted should ensure that the right granted to the testator to choose the governing law should not 'contravene the fundamental principles of reserving a proportion of the estate for the deceased person's closest relatives laid down by the law objectively applicable to the succession' (OJ 2006 no. C314E, 21 December 2006, p. 346).

the transfer of residence abroad. Furthermore, it must not be forgotten that, absent any choice by the testator, the ESR subjects the succession to the law of the country of his or her last habitual residence. It follows that, also in this case, protection is far from being assured to the expectations of family members against the unfavourable effects that may result from a transfer of residence to a foreign State. At any rate, the possibility of invoking the *ordre public* clause or, insofar as EU law and the law of the Member State concerned permit it, the instrument of *fraude à la loi*,[110] should in principle be sufficient in order to counter any abuses.

The granting of the right under consideration to the testator would on the other hand have entailed some important advantages. It would first have enabled persons who are fully integrated into the social and economic environment of the country in which they reside and who legitimately wish to organise their succession in accordance with the local law rather than with their own national law, with which they may even have lost all contact, to avoid the condition of instability and uncertainty liable to be caused by a transfer abroad. This would have resulted in a clear benefit for the exercise of the freedoms of movement and establishment of European citizens within the Union. Secondly, the ability to choose the law of the country of habitual residence at the time of the designation would have considerably favoured the coordination – which, as is known, is often difficult in international settings – between the rules applicable to the succession and the matrimonial property regime of the deceased, enabling both to be subject to the same law in a high number of

[110] The possibility of invoking *fraude à la loi* is explicitly mentioned in recital 26, albeit without specific reference to the particular problem discussed here. As far as the use of *ordre public* or the public policy clause (contained in article 35 of the ESR) is concerned, it must however be pointed out that the case law of States, be they Member or not, the laws of which grant compulsory heirship rights to the close relatives of the deceased has shown not to confer a truly essential value to the need to protect those rights against the effects of the application of a foreign law that does not recognise them, since most of the decisions given on the topic have refrained from resorting to this clause: see, e.g., in Italian case law, Corte di cassazione 24 June 1996, no. 5832, *Nuova giur civ* (1997), pp. 167–169; in Spain Tribunal Supremo 15 November 1996, *Lowenthal, Rev esp der int* (1997), p. 264, and 21 May 1999, *Denney, Rev esp der int* (1999), p. 756; in Switzerland Tribunal fédéral 17 August 1976, *Hirsch* v. *Cohen, Arrêts du Tribunal fédéral*, vol. 102, p. 136; also in France and Germany the case law of the lower courts has largely held that foreign laws that do not grant family members a reserved portion are not contrary to public policy. For a well-known example of the application of the concept of *fraude à la loi* see the decision issued in France by the Cour d'appel Aix-en-Provence 9 March 1982, *Rev crit dr int priv* (1983), p. 296 *et seq* in the *Caron* case, which was subsequently confirmed by the Cour de Cassation 20 March 1985, *Rev crit dr int priv* (1986), p. 66 *et seq*.

cases. In fact, according to the new EU regulations recently adopted on the subject, the law which is to govern the matrimonial property regime will be that of the country of the first common habitual residence of the spouses after the marriage, and the respective legislation of many Member States already follow the same principle of immutability over time.[111]

40. A significant change made by article 22.2 of the final text of the ESR to the original Commission proposal involves the acceptance, alongside the possibility of a choice of law 'made expressly in a declaration in the form of a disposition of property upon death', also of an implied choice 'demonstrated by the terms of such a disposition'. The main elements that the advocates of this approach generally consider to be capable of enabling the existence of an implicit intention on the part of the testator to subject the succession to a given law to be inferred are comprised of references contained in a disposition of last will to provisions, institutions or concepts that are peculiar to the law in question, as it occurs in the classic example of the establishment of a testamentary trust by a citizen of a common law country; also the recital 39 of the regulation appears to follow such a trend.[112] The provision is undoubtedly destined to give rise to complex and delicate interpretative problems. In fact, it is often difficult to distinguish in practice between situations in which the testator has formulated his dispositions of last will in accordance with his national law simply because he assumed that it was objectively applicable and he was in any case obliged to adapt his dispositions to its content and situations in which he was by contrast inspired by a real intention to choose it, albeit implicitly, as the law regulating his succession. However, it is only in the latter case that an implicit choice may strictly speaking be deemed to have been made, so much so as in the former case the belief that the *lex patriae* applied could have resulted from various reasons, including in particular a mistake or the fact that, at the time the

[111] Pursuant to article 22.1(a) of regulation no. 2016/1103 cited in footnote 45, the solution to these coordination problems will however be facilitated, at least to a certain extent, in the Member States participating to the enhancing cooperation by the recognition to the spouses of the right to choose the law of the State of habitual residence of one of them at the time the choice was made as being applicable to their matrimonial property regime. Such coordination is envisaged also in article 22 of regulation no. 2016/1104 regarding the property consequences of registered partnerships (also cited in footnote 45).

[112] According to the recital '[a] choice of law could be regarded as demonstrated by a disposition of property upon death where, for instance, the deceased had referred in his disposition to specific provisions of the law of the State of his nationality or where he had otherwise mentioned that law'.

dispositions of property upon death at issue were drawn up, the testator was habitually resident in the country of which he or she was a national or even that the succession entirely lacked any international elements, whilst the transfer of the interested party's residence abroad occurred at a later stage. However, the proponents of the introduction of this provision into the ESR do not appear to have attached much weight to the distinction under consideration, as their main aim was not to establish the actual will of the testator but rather to set up a device intended mainly to safeguard the validity and efficacy of dispositions of last will adopted in accordance with the law which the testator, rightly or wrongly, considered to be applicable to his succession at the time of their confection.[113] When construed in a sense so broad as to include the first of the two hypotheses referred to earlier, an implicit *professio juris* would in practice end up turning into a full blown legal fiction with the sole objective of favouring as far as possible the validity and efficacy of dispositions of property upon death in international situations or, to put it otherwise, into a new type of 'escape clause' to be added to that contained in article 21.2, whilst nevertheless setting itself apart due to the substantive goal at which it is directed and the different conditions to which its application is subject. However, the benefits that it may bring are offset by the risks to the foreseeability of the applicable law and the resulting increase in litigation between persons with an interest in the succession which it would inevitably entail. Definitive clarification of these problems will only be provided by the preliminary ruling of the European Court of Justice.

[113] See, in particular, Max Planck Institute for Comparative and International Private Law, 'Comments', pp. 613–614, for the assertion of the existence of the need to take into account 'the testator's belief and intention' that a given law applies in order to avoid 'the risk of producing unjust results'; see also Dutta, 'Succession and Wills', p. 579, according to which 'a more liberal approach would give the courts some flexibility and enable them, for example, to assume an implied choice of law if the terms of a testamentary disposition are based on the presumption that a certain law applies'. It is significant that in the German and Swiss case law, which has found such interpretations to be admissible much more often than in other countries, the tacit premise for their acceptance has always consisted in the fact that the testamentary disposition in question is invalid or ineffective according to the law applicable absent any choice, and is, by contrast, valid and effective according to the different law which is assumed to have been designated implicitly by the testator; on the requirement for this condition, see in the German literature, explicitly, R. Birk, 'Art. 25', in *Münchener Kommentar zum Bürgerlichen Gesetzbuch*, vol. X, 3rd ed. (München, 1998), p. 1356; H. Dörner, 'Art. 25', in *J. von Staudingers Kommentar zum Bürgerlichen Gesetzbuch mit Einführungsgesetz und Nebengesetze, Internationales Erbrecht* (Berlin, 2007), p. 278.

41. As already mentioned,[114] also the provisions contained in articles 24 and 25, which respectively subject the admissibility and substantive validity of dispositions of property upon death other than agreements as to succession and the admissibility, substantive validity and the binding effects between the parties of the agreements as to succession to the so-called 'hypothetical' succession law – namely to the law which, under the ESR, would have been applicable to the succession of the person or the persons concerned at the time when those acts were made – serve mainly a purpose of legal certainty. This solution permits to avoid, although, as will be seen,[115] only to a certain extent, the precariousness and uncertainty in the validity and effectiveness of the aforesaid dispositions and agreements that could be brought about by their subjection to the law of the testator's last habitual residence, which is of course liable to remaining indeterminate and indeterminable until his or her death. The inconveniences that would have resulted from the adoption of the latter option would have been especially serious in relation to agreements as to succession which, in contrast to other dispositions of property upon death, immediately give rise to legal effects between the parties, which thus need to know exactly which law will be applicable without being required to wait until the succession is opened. In cases involving agreements as to the respective successions of two or more persons, it would even be necessary to wait until the death of the last survivor before being able to define the succession of those died previously. This consideration explains why article 18 of the original Commission proposal, which followed the example provided for under articles 9 and 10 of the Hague Convention of 1989 on the Law Applicable to Succession to the Estates of Deceased Persons, limited the applicability of the 'hypothetical' succession law only to agreements as to succession, whilst the extension of that rule to other dispositions of property upon death was decided upon during a subsequent stage of the *travaux préparatoires* for the ESR.[116]

The legal certainty provided by articles 24 and 25 of the final text of the instrument is enhanced by the fact that, when determining the hypothetical succession law, recourse to the 'exception clause' laid down by article 21.2 is seemingly to be excluded. Although this interpretation is

[114] See no. 32. [115] See no. 43.

[116] However, most of the national laws of the Member States which, at the time the ESR entered into force, subjected the substantive validity of dispositions of property upon death to the hypothetical succession law followed the same broad solution adopted by the regulation: see article 30 of the Austrian act on private international law, article 9.8 of the Spanish civil code and article 26.5 of the German EGBGB.

not shared by some commentators,[117] it is based on a clear indication to that effect in recital 51, which specifies that the hypothetical succession law must be regarded as the law of the country in which the deceased was habitually resident at the time the disposition or dispositions in question was or were adopted or, if he made a *professio juris*, the law chosen, without any reference to the exception clause.[118] Furthermore, the opposite interpretation would appear to be difficult to reconcile with the objectives of legal certainty and foreseeability pursued by those provisions.

42. The adoption by the ESR, within the limits set out previously, of the principle of the hypothetical succession law and, more generally, the overall regulation of the admissibility and substantive validity of dispositions of property upon death laid down in articles 24 and 25, do not however perform the sole function of enhancing legal certainty and the stability of the organisation in advance of the succession. A second objective is to make it easier for the individuals concerned to use inheritance planning instruments that are not permitted under the law of all States, including principally the agreements as to succession, which are widespread in some countries but prohibited in others where they are regarded as a dangerous source of conditioning upon testamentary freedom, and in addition other types of dispositions of property upon death such as joint wills or *fideicommissa*. The maintenance of the validity of legal acts which are regarded as admissible, and thus valid, under the law which would have been applicable to the succession at the time they were made but which might be unknown – or even prohibited – under the law of the new habitual residence of the testator is actually also conducive to

[117] See, e. g. I. Rodríguez-Uría Suárez, 'La ley aplicable a las sucesiones *mortis causa* en el Reglamento (UE) 650/2012', *InDret* (2013/2), p. 28; A. Bonomi, 'Article 24', in A. Bonomi and P. Wautelet, *Le droit européen des successions. Commentaire du Règlement n° 650/2012 du 4 juillet 2012* (Bruxelles, 2013), p. 387, which however is of the view that in this case the 'exception clause' should be applied with particular caution.

[118] According to the recital: '[w]here reference is made in this Regulation to the law which would have been applicable to the succession of the person making a disposition of property upon death if he had died on the day on which the disposition was, as the case may be, made, modified or revoked, such reference should be understood as a reference to either the law of the State of the habitual residence of the person concerned on that day or, if he had made a choice of law under this Regulation, the law of the State of his nationality on that day'. It is difficult to imagine that the failure to include a reference to the 'exception clause' could have resulted from an oversight, given that such an assumption would be tantamount to considering the clarification of the meaning of the concept of hypothetical succession law contained in the recital as nothing more than a truism devoid of any practical purpose.

achieving this goal, as is confirmed in relation to agreements as to succession by recital 49.[119] But also the right granted, respectively under articles 24.2 and 25.3, to the author of a disposition of last will or to the parties to an agreement as to succession to choose the national law of the person or of one of the persons whose estate is involved as the law which is to govern the admissibility and substantive validity of the disposition, or the admissibility, substantive validity and the binding effects between the parties of the agreement, is intended to achieve the same result. In fact, unlike the *professio juris* relating to the whole of the succession provided for under article 22, this form of a merely partial choice of law cannot have the purpose of protecting the organisation of the succession from the uncertainty and risks of instability caused by the possibility of changes in the habitual residence of the deceased, since this result is already assured by the use of the objective connecting factor of the hypothetical succession law, which is obviously not liable to change over time. Its function is thus primarily substantive in nature and, by increasing the number of laws amenable to application on an alternative basis, involves offering the interested parties greater scope for organising the allocation of their inheritance in advance using instruments and arrangements not permitted under the law of all States.[120] This liberalising purpose may be perceived with particular clarity in respect of agreements concerning the succession of several persons, for which article 25.3 permits the national law of any of the persons whose estate is involved to be chosen. The ESR thereby ends up allowing virtually any

[119] 'In order to make it easier for succession rights acquired as a result of an agreement as to succession to be accepted in the Member States, this Regulation should determine which law is to govern the admissibility of such agreements, their substantive validity and their binding effects between the parties, including the conditions for their dissolution'.

[120] Theoretically, the ESR leaves open the possibility for the courts of the Member State the legislation of which does not allow for particular types of dispositions of property upon death, or even prohibit their use, to invoke the bar of *ordre public* on the recognition of their validity or effects. However, this risk is rather limited, at least for the most important category of dispositions in question, consisting in agreements as to succession, since the case law of the countries whose laws do not accept them mostly excludes their incompatibility with *ordre public*: see, in relation to Italy, Trib. Bolzano 8 March 1968, *Rivista giuridica dell'Alto Adige* (1968), p. 220; as to France, Cour d'appel Aix-en-Provence 16 October 2003, *Rev crit dr int priv* (2004), p. 589 *et seq.*; see also Tribunal de première instance of the Principality of Monaco 23 February 1995, *Rev crit dr int priv* (1996), p. 440 *et seq.* Moreover, in these countries there is a clear tendency towards the progressive lessening of the prohibition of the agreements under consideration, as can be seen from the increasingly frequent introduction of exceptions to it. It may be added that the entry into force of the ESR will probably contribute to reinforcing this trend further.

of the concerned parties to conclude, on the basis of a law with which the party in question may not personally have any connection, an agreement as to the succession that may be inadmissible both under his or her own national law and under the law of his or her country of habitual residence.[121]

43. The narrowness of the limits of the reference made by articles 24 and 25 to the hypothetical succession law, restricted as it is to questions relating to the admissibility and substantive validity of dispositions of property upon death (and, for agreements as to succession, also to their binding effects between the parties), obviously entails that the objectives of facilitating and reinforcing certainty of succession planning pursued in this way by the ESR can only be achieved on a similarly limited scale. In particular, the crucial question regarding the restrictions imposed on the power of disposition of the testator by the mandatory rules that protect persons entitled to a compulsory share of the estate or other similar rights remains subject to the law – which is not always easy to predict – of the testator's habitual residence at the time of death or, alternatively, to the law as resulting from a subsequent *professio juris* made by him or her in accordance with article 22.[122] The ensuing loss of

[121] Article 18.2 of the Commission proposal was inspired by a policy favouring even to a greater extent the admissibility and validity of agreements concerning the succession of more than one person, as it stipulated that, absent any choice by the parties, such agreements would be admissible and valid subject to the sole condition that they were deemed to be such under any of the hypothetical succession laws of the persons whose estates were involved. Within relations between Member States the legislation of which permits agreements as to succession and those the laws of which stipulate the contrary, the adoption of this rule would in practice have led to the systematic exclusion of the application of the laws of the latter countries in all situations involving the successions of persons habitually resident in different countries falling respectively into one or the other of the two groups. The solution adopted by article 25.2 of the final text of the ESR is more balanced because it requires that, in the absence of a choice, such agreements be considered to be admissible under the hypothetical succession laws of all of the persons whose inheritances are involved, and only if this requirement is met subsequently subjects the substantive validity and binding effects of the aforesaid agreements to that between the laws in question which has the closest connection with the agreement under consideration. In making this regulatory provision, European lawmakers have endeavoured to strike a compromise between their stance in favour of the admissibility of agreements as to succession and the positions to the contrary adopted in that area by a number of Member States.

[122] The inclusion of this question amongst the aspects of succession that are to be governed by the law ordinarily applicable to it pursuant to articles 21 and 22 is clearly stipulated by article 23.2(h) and is also confirmed by recital 50, according to which '[t]he law which, under this Regulation, will govern the admissibility and substantive validity of a disposition of property upon death and, as regards agreements as to succession, the

certainty is probably greater than that which may result from disparities between national regulations concerning the admissibility and substantive validity of the dispositions of property upon death, as such regulations differ much less, at least with regard to ordinary testamentary provisions, than those concerning compulsory heirship rights, and will moreover end up applying only in a few cases. Within this context, the most serious problems of course affect agreements as to succession. The subjection of the question concerning the existence and scope of forced heirship rights to a future law which is not yet determinable at the time the aforementioned agreements are concluded has the effect of introducing a significant degree of uncertainty into the advance organisation of the succession through the recourse to this type of instruments. In particular, the deceased may end up exercising a power of disposition which he might not in actual fact possess under a different legal system that may subsequently become applicable to the succession, and similarly the potential beneficiaries of a compulsory share of the estate may waive rights which, under that very same law, could prove to be inalienable, at least until the time when succession is opened. Obviously, the risks inherent within the described situation affect primarily the beneficiaries of the dispositions of property upon death included in the agreements: they could, for example, have rendered performance in exchange or made other concessions, but would nonetheless be exposed to any unfavourable consequences of a change in the law which is to govern the succession, over the occurrence of which they do not have any control.

In order to avoid these inconveniences, it was proposed during the preparatory works for the instrument that a more liberal solution be adopted involving the extension of the application of the hypothetical succession law also to the issue of determining the effects of at least agreements as to succession by entrusting to the provisions of that law the task of protecting the persons claiming a compulsory share of the estate, and subject of course to the possible intervention as a last resort of the *ordre public* of the forum State.[123] However, the prevalence taken on by

binding effects of such an agreement as between the parties, should be without prejudice to the rights of any person who, under the law applicable to the succession, has a right to a reserved share or another right of which he cannot be deprived by the person whose estate is involved'.

[123] See in this regard A. Davì, 'L'autonomie de la volonté en droit international privé des successions dans la perspective d'une future réglementation européenne', in Deutsches Notarinstitut, *Conflict of Law of Succession*, p. 406, and *Riv dir int priv proc* (2004), p. 492 *et seq.*; Davì, 'Riflessioni', p. 333 *et seq.*; S. Álvarez González and I. Rodríguez-Uría Suárez, 'La ley aplicable a los pactos sucesorios en la Propuesta del Reglamento sobre

the position which favoured affording greater importance to the protection of the members of the deceased's family than to other needs or values stood in the way of the adoption of a more generous approach. The ESR thus remained consistent with the principled stance according to which the intangibility of the forced heirship rights of family members cannot be exposed to the risk of being set aside other than by virtue of a *professio juris* by the testator in favour of his national law.[124] The acceptance of this sole restriction was certainly facilitated by the circumstance that, at the time the ESR entered into force, most of the internal laws of the Member States subjected the succession to the national law of the deceased and also by the fact that nationality is generally more difficult to change than habitual residence. It may be added that, at least in the numerous cases in which the close relatives of the deceased asserting a right to a forced share have his same nationality, it would be difficult to see how they could claim to have a reasonable aspiration to obtain protection under private international law for hereditary expectations based on a law which derives its only ground for applicability from the fact that, at the time of death, the deceased had established his habitual residence in a country different from that of the nationality of all the persons concerned. However, the fact remains that, considered overall, the provisions laid down in the final version of the ESR deprive agreements as to succession and other similar acts of a significant part of the utility which they may have as tools for succession planning.[125]

D. Spatial Continuity of the Legal Regime Applicable to the Succession

44. As is known, the pursuit of spatial continuity of the legal regime governing relationships between individuals is generally regarded as one

sucesiones', *Diario La Ley* (2011, no 7726), pp. 6, 7. For the extension of the same proposition to all dispositions of property upon death see Dutta, 'Succession and Wills', pp. 587, 591; Max Planck Institute for Comparative and International Private Law, 'Comments', p. 617 *et seq.*

[124] In this regard see no. 39.

[125] On the other hand it must be acknowledged that a comparable protection of the forced heirship rights of the close relatives of the deceased was to be found in article 12.2 of the Hague Convention of 1989 on the Law Applicable to Succession to the Estates of Deceased Persons and article 9.8 of the Spanish civil code; similarly, article 26.5 of the German EGBGB and articles 63 and 64 of the Portuguese civil code limited the scope of the hypothetical succession law only to the admissibility and substantive validity of agreements as to succession.

of the main objectives of private international law, and by some even as the very foundation for its existence. The fundamental reason for the reciprocal openness of national legal systems to the application within them of the rules of others or to the recognition of decisions or other acts issued by judicial and non-judicial authorities operating under their aegis lies in fact in the aim of ensuring as orderly as possible an operation of the legal affairs of individuals despite their concomitant subjection to the power of different States having different laws. This international uniformity or continuity of regulation, to be attained without making any change to the diversity between internal substantive legislations, but by trying to ensure that all of the States involved apply the same law and/or recognise the decisions and legal acts issued in the others, may naturally be better achieved by groups of States (which may not necessarily be considerable in number) making a collective effort at codification by adopting instruments of uniform private international law on an international or supranational level rather than one single legal system operating only with the limited instruments available to it. The spatial continuity of regulation is thus an objective shared by all multilateral instruments of uniform private international law. Under EU private international law however, this objective takes on further significance in view of its functional link with the aims of the internal market and with the establishment of the European area of freedom, security and justice. As it has been said, whilst in the traditional private international law created by individual States through their respective legislation or by two or more States through international treaties the international mobility of persons is only a factual element and a prerequisite for the application of such regulations, within EU private international law it is first and foremost an end to be achieved.[126] The setting up of a single legal regime that is uniformly applicable to international successions in the Member States is specifically intended to promote and facilitate the freedom of movement of persons within the Union and their enjoyment of the other benefits of the internal market by removing the obstacles that could be imposed on the exercise of those liberties and rights by disparities between the national legislation of different States in the field. These objectives are clearly set forth in recitals 7, 37 and 80 of the ESR. The attainment of spatial continuity within the legal succession regime is thus

[126] For this observation see C. Kessedjian, 'Un code européen au regard des objectifs du droit international privé', in M. Fallon, P. Lagarde and S. Poillot-Peruzzetto (eds), *Quelle architecture pour un code européen de droit international privé?* (Bruxelles, 2011), p. 119.

at the same time the main purpose of the instrument as well as the means used by it in order to achieve all of its other purposes.

45. Due to the completeness of the ESR described earlier,[127] the spatial continuity created by it applies to all private international law aspects of the regulation of succession and, in particular, to its two fundamental elements, that is the determination of the applicable law, which is the same throughout all Member States, and the recognition of judicial decisions; alongside these elements it is necessary to add also the acceptance and enforceability of authentic instruments, the enforceability of court settlements and the creation and efficacy in all Member States of the European Certificate of Succession. As regards the first aspect, the unification of the conflict of laws rules applicable within the Member States contributes to removing the obstacles to freedom of movement and the establishment of persons within the Union by offering the deceased the ability to organise his succession in advance and with a fair degree of certainty, as he may rely on the fact that the law designated to govern it will always be the same, irrespective of the Member State whose courts might have jurisdiction in future to rule on it.[128] The legal certainty and foreseeability thereby obtained are moreover increased, albeit indirectly, by the centralisation in principle of the vesting of jurisdiction within one single court, which renders one single law *de facto* applicable also to questions related to succession matters that may arise in the course of judicial proceedings, such as those relating to matrimonial property regimes or the property consequences of registered partnerships, as well as preliminary questions of family law, to which the Member States at present largely apply differing conflict of laws rules.[129] The high level of legal certainty thereby obtained during the stage before the succession is opened is matched by comparable achievements with regard to all matters relating to the subsequent stage of its devolution, administration and transmission in which a broad level of spatial continuity of regulation is likewise assured. The essential basis for reaching this result is provided by the obligation imposed by the ESR on all

[127] See nos. 14 and 15.

[128] The importance of realising this objective is stressed in recital 37: 'In order to allow citizens to avail themselves, with all legal certainty, of the benefits offered by the internal market, this Regulation should enable them to know in advance which law will apply to their succession. Harmonised conflict of laws rules should be introduced in order to avoid contradictory results'. See also Lagarde, 'Les principes de base', p. 697: 'Le futur défunt. . .ne sera pas freiné pour des raisons d'ordre successoral dans son désir de circuler d'un Etat membre dans un autre'.

[129] See in this regard no. 15.

Member States to recognise automatically, subject to the small number of conditions laid down in article 40, the decisions issued by other Member States' courts in matters of succession, both in contentious and non-contentious proceedings, and to render those decisions enforceable within their respective legal orders, pursuant to articles 45 to 58, on simple presentation by the interested party to the local court of competent authority of an application accompanied by some documents.[130] A declaration of enforceability may also be obtained – based on the same conditions and according to the same procedure – by any interested party with respect to authentic instruments and court settlements, provided, of course, that they are equally enforceable in the Member State of origin (articles 60 and 61). The provision of this set of facilities helps to foster the enjoyment by the citizens of the benefits of the internal market by making easier and faster to heirs, legatees, administrators and creditors of the succession the transboundary assertion of their respective qualities, rights and powers within the space of the Union.

A significant contribution to the same end is furthermore given by the rules on acceptance of authentic instruments (article 59) and on the creation of the European Certificate of Succession (articles 62 to 73). The function of authentic instruments and certificates of succession consists essentially in facilitating the provision of evidence concerning the status of the persons entitled to claim rights against or to exercise powers of administration over the estate. However, the characteristics

[130] As regards both the recognition and the declaration of enforceability of decisions, the ESR, having been adopted shortly before the completion of the procedure to review regulation no. 44/2001 on jurisdiction and the recognition and enforcement of judgments in civil and commercial matters (Brussels I) by regulation no. 1215/2012 (Brussels I-*bis*), essentially reiterates, the rules stated in the former without having been able to take account of the amendments made to it by the latter which, *inter alia*, has now rendered also enforceability automatic. Pursuant to article 52 ESR, the grounds for the refusal or revocation of a declaration of enforceability are the same which, according to article 40, prevent automatic recognition. Their existence may be established on appeal by the party against whom enforcement is sought. The grounds consist in the manifest incompatibility of the enforcement of the decision with the public policy (*ordre public*) of the forum, the serious violation of the rules on the right to a defence of the defendant and the irreconcilability of the decision to be enforced with an earlier decision given in the same Member State in which enforcement is sought or in another Member or non-Member State, provided that the earlier decision fulfils the conditions necessary for its recognition in the Member State in which enforcement is sought. Based on the experience of the application of the previous EU regulations on judicial cooperation in civil matters, it may be expected that in most cases none of these obstacles will arise and that therefore the recognition and enforcement of decisions will almost always be assured also in the area of succession.

and content of these acts vary considerably from one legal system to another. They may be issued by a court, a notary or another authority and in certain countries may even be replaced by documents or declarations drawn up by the interested parties themselves; consequently, they have different degrees of reliability and do not give rise to the same evidentiary effects in all States. It follows that in cross-border situations the possibility that such acts may not be deemed to be equivalent to the certification required under local law where they have been drawn up in a foreign country may often be a source of complications, additional costs and time delays.[131]

In order to remove or at least reduce these difficulties, article 59 of the ESR in the first place subjects the Member States to an obligation of mutual acceptance of the authentic instruments executed in each of them, specifying that those instruments shall have the same evidentiary effects in Member States other than that of origin that they produce in the latter or, if the effects in question are unknown under the law of one of the former States, 'the most comparable effects' (provided that this is not contrary to public policy in the Member State concerned). As highlighted by recital 61, the evidentiary effects which an authentic instrument will produce in another Member State will therefore mainly depend on the law of the Member State of origin. The use of the term 'acceptance' by the ESR in place of the term 'recognition' is due to the concern to distinguish between the efficacy of authentic instruments and that of judicial decisions, which are generally vested with the authority of *res judicata*, the recognition of which may moreover only be refused on the grounds stated in article 40, which do not include the possibility for the control either of the substantive validity or the authenticity of a document. Pursuant to article 59, these may be challenged, respectively, before the courts having jurisdiction under the ESR to rule on the succession and before the courts of the State of origin of the authentic instrument.[132] Secondly, the ESR establishes the European Certificate of Succession,

[131] See on these problems Bonomi, 'Successions internationales', pp. 405–406; Davì and Zanobetti, *Il nuovo diritto internazionale privato europeo*, p. 231 *et seq.*

[132] Conversely, according to article 46 of regulation no. 2201/2003 concerning jurisdiction and the recognition and enforcement of judgments in matrimonial matters and the matters of parental responsibility (Brussels II-*bis*), both authentic instruments and agreements between the parties that are enforceable in the Member State in which they have been drawn up or registered or, respectively, concluded 'shall be recognized and declared enforceable under the same conditions as judgments'. This provision has been criticized for the reasons stated above. See on this matter Lagarde, 'Les principes de base', pp. 731–732.

which is the first example of a public document created and entirely governed by EU legislation. The utility of this document, the use of which is not mandatory but merely optional, depends essentially on the fact that it gives rise to the same legal effects in all Member States and is therefore suitable to replace as a means of proof any similar act or document that may be required by the internal law of one of them. It thereby further facilitates individuals with an interest in demonstrating their respective capacities, rights or powers of administration in cases in which operations relating to the administration and/or transmission of the succession must be carried out in two or more Member States and the documents that may be issued by the competent authorities of one of them under its own national law do not have the same legal effects as those required under the law of another. Article 69 provides that the Certificate shall produce its effects in all Member States without any special procedure being required, that these effects consist in the presumption that it accurately demonstrates elements established under the law applicable to the succession or under any other law applicable to specific elements, and, in particular, that third parties may legitimately rely on the information contained in it in order to make payments or hand over assets (unless they are aware that its contents are not accurate or are unaware of such inaccuracy due to gross negligence) and that it shall constitute a valid document for the recording of succession property in the relevant register of a Member State.

46. The ESR has not only achieved almost absolute spatial continuity for the legal regime of succession within the Member States but has also endeavoured to achieve a certain level of coordination with the private international law systems of non-Member States. The provisions laid down by the ESR to this effect constitute an important step in completing the unification brought about by it within the Union framework since, with respect to international successions involving both Member and non-Member States, it is difficult to achieve the objectives of legal certainty and foreseeability and of effective protection of the rights of heirs, legatees and creditors of the estate pursued by the regulation without taking account, at least to some extent, of the positions under the legal systems of the latter States. In particular, in situations in which, due to the existence of such concomitant ties, the courts of the States falling respectively into one or the other of the two groups are vested with concurrent jurisdiction, it is possible that, under their various systems of private international law, they may apply different substantive laws leading to conflicting results and that the decisions issued in one country may not be eligible for recognition in the others. In order to limit as far as possible the occurrence of these difficulties the ESR uses two of the more traditional instruments for coordination in the field of conflict of laws: the admission of *renvoi* and the application of overriding mandatory rules or other similar rules contained in a foreign law different from that normally competent to regulate the succession, which are defined by article 30 as 'special rules' laid down by the law of the State in which certain assets belonging to the estate are located and which, according to that law, 'are applicable irrespective of the law applicable to the succession'. As regards *renvoi* by the law of a non-Member State, article 34 provides that it must be followed when it refers to the law of a Member State or the law of another non-Member State which would in turn apply its own provisions, and recital 57 specifies that in both of these cases the admission of *renvoi* is intended 'to ensure international consistency'. As regards the 'special rules' covered by article 30, they are more specifically those included in the law of the country where 'certain immovable property, certain enterprises or other special categories of assets are located', which 'for economic, family or social considerations, impose restrictions concerning or affecting the succession in respect of those assets'; they may be contained in the law of the Member State of the forum, in that of another Member State or in that of a third State, and obviously only in this last case amount to an instrument for coordination with the outside of the Union. The reason why article 30 refrained from using the expression 'overriding mandatory provisions' (*lois de police, Eingriffsnormen*), which was by contrast adopted by other EU private international law instruments, consists in the fact that certain legal systems may contain provisions of the type under consideration which, whilst being 'applicable irrespective of the law applicable to the succession', are not necessarily binding on the private parties and may be set aside by a will or an agreement as to succession. However, the requirement that such provisions must have the first characteristic is probably sufficient to enable them to be allocated to the category in question or, at least, clearly indicates the intention of the ESR to subject their application to the fulfilment of a condition which is absolutely typical of it.[133]

[133] On the use of the phrase 'overriding mandatory provisions' see, in particular, article 9 of regulation no. 593/2008 on the law applicable to contractual obligations (Rome I) and article 16 of regulation no. 864/2007 on the law applicable to non-contractual obligations (Rome II); the French text of the latter adopts, even more significantly, the formulation 'dispositions impératives dérogatoires'. Although, as mentioned in no. 8, article 30 ESR is modelled on article 15 of the Hague Convention of 1989 on the Law Applicable to

As regards relations with the legal systems of third countries, the introduction of this exception to the application of the law designated by the ESR as being ordinarily competent to regulate the succession enables to avoid a potential positive conflict of laws in respect of which the viewpoint of the local State would inevitably prevail, given the exclusive material control which it is able to exercise over the assets located in its territory.

Also concerning the exercise of jurisdiction the regulation did not fail to take account, to a certain extent, of the positions of the legal systems of non-Member States in article 12, which, as mentioned earlier,[134] empowers the court seised to decide, at the request of one of the parties, not to rule on the assets located in one of those States if it may be expected that its decisions in respect of such assets would not be recognized and/or declared enforceable in the State of the *situs*. As it is intended to prevent the emergence of a positive conflict with the legal system of the third State in which the assets involved are located, this provision may be in some sense regarded as a procedural equivalent of article 30. It will probably be applied most frequently within relations with the 'scissionist' countries which require exclusive jurisdiction for their own courts to rule on the succession in relation to the immovable property situated in their territories, as is generally the case for common law States, although it may also be applied in other cases, since it does not distinguish between movable and immovable property or on the basis of the reason why the third State concerned might refuse to recognise or enforce the decision.

Overall, ESR demonstrates a readiness to coordinate with the positions of the legal systems of non-Member States, which is considerably greater

Succession to the Estates of Deceased Persons, in contrast to the former, the latter provision does not require that the 'special rules' to which it relates are 'applicable irrespective of the law applicable to the succession'. This omission is due to the deliberate choice made during the *travaux préparatoires* for the convention, owing to the differences of opinion which emerged in this regard, to leave unresolved the question as to whether or not the special rules under examination should have mandatory status: see thereon the explanatory report by D. W. M. Waters, in Hague Conference on private international law, *Proceedings of the Sixteenth Session*, vol. II, *Succession to estates – applicable law* (The Hague, 1990), pp. 589, 591, and, for the discussions among the government delegates to the Conference, p. 422 *et seq*. Most commentators on the ESR are in agreement in concluding that the special rules covered by article 30 must have the status of *lois de police*: see, e.g., P. Wautelet, 'Article 30', in A. Bonomi and P. Wautelet, *Le droit européen des successions. Commentaire du Règlement n° 650/2012 du 4 juillet 2012* (Bruxelles, 2013), p. 476 *et seq.*; D. Damascelli, *Diritto internazionale privato delle successioni a causa di morte* (Milano, 2013), p. 78.

[134] See no. 31.

than that which may be observed in the other private international law instruments hitherto adopted within the framework of EU judicial cooperation in civil matters. In particular, the ESR is the first of such instruments to have admitted *renvoi* in general terms, albeit with various exceptions, and also with regard to foreign overriding mandatory rules its position is more generous than that of earlier acts.[135] This is a feature that deserves to be welcomed because, in a transnational context in which the movement of persons and goods is, of course, not limited to the Member States, the objectives underlying the construction of the European area of freedom, security and justice cannot be fully achieved without searching at least for some degree of legal harmony in relations with the outside world.[136]

[135] The admission of *renvoi* is expressly precluded by article 20 of regulation no. 593/2008 on the law applicable to contractual obligations (Rome I), article 24 of regulation no. 864/2007 on the law applicable to non-contractual obligations (Rome II) and article 11 of regulation no. 1259/2010 implementing enhanced cooperation in the area of the law applicable to divorce and legal separation (Rome III), although article 7.3 of the first regulation provides for a small exception for insurance contracts. These exclusions should not, however, be interpreted as an expression of an attitude contrary to the principle of *renvoi* which the ESR has reversed, but are rather due to specific reasons relating to each individual instrument: [see art. 34 no. 4]. As regards the overriding mandatory provisions of a State other than the forum State, it is sufficient to recall that the Rome II (article 16) and Rome III regulations refuse outright to take account of these and that article 9.3 of the Rome I regulation considerably reduces the scope for their application compared to article 7.1 of the Rome Convention on the law applicable to contractual obligations, by limiting it to provisions of the type in question contained in the law of the country where the obligations arising out of the contract have to be or have been performed insofar as those provisions render the performance of the contract unlawful: see, for some critical observations on this restriction, A. Bonomi, 'Le régime des règles impératives et des lois de police dans le Règlement 'Rome I' sur la loi applicable aux contrats', in E. Cashin Ritaine and A. Bonomi (eds), *Le nouveau règlement européen 'Rome I' relatif à la loi applicable aux obligations contractuelles* (Zurich-Bâle, 2008), p. 232 *et seq*. Furthermore, article 30 ESR provides for the compulsory application of the 'special rules' to which it refers, whilst article 9.3 of the Rome I regulation is limited to granting the court a discretionary power.

[136] See on this subject, for further analysis, A. Davì, 'Le renvoi en droit international privé contemporain', *Hague Recueil*, vol. 352 (2010), p. 290 *et seq*.

CHAPTER I

Scope and Definitions

Article 1

Scope

MATTHIAS WELLER

1. This Regulation shall apply to succession to the estates of deceased persons. It shall not apply to revenue, customs or administrative matters.
2. The following shall be excluded from the scope of this Regulation:
   (a) the status of natural persons, as well as family relationships and relationships deemed by the law applicable to such relationships to have comparable effects;
   (b) the legal capacity of natural persons, without prejudice to point (c) of Article 23(2) and to Article 26;
   (c) questions relating to the disappearance, absence or presumed death of a natural person;
   (d) questions relating to matrimonial property regimes and property regimes of relationships deemed by the law applicable to such relationships to have comparable effects to marriage;
   (e) maintenance obligations other than those arising by reason of death;
   (f) the formal validity of dispositions of property upon death made orally;
   (g) property rights, interests and assets created or transferred otherwise than by succession, for instance by way of gifts, joint ownership with a right of survivorship, pension plans, insurance contracts and arrangements of a similar nature, without prejudice to point (i) of Article 23(2);
   (h) questions governed by the law of companies and other bodies, corporate or unincorporated, such as clauses in the memoranda of association and articles of association of companies and other bodies, corporate or unincorporated, which determine what will happen to the shares upon the death of the Members;
   (i) the dissolution, extinction and merger of companies and other bodies, corporate or unincorporated;
   (j) the creation, administration and dissolution of trusts;
   (k) the nature of rights in rem; and
   (l) any recording in a register of rights in immovable or movable property, including the legal requirements for such recording, and the effects of recording or failing to record such rights in a register.

Summary

I. OVERVIEW *page* 74
II. SUCCESSION 76
III. EXCLUSION OF PUBLIC MATTERS 77
IV. EXCLUSION OF CIVIL MATTERS 79
A. Status of Natural Persons and Family Relations (point (a)) 80
1. Status of Natural Persons 80
2. Family Relationships 83
3. Relationships Comparable to Family Relationships 84
B. Legal Capacity of Natural Persons (point (b)) 84
C. Disappearance, Absence, Presumed Death of a natural person (point (c)) 85
D. Matrimonial Property Regimes and Comparable Regimes (point (d)) 86
E. Maintenance Obligations Other than those Arising by Reason of Death (point (e)) 93
F. Formal Validity of Dispositions of Property upon Death Made orally (point (f)) 94
G. Property Rights, Interests and Assets Created or Transferred Otherwise than by Succession (point (g)) 95
H. Questions Governed by the Law of Companies (point (h)) 98
I. Further Questions Governed by the Law of Companies (point (i)) 101
J. Creation, Administration and Dissolution of Trusts (point (j)) 101
K. Nature of Rights *in Rem* (point (k)) 104
L. Recording in a Register of Rights in Property (point (l)) 108

I. Overview

1. Article 1 defines the material scope of the ESR. According to the first sentence of article 1.1, the ESR applies to 'succession to the estates of deceased persons'. The second sentence excludes central matters of public law. Paragraph 2 of the provision excludes certain matters of private law with links to succession matters. The main objective of this paragraph is the coordination of the ESR with other EU regulations. In addition, some matters are excluded because there was no sufficient consent on how to regulate them on the level of harmonised EU law. Since the ESR brings together 'provisions on jurisdiction, on applicable law, on recognition or, as the case may be, acceptance, enforceability and enforcement of decisions, authentic instruments and court settlements and on the creation of a European Certificate of Succession'[1] in order to facilitate

[1] Recital 8 ESR.

'[t]he proper functioning of the internal market ... by removing the obstacles to the free movement of persons who currently face difficulties in asserting their rights in the context of a succession having cross-border implications',[2] it goes without saying in article 1 that the application of the ESR requires a conflict of laws.[3]

2. Legal terms and notions to which the ESR makes reference are to be interpreted autonomously. Legal terms and notions of other instruments of the European law must be taken into account in order to achieve a coherent interpretation, in particular for legal terms and notions relating to the material scope of other instruments, because both the definition of the material scope for this instrument in article 1.1 ESR as well as several of the exclusions in article 1.2 ESR aim at coordinating the numerous instruments of European private international law. This coordination includes instruments on procedural law as well as instruments on the choice of law. Last not least, the definition of the material scope in article 1 ESR determines the applicability *ratione materiae* of the European Certificate of Succession in article 63 *et seq.* ESR [see art. 63 *et seq.*].

3. For example, article 1.2(f) Brussels I-*bis* regulation[4] should be interpreted to the effect that there be neither an overlap nor a *lacuna.*[5] Civil matters involving an incidental question on succession law, e.g. the acquisition of the claim in question by succession, appear to be covered by the Brussels I-*bis* regulation.[6] The incidental question should be determined according to the law selected by the ESR in order to produce the same result irrespective of which Member State's authorities decide about the claim.[7] The ESR applies, in turn, if a question of succession law

[2] Recital 7, sentence 1.

[3] A. Davì and A. Zanobetti, *Il nuovo diritto internazionale privato europeo delle successioni* (Torino, 2014), p. 25; J. Carrascosa González, *El Reglamento Sucesorio Europeo 650/2012 de 4 julio 2012: Análisis crítico* (Granada, 2014), p. 23.

[4] Regulation (EU) no. 1215/2012 of the European Parliament and of the Council of 12 December 2012 on jurisdiction and the recognition and enforcement of judgments in civil and commercial matters (recast), OJ 2012 no. L351, 20 December 2012.

[5] A. Dutta, 'Art. 1 EuErbVO', Kommentierung der europäischen Erbrechtsverordnung, *in* Münchener Kommentar BGB, 6th ed., vol. X (München, 2015), para. 4.

[6] ECJ, case C-347/08, *Vorarlberger Gebietskrankenkasse* v. *WGV-Schwäbische Allgemeine Versicherungs AG* [2009] ERC I-08661, para. 44, *per obiter dictum*: 'where the statutory assignee of the rights of the directly injured party may himself be considered to be a weaker party, such an assignee should be able to benefit from special rules on the jurisdiction of courts laid down in those provisions. This is particularly the situation, as the Spanish Government states, of the heirs of the person injured in an accident'.

[7] Dutta, 'Art. 1 EuErbVO', para. 4.

constitutes the main question of the proceedings, for example proceedings for a negative declaratory judgment that the defendant is not an heir or otherwise beneficiary.

4. In regulating international jurisdiction as well as choice of law, the ESR may be considered a new generation of EU instruments on private international law that so far mainly focused either on the one or the other subject.[8] The comprehensive approach of private international law instruments[9] continues in respect of the instruments on matrimonial property regimes and property consequences of registered partnerships.[10] Under such a comprehensive approach the interpretation of legal terms and notions on the level of jurisdiction and on the level of choice of law tends to blur.[11] Nevertheless, it may remain necessary to make distinctions for both of these levels of private international law, even if the respective terms or notions have an identical wording or are defined generally for a comprehensive instrument.

II. Succession

5. According to article 1.1, sentence 1, the ESR applies to succession to the estates of deceased persons. Recital 9 explains that the scope of the ESR should include 'all civil-law aspects of succession'.[12] These are 'all forms of transfer of assets, rights and obligations by reason of death, whether by way of a voluntary transfer under a disposition of property upon death or a transfer through intestate succession'. On the basis of this explanation, article 3.1(a) ESR defines 'succession' as covering all

[8] Council Regulation (EC) no. 1346/2000 of 29 May 2000 on insolvency proceedings, OJ 2000 no. L160, 30 June 2000 (that will be replaced as from 26 June 2017 by Regulation (EU) no. 2015/848 of the European Parliament and of the Council of 20 May 2015 on insolvency proceedings (recast), OJ 2015 no. L141, 6 June 2015) already includes jurisdiction, recognition as well as choice of law.

[9] See e.g. Carrascosa González, *El Reglamento Sucesorio Europeo*, p. 22: 'Reglamento triple'.

[10] Council Regulation (EU) 2016/1103 of 24 June 2016 implementing enhanced cooperation in the area of jurisdiction, applicable law and the recognition and enforcement of decisions in matters of matrimonial property regimes; Council Regulation (EU) 2016/1104 of 24 June 2016 implementing enhanced cooperation in the area of jurisdiction, applicable law and the recognition and enforcement of decisions in matters of the property consequences of registered partnerships. Both regulations will be applicable as of 29 January 2019 in the Member States participating to the enhanced cooperation, i.e. Belgium, Bulgaria, Cyprus, the Czech Republic, Germany, Greece, Spain, France, Croatia, Italy, Luxembourg, Malta, the Netherlands, Austria, Portugal, Slovenia, Finland and Sweden.

[11] Dutta, 'Art. 1 EuErbVO', para. 1.

[12] Carrascosa González, *El Reglamento Sucesorio Europeo*, p. 29: 'concepto omnicomprensivo'.

forms of transfer of assets, rights and obligations by reason of death, either by voluntary transfer, such as by will or testamentary contract, or intestate succession. Article 23.2 ESR supplements this definition by providing a non-exclusive list of issues that are covered by succession law. Article 24 *et seq.* ESR provide for special choice-of-law rules in relation to issues that form part of 'succession' in the sense of article 1.1 ESR.

6. Recital 11 makes clear that the ESR should only apply to succession matters, not to other matters of civil law potentially related with succession matters. In order to clarify this limitation article 1.2 ESR contains a list of those matters of civil law that are often raised in connection with succession matters but that are excluded from the scope of the ESR. Finally, 'succession' should be interpreted consistently with 'wills and succession' in the sense of article 1.2(a) Brussels I and I-*bis* regulations. Any matter excluded from the scope of the ESR must be connected to the applicable law by recourse to the national choice-of-law rules of the Member States including, as the case may be, those emerging from international treaties implemented in the respective Member States. Nothing prevents the Member States from making use of the choice-of-law rules of the ESR for issues excluded from the material scope of the ESR. The application of the ESR, however, then entirely grounds on the respective national legal order, for example by way of analogy in order to close a *lacuna* in the national choice-of-law rules.

III. Exclusion of Public Matters

7. Article 1.1, sentence 2, excludes revenue, customs or administrative matters. Recital 10 explains that these matters are excluded insofar as they are 'of a public nature'. In particular, it is for national law to determine how taxes and other liabilities of a public-law nature are calculated and paid, whether these be taxes payable by the deceased at the time of death or any type of succession-related tax to be paid by the estate or the beneficiaries. Article 23.2(g) ESR does not apply for such 'debts under the succession' [see art. 23 no. 12]. Likewise, it is for the national law to decide whether the release of succession property to beneficiaries or the recording of succession property in a register may be made subject to the payment of taxes. This list of tax issues in recital 10 is not exclusive but only identifies the most typical succession-related tax matters.

8. Beyond these specific succession-related matters of public law, the terms 'revenue', 'customs' and 'administrative matters' should be interpreted consistently with the same terms in article 1.1, sentence 2, Rome I regulation;[13] article 1.1, sentence 2, Rome II regulation;[14] and article 1.1, sentence 2, Brussels I and I-*bis* regulations.[15] All of these instruments restrict themselves to civil matters because article 81 TFEU empowers the EU to enact measures for judicial cooperation (only) in 'civil matters'. The autonomous distinction between civil and public matters relies on the question whether one party of the legal relationship acted in exercise of specific powers vested to it as a body of public law or on the grounds of a public competence as opposed to powers vested in any (private) person, i.e. 'powers falling outside the scope of the ordinary legal rules applicable to relationships between private individuals'.[16] Articles 1.1, sentence 2, of the respective EU instruments make reference to the most apparent and most widely accepted examples of such powers. It is the function rather than the legal form or employment of the person exercising the power in question that determines the decision between public and private matters.[17] For example, claims arising from social welfare upon death of the deceased are administrative matters in the sense of article 1.1, sentence 2, ESR. Article 30 ESR provides in this respect that where the law of the State in which certain immovable property, certain enterprises or other special categories of assets are located contains special rules which, for economic, family or social considerations, impose restrictions concerning or affecting the succession in respect of those assets, those special rules shall apply to the succession in so far as, under the law of that State,

[13] Regulation (EC) no. 593/2008 of the European Parliament and of the Council of 17 June 2008 on the law applicable to contractual obligations (Rome I), OJ 2008 no. L177, 4 July 2008.

[14] Regulation (EC) no. 864/2007 of the European Parliament and of the Council of 11 July 2007 on the law applicable to non-contractual obligations (Rome II), OJ 2007 no. L199, 31 July 2007.

[15] See footnote 4.

[16] ECJ, case C-292/05, *Lechouritou and Others* v. *Dimosio tis Omospondiakis Dimokratias tis Germanias* [2007] ECR I-01519, para. 34; ECJ, case C-265/02, *Frahuil SA* v. *Assitalia SpA* [2004] ECR I-01543, para. 21; ECJ, case C-266/01, *Préservatrice foncière TIARD SA* v. *Staat der Nederlanden* [2003] ECR I-04867, para. 30; ECJ, case C-172/91, *Volker Sonntag* v. *Hans Waidmann, Elisabeth Waidmann and Stefan Waidmann* [1993] ECR I-01963, para. 20 *et seq.*

[17] ECJ, case 172/91, *Volker Sonntag* v. *Hans Waidmann, Elisabeth Waidmann and Stefan Waidmann* [1993] ECR I-01963, para. 23, with respect to the function of a teacher vis-à-vis his pupils as being outside the exercise of sovereign powers, irrespective of his status as a civil servant under public law in the legal system of a Member State.

they are applicable irrespective of the law applicable to the succession [see art. 30].

9. Furthermore, the nature of a matter does not change by transfer of a claim from one person to another.[18] For example, a claim based on public law does not change into a claim of private law just by assignment or succession.

IV. Exclusion of Civil Matters

10. Article 1.2 ESR contains a list of twelve subject matters of a civil law nature that are excluded from the scope of the ESR. These subject-matters often appear in connection with succession matters[19] but they are not to be dealt with by the ESR because according to recital 11 the ESR 'should not apply to areas of civil law other than succession'. The list of excluded matters is exhaustive.[20] Thus, civil matters outside the list of article 1.2 ESR but also outside 'succession' in the sense of article 1.1, sentence 1, ESR are equally outside the material scope of the ESR. This applies, for example, to the question whether and to what extent and in what way rights, claims, debts and property exist that form part of the estate.[21]

11. The list in article 1.2 ESR partly contains matters that are already dealt with by other EU instruments. This applies, for example, to point (e) (maintenance obligations).[22] One of the excluded matters (matrimonial property and property consequences of partnerships) has been, subsequently to the adoption of ESR, dealt with by other EU instruments and others might be in the future.[23] Finally, there is a number of matters that, at least at the moment, are deliberately left to the respective national conflict rules.

[18] M. Weller, 'Art. 1 Rome I Regulation', in G.-P. Calliess (ed), *Rome Regulations: Commentary on the European Rules of the Conflict of Laws* (Alphen aan den Rijn, 2015), para. 8.

[19] Davì and Zanobetti, *Il nuovo diritto internazionale privato europeo*, p. 26.

[20] Compare the wording of the non-exclusive list in article 23.2 ESR: 'in particular', '*notamment*', '*insbesondere*', A. Bonomi, 'Article 1', in A. Bonomi and P. Wautelet, *Le droit européen des successions. Commentaire du Règlement nº 650/2012 du 4 juillet 2012* (Bruxelles, 2013), p. 74.

[21] Bonomi, 'Article 1', p. 74.

[22] Council Regulation (EC) no. 4/2009 of 18 December 2008 on jurisdiction, applicable law, recognition and enforcement of decisions and cooperation in matters relating to maintenance obligations, OJ 2009 no. L7, 10 January 2009.

[23] See the regulations quoted in footnote 10.

12. As far as issues are outside the material scope of 'succession' for the purposes of the ESR, the Member States' law applies, unless there is another EU instrument. The Member States are free to characterise such issues as succession law by virtue of their own legal order and to apply to these issues their own national conflicts law. If a Member State removes the national conflicts law on succession, it is likely that such a Member States seeks to adjust its own law exactly along the lines of 'succession' in the sense of the ESR.[24] It may also be the case that such a Member State refers to the choice-of-law rules of the ESR for issues not covered by 'succession' under the ESR but covered by 'succession' as understood by the national law.[25] In that latter case the Member State makes use of the ESR by virtue of its own national law. It is a matter of interpretation of the national law which of these options has been chosen.

A. *Status of Natural Persons and Family Relations (point (a))*

13. Article 1.2(a) excludes the status of natural persons from the scope of the ESR, as well as it excludes family relationships and functionally comparable relationships. Both provisions should be interpreted consistently with article 1.2(a) and (b) Rome I regulation, article 1.2(a) Brussels I-*bis* regulation, and, as far as the natural status is concerned, with article 1.2(a) Brussels I regulation, and finally, as far as family relations and comparable relations are concerned, with article 1.2(a) Rome II regulation.

1. Status of Natural Persons

14. The concepts for determining the civil status – e.g. mother, father, child, married, divorced etc. – of natural persons differ strongly amongst the Member States.[26] In its green paper on the recognition of the effects of civil status records, the European Commission discussed the option of such a recognition on the basis of harmonised choice-of-law rules.[27] So far, however, there are no such rules in sight. Therefore, the EU legislator left this issue to the Member States' choice-of-law rules.

[24] Dutta, 'Art. 1 EuErbVO', para. 9.

[25] Davì and Zanobetti, *Il nuovo diritto internazionale privato europeo delle successioni*, p. 25.

[26] European Commission, green paper, 'Less Bureaucracy for Citizens: Promoting Free Movement of Public Documents and Recognition of the Effects of Civil Status Records', COM(2010) 747 final, 15 December 2010, para. 4.1, p. 11.

[27] European Commission, green paper, 'Less Bureaucracy for Citizens' (see footnote 26), para. 4.3(c) and question 9, p. 15.

The connection used by these rules varies between nationality, domicile and habitual residence.[28]

15. The status of natural persons often occurs as a preliminary question in connection with succession matters, in particular for the question of who is beneficiary (article 23.2(b) ESR) and whether there are reserved shares and other restrictions on the disposal of property upon death as well as claims which persons close to the deceased may have against the estate or the heirs (article 23.2(h) ESR). The exclusion is understood to cover the status of natural persons in particular in respect to such incidental questions to succession matters.[29] For example, it is the succession law determined by the ESR that decides whether an adoption or a registered partnership results in the position of a beneficiary whereas the question whether the respective person is validly adopted or whether there is a valid registered partnership is not dealt with by the ESR.

16. A follow-up question is how the incidental questions (of status or of other issues) should be dealt with. Basically, two approaches are discussed, namely either applying the choice-of-law rules of the *lex causae*, i.e. the choice-of-law rules of the law applicable to the main question ('dependent connection' because the selection of the applicable law to the incidental question depends on the *lex causae*), or the choice-of-law rules of the *lex fori* ('independent connection'). As far as the courts or even the legislator of the Member States explain themselves on this issue (which is hardly ever the case) there seems to be an overall tendency to resort to the choice-of-law rules of the *lex fori* rather than to those of the *lex causae*.[30] Under this approach, the incidental question will always be decided in the same way before the courts of the respective Member State, irrespective of the main question that raised the incidental question. Thus, the legal order of the respective Member State remains as coherent as possible in that a 'marriage' of two particular spouses is always regarded as a valid marriage irrespective of the context in which this question arises ('internal harmony').

17. However, such an internal harmony results in international disharmony in respect to the main question because the courts of different Member States will come to different results depending on their respective decisions on the incidental question. It is argued, therefore, that incidental questions should be decided according to the choice-of-law rules of the *lex causae*, i.e. those of the applicable succession law. This

[28] Bonomi, 'Article 1', p. 76.
[29] Bonomi, 'Article 1', p. 76.
[30] Bonomi, 'Article 1', p. 77.

would have the effect that from the perspective of substantive law, the incidental question will always be decided as if it had to be decided by the courts of the State that provides for the *lex causae*. Of course, procedural differences will remain from State to State and may still result in different decisions. Thus, 'international harmony' cannot be guaranteed by resorting to the choice-of-law rules of the *lex causae*.

There is no express rule in the ESR on how incidental questions should be dealt with. One may conclude that the Member States may choose as they wish.[31] One may suggest that both approaches should be used alternatively in order to enhance the chances for a positive result, for example, on the preliminary question of 'fatherhood' to the benefit of the 'child'.[32] But such a *favour validitatis* for assessing parentage may be unjustified if third persons, for example other children of the deceased person, would suffer disadvantages. One may further hold that by resorting to the choice-of-law rules of the *lex causae* the testator receives the possibility to choose the applicable law for his family relations via choosing the applicable succession law although a direct choice is usually not allowed.[33] But it would appear somewhat illogical to opt for a dependent connection only if there is no choice of law for the succession issues.[34] Rather, one should develop a general approach.

18. In principle, the most promising general approach in European private international law appears to be an independent connection because the more European conflicts rules (for the main question) come into existence, the more an independent connection of the incidental questions that makes use of these European conflicts rules also for incidental questions stabilise the uniformity of decisions within the internal market and furthers the relevance of the European conflicts rules.[35] For example, if an incidental question appears in the wording of a European choice-of-law rule for selecting the applicable law and if there is already another European choice-of-law rule that deals with this incidental question for the case that this question appears as main question, it should be a matter of coherence to resort to the European choice-of-law rule in both cases.

[31] Bonomi, 'Article 1', p. 78.

[32] For example, P. Lagarde, 'Observations sur l'articulation des questions de statut personnel et des questions alimentaires dans l'application des conventions de droit international privé', in A. E. von Overbeck (ed), *Conflits et harmonisation – Kollision und Vereinheitlichung – Conflicts and Harmonization* (Freiburg, 1990), p. 521 *et seq.*

[33] Bonomi, 'Article 1', p. 78. [34] But compare Bonomi, 'Article 1', p. 78.

[35] M. Weller, 'Europäisches Internationales Privatrecht, Allgemeiner Teil', in C. Teichmann and M. Gebauer (eds), *Enzyklopädie Europarecht – Europäisches Privat- und Unternehmensrecht* (Baden-Baden, 2015), § 8, paras. 72–82.

The effect is that the legal relationship in question is always dealt with according to the same substantive law irrespective of whether it appears as incidental question or main question. On the other hand, if an incidental question in the applicable substantive law selected by a European choice-of-law rule were to be connected by the choice-of-law rules of the legal order of the selected substantive law, recurring incidental questions may be decided differently depending on the context in which they appear.

19. However, in areas where there is not yet European conflicts law the picture may change.[36] In the context of the ESR, this may be particularly the case in respect to the function of the European Certificate of Succession.[37] To the extent that a dependent connection of incidental questions, i.e. resorting to the choice-of-law rules of the legal order selected by the ESR for the main question, furthers the uniformity of decisions more than an independent connection, a dependent connection should be applied. For the time being, it might be necessary to distinguish between incidental questions for which European choice-of-law rules already exist (independent) and others (dependent). Of course all these intricate questions will have to be submitted to the European Court of Justice for preliminary rulings.[38]

20. As soon as the *lex fori* and *lex causae* are congruent, these questions are of no practical relevance anymore because under both approaches the same substantive law would be applied to the incidental question.

2. Family Relationships

21. There is no definition of 'family relationships', neither in article 3 ESR, nor in the recitals. Family relationships must be determined in accordance with the interpretation of family relationships in article 1.2 (b) Rome I regulation and article 1.2(a) Rome II regulation. According to recital 8 Rome I regulation and recital 10 Rome II regulation 'family relationships' cover parentage, marriage, affinity and collateral relatives. Parentage covers, for example, the relation of a father to his (illegitimate) child[39] or issues of adoption.

[36] Weller, 'Europäisches Internationales Privatrecht, Allgemeiner Teil', § 8 para. 82.

[37] Dutta, 'Art. 1 EuErbVO', para. 28.

[38] Weller, 'Europäisches Internationales Privatrecht, Allgemeiner Teil', § 8 para. 82.

[39] Weller, 'Art. 1 Rome I Regulation', para. 24; R. Plender and M. Wilderspin, *European Private International Law of Obligations* (London, 2009), paras. 5–10.

3. Relationships Comparable to Family Relationships

22. Recital 8 Rome I regulation and recital 10 Rome II regulation make clear that the question whether a personal relationship has comparable effects to marriage and other family relationships is to be interpreted in accordance with the *lex fori*. This amendment primarily relates to (registered or unregistered) civil partnerships or specific same sex partnerships.[40] A Member State court seised with a matter involving personal relationships potentially having comparable effects to marriage and other family relationships first needs to determine the applicable *lex causae* according to the choice-of-law rules of the forum and then needs to compare the legal effects of the relationship in question with the autonomous notion of a 'family relationship' under the ESR, although this autonomous notion is still rather elusive. Presumably, the court will have to take notice of at least the major legal effects attributed to the personal relationship in question including issues outside the concrete case at hand such as tax matters and issues of criminal law.

B. Legal Capacity of Natural Persons (point (b))

23. Article 1.2(b) excludes issues relating to the legal capacity of natural persons, however without prejudice to article 23.2(c) and article 26 ESR. According to article 23 ESR the law selected by articles 21 and 22 ESR shall govern 'the succession as a whole' and, in particular, the capacity to inherit according to article 23.2(c) ESR [see art. 23 no. 8]. If the applicable succession law refers to the general capacity of the deceased, an incidental question arises as to whether the deceased had this general capacity according to the applicable law. Article 26 ESR deals with the substantive validity of dispositions of property upon death and agreements as to succession. Articles 26.1(a) to (e) ESR provide that the capacity of the person making the disposition of property upon death to make such a disposition pertains to the 'substantive validity' in the sense of article 24 and 25 ESR (point (a)) as well as the particular causes which bar the person making the disposition from disposing in favour of certain persons (point (b)) and the admissibility of representation for the purpose of

[40] For example, the French *pacte civil de solidarité* according to article 515–1 *et seq. code civil* or the German *Lebenspartnerschaft* according to the *Lebenspartnerschaftsgesetz (LPartG)*; J. Schmidt, 'Art. 1 EuErbVO', in *Beck-Online Großkommentar* (München, 2015), para. 16; Weller, 'Art. 1 Rome I Regulation', para. 27.

making a disposition of property upon death (point (c)) [see art. 26].[41] Apart from these specific reservations relating to a special capacity in succession matters, all issues of legal capacity of a natural person are to be excluded. These issues are to be identified in accordance with article 1.2 (a) Rome I regulation and article 1.2(a) Rome III regulation. This includes, for example, the protection and/or representation of minors and other persons who are, partly or fully, legally incapable in respect to any legal act that may have effect on succession matters such as accepting or waiving the rights as a beneficiary or opening the succession or the like.[42] In general, the Hague Conventions on the Protection of Minors[43] and Adults[44] may be relevant for cases touching upon these issues. Further, personality rights *post mortem* are covered by the exception as well as all questions affecting the deceased as a person other than those that relate to the consequences for the estate such as rules for dealing with the corpse.[45]

C. *Disappearance, Absence, Presumed Death of a Natural Person (point (c))*

24. Questions relating to the disappearance, absence or presumed death of a natural person are excluded by point (c). Disappearance, absence and presumed death are incidents that typically give rise to instituting succession proceedings and thus may be one of the causes of the opening of the succession in the sense of article 23.2(a) ESR if the applicable succession law provides so [see art. 23 no. 6]. However, the conditions of disappearance, absence or presumed death, in particular the prerequisites and procedures for assessing and declaring these incidents officially, are not governed by the ESR but are incidental questions. In addition, many legal systems characterise these questions as part of the civil or personal status of a natural person (whereas English common law seems to characterise these issues as procedural).[46] Since issues of civil

[41] Points (d) and (e) relate to the interpretation of such dispositions and their validity in case of fraud, duress or other impairments of the free will and thus are anyway no issues of legal capacity in the sense of article 1.2(b).

[42] Bonomi, 'Article 1', p. 80.

[43] Convention on Jurisdiction, Applicable Law, Recognition, Enforcement and Co-operation in Respect of Parental Responsibility and Measures for the Protection of Children, The Hague, 19 October 1996.

[44] Convention on the International Protection of Adults, The Hague, 13 January 2000.

[45] Dutta, 'Art. 1 EuErbVO', para. 13.

[46] Max Planck Institute for Comparative and International Private Law, 'Comments on the European Commission's Proposal for a Regulation of the European Parliament and of the

status are excluded by point (a), the questions listed under point (c) should likewise be excluded. The conditions for assessing the moment of death (e.g. in case of 'brain death') may be seen as part of the applicable succession law[47] or be understood as excluded under point (c).[48] Article 23.2(a) ESR does not answer this question,[49] because it merely refers to the time for opening the succession proceedings, not to the legal conditions for the 'death' of the deceased. Under an independent connection, the incidental questions excluded by point (c) are governed by the respective choice-of-law rules of the Member States. They usually select the law of the nationality, domicile or habitual residence.[50]

25. Article 32 ESR deals with *commorientes* and provides that those shall not have any rights to the succession of the other or others if their respective successions are governed by different laws and these laws provide differently for *commorientes*. For the sake of clarity, article 1.2(c) ESR should have made an express reservation for article 32 ESR as does article 1.2(b) for article 23.2(c) and article 26 ESR [see art. 32].

D. Matrimonial Property Regimes and Comparable Regimes (point (d))

26. Questions relating to matrimonial property regimes and property regimes of relationships deemed by the law applicable to such relationships to have comparable effects to marriage are excluded by point (d). This provision should be interpreted in accordance with article 1.2(c) Rome I regulation and article 1.2(b) Rome II regulation. Relationships deemed to have comparable effects to marriage according to the applicable law should be determined in accordance with article 1.2 ESR.

27. The exclusion of property issues of this kind from all of these instruments reacts to the works on instruments on the choice of law on matrimonial property and on property consequences of registered partnerships, that were under preparation during the negotiation of the ESR and have been subsequently adopted.[51] The text of these new instruments excludes in article 1.2(d) (marriage) and article 1.2(d) (partnership) 'the succession rights' of the surviving spouse or partner. Apart from these

Council on jurisdiction, applicable law, recognition and enforcement of decisions and authentic instruments in matters of succession and the creation of a European Certificate of Succession', *RabelsZ* (2010), pp. 522, 550, para. 31.

47 Dutta, 'Art. 1 EuErbVO', para. 14. 48 Bonomi, 'Article 1', p. 81.

49 But compare Dutta, 'Art. 1 EuErbVO', para. 14. 50 Bonomi, 'Article 1', p. 81.

51 See the regulations quoted in footnote 10.

instruments, there is the Hague Convention on Matrimonial Property.[52] However, only three Member States are contracting States.[53]

28. According to recital 12 ESR, matrimonial property regimes include marriage settlements to the extent that such settlements do not deal with succession matters. Recital 12 explains that authorities dealing with a succession should take into account the winding-up of the matrimonial (or comparable) property regime of the deceased when determining the estate of the deceased and the respective shares of the beneficiaries. The rather vague task of 'taking account' of the winding-up of the matrimonial property regime obviously seeks to grant sufficient flexibility for coordinating succession law and the applicable matrimonial property law regime in cases where each of these regimes come from the laws of different States.

29. The distinction between succession law and matrimonial property law is a classical problem of characterisation because at the moment of a spouse's death his or her matrimonial property regime usually comes to an end as well and needs to be wound up. Some jurisdictions protect the surviving spouse primarily under matrimonial property law whereas other jurisdictions protect the spouse by recourse to instruments from succession law, for example by increasing the spouse's share.[54]

30. However, now that the ESR is put into place it is the ESR that determines this characterisation as far as the scope of succession law is concerned.[55] In turn, the scope of autonomous choice-of-law rules on matrimonial property may have to be limited accordingly, if and to the extent that they cover issues that are now characterised as succession law in the sense of the ESR.[56]

31. Therefore, it is necessary to further clarify the scope of 'succession law' under the ESR in relation to issues of matrimonial property. According to article 3.1(a) ESR, 'succession' means the succession to the estate of a deceased person and covers all forms of transfer of assets, rights and obligations 'by reason of death, whether by way of a voluntary transfer under a disposition of property upon death or a transfer through

[52] Convention on the Law Applicable to Matrimonial Property Regimes, The Hague, 14 March 1978, in force 1 September 1992.

[53] France, Luxembourg, the Netherlands; Austria and Portugal are (only) signatory States.

[54] Max Planck Institute, 'Comments', pp. 522, 527, para. 9.

[55] H. Dörner, 'Die Abgrenzung des Erbstatuts vom Güterstatut', in A. Dutta and S. Herrler (eds), *Die europäische Erbrechtsverordnung* (München, 2014), pp. 73, 74, para. 4.

[56] H. Dörner, 'EuErbVO: Die Verordnung zum Internationalen Erb- und Erbverfahrensrecht ist in Kraft!', *ZEV* (2012), pp. 505, 507.

intestate succession' [see art. 3 no. 2]. This includes the decision about who is a beneficiary. Article 23.2(b) ESR explains on this point that succession law shall govern the determination of the beneficiaries, of their respective shares and of the obligations which may be imposed on them by the deceased, and the determination of other succession rights, 'including the succession rights of the surviving spouse or partner' [see art. 23 no. 7]. No further details are provided by the recitals in this respect, except for recital 12 that states the obvious that marriage settlements are excluded from the scope of the ESR 'to the extent that such settlements do not deal with succession matters'.

32. In a first step one may consider that 'the succession rights of the surviving spouse or partner' in the sense of article 23.2(b) ESR covers any right of a surviving spouse upon death of the other spouse, including rights that aim at distributing property acquired during the marriage after the dissolution of the marriage by death of one spouse.[57] However, the most convincing suggestion currently discussed for characterising succession as opposed to matrimonial property seems to be a functional approach.[58] Succession law aims at attributing the deceased's rights and assets to beneficiaries. This attribution may ground either on the deceased's explicit will or on the deceased's presumed will as laid down by legislation with a view to typically close personal connections of the beneficiary to the deceased, and such a personal connection may of course also be presumed in favour of the surviving spouse.

33. If the surviving spouse is to acquire rights or assets on these grounds, the respective rules should be characterised as succession law no matter where these rules may be systematically placed within the legal system of the applicable succession law. On the other hand, where a provision 'is solely concerned with dividing property between the

[57] See e.g. section 1371 German BGB. For details on the characterisation of this provision, see following.

[58] ECJ, case C-220/95, *Antonius van den Boogard* v. *Paula Laumen* [1997] ECR I-01147, para. 21 *et seq.*, in respect to the distinction between 'matrimonial relationships' and 'matters of maintenance' for the purposes of article 5.2 Brussels Convention; see also, directly to the judgment of the ECJ, M. Weller, 'Zur Abgrenzung von ehelichem Güterrecht und Unterhaltsrecht im EuGVÜ, zu EuGH 27. 2. 1997 – Van den Boogard / Laumen', *IPRax* (1999), p. 14; see further and in the same sense but with a view to the ESR, K. Thorn, 'Art. 1 EuErbVO', in *Palandt Bürgerliches Gesetzbuch*, 74th ed. (München, 2015), para. 8; Dörner, 'Die Abgrenzung des Erbstatuts vom Güterstatut', pp. 73, 75, para. 5; P. Mankowski, 'Das erbrechtliche Viertel nach § 1371 Abs. 1 BGB im deutschen und europäischen Internationalen Privatrecht', *ZEV* (2014), pp. 121, 127; Dutta, 'Art. 1 EuErbVO', para. 16.

spouses',[59] such a provision will be concerned with rights in property arising out of a matrimonial relationship. Matrimonial property law seeks to divide the property for compensating one spouse's contributions to the marriage in relation to the other spouse's contributions.[60]

34. On this basis, the following characterisations of provisions of national law are suggested:

For example, section 1931 German BGB is to be characterised as succession law.[61] This provision deals with intestate succession of the spouse. It provides, subject to certain conditions and modifications, that the surviving spouse as an heir on intestacy is entitled to one quarter of the inheritance together with relatives of the first degree, and to one half of the inheritance together with relatives of the second degree or together with grandparents.

35. Further, section 1932 German BGB is to be characterised as succession law,[62] as it has been characterised under autonomous German conflicts laws. This rule provides for certain preferential benefits for the surviving spouse. If the surviving spouse is an heir on intestacy together with relatives of the second degree or together with grandparents, the spouse has a right, in addition to the shares of the inheritance, to the objects belonging to the marital household, to the extent that these are not accessories to a plot of land, and to the wedding presents, as a preferential benefit. If the surviving spouse is an heir on intestacy together with relatives of the first degree, the spouse has a right to these objects to the extent that he needs them to maintain a reasonable household. These preferential benefits are governed by the provisions applying to legacies.

36. Section 1371 of the German BGB deals with the compensation of contributions of the spouses in case of death of one spouse. In case of divorce, the gains of both spouses during the marriage are equalised. In case of the termination of the marriage by death of one of the spouses rather than divorce, the provision provides in subsection 1 that the equalisation of the accrued gains is effected by the share of the inheritance on intestacy of the surviving spouse being increased by one quarter of the inheritance. It is of no relevance in this case, whether in the individual case the spouses did in fact accrue gains. Thus, the winding-up of the

[59] ECJ, case C-220/95 (see footnote 58), para. 22.

[60] Dörner, 'Die Abgrenzung des Erbstatuts vom Güterstatut', pp. 73, 75, para. 6.

[61] Dutta, 'Art. 1 EuErbVO', para. 16; Dörner, 'Die Abgrenzung des Erbstatuts vom Güterstatut', pp. 73, 76, para. 9.

[62] Dörner, 'Die Abgrenzung des Erbstatuts vom Güterstatut', pp. 73, 76, para. 9.

matrimonial property regime upon termination of the marriage is implemented by recourse to a tool taken from succession law. Nevertheless and with a view to its aim, this rule has been rightly characterised as a rule of matrimonial property law in Germany.[63] Again with a view to the aim of this rule, it should likewise be characterised as matrimonial property law for the purposes of the ESR.[64] If the surviving spouse does not become an heir and has no right to a legacy, he or she may under subsection 2 demand equalisation of the accrued gains under the provisions of sections 1373–1383 and section 1390 German BGB, i.e. according to the rules on winding-up of the matrimonial property regime in case of divorce. This rule evidently is a rule of matrimonial property law.

37. If under this characterisation the deceased spouse had, at the time of death, his habitual residence in Germany, German succession law will apply according to article 21 ESR. If additionally German matrimonial property law applies, no problems arise since there are no frictions between German succession law and German matrimonial property law. If, however, the deceased spouse had his habitual residence outside Germany, it is more likely that a succession law other than German law will have to be combined with German matrimonial property law. In this case, difficult problems of substitution and adjustment may arise.

38. For example, section 1371.1 German BGB provides for the equalisation of the accrued gains by increasing the share of the inheritance on intestacy of the surviving spouse by one quarter of the inheritance. Evidently, this provision runs into difficulties if the applicable succession law does not grant shares in the estate but provides for e.g. a beneficial interest (usufruct, *usufructus*). Further, if the surviving spouse receives from the combination of German matrimonial property law and the succession law of another State more than he or she would

[63] See, *per obiter dictum*, Bundesgerichtshof 12 September 2012, IV ZB 12/12, *ZEV 2012*, pp. 590, 591; Bundesgerichtshof 21 June 1963, V ZB 3/63, *NJW 1963*, pp. 1975, 1976; Oberlandesgericht of Schleswig-Holstein 19 August 2013, 3 WX 60/13, *NJW 2014*, p. 88 *et seq.*; Oberlandesgericht of Stuttgart 8 March 2005, 8 W 96/04, *IPRax 2005*, p. 549; H. Dörner, 'Art. 25 EGBGB' in *Staudinger Kommentar zum Bürgerlichen Gesetzbuch mit Einführungsgesetz und Nebengesetzen – EGBGB/IPR Art 25, 26 EGBGB (Internationales Erbrecht)* (Berlin, 2007), para. 34 *et seq.*

[64] Dutta, 'Art. 1 EuErbVO', para. 16; B. Walther, 'Die Qualifikation des § 1371 Abs. 1 BGB im Rahmen der europäischen Erb- und Güterrechtsverordnung', *GPR* (2014), pp. 325, 329; Dörner, 'Die Abgrenzung des Erbstatuts vom Güterstatut', pp. 73, 77, para. 13; but compare e.g. J. Kleinschmidt, 'Optionales Erbrecht: Das Europäische Nachlasszeugnis als Herausforderung an das Kollisionsrecht', *RabelsZ* (2013), p. 723 *et seq.*, esp. p. 757 *et seq.*

have received either under German or the other State's law alone, then evidently there is the need for adjustment.

39. In general, if the combination of two different legal orders for matrimonial property and succession results in an undue cumulation or a lack of protection of the spouse, there is the imminent need for adjustment.[65] To this end, recital 12 reminds the Member States that the authorities dealing with a given succession should 'take into account' the winding-up of the matrimonial property regime. When the instruments on the choice of law on matrimonial property and property consequences of registered partnerships will become applicable,[66] the danger of contradicting norms may be reduced – at least in the participating Member States – by the respective options for choosing the applicable law. Yet, article 22 ESR restricts this choice to the law of the nationality at the time of making the choice or at the time of death.[67] In the absence of a choice, the law of the last habitual residence of the deceased applies for succession[68] whereas the first common habitual residence of the spouses after marriage will determine the applicable law to matrimonial property.[69] This creates difficulties in particular for mobile spouses even though the European instruments should reduce obstacles to mobility. These difficulties should be taken care of in a future revision of the respective instruments, possibly to the effect that both regimes are selected or could be selected congruently.[70]

40. According to article 68(h) ESR, the European Certificate of Succession contains information concerning a marriage (or comparable) contract entered into by the deceased as well as information concerning the matrimonial (or comparable) property regime [see art. 68]. It is an open question whether the share for the surviving spouse arising from

[65] Bonomi, 'Article 1', p. 85. [66] See the regulations quoted in footnote 10.

[67] On this point see e.g. Mankowski, 'Das erbrechtliche Viertel', p. 121 *et seq.*, esp. p. 127 *et seq.*; C. Kohler, 'L'autonomie de la volonté en droit international privé: un principe universel entre libéralisme et étatisme', *Hague Recueil*, vol. 359 (2013), p. 289 *et seq.*, esp. p. 462 *et seq.*, para. 131 *et seq.*; A. Bonomi, 'The interaction among the future EU instruments on matrimonial property, registered partnerships and successions', *YPIL* (2011), p. 217 *et seq.*, esp. p. 230 *et seq.*

[68] Article 21.1 ESR.

[69] Article 26 of the regulation on matrimonial property regimes (quoted in footnote 10); article 26 of the regulation on property consequences of registered partnerships (quoted in footnote 10) states that in the absence of a choice the applicable law is the law of the State under whose law the registered partnership was created.

[70] Bonomi, 'Article 1', p. 86; B. Hess, E. Jayme and T. Pfeiffer, *Stellungnahme zum Vorschlag für eine Europäische Erbrechtsverordnung Version 2009/157 (COD) vom 16.1.2012* (Bruxelles, 2012), p. 32.

matrimonial property law such as e.g. according to section 1371.1 German BGB can be included in the Certificate. Since this share influences the entire distribution of the estate it should be possible to include it as a matter of an *effet utile.*[71]

41. Common law jurisdictions may provide for annulation of an earlier will upon death if the testator marries a second time. Obviously such rules aim at protecting the new spouse. In England, such rules traditionally seem to be characterised as matrimonial property,[72] whereas US-American commentators characterise them as succession law with a view to the nullifying effect on the will.[73]

42. Another difficult issue is the characterisation of advantages for a spouse upon death of the other spouse in marriage settlements. According to recital 12, the ESR is not applicable to marriage settlements 'to the extent that such settlements do not deal with succession matters'. Thus, a characterisation of such advantages in marriage settlements as an issue of succession seems to be not excluded, if not envisaged, by the ESR.[74]

43. In respect to procedural law the division between succession and matrimonial or partnership's property will presumably be easier once the two instruments on matrimonial property regime and on property consequences of registered partnerships will apply,[75] because article 4 of the regulation on matrimonial property and article 4 of the regulation on partnerships both refer to the jurisdictional rules for succession matters under the ESR. As long as these instruments do not yet apply, national law governs the jurisdiction for such property issues. Recital 12, sentence 2, may be read as explaining that a court exercising its jurisdiction for succession matters may 'take into account the winding-up of the matrimonial property regime'.[76] As far as the winding-up appears as incidental question to the succession matter it

[71] Dutta, 'Art. 1 EuErbVO', para. 18; Dörner, 'Die Abgrenzung des Erbstatuts vom Güterstatut', pp. 73, 81, para. 21.

[72] L. Collins et al. (eds), *Dicey, Morris & Collins on the Conflict of Laws*, 15th ed. (London, 2012), rule 159, para. 27–089, with reference to the judgment *In bonis Reid* (1866) LR 1 P & D 74, according to which the question whether a marriage revokes a will is determined by the law of the domicile *at the time of the marriage* rather than at the time of the death of the deceased.

[73] E. F. Scoles, P. Hay and S. C. Symeonides, *Conflict of Laws*, 4th ed. (St. Paul, 2004), § 20.12, p. 1130: 'Most courts . . . have . . . quite rigidly applied the law of the last domicile' [of the deceased, not the domicile at the time of divorce or remarriage].

[74] Bonomi, 'Article 1', p. 85. [75] See the regulations quoted in footnote 10.

[76] Dutta, 'Art. 1 EuErbVO', para. 17.

would be quite clear anyway that such an incidental issue falls within the jurisdiction of the succession court.

E. Maintenance Obligations Other Than Those Arising by Reason of Death (point (e))

44. Point (e) excludes maintenance obligations unless they arise by reason of death. 'Maintenance obligations' in this sense should be interpreted in accordance with article 1.2(b) Rome I regulation, article 1.2(a) Rome II regulation and article 1.2(g) Rome III regulation, because maintenance matters are now dealt with by the Maintenance regulation (as far as applicable to the participating Member States)[77] in connection with the Hague Maintenance Protocol[78] as far as choice of law is concerned.[79] Therefore, all exclusions in other instruments should be interpreted in accordance with article 1.1 and recital 11 of the EU Maintenance regulation according to which that regulation applies to maintenance obligations arising from a family relationship, parentage, marriage or affinity.

45. Maintenance obligations arising by reason of death fall within the scope of the ESR.[80] These are obligations that did not exist prior to death. Such obligations are often functionally equivalent to the reservation of shares for persons close to the deceased[81] or granted for persons not eligible for reserved shares,[82] thereby relating to 'claims which persons close to the deceased may have against the estate or the heirs' in the sense of article 23.2(h) ESR [see art. 23 no. 13].

46. The applicable law to maintenance obligations decides whether and on which conditions the obligation persists after the debtor's death,[83] whereas the succession law designated by the ESR decides if and to what

[77] See the reference in footnote 22.

[78] Hague Protocol of 23 November 2007 on the law applicable to maintenance obligations.

[79] Article 15 of the Maintenance regulation refers to the Protocol.

[80] See e.g. section 1969 German BGB according to which the heir is obliged to pay maintenance to family Members and persons in the house of the deceased for thirty days after the death to the same extent the deceased was obliged to maintain them.

[81] See e.g. article 684 civil code of Québec: 'Tout créancier d'aliments peut, dans les six mois qui suivent le décès, réclamer de la succession une contribution financière à titre d'aliments.', Bonomi, 'Article 1', p. 87.

[82] See e.g. article 767 French civil code in respect to the spouse concurring with descendants: 'La succession de l'époux prédécédé doit une pension au conjoint successible qui est dans le besoin', Bonomi, 'Article 1', p. 87.

[83] Bonomi, 'Article 1', p. 87.

extent a maintenance obligation emerges from and by reason of death[84] and whether it can be transferred.[85] A claim for maintenance is treated like any other claim against the estate and/or the beneficiaries. Succession law decides whether the claim is to be raised against the estate or (one of) the beneficiaries and whether the beneficiary has a right of recourse against his co-beneficiaries.

F. Formal Validity of Dispositions of Property upon Death Made Orally (point (f))

47. Point (f) excludes the question of formal validity of dispositions of property upon death, as defined in article 3.1(d) ESR, if made orally. This includes dispositions recorded by video or audio devices [see art. 3 no. 7].[86]

48. The Commission's proposal for the ESR[87] did not contain any rule on form. Article 27 ESR now deals with the formal validity of dispositions of property upon death made in writing [see art. 27]. This rule mirrors the 1961 Hague Convention on the form of testamentary dispositions.[88] The Hague Convention applies for contracting States amongst the Member States according to article 75.1, subparagraph 2, ESR and thereby preempts article 27 ESR [see art. 75 no. 2].

49. According to article 10 of the 1961 Hague Convention each contracting State may reserve the right not to recognise testamentary dispositions made orally, save in exceptional circumstances, by one of its nationals possessing no other nationality. This reservation, made by several Member States,[89] reflects the distrust of many jurisdictions against oral dispositions. Correspondingly, the exclusion in article 1.2(f) ESR reflects this distrust and leaves it to each Member State to regulate oral dispositions. Some jurisdictions[90] allow oral dispositions

[84] See e.g. section 1969.1, sentence 1, or sections 1586b.1, 1318.2, 1933, sentence 3, German BGB.

[85] Dutta, 'Art. 1 EuErbVO', para. 19. [86] Thorn, 'Art. 27 EuErbVO', para 2.

[87] Proposal for a Regulation of the European Parliament and of the Council on jurisdiction, applicable law, recognition and enforcement of decisions and authentic instruments in matters of succession and the creation of a European Certificate of Succession of 14 October 2009, COM(2009) 154 final.

[88] Convention on the Conflicts of Laws Relating to the Form of Testamentary Dispositions, The Hague, 5 October 1961, in force 5 January 1964.

[89] Belgium, Estonia, France, Luxembourg, the Netherlands.

[90] See e.g. section 587 *et seq.* Austrian civil code (*Allgemeines Bürgerliches Gesetzbuch, ABGB*): 'Der Erblasser kann auch vor einem Gerichte schriftlich oder mündlich testiren'.

generally, however usually on condition of the presence of witnesses and/or a written protocol, whereas other jurisdictions allow oral dispositions in cases of urgency.[91] The exclusion established by the ESR covers the formal validity of any oral disposition and thus even those made in cases of urgency. Therefore this issue is governed entirely by the autonomous choice-of-law rules of the Member States including, as the case may be, those from the Hague Convention.

50. According to article 1 of the Hague Convention, there is a strong *favour validitatis*: a testamentary disposition shall be valid as regards form if its form complies with the internal law (a) of the place where the testator made it, or (b) of a nationality possessed by the testator, either at the time when he made the disposition or at the time of his death or (c) of a place in which the testator had his domicile either at the time when he made the disposition, or at the time of his death, or (d) of the place in which the testator had his habitual residence either at the time when he made the disposition, or at the time of his death, or (e) so far as immovables are concerned, of the place where they are situated.

G. *Property Rights, Interests and Assets Created or Transferred Otherwise Than by Succession (point (g))*

51. Point (g), closely following article 1.2(d) of the Hague Convention of 1989 on the applicable law on succession,[92] excludes 'property rights, interests and assets created or transferred otherwise than by succession, for instance by way of gifts, joint ownership with a right of survivorship, pension plans, insurance contracts and arrangements of a similar nature,[93] without prejudice to point (i) of article 23 (2)'. According to the latter provision succession law shall govern any obligation to restore or account for gifts, advancements or legacies when determining the shares of the different beneficiaries. Recital 14, sentence 2, ESR confirms that the applicable succession law should decide on such 'claw backs', i.e. whether gifts or other forms of dispositions *inter vivos* giving rise to a right *in rem* prior to death should be restored or accounted for the purposes of determining the shares of the beneficiaries in accordance with the law applicable to the succession.

[91] Bonomi, 'Article 1', p. 88.

[92] Convention on the Law Applicable to Succession to the Estates of Deceased Persons, The Hague, 1 August 1989, not yet in force.

[93] The list is evidently non-exhaustive, Bonomi, 'Article 1', p. 90, and would easily cover trusts, if these were not expressly excluded by the exception in point (j).

52. Obligations arising from gifts fall, since 'freely assumed' by the donor,[94] under the Rome I regulation. The donor may freely choose the applicable law. In the absence of such a choice, article 4 Rome I regulation applies. In case of the donation of movable property, the law of the donor's habitual residence governs the obligation, pursuant to article 4.2 Rome I regulation. This will often coincide with the applicable succession law. In case of immovable property, the law of the *situs* applies according to article 4.1(c) Rome I regulation.

53. The transfer of ownership in execution of such an obligation is, if conceived separately from the creation of the obligation (such as in German and Austrian law), outside the existing European choice-of-law instruments and is, as far as movable and immovable property is concerned, governed by the *lex rei sitae*. This includes legacies that create obligations to transfer property: whereas the question if there is such a legacy is governed by the applicable *lex successionis*, the execution of the obligation is governed by the *lex rei sitae* if this obligation is one to transfer property.[95] As far as the transfer of rights is concerned, article 14 Rome I regulation may apply.

54. Special obligations arising from 'informal' gifts between spouses or registered partners such as the *unbenannte Zuwendung* under German law will be governed by the future regulations on matrimonial property or on property of registered partnerships.

55. Obligations for gifts on condition of the death of the donor in the sense of e.g. section 2301 German BGB (*Schenkungen von Todes wegen*)[96] are governed under German substantive law by succession law. Likewise,

[94] See e.g. ECJ, case C-26/91, *Handte & Co. GmbH* v. *Traitements Mécano-chimiques des Surfaces SA* [1992] ECR I-03967, para. 15; ECJ, case C-51/97, *Réunion européenne SA and Others* v. *Spliethoff's Bevrachtingskantoor BV and the Master of the vessel Alblasgracht V002* [1998] ECR I-06511, para. 17; ECJ, case C-334/00, *Fonderie Officine Meccaniche Tacconi SpA* v. *Heinrich Wagner Sinto Maschinenfabrik GmbH (HWS)* [2002] ECR I-07357, para. 23; ECJ, case C-265/02, *Frahuil SA* v. *Assitalia SpA* [2004] ECR I-01543, para. 24; ECJ, case C-27/02, *Petra Engler* v. *Janus Versand GmbH* [2005] ECR I-00481, para. 51, each on the distinction between 'contractual' and 'non-contractual' obligations under article 5, no. 1 and no. 3, Brussels Convention/regulation, see generally Weller, 'Art. 1 Rome I Regulation', para. 13.

[95] H.-P. Mansel, 'Art. 43 EGBGB', in *Staudinger Kommentar zum Bürgerlichen Gesetzbuch mit Einführungsgesetz und Nebengesetzen – EGBGB/IPR Art 43–446 (Internationales Sachenrecht)* (Berlin, 2015), para. 244.

[96] Section 2301 German BGB: 'Promise of donation mortis causa: (1) A promise of a donation made subject to the condition that the donee survives the donor is governed by the provisions concerning dispositions mortis causa.... (2) If the donor executes the donation by delivery of the object given, the provisions concerning gifts inter vivos apply.'

German conflicts law so far characterised such a gift as a matter of succession law. This characterisation should be continued under the ESR as a result of an autonomous interpretation of the regulation, be it as a kind of 'agreement as to succession' in the sense of article 3.1(b) ESR, be it otherwise succession law, as long as this promise for a gift has not been executed by the donor during his lifetime.[97] In tune with this characterisation, recital 14 generally suggests that donations resulting in rights *in rem* prior to the donor's death should be regarded as donations *inter vivos*.

56. The extent to which gifts are taken into account when it comes to calculating the disposable parts of the estate or claims of persons close to the deceased in the sense of article 23.2(h) ESR is governed by succession law.[98] This is made clear by recital 14, sentence 2, and article 23.2(i) ESR according to which any obligation to restore or account for gifts etc. when determining the shares of the different beneficiaries is governed by succession law [see art. 23 no. 16].

Common law joint ownerships or joint tenancies are types of shared ownership of property. Each owner usually holds an undivided interest in the property. The property includes a right of survivorship by which the surviving owner absorbs the deceased owner's interest. This 'absorption' will presumably have to be characterised as a transfer by death rather than an aspect of this particular type of property and will thus be governed by succession law.[99]

57. Pension plans ground on contractual obligations and thus fall within the scope of the Rome I regulation.[100] The same applies for insurance contracts.[101]

'Arrangements of a similar nature' are likewise excluded and are understood as covering e.g. accounts or portfolios payable on death and transfers on death (TOD) deeds or transfer on death securities under US-American laws.[102] The TOD deed is a special type of deed that can be used in a growing number of US States to transfer ownership of real estate outside of probate to the beneficiaries named in the deed.[103]

[97] Dutta, 'Art. 1 EuErbVO', para. 23; Schmidt, 'Art. 1 EuErbVO', para. 28. But compare Bonomi, 'Article 1', p. 103: characterisation *lege causae*.
[98] Bonomi, 'Article 1', p. 91. [99] Mansel, 'Art. 43 EGBGB', para. 255.
[100] Schmidt, 'Art. 1 EuErbVO', para. 30. [101] Schmidt, 'Art. 1 EuErbVO', para. 31.
[102] Bonomi, 'Article 1', p. 107.
[103] See generally the definition for payment on death (P.O.D) designations in § 6–201 (8) Uniform Probate Code 1969 (rev. 2010), at www.uniformlaws.org/shared/docs/probate%20code/2014_UPC_Final_apr23.pdf (30 June 2016).

In general, will substitutes in the sense of US laws,[104] including both pure will substitutes (the donor remains free to dispose of his assets) as well as imperfect substitutes (the donor is bound and cannot undo the disposition unilaterally) are understood as being covered from the exception, even though the applicable national choice-of-law rules may characterise such substitutes, in particular pure will substitutes, as issues of succession law and may even make use of the choice-of-law rules provided for in the ESR. Nothing of the ESR, however, prevents Member States from making use of these rules if they wish so as a matter of their own legal order.

58. All property rights, interests and assets created or transferred otherwise than by succession in the sense of point (g) may be restricted by mandatory rules of the applicable succession law, in particular rules protecting the claims of persons close to the deceased or reserved shares etc. in the sense of article 23.2(h) ESR and in particular any obligations to restore or account for gifts etc. in the sense of article 23.2(i) ESR [see art. 23 no. 13 *et seq.*, esp. 16].

H. *Questions Governed by the Law of Companies (point (h))*

59. Point (h) excludes questions governed by the law of companies. Point (i) supplements this exclusion in respect to the dissolution, extinction and merger of companies. As far as the scope of the 'law of companies' is concerned, the exclusion should be interpreted in accordance with article 1.2(f) Rome I regulation and article 1.2(d) Rome II regulation.

60. The reason for the exclusion in point (h) is that questions relating to the succession of shares and the consequences of death of shareholders or members are generally regarded as questions of company law rather than succession law, even though shares and memberships are of course part of the estate and thus in principle fall under the transfer of assets by reason of death.[105] Nevertheless, in many Member States the transfer of such company-related assets is governed by the *lex societatis*. The *lex successionis* and the *lex societatis* often do not coincide: whereas

[104] See section 7.1(a) Restatement Third on Property, Wills and Other Donative Transfers: 'A will substitute is an arrangement respecting property or contract rights that is established during the donor's life, under which the right to possession or enjoyment of the property or contractual payment shifts outside the probate to the done at the donor's death; and substantial lifetime rights of dominion, control, possession, or enjoyment are retained with the donor'; comment (a) explains that a will substitute serves the purposes of a will but nevertheless does not need to be executed in compliance with the statutory formalities required for a will.

[105] Bonomi, 'Article 1', p. 102.

the *lex successionis* is typically the law of the last habitual residence of the deceased, the *lex societatis* is, as a matter of national law, determined by the law of the incorporation or of the seat (subject to influences from the fundamental freedom of establishment as the case may be).[106] At the same time, both the substantive company law and the choice-of-law rules for companies have not yet been harmonised horizontally even though there are of course numerous instruments of secondary law on certain points of company law in the internal market. The consequence of the exception in point (h) is that some parts of the estate are transferred by the governing company law as opposed to the other parts of the estate.[107] Typically, company law provides for special rules for the succession of shares only of private companies and partnerships. Thus, such shares will be transferred upon death of a shareholder under the applicable company law[108] whereas other shares, in particular of public companies, will be transferred as any other part of the estate according to the applicable succession law.

61. Both corporate and unincorporated companies are covered.[109] This includes both public (e.g. the German *Kapitalgesellschaften*)[110] and private companies (e.g. *Personengesellschaften*)[111] of all kinds as well as cooperative societies (e.g. *Genossenschaften*),[112] associations (e.g. *Vereine*)[113] and foundations (e.g. *Stiftungen*).[114] On the other hand, single-person businesses (e.g. *Einzelkaufleute*) and undisclosed partnerships (e.g. *reine Innengesellschaften*) are not covered. [115]

62. As the text of the provision spells out, the exclusion primarily aims at clauses in the memoranda or articles of associations and articles of association of companies that provide for the case of death of a member, in particular on the question of what should happen to the share or membership of the deceased (e.g. *Nachfolgeklauseln*). Thus, it is

[106] See in particular ECJ, case C-212/97, *Centros Ltd* v. *Erhvervs- og Selskabsstyrelsen* [1999] ECR I-01459; ECJ, case C-208/00, *Überseering BV* v. *Nordic Construction Company Baumanagement GmbH (NCC)* [2002] ECR I-09919; ECJ, case C-167/01, *Kamer van Koophandel en Fabrieken voor Amsterdam* v. *Inspire Art Ltd* [2003] ECR I-10155.

[107] Bonomi, 'Article 1', p. 102.

[108] This result may also be seen as produced by the freedom of establishment, if applicable to the company, see Max Planck Institute, 'Comments', pp. 522, 554.

[109] Schmidt, 'Art. 1 EuErbVO', para. 35; Bonomi, 'Article 1', p. 102.

[110] M. Leitzen, 'EuErbVO: Praxisfragen an der Schnittstelle zwischen Erb- und Gesellschaftsrecht', *ZEV* (2012), p. 520.

[111] Leitzen, 'EuErbVO', p. 520. [112] Leitzen, 'EuErbVO', p. 520.

[113] Leitzen, 'EuErbVO', p. 520. [114] Leitzen, 'EuErbVO', p. 520.

[115] Schmidt, 'Art. 1 EuErbVO', para. 35; Leitzen, 'EuErbVO', p. 520.

the applicable company law that decides whether such clauses provide for a right of a third person to join in or for an immediate replacement of the deceased shareholder, partner or member[116] or whether any third person or only persons subject to certain qualifications are eligible (e.g. *qualifizierte Nachfolgeklauseln*)[117] and if and to what extent such clauses are valid under the applicable company law.[118]

63. Further and in the absence of specific clauses seeking to regulate the death of a shareholder or member, company law decides whether the company is dissolved upon death of one of the partners or whether the company continues to exist without the deceased[119] and whether any compensation is owed to the beneficiaries,[120] whether a share may be transferred[121] and if so to which beneficiary[122] and on which conditions such as approval by the other shareholders or members, if and how a group of beneficiaries may join in,[123] if and how a beneficiary who has joined in is liable for debts of the company,[124] and whether administration of a share/membership is possible.

64. If there are no such special rules in the applicable company law for regulating an issue related to the death of a member or shareholder, succession law governs this issue.[125] Thus, the exclusion in point (h) may also be conceived as providing for a 'double characterisation' of the issues covered as being both company and succession law under which company law pre-empts succession law. [126] Incidental questions of succession such as the status of a beneficiary that arise under the applicable company

[116] A. Everts, 'Neue Perspektiven zur Pflichtteilsdämpfung aufgrund der EuErbVO?', *ZEV* (2013), p. 124 *et seq.*, esp. p. 127; Leitzen, 'EuErbVO', p. 520.

[117] M. Volmer, 'Die EU-Erbrechtsverordnung – erste Fragen an Dogmatik und Forensik', *Der Deutsche Rechtspfleger* (2013), p. 421 *et seq.*, esp. p. 427.

[118] See e.g. article L-223-13 (2) French *code de commerce*; Bonomi, 'Article 1', p. 103.

[119] See e.g. section 177 German *Handelsgesetzbuch* (*HGB*), in respect to the private limited partnership (*Kommanditgesellschaft*).

[120] See e.g. article 252 Belgian *code des societés*, relating to private limited companies; C. Hertel, 'Die Abgrenzung des Erbstatuts vom Sachstatut und Gesellschaftsstatut', in A. Dutta and S. Herrler (eds), *Die europäische Erbrechtsverordnung* (München, 2014), p. 85 *et seq.*, esp. p. 105, para. 64; Dutta, 'Art. 1 EuErbVO', para. 26; W. Burandt, 'Das europäische Erbrecht im Wandel (Teil 2)', *Familie und Recht* (2013), p. 377 *et seq.*, esp. p. 379.

[121] See e.g. section 15.1 German limited liability company act (*Gesetz betreffend die Gesellschaften mit beschränkter Haftung, GmbHG*); article L-223-13(1) French *code de commerce*; article 249 Belgian *code des sociétés*, relating to private limited companies.

[122] Hertel, 'Die Abgrenzung des Erbstatuts vom Sachstatut und Gesellschaftsstatut', p. 85 *et seq.*, esp. p. 105, para. 64.

[123] Schmidt, 'Art. 1 EuErbVO', para. 38.

[124] Schmidt, 'Art. 1 EuErbVO', para. 38.

[125] Dutta, 'Art. 1 EuErbVO', para. 27.

[126] Dutta, 'Art. 1 EuErbVO', para. 27.

law should be connected independently and thus, if a court of a Member State is seised with the matter, to the law designated by the ESR.

65. Questions relating to the dissolution of companies, however, formally fall under the following exception in point (i). When it comes to the evaluation of shares in the context of distributing the estate amongst the beneficiaries or for assessing the rights and claims of non-beneficiaries, this evaluation in relation to other assets of the estate is governed by succession law but of course the balance sheets, for example, to base this evaluation on, are not governed by the law designated by the ESR.[127]

66. As far as a registered company is concerned, the exception in point (l) may also be of relevance. Issues of registration in connection with the transfer of shares and other company-related rights are not covered by succession law, but by the *lex registrationis.*[128]

I. Further Questions Governed by the Law of Companies (point (i))

67. Point (i) excludes the dissolution, extinction and merger of companies and other bodies, corporate or unincorporated. This exclusion supplements point (h) in respect to certain consequences of company law regularly occurring upon the death of a member, partner or shareholder of a company and makes crystal clear that these issues are governed by the applicable company law. Even without this clarification there could have been no doubt that the dissolution, extinction and merger of companies as such are governed by company law and point (h) makes it sufficiently clear that dissolutions, extinctions and mergers of companies on the occasion of the death of a member, partner or shareholder is likewise governed by company law, not by succession law. There seems to be little, if at all, benefit in point (i), but of course there is also no harm.

J. Creation, Administration and Dissolution of Trusts (point (j))

68. Trusts are important instruments in common law jurisdictions for planning and designing a succession during lifetime, be it by a trust *inter vivos* taking effect already during lifetime, or by a testamentary trust.

[127] Bonomi, 'Article 1', p. 105.

[128] Hertel, 'Die Abgrenzung des Erbstatuts vom Sachstatut und Gesellschaftsstatut', pp. 85, 106, para 64.

69. Point (j) excludes all issues on the creation, administration and dissolution of trusts. Recital 13, sentence 2, explains that this exclusion should not be understood as a general exclusion of trusts. Where a trust is created under a will or by operation of the law as a legal consequence of intestate succession, the applicable succession law should apply with respect to the devolution of the assets and the determination of the beneficiaries. The same applies to trusts by judicial act. Thus, point (j) only excludes trusts created voluntarily by a legal act of the settlor.[129] For example, trusts emerging after the death of one of two testators who established a mutual will are not covered by the exception, at least not 'with respect to the devolution of the assets'.[130] Further, even in respect to voluntarily created trusts succession law should remain applicable for issues other than the creation, administration and dissolution of trusts such as the interpretation of the disposition upon death by the settlor or the identification of the beneficiaries.[131] Even the creation by testamentary disposition as such may be seen as covered by succession law.[132]

70. 'Trust' should be interpreted in accordance with article 1.2(h) Rome I regulation and article 1.2(e) Rome II regulation, as well as with article 1.2(h) Rome III regulation. In addition, trusts are the subject of articles 7.6 and 25.3 Brussels I-*bis* regulation. Since all these provisions are specifically designed to take care of the trust as known under common law, the autonomous interpretation of trust in instruments of the European Union will strongly rely on the understanding of trusts in common law jurisdictions.[133] In addition, guidance may be found in the Hague Trust Convention.[134] Article 2.1 of that Convention defines trusts as referring to the legal relationships created (*inter vivos* or upon death) by a person, the settlor, when assets have been placed under the control of a trustee for the benefit of a beneficiary or for a specified purpose. According to article 2.2 of the Convention, a trust has the following characteristics: (a) the assets constitute a separate fund and

[129] Bonomi, 'Article 1', p. 109. [130] Recital 13, sentence 3, ESR.

[131] Bonomi, 'Article 1', p. 110.

[132] Thorn, 'Art. 1 EuErbVO', para. 14; Mansel, 'Art. 43 EGBGB', para. 254.

[133] See e.g. *Gomez* v. *Encarnación Gomez-Monche Vives* [2008] All ER (D) 31, interpreting in that way article 5.6 Brussels I regulation.

[134] Convention on the Law Applicable to Trusts and on their Recognition, The Hague, 1 July 1985. As of 30 June 2015, this Convention is in force only in a few Member States bound by the ESR (Italy, Luxembourg, Malta and the Netherlands). Other contracting States are Australia, Canada, China (only in respect to Hong Kong), Liechtenstein, Monaco, San Marino, Switzerland and the United Kingdom. Signatory States are Cyprus, France and the United States of America.

are not a part of the trustee's own estate; (b) title to the trust assets stands in the name of the trustee or in the name of another person on behalf of the trustee; (c) the trustee has the power and the duty, in respect of which he is accountable, to manage, employ or dispose of the assets in accordance with the terms of the trust and the special duties imposed upon him by law.

71. As far as trusts in this sense are excluded from the ESR, national choice-of-law rules apply. The law applicable to the trust may differ entirely from the succession law selected by the ESR. Where the Hague Trust Convention applies, article 6 provides that a trust shall be governed by the law chosen by the settlor. As opposed to article 22 ESR, the settlor may choose any law, subject only to internationally mandatory rules and public policy as defined by articles 16 and 18 of the Convention. In the absence of such a choice, article 7 of the Convention provides that the law of the closest connection shall apply. According to article 7(a) to (d), relevant factors are the place of administration designated by the settlor, the *situs* of the assets of the trust, the place of residence or business of the trustee and the objects of the trust and the places where they are to be fulfilled. Article 15 of the Convention provides that, by establishing a trust, the settlor cannot derogate from certain mandatory rules including (a) the protection of minors and incapable parties; (b) the personal and proprietary effects of marriage; (c) succession rights, testate and intestate, especially the indefeasible shares of spouses and relatives; (d) the transfer of title to property and security interests in property; (e) the protection of creditors in matters of insolvency; and (f) the protection, in other respects, of third parties acting in good faith.

72. Article 4 provides that the Convention does not apply to preliminary issues relating to the validity of wills or of other acts by virtue of which assets are transferred to the trustee. Thus, the constitution of a testamentary trust is considered not to be covered by the Convention.[135] This may even include the question whether a trust can at all validly be created by will. However, if this view leads to the consequence that trusts cannot be validly created by will whenever the applicable succession law is that of a civil law country non containing rules or notions for trusts, the Convention seems to be violated and it appears more convincing to restrict article 4 to the sole question whether the will as such is valid.[136]

[135] Bonomi, 'Article 1', p. 113. [136] Bonomi, 'Article 1', p. 113.

73. In non-contracting States, a testamentary trust may be characterised as an issue of succession law by the national choice-of-law rules.[137] If these are removed in view of the ESR,[138] there are no directly applicable choice-of-law rules for a testamentary trust.[139] In this case, either ad-hoc rules by case law will have to be applied or the ESR could be applied by analogy. However, the applicable succession law may limit the testamentary dispositions to certain types of dispositions (*numerus clausus*) such as in Germany, France or Spain. In that case, it appears adequate either to infer from the disposition an implied choice of law[140] or to reinterpret the testator's will as aiming at the closest equivalent to a trust such as an execution of the will (*Testamentsvollstreckung; nomination d'un exécuteur testamentaire*). Whether such an interpretation is possible is a question of the interpretation of the will in its entirety and as such governed by the succession law as determined according to the ESR.[141]

K. *Nature of Rights* In Rem *(point (k))*

74. The division between the *lex rei sitae* and the *lex successionis* was one of the most intensely debated issues during the legislative process.[142]

137 For Germany see e.g. Bundesgerichtshof 2 June 1976, IV ZR 162/74, *WM 1976*, pp. 811, 812; Dörner, 'Art. 25 EGBGB', para. 427; C. Wendehorst, 'Art. 43 EGBGB', in *Münchener Kommentar BGB*, 6th ed., vol. XI (München, 2015), para. 49; for France see e.g. Cour de cassation 3 November 1983, *Rev crit dir int priv* (1984), p. 336; see also Bonomi, 'Article 1', p. 113.

138 As is generally known, EU regulations automatically pre-empt national law. Thus, national choice-of-law rules on succession would be pre-empted by the ESR. No issue of implementation arises. Nevertheless, the view is taken that contradicting and even merely repeating national rules must be removed for the sake of clarity, see e.g., in relation to the Rome regulations and the respective German national choice-of-law rules, R. Wagner, 'Änderungsbedarf im autonomen deutschen internationalen Privatrecht aufgrund der Rom II-Verordnung? Ein Überblick über den Regierungsentwurf eines Gesetzes zur Anpassung der Vorschriften des Internationalen Privatrechts an die Rom II-Verordnung', *IPRax* (2008), p. 314.

139 P. Richters, 'Anwendungsprobleme der EuErbVO im deutsch-britischen Rechtsverkehr', *ZEV* (2012), pp. 576, 577.

140 Max Planck Institute, 'Comments', pp. 522, 558.

141 Bonomi, 'Article 1', p. 114.

142 See e.g. C. Döbereiner, 'Vindikationslegate unter Geltung der EU-Erbrechtsverordnung', *Zeitschrift für das Privatrecht der Europäischen Union* (2014), p. 42; K. Lechner, 'Die EuErbVO im Spannungsfeld zwischen Erbstatut und Sachenrecht', *IPRax* (2013), p. 497; B. Laukemann, in E. Jayme, B. Hess and T. Pfeiffer, *Stellungnahme zum Vorschlag für eine europäische Erbrechtsverordnung Version 2009/157 (COD) vom 16.1.2012* (Bruxelles, 2012), p. 32.

Despite this debate (or perhaps better: because of this debate), the regulation of this issue resulted in somewhat opaque rules.[143]

75. According to point (k), (only) the 'nature' of rights *in rem* is excluded from the scope of the ESR. This nature of rights *in rem* is governed by the national *lex rei sitae* of the respective Member State.[144] The nature of a right *in rem* is mainly determined by its prerogatives granted to the rightholder and the effects vis-à-vis third persons. However, it is not evident what exactly the 'nature' of a right *in rem* includes because there are different national concepts as to what constitutes a 'type' of a right *in rem*.[145] Yet, it appears clear that the *lex rei sitae* decides which type of right *in rem* is in question.[146] And generally it seems appropriate to restrict the understanding of the 'nature' of a right *in rem* to the existence of the type of right in order to contribute to the overall objective of the ESR to provide for a uniform succession law as far as possible. This would mean that the 'nature' or 'type' of a right *in rem* does not include the mode of acquisition.[147]

76. The 'transfer' of rights *in rem* by succession is governed by the applicable succession law. [148] Along the preceding lines, this should include the mode of acquisition, subject only to requirements and effects of the recording of the respective rights in registers. These requirements are excluded from the ESR by article 1.2(l) ESR. Article 69.5 ESR states accordingly that the European Succession Certificate shall constitute a valid document for the recording of succession property in the relevant register of a Member State only without prejudice to points (k) and (l).

77. Recital 15 further explains that the ESR allows for the creation or the transfer by succession of a right *in rem* as provided for in the applicable succession law. And indeed, according to article 23.2(e) ESR, it is succession law that governs the transfer of assets, rights and obligations forming part of the estate to the heirs or legatees. Succession law

[143] B. Laukemann, 'Die lex rei sitae in der Europäischen Erbrechtsverordnung – Inhalt, Schranken und Funktion', in *Ars aequi et boni in mundo. Festschrift für Rolf A. Schütze zum 80. Geburtstag* (München, 2014), pp. 325, 326 (also available in Max Planck Institute Luxembourg for International, European and Regulatory Procedural Law, *Working Paper Series 2/2014*, at www.mpi.lu).

[144] Bonomi, 'Article 1', p. 120. [145] Laukemann, 'Die lex rei sitae', *Working Paper*, p. 22.

[146] Mansel, 'Art. 43 EGBGB', para. 229.

[147] Mansel, 'Art. 43 EGBGB', para. 234; but compare e.g. G. Hohloch, 'Art. 1 EuErbrVO', in *Erman BGB*, 14th ed., vol. II (Köln, 2014), para. 13; Dörner, 'EuErbVO', pp. 505, 509.

[148] See article 3.1(a) ESR [see art. 3 no. 2] and article 23.2(e) ESR. [see art. 23 no. 10].

thus determines, for example, the 'entitlement',[149] i.e. identifies the person who acquires the right *in rem* by reason of death. Thus, the question whether a legacy creates an immediate right *in rem* (such as the *Vindikationslegat*) is to be determined by succession law.[150] The decision of whom is entitled to a *res* and until what moment in time does not touch upon the 'type' of the right *in rem* that forms the object of the legacy.[151] Further, succession law determines the scope of the right *in rem* to be acquired by this person, e.g. either full property or only usufruct or other limitations.[152]

78. Thus, the exception in favour of property law is to be understood rather narrowly[153] because the ESR evidently aims at providing for an application of succession law as comprehensively as possible.[154]

79. Yet, the ESR is not to affect the *numerus clausus* of rights *in rem* in the national laws of the Member States. Consequently, the ESR does not require a Member State to recognise a right *in rem* to property located in that Member State if the right *in rem* in question is not known in its legal system. For example, usufruct cannot be introduced under the applicable succession law of one Member State in another Member State that does not recognise it.[155] Rather, as recital 16 continues to explain and as article 31 provides, the ESR requires such a Member State (only) to provide for the adaptation of an unknown right *in rem*

[149] Dutta, 'Art.1 EuErbVO', para. 29: '*Berechtigung*'; Laukemann, 'Die lex rei sitae', *Working Paper*, p. 14: '*Zuweisung*'.

[150] For example, at least the following legal systems are understood as creating such immediate rights *in rem* by legacy, at least by certain types of legacy: France, Italy, Portugal, Spain, Hungary, Romania; see e.g. M. G. Cubbedu Wiedemann and A. Wiedemann, 'Erbrecht in Italien', in R. Süß (ed), *Erbrecht in Europa*, 2nd ed. (Bonn, 2007), para. 61; E. Huzel, B. Löber and I. Wollmann, 'Erbrecht in Portugal', in R. Süß (ed), *Erbrecht in Europa*, 2nd ed. (Bonn, 2007), para. 72; B. Löber and E. Huzel, 'Erbrecht in Spanien', in R. Süß (ed.), *Erbrecht in Europa*, 2nd ed. (Bonn, 2007), para. 75; see generally J. P. Schmidt, 'Ausländische Vindikationslegate über im Inland belegene Immobilien – zur Bedeutung des Art. 1 Abs. 2 lit. l EuErbVO', *ZEV* (2014), p. 133; R. Süß, 'Die Vindikationslage im internationalen Privatrecht', *RabelsZ* (2001), p. 244 *et seq.*, esp. p. 246 *et seq.* On the other hand, the legal systems of the following countries for example are understood as creating by legacy (or at least providing for such a type of legacy) merely claims against the estate: Austria, China, Germany, the Netherlands, Switzerland.

[151] Mansel, 'Art. 43 EGBGB', para. 234. [152] Bonomi, 'Article 1', p. 121.

[153] H.-P. Mansel, K. Thorn and R. Wagner, 'Europäisches Kollisionsrecht 2012: Voranschreiten des Kodifiktationsprozesses – Flickenteppich des Einheitsrechts', *IPRax* (2013), pp. 1, 7: property law excluded merely 'in principle'; but compare e.g. Döbereiner, 'Vindikationslegate', p. 42.

[154] Mansel, 'Art. 43 EGBGB', para. 227; Dutta, 'Art. 1 EuErbVO', para. 32.

[155] See the European Commission Proposal, quoted in footnote 87, para. 4.1., p. 5.

to the closest equivalent right *in rem* under the law of that Member State in order to allow the beneficiaries to enjoy the rights *in rem* created or transferred to him by succession under the applicable succession law irrespective of where the property is located and whether the jurisdiction there knows such a right or not [see art. 31].

80. On the other hand, a legacy that creates an immediate entitlement (*Vindikationslegat*) under the applicable succession law must not be adapted to the *lex rei sitae* if that law does not know such legacy but only legacies that create obligations (*Damnationslegat*). Rather, the *Vindikationslegat* is to be recognised as such because it does not touch upon the type of right *in rem* (the type of the right *in rem* in question is the same in both types of legacies), and the *Vindikationslegat* must be listed in the European Succession Certificate according to article 63.2(a) ESR as the 'right of a legatee'.

81. The principles of adaptation under article 31 ESR equally apply to intellectual property.[156] Accordingly, succession law determines who acquires a right upon death and the mode of acquisition whereas the question whether the right in question can at all be transferred upon death and how the death affects the right as such is seen as a matter of the applicable property, e.g. copyright law. However, if the intellectual property law provides for special rules for the death of the right holders,[157] these rules are understood to preempt succession law.[158]

82. In respect to adaptation account should be taken of the aims and the interests pursued by the specific right *in rem* and the effects attached to it. According to recital 15, sentence 3, ESR, the authorities or competent persons of the Member State whose succession law applies and has created or transferred the right unknown in the other Member State may be contacted for further information on the nature and effects of that right, in particular via the existing networks in the area of judicial cooperation in civil and commercial matters, but also any other available means facilitating the understanding of foreign law.

[156] Dutta, 'Art. 1 EuErbVO', para. 34.

[157] For an example see e.g. ECJ, case C-518/08, *Fundación Gala-Salvador Dalí and Visual Entidad de Gestión de Artistas Plásticos (VEGAP)* v. *Société des auteurs dans les arts graphiques et plastiques (ADAGP) and Others* [2010] ECR I-03091, para. 33, on special rules for the death of the artist in respect to the artist's resale right according to directive 2001/84/EC of the European Parliament and of the Council of 27 September 2001 on the resale right of an author of an original work of art, OJ 2001 no. L272, 13 October 2001.

[158] Dutta, 'Art. 1 EuErbVO', para. 34; Max Planck Institute, 'Comments', pp. 522, 560.

83. This adaptation will practically be of importance because the general choice-of-law rules for determining the applicable succession law cover all kinds of assets of the estate including immovable property. There is no special choice-of-law rule for immovable property that would point to the succession law of the *situs* thereby making congruent succession law and property law for this particular class of assets.[159]

84. From a general viewpoint, recital 16 and article 31 are of high relevance because they acknowledge the need for adaptation in a specific constellation. Recital 17 is even more relevant in that it makes clear that the reference to adaptation in this constellation does not preclude the recourse to this method in the course of the application of foreign law in any other context of the ESR. This explanation may certainly be generalised beyond the scope of the ESR. Adaptation has thus become a normatively recognised tool of European choice-of-law methodology.

85. If a legatee does not directly acquire a right *in rem* under the applicable succession law but needs to claim execution of the transfer or property from the estate against the heirs,[160] this transfer or property is not governed by the ESR but by the applicable property law according to the *lex rei sitae.*[161]

86. Acquisitions on the occasion of death or on the basis of death as *causa* for a transfer do not fall within the scope of the ESR as long as they count as transfers 'otherwise than by succession' in the sense of article 1.2 (g) ESR.

L. Recording in a Register of Rights in Property (point (l))

87. Point (l) excludes the recording in a register of rights in immovable or movable property, including, but not limited to,[162] the legal requirements for such recording, and the effects of recording or failing to record such rights in a register. The Commission's proposal had suggested excluding merely the 'publicising' of 'these rights'.[163]

159 Bonomi, 'Article 1', p. 119.

160 See e.g. section 2174 German BGB; article 1004 *et seq.* French *code civil.*

161 Bonomi, 'Article 1', p. 122; M. Buschbaum, 'Die künftige Erbrechtsverordnung – Wegbereiter für den acquis im europäischen Kollisionsrecht', in R. M. Beckmann and A. Matusche-Beckmann (eds), *Weitsicht in Versicherung und Wirtschaft – Gedächtnisschrift für Ulrich Hübner* (Heidelberg, 2012), pp. 589, 596.

162 Bonomi, 'Article 1', p. 126.

163 European Commission proposal, article 1.2(j).

88. 'Register' means registers publicly organised by law, including national and international,[164] as well as those for movable, intellectual or immovable property, as well as fully electronic registers.[165]

89. Recital 18 explains that the law of the Member State in which the register is kept determines under what legal conditions and how the recording must be carried out and which authorities (e.g. land registers or notaries) are in charge of checking that all requirements are met and that the documentation presented or established is sufficient or contains the necessary information. The *lex registrationis* often, but not necessarily, coincides with the *lex rei sitae.*[166] Thus, the reference to the *lex rei sitae* in recital 18 should be understood as referring to the *lex registrationis.*[167]

90. Recital 19, sentence 1, explains that the effects of the recording of a right in a register should be excluded from the scope of the ESR. Consequently, the *lex registrationis* should not only determine the formal and procedural conditions for registration but also its effects such as, for example, whether and in what moment of time the registration creates effect *inter partes* or *erga omnes*, as recital 19, sentences 2 and 3, makes clear. This goes beyond the typical scope of the *lex registrationis* that is usually restricted to formal conditions and procedures for registration. In addition, it must be noted that the *lex registrationis* and the *lex rei sitae* do not necessarily coincide. Thus, recital 19 is only correct on the assumption that both *leges* do coincide as it is (presumably) always the case in respect to immovable property.[168]

91. The conditions for registration include, e.g., the period of time in which the registration must be effectuated,[169] but also the question which legal transactions, for example a contractual agreement under private law, can be registered, what the fees for registration are and whether there is an option for electronic registration.[170] In particular, however, these conditions relate to formal requirements for registration. In that respect, the competent authorities of the Member State of registration may check that the right of the deceased to the succession property mentioned in the document presented for registration is a right which is recorded as such in the register or which is otherwise demonstrated in accordance with the

[164] Such as e.g. the register for the Cape Town Convention, see e.g. S. van Erp, 'The new Succession Regulation: The *lex rei sitae* rule in need of reappraisal?', *European Property Law Journal* (2012), pp. 187, 188.

[165] Bonomi, 'Article 1', p. 125. [166] Bonomi, 'Article 1', p. 126.

[168] Mansel, 'Art. 43 EGBGB', para. 241. [169] Bonomi, 'Article 1', p. 126.

[170] Bonomi, 'Article 1', p. 128.

law of the Member State of registration. In doing so, the registration authorities should, according to recital 18, sentence 4, accept such documents drawn up in another Member State by the competent authorities whose circulation is provided for by the ESR, in particular the European Certificate of Succession, in order to avoid duplication of documents.

92. According to article 69.5 ESR the European Succession Certificate shall constitute a valid document for the recording of succession property in the relevant register of a Member State, however without prejudice to points (k) and (l) of article 1.2 ESR.

93. In addition to that Certificate, all other documents are to be taken into account even if the *lex registrationis* allows only for registration on the basis of, e.g., notarial deeds from its own State.[171] On the other hand, the registration authorities are not precluded from asking for additional documentation as prescribed by the law of the Member State of registration, such as documents relating to the payment of revenue.

94. Likewise, the effects of registration are governed by the law of the Member State of registration, whereas the mode of transfer as such seems to remain part of succession law.[172] However, this is a matter of intense debate. It is argued that the exception in point (l) should cover entirely the conditions for acquisition.[173] Some argue that at least where the *lex registrationis/lex rei sitae* contains conditions that are designed to protect the reliability of legal transactions in cases of acquisition of property by death, these conditions should apply on the grounds of point (k) whereas succession law applies if the property law of the *lex registrationis* only fulfills a supportive and 'technical' function for implementing the decisions of the succession law ('functional approach').[174]

[171] See e.g. article 710–1 French *code civil*: 'Tout acte du droit doit, pour donner lieu aux formalités des publicités foncières, résulter d'un acte reçu en la forme authentique par un notaire exerçant en France . . .'.

[172] Dutta, 'Art. 1 EuErbVO', para. 32; Mansel, 'Art. 43 EGBGB', para. 234; Thorn, 'Art. 1 EuErbVO', para. 16; Kleinschmidt, 'Optionales Erbrecht', pp. 723, 763; van Erp, 'The new Succession Regulation', p. 187 *et seq.*, esp. p. 188 *et seq.*

[173] See e.g. Lechner, 'EuErbVO im Spannungsfeld', p. 497 *et seq.*, esp. p. 499 *et seq.*; P. Lagarde, 'Les principes de base du nouveau règlement européen sur les successions', *Rev crit dr int priv* (2012), pp. 691, 730; C. Döbereiner, 'Das internationale Erbrecht nach der EU-Erbrechtsverordnung (Teil I)', *MittBayNot* (2013), p. 358 *et seq.*, esp. p. 360 *et seq.*; W. H. Rechberger, 'Das Europäische Nachlasszeugnis und seine Wirkungen', *Österreichische Juristen-Zeitung* (2012), p. 14 *et seq.*, esp. p. 16 *et seq.*; U. Simon and M. Buschbaum, 'Die neue EU-Erbrechtsverordnung', *NJW* (2012), pp. 2393, 2397.

[174] Laukemann, 'Die lex rei sitae', *Working Paper*, p. 18.

95. Recital 19 explains that where the acquisition of a right in immovable property requires a recording in order to ensure the *erga omnes* effect of registers or to protect legal transactions, the moment of the *erga omnes* effect is governed by the law of that Member State whereas the acquisition *inter partes* is determined according to the applicable succession law.[175] In any case, the registration agency will have to apply foreign law as the applicable succession law for assessing whether the transfer as such is valid. This will potentially increase the costs of registration unless this effect is undone by the use of the European Succession Certificate.[176]

96. In legal systems in which registration is constitutive rather than declaratory, the question arises what happens if the applicable succession law provides for an immediate transfer to one of the beneficiaries but the *lex registrationis* requires registration for the transfer to be valid and such registration did not take place.[177] In such a case of conflict between the *lex successionis* and the *lex registrationis*, the succession law presumably only decides about the transfer by succession of the beneficiary but not about the validity of that transfer for particular assets of the estate in respect to conditions under the *lex registrationis*.[178] The *lex registrationis* thus trumps the *lex successionis* but this appears to be the objective of the exclusion under article 1.2(l).

[175] Schmidt, 'Ausländische Vindikationslegate', pp. 133, 135; Mansel, 'Art. 43 EGBGB', para. 242: 'cumulative application' of succession law and property law.
[176] Dutta, 'Art. 1 EuErbVO', para. 32. [177] Bonomi, 'Article 1', p. 129.
[178] Mansel, 'Art. 43 EGBGB', para. 242; Bonomi, 'Article 1', p. 129; van Erp, 'The new Succession Regulation', pp. 187, 188.

Article 2

Competence in Matters of Succession within the Member States

MATTHIAS WELLER

> This Regulation shall not affect the competence of the authorities of the Member States to deal with matters of succession.

1. Article 2 ESR makes clear that the ESR does not interfere with the competence of the Member States to regulate matters of succession in general. Rather, the ESR confines itself to regulating cross-border matters of succession.[1] One might have expected this central confinement to be mentioned in article 1 already.[2] At the same time, the limitation to international aspects appears self-evident given the ground of competence in article 81.2 TFEU on which the ESR is based. Yet, there are provisions of (special) substantive succession law (for international cases) such as article 32 on *commorientes* and article 33 on estates without a claimant as there are such provisions in other instruments of European private international law [see art. 32 and 33].[3]

2. More importantly but still quite self-evident,[4] article 2 clarifies that the ESR does not generally interfere with rules of local or regional

[1] G. Hohloch, 'Art. 3 EuErbrVO', in *Erman BGB*, 14th ed., vol. II (Köln, 2014), para. 1.

[2] Compare e.g. article 1.1 Regulation (EC) no. 593/2008 of the European Parliament and of the Council of 17 June 2008 on the law applicable to contractual obligations (Rome I), OJ 2008 no. L177, 4 July 2008 (Rome I): 'situations involving a conflict of laws'; article 1.1 Regulation (EC) no. 864/2007 of the European Parliament and of the Council of 11 July 2007 on the law applicable to non-contractual obligations (Rome II), OJ 2007 no. L199, 31 July 2007 (Rome II); article 1.1 Council Regulation (EU) no. 1259/2010 of 20 December 2010 implementing enhanced cooperation in the area of the law applicable to divorce and legal separation, OJ 2010 no. L342, 29 December 2010 (Rome III).

[3] See Council Regulation (EC) no. 1346/2000 of 29 May 2000 on insolvency proceedings, OJ 2000 no. L160, 30 June 2000 (that will be replaced as from 26 June 2017 by Regulation (EU) no. 2015/848 of the European Parliament and of the Council of 20 May 2015 on insolvency proceedings (recast), OJ 2015 no. L141, 6 June 2015), already includes jurisdiction, recognition as well as choice of law.

[4] The Commission's Proposal for a Regulation of the European Parliament and of the Council on jurisdiction, applicable law, recognition and enforcement of decisions and

jurisdiction and competence within a Member State,[5] including the allocation of competence within the various branches of the judiciary and with notaries, as the case may be.[6] Yet some provisions of the ESR do affect local jurisdiction. In particular, article 45 ESR expressly addresses the issue of 'jurisdiction of local courts' and provides, in subsection (1), that the application for a declaration of enforceability of another Member State court's decision shall be submitted to the court or competent authority of the Member State of enforcement as communicated by that Member State according to article 78 ESR. Subsection (2) determines local jurisdiction by reference to the place of domicile of the party against whom enforcement is sought, or to the place of enforcement.

3. Further, choice-of-court agreements may designate the jurisdiction of a specific court within a Member State and thereby determine international as well as local jurisdiction [see art. 5 no 4].

4. Finally and as a matter of the general principle of *effet utile*, if the ESR allocates international jurisdiction to a Member State, this Member State must provide for local jurisdiction somewhere within its territory irrespective of its internal rules.

authentic instruments in matters of succession and the creation of a European Certificate of Succession of 14 October 2009, COM(2009) 154 final, did not contain an equivalent provision.

[5] A. Dutta, 'Art. 2 EuErbVO', *Kommentierung der europäischen Erbrechtsverordnung*, in *Münchener Kommentar BGB*, 6th ed., vol. X (München, 2015), para. 1; A. Bonomi, 'Article 2', in A. Bonomi and P. Wautelet, *Le droit européen des successions. Commentaire du Règlement n° 650/2012 du 4 juillet 2012* (Bruxelles, 2013), p. 132.

[6] A. Bonomi, 'Article 2', p. 132.

Article 3

Definitions

MATHIAS WELLER

1. For the purposes of this Regulation:
   (a) 'succession' means succession to the estate of a deceased person and covers all forms of transfer of assets, rights and obligations by reason of death, whether by way of a voluntary transfer under a disposition of property upon death or a transfer through intestate succession;
   (b) 'agreement as to succession' means an agreement, including an agreement resulting from mutual wills, which, with or without consideration, creates, modifies or terminates rights to the future estate or estates of one or more persons party to the agreement;
   (c) 'joint will' means a will drawn up in one instrument by two or more persons;
   (d) 'disposition of property upon death' means a will, a joint will or an agreement as to succession;
   (e) 'Member State of origin' means the Member State in which the decision has been given, the court settlement approved or concluded, the authentic instrument established or the European Certificate of Succession issued;
   (f) 'Member State of enforcement' means the Member State in which the declaration of enforceability or the enforcement of the decision, court settlement or authentic instrument is sought;
   (g) 'decision' means any decision in a matter of succession given by a court of a Member State, whatever the decision may be called, including a decision on the determination of costs or expenses by an officer of the court;
   (h) 'court settlement' means a settlement in a matter of succession which has been approved by a court or concluded before a court in the course of proceedings;
   (i) 'authentic instrument' means a document in a matter of succession which has been formally drawn up or registered as an authentic instrument in a Member State and the authenticity of which:

(i) relates to the signature and the content of the authentic instrument; and
(ii) has been established by a public authority or other authority empowered for that purpose by the Member State of origin.

2. For the purposes of this Regulation, the term 'court' means any judicial authority and all other authorities and legal professionals with competence in matters of succession which exercise judicial functions or act pursuant to a delegation of power by a judicial authority or act under the control of a judicial authority, provided that such other authorities and legal professionals offer guarantees with regard to impartiality and the right of all parties to be heard and provided that their decisions under the law of the Member State in which they operate:
(a) may be made the subject of an appeal to or review by a judicial authority; and
(b) have a similar force and effect as a decision of a judicial authority on the same matter.

The Member States shall notify the Commission of the other authorities and legal professionals referred to in the first subparagraph in accordance with Article 79.

Summary

I. OVERVIEW *page* 115
II. THE DEFINITIONS 116
A. Succession 116
B. Agreement as to Succession 117
C. Joint Will 118
D. Disposition of Property upon Death 119
E. Member State of Origin 119
F. Member State of Enforcement 120
G. Decision 120
H. Court Settlement 121
I. Authentic Instrument 121
III. DEFINITION OF 'COURT' 122

I. Overview

1. Article 3.1 contains numerous definitions for core terms used later in the text of the ESR. This somewhat 'American' style of rule-making can be observed more and more in the legal instruments of the

European Union. One general function of such a list of core terms may indeed be to secure those legal terms to be interpreted autonomously.[1] Of course, other legal terms outside the list of definitions are to be interpreted autonomously as well. Article 3.1 ESR contains, in points (a) to (d), definitions of general relevance for the material scope of the ESR, and in points (e) to (i) definitions relating to recognition and enforcement. Article 3.2 provides for a special definition of courts and requires the Member States to notify to the European Commission certain structures and competencies of their respective judiciaries.

II. The Definitions

A. *Succession*

2. Article 3.1(a) ESR defines the most central term of 'succession' – by using first of all the term succession. On a formal level, this is of course logically defective. The *definiens* must not be identical with the *definiendum*.[2] On the level of contents, the explanation of the core term of the instrument that determines the entire material scope for jurisdiction, recognition and enforcement as well as choice of law is a little disappointing in that it states no more than the obvious. The user of the instrument merely learns that the instrument covers all forms of transfer of all kinds of assets and obligations by death, be it by 'disposition of property upon death' in the sense of article 3.1(d) ESR, be it through intestate succession. This definition is reiterated in recital 9 without any substantial additions. 'Intestate succession' includes, without spelling it out, acquisition of assets via reserved shares as mentioned in article 23.2(h) ESR.[3] It is a general characteristic of the ESR that articles 1 and 23 ESR on the scope of the applicable law are far more telling on how 'succession' should be understood than the express definition of that core term in article 3.1(a) ESR. But some more information is provided in the following definitions.

[1] A. Bonomi, 'Article 3', in A. Bonomi and P. Wautelet, *Le droit européen des successions. Commentaire du Règlement n° 650/2012 du 4 juillet 2012* (Bruxelles, 2013), p. 135.

[2] See e.g. C. Gratton, *Infinite Regress Arguments* (Dordrecht, 2010), p. 140.

[3] A. Dutta, 'Art. 3 EuErbVO', Kommentierung der europäischen Erbrechtsverordnung, *in* Münchener Kommentar BGB, 6th ed., vol. X (München, 2015), para. 2.

B. *Agreement as to Succession*

3. Article 3.1(b) ESR defines agreements as to succession as any agreement affecting rights, including third-party rights,[4] to the future estate. Article 25 ESR contains a special choice-of-law rule for these agreements [see art. 25]. The definition in article 3.1(b) ESR is designed along the lines of article 8 of the Hague Convention of 1989 on the law applicable to succession[5] and expressly includes mutual wills. As opposed to 'joint wills' in article 3.1(c) ESR, that requires the joint will to be drawn up in one instrument, the definition of succession agreements does not include any formal requirements.[6]

4. The understanding of succession agreements appears rather broad, in that it covers e.g. agreements to waive rights from legitimate shares, gifts on condition of death, the *donation-partage*[7] in French, Belgian and Portuguese law[8] and, according to most commentators, even contracts to make or not to make or to revoke or not to revoke a will, although these contracts do not directly affect rights but only oblige the testator to exercise his or her freedom to make a will in a certain way.[9] It is of no relevance whether there is a consideration or not. On the other hand, as soon as the deceased avoids any binding effect, for example in a joint will,[10] there is no longer an 'agreement' in the sense of the definition. If there is an agreement by virtue of a binding effect, the entire disposition is considered as 'agreement' even in respect to its non-binding parts,[11] whereas an obligation does not become part of the succession agreement merely because it is assumed as a consideration. Rather, such an obligation, even though part of the agreement but typically outside the material scope of the ESR since being assumed

[4] Dutta, 'Art. 3 EuErbVO', para. 8.

[5] Convention on the Law Applicable to Succession to the Estates of Deceased Persons, The Hague, 1 August 1989, not yet in force. Article 8 reads: 'For the purposes of this Chapter an agreement as to succession is an agreement created in writing or resulting from mutual wills which, with or without consideration, creates, varies or terminates rights in the future estate or estates of one or more persons parties to such agreement'.

[6] Compare article 8 of the Hague Convention: 'in writing'. [7] Bonomi, 'Article 3', p. 144.

[8] See e.g. section 1076 *et seq.* French *code civil.*

[9] Dutta, 'Art. 3 EuErbVO', para. 9; Bonomi, 'Article 3', p. 145: functional understanding of succession agreements; see also at p. 143; but compare A. Daví, 'L'autonomie de la volonté en droit international privé des successions dans la perspective d'une future réglementation européenne', *Riv dir int priv proc* (2004), pp. 473, 489.

[10] K. Lechner, 'Erbverträge und gemeinschaftliche Testamente in der neuen EU-Erbrechtsverordnung', *NJW* (2013), pp. 26, 27.

[11] Dutta, 'Article 3 EuErbVO', para. 9.

inter vivos, follows its own choice-of-law rules,[12] for example those of the Rome I regulation[13] or those dictated for maintenance obligations.[14] However, article 4.3 Rome I regulation appears to allow the application of the succession law.[15]

5. Clearly outside article 3.1(c) ESR are agreements to buy the (entire) estate or comparable transactions including those on the acquisition of assets out of the estate in the course of the distribution of the estate. Agreements on gifts, joint ownership with a right of survivorship, pension plans, insurance contracts and arrangements of similar nature are expressly excluded from the material scope of the ESR by article 1.2(g) ESR. Agreements by spouses on matrimonial property (article 1.2(d) ESR) and maintenance (article 1.2(e) ESR), sometimes agreed upon on the occasion of the establishment of a succession agreement, remain outside the definition of succession agreements even if drawn up in one single instrument.

C. *Joint Will*

6. There is no definition of 'will'. However, it appears to be common ground that wills relate to unilateral legal acts by which a person expresses his or her last will concerning his or her succession. 'Joint wills' in the sense of article 3.1(c) ESR are wills drawn up by at least two persons in one single instrument whereas mutual wills may well appear in separate instruments but may of course also appear in one instrument. Thus, a joint will may qualify as a succession agreement if there is a binding effect, i.e. if the joint will contains an agreement. Conversely, a succession agreement may at the same time be a joint will if the agreement is drawn up in one single instrument. Thus, article 24 ESR or article 25 ESR may apply to joint wills depending on whether the joint will includes an agreement (and is then submitted to article 25 ESR), or not (then article 24 ESR applies) [see art. 25; art. 24 no. 3 *et seq.*].

[12] C. F. Nordmeier, 'Erbverträge und nachlassbezogene Rechtsgeschäfte in der EuErbVO – eine Begriffsklärung', *ZEV* (2013), p. 117, 119; but compare Bonomi, 'Article 3', p. 142: '*lex successionis*'.

[13] Regulation (EC) no. 593/2008 of the European Parliament and of the Council of 17 June 2008 on the law applicable to contractual obligations (Rome I), OJ 2008 no. L177, 4 July 2008.

[14] Another category of considerations may be that of assuming maintenance obligations.

[15] Nordmeier, 'Erbverträge und nachlassbezogene Rechtsgeschäfte in der EuErbVO', pp. 117, 119.

D. *Disposition of Property upon Death*

7. The 'disposition of property upon death' in the sense of article 3.1(d) ESR is the generic term for any willful disposition upon death drawn up by the deceased, including all recognised types of legal acts by the deceased, namely the will, the joint will and the succession agreement. However, the definition simply names these examples but does not offer a common denominator. Thus, there is no criterion to distinguish dispositions upon death from those *inter vivos* in the sense of article 1.2(g) ESR.[16] Neither is there a reference to 'material' or 'substantive' forms of typical or less typical dispositions such as e.g. the designation of an heir, the establishment of a legacy or the provision for an execution of the will. Thus, it may become a matter of doubt whether the admissibility and the validity of such dispositions is governed by the general law of succession according to article 21 *et seq.* ESR or the special rules for dispositions under article 24 *et seq.* ESR.[17] It appears fair to say that this definition should have been drafted more accurately.

8. Article 24 *et seq.* ESR provide for special choice-of-law rules for dispositions upon death. Article 22.2 makes also reference to the disposition of property upon death in that it subjects the formal requirements of a choice of law to those for a disposition of property upon death according to article 27. Given the general character of the definition for dispositions of property upon death, it would have been more logical to place it further above, in particular in front of the definitions of the more specific dispositions by succession agreement and joint will.[18]

E. *Member State of Origin*

9. The following definitions in points (e) to (i) and in article 3.2 relate to procedure and aim at supporting the free circulation of judgments and other court decisions, authentic instruments and the European Certificate of Succession. First of all, article 3.1(e) ESR defines the Member State of origin for the purposes of recognition and enforcement and designates the Member State in which the decision in question has been rendered, the settlement in question has been approved of or the European Certificate of Succession has been issued. Neither article 1 nor article 3 ESR defines 'Member State' as such. Recital 82 explains that the United Kingdom and Ireland are not bound by the ESR, while recital 83

[16] Bonomi, 'Article 3', p. 138.
[17] Bonomi, 'Article 3', p. 138, and 'Article 24', p. 378.
[18] Bonomi, 'Article 3', p. 137.

makes clear that Denmark is likewise, but for different reasons, not bound by the ESR.

F. *Member State of Enforcement*

10. Article 3.1(f) ESR mirrors point (e) in that it designates the Member State of 'destination', i.e. the Member State in which enforcement is sought in respect to the aforementioned decisions and settlements or in respect to a European Certificate of Succession.

G. *Decision*

11. Article 3.1(g) ESR defines decisions as any decision by a 'court'[19] of a Member State irrespective of its denomination including decisions on costs or expenses taken by an officer of a Member State court.

12. Declarations received by a court will not count as 'decisions'. For example, article 13 ESR deals with acceptance and waiver of the succession, of a legacy or of a reserved share and provides that the Member State courts of the habitual residence – in addition to the general jurisdiction of the Member State courts for succession matters according to article 4 *et seq.* ESR – have jurisdiction to receive declarations on such acceptance or waiver. Such receiving of a decision which is essentially passive should be distinguished from actively rendering a 'decision' in the sense of article 3.1(g) ESR [see art. 13 no. 10].

13. It appears unsettled whether a national certificate of succession counts as a 'decision'.[20] As long as the certificate originates from a 'court' in the sense of article 3.2 ESR, however, it appears preferable to understand such a certificate as 'decision', at least if it did not originate from an *ex-parte* proceeding.[21] Documents relating to succession matters that do not fulfill these conditions may still qualify as 'authentic instruments' in the sense of articles 3.1(i) and 59 ESR [see art. 59].

[19] As defined by article 3.2 ESR.

[20] See e.g. H. Dörner, 'EuErbVO: Die Verordnung zum Internationalen Erb- und Erbverfahrensrecht ist in Kraft!', *ZEV* (2012), pp. 505, 512: no 'decision'; C. Hertel, 'Zum Nachweis der Erbfolge im Grundbuchverfahren mittels im Ausland erstellten Erbscheinen', *DNotZ* (2012), p. 688; but compare e.g. M. Buschbaum and U. Simon, 'EuErbVO: Das Europäische Nachlasszeugnis', *ZEV* (2012), p. 525; T. Rauscher, 'Einführung EuErbVO', in T. Rauscher, *Europäisches Zivilprozessrecht / Europäisches Internationales Privatrecht, vol. IV* (München, 2010), para. 81.

[21] Dutta, 'Art. 3', para. 13; R. Geimer, 'Art. 1 EuErbVO', in *Zöller, Kommentar ZPO*, 30th ed. (Köln, 2014), annex II J, para. 17.

H. *Court Settlement*

14. Article 3.1(h) ESR defines court settlements, along the lines of article 2(b) Brussels I-*bis* regulation,[22] as those relating to succession matters and being concluded before a court or approved by a court in the course of proceedings. This includes settlements on the distribution of the estate.[23] Article 61 provides for free circulation of court settlements on succession matters [see art. 61].

I. *Authentic Instrument*

15. Article 3.1(i) ESR describes authentic instruments, along the lines of article 2(c) Brussels I-*bis* regulation, as documents in succession matters having been drawn up formally or registered as authentic instrument in a Member State. These authentic instruments must be distinguished from 'decision' by a 'court' in the sense of articles 3.1(g) and 3.2 ESR.[24]

16. The authenticity must relate to the signature and the contents and it must have been established by a public authority including non-public authorities empowered respectively by the Member State of origin. The autonomous concept of authenticity, as further developed autonomously in recital 62 but mirroring the Latin notary system, takes account of the genuineness of the instrument, the formal prerequisites, the powers of the authority drawing up the instrument and the procedure and it also covers, again according to recital 62, the factual elements recorded in the instrument, e.g. that the parties indicated in the instrument appeared before the authority on the date indicated and that these parties made the declarations laid down in the instrument. Finally, recital 62 explains that challenges against the authenticity of the instrument should be made at the Member State of origin under the law of that Member State. Thus, authenticity of an instrument emerges as a result from applying national rules for establishing authentic instruments under a minimum standard functionally defined by the ESR [see art. 59].

17. Authentic instruments in the sense of article 3.1(i) ESR have the same evidentiary effects in other Member States as in the Member State of origin, subject to a public policy control, under article 59 ESR.[25] Recital

[22] Regulation (EU) no. 1215/2012 of the European Parliament and of the Council of 12 December 2012 on jurisdiction and the recognition and enforcement of judgments in civil and commercial matters (recast), OJ 2012 no. L351, 20 December 2012.

[23] Bonomi, 'Article 3', p. 152.

[24] See above nos. 11–13.

[25] See also recital 61 ESR.

61 explains that the evidentiary effects in the Member State of enforcement should be as close as possible to those of the authentic instrument under the law of the Member State of origin. If the document in question does not qualify as an authentic instrument it may still have effects in other Member States, but these effects are governed by the *lex successionis.*

III. Definition of 'Court'

18. Article 3.2, subparagraph 1, ESR defines the term 'court' broadly as encompassing judicial authorities such as proper courts. Additionally, any other authority or even a legal professional – this is a true novelty in European private international law – with competence in succession matters qualifies as a court as long as these bodies or persons (a) exercise judicial functions or (b) act pursuant to a delegation of power by a judicial authority or (c) act under the control of a judicial authority. Further condition is that (d) impartiality and (e) the right of all parties to be heard is guaranteed. Finally, the decisions of such 'courts' must (f) be subject to appeal or otherwise judicial review and (g) have a similar force and effect as a decision of a judicial authority on the same type of matter. According to article 3.2, subparagraph 2, ESR the Member States are obliged to notify the Commission of those of their authorities that are functionally described in subparagraph 1.

19. Recital 20 explains that the ESR seeks to respect the different judicial systems of the Member States and therefore offers a broad definition of 'court', but all of these courts are to be bound by the jurisdictional rules of the ESR. Furthermore, non-judicial authorities of a Member State empowered under national law to deal with succession matters should not be regarded as 'courts', as long as they do not exercise judicial functions, 'such as the notaries in most Member States'. Indeed, if a notary merely establishes authentic acts, such a notary does not exercise judicial functions and the establishment of a notarial deed about a declaration of will relating to succession matters is not a 'decision' but simply fulfills formal requirements of the applicable law. In turn, if notaries do exercise judicial functions, they are bound by the jurisdictional rules of the ESR like any other court (recital 21), and the acts of those notaries should circulate freely in accordance with the rules on recognition and enforcement under the ESR (recital 22).

20. It appears to be an open question whether arbitral tribunals may count as 'courts' in the sense of article 3.2 ESR. Neither 'arbitration' as such nor arbitration agreements are expressly excluded from the material scope of the ESR.[26] Arbitral tribunals will regularly fulfill the procedural minimum standards set out in article 3.2, subparagraph 1, ESR. Yet it would appear strange if the arbitral tribunal for an arbitral succession matter was to be bound, as a 'court' in the sense of the ESR, by its rules on jurisdiction.[27] This would mean that the interested parties could only choose as a seat of the arbitral tribunal those places provided for by chapter II of the ESR. One may also hold that these jurisdictional rules do not apply *ratione materiae*.[28] Alternatively, one may take the view that arbitral tribunals are not meant to be courts at all but that ESR implicitly establishes a fully mandatory system that excludes the derogation of the jurisdiction of (Member) State courts. If the ESR allows derogation in favour of arbitration it will presumably require the arbitral tribunal to apply the ESR's choice-of-law rules.[29] Arbitrability will be a matter of the applicable national law. Recognition and enforcement of the arbitral award will not fall within chapter IV of the ESR.

[26] Compare e.g. article 1.2(d) Brussels I-*bis* regulation and article 1.2(e) Rome I regulation.
[27] Dutta, 'Art. 3 EuErbVO', para. 20.
[28] P. Mankowski, 'Erbrechtliche Schiedsgerichte in Fällen mit Auslandsbezug und die EuErbVO', *ZEV* (2014), p. 395 *et seq.*, esp. p. 398 *et seq.*
[29] Mankowski, 'Erbrechtliche Schiedsgerichte', p. 395 *et seq.*, esp. p. 398 *et seq.*

CHAPTER II

Jurisdiction

Article 4

General Jurisdiction

ALFONSO-LUIS CALVO CARAVACA

The courts of the Member State in which the deceased had his habitual residence at the time of death shall have jurisdiction to rule on the succession as a whole.

Summary

I. INTRODUCTION *page* 127
II. OPTION IN FAVOUR OF 'HABITUAL RESIDENCE' 128
III. CHARACTERISTICS OF THE GENERAL FORUM ESTABLISHED BY THE ESR 133
IV. ADVANTAGES AND DISADVANTAGES OF THE NEW RULES 136
V. DETERMINING HABITUAL RESIDENCE 140
VI. APPLICATION PROBLEMS 143
A. Forum Shopping 143
B. Multiple Habitual Residences 146
C. Exception Clause? 147

I. Introduction

1. International jurisdiction can be defined as the legal power of a State's courts and public authorities, considered as a whole, to hear disputes arising out of international private situations in contentious or non-contentious proceedings.[1] In other words, it is a case of determining, for example, in which cases and under which grounds and principles the German, Italian or Spanish courts and public authorities are able to hear disputes arising out of international successions.

2. In the absence of uniform rules, from international or supranational sources, each State is entirely free to determine the conditions and cases in which its courts are granted with international jurisdiction (PCIJ

[1] See A.-L. Calvo Caravaca and J. Carrascosa González, *Derecho Internacional Privado*, 15th ed., vol. I (Granada, 2014), p. 113 *et seq.*; A. Heldrich, *Internationale Zuständigkeit und anwendbares Recht* (Berlin, 1969), pp. 65–91.

judgment 7 September 1927, *Lotus*, PCIJ judgment 28 February 1939, *Panevezis-Saldutiskis*). Public international law ensures each State of the right to organise its judiciary and to exercise its jurisdiction as it consider appropriate.[2] This has various consequences:

1. *Multiple grounds for international jurisdiction.* The courts of different States can declare themselves competent in relation to the same matter. This encourages forum shopping: the parties will choose to litigate in the courts of the country where conducting the proceedings is more in their interests.[3]
2. *Lack of any international jurisdiction.* It is also possible, in any given case, for the courts in the different States involved all to decline jurisdiction. In such a case, the claimant could not initiate proceedings in any court anywhere in the world. In order to avoid such a result, which amounts to a 'denial of justice', recourse can be made to the *forum necessitatis* rule [see art. 11].

3. Determining which State's courts are competent is sometimes a difficult task; it is, however, an important one. It is a difficult task because some national legislation adopt *exclusive* or *exorbitant* grounds of jurisdictions, even though the general rule should be the distribution of the concurrent jurisdiction of the courts of different States based upon reasonable connections.[4] It is an important task, because it affects three questions: which rules apply to procedure (the *lex fori regit processum* rule), which private international law rules apply in the competent court (and indirectly therefore, which substantial law governs the case) and, finally, what language will proceedings be held in.[5]

II. The Option in Favour of 'Habitual Residence'

4. Article 4 ESR establishes as a general rule that the courts of the Member State in which the deceased had his or her habitual residence

[2] M. Stürner, 'Deutsch-italienische Erbfälle unter der kommenden Europäischen Erbrechtsverordnung', *Jahrbuch für Italienisches Recht* 26 (2013), p. 61.

[3] M. Kähr, *Der Kampf um den Gerichtsstand – Forum Shopping im internationalen Verfahrensrecht der Schweiz* (Zürich, St. Gallen, 2010), pp. 37–48; M. Meyer, *Die Gerichtsstände der Erbrechtsverordnung unter besonderer Berücksichtigung des Forum Shopping* (Frankfurt am Main, 2013), pp. 15–20.

[4] See D. P. Fernández Arroyo, 'Compétence exclusive et compétence exorbitante dans les relations privées internationales', *Hague Recueil*, vol. 323 (2006), pp. 36–41.

[5] See Stürner, 'Deutsch-italienische Erbfälle', pp. 62–63.

at the time of death shall have jurisdiction.[6] The European legislator confers international jurisdiction to the courts of the Member State in which the deceased had his last habitual residence – that is to say, the State in which a person's life is centred and this interests are located.[7] The concept of habitual residence in article 4 ESR is the same as in article 21.1 ESR and in essence corresponds to that used in other rules of EU private international law.[8]

5. 'Habitual residence' enjoyed a limited run in the field of succession. Various conventions of the Hague Conference on Private International Law used it, but as a connecting factor for legislative competence, not jurisdiction: the Convention of 5 October 1961 on the Conflict of Laws Relating to the Form of Testamentary Dispositions (article 1(d)) and the Convention, never entered into force, of 1 August 1989 on the Law Applicable to Succession to the Estates of Deceased Persons (articles 3.1 and 3.2). The Convention of 2 October 1973 Concerning the International

[6] See, in general, A. Bonomi, 'Article 4', in A. Bonomi and P. Wautelet, *Le droit européen des successions. Commentaire du Règlement n° 650/2012 du 4 juillet 2012* (Bruxelles, 2013), pp. 169–182; J. Carrascosa González, *El Reglamento Sucesorio Europeo 650/2012 de 4 de julio 2012: Análisis crítico* (Granada, 2014), pp. 78–96; E. Castellanos Ruiz, 'Sucesión hereditaria: Reglamento 650/2012 sobre sucesión internacional', in A.-L. Calvo Caravaca and Carrascosa González (eds), *Derecho Internacional Privado*, 15th ed., vol. II (Granada, 2014), pp. 554–557; D. Damascelli, *Diritto internazionale privato delle successioni a causa di morte (dalla l. n. 218/1995 al reg. UE n. 650/2012)* (Milano, 2013), pp. 47–53; A. Davì and A. Zanobetti, 'Il nuovo diritto internazionale privato delle successioni nell'Unione Europea', *CdT* 5/2 (2013), pp. 112–115; A. Davì and A. Zanobetti, *Il nuovo diritto internazionale privato europeo delle successioni* (Torino, 2014), pp. 195–201; G. Hohloch, 'Kommentierung der EuErbRVO', in W. Erman, *BGB: Kommentar*, 14th ed. (Köln, 2014), pp. 6690–6692; A. Leandro, 'La giurisdizione nel regolamento dell'Unione europea sulle successioni *mortis causa*', in P. Franzina and A. Leandro (eds), *Il diritto internazionale privato europeo delle successioni* mortis causa (Milano, 2013), pp. 61–67; Meyer, *Die Gerichtsstände*, pp. 59–74.

[7] It is worth noting that the State of the last habitual residence of the deceased has not been defined in general terms as the State 'in which the centre of interests of his family and his social life was located' (recital 24 ESR). I think that recital 24 refers only to a particular case: i.e. the specific hypothesis, which occurs when the deceased has transferred his residence abroad for professional reasons without been accompanied by his family. Therefore, the definition of residence as the centre of interests of his family and his social life should not be used to characterise the content of the concept of habitual residence in general (interpretive criterion: *Inclusio unius est exclusio alterius*). This notion must express a personal connection of the deceased – and not of his family – with a particular country.

[8] S. Herzog, 'Die EU-ErbVO', *ErbRErbR – Zeitschrift für die gesamte erbrechtliche Praxis* 1 (2013), p. 6; Hohloch, 'Kommentierung', p. 6693; P. Lagarde, 'Les principes de base du nouveau règlement européen sur les successions', *Rev crit dr int priv* (2012), p. 699; D. Lehmann, 'Die EU-Erbrechtsverordnung zur Abwicklung grenzüberschreitender Nachlässe', *DStR – Deutsches Steuerrecht* 41 (2012), pp. 2085–2086.

Administration of the Estates of Deceased Persons did indeed use 'habitual residence' as the forum for international jurisdiction (article 2), but that convention was a resounding failure: only three States have ratified it. The European Group for Private International Law (EGPIL) – a prestigious and influential think tank – also adopted habitual residence as a ground for jurisdiction, in a proposal for a convention drafted in 1993: 'Proposal for a Convention concerning jurisdiction and the enforcement of judgments in family and succession matters' (article 5.1): 'The courts or authorities of the Contracting State in which the deceased had his habitual residence at the time of his death shall have jurisdiction in matters relating to succession.'

6. The adoption of 'habitual residence' as the general forum in matters of succession in the ESR constitutes an *historic milestone*. It is the first time that so many States have agreed internationally to codify a legal sector over which so much diversity presides. This diversity is well illustrated by an overview of the rules in force in the EU Member States prior to the adoption of the ESR. *Example 1:* In Germany, following a legal reform towards the end of 1999, the FamFG admitted the *dual functionality principle* (*der Grundsatz der Doppelfunktionalität*), according to which the rules specifying internal jurisdiction (*örtliche Zuständigkeit*), such as § 343 FamFG on matters of succession, were also to be used to determine international jurisdiction (*internationale Zuständigkeit*) (§ 105 FamFG).[9] *Example 2:* In accordance with article 50 of the 1995 Italian law on private international law, Italian courts had international jurisdiction in matters of succession, when the deceased was an Italian citizen at the time of his death, and also when the succession opened in Italy, when the most valuable part of the assets of the estate were located in Italy, when the defendant was resident in Italy or had submitted to Italian jurisdiction (save when the claim related to immovable property located abroad) and, finally, when the claim concerned assets located in Italy.[10] *Example 3:* The 1985 Spanish constitutional law on the Judiciary (LOPJ) as well as Spanish case law admitted a variety of forums in matters of succession: express submission, under certain conditions, to the Spanish courts in order to hear disputes relating to international matters of succession (article 22.2 LOPJ), tacit

[9] Calvo Caravaca and Carrascosa González, *Derecho Internacional Privado*, vol. I, pp. 16–18 (exclusivity of private international law), 743–749 (rule *lex fori regit processum*); Stürner, 'Deutsch-italienische Erbfälle', p. 61.

[10] See D. Damascelli, 'La legge applicabile alla successione per causa di morte secondo il diritto internazionale privato italiano', *Riv dir int priv proc* (2003), pp. 85–108, 106–108.

submission (article 22.2 LOPJ), a special forum where the deceased was last resident in Spanish territory (article 22.3 LOPJ), and, finally, a special forum for the case that immovable property was located in Spanish territory (article 22.3 LOPJ).[11]

7. The system of grounds for international jurisdiction in the ESR is based upon the principles of 'proximity' and 'proper administration of justice'.[12] Recital 23 ESR reminds us that

> [i]n view of the increasing mobility of citizens and in order to ensure the proper administration of justice within the Union and to ensure that a genuine connecting factor exists between the succession and the Member State in which jurisdiction is exercised, this Regulation should provide that the general connecting factor for the purposes of determining both jurisdiction and the applicable law should be the habitual residence of the deceased at the time of death.

Consequently, courts of the Member States must be competent in order to be able to rule on succession matter and apply the ESR's conflict rules. This is not possible unless there is a *sufficient connection* between the dispute and the EU Member State's court: the last habitual residence of the deceased in a Member State (article 4 ESR), the deceased's nationality accompanied by choice of law and other conditions (articles 5, 6 and 7 ESR), the presence of assets of the estate in a territory belonging to the Member State (article 10 ESR), are all international grounds for jurisdiction which demonstrate a real and sufficient connection between the claim and the EU.[13] Even the *forum necessitatis* provided for in article 11 ESR requires a *sufficient connection* in the case of the court hearing the substantive matter.[14] *Example:* A Spanish court incorrectly declares itself competent to hear a claim made by a claimant domiciled in France, who requested, in his capacity as a natural child, part of the inheritance left by his father, a Greek of Romanian origin who was last domiciled in Italy,

[11] See Castellanos Ruiz, 'Sucesión hereditaria', pp. 517–586, 520–522.

[12] See, in general, Fernández Arroyo, 'Compétence exclusive et compétence exorbitante', pp. 42–49 (principle of proximity) and pp. 58–61 (good administration of justice).

[13] R. Geimer, 'Die europäische Erbrechtsverordnung im Überblick', in J. Hager (ed), *Die neue europäische Erbrechtsverordnung. Tagungsband* (Baden-Baden, 2013), pp. 19–20; in general, H.-P. Mansel, 'Das Staatsangehörigkeitsprinzip im deutschen und gemeinschaftlichen IPR: Schutz der kuturellen Identität oder Diskriminierung der Person?', in E. Jayme (ed), *Kulturelle Identität und internationales Privatrecht* (Heidelberg, 2003), p. 145.

[14] See Carrascosa González, *El Reglamento Sucesorio Europeo*, p. 102; Davì and Zanobetti, 'Il nuovo diritto internazionale privato', pp. 119–120; Davì and Zanobetti, *Il nuovo diritto internazionale privato europeo*, pp. 208–209; G. Novelli, *Compendio di diritto internazionale privato e processuale*, 7th ed. (Napoli, 2004), pp. 95–98.

against the Romanian widow domiciled in Italy, who administered the inheritance of the children born in wedlock. The deceased's last domicile or habitual residence was not in Spain. Nor did he have immovable property, money or movable property in Spain. The inheritance mainly comprised shares in Italian and Greek companies. The only connection which the deceased had with Spain was that, in the past, he acquired Spanish nationality (which he subsequently lost), had a domicile in Spain (which was also lost when he moved to Italy many years before his death) and that, every year, he returned to Spain for a couple of months in the winter to play golf. Two months a year for the purposes of playing golf cannot be considered to be either a domicile or an habitual residence. The court could not even take interim relief measures in the absence of assets located in the Spanish territory, such as movable or immovable property. Had the ESR been in force, article 4 would prevented the Spanish court to declare its competence.

It is necessary to remember that the reasons justifying the international jurisdiction of the courts are not the same as those which justify application of a particular law to a given international case. In order to ground the jurisdiction of the courts of a State, the dispute has to bear a 'sufficient connection' with that State. In order to make a particular law applicable to an international private matter, a sufficient connection between that international private matter and a State is not enough. The law which should govern such a matter should be the 'proper law', the law which has the 'strongest right to application'. That, generally, is the law of the country most closely linked to the actual matter being disputed.[15] *Example:* If a Swedish citizen had retired at 85 to the Côte d'Azur in France, where he died at the age of 90 after having worked all his life in Germany, bought an apartment in London and left Swedish heirs who live spread out over Sweden, Denmark and Finland, it is appropriate to question whether the jurisdiction of the French court would really be the 'centre of gravity' for the matter and in fact that could be seriously doubted.[16]

8. International jurisdiction is a *prerequisite* for proceedings; consequently, however cumbersome it is to verify the habitual residence of the

[15] Calvo Caravaca and Carrascosa González, *Derecho Internacional Privado*, vol. I, p. 139.

[16] See H. Gaudemet-Tallon, 'Quelques réflexions sur les propositions concernant la compétence judiciaire, la reconnaissance et l'exécution des décisions en matière successorale dans l'Union européenne', in Deutsches Notarinstitut (ed), *Les Successions Internationales dans l'Union Européenne – Perspectives pour une harmonisation* (Würzburg, 2004), p. 451.

deceased, the courts of the Member States are obliged to do so (recital 25 *in fine*, by analogy).[17] They cannot base their jurisdiction upon a different ground of jurisdiction, due to uncertainty regarding the establishment of the 'last habitual residence of the deceased'; rather, the courts must justify their jurisdiction on the basis of the deceased's last habitual residence in their country. *Example:* In the absence of the conditions set forth in article 5 *et seq.* ESR, a dispute regarding the succession of a person who died in Italy and who had Italian nationality, but habitually resided in France, cannot be brought before an Italian judge. The reason for this is simple: the ESR has adopted last habitual residence of the deceased as a general ground for international jurisdiction in order to create a uniform area from the point of view of private international law for matters of succession.[18]

III. Characteristics of the General Forum Established by the ESR

9. The forum set out in article 4 ESR has the following *characteristics*:

1) It is a *general* ground for international jurisdiction. It attributes jurisdiction to the courts of a Member State as a whole (German, Italian, Spanish courts), because, save for grounds of jurisdiction based upon articles 5 and 7 ESR [see art. 5 no. 4], the European legislator has not designated which particular court in the territory of a Member State is competent (= it is not a *special* international jurisdiction forum). The determination of the specific court within the Member State is a task to be performed in each Member State, which will designate a particular court in accordance with its own domestic rules on subject-matter jurisdiction, territorial jurisdiction and functional jurisdiction.[19]
2) The European legislator starts from the very reasonable view that, in principle, disputes in matters of succession should be heard by the courts of the Member State in which the deceased had his habitual residence at the time of his death. However, the courts of that country must cede jurisdiction to courts of the Member State whose law, under article 22 ESR, has been chosen by the deceased to govern his

[17] See Carrascosa González, *El Reglamento Sucesorio Europeo*, p. 91; Castellanos Ruiz, 'Sucesión hereditaria', p. 557.
[18] T. Ballarino, 'Il nuovo regolamento europeo sulle successioni', *Riv dir int* (2013), p. 1138.
[19] Bonomi, 'Article 4', p. 173.

succession in *three instances*: first, when, by means of a document which has been written, dated and signed by all the affected parties, agreement has been made under article 5 ESR to allocate jurisdiction to the courts of the State whose law was chosen by the deceased [see art. 5 ESR no. 4 *et seq.*]; second, when the court of the Member State of the deceased's last habitual residence to which the matter has been submitted considers, as set out in article 6 ESR, on the request of one of the parties to the proceedings, that the courts of the Member State whose law has been chosen are better placed to hear the case [see art. 6 ESR no. 2 *et seq.*]; third, when the parties to the proceedings have expressly accepted the jurisdiction of the court seised in the Member State whose law was chosen by the deceased [see art. 7 ESR nos. 8–9]. Otherwise, it must also cede jurisdiction when the parties to the proceedings agree to *settle out of court* in the Member State whose law on succession the deceased has chosen [see art. 8 ESR].

3) It is a forum established in order to respond to the requirements of a *unitary system for private international law on matters of succession*. The courts in the relevant Member State have jurisdiction to hear the entire succession matter (article 4 *in fine* ESR), regardless of the movable or immovable nature of the assets comprising the inheritance, or of their location. Nor is it relevant, as stated in article 3.2 ESR and in recital 20, whether the proceedings are contentious or non-contentious. In accordance with the rule *accessorium principali sequitur*, those courts will also have international jurisdiction to hear *incidental or preliminary matters* which must be resolved in order to settle the disputed matter of succession, even though their pronouncements on these issues lack the force of *res judicata*.[20]
4) It is a forum which fixes in time the variable circumstance which defines it. A person can have resided in different States: habitual residence may vary over time. What is relevant, for the purposes of fixing jurisdiction of the courts for disputes in matters of succession, is the *last habitual residence*: the one which the deceased possessed *at the time of death*.
5) Another feature of article 4 ESR can be inferred from the preceding characteristic: it is an international jurisdiction forum for *disputes in matters of succession stricto sensu*; that is to say, disputes concerning

[20] See Carrascosa González, *El Reglamento Sucesorio Europeo*, p. 79; Castellanos Ruiz, 'Sucesión hereditaria', p. 554; Gaudemet-Tallon, 'Quelques réflexions', pp. 449, 452 and 455–456.

succession arisen after the death of the deceased. Article 4 ESR does not apply to: (a) disputes which arise *before the deceased's death* and whose subject is, for example, an advance waiver of inheritance or the validity of an agreement as to succession.[21] Hence the proposal – which was not accepted – from the Max-Planck-Institut für ausländisches und internationales Privatrecht of Hamburg that the ESR established that disputes over the future succession of a person be submitted to the authorities of the country of that person's habitual residence.[22] Since these types of dispute are excluded also from the Brussels regulation I-*bis*,[23] as set out in its article 1.2(f), and neither article 4 ESR, nor the other rules of international jurisdiction provided by the ESR, apply to them, the internal private international law rules of the Member States will govern the international jurisdiction of its courts in these cases. Nevertheless, their decisions can indeed benefit from *automatic recognition* in the Member States as provided for in chapter IV of the ESR, since they are judicial decisions of Member State authorities on matters which fall under articles 1, 3 and 23 ESR.[24] (b) *Property disputes between creditors of the succession and the heirs* as well as *between debtors of the succession and the heirs:* The Brussels I-*bis* regulation is applicable to them.[25]

6) Finally, it is a forum which favours *parallelism between jurisdiction and applicable law* (= judges applying their own law),[26] because by virtue of article 4 ESR (last habitual residence as the ground for jurisdiction) and article 21.1 ESR (last habitual residence as the connecting factor), international jurisdiction and the law applicable to

[21] See Davì and Zanobetti, 'Il nuovo diritto internazionale privato', pp. 113–114; Davì and Zanobetti, *Il nuovo diritto internazionale privato europeo*, p. 198.

[22] Max Planck Institute for Comparative and International Private Law, 'Comments on the European Commission's Proposal for a Regulation of the European Parliament and of the Council on jurisdiction, applicable law, recognition and enforcement of decisions and authentic instruments in matters of succession and the creation of a European Certificate of Succession', *RabelsZ* (2010), pp. 570–571.

[23] Regulation (EU) no. 1215/2012 of the European Parliament and of the Council of 12 December 2012 on jurisdiction and the recognition and enforcement of judgments in civil and commercial matters (recast), OJ no. L 351, 20 December 2012, p. 1.

[24] See Davì and Zanobetti, 'Il nuovo diritto internazionale privato', pp. 113–114; Davì and Zanobetti, *Il nuovo diritto internazionale privato europeo*, p. 198.

[25] Gaudemet-Tallon, 'Quelques réflexions', p. 454.

[26] B. Walther, *Der Gleichlaufgrundsatz – Abkehr oder Rückkehr? Eine kritische Auseinandersetzung mit der Bestimmung der internationalen Zuständigkeit im Erbscheinsverfahren aus deutscher und europäischer Sicht* (Frankfurt am Main, 2013).

matters of succession coincide and, as such, the courts will apply their own law to these cases [see art. 21 no. 8].

IV. Advantages and Disadvantages of the New Rules

10. There are a whole host of arguments in favour of and against the European legislator's recourse to 'habitual residence' as the ground for international jurisdiction.[27] Many of these arguments are also employed in order to fuel the controversy surrounding its use as a connecting factor [see art. 21 ESR no. 9]. They are as follows:

11. In favour of using 'habitual residence' as the ground for international jurisdiction, we may observe that:

1) 'Habitual residence' as a ground for jurisdiction is more appropriate in the European internal market (article 26.2 TFEU) than the 'nationality' of the person, and it is more egalitarian as it does not discriminate persons on grounds of nationality, as forbidden by article 18 TFEU.[28] It is more democratic, as it permits the European citizens, by

[27] Bonomi, 'Article 4', pp. 170–172.

[28] See, on this contentious issue, which has its origin in the German doctrine of private international law of the seventies of the last century, when European integration was not as intense as today and German lawyers paid much more attention to conflicts of laws than to conflicts of jurisdictions, U. Drobnig, 'Verstößt das Staatsangehörigkeitsprinzip gegen das Diskriminierungsverbot des EWG-Vertrags?', *RabelsZ* 34 (1970), pp. 640, 642–644, 646; M. Greeske, *Die Kollisionsnormen der neuen EU-Erbrechtsverordnung* (Frankfurt am Main, 2014), pp. 36–46; C. Herweg, *Die Vereinheitlichung des Internationalen Erbrechts im Europäischen Binnenmarkt* (Baden-Baden, 2004), pp. 226–228; A. Junghardt, *Die Vereinheitlichung des Erb- und Testamentrechts im Rahmen einer europäischen Verordnung – Rom IV-VO* (Regensburg, 2009), pp. 67–68; P. Kindler, 'Vom Staatsangehörigkeits- zum Domizilprinzip: das künftige internationale Erbrecht der Europäischen Union', *IPRax* (2010), p. 47; D. Lehmann, *Die Reform des Internationalen Erb- und Erbprozessrechts im Rahmen der geplanten Brüssel-IV Verordnung* (Angelbachtal, 2006), pp. 62, 65; R. Michaels, 'Die europäische IPR-Revolution – Regulierung, Europäisierung, Mediatisierung', in *Die richtige Ordnung: Festschrift für Jan Kropholler zum 70. Geburtstag* (Tübingen, 2008), p. 166; T. Rauscher, 'Heimatlos in Europa? – Gedanken gegen eine Aufgabe des Staatsangehörigkeitsprinzips im IPR', in *Festschrift für Erik Jayme*, vol. I (München, 2004), pp. 731–732; M. Rohe, 'Staatsangehörigkeit oder Lebensmittelpunkt? – Anknüpfungsgerechtigkeit im Lichte neuerer Entwicklungen', in C. Engel and H. Weber (eds), *Festschrift für Dietrich Rothoeft zum 65. Geburtstag* (München, 1994), p. 12; W.-H. Roth, 'Der Einfluß des Europäischen Gemeinschaftsrechts auf das Internationale Privatrecht', *RabelsZ* 55 (1991), pp. 643–645; T. Troge, *Europarecht und das Staatsangehörigkeitsprinzip im internationalen Privatrecht* (Baden-Baden, 2009).

choosing where they live, to establish indirectly a close connection with the courts and the law of a Member State.[29]

2) Habitual residence is a ground for jurisdiction simpler than the nationality.[30] It is based on factual elements (the continuous presence on the territory of a State with a certain desire for permanence), which in principle does not require the application of any rule of law (= absence of legal qualification) and that, generally, are easily verifiable.[31] Conversely, setting the nationality of a person might in some cases be a far more complicated task; it may require accreditation of certain events (birth in a particular State territory, existence of a parent-child relationship etc.) and application of set of rules (the law of nationality of a State). The use of 'habitual residence' by the European legislator also avoids cases in which nationality, as a ground for jurisdiction, is impracticable (statelessness) or implies difficult alternatives (dual nationality).[32]
3) The European legislator has attributed a *dual function to 'habitual residence'*.[33] It is used both to ground international jurisdiction (article 4 ESR) and also to determine the applicable law (article 21 ESR). As a consequence of the *parallelism between jurisdiction and applicable law*, the courts apply their own law of succession (*Gleichlauf*): this is the law with which they are most familiar and which does not cause them additional problems with submissions and evidence, which is ultimately reflected in a better application of the law and a reduction in procedural costs.[34] The option chosen by the European legislator is a demonstration of the *legal streamlining principle* (*der Grundsatz der Rationalisierung des Rechts*) or a preference for fast and simple legal solutions which avoid errors.[35]

[29] M. Sonnentag, 'Das Europäische Internationale Erbrecht im Spannungsfeld zwischen der Anknüpfung an die Staatsangehörigkeit und den gewöhnlichen Aufenthalt', *Europäisches Wirtschafts- und Steuerrecht* (2012), pp. 457–469.

[30] *Vid.* Stürner, 'Deutsch-italienische Erbfälle', p. 64.

[31] D. Baetge, *Der gewöhnliche Aufenthalt im Internationalen Privatrecht* (Tübingen, 1994), p. 108.

[32] Baetge, *Der gewöhnliche Aufenthalt*, pp. 82–83.

[33] See Stürner, 'Deutsch-italienische Erbfälle', p. 64.

[34] Drobnig, 'Verstößt das Staatsangehörigkeitsprinzip', pp. 639–640, 644–645; P. Mankowski, '§7. Der Allgemeine Teil des deutschen Internationalen Privatrecht', in C.V. Bar and P. Mankowski, *Internationales Privatrecht*, 2nd ed., vol. I (München, 2003), p. 561; Sonnentag, 'Das Europäische Internationale Erbrecht', p. 460.

[35] See Greeske, *Die Kollisionsnormen*, pp. 17–18; W. Hallstein, 'Angleichung des Privat- und Prozessrechts in der Europäischen Wirtschaftsgemeinschaft', *RabelsZ* (1964), p. 215.

12. In opposition to the use of habitual residence as a ground for international jurisdiction, it has been noted that:

1) 'Habitual residence' is, as a consequence of its vagueness, an 'indefinite legal concept' (*unbestimmter Rechtsbegriff*) which may cause uncertainty.[36] If what is required is permanence and certainty, nationality would be a more permanent and foreseeable connection. In other words, from a practical point of view, nationality is stable, difficult to change and, in general, easy to verify.[37]
2) Habitual residence is a criterion which, ultimately, makes the possibility of determining the competent forum easily available to individuals.[38] When national legislations differ greatly from one another, this favours *forum shopping* or, at least, does not prevent it: in the end, despite the legislator's good intentions, the radical *lex fori* path is followed.[39]
3) The 'habitual residence' puts the *deceased's cultural identity* in peril, as opposed to 'nationality', which represents a stricter connection between the individual and his country.[40] According to those who defend this argument,[41] the European legislator could choose between the *principle of nationality* (*Staatsangehörigkeitsprinzip*) (= submission to the law and/or courts of the State whose nationality is held by the individual) and the *domicile principle* (*domicile-Prinzip*) (= submission to the law and/or courts in the State in which the individual is domiciled, understood, in principle, as a space [State territory] in which there is a physical element [*personal presence*] and a *mental attitude* [*intention to remain forever*]): either of these two principles would locate a person's legal relationships in their country, albeit to different

[36] See Stürner, 'Deutsch-italienische Erbfälle', p. 64. On the 'indeterminacy' (*Unbestimmheit*) of the concept of habitual residence, see Baetge, *Der gewöhnliche Aufenthalt*, p. 106, and J. Kropholler, *Internationales Privatrecht einschließlich der Grundbegriffe des Internationalen Privatrechts*, 6th ed. (Tübingen, 2006), p. 285.

[37] See Rauscher, 'Heimatlos in Europa?', p. 730.

[38] See D. Leipold, 'Ist unser Erbrecht noch zeitgemäß? Gedankensplitter zu einem großen Thema', *Juristenzeitung* (2010), p. 809; H.-P. Mansel, 'Vereinheitlichung des Internationalen Erbrechts in der Europäischen Gemeinschaft – Kompetenzfragen und Regelungsgrundsätze', in S. Arkan, A. Yongalik and B. Sit (eds), *Prof. Dr. Tuğrul Ansay'a armağan* (Ankara, 2006), pp. 208–209.

[39] See Rauscher, 'Heimatlos in Europa?', p. 736; Stürner, 'Deutsch-italienische Erbfälle', p. 64.

[40] See Stürner, 'Deutsch-italienische Erbfälle', p. 64.

[41] Rauscher, 'Heimatlos in Europa?', p. 727.

degrees.[42] However, and unfortunately in those authors' view, the EU ultimately opted for 'habitual residence', despite the fact that 'the new magic formula for Private International Law means nothing less than an abandonment of the principle of nationality and submission to the fast pace of temporary mobility, under the image of a man who can travel freely around all of Europe, but is stateless.'[43]

13. It is highly likely, in the coming years, that as cases applying the ESR arise, the controversy between habitual residence and nationality will rear its head, despite the European legislator's clear choice in favour of the former. At least until the European Court of Justice establishes and settles possible group cases, we must be prepared to hear and read the preceding arguments again. In particular we will hear that we have already been warned of the dangers of legal uncertainty raised by the 'habitual residence' notion. Personally I am of the opinion that first, just as is done in some State legislation – for example in Switzerland (article 20.1(b) of the 1987 Swiss act on private international law) – the European legislator should define the notion of habitual residence.[44] Second, ultimately – perhaps with some hesitation – the ECJ will have to assume this task. Third, the fact that in the vast majority of matters encountered in life it is easy to recognise and apply the concept of habitual residence works in its favour. These matters are the legal affairs of *ordinary people* who, most of the time, do not commence litigation. Fourth, whether dealings are progressing in or out of court, it is necessary to know in advance what will be the competent court and applicable law applying to an international matter of succession (in case a dispute arises). This can be easily found out in the *majority of cases*. It is to be expected that, for the *minority of cases* – that is to say, the least common, most exotic or most obscure, those which law professors have a particular liking for – the ECJ and the courts in the Member States will be involved in an interpretation task: dissecting, distinguishing and satisfactorily resolving the different groups of cases encountered in legal practice. Given that *hard cases make bad law,* I do not consider that these cases, nor the initial hesitation or contradictions of the courts, call the fundamental model chosen by the ESR into question. Fifth, and finally, until we have established case law,

[42] See Rauscher, 'Heimatlos in Europa?', p. 727.

[43] Rauscher, 'Heimatlos in Europa?', p. 727 (translation by the author).

[44] See the attempts that were made in this direction, illustrated by Davì and Zanobetti, 'Il nuovo diritto internazionale privato', p. 32, footnote 115; Davì and Zanobetti, *Il nuovo diritto internazionale privato europeo*, p. 47, footnote 14.

there will be an obligation to make the notion of habitual residence more specific, which is a necessary and useful task which absolutely cannot be postponed.

V. Determining Habitual Residence

14. When the EU codified the conflict of laws in some areas, it did not fail to define the meaning of 'habitual residence'. *Example:* Article 19.1, *in fine* of the Rome I regulation,[45] states: 'The habitual residence of a natural person acting in the course of his business activity shall be his principal place of business'. This is perhaps not much, but it is better than nothing. The EU legislator liked this definition so much that it repeated it in article 23.2 of Rome II regulation.[46]

15. It is surprising that a legal instrument, like the ESR, in which habitual residence is so important as to determine the jurisdiction of the courts as well as the applicable law, is lacking a definition: article 3 does not define what habitual residence is. Authors have proposed *two approaches* to the problem of determining the last habitual residence of the deceased in order to cover this lacuna in difficult cases: one approach, based upon the methodological presumption of *consistency* in the EU legal system, would consist in extending the impact of case law relating to the framework texts of the EU which also use the notion of habitual residence, to matters of succession. Another approach would consist in basing the notion upon the recitals set out in relation to the same ESR.

16. According to the second approach, the conceptual *nucleus* could be extrapolated from private international law relating to matters of succession. One German jurist has compared this casuistic and analogic procedure to a natural geological process: ultimately, the 'islands in the sea of un-unified law' will be converted into 'real archipelagos' (= the *leading cases* provide *framework groups*).[47] This first methodological approach has been tried in *various EU legal sectors*:

[45] Regulation (EC) no. 593/2008 of the European Parliament and of the Council of 17 June 2008 on the law applicable to contractual obligations (Rome I), OJ 2008 no. L177, 4 July 2008.

[46] Regulation (EC) no. 864/2007 of the European Parliament and of the Council of 11 July 2007 on the law applicable to non-contractual obligations (Rome II), OJ 2007 no. L199, 31 July 2007.

[47] See Stürner, 'Deutsch-italienische Erbfälle', p. 65.

1) *European private international law in matrimonial matters:* regulation no. 2201/2003 (known as the Brussels II-*bis* regulation) governs, amongst other issues, international jurisdiction relating to divorce, legal separation and marriage annulment. Its article 3 contains seven forums for international jurisdiction in the mentioned matters and six of them make use of the notion of habitual residence.[48] *Example:* Mrs Sundelind López, a Swedish citizen, married Mr López Lizazo, a Cuban national. The married couple lived in France. The wife, who was still living in France, petitioned the Swedish courts for divorce from her husband, who had moved to Cuba. The Swedish courts refused jurisdiction because other courts in another Member State, the French courts, were competent (article 3 regulation 2201/2003) (ECJ, case C-68/07, *Kerstin Sundelind López* v. *Miguel Enrique López Lizazo* [2007] ECR I-10403).[49]
2) *European private international law on the protection of minors:* regulation no. 2201/2003 also governs, amongst other matters, international jurisdiction relating to the attribution, performance, delegation, limitation or termination of parental responsibility for children. The authorities in the Member State in which the minor habitually resides at the time the matter is brought before the

[48] See A.-L. Calvo Caravaca and J. Carrascosa González, 'Crisis matrimoniales', in A.-L. Calvo Caravaca and J. Carrascosa González (eds), *Derecho Internacional Privado*, 15th ed., vol. II (Granada, 2014), p. 191–202; C. Campiglio, 'Il foro della residenza abituale del coniuge nel Regolamento (CE) N° 2201/2003: note a margine delle prime pronunce italiane', *CdT* 2/2 (2010), pp. 242–249; R. Gewaltig, *Von der nationalen zur europäischen Zuständigkeitsregelung im Familienrecht: die internationale Zuständigkeit nach den europäischen Verordnungen (EG) Nr. 1347/2000 und Nr. 2201/2003 (EuEheVo) in Deutschland und in den Niederlanden* (Frankfurt am Main, Berlin, Bern, Wien, 2008); P. Gröschl, *Internationale Zuständigkeit im europäischen Eheverfahrensrecht* (Konstanz, 2007); C. Hajnczyk, *Die Zuständigkeit für Entscheidungen in Ehesachen und in anderen Familiensachen aus Anlass von Ehesachen sowie deren Anerkennung und Vollstreckung in der EG und in der Schweiz* (Frankfurt am Main, 2003); R. Hausmann, *Internationales und europäisches Ehescheidungsrecht: mit Scheidungsfolgenrecht* (München, Basel, 2013); C. Ricci, 'Il foro della residenza abituale nel Regolamento n° 2201/2003 e nella proposta Roma III', in A.-L. Calvo Caravaca and E. Castellanos Ruíz (eds), *La Unión Europea ante el Derecho de la Globalización* (Madrid, 2008), pp. 421–431; A. Richez-Pons, 'La notion de résidence', in H. Fulchiron and C. Nourissat (eds), *Le nouveau droit communautaire du divorce et de la responsabilité parentale* (Paris, 2005), pp. 149–160; I. Sauer, *Internationale Zuständigkeit für die Auflösung und Lockerung des Ehebandes nach deutschem, französischem und europäischem Recht* (Regensburg, 2003).

[49] See F. F. Garau Sobrino, *Rev esp der int* (2007), pp. 763–766; U. Spellenberg, *Zeitschrift für Zivilprozess, Internationaler Teil* 12 (2007), pp. 233–242; A. Wittwer, 'EuGH-Debüt im europäischen Familienrecht', *European Law Reporter* (2008), pp. 67–69.

authority have jurisdiction over parental responsibility (article 8 regulation no. 2201/2003).[50]

3) Administrative law relating to EU officials and European social and employment law.[51] *Example:* In ECJ, case C-452/93 P, *Pedro Magdalena Fernández* v. *Commission of the European Communities* [1994] ECR I-04295, para. 22, when considering whether an official should be paid compensation due to a change in his habitual residence, it was necessary to determine what the relevance of his having an interruption of a few months (in which he lived in Torrevieja, Spain), or his remaining where he usually lived in Belgium would be, and what elements necessarily had to be considered in order to verify the place of habitual residence were: 'the place of habitual residence is that in which the official concerned has established, with the intention that it should be of a lasting character, the permanent or habitual centre of his interests. However, for the purposes of determining habitual residence, all the factual circumstances which constitute such residence must be taken into account'.

17. It is appropriate here to evaluate this first approach. It can be summarised in two ideas: one, it does not lead to any *new results*. We can

[50] See A.-L. Calvo Caravaca and J. Carrascosa González, 'Protección de menores', in A.-L. Calvo Caravaca and J. Carrascosa González (eds), *Derecho Internacional Privado*, 15th ed., vol. II (Granada, 2014), pp. 402–414; E. Gallant, *Rev crit dr int priv* (2009), pp. 802–813; Greeske, *Die Kollisionsnormen*, pp. 85–87; R. Lamont, 'Case C-523/07, A, Judgment of the Court of Justice (Third Chamber) of 2 April 2009, not yet reported', *CMLRev* (2010), pp. 235–244; P. Mankowski, 'Der gewöhnliche Aufenthalt eines verbrachten Kindes unter der Brüssel IIa-VO – Anmerkung zu EuGH, Urt. v. 22.12.2010 – Rs. C-497/10 PPU', *GPR – Zeitschrift für das Privatrecht der Europäischen Union* (2011), pp. 209–213; J. Pirrung, 'Der gewöhnliche Aufenthalt des Kindes in internationalen Sorgerechtssachen – zum Urteil des EuGH vom 2. April 2009 in der Rechtssache A – C-523/07', in J. F. Baur et al. (eds), *Festschrift für Gunther Kuhne zum 70. Geburtstag* (Frankfurt am Main, 2009), pp. 843–857; A. Richez-Pons, 'Commentaire CJCE, 4 avr. 2009, affaire C-523/07', *GPR – Zeitschrift für das Privatrecht der Europäischen Union* (2009), pp. 247–250; K. Siehr, 'Kindesentführung und EuEheVO – Vorfragen und gewöhnlicher Aufenthalt im Europäischen Kollisionsrecht', *IPRax* (2012), pp. 316–320.

[51] See D. Baetge, 'Auf dem Weg zu einem gemeinsamen europäischen Verständnis des gewöhnlichen Aufenthalts – Ein Beitrag zur Europäisierung des Internationalen Privat- und Verfahrensrechts', in D. Baetge, J. von Hein and M. von Hinden (eds), *Die richtige Ordnung: Festschrift für Jan Kropholler zum 70. Geburtstag* (Tübingen, 2008), p. 79; Greeske, *Die Kollisionsnormen*, pp. 84–85; E. Ioratti Ferrari, 'Draft Common Frame of Reference and Terminology', in L. Antoniolli and F. Fiorentini (eds), *A factual Assessment of the Draft Common Frame of Reference* (München, 2011), p. 328; B. Karl, *ZESAR Zeitschrift für europäisches Sozial- und Arbeitsrecht* (2005), pp. 188–192; R. Resch, 'Wohnsitzerfordernis bei beitragsunabhängigen Sonderleistungen', *European Law Reporter* (1999), pp. 188–189.

infer from it that the concept of 'habitual residence' was always identified as 'the centre of a person's life'.[52] Obviously a concept of habitual residence as the centre of the life and interests of a person does exist and is not different form the ordinary or common notion of 'habitual residence' used regularly in all uniform private international law texts, including the conventions adopted by the Hague Conference. Two, its *scope* is necessarily *limited.* The ECJ itself has confirmed the principle that the concept of habitual residence must be determined in each case 'in the light of the context of the provisions and the objective of the Regulation' the application of which is being dealt with and that, therefore, in order to determine such a concept in each unique sector, the case law of the court on the concept of as it relates to other EU legal sectors cannot be transposed directly (ECJ, case 523/07, *A* [2009] ECR I-02805, paras. 35 and 36). Consequently, the second approach will be much more useful for the case law which application of the ESR will generate.[53]

VI. Application Problems

A. *Forum Shopping*

18. It has been acknowledged that the objective of all legal unification is to prevent some of the consequences of State legislators unilaterally delimiting the extent of their courts' jurisdiction, such as *forum shopping*,[54] that is the planned selection of a jurisdiction from amongst various possible, so as to obtain technical advantages of a substantive or procedural nature which lead to success in the proceedings.[55] The issue is whether the *last habitual residence* of the deceased set out in article 4 ESR is an appropriate ground of jurisdiction, capable to 'resist' to fraudulent procedural manoeuvring.[56]

19. From a *theoretical perspective*, there are *three reasons to worry* about potential fraudulent procedural manoeuvring:

[52] See Bonomi, 'Article 4', pp. 174–175; Carrascosa González, *El Reglamento Sucesorio Europeo*, p. 82–83; Castellanos Ruiz, 'Sucesión hereditaria', p. 555; H. Dörner, 'EuErbVO: Die Verordnung zum Internationalen Erb- und Erbverfahrensrecht ist in Kraft!', *ZEV* (2012), p. 510; Lagarde, 'Les principes de base', pp. 699–700.

[53] For this special study see art. 21 nos. 4 and 5.

[54] Stürner, 'Deutsch-italienische Erbfälle', p. 61.

[55] Stürner, 'Deutsch-italienische Erbfälle', p. 71.

[56] Meyer, *Die Gerichtsstände*, pp. 119–121, 162–166, 188–189.

1) The notion of an habitual residence is, in itself, so imprecise that it permits the parties to a dispute in matters of succession to affirm (whether truthfully or not) that the last habitual residence of the deceased was in different States. That would not be out of the ordinary. This is what happened, for example, in the case of the ground for jurisdiction employed by EU international competition law: the debtor's Centre of Main Interest (COMI) (article 3.1 regulation no. 1346/2000), regarding which two different and opposing theories have arisen (the Mind-of-Management-Theory and the Business-Activity-Theory).[57]
2) The EU has been, until now, incapable of eradicating *torpedo actions. Torpedo actions* (*acciones torpedo, Torpedoklagen, actions torpille*) are proceedings actions initiated by a party faced with an imminent dispute, so as to establish the jurisdiction of the courts of a State known for the length of its trials. These actions torpedo the process and keep it bogged down before the courts of a State and, as the proceedings have already started, this prevents other courts in other Member States from hearing the case, even if they have jurisdiction on the matter or were chosen as the competent courts by the parties under a choice-of-court agreement: *torpedo actions* paralyse justice. Not even the current Brussels I-*bis* regulation constitutes an insurmountable barrier to this type of action. There are no reasons to be more optimistic in this regard in the context of the ESR, where there is little experience, than in that of the Brussels I-*bis* regulation.[58]

[57] Stürner, 'Deutsch-italienische Erbfälle', p. 72. On the different problems raised by the ascertainment of the debtor's COMI, see A.-L. Calvo Caravaca and J. Carrascosa González, 'Capítulo 3. Los contratos internacionales. Ante el concurso de acreedores', in M. Yzquierdo Tolsada (ed.), Contratos, t. XVIII *(Los contratos, ante el concurso de acreedores. Repercusiones tributarias del incumplimiento de los contratos)* (Pamplona, 2014), pp. 569–916, 920–930, 682–727, and J. Rodríguez Rodrigo, 'El centro de intereses principales, como foro de competencia internacional en el Reglamento 1346/2000, en el caso de un grupo de sociedades', *Anuario de Derecho concursal* 33 (2014), pp. 501–536.

[58] Meyer, *Die Gerichtsstände der Erbrechtsverordnung*, pp. 172–175, 184–185; Stürner, 'Deutsch-italienische Erbfälle', p. 72. On *torpedo actions* in general, see P. Blanco-Morales Limones, 'Acciones declarativas negativas y *forum delicti commissi*. ¿Galgos o podencos? La litispendencia. Comentario a la Sentencia del Tribunal de Justicia (Sala Primera) de 25 de octubre de 2012. Folien Fischer AG y Fofitec AG contra Ritrama SpA', *CdT* 5/1 (2013), pp. 240–253; Calvo Caravaca and Carrascosa González, *Derecho Internacional Privado*, vol. I, pp. 167, 231, 275–280; I. Carl, *Einstweiliger Rechtsschutz bei Torpedoklagen* (Frankfurt am Main, Berlin, Bern, Wien, 2007); T. Hartley, 'The 'Italian Torpedo' and Choice-of-Court Agreements: Sunk At Last?', in P. Lindskoug et al. (eds), *Essays in honour of Michael Bogdan* (Lund, 2013), pp. 95–104; W.G. Hauser, 'Torpedoschutz im Fürstentum', in *90 Jahre*

3) Finally, we hardly have an efficient legal arsenal to protect us from these dangers. It is true that the formation of European case law applying the ESR will help in clarifying the notion of the last habitual residence of the deceased as an autonomous concept.[59] However, this will take time. It is no less true that recital 26 ESR allows courts, which consider themselves so justified, to take action against fraudulent procedural manoeuvring. Nonetheless experience proves that this type of practice is difficult to detect, prove and eradicate in a field, such as the law of succession, in which large sums of money may be at issue.

20. From a *practical perspective,* however, the *forum shopping* problem which could result from the use of habitual residence as a ground criterion for jurisdiction, seems very limited to me due to the fact that the judges in the Member States should, in any event, all apply the same law. As regards *torpedo actions*, it should be borne in mind that, on the other hand, courts must always verify (of their own motion, if necessary) whether the deceased's last habitual residence was actually in the territory of their State; consequently, if the response to that question is in the affirmative, there would be no abuse on the part of the plaintiff or claimant and, if it is in the negative, the danger of *forum shopping* will not become a reality. In conclusion, there is little opportunity for fraudulent manoeuvring and the recital relating to evasion of the law (recital 26 ESR) should not often have cause to be used.

Fürstlicher Oberster Gerichtshof (Wien, 2013), pp. 355–374; R. Hye-Knudsen, *Marken-, Patent- und Urheberrechtsverletzungen im europäischen Internationalen Zivilprozessrecht* (Tübingen, 2005), pp. 170–188; C. Schmehl, *Parallelverfahren und Justizgewährung: zur Verfahrenskoordination nach europäischem und deutschem Zivilprozessrecht am Beispiel taktischer 'Torpedoklagen'* (Tübingen, 2011); J. Suderow, 'Cuestiones de jurisdicción internacional en torno a la aplicación privada del Derecho antitrust: forum shopping y "demandas torpedo"', *CdT* 2/2 (2010), pp. 315–331; *id.*, 'Nuevas normas de litispendencia y conexidad para Europa: ¿El ocaso del torpedo italiano? ¿Flexibilidad versus previsibilidad?', *CdT* 5/1 (2013), pp. 184–198; M. Teixeira de Sousa, 'Die Bekàmpfung der Torpedoklagen durch einen europàischen Rechtskrafteinwand', in R. Geimer and R.A. Schütze (eds), *Recht ohne Grenzen: Festschrift für Athanassios Kaissis zum 65. Geburtstag* (München, 2012), pp. 1017–1026; S. Weber, 'Von Torpedos. Tankern und deutsch-französischen Gefechten – Gerichte und Schiedsgerichte im Binnenmarkt -', in W. Meng, G. Ress and T. Stein (eds), *Europäische Integration und Globalisierung: Festschrift zum 60-jährigen Bestehen des Europa-Instituts* (Baden-Baden, 2011), pp. 607–624.

59 Stürner, 'Deutsch-italienische Erbfälle', p. 72.

B. *Multiple Habitual Residences*

21. Another issue which deserves consideration is the existence of *a deceased with two or more habitual residences.* Save in circumstances where there is a personal habitual residence and a professional habitual residence (recital 24 ESR), this is a hypothesis which the ESR neither foresees nor prohibits: some people live between two countries.

In principle, a person can hold various habitual residences simultaneously in different States.[60] Everything will depend on the type of dispute in question (Audiencia Provincial Madrid 5 July 2002).

The foreseeable consequence is the possible concurrent jurisdiction on the same matter of courts in different States. In order to resolve *parallel proceedings in different States* it will be necessary to distinguish two sets of circumstances:

1) *Both habitual residences in two Member States subject to the ESR:* There would be a general rule and at least one special rule. According to the *general rule*, the defendant could invoke the *prior in tempore, potior in iure* rule and oblige the second court to remove itself from the matter, provided the *lis alibi pendens* requirements as between Member States are fulfilled (article 17 ESR).[61] Consequently, the *first claimant* would choose the State of habitual residence relevant for the purposes of article 4 ESR. In accordance with the *special rule*, when the deceased had various habitual residences in Member States and was a national in one of those States, the habitual residence in the Member State in which he was a national would prevail for the purposes of article 4 ESR. This interpretation is supported by recital 24 ESR. Another *special rule* can perhaps be added (which is also provided for in recital 24 ESR): that the deceased's main assets were located in one of the two States.
2) *An habitual residence in a Member State subject to the ESR and another in an EU Member State which is not subject to the ESR or a third party State:* This possibility is not addressed by the ESR. It is possible to imagine two potential solutions. One, the court in the Member State can only declare itself competent by virtue of article 4 ESR: the *lis alibi pendens* exception provided at article 17 ESR applies only in dealings between Member States subject to the ESR, and not to relations with EU States which are not subject to the same (United

[60] See Carrascosa González, *El Reglamento Sucesorio Europeo*, pp. 89–90.
[61] See Bonomi, 'Article 4', pp. 179–180.

Kingdom, Ireland and Denmark) or third party States. Two, the claimant in the second proceedings can invoke the international *lis alibi pendens* regime provided for in the forum's private international law system. This is the more satisfactory solution.

C. *Exception Clause?*

22. The ESR, by way of exception, opts for the law of the State with the closest connections to the deceased, when all the elements of the case indicate that he or her were clearly more connected with that a State than with the country of his or her last habitual residence (cf. recital 25) [see art. 21, no. 11 *et seq*]. This would be the case for a deceased without permanent residence in a EU country, but with important roots in a Member State, or a short-term last habitual residence in one Member State but his or her life's centre of gravity in another. It has been considered whether, in these cases, it is appropriate to apply by analogy the exception clause provided for the determination of the applicable law also to the determination of the jurisdiction.[62] This would, essentially, entail the following reasoning: there is a lacuna in the law (= there is no rule of international jurisdiction which, like article 21.2 ESR, makes provision for the centre of gravity of a case being found in a different Member State than that of the habitual residence); however, there is no lacuna in the legal system (= the basic principle is that, in such cases, the real connection prevails over the formal connection); *ergo*, the exception clause affects by analogy the functioning of article 4 ESR.

23. In my opinion, this interpretation would not be possible for various reasons. First, there is no legal lacuna as such; the European legislator has opted for a system based upon predictable and certain grounds of jurisdiction. Going further than this would entail an interpretation *contra legem*. Second, if the European legislator had wanted this solution to this type of case, it would have provided for it expressly, as was done in article 21.2 ESR regarding the applicable law; however, it has not done so. In other words, the exception clause is only intended to affect the applicable law.[63] Third, the clause in article 21.2 ESR is an exception,

[62] See Carrascosa González, *El Reglamento Sucesorio Europeo*, pp. 92–93; Castellanos Ruiz, 'Sucesión hereditaria: Reglamento 650/2012', pp. 556–557.

[63] See Bonomi, 'Article 4', pp. 179, 180–181; *id.*, 'Article 21', in A. Bonomi and P. Wautelet (eds), *Le droit européen des successions. Commentaire du Règlement nº 650/2012 du 4 juillet 2012* (Bruxelles, 2013), pp. 291–292; Lagarde, 'Les principes de base', pp. 700–701.

a type of 'free verse' in the middle of the harmony of the system and, consequently, it must be interpreted restrictively and should not be extrapolated from the scope of applicable law issues to questions of international jurisdiction. The recourse to *fraude à la loi*, when appropriate, in cases where the person whose succession is concerned dies shortly after having moved his or her habitual residence to another State, is sufficient for what, after all, is more important: the solution to the merits. *Example:* An Italian doctor working in Milan accepts an offer from a Spanish clinic to move to Spain permanently with his family and work there, as a plastic surgeon, for much better pay and other improved conditions of work. Ten months after moving his family to Spain, the doctor dies. It is clear that the deceased is resident in Spain, was with his family and intended to live in Spain permanently. In principle, the Spanish courts would have jurisdiction over the succession, since the deceased's habitual residence was in Spain (article 4 ESR). Spanish courts should apply Spanish law to this succession for the same reason (article 21.1 ESR). However, this is a case in which the deceased moved his habitual residence to a Member State 'recently before his death' (recital 25). In the event that all the circumstances demonstrate that the deceased had a stronger connection to the State of origin (Italy), what should the Spanish courts do? The correct answer, as we have seen, would be the *dissociation of the international jurisdiction* (habitual residence) *and the applicable law* (the law with the closest connection to the deceased): the Spanish courts would be competent under article 4 ESR, but apply a foreign law (Italian) to the succession matter under article 21.2 ESR, and could not declare their lack of jurisdiction in favour of the courts in the deceased's Member State of origin.[64] In conclusion, the exceptional provision set out in article 21.2 has the advantage that it allows for application of the closest appropriate law, without entailing the loss of the competence which the authorities of Member State have in accordance with article 4 ESR.[65]

64 See Carrascosa González, *El Reglamento Sucesorio Europeo*, pp. 93, 158.

65 Dörner, 'EuErbVO', pp. 510–511; Greeske, *Die Kollisionsnormen*, p. 147. Article 64 ESR (ref: art. 64) refers to the jurisdiction grounds set out in article 4 (as well as in articles 7, 10 and 11 ESR) also for establishing the competence of the Member States' authorities in issuing the European Certificate of Succession.

Article 5

Choice-of-Court Agreement

FABRIZIO MARONGIU BUONAIUTI

1. Where the law chosen by the deceased to govern his succession pursuant to Article 22 is the law of a Member State, the parties concerned may agree that a court or the courts of that Member State are to have exclusive jurisdiction to rule on any succession matter.
2. Such a choice-of-court agreement shall be expressed in writing, dated and signed by the parties concerned. Any communication by electronic means which provides a durable record of the agreement shall be deemed equivalent to writing.

Summary

I. RELATIONSHIP BETWEEN PROFESSIO JURIS BY THE DECEASED AND PROFESSIO FORI BY THE PARTIES CONCERNED *page* 149
- A. Alternative Means of Re-establishing *Gleichlauf* following a *professio juris* by the Deceased 149
- B. The Solution Provided under Article 5 ESR 151

II. REQUIREMENTS FOR A VALID PROFESSIO FORI UNDER THE ESR 157
- A. Formal Validity 157
- B. Substantial Validity 158

III. CONFLICTS AMONG SUBSEQUENT CHOICE-OF-COURT AGREEMENTS 160

I. Relationship between *professio juris* by the Deceased and *professio fori* by the Parties Concerned

A. *Alternative Means of Re-establishing* Gleichlauf *Following a* professio juris *by the Deceased*

1. Within the scheme of the ESR, the role of party autonomy as regards the allocation of jurisdiction is conceived as strictly complementary to the role it has been granted in respect of choice of law [see art. 22]. In fact, the ability of the parties concerned to choose the forum in which any dispute arising from a succession will be decided is made subject to the deceased having, in turn, chosen the law applicable to the succession by means of a *professio juris*. The choice by the parties concerned may only be made in respect of a court or the courts of the Member State of the law chosen by the deceased. Accordingly, within the scheme of the ESR the parties may only accept, either expressly or impliedly, the jurisdiction of such courts [see art. 7 no. 8; art. 9 no. 3].[1] Within this framework, the main function of a *professio fori* by the parties concerned consists of the re-establishment of a so-called *Gleichlauf*, i.e. a parallelism between jurisdiction and applicable law, which, absent a *professio juris* by the deceased, would have been granted by having resort to the last habitual residence of the latter, both as a general rule of jurisdiction [see art. 4] and as a general choice-of-law rule [see art. 21].[2]

2. In fact, the exercise by the deceased of the possibility to make a *professio juris* in favour of the law of his or her nationality pursuant to article 22 ESR [see art. 22] brings with it the disruption of the desired *Gleichlauf* or coincidence between *forum* and *jus*. Actually, and by contrast to the solution contemplated by some domestic systems of private international law,[3] within the scheme of the ESR the deceased is not in a position to affect the jurisdiction of the courts which will be called upon

[1] Cf. A. Bonomi, 'Article 5', in A. Bonomi and P. Wautelet, *Le droit européen des successions. Commentaire du Règlement n° 650/2012 du 4 juillet 2012* (Bruxelles, 2013), p. 183 *et seq.*, esp. p. 184.

[2] Cf., *de jure condendo*, E.-M. Bajons, 'Internationale Zuständigkeit und anwendbares Recht in grenzüberschreitenden Erbrechtsfällen innerhalb des europäischen Justizraums', in *Festschrift für Andreas Heldrich zum 70. Geburtstag* (München, 2005), p. 495 *et seq.*; A. Davì, 'Riflessioni sul futuro diritto internazionale privato europeo delle successioni', *Riv dir int* (2005), p. 297 *et seq.*; A. Bonomi, 'Successions internationales: conflits de lois et de juridictions', *Hague Recueil*, vol. 350 (2010), p. 71 *et seq.*, esp. p. 367 *et seq.*; *de jure condito*, among others, A. Davì and A. Zanobetti, 'Il nuovo diritto internazionale privato delle successioni nell'Unione europea', *CdT* 5/2 (2013), p. 5 *et seq.*, esp. p. 29 *et seq.*, p. 114 *et seq.*; A. Davì and A. Zanobetti, *Il nuovo diritto internazionale privato europeo delle successioni* (Torino, 2014), pp. 44 *et seq.*, 199 *et seq.*; J. Carrascosa González, *El Reglamento Sucesorio Europeo 650/2012 de 4 de Julio 2012: Análisis crítico* (Granada, 2014), p. 78 *et seq.*; P. Franzina, 'Ragioni, valori e collocazione sistematica della disciplina internazional-privatistica delle successioni *mortis causa*', in P. Franzina and A. Leandro (eds), *Il diritto internazionale privato europeo delle successioni* mortis causa (Milano, 2013), p. 1 *et seq.*, esp. p. 10 *et seq.*

[3] Particularly, article 87, para. 2 of the Swiss federal private international law act of 1987, which reads as follows: 'The authorities at the place of origin always have jurisdiction when a Swiss national having his or her last domicile in a foreign country submits, in a will or an inheritance agreement, his or her entire estate or the portion thereof located in Switzerland to the jurisdiction or to the law of Switzerland. This provision does not affect Article 86, paragraph 2' (English translation from A. Bucher (ed), *Commentaire romand, Loi sur le droit international privé, Convention de Lugano* (Bâle, 2011)).

to decide on any dispute arising from the succession. The attitude adopted under the ESR reveals a disparity in respect of the situation in which the deceased him- or herself had decided to dispose of his or her succession by settling a trust, in which case a choice of forum within the trust instrument would be permitted pursuant to article 25.2 regulation no. 1215/2012 (s. c. 'Brussels I-*bis*')[4] providing for the recast of regulation no. 44/2001 (s. c. 'Brussels I').[5]

3. Admittedly, whereas granting the deceased the right to make a *professio fori* alongside a *professio juris* would have afforded him or her the largest possible power to regulate his or her succession, it is questionable whether granting the deceased the possibility of determining the country before whose courts any dispute arising from his or her succession should be brought would have been acceptable as a matter of principle. In fact, since such disputes are inherently liable to arise only after the passing away of the deceased, leaving him or her to decide the venue where subsequent disputes arising among other parties should be decided, would impose an unjustified restriction on the right of the parties themselves to decide. At the very least, absent any choice by the parties concerned, it would defeat their reasonable expectations of being able to litigate before the ordinarily competent courts.[6]

B. The Solution Provided under Article 5 ESR

4. The solution provided under article 5 ESR, aimed at re-establishing the desirable correspondence between jurisdiction and applicable law,

[4] Regulation (EU) no. 1215/2012 of the European Parliament and of the Council of 12 December 2012 on jurisdiction and the recognition and enforcement of judgments in civil and commercial matters (recast), *OJ* no. L 351, 20 December 2012, p. 1.

[5] Council Regulation (EC) no. 44/2001 of 22 December 2000 on jurisdiction and the recognition and enforcement of judgments in civil and commercial matters, *OJ* no. L 12, 16 January 2001, p. 1. Cf., with regard to the rule as contained in its article 23.2, G. Contaldi, *Il trust nel diritto internazionale privato italiano* (Milano, 2001), p. 303 *et seq.*; A. Dutta, 'Das neue internationale Erbrecht der Europäischen Union – Eine erste Lekture der Erbrechtsverordnung', *FamRZ* (2013), p. 4 *et seq.*, esp. p. 7; B. Hess, 'Die internationale Zuständigkeit nach der Erbrechtsverordnung', in A. Dutta and S. Herrler (eds), *Die Europäische Erbrechtsverordnung* (München, 2014), p. 131 *et seq.*, esp. p. 137 *et seq.*

[6] Cf., particularly, R. Magnus, 'Gerichtsstandsvereinbarungen im Erbrecht?' *IPRax* (2013), p. 393 *et seq.*, esp. p. 396 *et seq.*, who instead advocates the solution of granting the deceased the right to make a *professio fori* alongside a *professio juris*, more broadly, D. Coester-Waltjen, 'Parteiautonomie in der internationalen Zuständigkeit', in *Festschrift für Andreas Heldrich zum 70. Geburtstag* (München, 2005), p. 549 *et seq.*

disrupted by a *professio juris* made by a deceased in favour of his or her national law, certainly appears more sympathetic to the expectations of the actual parties to the disputes arising from a succession. This allows such parties to opt themselves, by means of a choice-of-court agreement, for the jurisdiction of either a specified court or, generally, the courts of the country of the law chosen by the deceased as applicable to the succession. Such jurisdiction, as clearly stated by article 5 ESR, shall be exclusive,[7] with the natural consequence that any other court seised in a different Member State shall have a duty to decline jurisdiction [see art. 6 no. 1].

5. More often than not, such a choice by the parties concerned with a succession will take place after the opening of the succession, since prior to that point the fact of the deceased having made a *professio juris* in favour of his or her national law might not be known to the parties concerned, the choice by the deceased having been made in the form of a testamentary disposition or at least resulting from the terms of such a disposition [see art. 22 no. 21 *et seq*.]. Nonetheless, there is no obstacle, in principle, preventing the parties from entering into a choice-of-court agreement, even before the opening of the succession, since the deceased him- or herself might have disclosed his or her intention of making a *professio juris* under article 22 ESR.[8] Naturally, in this case, the choice-of-court agreement will only produce effects after the opening of the succession, since it must be taken into account that the deceased might at any moment withdraw his *professio juris*.[9] Additionally, the identification of the law chosen by the deceased may be uncertain until the very moment of death in cases where the deceased had designated the law of the country of which he or she would have had the nationality at that moment.[10] In such a case, the choice-of-court agreement entered into by the parties concerned pursuant to article 5 ESR would be ineffective where the deceased possessed the nationality of a third country at the point of death.

[7] Unpersuasively, A. Dutta, 'Art. 5 EuErbVO', in *Münchener Kommentar zum BGB*, 6th ed. (München, 2015), para. 16, argues instead that the parties concerned may agree for the chosen court or courts to be vested with concurrent jurisdiction. This seems irreconcilable with the duty of the otherwise competent courts to decline jurisdiction under article 6 (b) ESR.

[8] Cf. Bonomi, 'Article 5', p. 188 *et seq*.; Dutta, 'Art. 5 EuErbVO', cit., para. 19.

[9] Cf. Bonomi, 'Article 5', p. 188.

[10] Cf., for similar considerations in respect of the applicability of the general rule of jurisdiction under article 4 ESR, Davì and Zanobetti, 'Il nuovo diritto internazionale privato delle successioni', p. 113 *et seq*.; Davì and Zanobetti, *Il nuovo diritto internazionale privato europeo*, p. 198.

6. A question which the ESR leaves unanswered is whether the possibility for the parties concerned to make a *professio fori* is conditional upon the deceased having his or her habitual residence at the moment of death in a Member State that is subject to the regulation. In fact, on the one hand, it is to be noted that the ESR, following the path already taken by regulation no. 4/2009 in matters of maintenance obligations[11] and initially followed in the proposal for a recast of the Brussels I regulation,[12] provides for a comprehensive set of rules concerning jurisdiction, intended to govern both cases where the deceased had his or her last habitual residence in a Member State pursuant to the general rule under article 4 [see art. 4] and cases where the latter was habitually resident in a third country at the time of death, in which case the subsidiary rules of jurisdiction provided by ESR will apply, to the exclusion of domestic rules of jurisdiction [see art. 10 nos. 1–3].[13] It would accordingly follow that each of the rules on jurisdiction contained in the ESR could in principle apply whenever it would lead to the jurisdiction of the courts of a Member State, absent any further condition for its applicability from a territorial perspective. Nonetheless, as noted already,[14] a *professio juris* by the parties concerned has been conceived within the scheme of the ESR as a means of re-establishing a *Gleichlauf*, or coincidence, between jurisdiction and applicable law, disrupted by the *professio juris* made by the deceased. Accordingly, no *Gleichlauf* could be restored which in reality never existed, since in cases where the deceased was latterly habitually resident in a third country, no court of a Member State would have jurisdiction under the ESR, except in the exceptional circumstances contemplated under article 10, or in the case of article 11 ESR. The subsidiary rules of jurisdiction under article 10 ESR may assist in answering the question just posed. These do not consider the nationality of the deceased, as such, as a sufficient ground for establishing the jurisdiction of a Member State's courts. In fact, in terms of the rule in

[11] Council Regulation (EC) no. 4/2009 of 18 December 2008 on jurisdiction, applicable law, recognition and enforcement of decisions and cooperation in matters relating to maintenance obligations, *OJ* no. L 7, 10 January 2009, p. 1.

[12] Doc. COM(2010) 748 final, of 14 December 2010, article 4.2. See, among others, F. Pocar, 'Révision de Bruxelles I et ordre juridique international: quelle approche uniforme?', *Riv dir int priv proc* (2011), p. 591 *et seq.*; J. Weber, 'Universal Jurisdiction and Third States in the Reform of the Brussels I Regulation', *RabelsZ* (2011), p. 619 *et seq.*

[13] See, with regard to the Commission proposal, M. Hellner, 'El futuro reglamento de la UE sobre sucesiones. La relación con terceros estados', *An esp der int priv*, vol. 10 (2010), p. 379 *et seq.*, esp. p. 380 *et seq.*

[14] See no. 1.

question, such a nationality serves merely as a circumstance likely to provide further support to the location of assets forming the subject of the succession as a residual ground of jurisdiction [see art. 10 no. 12]. Accordingly, the mere fact that the deceased was, at the moment of making a *professio juris* or at the moment of death, a national of a certain Member State, would appear to provide an insufficient ground for the establishment of the jurisdiction of the courts of that country through an agreement by the parties pursuant to article 5 ESR. Additionally, in consideration of the risk that third countries more substantially connected to the succession might refuse recognition to judgments handed down by a Member State's courts under such circumstances, the nationality of the deceased is rarely adopted as a ground of jurisdiction in succession matters.[15]

7. Finally, it appears clear that a *professio fori* by the parties concerned under article 5 ESR may take place only after a *professio juris* by the deceased pursuant to article 22, and not following other forms of expression of the intention of the deceased to provide for the law applicable to his or her succession, such as a choice of the law applicable to an agreement governing succession, pursuant to article 25.3 ESR [see art. 25 no. 8 *et seq.*].[16] In fact, although the latter rule refers, in respect of each of the parties, to the conditions for a *professio juris* as embodied in article 22 ESR, it must be considered that the choice, by the parties to an agreement as to succession, as to the law governing such an agreement, may not be considered as equivalent, in respect of each of them, to a *professio juris* made pursuant to article 22. Inevitably, the effects of a choice of the law applicable to an agreement governing succession are limited, as clearly stated by article 25.3, to issues inherent to the agreement itself, such as its admissibility, its substantial validity and its effects, and do not extend,

[15] A rather isolated example in this respect can be found in article 50 of the Italian private international law act (law no. 218 of 31 May 1995), which provides for the nationality of the deceased at the moment of death as the first among a series of alternative grounds of jurisdiction: cf. R. Clerici, 'Articolo 50', in F. Pocar et al. (eds), *Commentario del nuovo diritto internazionale privato* (Padova, 1996), p. 246 *et seq*. This rule should be considered as being superseded by the coming into force of the jurisdiction rules contained in the ESR, which leave no residual scope of application to domestic rules of jurisdiction in the field covered by ESR: see Davì and Zanobetti, 'Il nuovo diritto internazionale privato delle successioni', p. 112; Davì and Zanobetti, *Il nuovo diritto internazionale privato europeo*, p. 196.

[16] As considered admissible, instead, by Dutta, 'Das neue internationale Erbrecht', p. 6 *et seq.; id.*, 'Art. 5 EuErbVO', para. 5; *id.*, 'Die europäische Erbrechtsverordnung vor ihrem Anwendungsbeginn: Zehn ausgewählte Streitstandsminiaturen', *IPRax* (2015), p. 32 *et seq.*, esp. p. 35 *et seq.*

unlike a *professio juris* individually made by each of the parties, to their respective successions as a whole. Accordingly, allowing a *professio fori* by the parties concerned, on the basis of a choice of the law applicable to an agreement as to succession pursuant to article 25.3 ESR, could bring the risk, if the effects of such a *professio fori* were to be intended as limited to disputes arising out of the agreement governing the succession, of endangering the unity of the succession by introducing a situation of co-existence among concurrent jurisdictions. This is insofar as the issues posed by such an agreement are not entirely separable from other issues concerning the succession. Conversely, if the effects of a *professio fori* in such circumstances were to be considered as likely to extend to disputes concerning the whole of the succession, allowing it would have endangered the achievement of the objective of re-establishing *Gleichlauf*. This is from the perspective that the courts of the Member State of the deceased's nationality could have been called upon to decide on issues lying outside the scope of the succession agreement, in respect of which no choice of their law had been made.[17] Analogous reasons lead to an exclusion of the possibility for the parties concerned to enter into a choice-of-court agreement under article 5 ESR following a choice by the deceased of the law applicable to a disposition of property upon death pursuant to article 24.2 ESR [see art. 24 no. 11 *et seq.*], since the effects of such a choice are limited to the admissibility and substantive validity of such a disposition.[18]

8. The solution adopted by the ESR presents two fundamental difficulties. The first one is due to the different scope of application of the rules concerning jurisdiction and choice of law respectively. Whereas the rules contained in the ESR and in other EU instruments alike, in respect of choice of law, are deemed to have universal application, that is, they also apply in the event where they should lead to the application of the law of a third country [see art. 20], the rules concerning jurisdiction apply only insofar as they provide for the jurisdiction of the courts of a Member State. Provisions contained within an EU regulation could not, in fact, govern the jurisdiction of courts or the competence of authorities belonging to third countries, which would of course remain free to provide or

[17] See Bonomi, 'Article 5', p. 186; Davì and Zanobetti, 'Il nuovo diritto internazionale privato delle successioni', p. 118 *et seq.*; Davì and Zanobetti, *Il nuovo diritto internazionale privato europeo*, p. 206 *et seq.*

[18] The opposite solution is suggested by Dutta, 'Das neue internationale Erbrecht', p. 6 *et seq.; id.*, 'Art. 5 EuErbVO', para. 5; *id.*, 'Die europäische Erbrechtsverordnung', p. 32 *et seq.*, esp. p. 35 *et seq.*

not provide for their jurisdiction in the circumstances contemplated by such a regulation according to their own domestic laws.[19]

9. Accordingly, the re-establishment of the desired coincidence between jurisdiction and applicable law by means of a *professio fori*, as conceived by the ESR, may be achieved only insofar as the law having formed the subject of the *professio juris* by the deceased is that of a Member State. In this respect, it appears questionable why the ESR itself, in providing under article 6(b) for a duty of the courts seised notwithstanding a *professio fori* in favour of the courts of a different Member State, to decline jurisdiction, and even, under article 6(a), for a discretion of so doing in relation to a *professio juris* by the deceased *in favour* of the law of the Member State of his or her nationality [see art. 6 no. 2], does not provide for such an action to be taken by Member State courts in the event of a *professio juris* by the deceased in favour of the law of a third country, by itself plainly admissible pursuant to articles 20 and 22 ESR. This is independent of the fact of the *professio juris* being followed or not by a *professio fori* by the parties in favour of the courts of the same third country. Such a possibility appears simply not to be contemplated under the ESR, which, at the same time, does not provide any means to prevent all of the parties concerned from agreeing to submit their dispute to a third country court having jurisdiction pursuant to its own rules. This is in the absence, in particular, of any rule within the ESR addressing the recognition and enforcement by Member States of judgments delivered by third country courts in matters governed by the regulation.[20]

10. The second practical problem inherent in the mechanism contemplated under article 5 ESR lies in the inevitable difficulty of identifying with certainty from the outset the parties concerned by a succession. At the moment of concluding a choice-of-court agreement, the parties might, in fact, be unaware of the existence of other subjects having an

[19] Cf., for some considerations in this respect, C. F. Majer, 'Die Geltung der EU-Erbrechtsverordnung für reine Drittstaatensachverhälte', *ZEV* (2011), p. 445 *et seq.*; more generally, M. Fallon and Th. Kruger, 'The Spatial Scope of the EU's Rules on Jurisdiction and Enforcement of Judgments: From Bilateral Modus to Unilateral Universality?', *YPIL*, vol. XIV (2012/2013), p. 1 *et seq.*, esp. p. 16 *et seq.*

[20] In this respect a suggestion by Magnus, 'Gerichtsstandsvereinbarungen', p. 394 *et seq.*, to the effect that the ESR could have provided for the right of the parties concerned by the succession to derogate from the jurisdiction of the Member State courts having jurisdiction under the regulation in the case of a *professio juris* by the deceased in favour of the law of a third country, appears rather superfluous, insofar as the parties concerned by the succession refrain from seising a Member State court under the regulation.

interest in the succession, who may appear or be identified at a later stage. As will be seen, the ESR addresses this difficulty, which inevitably arises in practice with successions, under article 9 [see art. 9 no. 1].

II. Requirements for a Valid *professio fori* under the ESR

A. *Formal Validity*

11. Turning more closely to an examination of the requirements of article 5 ESR in terms of the validity of a *professio fori* by the parties concerned, it should be observed at the outset that, following a technique already adopted under other EU instruments containing rules in respect of choice-of-court agreements, starting from the originating model provided by the 1968 Brussels Convention on jurisdiction and the recognition and enforcement of judgments in civil and commercial matters, such requirements only address the formal validity of these agreements.

12. The formal requirements set out in article 5.2 ESR, are actually stricter than those provided for under either the Brussels I regulation or its recast. They also appear to be more strongly inspired by those provided for in respect of choice-of-court agreements under regulation no. 4/2009 concerning maintenance obligations, or, if such a comparison may be attempted, by those provided for choice of law agreements under regulation no. 1259/2010 establishing an enhanced cooperation in the field of the law applicable to divorce or personal separation (s. c. 'Rome III' regulation). The rule requires that the agreements in question must be concluded in writing, adding, as a further requirement, that they also need to be dated and signed. The latter specification, which appears to be taken from the corresponding provision of article 7 of the Rome III regulation in respect of choice of law agreements, appears rather tautological.

13. In terms of the need for the agreement to be signed by the parties, such a requirement is normally considered as being inherent in the requirement for the agreement to be concluded in writing. This is because in the absence of signing, a written agreement could hardly be considered as having been concluded by the parties and may appear to be just a draft. With regard to the requirement for the agreement to be dated, such a requirement is relevant for the purposes of legal certainty, in terms of determining the moment at which the agreement has been concluded. Nonetheless, apart from the basic consideration that it is common practice to date any agreement or other document at the point of signature, it does not appear that the ESR attributes a specific relevance to the moment at which a choice-of-court agreement pursuant to article 5 is actually concluded.[21]

14. In particular, the ESR does not specify that such an agreement has to be concluded before the commencement of proceedings in the courts of the Member State of the law chosen by the deceased. Nevertheless, this may be considered as being implied by the general rule embodied in article 15 ESR concerning examination as to jurisdiction, whereby any court seised in a Member State which finds that it has no jurisdiction shall of its own motion declare its lack of jurisdiction [see art. 15 no. 1].

15. Following a solution which first appeared in the Brussels I regulation reflecting the ongoing technological developments in the field of communications,[22] article 5.2 ESR considers an agreement concluded through electronic means as equivalent to an agreement concluded in writing, provided the means used provide a durable record of the agreement. In terms of the application to an agreement concluded through electronic means of the requirements for the agreement to be dated and signed, the former does not seem to pose particular difficulties, since all electronic means of communication normally record the date and frequently also the time when the communication was dispatched. The latter would require that the communications between the parties expressing their consent should include a digital signature or other technical means of securing the provenance of the communication from the person appearing as the sender.[23]

B. Substantial Validity

16. The ESR, like all previous EU instruments containing rules concerning choice-of-court agreements, does not regulate the substantial validity of such agreements. It is regrettable in this respect that the ESR has not included a provision comparable to that included within article

[21] Cf., however, no. 19, concerning the possibility of conflicts among subsequent choice-of-court agreements.

[22] See article 23.2 regulation no. 44/2001, and, accordingly, article 25.2 regulation no. 1215/2012.

[23] Cf., similarly, H. Gaudemet-Tallon, 'Les règles de compétence judiciaire dans le règlement européen sur les successions', in G. Khairallah and M. Revillard (eds), *Droit européen des successions internationales. Le règlement du 4 juillet 2012* (Paris, 2013), p. 127 *et seq.*, esp. p. 131; instead, assuming a digital signature or technical arrangements of the like are not necessary, J. Schmidt, 'EuErbVO Artikel 5', in C. Budzikiewicz, M. Weller and W. Wurmnest (eds), *Beck-online Grosskommentar, EuErbVO* (München, 2014), para. 16.

25.1 of regulation no. 1215/2012, which, resolving a heavily debated issue, provides, albeit in negative terms, for the substantial validity of choice-of-court agreements, pursuant to that regulation, to be determined in accordance with the law of the country of the chosen court.[24]

17. Nonetheless, it seems reasonable to expect that the solution adopted under the Brussels I-*bis* regulation will have some influence on the interpretation of article 5 ESR. In fact, the solution adopted under that regulation appears particularly apposite in the specific context of the ESR. Apart from the additional argument which might be made by analogy with the provision under article 22.3 ESR, which subjects the substantial validity of the act embodying the *professio juris* by the deceased to the chosen law [see art. 22 no. 17], it is to be considered that the solution of subjecting the substantial validity of the choice-of-court agreement to the law of the chosen court appears dictated by the already underlined logic lying behind such agreements within the ESR, whereby they operate as a means of restoring the correspondence between *forum* and *jus* disrupted by the *professio juris* by the deceased in favour of his or her national law. Due to the strict interrelationship within the scheme of the ESR between substance and procedure, and, accordingly, between *forum* and *jus*, it is just as if the parties to the choice-of-court agreement had, through such an agreement, expressed their intention to consider the legal order of the nationality of the deceased, whose law had been chosen by the latter as applicable to his or her succession, as the legal system globally competent to regulate the succession, both in terms of the applicable law and the jurisdiction of the courts. It therefore seems plainly logical to argue that the validity as to the substance of the agreement in question should be determined pursuant to the law of the same legal order.

[24] Cf., in respect of the innovation introduced in this respect in regulation no. 1215/2012, among others, I. Queirolo, 'Choice-of-Court Agreements in the New Brussels I-*bis* Regulation: A Critical Appraisal', *YPIL*, vol. 15 (2013/2014), p. 113 *et seq.*, esp. p. 118 *et seq.*; J.-P. Béraudo, 'Regards sur le nouveau règlement Bruxelles I sur la compétence juridictionnelle, la reconnaissance et l'exécution des décisions en matière civile et commerciale', *JDI* (2013), p. 741 *et seq.*, esp. p. 747 *et seq.*; H. Gaudemet-Tallon and C. Kessedjian, 'La refonte du règlement Bruxelles I', *Revue trimestrielle de droit européen* (2013), p. 435 *et seq.*, esp. p. 445; A. Leandro, 'Prime osservazioni sul regolamento (UE) n. 1215/2012 ('Bruxelles I-*bis*')', *Il giusto processo civile* (2013), p. 583 *et seq.*, esp. p. 595 *et seq.*; A. Nuyts, 'La refonte du règlement Bruxelles I', *Rev crit dr int priv* (2013), p. 1 *et seq.*, esp. p. 54 *et seq.*; F. Salerno, *Giurisdizione ed efficacia delle decisioni straniere nel regolamento (UE) n. 1215/2012 (rifusione)*, 4th ed. (Padova, 2015), p. 206 *et seq.*

18. Furthermore, it is worth noting that such a solution also appears advisable from a practical perspective, since the structure of actions in succession matters may be different from one Member State to another, with the inherent risk of different attitudes concerning, in particular, the proper identification of the parties to different sorts of proceedings in succession matters.[25]

III. Conflicts among Subsequent Choice-of-Court Agreements

19. An issue which the ESR does not expressly regulate is the possibility of different choice-of-court agreements being entered into regarding the same succession. In this respect, it is worth remembering that such agreements may only provide for the jurisdiction of the courts of the Member State of the law chosen by the deceased to govern the succession, so that there is no risk of inconsistency at least as regards the Member State whose courts may form the subject of the parties' choice. The ability granted to the parties under article 5 ESR to specify in the agreement which court belonging to the Member State of the chosen law is to have jurisdiction,[26] brings with it the inherent risk of different courts within the same Member State being specified in subsequent agreements. In such an event, as a general rule, the later agreement should prevail provided it is entered into by all of the parties to the earlier one. Beyond this, there might exist a probably more substantial risk of conflicts among subsequent agreements concerning different issues related to the succession and possibly involving different parties concerned in turn by the relevant issue.[27] In this respect, it should be noted that the ESR adopts the rather inappropriate solution of supplementing the provisions appearing in the text of the regulation itself with further specifications within the preamble to the ESR. Although these do not carry binding force, they are naturally to be taken into account

[25] Cf., particularly, Magnus, 'Gerichtsstandsvereinbarungen', p. 395 *et seq.*

[26] As noted by Bonomi, 'Article 5', p. 190, in this case the ESR regulates at the same time jurisdiction and local competence within the Member State concerned. This appears as an exception to the general rule under article 2 ESR, whereby questions concerning the competence of the authorities within the individual Member States are not affected by the ESR.

[27] Cf. Bonomi, 'Article 5', p. 191, pointing to the incoherence of admitting partial choice-of-court agreements with the objective of promoting concentration of jurisdiction on matters related to the succession before a single *forum*, which is inherent in the exclusive nature of jurisdiction granted by a choice-of-court agreement pursuant to article 5 ESR.

for the purposes of interpretation.[28] Recital 28 states, in somewhat ambiguous terms, that it should be decided on a case-by-case basis whether, depending on the issues covered by the choice-of-court agreement, such an agreement has to be concluded by all of the parties concerned by the succession or whether it might be concluded by some of the parties only, insofar as it addresses a specific issue concerning exclusively those parties. The criterion for the admissibility of such partial choice-of-court agreements consists of the fact that the decision to be taken by the chosen court on the issue forming the subject of such an agreement should not affect the rights of the other parties concerned by the succession [see art. 9 no. 2].[29]

[28] Cf., for some remarks concerning the extensive use of recitals as a means of integrating the provisions contained in more recent regulations adopted in the field of European private international law, Davì and Zanobetti, 'Il nuovo diritto internazionale privato delle successioni', p. 17, footnote 55; Davì and Zanobetti, *Il nuovo diritto internazionale privato europeo*, pp. 23–24, footnote 74.

[29] Cf. Dutta, 'Art. 5 EuErbVO', para. 14, allowing partial choice-of-court agreements only insofar as they address issues capable of forming the subject of an action presenting a sufficient degree of autonomy from the rest of the succession matters, so as not to trigger the application of the *lis alibi pendens* rule under article 17 ESR in respect of actions related to the succession pending before the otherwise competent courts.

Article 6

Declining of Jurisdiction in the Event of a Choice of Law

FABRIZIO MARONGIU BUONAIUTI

Where the law chosen by the deceased to govern his succession pursuant to Article 22 is the law of a Member State, the court seised pursuant to Article 4 or Article 10:

(a) may, at the request of one of the parties to the proceedings, decline jurisdiction if it considers that the courts of the Member State of the chosen law are better placed to rule on the succession, taking into account the practical circumstances of the succession, such as the habitual residence of the parties and the location of the assets; or

(b) shall decline jurisdiction if the parties to the proceedings have agreed, in accordance with Article 5, to confer jurisdiction on a court or the courts of the Member State of the chosen law.

Summary

I. EFFECTS OF A PROFESSIO FORI ON THE COMPETENCE OF THE COURTS OF OTHER MEMBER STATES *page* 162

II. EFFECTS OF THE EXISTENCE OF A PROFESSIO JURIS ON THE COMPETENCE OF THE COURTS OF OTHER MEMBER STATES: ROOM FOR A DISCRETIONARY ASSESSMENT BY THE COURT SEISED 163

A. The Earlier Reception of a Discretionary Mechanism within the Brussels II-*bis* Regulation, in Matters of Parental Responsibility: Similarities and Differences 164

B. Relevant Grounds for the Exercise of Discretion under Article 6(a) ESR 168

I. Effects of a *professio fori* on the Competence of the Courts of Other Member States

1. The exclusive nature of the jurisdiction conferred upon the chosen court by a choice-of-court agreement concluded pursuant to article 5 ESR [see art. 5 no. 4] is expressly confirmed by the rather tautological rule contained in article 6(b) ESR. This rule places a duty on any court seised, under either the general rule on jurisdiction contained in article 4 or the subsidiary rules under article 10, to decline jurisdiction whenever the parties to the proceedings have, pursuant to article 5 ESR, opted for the jurisdiction of the courts of the Member State of the law chosen by the deceased as applicable to the succession. In the case of a choice-of-court agreement concerning only a particular issue arising from the succession [see art. 5 no. 19], it appears clear that the duty of any other court seised to decline jurisdiction under article 6(b) applies only insofar as the dispute falls within the scope of the agreement in question. This is clearly without prejudice to the possibility for the parties to the proceedings who did not participate in the choice-of-court agreement to object to the jurisdiction of the chosen courts pursuant to article 9.2 ESR, with the effect of rendering the agreement substantially ineffective [see art. 9 no. 6].

II. Effects of the Existence of a *professio juris* on the Competence of the Courts of Other Member States: Room for a Discretionary Assessment by the Court Seised

2. In the absence of a *professio fori* by the parties concerned by a succession in favour of the courts of the Member State whose law had been chosen by the deceased, article 6(a) ESR pursues the objective of establishing a *Gleichlauf* or coincidence between *forum* and *jus*. It does so by making provision for a discretionary mechanism enabling the court seised under either the general rule or the subsidiary rules to decline jurisdiction in favour of the courts of the Member State of the chosen law. Such a possibility of establishing a sort of *forum legis* is, however, only exercised by way of a request being made by one of the parties to the proceedings. This suggests that even absent an agreement among the parties concerning the appropriateness of subjecting a dispute between them arising from the succession to the courts of the Member State of the law chosen by the deceased, a request to that effect by any of them, while being necessary, could also be sufficient to produce the same effect. This is provided the court seised is itself satisfied as to the appropriateness of such a solution.

3. A question which is not specifically settled by the ESR is whether a decision by the court seised to decline jurisdiction under article 6(a) ESR may be taken just in respect of a particular issue forming the subject of the actual dispute rather than in respect of the succession as a whole. Despite the argument by analogy which might be made on the basis of the admissibility of partial choice-of-court agreements under the ESR [see art. 5 no. 19], it seems that the rationale for establishing *Gleichlauf* and the overall consideration of the circumstances of the succession as a whole, which the rule under consideration presupposes, militate against allowing such a selective power of declining jurisdiction, which would unduly extend the scope of the discretion granted to the court seised and increase the risk of fragmentation of the litigation concerning the succession.[1] It does, however, remain to be considered whether the decision by a court seised under the general rules, to decline jurisdiction in favour of the courts of the Member State of the chosen law, is also to be considered as binding in respect of future actions which might be brought before the same court or other courts competent under the general rules in respect of the succession. On the one side, respect for the unity of the succession should suggest avoiding a situation of concurrence among jurisdictions in respect of one and the same succession. On the other side, attention must be paid to the limits of the material scope of a declaration as to jurisdiction, which are hardly likely to extend beyond the limits of the action in respect of which the decision concerning jurisdiction has been taken. This is confirmed by the corresponding provision under article 7(a) ESR, whereby the courts of the Member State of the chosen law will have jurisdiction following a decision by the court previously seised to decline jurisdiction 'in the same case' [see art. 7 nos. 5–6]. Nonetheless, since such a decision has to be taken on the basis of the circumstances of the succession as a whole, it is to be expected that a corresponding decision will be taken in a case where the same court is again seised of a different action concerning the same succession.

A. *The Earlier Reception of a Discretionary Mechanism within the Brussels II*-bis *Regulation, in Matters of Parental Responsibility: Similarities and Differences*

4. In terms of the grounds upon which the court seised is expected to decide upon the appropriateness of taking such a step, the rule as

[1] Cf., conversely, advocating such a possibility, A. Dutta, 'Art. 6 EuErbVO', in *Münchener Kommentar zum BGB*, 6th ed. (München, 2015), para. 8. Actually, the systematic arguments mentioned in the text also find support in a different wording of the relevant provisions: whereas under article 5 the parties concerned may confer on the chosen court or courts jurisdiction to rule 'on any succession matter', under article 6(a) the court seised may decline jurisdiction if it considers that the courts of the Member State of the chosen law are better placed to rule 'on the succession', thus suggesting that the rule presupposes a unitary consideration of the succession as a whole.

contained in article 6(a) ESR is expressed in terms which appear to be strongly influenced by an earlier example of a discretionary mechanism of allocation of jurisdiction provided by article 15 of regulation no. 2201/2003 (s. c. 'Brussels II-*bis*').[2] This sets out a similar mechanism allowing the courts of a Member State seised of an action in matters of parental responsibility to stay their proceedings and invite the parties to introduce their action before the courts of another Member State, or directly request such courts to exercise their competence in respect of the case. This is in a situation where such courts would be better placed to deal with the case, based on a particular connection between the minor and the relevant Member State and in light of the best interests of the minor him- or herself.[3] Secondly, and more recently, a discretionary mechanism enabling Member States' courts to stay their proceedings in favour of third country courts has been innovatively introduced under articles 33 and 34 of the Brussels I-*bis* regulation, in respect of cases of *lis alibi pendens* and of related actions pending before third country courts.[4] Lastly, within the same text of the ESR, a further discretionary mechanism has been introduced under article 12, allowing the Member States' courts seised of an action under the ESR to refrain from exercising jurisdiction on assets belonging to the estate of the deceased which are located within a third country [see art. 12].

[2] Regulation (EU) no. 1215/2012 of the European Parliament and of the Council of 12 December 2012 on jurisdiction and the recognition and enforcement of judgments in civil and commercial matters (recast), OJ no. L 351, 20 December 2012, p. 1.

[3] Cf., among others, F. Marongiu Buonaiuti, *Litispendenza e connessione internazionale. Strumenti di coordinamento tra giurisdizioni statali in materia civile* (Napoli, 2008), p. 476 *et seq.*; id., 'La tutela del diritto di accesso alla giustizia e della parità delle armi tra i litiganti nella proposta di revisione del regolamento n. 44/2001', in A. Di Stefano and R. Sapienza (eds), *La tutela dei diritti umani e il diritto internazionale* (Napoli 2012), p. 345 *et seq.*, at p. 359, in footnote; J. Weber, 'Universal Jurisdiction and Third States in the Reform of the Brussels I Regulation', *RabelsZ* (2011), p. 619 *et seq.*, esp. p. 636 *et seq.*; C. M. Mariottini, 'The Proposed Recast of the Brussels I Regulation and *Forum non conveniens* in the European Union Judicial Area', in F. Pocar, I. Viarengo and F. C. Villata (eds), *Recasting Brussels I* (Padova, 2012), p. 285 *et seq.*, esp. p. 294 *et seq.*

[4] Cf. F. Marongiu Buonaiuti, 'Lis Alibi Pendens and Related Actions in the Relationships With the Courts of Third Countries in the Recast of the Brussels I Regulation', *YPIL*, vol. 15 (2013/2014), p. 87 *et seq.*; previously, concerning the partly corresponding rules contained in the Commission's proposal, *id.*, 'La disciplina della litispendenza nei rapporti tra giudici di paesi membri e giudici di paesi terzi nella proposta di revisione del regolamento n. 44/2001', *Riv dir int* (2011), p. 496 *et seq.*; L. Fumagalli, '*Lis Alibi Pendens*. The Rules on Parallel Proceedings in the Reform of the Brussels I Regulation', in F. Pocar, I. Viarengo and F. C. Villata (eds), *Recasting Brussels I* (Padova, 2012), p. 237 *et seq.*, esp. p. 249 *et seq.*

5. The mechanism introduced under article 6(a) ESR appears to be more akin to the model provided by article 15 of the Brussels II-*bis* regulation. This is from the point of view that it operates only among Member States' courts and, by contrast to the rules on *lis alibi pendens* and related actions, it does not presuppose the existence of any proceedings already pending before the courts of a different Member State which are considered more appropriate to hear the case.[5] Nevertheless, the rule as embodied in the ESR demonstrates significant differences from that contained in the earlier regulation, both from a procedural and, inevitably, from a substantive perspective. This reflects the different objectives pursued by the two instruments of which each rule forms a part.

6. From a procedural perspective, there is a notable difference between the mechanism embodied in article 15 of the Brussels II-*bis* regulation and that provided for under article 6(a) ESR. The former presupposes a discretionary identification of the Member State to whose courts the case is to be referred, based upon the existence of a particular connection of the minor with the relevant Member State such as those contemplated under paragraph 3 of the rule. By contrast, the mechanism provided for under article 6(a) ESR is deemed to operate exclusively in favour of the courts of a pre-determined Member State, that is, the country of the deceased's nationality whose law had been chosen by the deceased him or herself through a *professio juris*. This is in accordance with the specific ratio of the mechanism, consisting of the maintenance, through a sort of *forum legis*, of a *Gleichlauf* between *forum* and *jus* following such a choice by the deceased.[6]

7. Furthermore, probably relying upon the existence of this qualified connection between the dispute and the Member State whose courts are deemed to be more appropriate to hear the case, the rule as contained in the ESR expressly gives the power to the otherwise competent courts to decline jurisdiction in favour of the courts of the

[5] Cf., as concerns the mechanism embodied in article 15 Council regulation (EC) no. 2201/2003 of 27 November 2003 concerning jurisdiction and the recognition and enforcement of judgments in matrimonial matters and the matters of parental responsibility, repealing regulation (EC) no. 1347/2000 (OJ no. L 338, 23 December 2003, p. 1) (s. c. Brussels II-*bis* regulation), Marongiu Buonaiuti, *Litispendenza e connessione internazionale*, p. 476 *et seq.*; J. Weber, 'Universal Jurisdiction and Third States', cit., p. 636 *et seq.*; Mariottini, 'The Proposed Recast', p. 294 *et seq.*

[6] Cf. A. Bonomi, 'Article 6', in A. Bonomi and P. Wautelet, *Le droit européen des successions. Commentaire du règlement n° 650/2012 du 4 juillet 2012* (Bruxelles, 2013), p. 193 *et seq.*, esp. p. 197.

Member State of the chosen law. This effectively assumes the availability of the latter courts to exercise their jurisdiction as conferred upon them under article 7 ESR, as a consequence of the decision of the originally seised court to decline jurisdiction. By contrast, the rule contained in article 15 of the Brussels II-*bis* regulation, probably reflecting the relatively greater degree of vagueness, despite the specifications contained in its paragraph 3, of the requirement of the existence of a particular connection between the minor and the Member State whose courts are deemed more appropriate to deal with the case, is conceived in sensibly more cautious terms. In fact, the rule under article 15, Brussels II-*bis* regulation merely provides the courts originally seised with the power to suspend proceedings and invite the parties to seise the court deemed more appropriate, or directly request that court to assume jurisdiction. This is under the proviso that the originally seised court may only decline jurisdiction once the court deemed more appropriate has decided to accept jurisdiction, and that, failing this, the originally seised court shall continue to exercise its jurisdiction.

8. The reliance placed upon the availability of the courts of the Member State of the law chosen by the deceased to exercise jurisdiction pursuant to article 7(a) ESR [see art. 7 nos. 5–6], reflects a more general principle of reciprocal faith among the courts of different Member States. The adoption of a mechanism whereby the originally seised court could have simply suspended proceedings until the court deemed more appropriate had accepted to exercise its jurisdiction would, however, have been more respectful to the procedural rights of the parties. Such a solution would have left the door open for a resumption of the proceedings before the originally seised court in the exceptional case where the other court refused to exercise jurisdiction in respect of the action due to inadmissibility or any other ground, without requiring the applicant to recommence proceedings afresh before the original court.[7]

[7] Cf. Bonomi, 'Article 6', p. 198; A. Davì and A. Zanobetti, 'Il nuovo diritto internazionale privato delle successioni nell'Unione europea', *CdT* 5/2 (2013), p. 118; A. Davì and A. Zanobetti, *Il nuovo diritto internazionale privato europeo delle successioni* (Torino, 2014), p. 205 *et seq*. Cf. also, for critical remarks concerning the absence from the ESR of rules establishing an adequate system of cooperation among the courts concerned, B. Hess, 'Die internationale Zuständigkeit nach der Erbrechtsverordnung', in A. Dutta and S. Herrler (eds), *Die Europäische Erbrechtsverordnung* (München, 2014), p. 131 *et seq*., esp. p. 140 *et seq*.; J. Carrascosa González, *El Reglamento Sucesorio Europeo 650/2012 de 4 de Julio 2012. Análisis crítico* (Granada, 2014), p. 74 *et seq*.

B. *Relevant Grounds for the Exercise of Discretion under Article 6(a) ESR*

9. From a substantive perspective, the grounds upon which the originally seised court in the Member State of the last habitual residence of the deceased, or in the country whose courts are competent under article 10 ESR, is to establish that the courts of the Member State of the deceased's nationality are better placed to hear the case also present significant differences from the grounds set out under article 15 of the Brussels II-*bis* regulation. This reflects the different interests at stake in the respective fields governed by each of the regulations. The decision which can be taken by the originally seised court under article 15 of the Brussels II-*bis* regulation is primarily based upon considerations relating to the person of the minor, who is the subject for the protection of whose interest the relevant rules contained in the said regulation are specifically devised.[8] By contrast, the corresponding assessment that the originally seised court is expected to make under article 6(a) ESR is based upon sensibly broader considerations.

10. These are likely to reflect the underlying objective of protecting not just the interests of one subject but rather, of securing, also for the purposes of a correct allocation of jurisdiction, a balanced treatment of the interests of all of the parties concerned by the succession.[9] In fact, under article 6(a) ESR the originally seised court may decide that the courts of the Member State of the law chosen by the deceased are in a better position to rule upon the succession taking into account the whole of the practical circumstances of the latter. Such circumstances include the habitual residence of the parties and the place where the assets pertaining to the succession are situated.[10] Furthermore, the courts seised under the general or the subsidiary rules might come to the conclusion that the courts of the Member State of the chosen law are in

[8] Cf., with regard to the requirements for a decision to refer the case to a court better placed to hear the case under article 15, Brussels II-*bis* regulation, among others, G. Biagioni, 'Il nuovo regolamento comunitario sulla giurisdizione e sull'efficacia delle decisioni in materia matrimoniale e di responsabilità dei genitori', *Riv dir int* (2004), p. 991 *et seq.*, esp. p. 1018 *et seq.*; E. Gallant, *Responsabilité parentale et protection des enfants en droit international privé* (Paris, 2004), p. 123 *et seq.*

[9] Cf., for general remarks concerning the role of substantial interests in the allocation of jurisdiction, A. Heldrich, 'Die Interessen bei der Regelung der internationalen Zuständigkeit', in *Festschrift für Hans G. Ficker* (Frankfurt, Berlin, 1967), p. 205 *et seq.*

[10] Cf. Bonomi, 'Article 6', p. 197 *et seq.*; Dutta, 'Art. 6 EuErbVO', para. 7, both pointing to proximity as an underlying rationale for the mechanism established under article 6 (a) ESR.

a better position to rule upon the succession whenever the law in question provides for special procedures to be applied for the purposes of the settlement of the succession. These procedures may be strictly related to institutions which are peculiar to the chosen law, such that the ordinarily competent courts would find themselves ill-equipped to apply such a law.[11]

11. Since the possibility of such a decision by the originally seised court comes up for consideration only in the event of a *professio juris* by the deceased in favour of his or her national law which is not followed by an agreement among the parties concerned by the succession conferring jurisdiction to the courts of the same Member State, an assessment by the originally seised court on whether such courts would be more suited to rule upon the succession necessarily requires an evaluation of whether the specific circumstances of the succession point to a genuine link with the Member State of the deceased's nationality. In fact, in spite of the deceased having made a *professio juris* in favour of the law of his or her nationality, the succession might not reveal a substantial connection with the Member State of the chosen law [see art. 22]. In such an event, despite the advantage of having the courts applying their own law, it would be inappropriate to litigate any dispute arising from the succession before the courts of that country.

12. Furthermore, the absence of any coincidence between the country of the habitual residence of the majority of the heirs and, in particular, of the legitimate heirs, and the country whose law has been chosen by the deceased might reveal an intent by the deceased to defeat the expectations of such heirs to benefit from a reserved share in the succession. This is from the perspective that such a share would have been granted to them under the law of the country of the habitual residence of the deceased at the time of death, assuming that the legitimate heirs also have their habitual residence in the same country.[12] As contemplated under article

[11] Cf. Bonomi, 'Article 6', p. 197 *et seq.*, with regard, as an example, to the common law procedure of probate, or to other peculiar forms of administration of the succession contemplated by some continental-European systems [see art. 29].

[12] Cf., concerning the possible abuses which may be made by the deceased of his or her right to choose the law applicable to his or her succession through a *professio juris* under the ESR, A. Bonomi, 'Le choix de la loi applicable à la succession dans la proposition de règlement européen', in A. Bonomi and C. Schmid (eds), *Successions internationales. Réflexions autour du futur règlement européen et de son impact pour la Suisse* (Zürich, 2010), p. 23 *et seq.*, esp. p. 34 *et seq.*; with regard to the influence of considerations pertaining to the material elements of the case other than the *professio juris* made by the deceased in the decision to be taken by the court seised pursuant to article 6(a) ESR,

6(a) ESR, the location of assets forming the subject of the succession may also acquire relevance in the context of an assessment of whether the courts of the Member State of the chosen law are better suited to rule on the succession than those ordinarily competent under the ESR. Inevitably, insofar as the court seised is requested to adopt measures in respect of assets pertaining to the succession, which are to be enforced in the Member State where the assets concerned are situated, it would certainly be more expedient to have the case decided by the courts of that country, whenever the country in question coincides with the Member State of the chosen law.

13. At the same time, the opportunity to ensure insofar as possible a *Gleichlauf*, or coincidence between *forum* and *jus*, would appear particularly evident whenever the court seised is requested to adopt measures affecting rights *in rem* inherent in any of the assets pertaining to the succession. This is in order to prevent any problem of adaptation of those rights, as contemplated under article 31 ESR [see art. 31].

Carrascosa González, *El Reglamento Sucesorio*, p. 76; Davì and Zanobetti, 'Il nuovo diritto internazionale privato delle successioni', p. 118; Davì and Zanobetti, *Il nuovo diritto internazionale privato europeo*, p. 205 *et seq*.

Article 7

Jurisdiction in the Event of a Choice of Law

FABRIZIO MARONGIU BUONAIUTI

The courts of a Member State whose law had been chosen by the deceased pursuant to Article 22 shall have jurisdiction to rule on the succession if:

(a) a court previously seised has declined jurisdiction in the same case pursuant to Article 6;

(b) the parties to the proceedings have agreed, in accordance with Article 5, to confer jurisdiction on a court or the courts of that Member State; or

(c) the parties to the proceedings have expressly accepted the jurisdiction of the court seised.

Summary

I. PROFESSIO JURIS AND FORUM LEGIS: EFFECTS OF A PROFESSIO JURIS BY THE DECEASED ON THE COMPETENCE OF THE JUDGES OF THE MEMBER STATE OF THE CHOSEN LAW *page* 171

II. EFFECTS OF A PROFESSIO FORI BY THE PARTIES CONCERNED ON THE JURISDICTION OF THE CHOSEN COURT 172

III. EFFECTS OF A DECISION BY THE COURT SEISED UNDER THE GENERAL RULES TO DECLINE JURISDICTION ON THE JURISDICTION OF THE COURTS OF THE MEMBER STATE OF THE CHOSEN LAW 174

IV. EFFECTS OF AN EXPRESS ACCEPTANCE BY THE PARTIES OF THE JURISDICTION OF THE COURTS OF THE MEMBER STATE OF THE CHOSEN LAW 175

I. *Professio juris* and *forum legis*: Effects of a *professio juris* by the Deceased on the Competence of the Judges of the Member State of the Chosen Law

1. The provisions contained in article 6 ESR concerning the negative effects, respectively, of a *professio fori* by the parties concerned by a succession or of just a *professio juris* by the deceased on the jurisdiction of the courts of Member States other than that having formed the subject of either form of choice [see art. 6 nos. 1–2], find a direct parallelism, in the system of allocation of jurisdiction devised by the ESR, in the provisions contained in article 7. This rule addresses the corresponding positive effects of either form of acts on the jurisdiction of the courts of the Member State having formed the subject of the choice. Obviously, the effects deriving from either sort of act on the jurisdiction of the courts of the relevant Member State do not coincide.

2. In fact, in the case of a *professio juris* by the deceased in favour of the law of his or her nationality, even when the chosen law is that of a Member State, the applicability of such a law to the succession does not automatically produce a sort of *forum legis*. This is notwithstanding that such a solution might have been desirable from the perspective of ensuring a *Gleichlauf* or coincidence between *forum* and *jus*.[1]

II. Effects of a *professio fori* by the Parties Concerned on the Jurisdiction of the Chosen Court

3. Conversely, in the case of a choice-of-court agreement directly concluded by the parties concerned by a succession under article 5 ESR, such an agreement, as noted already [see art. 5 no. 4], produces the effect of conferring exclusive jurisdiction upon the specific court chosen, or, more generally, on the courts of the Member State whose law had formed the subject of a *professio juris* by the deceased. This effect is mirrored by the duty of any court seised in a different Member State to decline jurisdiction pursuant to article 6(b) ESR [see art. 6 no. 1]. Nonetheless, it must be noted that the provision contained in article 7(b), while confirming that the designated court or courts shall be vested with jurisdiction, does not at the same time expressly impose a duty on such courts to exercise such a jurisdiction. The existence of such a duty is, nevertheless, to be considered as inherent in the scheme of the ESR, based upon the binding effect of its provisions but in the exceptional circumstances in which it expressly confers a discretion upon the courts it designates. In terms of the effects of a choice-of-court agreement entered into by the parties

[1] Inevitably, accepting such a solution would have substantially implied granting the deceased an implicit right to a *professio fori*, which, instead, the ESR has reserved for the parties concerned by the succession; however some authors have taken a stance in favour of the first option: cf., among others, B. Hess, 'Die internationale Zuständigkeit nach der Erbrechtsverordnung', in A. Dutta and S. Herrler (eds), *Die Europäische Erbrechtsverordnung* (München, 2014), p. 131 *et seq.*, esp. p. 137 *et seq.*; R. Magnus, 'Gerichtsstandsvereinbarungen im Erbrecht?', *IPRax* (2013), p. 393 *et seq.*, esp. p. 396 *et seq.*

concerned pursuant to article 5 ESR, it seems that the only circumstances in which the court or the courts designated in the agreement may refuse to exercise jurisdiction, which the ESR itself considers as exclusive, are those in which they find the agreement to be invalid or inapplicable to the dispute at hand, or, eventually, where they declare the action to be inadmissible.

4. The exclusive nature of the jurisdiction conferred by a choice-of-court agreement under article 5 ESR rules out the co-existence of a parallel jurisdiction of the otherwise competent courts in other Member States. In the event that such otherwise competent courts are seised notwithstanding the presence of the choice-of-court agreement, they are accordingly obliged to decline jurisdiction under article 6(b) ESR [see art. 5, no. 4; art. 6, no. 1]. These courts may, however, in turn, find the agreement in question to be invalid or inapplicable to the dispute at hand, and may accordingly decide to proceed with the action. In such circumstances, the ESR does not contemplate a solution corresponding to that introduced under article 31.2 regulation no. 1215/2012 (s. c. 'Brussels I-*bis*')[2] to the effect that any other court seised shall stay the proceedings once the designated court is seised and until the latter has decided that it has no jurisdiction under the agreement.[3] Accordingly, in such a set of circumstances, the rule on *lis alibi pendens* will compel the designated court, if subsequently seised, to stay its proceedings until the first court seised has decided on its jurisdiction. Should the first court seised find the agreement to be invalid or inapplicable to the dispute at hand and decide to exercise its jurisdiction pursuant to the ordinary rules under the ESR, the designated court would be bound to respect such a decision and decline jurisdiction [see art. 17 no. 18].

[2] Regulation (EU) no. 1215/2012 of the European Parliament and of the Council of 12 December 2012 on jurisdiction and the recognition and enforcement of judgments in civil and commercial matters (recast), OJ no. L351, 20 December 2012, p. 1.

[3] Cf I. Queirolo, 'Choice-of-Court Agreements in the New Brussels I-*bis* Regulation: A Critical Appraisal', *YPIL*, vol. 15 (2013/2014), p. 113 *et seq.*, esp. p. 127 *et seq.*; F. Salerno, *Giurisdizione ed efficacia delle decisioni straniere nel regolamento (UE) n. 1215/2012 (rifusione)*, 4th ed. (Padova, 2015), pp. 206, 272 *et seq.* The rule has been devised specifically to prevent abusive tactics based on a recourse to the *lis alibi pendens* rule as a means of defeating a choice-of-court agreement, as would have been open to the parties under the pre-existing Brussels I rules: cf. ECJ, case C-116/06, *Eric Gasser* v. *MISAT* [2003] ECR I-14693, and T. C. Hartley, 'Choice-of-court Agreements, *lis pendens*, Human Rights and the Realities of International Business: Reflections on the *Gasser* Case', in *Le droit international privé: esprit et méthodes. Mélanges en l'honneur de Paul Lagarde* (Paris, 2005), p. 383 *et seq.*, esp. p. 387 *et seq.*

III. Effects of a Decision by the Court Seised under the General Rules to Decline Jurisdiction on the Jurisdiction of the Courts of the Member State of the Chosen Law

5. It remains to be considered whether, conversely, in the case where a court, seised under the general rules earlier than the designated court or courts, has declined jurisdiction pursuant to article 6(b) ESR finding the choice of court agreement to be valid and applicable in respect of the action at hand, the designated court or courts are bound by its findings or whether they may, in turn, declare the agreement to be invalid or inapplicable to the matter at hand. In this case, as suggested elsewhere [see art. 5 nos. 16–17], both courts should in principle decide upon the validity and effects of the agreement applying the same law, that is, the law of the designated court, so that the risk of diverging outcomes concerning the validity and scope of application of the agreement appears limited. It also appears that the designated court or courts are to be considered as bound by the findings of the first court seised and may not declare the agreement to be invalid or inapplicable. This is because the latter option would result in a negative conflict of jurisdictions which could amount to an unacceptable denial of justice.[4]

6. Similar considerations apply in the event of a decision by the court originally seised in a different Member State to decline jurisdiction under the circumstances contemplated by article 6(a) ESR. Apart from the differences which undeniably exist between the two hypotheses, it is also to be considered that, in the latter case, the mere fact of giving rise to a negative conflict of jurisdiction, whereby each of the courts coming up for consideration would consider the other as more appropriate to decide the case, would undoubtedly be inconsistent with the twofold objective of an efficient allocation of jurisdiction in succession matters and of safeguarding the procedural rights of the parties, that the ESR must have been intended to pursue.[5] Accordingly, the issue just raised

[4] Cf., among others, A. Bonomi, 'Article 7', in A. Bonomi and P. Wautelet, *Le droit européen des successions. Commentaire du règlement n° 650/2012 du 4 juillet 2012* (Bruxelles, 2013), p. 203 *et seq.*, esp. p. 203; A. Dutta, 'Art. 7 EuErbVO', in *Münchener Kommentar zum BGB*, 6th ed. (München, 2015), para. 3.

[5] Cf. recital 81 ESR. See, generally, F. Salerno, 'Il diritto processuale civile internazionale comunitario e le garanzie processuali fondamentali', in P. Picone (ed), *Diritto internazionale privato e diritto comunitario* (Padova, 2004), p. 95 *et seq.*, esp. p. 102 *et seq.*; P. Kinsch, 'Droits de l'homme, droits fondamentaux et droit international privé', *Hague Recueil*, vol. 318 (2005), p. 9 *et seq.*, esp. pp. 43 *et seq.*, 65 *et seq.*; F. Marongiu Buonaiuti, 'La tutela del diritto di accesso alla giustizia e della parità delle armi tra i litiganti nella proposta di

must be resolved in the light of the general principles underlying the European system of judicial cooperation in civil matters as a whole. This starts with the principle of reciprocal faith, whereby the courts of the Member State of the deceased's nationality, in the circumstances at hand, are expected to rely on the assessment of their greater appropriateness to decide the case made by the court originally seised in another Member State and are accordingly obliged to accept to exercise the jurisdiction so conferred upon them.[6]

7. This, in turn, presupposes that the parties having originally seised the ordinarily competent courts in a different Member State, after the decision of such courts to decline jurisdiction pursuant to article 6(a) ESR, undertake the burden of seising the courts of the Member State of the deceased's nationality thus vested with jurisdiction.[7]

IV. Effects of an Express Acceptance by the Parties of the Jurisdiction of the Courts of the Member State of the Chosen Law

8. The last hypothesis contemplated by article 7 of the ESR, whereby a court belonging to the Member State whose law has formed the subject of a *professio juris* by the deceased may assume jurisdiction, is that of an express acceptance by the parties to the proceedings. Such an acceptance is substantially equivalent in its effects to a prior agreement between the parties concerned under article 5 ESR. The sole differences are that the acceptance will only produce effect regarding the specific proceedings commenced before the court actually seised, and will normally, albeit not necessarily,[8] take the form of an express declaration before that court. This will either be included in the parties' written submissions or made

revisione del regolamento n. 44/2001', in A. Di Stefano and R. Sapienza (eds), *La tutela dei diritti umani e il diritto internazionale* (Napoli, 2012), p. 345 *et seq.*, esp. p. 348 *et seq.*

6 Cf. Bonomi, 'Article 7', p. 203; Dutta, 'Art. 7 EuErbVO', paras. 3–5.

7 Cf. A. Davì and A. Zanobetti, 'Il nuovo diritto internazionale privato delle successioni nell'Unione europea', *CdT* 5/2 (2013), p. 119; A. Davì and A. Zanobetti, *Il nuovo diritto internazionale privato europeo delle successioni* (Torino, 2014), p. 207. Cf. also, criticising the absence from the ESR of rules providing for a system of cooperation among the courts concerned, Hess, 'Die internationale Zuständigkeit', p. 140 *et seq.*; J. Carrascosa González, *El Reglamento Sucesorio Europeo 650/2012 de 4 de Julio 2012. Análisis crítico* (Granada, 2014), p. 74 *et seq.*

8 Cf. Dutta, 'Art. 7 EuErbVO', n. 8, noting that article 7(c) ESR does not prescribe that the acceptance has to take the form of a procedural act (*Verfahrenshandlung*).

orally at a hearing of the proceedings, subject to the procedural formalities established by the law of the forum.[9]

9. By contrast with a prior agreement under article 5, an express acceptance by the actual parties to the proceedings, necessarily requiring to be performed after their commencement, will avoid the prospective difficulty inherent in such an agreement, whereby, as noted already, not all of the subjects concerned may be known to the parties to the agreement at the time the agreement is entered into [see art. 5 no. 10]. In this respect, it must be noted that an express acceptance by the parties to the proceedings, who were not parties to an agreement concluded under article 5 ESR, produces an effect equivalent to that produced by an implied acceptance under article 9 ESR [see art. 9 no. 5]. Furthermore, it is worth considering that an express acceptance pursuant to article 7(c) ESR, consisting of a unilateral declaration, may also be resorted to in single-party proceedings, such as in matters of non-contentious jurisdiction as contemplated for the most part in continental-European countries.[10]

[9] Cf. Bonomi, 'Article 7', p. 204, noting that the procedural formalities established by the law of the *forum*, with particular regard to terms for the acceptance of jurisdiction, must not challenge the *effet utile* of the rule.

[10] Dutta, 'Art. 7 EuErbVO', para. 8.

Article 8

Closing of Own-Motion Proceedings in the Event of a Choice of Law

FABRIZIO MARONGIU BUONAIUTI

A court which has opened succession proceedings of its own motion under Article 4 or Article 10 shall close the proceedings if the parties to the proceedings have agreed to settle the succession amicably out of court in the Member State whose law had been chosen by the deceased pursuant to Article 22.

Summary

I. EFFECTS OF AN AGREEMENT BY THE PARTIES TO SETTLE THE SUCCESSION AMICABLY IN THE MEMBER STATE OF THE CHOSEN LAW ON PROCEEDINGS PENDING BEFORE OTHER MEMBER STATES' COURTS *page* 177

II. RELEVANCE OF THE PLACE WHERE AN OUT-OF-COURT SETTLEMENT IS ENTERED INTO FOR THE PURPOSES OF THE RULE UNDER ARTICLE 8 ESR 178

I. Effects of an Agreement by the Parties to Settle the Succession Amicably in the Member State of the Chosen Law on Proceedings Pending before Other Member States' Courts

1. Another way in which the ESR strives to ensure the desired *Gleichlauf* between *forum* and *jus* following a *professio juris* by the deceased in favour of the law of his or her nationality, is by placing a duty, under article 8, upon the courts of a Member State competent under the general rules of the ESR which have opened *ex officio* proceedings concerning the succession, to close such proceedings in cases where the parties have agreed to settle the succession amicably out of court in the Member State of the chosen law.[1]

[1] An amicable out-of court settlement does not appear to encompass an agreement by the parties to submit the dispute to arbitration, as suggested instead by B. Hess, 'Die internationale Zuständigkeit nach der Erbrechtsverordnung', in A. Dutta and S. Herrler (eds),

2. Actually, the provision raises some doubts as to why it has been included within a section of the ESR devoted to jurisdiction. In fact, the effects of such a settlement of the succession by the parties are deemed to affect the merits of the case, by extinguishing the interest of the parties, if not the supposed public interest which justified the opening *ex officio* of the proceedings, in the continuation of those proceedings, rather than, strictly speaking, the jurisdiction of the courts.[2]

II. Relevance of the Place Where an Out-of-Court Settlement Is Entered into for the Purposes of the Rule under Article 8 ESR

3. Secondly, and more substantially, it seems that in the case that the succession is regulated amicably by means of an out-of court settlement, a real issue of coincidence between *forum* and *jus* will hardly come up for consideration. Unlike a settlement approved by the court, which would require, at least to a certain extent, an intervention by the judiciary in terms of control of the agreement reached by the parties, an out-of-court settlement by definition takes place outside the purview of the courts. The place where such a settlement is concluded is therefore hardly relevant in terms of forum. The place where an out-of-court settlement is actually concluded would come up for consideration, in terms of the applicable law, only in respect of issues related to its formal validity. The fact of its having been concluded in the Member State of the law chosen by the deceased as applicable to the succession, does not, therefore, seem to merit different treatment under the ESR than a comparable

Die Europäische Erbrechtsverordnung (München, 2014), p. 131 *et seq.*, esp. p. 141, and, albeit with doubt, by R. Magnus, 'Gerichtsstandsvereinbarungen im Erbrecht?', *IPRax* (2013), p. 393 *et seq.*, esp. p. 398. An indication appearing to exclude such an interpretation, besides the current meaning of the terms used in the provision, comes from recital 29 ESR, which refers as an example, to an out-of-court settlement entered into before a notary. Cf. A. Dutta, 'Art. 8 EuErbVO', in *Münchener Kommentar zum BGB*, 6th ed. (München, 2015), para. 11, pointing to the fact that a settlement by arbitration, although taking place out of court, would not qualify as amicable.

2 Cf. A. Bonomi, 'Article 8', in A. Bonomi and P. Wautelet, *Le droit européen des successions. Commentaire du règlement n° 650/2012 du 4 juillet 2012* (Bruxelles, 2013), p. 205 *et seq.*, esp. p. 205; Dutta, 'Art. 8 EuErbVO', para. 1. In fact, the circumstance contemplated under article 8 ESR is likely to raise an issue of admissibility or preclusion of the action, which is left to the domestic laws of the Member States to regulate. These may not prejudice the *effet utile* of the ESR: cf., with regard to the Brussels Convention on jurisdiction and the enforcement of judgments in civil and commercial matters of 28 September 1968, ECJ, case C-365/88, *Kongress Agentur Hagen GmbH* v. *Zeehaghe BV* [1990] ECR I-1845, para. 17 *et seq.*

settlement entered into elsewhere. In fact, since the effects produced by an out-of-court settlement concerning the succession fall to be governed by the *lex successionis*, once under that law a settlement concluded by the parties is likely to completely dispose of any issue raised by the succession, any court seised of an action concerning the succession is likely to close the proceedings once it is satisfied of both the formal and substantive validity of the agreement embodying the settlement.[3]

4. Accordingly, the only meaningful reason justifying the reference contained within article 8 ESR to the Member State whose law has been chosen by the deceased, seems to be found in the need to ensure that the dispute is amenable to an amicable out-of-court settlement from the perspective of the chosen law. This need appears justified from the perspective that when proceedings are opened *ex officio*, this normally presupposes the involvement of an interest which does not fall entirely within the purview of the powers at the disposal of the parties.[4] This interpretation appears to be confirmed by recital 29 ESR, which clarifies that, conversely, in the case of proceedings commenced *ex parte*, the parties would be free to settle the dispute amicably, out of court, in any Member State of their choice, provided this is allowed under the law of that Member State, and even if the law applicable to the succession is not the law of that Member State.

5. The wording of the recital in this respect is actually unclear, since it would appear to be more accurate to argue that the question of the admissibility as well as the substantive validity of an out-of-court settlement of the succession, being a question of substance, is a matter governed by the *lex successionis*, and not by the law of the place where the out-of-court settlement is entered into. As noted already, the place where the out-of-court settlement has been entered into could only come up for consideration in respect of the agreement's formal validity, as might be argued by drawing an analogy with the rules contained in the ESR in respect of the law applicable to the formal validity of dispositions of property upon death or of agreements as to succession [see art. 27]. In terms of the specific scenario contemplated by article 8 ESR, the rationale behind the rule, as underlined above, would suggest that it should be for the law chosen by the deceased as applicable to the succession to govern all aspects of an out-of-court settlement, from its

[3] Cf. E.-M. Bajons, 'Internationale Zuständigkeit und anwendbares Recht in Erbsachen', in M. Schauer and E. Scheuba (eds), *Europäische Erbrechtsverordnung (2012/650/EU vom 4. Juli 2012)* (Wien, 2014), p. 29 *et seq.*, esp. p. 35. Cf., also, recital 29 ESR.

[4] Cf. Bonomi, 'Article 8', p. 205, footnote 2; Dutta, 'Art. 8 EuErbVo', para. 13.

admissibility and its validity – both with regard to its substance and form – to its effects.[5]

6. In the same vein, there does not appear to be much justification for only taking into account out-of-court settlements concluded in the country of the chosen law when the country in question is a Member State subject to the ESR. As noted already, out-of-court settlements do not pose a real issue in terms of jurisdiction, and, as far as the applicable law is concerned, the relevant provisions contained in the ESR, pursuant to which a court in a Member State is deemed to identify the law governing the validity in terms of the substance and form of such a settlement as well as its effects, are deemed to apply universally [see art. 20]. Taking this into consideration, there would not appear to be any justification for refusing, as a matter of principle, to take into account out-of-court settlements ultimately concluded in a third country, when, in the cases falling under article 8 ESR, the law of such a country has been chosen by the deceased as applicable to the succession.

7. Finally, it is worth considering which courts should have jurisdiction in respect of any dispute which might arise concerning either the admissibility, the validity, or the effects of an out-of-court settlement entered into pursuant to article 8 ESR. In principle, any such dispute should be resolved by the same court which has opened *ex officio* the proceedings which the out-of-court settlement entered into by the parties would be aimed at closing. The rule expressly identifies such a court as a court which would be competent under either the general rule contained in article 4 ESR [see art. 4] or under the subsidiary rules contemplated by article 10 [see art. 10]. This would not preclude the possibility for the parties to agree in their out-of court settlement that a court or the courts of the Member State of the law chosen by the deceased are to have jurisdiction to hear any dispute arising from the settlement itself, since such an agreement would be admissible under article 5 ESR and would achieve a *Gleichlauf* between *forum* and *jus* with regard to the dispute [see art. 5].

8. The same result could be achieved even in the absence of such a specific choice-of-court clause. This is on the basis that disputes concerning an out-of-court settlement entered into under article 8 ESR, being succession matters, would fall under the purview of a choice of

[5] Cf. Bonomi, 'Article 8', p. 206; Dutta, 'Art. 8 EuErbVO', para. 15; *id.*, 'Das neue internationale Erbrecht der Europäischen Union – Eine erste Lektüre der Erbrechtsverordnung', *FamRZ* (2013), p. 4 *et seq.*, esp. p. 6.

court agreement concerning the succession as a whole, separately entered into by the parties pursuant to article 5 ESR, with the inherent duty of the ordinarily competent courts to decline jurisdiction in respect of the dispute [see art. 5 no. 4].[6] Similarly, even absent any agreement whatsoever by the parties, the court seised under the general rules on disputes concerning the admissibility, validity or effects of an out-of-court settlement pursuant to article 8 ESR, may consider that the courts of the Member State of the law chosen by the deceased are better placed to hear the dispute, and may accordingly decline jurisdiction under article 6 (a) ESR [see art. 6 no. 2].[7] This would be based upon the consideration, among others, that the dispute in question will be governed by the law of such courts.

6 See Dutta, 'Art. 8 EuErbVO', para. 16, pointing out that the rule under article 8 ESR dos not *per se* confer jurisdiction upon the courts of the Member State of the chosen law (*keine Prorogationswirkung*).

7 Cf. Bonomi, 'Article 8', p. 206; Dutta, 'Art. 8 EuErbVO', para. 17.

Article 9

Jurisdiction Based on Appearance

FABRIZIO MARONGIU BUONAIUTI

1. Where, in the course of proceedings before a court of a Member State exercising jurisdiction pursuant to Article 7, it appears that not all the parties to those proceedings were party to the choice-of-court agreement, the court shall continue to exercise jurisdiction if the parties to the proceedings who were not party to the agreement enter an appearance without contesting the jurisdiction of the court.
2. If the jurisdiction of the court referred to in paragraph 1 is contested by parties to the proceedings who were not party to the agreement, the court shall decline jurisdiction.

   In that event, jurisdiction to rule on the succession shall lie with the courts having jurisdiction pursuant to Article 4 or Article 10.

Summary

I. THE POSITION OF SUBJECTS HAVING AN INTEREST IN THE SUCCESSION WHO ARE NOT PARTIES TO THE AGREEMENT EMBODYING THE PROFESSIO FORI *page* 182
II. RELATIONSHIPS WITH AN EXPRESS ACCEPTANCE BY THE PARTIES OF THE JURISDICTION OF THE COURTS OF THE MEMBER STATE OF THE CHOSEN LAW UNDER ARTICLE 7(C) ESR 184
III. CONSEQUENCES OF AN OBJECTION TO THE JURISDICTION OF THE COURTS OF THE MEMBER STATE OF THE CHOSEN LAW BY ANY OF THE PARTIES TO THE PROCEEDINGS WHO HAVE NOT PARTICIPATED IN THE AGREEMENT 185

I. The Position of Subjects Having an Interest in the Succession Who Are Not Parties to the Agreement Embodying the *professio fori*

1. As stated already [see art. 5 no 19], one of the inherent limitations to the *professio fori* as devised under the ESR, consists of the difficulty in identifying with certainty from the outset, that is, from the point of the opening of the succession upon the passing away of the deceased, all of the subjects having an interest in the succession.

2. In this respect, it is clear that the option made by the parties to the choice-of-court agreement contemplated under article 5 ESR cannot be imposed upon other subjects having an interest in the succession, who did not participate in the agreement in question, either because their existence was simply not known to the parties to the agreement, or due to an alleged intent by the parties to fraudulently exclude such other subjects from their arrangements concerning the succession. At the same time, it also seems reasonable that such an agreement, which, as noted already, pursues the desirable objective of re-establishing the *Gleichlauf* or correspondence between jurisdiction and applicable law jeopardized by the *professio juris* made by the deceased, should not be automatically nullified as a consequence of the subsequent identification of other subjects having an interest in the succession. Accordingly, the judicial process pursued up to that point before the court seised pursuant to such an agreement, should not be *ipso facto* invalidated, since it may well be within the interests of the subjects in question to submit the dispute to the jurisdiction of the chosen court.

3. Article 9 ESR satisfactorily caters for this possibility by providing that in the case of such a constellation, the choice-of-court agreement entered into by some of the parties concerned by the succession remains effective, if the other subjects concerned who have not participated in the agreement accept the jurisdiction of the chosen court, by entering an appearance before such a court without contesting its jurisdiction.

4. The mechanism of an implied acceptance of jurisdiction is not unknown with regard to other EU acts adopted in the field of judicial cooperation in civil matters.[1] It is noteworthy, however, that, within

[1] Cf., most notably, article 26.1 Regulation (EU) no. 1215/2012 of the European Parliament and of the Council of 12 December 2012 on jurisdiction and the recognition and enforcement of judgments in civil and commercial matters (recast), OJ no. L351, 20 December 2012, p. 1 (s. c. 'Brussels I-*bis*'), which reproduces the corresponding provision previously contained in article 24 Regulation (EC) no. 44/2001 of 22 December 2000 on jurisdiction and the recognition and enforcement of judgments in civil and commercial matters, OJ no. L12, 16 January 2001, p. 1 (s. c. 'Brussels I'), which has been replicated in turn by article 5 Council Regulation (EC) no. 4/2009 of 18 December 2008 on jurisdiction, applicable law, recognition and enforcement of decisions and cooperation in matters relating to maintenance obligations, OJ no. L7, 10 January 2009, p.1. A more restrictive attitude is instead adopted by Council Regulation (EC) no. 2201/2003 of 27 November 2003 concerning jurisdiction and the recognition and enforcement of judgments in matrimonial matters and the matters of

the scheme of the ESR, such a mechanism applies only in the specific circumstances identified under article 9. That is, exclusively in favour of a court or the courts of the Member State of the law chosen by the deceased, which have in turn formed the subject of a choice-of-court agreement by some of the parties concerned under article 5 ESR and have actually been seised by any of the parties to such an agreement. Accordingly, this provision cannot be resorted to in order to found the jurisdiction of the courts of any other Member State. Therefore, except in the circumstances contemplated under article 9, a court in any Member State having been seised of an action concerning a succession in respect of which it has no jurisdiction under the ESR, is obliged to dismiss the action pursuant to article 15 ESR irrespective of the fact of any of the defendants having entered an appearance before such a court without contesting its jurisdiction [see art. 15 no. 2].[2]

II. Relationships with an Express Acceptance by the Parties of the Jurisdiction of the Courts of the Member State of the Chosen Law under Article 7(c) ESR

5. As already mentioned, this possibility of an implied acceptance of the jurisdiction of the chosen court by the subjects concerned who were not parties to a choice-of-court agreement concluded under article 5 ESR, comes together with the possibility, envisaged under article 7(c) ESR, for the parties to the proceedings to expressly accept the jurisdiction of the court seised in the Member State of the law chosen by the deceased as applicable to the succession. By contrast to an implied acceptance under article 9, an express acceptance under article 7(c) ESR may be made independently of a choice-of-court agreement having been concluded by any of the parties concerned by the succession [see art. 7 no. 9].[3]

parental responsibility, repealing regulation (EC) no. 1347/2000, OJ no. L 338, 23 December 2003, p. 1 (s. c. 'Brussels II-*bis*'), which permits an implied acceptance of jurisdiction, on the basis of entering an appearance, only in respect of actions concerning access rights in the limited circumstances contemplated under article 9.2.

[2] Cf. A. Bonomi, 'Article 9', in A. Bonomi and P. Wautelet, *Le droit européen des successions. Commentaire du règlement n° 650/2012 du 4 juillet 2012* (Bruxelles, 2013), p. 207 *et seq.*, esp. p. 207.

[3] Cf. Bonomi, 'Article 9', p. 208; A. Dutta, 'Art. 9 EuErbVO', in *Münchener Kommentar zum BGB*, 6th ed. (München, 2015), para. 10.

III. Consequences of an Objection to the Jurisdiction of the Courts of the Member State of the Chosen Law by Any of the Parties to the Proceedings Who Have Not Participated in the Agreement

6. Clearly, as rather tautologically specified by article 9.2 ESR, in the case of any of the other parties to the proceedings who did not participate in the choice-of-court agreement contesting the jurisdiction of the chosen court, the agreement becomes ineffective and the chosen court is obliged to decline jurisdiction. In such a case, jurisdiction reverts to the otherwise competent courts pursuant to either the general rule under article 4 ESR, or the subsidiary rules under article 10. The ESR remains silent with regard to the effects of measures, which the court designated in the choice-of-court agreement might have adopted prior to declining jurisdiction under article 9.2 ESR. In this respect, it appears that it is for the ordinarily competent court to decide whether such measures should be maintained or should be replaced by new measures. This essentially depends upon whether the measures in question affect the interests of the parties which contested the jurisdiction of the other court.[4]

7. The solution contemplated under article 9.2 ESR does, in fact, seem to be inescapable,[5] unless it is proved, depending on the object of the proceedings, that the legal interests of the parties which participated in the choice-of-court agreement are separable from those of the other parties, so that the proceedings might continue before the designated court only as among the parties to the agreement without affecting the legal interests of the others. This last possibility is contemplated by recital 28 ESR, which refers to the possibility of choice-of-court agreements being entered into in respect of a specific issue by the parties individually concerned [see art. 5 no. 19].[6]

[4] Cf. Dutta, 'Art. 9 EuErbVO', para. 13, observing that the decision by the chosen court to decline jurisdiction under article 9.2 ESR as a matter of principle produces effects *ex nunc* only.

[5] Cf., instead, B. Hess, 'Die internationale Zuständigkeit nach der Erbrechtsverordnung', in A. Dutta and S. Herrler (eds), *Die Europäische Erbrechtsverordnung* (München, 2014), p. 131 *et seq*., esp. p. 138, who points out that more articulated solutions could have been foreseen, such as a referral of the action by the chosen court to the otherwise competent court, a solution which would have been more suitable within the context of the close integration and mutual trust inherent in the European judicial area.

[6] Cf. recital 28 ESR, which reads in the relevant part as follows: 'It would have to be determined on a case-by-case basis, depending in particular on the issue covered by the choice-of-court agreement, whether the agreement would have to be concluded between all parties concerned by the succession or whether some of them could agree to bring a specific issue before the chosen court in a situation where the decision by that court on that issue would not affect the rights of the other parties to the succession.'

Article 10

Subsidiary Jurisdiction

FABRIZIO MARONGIU BUONAIUTI

1. Where the habitual residence of the deceased at the time of death is not located in a Member State, the courts of a Member State in which assets of the estate are located shall nevertheless have jurisdiction to rule on the succession as a whole in so far as:
   (a) the deceased had the nationality of that Member State at the time of death; or, failing that,
   (b) the deceased had his previous habitual residence in that Member State, provided that, at the time the court is seised, a period of not more than five years has elapsed since that habitual residence changed.
2. Where no court in a Member State has jurisdiction pursuant to paragraph 1, the courts of the Member State in which assets of the estate are located shall nevertheless have jurisdiction to rule on those assets.

Summary

I. THE ROLE OF SUBSIDIARY JURISDICTION RULES WITHIN THE SYSTEM OF ALLOCATION OF JURISDICTION UNDER THE ESR *page* 187

II. SUBSIDIARY JURISDICTION OF THE COURTS OF A MEMBER STATE WHERE ASSETS BELONGING TO THE ESTATE OF THE DECEASED ARE LOCATED: GROUNDS FOR SUCH A RULE AND PROBLEMS INHERENT IN THE LOCATION OF ASSETS 188

III. CIRCUMSTANCES IN WHICH THE COURTS OF A MEMBER STATE WHERE ASSETS BELONGING TO THE ESTATE OF THE DECEASED ARE LOCATED MAY EXERCISE GENERAL JURISDICTION IN RESPECT OF THE SUCCESSION 193

A. Where the Deceased Possessed the Nationality of Such a Member State: Issues Raised by Double or Multiple Nationalities 193

B. Where the Deceased Was Previously Habitually Resident in the Relevant Member State: Issues Raised by the Temporal Requirement Contained in the Rule 194

IV. CASES IN WHICH JURISDICTION IS LIMITED TO DISPUTES CONCERNING ASSETS LOCATED WITHIN THE MEMBER STATE OF THE FORUM: ISSUES OF DELIMITATION AND DISADVANTAGES OF A FRAGMENTATION OF JURISDICTION IN RESPECT OF THE SUCCESSION 196

I. The Role of Subsidiary Jurisdiction Rules within the System of Allocation of Jurisdiction under the ESR

1. The underlying rationale behind the system of allocation of jurisdiction contained in the ESR, is that the regulation should provide an exhaustive set of rules determining the jurisdiction of the courts of the Member States to rule on any succession matter falling within the relevant scope of application, without leaving any room for the application of domestic rules of jurisdiction.[1]

2. Such a solution is not new of the ESR, having already been adopted by EC regulation no. 4/2009 in matters of maintenance obligations[2] and having also inspired the initial proposal for a recast of the Brussels I regulation,[3] even though, with regard to the latter, it has largely been set aside in the final text of EU regulation no. 1215/2012.[4]

1 Cf., among others, A. Bonomi, 'Introduction au Chapitre II – Compétence', in A. Bonomi and P. Wautelet, *Le droit européen des successions. Commentaire du règlement n° 650/2012 du 4 juillet 2012* (Bruxelles, 2013), p. 165 *et seq.*; A. Davì and A. Zanobetti, 'Il nuovo diritto internazionale privato delle successioni nell'Unione europea', *CdT* 5/2 (2013), p. 12 *et seq.*; A. Davì and A. Zanobetti, *Il nuovo diritto internazionale privato europeo delle successioni* (Torino, 2014), p. 195 *et seq.*; A. Dutta, 'Das neue internationale Erbrecht der Europäischen Union – Eine erste Lektüre der Erbrechtsverordnung', *FamRZ* (2013), p. 4 *et seq.*, esp. p. 6; H. Gaudemet-Tallon, 'Les règles de compétence judiciaire dans le règlement européen sur les successions', in G. Khairallah and M. Revillard (eds), *Droit européen des successions internationales. Le règlement du 4 juillet 2012* (Paris, 2013), p. 127 *et seq.*, esp. p. 130; B. Hess, 'Die internationale Zuständigkeit nach der Erbrechtsverordnung', in A. Dutta and S. Herrler (eds), *Die Europäische Erbrechtsverordnung* (München, 2014), p. 131 *et seq.*, esp. p. 133 *et seq.*

2 Cf. articles 6 and 7 Council Regulation (EC) no. 4/2009 of 18 December 2008 on jurisdiction, applicable law, recognition and enforcement of decisions and cooperation in matters relating to maintenance obligations, OJ no. L 7, 10 January 2009, p. 1, providing for subsidiary jurisdiction and *forum necessitatis* respectively. Cf., among others, M. Castellaneta and A. Leandro, 'Il regolamento CE n. 4/2009 relativo alle obbligazioni alimentari', *N l civ comm* (2009), p. 1051 *et seq.*, esp. p. 1073 *et seq.*; B. Ancel and H. Muir-Watt, 'Aliments sans frontières. Le règlement n° 4/2009 du 18 décembre 2008 relatif à la compétence, la loi applicable, la reconnaissance et l'exécution des décisions et la coopération en matière d'obligations alimentaires', *Rev crit dr int priv* (2010), p. 457 *et seq.*, esp. p. 463 *et seq.*

3 Doc. COM(2010) 748 final, of 14 December 2010, article 4.2. Cf., among others, F. Pocar, 'Révision de Bruxelles I et ordre juridique international: quelle approche uniforme?', *Riv dir int priv proc* (2011), p. 591 *et seq.*; J. Weber, 'Universal Jurisdiction and Third States in the Reform of the Brussels I Regulation', *RabelsZ* (2011), p. 619 *et seq.*

4 Cf. article 6 Regulation (EU) no. 1215/2012 of the European Parliament and of the Council of 12 December 2012 on jurisdiction and the recognition and enforcement of judgments in civil and commercial matters (recast), OJ no. L 351, 20 December 2012, p. 1; among others, H. Gaudemet-Tallon and C. Kessedjian, 'La refonte du règlement Bruxelles I', *Rev trim dr eur* (2013), p. 435 *et seq.*, esp. p. 439 *et seq.*; A. Leandro, 'Prime osservazioni sul regolamento

3. The solution adopted under the ESR, and the Maintenance regulation alike, brings with it the undeniable advantage of having the courts, in the Member States subject to the relevant regulation, apply a single set of rules of jurisdiction. With this comes the inherent advantage of pursuing to a greater extent the objective of uniformity with regard to the allocation of jurisdiction which each of the regulations pursues in respect of matters falling within their respective scope of application. The solution adopted by both regulations presents a further advantage, in that it overcomes the difficulties inherent in the delimitation of the respective scope of application of the uniform rules of jurisdiction and of the domestic rules, which the opposite system based on a co-existence of the two sets of rules inevitably poses.[5]

II. Subsidiary Jurisdiction of the Courts of a Member State Where Assets Belonging to the Estate of the Deceased are Located: Grounds for Such a Rule and Problems Inherent in the Location of Assets

4. Within the scheme of the ESR, the above-mentioned objective of providing uniform subsidiary rules of jurisdiction to be applied in lieu of a reference to the domestic rules of jurisdiction in succession matters whenever jurisdiction of a court in a Member State cannot be established pursuant to the general rule under article 4 ESR, is pursued by the rules contained in article 10. These rules are based upon the location of assets belonging to the estate of the deceased. As will be highlighted at a later stage, this operates either as a general ground of jurisdiction, concerning the whole of the succession as under the general rule embodied in article 4 ESR, or, alternatively, as a limited ground of jurisdiction of a strictly territorial nature, depending upon the existence of further elements establishing a stronger connection between the

(UE) n. 1215/2012 ("Bruxelles I bis")', *Il giusto processo civile* (2013), p. 583 *et seq.*, esp. p. 585 *et seq.*; A. Nuyts, 'La refonte du règlement Bruxelles I', *Rev crit dr int priv* (2013), p. 1 *et seq.*, esp. p. 4 *et seq.*; F. Salerno, *Giurisdizione ed efficacia delle decisioni straniere nel regolamento (UE) n. 1215/2012 (rifusione)*, 4th ed. (Padova, 2015), p. 81 *et seq.*

5 Cf., for some general remarks in this respect, A. Bonomi, 'Sull'opportunità e le possibili modalità di una regolamentazione comunitaria della competenza giurisdizionale applicabile *erga omnes*', *Riv dir int priv proc* (2007), p. 313 *et seq.*; F. Pocar, 'Faut-il remplacer le renvoi au droit national par des règles uniformes dans l'article 4 du règlement No. 44/2001?', in *Vers des nouveaux équilibres entre ordres juridiques. Liber amicorum Hélène Gaudemet-Tallon* (Paris, 2008), p. 573 *et seq.*

succession and one or more Member States where such assets are located.[6]

5. The opting for such a rule is, again, certainly not novel for the ESR, since it could be traced back to dated domestic rules of jurisdiction present in some Member States, where *forum patrimonii* or *forum arresti* were used as grounds of jurisdiction also beyond the domain of succession disputes.[7] The rule, as such, indeed reflects the prevailing material object of any dispute in succession matters, that is, the devolution of the estate of the deceased. As such, it can be considered as being inspired by the principle of proximity as a guiding rule in the allocation of jurisdiction, since, inevitably, the courts of a Member State where assets belonging to the estate of the deceased are located are, in principle, in a better position to rule upon devolution and transmission of those assets than those sitting in another country where the deceased left no assets whatsoever. Alongside proximity, the location of assets belonging to the estate of the deceased as a ground of jurisdiction presents the advantage of promoting the effectiveness of judicial protection of rights. This is in the sense that, in principle, the enforcement of a court decision is more expedient in respect of property present within the jurisdiction of the court than in respect of assets located abroad.[8]

6. With regard to the latter consideration, it is worth mentioning that if its relevance as among Member States may be considered as negligible in a system such as that established by the ESR, where recognition of judgments as among Member States is automatic and the enforceability

[6] Cf., particularly, A. Bonomi, 'Article 10', in A. Bonomi and P. Wautelet (eds), *Le droit européen des successions. Commentaire du règlement n° 650/2012 du 4 juillet 2012* (Bruxelles, 2013), p. 211 *et seq.*, esp. p. 215 *et seq.*; A. Dutta, 'Art. 10 EuErbVO', in *Münchener Kommentar zum BGB*, 6th ed. (München, 2015), para. 4 *et seq.*

[7] Cf., particularly, in Germany, § 23 *ZPO*, providing for *forum patrimonii*, and, historically, § 34 *Anhang zur Preussischen Allgemeinen Gerichtsordnung*, providing for *forum arresti*. Cf. R. Geimer, *Internationales Zivilprozessrecht*, 5th ed. (Köln, 2005), p. 430 *et seq.* Note that § 23 *ZPO* figured among the grounds of jurisdiction listed in annex I to the Council Regulation (EC) no. 44/2001 of 22 December 2000 on jurisdiction and the recognition and enforcement of judgments in civil and commercial matters, OJ no. L 12, 16 January 2001, p. 1 (s. c. 'Brussels I'), the application of which was excluded as against EU domiciled defendants under art. 3.2 of the regulation, being considered as an exorbitant ground of jurisdiction. Cf. currently art. 5.2 Brussels I-*bis* regulation, establishing a duty for the Member States to notify the European Commission of such grounds of jurisdiction, pursuant to article 76 of the regulation.

[8] Cf., on the rationale of the rule, among others, Bonomi, 'Article 10', p. 213 *et seq.*; Davì and Zanobetti, 'Il nuovo diritto internazionale privato delle successioni', p. 116 *et seq.*; Davì and Zanobetti, *Il nuovo diritto internazionale privato europeo*, p. 202 *et seq.*; Dutta, 'Art. 10 EuErbVO', para. 4; *id.*, 'Das neue internationale Erbrecht der Europäischen Union', p. 6.

of decisions can be refused only upon appeal based on a limited number of grounds [see arts. 39–40, 50], it still preserves its importance with regard to situations involving third countries. Such countries would be at liberty to refuse recognition or enforcement of a judgment handed down in a Member State affecting property under their jurisdiction according to their own domestic law. This concern is reflected in the ESR, which, under its article 12, provides for the power of a court in a Member State, having jurisdiction pursuant to the regulation, to refrain from ruling on assets belonging to the estate of the deceased which are located in a third country, whenever it may be presumed that the recognition or enforcement of the judgment to be delivered might be refused in the third country where the relevant assets are located [see art. 12 no. 1].

7. At the same time, location of assets belonging to the estate of the deceased as a subsidiary ground of jurisdiction has some undeniable disadvantages. The first is inherent in its ubiquitous nature. The deceased might well have left assets in different countries, be those Member States or third countries. Even though, naturally, the rule as a ground of jurisdiction only operates in respect of assets located in Member States subject to the regulation, it may give rise to a situation of concurrent jurisdictions among such states. This is because, as conceived under article 10.1 ESR, the rule operates irrespective of the value or of the comparable importance of the assets, in principle placing the courts of every Member State where any assets belonging to the estate of the deceased are located on an equal footing.[9] This, as will be seen shortly, is essentially the reason why the rule presupposes the existence of additional connecting factors also establishing a personal link of the deceased with the relevant Member State in order for the courts of that Member State to be vested with general jurisdiction in respect of the whole of the succession.[10]

8. A further difficulty posed by the subsidiary jurisdiction rule under consideration, is intrinsic to the location of the assets belonging to the estate of the deceased. Firstly, the rule under article 10 ESR, does not specify the relevant moment at which the locating of the assets, with regard, essentially, to moveable property, is deemed to take place. In this respect, it seems that the question should be resolved according to

[9] Cf., pointing to this disadvantage inherent in the rule, Bonomi, 'Article 10', p. 213; Davì and Zanobetti, 'Il nuovo diritto internazionale privato delle successioni', p. 116 *et seq.*; Davì and Zanobetti, *Il nuovo diritto internazionale privato europeo*, p. 203 *et seq.*; Dutta, 'Art. 10 EuErbVO', para. 12.

[10] Still, as will be seen, no. 11 *et seq.*, those additional connecting factors may in turn prove ubiquitous.

a general principle of procedural law, consisting of *perpetuatio jurisdictionis*, whereby jurisdiction is to be determined having regard to the legal framework and the conditions of fact existing at the moment of seising the court.[11] This, in turn, is to be determined pursuant to the autonomous rule under article 14 ESR [see art. 14 no. 1]. Subsequent changes in the circumstances existing at that point should not affect the jurisdiction of the courts which were competently seised at the time.[12] This solution is also in accordance with the general principle, developed within the European system of private international law, of legal certainty and foreseeability with regard to the establishment of jurisdiction.[13]

9. Secondly, problems may arise with regard to the locating of certain types of assets, which should, in turn, be resolved according to autonomous rules to be deduced from principles developed within the European system of private international law, or, failing such principles, drawing upon the common legal traditions of the Member States.[14] Among these, following a solution adopted in the European Insolvency regulation, it appears that moveable assets subject to registration, such as vehicles, ships and aircrafts, are to be considered as being located in the Member State where they are registered. This is the case even if, at the relevant

[11] Cf. in respect of this rule, which in Italian law is contemplated under article 5 Code of Civil Procedure, among others, G. Morelli, *Diritto processuale civile internazionale*, 2nd ed. (Padova, 1954), p. 157 *et seq.*; M. Giuliano, *La giurisdizione civile italiana e lo straniero*, 2nd ed. (Milano, 1970), p. 165 *et seq.*; a corresponding rule applies, as concerns domestic competence, but at the same time, albeit indirectly, also concerning jurisdiction, in Germany under section 261, paragraph 3.2, Zivilprozessordnung. Cf. Geimer, *Internationales Zivilprozessrecht*, p. 570 *et seq.*, and, with regard to its application in the present case, Dutta, 'Art. 10 EuErbVO', para. 9.

[12] A controversial issue is whether supervening changes to the relevant rules or circumstances of fact having the effect of founding jurisdiction should be taken into account: cf. Morelli, *Diritto processuale civile internazionale*, p. 165 *et seq*. This solution has been adopted under art. 8 of the Italian Private International Law Act of 1995, no. 218.

[13] Cf., among others, ECJ, case C-440/97, *GIE Groupe Concorde* v. *The Master of the vessel 'Suhadiwarno Panjan'* [1999] ECR I-6307, at 23; case C-256/00, *Besix* v. *Wasserreinigungsbau Kretzschmar* [2002] ECR I-1699, at 24; case C-281/02, *Andrew Owusu* v. *N. B. Jackson* [2005] ECR I-1383, at 38 *et seq.*; A. Dickinson, 'Legal Certainty and the Brussels Convention – Too Much of a Good Thing?', in P. de Vareilles-Sommières (ed), *Forum Shopping in the European Judicial Area* (Oxford; Portland, OR, 2007), p. 115 *et seq.*

[14] Cf. generally, among others, M. Audit, 'L'interprétation autonome du droit international privé communautaire', *JDI* (2004), p. 789 *et seq.*; R. Baratta, 'The Process of Characterization in the EC Conflict of Laws: Suggesting a Flexible Approach', *YPIL*, VI (2004), p. 155 *et seq.*; S. Bariatti, 'Qualificazione e interpretazione del diritto internazionale privato comunitario: prime riflessioni', *Riv dir int priv proc* (2006), p. 361 *et seq.*; specifically, Bonomi, 'Article 10', p. 216; Dutta, 'Art. 10 EuErbVO', para. 5.

time, they happen to be situated elsewhere.[15] Non-corporeal assets, such as intellectual property rights subject to registration, are treated the same way, with the Member State where they are registered being considered, albeit artificially, as the State in which they were located.[16] With regard to intellectual property rights having a unitary nature and producing EU-wide effects, such rights are to be located as property rights in accordance with the relevant establishing instruments.[17] The locating of intellectual property rights not subject to registration, such as copyright, may prove to be more controversial. With regard to such rights, reference may be made to the Member State in respect of which protection is required, reflecting the solution adopted for the purposes of determining the law applicable to infringements of such rights under article 8 of the Rome II regulation. This is so, even though such a rule may in turn prove ubiquitous, in the case of rights of the said type, protection of which can be claimed in respect of more Member States.[18]

10. With regard to credits, reference may be made once more to the criteria contemplated within the European Insolvency regulation no. 1346/2000, which, under article 2(g), refers to the Member State where the debtor has the centre of his or her main interests as intended under article 3.1 of the same regulation.[19] Further issues may arise concerning the locating of non-registered shares in companies, which are to be located in the Member State where the company itself is considered as being located.[20]

[15] Cf. article 2(g), second indent, regulation (EC) no. 1346/2000 on insolvency proceedings; Dutta, 'Art. 10 EuErbVO', no. 6. Cf., prospectively, also article 2.9(iv) EU regulation 848/2015 of 20 May 2015 on insolvency proceedings (recast), which will apply to insolvency proceedings opened after 26 June 2017.

[16] Cf., again, article 2(g), second indent, regulation (EC) no. 1346/2000; Dutta, 'Art. 10 EuErbVO', para. 6. This case would fall under article 2.9(iv) EU regulation no. 848/2015.

[17] Cf. art. 16, regulation (EC) no. 207/2009 on the community trademark; art. 27, regulation (EC) no. 6/2002 on community designs; art. 22, regulation (EC) no. 2100/1994 on community plant variety rights; Dutta, 'Art. 10 EuErbVO', no. 7; lastly, art. 7 regulation (EU) no. 1257/2012, implementing an enhanced cooperation in the area of unitary patent protection.

[18] Cf. Dutta, 'Art. 10 EuErbVO', no. 8; concerning the solution adopted in respect of choice of law under article 8 regulation (EC) no. 864/2007, s. c. 'Rome II', on the law applicable to non-contractual obligations, among others, N. Boschiero, 'Beni immateriali (diritto internazionale privato e processuale)', in *Enciclopedia del diritto, Annali*, II.2 (Milano, 2008), p. 115 *et seq.*, esp. p. 131 *et seq.*; A. Dickinson, *The Rome II Regulation* (Oxford, 2008), p. 447 *et seq.*; F. Marongiu Buonaiuti, *Le obbligazioni non contrattuali nel diritto internazionale privato* (Milano, 2013), p. 133 *et seq.* It should be noted that EU regulation 848/2015 provides under article 2.9(iv) for a different solution, pointing to the country where the owner of such rights has its habitual residence or registered office.

[19] Cf. Dutta, 'Art. 10 EuErbVO', para. 6.

[20] Cf. Dutta, 'Art. 10 EuErbVO', para. 8.

III. Circumstances in Which the Courts of a Member State Where Assets Belonging to the Estate of the Deceased Are Located May Exercise General Jurisdiction in Respect of the Succession

11. The additional connecting factors contemplated under article 10.1 ESR, in order for the subsidiary rule based on the location of assets belonging to the estate of the deceased to operate as a general ground of jurisdiction,[21] are placed in a hierarchical order. This means that the latter criterion may come up for consideration only in cases where the former is not met, so as to reduce, to the largest extent possible, the risk that the rule as a whole may give rise to a situation of concurrent jurisdictions.[22]

A. *Where the Deceased Possessed the Nationality of Such a Member State: Issues Raised by Double or Multiple Nationalities*

12. The first additional connecting factor contemplated under article 10.1(a) ESR, is the nationality of the deceased at the moment of death. As a matter of principle, the solution adopted in this respect appears reasonable, since it points to the nationality of the deceased as a subsidiary connecting factor to be resorted to in those cases where the main factor, habitual residence, does not apply since it would lead to a third country having jurisdiction. At the same time, the weaker degree of effectiveness of the connection with the relevant Member State which nationality as a connecting factor is likely to guarantee as compared with habitual residence, is balanced by its coincidence, which the rule presupposes, with the location of assets belonging to the estate of the deceased in the Member State concerned.

13. It is true, however, that the ubiquitous character of the latter ground of jurisdiction is not entirely eliminated by the cumulative reference to the nationality of the deceased at the moment of death,

[21] Cf. section II.

[22] The hierarchy existing between the two rules respectively contemplated under art. 10.1(a) and (b) ESR is also highlighted by the words 'failing that' at the end of lit. (a) and confirmed by recital 30 ESR. Cf., among others, Bonomi, 'Article 10', p. 218 *et seq.*; Davì and Zanobetti, 'Il nuovo diritto internazionale privato delle successioni', p. 116; Davì and Zanobetti, *Il nuovo diritto internazionale privato europeo*, p. 202; Dutta, 'Art. 10 EuErbVO', no. 11; by contrast, unpersuasively suggesting that a concurrence might exist between the jurisdictions of courts respectively competent under article 10.1(a) and (b), A. Leandro, 'La giurisdizione nel regolamento dell'Unione europea sulle successioni *mortis causa*', in P. Franzina and A. Leandro (eds), *Il diritto internazionale privato europeo delle successioni* mortis causa (Milano, 2013), p. 59 *et seq.*, esp. p. 73 *et seq.*

since the deceased might well have possessed the nationality of more than one Member State. In such a case, provided, obviously, that assets belonging to the estate of the deceased are at the same time present in the States in question, the ESR does not contain a solution to resolve cases of double or multiple nationalities. In the face of the silence of the ESR on this matter, it would seem arbitrary to attribute to any of the concurrent nationalities a prevalence based upon a more effective connection of the deceased with one of the Member States the nationality of which he or she possessed.[23] The ECJ has, in fact, excluded the possibility of relying on this sort of reasoning with regard to problems posed by double nationalities under EC regulation no. 2201/2003, s. c. 'Brussels II-*bis*', which is in turn silent in this respect.[24] Nor would it be feasible to grant prevalence to the Member State of which the deceased had the nationality at the moment of death where the largest part of his or her assets are located, since, as noted already, the ESR does not give relevance to the value or comparable relevance of assets present within different Member States.[25]

B. Where the Deceased Was Previously Habitually Resident in the Relevant Member State: Issues Raised by the Temporal Requirement Contained in the Rule

14. In the case where the deceased, at the moment of death, did not possess the nationality of any Member State where assets belonging to his or her estate are present, the ESR still provides for the location of such assets in a Member State to operate as a general ground of jurisdiction where he or she had previously been habitually resident in any such Member State. In fact, since in the situation contemplated under article 10.1(b) ESR, the deceased does not, at the moment of death, have

[23] Cf., among others, Bonomi, 'Article 10', p. 218; Davì and Zanobetti, 'Il nuovo diritto internazionale privato delle successioni', p. 116; Davì and Zanobetti, *Il nuovo diritto internazionale privato europeo*, p. 203; Dutta, 'Art. 10 EuErbVO', para. 12.

[24] Cf. ECJ, case C-168/08, *Laszlo Hadadi (Hadady)* v. *Csilla Marta Mesko, married name Hadadi (Hadady)* [2009] ECR I-6871, para. 44 *et seq*. It must be considered that the position adopted by the ECJ in that case was at least to a certain extent influenced by the context of the Brussels II-*bis* regulation, where the various grounds of jurisdiction in matrimonial matters are purely alternative to one another in order to grant, to the largest extent possible, applicants for divorce or personal separation the availability of a *forum*, differently from what happens under article 10.1 ESR, where, as noted already, the two grounds under points (a) and (b) are set out in a hierarchical order, pursuing the goal, insofar as possible, of concentrating succession disputes before a single *forum*.

[25] Cf. no. 4 *et seq*.

a current personal connection with any Member State in terms of his or her habitual residence, and with any Member State where assets belonging to his or her estate may be found with regard to his or her nationality, residually, reference is made to a previous habitual residence. Such a previous habitual residence, unlike the current habitual residence at the moment of death pursuant to the general rule under article 4, will be taken into account only insofar as it refers to a Member State where assets belonging to the estate of the deceased are located.[26]

15. The ESR, nonetheless, in order to ensure that such a previous habitual residence of the deceased, though cumulated with the presence of assets of his or her estate, does not represent too remote a connection between the deceased and the relevant Member State, only allows a previous habitual residence dating back no longer than five years at the moment the court is seised to be taken into account. In this respect, it has been questioned by some authors whether it would have been more appropriate to fix as a date *ad quem* the moment of death. Referring the end of the five-year period to the moment of seisure of the court implies a variable length of the maximum period running from the moment of the deceased having changed his or her habitual residence to the moment of death, depending upon how soon after the opening of the succession an action is commenced. Actually, subject to the applicable limitation periods, in the case of an action concerning the succession being commenced not earlier than five years after the opening of the succession, the rule as formulated in article 10.1(b) would become totally inapplicable. This is because any change in the habitual residence of the deceased occurring even shortly before his or her death would fall beyond the five-year period allowed under the rule.[27]

16. A further issue arises with regard to the correct identification of the moment when a change in the habitual residence of the deceased is to be considered as having taken place. As already noted by some commentators, habitual residence as a factual criterion establishing a connection between a person and a given country is the result of a process consisting of the building up over time of a series of personal, professional and family links of one person to a country, the establishment or relinquishment of which, by contrast to simple residence or domicile, which may

[26] As noted already, nos. 12 and 13, in respect of the nationality of the deceased at the moment of death, either connecting factor operates as a circumstance supporting the subsidiary ground of jurisdiction consisting of the presence of assets belonging to the estate of the deceased.

[27] Cf. Bonomi, 'Article 10', p. 219; Dutta, 'Art. 10 EuErbVO', para. 11.

normally be traced through public records, can hardly be referred to an exact moment in time.[28] Lastly, the rule as contained in article 10.1(b) ESR does not specify that the previous habitual residence of the deceased being taken into account is necessarily intended to be that immediately preceding the one he or she possessed at the moment of death. Nevertheless, the rationale for the rule, which, as already noted, is to be identified in the establishment of a not too remote connection of the deceased with the relevant Member State and in the need to avoid as far as possible cases of concurrent jurisdiction, suggests that the previous habitual residence to be taken into account is intended to be that immediately preceding the one that the deceased possessed at the moment of death.[29]

IV. Cases in Which Jurisdiction Is Limited to Disputes Concerning Assets Located within the Member State of the *forum*: Issues of Delimitation and Disadvantages of a Fragmentation of Jurisdiction in Respect of the Succession

17. In case none of the personal connections of the deceased provided for under article 10.1(a) or (b) ESR subsists with a Member State where assets belonging to his or her estate are located, article 10.2 provides for a jurisdiction of the courts of any Member States where such assets are located. This is limited to actions concerning those assets which are located in the Member State of the court seised. Such a ground of jurisdiction can be considered as a sort of last resort rule even though, unlike the *forum necessitatis* rule contemplated under article 11 ESR [see art. 11 no. 6], it does not presuppose that proceedings cannot be

[28] Cf. again Bonomi, 'Article 10', p. 220, arguing that where the previous habitual residence of the deceased cannot be established with sufficient certainty, the rule should be considered as inapplicable and, accordingly, the court should limit its jurisdiction to questions concerning assets present within its jurisdiction under art. 10.2 ESR; Dutta, 'Art. 10 EuErbVO', para. 11.

[29] Cf. Bonomi, 'Article 10', p. 219 *et seq*. This reading of the rule also appears to be suggested by its formulation, which refers to 'his previous habitual residence', which would imply that only the one immediately preceding that possessed at the moment of death comes into consideration. By contrast, arguing for a broader interpretation, Davì and Zanobetti, 'Il nuovo diritto internazionale privato delle successioni', p. 116, footnote 443; Davì and Zanobetti, *Il nuovo diritto internazionale privato europeo*, p. 203, note 19; Dutta, 'Art. 10 EuErbVO', para. 12; cf. also Gaudemet-Tallon, 'Les règles de compétence judiciaire', p. 139, also advancing the hypothesis of the courts of different Member States claiming jurisdiction under this head, based on a different appreciation of the circumstances determining such a previous habitual residence.

entertained before third country courts which might have jurisdiction to rule on the succession pursuant to their own domestic law.[30] The rule is, however, likely to give rise to some practical problems in terms of its application as well as to perplexities concerning its compatibility with the underlying rationale of the system of allocation of jurisdiction embodied in the ESR.

18. The main difficulty with regard to the application of such a rule is inherent in the delimitation of the scope of actions falling under the jurisdiction it establishes. In fact, there are actions which can be considered as strictly limited in their scope to specified assets belonging to the estate of the deceased, such as an action concerning the execution of a testamentary disposition or the reduction of a donation made by the deceased during his or her lifetime in respect of a specific asset located in one Member State. Equally, however, there may be cases where the action would not lend itself to such a straightforward delimitation based on the location of the assets involved. Particular problems would arise, in fact, with an action challenging the validity of a will affecting the whole of the estate of the deceased, comprising assets located in different Member States, not to mention in third countries as well.[31]

19. Furthermore, as already noted, the rule under article 10.2 ESR raises a more general question of consistency with the underlying rationale of the system of allocation of jurisdiction within the ESR, based as it is on unity of the succession both in terms of jurisdiction and applicable law and, as stressed elsewhere [see arts. 4, 5 nos. 2–4], on the objective of establishing as far as possible a *Gleichlauf* or coincidence between jurisdiction and applicable law. In fact, the rule, for all that the circumstances in which it will apply may appear exceptional, introduces an undesirable fragmentation of succession in terms of jurisdiction. It brings the already underlined risks of giving rise to situations of concurrent jurisdiction and, possibly, to situations decided divergently within different Member States. At the same time, it creates a situation, not unlike that which would arise in at least some cases under article 10.1, whereby the courts sitting in a Member State will be called upon to rule on the

[30] Cf. Davì and Zanobetti, *Il nuovo diritto internazionale privato europeo*, p. 203, pointing to the aim pursued by the rule of preventing a denial of justice in case the third country courts which would have jurisdiction in respect of the succession under their own domestic rules would, pursuant to such rules, only decide in respect of assets located within their jurisdiction.

[31] Cf. Bonomi, 'Article 10', p. 221; Davì and Zanobetti, *Il nuovo diritto internazionale privato europeo*, p. 203 *et seq.*; Dutta, 'Art. 10 EuErbVO', para. 13.

succession or, rather, a part of it, applying the law of a third country, insofar as such a law does not refer back to the law of a Member State under the rule on *renvoi* contained in the ESR [see art. 34].

20. The situations contemplated under article 10.1 ESR are already such that the main connecting factor consisting of the habitual residence of the deceased is located in a third country. Those contemplated under article 10.2 are undoubtedly even more strongly connected with a third country and, as such, raise to a greater extent the problem inherent in the different perspectives from which the rules contained in the ESR with regard to jurisdiction and applicable law respectively operate. Indeed, whereas the latter apply *erga omnes* [see art. 20], the rules of jurisdiction as contained in the ESR are not only applicable exclusively *inter partes*, but, critically, do not, except for the purposes of *forum necessitatis* [see art. 11 nos. 7–12] and for the possibility of a limitation of actions under article 12 ESR [see art. 12 nos. 9–14], take into any account the attitude taken by third country courts pursuant to their own domestic rules. This is particularly critical in those cases where such an attitude would have an impact on the exercise by Member State courts of jurisdiction of which they would be vested pursuant to the ESR. In terms of article 10.2, the ESR could have made the rather inconvenient solution of providing for a jurisdiction, which is limited to assets located within the *forum*, subject to the unavailability of third country courts having jurisdiction in respect of the succession to also rule upon those assets.[32]

[32] Cf. article 88.1 of the Swiss Private International Law Act of 1987, which provides that the Swiss courts shall exercise jurisdiction in succession matters in respect of assets left in Switzerland by a foreigner domiciled abroad at the moment of death, only insofar as the foreign courts would not exercise jurisdiction in respect of such assets; Bonomi, 'Article 10', p. 222.

Article 11

Forum Necessitatis

FABRIZIO MARONGIU BUONAIUTI

Where no court of a Member State has jurisdiction pursuant to other provisions of this Regulation, the courts of a Member State may, on an exceptional basis, rule on the succession if proceedings cannot reasonably be brought or conducted or would be impossible in a third State with which the case is closely connected.

The case must have a sufficient connection with the Member State of the court seised.

Summary

I. THE RATIONALE FOR THE RULE WITHIN THE SYSTEM OF ALLOCATION OF JURISDICTION UNDER THE ESR AND ITS PRECEDENTS *page* 200

II. ABSENCE OF ANY OTHER GROUND OF JURISDICTION UNDER THE ESR 201

III. EXISTENCE OF A CLOSE CONNECTION OF THE CASE WITH A THIRD COUNTRY WHERE THE ENTERTAINMENT OF AN ACTION WOULD PROVE IMPOSSIBLE OR UNREASONABLE 202

IV. CIRCUMSTANCES DETERMINING THE IMPOSSIBILITY OR THE UNREASONABLENESS OF BRINGING OR CONDUCTING PROCEEDINGS BEFORE THE COURTS OF SUCH A THIRD COUNTRY 203

- A. Where No Court in a Third Country with Which the Case Is Closely Connected Would Have Jurisdiction to Decide the Case 203
- B. Where the Action, though Falling within the Jurisdiction of the Courts of Such a Country, Would Prove Inadmissible on a Point of Law 204
- C. Where Local Circumstances Would Materially Make It Impossible or Unreasonable for the Plaintiff to Bring or Conduct His Case before Such a Court 205

V. THE REQUIREMENT OF A SUFFICIENT CONNECTION OF THE CASE WITH THE MEMBER STATE OF THE COURT SEISED 207

I. The Rationale for the Rule within the System of Allocation of Jurisdiction under the ESR and Its Precedents

1. The system of allocation of jurisdiction in succession matters as set out under the ESR is completed by a provision for a *forum necessitatis*. Such a rule, which is identical to that contained under article 7 regulation no. 4/2009 concerning maintenance obligations[1] and to a corresponding provision initially included in the proposal for a recast of the Brussels I regulation,[2] provides an exceptional ground of jurisdiction for the courts of a Member State which has a sufficient connection with the dispute in question. Such a ground of jurisdiction, which is subsidiary to any other ground of jurisdiction contemplated under the ESR, including the residual rules under its article 10, is only to be resorted to in cases where the action in question could not be entertained by the courts of a third country with which the case would be closely connected.[3]

2. The rule serves the same function as those established for corresponding purposes under domestic systems of private international law, such as the Swiss federal act on private international law (LDIP)[4] or the Belgian code of private international law,[5] which are aimed at the prevention of a denial of justice. This is in accordance with the already

[1] Cf. P. Franzina, 'Sul *forum necessitatis* nello spazio giudiziario europeo', *Riv dir int* (2009), p. 1121 *et seq.*; G. Rossolillo, '*Forum necessitatis* e flessibilità dei criteri di giurisdizione nel diritto internazionale privato nazionale e dell'Unione europea', *CdT* 2/1 (2010), p. 403 *et seq.*, esp. p. 413 *et seq.*

[2] Cf. article 26, doc. COM(2010) 748 final, and F. Marongiu Buonaiuti, 'La tutela del diritto di accesso alla giustizia e della parità delle armi tra i litiganti nella proposta di revisione del regolamento n. 44/2001', in A. Di Stefano and R. Sapienza (eds), *La tutela dei diritti umani e il diritto internazionale, XVI Convegno, Catania, 23–24 giugno 2011* (Napoli, 2012), p. 345 *et seq.*, esp. p. 355 *et seq.*

[3] Cf., among others, A. Bonomi, 'Article 11', in A. Bonomi and P. Wautelet, *Le droit européen des successions. Commentaire du règlement n° 650/2012 du 4 juillet 2012* (Bruxelles, 2013), p. 225 *et seq.*; A. Davì and A. Zanobetti, 'Il nuovo diritto internazionale privato delle successioni nell'Unione europea', *CdT* 5/2 (2013), p. 5 *et seq.*, esp. p. 119 *et seq.*; A. Davì and A. Zanobetti, *Il nuovo diritto internazionale privato europeo delle successioni* (Torino, 2014), p. 208 *et seq.*; A. Dutta, 'Art. 11 EuErbVO', in *Münchener Kommentar zum BGB*, 6th ed. (München, 2015), para. 1 *et seq.*

[4] Art. 3. Cf., among others, S. Othenin-Girard, 'Quelques observations sur le for de nécessité en droit international privé suisse', *RSuisseDIE* (1999), p. 251 *et seq.*; P. Volken, 'Art. 3', in D. Girsberger et al. (eds), *Zürcher Kommentar zum IPRG*, 2nd ed. (Zürich, 2004), p. 48 *et seq.*

[5] Art. 11. Cf. A. Nuyts, 'Article 11', in J. Erauw et al. (eds), *Het Wetboek internationaal Privaatrecht becommentarieerd – Le code de droit international privé commenté* (Oxford, Bruxelles, 2006), p. 64 *et seq.*; for a broader comparative survey, V. Rétornaz and B. Volders, 'Le for de nécessité: tableau comparatif et évolutif', *Rev crit dr int priv* (2008), p. 225 *et seq.*

highlighted choice of the EU legislator to include within the ESR an exhaustive set of rules of jurisdiction, which leave no room for resorting to domestic rules in those cases where jurisdiction of the courts sitting in a Member State could not be established on the grounds contemplated by the ESR [see art. 10 nos. 1–3]. This choice inevitably increases the risk of negative conflicts of jurisdictions. In fact, it cannot be denied that the system of allocation of jurisdiction set out in the ESR, distributive as it is as among Member States, operates unilaterally vis-à-vis third country courts. Such courts are not subject to the regulation's rules and are accordingly free to provide or not provide for their jurisdiction under their domestic law in those cases where no Member State court would have jurisdiction pursuant to the ESR.[6]

II. Absence of Any Other Ground of Jurisdiction under the ESR

3. The rule under article 11 ESR logically implies an extension of the scope of the jurisdiction of Member States' courts beyond the limits normally envisaged by the regulation itself, in cases which are inherently more closely connected with one or more third countries. In fact, the relatively rare cases in which the rule may apply, are cases where none of the grounds of jurisdiction contemplated under either article 4 or article 10 ESR would apply. This means not only that the deceased did not have his or her habitual residence in a Member State at the time of death, but also that he or she did not have the nationality of any Member State where assets belonging to his or her estate were located, nor a previous habitual residence dating back no longer than five years in any such Member State[7] [see art. 10, nos. 12–13 and 14–16].

4. It is therefore evident that those cases in which the rule is likely to apply are cases which should normally fall within the jurisdiction of

[6] Cf., noting the absence of any consideration within the ESR proposal of the exercise of jurisdiction by third country courts concerning successions connected with third countries, M. Hellner, 'El futuro reglamento de la UE sobre sucesiones. La relación con terceros estados', *An esp der int priv*, vol. 10 (2010), p. 379 *et seq.*, esp. p. 386 *et seq.*

[7] Cf. P. Lagarde, 'Les principes de base du nouveau règlement européen sur les successions', *Rev crit dr int priv* (2012), p. 691 *et seq.*, esp. p. 703 *et seq.*, arguing that whenever assets belonging to the estate of the deceased are located in a Member State, even absent the further connecting factors contemplated under article 10.1 ESR, a real need for a *forum necessitatis* does not exist, since the courts of the Member State where the said assets are located would have jurisdiction. Still, as conceded by the author, such a jurisdiction would be limited to the assets located in such a Member State and may not entirely cover the object of the action: cf. also Dutta, 'Art. 11 EuErbVO', para. 1.

a third country court, and, accordingly, Member States' courts should, in principle, be reluctant to exercise jurisdiction so as not to give rise to conflicts of jurisdiction with any such court, something which the ESR is not equipped to regulate. In fact, within the ESR no provision is made for cases of *lis alibi pendens* or related actions pending before third country courts, which are, by contrast, contemplated under regulation no. 1215/2012 (s. c. Brussels I-*bis* regulation).[8]

5. It must, furthermore, be considered that the rule under article 11 ESR is specifically conceived with a view to providing a remedy in respect of the unavailability or inability of third country courts to entertain the action, and not with regard to comparable situations which might arise before other Member States' courts.[9] In fact, it must be considered that an application of the rule as among Member States, besides being excluded by the clear wording of the provision, would risk altering the allocation of jurisdiction in succession matters as among Member States' courts devised by the ESR and would be incompatible with the principle of reciprocal faith, which prevents Member State courts from reviewing the reliability of other Member States' judicial systems.[10]

III. Existence of a Close Connection of the Case with a Third Country Where the Entertainment of an Action Would Prove Impossible or Unreasonable

6. Article 11 ESR, in referring to the impossibility or the unreasonableness of proceedings being entertained by the courts of a third country,

[8] Regulation (EU) no. 1215/2012 of the European Parliament and of the Council of 12 December 2012 on jurisdiction and the recognition and enforcement of judgments in civil and commercial matters (recast), OJ no. L 351, 20 December 2012, p. 1; cf. F. Marongiu Buonaiuti, '*Lis alibi pendens* and Related Actions in the Relationships with the Courts of Third Countries in the Recast of the Brussels I Regulation', *YPIL* (2013/2014), p. 87 *et seq.*, esp. p. 91 *et seq.* See also comments to articles 17 and 18 [see art. 17, nos. 19–20; art.18, no. 13].

[9] Cf., by contrast, arguing that the rule might also be applicable in such situations, Bonomi, 'Article 11', p. 226 *et seq.*

[10] Cf. ECJ, case C-116/02, *Gasser* v. *MISAT* [2003] ECR I-14693, at 55 *et seq.*, excluding the possibility that the excessive average length of judicial proceedings in the Member State of the court first seised may cause an exception to the application of the rules on *lis alibi pendens* as then embodied in the 1968 Brussels Convention. Cf., among others, Th. Schilling, 'Internationale Rechtshängigkeit vs. Entscheidung binnen angemessener Frist. Zum Zusammenspiel von Art. 6 I EMRK, Art. 307 EGV und Art. 27 EuGVV', *IPRax* (2004), p. 294 *et seq.*; R. Fentiman, 'Access to Justice and Parallel Proceedings in Europe', *CLJ* (2005), p. 312 *et seq.*; J. J. Fawcett, 'The Impact of Article 6(1) of the ECHR on Private International Law', ICLQ (2007), p. 1 *et seq.*, esp. p. 13 *et seq.*

identifies the country in question as one with which the case is closely connected. The regulation carefully avoids specifying the nature of the relevant connections, a specification which would have proved unduly restrictive and inconsistent with the rationale behind the rule, since it would have risked precluding the rule's application in cases not falling within any of the contemplated circumstances. Furthermore, it does not identify the relevant country as that with which the case, or the succession as a whole, is most closely connected. The rule could also therefore apply in cases in which there is a close connection with more than one third country, e.g. because the deceased was, at the time of death, habitually resident in a third country and possessed the nationality of another. In such a situation, the rule on *forum necessitatis* may come up for consideration only where the requirements for its application are satisfied in respect of all of the third countries with which the case has a close connection.[11] Similarly, it seems that the application of article 11 ESR would be ruled out whenever a court of a third country possessing a comparable provision on *forum necessitatis*, as could be the case, e.g., with Switzerland, would be available to exercise jurisdiction based on a more tenuous connection with the case.[12]

IV. Circumstances Determining the Impossibility or the Unreasonableness of Bringing or Conducting Proceedings before the Courts of Such a Third Country

A. *Where No Court in a Third Country with Which the Case Is Closely Connected Would Have Jurisdiction to Decide the Case*

7. Starting with the actual impossibility of filing an action in the third country court concerned, such an impossibility may be due either to circumstances of law or of fact. In terms of the former, the most obvious example would be that where the third country courts would not have jurisdiction under their own domestic rules.[13] Such a case of negative

[11] Cf. Lagarde, 'Les principes de base', p. 703; Bonomi, 'Article 11', p. 228 *et seq.*, noting that in the case where a third country court is available to exercise jurisdiction only in respect of assets located in that country, the Member State court seised under article 11 ESR may exercise jurisdiction only in respect of the remaining part of the succession. Cf. also Dutta, 'Art. 11 EuErbVO', para. 1.

[12] Cf. no. 2, footnote 4.

[13] Cf. Bonomi, 'Article 11', p. 227; Davì and Zanobetti, 'Il nuovo diritto internazionale privato delle successioni', p. 120; Davì and Zanobetti, *Il nuovo diritto internazionale privato europeo*, p. 209.

conflict of jurisdictions can be considered to be a natural consequence of the co-existence of different approaches to jurisdiction in succession matters. This means that in the absence of any coordination, it may well occur that in individual cases no court either in a Member State under the ESR or in a third country under its domestic rules would have jurisdiction.[14]

B. Where the Action, though Falling within the Jurisdiction of the Courts of Such a Country, Would Prove Inadmissible on a Point of Law

8. More controversial are those cases where an action before a third country court would be impossible on different legal grounds, such as through lack of admissibility.[15] A typical example would be the case of an action by a son born out of wedlock claiming his rights to the succession of his parent. Such an action would be inadmissible, in particular, in Islamic countries, due to the fact that under the legal systems of such countries no rights of succession are contemplated in favour of natural descendants.[16] Another example would be an action by a same-sex spouse claiming his or her rights to the estate of the other spouse. This could be held to be inadmissible in a third country which does not recognise same-sex marriages.[17] Nonetheless, issues of admissibility must be distinguished from issues concerning the substance of a case, as otherwise, the rule on *forum necessitatis* could leave itself open to abuse. This would occur if the rule on *forum necessitatis* is resorted to in order to allow the court seised under that rule to substitute its own views

[14] Cf. no. I.2.

[15] Cf., affirming that a decision declaring an action inadmissible, though leaving the right of access to a court unaffected, may entail prejudicing the right to obtain a judgment as to the substance of the claim under article 6 ECHR, ECtHR, *Prince Hans-Adam II of Liechtenstein* v. *Germany*, Judgment of 12 July 2001, no. 42527/98; *Kutic* v. *Croatia*, Judgment of 1st March 2002, no. 48778/99; cf. F. Marchadier, *Les objectives généraux du droit international privé à l'épreuve de la Convention européenne des droits de l'homme* (Bruxelles, 2007), p. 92 *et seq.*

[16] Cf. Davì and Zanobetti, 'Il nuovo diritto internazionale privato delle successioni', p. 120 *et seq.*; Davì and Zanobetti, *Il nuovo diritto internazionale privato europeo*, p. 209 *et seq.*

[17] Cf. Rossolillo, '*Forum necessitatis* e flessibilità dei criteri di giurisdizione', p. 409, pointing to some recent examples offered by domestic legislation concerning same-sex marriages or registered partnerships, which provide for the jurisdiction of the relevant domestic courts whenever an action based on that legislation would not be admissible before foreign courts that do not contemplate such institutions.

with regard to the law applicable to the substance of the case for those of the third country court having jurisdiction to rule on the dispute.[18]

9. It must be considered, in this respect, that *forum necessitatis* operates as an instrument intended to secure for the plaintiff a court where his or her action may be entertained, but not necessarily one that will uphold his or her rights as to the merits of the case.[19] This has also been clearly underlined by domestic case law founding jurisdiction upon the prevention of a denial of justice, particularly in terms of French case law concerning jurisdiction based on *déni de justice*. In a well-known decision, the *Cour d'appel* de Paris held that the French *forum* based on such a ground could not be relied upon when the action in question would be bound to fail in terms of its substance under the applicable foreign law, unless the plaintiff's claim appeared as deserving of enforcement as a matter of French public policy.[20] Subsequent developments within French case law actually appear to have broadened the exceptional assumption of jurisdiction by French courts in such circumstances, irrespective of the relevance of the claim under French public policy.[21]

C. Where Local Circumstances Would Materially Make It Impossible or Unreasonable for the Plaintiff to Bring or Conduct His Case before Such a Court

10. The rule under article 11 ESR may also come into consideration in those cases where an action before the third country courts having jurisdiction to rule upon the dispute in question would prove impossible or unreasonable due to other circumstances of law or of fact that would make it unfeasible for the plaintiff to seise such courts. In terms of the

[18] Cf. L. Corbion, *Le déni de justice en droit international privé* (Aix – Marseille, 2004), p. 204 *et seq.*, who seems to admit this possibility only in the extreme case where the law applied by a foreign court in order to dismiss the action would be contrary to French public policy. As noted by the author, nonetheless, the objective pursued in such a case by the courts offering to exercise their jurisdiction in order to allow the claim, appears to be more of a policy objective, rather than strictly speaking an objective of justice.

[19] Cf. Corbion, *Le déni de justice*, p. 202 *et seq.*

[20] Cour d'appel de Paris 10 November 1959, *Dawn Addams épouse Massimo* v. *Massimo*, *Rev crit dr int priv*, 1960, p. 218, noted by Ph. Francescakis, p. 221.

[21] Cour de cassation 3 February 1987, *Soc. La Boissière Beauchamp* v. *Soc. Messerschmitt-Balkow-Blohm Gmbh*, *Rev crit dr int priv* (1987), p. 617, noted by P.-Y. Gautier, concerning a case which the French Court of Cassation considered as subject to the 1968 Brussels Convention, which, according to the court, precluded the application of the French public policy considerations which had been relied upon in the earlier case law (cf. p. 619). Cf. Rossolillo, '*Forum necessitatis*', p. 408 *et seq.*

former, the third country court might impose, upon foreigners, an unreasonably high *cautio pro expenses* that the plaintiff could not afford to pay or might place other discriminatory restrictions upon their right of access to the courts, likely to either bar such access completely or make it unreasonably burdensome.[22] As for factual circumstances, these may, in turn, make the action impossible, whenever local circumstances of a natural or political nature would cause the judicial system of the third country not to operate at all, for example as a consequence of a serious natural catastrophe, a civil war or grave political turmoil in the country concerned.[23] Alternatively, factual circumstances could make it unreasonable for the parties to embark upon a trial in such a country. This might be the case where, due to corruption, bias or other mishandling of justice, the local courts may not be expected to guarantee a fair hearing of the dispute.[24]

11. Naturally, the rule grants a discretion to the Member State courts called upon to apply it, with regard, in particular, to the unreasonableness confronting the parties in attempting an action before a third country court. In order to prevent abuses of the rule and to avoid Member State courts ruling upon successions more closely connected to one or more third countries without a genuine need for invoking their jurisdiction, the requirements set out under the rule should be interpreted narrowly. The rule should, in fact, only be invoked where the plaintiff would face an actual risk of denial of justice before the courts of a third country with which the case is closely connected, and not simply because it would be more convenient for the parties to have their action heard by a Member State court rather than that of a third country.[25] In order to deprive the assessment that the Member State court is expected to make of any arbitrariness, the rule, as appears to be suggested in general terms by the Preamble to the ESR, should be interpreted in the light of the rules concerning fair trial as embodied by article 47 of the EU Charter of Fundamental Rights and article 6.1 ECHR. Particular regard should be

[22] Cf. Bonomi, 'Article 11', p. 227.

[23] Cf. recital 31 ESR, pointing to a civil war as an example of a situation likely to make access to the courts of a third country impossible.

[24] Cf. Bonomi, 'Article 11', p. 228.

[25] The need to adopt a narrow interpretation of the rule is also made clear in terms of its wording, whereby the rule states that it is to be resorted to 'on an exceptional basis', as also stressed in recital 31 ESR. Accordingly, under article 11 ESR there is no room for a broader assessment of the appropriateness of the exercise of jurisdiction such as is available under article 6(a)ESR [see art. 6 nos. 1–3].

had to the extensive case law of the European Court of Human Rights concerning the latter provision.[26]

12. The requirement for the entertainment of an action by a third country court to be deemed unreasonable would appear to be met in those cases where it can be expected that the judgment, to be delivered by a third country court, would not be amenable to recognition and enforcement elsewhere, including in the Member State of the court seised under *forum necessitatis*, whenever the recognition and enforcement of such a judgment in countries other than that where it is delivered are necessary for a complete disposal of the case.[27] In fact, it is worth remembering that the right of access to a court as interpreted by the European Court of Human Rights includes the right to a final judgment on the merits of the case, and, where necessary, to a judgment which is capable of enforcement, so as not to make the right in question purely theoretical or illusory.[28]

V. The Requirement of a Sufficient Connection of the Case with the Member State of the Court Seised

13. Self-restraint by Member State courts in resorting to the rule is also suggested by the further requirement stipulated in its second sentence, which states that the dispute must have a sufficient connection with the Member State of the court seised.[29] Excluding those connecting factors

[26] Cf. recital 81 ESR. A reference to the extensive body of case law of the ECtHR concerning the guarantees of a fair trial under article 6.1 ECHR also appears appropriate in respect of the corresponding guarantees under article 47 EU Charter of Fundamental Rights, based on the general rule under article 52.3 of the Charter. Cf., among others, ECJ, case C-400/10 PPU, *J. McB.* v. *L.E.* [2010] ECR I-8965, at 53; case C-279/09, *DEB* v. *Bundesrepublik Deutschland*, [2010] ECR I-13849, at 35, and Marongiu Buonaiuti, 'La tutela del diritto di accesso alla giustizia', p. 347.

[27] Cf., with regard to the forum based on the prevention of a denial of justice under French law, Corbion, *Le déni de justice*, p. 206 *et seq.*; with regard to article 11 ESR, Bonomi, 'Article 11', p. 228.

[28] Cf. ECtHR, *Hornsby* v. *Greece*, Judgment of 19 March 1997, no. 18357/91, and, among others, D. Harris *et al.* (eds), *Harris, O'Boyle & Warbrick: Law of the European Convention on Human Rights*, 2nd ed. (Oxford, 2009), p. 233 *et seq.*; M. Kloth, *Immunities and the Right of Access to Court under Article 6 of the European Convention on Human Rights* (Leiden; Boston, 2010), p. 88 *et seq.*; F. Marongiu Buonaiuti, 'Rinuncia all'immunità dello Stato estero dalle misure coercitive e tutela del diritto di accesso alla giustizia in alcune pronunce recenti della *Cour de cassation* francese', *Diritti umani e diritto internazionale* (2013), p. 615 *et seq.*, esp. p. 636 *et seq.*

[29] Cf., with regard to the corresponding requirement for the exercise of jurisdiction by French courts based on the prevention of a denial of justice, Corbion, *Le déni de justice*, p. 199 *et seq.*

upon which the jurisdiction of a Member State court could be founded under the other provisions of the regulation, any other connection not being purely fictitious, including the habitual residence of any of the heirs or of the other persons having an interest in the succession, and, in particular, of the parties to the dispute, would appear likely to qualify as such.[30]

14. This requirement, in turn, appears to be aimed at ensuring that Member States' courts are not called upon to exercise a jurisdiction which would be exorbitant and which could probably lead to the handing down of a judgment the recognition or enforcement of which could be denied in a third country with which the succession is closely connected.[31] The rule also tends to reduce *forum shopping*, by ensuring that the plaintiff does not arbitrarily choose the Member State whose courts he or she decides to seise as a *forum necessitatis*. Additionally, even though the case may have a sufficient connection with more than one Member State, the rule reduces the risk of the courts of more Member States being called upon to exercise jurisdiction under the rule. Such cases would, nevertheless, be dealt with under the rules concerning *lis pendens* and related actions contained in the regulation [see art. 17, no. 8; art. 18, no. 3].

[30] Cf., among others, Bonomi, 'Article 11', p. 228; Davì and Zanobetti, 'Il nuovo diritto internazionale privato delle successioni', p. 120; Davì and Zanobetti, *Il nuovo diritto internazionale privato europeo*, p. 209; Dutta, 'Art. 11 EuErbVO', para. 2.

[31] Cf. Davì and Zanobetti, 'Il nuovo diritto internazionale privato delle successioni', p. 121; Davì and Zanobetti, *Il nuovo diritto internazionale privato europeo*, p. 210, pointing to the possibility for the court seised under article 11 ESR to reduce this risk by excluding from its jurisdiction assets located within the third country concerned, as contemplated under article 12 ESR [see art. 12 nos. 1 and 15]. This, as suggested by Bonomi, 'Article 11', p. 229, would also prevent positive conflicts of jurisdiction with the courts of that country.

Article 12

Limitation of Proceedings

FABRIZIO MARONGIU BUONAIUTI

1. Where the estate of the deceased comprises assets located in a third State, the court seised to rule on the succession may, at the request of one of the parties, decide not to rule on one or more of such assets if it may be expected that its decision in respect of those assets will not be recognised and, where applicable, declared enforceable in that third State.
2. Paragraph 1 shall not affect the right of the parties to limit the scope of the proceedings under the law of the Member State of the court seised.

Summary

I. THE RATIONALE FOR THE RULE UNDER ARTICLE 12.1 AND ITS PRECEDENTS *page* 210

II. LOCATION OF ASSETS BELONGING TO THE ESTATE OF THE DECEASED IN A THIRD COUNTRY 212

III. NECESSITY OF HAVING THE JUDGMENT DELIVERED BY A MEMBER STATE COURT RECOGNISED OR ENFORCED IN A THIRD COUNTRY 213

IV. CIRCUMSTANCES IN WHICH THE COURT SEISED MUST SUBSTANTIATE ITS VIEWS AS TO THE LIKELIHOOD OF A DENIAL OF RECOGNITION OR ENFORCEMENT IN THE THIRD COUNTRY CONCERNED AND FURTHER GROUNDS FOR THE EXERCISE OF DISCRETION 214

A. Exclusive Jurisdiction of the Courts of the Third Country Where the Assets Concerned Are Located 214

B. Other Grounds for Denial of Recognition or Enforcement Likely to Form the Subject of a Predictive Assessment 216

C. Relevance of Considerations Relating to the Availability of the Courts of the Third Country Concerned to Decide Effectively in Respect of Those Assets 218

V. THE RIGHT OF THE PARTIES THEMSELVES TO LIMIT THE SCOPE OF THE PROCEEDINGS UNDER THE LEX FORI, PURSUANT TO ARTICLE 12.2 219

I. The Rationale for the Rule under Article 12.1 and Its Precedents

1. Article 12.1 ESR is the second provision within the section of the regulation concerning jurisdiction which specifically addresses the problems inherent in the coordination of the system of jurisdiction set out in the ESR in terms of its strictly *inter partes* approach to the role of third country courts in the adjudication of disputes concerning successions. Unlike article 11 ESR, which provides, in exceptional circumstances, for an extension of the scope of the jurisdiction normally allocated to Member States' courts due to the unavailability or inability of third country courts to exercise their jurisdiction [see art. 11 nos. 7–12], article 12.1 ESR, conversely, provides for the possibility of a limitation of the scope of the action pending before a Member State court in succession matters. This is insofar as the action involves assets located in a third country that would not recognise the judgment delivered by the Member State court seised with regard to those assets.[1]

2. There are precedents for this rule, which was not contemplated in the Commission's proposal and which was introduced into the text of the ESR at a later stage of its legislative process. Such precedents can be found within provisions, based upon a similar rationale, of domestic legislation concerning jurisdiction in succession matters[2] and in an almost corresponding rule contained within the proposal for a convention on jurisdiction and enforcement of judgments in family and succession matters drawn up by the European Group of Private International Law.[3] Like

[1] Cf., among others, A. Bonomi, 'Article 12', in A. Bonomi and P. Wautelet, *Le droit européen des successions. Commentaire du règlement n° 650/2012 du 4 juillet 2012* (Bruxelles, 2013), p. 231 *et seq.*; J. Carrascosa González, *El Reglamento Sucesorio Europeo 650/2012 de 4 de julio 2012. Análisis crítico* (Granada, 2014), p. 105 *et seq.*, A. Davì and A. Zanobetti, 'Il nuovo diritto internazionale privato delle successioni nell'Unione europea', *CdT* 5/2 (2013), p. 5 *et seq.*, esp. p. 121; A. Davì and A. Zanobetti, *Il nuovo diritto internazionale privato europeo delle successioni* (Torino, 2014), p. 211 *et seq.*; A. Dutta, 'Art. 12 EuErbVO', in *Münchener Kommentar zum BGB*, 6th ed. (München, 2015), para. 1 *et seq.*; H. Gaudemet-Tallon, 'Les règles de compétence judiciaire dans le règlement européen sur les successions', in G. Khairallah and M. Revillard (eds), *Droit européen des successions internationales. Le règlement du 4 juillet 2012* (Paris, 2013), p. 127 *et seq.*, esp. p. 136.

[2] Cf. art. 86.2 Swiss Federal Act on Private International Law of 18 December 1987 (LDIP), and A. Bucher, 'Art. 86', in A. Bucher (ed), *Loi sur le droit international privé. Convention de Lugano. Commentaire Romand* (Bâle, 2011), p. 791 *et seq.*

[3] Groupe européen de droit international privé. Réunion de Heidelberg (30 septembre-2 octobre 1993), 'Proposal for a convention concerning jurisdiction and the enforcement of judgments in family and succession matters', in *Rev crit dr int priv* (1993), p. 841 *et seq.*, also available at www.gedip-egpil.eu (last accessed 30 June 2016), article 5.4.

those provisions, but expressing the point more explicitly, the rule as contained within article 12.1 ESR reflects the need to ensure that the jurisdiction of Member States' courts is not exercised in vain, ending up with a judgment which the third country in which the assets concerned are located might refuse to recognise or enforce.[4] This could be either because, as specified in the proposal by the European Group of Private International Law, the domestic provisions of the third country in question provide for the exclusive jurisdiction of its own courts in respect of such assets, or for any other ground.[5] A similar concern, with regard to the law applicable to succession, appears to underpin the provision under article 30 ESR, whereby special rules of the *lex rei sitae*, providing for restrictions with regard to succession in respect of certain categories of assets, shall apply to the succession, provided such rules are considered under the same law as applicable irrespective of the law governing the succession [see art. 30].

3. The solution adopted under the rule is not entirely unproblematic. In fact, supposing the estate of the deceased is not composed uniquely of assets located in a third country which can be expected to deny recognition or enforcement of a judgment delivered by a Member State court in respect of such assets, the application of the rule inevitably implies a fragmentation of the succession. This is both with regard to jurisdiction, and, by implication, with regard to applicable law, since it can be expected that the third country courts which would exercise jurisdiction in respect of the assets located in such a country will apply the law designated under the country's own rules on conflict of laws. This outcome goes against the objective of unity with regard to the handling of successions, which the ESR pursues by adopting a unitary approach, avoiding any distinction among the assets of a succession based upon their nature and location, as would be inevitable under a dualist approach.[6] Taking into account this substantial drawback inherent in

[4] Cf. Bonomi, 'Article 12', p. 232; by contrast, Dutta, 'Art. 12 EuErbVO', para. 1, arguing that if the main justification for the rule was to be identified as the prevention of pointless judgments or with considerations of comity towards third countries, then the rule ought to have been conceived as binding and applicable *ex officio*.

[5] Cf. Bonomi, 'Article 12', p. 232, noting that in terms of its broad formulation, the rule under article 12 ESR might also apply in cases other than those in which the courts of the third country where the relevant assets are located claim exclusive jurisdiction in respect of such assets.

[6] Cf. Bonomi, 'Article 12', p. 235 *et seq*; Davì and Zanobetti, 'Il nuovo diritto internazionale privato delle successioni', p. 121; Davì and Zanobetti, *Il nuovo diritto internazionale privato europeo*, p. 211.

the rule, it appears reasonable that its application is subject, on the one hand, to a request by one of the parties, and, on the other hand, to a discretionary assessment by the judge seised of the action.[7]

II. Location of Assets Belonging to the Estate of the Deceased in a Third Country

4. The rule presupposes that the action filed before a Member State court having jurisdiction under the ESR also concerns assets belonging to the estate of the deceased which are located within a third country, irrespective of the value of such assets and of their comparable importance in relation to the other assets located within one or more Member States. Unlike the solution which had been put forward in the aforementioned proposal by the European Group of Private International Law, which concerned just immoveable property, the rule under article 12.1 ESR refers to any assets belonging to the succession of the deceased, thus raising at the outset an issue of location of the relevant assets not unlike the corresponding issue which arises under the subsidiary jurisdiction rules contemplated by article 10 ESR [see art. 10 nos. 8–10].

5. In terms of the latter provision, it appears clear that the location of assets belonging to the estate of the deceased within a Member State has to be established autonomously, so as to prevent inconsistencies and conflicts among the courts of different Member States claiming jurisdiction based upon different assumptions concerning the location of the same assets [see art. 10 no. 9]. It does seem, however, that a different solution has to be adopted with regard to the location of assets in a third country for the purposes of the rule under article 12.1 ESR. In fact, the purpose of the latter rule is not to provide a ground of jurisdiction for the courts of a Member State, but to prevent the denial of recognition or enforcement in a third country of a judgment handed down by a Member State court, essentially due to the fact that the judgment affects assets located in such a country. It would, therefore, appear reasonable that, for the specific purposes of the rule under examination, the location of the relevant assets

[7] Cf., underlining that the discretion by the Member State court seised should be exercised prudently, Bonomi, 'Article 12', p. 234; Dutta, 'Art. 12 EuErbVO', para. 8; A. Dutta, 'Das neue internationale Erbrecht der Europäischen Union – Eine erste Lektüre der Erbrechtsverordnung', *FamRZ* (2013), p. 4 *et seq.*, esp. p. 7.

within a third country should be established based upon the law of such a country.[8]

6. A third country court would not, in fact, be bound by a different finding of a Member State court concerning the location of assets that it would consider as being located within its *forum* and would accordingly be free to deny recognition or enforcement of a judgment delivered by a Member State court irrespective of the fact that such a court considered the relevant assets as being located elsewhere. In this respect, even though it must be considered that the third country where a denial of recognition or enforcement is to be feared under the rule is that which the Member State court seised considers as the third country where the relevant assets are located, in deciding upon whether such a third country is likely to deny recognition or enforcement of its judgment with regard to those assets, the Member State court seised should still, in the first instance, ensure that the courts of such a country would consider the relevant assets as being located within their *forum*. Otherwise, there would appear to be no reasonable ground upon which the courts of the third country concerned would refuse to recognise or enforce a Member State court judgment specifically concerning some assets, if they would consider them as being located in another country.[9]

III. Necessity of Having the Judgment Delivered by a Member State Court Recognised or Enforced in a Third Country

7. For the likelihood of a denial of recognition or enforcement of the judgment to be delivered by a Member State court in the third country court where the relevant assets are located to be material and, accordingly, to justify a decision by the Member State court seised not to rule in respect of such assets, it does not suffice that the judgment to be delivered by the Member State court generally concerns those assets, for example by taking them into account as part of the estate of the deceased for the purposes of determining the amount of a reserved share of the succession. Rather, it appears necessary that the judgment, to be delivered by the Member State court seised, contains concrete dispositions in respect

[8] As suggested by Bonomi, 'Article 12', p. 233; cf. to the contrary, arguing that the location of the relevant assets should be made autonomously, just as for the purposes of the rule under article 10.2 ESR, Dutta, 'Art. 12 EuErbVO', para. 4.

[9] Cf., considering the *lex rei sitae* as relevant for the classification of an asset as immoveable for the purposes of the rule contained under article 86.2 of the Swiss federal act on private international law (LDIP), Bucher, 'Art. 86', p. 794.

of the assets in question, for example by assigning them to one or more heirs or assignees. This is so that recognition and, in case, enforcement of the judgment in the third country where the relevant assets are located are necessary in order for the dispositions contained within the judgment with regard to such assets to produce their effects.[10]

8. A narrow interpretation of the requirements for the application of the rule appears to be warranted in consideration of the already underlined disadvantages inherent in its application, to be found essentially in a fragmentation of the litigation concerning the succession, most of all between a Member State and a third country in respect of which the mechanisms of coordination among concurrent jurisdictions established by the ESR are not available [see art. 17 nos. 19–20; art. 18 no. 13]. Accordingly, it appears to follow that in the case where a Member State court decides not to rule upon assets located in a third country under article 12.1 ESR, it still reserves the power to take those assets into account for the purposes of the other rulings which it is expected to make concerning the remaining part of the succession. This is particularly so with regard to the determination of reserved shares in the succession, so that the overall disposal of the succession is not affected by a decision taken under the rule.[11]

IV. Circumstances in Which the Court Seised Must Substantiate Its Views as to the Likelihood of a Denial of Recognition or Enforcement in the Third Country Concerned and Further Grounds for the Exercise of Discretion

A. *Exclusive Jurisdiction of the Courts of the Third Country Where the Assets Concerned Are Located*

9. The rule under article 12.1 ESR, with the clear intent of granting the Member State court seised a sufficiently broad discretion, does not specify the circumstances in which such a court is to decide that the judgment to be delivered is not likely to be recognised or enforced in

[10] Cf. Dutta, 'Art. 12 EuErbVO', para. 7.

[11] Cf. Bonomi, 'Article 12', p. 236; Dutta, 'Art. 12 EuErbVO', para. 7; Davì and Zanobetti, 'Il nuovo diritto internazionale privato delle successioni', p. 121; Davì and Zanobetti, *Il nuovo diritto internazionale privato europeo*, p. 211, suggesting that considerations related to the interests of preserving the unity of the succession in the discretionary evaluation to be performed by the Member State court seised might outweigh those related to the risk of a denial of recognition or enforcement of the judgment in the third country concerned.

a third country where assets belonging to the estate of the deceased are located. Nonetheless, as clearly pointed out in the aforementioned proposal by the European Group of Private International Law and as set out even more straightforwardly in a provision contained within the Swiss federal private international law act of 1987 for the same purposes, the primary ground upon which such an assumption is likely to be founded is that the third country concerned might provide in its domestic rules for the exclusive jurisdiction of its own courts in respect of succession disputes concerning assets located within its territory.[12] Such an exclusive jurisdiction of the local courts would inherently bar the recognition or enforcement of a judgment delivered abroad concerning such assets, due to the *Spiegelbildprinzip* which generally underpins domestic rules on recognition and enforcement of foreign judgments, in terms of the requirement of a correct assertion of jurisdiction by the foreign court having delivered the judgment to be recognised.[13]

10. The latter, which will constitute by far the most likely ground upon which a Member State court will decide to have recourse to the rule under article 12.1 ESR, has the undeniable advantage, from the perspective of legal certainty, of consisting of a ground for denial of recognition or enforcement of the prospective judgment which is comparably easy to ascertain. This is because jurisdiction rules in any given country are normally either contained within legislative provisions or, with regard to (for the most part) common law countries, clearly established through a consolidated body of case law.

[12] Cf. Groupe européen de droit international privé, 'Proposal for a convention concerning jurisdiction and the enforcement of judgments in family and succession matters', art. 5.4; article 86.2 LDIP; among the countries which contemplate the exclusive jurisdiction of their own courts, notably in respect of immoveables located within their territory, are, apart from some Member States (most notably France, whose rules are superseded by the ESR), also third countries inspired by the common law tradition: cf. A. Bonomi, 'Successions internationales: conflits de lois et de juridictions', *Hague Recueil*, vol. 350 (2010), p. 9 *et seq.*, esp. p. 370 *et seq.*; A. Heini, 'Art. 86', in D. Girsberger et al. (eds), *Zürcher Kommentar zum IPRG*, 2nd ed. (Zürich, 2004), p. 1022 *et seq.*, esp. p. 1025; A. E. von Overbeck, 'Les règimes matrimoniaux et les successions dans le nouveau droit international privé suisse', in F. Dessemontet (ed), *Le nouveau droit international privé suisse* (Lausanne, 1989), p. 59 *et seq.*, esp. p. 71 *et seq.*

[13] Cf., with regard to the s. c. *Spiegelbildprinzip* in respect of the correct assertion of jurisdiction by a foreign court for the purposes of the recognition of foreign judgments, R. Geimer, *Internationales Zivilprozessrecht*, 5th ed. (Köln, 2005), p. 902 *et seq.*

B. *Other Grounds for Denial of Recognition or Enforcement Likely to Form the Subject of a Predictive Assessment*

11. As already noted, article 12.1 ESR does not limit the grounds, upon which the Member State court seised is to assume that its judgment will be denied recognition or enforcement in such a country, to the situation of the courts of the third country where the relevant assets are located claiming exclusive jurisdiction. Accordingly, in principle, any other ground of denial of recognition or enforcement of foreign judgments, as contemplated under the law of the third country concerned, is likely to be taken into account, insofar as its existence can be foreseen with sufficient certainty at the point when the action is still pending before the Member State court.[14]

12. The inherent difficulty of foreseeing with sufficient certainty the existence of grounds of denial of recognition or enforcement of a judgment, before the judgment itself is materially handed down, is not new to article 12.1 ESR.[15] It is widely accepted, with regard to the predictive assessment to be performed in respect of the recognition of a foreign judgment in the *forum* in the reversed scenario of *lis alibi pendens*, that such an evaluation is by definition incomplete, since it may concern only those aspects of the judgment to be recognised or enforced which are likely to be assessed in advance with a sufficient degree of certainty. Among the most commonly contemplated grounds of denial of recognition or enforcement of foreign judgments, apart from the aforementioned ground relating to the criteria on which the jurisdiction of the court is based, those which are likely to form the subject of an assessment at the stage when the action is still pending concern the regularity of the introduction of the proceedings. This is particularly with regard to service of process on defaulting defendants. Furthermore, the ability of proceedings before the third country court to satisfy due process standards, especially regarding

[14] Cf. Bonomi, 'Article 12', p. 234; Dutta, 'Art. 12 EuErbVO', para. 6.

[15] In fact, the mechanism of a s. c. *Anerkennungsprognose* was first contemplated by German case law admitting the application of domestic rules on *lis alibi pendens* as contained in the ZPO in respect of proceedings pending abroad, a solution adopted in turn under French case law and later by domestic legislation, including the Swiss (article 9, federal private international law act (LDIP)), the Italian (article 7, law of 31 May 1995, no. 218) and the Belgian (article 14, code of private international law) ones, culminating in the rules introduced in the Brussels I-*bis* regulation concerning *lis alibi pendens* and related actions pending before third country courts (articles 33–34, Regulation (EU) no. 1215/2012 of the European Parliament and of the Council of 12 December 2012 on jurisdiction and the recognition and enforcement of judgments in civil and commercial matters (recast), OJ no. L351, 20 December 2012, p. 1).

the right to contradict throughout the proceedings, will come into account within the scope of such an assessment. In fact, these grounds should not, in principle, be a matter of particular concern in respect of Member State courts, which are bound to respect the due process standards contemplated under article 6.1 ECHR and article 47 EU Charter of Fundamental Rights.[16]

13. Rather, depending upon the peculiarities of the provisions concerning the recognition and enforcement of foreign judgments in the third country concerned, more concrete obstacles could be posed by a rule subjecting the recognition of a foreign judgment to the application of the same law as would have applied under the third country's conflict of laws rules. This is particularly the case where such rules are underpinned by different principles than those adopted under the ESR.[17]

14. Conversely, other more common grounds of denial of recognition or enforcement of foreign judgments, such as the irreconcilability of the judgment with domestic public policy, or its conflict with a domestic judgment or with an earlier foreign judgment recognised or enforceable in the forum, are normally considered likely to appear only once the judgment has been delivered. Nonetheless, there may be instances where the fact that proceedings will result in a judgment which will be incompatible with the public policy of the third country concerned, will already appear with sufficient clarity at the stage when the action is still pending. This might be, for example, because the court is due to decide the case applying a law which would consider as a heir somebody bound to the deceased by a sort of family relationship, the recognition of which would be incompatible with the public policy of the country in question.[18]

[16] Cf. recital 81 ESR, which underlines, rather tautologically, that the courts and other authorities in the Member States shall apply the rules contained in the regulation consistently with fundamental rights and with the principles enshrined in the EU Charter of Fundamental Rights.

[17] Such a requirement, which was traditionally present in some domestic systems of private international law, has been progressively abolished, most notably, in Germany, since the reform introduced by the *Gesetz zur Neuregelung des internationalen Privatrechts* (*IPR-Gesetz*) of 25 July 1986, and in France, after Cour de cassation, 1re Ch. civ. 20 February 2007, *Cornelissen c. Soc. Avianca Inc.*, *Dalloz* (2007) p. 1115 *et seq.*, noted L. d'Avout; *Rev crit dr int priv* (2007), p. 420 *et seq.*, noted B. Ancel and H. Muir-Watt; it may, nonetheless, still be present in some third country statutes concerning recognition of foreign judgments following that model.

[18] For example, a same-sex spouse or partner, who under the law applied by the Member State court seised pursuant to the ESR would be entitled to claim rights as to the succession, a result which might be incompatible with the public policy of a third country not recognising same-sex marriages or partnerships. Such an obstacle is actually also

Similarly, a firm risk of a denial of recognition may become clear at a stage when the action is still pending before the Member State court seised, whenever any of the parties has notice of the fact that a judgment on the case has already been handed down, or that proceedings are pending before the courts of the third country in question, on the same case, and are likely to result in a judgment which would bar the recognition of the judgment which will be delivered by the Member State court.[19]

C. *Relevance of Considerations Relating to the Availability of the Courts of the Third Country Concerned to Decide Effectively in Respect of Those Assets*

15. A prerequisite, which might appear inherent in the rationale for the rule under article 12.1 ESR, is that the courts of the third country, where assets belonging to the estate of the deceased are located and where the judgment to be delivered by the Member State court seised would risk facing a denial of recognition or enforcement, are available to exercise their jurisdiction in respect of those assets and are capable of securing a fair trial of the action. This would mean that the decision by the Member State court seised not to rule in respect of those assets does not entail a denial of justice with regard to the relevant claims. Actually, it must be considered that *forum necessitatis* considerations are rather alien to the logic of the rule, since, on the one hand, unlike article 11 ESR, the rule addresses situations in which a Member State court has jurisdiction under the ESR. On the other hand, the decision by a Member State court to also exercise its jurisdiction in respect of assets located within a third country, notwithstanding the appearance that its judgment will not be recognised or enforced in such a country, would not offer an effective remedy to the unavailability or inability of the courts of the third country concerned to secure a fair trial of the action [see art. 11 no. 14].

16. In fact, the rule presupposes that the judgment to be delivered by the Member State court seised would not be recognised or enforced in the

present as among Member States, due account being taken of the fact that the ESR leaves unaffected issues concerning personal status or family relationships which may give rise to succession rights [see art. 1 no. 13 *et seq.*; 21; 22].

19 Cf. Bonomi, 'Article 12', p. 234; Dutta, 'Art. 12 EuErbVO', para. 6, pointing to further circumstances in which the risk of denial of recognition or enforcement of the judgment in the third country concerned may appear clearly in advance, such as where that country does not recognise foreign judgments as a matter of principle or would not recognise judgments from the Member State of the court seised due to lack of reciprocity.

third country where assets belonging to the estate of the deceased are located. This, in turn, implies that even in the case where there should be a concern that the plaintiff would risk facing a denial of justice or undergoing a trial not fully in compliance with due process standards before the courts of the third country concerned, the decision by the Member State court seised to entertain the action also in respect of assets located in such a third country would be of no avail, specifically in terms of measures to be taken in respect of those assets.[20] Actually, as noted earlier, the application of the rule appears to be justified at all, only insofar as the circumstances of the case make the recognition or enforcement of the judgment in the third country concerned necessary for an effective disposal of the case as regards assets located within such a country.[21]

V. The Right of the Parties Themselves to Limit the Scope of the Proceedings under the *lex fori*, Pursuant to Article 12.2

17. Article 12.2 ESR provides that the power granted under paragraph 1 of the rule to the Member State court seised to decide, albeit upon request by one of the parties, to limit the scope of the proceedings by abstaining from ruling in respect of assets located in a third country in the circumstances discussed above, does not prejudice the right of the parties themselves to limit the scope of the proceedings, insofar as this is consistent with the law of the Member State of the court seised. Doubts might actually arise with regard to the actual need for such a rule, considering that the possibility for the parties to limit the scope of the proceedings is, in principle, a matter of domestic law, which, in a regulation addressing, in terms of jurisdiction, purely issues of international civil procedure, should normally be left to the domestic rules of either substantive or

[20] This is naturally without prejudice to the possibility for the Member State court seised to decide, of its own motion, to rule upon the succession as a whole, notwithstanding the risk of a denial of recognition or enforcement of the judgment in the third country concerned. Such a decision might be taken by the Member State court seised in order to preserve the unity of the succession, as suggested by Davì and Zanobetti, 'Il nuovo diritto internazionale privato delle successioni', p. 121; Davì and Zanobetti, *Il nuovo diritto internazionale privato europeo*, p. 211. In any event, a decision taken under the rule would not affect the possibility for the Member State court seised to take into account assets located within a third country for the purposes of the judgment it is expected to hand down concerning the remaining part of the succession, as suggested by Bonomi, 'Article 12', p. 236; Dutta, 'Art. 12 EuErbVO', para. 7.

[21] Cf. nos. 7–8.

procedural law to regulate. Clearly, this is subject to an inherent limitation due to the need for the application of such rules not to hinder the *effet utile* of the regulation.[22]

18. In order to give the rule under article 12.2 a purposive interpretation, its existence may be considered justified on the basis that it clarifies that domestic rules allowing the parties to limit the scope of the proceedings are not, as such, inconsistent with the special mechanism devised under paragraph 1 of the rule, which, as suggested by one author, can actually be resorted to only when the parties could not or, in any event, have not themselves limited the scope of the proceedings under the *lex fori*.[23] In fact, it must be considered that the prerequisites and the effects of a limitation of the scope of the proceedings under either rule do not coincide. On the one hand, article 12.2 presupposes the agreement of all of the parties, whereas the rule under paragraph 1 allows just one of them to apply for a limitation by the court seised, which, even when the relevant requirements are met, preserves a discretion as to whether to provide for such a limitation.[24] On the other hand, whereas a limitation of the proceedings by agreement of the parties under paragraph 2 may take place in whichever circumstances and concerning whichever issue forming the subject of the proceedings as allowed under the *lex fori*, a limitation by the court seised pursuant to paragraph 1 may take place only in respect of assets located in a third country and in the circumstances contemplated under the rule.

[22] Cf., concerning the need for domestic rules on admissibility of actions not to challenge the *effet utile* of the system of allocation of jurisdiction as among Member States' courts as then embodied in the 1968 Brussels Convention, ECJ, case C-365/88, *Kongress Agentur Hagen GmbH* v. *Zeehaghe BV* [1990] ECR I-1845, para 17 *et seq.*

[23] Cf. Bonomi, 'Article 12', p. 237. [24] Cf. no 3.

Article 13

Acceptance or Waiver of the Succession, of a Legacy or of a Reserved Share

ALESSANDRA ZANOBETTI

In addition to the court having jurisdiction to rule on the succession pursuant to this Regulation, the courts of the Member State of the habitual residence of any person who, under the law applicable to the succession, may make, before a court, a declaration concerning the acceptance or waiver of the succession, of a legacy or of a reserved share, or a declaration designed to limit the liability of the person concerned in respect of the liabilities under the succession, shall have jurisdiction to receive such declarations where, under the law of that Member State, such declarations may be made before a court.

Summary

I. SCOPE OF THE PROVISION AND RATIONALE *page* 222
II. A COMPARATIVE SURVEY OF THE PROCEDURES FOLLOWED FOR THE ACCEPTANCE, WAIVER OR LIMITATION OF LIABILITY IN THE VARIOUS LEGAL SYSTEMS 223
III. THE 'PERSONS' COVERED BY THE PROVISION, THE ASCERTAINMENT OF THEIR LEGAL CAPACITY AND THE IDENTIFICATION OF THEIR HABITUAL RESIDENCE 226
IV. SCOPE OF APPLICATION OF THE PROVISION: THE NEED TO DISTINGUISH BETWEEN 'DECLARATIONS' AND 'LEGAL PROCEEDINGS' 228
V. NON-APPLICABILITY OF ARTICLE 13 TO DECLARATIONS MADE PRIOR TO THE OPENING OF THE SUCCESSION 230
VI. THE CONCEPT OF A 'COURT' 231
VII. FORMAL VALIDITY OF DECLARATIONS 231
VIII. COMMUNICATION OF DECLARATIONS TO THE AUTHORITY 'WHICH IS OR WILL BE DEALING WITH THE SUCCESSION' 232

I. Scope of the Provision and Rationale

1. Article 13 introduces a special ground of jurisdiction in addition to those set out in article 4 *et seq.* ESR. It enables a person intending to make a declaration 'concerning the acceptance or waiver of the succession, of a legacy or of a reserved share' or a declaration designed to limit their liability 'in respect of the liabilities under the succession' to have recourse to the authorities of the State in which they have their habitual residence.

2. As recital 32 makes clear, the purpose of article 13 is 'to simplify the lives of heirs and legatees', and it does so by creating an easier and probably more economical route for a person required to make the type of declaration catered for by permitting them to address the competent authorities in their country of habitual residence rather than those with jurisdiction over the succession as a whole.[1] This mechanism undoubtedly is a source of simplification, but, as we will see, this is counterbalanced in certain situations by difficulties in application in connection, in particular, to the demarcation of the specific subject matter, to establishing the law that applies to the actual substance of the act and to coordination with any procedure regarding administration and devolution of the estate. In more complex cases, the result is that the advisable step may well be to discard this additional forum in order to avoid errors being made that could potentially result in rights being forfeited with serious consequences as a result.

3. The additional ground of jurisdiction introduced by article 13 is compulsory for the courts in all Member States; the courts in a Member State that participates to the ESR are, therefore, duty bound to receive declarations made by persons resident within their territory, regardless of whether the rules in force on a national level make any provision for this type of jurisdiction.

The final part of the provision nevertheless provides clarification to the effect that the courts must receive the declarations in question

[1] Commenting on the proposal submitted by the European Commission in 2009 (Proposal for a Regulation of the European Parliament and of the Council on jurisdiction, applicable law, recognition and enforcement of decisions and authentic instruments in matters of succession and the creation of a European Certificate of Succession, COM(2009)154 final), the Max-Planck-Institut für ausländisches und internationales Privatrecht of Hamburg drew particular attention to the significant saving in costs, including legal costs, that the introduction of this additional ground of jurisdiction would bring about: see 'Comments on the European Commission's Proposal for a Regulation of the European Parliament and of the Council on jurisdiction, applicable law, recognition and enforcement of decisions and authentic instruments in matters of succession and the creation of a European Certificate of Succession', *RabelsZ* (2010), p. 593.

'where, under the law of that Member State, such declarations may be made before a court'. Article 13 therefore limits its effects to jurisdiction, whereas the power of the courts to receive the declarations in question has to be established by local law. Where this is not the case, the parties involved are required to address the authorities that are competent to deal with the succession pursuant to article 4 *et seq.* ESR. The substantive validity of the declarations made, and, in particular, the possibility to take the step required (acceptance, waiver or limitation of liability) by making a simple declaration rather than via legal proceedings, are governed by the succession law, as we will see in more detail (see no. 10). Where the formal validity of declarations is concerned, this is governed by the ESR in article 28 (see no. 18) [see art. 28].

II. A Comparative Survey of the Procedures Followed for the Acceptance, Waiver or Limitation of Liability in the Various Legal Systems

4. As expressly established by article 23.2, points (e) and (g) respectively, 'conditions and effects of the acceptance or waiver of the succession or of a legacy' and 'liability for the debts under the succession' are governed by the law that applies to the succession [see art. 23 nos. 10 and 12].

Significant differences can be identified in the legislation in force in the various States in terms of a requirement that the succession or a legacy be accepted and the relevant procedures and effects; this is also the case for the rules governing a waiver as well as the manner in which the liability of heirs and legatees can be limited in relation to the liabilities under the succession, and the relevant effects.[2]

In certain States, heirs and legatees acquire their succession rights by virtue of an order issued by the relevant authority, while in other States no specific ruling is required. The former group principally comprises systems in which the estate does not pass directly to the heirs; this is the position in common law countries, where the phase that starts with the

[2] As far as the Member States are concerned, these differences have already been highlighted in the 'Étude de droit comparé sur les règles de conflits de juridictions et de conflits de lois relatives aux testaments et successions dans les États membres de l'Union Européenne', published in 2002 by the Deutsches Notarinstitut at the request of the European Commission, in Deutsches Notarinstitut (ed), *Conflict of Law of Succession in the European Union. Perspectives for a Harmonisation* (Würzburg, 2004), also available at www.successions.org, p. 115 *et seq.*

opening of the succession and ends with devolution of the estate upon the beneficiaries is administered by a 'personal representative' or an 'executor'. No 'acceptance' on the part of the heirs and legatees is required, although they are able to waive their share of the estate or their legacy by means of a 'disclaimer of interest' or a 'renunciation'; these declarations generally have to be made in writing before a competent authority. The fact that the personal representative steps in with a duty to pay the debts of the estate in full means that any limitation of liability by the heirs or legatees is clearly redundant. In terms of its effects, the system in place in common law countries is not entirely dissimilar to that found in the Scandinavian States. In Sweden, for example, the estate is treated as a legal entity administered by an administrator or by the heirs themselves until devolution of the shares upon the beneficiaries, without any specific acceptance being called for (article 18 *et seq. Ärvdabalk*); as the estate itself is liable for any debts, including tax, no specific limitation of liability is required in these countries either. The legislation in force in an additional group of countries instead provides that title to the deceased's assets passes directly to the heirs and legatees. In certain cases, this takes place at the point in time at which the succession opens: this is the position, for example, in France (article 724 of the civil code), Belgium (article 724 of the civil code) and Luxembourg (article 724 of the civil code).[3] Other systems, such as those in place in Bulgaria, Greece, Italy, Lithuania, Portugal and Spain, instead require acceptance; this can, however, be tacit and, in particular, can be assumed on the basis of certain steps taken by the heirs. Where these particular systems are concerned, it is, therefore, extremely important for anyone intending not to accept an inheritance to complete the necessary formalities within the timescales imposed, which vary enormously from country to country (ranging from ten years under Italian law[4] to just four months under Greek law[5]). A perfect example of the difference between the two subtypes is provided by a comparison between French law and the law in force in Italy: in the former, someone who takes no action whatsoever for

[3] These laws stipulate, however, that in order to become an heir, the State 'doit se faire envoyer en possession'.

[4] Article 480 of the Italian civil code; the deadline can be shortened by court order issued on the application of an interested party.

[5] Article 1847 of the Greek civil code; the deadline, which runs from when the succession opens or, where there is a will, from the date of publication of the will, is extended to one year where the deceased was living abroad at the time of death, or where the beneficiaries were living abroad.

more than ten years, failing to exercise the *droit d'option* granted to him, is treated as having waived his inheritance, while expiry of the ten-year deadline in Italy means that the right to accept is lost. In the former case, the person waives their right to remain an heir, while in the latter case, the person decides not to become an heir at all. Some of the countries in this group also require a court order for someone to officially be declared a beneficiary, with Austrian law being a well-known example: article 797 AGBG provides that acquisition of the assets of the estate by the heirs and legatees is by means of a court order (*Einanwortung*) as the result of specific court proceedings. In other countries, such as Germany and Slovakia, succession rights pass to the beneficiaries upon the opening of the succession, but heirs and legatees have to be declared as such by means of a certificate of inheritance issued by the court; heirs and legatees who do not intend to accept their share of the estate are required to issue a waiver within a time limit that starts to run from the date on which they formally become beneficiaries.

In countries in which the beneficiaries are liable for the debts of the estate, it is generally possible to limit liability to the amount of the assets, with an inventory of the assets of the estate having to be drawn up; in many cases, actual court proceedings have to be launched in compliance with a peremptory and often rather tight deadline. The law in certain countries dictates that liability for debts is limited to the amount of the share of the inheritance (e.g. article 142 of the Slovenian inheritance act). Where assets are exceeded by liabilities, other legal systems instead provide other avenues of protection for the heirs, such as abandoning the estate to the creditors or the estate being declared insolvent (e.g. as provided for by § 130(3) of the Estonian law of succession act).

Switzerland has a particular position on this point: article 566.2 of the Swiss civil code establishes a presumption that inheritance is waived where the deceased was known to be insolvent or had been officially declared bankrupt at the time of death.

5. The huge variations that come to light when comparing legislation in the various different countries do of course mean that the task of establishing the succession law that governs these requirements is a priority; a failure to meet the generally absolute and inflexible deadlines imposed by the different laws in force can in fact result in it being impossible to accept – or, in other cases, impossible to waive – an inheritance, or having to shoulder unlimited liability for the debts of the estate.

III. The 'Persons' Covered by the Provision, the Ascertainment of Their Legal Capacity and the Identification of Their Habitual Residence

6. Article 13 refers to any 'person' who may make a declaration. This 'person' is usually a beneficiary of the estate. But, as we have seen, in certain legal systems a person only becomes a beneficiary upon acceptance, and where the decision is taken to waive inheritance, they do not become an heir or a legatee; it follows that it would be inappropriate for article 13 to make use of expressions that might give rise to problems of interpretation.[6]

7. Capacity to make declarations and the matter of any representation that might be called for where a minor or an incapable is involved are governed by the law applicable to capacity in accordance with the conflict-of-laws provisions in place in the State of the forum and which might also be found in uniform private international law instruments.[7] The capacity to make declarations of this type does not in fact fall within the concept of 'capacity to inherit' which, pursuant to article 23.2(c) ESR, is subject to the law that governs the succession and is in fact excluded from the scope of application of the regulation pursuant to article 1.2(b). The conflict-of-laws provisions to be applied should be those in force in the country in which the declarations are made; the ESR therefore appears to embrace the possibility of this aspect being governed differently depending on whether the declarations are made in the forum dealing with the succession or in the additional forum. The fact that EU international private law is still a work in progress means that this is, however, the only solution possible. In addition, the drawbacks of this situation are mitigated by the fact that where the legal representation of children is concerned, the Hague Convention of 19 October 1996 on Jurisdiction, Applicable Law, Recognition, Enforcement and Co-operation in Respect of Parental Responsibility and Measures for the Protection of Children applies in all Member States,[8] while in terms of incapable adults, six Member States bound by the ESR have already

[6] The proposal presented by the Commission in 2009 (cited in footnote 1) instead referred to a person who was an 'heir' or 'legatee'.

[7] See F. Sauvage, 'L'option et la transmission du passif dans les successions internationales au regard du règlement européen du 4 juillet 2012', in G. Khairallah and M. Revillard, *Droit européen des successions internationales. Le règlement du 4 juillet 2012* (Paris, 2013), p. 110 *et seq.*; see also, albeit in relation to article 28, Wautelet, 'Article 28', p. 443.

[8] All EU Member States are currently parties to this convention.

ratified the Hague Convention of 13 January 2000 on the International Protection of Adults.[9]

8. Article 13 only comes into operation where the person required to provide a declaration falling within its scope of application habitually resides in a Member State, meaning a Member State that participates to the ESR. Where the person resides in a third State (or in a Member State that does not participate to the regulation), the only authorities that are competent to receive the declarations in question are those in the member country identified on the basis of article 4 *et seq.* ESR. Where the person resides in the same Member State that is home to those authorities, then article 13 is clearly redundant.

9. Establishing the habitual residence of the person making a declaration involves a finding of fact by the bodies that are competent to deal with the succession as a whole, because the ESR does not contemplate investigations of this nature, as well as for the respect for the principle of mutual trust between the authorities in the EU Member States. In addition, this finding has no impact on the substantive validity of the declaration itself (this being subject in any event to the succession law) and only has a bearing on whether the authority in question has the power to deal with it, although consequences might also rise in terms of the formal validity of the declaration (see no. 18) [see art. 28].

It is an accepted principle of European Union law that the decision establishing a person's habitual residence 'must be made in the light of the context of the provisions and the objective' of the regulation to be applied.[10] The reasoning behind the absence of any definition of this concept is in fact to leave room for it to be adapted to the context in which the problem in question arises, bearing in mind the particular characteristics of the matter to be regulated or the particular issue to be resolved.[11] In the scenario that we are concerned with, the purpose of article 13, as defined by recital 32, is to 'simplify the lives of heirs and legatees'; it would seem reasonable, therefore, that when dealing with cases in which the determination of the habitual residence is not crystal clear, the requirement for simplification that the provisions sets out to meet can

[9] The following ESR participant Member States had ratified the convention as at 30 June 2016: Austria, Czech Republic, Estonia, Finland, France and Germany.

[10] ECJ, case C-523/07, *A* [2009] ECR I-02805, para. 35.

[11] See A. Davì and A. Zanobetti, 'Il nuovo diritto internazionale privato delle successioni nell'Unione europea', *CdT* 5/2 (2013), p. 33 and footnote 117; A. Davì and A. Zanobetti, *Il nuovo diritto internazionale privato europeo delle successioni* (Torino, 2014), p. 49 and footnote 16.

operate as a guideline. In addition, it is obvious that in order for article 13 to function as intended, the concept of habitual residence need not necessarily be interpreted in the same manner as that adopted when establishing the last habitual residence of the deceased.[12]

IV. Scope of Application of the Provision: The Need to Distinguish between 'Declarations' and 'Legal Proceedings'

10. Article 13 concerns 'declarations'. This term refers to statements taken by the competent authority passively, i.e. at the request of the party making the declaration, as suggested by the use of the expression 'receive'. This is where the authority, which might in fact be a court, simply makes the declaration official and provides a guarantee in law in relation to steps taken at the behest of private individuals.[13] Where, however, the competent authority plays an active role (regardless of whether it takes the form of an administrative body or a court) then legal proceedings are involved, which fall outside the scope of application of article 13, as is confirmed by recital 33, which distinguishes between 'mere declarations' and 'legal proceedings'.[14] An evaluation of the steps to be taken is to be carried out with reference to the succession law alone; as a result, where, pursuant to the law in force in the place in which a person has his or her habitual residence, certain requirements have to

[12] But see P. Wautelet, 'Article 13', in A. Bonomi and P. Wautelet (eds), *Le droit européen des successions. Commentaire du Règlement n° 650/2012 du 4 juillet 2012* (Bruxelles, 2013), p. 241; this view cannot be accepted, on the basis that, in the case of someone who is still alive, it is arguably inappropriate to use the interpretative criteria suggested by recitals 23 and 24, which, as is clear from the actual wording of those two recitals where they refer to determining the 'habitual residence of the *deceased at the moment of death*', are designed to come into play when establishing the habitual residence of someone who has died.

[13] What is involved here, therefore, are steps of an administrative nature, including where the declaration has to be made before a court; see G. Biagioni, 'L'ambito di applicazione del regolamento successioni', in P. Franzina and A. Leandro, *Il diritto internazionale privato europeo delle successioni* mortis causa (Milano, 2013), p. 30; A. Leandro, 'La giurisdizione nel regolamento dell'Unione europea sulle successioni *mortis causa*', *ibid.*, p. 77; for the distinction between the work carried out by the courts that is treated as non-contentious and that classed as administrative, see F. Salerno, 'La giurisdizione volontaria nella legge di riforma di diritto internazionale privato', *Riv dir int* (2005), p. 624. In contrast, Wautelet, 'Article 13', p. 240, classes the receipt of declarations as a non-contentious step; this classification is difficult to accept, as steps that are simply taken passively such as those set out in article 13 cannot be compared to the exercise of jurisdiction, even where this is on a non-contentious basis.

[14] The recital adds that 'documents instituting the legal proceedings' should not 'be regarded as declarations for the purposes of this Regulation'.

be met by means of a declaration, but the succession law requires legal proceedings to be commenced, the route to the additional forum is shut off.

11. Where the succession law does not require the declarations in question to be made before a court or other authority but is content with what are simply private certifications (albeit made by way of public deed), article 13 does not apply. One example here is the position under Italian law: acceptance can take the form of a simple private statement in writing (article 475 of the Italian civil code); where the succession is governed by Italian law, those intending to accept their inheritance are not therefore required to address any particular authority, regardless of where they reside.

12. Recital 33 states in particular that a person who wishes to limit his liability for the debts under the succession cannot resort to a mere declaration to that effect before the competent authorities of the Member State of his habitual residence, even if this is possible under the law of that Member State, 'where the law applicable to the succession requires him to initiate specific legal proceedings, for instance inventory proceedings, before the competent court'. The recital goes on to add that a declaration 'made in such circumstances by a person in the Member State of his habitual residence in the form provided for by the law of that Member State should therefore not be formally valid for the purposes of this Regulation'. The recital makes improper reference to the declaration being 'formally valid', whereas the distinction between 'declarations' and 'specific legal proceedings' concerns substantive validity, which is submitted to the law governing the succession. The provision must, therefore, be properly taken to mean that a declaration made with reference to an inheritance governed by a succession law that requires legal proceedings to be launched in order to properly accept or waiver an inheritance or limit liability is null and void.

13. On the other hand, the fact that legal proceedings regarding the administration of the succession feature substance and procedure intertwined can give rise to well-known problems with application that prompted the European legislator to engineer a situation in which, to the extent possible, competent court and applicable law coincide with one another.[15] It is easy to understand the firm intention of avoiding

[15] Looking in particular at limitations of liability, an illustration of these problems is provided by the well-known *Zannantonio* case. Decided by the Bavarian Oberlandesgericht 2 December 1965, *Neue juristische Wochenschrift* (1967), p. 447 *et seq.*, this concerned an Italian citizen who had lived all his life in Bavaria and died *ab*

difficulties of this type in taking the decision to channel all legal proceedings in the direction of the competent court on the basis of article 4 *et seq.* ESR, with any alternative or additional court being avoided.

14. Article 13 also applies to the revocation of the declarations in question where the succession law allows this step and, of course, where the revocation itself also takes the form of a simple declaration;[16] article 13 in fact specifically refers to declarations '*concerning* the acceptance or waiver of the succession, or a legacy or of a reserved share', leaving no room for doubt that a revocation is included here.

V. Non-applicability of Article 13 to Declarations Made Prior to the Opening of the Succession

15. In certain countries, the law also allows declarations in relation to the succession and, in particular, waivers of an inheritance or of a reserved share, to be made before the opening of the succession itself. Article 13 cannot, however, be used as a basis on which to claim that the declarant's country of habitual residence is competent to receive such declarations: the ESR provisions regarding jurisdiction are only designed to operate once the succession has opened. Article 13 in fact starts out with the wording 'In addition to the courts having jurisdiction . . .'; this confirms that the forum in question is one that is additional to the court that has jurisdiction to deal with the succession as a whole and can only operate where the other provisions regarding jurisdiction also come into operation.

intestato. He left assets located in Germany and his heirs were his children, who were still minors. The problems caused as a result of the succession to his estate being subject to Italian law (this being the law of the nationality of the *de cujus*) resulted from the fact that under Italian law, minors can only accept with the benefit of inventory, this being a particular concept that plays no part in German law. As a result, the German court hearing the matter at first instance had been forced to declare that it lacked jurisdiction to deal with this aspect. But the Italian courts also declared that they lacked jurisdiction: pursuant to Italian law, the inventory can only be received by the authorities in the place where the succession was opened. In order to avoid justice being denied, the Bayerisches Oberlandesgericht therefore decided to recognise that the inventory drawn up pursuant to German procedural rules had the substantive effects that would be produced under Italian law. This case provides an example of the problems that can be faced when measures are adopted abroad that relate to the transfer of assets in the estate and which are common to certain legal systems but prove difficult to implement in others.

16 For a claim on similar lines in relation to the scope of application of article 28, see P. Wautelet, 'Article 28', in A. Bonomi and P. Wautelet, *Le droit européen des successions. Commentaire du Règlement n° 650/2012 du 4 juillet 2012* (Bruxelles, 2013), p. 438.

VI. The Concept of 'Court'

16. When referring to the authority that is competent to receive the declarations that fall within its scope of application, article 13 uses the term 'court'. Recital 32 states that such declarations can also be made 'before other authorities . . . which are competent to receive declarations under national law' in the Member State where the declaring person habitually resides. This clarification is useful: the definition of 'court' provided by article 3.2 ESR would appear to be irrelevant here, precisely because the steps involved in simply receiving a declaration do not match the definition of 'court' provided by that provision.

It must be the case, however, that the declarations in question can be made before an authority other than a court (a notary, for example), where this is possible in the State in which the party making the declaration resides; otherwise, article 13 would be largely redundant.

17. Reference in the wording of article 13 to a 'court' that receives the declarations suggests, however, that it does not apply to simple steps taken by the beneficiaries of the estate, even though such steps might have consequences in the eyes of the law [see art. 28].

VII. Formal Validity of Declarations: The Link between Article 13 and Article 28 ESR

18. As far as form is concerned, the ESR is careful to minimise, to the extent possible, the difficulties prompted by the different approaches that may be adopted in this area by the succession law and the law in force in the country in which the parties making the declarations have their habitual residence, with article 28 providing that declarations regarding acceptance, waiver and a limitation of liability are valid 'as to form' when they meet the requirements imposed by the 'law applicable to the succession pursuant to Article 21 or Article 22', or by 'the law of the State in which the person making the declaration has his habitual residence'. Declarations received by an authority exercising its jurisdiction on the basis of the additional forum contemplated by article 13 can, therefore, be made in the form permitted by local law [see art. 28].

VIII. Communication of Declarations to the Authority 'Which Is or Will Be Dealing with the Succession'

19. A declaration made in the beneficiaries' country of habitual residence is, in many cases, sufficient for the purposes of the administration and devolution of the estate: on the basis that no challenges are raised, this is the position not only where all the assets in the estate are located in the country in which the party making the declaration is resident, but also where the estate includes assets situated in other Member States. When received by an authority, these declarations in fact take on the form of authentic instruments that all Member States are required to accept pursuant to article 59 ESR [see art. 59].

20. In certain cases, however, the declaration has to be forwarded to the authority that is competent to deal with the succession pursuant to article 4 *et seq.* ESR. This is the position mainly where a European Certificate of Succession is required or where legal proceedings are underway, for example because the succession is contested.

Declarations made without complying with the substantive provisions of the succession law, including the relevant time limits imposed, are of course null and void. It is therefore incumbent upon the party making the declaration to obtain the information required on the applicable law and, most importantly, to establish that in order to properly comply with the requirements in question, the applicable law does not call for actual legal proceedings to be launched. Also a mistake in establishing the actual law that applies might result in the declaration being invalid.

21. Turning now to transmission of declarations to the authority that is competent to deal with the succession, recital 32 states that persons who have made such declarations before the competent authority in the country in which they habitually reside 'should themselves inform the court or authority which is or will be dealing with the succession of the existence of such declarations within any time limit set by the law applicable to the succession'.

The ESR does not establish any particular procedure to be followed when providing this information; in the absence of any specific provisions adopted by the Member States, this step would appear to be one that the party making the declaration is required himself to take, which is in fact what the recital suggests.[17] Where declarations are made in

[17] The duty of the parties involved to transmit these declarations has to be coordinated with the duties on the part of the authorities dealing with the succession. As far as the issue of a European Certificate of Succession is concerned, for example, article 65 *et seq.* ESR

compliance with the requirements regarding substantive and formal validity as established respectively by the succession law and by the laws referred to by article 28 ESR, it cannot be the case that a failure to communicate or a delay in doing so will result in the compliance being found to have fallen short or resulting in foreclosure; given the silence on the part of the ESR on this point, the consequences of a failure or delay will be those established by the substantive law that applies.[18]

require the application for this certificate to be accompanied by certain information, which specifically includes information about the identity of 'other possible beneficiaries' (article 65.1(e)) and 'an indication of whether any of the beneficiaries has made a declaration concerning acceptance or waiver of the succession' (article 65.1(k)). The issuing authority is required to verify the response provided and, where necessary, ask the applicant to provide additional information (article 66.1) [see art. 65 *et seq.*].

18 For a conclusion on similar lines, see Wautelet, 'Article 13', p. 244.

Article 14

Seising of a Court

FABRIZIO MARONGIU BUONAIUTI

For the purposes of this chapter, a court shall be deemed to be seised:

(a) at the time when the document instituting the proceedings or an equivalent document is lodged with the court, provided that the applicant has not subsequently failed to take the steps he was required to take to have service effected on the defendant;

(b) if the document has to be served before being lodged with the court, at the time when it is received by the authority responsible for service, provided that the applicant has not subsequently failed to take the steps he was required to take to have the document lodged with the court; or

(c) if the proceedings are opened of the court's own motion, at the time when the decision to open the proceedings is taken by the court, or, where such a decision is not required, at the time when the case is registered by the court.

Summary

I. SCOPE OF APPLICATION OF THE RULE AND PARALLELISM WITH ANALOGOUS SOLUTIONS CONTEMPLATED UNDER OTHER EU REGULATIONS *page* 234

II. RULES APPLICABLE TO EX PARTE ACTIONS AND THEIR APPLICATION IN RESPECT OF BOTH CONTENTIOUS AND NON-CONTENTIOUS PROCEEDINGS 236

III. THE RULE APPLICABLE AS REGARDS PROCEEDINGS COMMENCED EX OFFICIO 239

I. Scope of Application of the Rule and Parallelism with Analogous Solutions Contemplated under Other EU Regulations

1. The rules concerning jurisdiction set out in chapter II ESR are completed by a series of general provisions concerning the exercise of jurisdiction under any of the grounds contemplated under the regulation.[1] The

[1] H. Gaudemet-Tallon, 'Les règles de compétence judiciaire dans le règlement européen sur les successions', in G. Khairallah and M. Revillard (eds), *Droit européen des successions*

first of these rules is contained in article 14 ESR, which sets out autonomous criteria for determining the point at which a Member State court is to be considered as being seised for the purposes of the rules contained within that chapter of the ESR.

2. In particular, the rules contained within the provision under discussion will be relevant in respect of the application of the rules on *lis alibi pendens* and related actions contained in articles 17 and 18 ESR, which, like analogous rules contained in other EU regulations adopted in the field of judicial cooperation in civil matters following the originating model offered by the 1968 Brussels Convention, are based on a mechanism of temporal priority. This requires the adoption of clear criteria for a consistent determination of the point at which each of the courts exercising a concurrent jurisdiction is to be considered as being seised, in order to prevent conflicts between courts both claiming to have been seised first, based on the application of different procedural rules [see art. 17 no. 16; art. 18 nos. 6–7].[2]

3. Among the other provisions contained within chapter II ESR, the determination of the moment when a court has been seised appears to be relevant for the purposes of the rule under article 7(a) ESR, which provides for the jurisdiction of the courts of the Member State of the law chosen by the deceased as applicable to the succession, when a court previously seised has declined jurisdiction under article 6 [see art. 7 nos. 5–6]. The same determination is relevant in respect of the rule under article 10.1(b) ESR. This refers to the moment of seizure of the court as *dies ad quem* for calculating the five-year period up to which a previous habitual residence of the deceased in a Member State where assets belonging to his or her succession are located may be relevant for the purposes of establishing jurisdiction over the succession as a whole [see art. 10 no. 15]. For purposes other than the application of the rules contained within chapter II ESR, the rule under article 14 does not apply, since, as concerns issues governed by domestic law, such as the effects deriving from the seizure of a court in respect of limitation

internationales. Le règlement du 4 juillet 2012 (Paris, 2013), p. 127 *et seq.*, at p. 136 classifies such rules as 'règles procédurales concernant la compétence'. Cf. also, in somewhat vaguer terms, recital 34 ESR, classifying such provisions as 'general procedural rules'.

[2] As clearly shown by ECJ, case 129/83, *Zelger* v. *Salinitri* [1984] ECR 2397, concerning the application of the temporal priority requirement for the purposes of the rule on *lis alibi pendens* as embodied in article 21 of the 1968 Brussels Convention, which did not contemplate specific rules for the determination of the moment when a court was to be considered as being seised.

periods, the relevant criteria provided for under the law of the Member State concerned shall apply.[3]

4. The rules for determining the point at which a court in a Member State is to be considered as being seised, as set out in article 14 ESR, except for the rule under lit. (c) concerning proceedings commenced *ex officio*, are actually identical to the rules contained for the same purposes within the other regulations adopted in the field of judicial cooperation in civil matters in respect of which the same issue is relevant, such as article 30 regulation no. 44/2001 (s. c. 'Brussels I'), article 16 regulation no. 2201/2003 (s. c. 'Brussels II-*bis*'), article 9 regulation no. 4/2009 on maintenance obligations, and, lastly, apart from some specifications which will be mentioned in due course, article 32 regulation no. 1215/2012 (s. c. 'Brussels I-*bis*'). Even though the technique of adopting corresponding solutions throughout the various instruments, addressing the same issues in the respective fields concerned, presents the undeniable advantage of simplicity and consistency, it has been questioned whether the peculiarities of actions in succession matters, in particular with regard to the frequent recourse in such matters to non-contentious proceedings as contemplated under the law of some Member States, might have required some adaptations to the said rules in order to ease their application in respect of that type of proceedings.[4]

II. Rules Applicable to *ex parte* Actions and Their Application in Respect of Both Contentious and Non-contentious Proceedings

5. The rules contained in article 14(a) and (b) ESR for the purposes of determining the moment at which a court is to be considered as being seised of an *ex parte* action, just like the corresponding rules contained in the other EU regulations in the field of judicial cooperation in civil matters previously mentioned, are based on the assumption that the relevant moment is that when the first act contemplated under the *lex*

[3] Cf. A. Bonomi, 'Article 14', in A. Bonomi and P. Wautelet, *Le droit européen des successions. Commentaire du règlement n° 650/2012 du 4 juillet 2012* (Bruxelles, 2013), p. 245 *et seq.*, esp. p. 246.

[4] Cf., among others, A. Dutta, 'Art. 14 EuErbVO', in *Münchener Kommentar zum BGB*, 6th ed. (München, 2015), para. 1 *et seq.*, esp. paras. 3–4; A. Dutta, 'Das neue internationale Erbrecht der Europäischen Union – Eine erste Lektüre der Erbrechtsverordnung', *FamRZ* (2013), p. 4 *et seq.*, esp. p. 8; B. Hess, 'Die internationale Zuständigkeit nach der Erbrechtsverordnung', in A. Dutta and S. Herrler (eds), *Die Europäische Erbrechtsverordnung* (München, 2014), p. 131 *et seq.*, esp. p. 141.

fori for the purposes of introducing proceedings has been performed by the plaintiff. This is subject to the proviso that the latter does not neglect to attend to the subsequent procedural steps which are necessary under the same law for the purposes of completing the introductory phase of the proceedings. Inevitably, due account being taken of the fact that the introductory phase of the proceedings is conceived differently in the various Member States and, frequently, even within the same Member State different modalities may be contemplated depending upon the nature or the subject matter of the relevant proceedings, the rule contemplates two alternative solutions. These depend upon whether, under the *lex fori*, the document instituting proceedings must first be lodged with the court and subsequently served upon the defendant, or whether, conversely, such a document must be served upon the defendant before being lodged with the court.[5]

6. In the first case, article 14(a) ESR accordingly provides that a court is to be considered as being seised when the document introducing proceedings is lodged with the court, provided the plaintiff does not subsequently omit such procedural steps as are necessary in order to ensure that the document itself is served upon the defendant.

7. In the second case, article 14(b) ESR reciprocally provides that the relevant moment is that when the authority responsible for service of the document upon the defendant has received it, provided the plaintiff does not subsequently neglect to take the necessary procedural steps for ensuring that the document itself is lodged with the court. Like the corresponding rules figuring in other EU regulations, article 14(b) ESR refers to the moment when the authority responsible for service receives the document instituting proceedings, and not to the point at which the said document is actually served upon the defendant This is in order to prevent the plaintiff being prejudiced by possible delays in the performance of service by the competent authority, on which the plaintiff him or herself, once he or she has delivered the document to be served, hardly has any influence. It is regrettable, in this respect, that the rule as contained in the ESR has omitted to specify that the 'authority responsible for service' for the purposes of the rule is the first authority receiving the

[5] As noted in F. Marongiu Buonaiuti, *Litispendenza e connessione internazionale. Strumenti di coordinamento tra giurisdizioni statali in materia civile* (Naples, 2008), p. 243 *et seq.*; F. Marongiu Buonaiuti, '*Lis alibi pendens* and Related Actions in Civil and Commercial Matters Within the European Judicial Area', *YPIL* (2009), p. 511 *et seq.*, esp. p. 546 *et seq.*, an entirely uniform solution can hardly be achieved in this respect, due to the co-existence of different procedural models among the EU Member States.

documents to be served, as specified instead under article 32.1, second sentence, regulation no. 1215/2012 (s. c. 'Brussels I-*bis*').[6] Such a specification, which is particularly relevant in those cases where the document instituting proceedings must be served in a different Member State or even in a third country insofar as the dispute falls within the scope of application of the regulation, may, nonetheless, probably be read into the rule as contained in the ESR, since it appears entirely consonant with the said rationale of ensuring that the plaintiff is not prejudiced by possible delays affecting service procedures.[7]

8. The same rationale for the rules contemplated under article 14(a) and (b) ESR suggests that in those cases where, subject to the *lex fori*, the introduction of contentious proceedings is to be preceded by a conciliation procedure, the same rules shall apply in respect of the document instituting such a procedure, depending on the mode in which it is devised under the same law.[8]

9. As regards the application of the said criteria, which appear to be clearly devised for contentious proceedings, where the document instituting proceedings is normally to be served on one or more defendants either before or after being lodged with the court, in the different context of proceedings of a non-contentious nature as are frequently contemplated in succession matters under the law of some Member States, it appears that the difficulties likely to arise in such a case should not be overestimated. In fact, it appears abundantly clear that non-contentious proceedings, which are normally commenced by means of an application to the court by a person having an interest in obtaining some form of declaration by the court seised, may easily fall under the rule contemplated under article 14 (a) ESR, insofar as it refers to the moment when such an application is lodged with the court.[9]

[6] Cf., among others, H. Gaudemet-Tallon and C. Kessedjian, 'La refonte du règlement Bruxelles I', *Revue trimestrielle de droit européen* (2013), p. 435 *et seq.*, esp. p. 447; A. Leandro, 'Prime osservazioni sul regolamento (UE) n. 1215/2012 ("Bruxelles I *bis*")', *Il giusto processo civile* (2003), p. 583 *et seq.*, esp. p. 601 *et seq.*; F. Marongiu Buonaiuti, 'Per una prima lettura del regolamento "Bruxelles I *bis*": il nuovo regime della litispendenza e della connessione privativa', www.aldricus.com (last accessed 30 June 2016) (19 December 2012, no. 2); A. Nuyts, 'La refonte du règlement Bruxelles I', *Rev crit dr int priv* (2013), p. 1 *et seq.*, esp. p. 61.; F. Salerno, *Giurisdizione ed efficacia delle decisioni straniere nel regolamento (UE) n. 1215/2012 (rifusione)*, 4th ed, (Padova, 2015), p. 282 *et seq.*

[7] As we proposed with regard to article 30 regulation no. 44/2001 (s. c. 'Brussels I') which was equally silent in this respect: cf. Marongiu Buonaiuti, *Litispendenza e connessione internazionale*, p. 246; Marongiu Buonaiuti, 'Lis alibi pendens and Related Actions', p. 548 et seq.

[8] Cf. Bonomi, 'Article 14', p. 246.

[9] Cf. Dutta, 'Art. 12 EuErbVO', para. 4.

III. The Rule Applicable as Regards Proceedings Commenced *ex officio*

10. Clearly, neither of the rules under article 14(a) or (b) could lend itself to being adapted to the different case of proceedings commenced *ex officio*, as may be contemplated in succession matters under the law of some Member States [see art. 8 nos. 4–5], since in such proceedings, there is, by definition, no initiative by any of the parties or persons having an interest in the succession. Reflecting, in turn, the co-existence of different modalities under which such proceedings are commenced under the laws of the Member States contemplating them, article 14(c) ESR, adopts a rather flexible solution, providing as a general rule that the court is to be considered as being seised once the decision opening the proceedings is taken. In the case that no such decision is contemplated under the law of the relevant Member State, the rule refers as a residual solution to the moment when the case is registered at the court's docket, which in such a case would provide the first evidence of the proceedings having been commenced.[10]

[10] Cf. Bonomi, 'Article 12', p. 246; Dutta, 'Art. 12 EuErbVO', paras. 5–6.

Article 15

Examination as to Jurisdiction

FABRIZIO MARONGIU BUONAIUTI

Where a court of a Member State is seised of a succession matter over which it has no jurisdiction under this Regulation, it shall declare of its own motion that it has no jurisdiction.

Summary

I. RATIONALE FOR THE RULE AND COMPARISON WITH ANALOGOUS PROVISIONS CONTAINED IN OTHER EU REGULATIONS *page* 240

II. COORDINATION OF THE RULE WITH SPECIAL PROVISIONS CONCERNING THE DECLINING OF JURISDICTION UNDER THE ESR 243

I. Rationale for the Rule and Comparison with Analogous Provisions Contained in Other EU Regulations

1. The rule under article 15 ESR makes the allocation of jurisdiction in succession matters as amongst Member States' courts mandatory, by providing that a court seised of a dispute, in respect of which it has no jurisdiction under the regulation, is under a duty to declare of its own motion that it has no jurisdiction. Such a duty is expressed in absolute terms under the rule, such that it applies irrespective of the conduct of the parties, including in the case where the defendant enters an appearance without raising any objection to the jurisdiction of the court, as well as, subject to article 16 ESR [see art. 16 no. 2], in the case where the defendant fails to appear.[1]

[1] Cf., among others, A. Bonomi, 'Article 15', in A. Bonomi and P. Wautelet, *Le droit européen des successions. Commentaire du règlement n° 650/2012 du 4 juillet 2012* (Bruxelles, 2013), p. 247 *et seq.*; J. Carrascosa González, *El Reglamento Sucesorio Europeo 650/2012 de 4 de julio 2012. Análisis crítico* (Granada, 2014), p. 108 *et seq.*; A. Dutta, 'Art. 15 EuErbVO', in *Münchener Kommentar zum BGB*, 6th ed (München, 2015), para. 1 *et seq.*; H. Gaudemet-Tallon, 'Les règles de compétence judiciaire dans le règlement européen

2. The rather rigid solution adopted under the ESR, which corresponds to that adopted under other EU regulations which also contemplate a substantially mandatory distribution of jurisdiction as amongst the courts of the Member States, such as regulation no. 2201/2003 concerning jurisdiction and the recognition and enforcement of judgments in matrimonial matters and the matters of parental responsibility (s. c. 'Brussels II-*bis*')[2] and regulation no. 4/2009 on jurisdiction, applicable law, recognition and enforcement of decisions and cooperation in matters relating to maintenance obligations,[3] tallies with the limited role granted to party autonomy under the ESR with regard to the allocation of jurisdiction. In fact, as already noted [see art. 5 nos. 1 and 7], under the ESR a choice of *forum* by the parties concerned by the succession is only allowed in the case where the deceased has made a *professio juris* in favour of the law of the Member State the nationality of which he or she possessed, and may only relate to a court or the courts of that Member State. Accordingly, the extent to which a tacit acceptance of the jurisdiction of the courts of a Member State would be allowed is extremely narrow. In fact, such an implied acceptance may only take place where it is by the parties concerned by the succession who were not parties to a choice-of-court agreement and may only operate in favour of the court or courts designated under such an agreement [see art. 9 no. 4].[4]

3. While the solution adopted under article 15 ESR corresponds with those adopted under the two previously-mentioned regulations governing jurisdiction within the domain of family law matters, it is, by contrast, different from that adopted in civil and commercial matters under regulation no. 1215/2012 on jurisdiction and the recognition and enforcement of judgments in civil and commercial matters (recast) (s. c. 'Brussels I-*bis*') – as well as under the pre-existing regulation no. 44/2001 on jurisdiction and the recognition and enforcement of judgments in civil and commercial matters (s. c. 'Brussels I') – which places a duty upon the court seised to declare of its own motion its lack of jurisdiction only in cases where the courts of a different Member State have exclusive jurisdiction under the regulation. This corresponds with the sensibly broader role granted to party autonomy with regard to jurisdiction under the Brussels I system. Under that system, as a general rule, the parties are free to agree, under a choice-of-court agreement, upon the

sur les successions', in G. Khairallah and M. Revillard (eds), *Droit européen des successions internationales. Le règlement du 4 juillet 2012* (Paris, 2013), p. 127 *et seq.*, esp. p. 137.

[2] Cf. article 17. [3] Cf. article 10. [4] Cf. Bonomi, 'Article 15', p. 249.

jurisdiction of a court or the courts of whichever Member State, except in cases where the exclusive jurisdiction of the courts of a Member State is at stake or in cases falling within the ambit of special rules specifically devised for the protection of weaker parties. Accordingly, under such a system, jurisdiction may generally be based upon an implied acceptance by the defendant, except, again, in cases of exclusive jurisdiction and, subject to some caveats, introduced under regulation no. 1215/2012 (s. c. 'Brussels I-*bis*'), in cases governed by the above-mentioned rules protecting weaker parties.[5]

4. At the same time, an important difference must be noted. Under the Brussels I system, in cases where the Member State court which ought to have declared *ex officio* its lack of jurisdiction continues with a case, a violation of the exclusive jurisdiction of the courts of a different Member State can represent, albeit exceptionally, a ground for refusal of recognition or enforcement of the judgment involving such a violation.[6] By contrast, under the scheme of the ESR, a violation of the rules on jurisdiction is not in any way contemplated as a ground for refusal of recognition or enforcement of judgments [see art. 40]. As noted by one author, this is consistent with the non-exclusive nature of the grounds of jurisdiction contemplated under the ESR and reflects the corresponding attitude taken under both the Brussels II-*bis* and the Maintenance regulations, which, similarly, do not contemplate exclusive grounds of jurisdiction.[7] Equally, unlike the previously-mentioned regulations, it is the case that the grounds of jurisdiction contemplated under the ESR, though formally not of an exclusive nature, do not essentially operate very differently from exclusive grounds of jurisdiction as are contemplated under the Brussels I and, currently, the Brussels I-*bis* regulation. In fact, the ESR, in principle, excludes the co-existence of alternative grounds of jurisdiction, by putting the different grounds contemplated into a strict hierarchical order. This is particularly evident

[5] Cf. articles 25–26 regulation no. 1215/2012, and, previously, articles 23–24 regulation no. 44/2001; concerning the innovations introduced in this respect under the recast regulation, among others, H. Gaudemet-Tallon and C. Kessedjian, 'La refonte du règlement Bruxelles I', *Revue trimestrielle de droit européen* (2013), p. 435 *et seq.*, esp. p. 444 *et seq*; A. Leandro, 'Prime osservazioni sul regolamento (UE) n. 1215/2012 ("Bruxelles I bis")', *Il giusto processo civile* (2003), p. 583 *et seq.*, esp. p. 595 *et seq.*; A. Nuyts, 'La refonte du règlement Bruxelles I', *Rev crit dr int priv* (2013), p. 1 *et seq.*, esp. p. 49 *et seq.*

[6] Cf. article 45.1(e) regulation no. 1215/2012, and, previously, article 35.1 regulation no. 44/2001.

[7] Cf. article 24 regulation no. 2201/2003; within regulation no. 4/2009 no ground for refusal of recognition or enforcement is provided in this respect: cf. Bonomi, 'Article 15', p. 246 *et seq.*

with regard to the relationships between the general ground of jurisdiction under article 4 ESR and the subsidiary grounds contemplated under article 10 ESR [see art. 10 nos. 4 and 14] as well as concerning the effects deriving from a choice-of-court agreement under article 5 ESR [see art. 5, no. 4; art. 6, no. 1].

II. Coordination of the Rule with Special Provisions Concerning the Declining of Jurisdiction under the ESR

5. The rule contained in article 15 ESR, in general terms, applies without prejudice to other provisions contained within chapter II of the regulation, which provide for special circumstances under which a court of a Member State may decline jurisdiction. The first case is that contemplated under article 6 ESR, which actually concerns cases where the Member State court seised would have jurisdiction under the ordinary rules of the ESR but would either be under a duty to decline jurisdiction due to a choice-of-court agreement pursuant to article 5 ESR, or would be vested with a discretionary power to do so in favour of the courts of the Member State the law of which has been chosen by the deceased as being applicable to the succession [see art. 6 nos. 1–2]. Secondly, a duty upon a Member State court to decline jurisdiction is contemplated under article 9 ESR in the aforementioned circumstances of a choice-of-court agreement having been entered into by some, but not all, of the parties concerned by the succession, when any of the parties to the dispute who has not participated in the choice of court agreement objects to the jurisdiction of the chosen court [see art. 9 nos. 6–7].[8]

6. The general rule under article 15 ESR has a further distinguishing feature from the mechanisms contemplated under either article 6 or article 9. In fact, the latter operate with the aim of providing coordination amongst the courts of different Member States, so that the provision for the ability, or, as the case may be, the duty of the courts of a Member State to decline jurisdiction, is followed by a provision for the courts of another Member State to assume jurisdiction. For example, in the case of article 6 ESR, this is the courts of the Member State of the chosen law based on the corresponding provision under article 7(a) [see art. 7 nos. 5–6]. Under article 9.2, it is the courts which would be normally competent under either article 4 or 10 [see art. 9 no. 6]. By contrast, the rule contained in article 15 ESR appears to be conceived in a strictly unilateral fashion, only

[8] Cf. Bonomi, 'Article 15', p. 249.

addressing the conduct to be taken by the Member State court finding that it has no jurisdiction. In this respect, even though the noted absence of coordination may give rise to negative conflicts of jurisdiction[9] – such as where the courts of two Member States where the deceased had alternately spent the last part of his or her life would both consider that he or she was not habitually resident in either of them – it must be taken into account that the ESR satisfactorily caters for such a scenario through its rules on subsidiary jurisdiction [see art. 10 nos. 1–3] and, in exceptional cases, through its provision for a *forum necessitatis* [see art. 11 nos. 3–5].

[9] Cf. Dutta, 'Art. 15 EuErbVO', para. 3.

Article 16

Examination as to Admissibility

FABRIZIO MARONGIU BUONAIUTI

1. Where a defendant habitually resident in a State other than the Member State where the action was brought does not enter an appearance, the court having jurisdiction shall stay the proceedings so long as it is not shown that the defendant has been able to receive the document instituting the proceedings or an equivalent document in time to arrange for his defence, or that all necessary steps have been taken to that end.
2. Article 19 of Regulation (EC) No 1393/2007 of the European Parliament and of the Council of 13 November 2007 on the service in the Member States of judicial and extrajudicial documents in civil or commercial matters (service of documents) shall apply instead of paragraph 1 of this article if the document instituting the proceedings or an equivalent document had to be transmitted from one Member State to another pursuant to that Regulation.
3. Where Regulation (EC) No 1393/2007 is not applicable, article 15 of the Hague Convention of 15 November 1965 on the Service Abroad of Judicial and Extrajudicial Documents in Civil or Commercial Matters shall apply if the document instituting the proceedings or an equivalent document had to be transmitted abroad pursuant to that Convention.

Summary

I. RATIONALE FOR THE RULE AND ITS PRECEDENTS IN ANALOGOUS PROVISIONS CONTAINED WITHIN OTHER EU REGULATIONS *page* 245

II. DIFFERENCES BETWEEN THE GENERAL RULE UNDER PARAGRAPH 1 AND THE SPECIAL REGIMES PROVIDED FOR UNDER REGULATION 1393/2007 OR THE 1965 HAGUE CONVENTION 248

I. Rationale for the Rule and Its Precedents in Analogous Provisions Contained within Other EU Regulations

1. The rule under article 16 ESR appears to follow corresponding provisions contained within other EU regulations adopted in the field of judicial cooperation in civil matters, such as article 26, paragraphs 2–4, regulation no. 44/2001 on jurisdiction and the recognition and enforcement of judgments in civil and commercial matters (s. c. 'Brussels I') and currently article 28, paragraphs 2–4, on jurisdiction and the recognition and enforcement of judgments in civil and commercial matters (recast) (s. c. 'Brussels I-*bis*'), article 18 regulation no. 2201/2003 concerning jurisdiction and the recognition and enforcement of judgments in matrimonial matters and the matters of parental responsibility (s. c. 'Brussels II-*bis*') and article 11 regulation no. 4/2009 on jurisdiction, applicable law, recognition and enforcement of decisions and cooperation in matters relating to maintenance obligations.

2. Like the analogous provisions contained in other regulations, the rule pursues the objective of ensuring that a defendant who fails to appear is made aware of the commencement of proceedings against him or her and of the content of the plaintiff's claim in such a way as to provide him or her with sufficient opportunity and time to prepare for his or her defence. It does so by providing, under the general rule contained within its paragraph 1, that the Member State court seised shall stay its proceedings as long as is not proved that the defendant was placed in a position to timely arrange for his or her defence. As has been noted by some commentators, the rule aims at ensuring the effectiveness of the service of the document instituting proceedings on the defendant, rather than, strictly speaking, its regularity, that is, its conformity with the relevant provisions contemplated by the law of the country where service is to be effected or with autonomous rules contained in an EU instrument or an international convention.[1] In fact, also in terms of the duty to ensure respect for the guarantees of due process enshrined in article 6.1 ECHR and article 47 EU Charter of Fundamental Rights, which, as referred to in the preamble to the ESR, the Member States are required to comply with when applying the rules contained in the regulation, what appears to be of the essence is that the defendant is afforded sufficient opportunity and time to arrange for his or her defence, rather than a strict compliance with the procedural formalities prescribed under the domestic law of the relevant Member State.[2]

[1] Cf., A. Bonomi, 'Article 16', in A. Bonomi and P. Wautelet, *Le droit européen des successions. Commentaire du règlement n° 650/2012 du 4 juillet 2012* (Bruxelles, 2013), p. 251 *et seq.*, esp. p. 252; A. Dutta, 'Art. 16 EuErbVO', in *Münchener Kommentar zum BGB*, 6th ed. (München, 2015), para. 1 *et seq.*

[2] Cf. recital 81 ESR; Dutta, 'Art. 16 EuErbVO', para. 1.

3. The rule under article 16.1 applies only insofar as the defendant is habitually resident in a country, be it a Member State or a third country,[3] which is not the Member State where proceedings are being instituted. This is on the assumption that, otherwise, the matter will be dealt with at a domestic level under the relevant rules contemplated by the law of the *forum*. In the same vein, the rule applies only insofar as the defendant does not appear, since it can be assumed that in the case that he or she enters an appearance, he or she may apply for any failure affecting the service of the document instituting proceedings to be remedied as provided for under the law governing the conduct of the proceedings.[4]

4. Not unlike that which has been noted in respect of article 14 ESR [see art. 14 no. 9], some questions have been raised concerning the application of the rule under article 16.1 in relation to non-contentious proceedings, where the use of the term 'defendant' is inappropriate.[5] Nonetheless, also with regard to the rule presently under discussion, it is to be assumed that the inherent problems of adaptation of a provision clearly devised within the context of a standard model of contentious proceedings to the different context of non-contentious proceedings as may be contemplated under the laws of some Member States may be easily resolved by interpreting the expressions used in the regulation with a necessary degree of flexibility. Accordingly, it seems sufficiently clear that the term 'defendant', adopted under the rule, may simply be intended as meaning any such person which under the law of the *forum* is to receive notice of the document instituting proceedings, irrespective of the peculiarities of the domestic legal systems of the individual Member States.[6]

5. In the same vein, the terms used within the rule, clearly conceived to reflect the model of *ex parte* proceedings, appear capable of being adapted to the peculiarities of proceedings commenced *ex officio* as may be contemplated under the law of some Member States. This is

[3] In can be observed that the application of the rule with regard to a defendant habitually resident, or, rather, domiciled in a third country is not contemplated under either article 26 regulation no. 44/2001 or, currently, article 28 regulation no. 1215/2012.

[4] Cf. Bonomi, 'Article 16', p. 251.

[5] Cf. Dutta, 'Art. 16 EuErbVO', para. 3; in respect of the same question concerning the use of the term 'defendant' under article 14 ESR, A. Dutta, 'Das neue internationale Erbrecht der Europäischen Union – Eine erste Lektüre der Erbrechtsverordnung', *FamRZ* (2013), p. 4 *et seq.*, esp. p. 8; B. Hess, 'Die internationale Zuständigkeit nach der Erbrechtsverordnung', in A. Dutta and S. Herrler (eds), *Die Europäische Erbrechtsverordnung* (München, 2014), p. 131 *et seq.*, esp. p. 141.

[6] Cf. Dutta, 'Art. 16 EuErbVO', para. 4.

particularly the case, with regard to service, on persons concerned by the succession, of a notice of the commencement of such proceedings or of an invitation to appear or present submissions before the court, subject to the modalities contemplated under the law of the relevant Member State.[7]

II. Differences between the General Rule under Paragraph 1 and the Special Regimes Provided for under Regulation no. 1393/2007 or the 1965 Hague Convention

6. Article 16.2 ESR recognises the priority as *lex specialis* of the rules specifically contained within article 19 regulation no. 1393/2007 concerning the service in the Member States of judicial and extra-judicial documents in civil and commercial matters (s. c. Service regulation). Such rules, in those cases where the document instituting proceedings is to be served or communicated from one Member State to another, expressly regulate the course of action to be taken by the court seised in the case that the defendant has not appeared.[8]

7. The rule contained in article 19 of the Service regulation actually provides for more stringent standards than the general rule contained in article 16.1 ESR. In fact, instead of relying upon a standard of mere effectiveness of service, the rule contained in the Service regulation appears to be based upon a criterion of regularity of service.[9] Indeed, the rule provides that in case of default by the defendant the court seised shall not deliver a judgment until it is satisfied that the document instituting proceedings has been served on the defendant in accordance with the rules contemplated under the domestic law of the Member State where service is to be performed, that is, where the defendant him- or herself is present. As an alternative, the rule lays down the condition that service is actually effected upon the defendant or at his or her residence in any other form as contemplated by the Service regulation itself, adding, as a further requirement applicable in either case, that service has at the same time been effective in the same sense as contemplated under the general rule under article 16.1 ESR. The rule contained under article 19.2

[7] Cf. Dutta, 'Art. 16 EuErbVO', para. 5.

[8] Cf., concerning the corresponding rules contained within article 19 of the previous regulation no. 1348/2000, subsequently replaced by the current regulation no. 1393/2007, M. Frigo and L. Fumagalli, *L'assistenza giudiziaria internazionale in materia civile* (Padova, 2003), p. 85 *et seq.*

[9] As noted by Bonomi, 'Article 16', p. 253.

of the Service regulation does, nonetheless, with a view to relaxing to some extent the strict requirements that it sets out, allow for the possibility for the individual Member States to make a declaration pursuant to article 23 of the same regulation, whereby comparably less stringent standards may be relied upon by the courts of the relevant Member States, among a series of alternative requirements contemplated under the rule.[10]

8. In respect of those cases where the document instituting proceedings must be served or communicated as between a Member State and a third country and the Hague Convention of 15 November 1965 on the service abroad of judicial and extra-judicial documents in civil or commercial matters (s.c. Hague Service Convention) would apply,[11] article 16.3 ESR refers alternatively to the rules contained for the same purposes within article 15 of that convention. Article 15 of the Hague Service Convention actually sets out requirements for regularity of service to be resorted to by the court seised in case of default by the defendant, which substantially correspond to those contemplated under article 19 of the Service regulation. The latter, in fact, appears to be closely modelled on the earlier rule contained in the convention.[12] The rule under article 16 ESR could, for the sake of clarity, probably have been conceived in a more straightforward way, by placing the three provisions in which it is articulated into their correct hierarchical order, moving the residual rule contemplated under paragraph 1 behind the provisions referring to the special regimes contemplated under the Service regulation and the Hague Service Convention respectively.[13]

10 Cf. more extensively, Frigo and Fumagalli, *L'assistenza giudiziaria internazionale*, p. 85 *et seq*.

11 That is, substantially, as between contracting parties to the Hague Convention of 15 November 1965, provided such parties are not both at the same time Member States, including Denmark pursuant to a declaration under article 3.2 of the Agreement between the EC and Denmark concerning service of judicial and extra-judicial documents in civil and commercial matters (OJ 2008 no. L331, 10 December 2008, p. 21). In the latter case, the Service regulation prevails, pursuant to its article 20.1, which establishes its priority in respect of agreements concluded by the Member States with regard to matters to which it applies. The *status* table of the Hague Convention, featuring 71 contracting States, is available at the website of the Hague Conference on Private International Law: www.hcch.net (last accessed 30 June 2016).

12 Cf. Bonomi, 'Article 16', p. 253; as concerns the rules contained in Art. 15 of the 1965 Hague Convention, Frigo and Fumagalli, *L'assistenza giudiziaria internazionale*, p. 43 *et seq*.

13 In fact, the rule contained in article 16.1 applies residually when neither article 19 Service regulation, nor article 15 Hague Service Convention, apply. The references made to the latter rules in article 16, paragraphs 2 and 3, are therefore not truly 'complementary' rules,

9. Nonetheless, it is worth mentioning that the inherent difference between the requirements to be satisfied under the general rule contemplated under article 16.1 ESR and under the special rules contemplated by article 19 Service regulation, and article 15 Hague Service Convention, respectively, is overcome at the recognition and enforcement of judgments stage. In fact, article 40(b) ESR, contemplates as a ground for refusal of recognition of a judgment by default, the mere violation of the requirement relating to the effectiveness of service, in the same terms as contemplated under article 16.1, without attributing relevance to strict regularity requirements, as set out, by contrast, under either article 19 of the Service regulation or article 15 of the Hague Service Convention [see art. 40].[14]

as suggested instead by J. Carrascosa González, *El Reglamento Sucesorio Europeo 650/2012 de 4 julio 2012. Análisis crítico* (Granada, 2014), p. 109 *et seq.*

[14] Cf. Bonomi, 'Article 16', p. 253.

Article 17

Lis Pendens

FABRIZIO MARONGIU BUONAIUTI

1. Where proceedings involving the same cause of action and between the same parties are brought in the courts of different Member States, any court other than the court first seised shall of its own motion stay its proceedings until such time as the jurisdiction of the court first seised is established.
2. Where the jurisdiction of the court first seised is established, any court other than the court first seised shall decline jurisdiction in favour of that court.

Summary

I. RATIONALE FOR THE RULE AND COMPARISON WITH ANALOGOUS PROVISIONS CONTAINED IN OTHER EU REGULATIONS *page* 251

II. LOW LIKELIHOOD OF COURTS BELONGING TO DIFFERENT MEMBER STATES HAVING CONCURRENT JURISDICTION UNDER THE ESR 254

III. APPLICATION OF THE TRADITIONAL REQUIREMENTS OF LIS PENDENS AS DEVISED IN EARLIER INSTRUMENTS TO THE SPECIFIC CONTEXT OF SUCCESSION DISPUTES 257

A. Identical Cause of Action 258

B. Identical Parties 259

C. Temporal Priority 263

IV. EFFECTS DERIVING FROM THE APPLICATION OF THE RULE 263

V. ABSENCE OF A RULE ADDRESSING CASES WHERE PARALLEL PROCEEDINGS ARE PENDING BEFORE A THIRD COUNTRY COURT 265

I. Rationale for the Rule and Comparison with Analogous Provisions Contained in Other EU Regulations

1. The rule under article 17 ESR concerning *lis pendens* is closely modelled on the provisions included for the same purposes in previous EU instruments containing rules on jurisdiction and the enforcement of judgments. These include article 27 regulation no. 44/2001 (s. c. 'Brussels I'),[1] article 12 regulation no. 4/2009 concerning maintenance obligations,[2] and, subject to some differences concerning the relevant requirements reflecting the peculiarities of the field in which it operates, article 19 regulation no. 2201/2003 (s. c. 'Brussels II-*bis*').[3] Regrettably, despite having been adopted just a few months ahead of regulation no. 1215/2012 (s. c. 'Brussels I-*bis*'), article 17 of the ESR reflects the previous formulation of the rules on *lis pendens* as contained in the Brussels I regulation. It would have been preferable to adopt the current formulation of those rules as contained under the Brussels I-*bis* regulation, which introduces some innovations in respect of those rules, most notably with regard to proceedings pending before third country courts.[4]

2. The rules on *lis pendens* as contained in article 17 ESR, like those concerning related actions under article 18 ESR [see art. 18 no. 2], and those contained in the other above-mentioned regulations, are aimed at preventing an unwelcome duplication of proceedings before the courts of different Member States, which could result in the handing down of irreconcilable judgments.[5] In fact, within the context of the strongly inter-related structure of the ESR, the rules concerning jurisdiction form a unitary system along with those concerning the applicable law and those addressing the recognition and enforcement of judgments. In such a system, which, again, is common to the other regulations just mentioned, the incompatibility of a judgment delivered in a different

[1] Council Regulation (EC) no. 44/2001 of 22 December 2000 on jurisdiction and the recognition and enforcement of judgments in civil and commercial matters, OJ no. L 12, 16 January 2001, p. 1.

[2] Council Regulation (EC) no. 4/2009 of 18 December 2008 on jurisdiction, applicable law, recognition and enforcement of decisions and cooperation in matters relating to maintenance obligations, OJ no. L 7, 10 January 2009, p. 1.

[3] Regulation (EU) no. 1215/2012 of the European Parliament and of the Council of 12 December 2012 on jurisdiction and the recognition and enforcement of judgments in civil and commercial matters (recast), OJ no. L 351, 20 December 2012, p. 1.

[4] Cf., concerning in particular this feature of the rules as contained in the Brussels I-*bis* regulation, F. Marongiu Buonaiuti, '*Lis alibi pendens* and Related Actions in the Relationships with the Courts of Third Countries in the Recast of the Brussels I Regulation', *YPIL*, vol. 15 (2013/2014), p. 87 *et seq.*; more extensively on this point in section V.

[5] Cf. generally, on the functional relationship between rules on *lis pendens* and on the recognition of foreign judgments, among others, R. Geimer, *Internationales Zivilprozessrecht*, 5th ed. (Köln, 2005), p. 831 *et seq.*; F. Marongiu Buonaiuti, *Litispendenza e connessione internazionale. Strumenti di coordinamento tra giurisdizioni statali in materia civile* (Napoli, 2008), p. 31 *et seq.*; V. Moissinac-Massénat, *Les conflits de procédures et de décisions en droit international privé* (Paris, 2007), p. 25 *et seq.*

Member State with a domestic judgment, or with a judgment previously delivered in another Member State or in a third country which is recognised in the *forum*, is considered to constitute a ground for denial of recognition [see art. 40].[6]

3. The risk of the courts of different Member States coming up with incompatible judgments which the rules on *lis pendens* aim to reduce, if not eliminate altogether, is not totally excluded by the inclusion within the ESR of a common set of rules setting out the law applicable to individual successions. In fact, even if, pursuant to such rules, the courts of different Member States should, in principle, apply the same law to one and the same succession, it must be considered that, on occasion, the relevant connecting factors, such as, for example, that of the habitual residence of the deceased at the moment of death, may be susceptible to being interpreted in different ways by courts belonging to different Member States [see art. 4; art. 10 nos. 14–16; art. 21]. Furthermore, even in the case that the courts seised in different Member States should apply the same law, differences in the interpretation of the relevant provisions of such a law and in their application to the facts of the case may also lead to irreconcilable results. Ultimately, it must also be considered that even in the event that the courts simultaneously seised in different Member States came up with results that were materially the same, a duplication of proceedings would still be incompatible with an efficient discharging of judicial functions in the Member States concerned and with the principle of reciprocal faith inherent in the functioning of the European judicial area.[7]

[6] Cf., with regard to the purpose of the rule on *lis pendens* within the framework of the ESR, among others, A. Bonomi, 'Article 17', in A. Bonomi and P. Wautelet, *Le droit européen des successions. Commentaire du Règlement n° 650/2012 du 4 juillet 2012* (Bruxelles, 2013), p. 255; A. Dutta, 'Art. 17 EuErbVO', in *Münchener Kommentar zum BGB*, 6th ed. (München, 2015), para. 1.

[7] Under such a principle, Member State courts are expected to place reliance upon the exercise of jurisdiction by other Member States' courts, based upon the rules contained in an EU instrument, as leading to a judgment likely to be recognised and, as the case may be, enforced in the *forum*. Cf., for various references to such a principle in ECJ case law, ECJ, case C-116/02, *Gasser* v. *MISAT Srl* [2003] ECR I-14693, para. 48; case C-159/02, *Turner* v. *Grovit* [2004] ECR I-3565, para. 24; case C-185/07, *Allianz SpA (formerly Riunione Adriatica di Sicurtà SpA)* v. *West Tankers Inc.* [2009] ECR I-663, para. 30; on the latter, F. Marongiu Buonaiuti, 'Emanazione di provvedimenti inibitori a sostegno della competenza arbitrale e reciproca fiducia tra i sistemi giurisdizionali degli Stati membri dell'Unione europea', *Rivista dell'arbitrato* (2009), p. 245 *et seq.*

II. Low Likelihood of Courts Belonging to Different Member States Having Concurrent Jurisdiction under the ESR

4. If the rationale for the rule is basically the same as that underlying analogous provisions contained within other EU regulations adopted in the field of judicial cooperation in civil matters, the context in which the rule operates is still, to a certain extent, different from that in respect of which it was originally conceived. In fact, the rule on *lis pendens* as initially adopted under article 21 of the 1968 Brussels Convention and subsequently replicated under article 27 regulation no. 44/2001 was designed to operate within a system based on the co-existence of alternative grounds of jurisdiction, whereby courts belonging to different Member States could frequently be vested with jurisdiction in respect of the same dispute.[8] A similar situation could arise in the context of the other two instruments in which the rule on *lis pendens* was subsequently replicated, since both regulation no. 2201/2003 (s. c. 'Brussels II-*bis*'), in respect of matrimonial disputes,[9] and regulation no. 4/2009, concerning maintenance obligations, are based on the co-existence of alternative grounds of jurisdiction.[10]

5. The system of allocation of jurisdiction as among the courts of the Member States as devised under the ESR, is, instead, based upon the opposite model which can already be found in the provisions concerning jurisdiction in matters of parental responsibility contained within the

[8] The same applies in respect of the rules on jurisdiction as currently set out in EU regulation no. 1215/2012 (s. c. 'Brussels I-*bis*'): cf., among others, H. Gaudemet-Tallon and C. Kessedjian, 'La refonte du règlement Bruxelles I', *Rev trim dr eur* (2013), p. 435 *et seq*., esp. p. 438 *et seq*.; A. Leandro, 'Prime osservazioni sul regolamento (UE) no. 1215/ 2012 («Bruxelles I bis»)', *Il giusto processo civile* (2013), p. 583 *et seq*., esp. p. 594 *et seq*.; A. Nuyts, 'La refonte du règlement Bruxelles I', *Rev crit dr int priv* (2013), p. 1 *et seq*., esp. p. 49 *et seq*.; F. Salerno, *Giurisdizione ed efficacia delle decisioni straniere nel Regolamento (UE) n. 1215/2012 (rifusione)*, 4th ed. (Padova, 2015), p. 107 *et seq*.

[9] Cf. article 3, Council Regulation (EC) no. 2201/2003 of 27 November 2003 concerning jurisdiction and the recognition and enforcement of judgments in matrimonial matters and the matters of parental responsibility, repealing Regulation (EC) no. 1347/2000, OJ no. L 338, 23 December 2003, p. 1, providing for seven alternative grounds of jurisdiction; P. McEleavy, 'Brussels II *bis*: Matrimonial Matters, Parental Responsibility, Child Abduction and Mutual Recognition', *ICLQ* (2004), p. 503 *et seq*., esp. p. 505 *et seq*.

[10] Cf. art. 3, EC regulation no. 4/2009, providing for four alternative grounds of jurisdiction; B. Ancel and H. Muir-Watt, 'Aliments sans frontières. Le règlement n° 4/2009 du 18 décembre 2008 relatif à la compétence, la loi applicable, la reconnaissance et l'exécution des décisions et la coopération en matière d'obligations alimentaires', *Rev crit dr int priv* (2010), p. 457 *et seq*., esp. p. 463 *et seq*.

Brussels II-*bis* regulation.[11] Under these provisions, jurisdiction is in principle to vest with the courts of the Member State designated under a general rule, whereby the other rules contemplated are deemed to apply either residually or as an exception, so that the possibility for the courts of different Member States having concurrent jurisdiction in respect of the same dispute is ruled out altogether [see art. 10 nos. 1–3]. This goes alongside the duty of a Member State court seised, which finds that it has no jurisdiction under the regulation, to declare *ex officio* its lack of jurisdiction [see art. 15 nos. 1–2], and with the strictly limited scope within which the parties might found the jurisdiction of the courts of a Member State by entering an appearance before such courts [see art. 9 no. 4].

6. Taking into account the effects that the ESR gives to choice-of-court agreements entered into by the parties having an interest in a succession on the jurisdiction of other Member States' courts, which are under a duty to decline jurisdiction [see art. 5 no. 4; art. 6 no. 1], it must be considered that the only circumstances in which the courts of more than one Member States might concurrently consider themselves as having jurisdiction under the ESR, are those where, in the specific circumstances of the case, the relevant ground of jurisdiction should prove to be ubiquitous. This possibility exists under article 10.1(a), which points to the Member State of the deceased's nationality at the moment of death. Even though the availability of this ground is still subject to the presence of assets pertaining to the estate of the deceased in the relevant Member States, in the case of dual nationality, the courts of more Member States may found jurisdiction. This is on the basis that the ESR does not provide any ground for establishing priority among competing nationalities [see art. 10 no. 13].[12] Furthermore, the possibility exists for a ground of jurisdiction contemplated by the ESR to be interpreted differently by the courts of different Member States. This could happen in respect of the last habitual residence of the deceased under the general rule of jurisdiction contained in article 4 ESR, or, of his or her previous habitual residence under article 10.1(b) ESR, even assuming

[11] Cf. articles 8–15, EC regulation no. 2201/2003; McEleavy, 'Brussels II *bis*: Matrimonial Matters, Parental Responsibility', p. 506 *et seq.*; R. Espinosa Calabuig, *Custodia y visita de menores en el espacio judicial europeo* (Madrid, 2007), p. 121 *et seq.*

[12] Cf. Bonomi, 'Article 17', p. 256 *et seq.*; A. Davì and A. Zanobetti, 'Il nuovo diritto internazionale privato delle successioni nell'Unione europea', *CdT* 5/2 (2013), p. 5 *et seq.*, esp. p. 123; A. Davì and A. Zanobetti, *Il nuovo diritto internazionale privato europeo delle successioni* (Torino, 2014), p. 215.

that, as such, only the habitual residence immediately preceding that possessed by the deceased at the moment of death is to be taken into account under the rule [see art. 10 no. 16]. Nonetheless, with regard to such a possibility, it must be considered that, pursuant to the principle of reciprocal faith, once a court sitting in a Member State has been seised, based on the last, or, respectively, the previous habitual residence of the deceased being located in that Member State, courts sitting in other Member States which might be concurrently seised under the same ground are under a duty to rely on the ability of the court first seised to correctly apply the rules of jurisdiction contained in the ESR and stay their proceedings until that court has ruled upon its jurisdiction.[13]

7. The possibility of an actual exercise of concurrent jurisdiction by the courts of different Member States in respect of the same succession dispute being likely to give rise to a situation of *lis pendens* can, by contrast, be excluded in respect of article 10.2 ESR. This is because jurisdiction under that rule is limited to assets located within the relevant Member State [see art. 10 no. 19], so that the subject matter of the dispute would not coincide for the purposes of the rule on *lis pendens*.[14] The only possibility of an actual coincidence of cause of action between proceedings commenced in different Member States under article 10.2 ESR, would appear to lie in the rather infrequent scenario of actions being introduced in different Member States concerning an intellectual property right granted pursuant to an EU instrument that provides that the right in question has a unitary effect across the entire Union.[15] This would, nevertheless, not preclude that in any other set of circumstances, actions pending before the courts of different Member States seised under article 10.2, might be considered as related for the purposes of the rule under article 18 ESR, which, within the system of allocation of

[13] Cf., with regard to the Brussels I system, as then embodied in the 1968 Brussels Convention, ECJ, case C-351/89, *Overseas Union Insurance Ltd* v. *New Hampshire Insurance Co.* [1991] ECR I-3317, para 23; Marongiu Buonaiuti, *Litispendenza e connessione internazionale*, p. 396 *et seq.*, p. 427 *et seq.*; H. Gaudemet-Tallon, *Compétence et exécution des jugements en Europe*, 4th ed. (Paris, 2010), p. 351 *et seq.*; concerning the application of the same rule in respect of the ESR, Davì and Zanobetti, 'Il nuovo diritto internazionale privato delle successioni', p. 123 *et seq.*; Davì and Zanobetti, *Il nuovo diritto internazionale privato europeo*, p. 216.

[14] Cf. Bonomi, 'Article 17', p. 257.

[15] Such as under regulation (EC) no. 207/2009 on the Community trademark; regulation (EC) no. 6/2002 on Community designs; regulation (EC) no. 2100/1994 on Community plant variety rights; and regulation (EU) no. 1257/2012, implementing an enhanced cooperation in the area of unitary patent protection.

jurisdiction set out in the ESR, is probably likely to have greater chances of application than the strict *lis pendens* rule [see art. 18 no. 3].[16]

8. Finally, the scenario of courts of different Member States being seised of the same succession dispute based on *forum necessitatis* under article 11 ESR, would appear to be a rather hypothetical one. In fact, considering that the rule is only to be resorted to in exceptional circumstances and for the purposes of preventing a denial of justice which the plaintiff would incur before the courts of a third country with which the succession is closely connected, the mere fact of a court in a Member State with which the case presents a sufficient connection being available to hear the case under the rule would exclude the situation of necessity justifying the assumption of jurisdiction by the courts of other Member States [see art. 11 no. 14]. Nonetheless, assuming both courts are seised almost simultaneously and that at the moment of being seised neither is aware of the parallel seizure of another court in a different Member State, the rule on *lis pendens* would still help to resolve potential conflicts which might arise in such circumstances.[17]

III. Application of the Traditional Requirements of *lis pendens* as Devised in Earlier Instruments to the Specific Context of Succession Disputes

9. For a situation of *lis pendens* to actually arise under the rule contained in article 17 ESR, the same requirements as are set out under the Brussels I model must be satisfied, namely, both sets of proceedings involve the same cause of action, they are pending between the same parties and the other Member State's court has been seised first.[18]

[16] As noted by H. Gaudemet-Tallon, 'Les règles de compétence judiciaire dans le règlement européen sur les successions', in G. Khairallah and M. Revillard (eds), *Droit européen des successions internationales. Le règlement du 4 juillet 2012* (Paris, 2013), p. 127 *et seq.*, esp. p. 139.

[17] Cf., considering article 11 ESR among the rules likely to give rise to a concurrent jurisdiction among the courts of different Member States, Davì and Zanobetti, 'Il nuovo diritto internazionale privato delle successioni', p. 123; Davì and Zanobetti, *Il nuovo diritto internazionale privato europeo*, p. 215.

[18] Cf., for an overview of the requirements contemplated under the *lis pendens* rule embodied in the Brussels I regulation, F. Marongiu Buonaiuti, '*Lis alibi pendens* and Related Actions in Civil and Commercial Matters in the European Judicial Area', *YPIL*, vol. 11 (2009), p. 511 *et seq.*, esp. p. 517 *et seq.*; on the amendments introduced by regulation no. 1215/2012 ('Brussels I-*bis*'), in the terms contemplated under the European Commission's proposal, L. Fumagalli, '*Lis Alibi Pendens.* The Rules on Parallel Proceedings in the Reform of the Brussels I Regulation', in F. Pocar,

A. *Identical Cause of Action*

10. In terms of the first requirement relating to the identity of the cause of action, it would appear reasonable that a relative degree of flexibility is applied in its interpretation as has been adopted by the ECJ in its case law concerning the interpretation of the corresponding requirement contained firstly in article 21 of the Brussels Convention on jurisdiction and the enforcement of judgments in civil and commercial matters of 28 September 1968 and then in article 27 EC regulation no. 44/2001 (s. c. 'Brussels I').[19] There are two basic elements behind the rationale for the adoption of an autonomous and sufficiently broad interpretation of the said requirement. On the one hand, it reflects the difference between the conceptions of the various Member States with regard to the identification of the object of the proceedings, which, in itself, would make the establishment of an identical cause of action for the purposes of the rule particularly difficult. On the other hand, it is based upon the objective pursued by the rule. As already noted, the rules on *lis pendens* as contained firstly in the 1968 Brussels Convention and subsequently in the various EU instruments governing jurisdiction and the recognition and enforcement of judgments, actually have as their primary objective the prevention of the handing down of contradictory judgments. As clearly underlined by the ECJ in its case law, the aforementioned rules are more capable of securing the achievement of this aim if they are interpreted with a sufficient degree of flexibility, so as to encompass all cases where the same legal relationship forms the subject of both sets of proceedings. This is irrespective of the plaintiff in one set of proceedings claiming the enforcement of the relevant legal relationship and the plaintiff in the other claiming its discharge, and irrespective of which of the claims is brought to court first.[20]

I. Viarengo, F. C. Villata (eds), *Recasting Brussels I* (Padova, 2012), p. 237 *et seq.*; as contained in the final text of the regulation, F. Marongiu Buonaiuti, 'Per una prima lettura del regolamento "Bruxelles I-*bis*": il nuovo regime della litispendenza e della connessione privativa', http://aldricus.com (last accessed 30 June 2016) 19 December 2012; Salerno, *Giurisdizione ed efficacia delle decisioni straniere*, p. 262 *et seq.*

[19] Cf. ECJ, case 144/86, *Gubisch Maschinenfabrik* v. *Palumbo* [1987] ECR 4861; case C-406/02, *Tatry (Owners of the cargo lately laden on board the ship)* v. *Maciej Rataj (Owners of the ship)* [1994] ECR I-5439; case C-111/01, *Gantner Electronic GmbH* v. *Basch Exploitatie Maatschappij BV* [2003] ECR I-4207; case C-39/02, *Maersk Olie & Gas A/S* v. *Firma M. de Haan en W. de Boer* [2004] ECR I-9657; Marongiu Buonaiuti, '*Lis alibi pendens* and Related Actions', p. 528 *et seq.*, also for further references.

[20] Cf., especially, ECJ, case 144/86, *Gubisch Maschinenfabrik*, para. 16 *et seq.*; case C-406/02, *Tatry*, para. 41 *et seq.*

11. Applying the broad interpretation of the requirement under discussion, as adopted by the ECJ in respect of the *lis pendens* rules contained in the Brussels I model to the specific context of succession disputes, it appears that the requirement relating to the identity of the causes of action should be considered as being met in the case of disputes concerning the same testamentary disposition, irrespective of the fact of the enforcement of the disposition being claimed before the court seised in one Member State and its validity or effectiveness being challenged in the other and whichever of the two claims has been introduced first. Accordingly, disputes concerning the eligibility of a particular individual as an heir or a beneficiary of the same testamentary disposition, should be considered to involve the same cause of action for the purposes of the rule. This is irrespective of whether the claims in question are aimed at affirming, or, conversely, denying the eligibility of the person concerned. Similarly, disputes concerning the passing on of the same assets pertaining to the estate of the deceased should be considered as involving the same cause of action, irrespective of the difference in the modalities of the passing on claimed by the respective plaintiffs in the two sets of proceedings.[21]

B. *Identical Parties*

12. A similar degree of flexibility should be applied with regard to the interpretation of the additional requirement related to the parties being identical. In this matter as well, the ECJ case law concerning the interpretation of the corresponding requirement as embodied in article 21 of the 1968 Brussels Convention and subsequently article 27 of the Brussels I regulation may provide some guidance. In respect of those rules, the ECJ stressed in an earlier case that in the case of multi-party proceedings the rules on *lis pendens* may apply only in respect of those parties which are common to the two sets of proceedings and that the proceedings pending before the court seised second should continue in respect of the

[21] Cf., in favour of a sufficiently flexible interpretation of the requirement of identical causes of action for the purposes of the *lis pendens* rule as embodied in the ESR, M. Álvarez Torné, *La autoridad competente en materia de sucesiones internacionales: el nuevo reglamento de la UE* (Madrid, 2013), p. 189 *et seq.*; Bonomi, 'Article 17', p. 260 *et seq.*; Davì and Zanobetti, 'Il nuovo diritto internazionale privato delle successioni', p. 124; Davì and A. Zanobetti, *Il nuovo diritto internazionale privato europeo*, p. 216 *et seq.*; Dutta, 'Art. 17 EuErbVO', para. 2.; S. M. Weber, *Das Internationale Zivilprozessrecht erbrechtlicher Streitigkeiten* (Sipplingen, 2012), p. 263 *et seq.*

parties which are not involved in the proceedings pending before the court first seised.[22] Such a logical solution can also be easily applied to the specific context of succession disputes, where it would not be uncommon for disputes to arise among a plurality of heirs or other persons having an interest in the succession, not all of whom may simultaneously be parties to different actions arising from the succession.[23]

13. More interesting, and likely to be relevant within the specific context of succession disputes, is a further direction provided by the ECJ with regard to the interpretation of the requirement of identical parties for the purposes of the *lis pendens* rules as formerly contained in the 1968 Brussels Convention. In that context, the ECJ gave a clear direction in favour of attaching a wide meaning to the notion of 'party' rather than just a narrow, formal one. In the case in question, an action where the insurer of a ship-owner had appeared as a party against the party claiming damages arising from a navigation incident, the court held that the parties to the action could be considered to be the same as an action in which the party claiming damages was suing the ship-owner personally. This was subject to the proviso that it could be established that the insurer in one set of proceedings and the insured in the other, were acting in pursuance of the same and indivisible legal interest.[24] The solution adopted by the ECJ, which appears to follow the same logic of flexibility which underpinned the solutions upheld in respect of the requirement of the identity of the cause of action, could also be applied in the context of succession disputes. This would be the case, where the parties to concurrent actions are held to be substantially the same, despite not constituting the same parties in formal terms, based upon the consideration that the formally different parties would, materially, be subject to the effects of the judgments to be delivered in both sets of proceedings.[25]

[22] ECJ, case C-406/02, *Tatry (Owners of the cargo lately laden on board the ship) v. Maciej Rataj (Owners of the ship)*, paras 29 *et seq*. Cf. Marongiu Buonaiuti, '*Lis alibi pendens* and Related Actions', p. 542 *et seq*., also for further references.

[23] Cf. Bonomi, 'Article 17', p. 261 *et seq*.; Davì and Zanobetti, 'Il nuovo diritto internazionale privato delle successioni', p. 124; Davì and A. Zanobetti, *Il nuovo diritto internazionale privato europeo*, p. 216 *et seq*.

[24] ECJ, case C-351/96, *Druot assurances S.A.* v. *Consolidated Metallurgical Industries* [1998] ECR I-3075, para. 19 et seq.; cf. Marongiu Buonaiuti, '*Lis alibi pendens* and Related Actions', p. 543 *et seq*.; F. Persano, 'Il rilievo della litispendenza internazionale nella convenzione di Bruxelles del 1968: la nozione di «stesse parti»', *Riv dir int priv proc* (2000), p. 713 *et seq*.; F. Seatzu, 'The meaning of «same parties» in Article 21 of the Brussels Jurisdiction and Judgments Convention', *ELRev* (1999), p. 540 *et seq*.

[25] Cf. Weber, *Das Internationale Zivilprozessrecht*, p. 284 *et seq*.

Such a situation appears to be likely to arise within the domain of succession disputes, where all of the heirs appear as parties in one set of proceedings, whereas, subject to the relevant domestic law provisions which may so permit, the estate of the deceased appears in the other. This is unless it appears that, again subject to the applicable law, each of the heirs which are parties to the first action, would not be subject to the effects of the judgment to be delivered in respect of that action beyond the limits of their own share in the succession.[26] Inevitably, the establishment of an autonomous notion of identical parties for the purposes of the ESR is limited in a number of respects, namely, concerning entitlement to appear as a party to an action and the extent and limits within which each of the heirs and other persons having an interest in a succession may be subject to the effects of judgments delivered in respect of the succession itself, which fall to be governed by the *lex successionis*. It must, at least, be considered that such a law is to be determined, as among the Member States subject to the ESR, in accordance with the same conflict of laws rules, something which will, to some extent, ease the establishment of the requirement concerned [see art. 23].[27] A further scenario where a substantial identity of the parties to two sets of proceedings may be found despite their formal non-coincidence, might arise where the heirs are parties to one set of proceedings, whereas an administrator of the succession is a party to the other.[28] Obviously, in this case, the assessment to be performed for the purposes of establishing whether the parties are identical may prove more complex, since it appears likely to involve issues pertaining to the powers and entitlements of administrators of the succession, in respect of which the special conflict of laws rules under article 29 ESR envisage a careful balancing between the *lex successionis* and the *lex fori* in case the two should not coincide [see art. 29].

14. A further issue to be considered is the applicability of the requirement concerning the identity of the parties in relation to non-contentious proceedings, where the mere use of the term 'parties' is inappropriate. In fact, as already noted with regard to other provisions of the ESR posing similar problems of adaptation [see art. 14 no. 9], such proceedings are

[26] Cf. Weber, *Das Internationale Zivilprozessrecht*, p. 290 *et seq.*

[27] Cf. Bonomi, 'Article 17', p. 261 *et seq.*, pointing to article 23 ESR, under which the *lex successionis* regulates, among other matters, the determination of the beneficiaries and of other succession rights (paragraph 2(b)), as well as the powers of the heirs, executors of the wills and administrators of the estate (paragraph 2(f)), with the exception of cases provided for under article 29, paragraphs 2 and 3.

[28] Cf. Weber, *Das Internationale Zivilprozessrecht*, p. 293.

normally commenced by means of a unilateral application by one or more subjects, having an interest to obtain some form of declaration, who do not necessarily become a party to such proceedings, subject to the format which non-contentious proceedings take under domestic procedural law. In this respect, it must be noted that, in the field under discussion, procedural law aspects are closely intertwined with substantive ones, so that a *Gleichlauf* or correspondence between *forum* and *ius* appears to be particularly important.[29] It is probably also the case, here, that the substantive interpretation of the requirement concerning the identity of the parties adopted by the ECJ in respect of contentious proceedings would provide a solution. This is in the sense that it would lead to the requirement of identical parties having been met in respect of non-contentious proceedings brought in different Member States, whenever the declaratory relief sought would have effects for the same people, irrespective of their formally having been parties to the relevant proceedings.[30]

15. More complex might be a finding of subjectively identical parties between contentious and non-contentious proceedings, from the perspective of the structural differences between the two types of proceedings. In fact, since the presence of contentious proceedings before the courts of a Member State presupposes the existence of a dispute between the parties, it appears unlikely that all of the parties to such proceedings may at the same time be parties, even in the merely substantial terms specified above, to non-contentious proceedings in another Member State. This is because such proceedings by definition presuppose the absence of any dispute among the subjects concerned, at least in respect of the issue forming the subject of the declaratory relief sought. At the same time, it must be considered that a judgment to be delivered in contentious proceedings pending in one Member State, could have an impact on the contents of a declaration to be made by a court in non-contentious proceedings introduced in another Member State, even if the parties are not – or not entirely – the same. This is reflected in the peculiar context of the procedure introduced by the ESR for the issuing of a European Certificate of Succession, whereby the applicant is

[29] Cf. Dutta, 'Art. 17 EuErbVO', para. 3 *et seq.*

[30] Cf. ECJ, case C-351/96, *Druot assurances*, para. 19; also in favour of the adoption of a similar solution in respect of the case under discussion, Álvarez Torné, *La autoridad competente*, p. 189 *et seq.*; Dutta, 'Art. 17 EuErbVO', para. 4; D. Lübke, *Das neue europäische Internationale Nachlassverfahrensrecht* (Baden-Baden, 2013), p. 455 *et seq.*; Weber, *Das Internationale Zivilprozessrecht*, p. 269 *et seq.*

requested to specify in the relevant application that, to the best of his or her knowledge, no dispute is pending concerning the facts to be certified [see art. 65], and, accordingly, the authority competent for issuing the certificate shall not issue it if the facts to be certified are disputed or if the certificate would be contrary to a judgment concerning the same facts [see art. 67].[31] It is probably the case, considering the low likelihood of a full coincidence in terms of the parties and the cause of action between contentious and non-contentious proceedings pending in different Member States with regard to the same succession, that such cases are more likely to be dealt with under article 18 ESR concerning related actions. This grants a broader discretion to the court seised second in assessing the risk of irreconcilable results being reached in the concurrent proceedings [see art. 18 nos. 4–5].[32]

C. *Temporal Priority*

16. The operation of the rule on *lis pendens* as contained in the ESR is based upon the traditional logic of temporal priority, whereby it is for the court first seised to continue with the case whereas the court seised second is obliged to either suspend or, subject to the further requirements contemplated by the rule, decline jurisdiction in favour of the court first seised. In consideration of the relevance of this issue also in respect of other provisions of the ESR, the rules for determining the moment at which a court is to be deemed as being seised are set out separately under article 14 ESR [see art. 14 no. 2].

IV. Effects Deriving from the Application of the Rule

17. The rule on *lis pendens* contained in article 17 ESR also appears to closely follow the Brussels I model with regard to the effects deriving from its application for the court seised second.[33] The mechanism set out under the rule is, in fact, identical to that introduced initially under article 21 of the 1988 Lugano Convention and then replicated in the 1989 San Sebastian Convention, providing for the accession of Spain and Portugal to the 1968 Brussels Convention, which amended the existing article 21

[31] Cf. Weber, *Das Internationale Zivilprozessrecht*, p. 270 *et seq.*

[32] Cf. Lübke, *Das neue europäische Internationale Nachlassverfahrensrecht*, p. 457.

[33] For an overview of the effects deriving from the application of the rule on *lis pendens* under the Brussels I regulation we refer to Marongiu Buonaiuti, '*Lis alibi pendens* and Related Actions', p. 521 *et seq.*

of the latter convention in order to bring it in line with the more updated regime contemplated under the Lugano Convention.[34] The earlier system, which had been contemplated under the 1968 Brussels Convention, provided for a duty upon the court seised second to decline jurisdiction unless the jurisdiction of the court first seised was challenged.[35] By contrast, the current solution, which appears to be in the same terms in all the rules on *lis pendens* contained in the various EU instruments concerning jurisdiction up to the ESR, provides, under paragraph 1, for a duty upon the court seised second to stay its proceedings of its own motion until such time as the court first seised has established that it has jurisdiction. Once the court first seised has established its jurisdiction, the court seised second is obliged to decline jurisdiction in favour of that court. The *rationale* for such a two-step mechanism lies in preventing the plaintiff who sued before the court seised second from having to recommence proceedings afresh in the event that the court first seised finds that it has no jurisdiction. Such a scenario would carry an inherent risk of the possibility of recommencing proceedings being barred by the elapsing of limitation periods or by the possible preclusive effects produced under the *lex fori* by an earlier decision to decline jurisdiction in respect of the same case.[36]

18. At first sight, it might appear regrettable that the rule as contained under article 17 ESR, does not reflect the same specifications of the Brussels I *lis pendens* rules as have been introduced under EU regulation no. 1215/2012 (s. c. 'Brussels I-*bis*'), in particular concerning those cases where the court seised second is vested with exclusive jurisdiction pursuant to a choice-of-court agreement.[37] In this respect, the rule under article 31.2 Brussels I-*bis* regulation, provides for a duty upon any court seised other than that or those designated under a choice-of-court agreement, to stay its proceedings when the designated court is seised

[34] Cf. Marongiu Buonaiuti, *Litispendenza e connessione internazionale*, p. 110 *et seq.*

[35] Cf., for some critiques of the earlier, less cautious formulation of the rule, as contained in the original version of article 21 of the 1968 Brussels Convention, S. M. Carbone, 'Il regime della litispendenza nelle convenzioni dell'Aja e di Bruxelles', in *L'efficacia delle sentenze straniere nelle convenzioni multilaterali dell'Aja e della C.E.E.* (Padova, 1969), p. 107 *et seq.*; G. A. L. Droz, *Compétence judiciaire et effets des jugements dans le marché commun (Etude de la Convention de Bruxelles du 27 septembre 1968)* (Paris, 1972), p. 188 *et seq.*; P. Gothot and D. Holleaux, *La convention de Bruxelles du 27.9.1968, Compétence judiciaire et effets des jugements dans la CEE* (Paris, 1985), p. 123 *et seq.*

[36] Cf., for an extensive discussion of this issue, Marongiu Buonaiuti, *Litispendenza e connessione internazionale*, p. 515 *et seq.*

[37] Cf. Gaudemet-Tallon, 'Les règles de compétence judiciaire', p. 137 *et seq.*

and until such time as the latter finds that it has no jurisdiction under the agreement.[38] The rule as devised in the Brussels I-*bis* regulation, has been specifically designed to resolve the problem revealed by the ECJ judgment in the well-known *Gasser* case, whereby a court in a Member State, which had been designated in a choice-of-court agreement, had to stay its proceedings, until such time as the court seised first in a different Member State decided upon the validity and on the applicability of the choice-of-court agreement in respect of the dispute.[39] Nonetheless, it must be considered that, within the context of the ESR, the problem in question is specifically resolved in general terms under article 6(b), which, irrespective of the designated court having been seised or not, places a general duty upon any other court seised to decline jurisdiction, based on a choice-of-court agreement under article 5 ESR. The essential difference between the two regimes lies in the identification of the court competent to decide upon the validity and applicability of the agreement. In fact, whereas in terms of the rule introduced under the Brussels I-*bis* regulation, it will be for the designated court, provided it is seised, to rule upon the validity and applicability of the agreement, under the ESR it will be for the court seised under the general rules to do so, in order to decide upon whether it must actually decline jurisdiction under the rule [see art. 6 no. 1].

V. Absence of a Rule Addressing Cases Where Parallel Proceedings Are Pending before a Third Country Court

19. A further and more substantial lack of coordination between the ESR and the Brussels I-*bis* regulation lies in the absence within the former of any rule concerning situations of *lis pendens*, or of related actions,

[38] Cf. article 31.2 regulation no. 1215/2012; among others, Gaudemet-Tallon and Kessedjian, 'La refonte du règlement Bruxelles I', p. 446 *et seq.*; Leandro, 'Prime osservazioni sul regolamento', p. 597 *et seq.*; Marongiu Buonaiuti, 'Per una prima lettura del regolamento «Bruxelles I-*bis*»', no. 1; Nuyts, 'La refonte du règlement Bruxelles I', p. 50 *et seq.*; Salerno, *Giurisdizione ed efficacia delle decisioni straniere*, p. 272 *et seq.*

[39] ECJ, case C-116/02, *Erich Gasser GmbH.* v. *MISAT S.r.l.* [2003] ECR I-14693, paras 41 *et seq.*; cf., for critical comments, T. C. Hartley, 'Choice-of-court Agreements, lis pendens, Human Rights and the Realities of International Business: Reflections on the *Gasser* Case', in *Le droit international privé: esprit et méthodes, Mélanges en l'honneur de Paul Lagarde* (Paris, 2005), p. 383 *et seq.*, esp. p. 387 *et seq.*; L. Merrett, 'The Enforcement of Jurisdiction Agreements Within the Brussels Regime', *ICLQ* (2006), p. 315 *et seq.*; R. Fentiman, 'Parallel Proceedings and Jurisdiction Agreements in Europe', in P. de Vareilles-Sommières (ed), *Forum Shopping in the European Judicial Area* (Oxford – Portland, Or. 2007), p. 27 *et seq.*, esp. p. 31 *et seq.*

arising between a Member State court and a court sitting in a third country, as included, by contrast, under EU regulation no. 1215/2012.[40] The absence of any rule in this respect within the ESR is particularly regrettable, since, due to the obvious inapplicability of the rules on jurisdiction contained in the ESR with regard to third country courts, the likelihood of parallel proceedings being commenced before a Member State court and a third country court is actually stronger, in respect of successions simultaneously presenting connections with Member States and third countries, than in respect of concurrent proceedings as among Member States only. This is due to the already underlined peculiarities of the system of allocation of jurisdiction under the ESR, which tends to exclude the co-existence of parallel grounds of jurisdiction as among different Member States' courts.[41] Within the ESR, the problem of coordination with third country courts is actually addressed, albeit in an incomplete manner and from a purely unilateral perspective, under article 12. This provision grants Member States' courts the power to refrain from ruling upon assets belonging to the estate of the deceased which are located in a third country, whenever the judgment to be delivered would risk being denied recognition in respect of those assets in the third country concerned [ref: art. 12 no. 1].

20. The absence of any rule within the ESR concerning *lis pendens* and related actions pending before third country courts does not preclude the possibility for Member States' courts to apply domestic rules providing for *lis pendens* or, less frequently, for related actions pending before foreign courts.[42] In fact, notwithstanding the doubts which had been raised in respect of the Brussels I system after the well-known ECJ judgment in the *Owusu* case concerning the compatibility with that system of the resort by Member States' courts to domestic rules for the purposes of declining jurisdiction in favour of a third country court[43], it appears sufficiently clear that the negative attitude adopted by the ECJ in

[40] Cf., respectively, articles 33 and 34 regulation no. 1215/2012; Marongiu Buonaiuti, '*Lis alibi pendens* and Related Actions in the Relationships with the Courts of Third Countries', p. 91 *et seq.*; P. Franzina, '*Lis Pendens* Involving a Third Country Under the Brussels I-*bis* Regulation: An Overview', *Riv dir int priv proc* (2014), p. 23 *et seq.*; Salerno, *Giurisdizione ed efficacia delle decisioni straniere*, p. 284 *et seq.*

[41] Cf. Gaudemet-Tallon, 'Les règles de compétence judiciaire', p. 139.

[42] Cf. Bonomi, 'Article 17', p. 259 *et seq.*; Davì and Zanobetti, *Il nuovo diritto internazionale privato europeo delle successioni*, p. 214 *et seq.*

[43] ECJ, case C-281/02, *Andrew Owusu* v. *N. B. Jackson, trading as 'Villa Holidays Bal-Inn Villas' and Others* [2005] ECR 2005 I-1383, para. 37 *et seq.*; cf., among others, B. Audit and G. A. Bermann, 'The Application of Private International Norms to "Third Countries":

that case specifically concerned the common law doctrine of *forum non conveniens*, due, essentially, to the broadly discretionary nature of such a doctrine. As such, the position taken by the ECJ in that case would not justify preventing Member States' courts from relying upon domestic provisions based upon the same logic as those contained within the ESR for the purposes of achieving – on a broader scale – the same objectives of coordination and prevention of the handing down of contradictory judgments which are pursued, as among Member States, by the corresponding rules contained in the ESR.[44]

The Jurisdiction and Judgments Example', in A. Nuyts and N. Watté (eds), *International Civil Litigation in Europe and Relations With Third States* (Bruxelles, 2005), p. 55 *et seq.*, esp. p. 78 *et seq.*; R. Fentiman, 'National Law and the European Jurisdiction Regime', *ibid.*, p. 83 *et seq.*, esp. p. 101 *et seq.*; Th. Kruger, *Civil Jurisdiction Rules of the EU and Their Impact on Third States* (Oxford, 2008), p. 265 *et seq.*; P. de Vareilles-Sommières, 'The Mandatory Nature of article 2 of the Brussels Convention and Derogation from the Rule It Lays Down', in P. de Vareilles-Sommières (ed), *Forum Shopping in the European Judicial Area* (Oxford; Portland, OR, 2007), p. 101 *et seq.*

[44] Cf. Bonomi, 'Article 17', p. 259; for an analogous solution concerning disputes subject to the pre-existing Brussels I regulation, Marongiu Buonaiuti, '*Lis alibi pendens* and Related Actions in the Relationships with the Courts of Third Countries', p. 104 *et seq.*

Article 18

Related Actions

FABRIZIO MARONGIU BUONAIUTI

1. Where related actions are pending in the courts of different Member States, any court other than the court first seised may stay its proceedings.
2. Where those actions are pending at first instance, any court other than the court first seised may also, on the application of one of the parties, decline jurisdiction if the court first seised has jurisdiction over the actions in question and its law permits the consolidation thereof.
3. For the purposes of this Article, actions are deemed to be related where they are so closely connected that it is expedient to hear and determine them together to avoid the risk of irreconcilable decisions resulting from separate proceedings.

Summary

I. RATIONALE FOR THE RULE WITHIN THE SYSTEM OF THE ESR AND COMPARISON WITH ANALOGOUS PROVISIONS CONTAINED IN OTHER EU REGULATIONS *page* 269
II. REQUIREMENTS FOR THE APPLICATION OF THE RULE 271
A. Autonomous Definition of Related Actions and Relationships with Cases of *lis pendens* 271
B. Temporal Priority 273
C. Additional Requirements for a Decision to Decline Jurisdiction under Paragraph 2 of the Rule 273
III. EFFECTS DERIVING FROM THE APPLICATION OF THE RULE 275
IV. ABSENCE OF A RULE ADDRESSING CASES WHERE RELATED ACTIONS ARE PENDING BEFORE A THIRD COUNTRY COURT 277
V. THE SOLUTION PROPOSED IN THE PREAMBLE FOR CASES OF CONCURRENCE BETWEEN JUDICIAL AND EXTRA-JUDICIAL MEANS OF SETTLEMENT OF SUCCESSION DISPUTES 278

I. Rationale for the Rule within the System of the ESR and Comparison with Analogous Provisions Contained in Other EU Regulations

1. The model provided by regulation no. 44/2001 (s. c. 'Brussels I')[1] for resolving general problems related to the application of the rules on jurisdiction is followed closely in the ESR also for dealing with cases of related actions pending before the courts of different Member States. In fact, article 18 ESR is, in turn, identical to the corresponding provision contained in article 28 Brussels I regulation, which has already been replicated in article 13 EC regulation no. 4/2009, concerning maintenance obligations.[2] Similarly to what happened in respect of other rules also based on the Brussels I model, article 18 ESR follows the earlier formulation of the rules on related actions as contained in the Brussels I regulation, rather than the current formulation of those rules as now contained in regulation no. 1215/2012 (s. c. 'Brussels I-*bis*').[3] As will be noted later, the difference between the two formulations concerns specifically the requirements for a decision by any court other than the one first seised to decline jurisdiction under paragraph 2 of the rule.[4]

2. The rule as contained in article 18 ESR, like the corresponding provisions contained in the other EU instruments just mentioned, pursues the same objective of achieving a coordination in the exercise of jurisdiction within the European judicial area, in order to prevent a duplication and fragmentation of litigation concerning the same or related legal relationships. Such a duplication and fragmentation carries the inherent risk of contradictory or, at least, irreconcilable judgments being delivered by the courts of different Member States and of judicial resources within the states in question being used inefficiently. In terms of the objective pursued, the rules concerning related actions are aimed at complementing those addressing situations of *lis pendens*, by achieving the above-mentioned coordination in the exercise of judicial activities as

[1] Council Regulation (EC) no. 44/2001 of 22 December 2000 on jurisdiction and the recognition and enforcement of judgments in civil and commercial matters, OJ no. L 12, 16 January 2001, p. 1.

[2] Council Regulation (EC) no. 4/2009 of 18 December 2008 on jurisdiction, applicable law, recognition and enforcement of decisions and cooperation in matters relating to maintenance obligations, OJ no. L 7, 10 January 2009, p. 1.

[3] Regulation (EU) no. 1215/2012 of the European Parliament and of the Council of 12 December 2012 on jurisdiction and the recognition and enforcement of judgments in civil and commercial matters (recast), OJ no. L 351, 20 December 2012, p. 1.

[4] See no. 10.

among the courts of different Member States. This is not just in those cases where such courts are concurrently seised of the same dispute, but also in those cases where the disputes pending before the courts of different Member States, though not identical, present close ties. Such ties would, as specifically noted in the autonomous definition of related actions embodied in paragraph 3 of the rule, make it more expedient for such cases to be treated jointly before the courts of the same Member State.[5]

3. Specifically with regard to the function of the rule concerning related actions within the peculiar context of the ESR, it is worth mentioning that whereas, due to the peculiarities of the system of allocation of jurisdiction under the regulation, cases in which the courts of different Member States are likely to be concurrently seised of the same action appear rather infrequent [see art. 17 nos. 4–8], the rule set out under article 18 concerning related actions appears likely, by contrast, to have a slightly broader scope of application. The system of allocation of jurisdiction embodied in the ESR by itself, as a matter of principle, promotes the concentration of all disputes concerning the succession of a particular person before a single forum that will normally have jurisdiction in respect of the entire succession. Taking due account of this, the rule concerning related actions will, in principle, only be likely to come up for consideration in those exceptional cases, where the courts of more than one Member State would have jurisdiction in respect of different issues related to the succession. As noted already, this appears to be most likely with regard to the subsidiary ground of jurisdiction contemplated under article 10.2 ESR. This subsidiary ground, as an exception to the above mentioned principle of unity of the succession, permits that, absent the further connecting factors related to the person of the deceased as contemplated under paragraph 1 of the rule, the courts of the Member States where assets belonging to the estate of the deceased

[5] Cf., among others, with regard to the functional relationships between rules on *lis pendens* and on related actions, in general terms and with specific regard to the role of both instruments in the European judicial area, R. Geimer, *Internationales Zivilprozessrecht*, 5th ed. (Köln, 2005), p. 838 *et seq.*; F. Marongiu Buonaiuti, *Litispendenza e connessione internazionale. Strumenti di coordinamento tra giurisdizioni statali in materia civile* (Napoli, 2008), p. 55 *et seq.*, p. 365 *et seq.*; F. Marongiu Buonaiuti, '*Lis alibi pendens* and Related Actions in Civil and Commercial Matters in the European Judicial Area', *YPIL*, 11 (2009), p. 511 *et seq.*, esp. p. 525 *et seq.*; F. Salerno, *Giurisdizione ed efficacia delle decisioni straniere nel Regolamento (UE) n. 1215/2012 (rifusione)*, 4th ed. (Padova, 2015), p. 275 *et seq.*; on the definition of related actions embodied by the rule, no. 4.

are located, may exercise jurisdiction only in respect of assets which are located there [see art. 10 no. 19].[6]

II. Requirements for the Application of the Rule

A. *Autonomous Definition of Related Actions and Relationships with Cases of* lis pendens

4. In terms of the requirements for the application of the rule set out in article 18 ESR, it should be noted that the provision is built around the same autonomous definition of related actions as is present within the Brussels I regulation and was previously adopted in the 1968 Brussels Convention. According to such a definition, different actions are to be considered as being related when they have such a close connection, that it would be more expedient for them to be heard and decided jointly, in order to prevent the handing down of irreconcilable judgments as a consequence of the actions being dealt with in separate proceedings. In terms of the definition as it was formerly articulated in the Brussels Convention, the ECJ has clarified, in its case law, that the objective of avoiding the handing down of irreconcilable judgments, is intended to be construed in somewhat broader terms than just the prevention of strictly conflicting or contradictory judgments. The presence of the latter would justify the denial of recognition or enforcement of a judgment delivered in another Member State under the relevant rules as then contained in the convention and now similarly set out in the ESR.[7] In fact, as specified by

[6] Cf., among others, on the role of the rule on related actions within the specific context of the ESR, M. Álvarez Torné, *La autoridad competente en materia de sucesiones internacionales. El nuevo reglamento de la UE* (Madrid, 2013), p. 191 *et seq.*; A. Bonomi, 'Article 18', in A. Bonomi and P. Wautelet, *Le droit européen des successions. Commentaire du Règlement n° 650/2012 du 4 juillet 2012* (Bruxelles, 2013), p. 269 *et seq.*, esp. p. 270; A. Davì and A. Zanobetti, 'Il nuovo diritto internazionale privato delle successioni nell'Unione europea', *CdT* 5/2 (2013), p. 5 *et seq.*, esp. p. 124 *et seq.*; A. Davì and A. Zanobetti, *Il nuovo diritto internazionale privato europeo delle successioni* (Torino, 2014), p. 217; A. Dutta, 'Art. 18 EuErbVO', in *Münchener Kommentar zum BGB*, 6th ed. (München, 2015), para. 1 *et seq.*; H. Gaudemet-Tallon, 'Les règles de compétence judiciaire dans le règlement européen sur les successions', in G. Khairallah and M. Revillard (eds), *Droit européen des successions internationales. Le règlement du 4 juillet 2012* (Paris, 2013), p. 127 *et seq.*, esp. p. 139 *et seq.*; S. M. Weber, *Das Internationale Zivilprozessrecht erbrechtlicher Steritigkeiten* (Sipplingen, 2012), pp. 272 *et seq.*, 300 *et seq.*

[7] Cf. ECJ, case C-406/02, *Tatry (Owners of the cargo lately laden on board the ship the ship)* v. *Maciej Rataj (Owners of the ship)* [1994] ECR I-5439, at 51 *et seq.*; among others, Bonomi, 'Article 12', p. 270; Gaudemet-Tallon, 'Les règles de compétence judiciaire', p. 139 *et seq.*; D. Lübke, *Das neue europäische Internationale Nachlassverfahrensrecht*

the ECJ, the definition of related actions as then articulated in the Brussels Convention is to be interpreted in broad terms, so as to encompass all cases where there is a risk of conflicting decisions. This is the case even if the judgments resulting from separate proceedings in the different actions would not be mutually exclusive in their legal consequences and would be capable of separate enforcement.[8]

5. The clarification provided by the ECJ in its case law, in turn, reflects the distinction to be maintained between cases where two or more actions are related and cases where they are identical, as assumed, by contrast, though with a necessary degree of flexibility, by the rules on *lis pendens*. In that case, in the event that the actions are treated separately, the possibility for the ensuing judgments to coexist and be separately enforced appears to be excluded altogether [see art. 17 nos. 2–3]. Turning to the specific context of the ESR, in the previously-mentioned case where, under article 10.2 ESR, the courts of different Member States might be called to rule in respect of different assets belonging to the estate of the deceased, such actions are likely to be considered as being related. This is because the same legal issues may arise in such actions with regard to the passing on of the relevant assets. Due account must also be taken of the fact that, in principle, those issues will have to be dealt with under the same law as identified under the relevant provisions of the ESR, and may, albeit not necessarily, involve the same parties [see art. 10 nos. 17–19]. Obviously, insofar as some elements of the actions – to begin with, in the case just mentioned, the assets concerned – do not coincide, such matters could, in principle, also be treated and decided separately, without this leading to the handing down of mutually exclusive judgments. Accordingly, unlike the rule on *lis pendens*, the application of which is binding once the relevant requirements are met [see art. 17 no. 17], the application of the rule concerning related actions is left to the discretion of the court concerned.[9]

(Baden-Baden, 2013), p. 457; Marongiu Buonaiuti, *Litispendenza e connessione internazionale*, p. 374 *et seq.*; Marongiu Buonaiuti, '*Lis alibi pendens* and Related Actions', p. 525 *et seq.*

8 ECJ, case C-406/02, *Tatry*, at 53–57, distinguishing the situation from the different scenario addressed in ECJ, case 145/86, *Hoffmann* v. *Krieg* [1988] ECR 645, para 22 *et seq.*, where, with regard to the ground for denial of recognition of a judgment delivered in another contracting state as then contemplated under article 27, paragraph 3, of the 1968 Brussels Convention, the court stressed that in order to establish that two judgments are irreconcilable for the purposes of the said provision, it must be assessed whether they entail legal consequences which are mutually exclusive.

9 Cf., among others, Bonomi, 'Article 18', p. 270 *et seq.*; concerning the corresponding solution adopted under the Brussels I system, Marongiu Buonaiuti, *Litispendenza*

B. *Temporal Priority*

6. The rule concerning related actions as contained in article 18 ESR, although, as just noted, addressing a different set of circumstances than those forming the subject of the rule on *lis pendens*, also appears to nonetheless have been conceived on a very similar basis from a procedural perspective. The rule is, in fact, based in turn on the priority rule, whereby it is for the court first seised to proceed with the hearing of the action pending before it and for any other court seised with a related action, to stay its proceedings or, if the further requirements contemplated under paragraph 2 of the rule are met, to decline jurisdiction. Actually, since the actions pending before the different courts concerned are not identical and the application of the rule presupposes a discretionary evaluation of the circumstances of the case, it might be questioned whether the choice of automatically granting priority to the court first seised is appropriate. This is particularly the case from the perspective that the rule does not contemplate exceptions for cases where a different solution would be more expedient.[10]

7. In terms of the means by which temporal priority is to be established, the point at which each of the courts concerned is to be deemed as being seised of the relevant action, is to be determined, just as for the purposes of *lis pendens* [see art. 17 no. 16], pursuant to the general rule under article 14 ESR [see art. 14 no. 2].

C. *Additional Requirements for a Decision to Decline Jurisdiction under Paragraph 2 of the Rule*

8. Article 18.2 ESR introduces further requirements for the purposes of a decision by any court other than the one first seised to decline jurisdiction in favour of that court. Such a decision, unlike a decision to merely stay proceedings under paragraph 1 of the rule, may be taken only upon an application by one of the parties. These requirements clearly reflect the fact that, unlike in cases of *lis pendens*, related actions are inherently non identical, and, therefore, the action pending before the court first seised

e connessione internazionale, p. 469 *et seq.*; Marongiu Buonaiuti, '*Lis alibi pendens* and Related Actions', p. 527 *et seq.*; Salerno, *Giurisdizione ed efficacia delle decisioni straniere*, p. 278 *et seq.* More extensively on the effects deriving from the application of the rule in no. 11 *et seq.*

[10] Cf., noting that the rule as it is conceived does not grant any power of initiative to the court first seised, Bonomi, 'Article 18', p. 270; Dutta, 'Art. 18 EuErbVO', para. 1. More extensively on this point in no. 11.

may not automatically encompass within its scope the claims forming the subject of the actions pending before other courts. The rule therefore subjects the exercise of the discretion by the court intending to decline jurisdiction under the rule to the twofold requirement of the court first seised also being competent with regard to the claims forming the subject of the concurrent actions and of the law of such a court allowing the consolidation of the actions.[11]

9. The first of these requirements could actually reduce the practical application of this part of the rule within the context of the ESR, since, as noted already, the regulation's system of allocation of jurisdiction in principle aims to exclude the co-existence of multiple *fora*. Furthermore, even where such *fora* are exceptionally contemplated, such as in the afore-mentioned circumstances under article 10.2 ESR, the jurisdiction of each of the courts concerned is limited to claims possessing the relevant territorial connection with the *forum* [see art. 10 nos. 17–18]. The requirement under consideration will probably be met more easily in those – albeit exceptional – circumstances where the courts of more Member States might happen to be concurrently seised of related actions under a ground of general jurisdiction. This might occur, for example, where, at the point of death, the deceased possessed the nationality of more than one Member State, in the circumstances specified in article 10.1(a) [see art. 10 no. 13].

10. The rule set out in article 18.2 ESR provides, as a further requirement, for any court other than that first seised to decline jurisdiction in favour of the court first seised, that the actions concerned must be pending at first instance. The rule reflects the need to ensure that a decision adopted pursuant to it does not prejudice the right of the parties to the action, which is deemed to be consolidated with that pending before the court first seised, to a second degree of judgment, as could happen in the case that the latter action was pending at the appeal stage.[12] This requirement has been loosened, to a certain extent, within the Brussels I system under article 30.2 regulation no. 1215/2012, which

[11] Cf., doubting the appropriateness of the last requirement, considering that the consolidation of the two actions before the court first seised could also have been imposed by the ESR in the case that it was not contemplated under domestic law, Gaudemet-Tallon, 'Les règles de compétence judiciaire', p. 140, referring to an analogous opinion expressed in respect of the rule on related actions under article 22 of the 1968 Brussels Convention by P. Gothot and D. Holleaux, *La convention de Bruxelles du 27 septembre 1968: Compétence judiciaire et effets des jugements dans la CEE* (Paris, 1985), p. 127 *et seq.*

[12] Cf. Bonomi, 'Article 18', p. 271.

requires only that the action before the court first seised is pending at first instance. In fact, since the rule provides for a consolidation of the actions before the court first seised, the afore-mentioned risk only arises in the case that the action before such a court is pending at the appeal stage, whereas that before the other court is pending at first instance, and not in the opposite scenario.[13] Nonetheless, also in the opposite scenario, where proceedings before the court seised second were pending at the appeal stage whereas those before the court first seised were pending at first instance, a consolidation of both actions before the latter might cause the inconvenience of unreasonably prolonging the overall duration of the action which had been brought before the court seised second. It should therefore be considered appropriate that a decision to decline jurisdiction under paragraph 2 of the rule is also subject to the discretion of the court seised second, which will have to take into account the consequences deriving from such a decision for an efficient judicial protection of the parties' rights.

III. Effects Deriving from the Application of the Rule

11. Accordingly, the court seised second, even in the presence of significant connections between the actions, may consider it unnecessary or inappropriate to stay its proceedings or, upon application by one of the parties and provided the further requirements contemplated under paragraph 2 of the rule are met, to decline jurisdiction in favour of the court first seised. In practice, the rule may give rise to three different situations: in the first one, the two, or, hypothetically, more actions pending before courts of different Member States, will proceed independently, naturally leading to separate judgments. This would be on the assumption, which, as noted, is inherent in the situation of the actions being related for the purposes of the rule, that even in the case that the judgments should contain irreconcilable statements, the lack of coincidence between the object of the actions, or the parties, or both, would prevent an actual conflict from arising between the judgments in question.[14] In the second scenario, the court seised second may decide that the connections between the actions are so significant as to justify a stay of the

[13] Cf., among others, A. Leandro, 'Prime osservazioni sul regolamento (UE) n. 1215/2012 ("Bruxelles I *bis*")', *Il giusto processo civile* (2013), p. 583 *et seq.*, esp. p. 602; A. Nuyts, 'La refonte du règlement Bruxelles I', *Rev crit dr int priv* (2013), p. 1 *et seq.*, esp. p. 63; Salerno, *Giurisdizione ed efficacia delle decisioni straniere*, p. 279 *et seq.*

[14] Cf. no. 9.

proceedings. Consequently, the court seised second would be in a position to take account of the decision handed down by the court first seised in respect of the related action for the purposes of its own judgment.[15] Such a solution would appear to be particularly appropriate in those cases where the court first seised is called upon to decide on an issue which is of a preliminary nature in respect of the subject of the action pending before the court seised second. Clearly, due to the rigidity of the temporal priority mechanism underpinning the rule, a stay of the proceedings by the court seised second would be pointless in the opposite case where it was for the action pending before such a court to address a preliminary issue in respect of the claims forming the subject of the action pending before the court first seised.[16]

12. Probably of greater impact from the point of view of an efficient coordination of the exercise of jurisdiction as among Member States' courts, are the effects of a decision by the court seised second to decline jurisdiction under paragraph 2 of the rule. In fact, by contrast to the case of *lis pendens* where the concurrent actions are assumed to be identical and therefore reciprocally fungible [see art. 17 nos. 1–3, 10–15], such a decision presupposes a consolidation of both actions before the court first seised. This justifies the provision in respect of such a case of the further requirements examined previously, aimed at ensuring that such a solution is actually feasible both as concerns the jurisdiction of the court first seised and the admissibility of a consolidation of the two actions. The last requirement, just as in the corresponding Brussels I rule, is left to the domestic procedural law of the court first seised.[17] Unlike those cases where a corresponding rule, such as that currently contemplated under the Brussels I-*bis* regulation, applies in respect of actions concerning issues not yet subject to uniform conflict of laws rules adopted at EU

[15] Cf. Bonomi, 'Article 18', p. 270, pointing to the likelihood that the court first seised will deliver, within a reasonable time, a judgment likely to be recognised in the forum as an element to be taken into account by the court seised second for the purposes of a decision to stay its proceedings under the rule. For similar considerations in respect of a stay of proceedings under the corresponding rule contained in the Brussels I regulation, Marongiu Buonaiuti, *Litispendenza e connessione internazionale*, p. 479 *et seq.*, with reference to a decision by Oberlandesgericht Frankfurt a. M. 19 June 2000, *IPRax* 2001, p. 227, noted R. Geimer, 'Entscheidungsarmonie in Europa per Entscheidungsstop', p. 191 *et seq.*

[16] Cf. no. 6, concerning the rigidity of the temporal priority mechanism embodied in the rule and the appropriateness of a more flexible solution in respect of related actions than in strict *lis pendens* cases; see also Bonomi, 'Article 18', p. 270; Dutta, 'Art. 18 EuErbVO', para. 1.

[17] Cf. section II.C, and Gaudemet-Tallon, 'Les règles de compétence judiciaire', p. 140.

level, within the context of the ESR the consolidation of the related actions before the court first seised is not likely to have an impact on the law to be applied in deciding upon the action which has been brought before the court seised second. This is because both courts are subject to the same conflict of laws rules as are embodied in the ESR.[18]

IV. Absence of a Rule Addressing Cases Where Related Actions Are Pending before a Third Country Court

13. Similarly to the rule on *lis pendens* under article 17 ESR, the rule concerning related actions under article 18 ESR only makes provision for cases where related actions are pending before the courts of different Member States. Unlike the Brussels I-*bis* regulation, which contains specific provisions addressing cases of *lis pendens* and related actions pending before third country courts, with rather significant adaptations of the ordinary rules concerning the corresponding situations arising as among EU Member States only,[19] the ESR does not cover such situations. Given that the ESR is silent on the matter, with the only mechanism for attempting a coordination with third country courts being set out under article 12 ESR [see art. 12 nos. 1–3], it must be assumed that such situations will be dealt with under the corresponding domestic provisions concerning, respectively, *lis pendens* and related actions pending before foreign courts [see art. 17 no. 20].[20] In this respect, it must be

[18] Which pursues the two-fold objective of ensuring unity of the succession, both in terms of jurisdiction and applicable law, and of promoting, insofar as possibile, a *Gleichlauf, i. e.* a parallelism, between jurisdiction and applicable law: cf., among others, Davì and Zanobetti, 'Il nuovo diritto internazionale privato delle successioni', pp. 29 *et seq.*, 114 *et seq.*; Davì and Zanobetti, *Il nuovo diritto internazionale privato europeo*, pp. 44 *et seq.*, 199 *et seq.*; J. Carrascosa González, *El Reglamento Sucesorio Europeo 650/2012 de 4 de Julio 2012. Análisis crítico* (Granada, 2014), p. 78 *et seq.*; P. Franzina, 'Ragioni, valori e collocazione sistematica della disciplina internazionalprivatistica delle successioni *mortis causa*', in P. Franzina and A. Leandro (eds), *Il diritto internazionale privato europeo delle successioni* mortis causa (Milano, 2013), p. 1 *et seq.*, esp. p. 10 *et seq.*; P. Lagarde, 'Les principes de base du nouveau règlement européen sur les successions', *Rev crit dr int pr* (2012), p. 691 *et seq.*, esp. p. 694 *et seq.*

[19] Cf., respectively, articles 33 and 34 regulation no. 1215/2012; F. Marongiu Buonaiuti, '*Lis alibi pendens* and Related Actions in the Relationships with the Courts of Third Countries in the Recast of the Brussels I Regulation', *YPIL* (2013/14), p. 87 *et seq.*; P. Franzina, '*Lis Pendens* Involving a Third Country Under the Brussels I-*bis* Regulation: An Overview', *Riv dir int priv proc* (2014), p. 23 *et seq.*; Salerno, *Giurisdizione ed efficacia delle decisioni straniere*, p. 284 *et seq.*

[20] Cf. Bonomi, 'Article 18', p. 269; Davì and Zanobetti, *Il nuovo diritto internazionale privato europeo delle successioni*, p. 214 *et seq.*

noted that whereas many of the Member States provide in their domestic law for cases of *lis pendens* before a foreign court, domestic provisions in respect of related actions pending before foreign courts are comparably less frequent,[21] or may, eventually, be limited to cases where the action pending before a foreign court presents a special relationship to that pending in the forum, such as where such an action concerns a preliminary issue in respect of the action pending in the *forum*.[22]

V. The Solution Proposed in the Preamble for Cases of Concurrence between Judicial and Extra-Judicial Means of Settlement of Succession Disputes

14. To complete the examination of the provisions within the ESR which are aimed at coordinating concurrent proceedings pending in different Member States in succession matters, it is worth mentioning that a further suggestion, devoid as such of binding effect, is contained in this respect in the preamble to the ESR. The preamble supplements the text of the ESR with further indications, aimed more at integrating the content of the regulation rather than simply explaining the rationale and providing guidance on the interpretation of the various provisions contained within the regulation.[23] Recital 36, in fact, addresses those cases where subjects having an interest in a succession have commenced an action before the courts of a Member State while in another Member

[21] As an example, the Belgian code of private international law of 2004, while providing under article 14 for cases of *lis pendens* before foreign courts, under article 9 only contemplates the possibility of an extension of Belgian jurisdiction for actions which are related to those falling under the jurisdiction of Belgian courts, without addressing the circumstances where related actions are pending before foreign courts. Cf. P. Wautelet, 'Article 14. Litispendance internationale', in J. Erauw *et al.* (eds), *Het Wetboek Internationaal Privaatrecht becommentarieerd – Le Code de droit international privé commenté* (Antwerpen, Oxford, Brussels, 2006), p. 78 *et seq.*

[22] Such as, in Italy, under article 7, paragraph 3, law of 31 May 1995, no. 218, providing for the reform of the Italian system of private international law, which grants Italian courts a discretion to stay proceedings in the case where an action concerning a preliminary issue is pending before a foreign court, provided it can be expected that the foreign court will render a judgment that is likely to be recognised in the *forum*: cf., among others, C. Consolo, 'Profili della litispendenza internazionale', *Riv dir int* (1997), p. 5 *et seq.*, esp. p. 67 *et seq.*; M. A. Lupoi, *Conflitti transnazionali di giurisdizioni* (Milano, 2002), p. 853 *et seq.*; Marongiu Buonaiuti, *Litispendenza e connessione internazionale*, p. 61 *et seq.*, p. 383 *et seq.*

[23] Cf. Davì and Zanobetti, 'Il nuovo diritto internazionale privato delle successioni', p. 17, footnote 55; Davì and Zanobetti, *Il nuovo diritto internazionale privato europeo*, p. 23 *et seq.*, footnote 74.

State an extrajudicial form of settlement of the succession is being resorted to, or, alternatively, parallel extrajudicial settlements are being pursued in different Member States. In terms of these cases, the rules contained within the ESR concerning either *lis pendens* or related actions would be of no avail, since both rules apply, by definition, in respect of parallel court proceedings only. Such cases may be rather frequent, due to the fact that non-judicial bodies, such as notaries, before whom the settlements in question may be entered into – unless they are called to exercise judicial functions under article 3.2 ESR [see art. 3 nos. 18–19] – are not subject to the rules on jurisdiction contained within the regulation. Such rules, in principle, aim to exclude the possibility of courts of different Member States having concurrent jurisdiction in respect of the same succession [see art. 17 nos. 4–8]. In these cases, the preamble to the ESR suggests that it will be for the parties concerned, once they have received notice of the parallel initiatives undertaken in other Member States, to agree on how to proceed. Rather obviously, the preamble specifies that in the event that no agreement is found, it will be for the courts having jurisdiction under the regulation to rule upon the succession.[24]

[24] Cf., on the solutions proposed in the preamble to the ESR, recital 36, in respect of cases of parallel recourse to judicial and non-judicial means of settlement of succession issues, among others, Álvarez Torné, *La autoridad competente en materia de sucesiones internacionales*, p. 190; Davì and Zanobetti, 'Il nuovo diritto internazionale privato delle successioni', p. 125; Davì and Zanobetti, *Il nuovo diritto internazionale privato europeo*, p. 218; Dutta, 'Art. 17 EuErbVO', para. 6.

Article 19

Provisional, Including Protective, Measures

PASQUALINA FARINA

Application may be made to the courts of a Member State for such provisional, including protective, measures as may be available under the law of that State, even if, under this Regulation, the courts of another Member State have jurisdiction as to the substance of the matter.

Summary

I. INTRODUCTION *page* 280
II. THE RATIO BEHIND ARTICLE 19 ESR: THE ROLE OF FORUM LOCI EXECUTIONIS 282
III. THE CIRCULATION OF DECISIONS ADOPTING PROVISIONAL, INCLUDING PROTECTIVE, MEASURES AND COMPLIANCE WITH THE AUDI ALTERAM PARTEM PRINCIPLE 284
IV. THE NOTION OF 'PROVISIONAL, INCLUDING PROTECTIVE, MEASURES' IN ECJ CASE LAW 286

I. Introduction

1. Article 19 grants the courts in each Member State the power to order, in matters involving succession, 'provisional, including protective, measures' that are available pursuant to the law of that State. This includes where the courts of another Member State have jurisdiction in relation to succession proceedings pursuant to article 4 *et seq.* ESR.[1] Article 19 therefore ensures that domestic law governing interim relief in each Member State continues to operate.

[1] P. Wautelet, 'Article 19', in A. Bonomi and P. Wautelet, *Le droit européen des successions. Commentaire du Règlement n° 650/2012 du 4 juillet 2012* (Bruxelles, 2013), p. 273; A. Davì and A. Zanobetti, 'Il nuovo diritto internazionale privato delle successioni nell'Unione Europea', *CdT* 5/2 (2013), p. 122 *et seq.*; A. Davì and A. Zanobetti, *Il nuovo diritto internazionale privato europeo delle successioni* (Torino, 2014), p. 213 *et seq.*

2. Article 19 reproduces article 31 of regulation (EC) no. 44/2001 on jurisdiction and the recognition and enforcement of judgments in civil and commercial matters (s. c. Brussels I regulation). Given the extent to which the provisions of the two regulations essentially echo one another, when interpreting the provisions of the ESR it is in fact allowed to refer to the standard practice followed in the application of the latter regulation and, in particular, to judgments by the ECJ concerning the interpretation of the corresponding provisions contained in article 31 of the said regulation as well as in article 24 of its direct antecedent, the Brussels Convention on jurisdiction and the enforcement of judgments in civil and commercial matters of 28 September 1968. This of course insofar as the standard practice and judgments just mentioned are compatible with the peculiarities of succession matters.

Article 35 of the recent regulation (EU) no. 1215/2012 on jurisdiction and the recognition and enforcement of judgments in civil and commercial matters (recast) (s. c. Brussels I-*bis* regulation), which took the place of regulation no. 44/2001 with effect from 10 January 2015, contains a provision that corresponds with article 31 of the Brussels I regulation and article 24 of the 1968 Brussels Convention. The preamble to regulation no. 1215/2012 includes a recital that is not to be found in the legislation that came before it and which states as follows: '[w]here provisional, including protective, measures are ordered by a court of a Member State not having jurisdiction as to the substance of the matter, the effect of such measures should be confined, under this Regulation, to the territory of that Member State' (recital 33). This is followed by some specifications introduced in the definition of 'judgment' under article 2(a) of the said regulation, whereby it is specified that as a judgment capable of recognition and enforcement under chapter III of the regulation only such provisional, including protective, measures may be intended as are delivered by a court having jurisdiction as to the merits and with the exclusion of measures given *inaudita altera parte*.[2] While this regulation was adopted at a point in time after adoption of the ESR and, therefore, cannot be put to direct use when interpreting ESR's article 19, it is, however, based on ECJ case law concerning the interpretation of formerly article 24 of the Brussels Convention and later article 31 of regulation no. 44/2001, as we shall see.

3. Exercise of the jurisdiction to deliver interim measures granted by article 19 ESR is optional, leaving open the possibility of applying for

[2] Cf. F. Salerno, *Giurisdizione ed efficacia delle decisioni straniere nel Regolamento (UE) n. 1215/2012 (rifusione)*, 4th ed. (Padova, 2015), p. 293 *et seq.*

such measures to the courts having jurisdiction as to the merits of the case.[3] Jurisdiction pursuant to article 19 may be invoked independently from other grounds of jurisdiction[4] and clearly does not extend to the actual substance of the dispute, which the courts in the country identified on the basis of article 4 *et seq.* ESR are left to deal with.[5]

II. The *ratio* behind Article 19 ESR: The Role of *forum loci executionis*

4. The purpose of the additional *forum* established by article 19 ESR, which, as we have seen, co-exists with the *forum* vested with jurisdiction to hear the substance of the case pursuant to article 4 *et seq.* ESR, is to ensure that an effective protection of the rights forming the subject of a dispute is afforded by the courts.

A considerable number of Member States have legal systems in which orders providing for protective or preventive measures come under the jurisdiction of the courts in the country where the order applied for is to be enforced. The fact that the courts in the territorial country have jurisdiction to order interim relief means that the *exequatur* stage can be avoided, with the result that matters can be dealt with swiftly: where interim relief is concerned, time is, or course, of the essence.[6]

[3] In relation to the corresponding article 31 of regulation 44/2001 and article 24 of the Brussels Convention of 1968, see L. Pålsson, 'Interim Relief under the Brussels and Lugano Conventions', in *Private Law in the International Arena – Liber amicorum Kurt Siehr* (The Hague, 2000), p. 623, which defines the jurisdiction established by these provisions as 'additional'; M. Pertegás Sender, 'Article 31', in U. Magnus and P. Mankowski (eds), *Brussels I Regulation* (München, 2007), p. 524; H. Gaudemet-Tallon, *Compétence et exécution des jugements en Europe*, 4th ed. (Paris, 2010), p. 318 *et seq.*

[4] See S. M. Carbone, *Lo spazio giudiziario europeo in materia civile e commerciale*, 6th ed. (Torino, 2009), p. 190; according to L. Mari, *Il diritto processuale civile della Convenzione di Bruxelles* (Padova, 1999), p. 714, the ECJ has defined orders of this nature as "*essentially independent*", with the result that an order only comes under the umbrella of the jurisdiction to hear an application for interim relief established by article 31 of the Brussels I regulation and article 24 of the Brussels Convention where it satisfies a two-part test: (i) it must meet the requirements imposed by the procedural system in the court hearing the application for the order and (ii) it must meet the requirements imposed by the provision as established by case law emanating from the ECJ. See, on the same lines, L. Sandrini, *Tutela cautelare in funzione di giudizi esteri* (Padova, 2012), p. 135.

[5] Gaudemet-Tallon, *Compétence et exécution*, p. 320.

[6] E. Merlin, 'Le misure provvisorie e cautelari nello spazio giudiziario europeo: criteri di giurisdizione e limiti alla circolazione', in *Le discipline comunitarie relative al processo civile* (Milano, 2002), p. 241 *et seq.*

5. The role played by *forum loci executionis* in terms of interim relief has been highlighted by the ECJ in its judgment on a preliminary ruling in the 1980 *Denilauler* case in relation to article 24 of the 1968 Brussels Convention,[7] where the ECJ stated that the courts of the Member State where the assets subject to the measures sought are located 'are those best able to assess the circumstances which may lead to the grant or refusal of the measures sought' as well as 'to the laying down of procedures and conditions which the plaintiff must observe in order to guarantee the provisional and protective character of the measures ordered'[8]. In two subsequent decisions (the *Van Uden*[9] case in 1998 and the *Mietz*[10] case in 1999), the ECJ took the opportunity to repeat that this is the main *raison d'être* of this ground of jurisdiction. It would, therefore, seem reasonable to conclude that the courts in a Member State can only order interim relief where the measures in question have to be enforced within their own territory. This point, however, is open to debate.[11] The first argument to be raised in this respect is that there is no evidence of this specific requirement in the wording of the provision in question. In addition, the territorial principle may prove inadequate where the measures applied for concern assets the location of which cannot be identified straightforwardly (such as Internet assets),[12] or where the ruling is to be enforced in part in the Member State in which it was issued and in part abroad. Guidance is provided here by some statements made by the ECJ in its judgment in the *Van Uden* case.[13] In relation

[7] ECJ, case C-125/79, *Denilauler* v. *Couchet Frères* [1980] ECR I-1553. [8] *Ibid.*, para 16.

[9] ECJ, case C-391/95, *Van Uden Maritime BV* v. *Deco-Line* [1998] ECR I-7091.

[10] ECJ, case C-99/96, *Mietz* v. *Intership Yachting Sneek BV* [1999] ECR I-2277. Of the vast amount of commentary to be found on the *Van Uden and Mietz* judgments, see: C. Consolo, '*Van Uden* e *Mietz*: un'evitabile Babele', *Int'l Lis* (2002), p. 30 *et seq.*; T. Hartley, 'Interim Measures Under the Brussels Jurisdiction and Judgments Convention', *ELR* (1999), p. 674 *et seq.*; J. Kropholler, *Europäisches Zivilprozeßrecht*, 6th ed. (Heidelberg, 1998), p. 311 *et seq.*; A. Marmisse and M. Wilderspin, 'Le régime jurisprudentiel des mesures provisoires à la lumière des arrêts *Van Uden* et *Mietz*', *Rev crit dr int priv* (1999), p. 669 *et seq.*; Pålsson, 'Interim Relief', p. 621 *et seq.*

[11] See C. Consolo, 'La tutela sommaria e la convenzione di Bruxelles: la "circolazione" cautelare dei provvedimenti cautelari e dei decreti ingiuntivi', *Riv dir int priv proc* (1991), p. 593 *et seq.; id.*, 'Van Uden e Mietz', pp. 31–32; Pertegás Sender, 'Article 31', p. 533; Sandrini, *Tutela cautelare in funzione di giudizi esteri*, p. 324 *et seq.*

[12] For an example of an order for interim relief regarding a domain name situated abroad, see Salerno, *Giurisdizione ed efficacia delle decisioni straniere nel regolamento (UE) n. 1215/2012*, p. 301 *et seq.*, where the view is expressed that the territorial link is represented by the headquarters of the provider, even though the court hearing the application for interim relief is unable to 'contain the effects of its decision within the borders of the territory under its jurisdiction'.

[13] See footnote 9.

to the actual nature of provisional and protective measures, the ECJ stated that exercise of jurisdiction to hear an application for interim relief by the courts of a Member State which lack jurisdiction to hear the substance of the dispute 'is conditional on, *inter alia*, the existence of a real connecting link between the subject-matter of the measures sought and the territorial jurisdiction of the Contracting State of the court before which those measures are sought'. While the 'real' connecting factor referred to by the ECJ is easy to identify where the measures in questions are to be enforced in the country in which the relevant order is issued,[14] issuing an order that is to be enforced abroad is a step that should, instead, be approached with caution. In fact, there is a balance to be struck between (i) the principles of equivalence of the courts in the Member States and the mutual trust on their part[15] and (ii) the need to avoid interference with the jurisdiction of the courts designated by the relevant provisions of EU legislation as competent in respect of the substance of the case. As concerns jurisdiction on the merits, where succession matters are concerned reference is to be made exclusively to the jurisdiction rules under chapter II ESR, which, as we have seen, lean towards identifying the courts of one Member State only as having jurisdiction as to the substance of the case [see art. 4 *et seq*].[16]

III. The Circulation of Decisions Adopting Provisional, Including Protective, Measures and Compliance with the *audi alteram partem* Principle

6. A decision on an application for interim relief taken by the courts in a Member State claiming jurisdiction on the basis of article 19 ESR can

[14] See Davì and Zanobetti, 'Il nuovo diritto internazionale privato delle successioni', p. 122 *et seq.*; Davì and Zanobetti, *Il nuovo diritto internazionale privato europeo*, p. 213 and, in relation to article 31 of regulation no. 44/2001 and article 24 of the Brussels Convention of 1968, Pertegás Sender, 'Article 31', p. 533.

[15] See P. Girerd, 'Les principes d'équivalence et d'effectivité: encadrement ou désencadrement de l'autonomie procédurale des États membres', *Revue trimestrielle de droit européen* (2002), p. 75; Gaudemet-Tallon, *Compétence et exécution*, p. 319 *et seq.*

[16] To be added here is that fact that, as mentioned earlier at no. 2, regulation no. 1215/2012, which replaced regulation no. 44/2001, now states, under article 2(a), that an order for interim relief adopted by a court that lacks jurisdiction as to the substance of the matter, as further underlined at recital 33, 'should be confined, under this Regulation, to the territory of that Member State'. While this statement cannot of course be used directly when tackling the interpretation of article 19 ESR, there can be no doubt that it was included by the EU legislator in order to restrict the cross-border effects of orders made by courts with jurisdiction to hear the application for interim relief alone, in line with case law from the ECJ as cited.

produce effect in other Member States where the requirements to be met for the purposes of recognition and enforcement pursuant to article 40 *et seq.* ESR are satisfied [see art. 40 *et seq*].

The ECJ has stated that in order for a decision of this type to be recognised and enforced in another Member State, the principle that both parties should be heard must have been complied with, so that orders given *inaudita altera parte* – as is frequently the case where interim relief is concerned, given that the application for interim measures is usually made as a matter of urgency – are not, therefore, entitled to recognition. Of particular interest here is the *Denilauler* case, where, in relation to the Brussels Convention of 1968, the ECJ established that the list of conditions to be satisfied in order for a foreign decision to be recognised includes compliance with the principle that both parties should be heard and that such a requirement is not likely to be satisfied by orders 'which, under the national law of a contracting State, are intended to be delivered in the absence of the party against whom they are directed and to be enforced without prior service on him'.[17]

This statement must surely apply also in succession matters. Where provisional or protective measures granted *inaudita altera parte* are concerned, the provisions of the ESR in respect of recognition and enforcement do not, therefore, apply. As fundamental principles of the EU judicial area, respect for the right to a defence and for the principle that both parties should be heard (in advance) mean that, also in matters of succession, recognition and enforcement shall only be granted in respect of preventive and protective measures that have been ordered or authorised once the party potentially subject to such measures has been summoned to appear.[18]

In order for measures providing for interim relief to be delivered and implemented with the speed they call for, and in order to preserve the related element of surprise that is a particular feature of such measures, the application for such measures should preferably be made to a court in the *forum loci executionis.*[19]

[17] ECJ, case 120/79, *Denilauler*, in footnote 7, para. 8.

[18] Where this particular aspect is concerned, here too, on similar lines to what we saw in footnote 16, regulation no. 1215/2012, which replaced regulation no. 44/2001, now contains, under article 2(a), a statement to the effect the interim relief ordered without the other party being heard, as further clarified at recital 33, 'should not be recognised and enforced under this Regulation unless the judgment containing the measure is served on the defendant prior to enforcement'.

[19] Davì and Zanobetti, 'Il nuovo diritto internazionale privato delle successioni', p. 122; Davì and Zanobetti, *Il nuovo diritto internazionale privato europeo*, p. 213.

IV. The Notion of 'Provisional, Including Protective Measures' in ECJ Case Law

7. In line with article 24 of the convention and article 31 of regulation no. 44/2001, article 19 ESR refrains from listing the orders that the requested court based on the special *forum* established by the rule may give, having adopted instead the technique of simply referring to the domestic law of such a court, in a field where the domestic laws of the Member States vary quite sensibly.[20] Consequently, for the purposes of delineating the category of orders that satisfy the 'preventive and protective' requirement, we are called upon once again to work on the basis of the case law from the ECJ. Within that case law, while the initial interpretation provided by the ECJ simply pointed to interim relief measures as falling within the category of ancillary measures, based on their similarity to decisions given in relation to the substance of the matter,[21] the ECJ subsequently stated that the rule as then contained in article 24 of the 1968 Brussels Convention only refers to measures that are necessary for the purposes of the decision to be given on the substance of the case by the court having jurisdiction in its respect. Accordingly, in its 2005 judgment in the *St. Paul Dairy Industries* case, the ECJ excluded from the category here concerned orders providing for the gathering of evidence to be used in future proceedings regarding the substance of the matter.[22] The most important decision on this point was, however, handed down in 1992 in the *Reichert II* case, where the ECJ expressed the view that the notion of provisional and protective measures as embodied in article 24 of the Brussels Convention refers to measures which 'are intended to preserve a factual or legal situation so as to safeguard rights the recognition of which is sought elsewhere from the court having jurisdiction as to the substance of the matter'. The ECJ therefore concluded that the *actio pauliana* contemplated under French law, which results in a debtor's property being affected irreversibly, does not fall within the scope of article 24 of the convention.[23] Accordingly,

[20] For a comparative analysis, see G. Cuniberti, *Les mesures conservatoires portant sur des biens situés à l'étranger* (Paris, 2000), p. 57 *et seq.*; Sandrini, *Tutela cautelare*, p. 35 *et seq.*

[21] ECJ, case C-120/79, *De Cavel* v. *De Cavel* [1992] ECR 731, para 7.

[22] ECJ, case C-104/03, *St. Paul Dairy Industries NV* v. *Unibel Exser BVBA* [2005] ECR I-3481.

[23] ECJ, case C-261/90, *Mario Reichert* v. *Dresdner Bank AG* [1992] ECR I-2149, paras 34–35; the court in fact held that the *actio pauliana* under French law involves 'the court [being able to] vary the legal situation of the assets of the debtor and that of the beneficiary by ordering the revocation as against the creditor of the disposition effected by the debtor in

the conclusion can be reached that measures of an anticipatory nature and having the effect of irreversibly modifying the legal situation of the debtor's assets – with one example here being, of course, the *actio pauliana* just mentioned – fall outside the scope of application of the special *forum* established by the rule under examination.

8. In the subsequent *Van Uden* judgment the ECJ stated that where, in order to ensure the practical effect of the decision on the substance of the case, measures are requested which require steps to be taken in advance of such a decision, such as payment in the interim of sums due pursuant to a contract (as in the *Van Uden* case), such measures do not qualify as protective measures 'unless . . . repayment to the defendant of the sum awarded is guaranteed if the plaintiff is unsuccessful as regards the substance of his claim'.[24] The ECJ reaffirmed its decision less than a year later in the *Mietz* judgment.[25] The posting of a bond or similar security by the applicant in order to guarantee repayment in fact points to the provisional measure as not likely to close the dispute, since the successful applicant for interim relief is under a duty to commence proceedings before the court having jurisdiction as to the substance of the case. The ECJ's intention was to counter attempts to elude the jurisdictional criteria established by the European legislator[26] and prevent the transfer of the dispute on the merits to *fora* other than the courts with jurisdiction to hear the substance of the matter.

Where succession matters are concerned, the correct application of the principles set out by the ECJ should, therefore, lead to the view that the posting of a bond or other security by an applicant for interim relief is not necessary (save where expressly required by domestic procedural rules) for the granting of the measures applied for pursuant to article 19 ESR, where those measures are mainly intended for the purposes of preservation of a legal or factual situation. This is the case where assets that form part of the estate are sealed up or seised or where a receiver is appointed in order to prevent losses, or the increase of losses already incurred, in relation to those assets (with regard, e.g., to the need to sell perishable

fraud of the creditor's rights'; see on this point Gaudemet-Tallon, *Compétence et exécution*, p. 320 *et seq.*; Pertegás Sander, 'Article 31', p. 532.

[24] ECJ, case C-391/95, *Van Uden*, in footnote 9, paras 41, 47. For comments on this judgment see footnote 10.

[25] ECJ, case C-99/96, *Mietz*, in footnote 9.

[26] Gaudemet-Tallon, *Compétence et exécution*, p. 330; J. F. Van Drooghenbroeck, 'Les compétences internationale et territoriale du juge du provisoire (Les mesures provisoires et le litige européen)', in J. van Campernolle and G. Tarzia (eds), *Les mesures provisoires en droit belge, français et italien* (Bruxelles, 1998), p. 485.

assets as quickly as possible). The posting of a bond or similar security should, however, be considered necessary whenever the protective measures applied for are also sought in advance of the final judgment or as a means of resolving the dispute altogether, despite being called for in order to ensure the practical effect of the decision on the substance of the case. In contrast, as noted already,[27] orders that have the effect of permanently modifying the debtor's assets are excluded from the scope of application of the additional *forum* established by the rule under examination.

[27] In no. 7.

CHAPTER III

Applicable Law

Article 20

Universal Application

ALFONSO-LUIS CALVO CARAVACA

Any law specified by this Regulation shall be applied whether or not it is the law of a Member State.

Summary

I. THE ESR AS AN ERGA OMNES LEGAL INSTRUMENT *page* 291
II. ESR APPLICABILITY TO SUCCESSIONS OUTSIDE OF THE EUROPEAN UNION 293
A. Uniform Conflict-of-Laws Rules 293
B. Universal Conflict-of-Laws Rules 295

I. The ESR as an *erga omnes* Legal Instrument

1. The ESR bears a universal character, i.e. it applies *erga omnes*;[1] this 'universal application', as defined in the heading of its article 20, has multiple meanings.

1) The ESR applies regardless of the nationality of the deceased, heirs or legatees, of the habitual residence of the heirs or legatees, or of any other circumstances that may affect the succession, such as the place where the assets are located or were the will was drawn up, or should be executed, etc. In other words, the ESR conflict-of-laws rules are not subject to any reciprocity: they apply, regardless of the personal or territorial

[1] See, in general, A. Bonomi, 'Article 20', in A. Bonomi and P. Wautelet (eds), *Le droit européen des successions. Commentaire du Règlement n° 650/2012 du 4 juillet 2012* (Bruxelles, 2013), pp. 279–281; J. Carrascosa González, *El Reglamento Sucesorio Europeo 650/2012 de 4 de julio 2012: Análisis crítico* (Granada, 2014), pp. 10–12, 49; E. Castellanos Ruiz, 'Sucesión hereditaria: Reglamento 650/2012 sobre sucesión internacional', in A.-L. Calvo Caravaca and J. Carrascosa González (eds), *Derecho Internacional Privado*, 15th ed., vol. II (Granada, 2014), pp. 534–537; M. Stürner, 'Deutsch-italienische Erbfälle unter der kommenden Europäischen Erbrechtsverordnung', *Jahrbuch für Italienisches Recht* 26 (2013), p. 73.

connections of the situation to be regulated, so long as the *ratione materiae* and *ratione temporis* conditions required by the ESR are met.[2]

2) The ESR likewise applies regardless of the law designated by its conflict-of-laws rules: accordingly, the ESR applies even if the law governing the succession is the law of a non-Member State, hence the reason why the ESR is an *erga omnes* legal instrument, one of 'universal application'.

2. As a result of this universal application, in the case of a succession that falls within the scope of the ESR, the private international law rules of the participating Member States shall not apply. For example, in the case of Spain, this means that the conflict-of-laws rules contained in article 9.8 of the Spanish civil code shall be 'inapplicable' because replaced by the ESR. This is due to the combination of the ESR's universal application and its primacy over the national law of Member States. As has been highlighted by the ECJ – and confirmed by several constitutional courts of the Member States – European law prevails over the national law of the Member States.[3]

3. However, the national conflict-of-laws rules of the Member States still apply in the following few cases:

1) In the case of internal or regional conflict of laws relating to successions that may not necessarily be covered by the ESR (*strictly domestic conflicts of laws on succession*): These national rules have not been derogated and are still in effect, enabling them to be applied to cases not covered by the ESR. Thus in Spain, for example, some *Comunidades autónomas* have their own succession law. The basic principle brought about by the ESR is that it does not apply to the successions giving rise to interregional conflict-of-laws problems [see arts. 36–38 no. 21]. Nonetheless, a Member State may decide to unilaterally apply the ESR also to its domestic 'interregional' conflicts of laws. With regards to Spain, given that it has never made any indication on this matter, the general principle applies and consequently, the law applicable to a succession in case of an interregional conflict-of-laws has to be determined in accordance with national

[2] O. Feraci, 'La nuova disciplina europea della competenza giurisdizionale in materia di successioni *mortis causa*', *CdT* 5/2 (2013), p. 296.

[3] See ECJ, case 6/64, *Costa* v. *ENEL* [1964] ECR 1141; ECJ, case 43/71, *Politi S.A.S.* v. *Ministry for Finance of the Italian Republic* [1971] ECR 1039; ECJ, case 48/71, *Commission* v. *Italy* [1972] ECR 529; ECJ, case C-106/77, *Amministrazione delle Finanze dello Stato* v. *Simmenthal SpA* [1978] ECR 629.

(Spanish) rules, i.e. article 9.8 of the Spanish civil code in relation with article 16 thereof.

2) Whenever the law governing the succession pursuant to the ESR is the law of a State which comprises more than one legal system, each of which has its own substantive rules in matter of succession applicable in different territorial units or to different categories of persons (*the 'ad extra' or 'ad intra' referrals to countries comprising more than one legal system)*: The general principle established in this regards by the ESR is the cumulative and successive applicability of the conflict rules of the ESR and the State conflict rules provided for regulating these internal or interlocal conflicts of laws [see arts. 36–38].
3) In the event of successions of persons who died before 17 August 2015: The ESR does not apply to such successions (but see the transitional rules in article 83 ESR [see art. 83]) and thus, the national conflict-of-laws rules shall continue to apply.

4. Lastly, conflict rules contained in international conventions adopted prior to the enactment of the ESR to which one or more of the Member States are parties can, in certain circumstances, continue to apply [see art. 75].[4]

II. The Application of the ESR to 'Non-EU' Successions

A. Uniform Conflict-of-Laws Rules

5. The EU has legislative competence to enact conflict-of-laws rules that regulate all international successions.[5] Several opinions were

[4] G. Hohloch, 'Kommentierung der EuErbRVO', in Erman, *BGB: Kommentar*, 14th ed. (Köln, 2014), pp. 6692–6693.

[5] On the *iter legis* adopted for conferring to the EU the competence to unify private international law in general, and in particular for drawing up the ESR, see Carrascosa González, *El Reglamento Sucesorio Europeo*, pp. 12–20; A. Davì and A. Zanobetti, 'Il nuovo diritto internazionale privato delle successioni nell'Unione Europea', *CdT* 5/2 (2013), pp. 14–15; A. Davì and A. Zanobetti, *Il nuovo diritto internazionale privato europeo delle successioni* (Torino, 2014), pp. 18–20; H. Dörner, C. Hertel, P. Lagarde and W. Riering, 'Auf dem Weg zu einem Europäischen Internationalen Erb- und Erbverfahrensrecht', *IPRax* (2005), p. 1; M. Greeske, *Die Kollisionsnormen der neuen EU-Erbrechtsverordnung* (Frankfurt am Main, 2014), pp. 4–6, 9–23; C. Herweg, *Die Vereinheitlichung des Internationalen Erbrechts im Europäischen Binnenmarkt* (Baden-Baden, 2004), pp. 154, 156, 183–188, 201, 208–212, 214–216, 219, 221–222, 232; A. Junghardt, *Die Vereinheitlichung des Erb- und Testamentrechts im Rahmen einer europäischen Verordnung – Rom IV-VO* (Regensburg, 2009), pp. 24–27, 38, 44, 51; P. Kindler, 'Vom Staatsangehörigkeits- zum Domizilprinzip: das künftige internationale Erbrecht der Europäischen Union', *IPRax* (2010), p. 48; C. Kohler and W. Pintens, 'Ehe

expressed for justifying the universal nature of the EU conflict-of-laws rules, in particular with reference to regulations no. 593/2008 on the law applicable to contractual obligations (Rome I) (article 2) and no. 864/2007 on the law applicable to non-contractual obligations (Rome II) (article 3) opinions which continue to be valid *mutatis mutandis*.

6. The EU holds legislative competence as established in articles 67.1, 67.4 and 81.2(c) TFEU, also recalled in recital 2 ESR. This competence must be exercised by way of *uniform conflict rules* because, as the majority of authors have pointed out, given the importance of the succession matter in the EU, an adequate legal framework is required to reach certain *objectives*: to attain an authentic area of freedom, security and justice, as well as to reinforce the security of inheritance planning by individuals (see recitals 1, 7 and 80 ESR).[6] As *the end does not justify the means*, said rules must meet the requirements of judicial cooperation in civil matters with cross-border implications (article 81.1 TFEU), especially when it is necessary for the proper functioning of the internal market (article 81.2 TFEU), and respect the principles of conferral (article 5.2 TEU), subsidiarity (article 5.3 TEU) and proportionality (article 5.4 TEU).

7. The existence of uniform conflict rules eliminates, or, at the very least, reduces the probability of *forum shopping*, given that any of the EU Member States' courts having jurisdiction on the matter shall apply the ESR and, thus, the same domestic succession law (= *international harmony of solutions).*[7] Accordingly, *forum shopping*, even in the few cases in

und Familien im europäischen Recht – Entwicklung und Tendenzen', *FamRZ* (2007), p. 1484; H.-P. Mansel, 'Vereinheitlichung des Internationalen Erbrechts in der Europäischen Gemeinschaft – Kompetenzfragen und Regelungsgrundsätze', in S. Arkan, A. Yongalik and B. Sit (eds), *Prof. Dr. Tuğrul Ansay'a armağan* (Ankara, 2006), pp. 191–197; K. Schilling, *Binnenmarktkollisionsrecht* (Berlin, 2006), pp. 8–9, 33–36, 39–41, 415–416; M. Stürner, 'Deutsch-italienische Erbfälle', p. 60–61; R. Süß, 'Der Vorschlag der EG-Kommission zu einer Erbrechtsverordnung (Rom IV-Verordnung) vom 14. Oktober 2009', *ZErb – Zeitschrift für die Steuer- und Erbrechtspraxis* (2009), p. 342.

[6] See the meticulous and exhaustive analysis of the purposes of the ESR in Carrascosa González, *El Reglamento Sucesorio Europeo*, pp. 18–20, and Davì and Zanobetti, 'Il nuovo diritto internazionale privato', pp. 14, 27, 29–30, 36, 55, 61–62, 79–80, 97–98, 101, 110, 118, 122–124, 128, 135; Davì and Zanobetti, *Il nuovo diritto internazionale privato europeo*, pp. 18–20, 42–43, 53–55, 84–86, 95–97, 125–128, 130–136, 154–165, 168–171.

[7] See Dörner, Hertel, Lagarde and Riering, 'Auf dem Weg', p. 2; Greeske, *Die Kollisionsnormen der neuen EU-Erbrechtsverordnung*, pp. 16–17; Herweg, *Die Vereinheitlichung des Internationalen Erbrechts*, p. 218; M. Meyer, *Die Gerichtsstände der Erbrechtsverordnung unter besonderer Berücksichtigung des Forum Shopping* (Frankfurt am Main, 2013); Schilling, *Binnenmarktkollisionsrecht*, pp. 34–35.

which it is possible according to the ESR's rules on jurisdiction, is to expected to occur marginally and decrease because of financial (litigation costs), procedural (rules of evidence, interim orders, periods of limitation, structure or duration of the process, assessment of damages, enforceability of the decision) or factual reasons.[8]

B. *Universal Conflict Rules*

8. That being said, it is one thing for the European legislator to have, as we have just seen, legislative competence to establish uniform conflict rules, but it is quite a different thing for such conflict rules to be applied to any international succession, regardless of its connections to the EU (*universell geltende Kollisionsnormen*). It amounts to opting for one of two possible legislative policies: a restrictive one, which considers that article 81 TFEU requires that the issue to be regulated has an effective connection with at least two Member States (*binnenmarktinterne Sachverhalten*), or an expansive one, according to which the conflict rules contained in the ESR would also be applicable to successions relating to only one Member State and one or more non-member States (*reine Drittstaatenkonstellationen*).[9]

9. There are three reasons that support the European legislator in the adoption of *universal conflict-of-rules*:

1) It may be often difficult to distinguish between 'non-European' and 'truly European' cases.[10]
2) It would be cumbersome to follow the previous route: the European legislator should enact different rules for the different groups of cases, and it would prove quite difficult for the courts and authorities of

[8] M. Kähr, *Der Kampf um den Gerichtsstand – Forum Shopping im internationalen Verfahrensrecht der Schweiz* (Zürich, St. Gallen, 2010), pp. 37–48.

[9] See Greeske, *Die Kollisionsnormen*, pp. 23–30; Junghardt, *Die Vereinheitlichung des Erb- und Testamentrechts*, p. 27; Mansel, 'Vereinheitlichung des Internationalen Erbrechts', pp. 195–197; T. Rauscher, 'Heimatlos in Europa? – Gedanken gegen eine Aufgabe des Staatsangehörigkeitsprinzips im IPR', in *Festschrift für Erik Jayme*, vol. I (München, 2004), p. 725; F. Wilke, 'Das internationale Erbrecht nach der neuen EU-Erbrechtsverodrnung', *RIW* (2012), p. 608. *Contra*, see Herweg, *Die Vereinheitlichung des Internationalen Erbrechts*, p. 232.

[10] See H. Dörner, 'Das Grünbuch "Erb- und Testamentsrecht" der Europäischen Kommission', *ZEV* (2005), p. 137; *id.*, 'Der Entwurf einer europäischen Verordnung zum Internationalen Erb- und Erbverfahrensrecht – Überblick und ausgewählte Probleme', *ZEV* (2010), p. 222; Mansel, 'Vereinheitlichung des Internationalen Erbrechts', p. 197.

Member States to decide which set of rules have to be applied in each pertinent situation.[11]

3) Even in the latter case, a legal loophole could still be considered: What conflict rule should apply to 'mixed' successions, that is, those successions connected to Member States bound by the ESR *and* to Member States that have opted out of the ESR (United Kingdom, Ireland and Denmark), or to *non*-Member States?

10. The broad perspective adopted by the European legislator, which accepts that the ESR must apply to all international successions brought before Member States' authorities, radically solves the described problem: It offers an *integral* or *complete conflict of laws solution* (*eine kollisionsrechtliche Totallösung*).[12] This perspective is grounded on the idea that all successions originating claims submitted to the courts of the Member States do impact on the proper functioning of the internal market. Furthermore, it is an interpretation that is even more sustainable under the current article 81 TFEU, given that, differently from its predecessor (i.e. article 65 EC Treaty), its text includes the expression 'particularly' (article 81.2): 'the European Parliament and the Council, acting in accordance with the ordinary legislative procedure, shall adopt measures, *particularly* when necessary for the proper functioning of the internal market'. This equates to a recognition that the EU institutions can adopt not only measures affecting the functioning of the internal market, but also measures that do *not* affect it.

11. For the previously-mentioned reasons, the ESR employs *universal conflict rules* to determine the law applicable to any international succession submitted to the Member States' authorities.[13]

12. Last but not least, the potential *legislative imperialism* of the EU is less real than what it appears, because in order to apply the ESR conflict rules, the courts of the Member States must have jurisdiction. This requires a sufficient connection between the lawsuit and the Member

[11] H. Gaudemet-Tallon, 'Quelques réflexions sur les propositions concernant la compétence judiciaire, la reconnaissance et l'exécution des décisions en matière successorale dans l'Union européenne', in Deutsches Notarinstitut (ed), *Les Successions Internationales dans l'Union Européenne – Perspectives pour une harmonisation* (Würzburg, 2004), p. 446, 447.

[12] R. Geimer, 'Die europäische Erbrechtsverordnung im Überblick', in J. Hager (ed), *Die neue europäische Erbrechtsverordnung. Tagungsband* (Baden-Baden, 2013), p. 19.

[13] See, in general, on the distinction between bilateral or multilateral conflict of laws rules and unilateral rules, A.-L. Calvo Caravaca and J. Carrascosa González, *Derecho Internacional Privado*, 15th ed., vol. I (Granada, 2014), pp. 349–357, 371–372, 384.

State: the habitual residence of the deceased in that Member State [see art. 4], his nationality together with a *professio juris* and other conditions [see arts. 5, 6 and 7], the presence of the estate assets in the territory of that State [see art. 10], that are all grounds of international jurisdiction showing a real and sufficient connection between the matter under litigation and the EU.[14] Even the *forum necessitatis* established by article 11 ESR requires the presence of a *sufficient connection* between the case and the country of the court seised.

[14] Geimer, 'Die europäische Erbrechtsverordnung', pp. 19–20; in general, H.-P. Mansel, 'Das Staatsangehörigkeitsprinzip im deutschen und gemeinschaftlichen IPR: Schutz der kuturellen Identität oder Diskriminierung der Person?', in E. Jayme (ed), *Kulturelle Identität und internationales Privatrecht* (Heidelberg, 2003), p. 145; Carrascosa González, *El Reglamento Sucesorio Europeo*, p. 102; Davì and Zanobetti, 'Il nuovo diritto internazionale privato', pp. 119–120; Davì and Zanobetti, *Il nuovo diritto internazionale privato europeo*, pp. 208–209; G. Novelli, *Compendio di Diritto internazionale privato e processuale*, 7th ed. (Napoli, 2004), pp. 95–98.

Article 21

General Rule

ALFONSO-LUIS CALVO CARAVACA

1. Unless otherwise provided for in this Regulation, the law applicable to the succession as a whole shall be the law of the State in which the deceased had his habitual residence at the time of death.
2. Where, by way of exception, it is clear from all the circumstances of the case that, at the time of death, the deceased was manifestly more closely connected with a State other than the State whose law would be applicable under paragraph 1, the law applicable to the succession shall be the law of that other State.

Summary

I. INTRODUCTION *page* 298
II. DETERMINING THE APPLICABLE LAW: THE OBJECTIVE CRITERION 299
A. The habitual Residence of the Decedent at the Time of Death 299
1. Concept of Habitual Residence 300
2. Case Groups 308
3. Advantages and Disadvantages of the New Rules 312
B. The Exception Clause 317

I. Introduction

1. The ESR contains provisions on international jurisdiction (articles 4 to 19) and recognition of decisions (articles 39 to 58) aimed at resolving so-called conflicts of jurisdiction, as well as rules on the law applicable to international successions (articles 20 to 38), dealing with the so-called conflict of laws. It follows thus the path of regulation no. 4/2009 on jurisdiction, applicable law, recognition and enforcement of decisions and cooperation in matters relating to maintenance obligations, which also contains rules on these three issues, differently from Rome I, Rome II and Rome III regulations, which only contain rules on the establishment of the applicable law, respectively on contractual obligations, on non-contractual obligations and on divorce and legal separation.

II. Determining the Applicable Law: The Objective Connecting Factor

2. For the determination of the law governing a succession, the ESR resorts to an *objective connecting factor*, applicable in the absence of a choice of law (*professio juris*) that can be made in accordance with article 22 ESR. This objective connection, which reflects the *principle of proximity*, consists in the *last habitual residence of the deceased* as a connecting factor (article 21.1), complemented by an *exception* (or *escape*) *clause* for exceptional cases in which, given all of the circumstances of the case at hand, it may be inferred that 'at the time of death, the deceased was manifestly more closely connected' with a different State, whose law will then be applicable (article 21.2).[1]

A. *The Habitual Residence of the Deceased at the Time of Death*

3. Article 21.1 ESR subjects successions to the law of the country of the habitual residence of the deceased at the time of death. Consequently, it established an *objective connecting factor* so that the legal framework thus put in place has three characteristics:

1) It formulates the *principle of unity and universality of the succession.* According to this principle, the law governing the succession applies

[1] See, in general, A. Bonomi, 'Article 21', in A. Bonomi and P. Wautelet (eds), *Le droit européen des successions. Commentaire du Règlement nº 650/2012 du 4 juillet 2012* (Bruxelles, 2013), pp. 283–296; J. Carrascosa González, *El Reglamento Sucesorio Europeo 650/2012 de 4 de julio 2012: Análisis crítico* (Granada, 2014), pp. 148–165; E. Castellanos Ruiz, 'Sucesión hereditaria: Reglamento 650/2012 sobre sucesión internacional', in A.-L. Calvo Caravaca and J. Carrascosa González (eds), *Derecho Internacional Privado*, 15th ed., vol. II (Granada, 2014), pp. 554–557, 576–580; A. Davì and A. Zanobetti, 'Il nuovo diritto internazionale privato delle successioni nell'Unione Europea', *CdT* 5/2 (2013), pp. 29–37; A. Davì and A. Zanobetti, *Il nuovo diritto internazionale privato europeo delle successioni* (Torino, 2014), pp. 42–55; M. Greeske, *Die Kollisionsnormen der neuen EU-Erbrechtsverordnung* (Frankfurt am Main, 2014), pp. 31–98; G. Hohloch, 'Kommentierung der EuErbRVO', in Erman, *BGB: Kommentar*, 14th ed. (Köln, 2014), pp. 6693–6695; B. Walther, *Der Gleichlaufgrundsatz – Abkehr oder Rückkehr? Eine kritische Auseinandersetzung mit der Bestimmung der internationalen Zuständigkeit im Erbscheinsverfahren aus deutscher und europäischer Sicht* (Frankfurt am Main, 2013), pp. 183–191.

to all of the assets, regardless of the country in which they are located or their classification as movable or immovable property. This produces a *revolutionary change* for countries such as France, which have traditionally followed the *principle of plurality and territoriality of the succession (principle of scission)*, according to which movable and immovable property are distinguished.

2) The *lex successionis* is determined according to the *habitual residence of the deceased* at the time of death. The choice of this connecting factor does not only encompass the choice between the *systems of unity and universality of the succession* – which usually adopt as a connection the nationality of the deceased – *and of plurality and territoriality of the succession*, but represents a sort of *tertium genus*: the habitual residence as an objective criterion. It thus confirms the 'inexorable ascent' of the notion of habitual residence already embraced by important EU regulations on conflict of laws, such as the Rome I regulation (articles 4.1, 5.1 and 5.2, 6.1, 7.2), the Rome II regulation (articles 4.2, 5.1, 10.2, 11.2) and the so-called Rome III regulation (article 8(a) and (b)).[2]
3) Furthermore, the *conflit mobile* that could result from a change in the habitual residence of the person whose succession is concerned is avoided, because for the determination of the applicable law, only the last habitual residence or, in the words of the ESR, the deceased's habitual residence 'at the time of death'.

1. Concept of *Habitual Residence*

4. Having established the habitual residence of the deceased as an objective connecting factor in matters of succession, it is necessary to ascertain *what exactly is the notion of habitual residence* used by the ESR: if it matches the notion of domicile, if the ESR offers a definition or if, at any rate, it does provide criteria which enable the domicile of the deceased to be determined. It is an issue that has given rise to great debate in political and scientific forums and which, essentially, may be refocused on the following ideas:

[2] D. Lehmann, *Die Reform des Internationalen Erb- und Erbprozessrechts im Rahmen der geplanten Brüssel-IV Verordnung* (Angelbachtal, 2006), p. 91; F. Wilke, 'Das internationale Erbrecht nach der neuen EU-Erbrechtsverordnung', *RIW* (2012), pp. 601–609, 604. The last habitual residence of the deceased is a connecting factor adopted – albeit with a different scope – also by the Hague Convention of 1 August 1989 on the Law Applicable to Succession to the Estates of Deceased Persons: see P. Lagarde, 'La nouvelle Convention de La Haye sur la loi applicable aux successions', *Rev crit dr int priv* (1989), pp. 249–275.

1) It is now the most frequently used connecting factor for personal issues – those that in the past were grouped under the concept of *personal status*. Firstly adopted by the Hague Guardianship Convention of 1902, it did not become firmly established until after the Second World War, when *nationality* as a connecting factor began to give way to the connection of *habitual residence* in the Hague Conference on Private International Law conventions, almost as a notion of domicile adapted to the needs of international life.[3]
2) However, if the introduction in these conventions of the habitual residence as a connecting factor struck a blow through the heart of nationality, thus marking the end of its hegemony first in international conventions on private international law and, later, in domestic private international law, it is no less certain that the wide acceptance of *habitual residence* as a connecting factor also entails the rejection of the notion of *domicile* adopted by English private international law – a notion so rigid that its legal regime more closely resembles that applicable to nationality than to the concept of domicile in continental European countries.[4]
3) The private international law regulations drafted by the EU have also accepted habitual residence as a connecting factor.
4) It may appear nonsensical that no definition of *habitual residence* exists in the multilateral conventions of the Hague Conference on Private International Law, or even in the EU private international law regulations. It is unsurprising, then, for one to ask *what is the difficulty* in defining the concept of *habitual residence* or to enquire *if the notion is the same* in the various international legal sources or, at least, in the EU's regulations on private international law.
5) When a legal solution appears to be lacking in logic, it usually has an *historical explanation*. This is the case for the notion of habitual residence. Thus, for example, in the Hague Guardianship Convention of 1902, it was considered inappropriate to refer to the domicile of a minor and, in its place, it was deemed better to resort to the habitual residence. The fact that it referred to *residence* excluded

[3] See Carrascosa González, *El Reglamento Sucesorio Europeo*, p. 83; D. F. Cavers, '"Habitual Residence": A Useful Concept?', *The American University Law Review* 21 (1972), p. 475–493 (also in *id., The Choice of Law, Selected Essays 1933–1983* [Durham, 1985], pp. 244–262).

[4] P. B. Carter, 'Domicile: The Case for Radical Reform in the United Kingdom', *ICLQ* (1987), pp. 713–728; D. Henrich, 'Der Domizilbegriff im englischen Internationalen Privatrecht', *RabelsZ* (1960), pp. 456–495.

the Anglo-Saxon notion of *domicile*, whilst the addition of the adjective *habitual* prevented confusion with mere residence. In short, as has been observed by some authors, the notion of habitual residence has an historical explanation as a factual criterion, to be verified on a case-by-case basis, avoiding the rigidity associated with the legal definitions of the concept of domicile in internal legal systems.[5]

6) With regard to EU regulations, the lack of a definition is not a legal loophole resulting from legislative oversight, but is rather the desired result: one is master to his silence and slave to his words. If *habitual residence* had been defined in any European regulation on private international law, this concept would have been constricted and probably automatically compared to the concept expressed in other regulations, although governing very different matters, thus producing in some cases unsatisfactory results.
7) In relation to the ESR, the lack in its provisions of an express definition of the notion of habitual residence is to be underlined. The European legislator's attitude in this respect has been praised by those who consider that any attempt at a definition would have been incomplete, as it would not possibly include the multitude of variable cases that could exist in practice, and, at most, would feature gaps and raise difficulties of interpretation capable to undermine legal certainty.[6] The absence of a legal definition of *habitual residence* in the ESR is, however, mitigated by three of its recitals (23, 24 and 25), which provide helpful hermeneutic criteria.

5. These recitals could have fitted in perfectly with the articles of the ESR. As we have seen, none of the ESR provisions defines the notion of *habitual residence*; the recitals do, however, convey several important ideas to this effect:

1) *Habitual residence* is more than the mere stay in the territory of a State. It is a *close and stable connection with a State* that requires for its determination an overall assessment on the specific circumstances of the case in question, in particular, the fact of the presence in the State, its status, regularity and duration until the moment of the death of the person whose succession is concerned, in addition to the reasons of the latter's presence in that State: "In order to

[5] Davì and Zanobetti, 'Il nuovo diritto internazionale privato delle successioni', p. 32; Davì and Zanobetti, *Il nuovo diritto internazionale privato europeo*, p. 48.

[6] Davì and Zanobetti, 'Il nuovo diritto internazionale privato delle successioni', pp. 32–33; Davì and Zanobetti, *Il nuovo diritto internazionale privato europeo*, pp. 47–49.

determine the habitual residence, the authority dealing with the succession should make an overall assessment of the circumstances of the life of the deceased during the years preceding his death and at the time of his death, taking account of all relevant factual elements, in particular the duration and regularity of the deceased's presence in the State concerned and the conditions and reasons for that presence. The habitual residence thus determined should reveal a close and stable connection with the State concerned taking into account the specific aims of this Regulation" (recital 23, *in fine*). The identification of the habitual residence of the deceased entails establishing a person's centre of life, taking into account the main location of his or her personal, family, professional and financial interests.[7] It is thus a notion very close to that of 'domicile' as utilised by French case law prior to the ESR when ascertaining the law governing succession of movable property: the notion of 'habitual residence' of the ESR, similarly to the French notion, is based on the concurrence of a *material or objective* element, i.e. the effective physical presence of the person for a certain period of time in the territory of a State (*domus colere*) and a *psychological or subjective element*, i.e. the will of the person to establish the centre of his or her interests in a specific place (*animus manendi*).[8]

Consequently, the ESR adopts an *overall, weighted, casuistic concept* of the notion of *habitual residence.*

As regards the *overall* concept, a range of indications needs to be verified. 'All relevant factual elements' are to be considered, generally amongst personal and professional criteria.[9] *Personal criteria* valued positively in this regard would include the presence of the deceased's family members, the rental or purchase of a house, schooling of

[7] Davì and Zanobetti, 'Il nuovo diritto internazionale privato delle successioni', p. 33; Davì and Zanobetti, *Il nuovo diritto internazionale privato europeo*, p. 48.

[8] See Carrascosa González, *El Reglamento Sucesorio Europeo*, pp. 84–91; Castellanos Ruiz, 'Sucesión hereditaria', p. 555; Greeske, *Die Kollisionsnormen*, pp. 51–53, 58–59, 61–63; P. Mayer and V. Heuzé, *Droit international privé*, pp. 593–594. Accordingly, the concept of 'habitual residence' should be intended as similar to the notion of 'domicile' of the French private international law concerning succession in moveable property before the ESR (see P. Mayer and V. Heuzé, *Droit international privé*, 11th ed. (Issy-les-Moulineaux, 2014), p. 609).

[9] See D. Baetge, 'Auf dem Weg zu einem gemeinsamen europäischen Verständnis des gewöhnlichen Aufenthalts – Ein Beitrag zur Europäisierung des Internationalen Privat- und Verfahrensrechts', in D. Baetge, J. V. Hein and M. v. Hinden (eds), *Die richtige Ordnung: Festschrift für Jan Kropholler zum 70. Geburtstag* (Tübingen, 2008), p. 81.

children, and the existence of administrative ties with the authorities of the State of residence.[10] All these factors 'express the intention of that person to confer a certain stability on the place of connection, by reason of the continuity arising from a way of life and the development of normal social and occupational relationships'.[11] Likewise, fluency in the language of the country, the existence of a network of friends and local acquaintances and participation as an active member of an association are considered as evidence of integration into the host State.[12] *Professional criteria* are also quite varied: the practice of professional activities, the rental of business premises to work on a self-employed basis, working in a company, attending professional training or university courses, the establishment of companies, the opening of a bank account in the host State, etc. *Example:* A special case is that of persons who live in a Member State during the last few years of their life, but in "closed national circles" without integrating into the country's society. This is the typical case of many English nationals who live on Greek or Spanish seaside resorts and do not mix with locals from the area, and also of many German retirees who live most of the year in Majorca. What is the State of their habitual residence? Some authors believe that the answer to this question is the host State: the persons in question *do* mix, albeit only amongst themselves, and are integrated in their own way.[13] Conversely, others consider that their State of habitual residence is the State of origin, so long as they regularly return there and live in an almost exclusively German (or English) environment, which proves that there is no integration within the State of sojourn.[14]

As regards the *weighted* concept, the importance of each element is to be assessed; in other words, the concurrence of two or more

[10] See Greeske, *Die Kollisionsnormen*, pp. 56–57.

[11] ECJ, case C-262/99, *Paraskevas Louloudakis* v. *Elliniko Dimosio* [2001] ECR I-5573, para. 55, commented by M. Cittadini, 'L'orientamento della Corte di Giustizia in materia di residenza a fini fiscali', *Giur it* (2002), pp. 869–872; T. Sanna, 'Steuerbefreiung bei der vorübergehenden Einfuhr von Kraftfahrzeugen aufgrund gewöhnlichen Wohnsitzes im Ausland', *European Law Reporter* (2001), pp. 369–372; M.G. Valente, 'Recenti pronunciamenti in tema di residenza fiscale delle persone fisiche', *Diritto e pratica tributaria* (2001), pp. 847–857.

[12] See Carrascosa González, *El Reglamento Sucesorio Europeo*, pp. 90–91; Greeske, *Die Kollisionsnormen*, p. 57.

[13] See Carrascosa González, *El Reglamento Sucesorio Europeo*, pp. 93–94.

[14] See Greeske, *Die Kollisionsnormen*, p. 57; R. Süß, 'Der Vorschlag der EG-Kommission zu einer Erbrechtsverordnung (Rom IV-Verordnung) vom 14. Oktober 2009', *ZErb – Zeitschrift für die Steuer- und Erbrechtspraxis* (2009), p. 344.

indicators does not automatically entail that the mere presence in a State equates to habitual residence.

Lastly, habitual residence it is a *casuistic* concept, given that the elements to be considered will always need to be analysed meticulously on a case-by-case basis, and such analysis cannot be replaced by vague references to *general categories* (e.g. the succession of an English citizen having a home in London and a second home in Marbella) or *presumptions* (e.g. the idea that at least five years must have passed for residence in a State to be considered the 'habitual' residence).

From the structure of the concept of habitual residence, several *practical consequences* may be drawn. First, although the ESR has no specific rule applicable to *infants*, it may be held that their habitual residence is that of the State in which their parents habitually reside. This accordingly leaves open the possibility that they may be born in one State and have their habitual residence in another – even in a country in which they might have never set foot.[15] Second, in the event of a person imprisoned or detained in a psychiatric facility in a given State, the wilful element lacks and, consequently, for the purposes of the ESR there is no habitual residence in that State, unless it existed before the internment.[16] Third, the term 'habitual' should not be understood as the opposite of 'unusual' or 'extraordinary', but rather in the sense that the deceased resided 'ordinarily', 'usually' or 'generally' (*in der Regel*) in a given country.[17] This permits to differentiate an 'habitual residence' from a 'mere residence' or from a 'brief stay'[18], that require only the effective physical presence in a location, for example for the attendance, for one or two months, of a foreign language summer course.[19] A decisive indicator for the residence in a State to be considered "habitual" is *time*: the more

15 See Greeske, *Die Kollisionsnormen*, p. 51; J. Kropholler *Internationales Privatrecht einschließlich der Grundbegriffe des Internationalen Privatrechts*, 6th ed. (Tübingen, 2006), p. 284. *Contra*, Carrascosa González, *El Reglamento Sucesorio Europeo*, p. 85. On this problem, which is sometimes linked to the issue of whether a person can acquire an habitual residence through the representation of another person, Greeske, *Die Kollisionsnormen*, pp. 64–66.

16 See Greeske, *Die Kollisionsnormen*, p. 52.

17 See Greeske, *Die Kollisionsnormen*, pp. 52–53; Kropholler, *Internationales Privatrecht*, p. 284.

18 See D. Baetge, *Der gewöhnliche Aufenthalt im Internationalen Privatrecht* (Tübingen, 1994), p. 120; *id.*, 'Auf dem Weg', pp. 81–82; Greeske, *Die Kollisionsnormen*, p. 53.

19 Carrascosa González, *El Reglamento Sucesorio Europeo*, pp. 85–86; Walther, *Der Gleichlaufgrundsatz*, p. 29.

time that passes between the start of the continued presence of an individual in the territory of a specific State, the more likely it is that the person will be considered as having habitual residence in that State.[20] The ESR, however, has not established a precise period of time beyond which the residence becomes habitual.[21] Comparative law shows diverse time periods, ranging from three months to seven years.[22] Accordingly, an agreement on this issue during the drafting of the ESR was not to be expected.[23]

2) The *ratio legis*, i.e. the justification for the ESR legislator's preference for the adoption of *habitual residence* as a connecting factor, is the desire 'to ensure that a genuine connecting factor exists between the succession and the Member State in which jurisdiction is exercised', so long as the determined habitual residence reveals 'a close and stable connection' (recital 23), which is an expression that may appear at first sight enigmatic, but underlines the need for the deceased's social life centre to be effectively located in that State.

3) The fact that, pursuant to recital 23, the habitual residence should present 'a close and stable connection' of the deceased with a given country, is a requirement that poses a problem: which law applies when the deceased habitually resided in a State, whilst maintaining a *close and stable connection* with another State? The ESR is very precise in this respect. First, it avoids ambiguity: it is one thing for the *centre of gravity* of the relationship in question to be located in a State other than that of the habitual residence (*displaced centre of gravity*), and it is quite a different thing for the *centre of gravity* of the relationship to be located in the State of the deceased's habitual residence, but the problem consist in establishing where the habitual residence was actually located (*undetermined centre of gravity*). Recital 24 ESR refers to this second hypothesis when it reminds that '[i]n certain cases, determining the deceased's habitual residence may prove complex'. Having said that, the recital then sets forth three possible problematic cases: that of the deceased that had a centre of family and

20 See Baetge, *Der gewöhnliche Aufenthalt*, pp. 108–113; *id.*, 'Auf dem Weg', p. 81; Greeske, *Die Kollisionsnormen*, p. 58. On the question of whether 'the immediate establishment of a habitual residence' is possible (*sofortige Begründung des gewöhnlichen Aufenthals*), see Baetge, 'Auf dem Weg', pp. 84–85; Greeske, *Die Kollisionsnormen*, pp. 66–71; Kropholler, *Internationales Privatrecht*, p. 284.

21 Kropholler, *Internationales Privatrecht*, p. 279.

22 Baetge, *Der gewöhnliche Aufenthalt*, p. 109; Kropholler, *Internationales Privatrecht*, p. 279; Greeske, *Die Kollisionsnormen*, pp. 58–59.

23 Greeske, *Die Kollisionsnormen*, p. 59.

a professional life in different States, that of the deceased that had habitual residence in two or more States simultaneously and, finally, that of the deceased that had no habitual residence in any State:

> Such a case may arise, in particular, where the deceased for professional or economic reasons had gone to live abroad to work there, sometimes for a long time, but had maintained a close and stable connection with his State of origin. In such a case, the deceased could, depending on the circumstances of the case, be considered still to have his habitual residence in his State of origin in which the centre of interests of his family and his social life was located. Other complex cases may arise where the deceased lived in several States alternately or travelled from one State to another without settling permanently in any of them. If the deceased was a national of one of those States or had all his main assets in one of those States, his nationality or the location of those assets could be a special factor in the overall assessment of all the factual circumstances [recital 24].

Second, the ESR provides a solution for the event that, once the deceased's habitual residence has been determined, there is in effect a closer and more stable connection with another State (*displaced centre of gravity*): the exception clause (article 21.2 ESR).

4) In order to determine the habitual residence of a deceased, the following 'specific objectives' of the ESR should be considered: to ensure the correct administration of justice in the EU; to facilitate the proper functioning of the internal market, removing the obstacles to free movement of persons who face difficulties in asserting their rights in the context of a succession having cross-border implications; to ensure in the European area of justice that citizens can organise their succession; and to guarantee effectively the rights of heirs and legatees of other persons close to the deceased, as well as of creditors of the succession (recitals 7 and 23, *in fine*).[24]
5) Last but not least, determining the State of the last habitual residence of the deceased does not depend on factors such as whether it is *legal* or *illegal*, whether it matches the *tax residency* or not, or if the person is registered in the *local electoral register*.[25] This is why 'habitual residence' is classified as a 'factual domicile' (*faktischer Wohnsitz*).[26]

[24] See Castellanos Ruiz, 'Sucesión hereditaria', p. 555.

[25] See Baetge, *Der gewöhnliche Aufenthalt*, pp. 118–119; *id.*, 'Auf dem Weg', pp. 83–84; Carrascosa González, *El Reglamento Sucesorio Europeo*, pp. 83–84, 94; Castellanos Ruiz, 'Sucesión hereditaria', p. 555; Greeske, *Die Kollisionsnormen*, pp. 59–61.

[26] P. Mankowski, '§ 7. Der Allgemeine Teil des deutschen Internationalen Privatrechts', in C. von Bar and P. Mankowski, *Internationales Privatrecht*, vol. I (*Allgemeine Lehren*), 2nd ed. (München, 2003), p. 564.

The reason for this interpretation is that the ESR does not make expressly or implicitly any such requirement and, given that no distinction is drawn, recourse has to be had to the interpretative criterion of *ubi lex non distinguit, nec nos distinguere debemus* (Digest, 6, 2, 8). *Example:* Following the death in France, in 2000, of Mr J. Pellegrin, Mrs E. Michel, his second wife, and Mr G. Pellegrin, son from his first marriage, seised the French courts, that made it clear from the start that the real estate of the succession was located in France and that inheritance rights in its respect was thus submitted to French law. They doubted, however, whether that law also applied to the succession of the movable property, given that the decedent had a tax residency in Switzerland, that he had elected in order to benefit from a less costly tax system than the French one. The *Cour de cassation* confirmed that French law applied also to the succession of the movable property, as it had been established from all of the factual circumstances that the last domicile of the deceased was in France, where he lived with his second wife and where his main interests were, and not in Switzerland, where the connecting factors were purely circumstantial and served the sole purpose of satisfying administrative regulations.[27]

2. Groups of Cases

6. According to recital 23 ESR, in order to determine the habitual residence 'an overall assessment of the circumstances of the life of the deceased during the years preceding his death and at the time of his death, taking account of all relevant factual elements, in particular the duration and regularity of the deceased's presence in the State concerned and the conditions and reasons for that presence' must be made. Thanks to this set of criteria, the courts will be able in most cases to identify the State of habitual residence of the decedent with no great difficulty. It is possible to qualify these cases as *simple cases.*[28]

7. In some cases, however, the establishment of the last habitual residence of the deceased may be a difficult task (recital 24 ESR). These are situations that we may designate as 'complex cases'. We may analyse three possible complex cases:

[27] Cour de cassation 30 October 2006, *Rev crit dr int priv* (2007), pp. 573–575, with a note by B. Ancel.

[28] See Castellanos Ruiz, 'Sucesión hereditaria', p. 554.

1) *Personal and family habitual residence* vs *professional habitual residence.*[29] If, for professional or economic reasons solely, the deceased had moved his or her domicile to another country, but had maintained a close and stable connection with the State of origin, it is presumed that the deceased had maintained his or her habitual residence in the latter, i.e. in the State in which the centre of his or her family interest and social life was located.
2) *Deceased with two or more habitual residences.*[30] It might be presumed – as do some national legislations regarding domicile – that a person could not have more than one single habitual residence. The ESR, however, does not contain any provision in this regard. Besides, there are situations in which a person may certainly have two or more habitual residences: this may be the case, for example, for the German retirees in Tuscany or Majorca, for seasonal or for immigrant workers, and for foreign students with no definite future plans.[31]

   To overcome this difficulty, in some cases recital 24 may be used as support:

> Other complex cases may arise where the deceased lived in several States alternately or travelled from one State to another without settling permanently in any of them. If the deceased was a national of one of those States or had all his main assets in one of those States, his nationality or the location of those assets could be a special factor in the overall assessment of all the factual circumstances.

[29] See Carrascosa González, *El Reglamento Sucesorio Europeo*, pp. 91–92; Castellanos Ruiz, 'Sucesión hereditaria', pp. 555–556.

[30] See, on this issue, Baetge, *Der gewöhnliche Aufenthalt*, pp. 137–142; R. Geimer, 'Anmerkung zu KG 3.3.1987', *NJW* (1988), p. 652; Castellanos Ruiz, 'Sucesión hereditaria', p. 556; H. Gutzler, 'Anmerkung zu LG Freiburg 4.11.1947 und LG Hamburg 10.10.1947', *NJW* (1949), p. 154; D. Henrich, 'Bericht zu OLG Hamm 13.3.1989', *IPRax* (1990), p. 59; H. Lange, 'Wohnsitz und Wohnung, einheitlicher und mehrfacher Wohnsitz bei Eltern und Kindern', in *Entwicklungstendenzen im Wirtschafts- und Unternehmensrecht: Festschrift für Horst Bartholomeyczik zum 70. Geburtstag* (Berlin, 1973), pp. 243–244; W. Lauterbach, 'Anmerkung zu RG 15.11.1941', *Deutsches Recht, Ausgabe A* (1942), p. 535; F.A. Mann, 'Der "gewöhnliche Aufenthalt" im Internationalen Privatrecht', *Juristenzeitung* (1956), p. 470; E. Riezler, *Internationales Zivilprozessrecht und prozessuales Fremdenrecht* (Berlin, 1949), p. 185; L. Scheucher, 'Das Haager Testamentsformabkommen', *ZfRV* (1965), pp. 216 and (1966), p. 95; M. Schwimann, 'Das neue internationale Eherecht Österreichs', *Juristische Blätter* (1979), p. 342; H. Stoll, 'Rezension zu "Der 'gewöhnliche Aufenthalt' im Internationalen Privatrecht", *JZ* (1956), pp. 466–470, of F.A. Mann', *RabelsZ* (1957), pp. 190; M. Wolff, *Das internationale Privatrecht Deutschlands*, 3rd ed. (Berlin, Göttingen, Heidelberg, 1954), p. 43.

[31] Stürner, 'Deutsch-italienische Erbfälle', p. 67.

Ultimately, for the case in which the deceased lived alternately in more than one country or travelled from one State to another, the recital lists two elements that can represent a 'special factor' in the general assessment of the objective circumstances: the fact that the deceased was a national of one of the relevant States, or the fact that his main assets are located in one of them. Yet a clear presumption is not established.

3) *Deceased with no habitual residence*[32]. There has been discussion as to whether or not such persons exist. Strictly speaking, only a true nomad, it has been said, lacks a habitual residence: 'Unless one led a nomadic life, one had to be habitually resident somewhere'.[33] It is not a matter of not living in a given city or village pertaining to the same State, but rather of not living in any State on a habitual basis. On the other hand, there has been discussion as to whether it is possible to lose a previous habitual residence, including the habitual residence of origin, without acquiring a new one. There is some case law in the area of international child abduction and divorce. *Example 1:* In 1987, a British couple had a son out of wedlock, who was born in Western Australia. On 21 March 1990, the mother left Australia for England and, unbeknownst to the father, took their son with her. On 12 April 1990, an Australian court granted custody to the father. A week later, the Australian authorities requested the minor's return from the English authorities. At the House of Lords, Lord Brandon of Oakbrook held that: 'A person may cease to be habitually resident in country A in a single day if he or she leaves it with a settled intention not to return ... Such a person cannot, however, become habitually resident in country B in a single day'.[34] *Example 2:* In 1964, a German woman resident in Germany married a Dutchman also resident in Germany. At the start of 1986, both moved to Holland. After a few weeks, the couple separated and the wife returned to Germany. A year later, she filed for divorce and pension rights adjustment (*Versorgungsausgleich).* In a very debatable ruling, the

[32] See, on this matter, P. Albrecht, *Die steuerliche Behandlung deutsch-englischer Erbfälle* (Köln, Berlin, Bonn, München, 1992), pp. 241–242; Baetge, *Der gewöhnliche Aufenthalt*, pp. 142–147; R. Fentiman, 'Domicile Revisited', *The Cambridge Law Journal* 50/3 (1991), pp. 445–463, p. 450 *et seq.*; Greeske, *Die Kollisionsnormen*, pp. 71–74; Henrich, 'Der Domizilbegriff', p. 459 *et seq.*

[33] *Hack* v. *Hack* [1976] 6 Fam. Law 177.

[34] *Re J* (A Minor) (Abduction: Custody Rights) [1990] 3 W.L.R. 445–459, 492, 504. See the commentary by Baetge, *Der gewöhnliche Aufenthalt*, pp. 144–145.

Bundesgerichtshof, which had to apply the law of common habitual residence, given that the spouses had different nationalities, confirmed that such common habitual residence did not exist – a few weeks were insufficient for the wife to have been able to acquire habitual residence in Holland whilst, due to various disputed circumstances, she had lost the habitual residence in Germany.[35]

Despite these qualms, these 'modern nomads' can actually exist. *Example 1:* In 1986, a young man from New Zealand who had been travelling around Europe for three years appeared on the news.[36] Let us imagine that this *imperfect clone of Forrest Gump* had died and, furthermore, had left a considerable estate: what should be done in these cases? Article 21.1 ESR clearly cannot be applied because the 'habitual residence' connecting factor is impracticable. The ESR does not explicitly provide for any subsidiary connection for these types of cases. The only solution would be to resort to the *exception clause* under article 21.2 ESR and apply the law of the State with which the deceased was most connected. In this case, it would not be a matter of correcting a legal solution, but rather filling in a legal loophole.[37] *Example 2:* A Brazilian man travels the world as a nuclear power plant technician. He resides in several EU and non-EU countries at different stages of the year. He holds real estate in five countries (including a residence in Majorca). He has professional offices in New York, Geneva, Barcelona and Paris. After his death, the following people dispute his succession: distant relatives of Brazilian nationality domiciled in Rio de Janeiro, his partner for the last few years (a French singer with habitual residence in Majorca) and a Spaniard resident in Majorca who claims to be his son. If the Spanish courts find that they have jurisdiction pursuant to article 10 ESR, Spanish law could be applied to this succession in virtue of the closer connection with Spain pursuant to article 21.2 ESR, given that the deceased held real estate in Spain, his partner habitually resided in Spain and the alleged Spanish son also habitually resided in Spain.[38] *Example 3:* It has been confirmed that, in the case of a professional tennis player who competes matches all over the world over the course of seven or eight

[35] Bundesgerichtshof 3 February 1993, *IPRax* (1994), p. 131. For a commentary, see Baetge, *Der gewöhnliche Aufenthalt*, pp. 145–147.

[36] See Greeske, *Die Kollisionsnormen*, p. 72.

[37] See Hohloch, 'Kommentierung', pp. 6694–6695; Carrascosa González, *El Reglamento Sucesorio Europeo*, pp. 157, 159.

[38] See Carrascosa González, *El Reglamento Sucesorio Europeo*, pp. 157, 159.

months per year, the centre of life is the place in which his or her family lives, which is where he or she feels 'at home'.[39]

3. Advantages and Disadvantages of the New Rules

8. There are several reasons favouring the deceased's habitual residence at the time of death as a connecting factor.[40]

1) In the majority of successions, the last habitual residence of the deceased is an *objective connection* that guarantees the greatest proximity between the *de facto* assumption and the applicable legislation (*principle of proximity, Prinzip der engsten Verbindung*).[41] In effect, it is in the State where said habitual residence is found, that is found also the deceased's centre of life, and where the majority of heirs, legatees, assets and creditors are usually located.[42]
2) The last habitual residence of the deceased is a *neutral connecting factor* which, in the case of a marriage between citizens of two different nationalities, not only does not discriminate any of them due to their sex, but rather focuses on what unites the spouses (habitual residence in a State) and not what separates them (nationalities of different States) (*argument of the group law*).
3) The fact that the EU has opted for the last habitual residence of the deceased favours the *parallelism between the forum and the jus (Gleichlauf)*: pursuant to article 4 ESR (the habitual residence as a ground for international jurisdiction) [see art. 4] and article 21.1 ESR (the habitual residence as a connecting factor), jurisdiction and the applicable succession law coincide and, thus, the competent courts shall apply their own law.[43] As specified in recital 27 ESR, 'The rules of this Regulation are devised so as to ensure that the authority dealing with the succession will, in most situations, be applying its own law'. This avoids further and complex application problems, such as *renvoi* or the procedural treatment of foreign law. The *Gleichlauf* favours legal certainty and the rationalisation of the law, as it allows for faster procedures, increases the quality of

[39] Baetge, *Der gewöhnliche Aufenthalt*, p. 143.

[40] See Bonomi, 'Article 21', pp. 285–287; Carrascosa González, *El Reglamento Sucesorio Europeo*, pp. 149–155.

[41] Kropholler, *Internationales Privatrecht*, p. 26.

[42] See P. Kindler, 'Vom Staatsangehörigkeits- zum Domizilprinzip: das künftige internationale Erbrecht der Europäischen Union', *IPRax* (2010), pp. 44–50, 47.

[43] Walther, *Der Gleichlaufgrundsatz*, p. 167 *et seq.*

decisions, saves costs for the parties and avoids coordination problems between substantive and procedural law, in particular in the phase of administration of the succession.[44]

4) Opting for the recourse to the law of the habitual residence of the deceased at the time of death, which in most cases matches the habitual residence of the surviving spouse, also favours the *coincidence between the law applicable to succession and the law applicable to matrimonial property regimes*, when the latter, either for lack of choice of law or as a sole connecting factor, is that of the common habitual residence of the spouses.[45] Thanks to the ESR, in such cases the courts of the deceased's last habitual residence not only will enjoy jurisdiction, but also apply their own substantive law to both the matrimonial property regime and the actual succession. This greatly simplifies the court's task, as the dissolution of the matrimonial regime falls prior to the devolution of succession, which on occasions gives rise to difficult adaptation problems, that are lessened or avoided altogether when the same law apply both to patrimonial issues and to succession matters.
5) A political argument currently supports the reference to the last habitual residence instead of nationality as a connecting factor for succession. According to the most persuasive literature, *nationality* is a connecting factor very closely associated with the notion of State sovereignty that replaced domicile in the State codifications of the nineteenth century, in the heyday of the *principle of nationalities* and the formation of new European States.[46] This entails the question as to whether it would be

[44] Greeske, *Die Kollisionsnormen*, p. 150.

[45] The Council Regulation (EU) 2016/1103 of 24 June 2016 implementing enhanced cooperation in the area of jurisdiction, applicable law and the recognition and enforcement of decisions in matters of matrimonial property regimes, that will be applicable as of 29 January 2019, states that the matrimonial property regime is governed by the law of the common habitual residence of the spouses or future spouses or by the law of the habitual residence of one of them in the following cases: article 22.1(a) (= choice, or change, of applicable law: the law of the State of the habitual residence of the spouses of future spouses, or one of them, at the time this choice is made); article 26.1(a) (= applicable law where no choice is made: the law of the State of the spouses' first common habitual residence after their marriage). See, albeit with reference to a previous proposal on the same matter presented by the EU Commission in 2011, G. Biagioni, 'L'ambito di applicazione del Regolamento sulle successioni', in P. Franzina and A. Leandro (eds), *Il diritto internazionale privato europeo delle successioni* mortis causa (Milano, 2013), pp. 25–58, 49–52; K. Dengel, *Die europäische Vereinheitlichung des internationalen Ehegüterrechts und des internationalen Güterrechts für eingetragene Partnerschaften* (Tübingen, 2014).

[46] Davì and Zanobetti, 'Il nuovo diritto internazionale privato delle successioni', p. 30; Davì and Zanobetti, *Il nuovo diritto internazionale privato europeo*, pp. 44–45.

rational to maintain the connecting factor of 'nationality' in the conflict of laws rules of States engaged in a process of supranational integration, bent on the establishment of a European judicial area in which the principle of nationality is "regressing", and the very idea of State sovereignty is under 'erosion'.[47] Whilst it is to be questioned whether 'nationality' as a connecting factor ends up discriminating against people who live in the same State, habitual residence produces precisely the opposite effect: it is a much better match than nationality with the idea of European integration and assures that all individuals living in the same State are subject to the same law.[48] In these circumstances, it makes no sense to maintain the legal importance bestowed to the connecting factor of nationality in family relations and international successions.[49]

6) Lastly, 'nationality' is at times a connection that is non-existent (as is the case of stateless persons), impractical (as is the case of refugees), or indeterminate (as is the case of persons with double nationality). On the contrary, as some authors maintain, it is more difficult for these types of application problems to arise with regard to the notion of 'habitual residence', which is well understood, as it may be presumed that generally every individual has a habitual residence, and only one.[50] However, this is not a clear-cut opinion. Rather, most of the literature agrees that 'habitual residence' is a malleable notion, one that may be adapted to the needs of the case and to the objectives of the legislator; whilst the notion of 'nationality' is rigid and inflexible (whether or not a determined nationality is held).[51] Nevertheless we may expect to see future cases governed by the ESR in which ascertaining the precise deceased's habitual residence will involve as many difficulties as verifying effective nationality has always done,

[47] Davì and Zanobetti, 'Il nuovo diritto internazionale privato delle successioni', p. 30; Davì and Zanobetti, *Il nuovo diritto internazionale privato europeo*, p. 45.

[48] See Greeske, *Die Kollisionsnormen*, pp. 41–42; Kindler, 'Vom Staatsangehörigkeits- zum Domizilprinzip', p. 47; H.-P. Mansel, 'Vereinheitlichung des Internationalen Erbrechts in der Europäischen Gemeinschaft – Kompetenzfragen und Regelungsgrundsätze', in S. Arkan, A. Yongalik and B. Sit (eds), *Prof. Dr. Tuğrul Ansay'a armağan* (Ankara, 2006), p. 210.

[49] H. Dörner, 'Das Grünbuch "Erb- und Testamentsrecht" der Europäischen Kommission', *ZEV* (2005), pp. 137–138, 138.

[50] See M. Rohe, 'Staatsangehörigkeit oder Lebensmittelpunkt? – Anknüpfungsgerechtigkeit im Lichte neuerer Entwicklungen', in C. Engel and H. Weber (eds), *Festschrift für Dietrich Rothoeft zum 65. Geburtstag* (München, 1994), pp. 19, 21.

[51] See Baetge, 'Auf dem Weg zu einem gemeinsamen europäischen Verständnis des gewöhnlichen Aufenthalts', p. 82.

regardless of the quality or feasibility of defining the habitual residence in question.[52]

9. One may ask whether nationality is not perhaps a more preferable connecting factor than habitual residence for regulating succession, as it is intended to ensure continuity and permanence within legal rights and interests.[53] This argument ties in with the traditional dispute between domicile and nationality as guiding connecting factors for issues of personal status: it is easier to change domicile (and thus, habitual residence) than it is to change nationality. In other words, an easy-to-change connecting factor undermines legal certainty in the planning of succession.[54] However, the point is not so much to answer the question as to what connecting factor is easier to change, which may in turn raise certain problems relating to application (*conflit mobile, fraude à la loi*), but rather to answer the question of *what is more representative of an individual's tie with a country: nationality* (= maintaining a connection with the State of origin), leading to the application of the *lex originis*, or *habitual residence* in a State in which the deceased had planned to live for several years (= recognising the connection with the host State, in which it is supposed that there is social integration). On occasions, this debate is considered from a *multicultural perspective*: supporters of nationality as a connecting factor maintain that law is a product of culture and that applying the national law guarantees the connection of the persons with their cultural roots.[55] This, however, is a half-truth, which depends on several factors (the so-called clash of civilisations, the processes of supranational integration, the duration of the stay abroad or the transfer of nationality according to the *jus sanguinis* criterion). When interpreted literally, the *principle of nationality* can lead to the application of the law of a State that bears no relation whatsoever with second and third generation immigrants. This is, furthermore, an issue that cannot be solved in abstract terms and calls for two clarifications. The first is that it can only be dealt with on a case-by-case basis and, even so, may end up

[52] See Greeske, *Die Kollisionsnormen*, p. 46.

[53] See Bonomi, 'Article 21', pp. 287–288; Carrascosa González, *El Reglamento Sucesorio Europeo*, pp. 155–156.

[54] See Kindler, 'Vom Staatsangehörigkeits- zum Domizilprinzip', p. 47.

[55] See, on this thorny problem, Greeske, *Die Kollisionsnormen*, pp. 32–36; A. Junghardt, *Die Vereinheitlichung des Erb- und Testamentrechts im Rahmen einer europäischen Verordnung – Rom IV-VO* (Regensburg, 2009), p. 60; Kindler, 'Vom Staatsangehörigkeits- zum Domizilprinzip', pp. 46–47; H.-P. Mansel, 'Vereinheitlichung des Internationalen Erbrechts', pp. 208–209.

as an individual psychological issue.[56] The second is that the opposition between the *objective connection* of habitual residence and the *subjective connection* of nationality must not be exaggerated as, subject to specific conditions, the ESR permits a person to opt for the application of his or her national law [see art. 22].[57] This allows a person to choose 'the best of both worlds' ('*das Beste beider Welten*').[58]

10. Recital 37 ESR claims that '[i]n order to allow citizens to avail themselves, with all legal certainty, of the benefits offered by the internal market, this Regulation should enable them to know in advance which law will apply to their succession'. The ESR therefore endeavours to simplify the planning of international successions. In the opinion of the EU legislator, the habitual residence of the deceased at the time of death is the appropriate connecting factor: 'The main rule should ensure that the succession is governed by a predictable law with which it is closely connected' (recital 37 ESR). But, is this entirely true? One can imagine *three possible situations* in which it is debatable whether the last habitual residence is representative of the closest connection possible between a State and the deceased.[59] First, when a person simultaneously has two or more habitual residences, that is, he or she divides out his or her time during the year into more or less equal periods, during which he or she lives in different States (= plurality of potential connecting factors of the same legal nature). Second, when a person maintains a connection with his or her country of origin, despite habitually residing for long periods in another country, whether for professional, educational, health reasons or otherwise (= plurality of potential connecting factors of different legal natures). *Example:* A cancer patient, Mr G. Loiseau, notary public in the Ivory Coast since 1953, who held French nationality, moved to Paris to receive medical treatment in 1991, remaining there until his death in 1994. He left a fortune made up of real estate in France and in the Ivory Coast and money held in a trust in the Cayman Islands. By way of a holographic will, he made his wife legatee and his three sons heirs. The widow claimed a quarter of the succession as legatee and the usufruct

[56] Davì and Zanobetti, 'Il nuovo diritto internazionale privato delle successioni', p. 31; Davì and Zanobetti, *Il nuovo diritto internazionale privato europeo*, p. 45.

[57] Davì and Zanobetti, 'Il nuovo diritto internazionale privato delle successioni', p. 31; Davì and Zanobetti, *Il nuovo diritto internazionale privato europeo*, pp. 45–46.

[58] M. Stürner, 'Deutsch-italienische Erbfälle unter der kommenden Europäischen Erbrechtsverordnung', *Jahrbuch für Italienisches Recht* 26 (2013), p. 75.

[59] Davì and Zanobetti, 'Il nuovo diritto internazionale privato delle successioni', p. 32; Davì and Zanobetti, *Il nuovo diritto internazionale privato europeo*, pp. 46–47.

of the other three quarters granted to her by French law. However, was French law applicable? The debate throughout the proceedings focused on identifying the domicile of the deceased in order to determine the law applicable to the succession. The *Cour d'appel* of Paris believed that all indications pointed to the deceased having wanted to keep his domicile in the Ivory Coast: he had maintained his apartment in Abidjan, he paid social security contributions there and had declared in his wealth tax declaration that he was domiciled in Abidjan. The ruling from the *Cour de cassation*, as important as it was controversial, endorsed this opinion: the deceased's establishment in France was, for these purposes, ineffective, even though it had continued for years.[60] Third, the case in which the deceased lived for a long period of time in one country and changed his or her habitual residence to another State shortly before his death (= potential *conflit mobile* or *fraude à la loi*).

B. The Exception Clause

11. According to article 21.2 ESR, 'Where, by way of exception, it is clear from all the circumstances of the case that, at the time of death, the deceased was manifestly more closely connected with a State other than the State whose law would be applicable under paragraph 1, the law applicable to the succession shall be the law of that other State'. This is the so-called *exception* or *escape clause* (*clause d'exception, clausola d'eccezione, Ausweichsklausel*), whose aim, as previously indicated, is to provide a solution for situations in which the deceased possessed a closer and more stable connection with a State other than that of his or her last habitual residence (what we have named *displaced centre of gravity*).

12. The introduction of this clause is *surprising, debatable and dangerous*. Let us look at each of these characteristics in turn:

1) The exception clause of the ESR's article 24.2 is *surprising*, given that it did not appear in the proposal drafted by the EU Commission. In order to appraise the *ratio legis* of the introduction of this clause into the ESR, we can see an example taken from recital 25 ESR, which provides a possible justification:

   > With regard to the determination of the law applicable to the succession the authority dealing with the succession may in exceptional cases – where, for instance, the deceased had moved to the State of his habitual

[60] Cour de cassation 7 December 2005, *Rev crit dr int priv* (2006), pp. 583–596, with a note by S. Godechot-Patris.

residence fairly recently before his death and all the circumstances of the case indicate that he was manifestly more closely connected with another State – arrive at the conclusion that the law applicable to the succession should not be the law of the State of the habitual residence of the deceased but rather the law of the State with which the deceased was manifestly more closely connected.

The described situation corresponds to one of the aforementioned problematic cases: that which arises when the person whose succession is concerned dies shortly after having moved to another country, in such a way that one may reasonably think that his or her connections with the State of previous habitual residence are stronger than those with the new State. And therein lays the fear of the United Kingdom or of other northern EU countries that their elderly citizens may acquire an habitual residence in a less expensive country were they have moved for benefitting of a better climate, subjecting their succession to another, quite different legal system (Spanish, Italian, French, etc.), without perhaps realising it; conversely other Member States may be concerned by the possibility that a change in the habitual residence of a person shortly before his or her death may endanger the rights of the heirs entitled to a reserved share under the law of the country of previous residence.

2) The exception clause of article 24.2 ESR is *debatable* for two reasons:
   (a) The connecting factor based on the *concept of habitual residence* employed by the ESR is an *overall, weighted and casuistic* one, thus enabling the core of the relationship to be focused on without any need to rely on the exception clause, which is generally inoperative or scarcely relevant.[61] In this sense, it is interesting that recital 25 gives only one single example. In fact, some authors believe that this constitutes the only example of possible recourse to the clause.[62] *Example 1:* As we shall see, one possible application of article 21.2 ESR is represented by the scenario in which the person whose succession is concerned dies after having moved with his or her family to another Member State for professional reasons, for a very limited time, and with the intention of

[61] See Greeske, *Die Kollisionsnormen*, p. 147, who considers it as a very exceptional legal tool and believes that the introduction of art. ESR 21.2 is 'extremely regrettable' (*äußerst bedauerlich*); C. Kohler and W. Pintens, 'Entwicklungen im europäischen Familien- und Erbrecht 2011–2012', *FamRZ* (2012), pp. 1425–1432, 1427, 1429.

[62] Davì and Zanobetti, 'Il nuovo diritto internazionale privato delle successioni', p. 36; Davì and Zanobetti, *Il nuovo diritto internazionale privato europeo*, p. 54.

returning to the country or origin immediately afterwards. However, as it has been underlined, the same result offered by the recourse to the exception clause could be achieved without classifying the situation under article 21.2: it would be sufficient to carry out a meticulous and methodical analysis of the notion of habitual residence in order to conclude that the person in question had not acquired habitual residence in the host State, given that he or she was not socially established there, died shortly after the relocation (recital 25 ESR) and spent so little time in the new State until death as to have been unable to lose the habitual residence in the State of origin, to acquire habitual residence in the new State (unless it is considered possible to establish 'instant habitual residence' [*sofortige Begründung des gewöhlichen Aufenthalts*]), or to break the connections with the old State.[63]

Example 2: The exception clause would allow the law of the State of origin to be applied to the succession of a diplomat or consul instead of the law of the country to which he had been accredited for several years: it could safely be said that the deceased had a closest connection with the State of origin. But, truth be told, it is not necessary to resort to the exception clause: whilst a certain degree of flexibility is permitted in ascertaining the concept of last 'habitual residence', it could easily be claimed that, for the purposes of succession, the diplomat or consul maintained his or her habitual residence in the country of origin.[64]

(b) The exception clause in *matters of succession* is *more problematic* than in other sectors: it can be observed, and rightly so, that the essential issue is not that of giving a more suitable location to a specific obligation, but rather of deciding the fate of all the assets comprising a person's estate or, according to the conception based upon Roman law, the continuation of that person's life.[65]

3) Last but not least, the exception laid down by article 24.2 ESR is *dangerous*, given that it could give rise to *two unwanted effects* which are incompatible with the ESR's objectives:

63 Greeske, *Die Kollisionsnormen*, pp. 147–149.

64 A. Bonomi, 'Article 4', in A. Bonomi and P. Wautelet (eds), *Le droit européen des successions. Commentaire du Règlement n° 650/2012 du 4 juillet 2012* (Bruxelles, 2013), p. 175 footnote 21; P. Lagarde, 'Les principes de base du nouveau règlement européen sur les successions', *Rev crit dr int priv* (2012), p. 701.

65 T. Ballarino, 'Il nuovo regolamento europeo sulle successioni', *Riv dir int* (2013), p. 1122.

(a) *Undermining legal certainty.*[66] The drafters of the ESR were aware of this danger when they indicated: '[t]hat manifestly closest connection should, however, not be resorted to as a subsidiary connecting factor whenever the determination of the habitual residence of the deceased at the time of death proves complex' (recital 25 ESR, *in fine*).[67] Under the exception clause, establishing the law ultimately applicable proves to be unpredictable, thus making it difficult for people to plan their successions, which is one of the objectives sought by the ESR.
(b) *Breaking the connection between forum and jus.*[68] A court that has based its jurisdiction on the habitual residence of the deceased at the time of death (article 4 ESR) shall have to apply the law of another State (article 21.2 ESR) rather than its own (article 21.1 ESR). The application of a foreign law to succession issues may give rise to problems (such as the ascertainment and proof of foreign law or recourse to the public policy exception of the forum, if applicable), which ends up complicating and prolonging the corresponding proceedings, thus increasing their cost.

13. The adoption by ESR of the *exception clause* is, accordingly, difficult to justify.[69] In a nutshell, the ESR creates a new problem – the difficult relationship between the two paragraphs of article 21 – in order to regulate the situation which is likely to occur when the deceased was more closely connected with a State other than that where he or she had the last habitual residence, a situation which could have been dealt with by legal mechanisms included in the ESR itself, or in the legislation of the Member States. The result ultimately achieved by article 21.2 ESR is not an improvement in attending to the interests of the person whose succession in concerned or of the persons concerned by the inheritance, but

[66] Greeske, *Die Kollisionsnormen*, p. 149.

[67] See H. Dörner, 'EuErbVO: Die Verordnung zum Internationalen Erb- und Erbverfahrensrecht ist in Kraft!', *ZEV* (2012), p. 511. *Contra*, see L. Kunz, 'Die neue Europäische Erbrechtsverordnung – ein Überblick, Teil I', *GPR – Zeitschrift für das Privatrecht der Europäischen Union* (2012), p. 210, who supports the systematic use of the exception clause, whenever it is not possible to establish the habitual residence of the deceased.

[68] Greeske, *Die Kollisionsnormen*, p. 150.

[69] There is little wonder, then, that Greeske, *Die Kollisionsnormen*, p. 150, simply proposes the deletion of article 21.2 ESR in a future reform of the ESR. For an interesting and antagonistic approach to Greeske, that I support, see Carrascosa González, *El Reglamento Sucesorio Europeo*, pp. 160–161.

rather entails the danger that the court may apply a law different from that which the parties involved might have expected.[70]

14. In order to understand how the exception clause under article 21.1 ESR operates, a distinction must be drawn between:

1) *Prerequisites*. It is only possible to rely on the exception clause when the following *three requirements* are simultaneously met. First, no law has been chosen, as the exception clause may only be invoked when the deceased had not elected the law applicable to the succession or when any choice made is invalid.[71] Second, the clause must be interpreted *restrictively*: in particular, the lack of a last habitual residence must not be equated to the mere difficulty in its identification,[72] as underlined by recital 25 ESR, *in fine*, '[t]hat manifestly closest connection should, however, not be resorted to as a subsidiary connecting factor whenever the determination of the habitual residence of the deceased at the time of death proves complex'. Third, it is necessary that 'all the circumstances of the case' make it clear that 'at the time of death, the deceased was manifestly more closely connected with a State other than the State' of his or her last habitual residence. If such a conclusion is not reached 'from all the circumstances of the case' (not just from some), or if there is a connection with another State, but this is not the 'manifestly closest connection', the exception clause cannot be invoked. Some authors have suggested situations in which the deceased would be more closely connected to a State other than that of habitual residence. *Example:* If the deceased moved with all his family for professional reasons, but his habitual residence in the host State had to be limited to a fixed period beforehand, and the family wanted to return to the country of origin at a later stage, the centre of gravity of the situation would lie in the latter country.[73]
2) *Legal consequences*. The exception clause is a *subsidiary* legal mechanism: it cannot be invoked in order to achieve the ESR's objectives when other legal instruments are already available. Thus, for example, when the person whose succession is concerned moves shortly before his or her death his residence to another country whose law is very different from that of the State of the previous habitual residence, and

[70] Greeske, *Die Kollisionsnormen*, p. 150.
[71] Carrascosa González, *El Reglamento Sucesorio Europeo*, p. 162.
[72] Carrascosa González, *El Reglamento Sucesorio Europeo*, p. 161.
[73] Dörner, 'EuErbVO', p. 511.

that person draws up a will valid according the law of the country of the new residence, this may be considered as an abuse of the law (*fraude à la loi*), that may be counteracted by recourse to the rules on the abuse of rights under certain national legislation, if the circumstances of the case so permit. What is not possible is the systematic recourse in such cases to the exception clause laid down by article 21.2 ESR.

3) *Procedural law*. The exception clause is not simply an exception which must be interpreted narrowly, but must also be *meticulously motivated*: the court must explain in detail the reasons that have led it to conclude that the situation is more connected to a State other than that of the deceased's last habitual residence, provide the evidence in support of this conclusion, establish that all the pre-requisites are met and that the legal consequences attributed to the succession are justified.[74]

It should be clarified, on the other hand, whether or not the exception clause needs to be invoked by a party in order for the court to apply it or if the court can do so *ex officio*. Some authors contend that these possibilities are not mutually exclusive: given the silence of the ESR regarding this matter, it is sufficient for one of the parties or to the court itself to take the initiative, as *ubi lex non distinguit, nec nos distinguere debemus* (Digest, 6, 2, 8).[75]

[74] Carrascosa González, *El Reglamento Sucesorio Europeo*, pp. 162–165.
[75] See Carrascosa González, *El Reglamento Sucesorio Europeo*, pp. 163–164; Castellanos Ruiz, 'Sucesión hereditaria', p. 578.

Article 22

Choice of Law

ESPERANZA CASTELLANOS RUIZ

1. A person may choose as the law to govern his succession as a whole the law of the State whose nationality he possesses at the time of making the choice or at the time of death.

   A person possessing multiple nationalities may choose the law of any of the States whose nationality he possesses at the time of making the choice or at the time of death.
2. The choice shall be made expressly in a declaration in the form of a disposition of property upon death or shall be demonstrated by the terms of such a disposition.
3. The substantive validity of the act whereby the choice of law was made shall be governed by the chosen law.
4. Any modification or revocation of the choice of law shall meet the requirements as to form for the modification or revocation of a disposition of property upon death.

Summary

I. THE LEGISLATIVE OPTION IN FAVOUR OF PROFESSIO JURIS *page* 323

II. ADVANTAGES AND DISADVANTAGES OF PROFESSIO JURIS 326

III. CONDITIONS FOR THE CHOICE OF APPLICABLE LAW: NATIONAL LAW OF THE PERSON WHOSE SUCCESSION IS CONCERNED 331

IV. EXPRESS CHOICE AND TACIT CHOICE 344

A. Express choice of law 344

B. Tacit choice of law 345

V. TRANSITIONAL PROVISIONS: PRESUMPTIVE CHOICE OF LAW 349

VI. SUBSTANTIVE AUTONOMY AND 'INCORPORATION BY REFERENCE' CLAUSES 349

I. The Legislative Option in Favour of *professio juris*

1. Article 22 ESR states that a person may choose his national law as the law applicable to his or her succession. This possibility, expression of the principle of autonomy, is referred to as *professio* *juris*.[1] The chosen law prevails over all other laws applicable to the succession, in accordance with ESR (articles 20 and 21).

2. For the majority of the European Union Member States participant to ESR, this is indisputably one of the most significant novelties brought in by the new conflict of laws rules in matters of succession.[2] *Professio juris* provides a person with the option to choose the law applicable to his succession, with a view of reconciling the alternative between the application of the national law and the law of the habitual residence of the deceased, though preserving the principle of the unity of succession.[3]

The admissibility of *professio juris* involves the acceptance of freedom of choice – although restricted to national law – in succession matters. Choice of law has traditionally not been admitted, or has been highly restricted, in these areas. The option to choose the law applicable to successions had already been enshrined in the Hague Convention of 1 August 1989 on the Law Applicable to the Estates of Deceased

[1] On the origin and meaning of the expression '*professio juris*', see A. Bonomi, 'Le choix de la loi applicable à la succession dans la proposition de règlement européen', *Cursos de Derecho Internacional y Relaciones Internacionales de Vitoria-Gasteiz* (Bilbao, 2010), pp. 241–272; P. De Cesari, *Autonomia della volontà e legge regolatrice delle successioni* (Padova, 2001), pp. 65–120; J. M. Fontanellas Morell, La *professio iuris* sucesoria (Madrid, 2010), pp. 29–55.

[2] See M. Greeske, *Die Kollisionsnormen der neuen EU-Erbrechtsverordnung* (Frankfurt am Main, 2014), pp. 100–102.

[3] Regarding freedom of choice in private international law in matters of succession, see A.-L. Calvo Caravaca, 'Artículo 9.8 del Código civil', *Comentarios al Código Civil y compilaciones forales*, tome I, vol. II, 2nd ed. (Madrid, 1995), p. 356; J. Carrascosa González, *El Reglamento sucesorio europeo 650/2012 de 4 de julio de 2012. Análisis crítico* (Granada, 2014), pp. 129–130; A. Davì, 'L'autonomie de la volonté en droit international privé des successions dans la perspective d'une future réglementation européenne', *Riv dir int priv proc* (2004), pp. 473–498; H. Dölle, 'Die Rechtswahl im internationalen Erbrecht', *RabelsZ* (1966), pp. 205–240; K. Dreher, *Die Rechtswahl im internationalen Erbrecht: unter besondere Berücksichtigung des italienischen IPR-Reformgesetzes n. 218 vom 31. Mai 1995* (Frankfurt, 1999); H. Hanisch, '*Professio juris*, réserve légale und Pflichtteil', *Mélanges Guy Flattet* (Lausanne, 1985), pp. 473–489; A. Heini, 'Der Grundsatz der Nachlasseinheit und das neue internationale Erbrecht der Schweiz', *Festschrift für Cyril Hegnauer zum 65. Geburtstag* (Bern, 1986), pp. 187–195; K. P. Hotz, *Die Rechtswahl in Erbrecht im interkantonalen und internationalen Verhältnis* (Zürich, 1969); K. Jacobsen, 'Die Rechtswahl im interlokalen Erbrecht Deutschlands', *Recht in Ost und West* (1983), pp. 97–107; G. Kühne, *Die Parteiautonomie im internationalen Erbrecht* (Bielefeld, 1973); *id.*, 'Testierfreiheit und Rechtswahl im internationalen Erbrecht. Die Parteiautonomie. Eine «basic rule» des Kollisionsrechts?', *JuristenZeitung* (1973), pp. 403–407; K. Siehr, 'Das internationale Erbrecht nach dem Gesetz zur Neuregelung des IPR', *IPrax* (1987), pp. 4–8; F. Sturm, 'Parteiautonomie als bestimmender Faktor im internationalen Familien und Erbrecht', *Recht und Rechtserkenntnis. Festschrift für Ernst Wolf zum 70. Geburtstag* (Berlin, Bonn, München, 1985), pp. 637–658.

Persons, whose articles 5 and 6 give a person the option to submit his succession to the law of the state whose nationality he possesses or in which he has his habitual residence, at the time the choice is made or at the time of his death. The Convention, however, never entered into force.

The Hague Convention's adoption of a possibility of choice in the determination of the *lex successionis* has a precedent in article 90.2 of the Swiss act on private international law of 1987, which was also followed, albeit with different modalities, by other domestic codifications of private international law, such as the German act on private international law of 1986 (article 25.2 EGBGB), the 1991 civil code of Quebec (article 3098.2), the 1992 Romanian act on private international law (article 68), the 1995 Italian act on private international law (article 46.2), and the 2004 Belgian code on private international law (article 79); a similar solution was also accepted by two resolutions adopted by the Institute of International Law (at the 1967 Nice session and at the 1987 Cairo session respectively).

However, even if they admit *professio juris*, none of the said legal systems recognises an absolute right to choose any law whatsoever to govern a person's international succession; rather they subject this choice to limits, similar to those set out in article 22 ESR.

The ESR imposes the following restrictions on *professio juris*:

a) Choice of one law to govern the succession as a whole. The exercise of *professio juris* allows a person to choose a single law, irrespective of the nature of the assets and regardless of whether they are located in another Member State or in a third State (recital 37 *in fine* in connection with recital 42).[4] The ESR has opted for a unitary system, which allows for the choice of one law for the entire succession, thereby avoiding the disadvantages of scissionist systems [see art. 23 no. 2].[5] It is not possible for different laws to be chosen in a given succession (*dépeçage*) for reasons of legal certainty and in order to avoid the fragmentation of the succession (recital 37 ESR).
b) Choice restricted to the national law of the person whose succession is concerned. The choice offered by the ESR is limited: a person can only

[4] E. Castellanos Ruiz, 'Sucesión hereditaria: Reglamento 650/2012 sobre sucesión internacional', in A.-L. Calvo Caravaca and J. Carrascosa González (eds), *Derecho Internacional Privado*, 15th ed., vol. II (Granada, 2014), p. 569.

[5] A. Bonomi, 'Successions internationales: conflits de lois et de juridictions', *Hague Recueil*, vol. 350 (2010), p. 241 *et seq.*; E. Castellanos Ruiz, *Unidad vs. pluralidad legal de la sucesión internacional* (Granada, 2001), pp. 6–8; Davì, 'L'autonomie de la volonté', p. 481 *et seq.*; M. Goré, 'La *professio juris*', *Defrénois* (2012), pp. 763–764.

choose the law of the State whose nationality he possesses at the time of making the choice or at the time of his death (article 22 ESR).[6] In the event that the person holds several nationalities, he can choose the law of any of the States whose nationality he possesses at the time the choice is made or at the time of his death (article 22.1 ESR). This choice of law prevails over all other laws applicable to the succession, in accordance with ESR (articles 20 and 21).

The ESR has thereby opted, in the alternative between the application of the law of the habitual residence and of the national law, to leave this choice in the hands of the person whose succession is concerned.[7]

II. Advantages and Disadvantages of *professio juris*

3. *Professio juris* can be considered a double-edged sword, depending upon how its use is viewed, whether from the point of view of the person whose succession is concerned or from that of the beneficiaries to the inheritance.

4. From the point of view of the person whose succession is concerned, *professio juris* provides significant advantages.[8]

First, it allows a person to choose the law which is materially more in his interests for the purpose of benefitting or favouring the legal position of those beneficiaries as he considers most suitable, or which is more connected with his succession. Although the general rule, in accordance with article

[6] L. Abadie, 'La loi applicable au sein du règlement', *Droit de la famille*, 10 (2013), p. 14; F. Boulanger, 'Révolution juridique ou compromis en trompe l'oeil? – À propos du nouveau règlement européen sur les successions internationales', *La semaine juridique* (2012), pp. 1120–1130; Greeske, *Die Kollisionsnormen*, pp. 98–145.

[7] Davì, 'L'autonomie de la volonté', pp. 473–498; *id.*, 'Riflessioni sul futuro diritto internazionale privato europeo delle successioni', *Riv dir int* (2005), pp. 297–341; E. Jayme, 'Party Autonomy in International Family and Succession Law: New Tendencies', *YPIL* (2009), pp. 1–21; P. Kindler, 'From Nationality to Habitual Residence: Some Brief Remarks on the Future EU Regulation on International Successions and Wills', in K. Boele-Woelki, T. Einhorn, D. Girsberger and S. Symeonides (eds), *Convergence and Divergence in Private International Law – Liber Amicorum Kurt Siehr* (Zürich, The Hague, 2010), pp. 251–258; *id.*, 'La legge regolatrice delle successioni nella proposta di regolamento dell'Unione europea: qualche riflessione in tema di carattere universale, rinvio e *professio iuris*', *Riv dir int* (2011), pp. 422–432; A. E. von Overbeck, 'La *professio juris* comme moyen de rapprocher les principes du domicile et de la nationalité en droit international privé', *Liber amicorum B.L. Fredericq*, vol. II (Gent, 1965), pp. 1085–1112.

[8] A. Bonomi, 'Article 22', in A. Bonomi and P. Wautelet, *Le droit européen des successions. Commentaire du Règlement n° 650/2012 du 4 juillet 2012* (Bruxelles, 2013), pp. 301–305; Greeske, *Die Kollisionsnormen*, pp. 124–127.

21.1 ESR, is to apply the law of the State where the deceased had his habitual residence at the time of death, as it is considered the law most closely connected with the succession, it is possible that the succession might be better connected to other, different laws. This may be the case, for example, particularly in relation to the succession of persons who, for professional or other reasons, frequently change their habitual residence, or to the succession of persons who, despite having changed their habitual residence, have maintained links, of a personal nature or through property, with their country of origin.[9] From the point of view of the search for the law best connected to the succession, the mechanical and abstract application of the law of the country of habitual residence of the deceased at the time of his death can give rise to unfair and arbitrary results. Consequently, with the aim of achieving the objective imposed by the ESR, i.e. subjecting the succession to a predictable law with which it maintains a close connection, article 22 ESR offers the option, however limited, to a person of choosing the law applicable to his succession.

Article 22 is a conflict of laws rule guided by substantive considerations, as it is the person whose succession is concerned who has the last word in organising his succession and is thus permitted to dispose of his succession in advance;[10] *professio juris* allows a person to plan and arrange his succession in accordance with the chosen law.[11] All aspects relating to the succession will be governed by the law chosen, guaranteeing coherence between the dispositions of property upon death and any other issues subject to the *lex successionis*, and avoiding any heir discrimination that might be caused by the application of different laws to the same international succession.

The European legislator has given the testator the possibility to use *professio juris* even in anticipation of the application of the ESR:, since article 83.2 ESR provides that

> where the deceased had chosen the law applicable to his succession prior to 17 August 2015, that choice shall be valid if it meets the conditions laid down in Chapter III or if it is valid in application of the rules of private international law which were in force, at the time the choice was made, in the State in which the deceased had his habitual residence or in any of the States whose nationality he possessed.

[9] A. Davì and A. Zanobetti, 'Il nuovo diritto internazionale privato delle successioni nell'Unione europea', *CdT*, 5/2 (2013), pp. 37–38; A. Davì and A. Zanobetti, *Il nuovo diritto internazionale privato europeo delle successioni* (Torino, 2014), pp. 55–56.

[10] P. Lagarde, 'Les principes de base du nouveau règlement européen sur les successions', *Rev crit dr int priv* (2012), p. 719.

[11] Goré, 'La *professio juris*', p. 764; C. Lisanti, 'La *professio iuris* dans le règlement successions du 4 juillet 2012', *Gaz Pal*, n° 165–166 (2013), p. 1577.

Accordingly, this choice will be valid under ESR rules only if that person died on 17 August 2015, date in which the ESR became applicable, or after that date [see art. 83 no. 8 *et seq.*].[12]

Second, the predictability and certainty of the law applicable to the international succession is ensured, both for the person whose succession is concerned as well as for the beneficiaries, thus avoiding the uncertainty caused by locating the habitual residence of the deceased.[13] 'Habitual residence' is a connecting factor which is subjective and personal and can change over time, which is why it may bring some insecurity for persons wishing to arrange their succession in advance. Consequently, admission of *professio juris* introduces a significant level of certainty and stability regarding the law applicable to the succession in all the Member States where the ESR applies.[14] Nevertheless, this certainty and predictability in relation to the applicable law can be undermined in cases where assets of the estate are located in third countries where there is a concurrent jurisdiction which is competent to hear the succession, if that country does not give effect to the *professio juris* made under article 22 ESR. In such circumstances, it is not possible to guarantee uniform results in all cases.[15]

Third, *professio juris* avoids problems related to the evasion of law (*fraude à la loi*) which can occur as a result of an artificial change of habitual residence as the objective connecting factor, applicable, in the absence of a choice, under article 21.1 ESR, because the *lex successionis* becomes 'fixed' even where the habitual residence is subsequently transferred to another State.[16] A similar fraudulent change is rendered almost impossible in cases where the connecting factor is nationality by the strict conditions generally posed by the different legal systems to the acquisition of their nationality.

[12] Abadie, 'La loi applicable au sein du règlement', p. 16; C. Schoppe, 'Die Übergangsbestimmungen zur Rechtswahl im internationalen Erbrecht: Anwendungsprobleme und Gestaltungspotential', *IPRax* (2014), pp. 27–33; Lisanti, 'La *professio iuris*', p. 1577; H. Rosoux, 'Arrêt sur le régime transitoire du règlement successions', *Revue de planification patrimoniale belge et internationale*, 2 (2014), pp. 161–162.

[13] G. Khairallah, 'La détermination de la loi applicable à la succession', in G. Khairallah and M. Revillard (eds), *Droit européen des successions internationales (Le Règlement du 4 juillet 2012)* (Paris, 2013), p. 53; Lisanti, 'La *professio iuris*', p. 1576; Rosoux, 'Arrêt sur le régime transitoire', p. 159.

[14] A. Dutta, 'Succession and Wills in the Conflict of Laws on the Eve of Europeanisation', *RabelsZ* (2009), p. 571 *et seq.*

[15] Davì and Zanobetti, 'Il nuovo diritto internazionale privato delle successioni', pp. 38–39; Davì and Zanobetti, *Il nuovo diritto internazionale privato europeo*, p. 58.

[16] Rosoux, 'Arrêt sur le régime transitoire', p. 159.

Fourth, as the law chosen applies to the succession as a whole, it eliminates problems relating to the qualification of the assets of the estate as movable or immovable, which could occur in the legal systems based on scission, such as Belgium or France, where different conflict of laws rules were applied before the entry into force of ESR depending on the nature of the assets concerned.

5. From the beneficiaries' point of view, however, the *professio juris* must be reasonably restricted so that the persons entitled to reserved shares are not defrauded, and in order to guarantee a connection between the deceased and the chosen law ('That choice should be limited to the law of a State of their nationality in order to ensure a connection between the deceased and the law chosen and to avoid a law being chosen with the intention of frustrating the legitimate expectations of persons entitled to a reserved share': recital 38).[17] In order to avoid evasion of the law, and to ensure a genuine connection of the law chosen with the succession, the option of a person is restricted to two laws which both are significantly connected to the succession: the law of the State whose nationality the person possesses at the time the choice was made or at the time of his death.[18] Article 22 ESR does not impose any restriction upon a person's right to make a choice of law in relation to its effects; in particular, persons entitled to a reserved share under the law objectively applicable to the succession are not protected against the effects of that choice.[19] This is the most obvious disadvantage which the *professio juris* might cause: the choice of law may be made with the precise intention of avoiding application of the mandatory rules which would have been applicable to the succession in the absence of a choice.[20]

6. Although the ESR does not govern expressly evasion of law, this is however considered in recital 26 which states that 'nothing in this Regulation should prevent a court from applying mechanisms designed

[17] A. Junghardt, *Die Vereinheitlichung des Erb- und Testamentsrechts im Rahmen einer Europäischen Verordnung – Rom IV-VO* (Regensburg, 2009), p. 167 *et seq.*; Max Planck Institute for Comparative and International Private Law, 'Comments on the European Commission's Proposal for a Regulation of the European Parliament and of the Council on jurisdiction, applicable law, recognition and enforcement of decisions and authentic instruments in matters of succession and the creation of a European Certificate of Succession', *RabelsZ* (2010), pp. 522–720, 608–609.

[18] Greeske, *Die Kollisionsnormen*, pp. 102–103; Lagarde, 'Les principes de base', pp. 719–720.

[19] T. Ballarino, 'Il nuovo regolamento europeo sulle successioni', *Riv dir int* (2013), pp.1123–1124.

[20] Bonomi, 'Article 22', p. 305; Carrascosa González, *El Reglamento Sucesorio*, pp. 130–132.

to tackle the evasion of the law, such as fraude à la loi in the context of private international law'. That being said, the choice of one of the permitted laws is valid even if the application of the particular substantive law of succession chosen by the deceased does not recognise reserved shares or gives preference to the legal position of some beneficiaries over that of others. The chosen law will determine whether the deceased can dispose of all his assets or only some, or whether a system recognising reserved shares applies, amongst various other questions relating to the succession. The judge cannot appreciate the strength of the links between the succession and the State whose law has been selected, because this would cause a significant uncertainty in relation to the validity of the *professio juris*, which would be incompatible with the objectives of article 22 ESR: i.e. to ensure the predictability and the stability of the applicable law.

It would be possible, however, to consider, pursuant to recital 26, that a choice of law is fraudulent where the deceased acquired nationality of a State with the sole intention of subjecting his succession to the law of that State.[21] It must be a voluntary, malicious and artificial change, for example changing nationality just before dying to create a false connection between the succession and that country. If we consider the conditions usually required in order to acquire the nationality of a country, such an artificial change will occur hardly ever and would be very difficult to prove. Apart those changes in nationality, the *professio juris* could be considered fraudulent in cases where, save for nationality, the deceased had no other connection with the chosen law, as could be the case, for example, for second or third generation immigrants who retain their families' nationality but have no other contact with that country.[22]

7. It is equally difficult to ground on the public policy clause, set out in article 35 ESR, the invalidity of a *professio juris*, when the law chosen does not recognise reserved shares, or assigns only very small portions to reserved heirs.[23] This would contradict the principle of the predictability of the applicable law and the liberal spirit of the ESR, endangering the

[21] Bonomi, 'Article 22', pp. 332–333.

[22] Bonomi, 'Article 22', p. 333; Carrascosa González, *El Reglamento Sucesorio*, p. 151; D. Damascelli, *Diritto internazionale privato delle successioni a causa di morte* (Milano, 2013), p. 54.

[23] M. Azavant, 'L'ordre public successoral', *Droit de la famille*, 10 (2013), p. 21; Carrascosa González, *El Reglamento Sucesorio*, p. 122.

effet utile of article 22 ESR.[24] It is however possible to reject application of particular provisions of a foreign law, when the application of those provisions is 'manifestly incompatible' with the public policy of the Member State concerned, as stated in article 35 and in recital 58 ESR.[25] So, for example, the public policy exception can be invoked if a legal system creates discrimination because it differentiates succession rights based upon whether children are natural or legitimate, or grants better rights of succession on the basis of sex or ethnicity or religion, or if heirs are obliged to convert to a particular religion in order to inherit [see art. 35].[26] However, the possibility to have recourse to the aforementioned exception must be evaluated in the particular case, since the same rule can either be contrary to the public policy of the forum or not, according to the circumstances. These possible instances of discrimination must be assessed with special care, as in certain legal systems women may be granted fewer rights of inheritance but are entitled to certain benefits as compared to the male beneficiaries.[27] Accordingly, this can be seen not as a discrimination, but rather as a different style of family organisation.[28]

III. Conditions for the Choice of Applicable Law: National Law of the Person Whose Succession Is Concerned

8. Article 22 ESR sets out the conditions required for *professio juris* to be valid. The conditions are as follows:

[24] Bonomi, 'Article 22', p. 332; Davì and Zanobetti, 'Il nuovo diritto internazionale privato delle successioni', p. 44; Davì and Zanobetti, *Il nuovo diritto internazionale privato europeo*, p. 67.

[25] Carrascosa González, *El Reglamento sucesorio*, p. 122; Castellanos Ruiz, *Unidad versus pluralidad*, pp. 81–88; Davì and Zanobetti, 'Il nuovo diritto internazionale privato delle successioni', pp. 44–45; Davì and Zanobetti, *Il nuovo diritto internazionale privato europeo*, pp. 67–68. Also the Spanish Supreme Court, in its decisions dated 18 November 1996 (*Lowenthal*) and 21 May 1999 (*Denney*), has stated that: 'La legítima . . . no pertenece a materia protegida por el orden publíco . . .'.

[26] Azavant, 'L'ordre public successoral', p. 19; Damascelli, *Diritto internazionale privato delle successioni*, pp. 102–104; Davì and Zanobetti, 'Il nuovo diritto internazionale privato delle successioni', p. 106; Davì and Zanobetti, *Il nuovo diritto internazionale privato europeo*, pp. 171–172.

[27] Carrascosa González, *El Reglamento sucesorio*, pp. 169–171.

[28] S. Rodríguez Sánchez, *Una introducción al Reglamento de Sucesiones de la UE (desde la perspectiva de los derechos reales sobre bienes inmuebles y el Registro de la Propiedad en España)* (Madrid, 2013), pp. 171–174.

1) *Professio juris restricted to national law.* The choice of law must fall on the national law of the person, at the time of the choice or at the time of his death. Several remarks are to be made in this regard:

a) It is not possible to choose a law other than that of the State whose nationality the deceased possessed, whether at the time of the choice or at the time of his death.[29] According to recital 38 ESR this excludes the choice of any other law which, theoretically, could be chosen to govern a person's succession, in order to guarantee a connection between the deceased and the chosen law and, most importantly, in order to avoid a law being chosen with the sole intention of frustrating the legitimate expectations of the persons entitled to a reserved share. However, this argument does not entirely justify the exclusion of the *professio juris* in favour of other laws which could be closely connected with the deceased's succession, as may be the case in respect of the law of the deceased's habitual residence at the time of his death or at the time of the choice, or the law of the place where the deceased's assets are located or the law applicable to his matrimonial property regime.[30] This is so even though there could have been advantages in permitting the choice of such laws through a *professio juris.*

Provision could have been made, within this limited faculty for choice of law, for the law of habitual residence of the deceased at the time of his death to be chosen.[31] This is the law objectively applicable to a succession even in the absence of a choice, in accordance with article 21.1 ESR, but it is also evident that, due to the escape clause established by article 21.2 ESR, or to *renvoi*, as set out in article 34.1 ESR, a law different to that of the deceased's habitual residence at the time of his death can nevertheless be applied. Consequently, although some authors consider that the choice of the law of habitual residence would be useless, it could permit to submit the succession to that law, thus avoiding the recourse to the escape clause or the operation of *renvoi* under a third State's private international law rules.[32]

29 Khairallah, 'La détermination de la loi applicable', pp. 54–55.

30 Damascelli, *Diritto internazionale privato delle successioni*, pp. 55–56; P. Lagarde, 'Présentation du règlement sur les successions', in G. Khairallah and M. Revillard (eds), *Droit européen des successions internationales (Le règlement du 4 juillet 2012)* (Paris, 2013), pp. 12–13.

31 Bonomi, 'Article 22', pp. 311–313; Lagarde, 'Les principes de base', p. 720.

32 In favour of a choice of the law of the State where the deceased has his habitual residence at the time of his death, see Lagarde, 'Les principes de base', p. 720; in opposition to this opinion on the basis that this choice is of no effect, see Abadie, 'La loi applicable au sein du règlement', pp. 14–15.

Nor is it possible to choose the law of habitual residence of the deceased at the time the choice is made. The reason for this is none other than to avoid a law being chosen with the intention of frustrating the legitimate expectations of the persons entitled to a reserved share, as is expressly stated in recital 38 ESR. However, the law of a previous habitual residence may apply by operation of the escape clause set out in article 21.2 ESR, when it is clear that it is manifestly more closely connected than the law of the State where the deceased had his final residence.[33]

On the other hand, the exclusion of the *professio juris* in favour of the law of the place where the assets of the estate are located, specifically in relation to immovable property, is a response to the need to avoid scission.[34]

One of the practical advantages of permitting a choice of law in succession's matters it that it may allow matching the law applicable to succession and the law applicable to the matrimonial property regime.[35] However, under the ESR this is not permitted. This can be justified on the basis that the conflict rules on the law applicable to matrimonial property regimes in Europe are not unified; each State applies its own conflict rules. Choosing a sole law to govern the matrimonial property regime and the succession of the spouses will be easier when the conflict rules relating to matrimonial property regimes in the European Union will be unified. Indeed, the EU has adopted on 24 June 2016 the Council Regulation (EU) 2016/1103 of 24 June 2016 implementing enhanced cooperation in the area of jurisdiction, applicable law and the recognition and enforcement of decisions in matters of matrimonial property regimes that will be applicable as of 29 January 2019. For the time being, and until the mentioned regulation will be applicable, in the absence of coordination between the law applicable to the succession and the law applicable to the matrimonial property regimes, different conflict rules apply and accordingly the two issues, although connected, could be governed by different laws.

b) If a person chooses the law of the State whose nationality he possesses at the time the choice is made, that choice does not change due to a subsequent loss of that nationality, or the acquisition of a new nationality alongside that which the deceased had when he made the choice. In other words, article 22 ESR does not incline towards application of the deceased's 'most effective' national law, that is to say, that with

[33] Davì and Zanobetti, 'Il nuovo diritto internazionale privato delle successioni', pp. 42–43; Davì and Zanobetti, *Il nuovo diritto internazionale privato europeo*, pp. 64–65.

[34] Bonomi, 'Article 22', pp. 313–314; Lagarde, 'Les principes de base', p. 721.

[35] Bonomi, 'Article 22', pp. 314–316.

which he had the closest connection. The ESR accepts the choice of the national law, which offered at the moment of the choice a connection with the deceased which is considered adequate.[36] We can formulate the following remarks on this respect. First, in practical terms, the need to determine the deceased's 'most effective' nationality could often endanger the certainty of the applicable law, which is precisely one of the principal objectives that the *professio juris* proposes to attain, and the more so where the choice of law was made many years before the deceased's death. Second, one of the fundamental elements for determining the 'most effective' nationality of a person is precisely his habitual residence: admitting only the application of the law of the nationality which matches the deceased's habitual residence at the time the choice was made, would have reduced the usefulness of the *professio juris*, limiting it almost exclusively to cases in which the deceased intended to change his residence to a foreign country outside the European Union.[37] Finally, the Court of Justice of the European Union's case law does not allow for any preferential order of, or discrimination between, the different nationalities of the European Union Member States.[38] It must be admitted, however, that the solution adopted by the ESR can sometimes entail the application of the law of a State with which the deceased had a limited connection, if any.[39]

c) If a person chooses the law of the State whose nationality he possesses at the time of his death, this is of course a choice of the law governing his succession made 'in anticipation'. So, on the one hand, the choice of law might be made taking into account a nationality which that person assumes he will still have when he dies, but which he might not actually possess at the time of his death. On the other hand, the deceased can also choose a nationality which he does not yet possess, but is certain he will possess at the time of his death. This is the so-called deceased's anticipated nationality.[40] In both cases if, at the time of his death, the deceased does not possess the nationality corresponding to the law chosen,

[36] Davì, 'L'autonomie de la volonté', p. 481.

[37] Davì and Zanobetti, 'Il nuovo diritto internazionale privato delle successioni', pp. 39–40; Davì and Zanobetti, *Il nuovo diritto internazionale privato europeo*, pp. 59–60.

[38] ECJ, case C-369/90, *Micheletti* [1992] p. I-4239; ECJ, case C-148/02, *Garcia Avello* [2003] ECR I-11613; ECJ, case C-168/08, *Hadadi* [2009] ECR I-4239; Davì and Zanobetti 'Il nuovo diritto internazionale privato delle successioni', p. 40; Davì and Zanobetti, *Il nuovo diritto internazionale privato europeo*, pp. 60–61.

[39] Davì and Zanobetti, 'Il nuovo diritto internazionale privato delle successioni', p. 40; Davì and Zanobetti, *Il nuovo diritto internazionale privato europeo*, pp. 60–61.

[40] Carrascosa González, *El Reglamento sucesorio*, p. 143.

the choice will not be valid. In order to avoid this problem it had been suggested that, instead of designating the particular applicable law relating to the nationality a person will possess at the time of his death, a generic reference could be made to the law of the State whose nationality the deceased will hold at the time of his death, without expressly stating whether it will be French or Italian, for example. In this case, however, the person whose succession is concerned should have sufficient knowledge of the substantive provisions of the different countries whose law might apply as the law of the State whose nationality he will have at the time of his death.[41] On the other hand, article 22 ESR does not, however, permit a simple indication by a person that his succession is governed by the law of the State whose nationality he possesses, without indicating the point in time to which this refers, whether it is when the choice is made or at the time of his death, because if a change of nationality occurs between the time the choice is made and the time of death, identifying the intention of the deceased would be very difficult. The legal consequence, in the event that this change occurs, is that the choice of law is invalidated and, therefore, the law of the deceased's habitual residence at the time of his death applies, as the objective connecting factor for determining the *lex successionis*, in accordance with article 21 ESR.[42] Accordingly, if the choice of law is made in favour of the law of the State whose nationality the deceased possessed at the time the choice was made, this law will apply even if he has lost that nationality. A different interpretation would go against the literal content of article 22 ESR, and would hinder its purpose of guaranteeing the stability and certainty of the law applicable to the succession.[43]

9. 2) *Unilateral declaration on the part of the deceased.* Only the deceased can make use of the *professio juris*. In particular, the possibility of heirs agreeing on the law applicable to a deceased's succession, whether at the time of the opening of the succession or subsequently, must be excluded.[44]

[41] F. M. Wilke, 'Das internationale Erbrecht nach der neuen EU-Erbrechtsverordnung', *RIW* (2012), p. 605 *et seq.*

[42] A. Wysocka, 'How can a valid *professio iuris* be made under the EU Succession Regulation?', *NIPR* (2012), p. 570.

[43] A. Bonomi, 'Prime considerazioni sulle proposta di regolamento sulle successioni', *Riv dir int priv proc* (2010), p. 895; Davì and Zanobetti, 'Il nuovo diritto internazionale privato delle successioni', p. 41; Davì and Zanobetti, *Il nuovo diritto internazionale privato europeo*, p. 62.

[44] Damascelli, *Diritto internazionale privato delle successioni*, p. 56.

10. 3) *Only one law.* Only one law can be chosen. Multiple laws cannot be applied cumulatively to the same succession, since that would counteract the principles of unity and universality upon which the ESR system is based. It is therefore not possible to make a partial choice of applicable law or to designate multiple different laws to apply to the same succession, and all forms of *dépeçage* are prohibited.[45] The ESR does, however, allow one significant exception, as regards a partial choice of law, both to govern the admissibility and substantive validity of wills (article 24.1 ESR) and to govern the admissibility, substantive validity and binding effects between the parties to agreements as to succession (article 25.3 ESR).

11. 4) *In favour of the substantive law.* The *professio juris* refers to the substantive law chosen, not the rules relating to conflict of laws. As article 34 ESR states, *renvoi* does not apply when a choice of law has been made [see art. 34 no. 13 *et seq.*],[46] since it could disregard the deceased's actual wishes by the application of conflict rules from other legal systems.[47] Therefore, when there is a choice of law, it refers to the substantive provisions and not to the conflict of laws rules of the chosen law.[48]

12. 5) *Any substantive law.* The chosen substantive law can be that of a Member State or of a third State due to the universal nature of the rules concerning the law applicable to the succession (article 20 ESR); reference must always be made to a law belonging to a State's legal system.[49] If the chosen law is that of a State having more than one legal system on

[45] I. Calvo Vidal, 'El Derecho de sucesiones en la Unión Europea. Ley aplicable y carácter universal de la nueva normativa en materia de sucesiones', *Noticias de la UE*, 328 (2012), p. 99; Carrascosa González, *El Reglamento Sucesorio*, p. 125; Davì and Zanobetti, 'Il nuovo diritto internazionale privato delle successioni', p. 38; Greeske, *Die Kollisionsnormen*, pp. 127–129; Lagarde, 'Les principes de base', p. 721; Max Planck Institute, 'Comments', pp. 522, 602, 609–610 y 613; Wilke, 'Das internationale Erbrecht', p. 607.

[46] A. Davì, 'Le renvoi en droit international privé contemporain', *Hague Recueil*, vol. 352 (2012), pp. 376–381; Davì and Zanobetti, 'Il nuovo diritto internazionale privato delle successioni', pp. 89–90; Davì and Zanobetti, *Il nuovo diritto internazionale privato europeo*, pp. 142–144.

[47] On the incompatibility of *renvoi* with the autonomy of the rules on conflict and the distinction between *renvoi* and the possibility or impossibility of choosing the designated law's conflict rules in place of the substantive law, see Davì, 'Le renvoi', pp. 376–381.

[48] Although it is a minority position, the *renvoi* exclusion in cases where *professio juris* has been exercised, set out in article 34 ESR, has been criticized: see D. Solomon, 'Die Renaissance des Renvoi im Europäischen Internationalen Privatrecht', in *Liber Amicorum Klaus Schurig* (München, 2012), p. 259 *et seq.*; Wilke, 'Das internationale Erbrecht', p. 608.

[49] Goré, 'La *professio juris*', p. 764.

territorial or personal basis, articles 36 and 37 ESR will apply [see arts. 36–38].

13. 6) *Conflit mobile.* The possible change in the connecting factor is addressed by article 22.1 ESR, fixing the nationality connection on a particular moment in time: 'at the time of making the choice' or 'at the time of death'.[50]

14. 7) *An incidental question: determination of nationality.* Determination of the deceased's nationality or multiple nationalities must be resolved as a preliminary question not governed by the ESR, since whether a person is considered to possess the nationality of a State is outside its scope, as stated by recital 41 ESR: '[t]he issue of considering a person as a national of a State falls outside the scope of this Regulation and is subject to national law, including, where applicable, international Conventions, in full observance of the general principles of the European Union'. Each State has the exclusive competence to determine which persons hold its nationality. Therefore, a court, before which the determination of the deceased's nationality is being considered in a dispute relating to succession, will have to apply its own law if the nationality concerned is that of the forum State, but if it is the nationality of another State, it will have to apply that other State's rules. Recital 41 indicates that determination of nationality must be made 'in full observance of the general principles of the European Union'. This is not to say that European law does govern the acquisition or loss of nationality of the Member States, it being a question which falls within their sovereign jurisdictions. European law only contains principles relating to the recognition of the effects which the attribution or loss of a State's nationality might have within that law. Accordingly, the European principles which affect the law of nationality must operate as a European public policy mechanism towards the application of the law, both of the Member States and third States.[51]

15. 8) *Plurality of nationalities.* In the event that the deceased holds several nationalities, he can choose the law of "any" of the States whose nationality he holds at the time the choice is made or at the time of his death (article 22.1 ESR, paragraph 2).[52] The person whose succession is concerned may choose between whichever of the multiple nationalities he holds: it is irrelevant whether the deceased chooses the law of the State

[50] Goré, 'La *professio juris*', p. 763; Greeske, *Die Kollisionsnormen*, pp. 131–133.

[51] Carrascosa González, *El Reglamento Sucesorio*, pp. 133–134.

[52] J. M. Fontanellas Morell, 'El nuevo Reglamento europeo en materia de sucesiones. Aspectos de Derecho internacional privado', *Rev esp der int* (2013), pp. 284–290.

whose 'effective nationality' he possesses, or that of his 'latent nationality', since the European legislator has been very liberal in that respect.[53] This solution puts an end to the risk of a forum prioritising its national law.[54] Even though it can give rise to the application of a law which has no real connection with the succession, this has the practical advantage of favouring the certainty of the applicable law, thus avoiding the difficulty of establishing suitable criteria in order to determine that one nationality should prevail over another.[55] Also, if a person has multiple nationalities, one of a Member State and another of a third State, he can opt for any of them. In other words, nationality of a Member State does not prevail over nationality of a third State, and it is to be recalled that the rules concerning the determination of the *lex successionis* are universal and have effects *erga omnes* (article 20 ESR).[56]

16. 9) *Valid choice independent of the provisions in the chosen law.* A choice of law made under the ESR will be valid even when the chosen law does not provide for such an option in matters of succession (recital 40). The validity (from the point of view of the admissibility) of the *professio juris*, therefore, is not dependent upon the chosen law but rather derives from the ESR itself which allows for that choice.[57]

17. 10) *Substantive validity of the choice; consent.* The substantive validity of the act whereby the choice of law was made shall be governed by the chosen law (article 22.3 ESR) even when the chosen law does not provide for such an option in matters of succession. That being said, it is indeed important to determine the substantive validity of the act by which the choice of law was made. Consent of the parties is governed by the law chosen, even when its rules do not provide for such an option in matters of succession (recital 40).[58]

18. 11) *Capacity to make the choice.* Article 22 ESR is silent on the law which should apply to the capacity of a person to exercise the *professio juris*. However, by analogy, we can apply the solution offered by the ESR at article 26.1(a) in relation to the capacity of the person

[53] A. Bonomi, 'Il regolamento europeo sulle successioni', *Riv dir int priv proc* (2013), p. 300; Damascelli, *Diritto internazionale privato delle successioni*, p. 54; Goré, 'La *professio juris*', p. 763.

[54] Lagarde, 'Les principes de base', p. 719.

[55] Damascelli, *Diritto internazionale privato delle successioni*, p. 54.

[56] Carrascosa González, *El Reglamento Sucesorio*, pp. 135–137; Castellanos Ruiz, 'Sucesión hereditaria', p. 572.

[57] Khairallah, 'La détermination de la loi applicable', pp. 55–56.

[58] Goré, 'La *professio juris*', p. 766; Lagarde, 'Les principes de base', p. 721.

making the disposition of property upon death to make such a disposition. Thus, the capacity of a person to make the choice of law must be governed by the law allegedly chosen by the person making the disposition (articles 22.3 ESR and 26.1(a) ESR).[59]

19. 12) *Modification or revocation of the act.* Modification and revocation of the choice of law are subject to the same requirements as to form as apply to the modification or revocation of dispositions of property upon death (article 22.4 ESR). This plain and simple provision gives rise, however, directly or by implication, to several problems of interpretation.[60] It is therefore necessary to clarify the various aspects which relate to the modification or revocation of the act by which the choice is made.[61]

a) The ESR does not expressly address the admissibility of the modification or revocation of the *professio juris*. The problem lies in determining whether these two issues are governed directly by the ESR or rather by the chosen law itself. It seems reasonable to think that it is possible to modify or revoke the choice of law, because that is implicitly allowed by article 22.4 ESR, which governs the requirements for the formal validity of modifications or revocations of acts by which a choice of law is made.[62] Therefore, it is irrelevant that the chosen law allows such a modification or revocation to be made and even that the new law applicable to the succession allows it.

b) Nor does the ESR state which law is applicable to the substantive validity of the act modifying or revoking a choice of law. Nevertheless, recital 40 *in fine* states that the substantive validity of the consent and capacity of the parties to modify or revoke the act by which the choice of

[59] Davì and Zanobetti, 'Il nuovo diritto internazionale privato delle successioni', p. 51; Davì and Zanobetti, *Il nuovo diritto internazionale privato europeo*, pp. 78–79; Carrascosa González, *El Reglamento Sucesorio*, p. 126.

[60] Carrascosa González, *El Reglamento Sucesorio*, p. 144.

[61] Davì and Zanobetti, 'Il nuovo diritto internazionale privato delle successioni', pp. 50–57; Davì and Zanobetti, *Il nuovo diritto internazionale privato europeo*, pp. 76–80.

[62] In favour of this position see Davì, 'L'autonomie de la volonté', p. 487; Davì and Zanobetti, 'Il nuovo diritto internazionale privato delle successioni', p. 53, in particular footnote 201; Davì and Zanobetti, *Il nuovo diritto internazionale privato europeo*, pp. 81–82, in particular footnote 100. However, there are other authors suggesting that, if the rule of conflict which recognises the faculty to choose the applicable law makes no express mention of modification or revocation of the chosen law, that problem must be resolved directly by the previously chosen law, whose modification or revocation is being attempted, as it is that law which governs the substantive validity of the act by which the choice has been made: see Bonomi, 'Successions internationales', p. 250 *et seq*.

law is made is governed by the law originally chosen even when that law does not provide for such an option in matters of succession.[63]

c) The ESR does not resolve the problem concerning the possibility of an implicit revocation or modification of the act by which the choice of law is made as a consequence of the modification or revocation of the will, or any other disposition of property upon death, which that act contains. The revocation of the act including the *professio juris* can occur, for example, by way of an express declaration, when new dispositions are drafted which are incompatible, completely or in part, with the previous dispositions, or by the material destruction of the document containing the act by which the choice of law was made.

Is it possible to consider that the *professio juris* is impliedly modified or revoked, when the will in which it is expressed is modified or revoked? Even though the ESR does not offer an express solution, there are in article 22 ESR sufficient elements which suggest answering in the negative.[64] On the one hand, unlike article 22.2 ESR, which allows for the *professio juris* both in an express and a tacit form, article 22.4 clearly excludes the possibility of a tacit modification or revocation which might result from the terms of a disposition of property upon death, as it calls for the requirements as to form necessary for the modification or revocation of such dispositions. On the other hand, article 27 ESR, which governs the formal validity of dispositions of property upon death and is indirectly referred to by article 22.4 ESR, only applies to dispositions of property upon death made 'in writing'. The only meaning which can be given with certainty to this restriction is that it emphasises the exclusion of 'the formal validity of dispositions of property upon death made orally' from the scope of the ESR, as also set out at article 1.2(f) ESR. The ESR's silence on how to address problems relating to the form of an implicit modification or revocation of the *professio juris* is difficult to interpret as being a tacit demonstration of the ESR's intention to submit that possibility to one of the laws set out at article 27 ESR, particularly if we take into account the fact that some of these laws might ignore or even prohibit the *professio juris*. In any case, for sake of security, the interested person should clearly specify in the act revoking his will – or disposition of property upon death – his wishes regarding the choice of law that he

[63] Davì and Zanobetti, 'Il nuovo diritto internazionale privato delle successioni', p. 53; Davì and Zanobetti, *Il nuovo diritto internazionale privato europeo*, p. 82.

[64] On this issue, see the extremely precise analysis made by Davì and Zanobetti, 'Il nuovo diritto internazionale privato delle successioni', p. 54; Davì and Zanobetti, *Il nuovo diritto internazionale privato europeo*, pp. 83–84.

may have made previously, simultaneously with, or separately from, the modified or revoked disposition of property upon death.[65]

d) Nor does the ESR tackle expressly the problem of the unilateral revocability of the act containing the choice of law attached to an agreement as to succession or enclosed therein. Even when the choice of law is included in such an agreement, the *professio juris* continues to be a unilateral act by the person (or one of the persons) whose inheritance it deals with, and is therefore, in principle, unilaterally revocable. This differentiates it from the act by which the law for the agreement as to succession is chosen, which constitutes a proper agreement between the parties, and which can therefore only be revoked with the consent of all the participants in the agreement as to succession. Taking into account, in addition, that the law applicable to the succession does not necessarily coincide with the law governing the agreement as to succession, revocation of the *professio juris* can exert a negative, and sometimes even destructive, influence over the effects of the agreement. This is because the ESR explicitly subordinates the recognition of these effects to its compatibility with the mandatory rules of the law governing the succession which restrict the deceased's freedom to make a disposition, taking particular account of the rules protecting persons entitled to a reserved share. Precisely in order to protect the rights of the agreement beneficiaries against such risks, in the course of the studies and debates which accompanied the adoption of the ESR, a proposal was made of inserting a provision stating that a *professio juris* incorporated in an agreement as to succession could only be revoked with the consent of all the parties to the agreement.[66]

Nevertheless, although the ESR is inspired by a moderate attitude in favour of agreements as to succession (as confirmed by recital 49 ESR),[67] despite the prohibition of these agreements in the legal systems of various

[65] Davì and Zanobetti, 'Il nuovo diritto internazionale privato delle successioni', pp. 54–55; Davì and Zanobetti, *Il nuovo diritto internazionale privato europeo*, p. 84.

[66] See Davì, 'L'autonomie de la volonté', p. 495; Bonomi, 'Successions internationales', p. 253. This problem can be considered in an almost identical form in relation to joint wills containing interdependent dispositions of property upon death. Since those will, which can be equated with agreements as to succession, the remarks relating to the revocability of the *professio juris* included in the latter must be understood to apply equally to the revocability of the *professio*included in the former. On this point see Davì and Zanobetti, 'Il nuovo diritto internazionale privato delle successioni', p. 56, footnote 213; Davì and Zanobetti, *Il nuovo diritto internazionale privato europeo*, p. 87, footnote 212.

[67] Recital 49 states that: 'An agreement as to succession is a type of disposition of property upon death the admissibility and acceptance of which vary among the Member States. In order to make it easier for succession rights acquired as a result of an agreement as to succession to be accepted in the Member States, this Regulation should determine which

Member States, no provision in this regard has been included. The ESR prefers to leave intact the freedom of the person making the choice of law and at the same time to protect reserved heirs, which was one of the greatest preoccupations during the preparatory stages.[68] On the one hand, in fact, the ESR does not provide, in this case, for any kind of restriction upon revoking the *professio juris*. On the other hand, this unequivocally prioritises the rights of the persons entitled to reserved shares set out in the law governing the succession, when that law is different from the law governing agreements as to succession, over the rights of the beneficiaries under the agreement as to succession in question. Recital 50 ESR clarifies this issue by stating that the law applicable to the validity and effects of the agreements as to succession must be without prejudice to the rights of any person who, under the law applicable to the succession, has a right to a reserved share or another right of which he cannot be deprived by the person whose succession is involved. If we take into account the fact that, nevertheless, the beneficiaries under the agreements as to succession are not definitively protected by the ESR against the unfavourable effects which a change in the law governing the succession made by the deceased – due to a change in his country of habitual residence or via *professio juris* made *ex novo* after one of these agreements as to succession is concluded – might cause, it seems reasonable to infer that the aforementioned solution applies *mutatis mutandis* in relation to the revocation of a *professio juris* made at the same time as the agreements are concluded.[69]

e) The ESR makes no mention of the problems potentially raised by the revocation by operation of law of dispositions of property upon death devised under some legal systems, particularly common law systems. Some of these systems consider certain events in a person's life, such as

law is to govern the admissibility of such agreements, their substantive validity and their binding effects between the parties, including the conditions for their dissolution.'

[68] On this point see Davì and Zanobetti, 'Il nuovo diritto internazionale privato delle successioni', p. 56; Davì and Zanobetti, *Il nuovo diritto internazionale privato europeo*, pp. 87–88.

[69] In favour of this position, see Davì and Zanobetti, 'Il nuovo diritto internazionale privato delle successioni', p. 57; Davì and Zanobetti, *Il nuovo diritto internazionale privato europeo*, p. 88. For a different position see Wisocka, 'How can a valid *professio juris*', p. 574, who supports the opinion according to which the absence, in the conflict rule conferring the right to choose, or in the international private law to which the conflict rule governing the *professio juris* belongs, of restrictions on the revocability of the choice, must be interpreted as a demonstration of an implicit intention to subject the determination of those limits to the chosen law.

marriage, divorce, the birth or adoption of children, to be the cause of a revocation by operation of law of dispositions upon death made before those events. If the person does not replace the revoked dispositions with new ones, his succession will therefore be subject to the rules of intestacy.

When the disposition which is in question contained a choice of law in favour of the law operating the revocation, the problem arises of determining if also that choice has to be considered as annulled. If this were the case, the loss of effectiveness of the *professio juris* would subtract the disposition of last will to the chosen law and, therefore, also to the effect of revocation, with the further consequence that the succession would be governed by the law objectively applicable to it and not by the law that had been designated and that entails the loss of effectiveness of the disposition itself. As a result, the disposition of property upon death in question would not be affected by the revocation and would maintain its effects insofar as they are not contrary to the new law which has become objectively applicable. A correct interpretation of the ESR should, however, suggest to give to this problem a negative reply.[70] Indeed, we have seen that the ESR resolves autonomously, albeit at times implicitly, all problems relating to private international law issues connected with the *professio juris*, and that it submit to the designated law only the regulation of substantive law issues concerning the formal and substantive validity of the act itself. At any rate, it is certain that the ESR does not contain any rules relating to the loss of effectiveness of such a designation. Besides, the laws which make provision for that type of automatic revocation do not themselves extend their effects to the *professio juris*; and this, not only for the obvious reason that this institution is generally unknown to their majority, but also because the problems relating to the determination of the law governing the succession are of a different nature that those that dictate the revocation itself. Revocation by operation of law is in fact prescribed for the protection of the interests of the persons involved, or, more generally, for adapting the dispositions upon death to the new family situation of the person whose succession is concerned. It should finally be added that it is also possible that, notwithstanding the loss of effects of the previously adopted dispositions, the designated law continues to meet the intentions and expectations of the interested person,

[70] Davì and Zanobetti, 'Il nuovo diritto internazionale privato delle successioni', pp. 54–55; Davì and Zanobetti, *Il nuovo diritto internazionale privato europeo*, pp. 85–86. See, however, in opposition to this opinion, Wisocka, 'How can a valid *professio juris*', p. 573 *et seq.*, and, for a more general point of view, Bonomi, 'Successions internationales', p. 251 *et seq.*

who, in any event (and save in particular cases, such as the posthumous birth of children), maintains the possibility of reorganising the devolution of his estate in the manner that he deems most convenient.[71]

f) The formal validity of the modification or revocation of the choice of law is governed by the same law which is applicable to the form of dispositions of property upon death made in writing which modify or revoke a previous disposition, since article 22.4 ESR refers to article 27.2 ESR which governs the formal validity of these dispositions [see art. 27].[72]

20. 13) *Stateless persons.* Persons with no nationality, i.e. stateless persons, cannot make use of the *professio juris.* Their succession is governed by the law of the State of their habitual residence at the time of his death, pursuant to article 21.[73]

IV. Express Choice and Tacit Choice

21. 14) *Express or tacit choice.* The choice of law can be made 'expressly' in the form of a disposition of property upon death, or 'tacitly' when the choice is demonstrated by the terms of such a disposition (article 22.2 ESR).[74]

A. Express Choice of Law

22. *Express choice: declaration in the form of a 'disposition of property upon death'.* Article 3.1(d) ESR affirms that 'disposition of property upon death' means a will, a joint will – made by two or more persons in the same instrument – or an agreement as to succession – any agreement, including that resulting from reciprocal wills, creating, modifying or terminating, for or without consideration, rights relating to the succession or future successions of one or more persons who are party to that agreement. According to the ESR, therefore, the choice of law can be made expressly 'in the form' of a will, a joint will or an agreement as to succession.

[71] Davì and Zanobetti, 'Il nuovo diritto internazionale privato delle successioni', pp. 55–56; Davì and Zanobetti, *Il nuovo diritto internazionale privato europeo*, pp. 85–86.

[72] Davì and Zanobetti, 'Il nuovo diritto internazionale privato delle successioni', p. 52; Davì and Zanobetti, *Il nuovo diritto internazionale privato europeo*, pp. 80–81.

[73] Carrascosa González, *El Reglamento sucesorio*, p. 144.

[74] Abadie, 'La loi applicable au sein du règlement', p. 15; Greeske, *Die Kollisionsnormen*, pp. 142–144; Wilke, 'Das internationale Erbrecht', p. 606.

23. Formal validity of the act in which the choice is made will be governed by the law applicable to the form of the dispositions of property upon death. That is to say, if the choice of law is made in a will, the 1961 Hague Convention on the Conflicts of Laws Relating to the Form of Testamentary Dispositions will apply in those Member States which are parties to that Convention [see art. 75], and article 27 ESR will apply in the others. If the choice of law is made in the form of an agreement as to succession, then the law applicable to the form is governed by article 27 ESR in all Member States [see art. 27]. It must be underlined that it is not necessary for the choice of law to be made within a will, a joint will or an agreement, but, rather, the choice must meet the specific formal requirements for a disposition of property upon death.[75]

B. *Tacit Choice of Law*

24. *Tacit choice of law: arising from the terms of the disposition of property upon death.* The tacit choice of law must arise solely and exclusively from the terms of a will, joint will or agreement as to succession and should be clear and unequivocal.[76] However, the text of the ESR is not very precise on this respect.[77] This lack of precision might render more complex the assessment of the validity of the implicit choice.[78] Should the person making the choice of law be aware of the existence of a conflict of laws, and of the possibility of making a choice between them (*Rechtswahlbewusstsein*)? This would require a genuine 'choice consciousness' on the part of that person, who should comprehend that he is choosing between different laws. Or, rather, is it possible to consider that this awareness is not necessary for ascertaining that the person has a genuine intention to subject his succession to a particular legal system, even in the absence of knowledge as to the existence of a potential conflict of laws?[79]

[75] Calvo Vidal, 'El Derecho de sucesiones en la Unión Europea', p. 100.

[76] Goré, 'La *professio juris*', p. 765.

[77] Article 3.1 regulation no. 593/2008 on the law applicable to contractual obligations (Rome I) is much more precise, when it states that the freedom of choice by the parties 'shall be made expressly or clearly demonstrated by the terms of the contract or the circumstances of the case'; see Carrascosa González, *El Reglamento sucesorio*, p. 139.

[78] J. M. Fontanellas Morell, 'La forma de la designación de Ley en la propuesta de Reglamento europeo en materia de sucesiones', *Rev esp der int* (2011), pp. 123–127.

[79] Bonomi, 'Article 22', pp. 324–325; Davì and Zanobetti, 'Il nuovo diritto internazionale privato delle successioni', pp. 46–47; Davì and Zanobetti, *Il nuovo diritto internazionale privato europeo*, pp. 70–71.

In the literature and case law of countries which allow for an implicit *professio juris,* it is debated whether evidence of the person making the disposition's cognizance of a conflict of laws and the 'awareness to choose' between them is a necessary condition for its validity. Swiss authors unanimously answer this question in the negative, considering the person's intention to act in accordance with the law he might have chosen to be sufficient indication, even in the absence of evidence of a conscious intention to choose that law for that purpose.[80]

In turn, German authors, although their positions may appear to be more rigid, in practice reach similarly permissive conclusions. Even if a reference to rules, institutions or legal categories under a particular law is difficult to interpret as an unequivocal demonstration of an implicit choice of that law, the *favour validitatis* is used in order to consider that a disposition of property upon death, which would be invalid or ineffective under the objectively applicable law, is, on the contrary, valid and effective if it is so under the law considered to have been implicitly chosen. German judges extend the rule of the substantive German law on succession set out in paragraph 2084 BGB, according to which, if a disposition of property upon death is formulated in such a way that it allows for various interpretations, where there is any doubt, the preferred interpretation is the one which allows the disposition in question to be valid and take effect.[81] This solution is also reinforced by the trend of German courts of admitting that, even when the reference to the rules and concepts of German law relating to the entire succession are contrary

[80] See B. Dutoit, *Commentaire de la loi fédérale du 18 décembre 1987*, 2nd ed., (Bâle, Francfort-sur-le-Main, 1997), p. 248; A. Heini, 'Art. 90', en *Zürcher Kommentar zum IPRG*, 2nd ed. (Zürich, Basel, Genf, 2004), p. 1041 *et seq*; A. Bucher, *Commentaire romand. Loi sur le droit international privé. Convention de Lugano* (Bâle, 2011), p. 802. The Swiss Federal Court's case law appears, on the other hand, to be rather more demanding. Its leading decision in this area, dated 3 September 1998, *Arrêts du Tribunal fédéral*, vol. 125, III, p. 35 *et seq.*, relates to the will of a German citizen domiciled in Switzerland, drawn up in German by a German notary and containing significant references to the legal institutions of that country. The court, in fact, felt it necessary to explain the absence of an express *professio juris* in the act. On this point see Davì and Zanobetti, 'Il nuovo diritto internazionale privato delle successioni', p. 46 footnote 168; Davì and Zanobetti, *Il nuovo diritto internazionale privato europeo*, p. 71, footnote 67.

[81] See A. Tiedemann 'Die Rechtswahl im deutschen Internationalen Erbrecht', *RabelsZ* (1991), p. 30; R. Birk, 'Art. 25', in *Münchener Kommentar zum Bürgerlichen Gesetzbuch*, vol. X, *Einführungsgesetz*, 3rd ed. (München, 1998), p. 1356 *et seq.*; H. Dörner, 'Art. 25', in *J. von Staudingers Kommentar zum Bürgerliches Gesetzbuch mit Einführungsgesetz und Nebengesetzen, Internationales Erbrecht, Art. 25, 26 EGBGB* (Berlin, 2007), p. 278. For a more strict position, also see Landgericht Frankfurt a. M. 29 July 1997, *IPRechtssprechung* (1997), p. 233.

to article 25.2 EGBGB, which allows a choice of law only in relation to the part of the estate concerning immovable property located in Germany, the presumed implicit *professio juris,* nevertheless, preserves its value and effects, although only within the limits allowed by the rule in question.[82]

As we can see, in the approaches adopted by both countries' case law, implicit *professio juris* has substantially assumed the role of an instrument providing flexibility in conflict issues in matters of succession, whose use remains, in large part, a matter of the judges' discretion. It is a tool designed principally to protect, so far as possible, the validity and effectiveness of dispositions relating to a person's last wills adopted in accordance with the law which the person considered to be applicable when they were drawn up, from the harm which a mistaken evaluation of the legal context might have caused to the interested person, or which might result from a change in the objectively applicable law due to a subsequent change in residence to a foreign country, or other changes in the connecting factors.[83]

Since the EU legislator was aware of the problems of interpretation which the existence of a tacit choice of law in matters of succession might cause, recital 39 states that 'a choice of law could be regarded as demonstrated by a disposition of property upon death where, for instance, the deceased had referred in his disposition to specific provisions of the law of the State of his nationality or where he had otherwise mentioned that law'. The interpretation of the recital, with a view of alleviating the many and varied problems which might arise from the tacit choice of law, opens the possibility of two different situations. Firstly, a tacit choice of law can arise when a person has drawn up a disposition of property upon death in accordance with his national legislation, simply because he believed that this was the law objectively applicable to his succession. In this case, that law will be the law to be considered as tacitly chosen as applicable to the succession. Secondly, a tacit choice may derive from a simple error, or derive from the fact that the person resided in the same country whose nationality he possessed, or it may refer to a purely domestic succession, which, subsequently, acquires an international

[82] See Davì and Zanobetti, 'Il nuovo diritto internazionale privato delle successioni', p. 47, footnote 172; Davì and Zanobetti, *Il nuovo diritto internazionale privato europeo*, p. 72, footnote 71, where the following decisions are cited: Landgericht Hamburg 12 February 1991, *IPRechtsspechung* (1991), p. 264, Oberlandesgericht Zweibrücken 28 May 2002, *Zeitschrift für das gesamte Familienrecht* (2003), p. 1697.

[83] Davì and Zanobetti, 'Il nuovo diritto internazionale privato delle successioni', pp. 46–47; Davì and Zanobetti, *Il nuovo diritto internazionale privato europeo*, pp. 72–73.

character because the person whose succession is concerned moved his habitual residence to a country different from that of which he holds the nationality.[84] In short, the ESR appears to embrace a wide range of possibilities, without requiring a 'choice consciousness' on the part of the person, in order to overcome the ESR's possible inefficiencies *(favour validitatis)*.[85]

Some indicators are a sufficient proof of the existence of a tacit choice, while others, taken alone, are not sufficient.

1. *Sufficient indicators.* The following are clear examples of circumstances demonstrating a person's wish to submit the succession to the law of the State whose nationality he possesses: (a) When a person refers in his will to concepts or legal categories pertaining to his national law, which do not feature in the law of the state of his habitual residence:[86] for example, if the person is English and he constitutes a testamentary trust in accordance with English law, but he resides in a country where trusts are an unknown institution, there is clear evidence that the person intended to submit his succession to English law. (b) The conclusion of an agreement as to succession or the drawing up of joint wills can equally indicate the implicit wish of the person making the disposition to choose the law of the State whose nationality he possesses, when that law allows such dispositions to be admissible, contrary to the law of the State of his habitual residence.[87]

2. *Insufficient indications.* There are other circumstances which can be taken into account, although they are not sufficient in themselves to

[84] Davì and Zanobetti, 'Il nuovo diritto internazionale privato delle successioni', p. 46; Davì and Zanobetti, *Il nuovo diritto internazionale privato europeo*, p. 70.

[85] Davì and Zanobetti, 'Il nuovo diritto internazionale privato delle successioni nell'Unione europea', p. 48; Davì and Zanobetti, *Il nuovo diritto internazionale privato europeo*, p. 73. For emphasis on the opportunity to resort to using this tool in general terms, with the intention of avoiding 'the risk of producing unjust results', see Max Planck Institute, 'Comments', p. 614; similarly, in the sense that the adoption of a flexible and liberal focus in the field of *professio juris* will have provided the courts with the advantage of having greater flexibility and offering them, in particular, the option 'to assume an implied choice of law if the terms of a testamentary disposition are based on the presumption that a certain law applies', see Dutta, 'Succession and Wills', p. 579.

[86] Bonomi, 'Article 22', pp. 323–324; D. Damascelli, 'I criteri di collegamento impiegati dal regolamento n. 650/2012 per la designazione della legge regolatrice della successione a causa di morte', in P. Franzina and A. Leandro (eds), *Il diritto internazionale privato europeo delle successioni* mortis causa (Milano, 2013), p. 102; *id., Diritto internazionale privato delle successioni*, p. 57; Davì and Zanobetti, 'Il nuovo diritto internazionale privato delle successioni', p. 46; Davì and Zanobetti, *Il nuovo diritto internazionale privato europeo*, p. 69; Rosoux, 'Arrêt sur le régime transitoire', p. 163.

[87] Bonomi, 'Article 22', p. 324.

reveal a person's wish to choose the law of the State whose nationality he possesses as the *lex successionis*. So, for example: (a) if a notarized will is made, the fact of whether the notary is from the State whose nationality the person making the disposition possesses can be taken into account, particularly when the will is drawn up in accordance with the style and classifications characteristic of dispositions of property upon death in that state's notarial practices,[88] (b) the mere use of a particular language in drawing up the will or agreement as to succession does not appear to be sufficient to indicate the existence of a tacit choice of law, although, in addition to other indicators, it may corroborate the tacit choice of the national law of the person whose succession is concerned.[89]

V. Transitional Provisions: Presumptive Choice of Law

The 'transitional provisions' at article 83.4 ESR contemplate a particular case relating to circumstances in which the disposition of property upon death is made prior to 17 August 2015 (date in which the ESR became applicable) in accordance with the law which the person could have chosen under article 22 ESR. In this case, that law is considered to be the law applicable to the succession. This is to be considered rather as a legal fiction than as a tacit choice of law, since the law in question will be automatically applied to the entire succession without it being necessary to determine the wishes of the person making the disposition [see art. 83 no. 17 *et seq.*].[90]

VI. Substantive Autonomy and 'Incorporation by Reference' Clauses

25. The ESR allows a person to subject his succession solely to the law of the State whose nationality he possesses at the time of the choice or at the time of his death, but does not prevent the testator, in the exercise of his substantive autonomy, from incorporating the substantive rules of the

[88] Bonomi, 'Article 22', p. 324; Davì and Zanobetti, 'Il nuovo diritto internazionale privato delle successioni', p. 46.

[89] Damascelli, 'I criteri di collegamento', p. 102; *id., Diritto internazionale privato delle successioni*, p. 57; Davì and Zanobetti, 'Il nuovo diritto internazionale privato delle successioni nell'Unione europea', p. 46; Goré, 'La *professio juris*', pp. 762–766.

[90] Bonomi, 'Article 22', p. 323; D. Damascelli, 'I criteri di collegamento', pp. 103–104; *id., Diritto internazionale privato delle successioni*, p. 58.

law of succession of a particular legal system.[91] This reference or incorporation of substantive rules on succession which are part of a foreign law is distinct from *professio juris.*[92] Various remarks can be made:[93]

1) The *professio juris* is expression of the conflictual autonomy of a person in choosing the law applicable to his succession, whereas the recourse to the 'incorporation by reference' of substantive rules belonging to another foreign legal system, distinct from the national law of that person, is simply an exercise of the substantive autonomy granted to persons to include in their will any disposition that they consider most convenient in the organisation of their succession.

2) *'Incorporation by reference' clauses limited by the lex successionis.* However, the incorporation by reference of rules of a foreign legal system into a will or agreement as to succession, as with any example of substantive autonomy, cannot circumvent the mandatory rules of the law governing the succession under the ESR.

3) *Incorporation of rules belonging to the national law of the person making the disposition of property upon death.* When the rules incorporated into the will or the agreement as to succession belong to the legal system of the State whose nationality the person whose succession is concerned possesses, this reference may be an indicator of a tacit choice of law; if this is the case, the national law implicitly chosen will govern the succession as a whole.

[91] Davì and Zanobetti, 'Il nuovo diritto internazionale privato delle successioni', p. 46; Davì and Zanobetti, *Il nuovo diritto internazionale privato europeo*, p. 70; Tiedemann, 'Die Rechtswahl im deutschen Internationalen Erbrecht', p. 28.

[92] Damascelli, *Diritto internazionale privato delle successioni*, p. 59.

[93] Castellanos Ruiz, 'Sucesión hereditaria', p. 576.

Article 23

The Scope of the Applicable Law

ESPERANZA CASTELLANOS RUIZ

1. The law determined pursuant to Article 21 or Article 22 shall govern the succession as a whole.
2. That law shall govern in particular:
   (a) the causes, time and place of the opening of the succession;
   (b) the determination of the beneficiaries, of their respective shares and of the obligations which may be imposed on them by the deceased, and the determination of other succession rights, including the succession rights of the surviving spouse or partner;
   (c) the capacity to inherit;
   (d) disinheritance and disqualification by conduct;
   (e) the transfer to the heirs and, as the case may be, to the legatees of the assets, rights and obligations forming part of the estate, including the conditions and effects of the acceptance or waiver of the succession or of a legacy;
   (f) the powers of the heirs, the executors of the wills and other administrators of the estate, in particular as regards the sale of property and the payment of creditors, without prejudice to the powers referred to in Article 29(2) and (3);
   (g) liability for the debts under the succession;
   (h) the disposable part of the estate, the reserved shares and other restrictions on the disposal of property upon death as well as claims which persons close to the deceased may have against the estate or the heirs;
   (i) any obligation to restore or account for gifts, advancements or legacies when determining the shares of the different beneficiaries; and
   (j) the sharing-out of the estate.

Summary

I. GENERAL CONSIDERATIONS RELATING TO THE SCOPE OF THE APPLICABLE LAW *page* 352

II. ISSUES GOVERNED BY THE LEX SUCCESSIONIS 353

I. General Considerations Relating to the Scope of the Applicable Law

1. Article 23.1 ESR establishes the principles of *unity* and *universality*, when it states that the *lex successionis*, determined in accordance with article 21 ESR (general rule: the law of the State in which the deceased had his habitual residence at the time of death) or article 22 ESR (*professio juris* or choice of law: the law of the State whose nationality the deceased possessed at the time of making the choice or at the time of death), will govern the succession as a whole. Those principles aim to achieve legal certainty and avoid fragmentation of the succession,[1] as stated by recital 37 ESR, according to which the *lex successionis* should govern the succession as a whole, that is to say, all assets and rights forming part of the inheritance, independently of their nature and location in another Member State or in a third State, considering all the deceased's assets as a single estate subject, in principle, to one law only.[2]

2. This means, on the one hand, that the ESR intends to avoid the territorial scission of the succession, consisting in the application of different laws depending upon the nature and location of the assets of the estate. On the other hand, the ESR also aims to avoid a 'substantive' or 'functional' scission of the succession along substantive or functional lines, that is to say, the application of different laws to the different aspects of one sole succession; and, consequently, it establishes that the *lex successionis*, in principle, governs all issues which might arise from a succession, from its opening until ownership of the assets is transferred to its beneficiaries.[3] In this sense, recital 42 indicates that

> the law determined as the law applicable to the succession should govern the succession from the opening of the succession to the transfer of ownership of the assets forming part of the estate to the beneficiaries as determined by that law. It should include questions relating to the administration of the estate and to liability for the debts under the succession. The payment of the debts under the succession may, depending, in

[1] E. Castellanos Ruiz, 'Sucesión hereditaria: Reglamento 650/2012 sobre sucesión internacional', in A.-L. Calvo Caravaca and J. Carrascosa González (eds), *Derecho Internacional Privado*, 15th ed., vol. II (Granada, 2014), p. 580.

[2] G. Khairallah, 'La détermination de la loi applicable à la succession', in G. Khairallah and M. Revillard (eds), *Droit européen des successions internationales (Le Règlement du 4 juillet 2012)* (Paris, 2013), pp. 48–49.

[3] Regarding the 'territorial' scission and the 'substantive' or 'functional' scission, see M. Ferid, 'Le rattachement autonome de la transmission successorale en droit international privé', *Hague Recueil*, vol. 142 (1974), p. 110.

particular, on the law applicable to the succession, include the taking into account of a specific ranking of the creditors.[4]

Nevertheless, the ESR provides for exceptions both to the exclusion of the territorial scission in articles 30 and 32 ESR, and the exclusion of the functional scission in article 29 ESR.

II. Issues Governed by the *lex successionis*

3. Article 23.2 ESR governs the scope of the applicable law and enumerates the areas included within the wide scope of application of the *lex successionis*, in an attempt to include the succession as a whole. The list is illustrative and not exhaustive, since article 23.3 ESR indicates that the law applicable to the succession will govern 'in particular' the listed matters.[5]

4. In order to determine the scope of the law applicable to the succession, the EU legislator took inspiration from article 7 of the 1989 Hague Convention on the Law Applicable to Succession to the Estates of Deceased Persons and from articles 80 to 82 of the 2004 Belgian code of private international law.[6] However, the ESR differentiates itself clearly from the solutions contained in the 1989 Convention. On the one hand, the ESR has significantly increased the scope of application of the *lex successionis* compared to the 1989 Hague Convention: while article 7 of the Hague Convention enumerates five matters, article 23.2 ESR lists ten issues governed by the *lex successionis*, in line with its all-inclusive nature.[7] On the other hand, this is an indication of how the ESR has been profoundly innovative when compared with the Hague Convention, by including the administration and transfer of the inheritance within the scope of application of the *lex successionis*.

[4] A. Bonomi, 'Article 23, a)–d), h), i)', in A. Bonomi and P. Wautelet, *Le droit européen des successions. Commentaire du Règlement nº 650/2012 du 4 juillet 2012* (Bruxelles, 2013), pp. 338–339.

[5] Castellanos Ruiz, 'Sucesión hereditaria', p. 580; A. Davì and A. Zanobetti, 'Il nuovo diritto internazionale privato delle successioni nell'Unione europea', *CdT*, 5/2 (2013), p. 18; A. Davì and A. Zanobetti, *Il nuovo diritto internazionale privato europeo delle successioni* (Torino, 2014), pp. 26–27; G. Hohloch, 'Kommentierung der EuErbRVO' in Erman, *BGB: Kommentar*, 14th ed. (Köln, 2014), p. 6702.

[6] Bonomi, 'Article 23, a)–d), h), i)', p. 346; M. Revillard, 'Portée de la loi applicable', in G. Khairallah and M. Revillard (eds), *Droit européen des successions internationales (Le Règlement du 4 juillet 2012)* (Paris, 2013), pp. 69 and 74.

[7] D. Damascelli, *Diritto internazionale privato delle successioni a causa di morte* (Milano, 2013), p. 81; Revillard, 'Portée de la loi applicable', p. 71.

5. The study of the matters governed by the *lex successionis*, listed in article 23.2 ESR, must be done taking into account article 1.2 ESR, setting out the issues which are excluded from the *lex successionis*' scope.[8] Often the exclusion or inclusion of particular matters from or within the scope of application of the *lex successionis* are two sides of the same coin. In other words, article 1.2 ESR governs the scope of application in a negative sense and article 23.2 ESR in a positive sense.

Specifically, the law applicable to the succession will govern (article 23.2 ESR and recital 42):

6. a) *The causes, time and place of the opening of the succession.* Article 23.2(a) ESR subjects the causes, time and place of the opening of the succession to the *lex successionis*. In most national laws, death is the only circumstance which can cause the opening of a succession in relation to a foreign deceased. There are issues such as knowing whether a person is dead as well as determining the time of his death, for example in the case of brain death, which can arise as preliminary matters to the opening of the succession.[9] As these issues relating to the death of a person and the extinction of his legal personality are not matters of succession but rather matters which affect the civil status of such persons, they are excluded from the *lex successionis*, as article 1.2 (a) ESR expressly provides. These issues remain subject to the law personally applicable to the deceased according to the conflict of laws rules of the *forum*, whether that is the law of the State whose nationality he possesses, where he is domiciled or of his habitual residence. In the case of the latter, that coincides with the law objectively applicable to the succession.[10]

For cases where persons die during the same event and it is uncertain which persons predecease the others, article 32 ESR contains a special substantive rule, which states: 'where two or more persons whose successions are governed by different laws die in circumstances in which it is uncertain in what order their deaths occurred, and where those laws provide differently for that situation or make no provision for it at all,

[8] Damascelli, *Diritto internazionale privato delle successioni*, p. 40; Hohloch, 'Kommentierung der EuErbRVO', pp. 6698–6699.

[9] G. Biagioni, 'L'ambito di applicazione del regolamento sulle successioni', in P. Franzina and A. Leandro (eds), *Il diritto internazionale privato europeo delle successioni* mortis causa (Milano, 2013), pp. 44–45; Bonomi, 'Article 23', pp. 346–347.

[10] J. Carrascosa González, *El Reglamento sucesorio europeo 650/2012 de 4 de julio 2012. Análisis crítico* (Granada, 2014), pp. 167–168; Revillard, 'Portée de la loi applicable', pp. 71–72; Castellanos Ruiz, 'Sucesión hereditaria', p. 581.

none of the deceased persons shall have any rights to the succession of the other or others' [see art. 32].

In addition to death, in many legal systems the disappearance, absence or presumed death of a natural person are also causes for opening a succession, wherever the *lex successionis* makes such provisions.[11] Other reasons for the opening of the succession would probably raise the issue of their being in contrast with the public policy of the forum [ref: art. 35].

7. b) *The determination of the beneficiaries, of their respective shares and of the obligations which may be imposed on them by the deceased, and the determination of other succession rights, including the succession rights of the surviving spouse or partner.* Article 23.2(b) ESR states that the *lex successionis* determines the beneficiaries and their succession rights.[12] In this sense, recital 47 establishes that under most laws, the term 'beneficiaries' covers 'heirs and legatees and persons entitled to a reserved share although, for instance, the legal position of legatees is not the same under all laws.'[13] That position will depend upon the law applicable to the succession, under which it may be established that a legatee acquires 'only a claim against the heirs'. Devolution of estate is governed by the law of succession, which determines the amount of inheritance rights including the reserved shares, the heirs, the order of succession, the extent of the call to succession, the surviving spouse or partner's rights of succession, the modalities and limits of the succession by representation and the transfer of the right to accept the inheritance.[14] However, it is indeed possible to apply the public policy exception to the application of a foreign law which excludes from inheritance, or which reduces rights of inheritance, in relation to certain persons on the basis of discriminatory reasons such as their religion, ideology, belief, race or sex [see art. 35 no. 15 *et seq.*].[15]

Specifically, the law applicable to the succession will govern:[16] (i) whether the transfer of the assets is *ab intestato* or conversely is made

[11] Hohloch, 'Kommentierung der EuErbRVO', p. 6699.

[12] Hohloch, 'Kommentierung der EuErbRVO', p. 6699.

[13] Carrascosa González, *El Reglamento Sucesorio*, pp. 168–176; Revillard, 'Portée de la loi applicable', pp. 72–73.

[14] Damascelli, *Diritto internazionale privato delle successioni*, p. 82.

[15] M. Azavant, 'L'ordre public succesoral', *Droit de la famille*, no. 10 (2013), p. 19; A. Devaux, 'The European Regulations on Succession of July 2012: A Path Towards the End of the Succession Conflicts of Law in Europe, or not?', *The International Lawyer* (2013), p. 229.

[16] Bonomi, 'Article 23, a)–d), h), i)', pp. 348–350.

under a disposition of property upon death; (ii) in the case of intestate successions, the different categories of successors, generally grouped in grades of kinship, specifically which heirs are called to succeed and their order; (iii) in the case of a testate succession, the beneficiaries' rights and obligations, as well as the different categories of successors and the criteria for distinguishing between them (heirs instituted in the will or agreement as to succession, legatees) and the modalities of transfer of the assets of the estate (representation, substitution, etc.); (iv) whether a pupillary, exemplary, vulgar or trust substitution is possible; (v) the terms and effects of the succession proceedings by which the heirs, legatees and any other beneficiaries can enforce their expectations under the succession (declaration of heirs, distribution of inheritance, legatee petitions); (vi) the rights of all the successors, whether by virtue of familial relationship or any other connection with the deceased, including the surviving spouse and partner's rights of succession;[17] it should be underlined on that respect that the rights which apply to spouses or partners as a result of the dissolution of the matrimonial property regime or of the partnership are excluded from the *lex successionis*, as article 1.2 (d) ESR expressly states.

8. c) *The capacity to inherit.* Although article 1.2(b) ESR excludes the legal capacity of natural persons from the scope of application of the *lex successionis*, the capacity to inherit and the capacity of the person making a disposition of property upon death to make such a disposition are governed by the *lex successionis*, respectively under article 23.2(c) ESR and under article 26.1(a) ESR.[18] Article 23.3(c) ESR governs both the 'capacity' and 'incapacity' to inherit. Examples of issues included within the *lex successionis*:[19] (i) the inheritance rights of the conceived but unborn child; (ii) the requirements minors must fulfil in order for them to be able to inherit; (iii) incapacity or prohibitions on inheriting in particular circumstances, depending upon the different succession rights; (iv) capacity to inherit under a will.

9. d) *Disinheritance and disqualification by conduct.* Article 23.2(d) submits disinheritance and disqualification to the *lex successionis.*[20] Reasons provided for 'disinheritance' set out in the various legal

[17] Damascelli, *Diritto internazionale privato delle successioni*, pp. 82–83.

[18] For some perplexities in this respect, see P. Lagarde, 'Les principes de base du nouveau réglement européen sur les successions', *Rev crit dr int priv* (2012), pp. 707–708.

[19] Bonomi, 'Article 23, a)–d), h), i)', pp. 350–352; Carrascosa González, *El Reglamento Sucesorio*, pp. 176–178; p. 85; Hohloch, 'Kommentierung der EuErbRVO', p. 6699.

[20] Hohloch, 'Kommentierung der EuErbRVO', pp. 6699–6700.

systems are based upon particularly reprehensible, even criminal, behaviours. The law applicable to the succession governs, on the one hand, the methods of disinheritance – normally set out in the disposition of property upon death – as well as the disinherited parties means of opposing it; and, on the other hand, the effects of the disinheritance such as the possibility and forms of pardons.[21] Regarding 'disqualification by conduct', the *lex successionis* governs the effects of the indignity and whether or not they occur automatically, as well as their absolute character or the admissibility of a pardon on the part of the person whose succession is concerned.[22] Absolute incapacity to inherit, the reasons for disinheritance and the causes of indignity, as well as the reinstatement of the disqualified person by the person whose succession is concerned are questions which do not, in reality, affect the presumed heir's capacity, but rather the legal inheritance regime; they are therefore governed by the *lex successionis.*[23] Depending upon the reasons for the disinheritance and the causes of indignity set out in the law governing the succession, the public policy exception could play a role, under article 35 ESR [see art. 35 no. 22].[24]

10. e) *The transfer to the heirs and, as the case may be, to the legatees of the assets, rights and obligations forming part of the estate, including the conditions and effects of the acceptance or waiver of the succession or of a legacy.* Article 23.3(e) ESR covers a large number of issues:[25] the administration of the estate, the determination of the assets included in the estate, the legal regime for acceptance and renunciation of the inheritance and the legacy; the legal regime for the unclaimed estate; or

[21] Bonomi, 'Article 23, a)–d), h), i)', p. 353. [22] Bonomi, 'Article 23, a)–d), h), i)', p. 352.

[23] A.-L. Calvo Caravaca, 'Sucesión hereditaria', in J. D. González Campos et al., *Derecho internacional privado parte especial* (Madrid, 1995), pp. 393–422; *id.*, 'Artículo 9.8 Código civil', *Comentarios al Código Civil y a las Compilaciones forales*, vol. I, 2nd ed. (Madrid, 1995), pp. 350–391; *id.*, 'La sucesión hereditaria en el derecho internacional privado español', *Revista General de Derecho* (1986), pp. 3103–3138; Carrascosa González, *El Reglamento Sucesorio*, p. 178; Castellanos Ruiz, 'Sucesión hereditaria', p. 582.

[24] Azavant, 'L'ordre public succesoral', p. 19; Carrascosa González, *El Reglamento Sucesorio*, pp. 178–179; Revillard, 'Portée de la loi applicable', p. 73.

[25] P. Wautelet, 'Article 23, e)-g), j)', in A. Bonomi and P. Wautelet, *Le droit européen des successions. Commentaire du Règlement n° 650/2012 du 4 juillet 2012* (Bruxelles, 2013), pp. 354–360; Carrascosa González, *El Reglamento Sucesorio*, p. 179; Hohloch, 'Kommentierung der EuErbRVO', p. 6700; Castellanos Ruiz, 'Sucesión hereditaria', p. 584; Lagarde, 'Les principes de base', p. 711; Revillard, 'Portée de la loi applicable', pp. 74–75; F. Sauvage, 'L'option et la transmission du passif dans les successions internationales au regard du règlement européen', in G. Khairallah and M. Revillard (eds), *Droit européen des successions internationales (Le Règlement du 4 juillet 2012)* (Paris, 2013), p. 117.

the acquisition of the ownership of the assets being inherited.[26] Consequently, all transfers whether of assets or liabilities remain subject to the sole law of succession.[27]

There are two main systems for the administration of inheritance in comparative substantive succession law: the 'Latin system' followed by civil law countries, and the 'Anglo-Saxon system' followed in common law countries.[28] In the civil law system and, in general, in Latin countries, once the inheritance is accepted it produces a direct transfer of ownership from the deceased to the heirs, who can automatically proceed to administer the assets of the estate, save where the deceased has appointed an executor or a person to distribute the assets *ex professo*, or the judge, on application by an interested party, appoints an administrator.[29] In these countries there is no, or only minimal, legal control over the administration of the estate. Consequently, all problems relating to the administration of the estate are governed by the *lex successionis*. In common law countries, there is the intervention of an administrator or an executor, granted with extensive powers which are subject to rigorous judicial control to preserve and wind-up the deceased's estate in order to administer the estate and allocate its assets to the beneficiaries. In this sense, the Anglo-Saxon legal systems separate and distinguish problems strictly relating to succession from those relating to the administration of the estate, subjecting the latter to the *lex fori* – the law of the country where the administration is taking place and which is the law of the State from

[26] Carrascosa González, *El Reglamento Sucesorio*, p. 179.

[27] Wautelet, 'Article 23, e)–g), j)', p. 355; Lagarde, 'Les principes de base', pp. 712–715; Sauvage, 'L'option et la transmission du passif', p. 118.

[28] A. Rodríguez Benot, 'La acreditación de la cualidad de administrador de una herencia internacional: el certificado europeo de heredero', in R. Viñas and G. Garriga (eds), *Perspectivas del Derecho sucesorio en Europa* (Barcelona, 2009), pp. 175–218; Carrascosa González, *El Reglamento Sucesorio*, pp. 179–181.

[29] There are exceptions to the direct transfer of ownership from the deceased to the heirs in some civil law countries, such as the Austrian law proceedings in the *Einantwortung* matter, where transfer of ownership to the heirs did not occur directly but rather by means of special acceptance procedures. The death of the deceased is not sufficient for transfer of ownership of his assets to the heirs. Inheritance acceptance proceedings involving a judge are necessary. Under Austrian law, the transfer of the assets of the estate to the heirs is governed by the decision of a court. Until that court makes its decision, the heir does not take title to the deceased's rights and obligations. Between the opening of the succession and the heir's acceptance the inheritance is *unclaimed*, meaning that the court can even, if necessary, appoint an executor. When the heir accepts he is able to act as a representative for the succession, but there is no transfer of the assets of the estate until the *Einantwortung*. See A. Bonomi, 'Successions internationales: conflits de lois et de jurisdictions', *Hague Recueil*, vol. 350 (2010), pp. 333–334.

which the administrator's authority derives – or the law of the place where the assets are located. While countries with little organisation welcome, without difficulty, organised succession administration systems, it is more complicated for the reverse to be accepted: for example, an English judge will not hear a claim over a property located in England by a Spanish heir without a previous judicial authorization.[30]

In light of the significant differences in legal regulation amongst civil law and common law countries, the ESR opts for the solution offered by civil law countries and includes the administration of the estate within the scope of application of the *lex successionis*, subject, however, to specific rules relating to the appointment and the powers of administrators and executors, as set out in article 29 ESR and recital 43 ESR [see art. 29].[31]

Article 23 ESR also governs the acceptance and renunciation of the inheritance.[32] This provision refers to 'the conditions and effects of the acceptance or waiver of the succession or of a legacy': the law governing the succession determines whether the acquisition of the rights of succession occurs automatically on the opening of the succession and of the devolution of the estate, or if a formal acceptance is necessary, together with the legal regime for acceptance by legatees and whether it is possible or necessary to accept, partially or in its entirety, an inheritance with more liabilities than assets,[33] or the possibility of limiting the liability for the debts of the succession.[34]

[30] C. Baldus, 'Erbe und Vermächtnisnehmer nach der Erbrechtsverordnung', *GPR: Zeitschrift für Gemeinschaftsprivatrecht* (2012), pp. 312–215; *id.*, '¿Hacia un nuevo derecho sucesorio europeo?, *Anales de la Academia Matritense del Notariado*, no. 49 (2009), pp. 419–438. J. A. Carrillo Salcedo, 'La ley aplicable a la forma de las disposiciones testamentarias. Nota sobre el proyecto de Convenio adoptado por la Conferencia de La Haya de Derecho internacional privado', *Rev esp der int* (1961), pp. 169–194.

[31] Lagarde, 'Les principes de base', p. 714.

[32] Wautelet, 'Article 23, e)–g), j)', pp. 357–360.

[33] Carrascosa González, *El Reglamento Sucesorio*, p. 186; Sauvage, 'L'option et la transmission du passif', pp. 117–124; J.-P. Schmidt, 'Die kollisionsrechtliche Behandlung dinglich wirkender Vermächtnisse', *RabelsZ* (2013), pp. 1–30.

[34] In some legal systems, as, i.e., under article 1012 of the Spanish civil code and under articles 484–511 of the Italian civil code, an heir can accept an inheritance with the so called benefit of inventory, whose application in foreign countries where such a mechanism is an unknown legal institution can give rise to difficulties deriving from the lack of adequate procedural provisions in the forum. This institution has, for example, caused many problems for German judges, since the German legal system does not recognise acceptance under the benefit of inventory. This was the case in the Bayerisches Oberstes Landesgericht judgment of 2 December 1965, *Zannantonio, NJW* (1967), p. 447 *et seq.* On this point see Ferid, 'Le rattachement autonome', p. 125 *et seq.*;

The legal regime applicable to an unclaimed estate is also subject to the *lex successionis*. However, a special rule concerning the pretence of the State over an unclaimed estate is provided for in article 33 ESR [see art. 33].

Also the acquisition of ownership in the assets of the estate is a matter governed by the *lex successionis*, as is stated in article 23.2(e) ESR, in connection with recital 42, and can also be inferred from article 31 ESR and recitals 15.[35]

11. f) *The powers of the heirs, the executors of the wills and other administrators of the estate, in particular as regards the sale of property and the payment of creditors, without prejudice to the powers referred to in Article 29(2) and (3).* Article 23.2(f) ESR includes in the scope of the law applicable to the succession the administration of inheritance, without prejudice to the application of special rules relating to the administrators' appointment and authorities in particular situations set out in article 29 ESR.[36] The ESR adopts a unitary vision of administration of inheritance: the *lex successionis* governs the entirety of the succession proceedings, including the administration. This solution has the advantage of preserving the unity and coherence of the succession proceedings, avoiding their being dispersed.[37]

12. g) *Liability for the debts under the succession.* Liability for debts and charges which the succession entails is governed by the *lex successionis*. Article 23.2(g) ESR refers to liability for 'the debts under the succession' (the Spanish version mentions 'las deudas y cargas de la herencia', while versions in other language versions only refer to the debts). This is an ambiguous expression referring to the succession liabilities, that is to say, the debts which exist prior to the death of the deceased and the debts originated by the opening of the succession itself, including taxes.[38] Paragraph (g) must be read in connection with paragraph (e) of this same

A. Davì, 'Riflessioni sul futuro diritto internazionale privato europeo delle successioni', *Riv dir int* (2005), p. 337; Davì and Zanobetti, 'Il nuovo diritto internazionale privato delle successioni', p. 27, in particular footnote 96.

35 See Castellanos Ruiz, 'Sucesión hereditaria', pp. 587–588.

36 Wautelet, 'Article 23, e)–g), j)', pp. 360–366; S. Godechot-Patris, 'Le nouveau droit international privé des successions: entre satisfactions et craintes . . .', *Dalloz* (2012), pp. 2462–2469; *id.*, 'L'administration des successions', in G. Khairallah and M. Revillard (eds), *Droit européen des successions internationales (Le Règlement du 4 juillet 2012)* (Paris, 2013), pp. 87–104; Hohloch, 'Kommentierung der EuErbRVO', p. 6700; Revillard, 'Portée de la loi applicable', p. 75.

37 Godechot-Patris, 'L'administration des successions', p. 90.

38 Wautelet, 'Article 23, e)–g), j)', p. 363.

article 23 ESR, which refers to 'the transfer to the heirs and, as the case may be, to the legatees of the assets, rights and obligations forming part of the estate'.

Accordingly, the *lex successionis* governs:[39]

i) The determination of the amount of the deceased's debts for which the heirs, legatees or persons entitled to a reserved share are liable, and within what limits. In the different legal systems, liability can be *ultra vires hereditatis* if the heirs' liability is unlimited, or *intra vires hereditatis* if it is limited to the estate assets. When *lex successionis* provides for unlimited and personal liability on the part of the heirs, that law will also govern the ways of limiting that liability and, when applicable, acceptance under the benefit of inventory and cases in which this form of acceptance is mandatory in order to protect special categories of heirs, such as minors and incapables. The *lex successionis* will also determine whether the heirs' liability is joint and several or joint. Therefore, claims which the beneficiaries who have paid can make against the other beneficiaries are also subject to the *lex successionis.*
ii) Ways of protecting the deceased's creditors and persons entitled to a reserved share, in cases where there is confusion relating to the property of the deceased and the heirs' personal property, since this situation can create prejudice. Hence, if the *lex successionis* provides for unlimited liability, this gives rise to confusion over the heir's personal property and the estate. However, if the heirs' liability is limited there is a clear separation of property.[40]
iii) The 'payment of creditors' of the deceased is expressly provided for by way of example, amongst 'the powers of the heirs, the executors of the wills and other administrators of the estate, at paragraph (f) of article 23.2 ESR, subject to the *lex successionis*. However, the ESR does not seem to provide for the resolution of conflicts which can arise between the deceased's creditors in the event of more than one person accepting the same asset. The solution to this is ambiguous since recital 42 ESR states that 'the payment of the debts under the succession may, depending, in particular, on the law applicable to the

[39] Wautelet, 'Article 23, e)-g), j)', p. 365; Damascelli, *Diritto internazionale privato delle successioni,* pp. 85–86; Hohloch, 'Kommentierung der EuErbRVO', pp. 6700–6701; Revillard, 'Portée de la loi applicable', pp. 76–77; Sauvage, 'L'option et la transmission du passif', pp. 118–124.

[40] In this sense, for example, article 1003 of the Spanish civil code provides for the unlimited liability of heirs: see L. Díez-Picazo and A. Gullón, *Sistema de Derecho Civil,* vol. IV.2, *Derecho de sucesiones*, 11th ed. (Madrid, 2012), p. 253.

succession, include the taking into account of a specific ranking of the creditors'.[41] Similarly, the actions, enforcement and other specific measures which the creditors can take, fall outside the scope of the *lex successionis* since they usually deal with procedural issues governed by the law of the forum.

13. h) *The disposable part of the estate, the reserved shares and other restrictions on the disposal of property upon death as well as claims which persons close to the deceased may have against the estate or the heirs.* Article 23.2(h) ESR states that all issues relating to the reserved shares and any other restrictions on the freedom of a person in disposing of his estate upon death are governed by the *lex successionis*.[42] This is the only reference contained in ESR articles to persons entitled to a reserved share. The *lex successionis* reflects a close connection between the deceased, and his closest relatives, and the State whose law is declared applicable, so that the deceased's relatives should not be surprised by the substantive content of that law. The heirs normally know in advance whether they have a right to reserved shares, in accordance with the provisions of the *lex successionis*. A specific issue which might arise is where the *lex fori* is based upon a system where reserved shares are considered a matter of public policy under article 35 ESR. This is not to say that reserved shares are necessarily considered part of public policy, and therefore, must apply even though the *lex successionis* does not provide for them:[43] in most European legal systems, application of a foreign law which does not provide for a system of reserved shares should not be considered contrary to the public policy of the forum [see art. 35 no. 6 *et seq.*].[44]

[41] Wautelet, 'Article 23, e)–g), j)', p. 365.

[42] Bonomi, 'Article 23, a)–d), h), i)', pp. 366–371; Carrascosa González, *El Reglamento sucesorio europeo*, pp. 189–191; Hohloch, 'Kommentierung der EuErbRVO', p. 6701; Damascelli, *Diritto internazionale privato delle successioni*, pp. 87–90; Revillard, 'Portée de la loi applicable', p. 77.

[43] Carrascosa González, *El Reglamento Sucesorio*, p. 190; Damascelli, *Diritto internazionale privato delle successioni*, pp. 85–86; Lagarde, 'Les principes de base', pp. 709–710; A. Vaquer Aloy, 'Reflexiones sobre una eventual reforma de la legítima', *InDret* (2007), pp. 1–25.

[44] Damascelli, *Diritto internazionale privato delle successioni*, pp. 85–86; Davì and Zanobetti, 'Il nuovo diritto internazionale privato delle successioni', pp. 44–45; Davì and Zanobetti, *Il nuovo diritto internazionale privato europeo*, pp. 67–68. For the position of Spanish courts, see E. Castellanos Ruiz, *Unidad versus pluralidad legal de la sucesión internacional* (Granada, 2001), pp. 81–88. The Spanish position is made very clear in two Spanish Supreme Court judgments 18 November 1996 (*Lowenthal*) and 21 May 1999 (*Denney*) and also in the Malaga Provincial Court decision 13 March 2002. It is even clearer in the decision of the Alicante Provincial Court 27 February 2004, the decision of

Protection of the persons entitled to a reserved share was one of the reasons why the United Kingdom and Ireland did not *opt in*. These States wanted to avoid the application of a foreign *lex successionis* from restricting their testamentary freedom.[45] They also did not want to put the very significant amount which charities receive by virtue of wills at risk of legal clawback actions or recovery of the reserved shares by persons entitled to reserved shares under foreign laws which might be applicable in the United Kingdom and Ireland through the ESR.[46]

14. We must, however, take into account the fact that recital 50 ESR establishes that the law applicable to the validity of the dispositions of property upon death or the agreements as to succession must be without prejudice to the rights of any person who, under the *lex successionis*, has a right to a reserved share or another right of which he cannot be deprived by the person whose estate is concerned.[47] That is to say that the reserved shares are always governed by the *lex successionis*, determined in accordance with articles 21 and 22 ESR. Therefore, if the will or agreement as to succession made by the deceased does not make provision for reserved shares, the *lex successionis* would have to be applied in order to confirm what the consequences would be.[48] In this event, the preterition of a reserved heir does not entail the invalidity of the will, but rather the shares of the other heirs must be reduced for accommodating the reserved shares, unless the person entitled to a reserved share renounces, or unless there is any reason for disinheritance under the *lex successionis*.

15. Article 23.2(h) ESR also refers to 'other restrictions on the disposal of property upon death as well as claims which persons close to the deceased may have against the estate or the heirs'. In many legal systems,

the Tarragona Provincial Court 13 May 2004 and the decision of the Granada Provincial Court 19 July 2004. The latter decisions considers that the portion of reserved shares varies significantly between different legislation in the Spanish legal system, and cite the free distribution system practised in Aragon and Vizcaya and the invariable, single quota system followed in Catalonia as examples. Accordingly, it is not possible to consider the application of foreign laws providing for a different system of reserved shares to that set out in the Spanish civil code to be contrary to public policy, either when the reserved shares established by those laws is equal or similar to some of the Spanish local laws, or when no reserved share is provided for. Regarding the positions of courts in other European countries [see art. 35 no. 6 *et seq.*].

[45] Carrascosa González, *El Reglamento Sucesorio*, pp. 263–264; Lagarde, 'Les principes de base', pp. 710–711.

[46] Bonomi, 'Article 23, a)–d), h), i)', p. 372; Carrascosa González, *El Reglamento Sucesorio*, p. 48; Lagarde, 'Les principes de base', p. 709.

[47] Lagarde, 'Les principes de base', p. 711. [48] Lagarde, 'Les principes de base', p. 711.

reserved shares are completely unknown; however, these legal systems provide other mechanisms which restrict the testamentary freedom in order to protect certain persons.[49] One such example is the family provisions of English law.[50] Family provisions comprise certain persons' right to request that courts award them payment of an amount from the deceased's inheritance provided that: (a) that person is neither the heir nor the legatee nor in any other way a beneficiary of the inheritance or part thereof in respect of a reasonable amount judged from an economic point of view, whether under the will or any *ab intestato* statutory disposition; (b) the court, who has a very wide discretion in that respect, bearing in mind the circumstances of the particular case, considers the applicant's request reasonable. This process remedies the excesses of testamentary freedom, although the applicant has no genuine right but rather is dependent upon the judge's discretion.[51] Another protection mechanism similar to family provisions is the creation of a system based upon post mortem maintenance obligations in favour of certain of the deceased's family members, under Canadian law. The *lex successionis* applies to these maintenance obligations because they 'arise from the death', since obligations for maintenance which are not triggered by death are excluded from the scope of application of the *lex successionis*, under article 1.2(e) ESR. There are also other means of protection for certain relatives of the deceased, such as family allowance, homestead allowance or exempt property allowance, provided for in many states of the United States of America, which provide surviving spouses and, occasionally in the absence of a spouse, children, with the right to obtain certain hereditary rights, the value of which is set by law. Unlike the reserved shares, these amounts are not generally dependent upon the value of the assets being inherited. The allocation can consist in a sum of money or in the acquisition of certain of the deceased's assets, such as personal assets or those intended for use in the family home. Only assets in existence at the time of death are taken into account as a type of legacy provided for at law. Another protection mechanism, similar in this case to the reserved share, provided for in very different forms in the majority of common law countries is the elective share, in favour of the surviving

[49] S. Cámara Lapuente, '¿Derecho europeo de sucesiones? Un apunte', in S. Cámara Lapuente (ed), *Derecho privado europeo* (Madrid, 2003), p. 1219.

[50] Bonomi, 'Article 23, a)-d), h), i)', pp. 368–371; Carrascosa González, *El Reglamento Sucesorio*, pp. 5–6.

[51] On the discretion forming part of this measure, see: Vaquer Aloy, 'Reflexiones sobre una eventual reforma de la legítima', pp. 1–25.

spouse. This mechanism is an attempt to alleviate the inconveniences presented by those countries which do not provide for the concept of a 'matrimonial property regime', such as they are known in civil law countries. In these cases an authentic reserved share is calculated as such on an 'enlarged' estate which comprises not only the existing assets but also certain *inter vivos* gifts. The portion represented by the reserved share varies from one country to another: sometimes it is fixed and sometimes it depends upon the length of the marriage.[52]

16. i) *Any obligation to restore or account for gifts, advancements or legacies when determining the shares of the different beneficiaries.* The *lex successionis* does not apply to the validity or to the effects of *inter vivos* gifts. This is expressly provided for at article 1.2(g) ESR, when it excludes the following from the regulation's scope: 'property rights, interests and assets created or transferred otherwise than by succession', which includes by way of example, but is not limited to, 'gifts, joint ownership with a right of survivorship, pension plans, insurance contracts and arrangements of a similar nature'. These are assets, rights or interests created prior to the death of the deceased, otherwise than by succession, but which become due after death.

According to article 23.2(i) ESR, the *lex successionis* is only applied in order to identify gifts which are subject to 'clawback', that is to say, gifts made by the deceased which must be reintegrated into the estate in order to determine the shares due to the beneficiaries under the inheritance.[53] As is stated in recital 14, it must be the *lex successionis* 'which determines whether gifts or other forms of dispositions *inter vivos* giving rise to a right *in rem* prior to death should be restored or accounted for the purposes of determining the shares of the beneficiaries in accordance with the law applicable to the succession'.[54]

Provision is made for this 'clawback' obligation both in civil law systems and in common law countries. In the latter it is referred to as

[52] Bonomi, 'Article 23, a)–d), h), i)', pp. 370–371; T. Brandi, *Das Haager Abkommen von 1989 über das auf die Erbfolge anzuwendende Recht* (Berlin, 1996), p. 176 *et seq.*

[53] Hohloch, 'Kommentierung der EuErbRVO', p. 6701.

[54] For example, if the *lex successionis* were Spanish law, article 818 of the Spanish civil code provides that it is necessary to add the gifts made by the deceased, which are subject to 'clawback', to the assets of the estate. However, article 1041 of the Spanish civil code exempts certain gifts from clawback, such as expenses relating to support, education and the treatment of illnesses; see P. de Pablo Contreras, 'Legítimas y mejora: su satisfacción en la sucesión testada', in M. A. Pérez Álvarez (ed), *Curso de Derecho Civil (V) Derecho de sucesiones* (Madrid, 2013), pp. 312–319; Díez-Picazo and Gullón, *Sistema de Derecho Civil*, vol. IV, pp. 156 and 176–179.

hotchpot or advancement. However, this obligation is not recognised in Islamic legal systems. In addition, in countries which do indeed provide for the possibility of reintegrating gifts made by the deceased during his lifetime, this is governed in very different ways, both as regards the conditions required and the assets referred to, as well as the methods for calculating its allocation.[55]

The reduction of gifts when more is given or received *inter vivos* than could be given or received under a will, is a mechanism which allows beneficiaries to the inheritance to obtain their legal share, in order to remedy harm suffered.

It is necessary to take into account the fact that gifts are contracts governed by regulation (EC) no. 593/2008 of 17 June 2008 on the law applicable to contractual obligations (Rome I). However, not all gifts are governed by Rome I, since its article 1.2, at paragraphs (b) and (c), excludes from its scope obligations deriving from family relationships or relationships of comparable effect, from matrimonial property regimes or property regimes of relationships deemed by the law applicable to such relationships to have comparable effects to marriage, and from wills and succession; gifts *propter nuptias* or *mortis causa* should, accordingly, be excluded. Besides, in most cases, *mortis causa* gifts are considered to be agreements as to succession, and as such they are governed by article 25 ESR [see art. 25].

However, the obligation to reintegrate assets received by way of a gift into the estate, once the donor dies, is governed by the *lex successionis*, which can give rise to serious issues for the gift beneficiary. If the gift was validly made, in accordance with the applicable law as determined by Rome I rules, it is debateable whether, later, when the donor dies, the beneficiary must return part or all of the assets received, under the *lex successionis*.[56]

55 Bonomi, 'Article 23, a)–d), h), i)', p. 371.

56 Biagioni, 'L'ambito di applicazione del regolamento sulle successioni', pp. 38–39; P. Blanco-Morales Limones, 'El ámbito de la ley aplicable, incluida la administración de la sucesión', www.successions-europe.eu/event-downloads; *id.*, 'Las sucesiones internacionales y su régimen jurídico', *Revista de Derecho de la Unión Europea*, n. 22, (2012), pp. 67–98; *id.*, 'Consideraciones sobre el ámbito de la Ley aplicable a las sucesiones en la propuesta de Reglamento del Parlamento Europeo y del Consejo relativo a la competencia, la Ley aplicable, el reconocimiento y la ejecución de las resoluciones y los actos auténticos en materia de sucesiones y a la creación de un certificado sucesorio europeo', in C. Esplugues Mota y G. Palao Moreno (eds), *Nuevas fronteras del Derecho de la Unión Europea. Liber amicorum José Luis Iglesias Buhígues* (Valencia, 2012), pp. 413–431;

17. j) *The sharing-out of the estate*. Article 23.2(j) ESR subjects to the *lex successionis* the sharing-out of the estate, i.e. the final step in the winding-up of a succession.[57] The sharing-out is a legal act or transaction which extinguishes the unity of the estate and its joint ownership by the heirs, attributing assets and rights to the heirs in accordance to their corresponding shares. Their shares are thereby transformed into concrete assets and the joint ownership by the heirs disappears.[58] The sharing-out can be total, if it affects all the assets, or partial, if it only affects part of those assets and therefore the joint ownership by the heirs continues to exist in respect of the other assets, which will be shared-out subsequently.[59]

The persons authorised to request the inheritance be shared out and the possibility of the sharing-out taking place are also subject to the *lex successionis*.[60] The law applicable to the succession will also determine the voluntary and/or statutory methods used to share the inheritance out. However, the form and procedure relating to the sharing-out are procedural questions which are subject to the *lex fori*.[61] The most important operations in sharing-out of the estate are the inventory, the winding-up and the division of the assets into individual lots, that will be allocated to the heirs according to their respective shares. The division of the estate in lots is governed solely by the *lex successionis*, and not by the *lex rei sitae* as is the case in some legal systems such as the Dutch system where, for example, before the adoption of the ESR, the requirements relating to the property law of the place where the estate assets are located was taken into account.

Carrascosa González, *El Reglamento Sucesorio*, pp. 191–192; Revillard, 'Portée de la loi applicable', pp. 77–78.

[57] Wautelet, 'Article 23, e)–g), j)', pp. 372–374; Castellanos Ruiz, 'Sucesión hereditaria', p. 589; Hohloch, 'Kommentierung der EuErbRVO', p. 6701.

[58] Damascelli, *Diritto internazionale privato delle successioni*, p. 86; Díez-Picazo and Gullón, *Sistema de Derecho Civil*, vol. IV, p. 267. By way of example, this process is governed in the Spanish legal system by article 1068 of the Spanish civil code or in the French legal system by article 883 of the French civil code.

[59] Biagioni, 'L'ambito di applicazione del regolamento sulle successioni', pp. 39–40; C. Martínez de Aguirre Aldaz, 'Partición hereditaria: conceptos generales, operaciones particionales y tipos de partición', in M. A. Pérez Álvarez (ed), *Curso de Derecho Civil (V) Derecho de sucesiones* (Madrid, 2013), p. 444.

[60] Carrascosa González, *El Reglamento Sucesorio*, pp. 192–194; Revillard, 'Portée de la loi applicable', p. 78.

[61] Wautelet, 'Article 23, e)–g), j)', p. 373; Carrascosa González, *El Reglamento Sucesorio*, p. 194; Revillard, 'Portée de la loi applicable', p. 78.

A possible issue concerns the mandatory character of the submission of the sharing-out operation to the *lex successionis*, or whether the parties affected by the sharing-out itself can submit it to a different law, in cases where the sharing-out is carried out under contract. The ESR does not make any provision in this regard. Some authors do not consider freedom of choice of law to be possible in this final stage of the succession, not even when the sharing-out is conducted by means of negotiation between the joint heirs or legatees.[62] However, others believe that if the sharing-out of the estate is carried out under contract, the law which should govern that sharing-out is determined by the conflict rules applicable to contracts, specifically those in the Rome I regulation, whose article 3 permits a choice of law.[63] That being said, contracts dividing inheritance must comply with the asset allocation carried out by the *lex successionis* and it will only be possible to conclude such a contract in the cases and under the exceptions imposed by the *lex successionis*.[64]

Matters of form relating to the sharing-out are governed by the forum's conflict rules, save where the sharing-out is carried out under contract, when it is governed by article 11 of the Rome I regulation, based upon *favour negotii*.[65]

[62] Wautelet, 'Article 23, e)–g), j)', pp. 373–374; Damascelli, *Diritto internazionale privato delle successioni*, p. 86.

[63] Biagioni, 'L'ambito di applicazione del regolamento sulle successioni', p. 39; Carrascosa González, *El Reglamento Sucesorio*, p. 194.

[64] Carrascosa González, *El Reglamento Sucesorio*, p. 194.

[65] Biagioni, 'L'ambito di applicazione del regolamento sulle successioni', p. 40; Carrascosa González, *El Reglamento Sucesorio*, p. 194. For arguments against this solution and in favour of applying the *lex successionis* to formal matters relating to sharing-out the inheritance, see: Damascelli, *Diritto internazionale privato delle successioni*, p. 86.

Article 24

Dispositions of Property upon Death Other Than Agreements as to Succession

JULIANA RODRÍGUEZ RODRIGO

1. A disposition of property upon death other than an agreement as to succession shall be governed, as regards its admissibility and substantive validity, by the law which, under this Regulation, would have been applicable to the succession of the person who made the disposition if he had died on the day on which the disposition was made.
2. Notwithstanding paragraph 1, a person may choose as the law to govern his disposition of property upon death, as regards its admissibility and substantive validity, the law which that person could have chosen in accordance with Article 22 on the conditions set out therein.
3. Paragraph 1 shall apply, as appropriate, to the modification or revocation of a disposition of property upon death other than an agreement as to succession. In the event of a choice of law in accordance with paragraph 2, the modification or revocation shall be governed by the chosen law.

Summary

I. DISPOSITIONS OF PROPERTY UPON DEATH *page* 370

II. THE LAW APPLICABLE TO DISPOSITIONS OF PROPERTY UPON DEATH OTHER THAN AGREEMENTS TO SUCCESSION 372

A. Article 24.1. Substantive freedom of choice. The law applicable to the succession: law of habitual residence of the deceased at the time the will is drawn up 373

B. Article 24.2. Freedom of choice of law (*professio juris*) 375

III. MATTERS DEALT WITH BY ARTICLE 24 ESR 377

IV. THE LAW APPLICABLE TO MODIFICATION OR REVOCATION OF DISPOSITIONS OF PROPERTY UPON DEATH 378

I. Dispositions of Property upon Death

1. Dispositions of property upon death other than agreements as to succession are made in wills or joint wills, as defined by article 3.1(d) ESR. Accordingly, the ESR contemplates three different kinds of dispositions of property upon death: wills, joint wills and agreements as to succession. Article 24 ESR is dedicated to the first two, namely wills and joint wills, whereas article 25 ESR covers agreements as to succession.

2. *Wills.* The ESR does not offer a definition of wills. We can consider that a will is a document reflecting the private autonomy of the testator,[1] by which he decides in advance the future of his assets after his death. It is a unilateral act of will of a person.[2]

The will takes effect from the moment of the opening of the succession; until then, it represents in many legal systems the only expression of intent capable of affecting the assets of a person after his death.[3]

3. *Joint wills.* Article 3.1(c) of the ESR defines joint wills as wills drawn up in one legal act by two or more persons. A joint will means that two or more persons arrange their succession in one document, regardless of whether this is done through one single or two or more legal acts.[4] This definition corresponds with that given in some legal systems, both in countries were joint wills, under certain circumstances, are allowed, as in Germany, or forbidden, as in Spain. By way of example, sections 2265–2273 of the German BGB provide that two spouses can make a will together, in a public act or in a private document, such as a holographic will. Conversely, article 669 of the Spanish civil code forbids expressly joint wills, both in the form of a will made jointly or of more wills made in the same instrument, and irrespective of whether the persons wishing to make a joint will do so for their reciprocal benefit, or for the benefit of a third party. However, some Spanish *derechos forales*, such as those in Navarre and Aragon, consider joint wills as admissible.[5]

[1] M. Balloriani, R. De Rosa and S. Mezzanotte, *Manuale breve. Diritto civile* (Milano, 2012), p. 776.

[2] P. Malaurie, *Les successions. Les libéralités* (Paris, 2004), p. 245.

[3] G. Bonilini, 'Il negozio testamentario', in G. Bonilini (ed), *Trattato di diritto delle successioni e donazioni*, vol. II (Milano, 2009), p. 3.

[4] J. Carrascosa González, *El Reglamento sucesorio europeo 650/2012 de 4 de julio 2012. Análisis crítico* (Granada, 2014), p. 223.

[5] E. Zabalo Escudero, 'El testamento conjunto en derecho internacional privado. Especial referencia al testamento mancomunado aragonés', *Revista General de derecho* (1989), p. 6353. This has led the Spanish Supreme Court 8 October 2010 (RJ\2010\8009,

4. As already mentioned, there are two types of joint wills.[6] Firstly, testators can set out their last wishes independently albeit in the same document. In this case, the only connection between the wills is the common document in which they are drawn up. Secondly, testators may adopt reciprocal or mutual joint wills in which they express their final wishes conditional upon the wishes of the other testator or testators. This second kind of joint wills fits within the definition of agreements as to succession offered by article 3.1(b) ESR, according to which an agreement as to succession is 'an agreement, including an agreement resulting from mutual wills, which, with or without consideration, creates, modifies or terminates rights to the future estate or estates of one or more persons party to the agreement'. A reciprocal joint will, accordingly, falls under the provisions regulating agreements as to succession and as such its validity and admissibility are governed by article 25,[7] [see art. 25] contrarily to joint wills that do not respond to a mutual agreement of the testators and fall within the scope of article 24.[8]

5. *Agreements as to succession.* Finally, all dispositions upon death that fit in the definition of article 3.1(b) ESR that we have just mentioned

Repertorio de Jurisprudencia Aranzadi, Navarra) to refrain from recurring to the public policy exception against German law, thus concluding that irrevocability of a joint will was admissible. The Court was ruling on an appeal made to request that a joint will be deemed void due to the drawing up of a later will by the deceased, which revoked all previous instruments. The appellant invoked the public policy exception in favour of setting aside the German law rule that joint wills are irreversible since, under articles 737 and 739 of the Spanish civil code, wills are by essence reversible. The Spanish Supreme Court affirmed that the irrevocability of wills is not a matter of public policy, since, amongst other reasons, the possibility that the document could not be reversed was contemplated within the Spanish system in the *derechos forales* governing the joint will, and accordingly public policy could not be invoked in support of the setting aside of a foreign law which makes the same provision as a Spanish *derecho foral.* See also Audiencia Provincial de Alicante 17 January 2013, in which another appeal on the validity of a German joint will was decided (JUR\2013\116346, *Repertorio de Jurisprudencia Aranzadi*, Navarra).

[6] I. Rodríguez-Uría Suárez, 'La ley aplicable a las sucesiones *mortis causa* en el Reglamento (UE) 650/2012', *Indret* (2013), p. 26.

[7] Before the adoption of the ESR and the inclusion of joint wills within agreements as to succession, there were doubts in English literature as to whether these wills should be considered as governed by the law on succession or, rather, whether they should be considered as contracts and stay governed by the provisions particular to that area: see J. Harris, 'The Proposed EU Regulation on Succession and Wills: Prospects and Challenges', *Trust LI* (2008), p. 208.

[8] A. Davì and A. Zanobetti, 'Il nuovo diritto internazionale privato delle successioni nell'Unione Europea', *CdT* 5/2 (2013), p. 62; A. Davì and A. Zanobetti, *Il nuovo diritto internazionale privato europeo delle successioni* (Torino, 2014), p. 97; Zabalo Escudero, 'El testamento conjunto', pp. 6358–6359.

must be considered as agreements as to succession, whose admissibility and validity is submitted to the rules set forth in article 25 [see art. 25].[9]

6. The matters dealt with by article 24 ESR are the admissibility and substantive validity of the dispositions of property upon death other than agreements as to succession. The issues pertaining to the substantive validity of the dispositions of property upon death are listed in article 26 ESR [see art. 26]. As article 26.1(d) refers to the interpretation of dispositions of property upon death, it may be understood that the possible conversion of an invalid disposition into a valid one is governed by the law referred to in article 24 ESR, since this issue depends upon the interpretation of the testator's wishes.[10]

II. The Law Applicable to Dispositions of Property upon Death Other Than Agreements as to Succession

7. Article 24 ESR designates the law applicable to the admissibility and substantive validity of dispositions of property upon death other than agreements as to succession, that is the *hypothetical succession law*, i.e. the law which, under articles 21 and 22 ESR, would have been applicable to the succession of the person who made the disposition if he had died on the day on which the disposition was made. Article 24, accordingly, refers, albeit tacitly, to article 21 ESR (which provides that the law of habitual residence at the time of death will apply to legal or intestate succession) in its first paragraph, and to article 22 ESR (which permits a person, by way of a *professio juris*, to select the law applicable to his succession) in its second paragraph, adding the adjustments necessary for the specific purpose of this provision.

Consequently, the testator is able to know, at the time of confection of the will, which law applies to its admissibility and its substantive validity and, accordingly, is able to draft his last wishes in full awareness, thus avoiding the uncertainty to which a possible subsequent change of habitual residence (or nationality) would lead. Indeed, according to article 24, the law applicable to the admissibility and substantive validity of dispositions of property upon death other than agreements to succession – i.e., wills and joint wills – will be the law of the State (or of one of the States) of which the testator is a national at the time of their adoption,

[9] A. Bonomi, 'Article 24', in A. Bonomi and P. Wautelet, *Le droit européen des successions. Commentaire du Règlement n° 650/2012 du 4 juillet 2012* (Bruxelles, 2013), p. 378

[10] Bonomi, 'Article 24', p. 381.

when he has made a *professio juris*, or, in the absence of such a choice of law, the law of his habitual residence at that time.[11]

8. If a person decides to make use of his testamentary autonomy, the ESR offers him two means of doing so. On the one hand, he can make use of his conflictual autonomy by designating the law of a given State, whether it is a member of the European Union or not, as the governing law for his succession, on the conditions set out in article 22 [see art. 22]. On the other hand, he can exercise his substantive autonomy and draft clauses in the form of a will, which dispose of his assets as he considers appropriate. In this latter case, admissibility and substantive validity of these testamentary dispositions will be governed by the law set out in article 24.1 ESR, namely the law of the deceased's habitual residence, determined at the time the will is drawn up, or, according to article 24.2 ESR, the testator can also submit his will's the admissibility and substantive validity to the law of his nationality (or one of his nationalities) at that same moment.

A. *Article 24.1. Substantive Autonomy. Hypothetical Law: The Law Applicable to the Succession at the Time the Will Is Drawn Up*

9. Starting with substantive autonomy, which is dealt with in the first paragraph of article 24 ESR, a person can make a will with the purpose of organising his succession and the distribution of his assets as he sees fit. In order to establish whether this will is substantively valid, it is necessary to refer to the law which would be applicable to the succession at the time the will was drawn up (*hypothetisches Erbstatut*);[12] that is, the *lex successionis* adjusted to govern the substantive validity of the disposition of property upon death.[13] This law applies regardless of where the will was drawn up.[14]

[11] See recital 51 on this point.

[12] G. Hohloch, 'Kommentierung der EuErbRVO', in Erman, *BGB: Kommentar*, 14th ed. (Köln, 2014), p. 6703.

[13] In these cases, when applying the hypothetical succession law, namely the law of habitual residence at the time of drawing up the act, the exception clause contained in article 21.2 ESR must not be taken into account. Its applicability appears indeed to be explicitly ruled out by recital 51; moreover, its application would jeopardize the certainty and stability which the rule of the hypothetical succession law aims at; see Davì and Zanobetti, 'Il nuovo diritto internazionale privato delle successioni, p. 64; Davì and Zanobetti, *Il nuovo diritto internazionale privato europeo*, p. 100. Nevertheless, some authors consider that, in exceptional circumstances and depending upon the facts of the case, reference must be made to the law of the State with the closest connection to the deceased, in accordance with article 21.2 ESR, and the time for verification of the most closely connected State is when the will is executed, not when the deceased dies: see: Bonomi, 'Article 24', p. 386.

[14] Hohloch, 'Kommentierung der EuErbRVO', p. 6703.

Article 24 does not make specific provisions for joint wills. It appears reasonable to apply the laws of the habitual residences of each of the testators on a distributive basis, i.e. each pertinent law in relation to each of the persons whose succession is concerned.[15] As we have seen earlier in nos. 3 and 4, in joint wills the testators' wishes are not interdependent, otherwise the joint will would be considered as an agreement as to succession pursuant to article 3.1(b) ESR. Consequently, when assessing the substantive validity of a joint will, it will be necessary to analyse that validity in relation to each of the testators and to apply the law of the habitual residence (or the national law in case of *professio juris*) of each of them independently.[16]

10. Article 24.1 ESR has the effect of crystallising the law applicable to the succession, in such a way that, if the person whose succession is concerned, after drawing up the will, decides to choose, by way of a *professio juris*, the law applicable to his succession under article 22 ESR, that law can only be used to revoke an earlier will and make a new one which is subject to the chosen law.[17] If the new choice of law is not made with this intention, the chosen law will only govern the remaining matters listed in article 23, that is to say, the whole succession less the admissibility of the will and its substantive validity, which will both continue to be regulated by the law of the testator's habitual residence at the time the will is drawn up, under article 24.1 ESR.

11. The hypothetical law – i.e. the law of habitual residence of the testator at the time of the drawing up of the disposition – will govern the admissibility and substantive validity of the dispositions upon death. As stated in the preceding paragraph, if a choice of law has been made under article 22, the law chosen, or, in the absence of such choice, the law of the deceased's last habitual residence, will be applicable to the remaining matters listed in article 23.

[15] Davì and Zanobetti, 'Il nuovo diritto internazionale privato delle successioni', p. 62; Davì and Zanobetti, *Il nuovo diritto internazionale privato europeo*, p. 98; A. Bonomi, 'Article 3', in A. Bonomi and P. Wautelet, *Le droit européen des successions. Commentaire du Règlement nº 650/2012 du 4 juillet 2012* (Bruxelles, 2013), pp. 140–141.

[16] Other authors consider that the solution, in these cases, would be to apply the provisions relating to agreements as to succession by analogy, and conclude that the laws of the habitual residences of each of the deceased persons should be applied cumulatively (Hohloch, 'Kommentierung der EuErbRVO', pp. 6703–6704). Nevertheless, for each deceased person under a joint will, it hardly seems justifiable to render the validity of their will conditional upon the law of the habitual residence of the other testators with whom the only connection is the common document setting out their respective wishes.

[17] Bonomi, 'Article 24', p. 386.

B. *Article 24.2. Freedom of Choice of Law* (professio juris)

12. The ESR introduces freedom of choice of law into matters of succession [see art. 22 no. 1 *et seq.*]. Still, this freedom is limited, because the person whose succession is concerned can only choose his national law (or one of his national laws) at the time the choice is made or at the time of his death [see art. 22 nos. 5 and 8].[18]

For what concerns, however, admissibility and substantial validity of dispositions of property upon death, recital 51 indicates that when the ESR refers to the law applicable to dispositions of property upon death, whether in the form of a will or the form of an agreement as to succession, if the person whose succession is concerned has made use of his freedom of choice, the law which he can choose for these purposes is the law of the State of which he is a national *at the time that choice is made.*[19] Recital 51 states:

> Where reference is made in this Regulation to the law which would have been applicable to the succession of the person making a disposition of property upon death if he had died on the day on which the disposition was, as the case may be, made, modified or revoked, such reference should be understood as a reference to either the law of the State of the habitual residence of the person concerned on that day or, if he had made a choice of law under this Regulation, the law of the State of his nationality on that day.

This is justified by the lack of stability and predictability that the application of the national law that the testator possesses at the time of his death would entail.[20]

13. When the testator holds various nationalities, he may choose the law of any of the States of which he is a national as applicable to his succession (article 22.1 ESR). If he holds the nationality of a State with more than one legal system, articles 36 and 37 ESR will determine which territorial or personal unit must be considered for these purposes [see art. 36–38].

14. The choice of law, pursuant to article 22.2 ESR, may be made expressly in the form of a disposition of property upon death, or tacitly, in which case the choice shall be demonstrated by the terms of such

[18] R. Lafuente Sánchez, 'Hacia un sistema unitario europeo en materia de ley aplicable a las sucesiones internacionales', *CdT* 5/2 (2013), p. 359.

[19] See Davì and Zanobetti, 'Il nuovo diritto internazionale privato delle successioni', p. 64; Davì and Zanobetti, *Il nuovo diritto internazionale privato europeo*, p. 101; Bonomi, 'Article 24', p. 394.

[20] Bonomi, 'Article 24', p. 394.

a disposition [see art. 22 no. 21 *et seq.*]. Usually the will or the agreement as to succession is where the person whose succession is concerned makes the choice of the law of the State of which he is a national as the law to govern his succession.

15. In the case of a testamentary succession, the choice of law can also be made separately, whether or not by including a reference to the will in question.[21] When the will contains a choice of law, together with additional dispositions concerning the estate, the validity of the testamentary provisions is governed by the law chosen by the deceased (article 24.2 ESR). The same law will also determine the substantive validity of the choice of law clause, that is, whether the deceased had capacity and provided valid consent in respect of it (article 22.3 and recital 40); it must however be recalled that the possibility of making a choice of law is autonomously provided for by article 22 ESR and that it will be valid even when the chosen law does not admit such an option in matters of succession (recital 40) [see art. 22 no. 16].

16. The choice of law clause is independent of the disposition of property upon death to which it refers. Its validity is not dependent upon the validity of the will. The independence of the clause suggests that it is possible that a will could be void in accordance with the chosen law but that the choice of law clause itself could be valid.[22] In such cases, if the disposition of property upon death is invalid, the succession will be neither testamentary nor subject to an agreement as to succession, but rather intestate or statutory, though governed by the law chosen by the deceased.[23]

17. The exercise of the autonomy can be embodied in the will in question or in a prior will, provided, of course, that the choice of law has not been subsequently revoked.[24] In this sense, a choice of law made in a previous disposition of property upon death would be valid in order to regulate new dispositions made subsequently by the person whose succession is concerned.[25]

18. If the deceased had included a choice of law clause into the will, a problem arises as to the interpretation of that clause, depending upon whether the choice is made on the basis of article 24 ESR or article 22

[21] Hohloch, 'Kommentierung der EuErbRVO', p. 6704.

[22] Rodríguez-Uría Suárez, 'La ley aplicable a las sucesiones', p. 13.

[23] See on the issue of the faculty to choose a law in the event of an intestate succession, S. Álvarez González, 'Las legítimas en el Reglamento sobre sucesiones y testamentos', *An esp der int priv* 11 (2011), p. 381.

[24] Bonomi, 'Article 24', p. 388. [25] Bonomi, 'Article 24', p. 393.

ESR. The difference is important: if the clause is interpreted as having been made on the basis of the former, the law chosen will only govern the will's admissibility and substantive validity; conversely, if it is interpreted as having been made on the basis of the latter, that law will govern the whole succession. Thus, if the deceased did not make any specifications in relation to the choice of law, it must be inferred that he wished that law to apply to the whole succession;[26] in this way, the principle of unity of law which presides over the ESR is also respected.[27] Therefore, a choice of law contained in a will must be considered to have been made on the basis of article 22 ESR and will apply to the entire succession. If, on the contrary, the deceased specified that the chosen law should only apply to the will's admissibility and substantive validity, we are then dealing with freedom of choice exercised under article 24 ESR and, in this case, the law chosen only governs the areas referred to, while all other matters listed in article 23 will continue to be governed by the *lex successionis*, i.e. the law of the habitual residence of the deceased at the time of his death, or the law that the person has chosen if there has been a subsequent *professio juris* under article 22 ESR.[28]

III. Matters Dealt with by Article 24 ESR

19. The hypothetical law under article 24 ESR, whether that is the law of the testator's habitual residence at the time the will was drawn up, or the law of the State (or one of the States) of which the deceased was a national at that same moment, in case of a choice of law under article 24.2, will govern the admissibility and substantive validity of the testamentary provisions. The remaining succession matters are submitted to

[26] Bonomi, 'Article 24', p. 395.

[27] Regarding the principle of unity of succession, see P. Lagarde, 'Les principes de base du nouveau règlement européen sur les successions', *Rev. crit. dr. int. priv* (2012), p. 693; T. Ballarino, 'Il nuovo regolamento europeo sulle successioni', *Riv dir int* (2013), p. 1119; Davì and Zanobetti, 'Il nuovo diritto internazionale privato delle successioni', pp. 23–26; Davì and Zanobetti, *Il nuovo diritto internazionale privato europeo*, p. 16; E. Castellanos Ruiz, 'Sucesión hereditaria. Reglamento 650/2012 sobre sucesión internacional', in A.-L. Calvo Caravaca and J. Carrascosa González (eds), *Derecho Internacional Privado. Parte Especial*, 15th ed. (Granada, 2014), pp. 532–533. The first author cited considers that the ESR is based upon three principles: unity of succession, freedom of choice and continuity of the regime for successions (Lagarde, 'Les principes de base', pp. 692–693).

[28] On this point see: Davì and Zanobetti, 'Il nuovo diritto internazionale privato delle successioni', p. 59; Davì and Zanobetti, *Il nuovo diritto internazionale privato europeo*, pp. 100–101; E. Castellanos Ruiz, 'Sucesión hereditaria', p. 599; Bonomi, 'Article 24', p. 395.

the *lex successionis* under article 22 ESR, if there is a *professio juris,* or article 21 ESR if there is no choice of law. Therefore, there are two different possible laws which might apply to the succession. The reserved shares, for example, will be governed by the ordinary *lex successionis.* For that reason, if the deceased wishes to avoid the reserved shares being governed by the law of his habitual residence at the time of death, he can make use of the *professio juris* under article 22 ESR to ensure they are governed by the law of the State of which he is a national, either at the time of his death or at the time the choice is made [see art. 22 no. 8].

20. Article 24, unlike article 25 [see art. 25], makes no allusion to the effects of dispositions of property upon death other than agreements as to succession. It ensues that the law applicable under article 24 governs uniquely the admissibility and substantive validity of these dispositions.[29]

IV. The Law Applicable to Modification or Revocation of Dispositions of Property upon Death

21. Finally, article 24.3 ESR states that the same law which governs testamentary dispositions also governs their modification or revocation.

As regards modifications, some authors consider that the law of habitual residence of the testator at the time the will is drawn up will govern the admissibility of the modification, whereas the law of habitual residence at the time the modification is made will determine its validity.[30] We believe, conversely, that there are various reasons to maintain that a single law, the law of the habitual residence at the time of the modification, should apply both to admissibility and to substantive validity.[31] Indeed, on the one hand, as regards the admissibility of the modification or revocation, article 24.1 ESR makes no reference to the binding effects of testamentary dispositions – unlike the case of agreements as to succession under article 25 ESR – and thus, article 24.3 ESR provides that the law applicable under the first paragraph of the rule must also be used 'as appropriate', for the modification or revocation of the will, because these issues, namely modification and

[29] Cf. Bonomi, 'Article 24', p. 383, who nevertheless considers that, even though the article does not expressly say so, the law to which article 24 refers should be deemed as also applicable to at least some of the effects of those dispositions.

[30] Bonomi, 'Article 24', pp. 382–383.

[31] Davì and Zanobetti, 'Il nuovo diritto internazionale privato delle successioni', pp. 65–66; Davì and Zanobetti, *Il nuovo diritto internazionale privato europeo*, pp. 102–104.

revocation, refer to the binding effect of the disposition upon its author. Therefore, the possibility of modifying a testamentary disposition must remain governed by the law determined pursuant to article 24.1 at the time the modification is made. As regards the validity of the acts at issue, the fact that article 26.2 ESR states that, if a person has the capacity to adopt a valid disposition of property upon death in accordance with articles 24 and 25 ESR, that does not come to an end simply because there is a change in the law applicable at the time that disposition was modified or revoked, clearly supposes that, absent such clarification, the law applicable would have been the law which would have to be applied at the time the modification or revocation were made and not at the time of the confection of the original disposition. Therefore, in the absence of a *professio juris*, the law applicable to the validity of a disposition of property upon death will be that of the habitual residence of the deceased at the time the will is drawn up, and the law applicable to the modification or revocation of the disposition of property upon death will be different if the first applicable law has changed, that is, if the habitual residence of the deceased is elsewhere at the time of the modification or revocation of the disposition of property upon death, but not in any other case. The suggested solutions are confirmed by the fact that recital 51, referring to the drawing up, modification or revocation of a disposition of property upon death, provides that the applicable law must be that of the deceased's habitual residence as at the date of that drawing up, modification or revocation, or, in case a *professio juris* was made, the law of the State of which the person whose succession is concerned holds the nationality at that same time.

Article 25

Agreements as to Succession

JULIANA RODRÍGUEZ RODRIGO

1. An agreement as to succession regarding the succession of one person shall be governed, as regards its admissibility, its substantive validity and its binding effects between the parties, including the conditions for its dissolution, by the law which, under this Regulation, would have been applicable to the succession of that person if he had died on the day on which the agreement was concluded.
2. An agreement as to succession regarding the succession of several persons shall be admissible only if it is admissible under all the laws which, under this Regulation, would have governed the succession of all the persons involved if they had died on the day on which the agreement was concluded.

   An agreement as to succession which is admissible pursuant to the first subparagraph shall be governed, as regards its substantive validity and its binding effects between the parties, including the conditions for its dissolution, by the law, from among those referred to in the first subparagraph, with which it has the closest connection.
3. Notwithstanding paragraphs 1 and 2, the parties may choose as the law to govern their agreement as to succession, as regards its admissibility, its substantive validity and its binding effects between the parties, including the conditions for its dissolution, the law which the person or one of the persons whose estate is involved could have chosen in accordance with Article 22 on the conditions set out therein.

Summary

I. AGREEMENTS AS TO SUCCESSION *page* 381
  A. Definition 381
  B. Features 381
  C. Classification 382
  D. Comparative Law Survey 383
II. LAW APPLICABLE TO AGREEMENTS AS TO SUCCESSION 386
  A. Succession of a Sole Person (Articles 25.1 and 25.3 ESR) 387
  B. Succession of Several Persons (Articles 25.2 and 25.3 ESR) 389
III. AREAS DEALT WITH BY ARTICLE 25 ESR 392

I. Agreements as to Succession

A. *Definition*

1. An agreement as to succession is 'an agreement, including an agreement resulting from mutual wills, which, with or without consideration, creates, modifies or terminates rights to the future estate or estates of one or more persons party to the agreement' (article 3.1(b) ESR) [see art. 3 no. 3 *et seq.*].

We can include within this definition positive or acquisitive agreements, as well as negative or renunciation agreements, irrespective of whether they provide for a compensation;[1] the French *contrat de mariage* and the Italian *patto di famiglia*, which we discuss below, are to be considered as agreements as to succession for the purposes of the ESR.[2] Gifts upon death, the French *donation-partage* and various common law testamentary contracts are also deemed included in the definition.[3] Trusts, on the other hand, fall outside this definition because article 1.2 (j) ESR excludes them from its scope [see art. 1 no. 68 *et seq.*].

B. *Features*

2. The following features can be identified in agreements as to succession.[4] First, they are drawn up in order to organise a succession. Article 1.2(g) excludes the following from the ESR's scope: 'property rights, interests and assets created or transferred otherwise than by succession, for instance by way of gifts, joint ownership with a right of survivorship, pension plans, insurance contracts and arrangements of a similar nature' [see art. 1 no. 51 *et seq.*]. Therefore, an agreement as to succession, in order to be covered by the ESR, must transfer assets on the death of a person by succession. It is thus necessary to differentiate between *inter vivos* agreements, which take effect between living persons, and agreements taking effect upon death, even though some of their effects take place when they are drawn up. Only the latter can be

[1] See no. 3, for a definition of these types of agreements as to succession.

[2] E. Calò, 'El proyecto de Reglamento de la Unión Europea sobre la ley aplicable a las sucesiones: lo que no se ha dicho', *InDret* (3/2010), p. 4.

[3] A. Bonomi, 'Article 25', in A. Bonomi and Wautelet, *Le droit européen des successions. Commentaire du Règlement n° 650/2012 du 4 juillet 2012* (Bruxelles, 2013), p. 400; A. Davì and A. Zanobetti, 'Il nuovo diritto internazionale privato delle successioni nell'Unione Europea', *CdT* 5/2 (2013), p. 68; A. Davì and A. Zanobetti, *Il nuovo diritto internazionale private europeo delle succession* (Torino, 2014), pp. 106–107.

[4] A. Font i Segura, 'La ley aplicable a los pactos sucesorios', *InDret* (2/2009), pp. 7–8.

considered agreements as to succession. Consequently, although agreements as to succession are contracts, they affect successions and as such they fall outside the scope of application of regulation no. 593/2008 (Rome I).[5]

Second, an agreement as to succession becomes effective from the moment it is drawn up, even though its effects or some of them come into operation after the transferor has died. The agreement as to succession creates a legal bond between the parties from the moment it is concluded.

Third and finally, agreements as to succession cannot, by nature, be unilaterally revoked, since the agreement is multilateral and so this prevents any of the parties revoking the agreement unilaterally.

C. *Classification*

3. There are different types of agreements as to succession. Following a classifications based upon the purpose of the agreement, they can be divided into three categories.[6] First, we have 'inheritance agreements', which are positive or acquisitive and by virtue of which the deceased establishes that the other contracting party is an heir – 'institutional agreements' – or a legatee – 'designation agreements' – with that party's consent. Second, we have 'non-inheritance agreements', or abdication or renunciation agreements, according to which the heir or legatee renounces his rights over a succession. Finally, there are third party succession agreements, or *pacta de hereditate tertii*, by means of which heirs share out the inheritance due to them without the deceased's involvement. In this case, such agreements cannot be described as agreements as to succession under the ESR, since article 3.1(b) states that in order to be deemed 'agreement as to succession', an agreement must govern the succession of one or more persons who are parties to the same. Third party succession agreements are thus to be considered as contracts, governed by the *lex contractus*.[7]

[5] Regulation (EC) no. 593/2008 of the European Parliament and of the Council of 17 June 2008 on the law applicable to contractual obligations (Rome I), OJ no. L 177, 4 July 2008.

[6] T. Ballarino, 'Il nuovo regolamento europeo sulle successioni', *Riv dir int* (2013), p. 1143; M. Balloriani, R. de Rosa and S. Mezzanotte, *Manuale breve. Diritto civile* (Milano, 2012), p. 746; Font i Segura, 'La ley aplicable', p. 8.

[7] E. Castellanos Ruiz, 'Sucesión hereditaria', in A.-L. Calvo Caravaca and J. Carrascosa González, *Derecho Internacional Privado. Parte Especial*, 14th ed. (Granada, 2013), p. 555; Davì and Zanobetti, 'Il nuovo diritto internazionale privato delle successioni', p. 67; Davì and Zanobetti, *Il nuovo diritto internazionale privato europeo*, p. 106.

D. Comparative Law Survey

4. From a comparative perspective we can find examples of systems that do not allow this type of dispositions of property upon death and others that do.[8]

a) *Systems that do not provide for contractual succession.* These are Roman law systems, in which individual freedom prevails over group freedoms, in such a way that they consider that a person should be able to dispose of his assets upon death however and whenever he chooses, even when he has already stated his will in that regard. Such systems include for example Spanish *derecho común*, French law and Italian law. For this reason, these laws do not allow agreements as to succession, because they do not accept their irrevocability. Nevertheless, some of these systems do allow for agreements whose function is analogous to that played by agreements as to succession.

   In the Spanish system, agreements as to succession are forbidden under articles 658 and 1271 of the Spanish civil code. In this regard, article 1271 states that no contracts regarding a future inheritance may be entered into, other than those whose purpose is to perform the division of an estate *inter vivos* and other partitional dispositions. Notwithstanding the above, there are some references to this type of disposition of property upon death in the Spanish civil code. Article 826 refers to the promise to make or not to make betterment, made in a marriage agreement by public deed, which cannot be revoked by the testator.[9] For its part, article 827 refers to the fact that betterments made in a marriage agreement or by means of a contract made with a third party for valuable consideration, will be irrevocable. Finally, article 1341 covers the possibility of future spouses, under *capitulaciones matrimoniales*, giving one another future assets in the

[8] Bonomi, 'Article 25', pp. 398–399; J. Carrascosa González, *El Reglamento sucesorio europeo 650/2012 de 4 de julio 2012. Análisis crítico* (Granada, 2014), pp. 227–230. For more information on agreements as to succession in comparative law see A. Bonomi and M. Steiner (eds), *Les Pactes successoraux en droit comparé et en droit international privé. Nouveautés en droit français, italien ainsi qu'espagnol et implications pratiques pour la Suisse. Actes de la Journée d'étude de Lausanne du 5 mars 2007* (Genève, 2008); Y.-H. Leleu, 'Les pactes successoraux en droit comparé', in *Les relations contractuelles internationales. Le rôle du notaire* (Antwerpen-Apeldoorn, 1995), pp. 546–611.

[9] In Spanish law, two-thirds of the inheritance goes to the portion of the estate reserved to the heirs. One of those thirds is the betterment third, which the deceased can dispose in favour of one or some of his children or descendants, whether by birth or adoption (article 823 Spanish civil code).

event of death, in accordance with the provisions relating to testate succession.

The French system also forbids agreements as to succession. Nevertheless, there are various exceptions to this general prohibition. *Donation-partage* and the *contrat de mariage* are two such examples.[10] Thus, in relation to the latter, article 1390 of the French civil code (as amended by law no. 728 of 2006) allows spouses, when they agree the matrimonial property regime applicable in their *contrat de mariage*, to provide for the acquisition of the marriage assets by the survivor, upon the other spouse's death.[11]

The same occurs in Italy in the case of the *patto di famiglia*, defined by article 768(a) of the Italian civil code (introduced by law no. 55 of 2006) as the contract whereby a person transfers, in whole or in part, the company that he owns or its shares to one or more descendants.[12] The *patto di famiglia* aims to ensure the continuity of the family business and to avoid internal family disputes,[13] and provides an exception to the prohibition on agreements as to succession contained in article 458 Italian civil code.

As just mentioned, the *contrat de mariage* and the *patto di famiglia* fall within the ESR's definition of agreements as to succession.[14]

Agreements as to succession are forbidden also in Belgium, Greece, Luxembourg, the Netherlands and Portugal. Outside of the European Union, they are forbidden or unknown in Russia, China and various African and South American countries.[15]

5. It is to be underlined that in these systems, recourse is generally considered not to have to be made to the public policy of the forum in order to refuse the application of a foreign law which governs the

[10] P. Malaurie, *Les successions. Les libéralités* (Paris, 2004), p. 293.

[11] The provision allows the spouses to 'stipuler qu'à la dissolution du mariage par la mort de l'un d'eux, le survivant a la faculté d'acquérir ou, le cas échéant, de se faire attribuer dans le partage certains biens personnels du prédécédé, à charge d'en tenir compte à la succession, d'après la valeur qu'ils ont au jour où cette faculté sera exercée. La stipulation peut prévoir que l'époux survivant qui exerce cette faculté peut exiger des héritiers que lui soit consenti un bail portant sur l'immeuble dans lequel l'entreprise attribuée ou acquise est exploitée': see P. Catala, 'Préparer sa succession', *La Semaine Juridique, Édition Générale* 1–2 (10 janvier 2011), pp. 13–16.

[12] This is the definition of the *patto*: 'il contratto con cui, compatibilmente con le disposizioni in materia di impresa familiare e nel rispetto delle differenti tipologie societarie, l'imprenditore trasferisce, in tutto o in parte, l'azienda, e il titolare di partecipazioni societarie trasferisce, in tutto o in parte, le proprie quote, ad uno o più discendenti'.

[13] E. Calò, *Le successioni nel diritto internazionale privato* (Milanofiori Assago, 2007), p. 135; Carrascosa González, *El Reglamento Sucesorio Europeo*, p. 229.

[14] Calò, 'El proyecto de Reglamento'.

[15] Bonomi, 'Article 25', p. 399.

agreements as to succession, even though the legal system seised of the matter does not permit agreements of this kind [see art. 35 no. 24 *et seq.*].[16]

6. b) *Systems that do provide for contractual succession.* These systems are firstly those inspired by German legal tradition, in which group freedoms prevail over those of the individual. This is the case in Austria, Germany and Switzerland, but also in the Spanish autonomous communities of Catalonia, Aragon, the Balearics, Galicia, the Basque Country and Navarre.[17]

Thus, section 1941 of the German BGB provides an outline for contractual succession: the deceased may appoint an heir, grant legacies and impose testamentary burdens by contract (*Erbvertrag*), and the other party to the contract and a third party may be appointed as an heir (*Vertragserbe*) or as a legatee.[18] Subsequently, sections 2274–2302 are in-depth provisions relating to this type of agreements as to succession, which must be concluded before a notary; when made between spouses

[16] Davì and Zanobetti, 'Il nuovo diritto internazionale privato delle successioni', p. 73, nota 278; Davì and Zanobetti, *Il nuovo diritto internazionale privato europeo*, p. 115, nota 177, where authors cite, by way of a practical example, the Italian judgment from the Tribunale Bolzano 8 March 1968, *Rivista giuridica Alto Adige* (1968), p. 220, and the French judgment of the Cour d'appel Aix-en-Provence 16 October 2003, *Rev crit dr int priv* (2004), p. 589; see also A. Bonomi, 'Il regolamento europeo sulle successioni', *Riv dir int priv proc* (2013), pp. 315–316; Ballarino, 'Il nuovo regolamento', p. 1142; G. Khairallah, 'La détermination de la loi applicable à la succession', in G. Khairallah and M. Revillard (eds), *Droit européen des successions internationales. Le règlement du 4 juillet 2012*, Paris, 2013, p. 62. Regarding the Spanish system, where regional laws govern these agreements, see: Castellanos Ruiz, 'Sucesión hereditaria', pp. 556–557. The following Spanish judgments are also relevant: Tribunal Supremo 8 October 2010, RJ\2010\8009, Aranzadi (Navarra); Alicante Provincial Court 17 January 2013, JUR\2013\116346, Aranzadi (Navarra); although they refer to the impossibility of invoking the public policy clause against the recognition of a joint will as provided for under German law, it is possible to extrapolate their reasoning to agreements as to succession, as neither institution is provided for under ordinary Spanish law but both are under regional laws and, in this sense, should be treated similarly when opposing public policy against foreign laws.

[17] In the Spanish system, for example, contractual succession is governed by articles 377–404 of the 2011 Aragon *Código del Derecho Foral*; by articles 431-1 to 431-30 of the 2008 Catalonia *Código civil*; by articles 72–77 of the Balearic Islands 1990 *Compilación del Derecho Civil*; by articles 209–227 of the 2006 Galicia *Derecho civil*; by laws 171–183 1973 Navarre *Compilación del Derecho Civil Foral*, as amended in 1987; by articles 74–83 of the Bizkaia *Fuero Civil*; by articles 179–188 of the Basque country *Derecho Civil Foral*, as regards the Gipuzkoa *Fuero Civil*.

[18] The provision states that '(1) Der Erblasser kann durch Vertrag einen Erben einsetzen sowie Vermächtnisse und Auflagen anordnen (Erbvertrag). (2) Als Erbe (Vertragserbe) oder als Vermächtnisnehmer kann sowohl der andere Vertragschließende als ein Dritter bedacht werden'.

or members of a registered partnership, the form used for marriage contracts will be deemed sufficient (section 2276 BGB).

II. Law Applicable to Agreements as to Succession

7. Article 25 ESR establishes the law applicable to agreements as to succession, specifically to 'its admissibility, its substantive validity and its binding effects between the parties, including the conditions for its dissolution', when the agreement governs the succession of a single person (paragraph 1) and when it governs the succession of several persons (paragraph 2).

The special regime contained in article 25 ESR as regards agreements as to succession is very similar to that set out in article 24 ESR as regards wills and joint wills. Even though there certainly are similarities, there are also some differences between the two sets of rules. The Commission proposal,[19] by contrast, only covered agreements as to succession (article 18). In fact, in accordance with the 1989 Hague Convention,[20] the Commission had considered that only agreements as to succession needed a special regime differing from the general rules on matters of succession. Nevertheless, ultimately the ESR also includes special rules relating to dispositions of property upon death other than agreements as to succession in article 24 [see art. 24].

8. The general rule in the case of agreements as to succession is the same as that adopted in respect of wills, although with some adaptations for this type of contractual succession. The most important of these adaptations consists in the fact that the reference to the national law of the person whose succession is concerned (in case of a choice of the applicable law) or to the law of his habitual residence (in the absence of a choice of law) is 'crystallised' at the time the agreement is drawn up: this is the so-called anticipated or hypothetical succession law, as will be seen more extensively. Accordingly, as the applicable law is frozen at the time the agreement is established, the person whose succession is concerned can plan his succession in accordance with predictable legal provisions,

[19] Proposal for a Regulation of the European Parliament and of the Council on jurisdiction, applicable law, recognition and enforcement of decisions and authentic instruments in matters of succession and the creation of a European Certificate of Succession, COM (2009) 154 final.

[20] Articles 9 and 10 of the Hague Convention of 1 August 1989 on the Law Applicable to Succession to the Estates of Deceased Persons (not in force).

and will not leave the matter under the shadow of uncertainty which would be cast by his subsequent change of habitual residence or nationality.

9. If there is a choice of law, the clause in which that choice appears is independent of the disposition of property upon death to which it refers. Its validity is not dependent upon the validity of the agreement as to succession. The independence of the clause suggests that it is possible that an agreement as to succession could be void in accordance with the chosen law but that the choice of law clause itself could be valid.[21]

A. *Succession of a Sole Person (Articles 25.1 and 25.3 ESR)*

10. In this section a distinction must be made between the different areas being governed.

a) *Admissibility, substantive validity and binding effects between the parties.* These issues remain subject to the same law provided for in ESR articles 21 and 22, but the application of these rules is adjusted to this types of succession.

Therefore, if the parties have chosen a law, specifically the law of the State of which the deceased is a national at the time the choice is made, that law will apply to these issues. This choice of law is not a *professio juris* in the strictest sense, since it is an agreement between several persons and *professio juris* is a unilateral act.[22] On the other hand, at any time after the agreement as to succession has been drawn up, the deceased can choose the law of the State of which he is a national at the time the choice is made or at the time of his death to govern the remaining succession matters, by virtue of the *professio juris* set out in article 22 ESR.

Since agreements as to succession are binding upon parties the moment of their adoption, it is necessary to establish to which law they are submitted from that point; for this reason, the deceased cannot be allowed to choose the law of his future nationality at the time of his death, because this is not known at the time the agreement is drawn up and cannot be applied from that time. According to the

[21] I. Rodríguez-Uría Suárez, 'La ley aplicable a las sucesiones *mortis causa* en el Reglamento (UE) 650/2012', *InDret* (2/2013), p. 13.

[22] Rodríguez-Uría Suárez, 'La ley aplicable a las sucesiones', p. 32.

relevant literature, and considering also recital 51, the only time that must be taken into account with regard to agreements as to succession is when the agreement is drawn up.[23]

11. The choice of law must comply with the requirements laid down in article 22 ESR. Therefore, it must be made expressly in the form of a disposition of property upon death, or result from the terms of a disposition of that type (article 22.2 ESR), as exemplified by recital 39 ESR: 'A choice of law could be regarded as demonstrated by a disposition of property upon death where, for instance, the deceased had referred in his disposition to specific provisions of the law of the State of his nationality or where he had otherwise mentioned that law' [see art. 22 no. 24 *et seq.*].[24]

12. If, conversely, the parties have not chosen the applicable law, the agreement will be governed by the law of habitual residence of the deceased at the time the agreement as to succession is drawn up.

13. b) *The remaining succession matters.* The other matters listed under article 23 ESR are governed by the *lex successionis*, i.e. the law provided for under articles 21 or 22 ESR.

The same succession may, accordingly, be governed by two different laws, the so-called hypothetical *lex successionis*, applicable to the issues covered in article 25 ESR, and the actual *lex successionis*, applicable to the other issues. As already indicated, in order to avoid the reserved shares being governed by the law of the deceased's habitual residence at the time of his death, a person can choose, by means of a unilateral declaration made in the required form, a law to apply to his succession by virtue of article 22 ESR. In such a case, this chosen law would apply to all matters listed in article 23, including the reserved shares.[25]

[23] B. Barel, 'La disciplina dei patti successori', in P. Franzina and A. Leandro (eds), *Il diritto internazionale privato europeo delle successioni mortis causa* (Milano, 2013), pp. 126–127; Carrascosa González, *El Reglamento Sucesorio Europeo*, p. 232; Davì and Zanobetti, 'Il nuovo diritto internazionale', p. 75; Davì and Zanobetti, *Il nuovo diritto internazionale,* p. 119.

[24] For practical examples see Rodríguez-Uría Suárez, 'La ley aplicable a las sucesiones', p. 13.

[25] S. Álvarez González, 'Las legítimas en el Reglamento sobre sucesiones y testamentos', *An esp der int priv* 11 (2011), p. 385; P. Lagarde, 'Les principes de base du nouveau règlement européen sur les successions', *Rev crit dr int priv* (2012); Ballarino, 'Il nuovo regolamento', p. 1143, Davì and Zanobetti, 'Il nuovo diritto internazionale privato delle successioni', p. 75 *et seq.*; Rodríguez-Uría Suárez, 'La ley aplicable a las sucesiones', pp. 34–35; Castellanos Ruiz, 'Sucesión hereditaria. Reglamento 650/2012', p. 606; Davì and Zanobetti, *Il nuovo diritto internazionale privato europeo*, p. 118 *et seq.*

B. *Succession of Several Persons (Articles 25.2 and 25.3 ESR)*

14. A corresponding distinction applies with respect to agreements concerning the succession of several persons.

a) *Admissibility, substantive validity and effects inter partes.* Parties can submit these issues to the law of the State of which any of them is a national at the time the agreement is drawn up as the applicable law. In such cases, it might be possible that the aspects of the succession covered in article 25 ESR would be governed by a law with no connection to one of the persons whose succession is concerned, if the chosen law is the national law of another party to the agreement as to succession.

15. When no law is chosen, the admissibility of the agreement as to succession is governed by means of a cumulative application of the laws of the habitual residences of each of the persons whose succession is concerned by the agreement at the time the agreement is drawn up, whereas, once the agreement is deemed to be admissible, its substantive validity and *inter partes* effects, including the conditions for its dissolution, are governed by the law, amongst those of the countries in which the persons whose succession are concerned have their habitual residence, which has the closest connection with the agreement.

During the adoption of the ESR, various options had been proposed for determining the law applicable to agreements concerning the succession of several persons:[26] (a) either, the agreement would be admissible when all the applicable laws so allow (cumulative application); (b) or, the agreement would be admissible when any of the applicable laws so allow (alternative application); (c) or, the agreement would be valid, as regards each of the persons in question, when the law of their habitual residence considers it to be so (distributive application). In the last case, each law would apply to each person and would determine whether the agreement is admissible in relation to them. There could also be a fourth solution,[27] consisting in considering that the agreement is valid when the law of habitual residence of the first party to die so allows (distributive or fortuitous solution).

[26] Bonomi, 'Article 25', p. 409.

[27] Rodríguez-Uría Suárez, 'La ley aplicable a las sucesiones', pp. 29–31.

The ESR opts for the first option.[28] That is, unlike article 18.2 of the EU Commission proposal, which adopted an alternative application of the laws, the ESR chooses to apply the laws cumulatively. In this way, the agreement as to succession will only be valid if it is regarded as valid under the law of the habitual residence of each person whose succession is concerned and who is a party to the agreement.[29] The alternative application of one or another of these laws proposed by the Commission would entail the consequence that the validity of the agreement could have been governed by the law of the habitual residence of one of the parties even when that law had no relation whatsoever with other parties whose succession was concerned.[30] In addition, if the EU legislator had endorsed that alternative option, when an agreement as to succession would be valid under the law of the habitual residence of one of the parties, this automatically would exclude the application of the law of the habitual residences of the parties residing in countries whose legal systems do not permit agreements as to succession, and, inevitably, the position of those States which permit this kind of agreements would have prevailed.[31]

The solution adopted by the ESR is, accordingly, stricter than the alternative application provided for in the Commission's proposal.[32]

16. As regards the law applicable to the substantive validity and effects of agreements as to succession as between the parties, in the absence of a choice of law, as mentioned above, the ESR provides that the governing law will be that which, from amongst those applicable to the admissibility of the agreement (i.e. the laws of the countries of the

[28] This same cumulative solution is proposed by some authors in relation to the validity of joint wills: see: E. Zabalo Escudero, 'El testamento conjunto en Derecho internacional privado. Especial referencia al testamento mancomunado aragonés', *Revista General de Derecho* (1989), p. 6364.

[29] Barel, 'La disciplina dei patti successori', p. 125; Bonomi, 'Article 25', pp. 409–410; Bonomi, 'Il regolamento europeo sulle successioni', pp. 316–317; Lagarde, 'Les principes de base', p. 704; Davì and Zanobetti, 'Il nuovo diritto internazionale privato delle successioni', p. 72; Carrascosa González, *El Reglamento sucesorio europeo*, pp. 232–233; Davì and Zanobetti, *Il nuovo diritto internazionale privato europeo*, p. 114.

[30] Davì and Zanobetti, *Il nuovo diritto internazionale privato europeo*, p. 115.

[31] Davì and Zanobetti, *Il nuovo diritto internazionale privato europeo*, p. 115.

[32] The ESR provision is, however, less strict that the provision of article 10 of the 1989 Hague Convention on the Law Applicable to Succession to the Estates of Deceased Persons, stating that non only the admissibility, but also the effects of an agreement as to succession involving the estates of more than one person would be submitted to the cumulative application of the laws that would govern 'the succession to the estates of all those persons if each such person had died on the date of the agreement'.

respective habitual residences of the persons whose successions are concerned), has the closest connection with the agreement. When determining which law demonstrates the closest connection, various factors can be taken into account.[33] On the one hand, one important element in specifying which law is the most closely connected is the place where the agreement was made.[34] Generally, unlike what happens for mutual wills, legal systems that permit these agreements require specific formalities for their drawing up, with the result that the parties must recur to a notary or other authority in order to complete them. It can be presumed that, in the majority of cases, the country the parties select for the accomplishment of the agreement as to succession will have the closest connections with the agreement, provided obviously that its law is one of those applicable to the agreement under the first paragraph of article 25.2. Other factors to be taken into account when determining the most closely connected law can be the places of habitual residence of the persons making the disposition at the time the agreement is drawn up, their nationality, their habitual residence prior to that time, the location of the assets which are the subject of the agreement, and so on.[35]

Factors that take place after the agreement is drawn up can also be taken into account; however, care must be taken not to harm the parties' legitimate expectations by taking into account elements which they could not have been aware of when the agreement was established.[36]

17. In order to avoid the cumulative application of the laws of habitual residence of each of the deceased parties at the time the agreement is drawn up, and to ensure that the agreement is admissible in relation to all parties, as well as to avoid having to resort, for the substantive validity and *inter partes* effects of the agreement, to the law demonstrating the closest connection from amongst those mentioned above, the parties, as we have seen, can choose the applicable law under article 25.3 ESR.

18. b) *The remaining issues.* The remaining issues are governed by the actual *lex successionis* determined under article 21 or article 22 ESR.

As mentioned earlier, *professio juris* under article 22 ESR allows a person having entered into an agreement as to succession to choose the law of the state of which he is a national at the time of the choice or at the time of his death, to govern the other issues relating to his succession under article 23 ESR, including possible reserved shares.

[33] Bonomi, 'Article 25', p. 411.

[34] G. Hohloch, 'Kommentierung der EuErbRVO', in Erman, *BGB: Kommentar*, 14th ed. (Köln, 2014), p. 6706.

[35] Bonomi, 'Article 25', p. 411. [36] Bonomi, 'Article 25', p. 412.

In the absence of a choice of law, the remaining issues relating to the succession that are not covered by article 25 ESR remain subject to the *lex successionis* established pursuant to article 21 ESR. It is now appropriate to ask which law that will be when several persons make provision for succession by means of one agreement. Effectively, article 21 ESR refers to the law of habitual residence of the deceased at the time of death, but in this case there would be several deceased parties. The solution to this problem must be a distributive one, in the sense that the law of the last habitual residence is applied to each of the deceased parties in order to resolve all issues that are not subject to the law provided under article 25 ESR upon the death of each of them.

III. Areas Dealt with by Article 25 ESR

19. The preceding rule concerns the law applicable to the admissibility of the agreement, its substantive validity and the binding effects between the parties, including the conditions for their resolution.

The admissibility of the agreement is a condition for its validity. Indeed, if the applicable law or laws do not consider the agreement to be admissible, the resulting sanction is that the agreement will be void.[37] This law or laws will also determine any restrictions as regards the persons who can be party to the agreement and the assets to which it may relate. Thus, for example, a business is the only permissible asset to be included in an Italian *patto di famiglia*.

20. The list of issues pertaining to the substantive validity of an agreement as to succession can be found in article 26 ESR.

Notwithstanding the absence in article 26 of any provision to that effect, the possible conversion of an invalid disposition into a valid disposition is governed by the law referred to in article 25, since such conversion amounts to nothing more than the interpretation of the will of the deceased and the interpretation of the disposition of property upon death is one of the issues specifically included in the concept of substantive validity under article 26.[38]

21. The irrevocability of the agreement is one of the possible effects that can bind the parties. The legal systems admitting agreements as to succession usually provide that the parties cannot revoke certain clauses in the agreement, as is the case in Germany, for example. As regards reciprocal or mutual wills, irrevocability is a product of the

[37] Bonomi, 'Article 25', p. 402. [38] Bonomi, 'Article 25', p. 403.

interdependence of the dispositions made by the testators; however, some countries' legal systems allow such wills to be revoked, either in part or in their entirety – as is the case for example in Austria or France.

Agreements become irrevocable, generally speaking, when they are drawn up. However, in the case of mutual wills, this happens when the first testator dies.

22. Article 25 also provides that the conditions for dissolving the agreement are governed by the law referred to in the rule; the grounds for its annulment are also included.[39] Thus, the grounds for dissolving an agreement as to succession, whether upon the parties' consent or at the request of one of them, or as provided for by law irrespective of their wishes, remain subject to the law referred to in article 25 ESR.[40]

[39] Bonomi, 'Article 25', p. 404.

[40] Bonomi, 'Article 25', p. 404; Davì and Zanobetti, 'Il nuovo diritto internazionale privato delle successioni', pp. 62, 71; Carrascosa González, *El Reglamento sucesorio europeo*, pp. 232–233; Davì and Zanobetti, *Il nuovo diritto internazionale privato europeo*, pp. 97, 113; E. Fongaro, 'L'anticipation successorale à l'épreuve du "règlement successions"', *JDI* (2014), p. 477.

Article 26

Substantive Validity of Dispositions of Property upon Death

CELIA M. CAAMIÑA DOMÍNGUEZ

1. For the purposes of Articles 24 and 25 the following elements shall pertain to substantive validity:
   (a) the capacity of the person making the disposition of property upon death to make such a disposition;
   (b) the particular causes which bar the person making the disposition from disposing in favour of certain persons or which bar a person from receiving succession property from the person making the disposition;
   (c) the admissibility of representation for the purposes of making a disposition of property upon death;
   (d) the interpretation of the disposition;
   (e) fraud, duress, mistake and any other questions relating to the consent or intention of the person making the disposition.
2. Where a person has the capacity to make a disposition of property upon death under the law applicable pursuant to Article 24 or Article 25, a subsequent change of the law applicable shall not affect his capacity to modify or revoke such a disposition.

Summary

I. INTRODUCTION *page* 395
II. THE CAPACITY OF A PERSON TO MAKE A DISPOSITION OF PROPERTY UPON DEATH 395
III. THE PARTICULAR CAUSES WHICH BAR A PERSON FROM DISPOSING IN FAVOUR OF CERTAIN PERSONS OR FROM RECEIVING SUCCESSION PROPERTY FROM CERTAIN PERSONS 399
IV. THE ADMISSIBILITY OF REPRESENTATION FOR THE PURPOSES OF MAKING A DISPOSITION OF PROPERTY UPON DEATH 400
V. THE INTERPRETATION OF THE DISPOSITION 400
VI. FRAUD, DURESS, MISTAKE AND ANY OTHER QUESTIONS RELATING TO THE CONSENT OR INTENTION OF THE PERSON MAKING THE DISPOSITION 401

I. Introduction

1. The concept of the 'substantive validity' of dispositions of property upon death is defined in article 26 ESR. The first paragraph of the rule provides a list of the elements which, for the purposes of articles 24 and 25 ESR, are to be considered as components of the concept of 'substantive validity'.[1] The list should not to be considered as exhaustive, even though the wording of the rule appears to suggest the opposite ('the following elements shall pertain to substantive validity') especially when its wording is compared with the formulation of article 23.2 ('That law shall govern *in particular* . . .').[2] A literal interpretation of the list as exhaustive would, in fact, result in issues related to substantial validity which are not expressly listed in article 26 being governed by the law applicable to the succession; this, as has been underlined, would lead to inconsistent and unsatisfactory results.[3] The second paragraph of article 26 deals with the capacity of a person wishing to modify or revoke a previous disposition of property upon death.

II. The Capacity of a Person to Make a Disposition of Property upon Death

2. The Commission's green paper had illustrated the different solutions offered by the EU Member States legal systems for determining the capacity of a person making a disposition upon death.[4] Fundamentally, the following trends could be observed:[5] (a) submission of the capacity to make a disposition of property upon death to the personal law of the author of the disposition, as part of his or her personal status (e.g. in Spanish law, application of the national law of the person making the disposition at the time of its confection (article

[1] A. Bonomi, 'Article 26', in A. Bonomi and P. Wautelet, *Le droit européen des successions. Commentaire du Règlement nº 650/2012 du 4 juillet 2012* (Bruxelles, 2013), p. 417.

[2] Bonomi, 'Article 26', p. 416. [3] Bonomi, 'Article 26', p. 416.

[4] Commission of the European Communities, green paper 'Succession and Wills', Brussels, 1 March 2005, COM(2005) 65 final.

[5] See the summary of the solutions existing in the different laws of some of the Member States compiled by the German Deutsches Notarinstitut on behalf of the European Commission, Directorate General Justice and Home Affairs: 'Étude de droit comparé sur les règles de conflits de juridictions et de conflits de lois relatives aux testaments et successions dans les États membres de l'Union Européenne. Rapport Final: Synthèse et Conclusions', in Deutsches Notarinstitut (ed), *Conflict of Law of Succession in the European Union. Perspectives for a Harmonisation* (Würzburg, 2004), p. 47.

9.1 Spanish civil code));[6] (b) submission of capacity to the law governing the succession: for example, in English law, as regards movable property, the law of the State where the testator is domiciled at the time of drawing up his will governs the testator's capacity;[7] (c) alternative application of different laws in order to favour the capacity of a person to make a disposition of property upon death: this was the case in Austrian and Finnish law, respectively section 30 IPRG (Austrian act on private international law) and chapter 26(10) of the Finnish code of inheritance.

3. As article 26 ESR includes the 'capacity of the person making the disposition of property upon death' within the concept of 'substantive validity', that capacity is governed by article 24 or article 25 ESR, as applicable. Accordingly, as more extensively illustrated in the comment relating to the two mentioned provisions [see art. 24 and art. 25], the law applicable has to be determined as follows.

Dispositions of property upon death other than agreements as to succession are governed by (a) the law of the State of which the deceased was a national at the time the choice was made, when he had chosen that law in accordance with article 22 (whether it is a general choice of law applicable to the succession, or a choice which only applies to admissibility and substantive validity);[8] (b) in the absence of a choice, the law of the country in which the deceased was habitually resident when the disposition was made.[9] We consider, in the light of recital 51 ESR, that it is not appropriate in this case to make recourse to the escape clause provided for in article 21.2 ESR, so that, in the absence of a choice of law,

[6] See A.-L. Calvo Caravaca and J. Carrascosa González, 'Persona física', in A.-L. Calvo Caravaca and J. Carrascosa González (eds), *Derecho Internacional Privado*, 15th ed. (Granada, 2014), vol. II, p. 37.

[7] L. Collins (ed), *Dicey & Morris on the Conflict of Laws*, 13th ed. (London, 2000), vol. II, p. 1029; J. Harris, 'The Proposed EU Regulation on Succession and Wills: Prospects and Challenges', *Trust LI* (2008), pp. 214–215.

[8] A. Davì and A. Zanobetti, 'Il nuovo diritto internazionale privato delle successioni nell'Unione Europea', *CdT* 5/2 (2013), pp. 64–65; A. Davì and A. Zanobetti, *Il nuovo diritto internazionale privato europeo delle successioni* (Torino, 2014), pp. 100–102; J. Carrascosa González, *El Reglamento Sucesorio Europeo 650/2012 de 4 de julio 2012. Análisis crítico* (Granada, 2014), pp. 224–225.

[9] Articles 24.1 and 24.3 ESR. See also on this respect recital 51 ESR: 'Where reference is made in this Regulation to the law which would have been applicable to the succession of the person making a disposition of property upon death if he had died on the day on which the disposition was, as the case may be, made, modified or revoked, such reference should be understood as a reference to either the law of the State of the habitual residence of the person concerned on that day or, if he had made a choice of law under this Regulation, the law of the State of his nationality on that day'.

the law of the country in which the deceased was habitually resident when the disposition was made will always apply.[10] The exclusion of the recourse to the escape clause permits to evade the insecurity associated with its operation and is, therefore, consistent with the aim of providing greater certainty and stability to the arrangement of matters of succession, which is the objective sought by applying the law of the country where the deceased was habitually resident 'on the day on which the disposition was . . . made'. Also the fact that recital 51 does not make any reference to the escape clause supports this interpretation.[11]

As regards agreements as to succession, it is appropriate to bear in mind that article 26 only covers the capacity of a person making a disposition upon death and that, by virtue of article 1.2(b) ESR [see art. 1 no. 23], the status of natural persons, save as is provided for in article 26 under comment and in article 23.2(c) [see art. 23 no. 8], is excluded from the scope of the regulation and therefore is governed by the domestic law of the Member States. When the agreement concerns the succession of one person, the capacity of the person making the disposition will be governed (a) by the parties' chosen law (the parties may choose the law of the State of which the person whose succession is in question was a national at the time the choice was made, subject to the conditions set out in article 22) [see art. 22]; (b) in the absence of a choice of law, by the law of the habitual residence of the person whose succession is concerned, at the time the agreement is drawn up. When the agreement relates to the succession of several persons, the capacity of the persons making the disposition will be governed (a) by the parties' chosen law (the parties may choose the law of the State of which one of the persons whose succession is concerned is a national at the time the choice is made, in accordance with article 22); (b) in the absence of a choice of law, by the law from among the laws of the habitual residences of each of the persons whose succession is concerned at the time the agreement is drawn up, that has the closest connection with the agreement itself [see art. 25 no. 16 *et seq.*].

It is important to bear in mind the distinction between *admissibility* and *capacity* since, in order to determine whether an agreement as to

[10] See Davì and Zanobetti, 'Il nuovo diritto internazionale privato delle successioni', p. 64; Davì and Zanobetti, *Il nuovo diritto internazionale privato europeo*, p. 100. For a different opinion, affirming that the escape clause can operate also in this case, see Bonomi, 'Article 26', p. 387; I. Rodríguez-Uría Suárez, 'La ley aplicable a las sucesiones *mortis causa* en el Reglamento (UE) 650/2012', *Indret* (2013/2), p. 22.

[11] See Davì and Zanobetti, *Il nuovo diritto internazionale privato europeo*, p. 100. For the text of recital 51 see footnote 9.

succession relating to the succession of several people is admissible, in some cases several laws have to be applied cumulatively, pursuant to article 25.2.[12] Conversely, once confirmation that the agreement is admissible has been obtained, one sole law will govern the capacity of the persons making the disposition (along with the other issues which make up substantive validity).

4. Article 24.3 ESR states that capacity to make a modification or revocation of a disposition of property upon death is governed by the law applicable to substantive validity at the moment the modification or revocation is carried out, i.e. the chosen law according to article 22, or, in the absence of a choice of law, the law which would have been applicable if the author of the modification or revocation had died on the day on which the modification or revocation were carried out.[13]

Article 26.2 contains a derogation to article 26.3, that adds an important clarification as regards capacity to modify or revoke a disposition of property upon death. The provision states that when a person had adopted a disposition of property upon death for which he was capable under the then applicable law, he is to be considered as having maintained his capacity, if he subsequently wishes to modify or revoke that disposition. As has been underlined, it is a provision whose justification is self-evident.[14] In principle, as we have seen, according to article 24.3, the capacity is submitted to the law applicable to the modification or revocation at the moment in which these acts are made; in some cases it might however occur that, due to changes in the circumstances or in the applicable law, that person would not actually enjoy capacity to make that modification or revocation. In order to avoid this unsatisfactory result, article 26.2 states that a person to whom the applicable law, in accordance with articles 24 and 25, granted capacity to adopt a disposition of property upon death, will maintain in any event capacity to modify or revoke that disposition.[15]

[12] See article 25 [see art. 25 no. 15 *et seq.*]; see also Carrascosa González, *El Reglamento Sucesorio*, p. 232.

[13] On the problems of interpretation of article 24.3, see Davì and Zanobetti, 'Il nuovo diritto internazionale privato delle successioni', pp. 65–67; Davì and Zanobetti, *Il nuovo diritto internazionale privato europeo*, pp. 102–105.

[14] Bonomi, Article 26, p. 420; Rodríguez-Uría Suárez, 'La ley aplicable', p. 36, footnote 109.

[15] W. Burandt, 'EuErbVO: Europäische Erbrechtsverordnung (VO Nr. (EU) Nr. 650/2012)', in W. Burandt and D. Rojahn (eds), *Erbrecht*, 2nd ed. (München, 2014), pp. 1446–1447; Bonomi, 'Article 26', pp. 420–421.

III. The Particular Causes Which Bar a Person from Disposing in Favour of Certain Persons or from Receiving Succession Property from Certain Persons

5. The particular causes which prohibit a person to make a disposition in favour of certain persons or which bar a person from receiving succession property from a certain person, or, at any rate, that consider as null and void a disposition in favour of certain persons, are also included within the concept of 'substantive validity'. This is fundamentally a case of avoiding any possible external influence upon the will of a person when making a disposition upon death and protecting the freedom of the testator.[16] In comparative law, we see that dispositions of this kind are generally subject to the law applicable to the succession,[17] and it has been underlined that these provisions are essential especially in legal systems in which the law makes it difficult to obtain the annulment of a disposition of property upon death on the ground of irregularities in consent.[18] Examples of provisions that bar a person from making a disposition in favour of certain persons, or consider such a disposition as null and void, concern the priest to whom the deceased confessed during his or her final illness (article 752 Spanish civil code), the deceased's guardian, unless he or she is a close relative of the former (article 907.1 French civil code, article 596 Italian civil code, article 753 Spanish civil code), the notary public receiving a will (article 597 Italian civil code, article 754 Spanish civil code), members of the medical profession who have provided care to a person during his or her final illness (article 909 French civil code), witnesses to an open will (article 975 French civil code, article 597 Italian civil code, article 754 Spanish civil code); these prohibitions sometimes extend to close relatives of the persons mentioned earlier.[19] Conversely, other legal systems place greater emphasis in protecting the free will of testators on the recourse to general mechanisms,

[16] See M. Madriñán Vázquez, *El Derecho de Representación en la Sucesión Testada* (Cizur Menor, 2009), p. 58.

[17] See Deutsches Notarinstitut (ed), *Conflict of Law of Succession*, p. 47.

[18] M. P. García Rubio and M. Otero Crespo, 'Capacidad, incapacidad e indignidad para suceder', in M. C. Gete-Alonso and Calera (eds), *Tratado de Derecho de Sucesiones* (Cizur Menor, 2011), vol. I, pp. 230–231.

[19] Cf., e.g., articles 907.1 and 909.3 of the French civil code (see P. Malaurie, *Les successions. Les libéralités* (Paris, 2004), p. 172), and the comparative law study by García Rubio and Otero Crespo, 'Capacidad', pp. 231–233.

such as the German legal provision which states that legal acts contrary to public morality are void (section 138 BGB), or the doctrine of undue influence in English law.[20]

IV. The Admissibility of Representation for the Purposes of Making a Disposition of Property upon Death

6. The law applicable by virtue of articles 24 and 25 ESR will determine whether the dispositions of property upon death are strictly personal acts ('actos personalísimos' in Spanish law, 'actes strictement personnels' in French law) that cannot be made by a representative, or, conversely, if representation is admitted. For example, Spanish *derecho común* states that generally it is not possible to leave the confection of a will, whether in whole or in part, to the discretion of a third party, or to make a will through a representative or agent;[21] Italian law has a similar provision and does not allow representation.[22] Conversely, English law does indeed allow a person to grant a power of appointment to another person, who will dispose of that person's estate after his or her death.[23]

V. The Interpretation of the Disposition

7. Certain legal systems allow the person whose succession is concerned to choose the law governing the interpretation of the disposition of property upon death. Thus, in Portuguese law, testamentary dispositions would be governed by the law personally applicable to the person having made the disposition, save where he makes a different choice.[24]

By the inclusion of interpretation into the ESR concept of substantive validity, the law applicable pursuant to articles 24 and 25 ESR will

[20] In German law recourse has been made also to section 134 BGB (see García Rubio and Otero Crespo, 'Capacidad', pp. 233–236).

[21] A. Domínguez Luelmo, 'El testamento', in M. C. Gete-Alonso and Calera (eds), *Tratado de Derecho de Sucesiones* (Cizur Menor, 2011), vol. I, p. 378.

[22] Cf. articles 631 and 632 of Italian civil code: see G. Bonilini, 'Il negozio testamentario', in G. Bonilini (dir.), *Trattato di diritto delle successioni e donazioni* (Milano, 2009), vol. II, p. 37.

[23] See Deutsches Notarinstitut (ed), *Conflict of Law of Succession*, p. 51; Collins (ed), *Dicey & Morris*, pp. 1054–1056.

[24] Cf. article 64(a) of Portuguese *código civil*: see D. Moura Vicente, *Direito Internacional Privado. Textos normativos e fundamentais* (Coimbra, 2012); on English law, see Collins (ed), *Dicey & Morris*, pp. 1040–1042; Harris, 'The Proposed EU Regulation', p. 216.

determine which elements of interpretation can be used (literal, systematic, teleological, etc.); the means which can be employed in order to ascertain the will of the person making the disposition; and whether the incorporation of legal provisions into the will is appropriate and under what conditions.[25]

VI. Fraud, Duress, Mistake and Any Other Questions Relating to the Consent or Intention of the Person Making the Disposition

8. According to article 26.1(e) ESR, all issues related to the consent or intention of the testator that might influence the validity of the dispositions of property upon death are included into the concept of 'substantive validity' and are accordingly submitted to the hypothetic succession law, as determined pursuant to articles 24 and 25 ESR.[26] Article 26.1(e) expressly mentions fraud, duress and mistake; the provision also covers any other circumstances in which the intervention of a third person might have affected the free will of the disposing person, such as cases that fall under the doctrine of 'undue influence' which is traditionally employed in common law countries.[27]

[25] See, amongst others, B. Verdera Izquierdo, 'Interpretación del testamento (epígrafes I, II, III, IV, V.1, V.2, V.3 and IX)', and P. A. Munar Bernat, 'Interpretación del testamento (epígrafes V.4, VI, VII, VIII)', in M. C. Gete-Alonso and Calera (eds), *Tratado de Derecho de Sucesiones* (Cizur Menor, 2011), vol. I, p. 647 *et seq.*

[26] García Rubio and Otero Crespo, 'Capacidad', pp. 230–231.

[27] Bonomi, 'Article 26', p. 422.

Article 27

Formal Validity of Dispositions of Property upon Death Made in Writing

CELIA M. CAAMIÑA DOMÍNGUEZ

1. A disposition of property upon death made in writing shall be valid as regards form if its form complies with the law:
   (a) of the State in which the disposition was made or the agreement as succession concluded;
   (b) of a State whose nationality the testator or at least one of the persons whose succession is concerned by an agreement as to succession possessed, either at the time when the disposition was made or the agreement concluded, or at the time of death;
   (c) of a State in which the testator or at least one of the persons whose succession is concerned by an agreement as to succession had his domicile, either at the time when the disposition was made or the agreement concluded, or at the time of death;
   (d) of the State in which the testator or at least one of the persons whose succession is concerned by an agreement as to succession had his habitual residence, either at the time when the disposition was made or the agreement concluded, or at the time of death; or
   (e) in so far as immovable property is concerned, of the State in which that property is located.

   The determination of the question whether or not the testator or any person whose succession is concerned by the agreement as to succession had his domicile in a particular State shall be governed by the law of that State.
2. Paragraph 1 shall also apply to dispositions of property upon death modifying or revoking an earlier disposition. The modification or revocation shall also be valid as regards form if it complies with any one of the laws according to the terms of which, under paragraph 1, the disposition of property upon death which has been modified or revoked was valid.
3. For the purposes of this Article, any provision of law which limits the permitted forms of dispositions of property upon death by reference to the age, nationality or other personal conditions of the testator or of the persons whose succession is concerned by an agreement as to succession

shall be deemed to pertain to matters of form. The same rule shall apply to the qualifications to be possessed by any witnesses required for the validity of a disposition of property upon death.

Summary

I. INTRODUCTION *page* 403
II. FORMAL VALIDITY OF DISPOSITIONS OF PROPERTY UPON DEATH MADE IN WRITING 405
III. THE FORMAL VALIDITY OF DISPOSITIONS OF PROPERTY UPON DEATH MODIFYING OR REVOKING AN EARLIER DISPOSITION 409
IV. PROVISIONS OF LAW WHICH LIMIT THE PERMITTED FORMS ON THE BASIS OF PERSONAL CONDITIONS 409

I. Introduction

1. Prior to examining article 27, it is to be underlined that, in accordance with article 75 ESR, Member States which are parties to the 1961 Hague Convention on the Conflicts of Laws Relating to the Form of Testamentary Dispositions will continue to apply that convention, and not article 27 ESR, to the formal validity of wills and joint wills [see art. 75 no. 2].[1]

As the convention does not apply to the form of agreements as to succession, the form of such agreements is governed by the ESR rules for all Member States, whether or not they are parties to the convention.[2]

[1] T. Ballarino, 'Il nuovo regolamento europeo sulle successioni', *Riv dir int* (2013), p. 1144. In this respect, the Deutsches Notarinstitut believed that the regulation of the form of the dispositions upon death at the European level was not necessary: see 'Étude de droit comparé sur les règles de conflits de juridictions et de conflits de lois relatives aux testaments et successions dans les États membres de l'Union Européenne. Rapport Final: Synthèse et Conclusions', made on behalf of the European Commission, Directorate General for Justice and Home Affairs, in Deutsches Notarinstitut (ed), *Conflict of Law of Succession in the European Union. Perspectives for a Harmonisation* (Würzburg, 2004), p. 79; W. Burandt, 'EuErbVO: Europäische Erbrechtsverordnung (VO Nr. (EU) Nr. 650/ 2012)', in W. Burandt and D. Rojahn, *Erbrecht*, 2nd ed. (München, 2014), p. 1447.

[2] See, amongst others, A. Bonomi, 'Article 27', in A. Bonomi and P. Wautelet (eds), *Le droit européen des successions. Commentaire du Règlement nº 650/2012 du 4 juillet 2012* (Bruxelles, 2013), pp. 424–425; G. Biagioni, 'L'ambito di applicazione del regolamento sulle successioni', in P. Franzina and A. Leandro (eds), Il diritto internazionale privato europeo delle successioni *mortis causa* (Milano, 2013), pp. 25–58; E. Castellanos Ruiz, 'Sucesión hereditaria', in A.-L. Calvo Caravaca and J. Carrascosa González (eds), *Derecho Internacional Privado*, 15th ed. (Granada, 2014), vol. II, pp. 606–607; A. Davì and A. Zanobetti, 'Il nuovo diritto internazionale privato delle successioni nell'Unione europea', *CdT* 5/2 (2013), p. 79; A. Davì and A. Zanobetti, *Il nuovo diritto internazionale privato europeo delle successioni* (Torino, 2014), pp. 125–126; I. Rodríguez-Uría Suárez, 'La

Article 75 ESR itself indirectly refers to the convention's inapplicability to the form of agreements as to succession, since it states that the 1961 Hague Convention continues to apply – for Member States who are parties thereof – 'with regard to the formal validity of wills and joint wills'.[3] The absence of any reference to agreements as to succession reinforces the assumption that article 27 ESR applies to the formal validity of those agreements in all Member States.

Article 27 ESR refers solely to dispositions of property upon death made in writing; pursuant to article 1.2(f) ESR, the formal validity of dispositions of property upon death made orally is excluded from the scope of the regulation, and in each Member State continues, therefore, to be governed by the domestic conflict of laws rules [see art. 1 nos. 47 and 49].[4]

2. The following situations are thus to be distinguished: (a) for Member States parties to the 1961 Hague Convention, the form of wills is governed by that convention; (b) for Member States not parties to the 1961 Hague Convention, the form of wills is governed by article 27 ESR; and (c) for all Member States, the form of agreements as to succession is governed by article 27 ESR.[5]

3. It is to be reminded that article 22.2 ESR, which allows for a choice of law applicable to the succession, states that such a choice shall be made 'in the form of a disposition of property upon death' or demonstrated 'by the terms of such a disposition'. Therefore, it can be maintained that article 27 also governs the form in which this choice, referred to as *professio juris*, is made by way of a disposition of property upon death, and that it applies in connection with article 22.2 (choice of law for the succession as a whole), article 24.2 (choice of law as regards admissibility and substantive validity of dispositions of property upon death other than agreements to succession), as well as article 25.3 (choice of law as regards agreements as to succession).[6]

ley aplicable a las sucesiones *mortis causa* en el Reglamento (UE) 650/2012', *InDret* (2013/2), p. 40.

3 Rodríguez-Uría Suárez, 'La ley aplicable', p. 40.

4 Bonomi, 'Article 27', pp. 88–90.

5 Bonomi, 'Article 27', p. 426; Castellanos Ruiz, 'Sucesión', pp. 600–601, 607–608; J. Müller-Lukoschek, *Die neue EU-Erbrechtsverordnung: Einführung in die neue Rechtslage* (Bonn, 2013), p. 99.

6 Bonomi, 'Article 27', pp. 426–427; Davì and Zanobetti, 'Il nuovo diritto internazionale privato delle successioni', pp. 50–51. For a recommendation regarding recourse to a will received by a notary 'on the grounds that it brings security and it avoids will contests', see A. Devaux, 'The European Regulations on Succession of July 2012: A Path Towards the End of the Succession Conflicts of Law in Europe, or not?', *The International Lawyer* (2013), p. 235.

II. Formal Validity of Dispositions of Property upon Death Made in Writing

4. Article 27 governs the formalities required for the adoption of a disposition of property upon death. As noted previously, the provision governs the form of wills and joint wills for Member States that are not parties to the 1961 Hague Convention, and the form of agreements as to succession for all Member States.[7]

5. Article 3.1(c) ESR defines joint wills as wills drawn up in one instrument by two or more persons. They are forbidden in some legal systems, such as Spanish *derecho común* (article 669 Spanish civil code), Italian law (article 589 Italian civil code) and French law (article 968 French civil code), and permitted in others, such as in Germany (section 2265 *et seq.* BGB).[8]

In order to determine whether prohibitions such as those set out above constitute an issue of substantive validity or of formal validity, we must start with the distinction between joint wills and mutual wills.[9] While the former, according to article 3.1(c) ESR, are made by two or more persons in the same instrument, without any agreement as regards each person's succession rights, the latter are treated as agreements as to succession, defined under article 3.1(b) ESR as agreements that confer, modify or revoke (with or without consideration) rights relating to the succession or future successions of one or more persons who are party to that agreement.

As regards the inclusion of prohibition of making joint wills in article 24 or article 27 of the ESR, there are two possible views.

a) The first considers the admissibility of joint wills as a question of substance.[10] As article 24 ESR governs the 'admissibility' and 'substantive validity' of dispositions of property upon death other than

[7] Bonomi, 'Article 27', p. 426; Müller-Lukoschek, *Die neue EU-Erbrechtsverordnung*, p. 99.

[8] See, with respect to Italian law, G. Bonilini, 'Il negozio testamentario', in G. Bonilini (ed), *Trattato di diritto delle successioni e donazioni* (Milano, 2009), vol. II, pp. 37–39). It is appropriate here to specify that Spanish derecho común forbids joint wills, however they are allowed in Spain under certain regional laws (for examples see articles 187–195 of *Ley* 2/2006 de *Derecho Civil de Galicia*; article 406 *et seq.* of the *Código del Derecho Foral de Aragón*. There is also an exception to that prohibition under Italian law (see articles 768 (a)–(g) of the Italian civil code as regards the *patto di famiglia*). For a comparative law survey, see article 25, no. 4 [see art. 25 no. 4 *et seq.*].

[9] Bonomi, 'Article 27', pp. 431–432.

[10] See, amongst others, Davì and Zanobetti, 'Il nuovo diritto internazionale privato delle successioni', pp. 60–61; Davì and Zanobetti, *Il nuovo diritto internazionale privato europeo*, pp. 93–99; A. Dutta, 'Das neue internationale Erbrecht der Europäischen

agreements as to succession (and, as we have seen, pursuant article 3.1 (c) ESR, joint wills are not considered pertaining to this category), the admissibility (or prohibition) of joint wills should be governed by article 24 ESR.

b) According to the second opinion, whether a joint will can be made is a question of form, while a mutual will must be treated as an agreement as to succession.[11] Thus, the admissibility of a mutual will is governed by article 25 and, in the event that it is admissible, article 27 will determine the form it may take.[12] Conversely, as a joint will, according to article 3.1(c) ESR, is drawn up in one instrument by two or more persons, without any agreement as regards each person's succession rights, the circumstance that two or more persons have drawn up a will in the same instrument is a question of form.[13]

It is to be observed that according to this second opinion the issue of 'admissibility' (or 'prohibition') would receive a different treatment in the two cases, because when it concerns a mutual will, it would be governed by article 25 on admissibility and substantive validity, whereas the same issue in respect of joint wills would be governed by article 27 on formal validity. If, along with the definitions given by article 3 ESR, mutual wills are considered as agreements as to succession, and joint wills are seen as dispositions of property upon death other than agreements as to succession, we should rather conclude that the admissibility and substantial validity of a mutual will is governed by article 25 ESR, while the admissibility and substantive validity of a joint will fall within the scope of application of article 24 ESR.

6. The Commission's proposal did not include any provision concerning the form of dispositions of property upon death, which was introduced during the procedure of adoption of the ESR.[14]

Article 27.1 contains various alternative connecting factors. It must be underlined that the rule refers to the substantive internal laws, since article 34.2 ESR does not allow *renvoi* with respect to article 27; it

Union – Eine erste Lektüre der Erbrechtsverordnung', *Zeitschrift für das gesamte Familienrecht* (2013), p. 10 *et seq.*

11 Bonomi, 'Article 27', pp. 431–432. 12 Bonomi, 'Article 27', pp. 431–432.

13 Bonomi, 'Article 27', pp. 431–432.

14 Recital 19 of the Proposal for a Regulation of the European Parliament and of the Council on jurisdiction, applicable law, recognition and enforcement of decisions and authentic instruments in matters of succession and the creation of a European Certificate of Succession, COM(2009)154 final; see Davì and Zanobetti, 'Il nuovo diritto internazionale privato delle successioni', p. 15; Rodríguez-Uría Suárez, 'La ley aplicable', pp. 38–39.

would, in fact, not be appropriate to allow *renvoi* in this context, not even when it would permit to consider the disposition formally valid [see art. 34, no. 15].[15]

The extensive list of connecting factors aims at favouring the disposition's formal validity,[16] and it essentially reproduces the 1961 Hague Convention, with a view to achieve a uniform solution for all the Member States, whether or not they are parties to the convention.[17] The generous rules on the law applicable to formal validity set out in the ESR come up against the limits of fraud of the law, as alluded to by recital 52, which states: 'When determining whether a given disposition of property upon death is formally valid under this Regulation, the competent authority should disregard the fraudulent creation of an international element to circumvent the rules on formal validity'.

The alternative options set out in article 27.1 focus on three basic elements: (a) the place where the disposition was made or the agreement as to succession concluded; (b) circumstances relating to the testator or one of the persons whose succession is concerned by the agreement as to succession; (c) the place where the immovable property is located.

7. a) Law of the State in which the disposition was made or the agreement as to succession concluded (article 27.1(a)): the ESR does not provide a definition of the place where the disposition is made or the agreement as to succession is concluded, and this, although it does not normally pose difficulties in dispositions made before a notary, could cause problems of proof in the case of holographic wills.[18]

b) Law of the State where the testator or one of the persons whose succession is concerned by an agreement as to succession was a national, was domiciled or had his habitual residence: any of the circumstances mentioned (nationality, domicile or habitual residence) can change over time; the rule tries to resolve the possible change in the applicable law (*conflit mobile*) by taking account of these factors both at the time the disposition is made or the agreement as to succession is drawn up, and at the time of death. The likelihood of the form of the disposition being

[15] Bonomi, 'Article 27', p. 436.

[16] See Davì and Zanobetti, 'Il nuovo diritto internazionale privato delle successioni', p. 49; Burandt, 'Verordnung EU Nr. 650/2012', p. 1447; Müller-Lukoschek, *Die neue EU-Erbrechtsverordnung*, p. 99.

[17] Davì and Zanobetti, 'Il nuovo diritto internazionale privato delle successioni', p. 79; Davì and Zanobetti, *Il nuovo diritto internazionale privato europeo*, p. 127.

[18] *See* Bonomi, 'Article 27', p. 433; which, in the case of holographic wills, is considered to be the place stated in the will, so far as the interested party cannot prove that it is false.

valid is increased in cases involving multiple nationalities, given that it would be sufficient for the form to fall under the law of one of the nationalities, as indicated in article 27.1(b) ESR, similarly to the provision contained in article 1(b) of the 1961 Hague Convention.[19] As regards domicile, the ESR provides that, in order to determine whether the testator or one of the persons whose succession is concerned by an agreement as to succession was domiciled in a particular State, the law of that State will be applied. This is the same solution adopted by the 1961 Hague Convention (article 1 *in fine*). As noted in relation to nationality, it should be considered that, if the person making the disposition is domiciled in more than one State (a prospect whose likelihood is increased by the fact that, as stated by the last sentence of article 27.1 ESR, the determination of the domicile in a given State must me made in accordance with the law of that same State), the disposition will be deemed formally valid to the extent that the form of the disposition is admitted by the law of any of the States where the person making the disposition was domiciled.[20]

As we can see, the subjective connecting factors (nationality, domicile or habitual residence) have special characteristics which affect agreements as to succession concerning the succession of several people. In such a circumstance, the form of an agreement as to succession will be valid if it is admitted by the law of a State where one of the persons whose succession is concerned was a national, was domiciled or had his or her habitual residence, thus increasing the number of laws which can make the agreement as to succession formally valid. It is important to remember, however, that article 27 determines whether the agreement as to succession is formally valid but not, however, if it is admissible, since the admissibility falls under article 25 ESR [see art. 25 nos. 10 *et seq.* and 14 *et seq.*].

c) In respect of immovable property, law of the country where the property is situated:. as is set out in the literature, the concept of immovable property as well as its location must be determined by means of an autonomous assessment, thereby avoiding the competent court interpreting such concepts in accordance with the *lex fori*.[21]

[19] See, amongst others, Bonomi, 'Article 27', p. 434; Carrascosa González, *El Reglamento Sucesorio*, p. 240; Davì and Zanobetti, 'Il nuovo diritto internazionale privato delle successioni', p. 80.

[20] Bonomi, 'Article 27', p. 433.

[21] Bonomi, 'Article 27', pp. 434–435.

III. The Formal Validity of Dispositions of Property upon Death Modifying or Revoking an Earlier Disposition

8. Article 27.2 refers to the formal validity of dispositions of property upon death modifying or revoking an earlier disposition and accordingly the paragraph does not apply to new dispositions made by a person during the course of his life without revoking or modifying those made earlier, that fall under paragraph 1 of article 27.[22]

9. The ESR favours the formal validity of dispositions of property upon death modifying or revoking an earlier disposition.[23] The method chosen by the ESR consists in allowing the law which is applicable to the form to be one of those set out in the first paragraph (treating the modifying or revoking disposition as though it were a new disposition), or one of the laws that would be applicable as to the form to the modified or revoked disposition. So, for example, if the person making a disposition changes his nationality during his lifetime, his nationality will have the following effects: the disposition modifying or revoking an earlier disposition will be formally valid if it is valid under the law of (a) the State whose nationality the person making the disposition held when he made the disposition modifying or revoking the earlier disposition; (b) the State whose nationality he held when he made the modified or revoked disposition; or (c) the State whose nationality he held at the time of his death.

10. As noted earlier in no. 3, article 27 also applies to the form of the choice of law carried out by means of a disposition of property upon death. In this sense, when it refers to the modification or revocation of the choice of law, article 22.4 ESR stipulates that the formality requirements applicable to the modification or revocation of dispositions of property upon death must be met. Consequently, article 27.2 also applies to the modification or revocation of the choice of law.

IV. Provisions of Law Which Limit the Permitted Forms on the Basis of Personal Conditions

11. The third paragraph of article 27 states that provisions of law which limit the form of dispositions of property upon death made in writing on the basis of the personal conditions of the testator or any of the persons whose succession is concerned by an agreement as to succession, are

22 Bonomi, 'Article 27', p. 435. 23 Bonomi, 'Article 27', p. 435.

deemed to be 'matters of form'. This rule mentions, by way of example, conditions such as age and nationality. Qualifications to be possessed by any witnesses required for the validity of a disposition of property upon death are also deemed to be matters of form under this rule.

It must be recalled that the rule refers to provisions which limit the form of testamentary dispositions, on the basis of personal conditions such as age and nationality. This could create confusion with reference to age, for example, as a circumstance relating to capacity to make a will and, consequently, as a component of substantive validity (article 26), or as a component of formal validity. This issue is clarified in recital 53 ESR, which states that the law applicable to the formal validity of a disposition of property upon death should not determine whether a minor has capacity to make such a disposition. That capacity forms part of the concept of substantive validity. Conversely, article 27.3 refers to the provisions determining whether a personal qualification should bar a person from making a disposition of property upon death in a certain form.[24] It therefore deals with a person with capacity to make the disposition of property upon death, even though he cannot make it in a particular form. Article 2223 of the Portuguese civil code is worth citing by way of an example of such provisions, as it states that a will made by a Portuguese citizen in a foreign country in accordance with foreign law only has effect in Portugal if it has been adopted in a solemn form.[25]

As these conditions are deemed by the ESR to be 'matters of form', even if the relevant provisions are considered under domestic law as 'mandatory laws' (*lois de police, norme di applicazione necessaria*), their application cannot prevail over the alternative laws indicated by article 27, since the ESR does not provide for their application when dealing with matters of form. For what concern the operation of the public policy clause set out in article 35 ESR (ref: art. 35), it is to be underlined that article 27.1 contains alternative connecting factors, and accordingly the disposition of property upon death will be valid as to the form if it is valid pursuant to any of the laws referred to. As such, even though

[24] Bonomi, 'Article 27', p. 419.

[25] The provision states that 'O testamento feito por cidadão português em país estrangeiro com observância da lei estrangeira competente só produz efeitos em Portugal se tiver sido observada uma forma solene na sua feitura ou aprovação.' See the analysis of this rule carried out by L. de Lima Pinheiro, *Direito Internacional Privado. Direito de Conflitos. Parte especial*, 3rd ed. (Coimbra, 2009), vol. II, pp. 236–237.

one of these laws contains a provision restricting the form of a disposition upon death on the basis of the personal conditions of the testator or any of the persons whose succession is concerned by an agreement as to succession, such restriction will not operate to the extent that any other law referred to in article 27.1 does not contain such a restriction.

Article 28

Validity as to Form of a Declaration Concerning Acceptance or Waiver

ALESSANDRA ZANOBETTI

A declaration concerning the acceptance or waiver of the succession, of a legacy or of a reserved share, or a declaration designed to limit the liability of the person making the declaration, shall be valid as to form where it meets the requirements of:

(a) the law applicable to the succession pursuant to Article 21 or Article 22; or

(b) the law of the State in which the person making the declaration has his habitual residence.

Summary

I. THE ALTERNATIVE CONNECTION AS TO THE FORM OF DECLARATIONS OF HEIRS AND LEGATEES; CORRELATION WITH ARTICLE 13 ESR *page* 412

II. LIMITATIONS ON THE SCOPE OF APPLICATION: THE CONCEPT OF VALIDITY AS TO FORM 415

I. The Alternative Connection as to the Form of Declarations of Heirs and Legatees; Correlation with Article 13 ESR

1. Article 28 ESR governs the form of declarations 'concerning the acceptance or waiver of the succession, of a legacy or of a reserved share', or 'designed to limit the liability of the person making the declaration'.

As expressly established by article 23.2, points (e) and (g) respectively, 'conditions and effects of the acceptance or waiver of the succession or of a legacy' and 'liability for the debts under the succession' are, in terms of substance, governed by the law that applies to the succession [see art. 23 nos. 10 and 12]. Where form is concerned, however, on similar lines (albeit in less generous terms) to the provisions of article 27 regarding the formal validity of dispositions of property upon death [see art. 27], article 28 establishes two alternative connections, with the result that declarations falling within its scope of application are valid as to form where they meet the requirements established either by the law applicable to the succession or by the law of the country of habitual residence of the author of the declaration.

In order to favour the formal validity of the declarations in question, the European legislator decided to simplify the task faced by heirs and legatees by permitting them to follow either the provisions of the law governing the succession pursuant to articles 21 and 22 ESR, or those that apply in the country of their habitual residence: heirs and legatees are more likely to be familiar with these provisions to some degree or will find it easier to establish what exactly is required of them.[1]

2. Article 28 must be read in conjunction with article 13 ESR,[2] which introduces an additional forum for these declarations [see art. 13]. The result is that the task faced by the authorities in the Member State of habitual residence of the person making the declaration is also simplified, as they are able to work on the basis of the formal provisions established by their own *lex fori*.

The scope of application of article 28 is, however, broader than that of article 13. First and foremost, in contrast to article 13, article 28 applies also where the person making the declaration resides in a Member State not bound by the ESR or non member of the EU, as it refers to the law in the country in which that person has his habitual residence, without specifying that that country has to be a Member State.[3] It follows that a declaration received by the authority dealing with the succession as

1 As the intention was to lighten the burden in terms of formal validity of the declaration and to simplify the task faced by the heirs and legatees, then there is a further connecting factor that could have accompanied the alternatives established by article 28, i.e. the law in force in the country in which the declaration is to be issued. See the comments made by A. Dutta, 'Das neue internationale Erbrecht der Europäischen Union – Eine erste Lektüre der Erbrechtsverordnung', *Zeitschrift für das gesamte Familienrecht* (2013), p. 11. It is of course possible that the European legislator was against broadening the laws that might apply here to extend beyond the law governing the succession in general, wishing to avoid the unity of *forum* and *jus* that the regulation itself seeks to establish being decoupled on too many occasions. For a view on similar lines in relation to the fact that no *renvoi* applies to article 28(b), see article 34 no. 17 [see art. 34 no. 17].

2 See A. Davì and A. Zanobetti, 'Il nuovo diritto internazionale privato delle successioni nell'Unione europea', *CdT* 5/2 (2013), p. 81; A. Davì and A. Zanobetti, *Il nuovo diritto internazionale privato europeo delle successioni* (Torino, 2014), p. 129.

3 For that matter, pursuant to article 20 ESR the provisions of the ESR regarding the applicable law are of universal application in their entirety [see art. 20].

a whole will be valid where it is in the form required by the law of the country of habitual residence of the person making the declaration or, alternatively, in the form established by the law governing the succession.[4]

In addition, article 28 also applies to declarations which, in order to be valid, do not need to be received by an authority. Pursuant to Italian law, for example, acceptance of an inheritance can take the form of a simple private statement; this is a step which, therefore, article 28 applies to, but article 13 does not.

3. The connection between article 13 and article 28 means that in tackling the interpretation of the latter, the views set out in full in relation to the former also apply here.

This is principally the case when it comes to the distinction to be made, in light of the succession law, between simple declarations, which come under the umbrella of article 13 and article 28, and actual legal proceedings, which are excluded from the scope of application of these two provisions [see art. 13 no. 10 *et seq*.].

While in order to determine the law of succession articles 21 and 22 ESR are to be consulted [see arts. 21 and 22], establishing the law referred to by the second alternative connecting factor involves ascertaining the habitual residence of the person making the declaration; as stated in the commentary on article 13, this is a finding of fact, to be made on a case-by-case basis, 'in the light of the context of the provisions and the objective' of the regulation to be applied [see art. 13 no. 9].[5] It should be borne in mind that where the second connecting factor is concerned, article 34.2 specifically states that the *renvoi* does not apply [see art. 34 no. 17].

4. Article 28 only applies to declarations made after the succession has opened. Acceptances and waivers in relation to a succession that has not yet opened, where permitted pursuant to the applicable law, are in fact usually agreed with the person whose estate is involved and, on many occasions, with the potential co-heirs; they are, therefore, basically comparable to succession agreements.[6] The fact that article 28 refers to the

[4] See P. Wautelet, 'Article 28' in A. Bonomi and P. Wautelet, *Le droit européen des successions. Commentaire du Règlement n° 650/2012 du 4 juillet 2012)* (Bruxelles 2013) p. 445.

[5] ECJ, case C-523/07, 'A' [2009] ECR I-02805, paragraph 35.

[6] Certain legislations that consider that succession agreements are null and void make it possible, subject to strict limitations, for a presumed heir to a reserved share to waive that share in advance. Article 930 *et seq*. of the French civil code, for example, allow an advance waiver of the right to claim the reserved share, but this only takes effect with the consent of

succession law to be established on the basis of articles 21 and 22, and to that law alone (which can only be determined upon the opening of the succession), rather than to the anticipated or hypothetic succession law (which would be required if article 28 would apply also to declarations made before the succession opened) clearly confirms that article 28 does not concern this type of declarations.

II. Limitations on the Scope of Application: The Concept of Validity as to Form

5. In terms of the procedure to be followed, the time scales imposed, and the conditions that apply to the acceptance or waiver of an inheritance or to limitations on the liability of beneficiaries, the law in force in the various different countries varies to a certain extent.[7] Article 28 only applies, however, to validity as to form, and, therefore, to the requirements of a non-substantive nature that the declarations must meet, i.e. the procedure to be followed for the particular step in question to be exteriorised so that it is valid in the eyes of the law. Examples of provisions relating to form are: the requirement that the declaration be in writing or recorded in an authenticated document; certification of the date; signature by hand by the signatory; authentication of the signature, or signature in the presence of witnesses; the possibility to make recourse to new technologies and, where used, the technical measures to be implemented, such as digital signatures or certified e-mail.

6. In some legal systems, the law places certain steps taken by beneficiaries on an equal footing with tacit acceptance or waiver. Portuguese law, for example, states that steps taken that necessarily presuppose an intention to accept the inheritance constitute 'tacit' acceptance (article 2056 of the civil code).[8]

There is no room for doubt, however, that an acceptance or waiver of this nature is excluded from the scope of application of article 28. The very wording of article 28 itself supports this opinion: the term

the person whose succession is concerned. Under Finnish law, a presumed heir can waive his right to the reserved share by writing to the *de cujus* on condition that he is adequately compensated in return or that the will provides compensation for his spouse or descendants (chapter 17.1 of the inheritance code). Sweden has a similar rule (article 17.2 Ärvdabalk). Steps of this nature are clearly beyond the scope of application of article 28.

[7] For a brief comparative analysis, see article 13, no. 4 [ref: art. 13 no. 4].

[8] The civil codes in Belgium (article 778), Italy (article 476) and Spain (article 999) have similar provisions.

declarations that is used here would appear to refer to express forms of acceptance, waiver or limitation of liability alone. In addition, even where the laws in question refer to a tacit 'form', this is to the form of the acceptance or waiver and not to the form of the declaration of acceptance or waiver. Besides, article 28 is intended to simplify the execution of formal requirements weighing on the beneficiaries of the succession according to the law that the ESR states as applicable; as a result, where a different law, such as that in force in the place in which the person required to make the declaration resides, does not call for requirements of that type, this is irrelevant for the rationale of the provision.[9]

The presumptions established in this area by a considerable number of legislations, such as the expiry of time without any express waiver being made (which in many systems, such as in Italy and Portugal, implies acceptance), or the presumption of acceptance which, pursuant to article 778 of the French civil code, is the result of the concealment of assets that form part of the inheritance, or the presumed waiver pursuant to article 566.2 of the Swiss civil code where the deceased is known to be insolvent, must, for the same reasons and all the more so, also be treated as falling beyond the scope of application of article 28.[10]

[9] See Wautelet, 'Article 28', p. 439.

[10] See also Wautelet, 'Article 28', p. 440.

Article 29

Special Rules on the Appointment and Powers of an Administrator of the Estate in Certain Situations

GIANLUCA CONTALDI

1. Where the appointment of an administrator is mandatory or mandatory upon request under the law of the Member State whose courts have jurisdiction to rule on the succession pursuant to this Regulation and the law applicable to the succession is a foreign law, the courts of that Member State may, when seised, appoint one or more administrators of the estate under their own law, subject to the conditions laid down in this Article.

   The administrator(s) appointed pursuant to this paragraph shall be the person(s) entitled to execute the will of the deceased and/or to administer the estate under the law applicable to the succession. Where that law does not provide for the administration of the estate by a person who is not a beneficiary, the courts of the Member State in which the administrator is to be appointed may appoint a third-party administrator under their own law if that law so requires and there is a serious conflict of interests between the beneficiaries or between the beneficiaries and the creditors or other persons having guaranteed the debts of the deceased, a disagreement amongst the beneficiaries on the administration of the estate or a complex estate to administer due to the nature of the assets.

   The administrator(s) appointed pursuant to this paragraph shall be the only person(s) entitled to exercise the powers referred to in paragraph 2 or 3.
2. The person(s) appointed as administrator(s) pursuant to paragraph 1 shall exercise the powers to administer the estate which he or they may exercise under the law applicable to the succession. The appointing court may, in its decision, lay down specific conditions for the exercise of such powers in accordance with the law applicable to the succession.

   Where the law applicable to the succession does not provide for sufficient powers to preserve the assets of the estate or to protect the rights of the creditors or other persons having guaranteed the debts of the deceased, the appointing court may decide to allow the administrator(s) to exercise, on a residual basis, the powers provided to that end by its own law and may, in its decision, lay down specific conditions for the exercise of such powers in accordance with that law.

When exercising such residual powers, however, the administrator(s) shall respect the law applicable to the succession as regards transfer of ownership of succession property, liability for debts under the succession, rights of beneficiaries, including, where applicable, the right to accept or to waive the succession, and, where applicable, the powers of the executor of the will of the deceased.

3. Notwithstanding paragraph 2, the court appointing one or more administrators pursuant to paragraph 1 may, by way of exception, where the law applicable to the succession is the law of a third State, decide to vest in those administrators all the powers of administration provided for by the law of the Member State in which they are appointed.

When exercising such powers, however, the administrators shall respect, in particular, the determination of the beneficiaries and their succession rights, including their rights to a reserved share or claim against the estate or the heirs under the law applicable to the succession.

Summary

I. THE ADMINISTRATION OF ESTATES IN A COMPARATIVE PERSPECTIVE *page* 418

II. SCOPE OF APPLICATION OF ARTICLE 29 IN LIGHT OF THE NON-PARTICIPATION BY UNITED KINGDOM AND IRELAND IN THE ESR 421

III. ANALYSIS OF THE PREREQUISITES FOR THE APPLICATION OF A SPECIFIC LAW TO THE ADMINISTRATION OF ESTATES 423

IV. THE POSSIBILITY TO SETTLE THE DISPUTES AMICABLY IN COMPLIANCE WITH THE LAW GOVERNING THE SUCCESSION 427

V. THE LAW GOVERNING THE ADMINISTRATION WHEN THE LAW APPLICABLE TO THE SUCCESSION IS THAT OF A THIRD COUNTRY 428

I. The Administration of Estates in a Comparative Perspective

1. This provision deals with the problem of identifying the law applicable to the administration of the succession. From this point of view, the ESR differs from the solutions adopted in other international instruments. In details, the Hague Convention of 2 October 1973 Concerning the International Administration of the Estates of Deceased Persons,[1] far

[1] The Hague Convention of 2 October 1973 Concerning the International Administration of the Estates of Deceased Persons met very little success at international level, being it in force between the Czech Republic, Slovakia and Portugal. Pursuant to article 75.2, the ESR prevails over the convention [see art. 74 no. 3].

from adopting specific conflict rules, restricts itself to providing the issuing of an international certificate, i.e. a document capable of demonstrating, in a uniform manner for the contracting States, the person entitled to pay creditors and distribute the residual part of the estate. On the other hand, the issue of identifying the law governing the administration was intentionally omitted in the Hague Convention of 1 August 1989 on the Law Applicable to Succession to the Estates of Deceased Persons.[2]

2. The absence of specific conflict of law rules governing the administration of succession in international conventions is essentially due to the variety of mechanisms for its substantive regulation. One scheme, especially known in civil law jurisdictions (such as Italy, France, Germany and Spain), is generally defined as 'succession in the person'; in these legal systems the heir is considered to be the continuator of the deceased's property and financial relations. Therefore, without the need of any procedure, the deceased's assets and legal relationships are transmitted directly to the heir, who thus has the duty to distribute the legacies and pay the debts.

3. A second group of legal systems provides a sort of indirect transmission which is generally known as 'succession to the assets'. This mechanism is prevalent in common law jurisdictions and it provides for granting of probate by the court in order to verify the authenticity of a will and rendering it enforceable. Following that step, a further stage opens up, characterised by the appointment of a personal representative. Under strict judicial control, that figure undertakes a role similar to that

[2] Article 7.2 of the Hague Convention of 1 August 1989 on the Law Applicable to Succession to the Estates of Deceased Persons – which is not in force on an international level – provides that the law identified by the conflict-of-laws provisions governs – (a) the determination of the heirs, devisees and legatees, the respective shares of those persons and the obligations imposed upon them by the deceased, as well as other succession rights arising by reason of death including provision by a court or other authority out of the estate of the deceased in favour of persons close to the deceased; (b) disinheritance and disqualification by conduct; (c) any obligation to restore or account for gifts, advancements or legacies when determining the shares of heirs, devisees or legatees; (d) the disposable part of the estate, indefeasible interests and other restrictions on dispositions of property upon death; *e)* the material validity of testamentary dispositions; paragraph 3 of the article further adds that 'Paragraph 2 does not preclude the application in a Contracting State of the law applicable under this Convention to other matters which are considered by that State to be governed by the law of succession'. The Convention does not, therefore, specifically include administration amongst the matters governed by the *lex successionis*, leaving each contracting State the choice to extend the succession law to cater for this aspect as well.

of a trustee[3] and in particular performs the function of administering the succession, managing the assets, paying the creditors, and, only once those operations have been completed, he transmits the residual part of the estate to the heirs.[4] In legal systems of this kind, therefore, the heirs do not succeed in the legal position of the deceased as they succeed only to the remaining part of the assets of the deceased once that the tasks mentioned earlier have been performed.[5]

4. Finally, a third group of legal systems, although characterised by a tendency towards the continuity of legal personality of the deceased by the heir, require an intervention by the court having jurisdiction in order to transmit the residue to the heirs. In contrast to the first kind of systems examined above, in this case the measure adopted by the court has the function of 'constituting' the heir's rights.[6] In such cases the administration stage does not represent a necessary step (although frequently occurring in practice), but only a possible event in case the court is unable to provide in any other way.

5. There is a certain degree of non-communicability between the systems mentioned above and, in particular, between the civil law systems characterised by the continuity principle and the common law systems based on the principle of succession to the assets. That difficulty in the interaction between these two legal systems depends, to a large extent, also on the conflict of law rules. While common law jurisdictions usually apply the law of the deceased's domicile to succession to moveable assets and the *lex rei sitae* to succession to immoveable property, civil law systems (with some exceptions: as occurred *inter alia* in the French and the Belgian legal orders) often adopt a unitary approach and apply either the law of the country of last residence or, in some cases, national law (as occurred in particular in Italy, Germany and Spain). In the event that, after the entry into force of the ESR, the deceased has made a *professio juris* and therefore his national law governs the entire

[3] On the comparison between personal representative and trustee, see footnote 25.

[4] Where appointed by the testator in the will, the personal representative is referred to as the 'executor'; where appointed by the court, the term used is 'administrator'.

[5] For a comparison of the two systems, see S. Godechot-Patris, 'L'administration des successions', in G. Khairallah and Revillard (eds), *Droit européen des successions internationales* (Paris, 2013), p. 88 s.; P. Wautelet, 'Article 29', in A. Bonomi and P. Wautelet, *Le droit européen des successions. Commentaire du Règlement n° 650/2012 du 4 juillet 2012* (Bruxelles, 2013), p. 455.

[6] This is the functioning of the Austrian system, which provides the issue of a judicial provision named *Einantwortung*: see Y. H. Leleu, *La transmission de la succession en droit comparé* (Bruxelles, 1996), p. 187 *et seq.*

succession, a real conflict could arise: it could in fact be the case that an heir, appointed on the basis of a foreign legal system, intends to take possession of the assets situated in the United Kingdom, in which, on the other hand, the court has appointed an administrator who wishes to settle all the estate debts prior to transmitting the remaining part of the assets to the heirs.[7]

6. It is therefore appropriate to point out that the difficulty of coordination regards especially the common law jurisdictions, which generally exclude the heirs invested under the foreign law governing the succession from taking possession of the assets located in the territory.[8] This is due essentially to the judicial nature of probate and of the appointment of the personal representative, which contributes to conferring a territorial scope of application to the entire succession.[9] Difficulties in applying United Kingdom or North American law appear to be less pronounced in civil law systems, since in those jurisdictions the order for appointment and granting of powers to the administrator is usually automatically recognised, without need for any judicial procedure. Following that recognition, an executor appointed abroad may in fact freely exercise his or her own powers in the country concerned.[10]

II. Scope of Application of Article 29 in Light of the Non-participation by the United Kingdom and Ireland in the ESR

7. The provision in question therefore originates from the idea of facilitating accession to the ESR by the United Kingdom and Ireland. As it is an instrument adopted in the field of judicial cooperation in civil

[7] See A. Bonomi, 'Successions internationales: conflits de lois et de juridictions', *Hague Recueil*, vol. 350 (2010), p. 344 *et seq.*

[8] F. Boulanger, *Droit international des successions* (Paris, 2004), p. 168, points out that in the US legal system, testamentary executors appointed abroad are at times allowed to exercise their powers within the United States due to the principle of comity.

[9] M. Goré, *L'administration des successions en droit international privé français* (Paris, 2004), p. 42 *et seq.*

[10] This was in fact the position followed by French case law (see Cour de cassation, 1re civ., 6 June 1967, *Schapiro, Rev crit dr int priv* (1969), p. 75, with commentary by J. Deprez, and JDI (1967), p. 890, with commentary by J. D. Bredin; Cour de cassation, 1re civ., 3 November 1983, *Rev crit dr int priv* (1984), p. 336 with commentary by M. Revillard, and JDI (1985), p. 115, with commentary by B. Ancel) and Italian case law (see Corte di cassazione 13 April 1959, n. 1089, *Riv dir int* (1959), p. 620 *et seq.*, as well as Tribunale Bari 16 February 1974, *Riv dir int* (1975), p. 600 *et seq.*; Tribunale Genova 18 July 1989, *Riv dir int priv proc* (1990), p. 674 *et seq.*).

matters, those States may decide, on a case-by-case basis, whether or not to participate in the legislation enacted by the European institutions.[11]

8. Unfortunately, the provision under examination has not produced the desired effect, since neither the United Kingdom nor Ireland has acceded to the ESR. It cannot of course be ruled out that they will decide to take part at a later stage, as they can inform the Council and Commission of their decision 'at any time' after the adoption of a measure pursuant to article 81 TFEU. However, at the moment, the said countries do not appear so inclined, and this is even more unlikely to take place in the future, after the outcome of the British referendum of 23 June 2016, which compels the British government to withdraw from the EU.

On the other hand, the lack of participation was probably foreseeable, since the final wording of the provision appears even more restrictive, on the level of possibility to introduce derogations to the unitary nature of the law governing the succession, than the corresponding article 21.2, of the proposal submitted by the European Commission in 2009.[12] The draft provision established in fact that the law governing the succession shall not preclude

> the application of the law of the Member State in which the property is located where it: (a) subjects the administration and liquidation of the succession to the appointment of an administrator or executor of the will via an authority located in this Member State. The law applicable to the succession shall govern the determination of the persons, such as the heirs, legatees, executors or administrators of the will, who are likely to be appointed to administer and liquidate the succession.

9. While the proposed legislation prescribed the application of the law of the *situs* to all issues regarding the administration, the solution finally approved, on the contrary, allows the heirs and executors appointed on the basis of the *lex fori* to exercise the powers provided in the *lex successionis* also over the assets situated in the United Kingdom and Ireland. The application of the regulation in those countries, furthermore, would have exposed the heirs residing in the United Kingdom and Ireland to unlimited liability for debts under the law governing the succession, which is precisely the consequence that the system of judicial

[11] See article 3 of Protocol no. 21 on the position of the United Kingdom and Ireland in respect of the area of freedom, security and justice, attached to the Treaties establishing the European Union.

[12] EC Commission, Proposal for a Regulation of the European Parliament and of the Council on jurisdiction, applicable law, recognition and enforcement of decisions and authentic instruments in matters of succession and the creation of a European Certificate of Succession, Brussels, 14 October 2009, COM(2009) 154 final, p. 22.

administration of succession sought to prevent.[13] In other words, the application of the ESR in those countries would have an impact also on domestic law, since these Member States would no longer have the freedom to govern succession to the assets located on their respective territories according to their own laws.[14] The fact that the United Kingdom and Ireland have opted out of the ESR on succession largely deprives the provision in question of any practical importance.[15]

On the other hand, by not acceding to the ESR, these countries are not even required to recognise the powers of testamentary executors appointed in other European Member States.[16]

III. Analysis of the Prerequisites for the Application of a Specific Law to the Administration of Estates

10. By establishing a specific conflict of laws rule for administration, the provision in question introduces a derogation to the principle of unity of the law governing the succession.[17] Therefore it is a provision which has little relevance from the point of view of the continental-European law countries, which normally include the administration within the scope of application of the law governing the succession.[18] It is not hence a coincidence that, prior to the adoption of the ESR, some

[13] On these points see J. Harris, 'The Proposed EU Regulation on Succession and Wills: Prospects and Challenges', *Trust LI* (2008), pp. 181 *et seq.*, 190 *et seq.*; A. Bonomi, 'Prime considerazioni sulla proposta di regolamento sulle successioni', *Riv dir int priv proc* (2010), pp. 875 *et seq.*, 900.

[14] Certain commentators observed how, during the course of the negotiations, the United Kingdom and Ireland exercised a considerable degree of influence on some of the solutions adopted: see Godechot-Patris, 'L'administration des successions', p. 90; Wautelet, 'Article 29', p. 455.

[15] Save Cyprus, which, being a common law jurisdiction, adopts a similar approach to that followed in England: see A. Davì and A. Zanobetti, *Il nuovo diritto internazionale privato europeo delle successioni* (Torino, 2014), 181, footnote 322. Certain authors include Malta in this category (W. Burandt and D. Rjahn, *Erbrecht* (München, 2014), p. 1449), but it does not appear that courts in this country issue probates.

[16] T. Ballarino, 'Il nuovo regolamento europeo sulle successioni', *Riv dir int* (2013), p. 1127, observes that the European legislator could have made the European certificate the object of a separate regulation, thereby enabling the common law systems to participate to it.

[17] See Davì and Zanobetti, *Il nuovo diritto internazionale privato europeo*, p. 181.

[18] The suggestion, however, had been made in the past by certain authors that specific provisions be adopted governing the administration of successions. See M. Ferid, 'Le rattachement autonome de la transmission successorale en droit international privé', *Hague Recueil*, vol. 142 (1974), pp. 71 *et seq.*, 169 *et seq.*; Goré, *L'administration des successions*, p. 81 *et seq.*

commentators considered that a provision such as this should not be adopted, as it could potentially result in a reason for controversial and divergent applications.[19]

11. Given that premise, the provision in question is characterised by an extremely cautious attitude: the drafters of the ESR have in fact introduced a rule which merely provides for an option, allowing the courts of the Member States whose legal systems provide an administration stage, to apply a different law from that governing the succession, but certainly does not oblige them to do so.[20] As it is a special rule it can be assumed on the other hand that the European Court of Justice will construe it narrowly. The case law of the ECJ is well known to provide a narrow interpretation of exceptions when they may be considered detrimental to the unity and uniformity of application of EU law.[21]

12. The analysis of the provision under comment can be split into three parts: the first pertains to the prerequisites for the application of the exception; the second relates to appointment of administrators; the third concerns the powers which can be actually exercised by the subjects thus appointed.

13. The prerequisites for the application of the provision in question are threefold. The first is that the appointment of the administrator must be compulsorily provided by the *lex fori*. This certainly occurs in the common law systems, but also the Swedish and Finnish legal systems provide for a compulsory appointment of an administrator for the succession: with respect to those legal systems the mechanism under article 29 may consequently produce some effects.[22]

[19] See A. Dutta, 'Succession and Wills in the Conflict of Laws in the Eve of Europeanisation', *RabelsZ* (2009), pp. 547 *et seq*., 602.

[20] See J. Carrascosa González, *El Reglamento Sucesorio Europeo 650/2012 de 4 julio 2012. Anális crítico* (Granada, 2014), p. 199.

[21] This approach to interpretation adopted by the Court of Justice has been the subject of criticism, e.g. by A. Davì, *Comunità europee e sanzioni economiche internazionali* (Napoli, 1993), p. 234 *et seq*.

[22] See also A. Bonomi, 'Il regolamento europeo sulle successioni', *Riv dir int priv proc* (2013), pp. 293 *et seq*., 314. See, in addition, the *Country Reports* for Sweden and Finland annexed to the research carried out by *Deutsches Notarinstitut* (the results of which were published in *Les successions internationales dans l'UE. Perspectives pour une harmonisation* (Würzburg, 2004) and which can also be found at ec.europa.eu/civiljustice/publications/docs/report_conflits_suede.pdf (concerning Sweden; last accessed 5 July 2016) and ec.europa.eu/civiljustice/publications/docs/report_conflits_finland.pdf (concerning Finland, last accessed 5 July 2016). There is doubt, however, over whether the provision is operative in the legal systems of the third type mentioned earlier, no. 4, and in particular in Austria, where there is a phase of administration controlled by the court, with a subsequent order transferring title in the assets to the heirs: the reason for this is that

14. Secondly, it is necessary that the court seised is located in a different country from that whose law governs the succession. Since the ESR is based on the principle of substantial correspondence between applicable law and forum, the separation of these two aspects can occur only in limited situations. It takes place most frequently where the deceased has chosen his own national law to govern the succession instead of the law of his country of habitual residence, as specifically permitted by article 22 of the ESR.[23] Further hypothesis may arise where the criterion for jurisdiction is determined on the basis of the place where the assets are located (article 10) or in respect of the *forum necessitatis* (article 11).

15. Thirdly, it is necessary that the court seised is located in a 'Member State'. It must be noted, that, while, as regards the applicable law, the ESR has universal application (article 20), the same cannot be said in relation to the criteria for establishing jurisdiction, which of course operate only for the purpose of identifying as courts having jurisdiction those of a Member State. In that respect it is useful to point out that the term *Member State* must be considered as including a State participating in the ESR, so that for the purposes of the mechanism established by article 29, the United Kingdom, Ireland and Denmark are necessarily excluded. The courts in the said countries, therefore, shall continue to appoint the administrators for the assets located on their territory by virtue of the provisions provided for by the *lex fori* and not due to effect of the mechanism provided by article 29.

16. The persons eligible for appointment as administrators are in principle those identified by the *lex successionis*. In line with the practice previously followed in common law countries[24] the ESR introduces here

here the appointment of an administrator is not generally a compulsory step. In such circumstances, the assets in the estate find themselves in what might be described as being held in suspension, similarly to a legacy in abeyance: see M. Lowenthal and F. Schwank, 'Austria', in L. Garb and J. Wood (eds), *International Succession*, 3rd ed. (Oxford, 2010), p. 42. The following authors also rule out the provision in question from applying to the Austrian legal system: Wautelet, 'Article 29', p. 457; Bonomi, *Successions internationales*, p. 351, footnote 1046; M. Greeske, *Die Kollisionsnormen der neuen EU-Erbrechtverordnung* (Frankfurt am Main, 2014), p. 177 seems more inclined, however, to treat this system as being comparable with common law systems.

23 See P. Lagarde, 'Les principes de base du nouveau règlement européen sur les successions', *Rev crit dr int priv* (2012), pp. 691 *et seq*., 714.

24 See G. Droz, 'L'activité notariale internationale', *Hague Recueil*, vol. 280 (1999), p. 75; see also Max Planck Institute for Comparative and International Private Law, 'Comments on the European Commission Proposal's for a Regulation of the European Parliament of the European Parliament an of the Council on Jurisdiction, Applicable Law, Recognition and

a sort of concurrence between two different laws: a first one, that is, the *lex fori*, lays down the rule that the appointment of an administrator is mandatory and also governs the procedure to follow in order to fulfil that obligation; a second one, that is, the law governing the succession, identifies the persons who can fill the role of administrator. This concurrence between two laws in relation to different aspects of a procedure which appears conceptually unitary, in terms of recital 43, pursues the function of ensuring a smooth coordination between the two laws. In certain cases, a third party may also be appointed (i.e. other than the heirs or the executor designated in the will or by the law governing the succession) where provided for by the *lex fori* and when there is a conflict of interests between the beneficiaries or between the beneficiaries and creditors or when there is a disagreement between the beneficiaries regarding the administration of the estate.

17. Pursuant to article 29.2, the powers that the administrators may exercise are provided for by the *lex successionis*. In other words, in the event that the appointment is prescribed by the law of the court seised, the appointment of a specific person as administrator and the powers that he or she can exercise depend, more or less exclusively, on the law governing the succession. That provision, while perhaps not completely logical, aims at maintaining the law governing the succession as far as possible intact. It is however possible for the courts, when appointing an administrator, to impose some specific conditions for the performance of powers or to establish the 'residual' application of the *lex fori*; and they can do that, above all, where the law governing the succession does not provide sufficient powers to preserve the assets of the estate or to protect the creditors. Those residual powers, according to recital 44, could, for example, include the powers of 'establishing a list of the assets of the estate and the debts under the succession, informing creditors of the opening of the succession and inviting them to make their claims known'. This shall probably be the more usual instance for applying the *lex fori*, due to the fact that in legal systems following the principle of personal succession, the administrators are generally equated to mere agents of the deceased, while in common law systems they are regarded as the real proprietors who have powers commensurate to such status. Also in this case issues concerning transfer of assets, liability for debts under the succession and rights of the beneficiaries remain subject to application of

Enforcement of Decisions and Authentic Instruments in Matters of Succession and the Creation of a European Certificate of Succession', *RabelsZ* (2010), p. 641.

the law governing the succession. The practical result will be that, on each occasion, before proceeding with the sale of an asset or paying a legacy, the administrators will have to follow scrupulously the instructions provided by the *lex successionis* and obtain the legal authorisation which this law requires, also in relation to the assets which are located on the territory of the court which ordered the appointment.[25]

18. The joint application of the *lex fori* and the law governing the succession will necessarily require an effort of adaptation. In such cases it could even happen that the law governing succession provides for the exercise of powers unknown to the *lex fori*, such as, for example, the direct administration of the estate by the court or the attribution to the judge of administrative tasks, such as the duty to chair a meeting of heirs, legatees and creditors. In such situations, a case-by-case approach would be required, identifying the functionally corresponding powers within the scope of the *lex fori*.

IV. The Possibility to Settle the Disputes Amicably in Compliance with the Law Governing the Succession

19. Recital 43 contains an indication which is apparently redundant. It establishes that the appointment of administrators provided by the *lex fori* 'should be without prejudice to any choice made by the parties to settle the succession amicably out of court in another Member State where this is possible under the law of that Member State'. It appears obvious in fact that the parties, generally the heirs, can always settle any

[25] The personal representative is the owner of the assets in equity and his position has often been compared to that of a trustee: like a trustee, he has the right of ownership over the assets, whose scope is limited by the purpose of the trust. There are however various differences between these two figures. First and foremost, they have different tasks: while the trustee must ensure that the assets placed in trust are properly managed in such a way that the aim that the settlor had in mind is achieved, the personal representative is simply required to collect in the assets, pay the debts and distribute the remainder of the estate to the heirs. This functional difference gives rise to certain additional consequences in terms of procedures and liability: especially when minors are involved, while the trustee is required to obtain a leave of the court to carry out the extraordinary administration, the personal representative can proceed directly with the sale of the portfolio whether it is necessary in order to discharge the obligations of the estate. But the most significant differences between the two consist in the position of the beneficiaries: the beneficiaries of a trust are the owners in equity and, therefore, have considerable powers of control, whilst the heirs, until they receive the assets, have no real rights over the estate. For a comparison between these two institutions, see S. Godechot, *L'articulation du trust et du droit des successions* (Paris, 2004), p. 267 *et seq.*

dispute arising between them regarding the division of the estate, all the more so as the systematic positioning of that provision in a recital suggests that it adds nothing more than that which can be found in the letter of the ESR.

20. It is possible however to see recital 43 as the enunciation of a provision of a substantial nature. According to common law systems, in fact, a settlement between the heirs does not extinguish the duty of the personal representative to pay the estate creditors. On the other hand, in these systems, until the apportionment of the remaining part of the assets, the heirs themselves do not have rights as such, which can be exercised without restriction: until transmission of the residue they are vested with mere expectations.

21. In this context it appears reasonable to believe that the European legislator has decided to insert a rule of substantial nature into a recital, by virtue of which it may always be possible for the heirs to derogate from the law governing the administration and to settle any dispute which has arisen between them, even if, due to the particular structure of the *lex fori*, they could not exercise their rights at that specific moment. From this point of view, the rule in question appears to introduce a further derogation to the law governing administration. We are dealing, clearly, not with a choice-of-law rule, but with a provision of a substantive nature, which may apply whenever the *lex fori* does not provide for a similar possibility at a given stage of the administration process or, more simply, makes the effectiveness of the settlement dependent on the subsequent acquisition of the right.[26]

V. The Law Governing the Administration When the Law Applicable to the Succession Is That of a Third Country

22. Finally, article 29 contains a specific provision for the case in which the law applicable to the succession is that of a third country. This is obviously a possible eventuality since the ESR as concerns the applicable law is of universal application [see art. 20]. In such cases the court can decide 'by way of exception' to grant to the administrators all the powers provided by the *lex fori*.

23. This provision was probably dictated by the desire to offer a wider opening to common law countries in order to facilitate their

[26] The transaction concluded in one of the Member States is of course subject to recognition and a declaration of enforceability, pursuant to article 61 ESR.

participation. Notwithstanding the intention of the European legislator, the provision in question does not appear as entirely suitable, since it is not aimed at protecting the law of the European Union, nor its uniform application, but merely grants more space to the *lex fori*. Accordingly, the provision does not seem to deserve much approval, as it introduces more or less wider derogations depending on whether the *lex successionis* is that of a Member State or of a third country.

24. Such a provision, within the scope of a private international law regulation with universal application, introduces a differentiation for the determination of the limits to the law governing the succession, which may appear to be not entirely justified: consider the case in which the deceased, while leaving all his assets in a Member State in which he has spent most of his life, decides to spend the final part of his life in a non-EU country, to which he moved perhaps only to receive a particular medical treatment. This further exception in the operation of the rather intricate mechanism of article 29 may bring about some failings in the functioning of the ESR, which can depend on particular contingent factors which are not even entirely foreseeable at an earlier stage (i.e. when the will was drawn up).[27]

25. In conclusion, article 29 appears to be rather complex and it requires continuous efforts for reconciling different governing laws, without however effectively preserving the features of common law jurisdictions and without therefore completely achieving the purpose of favouring their participation to the ESR.

[27] See also the perplexities expressed by Godechot-Patris, 'L'administration des successions', p. 103.

Article 30

Special Rules Imposing Restrictions Concerning or Affecting the Succession in Respect of Certain Assets

GIANLUCA CONTALDI

Where the law of the State in which certain immovable property, certain enterprises or other special categories of assets are located contains special rules which, for economic, family or social considerations, impose restrictions concerning or affecting the succession in respect of those assets, those special rules shall apply to the succession in so far as, under the law of that State, they are applicable irrespective of the law applicable to the succession.

Summary

I. THE IMPACT OF THE LAW OF THE SITUS ON INTERNATIONAL REGULATION OF SUCCESSIONS *page* 430

II. THE PRINCIPAL TYPES OF RULES FALLING WITHIN THE SCOPE OF APPLICATION OF ARTICLE 30 432

III. PROBLEMS OF INTERPRETATION 438

I. The Impact of the Law of the *situs* on International Regulation of Successions

1. Article 30 deals with the effect of binding provisions in force in the place in which certain assets of the estate are located where the succession is governed by a different law.[1] It establishes that overriding mandatory provisions in the country in which certain immovable property, enterprises and other categories of assets are located shall prevail over the law governing the succession.[2]

[1] Article 30 reflects a solution previously adopted by article 15 of the Hague Convention of 1 August 1989 on the law applicable to successions. This convention is not in force on an international level: the only country that had ratified it is the Netherlands, who then denounced it on 17 December 2014, due to the adoption of the ESR.

[2] Despite the absence of any express definition, there would appear to be no doubt that national provisions that take effect as a result of article 30 must take the form of overriding mandatory provisions. The wording of article 30 itself makes it clear that the provisions must be treated by the law containing them as applicable 'irrespective of the law applicable

2. The solution adopted by article 30 appears appropriate considering that, in line with the principle of unity of the succession, the ESR generally excludes the *lex rei sitae* from applying, even where immovable property is concerned.[3] Had the European legislator deprived the overriding mandatory provisions of the law of the *situs* of any significance, where the assets in question are in a non-EU Member State whose legislation contains rules of this type, the conflict rules in the ESR would have had very little effect. It would in fact be difficult for judgments adopted in one Member State to be enforced in the country where the assets in question are located.[4]

3. National provisions that potentially take effect within the scope of article 30 must constitute a special set of rules that affect the succession, meaning that they must impose restrictions on the transferability of assets on death. For this purpose, it is worth pointing out a subtle difference between the various language versions of the article. While the Italian wording establishes that the special rules 'must impose a restriction' on the succession, the versions in other languages recognise that these provisions can also simply 'affect' how the succession is governed.[5] This is, however, an aspect that does not appear to have any practical consequences on the range of the provisions taken into

to the succession'. On these lines see A. Bonomi, 'Il regolamento europeo sulle successioni', *Riv dir int priv proc* (2013), p. 314; A. Devaux, 'The European Regulation on Succession of July 2012: A Path towards the End of the Succession Conflicts of Law in Europe, or Not?', *The International Lawyer* (2013), p. 243; N. Chikoc Barreda, 'Reflexiones sobre los regímenes especiales en derecho internacional privado sucesorio según el reglamento europeo 650/2012 de 4 Julio de 2012', *CdT* 6/1 (2014), p. 132.

[3] D. Martiny, 'Lex rei sitae as a connecting factor in EU Private International Law', *IPRax* (2012), p. 119 *et seq.*, had previously emphasised the requirement that the EU succession rules allow the law in force in the country housing the assets to have a voice to a certain extent.

[4] The assumption can in fact be made that where recognition of a foreign judgment is sought in one of these countries, the overriding mandatory provisions to be applied by the court come into play as principles of public policy. See A. Davì and A. Zanobetti, *Il nuovo diritto internazionale privato europeo delle successioni* (Torino, 2014), p. 180; J. Carrascosa González, *El reglamento sucesorio europeo 650/2012 de 4 julio 2012. Análisis crítico* (Granada, 2014), p. 203.

[5] The Italian version states that the provisions in question must be 'norme speciali che ... impongono restrizioni alla successione', while in the other language versions, the same expression is contained in a hendiadys. See the French wording: 'dispositions spéciales qui ... imposent des restrictions concernant la succession portant sur ces biens ou ayant une incidence sur celle-ci'; the Spanish text: 'disposiciones especiales que ... afecten o impongan restricciones a la sucesión de dichos bienes'; the German wording: 'beschränken oder berühren'; and, finally, the Portuguese version of the same provision: 'imponham restrições quanto à sucessão ou a afetem no respeitante a esses bens'.

consideration by article 30, which are in any event subject to the requirement that they introduce certain exceptions to the normal transferability of assets upon death.

4. In addition, the provisions must establish special succession rules that concern certain immovable property, certain enterprises or certain other categories of assets. The ESR does not offer any help in defining more precisely these concepts. Set against this backdrop, there is considerable merit in the argument that the task of delimiting the assets that come within the categories in question falls to the law in force where those assets are located.[6]

II. The Principal Types of Rules Falling within the Scope of Application of Article 30

5. In order to be taken into account as binding provisions by article 30, the rules referred to in the article must have a specific purpose. They are in fact identified on the basis of their function, with importance being attached to the objectives pursued, which must cater for needs of an economic, family or social nature.[7]

6. The category of rules classified as economic in nature principally comprises the provisions regarding the succession of agricultural and artisan businesses.[8] A comparative analysis reveals two different mechanisms that are widely used in order to place certain assets beyond the scope of the ordinary succession rules.

7. The first of these involves the provisions that establish an 'anomalous' succession: they dictate that, where the owner passes away, the business is allocated to those (where 'those' can mean individuals or a group) who already had a link with it or who are prepared to carry it on, despite not being party to the succession relationship in its strictest sense. This category includes the transmission of rural leases pursuant to French law, succession to the right to use the land, which is a common

[6] P. Wautelet, 'Article 30', in A. Bonomi and P. Wautelet, *Le droit européen des successions. Commentaire du Règlement n° 650/2012 du 4 juillet 2012* (Bruxelles 2013), p. 471.

[7] A. Davì and A. Zanobetti, 'Il nuovo diritto internazionale privato delle successioni nell'Unione europea', *CdT* 5/2 (2013), p. 109; Davì and Zanobetti, *Il nuovo diritto internazionale privato europeo*, p. 177.

[8] Bonomi, 'Il regolamento europeo sulle successioni', p. 314; Davì and Zanobetti, 'Il nuovo diritto internazionale privato delle successioni', p. 110; Davì and Zanobetti, *Il nuovo diritto internazionale privato europeo*, p. 177; Wautelet, 'Article 30', p. 469 *et seq.*; D. Damascelli, *Diritto internazionale privato delle successioni a causa di morte*, Milano (2013), p. 78 *et seq.*; Chikoc Barreda, 'Reflexiones sobre los regímenes especiales', p. 138 *et seq.*

feature of Spanish law, transmission of the ownership of an agricultural business pursuant to Slovenian law and succession to the 'maso chiuso' according to the legislation in force in the Italian province of Bolzano.[9] In such situations, the only interest which deserves protection is that of the group of people involved in preserving the business. The departure from the law governing the succession comes into play as a result of a particular requirement at a local level: the opportunity to preserve a specific agricultural establishment at a time in which the countryside is witnessing the gradual lessening of the population. Dividing up the ownership of these businesses would, in a number of cases, mean running the risk of them disappearing altogether: they would cease to be lucrative and, as a result, would have little appeal. In the absence of provisions that operate in order to keep the farm as one distinct unit, the heirs may well be tempted to abandon work in the agricultural sector in search of more remunerative employment. This scenario would, in turn, have serious social ramifications, resulting in a depletion of the territory that these businesses occupy.

8. The second type of mechanism, on the other hand, takes the form of provisions designed to encourage the passage of title in an asset or a group of assets to one single heir (usually the spouse or the descendent already working in the business). This result is achieved via an indirect mechanism that involves providing the person in question with the opportunity to acquire the co-heirs' shares in addition to his or her own, with compensation being provided if necessary in cash or in kind. In contrast to the first mechanism examined, these provisions do not involve a departure from the succession regime, simply by allowing certain heirs to acquire ownership of assets from others and buying out their shares; put differently, the provisions that this mechanism is concerned with establish what might be described as a right of first refusal in favour of a co-heir who, when the succession is opened, finds himself in

[9] See, respectively, article L. 411–34 of the French code rural et de la pêche maritime, providing that the lease can continue to the spouse or descendants who worked in the business in the five-year period prior to the opening of the succession; article 32 of the *Ley de Reforma y Desarrollo Agrario* (decree 118/1973, as amended by law 19/1995: here too, the spouse or descendants are placed first in line in terms of succession to the farming licence, on condition that they are farmers themselves); article 7 of the Slovenian law on agricultural businesses of 7 December 1995, which states that a testator can, by means of a will, designate up to a maximum of two heirs from a limited group of people; finally, in Italy, article 14 of law no. 17 of 28 November 2001 in the Province of Bolzano on the 'maso chiuso', which establishes that, in the absence of any directions provided by the testator, the business is passed on in accordance with an established order of preference.

a particular position in relation to a certain asset. The rules regarding preferential allocation under French law fall into this category, with similar systems also found in Austria, Belgium, Finland, Germany, Italy, Luxembourg, Norway, Poland and Switzerland.[10]

9. Another purpose which can be taken into consideration in article 30 is the social purpose. The provisions in question here relate to certain art collections or libraries which, given that they form one complete unit overall, are of historical value and importance, with the purpose behind the provisions being to keep them together as a whole. One example here is the mechanism whereby assets are returned to the ascendants where the donee dies without heirs.[11]

10. Still in the same area, certain other provisions can be found that are designed to preserve the nature of certain collections of historical interest as a unit. One particular scenario worth mentioning where the Italian legal system is concerned involves the archives belonging to the

[10] See articles 831–834 of the French civil code (it should be pointed out here that the French Cour de cassation has decided in favour of the internationally binding nature of the provisions regarding preferential allocation: see the references on this point below at footnote 21); article 832–1 of the Luxembourg civil code, which dictates that the business forms part of the share of the inheritance taken up by the person awarded the business, who is then required to compensate the other heirs to the extent; article 49 of Italian law no. 203 of 1982, 'Provisions regarding agricultural contracts', pursuant to which an heir who already works in the agricultural business has option rights in relation to the purchase of the business; Swiss federal law on land ownership (*loi fédérale sur le droit foncier rural* of 4 October 1991), which allows each heir to ask for the agricultural business to be allocated on a preferential basis; articles 1058–1062 of the Polish civil code, which allocate the agricultural business to the heirs in accordance with a predetermined order (the heirs who worked in the business; the heirs with skills in the agricultural sector; the heirs without employment elsewhere), but on condition that the piece of land measures at least one hectare. Other systems instead attach greater importance to the claim by an heir who meets more than one requirement or the heir designated in the will: see, for example, the Austrian *Bundesgesetz über besondere Vorschriften für die baüerliche Erbteilung* of 1958, which establishes allocation on a preferential basis to the heir who meets certain requirements established by law; and German law (*Höfeordnung*, of 24 April 1947), which dictates that an agricultural business be transmitted to one heir alone following the order established by section 5 of that law, in the absence of any provision to the contrary by the testator.

[11] Article 738–2 of the French civil code in fact states that where a donee dies without heirs, the donations are allocated to the donee's ascendants (so-called *droit de retour*; see Davì and Zanobetti, 'Il nuovo diritto internazionale privato delle successioni', p. 110; Davì and Zanobetti, *Il nuovo diritto internazionale privato europeo*, p. 178). Also included here is law no. 3/1992 in the Basque country regarding the 'troncalidad', which operates on similar lines, stating that where a person dies without heirs, his assets are restored to the original family unit (see Chikoc Barreda, 'Reflexiones sobre los regímenes especiales', p. 140 *et seq.*).

philosopher Benedetto Croce. In order to carry out the intentions expressed by Croce in his will, his heirs decided to leave to the public the collection of papers and documents (including letters) that he had built up over the course of his life, setting up a foundation for this purpose. Still today, the foundation manages the library and archives located in the apartment that the famous academic made his home. There are different rules in place, however, to govern (i) the library and (ii) the archives and Croce's personal correspondence. While the books were donated to the foundation when it was first established, the heirs retained ownership of the archives and correspondence, although in fact placing these with the foundation in trust. The particular provision in the foundation's constitution (which was given the force of law) and which establishes this particular set of rules can, it appears, be classed as an overriding mandatory provision of the type referred to in article 30: it is in fact a provision of the law that establishes special rules in order to achieve a social purpose (i.e. provide access to Croce's archives) and which affects specific assets. In relation to those assets, it establishes a departure at least from the standard rules governing the division of the estate and the extent to which the heirs can secure their respective shares.[12]

11. Turning finally to family considerations, this area involves provisions that establish succession by a spouse or cohabitee to a lease, especially where that person is elderly or suffering financial hardship.[13]

12. In terms of the category of national provisions that might take effect as a result of the mechanism established by article 30, it is doubtful whether this includes provisions that concern the possibility of other

[12] Article 14 of the Statute of the Foundation 'Biblioteca Benedetto Croce' approved by decree by the President of the Republic no. 1529 of 1956 states as follows: 'Senator Benedetto Croce's archives and correspondence placed with the Foundation in trust in perpetuity shall be kept by the Foundation on the premises of the library, with any decision regarding the consultation and publication of the documents that make up the said archives and correspondence being reserved to the heirs of Senator Benedetto Croce pursuant to law'.

[13] The cohabitee's right has been sometimes recognised on a Judicial basis even without any clear indication of the legislature. See, for example, in Italy, judgment by the Constitutional Court no. 404 of 7 April 1988, in *Foro it*, I (1988), p. 2515. In the sense that provisions that protect frail or deprived cohabitees and relatives are to be classed as overriding mandatory provisions and can prevail over the law governing the succession, see, specifically in relation to the system in France, Devaux, 'The European Regulation on Succession of July 2012', p. 243.

rights of a personal nature being transferable upon death.[14] Doubt has been expressed in literature also in relation to provisions (forming part of copyright law) that allow certain close relatives to object to the publication or amendment of a work once the author has died.[15] Provisions on these lines are often to be found in civil law systems, which generally establish that close relatives (the spouse or children) or the State are able to exercise certain of the prerogatives that originally fell to the author to exercise during his life.[16]

13. Whether the mechanism established by article 30 applies also to provisions of this latter type is not entirely clear. First and foremost, there is a degree of uncertainty over whether these provisions are overriding mandatory provisions, although a decision of the French *Cour de cassation* would appear to state that they are.[17] Secondly, in order for article 30

[14] Here, one author includes, in particular, noble titles (Carrascosa González, *El reglamento sucesorio*, p. 201). There is in fact some doubt as to whether noble titles (which in fact now no longer call into play the right to succession in relation to an asset but generally attribute only the right to use a certain name), can be classed as provisions that might be relevant as a result of article 30. In addition, it should be pointed out that foreign legislation that establishes rules on the transfer of noble titles may easily be considered as contrary to public policy in many countries. Several modern legal systems in fact refuse to recognise such titles: provisions that result in certain prerogatives arising as a result of the possession of a particular title or which restrict succession to the descendants to one of the sexes only could in fact prove to fall foul of public policy. In Spain, precisely in order to prevent discrimination, noble titles underwent reform as a result of law no. 33/2006, which, from the point of view of succession, placed the first-born daughter on a part with the first-born son.

[15] See Wautelet, 'Article 30', p. 471 *et seq.*; Carrascosa González, *El reglamento sucesorio*, p. 201.

[16] Moral rights, as a component of copyright (together with the right of economic use), are recognised by article 6-*bis* of the Berne Convention for the Protection of Literary and Artistic Works of 9 September 1886, paragraph 2 of which stipulates that the contracting States have the power to establish that certain moral prerogatives are extinguished upon the death of the author. The convention has been amended on a number of occasions and is currently in force in 168 countries (see www.wipo.int for a list). Civil law systems generally recognise close relatives as having the right to defend the authenticity of the work or to object to changes being made to it: see, in the case of Italy, articles 20 and 23 of law no. 633/41 on copyright; for France see article L 121–2 of the *code de la propriété intellectuelle*; section 29 of the German law on copyright (*Gesetz über Urheberrecht und verwandte Schutzrechte – Urheberrechtsgesetz*, of 9 September 1965) establishes that moral rights cannot be transferred, save by inheritance; finally, article 57 of the Portuguese *código de derecho de autor y derechos conexos* (law no. 45/85 of 17 September 1985) grants the State the power to defend copyright in works that have already been published. In contrast, in common law jurisdictions, moral rights can generally be transferred in the same manner as economic rights.

[17] See the judgment by the French Cour de cassation, 1ère civ., 28 May 1991, *Huston c. Turner Entertainment, Rev crit dr int priv* (1991), p. 752. This particular case involved

to apply, it would have to be established that the provisions impose restrictions on the succession of certain assets: however, the use of the term *assets* in the English version of the ESR appears to suggest that its scope should not be extended to cover rights over intangible assets. Finally, it is by no means certain that such provisions have any real impact on how the succession is governed. Views have been expressed in the literature to the effect that parties exercising certain moral prerogatives on the death of the author are asserting rights which are their own and which differ entirely from the rights originally held by the person whose estate is involved.[18] Taking into account the fact that the majority of legal systems that embrace this possibility establish first and foremost that moral rights cannot be transferred to persons other than the author. This view is, in reality, one that can be accepted.

14. It should be noted, however, that the provisions of the law of the *situs* regarding the procedures to be followed for the transfer of the asset to be valid and regarding registration in the land registers do not fall within the scope of application of article 30. The priority enjoyed by these provisions over the law governing the succession is in fact already guaranteed by points (k) and (l) of article 1.2 ESR [see art. 1 no. 74 *et seq*. and 87 *et seq*.], which exclude these issues from the scope of application of the ESRn.[19]

15. Finally, also to be found beyond the scope of application of the regulation are provisions which, as part of the articles of association of a company, establish the destination of shares held in the company by the

the heirs of the American film director J. Huston, who objected to a colour version of the film *The Asphalt Jungle* (originally made in black and white) being released in France. The moral rights and the right of economic use of the work had been validly assigned to Turner Entertainment in accordance with the law of the United States (which applied as the law of the country in which the film was originally made and released). The heirs were successful in court, however, on the basis of the premise that the provisions of French law regarding the protection of the moral rights were mandatory. On this case, see F. Vischer 'Das "Droit moral de l'auteur" aus rechtsvergleichendem und kollisionrechtlicher Sicht', in R. Frank (ed), *Recht und Kunst. Symposium aus Anlass des 89. Geburstages von Wolfram Müller-Freienfels* (Heidelberg, 1996), p. 85; D. Moura Vicente, 'La proprieté intellectuelle en droit international privé', *Hague Recueil*, vol. 335 (2008), pp. 127–128.

18 According to the majority view expressed in the literature, this is the position in the Italian system: L. C. Ubertazzi and M. Ammendola, *Il diritto d'autore* (Torino, 1993), p. 65; P. Auteri, *Diritto d'autore*, in P. Auteri, G. Floridia, V. Mangini, G. Olivieri, M. Ricolfi and P. Spada, *Diritto industriale. Proprietà e concorrenza*, 2nd ed. (Torino, 2005), p. 542.

19 T. Ballarino, 'Il nuovo regolamento europeo sulle successioni', *Riv dir int* (2013), p. 1128; B. Laukemann, 'Die lex rei sitae in der Europäischen Erbrechtsverordnung- Inhalt, Schranken und Funktion', *MPILux Working Paper*, 2 (2014), www.mpi.lu (last accessed 2 September 2015).

deceased (usually establishing a right of first refusal or an increase in the shares held by the other shareholders) [see art. 1 no. 59].[20]

III. Problems of Interpretation

16. The point should be made that the provisions of national law that might take effect as a result of article 30 ESR are not always mandatory on a domestic level. A departure from some of these provisions is in fact possible, with the testator or coheirs able to decide for themselves the best way in which to keep ownership of the asset or the business involved intact. Given the purpose of article 30, the possibility cannot be ruled out that even provisions that can be departed from on a domestic level are mandatory on the international stage in light of their specific socio-economic function. The issue has been resolved by implication in the affirmative by the French Supreme Court, specifically in relation to the provisions of French law regarding preferential allocation.[21] What is mandatory here on an international level is not so much the principle that the business per se must be preserved, but instead the provision of the possibility for one of the coheirs to ask for it to be allocated to him exclusively. The ability to freely dispose of inheritance rights or to waive them does not, therefore, dilute the mandatory character on an international level of the provisions that grant a beneficiary this power: it is precisely the abstract provision of the possibility of asking for the business to be allocated on an exclusive basis that achieves the purpose that the legislator sets out to achieve, i.e. preservation.

[20] Before the ESR came into force, there was an element of doubt over how these provisions were to be classified. There would appear to be considerable merit in the argument that the consequences of the death of the shareholder as far as the company is concerned are subject to the law that governs the company itself, while the effects in terms of succession would depend on the law that governs the succession (v. A. Dutta, 'Die Abgrenzung von Gesellschaftsstatut und Erbstatut beim Tod des Gesellschafters', *RabelsZ* (2009), p. 740 *et seq.*).

[21] See Cour de cassation, 1ère civ., 10 October 2012, *JDI* (2013), p. 119, with commentary by E. Fongaro. The provisions governing preferential allocation can, in fact be departed from on a national level, given that, pursuant to articles 832–1, 832–2 and 832–3 of the French civil code, where a number of preferential allocation claims are made by a number of heirs, the matter can be resolved by way of agreement between them. It was in fact precisely this feature which, before the judgment was handed down by the Cour de cassation, prompted certain authors to express the view that the provisions regarding preferential allocation did not belong to the category of mandatory provisions (see P. Lagarde, 'Successions', *Répertoire de droit international*, Dalloz, 2nd ed. (1998), V, para. 227).

17. Secondly, not only do the provisions of the law of the forum that are mandatory on an international level fall within the scope of application of article 30; those that might be contained in any foreign law also follow the same route. The mandatory provisions in place where certain assets are located may in fact come into play in a forum that is different to (i) the forum whose law governs the succession and (ii) the forum of the court hearing the matter.[22] Article 9.3 of regulation no. 593/2008 (Rome I) on the law applicable to contractual obligations[23] does of course establish that mandatory provisions in force in the place in which the obligations established by the contract are to be performed can be given effect, but makes this dependent upon a discretionary appreciation of the proceeding court. In contrast, within the context of the ESR, application of binding provisions in force in a third country is not subject to any discretionary view taken by the court. The provisions must in fact be applied automatically once it has been established that, pursuant to the law of the place in which the assets are located, those provisions are mandatory.

18. It should also be noted that article 30 does not open the door to all overriding mandatory provisions taking effect, since it concerns only those that establish a special regime and which have the specific purposes previously examined.[24] The possibility of overriding mandatory provisions taking effect that are not designed with those specific purposes must, therefore, be ruled out. In certain cases, the binding provisions in force in the forum having a different object, however, may take effect by virtue of article 35 ESR, on condition that they are in fact a direct or

[22] The same solution has also been adopted by Swiss law: section 19 of the Private International Law Act allows the overriding mandatory provisions regarding any matter that are in force in a third State to take effect, including where family relationships and relationships with regard to succession are concerned (see A. Bonomi, 'Successions internationales: conflits des lois et de juridictions', *Hague Recueil*, vol. 350 (2010), p. 149 *et seq.*).

[23] Regulation (EC) no. 593/2008 of the European Parliament and of the Council of 17 June 2008 on the law applicable to contractual obligations (Rome I), OJ L 177, 7 July 2008, p. 6.

[24] The Max Planck Institute for Comparative and International Private Law suggested replacing the current wording of the article with a provision styled on the basis of article 9.1 of regulation no. 593/08, precisely in order to include binding provisions that cannot be matched up with any of the purposes listed in article 30 ESR; see the Institute's 'Comments on the European Commission Proposal's for a Regulation of the European Parliament and of the Council on Jurisdiction, Applicable Law, Recognition and Enforcement of Decisions and Authentic Instruments in Matters of Succession and the Creation of a European Certificate of Succession', *RabelsZ* (2010), p. 646.

indirect expression of the principles of public policy of the forum State. But beyond that possible scenario, which is in fact rather uncommon, there is no room for any role to be played by binding provisions designed for a purpose other than those expressly referred to in article 30.[25]

19. Finally, it is to be recalled that recital 54 provides a pointer on general lines regarding interpretation, establishing that:

> this exception to the application of the law applicable to the succession requires a *strict interpretation* in order to remain compatible with the general objective of this Regulation. Therefore, neither conflict-of-laws rules subjecting immovable property to a law different from that applicable to movable property nor provisions providing for a reserved share of the estate greater than that provided for in the law applicable to the succession under this Regulation may be regarded as constituting special rules imposing restrictions concerning or affecting the succession in respect of certain assets.

20. The requirement for interpretation on restrictive lines can be justified in light of the purposes that the EU legislator set out to achieve. The number of exceptions to the unity of the succession law needs to be reigned in as far as possible in order not to thwart the objectives of the ESR in terms of harmonisation.[26] At any rate, it appears self-evident that neither the conflict of laws rules of scissionist countries that subject succession to immoveable property to a law different from that applicable to moveable goods, nor the substantive rules of the law of the *situs* concerning the extension of the reserved share, could be taken into consideration in applying article 30, given that both sets of rules cannot be regarded as special regimes covered by that provision, but pertain to the ordinary rules governing succession. The former, however, may fall

[25] It cannot of course be ruled out that binding provisions that do not directly relate to succession and, therefore, fall outside the scope of application of article 30, apply in any event on different grounds. In terms of the corresponding article 15 of the Hague Convention on the Law Applicable to Succession, the problem has been met in relation to the provisions regarding the preservation of a given State's cultural heritage. Certain authors took the view that such provisions were applicable in any event as part of the rules governing the assets rather than the rules governing the succession (see P. Lagarde, 'La nouvelle Convention de La Haye sur la loi applicable aux successions', *Rev crit dr int priv* (1989), p. 267; A. von Overbeck, 'La Convention du premier août 1989 sur la loi applicable aux successions pour cause de mort', *Annuaire suisse de droit international* (1989), p. 150 and, with reference to the ESR, see Damascelli, *Diritto internazionale privato delle successioni*, p. 79).

[26] See Davì and Zanobetti, 'Il nuovo diritto internazionale privato delle successioni nell'Unione europea', p. 110; Davì and Zanobetti, *Il nuovo diritto internazionale privato europeo*, p. 179.

within the scope of *renvoi* pursuant to article 34 ESR [see art. 34 no. 19]. The latter can obviously be applied when they are part of the law designated to govern succession by the ESR conflict of laws rules; they could also, in exceptional cases, be taken into account as expression of the principles of the public policy of the forum State, pursuant to article 35 [see art. 35 no. 6 *et seq.*]

Article 31

Adaptation of Rights in rem

ERMANNO CALZOLAIO AND LAURA VAGNI

Where a person invokes a right *in rem* to which he is entitled under the law applicable to the succession and the law of the Member State in which the right is invoked does not know the right *in rem* in question, that right shall, if necessary and to the extent possible, be adapted to the closest equivalent right *in rem* under the law of that State, taking into account the aims and the interests pursued by the specific right *in rem* and the effects attached to it.

Summary

I. INTRODUCTION: THE DISTINCTION BETWEEN REAL AND PERSONAL RIGHTS *page* 442
II. THE FIELD OF APPLICATION OF ARTICLE 31 ESR 444
III. UNKNOWN RIGHTS IN REM: CONTROVERSIAL ISSUES 447
A. Mutual Wills 448
B. Rights Acquired by Estoppel 450

I. Introduction: The Distinction between Real and Personal Rights

1. 'The nature of rights in rem' and 'the creation, administration and dissolution of trusts' are outside the field of application of the ESR [see art. 1 no. 74 *et seq.*, no. 68 *et seq.*]. Notwithstanding this exclusion, a very difficult and controversial problem arises when succession law recognises rights in relation to an asset, which are not recognised or do not correspond with equivalent rights in the State where they are invoked.

The Commission proposal did not address this issue, so the insertion of article 31 ESR, which aims to provide a solution, should be welcomed. This provides that 'if necessary and to the extent possible' the unrecognised right shall be 'adapted to the closest equivalent right *in rem*' under the law of the State in which it is invoked, 'taking into account the aims and the interests pursued by the specific right *in rem* and the effects attached to it'.

2. This provision is very interesting from a comparative point of view. The expression used in the English version of the ESR is 'rights *in rem*', whereas the French version talks about 'droits réels', the German 'dinglicher Recthe', the Italian 'diritti reali' and the Spanish 'derechos reales'.

The exact meaning of 'real' rights and the distinction between real and personal rights are among the most problematic issues in comparative law. The difference between the civil law and the common law traditions is particularly relevant in this field.

3. Even if among civil law countries there are differences in the conceptualisation of the various 'real rights', there is no doubt that common ground can be identified. That common ground lies in the division of patrimonial rights into two categories, personal rights and real rights, which have a different nature and different effects. This distinction is based upon a specific conceptualisation of 'property': in civil law countries, *propriété – proprietà – Eigentum – propriedad*, is intended as a right to own a physical asset in an absolute and exclusive way. The notion of a 'real right' is grounded in the relationship between a person and a material thing, whereas a 'personal right' is a right to obtain from another person the performance of an obligation.[1]

4. By contrast, the conceptualisation of property in English law is quite different, as it has a patrimonial nature, according to which property embraces all rights 'which are capable of being exchanged for the ownership of money'.[2] Therefore, incorporeal things (such as shares, or debts) are treated as objects: 'any thing which is object of commerce may be treated as an asset, just as much if it is an abstraction like a share in a company as if it is a physical object like a house or a car'.[3]

The distinction between 'real' and 'personal' rights is also well known within the common law tradition, however it is conceptualised differently and has different implications. The rights included within both of these categories can be the object of property. So the distinction is emptied of the systematic content it has within the civil law tradition.[4] As a result, the classification of property rights is highly problematic and

[1] L. Moccia, 'Riflessioni sull'idea di proprietà', *Riv trim dir proc civ* (2008), p. 21.

[2] T. C. Williams, 'The Terms Real and Personal in English Law', *LQR* (1888), p. 394.

[3] F. H. Lawson and B. Rudden, *The Law of Property*, 3rd ed. (Oxford, 2002), p. 21.

[4] L. Moccia, 'Basic Ways of Defining Property', in *Studi in memoria di Michele Giorgianni* (Napoli, 2007), p. 761.

the Roman law categories of rights *in rem* and rights *in personam* 'do not match English usage and are a constant source of confusion'.[5]

5. In the light of all of this, an initial difficulty arises in terms of identifying the rights covered by article 31 ESR, because the precise meaning of 'rights *in rem*' is not clear under common law and in any case, there is not an equivalence between 'rights *in rem*' and 'droits réels'. It is also because of this that there is virtually no harmonisation within the European Union in this field. Moreover, a further obstacle to the harmonisation of property law comes from article 345 TFEU, according to which 'the treaties shall in no way prejudice the rules in Member States governing the system of property ownership'. This provision is sometimes employed by Member States as a means of defending their own legal traditions, even beyond the scope of the article.[6]

A problem may arise whenever succession law is invoked in another Member State, which does not recognise the kind of right in question. In such cases, judges will have to find a solution so as to give effect to a right recognised by succession law, attempting to deal with concepts and categories which may be unfamiliar to his or her own legal system. The role of comparative law is of paramount importance in this regard, as will be shown in the following paragraphs.

II. The Field of Application of Article 31 ESR

6. Article 31 ESR applies if 'the law of the Member State in which the right is invoked does not know the right *in rem* in question'. It states that, under the conditions described, the judge shall adapt the unknown right to the closest equivalent right *in rem* under the law of the State where the right is invoked.

7. This provision was not included in the proposal for the ESR made by the Commission.[7] Conversely, the Commission's proposal excluded

[5] W. Swadling, 'Property: General Principles', in A. Burrows (ed), *English Private Law*, 3rd ed. (Oxford, 2013), p. 178. For a comprehensive analysis about the origins of the distinction between real and personal property and its implications, see Williams, 'The Terms Real and Personal', p. 394.

[6] J. Harris, 'The Proposed EU Regulation on Succession and Wills: Prospects and Challenges', *Trust LI* (2008), p. 203, claims that this article inhibits to recognise rights *in rem* which are unknown in the Member State where they are invoked. But see B. Akkermans and E. Ramaekers, 'Article 345 TFEU (ex art. 295 EC), Its Meanings and Interpretation', *European Law Journal* (2010), p. 292, for a comprehensive analysis about the origins and scope of article 345 TFEU.

[7] COM (2009) 154 def., see recital 10 and art. 1(j).

the list of the rights *in rem* relating to property and the nature of such rights from the scope of the ESR [see art. 1 no. 74 *et seq.*], as well as the recognition by *situs* States of a real right not known by the national law.[8] The Max Planck Institute suggested adding another paragraph to article 21 of the proposal,[9] which would address the problem of adaptation of rights *in rem*, not known as such in the *situs* State. The proposal was accepted, although the final version of article 31 ESR is formulated differently from the Max Planck Institute proposal.[10]

8. Article 31 ESR establishes two conditions of applicability. The first condition is that the right invoked is a right *in rem* according to the relevant succession law. This immediately raises a set of problems, as a result of what we discussed in nos. 1–5. Indeed, due to the different conceptualisations of property rights, it seems illogical to limit oneself to mere formal classifications, without investigating the kind of protection afforded to the beneficiary by the succession law in question. In other words, beyond the definitions and the classifications adopted by the relevant succession law, the judge will have to identify the substantial nature of the right in question. It may be the case that a 'personal' right has the firm characteristics of a 'proprietary' right according to the relevant succession law. A case-by-case approach is required, as will be shown in nos. 14–18 using practical examples.

9. The second condition for the application of article 31 ESR is the inexistence of the right *in rem* in question in the Member State where it is invoked. The meaning of the expression 'does not know' is controversial.

In this respect, an initial issue to be considered is the situation where the Member State 'knows' the right in question, but does not – unlike the relevant succession law – afford such right to the claimant. For example, under the Norwegian system, the *uskifte* grants a surviving cohabitant the right of usufruct over some assets of the entire estate, such as the home and the household effects. The same right is not recognised in Italy for

[8] Cf. A.-L. Calvo Caravaca and J. Carrascosa González, *Derecho internacional privado*, 15th ed. (Granada, 2014), vol. I, p. 416.

[9] Max Planck Institute for Comparative and International Private Law, 'Comments on the European Commission's Proposal for a Regulation of the European Parliament and of the Council on Jurisdiction, Applicable Law, Recognition and Enforcement of Decisions and Authentic Instruments in Matters of Succession and the Creation of a European Certificate of Succession', *RabelsZ* (2010), p. 649.

[10] The text of article 31 ESR is inspired by article 15.2 of the Hague Convention of 1 July 1985 on the Law Applicable to Trusts and on their Recognition; on this issue see A. Davì and A. Zanobetti, *Il nuovo diritto internazionale privato europeo delle successioni* (Torino, 2014), p. 30.

surviving cohabitees, although Italian private law does, of course, know the right of usufruct. If Norwegian law is the applicable succession law, the cohabitant of the deceased could invoke the usufruct over assets located in Italy. In this case, article 31 ESR should not apply, because the right is not 'unknown' in the Member State where it is invoked. Accordingly, the right invoked should be afforded to the claimant according to succession law, without requiring any kind of adaptation.

10. Another example concerns the different form that acquisition of legacy takes within the Member States. In France and in the legal systems following the French model (Belgium, Italy, etc.), the legatee is vested in a real right on the same day as the testator's death (article 1014 of the French civil code). By contrast, under the German legal system, the legatee only acquires a personal right, that is to say a right to obtain the object of legacy from the heir (*Damnationslegat*: section 2174 BGB). Some authors argue that article 31 ESR will be useful for solving this kind of problem, through the mechanism of adaptation.[11] In our opinion, however, article 31 ESR appears to be inapplicable in this case, because the right *in rem* recognised by the relevant succession law (that is to say *Eigentum*) is clearly well known in Germany. So the judge will have to grant it to the claimant, without reverting to any adaptation, but simply by applying the relevant succession law.[12]

11. A similar conclusion should be reached where the applicable succession law provides that the heir is vested in a right *in rem* whereas the law of the Member State where it is invoked does not. For example, according to article 734 of the Italian civil code, a testator is allowed to divide his or her assets between his or her heirs. In such an event, the heirs are automatically vested in the corresponding rights upon the testator's death. This rule is not shared by other Member States, but the result of the division of assets (i.e. acquisition of a property right) is clearly well known. There is therefore no need to revert to article 31 ESR, but simply to recognise the right according to succession law.[13]

12. By contrast, article 31 ESR will be applicable where the right recognised by the relevant succession law does not have the same content in the Member State where it is invoked. For example, the right of

[11] P. Lagarde, 'Les principes de base du nouveau règlement européen sur les successions', *Rev crit dr int privé* (2012), p. 691.

[12] In this sense, see P. Wautelet, 'Article 31', A. Bonomi and P. Wautelet, *Le droit européen des successions. Commentaire du Règlement n° 650/2012 du 4 juillet 2012* (Bruxelles, 2013), p. 485.

[13] In the same sense, cf. Wautelet, 'Article 31', p. 486.

'usufruct' is a well-known real right within civil law systems, but the contents of the right differ in some cases. The rule in most legal systems is that the usufructuary is not entitled to consume the object of the usufruct, except in the case of perishable things (see article 995 of the Italian civil code). The Dutch civil code, however, provides that the proprietor can grant the usufructuary the right to consume the encumbered assets entirely or partially (article 3:215 NBW). Does this classify the right as being 'unknown' in the other civil law systems? Some scholars argue that article 31 ESR should only apply if the differences affect the nature of the rights in question. They conclude that this occurs in the example of usufruct under Dutch law, but not in other cases where there are minor differences. In our opinion, this criterion for application appears to leave a degree of uncertainty.

13. It can be very difficult to distinguish between qualitative and quantitative differences. Indeed, even in cases of minor differences, the judge will be asked to adapt the right 'known' in his or her legal system in order to afford an equivalent protection to that given by the relevant succession law. Article 31 ESR is, accordingly, of great use in all cases where any kind of adaptation is needed.

The right of usufruct provides another useful example. Under German law, a usufruct may only be created in such a way that the usufructuary obtains the usufruct in the form of individual objects constituting assets belonging to one person (section 1085 BGB). By contrast, in other legal systems, a usufruct can also be created in respect of a 'universality of assets'. For example, under French law, a surviving conjoint can choose (in certain cases) to have a usufruct over all the assets belonging to the deceased (article 757 French civil code). If French law is to be applied in the same way as the relevant succession law in Germany, the judge will have to adapt the German rules in order to grant a right of usufruct over each individual asset.[14] This is another example which shows the usefulness of article 31 ESR.

III. Unknown Rights *in rem*: Controversial Issues

14. More thorny questions arise when the right *in rem* is not known at all in the Member State where it is invoked. Where the succession law of a common law country is to be applied in a civil law system, a judge may

[14] In this sense, Lagarde, 'Les principes de base', p. 693.

be required to compare completely different concepts. The application of equivalence may reveal some unexpected results.

According to article 31 ESR, the judge has to find the closest equivalent right *in rem* to the foreign right *in rem* invoked. The text accords with recital 16, which states: 'an unknown right *in rem* should be adapted to the closest equivalent right *in rem* under the law of that other Member State'. Under a literal interpretation, the judge should only choose among the rights *in rem* known by his or her legal system. In most cases, this means that the judge is limited by the list of real rights (*numerus clausus*). But it can occur that there is not an equivalent right *in rem* to the foreign right invoked. So a literal interpretation could lead to a lack of protection for the claimant, thus frustrating the aims of the ESR. For this reason, a purposive construction of article 31 ESR should be adopted, in order to ensure to the claimant an adequate protection of the right invoked. Recital 17 provides useful guidance, stating that 'the adaptation of unknown rights *in rem* as explicitly provided for by this Regulation should not preclude other forms of adaptation in the context of the application of this Regulation'. This means that the judge has wide margins of appreciation in order to identify the equivalent right. It is a challenge which requires an exercise of comparison, as will be shown by the following examples.

A. *Mutual Wills*

15. The law of trusts is a good area to use in terms of understanding the judge's role in the practical application of article 31 ESR.

In the law of trusts, fiduciary duties give rise to proprietary rights in a way which is not familiar to civil law systems. Most of these rights are located at the crossroads of the civil law distinction between personal and real rights. As a consequence, a judge dealing with a trust has to resolve difficult issues concerning the nature and classification of rights.

It may well happen that the law of a common law country is the applicable law according to the ESR, notwithstanding that 'the creation, administration and dissolution of trusts' are outside the field of application of the ESR [see art. 1 no. 68 *et seq*].

16. An example can be drawn from the issue of mutual wills. This expression is used generally to describe both joint wills and wills executed pursuant to a previous arrangement. These two kinds of wills are, however, different. In the case of the former, a single document states the wishes of two or more people, whereas in the latter case, separate wills are made by the parties according to a previous agreement. The conditions for the presence of this second type of mutual will are the existence of an arrangement between the testators and of two (or more) autonomous documents.

17. The validity and the effects of mutual wills are treated differently in the Member States.[15] Such wills are effective under English law, where the surviving party is not entitled to revoke the will. Consequently, the death of one party gives rise to a constructive trust and the surviving party (trustee) has to act in conformity with the arrangement reached with the deceased. The executors under mutual wills are beneficiaries of the trust and may invoke their beneficial interest against third parties. Therefore if, for example, the survivor revokes the will and makes a new will, the executors under the new will are vested in the legal ownership of the estate but the beneficiaries may oppose their equitable interest against them.

Under Italian law, joint wills are void according to article 589 of the civil code. Although the interpretation of this provision is debated, it is accepted that the surviving party has the right to revoke his or her will.

18. Assume that an Italian judge has to resolve a case about mutual wills governed by English law under the relevant conflict of law provisions of the ESR. In the example considered above, this may result in the beneficiaries invoking an equitable interest in respect of an asset located in Italy. Accordingly, the Italian judge will have to decide upon the dispute between the beneficiaries and the heirs of the surviving party pursuant to English law. In this context, article 31 ESR is a useful tool that should lead the judge to identify an equivalent right to that invoked by the claimant. In fact, in our opinion, the conditions for the application of article 31 ESR described above would be fully satisfied. The proprietary nature of the equitable interest classifies the interest as a right *in rem* for the purposes of the ESR. Given that this right is unknown in the Italian system, it should be adapted. The absence in Italian law of a 'closest equivalent right *in rem*' is unquestionable: neither the right to property nor a minor real right can be used for the adaptation, as a result of the difference in structure and content of these rights. This may require the

[15] For instance, mutual wills are valid and effective in English law (R. Kerridge, 'Succession', in A. Burrows (ed), *English Private Law*, p. 446) and in German law (section 2270 BGB), but their validity is debated or denied in other jurisdictions. Cf. J. A. Schoenblum, *Multistate and Multinational Estate Planning* (Chicago, 2009), vol. 1, p. 15–10 *et seq.*

judge to resort to a personal right or to a combination of more than one right in order to achieve the best adaptation.

B. Rights Acquired by Estoppel

19. The patrimonial conceptualisation of property accepted in common law countries and the distinction between legal rights and equitable interests, lead to constant problems of adaptation when a civil law judge is required to apply the succession law of a common law country.

An interesting example comes from the doctrine of proprietary estoppel. Proprietary estoppel is an equitable doctrine, developed in the system of equity, according to which detrimental reliance may be the root of a proprietary right. It was on this basis, for instance, that the House of Lords recognised the beneficial interest of a farmer in his uncle's farm.[16] The farmer had been working for many years on his uncle's farm without any payment, under the assurance that he would inherit the farm upon his uncle's death. The House of Lords held that the detriment suffered by the claimant in reliance upon his uncle's representation gave rise to a beneficial interest in the farm. Accordingly, the farmer was vested with a proprietary right even in the absence of a legal title.

20. The doctrine of proprietary estoppel gives rise to rights of various kinds (personal or proprietary) depending on the specific circumstances of the case. In the common law tradition, there is a debate about the nature of the rights acquired by estoppel, as the content and the nature of such rights depends upon the need to protect the claimant's reasonable reliance[17]. In English law, the Land Registration Act 2002, section 116, provides that equity by estoppel 'has effect from the time that the equity arises as an interest capable of binding successors in title'. This provision is, however, inconclusive as to the nature of the rights that a court may recognise.[18] Even a personal right could be enforced against third parties.

21. Problems of adaptation may arise when a right acquired by estoppel is invoked in a Member State which is a stranger to the common law mechanism of acquisition of rights.

Assume, for example, that a person resident in England dies intestate; according to article 20 ESR, English law governs his succession. The deceased's cousin invokes a right to live in a property of the deceased

[16] *Thorner* v. *Majors and others* [2009] UKHL 18.

[17] J. Bray, *Unlocking Land Law*, 4th ed. (New York, 2014), p. 204.

[18] See for a full discussion about this issue, see S. Bright and B. McFarlane, 'Proprietary Estoppel and Property Rights', *CLJ* (2005), p. 449.

for his lifetime, which is acquired by estoppel and relates to a lodge belonging to the deceased located in Normandy. The French judge has to apply English law and, consequently, must resolve a number of issues: firstly, what is the nature of the right vested in the claimant according to succession law; secondly, whether the right invoked is unknown in French law; and thirdly, which is the closest equivalent right in French law to the unknown right. There are no straightforward answers to these questions, as they depend upon the precise facts.

In this case, the judge has to investigate if the right invoked by the deceased's cousin is binding against a third party purchaser. This investigation requires a precise examination of English law. In fact, depending upon the specific circumstances, the right acquired by the cousin may be personal or proprietary. If it is binding against third parties, it is difficult not to consider it as a right *in rem*, independently of the classification as personal or proprietary. The judge will therefore have recourse to article 31 ESR in order to adapt the right to the closest equivalent right *in rem* in French law, so as to provide the claimant with adequate protection.

22. Appreciating equivalence does require the use of comparison, so as to identify a functional analogy between a right acquired by estoppel and a right 'known' in the French system. The judge could find a similarity with a *droit réel* (such as usufruct), but sometimes equivalence may prove to be difficult or even impossible to achieve. For instance, under English law, some rights acquired by estoppel (such as life-rents or annuities) do not have an equivalent in French law as *droits réels*. So the judge could try to refer to personal rights or to a combination of rights, in order to achieve a protection for the claimant.

23. In the light of all of the preceding analysis, the practical application of article 31 ESR and the realisation of equivalence will depend heavily upon judicial discretion. While article 31 ESR ensures a high degree of flexibility, it also leads to a divergence among the Member States. It is thus the task of jurists, by way of recourse to comparative methods, to make a synthesis between the needs of harmonization and the peculiarities of local legal traditions.

Article 32

Commorientes

ERMANNO CALZOLAIO

When two or more persons whose successions are governed by different laws die in circumstances in which it is uncertain in what order their deaths occurred, and where those laws provide differently for that situation or make no provision for it at all, none of the deceased persons shall have any rights to the succession of the other or others.

Summary

I. INTRODUCTION *page* 452
II. THE SOLUTION ADOPTED BY ARTICLE 32 ESR 454
III. CONDITIONS OF APPLICABILITY 455

I. Introduction

1. Article 32 ESR deals with a very difficult aspect of the law of succession. The Latin term *commorientes*, used in the English version of the ESR and translated in almost all the other versions,[1] refers to the phenomenon of two or more people who die in circumstances where the exact determination of the order of deaths is uncertain. This situation can occur in various cases, such as car accidents, shipwrecks, air accidents, natural disasters, and so on. In all such cases, it is practically impossible to establish which of the people involved died first.

2. In terms of the Roman sources, this issue is dealt with in various fragments of the Digest. Even if it is impossible to draw a common principle from such sources, what clearly emerges is the presence of a set of presumptions of survivorship. For instance, in the case of a father and a son dying during a war, the father is presumed to have died first, so as to enable the mother to inherit from her son, with preference towards the father's relatives. Conversely, in the case of the

[1] *Kommorienten* (German), *comourants* (French), *conmorientes* (Spanish), *commorienza* (Italian).

simultaneous deaths of a father and his pubescent son, the presumption is in favour of the survivorship of the father.[2]

3. The various presumptions laid down by the Roman sources are inherited and developed by the medieval jurists and, using their interpretation, are set out in the first codifications of the nineteenth century.

Article 720 of the original version of the French civil code of 1804 sets out a complex mechanism, essentially based upon age: for example, if the two people are less than fifteen years old, the elder is presumed to survive the younger; by contrast, if they are over sixty, the younger is presumed to survive the older. This system was strongly criticised as being artificial and overly complex. Partly for this reason, it was replaced in most civil law countries and the rules were simplified, providing that in cases of uncertainty, the law should consider that the people involved died simultaneously and do not succeed one another. This is the case in Germany (section 11 missing persons act), Italy (article 924 of the 1865 civil code and now article 4 of the civil code), Spain (article 33 of the civil code), and Netherlands (article 725–1(1) of the civil code).

Finally, a reform was also enacted in France in 2001. The new article 725 of the civil code provides that if the order of deaths cannot be established, none of the deceased persons shall have rights to the succession of the other.[3]

4. This new rule, which corresponds to that adopted by article 32 of the ESR, undoubtedly has the advantage of being far simpler. At the same time, the rule is perhaps even more fictitious than the presumptions previously settled upon in some legal systems, as it must be accepted that it is almost inconceivable that two people would die at exactly the same time. The solution thus seems quite arbitrary. Because of this, it tends to be widely accepted in every legal system, that the presumption of simultaneous death can be rebutted by evidence that one of the persons involved survived the other.

5. It is worth mentioning that English law continues to reflect the influence of *jus commune*. In fact, section 184 of the English Property Act 1925 provides that '[w]here two or more persons have died in circumstances rendering it uncertain which of them survived the other or others, such deaths shall (subject to any order of the court), for all purposes

[2] For a full analysis, see R. Luzzatto, 'Commorienza', in *Novissimo Digesto Italiano* (Torino, 1959), vol. III, p. 675.

[3] P. Malaurie, *Droit civil. Les successions, les libéralités*, 5th ed. (Paris, 2012), p. 43; A. M. Leroyer, *Droit des successions*, 2nd ed. (Paris, 2011), p. 25, R. Le Guidec and G. Chabot, 'Succession', in *Répertoire Droit Civil* (2013).

affecting the title to property, be presumed to have occurred in order of seniority, and accordingly the younger shall be deemed to have survived the elder'. The leading English case, in this respect, is *Hickman* v. *Peacey*,[4] in which it was established that the statutory presumption should apply unless there was certainty, beyond reasonable doubt, as to the order of deaths.

6. Other legal systems adopt neither a system of presumption of priority of deaths, nor a presumption of simultaneous death. This is the case in the United States, where the Uniform Simultaneous Death Act, originally enacted in 1940 and subsequently amended in 1993, provides that if two or more people die within 120 hours of one another, in the absence of specific provisions by a will or other documents, each one is considered to have predeceased the others.[5]

II. The Solution Adopted by Article 32 ESR

7. In the context just described, article 32 ESR provides that 'none of the deceased persons shall have any rights to the succession of the other or others'. This means that in the case of two people dying as a result of the same event, where the relevant succession laws are different, those laws will determine the rules governing the two successions. It will not, however, be possible to take into account the succession rights that either of them could claim according to his or her law.

8. Article 32 is clearly a substantive rule, in the sense that it does not resolve a problem of conflict of laws, but directly identifies a solution. It aims at avoiding the risk that the application of different laws to the establishment of the time of death of the people involved leads to contradictory results.[6]

9. The introduction of this substantive rule raises a problem of competence, because the ESR is grounded in article 81 TFEU, paragraph 2(c), which enables the enacting of measures on 'the compatibility of the rules applicable in the Member States concerning conflict of laws and of jurisdiction'. One could argue that a provision which does not concern conflict of laws, but which contains a substantive rule, is outside the competence of the European Union. This issue is, of course, a delicate

[4] *Hickman* v. *Peacey* [1945] A.C. 304.

[5] R. W. Harris, 'Federal Estate Consequences of Common Disasters or Closely Approximate Deaths', *Tax Lawyer* (1994), p. 763.

[6] A. Davì and A. Zanobetti, *Il nuovo diritto internazionale privato europeo delle successioni* (Torino, 2014), p. 183 *et seq.*

one. It has been suggested, however, that the rule set out in article 32 is necessary to ensure the correct application of a harmonised system of conflict of laws, and in the light of this argument it can be interpreted as being within the competence of the EU.[7]

III. Conditions of Applicability

10. A preliminary consideration to point out concerns the field of application of article 32 ESR, which does not concern the determination of the moment of death and the capacity to inherit. These aspects are devolved to the applicable succession law or laws (see article 23, points (a) and (c)). So article 32 will apply only if, according to the succession laws in question, it is not possible to determine the order of death.

When this is the case, there are three conditions for applicability of the rule.

1) *Successions governed by different laws.* The first condition to be satisfied is that the successions of the persons involved are not regulated by the same law, otherwise article 32 ESR will not apply and the case will be regulated according to the applicable law. It can happen, for example, that the persons involved had their respective habitual residence in different countries, or that, even if they both resided in the same country, one of them chose to submit his or her succession to the law of another country pursuant to article 22 ESR. In such cases, article 32 ESR will be applicable.
2) *Uncertainty about the order of deaths.* The second condition of applicability is that the order of deaths is uncertain. In fact, the text of article 32 ESR states that the rule is applicable in 'circumstances in which it is uncertain in what order their deaths occurred'. The most reasonable interpretation of this formulation is that it does not require an absolute impossibility of ascertaining the exact moment of death, but only that there is uncertainty as to the order of deaths.[8]
3) *Difference in the applicable provisions.* The third condition required for the application of article 32 ESR concerns the difference between the provisions of the applicable succession laws. This is more controversial. The relevant laws should 'provide differently for that

[7] P. Wautelet, 'Article 32', in A. Bonomi and P. Wautelet, *Le droit européen des successions. Commentaire du Règlement n° 650/2012 du 4 juillet 2012* (Bruxelles, 2013), p. 495.

[8] In this sense, cf. Wautelet, 'Article 32', p. 495.

> situation or make no provision for it at all'. No problem arises if the two applicable laws adopt the same rule, because in this case there is no difference between the applicable laws, so the problem will be easily resolved without referring to the solution provided by article 32 ESR, which is only applicable if there is a difference between the two laws.

Article 32 ESR refers to *different* provisions; according to a literal interpretation, it should therefore be applied in every case where there is a difference between the various applicable laws.

This solution, however, would prevent the application of domestic laws even where the difference between the laws applicable to *commorientes* does not lead to incompatible solutions. Take, for example, the case of an accident where a father and his son both die. The father had his habitual residence in Italy, whereas his son was married in England, which was also his country of habitual residence. Italian law is applicable to the succession of the father and English law is applicable to the succession of his son. According to Italian law, there is a presumption of simultaneous deaths and no one can inherit from the other. According to the English rule, the younger person (i.e. the son) is presumed to survive the father and will accordingly inherit from his father. In this case, the two applicable laws have different provisions, but the solutions provided by the relevant domestic laws are not incompatible. Italian law, that regulates the succession of the father, excludes the possibility that he is an heir, whereas English law, applicable to the son's succession, provides that the son succeeds his father.

In the light of these considerations, some authors argue that, despite the fact that the applicable laws have different provisions, the solutions are reconcilable, because the eldest person (e.g. the father in our example) has no right to succeed the other party in both cases.[9] According to this view, article 32 ESR would not be applicable in the above example, as its application would be limited to cases of substantial conflict, which only arise if the divergent assumptions lead to irreconcilable results. This occurs, for instance, when under both succession laws the respective other person survives and inherits from the other. This is the view adopted by the majority of scholars and it is in accordance with the

[9] A. Dutta, 'Succession and Wills in the Conflict of Laws on the Eve of Europeanisation', *RabelsZ* (2009), p. 599; Wautelet, 'Article 32', p. 497; see also Davì and Zanobetti, *Il nuovo diritto internazionale privato europeo delle successioni*, p. 184, who express support for this interpretation.

formulation of the original proposal of the Commission, which made reference to an incompatibility between the various applicable laws.[10]

It is worth noting, however, that the final text of the ESR seems to make a clear choice, as it refers to 'different provisions' and not to 'incompatible' results. In the various versions of the ESR there is always a reference to different provisions: 'provide differently' (English version), 'dispositions différentes' (French version), 'leggi [che] regolano la fattispecie in maniera differente' (Italian version), 'regeln diese Rechte diesen Sachverhalt unterschiedlich' (German version), 'mediante disposiciones diferentes' (Spanish version). For this reason it is at least questionable if the interpretation provided by the majority of scholars will be confirmed by case law, because it seems to be at odds with the words used by the European legislator. In this context, it should not be excluded that the construction of article 32 ESR will be that when the various succession laws involved have different provisions, none of the persons involved shall have any right of succession over the other.

[10] Max Planck Institute for Comparative and International Private Law, 'Comments on the European Commission's Proposal for a Regulation of the European Parliament and of the Council on Jurisdiction, Applicable Law, Recognition and Enforcement of Decisions and Authentic Instruments in Matters of Succession and the Creation of a European Certificate of Succession', *RabelsZ* (2010), p. 661.

Article 33

Estate without a Claimant

LAURA VAGNI

To the extent that, under the law applicable to the succession pursuant to this Regulation, there is no heir or legatee for any assets under a disposition of property upon death and no natural person is an heir by operation of law, the application of the law so determined shall not preclude the right of a Member State or of an entity appointed for that purpose by that Member State to appropriate under its own law the assets of the estate located on its territory, provided that the creditors are entitled to seek satisfaction of their claims out of the assets of the estate as a whole.

Summary

I. INTRODUCTION: THE STATE AS AN OWNER OR AS A FINAL HEIR *page* 458

II. DETERMINING THE STATE'S RIGHT IN CROSS-BORDER SUCCESSION CASES 460

III. THE SOLUTION PROVIDED BY ARTICLE 33 ESR 464

IV. PARTIALLY UNCLAIMED ESTATES 465

V. POSITIVE AND NEGATIVE CONFLICTS OF LAWS 466

I. Introduction: The State as an Owner or As a Final Heir

1. Article 33 ESR deals with the conflict of laws arising in the case of an estate without a claimant, the ownership of which is claimed by different States. The conflict of laws in this field is essentially due to a difference among national laws in determining the nature of the State's rights over heirless properties.

Some national laws provide that the State itself acquires heirless properties as a final heir, whereas other States follow the theory of 'eminent dominion' and classify estates without a claimant as *bona vacantia*. In the first case, the acquisition of the estate rests on a private law issue while in the second case, conversely, the appropriation of the estate is based on the public law principle of territorial sovereignty.[1]

[1] Among a large literature on this issue, see K. Lipstein, 'Private International Law – Bona Vacantia and Ultimus Heres', *CLJ* (1954), p. 22; M. F. J. Heckel, *Das Fiskuserbrecht im*

2. The difference between the theories of the 'final heir' State and of the 'appropriation' State has its origins in the modern age, whereas in the past European countries shared the common doctrine of eminent dominion, according to which the crown had the ultimate ownership of the lands within its own territory.[2] This approach has its roots in the feudal doctrine of escheat,[3] according to which, when a tenant in possession dies, the land reverts to the landlord or to the crown. In this case, the crown has a right to appropriate *bona vacantia*, in the absence of any other successors. The right of escheat developed from the interpretation of the Justinian *Corpus Iuris*[4] and it underpinned the ancestral idea that consanguinity was an essential condition for a person to qualify as an heir.

3. The theory of the 'final heir' State was first introduced by German historical scholars and was developed by the Pandectists towards the end of the nineteenth century, recovering classical Roman sources.[5] This new theory spread all over Europe and many European systems still follow it. Among the States in question, it is worth mentioning Germany, which was the cradle of a new scientific interpretation. Indeed, section 1936 of the BGB provides that in the case of an estate without a claimant the Federal government is the heir. A similar approach is shared by other EU Member States, such as Greece (article 1821 civil code), Italy (article 586 civil code), Poland (article 935 civil code), Portugal (article 2152 civil code) and Spain (article 956 civil code).

4. By contrast, in other European States this approach was rejected. The theory of the 'final heir' has always been repudiated by French scholars and ultimately, the rule provided under the French civil code is that the property of persons who die without heirs, or whose

Internationalen Privatrecht. Eine rechtsvergleichende Untersuchung im Hinblick auf ein künftiges europäisches Erbkollisionsrecht (Tübingen, 2006); A. Dutta, 'Succession and Wills in the Conflict of Laws on the Eve of Europeanization', *RabelsZ* (2009), p. 595.

[2] Cf. Lipstein, 'Private International Law – Bona Vacantia and Ultimus Heres', p. 23.

[3] Cf. W. Blackstone, *Commentaries on the Law of England*, 15th ed. (London, 1809), book II, para. 246, p. 245; E. Coke, *The First Institute of the Law of England*, 16th ed. (Dublin, 1809), vol. I, sec. 4, 13a, 92b; R. Huebner, *A History of Germanic Private Law*, Eng. trans. by S. F. Philbrick (New Jersey, 2000), book V, para. 109, p. 738.

[4] *Corpus Iuris Civilis Codex*, X. X. 1.

[5] See K. A. von Vangerow, *Lehrbuch der Pandekten*, 7th ed. (Hamburg, 1867), para. 564, p. 571; F. C. von Savigny, *Private International Law. A Treatise on the Conflict of Laws* (Edinburgh, 1869), para. 285, p. 235; B. Windscheid, *Lehrbuch des Pandektenrechts*, 8th ed. (Frankfurt, 1901), para. 507, p. 330, who quoted the *Lex Iulia et Papia*, under the emperor Augustus (L 4 C de bon. vac. 10.); for classical Roman sources, see Ulpiani, *Fragmenta*, 28, 7; on this issue cf. R. Astolfi, 'I beni vacanti e la legislazione caducaria', *Bullettino dell'istituto di diritto romano Vittorio Scialoja*, vol. 68 (1965), p. 323 *et seq.*

successions have been abandoned, belongs to the State (article 539).[6] In Europe, the appropriation theory is also followed in Belgium (article 539 civil code), Austria (section 760 ABGB), Sweden (section 1, chapter 5 of the Swedish succession act), Slovenia (article 9 of the Slovenian succession act), Netherlands (article 4:189 Dutch civil code) and England (section 46, Law of Property Act 1925). Furthermore, common law countries worldwide recognise the English doctrine on this issue and regard the State as an ultimate owner of the territory within its boundaries.

II. Determining the State's Right in Cross-Border Succession Cases

5. The difference between the two theories just described does not have great practical consequences from a national law perspective, as the rules governing the acquisition of heirless estates by the State are very similar in almost every legal system.[7] However, the different approaches in terms of substantive law produce significant effects in cross-border succession cases, giving rise to positive and negative conflicts of laws.

6. A positive conflict arises when a particular asset is claimed both by the State on whose territory it is situated and by the State considered to be the final heir in terms of the applicable law. Conversely, a negative conflict of laws occurs where the law governing the succession does not provide for the succession of the State and the State on whose territory the assets are situated does not have title to appropriate the assets in question.

7. By the end of the nineteenth century, there was a great debate among scholars about how to resolve these conflicts of laws. Some authors considered the nature of the State's right as a preliminary question and argued that the position of the State was to be classified according to the *lex fori*.[8] This approach was followed, for example, by the Court of Appeal of Alexandria in the case of *Olivo*, decided in 1956.[9] In that

[6] Article last modified by law no. 809, 13 August 2004, article 174.

[7] Lipstein, 'Private International Law – Bona Vacantia and Ultimus Heres', p. 25.

[8] The *lex fori* theory was proposed by F. Kahn, 'Gesetzeskollisionen. Ein Beitrag zur Lehre des IPR', *Jahrbücher für die Dogmatik des heutigen römischen und deutschen Privatrechts*, vol. XXX (1891), p. 1 *et seq.*; F. Bartin, *De l'impossibilité d'arriver à la suppression définitive des conflits de lois* (Paris, 1897), p. 225 *et seq.*; E. G. Lorenzen, 'The Qualification, Classification, or Characterization Problem in the Conflict of Laws', *Yale Law School Faculty Scholarship Series* (1941), paper 4584. For a qualification based on comparative law, see E. Rabel, 'Das Problem der Qualifikation', *RabelsZ* (1931), p. 241 *et seq.*

[9] Court of Appeal of Alexandria 17 May 1956, *Riv dir int* (1958), pp. 140–144.

case, the Italian State claimed the heirless estate left in Egypt by Mrs Olivo, who had died intestate and without relatives within the sixth degree. The applicable succession law was Italian law, but the court held that the position of the State with regard to the assets was to be determined according to Egyptian law (*lex fori*). In fact, article 10 of the Egyptian civil code states that Egyptian law alone will determine the nature of a legal relationship in order to ascertain the law applicable in cross-border cases.[10] As the *lex fori* did not include the State among the intestate heirs,[11] Italy had no title to acquire the assets located in Egypt.

8. The previously-mentioned debate was solved in the second half of the twentieth century, when other scholars demonstrated the incorrect use of such a system of 'characterization' and the warped effects on the operation of conflict of laws rules.[12] Indeed, the doctrine of 'characterization' or 'classification' aims at establishing whether ascertaining who is entitled to an estate and whether or not the latter is vacant falls within the competence of the law governing the succession or not. It does not, however, seek to determine the nature of the State's right to the estate. If the State's position in respect of the estate is characterised by the *lex fori*, the applicable law is replaced by a substantive rule of the *lex fori* and the classification that determined the applicable law is ruled out altogether.

9. The State's right to heirless assets was determined pursuant to the *lex causae* in the case of *Re Maldonado*, decided by the English Court of Appeal.[13] The deceased person was a Spanish citizen, domiciled in Spain, who had died intestate and without any successors, leaving movable property in England. The Spanish State gained a declaration of heirship in Spain on the basis of article 958 of the Spanish civil code and accordingly claimed the appropriation of the property. The UK Treasury solicitor, acting as a defendant, argued that the assets were situated in England and were vested in the Crown, according to a paramount right of State sovereignty; this also assumed that the right of Spain, regardless of the language of the Spanish civil code, was actually a right of appropriation based upon the principle of sovereignty, so the applicable law was the *lex rei sitae* and UK law should prevail. The Court of Appeal

[10] *Contra:* R. Quadri, 'La successione dello Stato nel diritto internazionale privato', *Riv dir int* (1958), p. 60, note 19, who argues that article 10 was not applicable to the case as there was not a conflict of classification.

[11] Article 18 of the Egyptian civil code; article 4, law no. 77, 4 October 1943.

[12] Quadri, 'La successione dello Stato', p. 58.

[13] *State of Spain* v. *Treasury Solicitor* [1953] 2 All ER 1579.

rejected these arguments and the case was decided in favour of Spain. The court held that the nature of the State's right must be established according to the *lex causae* (in this case Spanish law).[14] Therefore, if the *lex causae* includes the State among the heirs, the estate is not vacant, and the State could succeed to the deceased in the same way as any other heir. The eminent dominion right could eventually be exercised by a State within the limits of its own boundaries, where, after considering the possible intestate heirs according to the applicable succession law, the estate is vacant.[15]

10. In the European context, a similar solution is to be found in some private international law statutes, now superseded by the ESR provisions insofar as they cover the same subject matters, which expressly provide that the rights against estates (including a State's right) are to be governed by the law applicable to the succession. Article 28 of the Greek civil code states that the applicable succession law is decisive in all questions relating to the law of inheritance.[16] Additionally, the State's position towards heirless assets is expressly considered as a matter to be regulated by the law governing the succession under the Belgian code of private international law, whose article 80 provides that the law applicable to the succession determines the State's title to inheritance.[17] The new Romanian civil code of 2011 expressly provides that the law applicable to the succession governs the position of a State in relation to heirless assets.[18] Also article 92 of Switzerland's federal act on private

[14] *State of Spain* v. *Treasury Solicitor*, Morris J.L., 1585.

[15] A similar approach was followed by Belgian Cour de cassation (1e Ch.) 28 March 1952, *Rev crit dir int priv* (1953), p. 132, with a comment by Y. Loussouarn.

[16] Cf. L. Garb, *International Succession* (The Hague, 2004), vol. I, p. 266; L. Garb and J. Wood, *International Succession*, 3rd ed. (Oxford, 2010), p. 294 *et seq.*

[17] Belgian code of private international law of 2004; cf. Garb and Wood, *International Successions*, p. 74 *et seq.* For a critical appraisal of this provision as well as of the similar disposition contained in article 67(g) of the Romanian civil code of 2010, see Max Planck Institute for Comparative and International Private Law, 'Comments on the European Commission's Proposal for a Regulation of the European Parliament and of the Council on Jurisdiction, Applicable Law, Recognition and Enforcement of Decisions and Authentic Instruments in Matters of Succession and the Creation of a European Certificate of Succession', *RabelZ* (2010), p. 655, para. 288.

[18] Romanian civil code, article 67(g). The code full repealed the law no. 105 of 1992, which yet provided that the applicable law determines the position of the State to heirless assets; see M. F. Popa, 'Brief Overview of the Rules Governing the Conflict of Laws in Succession Matters According to the New Romanian Civil Code', in *International Conference: CKS 2013 – Challenges of the Knowledge Society* (Bucharest, 2013), p. 369; the new Romanian civil code, law no. 71 of 2011, in force since 1 October 2011, reformed the conflict of laws regime, the law applicable to international succession included, see C. Avasilencei, 'La

international law shares the same view and states that the applicable law shall determine who is entitled to the estate and to what extent.[19]

11. Nevertheless, the State considered as an heir by the applicable succession law is favoured in cross-border cases as it can invoke a right over assets located in foreign countries, with precedence over the *situs* State.

Some private international law statutes mitigate this result, preventing a State from inheriting heirless assets situated in foreign countries. This was the case, prior to the entry into force of the ESR, with article 29 of the Austrian private international law act of 1978, which regulated succession to heirless estates as a special issue. This provision stated that if a person died without heirs and a foreign State was entitled to acquire the estate as the legal heir under the national law of the deceased person, the *situs* State would prevail and acquire the assets within its territory.[20]

12. The same problem was addressed during the drafting of the Hague Convention of 1 August 1989 on the Law Applicable to Succession to the Estates of Deceased Persons (which never entered into force); the delegates considered three different possibilities: (a) a State can always appropriate the heirless assets located within its territory; (b) the applicable law determines whether the eminent dominion or the final heir theory is to prevail; (c) a State has the right to acquire immovable properties situated within its territory, but rights over movable property are determined by the applicable succession law.[21]

The first option was adopted in the preliminary draft of the convention (article 12). The text of the provision was retained in the final version, although during the sixteenth session of the Hague Conference on Private International Law the debate was reopened and alternative solutions were suggested.[22] Ultimately, article 16 of the Hague

codification des conflits de lois dans le nouveau Code civil roumain: une nouvelle forme en attente d'un contentieux', *Rev crit dr int priv* (2012), pp. 273–274. On the previous private international law system see D. A. Popescu, 'Some remarks on the applicable law to international succession in Romania', *YPIL* 9 (2007), p. 296 *et seq.*

19 B. Dutoit, *Droit international privé suisse. Commentaire de la loi fédérale du 18 Décembre 1987*, 4th ed. (Bâle, Genève, Munich, 2005), pp. 306–309.

20 Oberster Gerichtshof (OGH) 26 February 1985, *IPRax* (1986), p. 43.

21 D. W. M. Waters, 'Explanatory Report', in Hague Conference on Private International Law, *Acts and Proceedings of the Sixteenth Session (1988)*, vol. II, *Succession to Estates – Applicable Law* (The Hague, 1990), p. 591.

22 See the proposal from the Swiss delegation and the proposal from the Spanish delegation, Waters, 'Explanatory Report', p. 591.

Convention states that in the case of an estate without a claimant, the applicable law does not preclude a State from appropriating the assets of the estate that are situated within its own territory.

The Hague Convention provision had been incorporated into Dutch law in 2002, and included in article 10.145 of the new civil code, which provided that '[t]he law applicable to succession to a deceased's estate shall be designated by the Hague Convention on Succession 1989'.[23] This provision is obviously now superseded by the entry into force of the ESR insofar as it covers the same subject matter.

III. The Solution Provided by Article 33 ESR

13. Article 33 ESR follows the path of the Hague Convention, preventing the law governing the succession from precluding appropriation by a Member State within its territory, according to domestic law.[24] However, article 33 ESR introduces two significant differences with respect to article 16 of the Hague Convention.

14. Firstly, article 16 of the Hague Convention is applicable both to contracting States and to third countries, whereas the limitation of succession law in favour of domestic law, provided for by article 33 ESR, is applicable only where the estate is located within the territory of a Member State. Under article 33 ESR, heirless assets located within third countries are regulated by the relevant succession law. Nevertheless, a Member State that invokes its right over an heirless estate under the ESR could face the opposition of a third country claiming ownership of the assets located within its own territory.[25]

15. The second difference between article 16 of the Hague Convention and the text of article 33 ESR, confirmed by recital 56 of the ESR preamble, concerns the express reference to the protection

[23] Netherlands act of 19 May 2011, adopting and implementing book 10 (private international law) of Dutch civil code, in force as of 1 January 2012; cf. K. Boele-Woelki and D. van Iterson, 'The Dutch Private International Law Codification: Principles, Objectives and Opportunities', *Electronic Journal of Comparative Law* (2010), p. 1 *et seq.*

[24] As an example of a legislation of a Member State adopting this solution, see the Swedish act no. 81 (1937) on Conflicts of Law in Regard to Succession, whose article 11 provides that if a deceased person leaves properties within the realm, which by the law of the deceased's country would pass to the State, such property will be appropriated by the Swedish State Inheritance Fund.

[25] See P. Wautelet, 'Article 33', in A. Bonomi and P. Wautelet, *Le droit européen des successions. Commentaire du Règlement n° 650/2012 du 4 juillet 2012* (Bruxelles, 2013), p. 508; see also no. 20.

of the creditor's rights.[26] This provision is aimed at avoiding some difficulties which could derive from the application of different laws. In fact, article 33 ESR introduces an exception to the principle of unity of succession underlying the ESR, according to which one single succession law is applicable to the whole of the estate, wherever it is situated. The prevalence of the *lex rei sitae* splits up the unity of an estate with major risks for the recovery of assets by creditors.

IV. Partially Unclaimed Estates

16. The main condition for the application of article 33 ESR is that there is no legatee and testate or intestate physical heir for the estate. This condition is to be verified according to the law governing the succession.

17. The expression 'no heir or legatee for any assets' leaves uncertainty as to whether article 33 ESR is applicable in the case of a partially unclaimed estate, such as the case of a deceased who disposed of some, but not all of his assets, leaving no intestate physical heir (or heirs that have renounced to the succession). The literal meaning of the text and a comparison among the different linguistic official versions are not conclusive in terms of resolving this question, as some of them resemble the English version, referring to the absence of heirs and legatees 'for any assets', but other texts take a quite different form. The Italian version, for example, refers generally to the absence of dispositions which appoint heirs or legatees.

18. The same problem was addressed during the preparatory works of the Hague Convention, but the draft article 16 was not reworded in the final text of the convention. However, in the plenary session convened for the adoption of the text of the convention, it was pointed out that it was not the intention of the drafters to exclude the application of article 16 to partially unclaimed estates.[27] In fact, the common goal of the different national rules governing the acquisition of estates without a claimant is to increase the State returns and to limit litigation between private parties for the appropriation of *bona vacantia*. Therefore, the meaning of article 16 was to be coherent with this aim. Similarly, article 33 ESR should also be applied to partially unclaimed estates, as the literal meaning of the text does not prevent such a construction.

[26] The issue was not included in the Commission's proposal; see article 24, COM(2009) 154 final.

[27] Waters, 'Explanatory Report', p. 591.

V. Positive and Negative Conflicts of Laws

19. Article 33 ESR resolves the positive conflicts of laws, which may arise in cross-border cases, ensuring the precedence of the Member State where the assets are situated. One might take the example of a Greek citizen, who dies intestate and without successors, leaving some estate situated in France. If the applicable succession law is the law of Greece, the Greek State would succeed as final heir to all assets situated in Greece, but not upon those located within France. French law, which follows the doctrine of eminent dominion, will prevail over the law governing the succession, granting ownership of the assets situated within France to the French State (article 539 civil code).

20. As already mentioned, the same solution does not apply to third countries. Assume that an Italian citizen dies intestate and without heirs, leaving some assets in Argentina. If Italian law is the law applicable to the succession, the Italian State could invoke its right to inherit the estate even outside its boundaries, as the limitation to the operation of succession law set out in article 33 ESR is not applicable. However, Argentina could oppose the application of the *lex rei sitae* over immovable assets situated within Argentina. In fact, according to Argentinian law, the federal State, a province or the city of Buenos Aires escheat the estate left vacant (article 2648 civil and commerical code).[28]

21. Member States could appropriate the assets located on their respective territories within the limits prescribed by domestic law. Moreover, the precedence of the territorial Member State's law over the law governing the succession is limited to the assets located within that Member State's territory. The location of assets is thus decisive in resolving the conflict of laws issue. While the location of immovable properties is well established according to the principle of territorial sovereignty, the location of movable property raises some questions. In fact, the connection between a movable asset and the territory of a State is not always definite and the determination of the place where a movable asset is situated could itself give rise to a conflict of laws.

22. Article 33 ESR does not make any specific reference to the distinction between immovable and movable property and to the criteria

[28] See also articles 2441–2443 of Argentine civil and commerical code. Argentina follows a scissionist system in succession matters, see article 2644 civil and commerical code; on scissionist and unitary system in succession law, cf. A. Davì and A. Zanobetti, *Il nuovo diritto internazionale privato europeo delle successioni* (Torino, 2014), p. 7–10 [see art. 23 no. 2].

for establishing the location of the latter. It may be debatable, for example, where a bank account, a financial instrument, a copyright or other incorporeal forms of property are situated [see art. 10 nos. 7–10].[29] Moreover, the rules on localisation of corporeal assets appear unsatisfactory when compared with those on incorporeal assets, especially in the dematerialised world of the internet. As a result, different States could claim the ownership of an item of moveable property assuming it is situated within their own territories. The ESR leaves the resolution of this matter to the interpretation of the courts.

23. Some scholars suggest reverting to analogy and applying rules on localisation provided by EU legislation in other branches of private international law. In this respect, the ECJ could make reference to the rules provided under article 2(g) of the current EC regulation on insolvency proceedings.[30]

24. As far as negative conflicts of laws are concerned, article 33 ESR does not offer a solution. Assume that an Italian citizen has his habitual residence in France. If he dies intestate and without physical heirs, his estate situated in Italy may remain unclaimed by both France and Italy. In fact, as French law is the law governing the succession, the Italian State is not an heir. In this case, the estate located within Italy is vacant, but France cannot acquire the vacant estate on Italian territory, being, as it is, outside its sovereignty.

In the absence of any express provision on this point under article 33 ESR,[31] the estate remains unclaimed and the *situs* State can be entitled to

[29] See E. F. Scoles and P. Hay, *Conflict of laws*, 2nd ed. (St. Paul, 1992), p. 863; J. A. Schoenblum, *Multistate and Multinational Estate Planning*, vol. I (Chicago, 2009), para. 16.07 (16–49).

[30] Council regulation (EC) no. 1346/2000, 29 May 2000; its article 2(g) states that 'the Member State in which assets are situated' shall mean in the case of:
- tangible property, the Member State within the territory of which the property is situated,
- property and rights ownership of or entitlement to which must be entered in a public register, the Member State under the authority of which the register is kept,
- claims, the Member State within the territory of which the third party required to meet them has the centre of his main interests, as determined in Article 3(1)'.

Cf., prospectively, the more extensive specifications contained in article 2.9 EU regulation no. 848/2015 of 20 May 2015 on insolvency proceedings (recast), which will apply to insolvency proceedings opened after 26 June 2017.

See also Wautelet, 'Article 33', p. 507; A. Bonomi, 'Article 10', in A. Bonomi and P. Wautelet, *Le droit européen des successions*, p. 216.

[31] The European Commission's proposal for the ESR was criticised because of its failure to solve negative conflicts of this type. The Max Planck Institute for Comparative and International Private Law, 'Comments on the European Commission's Proposal', p. 605

acquire ownership insofar as it has a valid right to do so under different provisions of its own domestic law.

It is worth mentioning that in several legal systems the legislation provides that when a negative conflict arises, the estate is appropriated by the *situs* State. For example, according to article 49 of the Italian act on private international law of 1995, if, under the applicable law, there is no testate or intestate successors and the State is not an heir, the assets of the estate located within Italy shall be appropriated by the Italian State. A similar solution is adopted by article 92 of the Bulgarian private international law code of 2005.[32]

et seq., suggested modifying the text of the article and adopting the same version of article 29 of the Austrian private international law act (see no. 11).

[32] Bulgarian private international law code, law no. 42 of 2005, in force since 17 May 2005, then emended by law no. 59 of 2007; see C. Jessel-Holst, 'The Bulgarian Private International Law Code of 2005', *YPIL* (2007), p. 375 *et seq.*

Article 34

Renvoi

ANGELO DAVÌ

1. The application of the law of any third State specified by this Regulation shall mean the application of the rules of law in force in that State, including the rules of private international law in so far as those rules make a *renvoi*:
   (a) to the law of a Member State; or
   (b) to the law of another third State which would apply its own law.
2. No *renvoi* shall apply with respect to the laws referred to in Article 21 (2), Article 22, Article 27, point (b) of Article 28 and Article 30.

Summary

I. INTRODUCTION: THE ORIGINS, PURPOSE AND CONTENT OF THE RULE *page* 469
II. CASES IN WHICH THE ESR PROVIDES THAT A LAW OTHER THAN THE LAW OF THE FORUM IS APPLICABLE AND IN WHICH A RENVOI MAY THEREFORE OCCUR 475
III. EXCEPTIONS TO THE PRINCIPLE OF RENVOI BEING ADMITTED 479
IV. THE MOST FREQUENT CASES IN WHICH A RENVOI MAY OCCUR 487
V. THE TYPE OF RENVOI ADOPTED BY THE ESR 491
VI. SOLUTIONS FOR CASES WHERE RENVOI IS NOT ACCEPTED BY THE LAW OF THE NON-MEMBER STATE TO WHICH IT IS DIRECTED 499
VII. CONCLUDING REMARKS 503

I. Introduction: The Origins, Purpose and Content of the Rule

1. In order to secure a certain degree of coordination with the private international law systems in third States whose laws are referred to by the ESR, the regulation allows the conflict-of-laws rules contained in those laws to be taken into consideration. Article 34 therefore establishes the principle (albeit moderated by certain exceptions) according to which, where the laws of third States, that pursuant to the ESR conflict provisions are applicable, do not intend to govern by means of their material provisions the matters falling within their remit and instead make reference to the law of a Member State or to the law of another third State that would apply its own law, this reference or *renvoi* must be followed.

2. The concepts of 'Member State' and 'third State' employed by article 34 and, in fact, by the vast number of other provisions of the ESR that employ either one or the other or even both (e.g. articles 3–13, 39.1, 59.1, 60.1, 62.1 and 62.3) should be understood respectively to mean, more precisely, a State bound by the ESR and a State not bound by it. To bear in mind here is the fact that the three EU Member States that have not participated to the adoption of the ESR, i.e. Denmark, Ireland and the United Kingdom, are not subject to its provisions; for the purposes of the ESR, therefore, these States are to be put on the same footing as third States [see art. 3 no. 9]. Where *renvoi* in particular is concerned, precisely because the ESR does not apply to these three States, in matters of succession they have kept separate conflict rules in place in their own legal systems that potentially differ from those introduced by the ESR into the other Member States. These rules therefore allow their legal systems to operate on the same lines as non-EU countries, making *renvois* which the complete harmonisation in this field in the other Member States as a result of the ESR has made impossible in their dealings with one another; correspondingly, where a *renvoi* is directed towards them, they are entirely at liberty to decide at their own discretion whether to accept or reject it.[1]

3. The introduction into the ESR of a rule permitting a *renvoi* is the result of an amendment by the Council (agreed on an informal basis with the European Parliament) to the Commission's original 2009 proposal. The proposal in fact included an article 26 that rejected the *renvoi*

[1] Clarification to the effect that the EU Member States that are non bound by a regulation shall not be treated as 'Member States' for the purposes of its application can be found in all previous pieces of legislation adopted by the EU in the area of private international law. One example is article 1.4 of regulation no. 864/2007 on the law applicable to non-contractual obligations (Rome II), which establishes that '[f]or the purposes of this Regulation, "Member State" shall mean any Member State other than Denmark'. Similarly, article 1.4 of regulation no. 593/2008 on the law applicable to contractual obligations (Rome I) states that '[i]n this Regulation, the term "Member State" shall mean Member States to which this Regulation applies'. Similar clarification was also to be found in the ESR Proposal presented in 2009 by the Commission (Proposal for a Regulation of the European Parliament and of the Council on jurisdiction, applicable law, recognition and enforcement of decisions and authentic instruments in matters of succession and the creation of a European Certificate of Succession, COM (2009) 154 final), where article 1.2 reads as follows: 'In this Regulation "Member State" means all the Member States with the exception of Denmark [the United Kingdom and Ireland].' The omission of such a clarification in the finalised version of the ESR is unfortunate: see more widely introduction, no. 13; A. Bonomi, 'Introduction', in A. Bonomi and P. Wautelet, *Le droit européen des successions. Commentaire du Règlement n° 650/2012 du 4 juillet 2012* (Bruxelles, 2013), pp. 30–31.

outright.[2] Despite the novelty aspect, the amendment was not entirely unexpected, however: much of the feedback provided in response to the green paper published by the Commission in 2005, including the input from the governments of eight Member States, as well as the resolution adopted by the European Parliament in 2006 making certain recommendations to the Commission on the content of the piece of legislation on the drawing board at that time were in favour of *renvoi*.[3] In addition, throughout the course of the preparatory work and both before and after presentation of the Commission's proposal, similar positions in favour had been adopted by influential academic and scientific institutions and associations, such as the Groupe européen de droit international privé, the Deutscher Rat für internationales Privatrecht and the Max-Planck-Institut für ausländisches und internationales Privatrecht of Hamburg, with support also being lent by a large majority in the literature.[4]

[2] Proposal for a Regulation of the European Parliament and of the Council (*supra*, footnote 1), article 26: 'When this Regulation provides for the application of the law of a State, it means the rules of law in force in that State other than its rules of private international law'.

[3] The eight Member States expressing this view were Finland, Germany, Lithuania, Luxembourg, the Netherlands, Poland, Slovakia and the United Kingdom; only the governments of Estonia and Sweden were against *renvoi* being allowed. Recommendation 6 (on general issues regarding the applicable law) contained in the European Parliament Resolution with recommendations to the Commission on succession and wills of 16 November 2006, P6-TA(2006) 496, OJ 2006 C 314 E of 21 December 2006, p. 345, was drafted as follows: 'for the purpose of coordinating the Community system of conflict rules governing succession with those of third countries, the prospective regulation should lay down specific rules concerning *renvoi*, establishing that, where the law applicable to the succession is the law of a third country and that country's conflict rules designate the law of a Member State or the law of another third country which, according to the system of private international law, could also apply its own law to the case in question, the law of that other Member State or, if appropriate, of that other third country, should apply'.

[4] See 'Réponse du Groupe européen de droit international privé au livre vert de la Commission européenne sur les successions et testaments', point 2(g), www.gedip-egpil.eu; for a summary of the work by the Deutscher Rat für internationales Privatrecht on this topic see F. Bauer, 'Neues europäisches Kollisions- und Verfahrensrecht auf dem Weg: Stellungnahme des Deutschen Rates für IPR zum internationalen Erb- und Scheidungsrecht', *IPRax* (2006), p. 202 *et seq.*; for the position adopted by the Max Planck Institute of Hamburg, see its 'Comments on the European Commission's Proposal for a Regulation of the European Parliament and of the Council on jurisdiction, applicable law, recognition and enforcement of decisions and authentic instruments in matters of succession and the creation of a European Certificate of Succession', *RabelsZ* (2010), p. 656 *et seq.* For some of the authors in favour of the future regulation including a provision that allows *renvoi* in one form or another, see K. Siehr, 'General Problems of Private International Law in Modern Codifications – *De Lege Lata* and *De Lege Europea Ferenda*', *YPIL* (2005), p. 44, and *id.*, 'Connecting Factors, Party Autonomy and Renvoi', in A. Malatesta, S. Bariatti and F. Pocar (eds), *The External Dimension of EC Private*

4. The fact that the ESR opens the door to *renvoi* also represents a change of direction as compared to previous legislation adopted by the European Union in the area of private international law. Regulations no. 593/2008 and no. 864/2007, which concern the law applicable to contractual and non-contractual obligations respectively, and regulation no. 1259/2010 implementing enhanced cooperation in the area of the law applicable to divorce and legal separation, in fact rule it out of consideration in general terms.[5] This position is not, however, necessarily in conflict with the different solution adopted by the ESR, being most likely supported by reasons pertaining to the individual regulations themselves rather than being a matter of principle. Where regulations no. 593/2008 and no. 864/2007 are concerned, these reasons have taken the form of a widely adopted approach on the international front to the effect that it is inappropriate for *renvoi* to be allowed in the field of obligations. One explanation for this is the significant presence here of provisions that give rise to issues of compatibility with the use of *renvoi*, such as those that contain exception clauses, or rely on other methods involving a case-based search of the applicable law or leave it to the parties themselves to decide on the law that should apply, or provisions based mainly on concerns of substantive justice. In terms of regulation no. 1259/2010, the exclusion would largely appear to be the result of the EU legislator's intention to foster mobility within the EU to the fullest extent possible, allowing citizens to take advantage of the differences to be found in divorce legislation in the various Member States in order to dissolve their marriage in a quicker and easier way. Nevertheless, the fact that the ESR adopts the opposite

International Law in Family and Succession Matters (Padova, 2008), p. 262 *et seq.*; A. Davì, 'Riflessioni sul futuro diritto internazionale privato europeo delle successioni', *Riv dir int* (2005), p. 315; A. Borrás, 'L'approche du renvoi dans un système d'unité de la succession', in *Mélanges en l'honneur de Mariel Revillard* (Paris, 2007), p. 33; A. Dutta, 'Succession and Wills in the Conflict of Laws on the Eve of Europeanisation', *RabelsZ* (2009), p. 558 *et seq.*; A. Bonomi, 'Prime considerazioni sulla proposta di regolamento sulle successioni', *Riv dir int priv proc* (2010), p. 910 *et seq.*, 914; C. Nourissat, 'Le futur droit des successions internationales de l'Union européenne', *Defrénois* (2010), no. 13; K. Schurig, 'Das internationale Erbrecht wird europäisch – Bemerkungen zur kommenden Europäischen Verordnung', in *Festschrift für Ulrich Spellenberg zum 70. Geburtstag* (München, 2010), p. 347 *et seq.*; P. Kindler, 'La legge regolatrice delle successioni nella proposta di regolamento dell'Unione europea: qualche riflessione in tema di carattere universale, rinvio e *professio juris, Riv dir int* (2011), p. 428; H. J. Sonnenberger, 'Grenzen der Verweisung durch europäisches internationales Privatrecht', *IPRax* (2011), p. 330.

[5] Article 20 of regulation no. 593/2008, article 24 of regulation no. 864/2007, article 11 of regulation no. 1259/2010. Article 7.3 of regulation no. 593/2008 does, however, make a slight exception in the case of insurance contracts: see A. Davì, 'Le renvoi en droit international privé contemporain', *Hague Recueil*, vol. 352 (2010), p. 302 *et seq.*

solution now provides clear evidence of the absence of any hostility in principle on the part of EU private international law to this device being used.[6] Effectively, as the international circulation of people and property does not take place solely within the Member States, the European Union's internal area cannot be kept separate from what lies outside it. It follows that the objective of simplification of international legal life of individuals pursued by the progressive construction of a European system of private international law in the context of the 'area of freedom, security and justice' provided for by Title V TFEU (articles 67 *et seq.*) makes it practically indispensable to try to find in appropriate cases a reasonable degree of coordination with the rules of conflict of laws of third States. And it is precisely these attempts at coordination in dealings with countries outside the EU that the introduction of article 34 of the ESR carries out, as stated by recital 57 where it says that that '*renvoi* should be accepted in order to ensure international consistency'. Actually, in international successions that are not exclusively connected with the circle of the Member States but have also links with non-EU countries, the courts in the latter are often called upon by the provisions of their own legislation to rule on these matters concurrently with the courts in the Member States. In such circumstances, where different laws apply to the succession in each of the two groups of countries, it would be virtually impossible to predict which law would in the event be applied, creating ample opportunity for forum shopping and forum running and prompting a significant increase in the number of disputes between heirs or between heirs and other parties claiming interests on the inheritance. This situation would fundamentally conflict with the principal aims of the ESR.[7] The *renvoi* allowed by article 34 can effectively help to solve these problems, albeit only in the presence of favourable conditions, which, however, do exist in a significant number of cases.

5. As previously stated [see *supra* no. 1], article 34.1 provides that the *renvoi* by the law of a third State initially designated by the ESR conflict-

[6] The reasons of the exclusion of *renvoi* by the respective articles 32 of the two recent EU regulations no. 2016/1103 on matrimonial property regimes and no. 2016/1104 on the property consequences of registered partnerships are more difficult to define: see for a brief discussion of the subject, Davi, 'Le renvoi', p. 355 *et seq.*

[7] To the extent relevant here, these aims are illustrated in recital 37 as follows: 'In order to allow citizens to avail themselves, with all legal certainty, of the benefits offered by the internal market, this Regulation should enable them to know in advance which law will apply to their succession. Harmonised conflict-of-laws rules should be introduced in order to avoid contradictory results. The main rule should ensure that the succession is governed by a predictable law with which it is closely connected'.

of-laws provisions is to be followed in two situations: where the *renvoi* is to the law of a Member State (paragraph 1 (a) of the article) and where it is to the law of another third State that would apply its own law (paragraph 1 (b)). In the first situation, the general benefits of coordination are accompanied by an additional advantage of a practical nature: the possibility of applying the substantive law of the forum State or that of another Member State in place of the substantive provisions of the law of a third State originally designated, which in many instances might present a greater challenge in terms of ascertainment, interpretation and implementation. The second situation reflects the particular type of *renvoi* adopted by the Hague Convention of 1989 on the Law Applicable to Succession to the Estates of Deceased Persons (article 4) and by the respective legislation in force in certain Member States.[8] The main reason in favour of admitting *renvoi* in this case is the following: when the laws of at least two third States closely connected with the succession (and which very often might be those having the greatest interest in regulating it[9]) agree that the law of one of them should apply, if the Member States would insist on designating the law of the other third State, this would result in creating from the outside a conflict that in fact exists only from the point of view of the Member States themselves. Such a situation would be difficult to reconcile with the aims

[8] See article 17 of the Portuguese civil code of 1966 and article 13 of the Italian act on private international law of 1995. The solution decided upon by the Hague Convention is more restrictive than that adopted by the ESR: the former only allows a *renvoi* to the law of a third country (which is accepted by that law) and rejects a *renvoi* to the law of a State party to the convention. The explanation for this restriction is the requirement that came to light during the drafting of the convention for a compromise to be found between the positions adopted by the delegations in favour of allowing *renvoi* and the positions taken up by those who opposed that step, with Denmark being the main champion of the cause in the latter group: the Danish delegation in fact managed to secure the introduction into the convention of a particular provision (article 24.1(b)) allowing a State to lodge a reservation on the point. The literature has generally tended to criticise this approach, highlighting the fact that the need of coordination between the positions of the group of states participating to a collective work of codification and those of third countries is the same irrespective of the direction in which the *renvoi* operates: see P. Lagarde, 'La nouvelle Convention de La Haye sur la loi applicable aux successions', *Rev crit dr int priv* (1989), p. 259; Y. Lequette, 'Le droit international privé de la famille à l'épreuve des conventions internationales', *Hague Recueil*, vol. 246 (1994), p. 222 *et seq.*; Davì, 'Le renvoi', p. 280 *et seq.*, footnote 575.

[9] As we will see in the following paragraph, the majority of cases in which the conflict-of-laws rules contained in the ESR dictate that the law of a third State applies are those in which the jurisdiction of the courts in the Member States is only subsidiary in nature or is assumed on the exceptional basis of what is referred to as *forum necessitatis*.

of the ESR. It may be added that the harmony existing between the laws of at least two foreign countries to which the succession is connected provides Member States with a guarantee that, where they waive the conflict-of-laws rule which, at the outset, they considered preferable, this renunciation will be rewarded by the attainment of a considerable degree of international uniformity.

II. Cases in Which the ESR Provides That a Law Other Than the Law of the Forum Is Applicable and in Which a *Renvoi* May Therefore Occur

6. There are two conditions to be met for a *renvoi* to take place. The first is that the conflict-of-laws rules of the forum State initially refer the matter to a foreign law. The second is that the content of the conflict-of-laws provisions of the foreign law designated as being applicable differ from the content of the corresponding provisions in place in the forum, given that otherwise the former would clearly make no *renvoi*, but would agree with the latter. It follows from this that, within the scope of application of the ESR, the foreign law in question must be the law of a third State, since the conflict-of-laws rules in force in the Member States have been harmonised by this piece of legislation, leaving no room for a *renvoi* in dealings between their legal systems. It is, however, only in a limited number of situations that these two conditions will be satisfied. In fact one of the main features of the ESR is the parallelism between jurisdiction and applicable law that it creates through the adoption of the same connecting factor of the habitual residence of the deceased at the time of death as a general criterion for the determination of the one and the other (articles 4 and 21, respectively).[10] This parallelism (*Gleichlauf*) between *forum* and *jus* is intended to avoid as much as possible the well-known difficulties that are often encountered in the area of succession as a result of foreign law being applied to the administration, transmission and distribution of the estate, which are organised by each legal system in its own particular fashion and are often difficult to be put into operation within a different legal order. The role that *renvoi* can play within the ESR is therefore limited, despite the fact that, on outward

[10] The importance of the role played by this principle within the ESR is expressly set out in recital 27: 'The rules of this Regulation are devised so as to ensure that the authority dealing with the succession will, in most situations, be applying its own law' [see art. 21 no. 8].

appearances, article 34 would seem to permit it generally. In practice, it can only be called upon in cases in which the ESR establishes exceptions to the principle of unity of *forum* and *jus*. These exceptions can result either from the addition of further, secondary criteria to the main criterion of jurisdiction of the last habitual residence of the deceased established by article 4 or from the provision of special conflict-of-laws rules which, for the purposes of determining the law that applies to certain aspects of succession, adopt a different connecting factor. In both situations, obviously the law referred to as being applicable must be the law of a third country.[11]

7. There are three situations, or groups of situations, in which the decoupling of *forum* and *jus* that represents the first condition to be met for a *renvoi* to take place is the result of the ESR establishing jurisdictional criteria in addition to the general criterion of last habitual residence of the deceased: the cases of subsidiary jurisdiction listed in article 10; the so-called *forum necessitatis* created by article 11; the special jurisdictional criteria established by article 13 for declarations regarding the acceptance or waiver of the succession, of a legacy or of a reserved share and for declarations designed to limit the liability of the person concerned in respect of the liabilities under the succession.[12]

The group of cases coming under the subsidiary jurisdiction is by far the most important. Article 10.1 in fact provides that, even though the deceased's last habitual residence was in a non-Member State (whose law is, therefore, the law that would normally apply pursuant to article 21), the courts of the Member State in which assets of the estate are located shall nevertheless have jurisdiction to rule on the succession as a whole, provided that the deceased was a national of that State or, failing that, his or her habitual residence was in that State up to a date not more than five years prior to the court being seised of the matter; paragraph 2 of the article further adds that, in the absence of these two conditions, those courts shall nevertheless have jurisdiction to rule on the succession to the extent of those assets alone [see art. 10]. It is apparent that situations of this type are by no means infrequent where international successions are

[11] As we will see at no. 9 *et seq*., even where the conditions set out above are met, the ESR still makes admission of *renvoi* subject to a certain number of exceptions.

[12] Also the exercise of the faculty that article 22 grants a person to choose his national law as applicable to the succession can lead to *forum* and *jus* taking separate paths. In no circumstances, however, can this possibility give rise to a *renvoi*, since the choice of law by the deceased is one of the exceptions established by article 34.2 to *renvoi* being admitted: see no. 13.

concerned. The *forum necessitatis* provided for by article 11 is instead a criterion of much rarer application, as it is designed to come into play on an exceptional basis only where no court of a Member State can hear the matter pursuant to the ordinary rules of jurisdiction (including those set out in article 10) and where there is the danger of a substantial denial of justice due to the impossibility, or serious difficulty, for the party or parties concerned to initiate proceedings in a third State with which the case is closely connected [see art. 11]. The special jurisdictional criterion established by article 13 is also of limited significance. According to this provision, persons who, under the law that governs the succession, may or are required to make before a courts a declaration of acceptance or waiver of an inheritance or legacy or a declaration designed to limit their liability in relation to the liabilities under the succession, may make that declaration before the courts of the Member State in which they habitually reside, instead of the courts normally having jurisdiction pursuant to the ESR [see art. 13]. The practical significance of this case is further diminished by the fact that whilst the law that applies to the succession is not the same as that of the Member State in which the party making the declaration is habitually resident, it may well be the law of another Member State rather than the law of a third country. In this situation the possibility of a *renvoi* would obviously be ruled out.

8. Even more limited in scale is the number of cases in which the unity of *forum* and *jus* established by the regulation is broken up by special conflict-of-laws rules in the ESR which, by derogation from the general principle that the entire succession is subject to the law of the State in which the deceased had his habitual residence at the time of death, adopt different solutions in respect of certain issues. The only two possible situations in this group are those contemplated by articles 24 and 25. Respectively, these make the issue of admissibility and substantive validity of dispositions of property upon death other than agreements as to succession, and the issue of admissibility and substantive validity as well as the binding effects between the parties of agreements as to succession, subject to the 'hypothetical' or 'anticipated' succession law/s of the person or persons whose successions are involved, that is, the law or laws of the country or countries where they had their habitual residence at the time that the dispositions were made or the agreements were entered into, rather than at the time of death. Where these countries are not bound by the ESR, the fact that their respective laws apply, calling for the provisions of private international law that they contain to be taken into account, paves the way for a *renvoi.*[13] Such a situation can quite naturally arise where the laws in question use a connecting factor other than habitual residence (e.g. the nationality of the deceased or the location of the assets forming the estate or part of it) or as a result of the fact that, whilst adopting this same criterion, they do not acknowledge the principle of the 'hypothetical' or 'anticipated' succession law. Especially in the latter case there is some risk that the effect of *renvoi* would be in conflict with the purpose of articles 24 and 25, which primarily consists in supporting the validity of dispositions on death and of succession agreements, avoiding a situation in which, as a result of the testator moving his habitual residence abroad, a different law in fact applies, rendering the dispositions and agreements invalid, possibly betraying the expectations of the persons involved [see art. 24 and art. 25]. For this reason it has been suggested that a *renvoi* productive of such effects should not be followed despite its rejection is not included among the exceptions to its admission listed in article 34.2.[14] It is by no means certain that such a suggestion reflects the intentions of the ESR authors, not only because this ground for refusal of *renvoi* is not one of the exceptions to its admission established by article 34.2 (which, in fact, appears to have been very carefully drafted), but also because its refusal would, hand in hand with the advantage referred to, give rise to significant drawbacks, including the door being opened to forum shopping and forum running and the connected risk of conflicting decisions being handed down by the courts. In fact, if at the point in time at which dispositions on death were made or succession agreements were entered into, the person whose estate is involved was residing in a non-EU Member State, the situation will usually bear with the State in question sufficient contacts to ground the jurisdiction of its courts, which would apply a different law to the one

[13] It should be added that the theoretical possibility of a *renvoi* also exists as regards the special rule set out in article 28, which, in connection with article 13 (mentioned earlier at no. 7), submits alternatively formal validity of the declaration of acceptance or waiver of the succession or a legacy as well as formal validity of declarations designed to limit liability on the part of the person making the declaration to the law that ordinarily governs the succession or the law of the State in which the person making the declaration habitually resides. Nevertheless, as an exception to the general principle that a *renvoi* is allowed, article 34.2 (see no. 17) expressly rules out the *renvoi* that can be effected by the latter law, while the possibility of a *renvoi* by the former can quite naturally depend only on a court of a Member State assuming jurisdiction on the basis of a connecting factor other than the last habitual residence of the deceased.

[14] See A. Bonomi, 'Article 34', in A. Bonomi and P. Wautelet, *Le droit européen des successions. Commentaire du Règlement n° 650/2012 du 4 juillet 2012* (Bruxelles, 2013), p. 512 *et seq.*

that would be applicable in the Member States. It may be added that to conclude that the person making a disposition on death or the parties to an agreement regarding the succession of someone who, when the disposition was made or the agreement signed, was habitually residing in a non-EU Member State worked at all times on the basis of the private international law of the Member States and, therefore, relied on the succession being subject to the conflict-of-laws rules set out in articles 24 and 25 ESR is perhaps taking matters a little too far.

III. Exceptions to the Principle of *Renvoi* Being Admitted

9. As stated previously, even to the extent that the ESR allows the court with jurisdiction and the applicable law to be decoupled, *renvoi* does not always have to be followed. Article 34.2 sets out five different exceptions to *renvoi* applying. These are in fact connected to the use made by the ESR of types of conflict-of-laws rules and connecting factors which, from a technical point of view or from the standpoint of legislative policy, are generally seen as being difficult to reconcile with the use of this tool of coordination among legal systems. Similar exceptions can also be found in the legislation of many Member States. At times, these exceptions are listed in analytical detail by specific legislative provisions, such as article 13 of the Italian act on private international law, whose pattern is similar to that adopted by article 34.2 ESR itself. At times, they are part of a generic and indefinite formula such as that found in article 4 of German EGBGB, which dictates that *renvoi* must be rejected whenever its admission would be contrary to the 'spirit' of the reference to foreign law by a German conflict-of-laws rule (*sofern dies nicht dem Sinn der Verweisung widerspricht*).

10. The first of the exceptions referred to above concerns the situation in which the law that applies to the succession has been established by relying on the 'escape clause' or 'exception clause' contained in article 21.2. Use of the case-based method underlying this type of clause is difficult to reconcile with the rather mechanical, rigid nature of the operation of *renvoi*. The reasons for this are well known. On the one hand, if the law that has been identified by means of a flexible procedure like this is indeed the law which, taking all the circumstances of the case into account, demonstrates the strongest links with a particular succession, a subsequent *renvoi* would necessarily lead to a law being applied that has a more distant connection. The result of the effort made to identify the centre of gravity of the situation more accurately and precisely than by means of the automatic operation of a conflict-of-laws rule of a general and abstract nature would, therefore, inevitably be undermined. On the other hand, the willingness or unwillingness to be applied of the different laws with which the deceased had ties and therefore the *renvois* that each of them can operate to the others or receive from them, represent some of the most important factors to be taken into consideration when evaluating and comparing the respective significance of the relationships between the laws in question and the succession, given that the substance and effectiveness of those relationships can only be significantly strengthened or weakened by the presence or absence of a corresponding intention of each of the laws in question to apply. Consequently, to give any further consideration to *renvoi* would be pointless and even counterproductive as it would amount to reconsider the decision reached on the basis of an assessment of all the relevant circumstances, including the solutions adopted by the conflict-of-laws systems in all of the States that the succession has a connection with.[15]

11. There is another case in which the ESR uses the criterion of closest connection of the individual case, albeit as a connecting factor of an ordinary nature rather than by means of an 'exception clause'. This is when the law applicable to agreements as to succession regarding the succession of several persons has to be established. In fact, pursuant to article 25.2, the substantive validity and binding effects between the parties of these agreements are subject to the law that the agreement in question has the strongest ties with, provided that the agreement is admissible on the basis of the 'hypothetical' succession laws for all the persons involved (i.e. the laws that would have been applicable to their respective successions had they died on the same day on which they entered into the agreement) [see art. 25]. This case, however, is not included in the list of the exceptions that article 34.2 establishes to the general rule according to which *renvoi* is admitted. The explanation for the said exclusion is the fact that within the framework of article 25.2, the case-based method is only used on a partial basis. The sole points of contact which are taken into consideration in this case are those that exist between the agreement at issue and the 'hypothetical' succession laws for each of the persons involved (i.e. the laws of the countries in which they are habitually resident at the time that the agreement is entered into).

[15] See A. Davì and A. Zanobetti, 'Il nuovo diritto internazionale privato delle successioni nell'Unione europea', *CdT*, 5/2 (2013), p. 87 ss.; A. Davì and A. Zanobetti, *Il nuovo diritto internazionale privato europeo delle successioni* (Torino, 2014), p. 140; Bonomi, 'Article 34', pp. 519–520.

Links that might exist with the laws of other countries (e.g. the country whose nationality is held by one – or even all of – the persons whose inheritance is involved or the country in which the assets that the agreement concerns are located) are left entirely out of the picture during this assessment process. As a result, once the process had been concluded and, of the laws that have been compared with each other and those alone, the law that the agreement is most closely connected with has been identified, there is no reason not to follow the *renvoi* made by that law to the law of a third country. A solution to the contrary would in particular give rise to a situation in which agreements relating to the succession of a number of people and those that concern the succession of one person alone, in relation to which *renvoi* is certainly allowed, would not be treated in the same way. It is therefore only in the internal relationships between the laws whose links with the situation have already been appraised and compared that fresh consideration of the *renvoi* should be ruled out.[16]

12. The problem of the relationship between *renvoi* and a case-based search for the closest link can also arise, albeit from a particular standpoint, where the ESR's conflict-of-laws rules refer to the law of a State that has more than one legal system. Where this type of situation is concerned, the principle established by article 36.2(b) and article 37.3 is that, if the State in question does not have a centralised body of internal conflict-of-laws rules that establish which of the various different systems of law or set of rules composing its legal system is applicable, the system or set of rules with which the deceased had the closest connection shall apply [see art. 36 and art. 38 nos. 3, 14, 19 *et seq.*]. In situations such as these, it is clear that the case-based method is only used to identify the internal legal system or set of rules that is to apply, while the foreign legal system taken overall is determined on the basis of the ordinary connecting factors adopted by the ESR. As a result, there is no doubt that any *renvoi* to the law of a different State by the international conflict-of-laws rules contained in the composite legal system referred to, must be duly followed, whether those rules are centralised or are the rules of the specific legal unit that the deceased had the closest connection with.[17]

[16] For the different opinion to the effect that *renvoi* should be rejected also when it is to the law of a third country, see, however, G. Hohloch, 'Kommentierung der EuErbRVO', in W. Erman, *BGB: Kommentar*, 14th ed. (Köln, 2014), p. 6717.

[17] See also article 36 and article 38, no. 4, and, more generally, Davì, 'Le renvoi', p. 388–389.

13. The second exception that article 34.2 introduces to *renvoi* being allowed concerns the situation in which the deceased has availed himself of the faculty granted by article 22 to choose the law of the State (or one of the States) whose nationality he held as the law applicable to his succession. Exclusion of *renvoi* where a choice of law has been made is a solution widely accepted by the legal literature as well as by the legislation of the States and by the international conventions dealing with conflicts of laws.[18] In particular, where matters of succession are concerned, this exclusion is established by article 4 of the Hague Convention of 1989 on the Law Applicable to Succession to the Estates of Deceased Persons, which stipulates that *renvoi* can only be taken into consideration where it is effected by a law designated by means of one of the objective connecting factors listed in article 3. The admission of *renvoi* in the case under consideration would amount to giving priority to the position adopted by the chosen foreign law about its own application over the freedom of choice that the ESR grants on this point to the testator and would, therefore, conflict with the legislative intention of allowing the testator to subject his succession to the rules which, in his view, best suit his interests. It should furthermore be considered that whilst allowing *renvoi* could, on the one hand, produce results that are incompatible with the intention and expectations of the deceased, it could, on the other hand, in fact offer him the opportunity to exploit this mechanism in order to circumvent the limitations imposed on his power of choice by article 22, which restricts the options open to him to his national law (or one of his different national laws) alone. To avoid this risk, the ESR adds to the rejection of *renvoi* established by article 34.2 the prohibition implicitly made to the testator by article 22 to include himself in the object of his choice the rules of conflict of laws that can be contained in his national law.[19]

[18] In national legislation, see, for this exclusion as a general principle, e.g., article 19.2 of the Portuguese civil code of 1966 and article 13.2(a) of the Italian act on private international law of 1995. Article 6 of the Slovenian act on private international law goes even further, excluding *renvoi* in any areas in which the said act grants the parties the faculty to choose the applicable law, regardless of whether this faculty has in practice been exercised.

[19] A corresponding prohibition, either express or implied, can also be found in the majority of the respective laws of the Member States: see for example article 4.2 of the German EGBGB (*Soweit die Parteien das Recht eines Staates wählen können, können sie nur auf die Sachvorschriften verweisen*). Where the faculty to choose the applicable law that is granted to the parties involved does not take the form of a limited possibility of choice between a more or less restricted number of pre-established laws but can instead relate to any law at all (this usually being the position where choice of governing law for international

14. Whilst exclusion of *renvoi* by article 34.2 on the basis of a choice of law having been made would, at first glance, appear to concern only the *professio juris* relating to the entire succession allowed by article 22, it seems clear that it must also be taken to extend to the more specific cases of choice of law applicable to testamentary dispositions and agreements as to succession allowed by article 24.2 and article 25.3 respectively. This conclusion also finds adequate support in a literal construction, as the last two provisions make it clear that the choice that they contemplate has to be made 'in accordance with Article 22 on the conditions set out therein'. Among the conditions to which the choice of law on the succession as a whole is subject under article 22, there is however its subtraction to the mechanism of *renvoi*, since this article is supplemented by article 34.2, or at least it acquires its full meaning when seen in its relationship with the latter. It would, therefore, seem reasonable to conclude that the same solution must also apply to the choices of law of a more limited nature envisaged by article 24.2 and article 25.3. It should be added that an interpretation on opposing lines would produce consequences that one would struggle to accept had been those that the ESR legislator had in mind: firstly, the impossibility in many cases of subjecting, by virtue of one or more choices of law, dispositions of property upon death or agreements as to succession to the substantive provisions of the same law that governs the remaining aspects of the succession; and, secondly, the impossibility of preventing exploitation of *renvoi* for subtracting the said dispositions or agreements from the limitations imposed on the freedom of choice by article 24.2 and article 25.3, which, as with article 22, only allow national law to be chosen.[20]

15. The third exception established by article 34.2 concerns determining the law that governs the form of dispositions of property upon death, including agreements as to succession, as well as the form that

contracts is concerned), there are, however, no obstacles in principle to a choice being made that encompasses the conflict-of-laws provisions of the law chosen. Nevertheless, article 3 of regulation 593/2008 on the law applicable to contractual obligations (Rome I) is generally not interpreted in this broad sense.

[20] The interpretation suggested is supported almost unanimously by the literature: see A. Dutta, 'Das neue internationale Erbrecht der Europäischen Union – Eine erste Lektüre der Erbrechtsverordnung', *FamRZ* (2013), p. 12, footnote 70; Davì and Zanobetti, 'Il nuovo diritto internazionale privato delle successioni', p. 90; Davì and Zanobetti, *Il nuovo diritto internazionale privato europeo*, p. 144; Bonomi, 'Article 34', p. 521; Hohloch, 'Kommentierung der EuErbRVO', p. 6717; more hesitant: I. Rodríguez-Uría Suárez, 'La ley aplicable a las sucesiones mortis causa en el Reglamento (UE) 650/2012, *Indret* (2013/2), p. 42.

their modification or revocation may take. In support of the formal validity of these legal acts, article 27 establishes a list of eight different laws (borrowed from article 1 of the Hague Convention of 1961 on the Conflicts of Laws Relating to the Form of Testamentary Dispositions), stating that they are all alternatively applicable and that the acts in question are to be considered as formally valid where they meet the conditions required by any of the laws referred to [see art. 27 no. 6 *et seq.*]. Article 27 is thus making use of the conflict-of-laws method of the alternative connection designed to secure a certain material result. Use of this method is generally viewed as being irreconcilable or difficult to reconcile with *renvoi* being admitted. This is because in many cases the operation of *renvoi* might prevent the sought material result being achieved, either reducing (or even eliminating altogether) the alternatives available, where it takes place in the internal relationships between laws already included in the list of those designated directly, or leading to the application of a different law that operates contrary to the result intended, while the obtainment of the latter would have been permitted by the application of the substantive provisions of the law making the *renvoi*. Acceptance of the *renvoi* to a third law that works in support of the policy underlying the alternative reference rule also comes with drawbacks: it might upset the balance struck by that provision between various requirements, which include the need to keep within a reasonable limit the favour for the result at stake and the need to ensure that all the laws made applicable have an adequate connection with the case.

These observations of a general nature can be supplemented by two more specific reasons supporting the exclusion of *renvoi* in relation to the result-selective choice-of-law rules of the type under examination and concerning particularly article 27. The first is that this provision contains a list of alternatively applicable connecting factors that is so broad that, in practice, it includes nearly all of those that can be found in existing legislation. If *renvoi* was admitted here, it would, therefore, of necessity have an extremely reduced role to play.[21] The second is that

[21] One of the few possibilities not taken directly into account by article 27 is where the succession – or certain aspects of it – is subject to the same law that governs the deceased's marital property regime. In the Member States legislations, this solution was established, for example, by article 9.8 of the Spanish civil code only in relation to succession rights granted by law to the surviving spouse and by chapter 26, section 6, of the Finnish succession code, on the sole basis of the choice made to this effect by the testator; however, the former provision, since it concerned only rights arising directly from the law, had no influence on the formal validity of dispositions of property upon death.

the Hague Convention of 1961, whose content article 27 of the ESR merely reproduces with slight, unimportant textual changes, refuses in turn to take the *renvoi* into account.[22] Adoption of a different solution in the ESR would, therefore, have resulted in a discrepancy between the two legal instruments that would have been in conflict with the aim pursued by article 27 of harmonising the rules that govern the form of dispositions on death in dealings between the fourteen Member States parties to the convention and the eleven Member States only bound by the ESR [see art. 27 no 6].[23]

16. The last two exceptions are of lesser importance. One of the two cannot in fact even be described as an exception in the true sense of the word, as it deals with a situation in which the possibility of a *renvoi* is of necessity ruled out right at the very outset. Pursuant to article 30, where the law of the State in which certain immovable property, enterprises or other particular categories of assets are located has special provisions which, upon economic, family or social considerations, impose restrictions on the succession in relation to the assets in question, those provisions must take priority in application over the provisions of the law that would normally govern the succession; this is on condition that, on the basis of the law of the State that is home to the assets, the former provisions 'are applicable irrespective of the law applicable to the

[22] The formula used by article 1 of the convention in order to indicate the intention to exclude any reference to the rules of private international law contained in the laws that it states to be alternatively applicable consists in the expression 'internal law(s)' which, in the language adopted by the conventions drawn up at the Hague Conference in the decades immediately following the Second World War, in fact means that only the substantive rules of each of the laws in question have to be taken into account.

[23] It has to be observed that whilst, as mentioned previously, the convention does not directly allow *renvoi*, its article 3 permits the contracting States to maintain or adopt rules that recognise the validity of dispositions on death made in compliance with the formal requirements of a law other than a law included in the list of those stated to be alternatively applicable under its article 1 (which corresponds with article 27 ESR). It follows that, despite the fact that this point is rarely highlighted, the convention does not shut the door on the possibility of its contracting States to decide to take into account, on the basis of their national conflict-of-laws provisions, *renvois* that can be made to laws that are not included in the list established by article 1: see J. Derruppé, 'Le renvoi dans les conventions internationales', *Juris-classeur de droit international* (1993), fasc. 532–3, p. 3; Davì, 'Le renvoi', p. 269 *et seq.* The aim that the ESR sets out to achieve, being to secure, via reception of the essential content of the convention, harmonisation of the rules governing the formal validity of dispositions on death in all Member States, whether or not they are bound by the second instrument, leads to construing the provision of article 75.1, pursuant to which the Member States that are parties to the convention shall continue to apply its provisions instead of article 27 of the ESR, as meaning that it has deprived them of the freedom to avail themselves of this faculty also in the future.

succession' [see art. 30]. It is clear, therefore, that the specification in article 34.2 to the effect that the general rule admitting the *renvoi* does not operate in such cases is nothing more than a simple acknowledgement of the factual situation in place, given that, to the extent that the law in force in the country where the assets are located regards the special provisions mentioned in article 30 as being applicable, it makes no *renvoi*.[24]

17. The last remaining exception concerns the specific requirements as to form in article 28, regarding declarations of acceptance or waiver of the succession, of a legacy or of a reserved share, or declarations designed to limit liability for the deceased's debts. Pursuant to article 28, the formal validity of these declarations is subject either to the law ordinarily applicable to the succession as a whole in accordance with articles 21 and 22 or, alternatively, to the law of the place in which the person making the said declarations habitually resides. Article 34.2 rules out the *renvoi* in the latter of the two alternatives, thereby impliedly acknowledging it in the former. The exclusion, which entails even the rejection of the *renvoi* addressed to the *lex loci actus* as such,[25] probably reflects concerns raised about the need to minimise the instances of *forum* and *jus* being decoupled, in an area such as the formal validity of this type of acts, that are usually functionally connected with the administration and distribution of the estate, phases in which substance and procedure are often closely entwined, and accordingly the application of a law other than the law that governs the succession as a whole (or the *lex fori* itself) can at times give rise to difficulties. Given that, in addition to the courts that have general jurisdiction to rule on the succession, article 13 also grants jurisdiction to receive the declarations in question to the courts in the Member State in which the persons required to make the declarations habitually reside [see art. 13], it is in fact to be expected that the law of this State will coincide with the law of the forum in a large number of cases. Where, however, *renvoi* is effected by the law that governs the succession as a whole, the very fact that there is a *renvoi* can be seen as being sufficient to demonstrate the absence of any insuperable obstacles to the declaration being subject to a law other than that law.

[24] This observation is common among commentators: see D. Solomon, 'Die Renaissance des Renvoi im Europäischen Internationalen Privatrecht', in *Liber Amicorum Klaus Schurig* (München, 2012), p. 262; F. M. Wilke, 'Das internationale Erbrecht nach der neuen EU-Erbrechtsverordnung', *RIW* (2012), p. 608; Davì and Zanobetti, 'Il nuovo diritto internazionale privato delle successioni', p. 92; Davì and Zanobetti, *Il nuovo diritto internazionale privato europeo*, p. 147 *et seq.*; Bonomi, 'Article 34', p. 522.

[25] This rejection is criticised by Dutta, 'Das neue internationale Erbrecht', p. 15.

IV. The Most Frequent Cases in Which a *Renvoi* May Occur

18. Within the framework of the ESR, *renvoi* is likely to operate most frequently in cases involving the succession of citizens of the Member States whose last habitual residence was in a third country where the law in force, which, pursuant to the general rule in article 21, is the law designated to govern the succession, adopts instead the connecting factor of nationality and, therefore, refers back to the relevant person's national law. In situations such as this, in addition to the benefits of coordination with the positions taken up by the conflict-of-laws systems in non-Member States whose courts generally have jurisdiction in parallel with that of the forum state, admission of *renvoi* also offers important advantages of a practical nature connected to what a commentator has described as the 'repatriation' of the succession's regulation to the European Union.[26]

Among these advantages there is the re-establishment of the parallelism between *forum* and *jus*, whose preservation to the extent possible is one of the main objectives of the ESR, and that the recourse made by article 10.1(a) to the subsidiary jurisdictional ground of nationality of the deceased would negate in the event that there was no *renvoi* or the *renvoi* was not accepted. In the latter case, the courts in the Member States assuming jurisdiction on the basis of that provision should in fact apply the law of the non-Member State in which the deceased was last habitually resident, despite that this law does not consider itself as applicable.

An additional advantage is the opportunity to avoid having to tackle the various and often complex problems that can arise where the succession of citizens of European countries is subject to substantive regulations largely inappropriate as a result of their last habitual residence having been in one of the Asian or African countries where tradition and legal culture, especially if based on obedience to precepts rooted in religion, differ significantly from those found in countries in the Western world. These difficulties may especially include, firstly, that of having to take more frequently than usual delicate decisions on the compatibility of the foreign law to the public policy of the forum;[27] secondly, those that can arise from the existence in certain countries of interpersonal law systems with ethnic or religious roots which are subdivided into distinct and separate sub-systems whose applicability to individuals depends on

[26] See Nourissat, 'Le futur droit des successions', no. 13.

[27] Attention is drawn to this aspect, for example, by Bonomi, 'Prime considerazioni', p. 910; *id.*, 'Article 34', p. 516.

whether they belong to a particular community, without any catch-all safety net in place in the form of a non-denominational law or a law otherwise applicable on a residuary basis to the succession of foreign citizens who are not members of any particular community.[28] The possibility offered by *renvoi* of avoiding difficulties of this type is also what prompted the majority of the legal literature to criticise the fact that the Commission's proposal of 2009 had excluded it, and now leads most commentators to approve its inclusion in the finalised version of the ESR.[29]

19. Another situation in which we might expect to see *renvoi* frequently called upon is where the deceased's last habitual residence was in a non-Member State which, contrary to the ESR, adopts the dualist principle, or the principle of territorial scission of the succession, according to which only the succession of movable property is subject to the deceased's personal law (usually identified as the law of his last domicile or of his last residence but at times also as his national law), with succession in relation to immovable property being subject to the law of the country or countries in which this property is located. Before the ESR, in articles 4, 21.1 and 22.1, extended the opposing principle of unity and universality of the succession to all Member States, a scissionist approach was followed by some of them, such as Belgium, Bulgaria, Cyprus, France, Latvia, Lithuania, Luxembourg and Malta. Solutions of this type can currently be found in common law countries, Russia, China and certain countries in Asia, Africa and Latin America.[30] The chances of having to take account of a *renvoi* addressed by the law of a scissionist country to the *lex rei sitae* are much increased as a result of article 10.2 ESR, which deems the presence in a Member State of immovable

[28] Difficulties of this type can sometimes arise even for these countries themselves: see, for example, the decision handed down by the Supreme Court of Lebanon on 28 March 1998 in the *Philibert* case, JDI (2001), p. 873 *et seq.*, in which the court justified rejection of the *renvoi* by French law to Lebanese law in relation to the succession of a French citizen last domiciled in Lebanon, where also the immovable property assets in his estate were located, on the basis that Lebanon had no provisions on succession of a residuary character that could apply to foreigners; see on this subject in more detail Davì, 'Le renvoi', p. 115 *et seq.*

[29] See Bonomi, 'Prime considerazioni', pp. 910, 914; Nourissat, 'Le futur droit des successions', no. 13; Kindler, 'La legge regolatrice delle successioni', p. 428; P. Lagarde, 'Les principes de base du nouveau règlement européen sur les successions', *Rev crit dr int priv* (2012), p. 705.

[30] Some of these countries even apply the law of the *situs rei* to the succession in relation to movable property. For more information see Davì and Zanobetti, *Il nuovo diritto internazionale privato europeo*, p. 7 *et seq.*

property assets that are part of the estate to provide sufficient basis for the establishment of the jurisdiction of the courts in that State to rule on the devolution of those assets, including where no other connecting factors with the State in question can be found. But even when the courts in the Member States assume jurisdiction on the basis of criteria with more general scope when compared to the mere presence of individual assets, such as nationality or previous habitual residence of the deceased, pursuant to article 10.1(a) and (b), and the estate includes immovable property assets that are located in different countries, admission of *renvoi* made by the law of a country that adopts the scissionist principle results in a number of partial references that can be to the law of the forum State itself as well as to the law of other States, whether or not they are members. Through the operation of the *renvoi* mechanism, the fragmentation of the estate into a plurality of masses subject to different laws that is prompted by application of the principle of scission can thus take place in practice even within the internal judicial area of the European Union, despite the ESR in turn adopting the opposing principle of unity of succession.

Scission does of course present a considerable number of drawbacks. These include the possibility that differing views will be taken on the validity of the will pursuant to the various local laws (which has prompted the practice in common law countries of drawing up a number of separate wills, or multiple wills, as necessary), the difficulties encountered in allocating the debts of the deceased between the various parcels of the estate and unequal treatment of heirs as a result of differences in the succession laws that separately apply to protect forced heirs or to obligations to restore or account for gifts, advancements or legacies.[31] With these disadvantages in mind, during the course of the preparatory work for the ESR a certain number of authors had suggested that admission of *renvoi* be excluded in cases in which it would compromise the unity of succession.[32] The final version of article 34 does not, however, contain any restriction of this type, thus following the same

[31] On these and on other problems that practical application of the scissionist system can give rise to, see for example Haopei Li, 'Some Recent Developments in the Conflict of Laws of Succession', *Hague Recueil*, vol. 224 (1990), p. 55 *et seq.*; Davì, 'Riflessioni', p. 310 *et seq.*; Bonomi 'Successions internationales', p. 117 *et seq.*

[32] See Dutta, 'Succession and Wills', p. 558 *et seq.*; Bonomi, 'Prime considerazioni', p. 911; for a position against admission of *renvoi* when producing a scission see also Siehr, 'Connecting Factors', p. 265; in favour, including in this situation, see Max Planck Institute for Comparative and International Private Law, 'Comments', p. 660.

solution which had already been adopted by article 4 of the Hague Convention of 1989 on the Law Applicable to Succession to the Estates of Deceased Persons.[33] The authors of the ESR have therefore proven to give greater weight to the advantages of a general nature offered by the use of *renvoi* than to the wish to avoid as far as possible the inconveniences of scission. Moreover, there are other respects in which the stance adopted by the ESR would not appear to be one that is wholly against the principle of scission, given that it allows the seised court, in the absence of other jurisdictional criteria, to rule on the succession solely in relation to the assets that exist in the forum Member State (article 10.2) and to refrain from ruling on the devolution of assets that are located in a non-Member State where the latter is expected to refuse to recognise the decision (article 12.1). In addition, one effect of scission might equally be produced as a result of the application of article 30, which grants priority over the law that would normally govern the succession to the special rules which certain categories of assets are subject to, pursuant to the law in force in the place in which they are located.

20. Less frequent instances of *renvoi* can also arise in dealings with third countries adopting, in their conflict-of-laws rules on succession, connecting factors that are, on all appearances, similar or in fact identical to the connecting factor of the deceased's habitual residence used by article 21 of the ESR, such as domicile, residence or habitual residence itself, whilst, however, interpreting these concepts in a manner not perfectly coinciding with the meaning given to the notion of deceased's habitual residence by the ESR [see art. 21 no. 4 *et seq.*]. Situations of this type can especially occur in relation to the concept of domicile used by English law and, albeit with possible additional differences, by other common law countries. But the concept of domicile to be found in Swiss law, as defined by article 20 of Switzerland's act on private international law, also differs from the concept of habitual residence used by the ESR. The possibility that the conflict-of-laws system in one of the foreign States in question will consider that the deceased was domiciled or resident at the time of death in a country other than the one in which

[33] Before the ESR became applicable in the Member States, there was a tendency in the legislation or case law of a small number of Member States (such as France, Spain and Belgium) to reject or to admit *renvoi* depending on whether allowing it would lead to the disruption of the unity of succession, or, on the contrary, would permit this unity to be maintained or restored; all the remaining Member States with conflict-of-laws rules that admitted *renvoi* applied it regardless of the effects that it might produce in this respect: see Davì, 'Le renvoi', p. 471 *et seq.*

he should, pursuant to the ESR, be treated as having had his last habitual residence cannot, therefore, be ruled out.[34]

V. The Type of *Renvoi* Adopted by the ESR

21. The main problem of a general nature when interpreting article 34 consists doubtless in establishing whether the type of *renvoi* that it adopts is the 'single' or 'partial' *renvoi* or the 'total' or 'integral' or 'double' *renvoi*, also referred to in common law countries as the 'foreign court theory', according to which the judge in the forum required to apply the law of a foreign State must decide the case before him applying the same substantive provisions that a judge in that foreign State would apply.[35] This point is the subject of debate amongst the commentators of the provision, given that it fails to provide any explicit clarification thus leaving, perhaps intentionally, both options open.[36] For the purposes of establishing whether or not the designated foreign law makes a *renvoi*,

[34] On this possibility see also Schurig, 'Das internationale Erbrecht wird europäisch', p. 348. On the complex concept of domicile in English law see J. J. Fawcett, J. M Carruthers and P. M. North, *Cheshire, North & Fawcett: Private International Law*, 14th ed. (Oxford, 2008), p. 153 *et seq.*; P. Rogerson, *Collier's Conflict of Laws*, 4th ed. (Cambridge, 2013), p. 71 *et seq.*; for a survey by a foreign scholar see J. Carrascosa González, *El Reglamento Sucesorio Europeo 650/2012 de 4 de Julio 2012: Análisis crítico* (Granada, 2014), pp. 291–296. In Switzerland, where article 91 of the 1987 act on private international law dictates that the succession of someone who was last domiciled abroad is subject to the law designated by the conflict-of-laws rules of the foreign State in which the deceased was domiciled, article 20 of that act defines the State of domicile as that in which a person resides with the intention of settling (*dans lequel elle réside avec l'intention de s'y établir*); on this concept, which is similar in some respects to the 'domicile of choice' in English law, see A. Bucher, *Droit international privé suisse*, vol. II, *Personnes, Famille, Successions* (Bâle, 1992), p. 60 *et seq.*; M. Keller and J. Kren Kostkiewicz, 'Art. 20', in *Zürcher Kommentar zum IPRG*, 2nd ed. (Zürich, 2004), p. 305 *et seq.*

[35] See *Collier* v. *Rivaz* [1841] 2 Curteis 855, *per* Sir Herbert Jenner, for the famous statement that 'the Court sitting here . . . must consider itself sitting in Belgium under the particular circumstances of the case'. It should be noted, however, that even if one considers, as do some authors, including the author of this comment, that the type of *renvoi* adopted by the ESR is the total or integral version, such a *renvoi* would not entirely coincide with the 'foreign court theory' model, because, where *renvoi* is to the law of a non-Member State, article 34.1(b) makes its admission dependent upon the law referred to agreeing that it should be applied (see more on this at no. 5). In fact in the original version of that theory this is not a requirement.

[36] This want of clarity on the point has been highlighted by a number of commentators and indeed frowned upon by some of them: see Solomon, 'Die Renaissance des Renvoi', p. 241 *et seq.* (referring to the finalised text of the ESR's Proposal as amended in 2011); Davì and Zanobetti, 'Il nuovo diritto internazionale privato delle successioni', p. 96; Davì and Zanobetti, *Il nuovo diritto internazionale privato europeo*, p. 154; Bonomi, 'Article 34',

the first type of *renvoi*, as well known, does involve simply looking at that law's choice-of-law rules or reference rules. This therefore entails the exclusion of the taking into account of the rules that, in turn, it contains concerning *renvoi*, despite the fact that, within the conflict-of-laws system that they are part of, these latter rules obviously supplement the aforementioned choice-of-law rules, thus making a decisive contribution to establishing the meaning and extent of the reference that they make to a different law (the law of the forum itself or the law of a third State). Aiming at faithfully reconstructing the solution in fact adopted by the conflict-of-laws system in the foreign law referred to, the second type, instead, includes a consideration of the position adopted by that system as regards *renvoi*, thus avoiding the risk of that law being treated as intending to designate a different law where in fact such an intention does not exist.[37] The expressions 'partial' or 'total' *renvoi* do of course indicate the extent to which the appraisal of the provisions of the foreign private international law system is exhaustive (and, therefore, ultimately, the extent to which it is accurate) in the two models in question.[38]

22. The practical advantage of the single *renvoi* is that it favours to the utmost the application of the substantive rules of the *lex fori*, thus

p. 517; M. Greeske, *Die Kollisionsnormen der neuen EU-Erbrechtsverordnung* (Frankfurt a. M., 2014), p. 190.

[37] In the version of *renvoi* adopted by article 34.1(b), which, for the purposes of admission of *renvoi* to the law of a non-Member State, imposes an additional condition in the form of 'acceptance' of *renvoi* by the law referred to, i.e. the condition that this law in turn considers its own substantive provisions as applicable (see no. 5), the total *renvoi* calls for an equally exhaustive examination of the conflict-of-laws system established by the law in question, in order to also be able to take account of the position that it adopts in terms of *renvoi*; the same can be said for the conflict-of-laws systems to be found in additional laws that might be involved in the round of subsequent referrals: on this point see further at nos. 28 and 29.

For a detailed analysis of the two general models of *renvoi* mentioned above, carried out from a technical point of view as well as from the standpoint of legislative policy, see Davì, 'Le renvoi', pp. 146 *et seq.*, 170 *et seq.*, 208 *et seq.*; *id.*, 'Ancora sulle finalità (e sui due diversi modelli) del rinvio nel diritto internazionale privato contemporaneo, *Riv dir int* (2014), pp. 1032–1107.

[38] The expression 'double *renvoi*' as opposed to 'single *renvoi*' is instead basically a figure of speech to indicate that, in relationships between the law of the forum and the foreign law referred to, which, whilst in turn referring back to the former, does however accept the *renvoi* to it, the occurrence can be described as if there were two *renvois*, one of them being the *renvoi* which is made by the foreign law to the law of the forum and which extends to its conflict-of-laws provisions, whilst the other is the *renvoi* that the law of the forum then carries out through these letter when they are called upon to operate a second time around by the new reference made to them by the foreign law: on this expression being incorrect from a technical point of view, see Davì, 'Le renvoi', pp. 167–168.

reducing proportionately the need to address the various different problems often involved by the application of a foreign law.[39] The use of this type of *renvoi* in fact leads to the *lex fori* being applied even where the foreign law which, on first blush, refers back to it, in turn makes use of the same type of *renvoi* and, therefore, considers in fact its own material provisions as being applicable in preference to those of the law of the forum. In cases such as these, the advantage of returning to the law of the forum is, however, secured at the double price of a voluntary distortion of the true intention of the foreign law and of the sacrifice of a uniformity of regulation in the relationship to the latter that would be perfectly achievable if the decision was taken to persist in the designation of its substantive rules that was made at the outset, albeit on a conditional basis, and which also corresponds with its actual position. So what the single *renvoi* actually sets out to achieve is the indiscriminate extension of the scope of application of the *lex fori* rather than establishing consistency with the point of view of the foreign law. If the desired result was instead the latter, the reference back would have to be accepted only once it had been established that the foreign law making that reference would not do the same. And where *renvoi* is to the law of a third country which is a non-Member State, here too the single *renvoi* proves to be of little effect in terms of coordination, given that an only partial consideration of the respective conflict-of-laws systems in the States involved can in some cases result in the intention of those systems being distorted, with one or other of them incorrectly being interpreted as intending to make a *renvoi*, where this is not in fact the case, or rejecting a reference that instead it actually accepts.[40]

23. Turning now to the total *renvoi*, in allowing a faithful reconstruction of both the position adopted by the conflict-of-laws system of the

[39] For a brief illustration of some of these difficulties, see nos. 6 and 18.

[40] For example, say a ruling is required in a particular Member State on the succession of a British citizen who was habitually resident, owned immovable property, and was domiciled (from the point of view of English law) in a non-EU country such as Egypt or Syria, where the deceased's national law applies in matters of succession and *renvoi* is not admitted. If article 34 were construed as meaning that it adopts the partial *renvoi*, the view would have to be taken that the reference made by Egyptian or Syrian law, designated by article 21 ESR, to English law is not accepted, given that, pursuant to the English choice-of-law rules, the succession of movable property is subject to the law of domicile, with the succession of immovable property being subject to the *situs rei*. Such a conclusion would, however, be mistaken as in reality English law would take account of the *renvoi* to it by Egyptian or Syrian law and, therefore, would agree on the applicability of its own substantive provisions.

foreign law designated at the outset and the respective positions of the conflict-of-laws systems of other laws that might be involved in the chain of references, this in fact permits the legal system of the forum to effectively secure coordination with the approaches adopted by the laws in question whenever this can in practice be achieved. In particular, in the event of a reference back to the *lex fori*, adoption of the total *renvoi* ensures uniformity of decisions in dealings with foreign laws that do not in fact admit *renvoi*, as well as with those that use the single *renvoi*. This objective is in practice achieved with *renvoi* being accepted or not, depending on whether the foreign State does or does not accept it, with the possibility in the former case of establishing with certainty that there is, quite simply, no real reference to the *lex fori* at all. By contrast, the single *renvoi* only paves the way for uniform results when dealing with foreign laws that reject *renvoi* and moreover, by refusing to check their actual positions, even when it achieves this result, does so on a random basis only. In fact, in relationships between two laws which, having divergent conflict-of-laws rules, initially refer to one another, harmony can be re-established by means of *renvoi* only where the positions adopted by the laws involved also diverge in terms of the *renvoi* itself: what is required, in more precise terms, is that one of them rejects it while the other one accepts it, or one adopts the single *renvoi* while the other adopts the total *renvoi*. In cases such as these, uniformity is restored because the two inconsistencies are offset against one another and cancel each other out. Conversely, in dealings between two laws that both use the single *renvoi*, there is no harmony created, with a simple exchange of the initial solutions taking place. It should be added that, where *renvoi* is to the law of a third country, here too the exhaustive nature of the appraisal of the foreign conflict-of-laws systems involved as a result of using the total *renvoi* means that the forum State is able to achieve a genuine degree of coordination with the positions adopted by those systems whenever possible in practice, and that, where these positions prove to be divergent, its final choice can be the one that it considers most suitable, based on a consideration of all the relevant information, without running the risk of misunderstandings.[41]

It is only where both the law of the forum and the foreign law that it designates at the outset (or, in the case of a *renvoi* to the law of a third State, the two foreign laws involved) adopt the total *renvoi* principle, that *renvoi* can no longer usefully play its intended role in terms of

[41] See the example at footnote 40.

coordination. In effect, with these two laws having no intention of accepting *renvoi* until they have established that it actually exists, each of them needs to accurately reconstruct the approach taken towards it by the other; however, as the position of the latter is also dependant on the position adopted by the former, neither of the two is able to provide or obtain a response.[42]

Where a situation such as this arises, the only suitable way to tackle it from the standpoint of systems that use this type of *renvoi* should consist in remaining loyal to the initial designation that they had made (albeit on conditional terms) of the material provisions of the foreign law. The suggested solution should be considered a logical implication of the adoption of the type of *renvoi* in question, which has as its sole objective to secure better coordination with the actual positions of the foreign legal systems and, therefore, makes the decision to abandon the substantive provisions of a certain foreign law chosen at the outset conditional upon establishing that the foreign law in question instead considers the provisions of the law of the forum to apply. It follows that, in the absence of certainty that the condition imposed is met, either because the designated law uses the single *renvoi* and, therefore, agrees on the applicability of its own substantive provisions, or because it also adopts the total *renvoi* and, therefore, its ultimate position depends on the decision taken on the point by the law of the forum itself, there are no reasons to justify abandoning the choice made initially.[43]

[42] Situations of this type rarely arise in practice. The first reason for this is that not all legal systems admit *renvoi*; those that do admit it do not all use the same type of *renvoi* and do not all apply it in the same cases. The second reason is that the total *renvoi* is mainly (although not exclusively) followed by common law countries, which, in most fields, adopt, as their starting point, choice-of-law rules that are similar or identical, thus somewhat restricting the opportunity for the *renvoi* problem to arise when dealing with one another. In matters of succession, such a situation arises for example in the relationship between Swiss law and the law of Louisiana. As mentioned previously (see footnote 34), in Switzerland, pursuant to article 91 of the act on private international law, the succession of a person who, at the time of death, was domiciled in a foreign country is subject to the law designated by the conflict-of-laws rules in force in the country in question, while article 3534 of the civil code of Louisiana dictates that succession in terms of immovable property located abroad is governed by the law that the courts in the State in which those assets are located would apply. It follows that the succession of immovable property located in Switzerland belonging to a deceased who was last domiciled in Louisiana should, in accordance with the law of the former country, be governed by the law designated by the conflict-of-laws system in the latter country (including its rules regarding *renvoi*) and vice versa.

[43] The solution put forward is one that is generally accepted by the legal literature in common law as well as civil law countries: see, amongst the authors in the former

24. There are various arguments in support of the view that article 34 should be construed as intending to adopt the total *renvoi*.[44] First and foremost, a clear indication that this interpretation is correct is provided by recital 57. This specifies that the *renvoi* 'either to the law of a Member State or to the law of a third State which would apply its own law ... should be accepted in order to ensure international consistency', making it clear that the particular purpose in using this device (not its only

group of countries, W. W. Cook, *The Logical and Legal Bases of the Conflict of Laws* (Cambridge, Mass., 1942), p. 244; J. B. Collier, *Conflict of Laws*, 2nd ed. (Cambridge, 1994), p. 26, footnote 54; M. Davies, A. Bell and P. Le Gay Brereton, *Nygh's Conflict of Laws in Australia*, 8th ed. (Chatswood, N.S.W., 2010), p. 326; of those belonging to the second group, M. Keller and K. Siehr, *Allgemeine Lehren des internationalen Privatrechts* (Zürich, 1986), p. 477; Bucher, *Droit international privé suisse*, vol. I, 2, *Partie générale – Droit applicable*, p. 124; H. Kuhn, *Der Renvoi im internationalen Erbrecht der Schweiz* (Zürich, 1998), pp. 384, 404; M. Sonnentag, *Der Renvoi im internationalen Privatrecht* (Tübingen, 2001), p. 301 *et seq.* Confirmation that this solution is in line with the logic behind the operation of the total *renvoi* is also provided by the fact that it is adopted by article 18 of the Portuguese civil code of 1966, this being the oldest legislative provision in a continental European country to expressly admit the type of *renvoi* in question. On the basis of this provision, the reference back to Portuguese law by a foreign law has to be accepted only on condition that it is directed exclusively at its 'internal' or substantive provisions (*o direito interno português*) and does not, therefore, take the provisions of its private international law into account.

[44] In favour of this interpretation, see Davì and Zanobetti, 'Il nuovo diritto internazionale privato delle successioni', p. 101 *et seq.*; Davì and Zanobetti, *Il nuovo diritto internazionale privato europeo*, p. 162 *et seq.*; R. Hausmann, 'Art. 4 EGBGB', in *J. von Staudingers Kommentar zum Bürgerlichen Gesetzbuch mit Einführungsgesetz und Nebengesetzen*, 15th ed. (Berlin, 2013), p. 154; Carrascosa González, *El Reglamento Sucesorio Europeo*, p. 288; E. Castellanos Ruiz, 'Sucesión hereditaria: Reglamento 650/2012 sobre sucesión internacional', in A.-L. Calvo Caravaca and J. Carrascosa González (eds), *Derecho Internacional Privado*, 15th ed., vol. II (Granada, 2014), p. 625 *et seq.*; see also, in more general terms, for the opinion that the total *renvoi* is the type of *renvoi* that should always be adopted by EU legal instruments relating to private international law that use this device, Siehr, 'General Problems of Private International Law', p. 44. The opposite interpretation to the effect that article 34 intended to adopt solely the model of single *renvoi* regardless of the fact that the *renvoi* is to the law of a Member State or to that of a non-Member State is instead favoured by E.-M. Bajons, 'Internationale Zuständigkeit und anwendbares Recht in Erbsachen', in M. Schauer and E. Scheuba (eds), *Europäische Erbrechtsverordnung (2012/650 EU vom 4. Juli 2012)* (Wien, 2012), p. 37. For a midway position, where the view is that article 34 admits the single or total *renvoi* depending on whether the reference made by the foreign law designated at the outset by the ESR's conflict-of-laws rules is to the law of a Member State or the law of a third country, see, expressly or impliedly, Solomon, 'Die Renaissance des Renvoi', p. 253 *et seq.*; Bonomi, 'Article 34', pp. 517, 519, footnote 15; H. Schack, 'Was bleibt vom Renvoi?', *IPRax*, 2013, p. 319; Greeske, *Die Kollisionsnormen*, p. 190 *et seq.*; Hohloch, 'Kommentierung der EuErbRVO', pp. 6717–6718; P. Kindler, 'Der Aktionär im toskanischen Lebensabend – Zum Kollisionsrecht der Testamentsgestaltung bei Auslandsdomizil unter der neuen EU-Erbverordnung', in *Festschrift für Eberhard Stilz* (München, 2014), p. 352.

purpose, but certainly its main one at least) is to attempt to secure coordination with the conflict-of-laws systems in place in third countries. Instead, the main objective of the single *renvoi* is to extend the scope of application of the internal law of the forum, including where this is to the detriment of coordination that could quite easily be achieved by accepting to precisely reconstruct the actual standpoint adopted by the foreign legal systems. Where this type of *renvoi* is concerned, securing international consistency is, therefore, a fringe benefit at best, attainable, on a conditional basis, only where it can be reconciled with achieving the principal purpose. With the total *renvoi*, conversely, the relationship between the two objectives is turned on its head: search for uniformity of decisions is the paramount objective here, and the practical result of returning to applying the substantive law of the forum may well be warmly welcomed but is in fact only a collateral and secondary advantage that can always be sacrificed where necessary in order to achieve the main purpose. And so there should be no room for doubt that the total *renvoi* is the type of *renvoi* that corresponds best with the purpose set out in recital 57.

25. An additional point to be considered is the fact that article 34 requires *renvoi* to be taken into account (i) when it is to the law of a non-Member State, which in turn considers that its own law applies and therefore 'accepts', as is said, that designation, and (ii) when it is to the law of a Member State. In the first of these two situations at least, recourse to this device can clearly have the sole objective of attempting to secure international consistency. Consequently, it has to be seen as a total and not a simple *renvoi*, since, as we have already underlined, it is very often the case that real consistency can only be secured via an exhaustive evaluation of the interaction between, and of the ultimate positions adopted by, the conflict-of-laws systems in place in the foreign legal orders involved.[45]

This leaves us with those cases in which *renvoi* is to the law of a Member State. It should be emphasised here that where these cases are concerned, article 34 makes no distinction on the basis of whether the law referred to is the law of the State of the forum itself or that of a *different* Member State. This calls for the two possible situations to be

[45] See no. 22, and in particular the example provided at footnote 40. As stated in footnote 44, the opportunity, for this reason, to construe the *renvoi* to the law of a third State as a total *renvoi* is also acknowledged either expressly or implicitly by at least a certain number of the authors who support the opposite interpretation regarding the *renvoi* to the law of a Member State.

treated in the same way. It follows that the argument that it is easier and quicker to understand, interpret and implement the *lex fori* than it is to work with the foreign laws originally designated (this being the argument traditionally employed in support of using the *renvoi* to the former mainly as a means of extending its scope of application) loses much of its weight, as it cannot be relied upon correspondently with regard to the laws of other Member States. It is in fact by no means certain that the ascertainment of the exact content and the practical application of the substantive provisions of the laws of all twenty-five 'Member States' (in the sense that this expression is used by the ESR: see no. 2) is necessarily a quicker and easier task for the seised court than the ascertainment and application of the law of every third country. And it is at least as questionable that these hypothetical advantages are capable of justifying a use of *renvoi* based on the voluntary misinterpretation of the foreign conflict-of-laws systems or the decision to forego the international consistency that might otherwise be achieved. It is significant here that the suggestion that a solution of this type be expressly provided for, as put forward by the Max-Planck-Institut für ausländisches und internationales Privatrecht during the course of the ESR preparatory work, was not taken up. The Max-Planck-Institut had in particular recommended that the ESR simply regulate the situation in which there was a *renvoi* to the law of a Member State, expressly adopting the partial type of *renvoi*, and that it be left to the court hearing the matter to resolve, on a case-by-case basis, the problems relating to a *renvoi* to the law of a third State, not least in view of the fact that such problems rarely arise.[46] The failure to accept this proposal, together with the fact

[46] See Max Planck Institute for Comparative and International Private Law, 'Comments', p. 656 ss. The amendment suggested by the Institute to the wording of article 26 of the initial proposal tabled by the Commission (which corresponds with the current article 34 ESR) was drafted as follows: 'Where this Regulation provides for the application of the law of a non-Member State, the rules of private international law of that State shall apply where they designate, as to matters of succession, the law of any Member State; the law of that Member State shall apply except for its rules of private international law'. In making *renvoi* admissible only where it was to the law of a Member State, the amendment basically put forward a solution that was the exact opposite of that adopted by the Hague Convention of 1989 on the Law Applicable to Succession to the Estates of Deceased Persons whose article 4 (see no. 5 and footnote 8) only admits *renvoi* which is effected to the law of a third State and which that law accepts. The characterisation of the type of *renvoi* envisaged by the amendment as a single or partial *renvoi* resulted clearly from the final clarification to the effect that the law of the Member State referred to should in all cases be applied 'except for its rules of private international law'.

that article 34 makes no distinction on the basis of the direction that the *renvoi* takes and consequently appears to conceive it as a unity, would seem to lend support to the view that it should always be treated as a total *renvoi*. As a result, paragraph 1(a) of the provision, which stipulates acceptance of *renvoi* by third countries' conflict-of-laws rules to the law of a Member State, has to be construed as calling for verification of the real existence of this *renvoi* (i.e. that it originates from a law which, in turn, does not accept the reference originally made to the law in question by the ESR).

26. Further support for this conclusion can be found in the fact that article 34 admits *renvoi* even where its acceptance leads to the territorial scission of the succession. As we have seen, the fundamental objective in adopting *renvoi* in its single version is to simplify the task faced by the court hearing the matter by replacing application of the foreign law with application of the law of the forum, with the aim of securing international consistency appearing much further down the list of priorities.[47] On the other hand, however, the drawbacks that scission can create are often at least as important than the problems that application of the foreign law usually gives rise to.[48] It would therefore be reasonable to conclude that, if admission of *renvoi* to the laws of the Member States had only had this limited aim of simplification, it would most probably have been excluded where it leads to scission; and this all the more so as there was some support, during the course of the preparatory work for the ESR, for the introduction of a restriction of this type, and similar solutions were also followed by the courts or legislation in certain Member States.[49]

VI. Solutions for Cases Where *Renvoi* Is Not Accepted by the Law of the Non-Member State to Which It Is Directed

27. Where *renvoi* by the law of a non-Member State initially designated by the ESR's conflict-of-laws rules is to the law of another non-Member

[47] This is generally also acknowledged by authors who hold the view that the *renvoi* adopted by article 34 should be taken as being a single *renvoi*: see Solomon, 'Die Renaissance des Renvoi', p. 253; Bonomi, 'Article 34', p. 517; Greeske, *Die Kollisionsnormen*, p. 190.

[48] See no. 19.

[49] For the authors who, during the course of the preparatory work for the ESR, had expressed an opinion in favour of the rejection of a *renvoi* that resulted in scission, see for example Siehr, 'Connecting Factors', p. 265; Dutta, 'Succession and Wills', p. 558 *et seq.*; Bonomi, 'Prime considerazioni', p. 911; for details on case law and legislation in the Member States before the ESR came into force, see footnote 33.

State, article 34.1(b) only regulates explicitly the situation in which the *renvoi* is accepted. Therefore a brief examination is necessary of those cases in which such an acceptance is missing. Rejection of *renvoi* can of course depend either by the fact that the law that it is directed towards in turn considers the substantive provisions of the law referring to it as being applicable or (and this is a less frequent occurrence) by the fact that the law referred to instead designates the law of yet another State (which could also be the law of the forum itself). The solution to be adopted in all such cases is always based on one principle alone: as article 34 establishes that *renvoi* is to be taken into account only where the law that it refers to agrees that it should be applied, whenever this requirement is not satisfied, the only option is to apply the substantive provisions of the law originally designated by the ESR. Whilst article 34 does not expressly set out this solution, it can be logically inferred by it through a simple *argumentum a contrariis*; in addition, a confirmation can be found in the provisions of internal legislation or in international conventions that similarly make admission of *renvoi* subject to the same requirement.[50]

28. In the first of the two cases previously mentioned, that is, where the law of the non-Member State that the *renvoi* refers to considers the substantive provisions of the law making that *renvoi* as being applicable, no particular problems arise: as the requirement that *renvoi* be accepted has not been met, the *renvoi* is not to be followed.[51] Where the law of the non-Member State that the *renvoi* points towards refers, instead, to another law, matters are complicated by the possibility that not only will this second *renvoi* be accepted, but that also the law which is at the

[50] See, for example, article 4.3 of the Venezuelan act on private international law of 1983 (*deberá aplicarse el Derecho interno del Estado que declare competente la norma venezolana de conflicto*) and article 21.2 of the Hague Convention of 1996 on Jurisdiction, Applicable Law, Recognition, Enforcement and Co-operation in Respect of Parental Responsibility and Measures for the Protection of Children ('If that other non-Contracting State would not apply its own law, the applicable law is that designated by Article 16').

[51] It is of course perfectly possible that it is rather the law initially making the *renvoi* that accepts the reference to it made in turn by the second law and that, as a consequence, not only is acceptance of the original *renvoi* missing, also missing is the actual *renvoi* itself. In such circumstances, the end result in terms of seeking international consistency would in practice be no different to the end result if the first *renvoi* was accepted, given that all of the laws making up the circuit would adhere to the solution adopted by the ESR, which, as we have seen, would involve maintaining application of the substantive provisions of the law that it had designated at the outset. For an example of this kind in German case law, where the seised court followed the total *renvoi* principle, see Landgericht Frankfurt a. M. 29 July 1997, *IPRspr 1997*, p. 232.

start of the chain of subsequent references is willing to take it into account, thereby falling in line with the common position of the other two. Situations of this type are certainly rare. In matters of succession an example of this kind could however be offered by the following situation. The law of the country in which the deceased had his last habitual residence, designated by article 21 ESR, refers to the law of his nationality. Following the principle of scission, the law of his nationality in turn makes a *renvoi* to the different law of the place in which one or more immovable property assets in the estate are located. The *renvoi* is accepted by that law and, in addition, the first law agrees with that *renvoi*. In theory, we could conceive a potential scenario involving an even longer sequence of *renvois* in which all of the laws in the chain end up agreeing that the last of them is the law that applies. Such situations differ from that in which *renvoi* is immediately accepted by the first law that it points towards only for the largest number of foreign laws involved. Consequently, the taking into account of this series of *renvois* by the legal system of the State of the forum allows international consistency to be achieved to an even greater extent and therefore is perfectly in line with the whole purpose behind a provision such as article 34 ESR, which makes admission of *renvoi* subject to the requirement that it ensures that a substantial degree of international uniformity of solutions is achieved. For this reason, some ESR commentators have expressed their favour for this interpretation.[52] There is, however, an opposing opinion, which is based mainly on the purely literal argument that the 'clear' wording of article 34 authorises the taking into account only of a *renvoi* made by the law originally designated by the ESR's conflict-of-laws rules, and not also of the subsequent *renvois* that might be made by different laws.[53] In reality, once it is acknowledged that when *renvoi* is to the law of a non-Member State, article 34 adopts the total *renvoi*,[54] a technically correct construction of how it operates should lead to the conclusion that the first interpretation is wholly in line not only with the spirit, but also the letter

[52] See Solomon, 'Die Renaissance des Renvoi', p. 255; M. Sonnentag, 'Das Europäische Internationale Erbrecht im Spannungsfeld zwischen der Anknüpfung an die Staatsangehörigkeit und den gewöhnlichen Aufenthalt', *Europäisches Wirtschafts- und Steuerrecht* (2012), p. 468; Bonomi, 'Article 34', p 518 *et seq*.

[53] For this interpretation see R. Hausmann, 'Art. 4 EGBGB', pp. 153–154; M. Stürner, 'Deutsch-italienische Erbfälle unter der kommenden Europäischen Erbrechtsverordnung', *Jahrbuch für italienisches Recht* 26 (2013), pp. 77–78; Carrascosa González, *El Reglamento Sucesorio Europeo*, p. 278; Castellanos Ruiz, 'Sucesión hereditaria', pp. 620, 622.

[54] See nos. 24–26 and, in particular, the references in footnote 44.

of the provision. For the purposes of establishing its actual existence, use of this type of *renvoi* in fact calls for an exhaustive appraisal of the content of the foreign conflict-of-laws system responsible for the first reference made and of the way that it interacts with the other conflict-of-laws systems involved.[55] It follows that where there is a sequence of references that winds up with a law which is willing to apply and is designated by all of the laws further up the chain, it is difficult to see how it can be denied that this law is referred to by the first to the same extent that it is referred to by all of the others. The result, as far as the State of the forum is concerned, is in fact that the law that its conflict-of-laws rule had originally referred to as being applicable makes a *renvoi* to another law (albeit having taken one or more foreign conflict-of-laws systems into account) that is accepted by that other law. Also from this standpoint, admission of *renvoi* would thus appear to be a reasonable interpretation of article 34.

29. The same conclusion should be reached, and for the same reasons, where, in a sequence of three or more *renvois* between foreign laws, the last of these laws, instead of accepting that it is the designated law, refers back to an intermediate law, provided that the latter agrees to being applied and where the first law, as well as any others further up the chain, is also in agreement. It is only when interruptions arise in the series of successive references that the 'accepted transmission' mechanism (i.e., to quote article 34.1(b), the *renvoi* 'to the law of a third State which would apply its own law') no longer works, and the substantive provisions of the law initially designated by the conflict-of-laws rules in place in the State of the forum must remain applicable. It should also be pointed out that in the case of what can be described as an 'indirect reference back' or an 'indirect remission', that is, where the sequence of *renvois* between foreign laws winds up by referring back to the law of the forum, the logic of the total *renvoi* implies that application of the substantive rules of the law of the forum in place of those of the law that it initially designated is subject to establishing that it is in line with the actual intention of all the foreign laws involved: the purpose of this type of *renvoi* is not an indiscriminate extension of the scope of application of the *lex fori* but an attempt to secure international uniformity of solutions.[56]

[55] See nos. 21–23, and, in particular, the example in footnote 40.

[56] For further analysis of this last situation and for a discussion of an old Austrian decision, see Davì, 'Le renvoi', cit., p. 246 *et seq.*

VII. Concluding Remarks

30. The analysis set out above demonstrates that, when correctly construed and applied, the type of *renvoi* adopted by the ESR frequently paves the way for a significant degree of consistency to be achieved with the positions adopted by foreign legal systems, whether *renvoi* is to the law of the State of the forum (remission) or to the law of a different State, be it a member or non-Member State (transmission). In particular, this is the result that can be secured in the first situation in dealings with countries that simply do not admit *renvoi* as well as countries that adopt the single *renvoi*, while in the second situation it can be achieved whenever all the foreign laws involved are in agreement, but at times even when the agreement exists only between some of them.[57] In practice, it is almost only when there is a reference back to the law of the forum by a law which, in turn, uses the total *renvoi* that coordination between the respective positions has to be completely abandoned. This is, however, something that rarely happens,[58] and that we currently come across in the main in dealings with common law States in relation to successions involving immovable assets located in a Member State that are part of the estate of a deceased whose last habitual residence was in a State in the first group.[59] Since they follow the principle of scission, common law countries make succession in relation to immovable property located abroad subject to the law of the *situs*, and in addition they admit the *renvoi* on the foreign court theory design. On the other hand, these countries generally deny their courts jurisdiction to rule on successions that concern immovable property located abroad,[60] and never make recognition of decisions handed down by foreign courts subject to the requirement that their conflict-of-laws rules have been observed. It follows from this that the want of consistency with the positions adopted by their private international law systems will remain, in the majority of cases, devoid of

[57] On this possibility, see no. 29. [58] On this subject, see footnote 42.

[59] The cases discussed at no. 20, where the occurrence of a *renvoi* can be the result of a difference in meaning that concepts such as domicile, residence or habitual residence may assume in the law of certain non-Member States compared to the concept of habitual residence adopted by the ESR, are of course more rare.

[60] This rule is followed in particular in the United States, Canada and Australia. An exception is represented by the UK, where jurisdiction regarding succession is understood in terms of jurisdiction to appoint a personal representative of the deceased and the courts may also exercise this type of jurisdiction, where they consider it appropriate to do so, even when the estate includes immovable property located abroad: see Fawcett, Carruthers and North, *Cheshire, North & Fawcett: Private International Law*, p. 1255, and the cases cited *ibid.*, footnote 13.

practical impact.[61] In such situations, the only drawback when interpreting *renvoi* adopted by article 34 as being total is losing the advantage of replacing the foreign law originally designated by the conflict-of-laws rules contained in the ESR with the law of the forum. In practice, however, this is arguably offset to a large extent by the advantage of the possibility of avoiding the difficulties that would arise as a result of the scission of the succession that acceptance of *renvoi* would often entail.

[61] See for a similar observation Siehr, 'Connecting Factors', p. 266.

Article 35

Public Policy (ordre public)

GIANLUCA CONTALDI AND CRISTINA GRIECO

The application of a provision of the law of any State specified by this Regulation may be refused only if such application is manifestly incompatible with the public policy (*ordre public*) of the forum.

Summary

I. THE BACKGROUND *page* 505
II. THE RESERVED SHARE OF THE ESTATE AND THE PROTECTION OF FORCED HEIRS 507
III. CASES INVOLVING DISCRIMINATORY LEGISLATION 512
IV. HEIRS UNWORTHY OF INHERITING 516
V. AGREEMENTS AS TO SUCCESSION 517
VI. THE CONSEQUENCES OF RECOURSE TO THE PUBLIC POLICY CLAUSE 518

I. The Background

1. The purpose of a public policy clause is, as well known, to limit the extent to which provisions of foreign law that the forum legal system finds wholly unacceptable are allowed to have effect. However, this limitation cannot be called into play in the presence of a mere discrepancy in the material provisions that govern the facts in question. This interpretation is supported by the use in article 35 of the expression 'manifestly incompatible', which is already featured in most conventions drawn up by the Hague Conference on Private International Law[1] as well as the private international law instruments adopted by the EU institutions. Additionally, recital 58 ESR specifies that only 'considerations of

[1] In matters of succession, see article 7 of the Convention of 5 October 1961 on the Conflicts of Laws Relating to the Form of Testamentary Dispositions, article 17 of the Convention of 2 October 1973 Concerning the International Administration of the Estates of Deceased Persons and article 18 of the Convention of 1 August 1989 on the Law Applicable to Succession to the Estates of Deceased Persons.

public interest in exceptional circumstances' can result in the law designated by the ESR conflict-of-laws provisions not being applied.

2. It is worth pointing out that the EU legislator considered it unnecessary to draw up different rules depending on whether the foreign provisions in question originate from third countries or from Member States, with the result that the legislation in force in the latter group does not benefit from any special treatment.[2]

3. The need to safeguard the fundamental principles of the law of the forum arises whenever foreign legal values are to be taken into account within the forum legal system. It is on this basis that this exception can also be relied upon and operates in relation to judgments handed down in another State or authentic instruments drawn up in a foreign legal system.[3]

4. Although there are significant differences in the substantive law in force in the various countries, the exception on the grounds of public policy is likely to play a fairly limited role; this is explained firstly by the parallelism between *forum* and *jus* that the ESR sets out to achieve.[4] In practical terms, article 35 can only come into operation where the ESR grants jurisdiction to the court of a country other than that whose law is to govern the succession. This can come about as a result of a choice of applicable law [see art. 22], not accompanied by a choice of forum according to article 5 *et seq.*, or as a result of certain assets that form part of the estate being located in the State in which the court hearing the matter is sitting [see art. 10] or, finally, where jurisdiction is exercised on the basis of what is referred to as *forum necessitatis* [see art. 11].

5. But here, too, it is by no means certain that the public policy of the forum can in fact come into play. Whilst the wording of the ESR is silent on the point, it would be reasonable to conclude that the public policy clause can only operate where there is a sufficiently close connection

[2] J. Carrascosa González, *El Reglamento Sucesorio Europeo 650/2012 de 4 de julio 2012: Análisis crítico* (Granada, 2014), p. 260. For a restrictive interpretation of the public policy limitation in cases in which the law of another EU Member State is to be applied, see instead I. A. Calvo Vidal, 'El Derecho de sucesiones en la Unión Europea. Ley aplicable y carácter universal de la nueva normativa en materia de sucesiones', *Noticias de la Unión Europea* (2012), pp. 104–105.

[3] Cf. article 40 ESR, which concerns recognition of judgments handed down in other Member States; article 59.1, which deals with the evidentiary value of authentic instruments established in other Member States; article 60.3, on enforceability of foreign authentic instruments; article 61.3, which concerns enforceability of court settlements.

[4] A. Davì and A. Zanobetti, 'Il nuovo diritto internazionale privato delle successioni nell'Unione europea', *CdT* 5/2 (2013), p. 106; A. Davì and A. Zanobetti, *Il nuovo diritto internazionale privato europeo delle successioni* (Torino, 2014), p. 17 *et seq.*

between the legal relationship at issue and the forum itself (*Inlandsbeziehung*).[5] Where the link is too tenuous, it is difficult to envisage the fundamental values of the internal system being infringed. In conclusion, where the grounds for establishing jurisdictional competence are taken together with the provisions of article 35 ESR, the assumption can be made that where public policy steps in, this can certainly be justified when the State of the forum is the last habitual residence of the deceased or the country whose the deceased was a national, or houses some of the assets that make up the estate. Conversely, the public policy of the forum should only come into play with great caution in the absence of strong links with the case in question, as might at times occur where the jurisdiction is grounded on article 10 ESR (in particular when the jurisdiction is exercised also on assets not situated in the forum country) or on article 11 ESR (*forum necessitatis*).[6]

II. The Reserved Share of the Estate and the Protection of Forced Heirs

6. Let us now turn to the most relevant groups of cases in which public policy can come into play. One of the main areas of succession law in which public policy can have an impact concerns the rules on the reserved share. There is a difference here in terms of how civil law countries and common law jurisdictions operate. The former, albeit with variances, consider that part of the estate cannot be disposed of at will, while the latter place no restrictions on the freedom to dispose of one's estate and generally do not provide for reserved shares.

7. Although provisions regarding the reserved share are usually considered as mandatory, it is less certain that they form part of the public policy of the State which has enacted them.[7] The case law of the Member States courts would appear to lean away from treating foreign laws that do not establish a reserved share for the deceased's relatives as

[5] This theory was developed for the first time by F. Kahn, 'Die Lehre vom ordre public (Proibitivgesetze)', *Jherings Jahrbücher für die Dogmatik des bürgerlichen Rechts* (1898), p. 13, and then worked on by other authors (see M. Wolff, *Das Internationale Privatrecht Deutschlands* (Berlin, 1954), p. 66; P. Lagarde, *Recherches sur l'ordre public en droit international privé* (Paris, 1959), p. 59 *et seq.*).

[6] See A. Bonomi, 'Article 35', in A. Bonomi and P. Wautelet eds *Le droit européen des successions (Commentaire du Règlement n° 650/2012 du 4 juillet 2012)* (Bruxelles, 2013), pp. 572–528.

[7] G. Khairallah, 'La détermination de la loi applicable à la succession', in G. Khairallah and M. Revillard (eds), *Droit européen des successions internationales* (Paris, 2013), p. 56 *et seq.*

being absolutely contrary to public policy.[8] Despite this, the views expressed when the regulation was in the pipeline appear to differ somewhat on this point, and due account should, therefore, be taken of them.

8. The most radical position is that adopted by the French Senate and the French Society of Notaries, who, while the preparatory work was underway, claimed that the provisions governing the reserved share were mandatory for French citizens.[9] It should, however, be pointed out that in France the importance of public policy on a practical level as a means

[8] In Italian case law, a foreign law that did not establish a reserved share was considered contrary to public policy by the Tribunale Sanremo 31 December 1984, *Riv dir int priv proc* (1986), p. 341 and by the Corte d'appello di Milano 4 December 1992, *Riv dir int priv proc* (1994), p. 821. The latter decision was, however, overturned by the Corte di cassazione 24 June 1996, n. 5832, *Nuova giur civ* (1997), pp. 167–169, with the clarification that the reserved portion of the estate is not included in the list of provisions 'that go to make up public policy'. For decisions on the same lines as this ruling by the Supreme Court, see Tribunale Termini Imerese 15 July 1965, *Giurisprudenza siciliana* (1965), p. 784 *et seq.* and Tribunale Chiavari 25 February 1974, *Riv dir int priv proc* (1977), p. 379 *et seq.* German case law (Bundesgerichtshof 21 April 1993, *IPRax* (1994), p. 375 *et seq.*) takes the view that the absence in the foreign law of reserved portion cannot result in public policy being infringed. Nevertheless, the German Constitutional Court has said that the reserved share principle cannot be derogated where it is justified by the need to protect the State from claims by disinherited heirs who find themselves on the breadline, or where those entitled to the reserved portion are children: see Bundesverfassungsgericht 19 April 2005, *NJW* (2005), p. 1561. As for Spain, see, on the same line, the two decisions of the Tribunal supremo 15 November 1966, *Lowenthal, Rev esp der int* (1997), p. 264, and 21 May 1999, *Denney, Rev esp der int* (1999), p. 756. Also in Switzerland, the possibility of public policy operating here was ruled out in the well-known judgment of the Tribunal fédéral 17 August 1976, *Hirsch* v. *Cohen, Arrêts du Tribunal fédéral*, vol. 102, II, p. 136. In literature see E. Vitta, *Diritto internazionale privato*, vol. III (Torino, 1975), p. 132; S. Othenin-Girard, *La réserve d'ordre public en droit international privé suisse* (Zurich, 1999), p. 595; B. Audit, *Droit international privé* (Paris, 2000), p. 750 *et seq.*; M. Virgós Soriano and E. Rodríguez Pineau, 'Succession Law and Renvoi: the Spanish Solution', in *Festschrift für Erik Jayme* (München 2004), vol. I, p. 977 ss.; F. M. Wilke, 'Das internationale Erbrecht nach der neuen EU-Erbrechtsverordnung', *RIW* (2012), p. 607; Davì and Zanobetti, 'Il nuovo diritto internazionale privato delle successioni', pp. 108–109; Davì and Zanobetti, *Il nuovo diritto internazionale privato europeo*, pp. 175–176.

[9] During the course of the preparatory work for the ESR, having pointed out that 'le principe de la réserve héréditaire, traduction juridique d'un véritable devoir moral, constitue une règle essentielle du droit français' on 21 February 2006, the French Senate adopted a resolution calling upon the government to 'veiller à ce que le texte finalement adopté garantisse que l'application des règles déterminant la loi applicable ne puisse permettre à un ressortissant français de faire échapper sa succession au mécanisme de la réserve héréditaire'. In similar vein, it was stated in the proposals put forward by the 108th notaries' congress in France that 'il faudrait, pour que la réserve héréditaire puisse être opposée à l'application d'une loi étrangère, qu'elle soit considérée comme faisant partie de l'ordre public international' (see http://2012.congresdesnotaries.fr/l-ouvrage-du-108eme-congres, last accessed 30 June 2016).

of protecting the reserved share was, up until a short time ago, minimal, given the effect in this particular system of the mechanism known as *prélèvement,* which allowed French heirs to take over the assets located in France to the extent of the value of assets that, being located abroad, were beyond their reach.[10]

9. Positioned right at the other end of the spectrum is the theory that states that the provisions regarding the reserved share are not part of the public policy of the forum in any shape or form. On the basis of this approach, the provisions regarding the part of the estate that cannot be disposed of at will only apply where they form part of the law governing the succession.[11] Support for this conclusion would appear to be offered by the framework that the ESR seems to have established. Expectations of the heirs entitled to a forced share would in any event be poorly protected in a system that worked on the basis of the connecting factor of the habitual residence of the deceased. The testator could in fact always decide to establish residence in a country that makes no provision for reserved shares or recognises them only in part.[12] Added to this is the fact that the possibility pursuant to article 22 ESR to choose the applicable law

[10] This mechanism, which was recently declared unconstitutional by the Conseil constitutionnel 5 August 2011, no. 159, could also explain the lack of any established practice. Some relevance here has the well-known *Caron* case, Cour d'appel Aix-en-Provence 9 March 1982, *Rev crit dr int priv* (1983), p. 282 *et seq.*, with notes by G. Droz. The deceased, a former French citizen naturalised American, was domiciled in the Virgin Islands and owned real estate in France. He had set up a company in the Virgin Islands, with his capital contribution to this company taking the form of the real estate, with the result that, where his personal assets were concerned, that real estate was replaced by shares in the company; in contrast to the real estate transferred to the company, those shares, being securities, were subject to the law of the domicile, instead of the law of the *situs*. This somewhat complex series of steps had been put in train in order to avoid application of the provisions of French law concerning the reserve owed to the deceased's children (and of the *droit de prélèvement* enjoyed by the daughter having French citizenship). Such mechanism was anyway swept aside by the French judges, who declared the transfer of the real estate to the company to be of no effect in France as the whole purpose behind it was to circumvent the law.

[11] See T. Ballarino, 'Le successioni nel diritto internazionale privato italiano', *Riv not* (1986), pp. 1, 6; M. Revillard, *Droit international privé et communautaire: pratique notariale*, 7th ed. (Paris, 2010), no. 716; D. Bureau and H. Muir-Watt, *Droit international privé*, vol. II (Paris, 2007), no. 843. See also the position adopted by the European Group for Private International Law: 'Réponse du GEDIP au livre vert de la Commission européenne sur les successions et testaments', which can be found on the Group's website at www.gedip-egpil.eu/gedip_documents.html (last accessed 6 July 2016)

[12] A. Davì, 'Riflessioni sul futuro diritto internazionale privato europeo delle successioni', *Riv dir int* (2005), p. 324 *et seq.*

suggests that a law could be designated that also provides very little protection to the rights of the forced heirs. The decision of a person to submit the succession to his or her national law rather than to the law in force in the place of residence could be dictated precisely by the desire to choose a legislation that appears more flexible in this regard.[13]

10. There are signs that the EU legislator has accepted in principle the consequences of the freedom afforded to the testator to change the law governing the succession of his estate;[14] in striking a balance between the interests of the testator and those of his close relatives, it would then appear that the decision taken was in favour of the former.[15] Besides, this approach reflects trends that can be identified in many countries. A comparative analysis demonstrates that newly-introduced mechanisms allow the testator in many cases to plan his succession in advance, with the effects of the provisions regarding the reserved share of the estate being reduced or even cancelled altogether as a result.[16]

11. Nevertheless, also the approach that sees the protection of the reserved share being brought exclusively within the scope of the *lex causae* has met with a degree of disapproval. In this regard, the fact that the text of the ESR does not contain a specific reference to the problem of the reserved share is of some relevance. This aspect takes on particular significance when its final wording is set against the proposal submitted

[13] It is in any event fairly rare to come across a case in which the choice of law has in fact been dictated by a desire to shut the door on the heirs entitled to the reserved share: see A. Davì, 'L'autonomie de la volonté en droit international privé des successions dans la perspective d'une future réglementation européenne', in *Les successions internationales dans l'UE: perspectives pour une harmonisation* (Würzburg, 2004), p. 389.

[14] F. M. Wilke, 'Das internationale Erbrecht nach der neuen EU-Erbrechtsverordnung', *RIW* (2012), p. 601 *et seq.*

[15] Davì, 'Riflessioni', p. 324.

[16] These mechanisms may include: gifts *mortis causa*, contracts in favour of third parties, trusts, deposits, and life insurance policies in favour of third parties. In addition, legal systems that traditionally tend to reign in the testator's autonomy have, in recent times, introduced new possibilities, such as the Italian 'patto di famiglia' in relation to family business (introduced by law no. 55 of 2006) and, in France, the possibility of waiving in advance the right to take action to recover the reserved share (introduced by law no. 728 of 2006): see A. Braun, 'Towards a Greater Autonomy for Testators and Heirs: Some Reflections on Recent Reforms in France, Belgium and Italy', *ZeuP* (2012), p. 461 *et seq.* Introduction of new methods of dealing with succession in advance has been supported by the EU Commission: see Recommendation 94/1069/EC of 7 December 1994 on the transfer of small and medium-sized enterprises submitted by the Commission to the Member States on 7 December 1994, OJ L 385, 31 December 1994, p. 14 *et seq.* On this point, see also Davì and Zanobetti, 'Il nuovo diritto internazionale privato delle successioni', p. 110; Davì and Zanobetti, *Il nuovo diritto internazionale privato europeo*, p. 109.

in 2009 by the Commission, which, in article 27.2, specifically established that 'the application of a rule of the law determined by this Regulation may not be considered to be contrary to the public policy of the forum on the sole ground that its clauses regarding the reserved portion of an estate differ from those in force in the forum'.[17] The fact that this clause was deleted from the final text of the ESR suggests that the regulation is not wholly insensitive to the need to safeguard forced heirs. Proof of this can be found in recital 50, which clarifies that application of the law that governs the admissibility, substantive validity of dispositions upon death and the binding effect of agreements as to succession 'should be without prejudice to the rights of any person who, under the law applicable to the succession, has a right to a reserved share'.

12. Accordingly, consideration on a case-by-case basis is called for. In principle, public policy should not be called into play in the following situations: where the reserved share established by the governing law of the succession is smaller than that established by the law of the *forum*, unless it is significantly so; where the foreign law allows the usufruct of an asset that forms part of the estate rather than title to it;[18] where the foreign law establishes that there is an entitlement only to a monetary compensation, while the law of the *forum* recognises title to a share of the assets of the estate; where, whilst not allocating a share of the estate to someone who would, pursuant to the law of the forum, be entitled by law to inherit, the governing law acknowledges that he or she is, however, entitled to receive an allowance out of the estate;[19] where the methods established by the succession law for calculating the reserved share and the available hereditary mass differ from those established in the forum.[20]

13. Public policy is also incapable of preventing succession law from being applied where the categories of people thereby entitled to the reserved share differ from those established by the law of the forum. It should be pointed out here that, albeit in differing fashion, every

[17] This provision had met with criticism on the grounds that it was rather unclear and ambiguous. See on this point H. Dörner, 'Der Entwurf einer europäischen Verordnung zum internationalen Erb-und Erbverfahrensrecht- Überblick und ausgewählte Probleme', *ZEV* (2010), p. 221 *et seq*; A. Bonomi, 'Testamentary freedom or forced heirship? Balancing party autonomy and the protection of family members', *NIPR* (2010), p. 605 *et seq*.

[18] As established by legislation in certain countries – e.g. article 834 of the Spanish civil code – in favour of the surviving spouse.

[19] This is generally what happens in the German system: see section 2303 BGB.

[20] In Italy and in other legal systems, for example, gifts made during the lifetime of the deceased can be brought back into the estate by virtue of what is referred to as clawback.

legislation that provides safeguards for forced heirs does cater for descendants and, often the spouse (or, in certain cases, the partner).[21] Certain systems, however, also establish a reserve for ascendants and collateral relatives, often only in the absence of anyone else with succession rights; the very fact that such provisions generally have a subsidiary nature suggests that this is not a fundamental principle that might become relevant within the framework of the public policy exception.[22]

14. Things are different when the risk exists that the succession law ignoring the reserved share leaves without safeguard the two categories of relatives who are considered as deserving protection by the majority of the legal systems, i.e. children not of age and the surviving spouse. Here, steps need to be taken in order to establish whether, pursuant to the foreign law that has to be applied, sufficient protection can somehow still be secured, albeit via different mechanisms.[23] When this investigation gives a negative result, recourse to public policy can reasonably be considered not to be excluded.[24]

III. Cases Involving Discriminatory Legislation

15. Other situations in which we might see public policy invoked are where the governing law contains provisions that are discriminatory. Recital 58 ESR in fact refers specifically to article 21 of the Charter of Fundamental Rights of the European Union, which prohibits unfair

[21] For the relevant legislation, see Davì and Zanobetti, *Il nuovo diritto internazionale privato europeo*, p. 6, footnote 14.

[22] A. Bonomi, 'Il regolamento europeo sulle successioni', *Riv dir int priv proc* (2013), p. 293 *et seq.*

[23] For example, where during his lifetime, the testator made spontaneously, in one way or another, adequate provision for his close relatives, or where recourse can be had to the elective share mechanism used in the majority of the territorial legal systems in place in the United States, this being seen as an acceptable alternative to the reserved share. In common law systems that differ from that in the United States, family provisions are widely used: whilst not wholly comparable to the concept of the reserved share of the estate (see E. Calò, *Le successioni nel diritto internazionale privato* (Milano, 2007), p. 58), these nevertheless afford protection to the close relatives of the deceased. One example here is section 1 (1) of the Inheritance (Provision for Family and Dependants) Act (as amended in 1995) in force in England and Wales, which provides that a surviving spouse, child or anyone maintained by a person who, at the time of death, was domiciled in England or Wales can apply to the court for financial provision 'on the ground that the disposition of the deceased's estate effected by his will or the law relating to intestacy, or the combination of his will and that law, is not such as to make reasonable financial provision for the applicant'.

[24] See Davì, 'Riflessioni', p. 322.

discrimination.[25] In terms of succession, discrimination might in particular arise where, on the grounds of religion, sex, sexual orientation or, finally, membership of a particular social class, the law governing the succession rules out certain persons who would otherwise be entitled to succeed.[26] Discrimination on these lines can affect the categories of persons entitled to succeed as well as the allocation of the reserved shares of the estate.

16. Differences in the laws in force have become more accentuated over recent years as a result of certain States recognising same-sex couples. From the point of view of succession, legislation in countries that recognise such couples often – but not always – equate the partner to a spouse.[27] An examination of the effect of public policy here must take into consideration the ruling by the European Court of Human Rights in the well-known *Karner* case,[28] which established that legislation in a country that prevented a partner from succeeding to the tenancy of his homosexual cohabitee was in breach of articles 8 and 14 of the convention. As a consequence, in the case of EU countries that do not contemplate same-sex partnerships, the partner or spouse's succession rights established by the law governing succession should not to be treated as being in conflict with public policy.[29] The prohibition on discrimination on the grounds of sex or sexual orientation should, therefore, operate to prevent same-sex partnerships being stripped off any effect.[30] As matters currently

[25] This provision reads as follows: 'Any discrimination based on any ground such as sex, race, colour, ethnic or social origin, genetic features, language, religion or belief, political or any other opinion, membership of a national minority, property, birth, disability, age or sexual orientation shall be prohibited' ; see H. Gaudemet-Tallon, Le pluralisme en droit international privé: richesses et faiblesses, *'Hague Recueil'*, vol. 312 (2005), pp. 271 *et seq.*, 424–434; J. Meeusen, 'Le droit international privé et le principe de non-discrimination', *Hague Recueil*, vol. 353 (2012), p. 137 *et seq.*

[26] M. Revillard, 'Successions internationales: le règlement du Parlement européen et du Conseil du 4 juillet 2012 en matière de successions', *Defrenois* (2012), p. 749; M. Grimaldi, 'Brèves réflexions sur l'ordre public et la réserve héréditaire', *Defrenois* (2012), p. 757. For an analysis of the rules established in this respect by the Islamic succession law see A. Hussain, *The Islamic Law of Succession* (Riyadh, 2005); A. K. Pattar, *Islamisch inspiriertes Erbrecht und deutscher Ordre public. Die Erbrechtsordnungen von Ägypten, Tunesien und Marokko und ihre Anwendbarkeit im Inland* (Berlin, 2007), p. 20 *et seq.*

[27] See Davì and Zanobetti, *Il nuovo diritto internazionale privato europeo*, p. 5, footnote 11.

[28] ECtHR, judgment of 24 July 2003, *Karner* v. *Austria*, no. 40016/98, para. 41.

[29] In Italy, even before the adoption of a law on civil unions (law 20 May 2016, no. 76), the Corte di cassazione 5 March 2012, no. 4184, *Riv dir int priv proc* (2012), p. 747, stated that a homosexual couple is entitled to claim before the court a similar treatment to that guaranteed by the law to a married couple.

[30] Davì and Zanobetti, 'Il nuovo diritto internazionale privato delle successioni', p. 109 *et seq.*; Davì and Zanobetti, *Il nuovo diritto internazionale privato europeo*, p. 173.

stand, this approach finds also support in the adoption of the recent EU regulation on the property consequences of registered partnerships which clearly demonstrates, if there was still any doubt, that most Member States do not consider as contrary to public policy this type of legal relationships.[31] Moreover, it should be pointed out that a failure to recognise that a partner has succession rights might even amount to a restriction on the freedom of movement within the Union; this is in fact the situation that would arise in the event that succession rights acquired abroad by a partner are denied recognition.

17. Similarly, inheritance rights on the part of children of homosexual couples, including adopted children, should also be recognised, and this includes where the law of the forum does not open the door to these couples to adopt. Recognition of the succession rights that derive from this type of partnership does not in fact necessarily presuppose the recognition of the relationship itself.

18. A further issue concerns succession rights deriving from relationships foreign to the tradition of the Western legal systems, such as polygamous marriages, which are a source of discrimination towards women and thus directly contravene the principle enshrined by article 5 of Protocol No. 7 to the ECHR. However, this does not prevent those marriages from producing effects where succession is concerned.[32] First and foremost, excluding such succession rights would further aggravate a situation that is already discriminatory: if the second marriage entered into by the deceased was not given effect in this respect, the second wife would suffer prejudice twice, not only by being deprived of all rights over her husband's succession, but also as she would be unable to make a claim for maintenance against the estate.

19. Recognising the effects of a polygamous marriage might, however, not be sufficient; in some circumstances, the judge might also be called

[31] Council Regulation (EU) 2016/1104 of 24 June 2016 implementing enhanced cooperation in the area of jurisdiction, applicable law and the recognition and enforcement of decisions in matters of the property consequences of registered partnerships.

[32] On the succession rights recognised in France to the second wife in a polygamous marriage, see J. Déprez, 'Droit international privé et conflits de civilisations. Aspects méthodologiques. Les relations entre systèmes d'Europe occidentale et systèmes islamiques en matière de statut personnel', *Hague Recueil*, vol. 211 (1988), p. 163. In Italy, the Corte di cassazione 2 marzo 1999, n. 1739, *Riv dir int priv proc* (1999), p. 613 stated that the polygamous marriage does not exclude inheritance rights of the surviving wifes. In the literature, see G. Conetti, 'La successione del musulmano poligamo', *Studium Juris* (1997), p. 247 *et seq.*; V. Zambrano, 'Ordine pubblico e matrimonio contratto all'estero secondo il rito mussulmano', *Famiglia e diritto* (1999), p. 327 *et seq.*

upon to adapt the provisions of the internal legislation.[33] As is well known, adaptation is a complex procedure, and one that requires the courts to employ a certain degree of creativity. In addition, the success on a practical level of the efforts that can be done in this direction depends on a wide range of factors, including the amount of discretion afforded to the judges and the limitations imposed by the *lex causae* in shaping the succession. An exploration of this type of problems, however, falls largely outside the scope of an analysis of the ESR, as their solution mainly depends on the structure and general features of each individual law system.

20. Turning now to the relationship between parents and children, the European Court of Human Rights criticised a provision of French law that stipulated that children born out of wedlock were entitled to less favourable treatment in terms of succession.[34] This is an issue that could come to the fore today especially in relation to the application of laws based on Muslim traditions. Islamic law in fact only recognises legitimate filiation,[35] with the result that children born out of wedlock have no inheritance rights on their father's estate. In such circumstances, the court of a Member State should rule out application of the foreign law that prevents children born out of wedlock from having inheritance rights.

21. Certain situations can also arise in Muslim countries that involve discrimination on the grounds of religion. In many of these States, a clear distinction is made between the persons entitled to succeed, depending on whether they follow the religion of Islam; generally, those who do not are deprived of any succession rights at all.[36] In European countries, discrimination based on religion is contrary both to the principle of

[33] For instance, in the well-known *Bendeddouche* case, which concerned the inheritance of the estate of a polygamous Muslim, the French Cour de cassation took the share reserved under French law for the surviving spouse (being one-third of the estate) and divided it equally between the deceased's two wives, awarding them one-sixth of the estate each (Cour de cassation 3 January 1980, *Rev crit dr int priv* (1980), p. 331).

[34] ECtHR, *Mazurek* v. *France*, 1 February 2000, no. 34406/97. France modified the law in 2001; the European Court of Human Rights further ruled that the right to inherit had to be granted also to children born under the old regime (ECtHR, *Fabris* v. *France*, 7 February 2013, no. 16574/08).

[35] Also adoption is forbidden by the Koran (sura XXXIII: 'God has not made for any man two hearts in his inside ... nor has He made your adopted sons your real sons'). To protect minors who are in need, the concept of *kafala* was established, which involves a *kafil* (or a *kafil* couple) undertaking – in the presence of a judge or a notary – to care for the child, but without any relationship of filiation being acquired: see C. Campiglio, 'Il diritto di famiglia islamico nella prassi italiana', *Riv dir int priv proc* (2008), p. 43 *et seq.*

[36] See the legislative provisions in force in some of these countries as set out in the volume S. Aldeeb Abu Sahlieh and A. Bonomi (eds), *Le droit musulman de la famille et des successions à l'épreuve des ordres juridiques occidentaux*, (Zurich, 1999), p. 309 *et seq.*

equality and to the right to freedom of religion.[37] It is therefore reasonable to believe that here, too, public policy can be invoked to set aside foreign law.

22. Finally, the legislation in Muslim countries that follow the Sharia affords different treatment to persons entitled to succeed, depending on their gender. The rules of the Koran in particular lay down that the children of the deceased are to be allocated different shares of the estate, depending on whether they are male or female.[38] This clear breach of the principle of equality does seem to justify a limitation based on public policy.[39]

IV. Heirs Unworthy of Inheriting

23. Turning now to the issue of heirs who are deemed unworthy of inheriting, public policy might arguably come into play where, in contrast to the law of the forum, the foreign law does not contemplate disinheritance as a result of conduct that is considered particularly despicable or offensive, such as an attempt on the life of the person whose estate is involved or one of his close relatives. Beyond this possible scenario, differences in the rules establishing the grounds on which an heir is considered unworthy of inheriting should not, as a rule, justify

[37] Bonomi, 'Article 35', p. 534. See, for example, in French case law Cour de cassation 21 November 2002, *JurisData* n. 2012–026552, which ruled that provisions that make succession rights subject to religious conversion and which disinherit heirs where they do not follow a certain religion, are in breach of the European Convention on Human Rights.

[38] The Koran 4:176 states in this regard that 'if there are brothers and sisters, the male will have twice the share of the female'.

[39] There is however little case law to consider here. One case of interest is Landgericht Hamburg 12 February 1991, *IPRechtssprechung 1991*, p. 264 ss., which held that the rule of Islamic law (this particular case involved Iranian law) that dictates that daughters receive half the amount allocated to sons does not fall foul of German public policy, at least when applied to persons who are members of that particular culture of their own choosing, on the basis that it is also possible under German law for a parent to leave different shares of their estate to each of their children by means of a will. These days, such provisions are also felt to a certain degree to be unfair in a number of Muslim countries; a parent can also get around the provisions at issue by making gifts to his children, given that under Islamic law the mechanism whereby certain *inter vivos* gifts are to be returned to the estate does not exist. This solution could also provide a remedy for the problems raised by the fact that a non-Muslim cannot inherit from a Muslim and to a non-Muslim wife therefore being excluded from the group of persons entitled to succeed. The relative lack of case law on this point might therefore also be explained by the fact that, without infringing the precepts of the Sharia, a Muslim is in any event at liberty to dispose of his assets by executing a will in relation to the disposable part or by resorting to gifts. See on this point Davì and Zanobetti, *Il nuovo diritto internazionale privato europeo*, p. 172.

recourse to public policy, simply amounting to a discrepancy in the substantive provisions that govern this concept.

V. Agreements as to Succession

24. The different degree of freedom enjoyed by the testator pursuant to the different legislations also affects the possibility of entering into agreements as to succession or organising other forms of estate planning. In certain legal systems, such mechanisms play an important role in the transmission of family wealth. The differences that can be identified here raise a question mark over the extent to which legal systems that are unfamiliar with these concepts or even expressly forbid them can invoke public policy as a remedy. Article 25 ESR establishes which law governs the admissibility and the validity of agreements as to succession [see art. 25]. This suggests that the intention of the European legislator was to pave the way for rights arising out of a succession agreement to be accepted also in Member States where this form of disposition is forbidden. Case law and legal literature in these countries generally lean towards such prohibition not being considered as part of public policy.[40] Also the preference displayed by the European legislator in favour of succession agreements does in fact support the most plausible

[40] In case law, see, in Italy, Tribunale Bolzano 8 March 1969, *Rivista giuridica dell'Alto Adige* (1968), p. 220; in France, Cour d'appel Aix-en-Provence 16 October 2003, *Rev crit dr int priv*, p. 589 with a comment by P. Lagarde. In the Italian literature, the fact that in Italy a foreign law allowing succession agreements is compatible with public policy is recognised by most authors: see P. Picone, 'La legge applicabile alle successioni', in *La riforma del diritto internazionale privato e i suoi riflessi sull'attività notarile* (Milano, 1991), p. 99; A. Migliazza, 'Successione – VII), Diritto internazionale privato e processuale', in *Enciclopedia Giuridica*, XXX (Roma, 1993), p. 6; P. De Cesari, *Autonomia della volontà e legge regolatrice delle successioni* (Padova, 2001), p. 171; Davì, 'Riflessioni', p. 330; B. Barel, 'La disciplina dei patti successori', in P. Franzina and A. Leandro (eds), *Il diritto internazionale privato europeo delle successioni* mortis causa (Milano, 2013), pp. 136–138. In France, by contrast, some authors would appear to lean towards succession agreements that are subject to foreign law being treated as being of no effect: see Grimaldi, 'Brèves réflexions sur l'ordre public', pp. 757–760, and, albeit in less clear-cut terms, J. Foyer, 'Reconnaissance, acceptation et exécution des jugements étrangers, des actes authentiques et des transaction judiciares', in G. Khairallah and M. Revillard (eds), *Droit européen des successions internationales*, p. 148. In Spain succession agreements are not considered as being contrary to public policy, with one reason being that they are permitted by the *derechos forales* in the Balearic Islands, Catalonia and Aragon: see S. Cámara Lapuente, 'New Developments in the Spanish Law of Succession', *InDret* (2007/4); E. Castellanos Ruiz, 'Sucesión hereditaria', in A.-L. Calvo Caravaca and J. Carrascosa González (eds), *Derecho internacional privado*, 13th ed., vol. II (Granada, 2012), p. 521.

interpretation, according to which these instruments of estate planning are not contrary to public policy [see art. 25 no. 5].[41]

V. The Consequences of Recourse to the Public Policy Clause

25. A further problem lies in the fact that the ESR does not set out the consequences of recourse to public policy. A first solution to this problem might involve having recourse to a different connecting factor other than the one that points to the inapplicable law. This route could be taken when the succession law was designated by the testator by means of an option in favour of his national law; where this law proves to be contrary to public policy, the law of the country of last habitual residence might apply on the basis that this is the law that applies to succession pursuant to the ESR in the absence of a choice by the testator.

26. However, the view that the ESR simply does not deal with the effects of the operation of public policy would appear to fit better with the structure and features of the regulation, in which the objective connecting factor of the deceased's last habitual residence and the choice of the applicable law made by him do not appear to have been designated to operate beside one another. Working on the basis of this different interpretation, the consequences of public policy being called upon as a remedy, in the absence of any direction being provided by the ESR, will thus depend upon the law of the forum, which might simply declare as applicable its own rules.[42]

[41] S. Marino, 'La proposta di regolamento sulla cooperazione giudiziaria in materia di successioni', *Riv dir int* (2010), p. 469.

[42] Carrascosa González, *El Reglamento Sucesorio*, p. 262.

Article 36

States with More Than One Legal System: Territorial Conflicts of Laws

CELIA M. CAAMIÑA DOMÍNGUEZ

1. Where the law specified by this Regulation is that of a State which comprises several territorial units each of which has its own rules of law in respect of succession, the internal conflict-of-laws rules of that State shall determine the relevant territorial unit whose rules of law are to apply.
2. In the absence of such internal conflict-of-laws rules:
   (a) any reference to the law of the State referred to in paragraph 1 shall, for the purposes of determining the law applicable pursuant to provisions referring to the habitual residence of the deceased, be construed as referring to the law of the territorial unit in which the deceased had his habitual residence at the time of death;
   (b) any reference to the law of the State referred to in paragraph 1 shall, for the purposes of determining the law applicable pursuant to provisions referring to the nationality of the deceased, be construed as referring to the law of the territorial unit with which the deceased had the closest connection;
   (c) any reference to the law of the State referred to in paragraph 1 shall, for the purposes of determining the law applicable pursuant to any other provisions referring to other elements as connecting factors, be construed as referring to the law of the territorial unit in which the relevant element is located.
3. Notwithstanding paragraph 2, any reference to the law of the State referred to in paragraph 1 shall, for the purposes of determining the relevant law pursuant to Article 27, in the absence of internal conflict- of-laws rules in that State, be construed as referring to the law of the territorial unit with which the testator or the persons whose succession is concerned by the agreement as to succession had the closest connection.

Article 37

States with More Than One Legal System: Inter-personal Conflicts of Laws

In relation to a State which has two or more systems of law or sets of rules applicable to different categories of persons in respect of succession, any reference to the law of that State shall be construed as referring to the system of law or set of rules determined by the rules in force in that State. In the absence of such rules, the system of law or the set of rules with which the deceased had the closest connection shall apply.

Article 38

Non-application of This Regulation to Internal Conflicts of Laws

A Member State which comprises several territorial units each of which has its own rules of law in respect of succession shall not be required to apply this Regulation to conflicts of laws arising between such units only.

Summary

I. INTRODUCTION *page* 521
II. TERRITORY-BASED NON-UNIFIED LEGAL SYSTEMS 522
A. General Rules for Territory-Based Non-unified Legal Systems 522
B. Rules Applicable to Territory-Based Non-unified Legal Systems in Relation to the Form of Dispositions of Property upon Death 527
III. PERSON-BASED NON-UNIFIED LEGAL SYSTEMS 528
IV. INTERNAL CONFLICTS OF LAWS 529

I. Introduction

1. Articles 36 and 37 ESR deal with reference by the ESR conflict-of-laws rule to the law of States whose legal systems are not unified and are thus characterised by legal pluralism (*Etats plurilégilsatifs, ordenamientos plurilegislativos, Staaten mit mehr als einem Rechtssystem*), and draw a distinction between two types of systems: (a) inter-territorial non-unified systems, that is, States comprising several territorial units, to which different systems of law or sets of different rules apply (amongst others, Spain, the United Kingdom, the United States of America and other federal States such as Australia and Canada);[1] and (b) inter-personal non-unified systems, that is to say, States which have various systems of law or sets of rules applicable to different categories of persons

[1] See, amongst others, in Spain, Tribunal Supremo 5 November 1996 (*Lowenthal*) (RJ 1996 \8212) (US citizen); Tribunal Supremo 21 May 1999 (*Denney*) (RJ\1999\4580) (British citizen from England); Audiencia Provincial Alicante 10 May 2003 (JUR\2003\197311) (British citizen from Scotland); in England, Re Cutcliffe's Trusts [1940] Ch. 565, 56 T.L.R. 53 (Canadian citizen); in Portugal, Tribunal da Relação de Évora 6 November 2008 (available at www.dgsi.pt) (British citizen from England).

(e.g. India, Lebanon, Morocco and Syria, as well as several other African and Asian States).[2] Article 38, as we will see, restricts itself to stating that the ESR does not apply to internal conflicts of laws.

II. Territory-Based Non-unified Legal Systems

A. *General Rules for Territory-Based Non-unified Legal Systems*

2. When the applicable law designated by the ESR is that of a State comprising various territorial units, where all or part of these have their own rules relating to matters of succession, the matter should proceed in accordance with the rules provided by articles 36.1 and 36.2. As will be discussed in no. 16 *et seq.*, these provisions do not apply within the scope of article 27, relating to the form of dispositions of property upon death, since the ESR deals with reference to non-unified States in such cases under article 36.3. Therefore, we will call the rules set out in articles 36.1 and 2, for the purposes of our study, 'general rules', as the only aspect excluded from their application are matters relating to the form of dispositions of property upon death.

3. The solutions offered by articles 36.1 and 36.2 are as follows.

1) If the non-unified State has its own internal conflict-of-laws rules which govern this issue, those rules will decide which territorial unit's law is applicable. We thus find ourselves faced with an indirect reference rule.[3] The ESR does not allow each territorial unit to be considered as though it were a country for the purposes of determining the law applicable in accordance with the same.
2) In the absence of any such rules in the non-unified State itself, the ESR sets out a series of solutions, which depend upon the connecting factor employed by the ESR conflict rule which operates the reference in the first place: (a) if the connecting factor is the last habitual

[2] See 'Étude de droit comparé sur les règles de conflits de juridictions et de conflits de lois relatives aux testaments et successions dans les États membres de l'Union Européenne', in Deutsches Notarinstitut (ed), *Conflict of Law of Succession in the European Union. Perspectives for a Harmonisation* (Würzburg, 2004), pp. 60–61; A. Bonomi, 'Articles 36 à 38', in A. Bonomi and P. Wautelet (eds), *Le droit européen des successions. Commentaire du Règlement nº 650/2012 du 4 juillet 2012* (Bruxelles, 2013), pp. 553–554.

[3] J. Carrascosa González, *El Reglamento Sucesorio Europeo 650/2012 de 4 de julio 2012. Análisis crítico* (Granada, 2014), p. 267. See the analysis of different models for reference to systems with more than one law carried out by P. Quinzá Redondo and G. Christandl, 'Ordenamientos plurilegislativos en el Reglamento (UE) de Sucesiones con especial referencia al ordenamiento jurídico español', *Indret* (2013/3), pp. 6–11.

residence of the deceased, it is understood that reference has to be made to the territorial unit in which the deceased had his habitual residence at the time of his death; (b) if the connecting factor is nationality, it is understood as referring to the territorial unit with which the deceased had the closest connection; (c) if the connecting factor is any other element, it is understood that reference is made to the territorial unit in which the element in question is located.

4. For example, in the case of the United Kingdom, the rules that apply in order to determine reference to their non-unified system are equivalent to those which govern international cases, with the result that in matter of succession the law of the deceased's last domicile is applied to movable property while the law applicable to immovable property is that of the place where it is located.[4]

It has to be underlined that cases of reference to a non-unified legal system are not excluded from *renvoi* under article 34.2 of the ESR [see art. 34 no. 12]. Therefore, when the ESR conflict-of-laws rules refer to the legal system of a specific territorial unit that has its own system of private international law (as is the case in common law countries), it is necessary to take into account the *renvoi* that the territorial unit's conflict rules may address to the law of a Member State or to the law of a third State which would apply its own law.[5]

5. In the case of Spain, for example, part of the territorial units which constitute the Spanish State (*Comunidades Autónomas*) have their own law in matter of succession (*derechos forales*), while others apply ordinary Spanish law. The Spanish system has its own rules that govern the internal conflict of laws. Specifically, under articles 16 and 9.8 of the Spanish civil code, the law of the deceased's *vecindad civil* applies. So, in the event that the ESR conflict rules refer to Spanish law, the question of whether ordinary civil law or the law of one of the *Comunidades Autónomas* with its own rules in matters of succession applies will be determined by considering the deceased's *vecindad civil*, as defined by the relevant Spanish law.[6]

6. As we know, article 22 of the ESR allows the law of the State of which the deceased was a national at the time of making such a choice or

[4] See Deutsches Notarinstitut (ed), 'Étude', p. 60. On the fragmentation of the applicable law which this can cause, see Bonomi, 'Articles 36 à 38', pp. 556–557.

[5] On acceptance of *renvoi* in the case of reference to a non-unified legal system, see A. Davì, 'Le renvoi en droit international privé contemporain', *Hague Recueil*, vol. 352 (2010), pp. 388–389.

[6] On determination of *vecindad civil*, see articles 14 and 15 of the Spanish civil code.

at the time of his death to be elected as the applicable law by way of a *professio juris*. In such an eventuality, if the person chooses his national law when he is a national of a non-unified State, recourse has to be made to articles 36.1 and 36.2 in order to identify the law of the specific territorial unit that is applicable.[7]

7. It is also necessary to consider what happens if a person has made a *professio juris* in favour of the law of a specific territorial unit, in which case we deem that, as article 22 refers to the choice of the law of a State of 'nationality', the specification of a territorial unit must be determined by articles 36.1 and 36.2. As such, the choice of the law of a specific territorial unit that does not fall under the solutions provided by articles 36.1 and 36.2 will not be valid.[8] It is possible to consider that if the choice of law refers to a specific territorial unit, for the purposes of the ESR it must be assumed that the choice relates to the State of which the territorial unit forms part, after which, in accordance with articles 36.1 and 36.2, it will be necessary to check whether the law of the territorial unit is actually applicable. It is clear, however, that the succession might then be governed by a law different from the one selected by the deceased.[9] For example, this will occur when, in applying article 36.1, where the non-unified system has its own internal rules on conflict of laws, these rules do not allow for the choice of law to be that of one particular territorial unit, and the solutions adopted by contrast lead to the application of a different territorial unit's law.

8. On the other hand, in some cases it may happen that the non-unified State possesses rules for determining the specific territorial unit, but those rules do not offer a solution for a specific situation. By way of example, we can focus on the case of the Spanish system which, as we have stated, has its own rules on this respect, which, in accordance with articles 16 and 9.8 of the Spanish civil code, result in the application of the law of the deceased's place of *vecindad civil*. This rule, however, cannot operate when the deceased was a foreigner who never acquired Spanish nationality. In these cases, it is not possible to specify which Spanish territorial unit's legal system applies, since a foreign citizen has no *vecindad civil*.[10]

7 E. Castellanos Ruiz, 'Sucesión hereditaria', in A.-L. Calvo Caravaca and J. Carrascosa González (eds), *Derecho Internacional Privado*, 15th ed. (Granada, 2014), vol. II, p. 571.

8 See, amongst others, Bonomi, 'Articles 36 à 38', p. 557; J. Heinig, 'Rechtswahlen in Verfügungen von Todes wegen nach der EU-Erbrechts-Verordnung', *RNotZ* (2014), p. 197 *et seq*.

9 Bonomi, 'Articles 36 à 38', p. 557.

10 On determination of *vecindad civil*, see articles 14 and 15 of the Spanish civil code.

9. There is more than one possible answer to this problem.[11] In that regard, it is appropriate to consider whether the matter under consideration falls under article 36.1 or 36.2. We have thus to analyse, within the scope of the ESR, the meaning of the words 'In the absence of such internal conflict-of-laws rules' at the start of article 36.2. Specifically, it is necessary to decide whether article 36.2 comes into play when the non-unified system lacks any provision whatsoever relating to that reference or also in the event that such country has rules for resolving the internal conflict that, however, do not offer a solution for a specific hypothesis, as is the case, in the above example, with the Spanish system.

10. The options are as follows: (a) If article 36.2 is not deemed as applicable when a non-unified system has its own rules for the reference to the specific territorial unit, then the problem raised by *vecindad civil* in the Spanish system must be resolved using the mechanisms of the Spanish system itself (without reverting to the ESR). Along these lines, some authors propose applying article 9.10 of the Spanish civil code by analogy, which would solve the problem of the foreigner's lack of *vecindad civil* by applying the law of the territorial unit where the deceased's habitual residence was located. In this case, once article 36.1 of the ESR leads to the application of the rules for resolving the internal conflict of laws, the solution has to be found in the non-unified system itself.[12] (b) We are, however, in favour of a different option: the phrase 'In the absence of such internal conflict-of-laws rules' can be taken to mean that article 36.2 apply also when the rules exist, but do not settle the matter in question. Thus, as the Spanish system does not resolve the case of the aforementioned deceased foreigner because he lacks *vecindad civil*, we believe that recourse must be made to the subsidiary rules of article 36.2.[13]

11. Another problem arises if the non-unified State with more than one legal system does not have internal conflict-of-laws rules, but each territorial unit has its own (as is the case in the United States of America).[14] From our point of view, it is correct to apply the subsidiary provisions of article 36.2 to such cases.[15]

[11] See the summary of the possible solutions by Carrascosa González, *El Reglamento Sucesorio*, pp. 267–268; Quinzá Redondo and Christandl, 'Ordenamientos plurilegislativos', pp. 17–20.

[12] See Carrascosa González, *El Reglamento Sucesorio*, p. 268, which considers that this might perhaps be the best solution.

[13] See Quinzá Redondo and Christandl, 'Ordenamientos plurilegislativos', pp. 19–20; Rodríguez-Uría Suárez, 'La ley aplicable', pp. 45–46.

[14] Bonomi, 'Articles 36 à 38', p. 556.

[15] For another approach see Bonomi, 'Articles 36 à 38', p. 556.

12. The following clarifications have to be made in respect of the subsidiary solutions.

13. a) As regards the 'habitual residence' connection, article 36.2 provides that the reference must be deemed to be made to the law of the territorial unit where the deceased had his habitual residence 'at the time of his death'. However, we must bear in mind the circumstances set out in articles 24 and 25 ESR in which the law of the deceased's habitual residence at the time a disposition of property is drawn up, amended or revoked is applicable [see art 24 and art. 25]. In such cases, if reference is made to the law of a non-unified country to be resolved in accordance with article 36.2 (a), the law of the territorial unit of the deceased's habitual residence at the time a disposition of property is drawn up, amended or revoked will apply, as appropriate.[16]

14. b) Likewise, as regards the 'nationality' connection, the specification in recital 51 must also be borne in mind, within the scope of articles 24 and 25, with the result that, in certain circumstances, the choice of law refers to the State of which the deceased was a national at that time.[17] In such cases, if reference is made to a non-unified system to be resolved in accordance with article 36.2(a), in the same way as has been explained in relation to habitual residence, the law of the territorial unit of which the deceased was a national on that date, and with which the deceased would therefore have had the closest connection, will apply.[18]

As we have noted, if a person chooses his or her national law (within the scope of article 22), we must refer to articles 36 and 37 in order to determine which particular territorial unit's law applies, in the event that the person is a national of a non-unified State.[19] We have also explained that, even though a person may directly choose the law of a particular territorial unit of the State of which he is a national, the identification of the territorial unit must be determined by articles 36 and 37, such that any choice in favour of a territorial unit that does not fall under the solutions offered by articles 36 and 37 will not be valid.[20] As already noted, succession might then be governed by a law which the deceased did not want.[21]

[16] Bonomi, 'Articles 36 à 38', p. 559.

[17] Again, on the cited recital, see Davì and Zanobetti, 'Il nuovo diritto internazionale privato delle successioni nell'Unione europea', p. 64; A. Davì and A. Zanobetti, *Il nuovo diritto internazionale privato europeo delle successioni* (Torino, 2014), p. 100.

[18] Bonomi, 'Articles 36 à 38', p. 559. [19] Castellanos Ruiz, 'Sucesión', p. 571.

[20] See, amongst others, Bonomi, 'Articles 36 à 38', p. 557; Heinig, 'Rechtswahlen in Verfügungen von Todes wegen', p. 197 *et seq.*

[21] Bonomi, 'Articles 36 à 38', p. 557.

However, within the scope of article 36.2, we consider that the choice of the law of a particular territorial unit ought to be taken into consideration as one of the elements enabling the closest connection to be determined.[22]

15. c) Finally, in the event that the connecting factor which operates the reference to the non-unified State is neither the deceased's habitual residence nor his nationality, the law of the territorial unit in which the element in question is located will then apply, pursuant to article 36.2(c). This will occur where the connecting factor are the habitual residence of the person making the declaration (article 28) and the country in which immovable property is located (articles 30, 31 and 33 ESR).[23]

B. Rules Applicable to Territory-Based Non-unified Legal Systems in Relation to the Form of Dispositions of Property upon Death

16. When the reference to the non-unified legal system occurs within the scope of article 27, on the form of dispositions *mortis causa*, in the absence of internal conflict-of-laws rules article 36.3 of the ESR applies. Accordingly, article 36.3 is applicable when the conflict-of-laws rules refers to a State with territory-based multiple legal systems within the context of the form of dispositions of property upon death, while article 36.2 apply in all other cases. It must also be recalled that, in accordance with article 75 of the ESR, the 1961 Hague Convention on the form of testamentary dispositions continues to apply for Member States which are parties thereof 'with regard to the formal validity of wills and joint wills'.

17. Therefore, in line with the comments made in relation to article 27 ESR regarding dispositions of property upon death made in writing, we must remember that (a) for Member States that are parties to the 1961 Hague Convention, the form of wills is governed by that Convention and, therefore, reference to a non-unified State must be resolved in accordance with the relevant provisions of the convention; (b) for Member States that are not parties to the 1961 Hague Convention, the form of wills is governed by the ESR and, consequently, any reference to a non-unified State must be resolved in accordance with paragraphs 1 and 3 of article 36; (c) for all Member States, the form of agreements as to

[22] Bonomi, 'Articles 36 à 38', p. 560.

[23] Davì and Zanobetti, *Il nuovo diritto internazionale privato europeo delle successioni*, pp. 191–192.

succession is governed by the ESR, and therefore any such issue must be resolved in accordance with paragraphs 1 and 3 of article 36.[24]

18. Member States that are parties to the 1961 Hague Convention will, in respect of reference to a non-unified State operated by connecting factors relating to a 'place', as, for example, does article 1(a), which refers to the law 'of the place' where the testator made the disposition, apply the law of that particular territorial unit directly; whereas, when the connecting factor does not refer to a 'place', as is the case in article 1(b), which makes recourse to nationality as a connection, they will apply, first, the internal conflict-of-laws rules of the country concerned and, in absence of such rules, will refer, as prescribed by article 1.II of the 1961 Hague Convention, to the law of the unit presenting 'the most real connexion which the testator had with any one of the various laws within that system'.[25]

19. The solutions offered by the ESR are as follows:

1) If the State has internal conflict-of-laws rules, pursuant to article 36.1, those rules will determine which territorial unit's law is applicable. We thus find ourselves faced, once again, with an indirect reference rule.[26]
2) In the absence of such rules, article 36.3 prescribes the application of the law of the territorial unit with which the testator, or the persons whose succession is concerned by an agreement, had the closest connection. In this case, we can see that the ESR's provision coincides with article 1.II of the 1961 Hague Convention, with the result that the solution is the same both for Member States that are parties to the convention and for those that are not.

III. Person-Based Non-unified Legal Systems

20. When dealing with a person-based non-unified legal system, that is to say, in the event that there are different groups of rules in a State, the application of which is determined not by a territorial connection, but rather on the basis of personal categories (e.g. the religion which an

[24] A. Bonomi, 'Article 27', in A. Bonomi and P. Wautelet, *Le droit européen des successions. Commentaire du Règlement nº 650/2012 du 4 juillet 2012* (Bruxelles, 2013), p. 426.

[25] See Quinzá Redondo and Christandl, 'Ordenamientos plurilegislativos', pp. 20–21, which consider that the ESR solution does not sufficiently favour the *favour validitatis* principle.

[26] See Carrascosa González, *El Reglamento Sucesorio*, p. 267; Quinzá Redondo and Christandl, 'Ordenamientos plurilegislativos', pp. 6–11.

individual practises, or the ethnic community to which he pertains),[27] the solutions are as follows: (1) If the State has rules for the internal conflict of laws, those rules will decide which group of personal rules is applicable. We are thus confronted once again with an indirect reference rule.[28] (2) In the absence of such rules, the group of personal rules with which the deceased would have had the closest connection will apply. We therefore see that, while in the event of a reference to a territory-based non-unified State, the ESR considers different subsidiary solutions, on the basis of the connecting factor used by the relevant conflict rule, when the reference concerns a person-based system, there is only one subsidiary solution.

IV. Internal Conflicts of Laws

21. Pursuant to article 38 ESR, the application of the ESR international conflicts of laws rules to internal rules on conflicts of laws (that is to say, to those arising exclusively between a State's territorial units) is optional for each Member State.[29]

So, as a general rule, the ESR will not apply in such cases, unless the Member State in question so decides. It has therefore been stated that this is a 'national policy decision'.[30]

[27] See Audiencia Provincial Madrid 27 September 2013 (JUR\2014\5518) (Moroccan national who was a practising Jew).

[28] Carrascosa González, *El Reglamento Sucesorio*, p. 267.

[29] On criticism dealing with this rule, *see* Quinzá Redondo and Christandl, 'Ordenamientos plurilegislativos', pp. 16–17.

[30] Carrascosa González, *El Reglamento Sucesorio*, p. 32. It should be mentioned here that to date the only Member State participant to the ESR that is in this position is Spain, that has made no indication in this respect. Accordingly, domestic rules continue to apply to Spanish 'interregional' conflicts in matters of succession [see art. 20 no. 3].

CHAPTER IV

Recognition, Enforceability and Enforcement of Decisions

Article 39

Recognition

ELENA D'ALESSANDRO

1. A decision given in a Member State shall be recognised in the other Member States without any special procedure being required.
2. Any interested party who raises the recognition of a decision as the principal issue in a dispute may, in accordance with the procedure provided for in Articles 45 to 58, apply for that decision to be recognised.
3. If the outcome of the proceedings in a court of a Member State depends on the determination of an incidental question of recognition, that court shall have jurisdiction over that question.

Summary

I. THE CONCEPT OF RECOGNITION OF A DECISION GIVEN IN ANOTHER MEMBER STATE *page* 533

II. DECLARATORY PROCEEDINGS 538

III. RECOGNITION AS AN INCIDENTAL ISSUE 540

I. The Concept of Recognition of a Decision Given in Another Member State

1. Among the principal new features introduced by the ESR are the uniform rules on recognition and enforcement of decisions on matters of succession. Previously such judgments were excluded from the scope of European judicial cooperation in civil matters.[1]

The provisions of chapter IV of the ESR are modelled on those of regulation no. 44/2001[2] so that, *mutatis mutandis,* it will be possible to

[1] This is also pointed out by A. Davì and A. Zanobetti, 'Il nuovo diritto internazionale privato delle successioni nell'Unione europea', *CdT* 5/2 (2013), p. 125; I. Pretelli, 'Reconnaissance, force exécutoire et exécution des décisions', in A. Bonomi and P. Wautelet, *Le droit européen des successions. Commentaire du Règlement n° 650/2012 du 4 juillet 2012* (Bruxelles, 2013), p. 565.

[2] Council Regulation (EC) no. 44/2001 of 22 December 2000 on jurisdiction and the recognition and enforcement of judgments in civil and commercial matters, OJ no. L12,

apply the case law of the European Court of Justice with reference to the rules on recognition contained in the Brussels Convention on jurisdiction and the enforcement of judgments in civil and commercial matters of 28 September 1968 and in regulation no. 44/2001.
Article 39 ESR, in particular, stipulates that decisions on matters of succession given in a Member State and falling within the scope of application of the ESR as outlined in article 1 [see art. 1 no. 5 *et seq.*] are automatically recognised in the other Member States. In order for article 39 to apply it is not necessary that the decision resolves a cross-border dispute nor that the court which delivered its decision based its competence on the rules set forth in chapter II ESR, it being sufficient that it is a judgment delivered by a court of a Member State.[3]
In order to be allowed to circulate pursuant to article 39 ESR, decisions must be able to produce effects outside the proceedings in which they were pronounced.

2. The definition of the word 'decision' is provided under article 3(g) of the ESR as any decision on an issue of succession 'given by a court of a Member State, whatever the decision may be called, including a decision on the determination of costs or expenses by an officer of the court' [see art. 3 no. 11 *et seq.*].[4] The word 'court', as can be seen from

16 January 2001, p. 1 (replaced as from 10 January 2015 by Regulation (EU) no. 1215/2012 of the European Parliament and of the Council of 12 December 2012 on jurisdiction and the recognition and enforcement of judgments in civil and commercial matters (recast), OJ no. L351, 20 December 2012, p. 1).

[3] Davì and Zanobetti, 'Il nuovo diritto internazionale privato delle successioni', p. 126; Pretelli, 'Reconnaissance', p. 566 *et seq.*; A. Davì and A. Zanobetti, *Il nuovo diritto internazionale privato europeo delle successioni* (Torino, 2014), p. 220.

[4] When interpreting article 3(g) ESR, however, account has to be taken of the ruling in relation to regulation no. 44/2001 by the ECJ, case C-456/11, *Gothaer Allgemeine Versicherung* v. *Samskip GmbH* [2012] ECLI:EU:C:2012:719, where the court stated that the concept of decision 'must be interpreted as meaning that it also covers a judgment by which the court of a Member State declines jurisdiction on the basis of a jurisdiction clause, irrespective of how that judgment is categorised under the law of another Member State' (para. 32). The ECJ also stated that 'the court before which recognition is sought of a judgment by which a court of another Member State has declined jurisdiction on the basis of a jurisdiction clause is bound by the finding – made in the grounds of a judgment, which has since become final, declaring the action inadmissible – regarding the validity of that clause' (para. 33). On this decision, see comments by I. Bach, 'Deine Rechtskraft? Meine Rechtskraft! Zur Entscheidung des EuGH, den Unionsrechtlichen Rechtskraftbegriff auf zivilrechtliche Entscheidungen nationaler Gerichte anzuwenden', *EuZW* (2013), p. 56; E. D'Alessandro,'Pronunce declinatorie di giurisdizione: la Corte di giustizia impone limiti di efficacia europei', *Foro it* (2013), IV, pp. 42–45; M. Nioche, 'Reconnaissance d'une décision étrangère d'incompétence prise sur le fondement d'une clause attributive de juridiction', *Rev crit dr int priv* (2013), p. 686; A. Henke, 'Verso una

the drafts of the ESR, in particular the proposal for a regulation in matters of succession by the European Parliament and the Council,[5] is to be understood in the broadest sense to include also 'notaries and court clerks'.

The decision may be given at the outcome of interim proceedings or proceedings on the merits. It cannot however be a judicial settlement[6] as recognition and enforcement in that respect are covered by article 61 [see art. 61].

The wording of recital 59 ESR (which ensures for the ESR the elimination of the doubts about interpretation which arose in relation to regulation 44/2001) indicates that it can deal with decisions given in both contentious and non-contentious cases: 'irrespective of whether such decisions were given in contentious or non-contentious proceedings', such as an order to draw up an inventory, or an order excluding creditors from claiming against the estate of the deceased.[7]

3. The following, however, are typical examples of decisions given in contentious proceedings eligible for recognition pursuant to article 39 ESR: orders settling disputes arising between parties having claims in respect of the succession, for instance between heirs, or between one heir (or heirs) and one or more legatees and concerning the validity of a will or its interpretation; decisions handed down at the end of proceedings for proving of heirs or a definitive judgment of abatement of legacies; rulings which find unfitness to inherit or which confirm that some assets do not form part of the estate.

4. Accordingly, in order to be permitted to circulate in the European judicial area in terms of article 39 ESR, decisions must satisfy the

nozione europea di *res judicata*: l'efficacia extraprocessuale della declinatoria di giurisdizione e il giudicato sui motivi', *Diritto del commercio internazionale* (2013), p. 1085; H. Roth, 'Europäischer Rechtskraftbegriff im Zuständigkeitsrecht?' *IPRax* (2014), p. 136.

5 Proposal for a Regulation of the European Parliament and of the Council, Bruxelles, 14.10.2009, COM(2009) 154, final, section 4.1, chapter 1, article 1.

6 As clarified, in relation to the Brussels Convention of 1968, by the ECJ, case C-414/92, *Solo Kleinmotoren GmbH* v. *Emilio Boch* [1994] ECR I-2237, paras. 17–18.

7 Deutsches Notarinstitut (ed), *Conflict of Law of Succession in the European Union. Perspectives for a Harmonisation* (Würzburg, 2004), p. 37; Davì and Zanobetti, 'Il nuovo diritto internazionale privato delle successioni', p. 126; J. Foyer, 'Reconnaissance, acceptation et exécution des jugements étrangers, des actes authentiques et des transactions judiciaires?', in G. Khairallah and M. Revillard (eds), *Droit européen des successions internationales. Le règlement du 4 juillet 2012* (Paris, 2013), p. 143; W. Burandt, in *Beckische kurz Kommentare. Erbrecht*, 2nd ed. (München, 2014), p. 1452; Davì and Zanobetti, *Il nuovo diritto internazionale privato europeo*, p. 220.

prerequisites set forth in article 3(g) ESR and at the same time must relate directly to succession matters [see art. 1 no. 5 *et seq.*]. Therefore, the following are excluded from the scope of application of article 39 ESR insofar as not directly concerning succession matters: decisions concerning relationships between the deceased's creditors and the heirs, for example, repayment of a loan to the deceased; decisions regarding relationships between the debtors of the deceased and the heirs;[8] orders and decisions relating to gifts.[9] Those orders are in fact merely ascribable to civil and commercial matters, thus capable of circulating pursuant to regulation 44/2001 and, if given in proceedings commenced dating from 10 January 2015, pursuant to regulation 1215/2012.

A different conclusion would appear to be reached in relation to decisions regarding the validity of settlements aimed at putting an end to disputes regarding the succession. Prior to the entry into force of the ESR attempts had been made to bring that type of disputes within the scope of regulation 44/2001, based on the fact that such a pronouncement did not relate 'directly' to the rights and actions deriving from the succession.[10] However, since a succession matter constitutes the subject of the settlement declared valid or invalid by the court decision which must circulate, it appears preferable to bring that type of decision within the scope of the ESR.

5. Similarly, declarations of acceptance or waiver of inheritance received by a court pursuant to article 13 ESR [see art. 13 no. 10] cannot circulate pursuant to article 39 ESR, as they do not meet the prerequisites under article 3(g) ESR. These are not, in fact, 'decisions', as also shown by the terminology used in article 13 ESR, which describes them as 'declarations'.

[8] In the sense that recognition of these decisions was governed by regulation no. 44/2001 (and currently by regulation no. 1215/2012): S. M. Carbone, *Lo spazio giudiziario europeo in materia civile e commerciale. Da Bruxelles I al regolamento CE n. 805/*2004, 6th ed. (Torino, 2009), p. 25; H. Gaudemet-Tallon, *Compétence et exécution des jugements en Europe*, 4th ed. (Paris, 2010), p. 65 *et seq.*; J. Kropholler and J. von Hein, *Europäisches Zivilprozessrecht*, 9th ed. (Frankfurt am Main, 2011), p. 102; P. Schlosser, *EU-Zivilprozessrecht*, 3rd ed. (München, 2009), pp. 30–31.

[9] G. Droz, *Compétence judiciaire et effets des jugements dans le marché commun (Étude de la Convention de Bruxelles du 27 septembre 1968)* (Paris, 1972) p. 35; L. Mari, *Il diritto processuale civile della Convenzione di Bruxelles* (Padova, 1999), p. 98.

[10] A. Layton A. and H. Mercer, *European Civil Practice*, 2nd ed., vol. I (London, 2004), p. 355; Mari, *Il diritto processuale civile*, p. 98; F. Salerno, *Giurisdizione ed efficacia delle decisioni straniere*, 3rd ed. (Padova, 2006), pp. 80–81 and, in Italian case law, Tribunale Roma 13 December 1991, *Riv dir int priv proc* (1995), p. 673.

6. The technique of recognition chosen is – as usual in EU private international law instruments – automatic recognition, on the basis of which the effects produced by the decision in the Member State of origin from the time they arise extend their validity automatically into the European judicial area (extension of effects, *Wirkungserstreckung*).[11]

Specifically, the following can be automatically recognised: declaratory effect (*Feststellungswirkung*), constitutive effect, consisting of the creation, modification or extinction of a legal relationship (*Gestaltungswirkung*) and, more generally, any other type of effect, other than enforcement, produced by a foreign decision on the merits in succession matters (for example: *Interventionswirkung* and *Streitverkündungswirkung*).

The objective, subjective and time limits for determining the effects of the foreign decision recognised pursuant to article 39 ESR are governed by the procedural law of the Member State of origin of the decision itself.

7. In order to use a foreign decision as an enforceable title in the Member State in which enforcement is sought it will be necessary to commence an *exequatur* procedure governed by articles 43 *et seq.* ESR [see art. 43] similar to that contemplated in general terms for civil and commercial matters under regulation no. 44/2001 (i.e. the regulation that

[11] In relation to the Brussels Convention of 1968, the Court of Justice of the European Union has in fact specified that 'a foreign judgment which has been recognized by virtue of article 26 of the Convention must in principle have the same effects in the State in which enforcement is sought as it does in the State in which judgment was given': ECJ, case 145/86, *Hoffmann* v. *Krieg* [1988] ECR 645, paras. 10–11. Where it exceeds the effects accorded to a corresponding internal ruling, however, it is doubtful whether this extent of effect (*Wirkungserstreckung*) can be 'limited' by the State in which enforcement is sought (*Kumulationstheorie*). In relation to regulation no. 44/2001, negative opinions have been expressed by P. Gottwald, in *Münchener Kommentar zur Zivilprozessordnung*, vol. III, 4th ed. (München, 2013), p. 1879, and Kropholler and von Hein, *Europäisches Zivilprozessrecht*, p. 551 *et seq.* Support for the *Kumulationstheorie* is offered by H. Schack, *Internationales Zivilverfahrensrecht*, 6th ed. (München, 2014), p. 332. The ECJ did not appear to provide any firm directions on this point in ECJ, case C-420/07, *Apostolides* v. *Orams* [2009] ECR I-3571, para. 66, and ECJ, case C-139/10, *Prism Investments BV* v. *Van der Meer* [2011] ECR 1, para. 38, in which it stated that 'although recognition must have the effect, in principle, of conferring on judgments the authority and effectiveness accorded to them in the Member State in which they were delivered . . ., there is, however, no reason for granting to a judgment, when it is enforced, rights which it does not have in the Member State of origin or effects that a similar judgment given directly in the Member State in which enforcement is sought would not have'; these decisions refer to the possibility of limiting the effects of enforcement which, in the system established by regulation no. 44/2001, just as in the ESR, are not automatically recognised but are instead created *ex novo* by the Member State in which enforcement is sought.

was in force when the ESR was enacted). At that time, however, it was already known that regulation no. 44/2001 would be replaced by regulation no. 1215/2012, which implements the same solution as the European enforcement order established by regulation no. 805/2004, consequently abolishing the *exequatur* system. The European legislator therefore intentionally chose to exclude succession from the scope within which this solution applies.

8. The delivery of an *exequatur* is necessary only in order to grant enforceability and therefore does not constitute a necessary condition for the purposes of entering a decision in succession matters emanating from another Member State in the immovable property registers (where such formality is required by the Member State where the property is situated). Automatic recognition pursuant to article 39 ESR will be sufficient for that purpose.

II. Declaratory Proceedings

9. Similarly to the provisions under article 33.2 regulation no. 44/2001 and now article 36.2 regulation no. 1215/2012, article 39.2 ESR establishes that, where disputes arise regarding recognition of a decision in succession matters emanating from another Member State, it will be possible to bring proceedings for a declaration of effectiveness of that decision in the Member State where enforcement is sought. The court or administrative authority competent for that case can be identified on the basis of the criteria set forth in article 45.1 ESR [see art. 44 and art. 45 no. 2].

10. The party with standing to bring the declaratory action will be any subject bound by the effects of the foreign decision, even if he did not take part in the proceedings in which the decision was given.[12] The party with standing to be sued will be the party against whom it is intended to enforce the decision in the Member State where enforcement is sought. Similarly to article 33.2 of regulation no. 44/2001 and article 36.2 of regulation no. 1215/2012, article 39 ESR merely specifies that, in order for the action to be brought, it is necessary that an objection is raised regarding recognition of a decision from another Member State. The rule, at least in principle, appears to refer to the procedural rules of the *lex fori* regarding the existence of legal interest in bringing proceedings (*interesse necessario ad agire in giudizio, Rechtsschutzinteresse*), that

[12] In agreement with this is Pretelli, 'Article 39', p. 578.

is, regarding the requirements for the admissibility of the claim, even though some commentators, who wish to render the procedure as uniform as possible, have argued that it should not be subject to any review as to its admissibility under the *lex fori*.[13]

11. The court with local jurisdiction to hear the case referred to in article 39.2 ESR will be identified on the basis of the ground indicated in article 45.2 ESR, adapted to the circumstances of the case at hand [see art. 44 and art. 45 no. 2].

Article 45.2 ESR establishes in fact that 'the local jurisdiction shall be determined by reference to the place of domicile of the party against whom enforcement is sought, or to the place of enforcement'. In cases falling under article 39 ESR, which relates to automatic recognition only of declaratory or constitutive decisions, there is no indication as to where the decision must be, properly speaking, enforced. Therefore, it is necessary to consider the place of domicile of the party against whom the applicant intends to avail himself of the decision.[14] In the event that a decision is to take effect against more than one party domiciled in different places in the same Member State, it should be possible for the interested party to bring the proceedings before the court in a place where any of the parties against whom the decision is to produce its effects is domiciled.[15]

The proceedings will be articulated in two stages, the first of which will be *ex parte* and the second will imply a hearing on the merits according to the procedure set forth in article 46 *et seq.* ESR [see art. 46 and art. 49].

12. Lastly, the ESR makes no mention of the possibility for the party against whom a decision in succession matters may be called to produce its effects to bring an action for negative declaratory relief with a view to

[13] Pretelli, 'Article 39', p. 578. In relation to regulation no. 44/2001, Gaudemet-Tallon, *Compétence et exécution*, p. 460, expresses the hope that a 'European' concept of interest in acting will be created.

[14] For support for this solution where article 39.2 of regulation no. 44/2001 is concerned, see Carbone, *Lo spazio giudiziario europeo*, p. 225; Gaudemet-Tallon, *Compétence et exécution*, p. 459; R. Geimer, *Europäisches Zivilverfahrensrecht*, 3rd ed. (München, 2010), p. 747; Salerno, *Giurisdizione ed efficacia*, p. 343 *et seq.*; Kropholler and von Hein, *Europäisches Zivilprozessrecht*, p. 624 *et seq.*; Schlosser, *EU- Zivilprozessrecht*, p. 264.

[15] In relation to regulation no. 44/2001, see Gaudemet-Tallon, *Compétence et exécution*, p. 459: 'La meilleure solution serait sans doute alors de permettre à la partie qui forme une demande principale en reconnaissance d'agir au siège du tribunal de grande instance de son choix dans l'État requis, pourvu que ce choix soit conforme à une bonne administration de la justice'.

having the decision declared unrecognisable pursuant to article 39 ESR. As this issue is not governed by the European legislator it remains subject to the procedural law of the individual Member State.[16]

III. Recognition as an Incidental Issue

13. In similar terms to those presently contained under article 36.3 regulation no. 1215/2012 and previously under article 33.3 regulation no. 44/2001, article 39.3 ESR provides that, in case the declaratory or constitutive effects produced by a decision in matters of succession are raised in the course of proceedings on the merits pending in a Member State other than that in which the decision was made, considering that its content is capable of affecting the substance of the decision requested of the court seised, the latter has jurisdiction to evaluate whether that decision can be recognised. Therefore, prior to basing its decision on a judgment from another Member State, the court shall verify of its own motion (i.e. even where neither party raises an objection in that respect) whether the decision can be recognised. The court must verify that none of the conditions exist which would preclude recognition pursuant to article 40 ESR. The control by the court regarding recognisability of a decision in matters of succession in such a case must be reconciled (i.e. its scope is *de facto* limited) with the general rule that, analogously to recognition ordinarily requested pursuant to article 39.2 ESR, the burden of alleging and proving the facts which prevent recognition rests with the

[16] See Pretelli, 'Article 39', p. 580. It is in fact possible in a number of Member States to commence proceedings to secure a negative declaration in relation to the recognition of a foreign decision. In Germany, for example, such proceedings can be launched pursuant to section 256 ZPO; see Kropholler and von Hein, *Europäisches Zivilprozessrecht*, p. 557 *et seq*. In relation to regulation no. 44/2001, in France, an *action en inopposabilité* concerning a foreign ruling can generally be commenced: see J. P. Béraudo, 'Convention de Bruxelles, Conventions de Lugano et règlement (CE) n° 44/2001 – Reconnaissance des décisions juridictionnelles', *Juris Classeur Procédure civile*, fasc. 52–50 (Paris, 2010), p. 1 *et seq*., spec. No. 77; D. Bureau and H. Muir-Watt, *Droit international privé*, vol. I, 3rd ed. (Paris, 2014), p. 332 *et seq*.; Gaudemet-Tallon, *Compétence et exécution*, p. 457. The same possibility is also widely acknowledged in Italy: see, e.g., O. Lopes Pegna, *I procedimenti relativi all'efficacia delle decisioni straniere in materia civile* (Padova, 2009), p. 122 *et seq*. The courts have at times held the opposite view, although with reference to a negative declaration in relation to a decision capable of recognition pursuant to the Italian private international law act of 1995: Appello Venezia 27 May 1997, *Foro Padano* (1998), I, p. 197; Appello Milano 13 March 1998, *Riv dir int priv proc* (1999) p. 570.

party who has an interest in demonstrating the non-recognisability of the decision [see art. 40 and art. 41 no. 3 *et seq.*].[17]
The effects of the control performed by the court incidentally within the pending proceedings will be limited to those proceedings[18] and therefore will not preclude in any way the subsequent bringing of an action seeking a ruling on the eligibility of the foreign decision for recognition pursuant to article 39.2 ESR.

14. Similarly, if objections are raised between the parties regarding the recognition under the ESR of a foreign decision in succession matters within proceedings pending in the Member State where recognition of such a decision is sought, the party having an interest in relying upon the effects of the decision may request the court to declare whether that decision is recognisable pursuant to the ESR. Also in such a case, the effects of the declaration will be limited to those proceedings. The burden of proof relating to the facts precluding recognition shall once again lie with the party challenging the recognisability of the decision [see art. 40 and art. 41 no. 3 *et seq*].

15. Finally, when the *lex fori* of the Member State in which enforcement is sought allows new claims to be brought during the course of the proceedings,[19] if a challenge is filed by the opposing party, the party interested in relying upon the effects of the foreign decision may also request the court to decide with *res judicata* effect whether the decision in succession matters upon whose effects that party intends to rely is automatically recognisable. The wording of article 39.3 ESR appears to be open to the conclusion that, in such a case, the court seised will have jurisdiction to decide also on that new request.[20]

[17] Bureau and Muir-Watt, *Droit international privé*, p. 335.

[18] Kropholler and von Hein, *Europäisches Zivilprozessrecht*, p. 559.

[19] As it is the case, for example, under Italian civil procedural law pursuant to article 34 of the Italian code of civil procedure, and under German civil procedural law pursuant to section 256 abs. 2 of the German civil procedure code (ZPO).

[20] Compare with the interpertation suggested, in relation to the regulation no. 44/2001 by S. Leible, 'Brussels I-VO', in T. Rauscher, *Europäisches Zivilprozess und Kollisionsrecht* (München, 2011), p. 724; Schlosser, *EU- Zivilprozessrecht*, p. 264. *Contra*: P. Gottwald, 'Art. 34 EuGVO', in *Münchener Kommentar zur Zivilprozessordnung*, vol. 3 (München, 2013), p. 1883.

Article 40

Grounds of Non-recognition

ELENA D'ALESSANDRO

A decision shall not be recognised:

(a) if such recognition is manifestly contrary to public policy (*ordre public*) in the Member State in which recognition is sought;

(b) where it was given in default of appearance, if the defendant was not served with the document which instituted the proceedings or with an equivalent document in sufficient time and in such a way as to enable him to arrange for his defence, unless the defendant failed to commence proceedings to challenge the decision when it was possible for him to do so;

(c) if it is irreconcilable with a decision given in proceedings between the same parties in the Member State in which recognition is sought;

(d) if it is irreconcilable with an earlier decision given in another Member State or in a third State in proceedings involving the same cause of action and between the same parties, provided that the earlier decision fulfils the conditions necessary for its recognition in the Member State in which recognition is sought.

Article 41

No Review as to the Substance

Under no circumstances may a decision given in a Member State be reviewed as to its substance.

Summary

I. PRELIMINARY REMARKS: THE GROUNDS OF NON-RECOGNITION AND THE EXCLUSION OF A REVIEW AS TO THE SUBSTANCE *page* 543

II. SUBSTANTIVE PUBLIC POLICY 546

II. PROCEDURAL PUBLIC POLICY 552

III. DECISIONS GIVEN IN DEFAULT OF APPEARANCE 554

IV. IRRECONCILABILITY OF THE DECISION WITH OTHER DECISIONS 557

I. Preliminary Remarks: The Grounds of Non-recognition and the Exclusion of a Review as to the Substance

1. As stated in its article 39.1, the ESR has opted for the automatic recognition of decisions rendered in another Member State [see art. 39 no. 1]. It follows that the only obstacle to recognition of such a decision is the existence of one of the grounds for non-recognition included in the exhaustive list set out under article 40 ESR.[1]

2. As established under article 41 ESR,[2] in no circumstances can a decision handed down in another Member State be reviewed as to its

[1] See on similar lines I. Pretelli, 'Article 40', in A. Bonomi and P. Wautelet, *Le droit européen des successions. Commentaire du Règlement n° 650/2012 du 4 juillet 2012* (Bruxelles, 2013), p. 584.

[2] Article 41 ESR prevents the judge in the State in which recognition is sought from examining whether the decision rendered in another Member State is correct. As Pretelli points out in 'Article 40', p. 606, there is, however, nothing to prevent the judge in the Member State in which recognition is sought from examining whether the factual information set out in the attestation issued by the court or competent authority in the originating Member State and which, pursuant to article 46(b) ESR, has to be submitted along with the application for enforcement or for an order that the decision should be recognised, is correct. As clarified by the European Court of Justice in the *Trade Agency* case, in relation to regulation no. 44/2001, which also prohibits a review of the decision in

substance. The grounds for non-recognition under article 41 ESR in fact close the door firmly on any new ruling on the substance being made by the courts of the Member State in which recognition is sought.

3. In proceedings launched as the result of a dispute over recognition of a decision pursuant to article 39.2 ESR, it is for the party asserting that a decision from another Member State should not be recognised to allege and proof that one of the grounds for non-recognition applies [see art. 39].[3] While article 48 ESR [see art. 48 no. 3] expressly provides that the courts must issue the *exequatur* without carrying out a review under article 40 ESR, the regulation is silent on whether, at the appeal stage referred to in article 50 ESR, it is open to the court to rule, of its own motion, that a ground for non-recognition applies that is different from the ground or grounds actually alleged by the interested party [see art. 50].

To the extent that the value of the free circulation of decisions within the European judicial area is to be promoted, the silence maintained here by the ESR can be taken as a sign of an intention to rule out the existence of powers to control the grounds for refusal on the court's own motion[4].

Nevertheless, these grounds include one – recognition being manifestly contrary to public policy, as established by article 40(a) ESR [see art. 40 no. 6] – which is intended to safeguard the public interest. For this reason, the check of the existence of this ground for non-recognition cannot depend solely on one of the parties requesting that such an investigation be carried out (with this only being possible, however, in

terms of substance, 'no provision of regulation 44/2001 expressly prohibits the court of the Member State in which enforcement is sought from verifying the accuracy of the factual information contained in the certificate': ECJ, case C-619/10, *Trade Agency Ltd* v. *Seramico Investments Ltd* [2012] ECLI:EU:C:2012:531, para. 35, commented on by L. Idot, 'Exécution d'un jugement rendu par défaut, ordre public et droits fondamentaux', *Europe* (2012/11), p. 50; M. Stella, 'Default judgments inglesi alla prova dell'ordine pubblico processuale europeo, tra aneliti deflattivi esasperati e superiori istanze di un'equa tutela del contumace', *Int'l Lis* (2012) p. 171; H. Roth, 'Der Einwand der Nichtzustellung des verfahrenseinleitenden Schriftstücks (Art. 34 Nr. 2, 54 EuGVVO) und die Anforderungen an Versäumnisurteile im Lichte des Art. 34 Nr. 1 EuGVVO', *IPRax* (2013), p. 402; R. Caro Gàndara, *An esp der int priv* XII (2012), p. 1029.

[3] See A. Davì and A. Zanobetti, 'Il nuovo diritto internazionale privato delle successioni nell'Unione europea', *CdT* 5/2 (2013), p. 128.

[4] See Davì and Zanobetti, 'Il nuovo diritto internazionale privato delle successioni', p. 129; Pretelli, 'Article 40', p. 585. Alternatively, this silence on the part of the European legislator regarding the power of a national court to consider of its own motion grounds of refusal of recognition could be interpreted as a reference to the *lex fori*: this is the view held in relation to regulation no. 44/2001 by H. Gaudemet-Tallon, *Compétence et exécution des jugements en Europe*, 4th ed. (Paris, 2010), p. 474.

the so-called appeal phase governed by article 50 ESR).[5] Putting it differently: bound by a duty to respect the fundamental rights protected by the Charter of Fundamental Rights of the European Union and by the European Convention on Human Rights, in proceedings under article 50 ESR a Member State court should, therefore, on its own motion evaluate whether a foreign decision is contrary to European public policy. As in fact clarified by the European Court of Human Rights in the *Pellegrini* case,[6] recognition of a decision rendered in a country that is not a party to the ECHR that breaches these fundamental rights results in the court in a State party that recognises such a decision as a breach of those rights itself.

The chances of this type of situation arising would, however, appear to be extremely slim. A judge in another Member State would have to have delivered a decision that was in breach of the fundamental rights of the European Union (which should be excluded pursuant to article 35 ESR [see art. 35]). Then proceedings would need to be launched in order to guarantee recognition or enforcement of the foreign decision pursuant to article 50 ESR. And then the party against whom the decision is to be enforced would have to fail to rely on this ground for refusal.

4. The grounds for non-recognition under article 40 ESR have a dual nature: not only do they form the basis for a refusal to recognise a foreign decision, but they also operate as adequate reasons for refusing or revoking a declaration of enforceability [see art. 52]. Such a declaration, as we have already seen [see no. 3], in the perspective of promoting the circulation of decisions within the European legal space, is granted under article 48 ESR without any investigations taking place pursuant to article 40 ESR [see art. 48].

5. In terms of their content, the grounds for non-recognition under article 40 ESR correspond to those set out under article 34 of regulation no. 44/2001 (and now they reflect the grounds under article

[5] In fact, as pointed out by J. Foyer, 'Reconnaissance, acceptation et exécution des jugements étrangers, des actes authentiques et des transactions judiciaires', in G. Khairallah and M. Revillard (eds), *Droit européen des successions internationales* (Paris, 2013), p. 156: 'Il peut sembler léger de laisser à la disposition des parties des éléments aussi importants que, par exemple, la contrariété de la décision étrangère à l'ordre public'. In relation to regulation no. 44/2001, the German literature leans towards this view, claiming that the grounds for non-recognition can be *ex officio* detected by the court during the procedural phase referred to in article 43 *et seq.* regulation no. 44/2001; among others see P. Schlosser, *EU- Zivilprozessrecht,* 3rd ed. (München, 2009), p. 190; J. Kropholler and J. von Hein, *Europäisches Zivilprozessrecht*, 9th ed. (Frankfurt am Main, 2011), p. 548.

[6] ECtHR, *Pellegrini* v. *Italy,* Judgment of 20 July, 2001, no. 30882/96.

45 of regulation no. 1215/2012).[7] Case law from the ECJ concerning article 34 of regulation no. 44/2001 must, therefore, be considered as applicable insofar as relevant.

II. Substantive Public Policy

6. Article 40(a) ESR establishes that a decision originating from another Member State regarding succession shall not be granted recognition in the *forum* where its effects are manifestly contrary to public policy in the Member State in which recognition is sought.

The concept of public policy that article 40 ESR refers to covers both substantive public policy and procedural public policy.[8]

7. As a general principle, the concept of substantive public policy needs to be established on a national level,[9] and should take into account the fundamental legal values in place in the Member State in which recognition is sought. To be added to these are the values enshrined in the Charter of Fundamental Rights of the European Union, which has the

[7] Council Regulation (EC) no. 44/2001 of 22 December 2000 on jurisdiction and the recognition and enforcement of judgments in civil and commercial matters, OJ no. L12, 16 January 2001, p. 1 (replaced as from 10 January 2015 by regulation (EU) no. 1215/2012 of the European Parliament and of the Council of 12 December 2012 on jurisdiction and the recognition and enforcement of judgments in civil and commercial matters (recast), OJ no. L351, 20 December 2012, p. 1).

[8] See Davì and Zanobetti, 'Il nuovo diritto internazionale privato delle successioni', p. 128; Foyer, 'Reconnaissance, acceptation et exécution', p. 15; Pretelli, 'Article 40', p. 589 *et seq.* It follows that in order to define the scope of application of article 40(a) ESR, reference can be made to rulings by the Court of Justice regarding the public policy clause referred to in article 27.1 of the Brussels Convention of 1968 and article 34.1 regulation no. 44/2001, including, *in primis*: (i) ECJ, case C-7/98, *Krombach* v. *Bambersky* [2000] ECR I-1935, annotated by H. Muir Watt, *Rev crit dr int priv* (2000), pp. 489–497; R. González González, 'Límites a la construcción de un "orden público europeo" en materia de derechos fundamentales (A propósito de la sentencia del TJCE Krombach c. Bamberski, de 28 de marzo de 2000)', *Rev der com eur* (2000), pp. 593–617; G. Biagioni, 'L'art. 6 della Convenzione europea dei diritti dell'uomo e l'ordine pubblico processuale nel sistema della Convenzione di Bruxelles', *Riv dir int* (2001) pp. 723–737; (ii) ECJ, case C-394/07, *Gambazzi* v. *DaimlerChrysler Canada Inc. et al.* [2009] ECR I-2563, annotated by B. Sujecki, 'Unverhältnismäßige Beeinträchtigung des Anspruchs auf rechtliches Gehör', *EuZW* (2009), p. 424; F. Jault-Seseke, 'Conflit de juridictions. Les règles communautaires', *Dalloz* (2010), p. 1593; G. Cuniberti, 'Debarment from Defending, Default Judgments and Public Policy', *IPRax* (2010), p. 148; E. D'Alessandro, 'Provvedimento inglese di esclusione dal processo e diniego di riconoscimento per contrarietà all'ordine pubblico processuale. La Corte di giustizia si pronuncia sul caso "Gambazzi"', *Foro it* (2009), IV, p. 384.

[9] M. Stürner, 'Deutsch-italienische Erbfälle unter der kommenden Europäischen Erbrechtsverordnung', *Jahrbuch für italienisches Recht* (2013), p. 78.

same force as the EU treaties, as well as those set out in the European Convention of Human Rights.

When tackling the interpretation of the European Union treaties – a task assigned to it by article 267 of the Treaty on the Functioning of the European Union – the ECJ can do no more than check that the courts in the Member State in which recognition is sought do not rely on the public policy ground for the purposes of a denial of recognition simply in order to close the door on a foreign ruling being introduced in that forum, thereby making improper use of the grounds for non-recognition.[10] We find this rule confirmed under recital 58 ESR: 'the courts or other competent authorities should not be able to apply the public-policy exception in order to set aside the law of another State or to refuse to recognise or, as the case may be, accept or enforce a decision, an authentic instrument or a court settlement from another Member State when doing so would be contrary to the Charter of Fundamental Rights of the European Union, and in particular article 21 thereof, which prohibits all forms of discrimination'.

8. The ground for non-recognition that appears under article 40(a) ESR is drafted on the same lines as article 35 ESR, which, of course, refers to provisions of the law of any State specified by the regulation [see art. 35]. Both article 40(a) and article 35 ESR in fact refer to 'manifest incompatibility' with the *forum*'s public policy. But whilst the wording of the two provisions might be identical, differences can be identified in their scope of application. It should in fact be noted that:

(1) in contrast to article 40, the scope of application of article 35 ESR should (at least in the mind of the European legislator) be 'marginal' given that, as recital 27 points out, the rules of the ESR 'are devised so as to ensure that the authority dealing with the succession will, in most situations, be applying its own law';[11]
(2) article 40(a) ESR makes reference to procedural as well as to substantive public policy;

[10] ECJ, case C-7/98, *Krombach* v. *Bambersky* [2000] ECR I-1935, on which see the authors cited at footnote 8; ECJ, case C-38/1998, *Régie nationale des usines Renault Maxicar SpA* v. *Orazio Formento* [2000] ECR I-2973, annotated by B. Hess, 'Urteilsfreizügigkeit und ordre public-Vorbehalt bei Verstößen gegen Verfahrensgrundrechte und Marktfreiheiten', *IPRax* (2001), p. 301; I. Donzallaz, 'Le renouveau de l'ordre public dans la CB/CL au regard des ACJCE Krombach et Renault et de la révision de ces traités', AJP (2001), p. 160; ECJ, case C-302/13, *FlyLAL-Lithuanian Airlines AS* v. *Starptautiska lidosta Riga VAS, Air Baltic Corporation AS* [2014] ECLI:EU:C:2014:2319, at 47.

[11] Davì and Zanobetti, 'Il nuovo diritto internazionale privato delle successioni', p. 106.

(3) where substantive public policy is concerned, the established view expressed in literature is that the extent of this concept is narrower where the recognition of acquired rights that derive from foreign decisions is involved (rather than in respect of the application of foreign law).

The French use the expression *effet atténué de l'ordre public* in discussions on this point,[12] and literature in Spain refers to *orden público internacional atenuado*.[13]

German literature has identified a practical answer that basically takes a different route by emphasising the strictly local nature of public policy. This leads to the claim being made that substantive public policy can only be relied upon as a ground of non-recognition when a link can be identified between the forum and the decision to be recognised (*Inlandsbeziehung*).[14]

9. Legal literature identifies three distinct types of decisions that might potentially give rise to problems of compatibility with public policy. These are detailed as follows.

1) Decisions delivered in a Member State which, by virtue of the legislation that applies to the particular dispute, for example the law in force in an Islamic country, result in inequality, with the heirs of the deceased being treated differently on the basis of sex, religion or *status* (children born in or out of wedlock).[15]

[12] Among others, H. Batiffol, *Droit international privé*, vol. I (Paris, 1974), p. 415 *et seq.*; B. Audit, *Droit international privé* (Paris, 2000), p. 405 *et seq.*; D. Bureau and H. Muir Watt, *Droit international privé. Partie générale*, vol. I, 3rd ed. (Paris, 2014), p. 306. In case law see the French Cour de cassation 17 April 1953, *Rivière, Rev cr dr int priv* (1953), p. 412, with comment by H. Batiffol; Cour de cassation 12 mars 2009, no. 08–10974, www.legifrance.gouv.fr.

[13] A.-L. Calvo Caravaca and J. Carrascosa González, *Derecho internacional privado*, 15th ed. (Granada, 2014), vol. I, p. 539 *et seq.*

[14] Among others, E. Zitelmann, *Internationales Privatrecht*, vol. I (Leipzig, 1897), p. 363 *et seq.*; F. Kahn, *Die Lehre vom ordre public (Prohibitivgesetze)*, in *Jherings Jahrbücher für die Dogmatik des bürgerlichen Rechts*, 39 (Jena, 1898), p. 9 *et seq.*; D. Martiny, *Handbuch des Internationalen Zivilverfahrensrechts*, vol. III/1 (Tübingen, 1984), p. 465 *et seq.*; R. Geimer, in R. Geimer and R. Schütze, *Internationale Urteilsanerkennung*, I (München, 1984), p. 1583. On similar lines in conceptual terms we have the French theory of 'ordre public de proximité' developed by the more modern day French literature, on which, out of all those who have written on the point, see P. Courbe, 'L'ordre public de proximité', in Le droit international privé: esprit et méthodes. Mélanges en l'honneur de Paul Lagarde (Paris, 2005), p. 227 *et seq.*

[15] This example is used by Foyer, 'Reconnaissance, acceptation et exécution', p. 157, and by Pretelli, 'Article 40', p. 590, who, in particular, refers to a German judgment, renedered by default, applying the law of Kuwait and to be recognised in France. A case of this type was

There would appear to be no argument against the view expressed here that decisions on these lines cannot be recognised, being contrary to public policy. They are in fact in clear conflict with the fundamental principles that originated on a European level and which, as such, are of uniform application in the European judicial area. More specifically, decisions of this type conflict with:

(i) the provisions under articles 8–10 of the Treaty on the Functioning of the European Union;
(ii) the provisions set out under Protocol XII, article 1, of the European Convention on Human Rights;
(iii) the provisions under article 21 of the Charter of Fundamental Rights of the European Union.[16]

The ESR should in fact be capable of preventing such decisions from being handed down anywhere within the EU judicial area, with article 40 (a) ESR in practice being of residual application as a result. By virtue of the supremacy of EU law, a judge in a Member State applying his or her national law will be duty bound to disapply any provision of the law regarding succession that sits unhappily with the provisions previously set out at (i), (ii) and (iii).

also decided by the Landgericht Hamburg 12 February 1991, *IPRspr* (1991), p. 264, which took the view that the rule established by Iranian law that limits the amount of a father's estate to devolve upon his daughters to half the amount allocated to the sons was not against public policy, as German law also gave a parent the power to differentiate between the shares due to their children by means of a testamentary disposition using the 'available share'.

Slight differences can be found, however, with the possible situation considered by H. Gaudemet-Tallon, 'Quelques réflexions sur les propositions concernant la compétence judiciaire, la reconnaissance et l'exécution des décisions en matière successorale dans l'Union européenne', in Deutsches Notarinstitut (ed), *Les successions internationales dans l'UE. Perspectives pour une harmonisation* (Würzburg, 2004), pp. 455–456, who examines the hypothetical situation in which a decision is handed down in a country that is not bound by the ESR, i.e. the French province of Mayotte; in that State, applying Muslim law, the judge dismissed the succession claims made by the natural son. In describing the case, the author points out that the Cour de cassation has treated the decision (to be recognised in accordance with the local provisions of international civil procedure) as being in line with international public policy: Cour de cassation 25 February 1997, N-94–19321, *Bull civ* (1997), I, no. 67.

[16] Pretelli, 'Article 40', pp. 590–591; Foyer, 'Reconnaissance, acceptation et exécution', p. 157. For thoughts on similar lines see A. K. Pattar, *Islamisch inspiriertes Erbrecht und deutscher Ordre public: Die Erbrechtsordnungen von Ägypten, Tunesien und Marokko und ihre Anwendbarkeit im Inland* (Berlin, 2007), p. 473 *et seq.*

Required by the ESR conflict of laws provisions to apply foreign law designed on such lines, the judge would have to refrain from doing so by virtue of the public policy clause under article 35 ESR [see art. 35].

10. 2) The second category of decisions can be sub-divided as follows:

(a) decisions pronounced in a Member State which, where there is a polygamous marriage, allocate succession rights to the second wife of the deceased and/or their children,[17] and
(b) decisions that allocate succession rights to the deceased's same-sex spouse or partner and/or their children.[18]

As concerns a decision that, in case of a polygamous marriage, grants the second wife of the deceased succession rights, the view has generally been held for some time now that this situation is not one that is contrary to public policy. Recognising such a decision in fact translates only into allowing the woman to exercise her succession rights in the Member State in which recognition is sought, while the 'polygamous marriage' itself only continues to take effect in the State of origin, that is beyond the boundaries of the State being asked to recognise the decision.[19]

[17] For this example, see Pretelli, 'Article 40', p. 591.

[18] This example is one put forward by: Davì and Zanobetti, 'Il nuovo diritto internazionale privato delle successioni', p. 107 *et seq.*; Foyer, 'Reconnaissance, acceptation et exécution', p. 157; Pretelli, 'Article 40', p. 592.

[19] A. Davì, *L'adozione nel diritto internazionale privato italiano* (Milano, 1981), p. 335, footnote 98; C. A. Esplugues, 'Legal Recognition of Polygamous Marriages', *The Comparative and International Law Journal of Southern Africa* (1984), p. 302 *et seq.*; P. Lagarde, 'La théorie de l'ordre public international face à la polygamie et à la répudiation: l'expérience française', in *Nouveaux itinéraires en droit: hommage à François Rigaux* (Bruxelles, 1993), p. 263 *et seq.*; F. Guillame, 'O tempora! O mores!: l'effet du temps sur l'ordre public en droit international privé, in P. Zen-Ruffinen, in *Le temps et le droit. Recueil de travaux offerts à la journée de la société suisse des juristes 2008* (Bâle, 2008), p. 108 *et seq.*; D. Bureau and H. Muir Watt, *Droit international privé. Partie générale*, vol. I, 3rd ed. (Paris, 2014), p. 535 *et seq.* The French courts have had to tackle the issue flagged up earlier on a number of occasions, with French case law featuring the well-known *Bendeddouch* case. Decided by the Cour de cassation with judgment 78–13762 of 3 January 1980, *Rev crit dr int priv* (1980), p. 331, the case involved the succession of a polygamous Muslim. The Cour de cassation had to carve up the share reserved by French law to the surviving spouse (i.e. a third of the estate) into equal parts between the two wives, who each received one sixth of the estate. In Italian case law see Corte di cassazione 2 March 1999, no. 1739, *Foro it.* (1999), I, p. 1458 e *Famiglia e dir.* (1999), p. 327, with note by V. Zambrano, 'Ordine pubblico e matrimonio contratto all'estero secondo il rito mussulmano'.

On an EU level, see the recent decision by the Civil Service Tribunal (Full Court), case F-45/07, *Wolfgang Mandt* v. *European Parliament* [2010] ECLI:EU:F:2010:72, particularly at 87 where it states that 'the fact that ... a Union institution recognises that two

It would appear that the issue of whether the decisions in group 2(b) can be afforded recognition are to be resolved in the same way. Looking at the public policy clause under article 35 ESR, the opportunity has been taken in the literature to clarify that a foreign law that grants succession rights to a same-sex spouse or partner cannot be treated as being contrary to substantive public policy for the very reason that discrimination on the grounds of sex is prohibited [see art. 35 no. 16]. The same applies, *mutatis mutandis,* to decisions awarding succession rights to a same-sex spouse or partner, and all the more so: here too, in exactly the same way as with a polygamous marriage, the marriage or union between persons of the same sex is not the subject of the application for recognition, with that partnership continuing to be valid in the State of origin and not in the State in which recognition is sought.

11. 3) The third type of decision is one that originates from another Member State where the court has applied substantive law that does not provide that part of the estate must of necessity devolve upon the legitimate heirs, or has applied a law that does so stipulate but on the basis of criteria that differ from those established by the succession law in the Member State in which recognition is sought. Whilst the definitive test in the ESR does not contain the specific provision that can be found in article 27.2 of the European Commission's Proposal,[20] which provided that 'the application of a rule of the law determined by the regulation may not be considered to be contrary to the public policy of the forum on the sole ground that its clauses regarding the reserved portion of an estate differ from those in force in the forum', the view adopted by the majority of those who have written on the point is that this is not an inconsistency that is capable of bringing the ground of non-recognition under article 40(a) ESR into play. If such inconsistencies were, as of themselves, seen as being capable of doing so, the whole *raison d'être* of the ESR itself would be undermined [see art. 35 no. 6 *et seq.*].[21] The wording of the ESR would appear to support this

persons have the status of surviving spouse of one and the same deceased former official, for the purposes of granting a pecuniary benefit, does not in any way constitute even implicit acceptance at Union level of multiple marriage, an acceptance that might raise a question of compatibility with higher principles and rules of law, in particular if each of the persons concerned was in receipt of the entire pecuniary benefit provided for "the surviving spouse"'.

20 COM(2009) 154 final.

21 Davì and Zanobetti, 'Il nuovo diritto internazionale privato delle successioni', p. 44, text and footnote 164; Pretelli, 'Article 40', pp. 594–595; Stürner, 'Deutsch-italienische Erbfälle', pp. 78–79, who points out that there could, however, be a material breach of

conclusion, to the extent that it allows, as a matter of principle, succession agreements to be entered into pursuant to article 25 ESR [see art. 25]. If, as it would appear, judgments that concern the validity and effect of these succession agreements are capable of circulating within the European judicial area pursuant to article 39 ESR without any possibility of being denied recognition on the grounds that they are contrary to substantive public policy[22], then, *a fortiori*, judgments that apply different rules in relation to that part of the estate which, of necessity, devolves upon the closest relatives, must also be capable of circulating alike.

II. Procedural Public Policy

12. As concerns procedural public policy, in order for a foreign ruling not to be denied recognition, it must be ensured that, in the course of the proceedings in another Member State against a defendant who did not enter an appearance and was not unintentionally absent, the procedural safeguards established by article 6 of the European Convention on Human Rights and article 47 of the Charter of Fundamental Rights of the European Union were in place. These must include the right to be informed of the reasons for a particular ruling by the court, so that the losing party can understand why there has been a finding against them and, if appropriate, launch an appeal.[23]

public policy where, as a result of what is referred to as disinheritance, someone in the category of weak subjects afforded protected by the Charter of Fundamental Rights of the European Union (e.g. a child) suffers a breach of their fundamental rights; see G. Khairallah, 'La détermination de la loi applicable à la succession', in G. Khairallah and M. Revillard (eds), *Droit europeén des successions internationales* (Paris, 2013), p. 57.

As pointed out by Davì and Zanobetti, 'Il nuovo diritto internazionale privato delle successioni', p. 44, text and footnote 164, this approach is taken by national case law, in Spain and Italy at least. See in fact, in Spanish case law: Trib. supremo 15 November 1996 (Lowenthal), *Rev esp der int* (1997), p. 264, and Trib. Supremo 21 May 1999 (Denney), *Rev esp der int* (1999), p. 756 *et seq.*, commented on by M. Virgós Soriano and E. Rodríguez Pineau, 'Succession Law and Renvoi: the Spanish Solution', in *Festschrift für Erik Jayme* (München, 2004), vol. I, p. 977 *et seq.*; in Italy, Corte di cassazione 24 June 1996, no. 5832, *N giur civ comm* (1997), I, p. 164, with note by E. Calò, 'L'etica dell'ordine pubblico internazionale e lo spirito della successione necessaria'.

[22] Pretelli, 'Article 40', p. 595.

[23] ECJ, case C-619/10, *Trade Agency* v. *Seramico*, in footnote 2; ECJ, case C-302/13, *FlyLAL-Lithuanian Airlines AS* v. *Starptautiska lidosta Riga VAS, Air Baltic Corporaition AS* [2014] ECLI:EU:C:2014:2319, at 51.

On more general lines, reference should be made to the concept of procedural public policy drawn up by the ECJ with reference to the Brussels Convention of 1968 and regulation no. 44/2001.[24]

13. It should be noted, in addition, that the grounds of non-recognition under article 40 ESR provide no opportunity, albeit even on a limited basis, to examine whether, pursuant to the ESR, the originating court in fact had jurisdiction to issue the decision recognition of which is sought.

Nor can any corresponding provision be found under article 35.3 of regulation no. 44/2001 (and now under article 45.3 of regulation no. 1215/2012), which dictates that the jurisdiction of the courts in the Member State of origin is not a factor to be included in the equation when assessing whether the foreign proceedings pass the public policy test.

The silence of the ESR on this point would appear to be justified by the fact that, in contrast to regulations no. 44/2001 and no. 1215/2012, in the case of the ESR the provisions governing jurisdiction are entirely the same for all the Member States subject to the ESR. The ESR, in fact, makes no reference at all to the provisions governing jurisdiction in the various individual national procedural systems.

Consequently, precisely because none of the grounds of non-recognition under article 40 ESR expressly require an assessment of whether the court that issued the relevant ruling in fact had jurisdiction to do so, it is reasonable to conclude that, where succession is concerned, the rule that applies here is one that dictates that provisions regarding jurisdiction do not concern procedural public policy. In other words, the mutual trust between Member States, whose courts apply the same ESR provisions regarding jurisdiction, means that the courts in the Member

[24] On the concept of European procedural public policy, as delineated by the Court of Justice, and in addition to the authors referred to footnotes 8 and 10, see D. Martiny, *Handbuch des Internationalen Zivilverfahrensrechts*, vol. III/2, p. 50 *et seq.*; J. Fölisch, *Der Gemeineuropäische ordre public* (Frankfurt am Main, 1997), p. 15 *et seq.*; C. Picheral, *L'ordre public européen* (Paris, 2001), p. 14 *et seq.*; J. Basedow, 'Recherches sur la formation de l'ordre public européen dans la jurisprudence' in *Mélanges en l'honneur de Paul Lagarde* (Paris, 2005), pp. 55–74; Schlosser, *EU-Zivilprozessrecht*, p. 180 *et seq.*; R. Fentiman, *International Commercial Litigation* (Oxford, 2010), p. 714 *et seq.*; Gaudemet-Tallon, *Compétence et exécution des jugements en Europe*, p. 416 *et seq.*; Kropholler and von Hein, *Europäisches Zivilprozessrecht*, p. 566 *et seq.*; Calvo Caravaca and Carrascosa González, *Derecho internacional privado*, p. 596 *et seq.;* O. Feraci, *L'ordine pubblico nel diritto dell'Unione europea* (Milano, 2012), pp. 138 *et seq.*, 388 *et seq.*; Bureau and Muir Watt, *Droit international privé*, p. 312 *et seq.*

State in which recognition is sought are not at liberty to check whether the judicial authority that issued the original ruling in fact had jurisdiction in respect of the dispute.[25]

14. The fact that the possibility of a control by the Member State in which recognition is sought on whether the court that issued the decision to be recognised had jurisdiction to do so is excluded altogether takes on particular significance when it comes to the circulation of protective measures. Article 19 ESR in fact dictates that protective measures can also be ordered by a judge who lacks jurisdiction as to the substance of the matter; in addition, and on similar lines to regulation no. 44/2001, there is no express provision to be found in the ESR that prohibits the circulation of protective measures issued by a judge lacking jurisdiction regarding the substance of the case [see art. 19].

It follows that, under the ESR – *a fortiori* as the Member State in which recognition is sought has no opportunity whatsoever to check whether the court which issued the ruling had jurisdiction to do so – protective measures can circulate regardless of whether they were issued by a court with or without jurisdiction to deal with the substance of the matter. What we have here is a significant imbalance when set against article 2(a) of regulation no. 1215/2012, which only allows protective measures ordered by a court having jurisdiction on the merits of the case to circulate within the EU judicial area (and as we will see in no. 15, this is on condition that, when the ruling was ordered, both parties were heard [see art. 19 no. 6]).

III. Decisions Given in Default of Appearance

15. The wording of article 40(b) ESR reflects article 34.2 of regulation no. 44/2001 (and now article 45(b) of regulation no. 1215/2012). Article 40(b) establishes that there is no room for recognition where the document instituting the proceedings or an equivalent document was not served on the defendant in sufficient time and in such a way as to enable

[25] On the same lines, see Pretelli, 'Article 40', pp. 570–571 and 597; Foyer, 'Reconnaissance, acceptation et exécution', p. 157, footnote 62, who makes the point that we have already seen above: in contrast with article 30 of the proposal COM (2009) 154 final, the finalised version of the ESR does not specify that the provisions regarding jurisdiction of the courts of the originating Member State cannot be taken into consideration for the purposes of assessing the extent to which the foreign decision complies with procedural public policy criteria. In Foyer's view, removal of this clarification can be explained by the fact that it was considered superfluous.

him to submit his defence,[26] unless the defendant failed to appeal the decision, despite being in a position to do so.

In terms of the circulation of protective measures, the provision must be taken as excluding automatic recognition of the order issued without the other party being heard [see art. 19 no. 6].

When applying article 40(b) ESR, it is open to the courts to refer to judgments handed down by the ECJ and to opinions expressed in the legal literature regarding the provision under article 34.2 of regulation 44/2001, given that the latter corresponds with that being applied under the ESR.[27]

16. It is in fact perfectly clear from its wording that the provision under article 40(b) ESR refers exclusively to the situation in which an absent defendant's right to a defence has been infringed, as long as the defendant was unable to remedy this infringement using the procedural tools in place for this purpose in the originating Member State. For this reason, when completing the attestation under annex 1 of regulation no. 1329/2014 (which contains the forms referred to in the ESR) the court that handed down the decision is required to state that the ruling was given in default of appearance.[28]

In contrast, as was already the case with article 43.2 of regulation no. 44/2001 (and as is the case currently with article 45 (b) of regulation

[26] In addition, the provision of article 40(b) ESR has to be coordinated with that of article 16 ESR [see art. 16], which is designed to prevent a ruling against an absent party who is unaware of the proceedings against him.

[27] On which see, *ex multis*, E. Merlin, 'Riconoscimento ed esecutività della decisione straniera nel Reg. "Bruxelles I"', *Riv dir proc* (2001), p. 439; J. Kropholler, *Europäisches Zivilprozessrecht*, 8th ed. (Frankfurt am Main, 2005) p. 412 *et seq.*; M. De Cristofaro, 'L'onere di impugnazione della sentenza quale limite al rilievo dei vizi nella fase introduttiva del giudizio chiuso da sentenza contumaciale: tra diritto di difesa e full faith and credit', *Int'l Lis* (2007), p. 7 *et seq.*; P. Gottwald, *Münchener Kommentar zur Zivilprozessordnung*, vol. 3 (München, 2008), art. 34 EuGVO, nos. 15–17; Gaudemet-Tallon, *Compétence et exécution des jugements en Europe*, p. 433 *et seq.*; Kropholler and von Hein, *Europäisches Zivilprozessrecht*, p. 551 *et seq.*; S. Leible, 'Brussels I-VO', in T. Rauscher, *Europäisches Zivilprozess und Kollisionsrecht* (München, 2011), p. 743 *et seq.*; P. Rogerson, *Collier's Conflict of Laws*, 4th ed. (Cambridge, 2013), p. 229 *et seq.* In case law see BGH 12 December 2007-XII ZB 240/05, *NJW-RR*, 2008, p. 586; BGH 6 October 2005 – IX ZB 27/02, *IHR*, 2006, p. 259.

[28] Commission Implementing Regulation (EU) no. 1329/2014 of 9 December 2014 establishing the Forms referred to in Regulation (EU) no. 650/2012 of the European Parliament and of the Council on jurisdiction, applicable law, recognition and enforcement of decisions and acceptance and enforcement of authentic instruments in matters of succession and on the creation of a European Certificate of Succession, OJ L 359/30, 16 December 2014.

no. 1215/2012), article 40(b) ESR does not concern situations in which the boundaries of the category of parties affected by a judgment handed down in another Member State are more extensive when compared to those that would be in place had the decision been made in the home courts. Reference is made in particular here to the situation in which the decision to be granted recognition produces effect *erga omnes*, that is, it also produces effect as against third parties who were not in a position to be involved in the proceedings in which the decision was given.

In circumstances such as these, a 'limitation' on the extent to which the foreign court's decision affects parties in the forum will, however, arise, either as a result of the application of the *Kumulationstheorie* – that is, the German theory whereby the effects of a recognised foreign decision can never extend further than those of a corresponding decision at home[29] – or at the very least by applying the ground for non-recognition under article 40(a) ESR and, chiefly, given the need to comply with the *forum*'s procedural public policy.[30] As we have sought to demonstrate elsewhere,[31] it is in fact the case that the safeguards in the form of the right for both parties to be heard require that, as a rule, a decision only produces *inter partes* effects (the *res judicata* effect of a judgment is limited to the parties to the action and to those persons who have a certain, specified legal relationship with one of the parties). For this reason, a judgment handed down in another Member State that produces *erga omnes* effects will be recognised in the State in which recognition is sought, but, within that legal system, it will produce only *inter partes* effects. Just where a domestic decision of the Member State

[29] With the *Kumulationstheorie*, the procedural rules in place in the State in which recognition is sought regarding the limitations of the effects of the decision are used in order to 'stem' the extent to which the foreign judgment takes effect. Nevertheless, the majority of German authors who drew up and lend their name to the *Kumulationstheorie* limit its effect to national legislation on the recognition of foreign judgments, ruling out application of the *Kumulationstheorie* where recognition of the foreign judgment is as a result of regulation 44/2001. See to this effect Schlosser, *EU- Zivilprozessrecht*, p. 170; Kropholler and von Hein, *Europäisches Zivilprozessrecht*, p. 551 *et seq*. For the opposite view, i.e. that reference can also be made to the *Kumulationstheorie* when recognition of foreign decisions is governed by the European legislator, see H. Schack, *Internationales Zivilverfahrensrecht*, 6th ed. (München, 2014), p. 332.

[30] In relation to the proposal for the regulation, a result on similar lines is reached in 'Comments on the European Commission's Proposal for a Regulation of the European Parliament and of the Council on jurisdiction, applicable law, recognition and enforcement of decisions and authentic instruments in matters of succession and the creation of a European Certificate of Succession', drawn up by the Max Planck Institute for Comparative and International Private Law of Hamburg, in *RabelsZ* (2010), pp. 667–668.

[31] E. D'Alessandro, *Il riconoscimento delle sentenze straniere* (Torino, 2007), p. 200 *et seq.*

requested with the same content would produce *erga omnes* effects, can a decision producing *erga omnes* effects in the Member State of origin be recognised with corresponding effects in the Member State requested.

IV. Irreconcilability of the Decision with Other Decisions

17. The grounds of non-recognition under article 40(c) and (d) ESR appear at first blush to coincide with those established by article 34.3 and 34.4 of regulation no. 44/2001 (now corresponding to article 45(c) and (d) of regulation no. 1215/2012).[32] Pursuant to article 40(c) and (d), a foreign decision shall not be recognised where it conflicts with a decision in proceedings between the same parties in the Member State in which recognition is sought or where it is irreconcilable with an earlier decision given in another Member State or in a third state in proceedings involving the same cause of action and between the same parties, on condition that the earlier decision meets the conditions necessary for recognition in the Member State in which recognition is sought.

Closer examination reveals the following point, however. In order to repeat the fact that judgments capable of circulation pursuant to the ESR in matters of succession include those handed down in non-contentious proceedings, as can be seen from a reading of recital 59 ESR,[33] using an expression that cannot be found under article 45(c) of regulation no. 1215/2012 or article 34.3 of regulation no. 44/2001, article 40(c) ESR states that a decision shall not be recognised if in conflict with another judgment handed down in 'proceedings' between the same parties in the Member State in which recognition is sought. This insertion is best appreciated when consulting the English version of the ESR.

In contrast with the French, German, Spanish and Italian versions, the English wording of article 34.3 of regulation no. 44/2001 (but not the wording of article 45(d) of regulation no. 1215/2012) in fact states that the conflicting decision must have been given 'in a dispute', reference therefore being made to contentious matters alone.

[32] See U. Simon and M. Buschbaum, 'Die neue EU-Erbrechtsverordnung', *NJW* (2012), p. 2397.

[33] An observation made by Davì and Zanobetti, 'Il nuovo diritto internazionale privato delle successioni', p. 128; Foyer, 'Reconnaissance, acceptation et exécution', p. 153; Pretelli, 'Article 40', p. 563.

Most likely for the same reason, article 40(d) ESR uses the expression *proceedings involving the same cause of action and between the same parties* rather than the word *dispute*, which is instead what we find in article 45(d) of regulation no. 1215/2012.

18. The two grounds of non-recognition that we have just mentioned, that is, article 40(c) and (d) ESR, make up the last resort in terms of ensuring consistency with the legal system of the forum.

As already pointed out by other authors,[34] it is far easier to envisage circumstances in which article 40(d) ESR might be applied than is the case with article 40(c) ESR. Conflict could in fact more frequently arise between a decision in matters of succession handed down in a Member State and another decision handed down in a third country, that has already been or is to be recognised in the Member State requested. The ground of non-recognition under article 40(c) ESR will, however, probably be of extremely limited application indeed. On the one hand, in fact, the grounds of jurisdiction contemplated by the ESR are generally grounds of exclusive jurisdiction (save in the case of article 10 ESR) [see art. 10], accompanied by a duty of the court seised to carry out an examination *ex officio* of its jurisdiction, whilst, on the other hand, the handing down of two decisions by judges in different Member States that conflict with one another might in fact be prevented naturally by applying the preventive mechanism in the form of the European *lis pendens* rule [see art. 17].

19. The concept of 'conflict' between decisions to be adopted when interpreting the grounds of non-recognition in question – although, as far as the ESR is concerned, rulings made in contentious proceedings as well as those in non-contentious proceedings can circulate – will coincide with the concept outlined by the ECJ in relation to paragraphs 3 and 4 of article 34 of regulation no. 44/2001: attention must be paid to the fact that the *res judicata* effects of the two judgments mutually annul one another.[35] Clearly, if the evaluation concerns *dicta* in non-contentious

[34] Davì and Zanobetti, 'Il nuovo diritto internazionale privato delle successioni', p. 128; Pretelli, 'Article 40', p. 604.

[35] ECJ, case 145/86, *Hoffmann* v. *Krieg* [1988] ECR 645, commented on by A. Huet, 'Chronique de jurisprudence de la Cour de justice des Communautés européennes. Convention de Bruxelles du 27 septembre 1968', *JDI* (1989), p. 449; H. Linke, 'Ungelöste Probleme des europäischen Zivilverfahrensrechts. Anderweitige Rechtshängigkeit – zusammenhängende Verfahren – unvereinbare Entscheidungen', *RIW* (1988), p. 822; ECJ, case C-420/07 *Apostolides* v. *Orams* [2009] ECR I-3571, commented on by H. Medainis, 'The Brussels I Regulation and the Cyprus problem before the Court of

proceedings[36], as decisions delivered in such proceedings do not – in principle – have *res judicata* effect, the *focus* must be on the constitutive effects, in terms of creation, modification or extinction of a legal relationship, of the two judgments alone.

20. The requirement under article 40(c) ESR will apply not only where decisions upon the conclusion of declaratory proceedings circulate or in the event of rulings in non-contentious proceedings, but it will also be of application where it is protective measures that circulate [see art. 19 and art. 39].

As in fact clarified by the ECJ in the *Italian Leather* judgment regarding article 27.3 of the 1968 Brussels Convention,[37] 'a foreign decision on

Justice. Comment on Apostolides v. Orams', *ELRev* (2009), p. 963; G. De Baere, *CMLRev* (2010), p. 1123. Other judgments handed down by the Court of Justice have looked at article 34.3 and 34.4 of regulation 44/2001 not just in order to define the concept of 'conflict of decisions' but mainly to delineate the scope of application of the two grounds of non-recognition. Here too, these judgments can be turned to for the purposes of interpreting article 40 (c) and (d) ESR. See in particular: (i) ECJ, case C-157/12, *Salzgitter Mannesmann Handel GmbH* v. *SC Laminorul SA* [2013] ECLI:EU:C:2013:597, annotated by G. Mäsch, 'Keine Anwendbarkeit von Artikel 34 Nummer 4 auf unvereinbare Entscheidungen aus demselben Mitgliedstaat', *EuZW* (2013), p. 905. In *Salzgitter*, the ECJ held that 'article 34(4) of Council Regulation (EC) no. 44/2001 of 22 December 2000 on jurisdiction and the recognition and enforcement of judgments in civil and commercial matters must be interpreted as not covering irreconcilable judgments given by courts of the same Member State'. (ii) ECJ, case C-414/92, *Solo Kleinmotoren* v. *Boch* [1994] ECR I-2237, annotated by A. Huet, *JDI* (1995), p. 466; B. von Hoffmann and W. Hau, 'Deutscher Prozeßvergleich kein Anerkennungshindernis nach Art. 27 Nr. 3 EuGVÜ, *IPRax* (1995), p. 217; G. Coscia, 'Contrasto fra decisioni e atti equiparati', *Foro it.* (1996), IV, p. 463 *et seq.* In this judgment, the Court of Justice provided clarification to the effect that article 27.3 of the Brussels Convention of 1986 then in force 'must be interpreted strictly, inasmuch as it constitutes an obstacle to the achievement of one of its fundamental objectives, which is to facilitate, to the greatest extent possible, the free movement of judgments by providing for a simple and rapid enforcement procedure. Hence article 27(3) of the convention is to be interpreted as meaning that an enforceable settlement reached before a court of the State in which recognition is sought in order to settle legal proceedings which are in progress does not constitute a 'judgment' within the meaning of that provision, 'given in a dispute between the same parties in the State in which recognition is sought' which, under the Convention, may preclude recognition and enforcement of a judgment given in another Contracting State'.

36 See P. Jenard, 'Report on the Convention of 27 September 1968 on jurisdiction and the enforcement of judgments in civil and commercial matters', JO C59, 5 March 1979, p. 9.

37 ECJ, case C-80/00, *Italian Leather s.p.a.* v. *Weco Polstermöbel GmbH & Co.* [2002] ECR I–4995. Commentary on this decision has been provided by C. Consolo and E. Merlin, 'Conflitto fra provvedimenti sommari-cautelari e diniego di riconoscimento: la *Italian Leather* segna una forzatura', *Int'l Lis* (2002), p. 110 *et seq.*; G. Biagioni, 'Interferenze tra provvedimenti provvisori o cautelari e decisioni di merito nella Convenzione di Bruxelles', *Riv dir int* (2002), p. 713 *et seq.*; C. Wolf and S. Lange, 'Das Europäische System des einstweiligen Rechtschutzes – doch noch kein System?', *RIW* (2003), p. 55;

interim measures ordering an obligor not to carry out certain acts is irreconcilable with a decision on interim measures refusing to grant such an order in a dispute between the same parties in the State where recognition is sought' (paragraph 47). Consequently, '[w]here a court of the State in which recognition is sought finds that a judgment of a court of another Contracting State is irreconcilable with a judgment given by a court of the former State in a dispute between the same parties, it is required to refuse to recognise the foreign judgment' (para. 52).

B. Hess, 'Konkurrierende Unterlassungsverfügungen im Europäischen Justizraum', *IPRax* (2005), p. 23.

Article 42

Staying of Recognition Proceedings

ELENA D'ALESSANDRO

A court of a Member State in which recognition is sought of a decision given in another Member State may stay the proceedings if an ordinary appeal against the decision has been lodged in the Member State of origin.

Summary

I. STAYING OF RECOGNITION PROCEEDINGS *page* 561
II. MEANING OF 'ORDINARY APPEAL' 565

I. Staying of Recognition Proceedings

1. Article 42 ESR establishes that the court seised to decide on the recognition of a foreign decision in matters of succession – without implying a declaration of enforceability of such a decision [see art. 43] – can stay proceedings pending before it where the decision has been challenged in the court of origin by the lodging of an 'ordinary appeal'.[1]

Such a situation could occur insofar as the ESR does not require a decision in matters of succession to be a final judgment (i.e. to be vested, e.g. with *formelle Rechtskraft, giudicato formale, cosa juzgada formal, autorité de la chose jugée*) in order to be able to circulate freely within the European legal space.

Thus, if the decision to be recognised is provisionally enforceable in the Member State of origin, as occurs for example in France where a judgment still open to appeal has *force de la chose jugée*,[2] that decision

[1] This is simply a power on the part of the judge hearing the matter, and one that can also be exercised automatically: for agreement on this see I. Pretelli, 'Article 40', in A. Bonomi and P. Wautelet, *Le droit européen des successions. Commentaire du Règlement n° 650/2012 du 4 juillet 2012* (Bruxelles, 2013), p. 608, where attention is drawn to the differences when compared to article 53 ESR [see art. 53], where instead a stay is mandatory.

[2] H. Gaudemet-Tallon, *Compétence et exécution des jugements en Europe*, 4th ed. (Paris, 2010), p. 373 *et seq.*; J. Kropholler and J. von Hein, *Europäisches Zivilprozessrecht*, 9th ed.

could circulate within other EU Member States legal systems pursuant to article 39 ESR [see art. 39]. Therefore, it is possible that a decision automatically recognised in another Member State may be appealed in the Member State of origin.

2. Once it is understood that article 42 ESR refers only to situations in which recognition is sought of a foreign decision in matters of succession appealed in the Member State of origin (similarly to that provided by article 37 of regulation no. 44/2001[3]) it must be established whether this applies:

i) solely to cases in which recognition is requested as a principal issue; or:
ii) where a stay can be ordered also by a Member State court in the course of pending proceedings in which one of the parties has raised a counterclaim seeking a declaration of enforceability of the foreign decision in that Member State; or, even:
iii) where a stay may be ordered in the event that the effects of a decision from another Member State are simply invoked in the course of pending proceedings without the court being requested to rule on the recognition of such a decision, that is, in cases where the court disposes of the issue incidentally, that is by a decision with effects limited to the pending proceedings.

This aspect also caused uncertainly regarding the implementation of article 37 of regulation no. 44/2001 (formerly article 30 of the Brussels Convention on jurisdiction and the enforcement of judgments in civil and commercial matters of 28 September 1968), that is, the rule which inspired the wording of article 42 ESR.

As concerns article 37 of regulation no. 44/2001, it is well-known that some commentators consider that a stay can be ordered only when recognition is requested as a principal issue,[4] while others are of the

(Frankfurt am Main, 2011), p. 551 *et seq.*; E. D'Alessandro, *Il riconoscimento delle sentenze straniere* (Torino, 2007), p. 124 *et seq.*

[3] Council regulation (EC) no. 44/2001 of 22 December 2000 on jurisdiction and the recognition and enforcement of judgments in civil and commercial matters, OJ no. L12, 16 January 2001, p. 1 (replaced as from 10 January 2015 by regulation (EU) no. 1215/2012 of the European Parliament and of the Council of 12 December 2012 on jurisdiction and the recognition and enforcement of judgments in civil and commercial matters (recast), OJ no. L351, 20 December 2012, p. 1).

[4] F. Salerno, *Giurisdizione ed efficacia delle decisioni straniere*, 3rd ed. (Padova, 2006), pp. 375, 377. Cf., concerning the corresponding rule appearing, with amendments, under article 38 regulation 1215/2012, F. Salerno, *Giurisdizione ed efficacia delle decisioni straniere*, 4th ed. (Padova, 2015), p. 367.

opinion that it can be ordered only in the event that recognition is sought as an incidental question.[5]

The Jenard Report on the 1968 Brussels Convention, in commenting on the corresponding article 30 of the convention, referred to a scenario in which an issue concerning the recognition of a decision handed down in another Member State may be raised before a court in the course of pending proceedings without need for that issue to be decided with effect of *res judicata*.[6]

It is therefore necessary to establish which of these two interpretations should be applied *mutatis mutandis* to article 42 ESR.

It would appear that in choosing between these interpretations it is necessary to consider the underlying rationale for staying proceedings pursuant to article 42 ESR.

The staying of recognition proceedings pending in the Member State requested is intended to prevent the court taking account of a decision on succession handed down in another Member State, whose effects:

a) have either been suspended pending the appeal (with reference to cases where the legal system of the Member State of origin provides that the lodging of an appeal suspends the provisional enforceability of the decision automatically, or upon motion by one of the parties); or
b) are enforceable, but are nonetheless subject to being overturned if the appeal is upheld.

If, indeed, this is the rationale for a stay under article 42 ESR, then the need to stay the proceedings in the Member State requested cannot be limited to situations in which recognition is claimed as a principal issue. This in order to prevent a pointless declaration of recognition being adopted, with a decision being declared effective in the Member State requested whilst it is later overturned in the Member State of origin (case

[5] O. Lopes Pegna, *I procedimenti relativi all'efficacia delle decisioni straniere in materia civile* (Padova, 2009), p. 206; P. Gottwald, 'Article 37', in *Münchener Kommentar zur Zivilprozessordnung*, vol. 3, 3rd ed. (München, 2008), para. 3; S. Leible, 'Brussels I-VO', in T. Rauscher (ed), *Europäisches Zivilprozess* (München, 2011), p. 769; J. Kropholler, *Europäisches Zivilprozessrecht*, 8th ed. (Frankfurt am Main, 2005), p. 442; Kropholler and von Hein, *Europäisches Zivilprozessrecht*, p. 606; P. Schlosser, *EU-Zivilprozessrecht*, 3th ed. (München, 2009), p. 196, based on the view that, in the event of recognition as a principal issue, article 46 of regulation no. 44/2011 would apply.

[6] P. Jenard, 'Report on the Convention of 27 September 1968 on jurisdiction and the enforcement of judgments in civil and commercial matters', *sub* art. 30, JO C59, 5 March 1979, p. 46; Gaudemet-Tallon, *Compétence et exécution*, p. 469.

b), or, conversely, to prevent recognition being refused due to a transient ground, such as where the effects of the decision have been temporarily suspended in the Member State of origin (case *a*).

The need to order a stay of proceedings could, instead, arise, perhaps even more significantly (for evident reasons) when the foreign judgment is invoked incidentally in the course of proceedings pending on a different issue, which is nonetheless closely dependent on the matter forming the subject of the decision to be recognised (i.e. in case of related actions). In such cases, the risk is that the court will decide on a dependent claim taking into account the content of a decision that is liable to be amended or overturned following the conclusion of appeal proceedings underway in the Member State of origin. Alternatively, it may be the case that the court refuses to take the foreign decision into account because its effects have been suspended following the lodging of an appeal in the Member State of origin. In such cases, the stay of the dependent action produces the result of coordinating the judgment issued in another Member State and the proceedings concerning a cause of action that is closely related to the issue forming the subject of the judgment to be recognised.

The said need of ensuring a coordination exists both in cases in which the interested party has requested a declaration recognising the effects of the foreign judgment in the Member State concerned and when the issue of the recognition of the foreign judgment is decided by a Member State court before which the issue is raised incidentally, and therefore with effects limited to the proceedings pending before it.

Therefore, it appears preferable to adopt the broadest possible interpretation of article 42 ESR.[7]

3. Moreover, from a critical perspective it must be observed that, rather than limiting itself to reproducing the wording of article 37.1 of regulation no. 44/2001, in drafting the wording of article 42 ESR the EU legislator could have clarified the said aspect, preferably opting unequivocally for the reading espoused here.

On the other hand, the choice of remaining true to the letter of article 37 regulation no. 44/2001 appears appropriate, particularly as concerns the decision made by the EU legislator not to allow a stay to be ordered also pending the time limit for the lodging of an appeal, since, according

[7] On similar lines, in relation to article 30 of the Brussels Convention of 1968, see M. De Cristofaro, 'Presupposti e rimedi per il provvedimento che "sospende" l'opposizione all'*exequatur* o il riconoscimento di una sentenza comunitaria', *Riv dir int priv proc* (1998), p. 754.

to the literature, such an extension of the circumstances in which a stay might have been granted would have encouraged the lodging of requests for a stay pursuing a dilatory intent.[8]

Moreover, the problems of coordination with proceedings pending in the State of enforcement arise at the moment of the lodging of an appeal in the Member State of origin, and not during the period in which such an appeal might be brought, since during that period there is no certainty that an appeal will eventually be brought.

II. Meaning of 'Ordinary Appeal'

4. In view of the fact that article 42 ESR is based on the wording of article 37.1 regulation no. 44/2001, an interpretation of the expression 'ordinary appeal' in article 42 ESR can be gleaned from the ECJ case law concerning article 37.1 of that regulation. In *Industrial Diamond* the ECJ had the opportunity to clarify with regard to article 30 of the Brussels Convention (corresponding to article 37 of regulation no. 44/2001) that, in order to establish whether or not an appeal can be considered ordinary, national law should not be consulted.[9] Indeed, 'if the concept of

[8] A. Layton and H. Mercer, *European Civil Practice*, 2nd ed., vol. I (London, 2004), pp. 944–945.

[9] ECJ, case 43/77, *Industrial Diamond. Supplies* v. *Luigi Riva* [1977] ECR 2175, paras. 37, 42. Comments on this judgment have been provided by T. C. Hartley, 'Procedure for Enforcement: Effect of Appeal in Judgment-granting State', *ELRev* (1978) p. 160 and by H. Gaudemet-Tallon, *Rev crit dr int priv* (1979) p. 433. Although it concerns the Brussels Convention of 1968, this judgment can be taken into consideration:

(i) when establishing whether ordering the stay pursuant to article 42 ESR is simply a power on the part of the judge hearing the claim that the decision issued and appealed in another Member State is effective or, instead, a duty. At point 32 of the judgment in the *Industrial Diamond* case, the ECJ in fact stated that 'the court before which the recognition or enforcement is sought is not under a duty to stay the proceedings but merely has the power to do so';
(ii) when establishing the factors to be taken into account by the court when granting the stay.

In the literature, on the concept of an 'ordinary appeal' within the context of the Brussels Convention and regulation no. 44/2001, see also N. Boschiero, 'La nozione di mezzo ordinario di impugnazione ai sensi degli artt. 30 e 38 della Convenzione di Bruxelles del 1968', in T. Ballarino (ed), *La Convenzione di Bruxelles del 1968 e la riforma del processo civile italiano* (Milano, 1985), p. 102 *et seq.*; D'Alessandro, *Il riconoscimento delle sentenze straniere*, p. 362 *et seq.*; Gaudemet Tallon, *Compétence et exécution*, p. 469, p. 478 *et seq.*; Kropholler and J. von Hein, *Europäisches Zivilprozessrecht*, p. 607 *et seq.*; P. Schlosser, *EU-Zivilprozessrecht*, p. 196, p. 223 *et seq.*; Salerno, *Giurisdizione ed efficacia*, p. 376 *et seq.*; T. C. Hartley, *International Commercial Litigation* (Cambridge, 2009), p. 323.

"ordinary appeal" were interpreted by reference to a national legal system, whether the legal system of the State in which the judgment was given or that of the State in which enforcement or recognition is sought, it would in certain cases be impossible to classify a specific appeal with the required degree of certainty for the purposes of articles 30 and 38 of the Brussels Convention' (para. 24).

An autonomous European criterion would be preferable. Significantly, the ECJ in *Industrial Diamond* stated that 'the expression "ordinary appeal" must be understood as meaning any appeal which forms part of the normal course of an action and which, as such, constitutes a procedural development which any party must reasonably expect' (para. 37). It was also specified that

> within the meaning of articles 30 and 38 of the Convention, any appeal which is such that it may result in the annulment or the amendment of the judgment which is the subject-matter of the procedure for recognition or enforcement according to the Convention and the lodging of which is bound, in the State in which the judgment was given, to a period which is laid down by the law and starts to run by virtue of that same judgment constitutes an 'ordinary appeal' which has been lodged or may be lodged against a foreign judgment [para. 42].

5. Once the proceedings have been stayed, in the absence of a uniform EU rule governing the procedures applicable to the resumption of the proceedings, the *lex fori* must be applied:

(i) to establish the time limit for the resumption of proceedings after the end of the stay once the appeal is concluded with a final judgment; and
(ii) to establish the procedure by which the resumption of proceedings must take place and, finally, the parties who can apply for it.

During the stay of the proceedings concerning the recognition of a judgment from another Member State, it will be possible to request provisional, including protective measures according to the procedural law of the Member State of enforcement, pursuant to article 54.1 ESR [see art. 54].

Article 43

Enforceability

LIVIA DI COLA

Decisions given in a Member State and enforceable in that State shall be enforceable in another Member State when, on the application of any interested party, they have been declared enforceable there in accordance with the procedure provided for in Articles 45 to 58.

Summary

I. INTRODUCTORY REMARKS: THE MECHANISM FOR ESTABLISHING ENFORCEABILITY *page* 567
II. DECISIONS SUBJECT TO THE EXEQUATUR PROCEDURE 569

I. Introductory Remarks: The Mechanism for Establishing Enforceability

1. The mechanism selected by the ESR for establishing enforceability is similar to that under regulation no. 44/2001 (Brussels I regulation).[1] A direct consequence of that similarity is the possibility to refer to the case law of the ECJ concerning the procedure provided for under article 36 *et seq.* of regulation no. 44/2001, as well as to its earlier case law regarding article 31 of the Brussels Convention on jurisdiction and the enforcement of judgments in civil and commercial matters of 28 September 1968. The appropriateness of this method of interpretation[2] is confirmed firstly by recital 59 ESR, which states:

[1] Council Regulation (EC) no. 44/2001 of 22 December 2000 on jurisdiction and the recognition and enforcement of judgments in civil and commercial matters, OJ no. L12, 16 January 2001, p. 1 (replaced as from 10 January 2015 by Regulation (EU) no. 1215/2012 of the European Parliament and of the Council of 12 December 2012 on jurisdiction and the recognition and enforcement of judgments in civil and commercial matters (recast), OJ no. L351, 20 December 2012, p. 1).

[2] A. Davì and A. Zanobetti, 'Il nuovo diritto internazionale privato delle successioni nell'Unione Europea', *CdT* 5/2 (2013), pp. 126–127; A. Davì and A. Zanobetti, *Il nuovo diritto internazionale privato europeo delle successioni* (Torino, 2014), pp. 220–221.

> In the light of its general objective, which is the mutual recognition of decisions given in the Member States in matters of succession, irrespective of whether such decisions were given in contentious or non-contentious proceedings, this regulation should lay down rules relating to the recognition, enforceability and enforcement of decisions similar to those of other Union instruments in the area of judicial cooperation in civil matters.

Secondly, as a further confirmation of the validity of this approach, the part of the European Commission's proposal[3] dedicated to a commentary of the articles of the proposed ESR states in respect of chapter IV that:

> The provisions contained in this Chapter are based on the corresponding rules contained in regulation (EC) No 44/2001. Provision is made for the recognition of all the decisions and legal transactions in order to give substance in succession matters to the principle of mutual recognition, which is based on the principle of mutual trust. The grounds for non-recognition have therefore been kept to the necessary minimum.

The concerns raised in the study conducted by *Deutsches Notarinstitut*,[4] in which it was agreed that *l'organisation d'une procédure simplifiée* was appropriate while *l'allègement du contrôle exercé sur la décision étrangère*[5] was not, have not been acted upon. The need was stressed to retain the control by the court in the Member State in which enforcement is sought over possible grounds of non-recognition also in the *ex parte* summary stage, given the often irreversible consequences of enforcement of a decision in matters of succession. The difficulty was also noted in distinguishing between matters of succession and other issues which are strictly connected but subject to different rules: such as, for example, obligations incumbent upon the estate to pay maintenance and disputes between creditors or debtors of the estate and the heirs.

On 10 January 2015, regulation no. 1215/2012 came into force, repealing regulation no. 44/2001, which, nonetheless, continues to apply in respect of

[3] Proposal for a regulation of the European Parliament and of the Council on jurisdiction, applicable law, recognition and enforcement of decisions and authentic instruments in matters of succession and the creation of a European Certificate of Succession, 14 October 2009, COM/2009/0154 final.

[4] Deutsches Notarinstitut (ed), *Conflict of Law of Succession in the European Union. Perspectives for a Harmonisation* (Würzburg, 2004).

[5] H. Gaudemet-Tallon, 'Quelques réflexions sur les propositions concernant la compétence judiciaire, la reconnaissance et l'exécution des décisions en matière successorale dans l'Union européenne', in Deutsches Notarinstitut (ed), *Conflict of Law of Succession in the European Union. Perspectives for a Harmonisation* (Würzburg, 2004), p. 445.

judgments given in proceedings commenced before that date. The main new features of this regulation include the abolition of the *exequatur* procedure in respect of judgments in civil and commercial matters falling under its scope of application, excluding, *inter alia*, wills and succession. Therefore that legislation does not address matters of succession.

II. Decisions Subject to the *Exequatur* Procedure

2. The concept of 'decision' for the purposes of the ESR is defined under article 3(g) as any decision issued by a court or officer of the court with authority to decide on costs and regardless of what the decision may be called. The ECJ, referring to the corresponding provision under the Brussels Convention, has held that provisions which limit themselves to declaring the intention of the parties cannot be classified as decisions[6]. For the purposes of the ESR, 'decision' means a ruling issued at the outcome of either contentious proceedings or non-contentious proceedings: that is not only expressly specified under recital 59 ESR, but can also be inferred from the preparatory works.[7] Indeed, the report accompanying the 2009 European Commission's Proposal,[8] under section 4.1, chapter I 'Scope of application and definitions', article 2, reads: 'Courts: More often than not, successions are settled out of court. The concept of courts used in this regulation is used in its broadest sense and includes other authorities where they exercise a function falling within the jurisdiction of the courts, in particular by means of delegation, including notaries and court clerks'. In that respect it must be borne in mind that notaries and court clerks feature strongly in the administration of non-contentious proceedings and at the summary stage of contentious proceedings such as for example the German *Mahnverfahren* procedure (summary order for payment). The possibility for bodies other than courts to hand down measures capable of enforcement under art. 43 ESR does not contrast with ECJ case law related to the Brussels Convention of 1968, according to which '... in order to be

[6] ECJ, case C-414/92, *Solo Kleinmotoren GmbH* v. *Emilio Boch* [1994] ECR I-2237, para 18; see Davì and Zanobetti, *Il nuovo diritto internazionale privato europeo delle successioni*, p. 220 *et seq*.

[7] Davì and Zanobetti, 'Il nuovo diritto internazionale privato delle successioni nell'Unione Europea', pp. 126–127; Davì and Zanobetti, *Il nuovo diritto internazionale privato europeo delle successioni*, p. 220 *et seq*.

[8] See footnote 3.

a "judgment" for the purposes of the Convention the decision must emanate from a judicial body of a Contracting State deciding on its own authority on the issues between the parties'.[9] Court clerks and notaries, in fact, may perform functions delegated by the court in proceedings or procedural stages in which there is no need to resolve any dispute.[10]

3. Therefore, within the context of the ESR, the doubts raised in the literature as to whether decisions given in non-contentious proceedings are to be excluded from the definition of 'decision' in terms of article 32 of regulation no. 44/2001[11] are to be ruled out altogether. The notion of a decision entitled to recognition [see art. 39] coincides only partially with that of a decision capable of enforcement: 'The enforcement procedure which relates solely to measures requiring material execution ... is designed to render the foreign judgment enforceable by means of a domestic order'.[12] Whilst the object of automatic recognition is the finding made in a court decision, decisions issued in non-contentious proceedings cannot fall within that definition, even though they may contain enforceable provisions. On the contrary, declaratory judgments and judgments *in rem* are recognisable but not enforceable. Nonetheless, such judgments can still be implemented other than through enforcement, for example by entry into public registers without any requirement for an *exequatur* procedure.

Provisional and protective measures [see art. 19] can also be declared enforceable provided that the following conditions are met: if delivered *ex parte*, the unsuccessful party has been summoned to appear;[13] the defendant is guaranteed reimbursement of any amount paid in the event that the claimant is unsuccessful in the proceedings on the merits;[14] or

[9] ECJ, case C-414/92, *Solo Kleinmotoren*, in footnote 3, para. 17; ECJ, case C-39/02, *Mærsk Olie & Gas A/S* v. *Firma M. de Haan & W. de Boer* [2004] ECR I-9657, para. 45.

[10] W. J. Habscheid, *Freiwillige Gerichtsbarkeit* (München, 1983), p. 22.

[11] F. Salerno, *Giurisdizione ed efficacia delle decisioni straniere nel regolamento (CE) n. 44/2001*, 3rd ed. (Padova, 2006), p. 65; with regard to regulation no. 1215/2012, F. Salerno, *Giurisdizione ed efficacia delle decisioni straniere nel regolamento (UE) n. 1215/2012 (rifusione)*, 4th ed. (Padova, 2015), p. 315 *et seq.*; S. M. Carbone, *Lo spazio giudiziario europeo in materia civile e commerciale*, 6th ed. (Torino, 2009), p. 220; H. Gaudemet-Tallon, *Compétence et exécution des jugements en Europe*, 4th ed. (Paris, 2010), p. 388.

[12] Opinion of Advocate General La Pergola, 28 May 1998, case C-267/97, *Eric Coursier* v. *Fortis Bank et al.* [1999] ECR I-2543, para. 13.

[13] ECJ, case C-125/79, *Denilauler* v. *Couchet Frères* [1980] ECR I-1553; ECJ, case C-474/93, *Hengst Import BV* v. *Anna Maria Campese* [1995] ECR I-2113.

[14] ECJ, case C-391/95, *Van Uden Maritime BV* v. *Deco-Line*, [1998] ECR I- 7091; ECJ, case C-99/96, *Mietz* v. *Intership Yachting Sneek BV* [1999] ECR I- 2277.

the proceedings concern protective measures.[15] An award of costs may be held to be enforceable insofar as it is an independent decision pursuant to article 3 ESR [see art. 3 no. 11], irrespective of any claim seeking to enforce the decision on the merits. No application for a declaration of enforceability can be made in respect of orders the effects of which are limited to the pending proceedings, such as measures of inquiry.

4. One prerequisite for a declaration of enforceability under the rule in question is that the decision is enforceable pursuant to the law of the country in which it is given:[16] the enforceability of the decision in the Member State of origin is a prerequisite for the enforcement of the decision in the Member State in which enforcement is sought.[17] It must be borne in mind that the decision must be accompanied by the enforcement order granted in the State of origin whenever this is required for the decision to be enforced at a domestic level, failing which it cannot be considered as an enforceable title. The Jenard Report, however, specified, in relation to article 31 of the Brussels Convention, that 'Article 31 does not purport to determine whether it is the judgment given in the State of origin, or the decision authorizing the issue of the enforcement order, which is enforceable in the State in which enforcement is sought'.[18] The ECJ held that, in an *exequatur* procedure, it is irrelevant whether a decision can materially be enforced on assets available to satisfy the claim[19] and whether it is actually enforced in the Member State of origin: the fact of the decision having already been enforced in the Member State of origin can only be invoked as a ground of opposition to enforcement measures undertaken following a declaration of enforceability in the Member State requested.[20] The court reached that conclusion starting from the assumption that the granting of a declaration of enforceability may be refused only based on the grounds contemplated under European Union law.

15 ECJ, case C-261/90, *Mario Reichert* v. *Dresdner Bank AG* [1992] ECR I- 2149, para. 34; ECJ, case C-391/95, *Van Uden*, in footnote 14, para. 37; ECJ, case C-104/03, *St. Paul Dairy Industries NV* v. *Unibel Exser BVBA* [2005] ECR I- 3481, para. 13.

16 P. Jenard, 'Report on the Convention of 27 September 1968 on jurisdiction and the enforcement of judgments in civil and commercial matters', OJ 1979 no. C59, 5 March 1979, pp. 1–48.

17 ECJ, case C-139/10, *Prism Investments BV* v. *Jaap Anne van der Meer/ Arilco Holland BV* [2011] ECR I- 9511, para. 38.

18 Jenard, 'Report', p. 49.

19 ECJ, case C-267/97, *Eric Coursier*, in footnote 12; ECJ, case C-420/07, *Meletis Apostolides* v. *David Charles Orams, Linda Elizabeth Orams* [2009] ECR I- 3571.

20 ECJ, case C-139/10, *Prism Investments*, above footnote 17, paras. 39–40, 43.

5. The basic equivalence of enforceability of the decision in the country of origin and in that in which enforcement is sought means that the *exequatur* procedure cannot provide the decision with broader effects than it had in its country of origin.[21] When called upon to interpret article 26 of the Brussels Convention, the ECJ clarified that the recognition of foreign judgments must 'have the result of conferring on judgments the authority and effectiveness accorded to them in the State in which they were given'.[22] In that respect, there are two principal conflicting models of the circulation of foreign judgments [see arts. 40–41]: that of the 'extension of the effects', endorsed within the case law mentioned above, and that of the 'assimilation of the effects', according to which the foreign decision must be given the same effect as the corresponding domestic decision.[23] A third and halfway construction known as '*doppia confinazione degli effetti*' [dual limitation of the effects] may be preferable to either of the two solutions put forward. According to that third model some interference by the legal system of the country where enforcement is requested should also be admitted in determining the scope of the effects attributable to the decision recognised:[24] following recognition, the effects of the foreign judgment would be limited to those which are common to both legal systems for judgments of the like.

6. The decision has to give rise to a title which is enforceable: i.e. it must involve a right which is clearly and unconditionally determined, so as to permit its effective enforcement in the State in which enforcement is sought.[25] In relation to article 38 of regulation no. 44/2001, it has been

[21] ECJ, case C-420/07, *Meletis Apostolides*, above footnote 19, para. 66.

[22] ECJ, case C-145/86, *Hoffmann* v. *Krieg* [1988] ECR I- 645, paras. 10, 11, 27; P. Jenard, 'Report', pp. 42–43. V. G. de Leval, 'Une harmonisation des procédures d'exécution dans l'Union européenne est-elle concevable?', in G. de Leval (ed), *Seizure and Overindebtedness in the European Union* (Den Haag, 1997), pp. 595–606.

[23] For a more in-depth look, see C. Consolo, 'Evoluzioni nel riconoscimento delle sentenze straniere', *Riv trim dir proc civ* (1997), p. 575; A. Carratta, 'La sentenza civile straniera tra "riconoscimento" ed "estensione dell'efficacia"', *Riv dir proc* (2006), p. 1148; E. D'Alessandro, *Il riconoscimento delle sentenze straniere* (Torino, 2007), p. 67 and footnote 38.

[24] C. Consolo, 'La tutela sommaria e la Convenzione di Bruxelles: la "circolazione" comunitaria dei provvedimenti cautelari e dei decreti ingiuntivi', *Riv dir int priv proc* (1991), p. 628 and footnote 75.

[25] G. Tarzia, 'Les titres exécutoires et le recouvrement des créances dans l'Union Européenne', *Actualité du droit/Annales de droit de Liège* (1995), p. 381; with reference to article 38 of the Brussels I regulation, the Court of Justice held that the term 'enforceable' 'is to be interpreted as referring solely to the enforceability, in formal terms, of foreign decisions and not to the circumstances in which such decisions may be executed in the State of origin' (ECJ, case C-267/97, *Eric Coursier*, in footnote 12, para. 33): see K. Kerameus, 'Article 38', in U. Magnus and P. Mankowski (eds), *Brussels I Regulation* (München, 2007), p. 646.

held that, as the procedure is intended to render a foreign decision equivalent in terms of enforceability to a domestic decision, it is necessary to ensure that the right is determinable with clarity also from the perspective of the Member State where enforcement is requested.[26]

Finally, a partial declaration of enforceability can most likely be sought, based on an application by analogy of article 48 of regulation no. 44/2001.

[26] C. Althammer, 'Art. 38', in T. Simons and R. Hausmann (eds), *Unalex Kommentar Brüssel I-Verordnung: Kommentar zur VO (EG) 44/2001 und zum Übereinkommen von Lugano* (Munich, 2012), p. 788.

Article 44

Determination of Domicile

LIVIA DI COLA

To determine whether, for the purposes of the procedure provided for in Articles 45 to 58, a party is domiciled in the Member State of enforcement, the court seised shall apply the internal law of that Member State.

Article 45

Jurisdiction of Local Courts

1. The application for a declaration of enforceability shall be submitted to the court or competent authority of the Member State of enforcement communicated by that Member State to the Commission in accordance with Article 78.
2. The local jurisdiction shall be determined by reference to the place of domicile of the party against whom enforcement is sought, or to the place of enforcement.

Summary

I. DOMICILE AND ITS DETERMINATION *page* 575
II. JURISDICTION 576

I. Domicile and Its Determination

1. The determination of the domicile of the person against whom enforcement is sought is fundamental for the purposes of a declaration of enforceability of a foreign decision under the ESR, since jurisdiction for that purpose is established on precisely that basis. Using a method common to the Brussels Convention on jurisdiction and the enforcement of judgments in civil and commercial matters of 28 September 1968 and regulation no. 44/2001 (Brussels I),[1] the EU legislator has not provided a definition of domicile, considering it sufficient to designate the law applicable for that purpose, i.e. the *lex fori*. As a difference from article 40 regulation no. 44/2001, and as is discussed in the relevant comment [see art. 46 and art. 49 no. 6], article 46 ESR does not require the applicant to have a postal address or an authorised representative in the Member State of enforcement.

[1] Council Regulation (EC) no. 44/2001 of 22 December 2000 on jurisdiction and the recognition and enforcement of judgments in civil and commercial matters, OJ no. L12, 16 January 2001, p. 1.

Similarly to article 41.3 regulation no. 1215/2012 (Brussels I-*bis*),[2] article 46 confirms a specific choice of legislative policy in that sense.[3] Under article 41.3 regulation Brussels I-*bis*, the appointment of an authorised representative in the Member State where enforcement is sought is required only in case it is mandatory according to the law of that Member State irrespective of the nationality or the domicile of the applicant.

II. Jurisdiction

2. In order to determine jurisdiction for the purposes of a declaration of enforceability of a decision given in another Member State, the criteria adopted by article 45 consist of the domicile of the party against whom enforcement is sought, or, alternatively, of the place of enforcement of the decision. In this way, problems relating to multiple domiciles of the person against whom enforcement is sought or difficulties in identifying his actual domicile can be avoided. In the event of multiple domiciles, the court seised of an application for a declaration of enforceability of a decision given in another Member State should rely on the notion of domicile established by the *lex fori* and ascertain, prior to the commencement of the proceedings, whether on the basis of domestic law the defendant has a domicile in that Member State. In cases involving a negative conflict of jurisdictions, the *impasse* may be overcome by referring to the courts of the place where enforcement is sought.[4] This alternative jurisdiction for the purposes of a declaration of enforceability of a foreign decision, which is also available under regulation no. 44/2001 and constitutes an innovation with respect to the Brussels Convention,[5] has been much appreciated by the literature,[6] which has stressed that the procedure of *exequatur* is nothing more than a precursor for the subsequent conduct of the enforcement procedure. Since jurisdiction over

[2] Regulation (EU) no. 1215/2012 of the European Parliament and of the Council of 12 December 2012 on jurisdiction and the recognition and enforcement of judgments in civil and commercial matters (recast), OJ no. L351, 20 December 2012, p. 1, which has replaced regulation no. 44/2001 as from 10 January 2015.

[3] I. Pretelli, 'Art. 46', in A. Bonomi and P. Wautelet, *Le droit européen des successions. Commentaire du Règlement nº 650/2012 du 4 juillet 2012* (Bruxelles, 2013), p. 619.

[4] I. Pretelli, 'Art. 44', in A. Bonomi and P. Wautelet, *Le droit européen des successions. Commentaire du Règlement nº 650/2012 du 4 juillet 2012* (Bruxelles, 2013), pp. 615–616.

[5] Pursuant to article 32.2, forum of execution was an alternative to forum of domicile.

[6] E. Merlin, 'Riconoscimento ed esecutività della decisione straniera nel regolamento Bruxelles I', *Riv dir proc* (2001), p. 444.

the enforcement procedure properly so called is determined on the basis of the location of the assets to be expropriated, it may happen that more than one court has jurisdiction. In that respect, it has been held that it is sufficient to demonstrate that the debtor's assets to be subject to enforcement are present within the jurisdiction of the court seised. However, it is not necessary to prove at the time the application is filed that enforcement will actually be possible.[7] The point in time with reference to which jurisdiction is to be established is the date on which the application is field. In compliance with a general rule of *perpetuatio jurisdictionis,* any subsequent changes in the material facts are not relevant. In fact, 'if the jurisdiction of the court seised were to be removed as a result of a change of residence of the debtor after the application was submitted, the debtor could easily evade enforcement proceedings merely by changing his residence'.[8] On the contrary, it is generally considered that an initial lack of jurisdiction may be remedied until the decision is issued.[9]

3. The application for a declaration of enforceability can be brought, subject to the domestic law of the Member State in which enforcement is sought, not only before the courts but also before the competent administrative authorities of that Member State, based on the information which the individual Member States are expected to communicate to the European Commission under article 78 ESR [see art. 77 and art. 79 no. 3], in a manner similar to that provided for under article 39.1 of regulation no. 44/2001. The European Commission is responsible for drawing up the list of authorities to which applications are to be filed in the individual Member States, based on the communications received from the Member States themselves.[10]

[7] C. Althammer, 'Art. 38', in T. Simons and R. Hausmann (eds), *Unalex Kommentar Brüssel I-Verordnung: Kommentar zur VO (EG) 44/2001 und zum Übereinkommen von Lugano* (München, 2012), pp. 780–781.

[8] *Opinion of Advocate General La Pergola*, case C-260/97, *Unibank A/S* v. *Flemming G. Christensen* [1999] ECR I-3717, para. 11; ECJ, case C-260/97, *Unibank A/S* [1999] ECR I-3715, para. 10.

[9] This is a general principle of application in all the EU Member States; see for example German case law (BGH 26 June 1997, *Unalex DE-418*; OLG Saarbrücken 5 March 1992, *Unalex DE-1991*; OLG Zweibrücken 14 September 1999, *Unalex DE-243*), as well as article 8 of the Italian private international law Act of 1995, which sets out the express provision that 'jurisdiction shall subsist where the facts and the provisions that establish it arise during the course of the proceedings'.

[10] The list of authorities resulting from the communications provided by the Member States to the European Commission pursuant to article 78 ESR is available online through the e-justice portal: e-justice.europa.eu/content_successions-166-en.do (last accessed 5 July 2016).

Article 46

Procedure

LIVIA DI COLA

1. The application procedure shall be governed by the law of the Member State of enforcement.
2. The applicant shall not be required to have a postal address or an authorised representative in the Member State of enforcement.
3. The application shall be accompanied by the following documents:
   (a) a copy of the decision which satisfies the conditions necessary to establish its authenticity;
   (b) the attestation issued by the court or competent authority of the Member State of origin using the form established in accordance with the advisory procedure referred to in Article 81(2), without prejudice to Article 47.

Article 47

Non-production of the Attestation

1. If the attestation referred to in point (b) of Article 46 (3) is not produced, the court or competent authority may specify a time for its production or accept an equivalent document or, if it considers that it has sufficient information before it, dispense with its production.
2. If the court or competent authority so requires, a translation of the documents shall be produced. The translation shall be done by a person qualified to do translations in one of the Member States.

Article 48

Declaration of Enforceability

The decision shall be declared enforceable immediately on completion of the formalities in Article 46 without any review under Article 40. The party against whom enforcement is sought shall not at this stage of the proceedings be entitled to make any submissions on the application.

Article 49

Notice of the Decision on the Application for a Declaration of Enforceability

1. The decision on the application for a declaration of enforceability shall forthwith be brought to the notice of the applicant in accordance with the procedure laid down by the law of the Member State of enforcement.
2. The declaration of enforceability shall be served on the party against whom enforcement is sought, accompanied by the decision, if not already served on that party.

Summary

I. THE STRUCTURE AND NATURE OF THE PROCEDURE *page* 581
II. PROCEDURAL ISSUES 586
A. The Initiating Application and Documents to Be Produced 586
B. Control by the Judge at the *inaudita altera parte* Stage 587
C. The Service of Notice of the Decision Granting or Refusing the *exequatur* procedure 588

I. The Nature of the Procedure

1. The purpose of the *exequatur* procedure is to render a foreign judgment enforceable in the state in which enforcement is sought, quickly and by way of a simple review of its formal validity. Indeed, considering the guarantees afforded to the defendant in the original proceedings by the uniform rules on jurisdiction as embodied in the ESR and the respect for defence rights which all Member States are under a duty to guarantee, a judgment given in another Member State benefits from a kind of presumption of regularity, even if it has not become *res judicata* in the Member State of origin.[1] Essentially, the procedure aims to make it easier for a gaining party in the Member State in which the decision on the merits was given to obtain a valid enforcement title. The structure of the procedure reflects the aim pursued: it is comprised of an initial *ex parte*

[1] ECJ, case C-125/79, *Denilauler* v. *Couchet Frères* [1980] ECR I-1553, para. 13.

stage in which the court merely examines the documents produced, and of an eventual second stage of a contradictory nature, which takes place in case the person against whom enforcement is sought brings an appeal against the declaration of enforceability within the relevant time limit. Such a second stage may involve a possible hearing of both parties, during which the person against whom enforcement is sought is placed in a position to raise all relevant arguments and claims to his defence [see art. 50]. In addition to the grounds for denial of recognition set out under article 40, an appeal can be based on the unenforceable nature of the decision,[2] on the fact that the title has already been enforced or on the lack of jurisdiction by the court seised; however, given the trust and respect that the legal system of the Member State in which enforcement is sought is expected to have for the sovereignty of the Member State of origin, any review as to the substance of the case is ruled out altogether [see art. 41], as it is for any attempt to challenge the jurisdiction of the foreign court which handed down the decision whose enforcement is sought.[3] That prohibition applies also in case the decision has not acquired the force of *res judicata*, i.e. it has not become definitive, in the Member State of origin: to that end, all the unsuccessful party can do is to appeal against the order in the Member State of origin. Only in case the enforceability of the decision is suspended as a consequence of an appeal in the Member State of origin can the court in the Member State of enforcement stay the proceedings for a declaration of enforceability upon application by the party against whom enforcement is sought [see art. 53]. The provisions of the ESR merely outline the framework for the procedure, leaving it to the domestic law of the Member State where enforcement is sought to make more detailed provision. The ESR, however, sets

[2] On the interpretation of the corresponding provisions regarding enforcement contained in the article in the Brussels Convention on jurisdiction and the enforcement of judgments in civil and commercial matters of 28 September 1968, being the direct antecedent of regulation no. 44/2001 (see footnote 5), on which the procedural part of the ESR is expressly based, see Report on the Convention on jurisdiction and the enforcement of judgments in civil and commercial matters signed at Brussels, 27 September 1968, drawn up by P. Jenard, OJ no. C59, 5 March 1979, p. 47: '[T]he Convention is based on the principle that a foreign judgment is presumed to be in order. It must, in principle, be possible to enforce it in the State in which enforcement is sought. Enforcement can be refused only if there is a ground for refusing recognition. The foreign judgment must, however, be enforceable in the State in which it was given in order to be enforceable in the State in which enforcement is sought'.

[3] Article 27.4 of the Brussels Convention and article 35 of regulation no. 44/2001, which do not have a corresponding provision in the ESR, contemplate a limited check on the respect for exclusive and imperative jurisdiction criteria.

down the fundamental points of the procedure, indicating first the type of documents to be produced and providing also, through an implementing regulation successively adopted by the European Commission, the standard form for the attestation by the competent authority in the Member State of origin to be produced alongside with the decision.[4]

2. Two theories may be recalled regarding the nature and subject of the procedure, which were formulated in respect of similar procedures contemplated under articles 39–42 of regulation no. 44/2001.[5] According to the first of these theories, the procedure under examination is to be considered as contentious from start to finish, and its aim is to establish the conditions necessary for the granting of *exequatur* at both the first and second stages. On the other hand, pursuant to the other view, the initial stage is being administrative in nature, while the second implies the exercise of contentious jurisdiction: the first stage involves a simple review of the formal validity of the documentation, while the second stage deals with the eventual failure to satisfy the requirements for enforceability. The Italian Court of Cassation had stated its views concerning the procedure provided for under article 31 *et seq.* of the Brussels Convention on jurisdiction and the enforcement of judgments in civil and commercial matters of 27 September 1968.[6] The court held that it was indeed a procedure of contentious jurisdiction, of the same nature as the ordinary *exequatur* procedure contemplated under Italian law as at the time in force, in respect of which it constituted a special procedure, involving, not differently form the ordinary one, the resolution of conflicting individual rights regarding the enforcement of a foreign judgment. The initial stage would also appear to be contentious in nature because, also at that stage, the court had, under the procedure as devised

[4] Cf. Commission Implementing Regulation (EU) no. 1329/2014 of 9 December 2014, establishing the forms referred to in Regulation (EU) no. 650/2012 of the European Parliament and of the Council on jurisdiction, applicable law, recognition and enforcement of decisions and acceptance and enforcement of authentic instruments in matters of succession and on the creation of a European Certificate of Succession, OJ 2014 no. L359, 16 December 2014, p. 30, annex I, form I.

[5] Council Regulation (EC) no. 44/2001 of 22 December 2000 on jurisdiction and the recognition and enforcement of judgments in civil and commercial matters, OJ no. L12, 16 January 2001 (replaced as from 10 January 2015 by Regulation (EU) no. 1215/2012 of the European Parliament and of the Council of 12 December 2012 on jurisdiction and the recognition and enforcement of judgments in civil and commercial matters (recast), OJ no. L351, 20 December 2012, p. 1).

[6] Corte di cassazione 9 June 1983, n. 3949, *Riv dir int priv proc* (1984), p. 162; Corte di cassazione 26 June 1986, n. 4253, *Riv dir int priv proc* (1987), p. 767; Corte di cassazione 16 July 1994, n. 6704, *Riv dir int priv proc* (1995), p. 727.

under the Brussels Convention, the power to establish whether the prerequisites for enforcement of the judgment had been met. It thus amounted to a merely potential and deferred adversarial procedure, in which the commencement of the properly adversarial phase was dependent on the raising of an appeal within the prescribed time limits, failing which the decision concerning the enforceability became definitive.

3. Regulation no. 44/2001 made significant amendments to the initial stage of the *exequatur* procedure, aimed at further restricting the competence of the court by removing the requirement for evidence of due service of the document instituting proceedings or of the decision on the absent party;[7] in addition, the court can no longer investigate at this stage of the procedure the existence of grounds for denial of recognition.[8] On the basis of the rules as contained under regulation no. 44/2001, it has been argued in the literature that the continuity between the first and second stages of the procedure in terms of subject matter and nature has been lost. The subject matter of the procedure in its first stage is of an essentially administrative nature and the competent court or administrative authority limits itself at this stage to reviewing the formal validity of the documentation produced. The second stage, however, is contentious in nature and aims to establish that the prerequisites for the recognisability have not been met or that the decision is not enforceable.[9] This theory is supported by the fact that it is possible to bring an application for *exequatur* before an administrative authority rather than the courts. It is argued elsewhere in the literature that, notwithstanding the amendments introduced by regulation no. 44/2001, the procedure retains its unitary nature and structure and is still aimed at making a positive finding that the prerequisites for the enforceability of the foreign judgment have been met. The foregoing applies both where the action taken pursuant to article 43 of the said regulation is classified as an opposition and when it is classified as an appeal.[10] The present writer favours the latter classification. The limitation of the

[7] Cf. article 53 regulation no. 44/2001, as compared to articles 46 and 47 of the Brussels Convention.

[8] Cf. article 41 regulation no. 44/2001, as compared to article 34.2, combined with articles 27 and 28 of the Brussels Convention.

[9] E. Merlin, 'Riconoscimento ed esecutività della decisione straniera nel regolamento Bruxelles I', *Riv dir proc* (2001), p. 450 *et seq.*; S. M. Carbone, *Lo spazio giudiziario europeo in materia civile e commerciale*, 6th ed. (Torino, 2009), pp. 231–233; H. Gaudemet-Tallon, *Compétence et exécution des jugements en Europe*, 4th ed. (Paris, 2010), pp. 470–471.

[10] For a more in-depth look on this point, see E. D'Alessando, *Il riconoscimento delle sentenze straniere* (Torino, 2007), p. 366 *et seq.; id.*, 'Exequatur secondo la Convenzione

control by the court at the summary stage, does not in fact affect the nature of the proceedings. In order to establish the solidity of that assertion it must be considered that there are two models within the EU Member States' legal systems of an application for a summary order for payment, involving an initial more or less summary stage which ends, in any event, with an order which can become *res judicata*. These are: the purely summary procedure (a well-known example is the German *Mahnverfahren*), where the applicant merely submits the application without any evidence whatsoever; and the summary order for payment, based on documentary evidence. A distinction may be drawn between the two procedures based on the scope of the court's investigation. In the former model, this is limited to considering the completeness and sufficiency of the application, while in the latter it extends also to the documentary evidence presented. However, both have the same structure and nature, as they are based on deferred adversarial proceedings, which may be initiated upon the initiative of the person against whom the order is sought, who, in bringing opposition against it, may give rise to a second stage of the procedure, involving a full examination of the merits. Failure by the person against whom the order is sought to enter an appearance will, in both types of summary procedure just mentioned, result in a definitive order being pronounced *ex parte.* Furthermore, the argument stressing the possibility of applying, as an alternative, to an administrative authority cannot be considered insurmountable. It is sufficient to bear in mind that in Germany the first stage of proceedings for a summary order for payment *(Mahnverfahren)* is administered by a court official; indeed, since 1 December 2008, an application to obtain an order for payment can only be lodged online and its formal validity is reviewed automatically using software.[11] Essentially, in such a procedure the administrative authority performs functions delegated by the court, which exercises its competence when the resolution of a dispute is necessary. Adhering to the theory of the unitary nature of the two stages means giving *res judicata* authority to decisions made *ex parte* that are not appealed,[12] without at the

di Bruxelles', *Int'l Lis* (2008), I, p. 24; R. Geimer, 'Art. 38–42', in R. Geimer and R. A. Schütze, *Europäisches Zivilverfahrensrecht*, 3rd ed. (München, 2010), pp. 713–766.

[11] U. Salten and K. Gräve, *Gerichtliches Mahnverfahren und Zwangsvollstreckung* (Köln, 2007); B. Sujecki, *Mahnverfahren: mit elektronischem und europäischen Mahnverfahren* (Heideberg-München-Landsberg-Berlin, 2007).

[12] R. Geimer, 'Art. 41', in R. Geimer and R. A. Schütze, *Europäisches Zivilverfahrensrecht*, 3rd ed. (München, 2010), p. 762.

same time granting them the definitive nature which is inherent in an administrative act.[13]

4. Finally, European Union law does not prohibit pre-emptive actions seeking a ruling declaring that a decision given in another Member State is not enforceable, provided this is allowed under the domestic law of the Member State where such a ruling is sought[14].

II. Procedural Issues

5. The procedure outlined by articles 46–48 is extremely concise and essential: it provides a mere framework to be filled in with the provisions of the *lex fori* (article 47.1 ESR).

A. *The Writ of Summons and the Documents to Be Produced*

6. The person with standing to bring an application is the person in whose favour the decision was given, or alternatively, the successors or assignees of the party in whose favour an enforceable copy of the decision has been delivered. More generally, in any event, the principle affirmed in the Jenard Report applies: 'The expression 'on the application of any interested party' implies that any person who is entitled to the benefit of the judgment in the State in which it was given has the right to apply for an order for its enforcement'.[15] The purpose of the procedure identifies the subjects with standing to apply: those who cannot seek enforcement must be excluded.[16] Nothing is said as to the form and content of the application, in respect of which, as a difference from regulation no. 44/2001, article 46.2 ESR provides that the applicant is not required to have a postal address or an authorised representative in the Member State of enforcement. Essentially, article 46.2 ESR contradicts the principle previously established by the ECJ in relation to similar actions governed by article 33 of the Brussels Convention, according to which, if the legal system of the Member States does not contemplate the possibility of

[13] Gaudemet-Tallon, *Compétence et exécution*, pp. 470–471; I. Pretelli, 'Art. 48', in A. Bonomi and P. Wautelet, *Le droit européen des successions. Commentaire du Règlement n° 650/2012 du 4 juillet 2012* (Bruxelles, 2013), p. 620.

[14] Gaudemet-Tallon, *Compétence et exécution*, p. 456, sets out this possibility in relation to the corresponding procedure governed by regulation 44/2001.

[15] Jenard, 'Report', p. 49. [16] Gaudemet-Tallon, *Compétence et exécution*, p. 460.

establishing an address for service, then the applicant is required to appoint a representative *ad litem*[17].

7. The application must be accompanied by certain additional documents. First, a certified copy is required of the decision of which enforcement is sought. As the EU legislator has given no indication regarding this point, the signature of the judge and the stamp of the court clerk appears to be considered as sufficient for the purposes of confirmation of the authenticity of the decision.[18] The attestation issued by the competent court in the State where enforcement is sought must be drawn up in the standard form set forth as annex I to Commission Implementing regulation no. 1329/2014.[19] The ECJ has specified in a fairly recent judgment that use of a standard form has the function of facilitating the declaration of enforceability, by rendering its issue more or less automatic,[20] as it embodies all the necessary information. However, in the same judgment the court added that, in any event, the information contained in the attestation is intended merely for guidance purposes: it is sufficient to note that the attestation does not necessarily have to be issued by the court which gave the decision the enforcement of which is sought.[21] The attestation should avoid the need for translation since the form and instructions are structured identically in all of the various language versions. Submission of the attestation is not mandatory, as can be inferred from article 47.1. Failure to submit the attestation does not necessarily prejudice the favourable outcome of the procedure as the court can accept equivalent documents or decide that they are simply superfluous. Documentary evidence of service or communication of the decision on or to the unsuccessful party is not required, and the date of service needs not to be shown in the attestation.

B. Control by the Court at the inaudita altera parte *Stage*

8. A combined reading of article 48 and article 40 ESR clearly shows that at the initial stage of the *exequatur* procedure the court must limit itself to a merely formal review of the documents filed, without

[17] ECJ, case C-198/85, *Carron* v. *Germany* [1986] ECR 2437, para. 9.

[18] I. Pretelli, 'Art. 46', in A. Bonomi A. and P. Wautelet, *Le droit européen des successions. Commentaire du Règlement nº 650/2012 du 4 juillet 2012* (Bruxelles, 2013), p. 620.

[19] See footnote 4.

[20] ECJ, case C-619/10, *Trade Agency Ltd* v. *Seramico Investments Ltd* [2012] ECLI: EU: C:2012:531, para. 41.

[21] *Ibid.*, para. 36.

examining the grounds for refusal of recognition. The reason for that has been explained on several occasions by the ECJ with reference to articles 38–52 of regulation no. 44/2001:

> The limited nature of that review is justified by the purpose of that procedure, which is not to initiate new proceedings, but rather to agree, on the basis of mutual trust in the administration of justice in the Member States, to the judgment delivered by a court or tribunal of a Member State other than the Member State in which enforcement is sought being enforced by means of incorporation into the latter Member State's legal order.[22]

However some further controls cannot be ruled out. Although the regulation makes no mention in that respect, it is reasonable to suppose that the court may declare of its own motion that it lacks jurisdiction in respect of the declaration of enforceability being sought,[23] as expressly provided under article 15 ESR as concerns jurisdiction on the merits [see art. 15]. In fact, there is no reason to exclude an analogous solution in respect of proceedings of *exequatur*, especially at the *inaudita altera parte* stage. On the other hand, the absence of a defendant at that stage necessarily implies that the powers of control by the judge will be enhanced also in contradictory proceedings when the defendant remains absent (see also article 26.1 of regulation no. 44/2001). Within this context, it is appropriate that the power of the court seised to review its jurisdiction on the application for a declaration of enforceability is exercised uniformly across all Member States. It is considered, furthermore, with reference to the corresponding procedure under regulation no. 44/2001, that at that stage the court should verify the necessary prerequisites for the enforceability of the foreign judgment, such as, for example, the determination or the determinability of the subject.[24]

C. *The Service or Communication of the Order Granting or Refusing* exequatur

9. The decision on conclusion of the *ex parte* stage of the procedure for a declaration of enforceability must be communicated to the applicant by

[22] ECJ, case C-139/10, *Prism Investments BV* v. *Jaap Anne van der Meer/ Arilco Holland BV* [2011] ECR I- 9511, para. 31.

[23] Gaudemet-Tallon, *Compétence et exécution*, pp. 458–459.

[24] C. Althammer, 'Art. 41', in T. Simons and R. Hausmann (eds), *Unalex Kommentar Brüssel I-Verordnung: Kommentar zur VO (EG) 44/2001 und zum Übereinkommen von Lugano* (München, 2012), p. 811.

the clerk of the court seised, irrespective of whether it allows or refuses the application; however, only the decision granting the enforceability must be served on the party against whom enforcement is sought, along with the decision declared enforceable, if this has not already been served or communicated to that party. These formalities are particularly important as their accomplishment determines the starting date for the time limit for an appeal pursuant to article 50 ESR. The service or communication must take place in accordance with the *lex fori*; the same law governs not only the procedure but also the grounds for invalidity or failure to effect service or communication, as well as any regularisation procedure. If the party against whom service has to be effected is domiciled in another Member State, however, regulation no. 1393/2007 on service of documents applies.[25] If that party is domiciled in a third country, international agreements such as the Hague Convention of 15 November 1965 on the Service Abroad of Judicial and Extrajudicial Documents in Civil or Commercial Matters may come for consideration. As concerns the communication to the applicant of the decision adopted on the application for a declaration of enforceability, this may prove to be difficult if the applicant him- or herself has not provided an address for service or has not appointed a representative in the Member State of enforcement. On the other hand, such an obligation is expressly excluded by article 46. In such cases, it may be necessary to effect the communication in the country in which the applicant is domiciled, and impliedly, if that country is a Member State, according to the procedures set forth in regulation no. 1393/2007.

10. The time limit for an appeal against the decision on the application for a declaration of enforceability pursuant to article 50 will not start to run in the event of invalid service or if service is not effected. In addition, mere knowledge of the order on the part of the applicant or of the party against whom enforcement is sought cannot be relied upon to that end.[26] As regards the right of defence of the party against whom enforcement is sought, the ECJ has held that

> First, the requirement that the decision authorising enforcement be served has a dual function: on the one hand, it serves to protect the rights of the

[25] Regulation (EC) no. 1393/2007 of the European Parliament and of the Council of 13 November 2007 on the service in the Member States of judicial and extrajudicial documents in civil or commercial matters (service of documents), and repealing Council Regulation (EC) no. 1348/2000, OJ L324, 10 December 2007, p. 79.

[26] ECJ, case C-3/05, *G. Verdoliva* v. *J. M. Van der Hoeven BV, Banco di Sardegna & San Paolo IMI SpA.* [2006] ECR I-1579, paras. 34–38.

> party against whom enforcement is sought and, on the other, it allows, in terms of evidence, the strict and mandatory time-limit for appealing provided for under that provision to be calculated precisely.[27] . . . Secondly, . . . if the sole issue were whether the document authorising enforcement came to the attention of the party against whom enforcement was sought, that could render the requirement of due service meaningless.[28] . . . Moreover, that would make the exact calculation of the time-limit provided for in that provision more difficult, thus thwarting the uniform application of the provisions of the Convention'.[29]

These requirements and guarantees are in fact required in respect of any of the parties entitled to appeal against the decision adopted on the application for a declaration of enforceability, who, faced with an unfavourable decision, has an interest in being informed of this fact quickly, in order to be able to file an appeal against it. For the purposes of service or communication of the said decision, it is therefore advisable that the applicant states an address in the application bringing the proceedings.

[27] *Ibid.*, para. 34. [28] *Ibid.*, para. 36. [29] *Ibid.*, para. 37.

Article 50

Appeal against the Decision on the Application for a Declaration of Enforceability

SALVATORE ZIINO

1. The decision on the application for a declaration of enforceability may be appealed against by either party.
2. The appeal shall be lodged with the court communicated by the Member State concerned to the Commission in accordance with Article 78.
3. The appeal shall be dealt with in accordance with the rules governing procedure in contradictory matters.
4. If the party against whom enforcement is sought fails to appear before the appellate court in proceedings concerning an appeal brought by the applicant, Article 16 shall apply even where the party against whom enforcement is sought is not domiciled in any of the Member States.
5. An appeal against the declaration of enforceability shall be lodged within 30 days of service thereof. If the party against whom enforcement is sought is domiciled in a Member State other than that in which the declaration of enforceability was given, the time for appealing shall be 60 days and shall run from the date of service, either on him in person or at his residence. No extension may be granted on account of distance.

Summary

I. INTRODUCTORY REMARKS *page* 591
II. MUTUAL RECOGNITION AND APPEAL: TIME LIMITS AND PARTIES 594
III. PROCEDURE 596

I. Introductory Remarks

1. The proposal for a regulation in matters of succession tabled by the European Commission in 2009 contained only five articles that dealt with the recognition and enforcement of decisions regarding succession.[1]

[1] See articles 29–33 of the Proposal for a regulation of the European Parliament and of the Council on jurisdiction, applicable law, recognition and enforcement of decisions and

In terms of the relevant procedure, those articles referred back to section 2 of chapter III, regulation no. 44/2001, specifically dedicated to the enforcement of judgments given in other Member States.[2]

During the legislative procedure leading to the adoption of the ESR, the preferred route was, however, to introduce specific procedural provisions regarding the recognition and enforcement of decisions involving succession; to a large extent, these provisions in fact reflect the content of the corresponding provisions under regulation no. 44/2001.[3] The manner in which these two pieces of legislation interact with one another is described by recital 34 ESR, which states that 'this Regulation should provide for general procedural rules similar to those of other Union instruments in the area of judicial cooperation in civil matters', and by recital 59, which states that

> in the light of its general objective, which is the mutual recognition of decisions given in the Member States in matters of succession, irrespective of whether such decisions were given in contentious or non-contentious proceedings, this Regulation should lay down rules relating to the recognition, enforceability and enforcement of decisions similar to those of other Union instruments in the area of judicial cooperation in civil matters.

The extent to which the provisions of the two regulations echo one another implies that when interpreting the provisions of the ESR, reference can be made to judgments handed down by the ECJ in respect of the

authentic instruments in matters of succession and the creation of a European Certificate of Succession, COM(2009)154 final. Back in 2004, the Deutsches Notarinstitut carried out research on behalf of the European Commission into the provisions governing succession in the various different countries in Europe and suggested that the mechanism established by 44/2001 (see footnote 2), involving the automatic recognition of decisions, should apply in this particular area. The research and proposals were published in Deutsches Notarinstitut (ed), *Conflict of Law of Succession in the European Union. Perspectives for a Harmonisation* (Würzburg, 2004) (also available at www.successions.org, last accessed 5 July 2016).

[2] Council Regulation (EC) no. 44/2001 of 22 December 2000 on jurisdiction and the recognition and enforcement of judgments in civil and commercial matters, OJ no. L12, 16 January 2001, p. 1 (replaced as from 10 January 2015 by Regulation (EU) no. 1215/2012 of the European Parliament and of the Council of 12 December 2012 on jurisdiction and the recognition and enforcement of judgments in civil and commercial matters (recast), OJ no. L351, 20 December 2012, p. 1).

[3] See J. Müller-Lukoschek, *Die neue EU-Erbrechtsverordnung* (Bonn, 2013), p. 131; A. Davì and A. Zanobetti, 'Il nuovo diritto internazionale privato delle successioni nell'Unione Europea', *CdT* (2013), p. 125; A. Davì and A. Zanobetti, *Il nuovo diritto internazionale privato europeo delle successioni* (Torino, 2014), p. 219. Regulation no. 1215/2012 (see footnote 2) is based on new principles and new rules: in particular, the *exequatur* is abolished and, pursuant to article 39, a decision issued 'in a Member State shall be enforceable in the other Member States without any declaration of enforceability being required'.

corresponding provisions under regulation no. 44/2001 as well as under its direct antecedent, the Brussels Convention of 1968;[4] this is of course on the proviso that these judgments are compatible with the peculiarities of succession matters.[5]

2. Pursuant to the ESR, decisions issued in other Member States 'shall be recognised in the other Member States without any special procedure being required' [see art. 39 no. 1]: the task of considering whether there are any obstacles to recognition is postponed to the appeal stage, if indeed an appeal is launched. The enforcement of decisions is instead dependant upon proceedings being commenced, although the initial phase is carried out without hearing the party against whom enforcement is sought, as stated in article 48 [see art. 46 and art. 49 no. 1].[6]

Article 50 ESR, which corresponds with article 43 of regulation no. 44/2001, governs appeals against decisions on declarations of enforceability. The five paragraphs that make up this article establish the right of either party to appeal; they refer to the communications by the individual Member States that identify the competent national court before which an appeal is to be lodged; they refer to the domestic rules of the individual Member States governing procedure in contentious matters; they provide for the application of article 16 ESR in respect of cases where the defendant to the enforcement proceedings does not appear, and, lastly, they establish the time limit for an appeal.

4 Convention on jurisdiction and the enforcement of judgments in civil and commercial matters, Brussels, 28 September 1968. The 'continuity between the Brussels Convention and this Regulation', which 'applies as regards the interpretation of the Brussels Convention by the Court of Justice of the European Communities', is expressly stated by recital 19 of regulation no. 44/2001.

5 Davì and Zanobetti, 'Il nuovo diritto internazionale privato delle successioni nell'Unione Europea', p. 126; Davì and Zanobetti, *Il nuovo diritto internazionale privato europeo*, p. 219.

6 Support for this decision had been expressed by the Max Planck Institute for Comparative and International Private Law, 'Comments on the European Commission's Proposal for a Regulation of the European Parliament and of the Council on jurisdiction, applicable law, recognition and enforcement of decisions and authentic instruments in matters of succession and the creation of a European Certificate of Succession', *RabelsZ* (2010), p. 667, para. 252. Given that matters of succession and family law are closely knit, and in light of the sometime irreversible consequences of decisions made regarding the former, the suggestion had instead been made that a different mechanism be introduced that was based on checks being carried out in advance (H. Gaudemet-Tallon, 'Quelques réflexions sur les propositions concernant la compétence judiciaire, la reconnaissance et l'exécution des décisions en matière successorale dans l'Union européenne', in Deutsches Notarinstitut (ed), *Conflict of Law of Succession in the European Union. Perspectives for a Harmonisation* (Würzburg, 2004), pp. 455–456).

II. Mutual Recognition and Appeal: Time Limits and Parties

3. An appeal against the decision on an application for a declaration of enforceability can be lodged by 'either party' and can, therefore, be launched by anyone who was a party to the proceedings heard in the originating Member State and in fact *only* by such parties. These provisions are mandatory, as confirmed by case law from the Court of Justice in relation to the corresponding article 43 of regulation no. 44/2001.[7]

Where the national court has declared the foreign decision enforceable, the party subject to the declaration of enforceability may appeal within a time limit, established under article 50.5 ESR, of thirty days, or sixty days where the party resides in another Member State. These time limits, which are peremptory, run from the date on which the decision on the application for a declaration of enforceability was served on the respondent directly or at his address.[8]

4. Article 50 ESR follows the example set by article 43 of regulation no. 44/2001 and article 36 of the Brussels Convention in laying down no specific rules as concerns the time limit for lodging an appeal in respect of cases where the party against whom enforcement is sought resides in a third country. It would, however, be unreasonable to assume from the silence on the part of article 43 that in such circumstances the appeal must be lodged within the thirty day time limit: this is a very tight time frame that would make it extremely difficult to exercise the right to a defence, this of course being a fundamental right enshrined in article 6 of the European Convention on Human Rights and in article 47 of the Charter of Fundamental Rights of the European Union.[9]

[7] ECJ, case 167/08, *Draka NK Cables Ltd* v. *Omnipol Ltd* [2009] ECR I-03477, which went as far as establishing that creditors who stand in their debtor's shoes and enforce rights directly are to be treated as third parties and are not entitled to lodge the appeal contemplated by article 43 of regulation no. 44/2001; see R. Bonatti, 'L'autonomia del diritto dell'Unione come cavallo di Troia per una nuova stagione di integrazione processuale: il caso della «nozione di parte»', *Int'Lis* (2010) 2, p. 69; H. Gaudemet-Tallon, *Compétence et exécution des jugements en Europe*, 4th ed. (Paris, 2010), p. 476; F. Ravidà, 'Il regolamento n. 44/2001 sulla competenza giurisdizionale, il riconoscimento e l'esecuzione delle decisioni in materia civile e commerciale', in S. Scarafoni (ed), *Il processo civile e la normativa comunitaria* (Torino, 2012), p. 270.

[8] Note that regulation no. 44/2001 sets out slightly different time limits for an appeal, being a month (instead of thirty days) and two months (instead of sixty days) respectively.

[9] In relation to the corresponding provision contained in article 43 of regulation no. 44/2001, see Gaudemet-Tallon, *Compétence et exécution*, p. 476.

The more logical conclusion would appear to be as follows: as these circumstances are not catered for by the uniform provisions, we have to work on the basis of the time limits established under the domestic law of the individual Member States,[10] with regard either to specific provisions expressly contemplating such cases or, in the absence of such provisions, to general rules of procedure.[11]

5. Article 50 establishes no time limit, however, in respect of cases where the appeal is lodged by the party whose application for a declaration of enforceability has been dismissed.[12] The report accompanying the Brussels Convention of 1968 explains that the reasoning behind the absence of a time limit was to allow the applicant to collect the documentation required in order to secure a declaration of enforceability.[13]

6. As mentioned earlier, article 50 ESR only allows the 'parties' to appeal, while third parties have no such power and, therefore, are left to

[10] Davì and Zanobetti, 'Il nuovo diritto internazionale privato delle successioni', p. 127, and Davì and Zanobetti, *Il nuovo diritto internazionale privato europeo*, p. 221 and footnote 54, where the view is expressed that in the case of a party domiciled in a non-Member State, the time limit could be extended on the grounds of distance, following the rules in force on this point in the Member State in which the declaration that the decision is enforceable has been issued, while this extension is not possible where the parties are domiciled in Member States; in relation to article 43 of regulation no. 44/2001, see on these lines Gaudemet-Tallon, *Compétence et exécution*, p. 476. This interpretation makes reference to claims made regarding the corresponding provisions in the Brussels Convention of 1968 by P. Jenard, 'Report on the Convention of 27 September 1968 on jurisdiction and the enforcement of judgments in civil and commercial matters', OJ 1979 no. C59, 5 March 1979, p. 51. Referring to that Report, K. Kerameus, 'Article 43', in U. Magnus and P. Mankowski (eds), *Brussels I Regulation* (München, 2007), p. 663, states: 'if the party taking the appeal is domiciled outside the Community territory, it is submitted that the time limit will be one month which may be extended on account of distance in accordance with the law of the Member State authorizing enforcement of the foreign judgment'.

[11] In Germany, for example, specific provisions govern this particular situation courtesy of article 55 of the law on recognition and enforcement of foreign decisions (*Anerkennungs- und Vollstreckungsausführungsgesetz, AVAG*), which establishes a two-month time limit for the appeal contemplated by article 43 of regulation no. 44/2001, including where the party subject to the decision resides in a non-Member State: see R. Geimer, 'Anerkennung und Vollstreckung', in R. Geimer and R. A. Schütze, *Europäisches Zivilverfahrensrecht*, 3rd ed. (Munich, 2010), pp. 775–776.

[12] The Italian Corte di cassazione 2 August 2007, no. 17005, *Riv dir int priv proc* (2009), p.175, instead erroneously stated that where the application for a declaration of enforceability is dismissed, pursuant to the Brussels Convention an appeal must be lodged within the same time limits as those that apply in the event that the application is granted.

[13] Jenard, 'Report', p. 53. In relation to the corresponding provisions of regulation no. 44/2001, certain Member States such as the UK and the Netherlands have introduced specific time limit in which to lodge an appeal against the dismissal of an application for a declaration of enforceability: see the references in Gaudemet-Tallon, *Compétence et exécution*, p. 477.

exercise their rights using other routes. On this point, the ECJ has stated that the enforcement proceedings properly intended, as distinct from the procedure for a declaration of enforceability, continue to be governed by the law of the Member State in which enforcement is sought; it follows that third parties can defend the enforcement proceedings using the mechanisms provided by the law of that country. This does not, of course, prevent them from taking action in the Member State in which the decision to be recognised was issued, relying on the various remedies established by the law of that country.[14]

III. Procedure

7. Each Member State has communicated to the Commission, details the court having jurisdiction to hear the appeal pursuant to article 50 ESR [see art. 77 and art. 79 no. 3].[15]

8. The appeal itself, including the format of the notice of appeal, the time limits for the parties to appear and the subsequent phases, is governed by the national provisions in force in the individual Member States in respect of contentious matters, as set out specifically in article 50.3 ESR.[16] This applies irrespective of whether the appeal is lodged by the party against whom the declaration of enforceability is sought or by the party whose application for a declaration of enforceability has been dismissed.

The parties are only required to have legal representation on appeal in those cases where the relevant provisions of the individual Member State in which enforcement is sought so provide.

9. Article 50.4 ESR, which corresponds with article 43.4 of regulation no. 44/2001, puts special safeguards in place where the appeal is lodged against a decision denying enforcement. Where the appeal is launched by

[14] ECJ, case C-167/08, *Draka NK Cables Ltd* v. *Omnipol Ltd* [2009] ECR I-03477; v. R. Geimer, 'Anerkennung und Vollstreckung', in R. Geimer and R. A. Schütze, *Europäisches Zivilverfahrensrecht*, p. 775; I. Pretelli, 'Article 50', in A. Bonomi and P. Wautelet, *Le droit européen des successions. Commentaire du Règlement n° 650/2012 du 4 juillet 2012* (Bruxelles, 2013), p. 633.

[15] The list of the authorities with competence to deal with appeals against decisions on applications in accordance with with article 50(2) is available on-line through the e-justice portal: https://e-justice.europa.eu/content_successions-166-en.do (last accessed 5 July 2016).

[16] In relation to the corresponding provisions of regulation no. 44/2001, see B. Hess, 'Free Movement of Judgments', in B. Hess, T. Pfeiffer and P. Schlosser (eds), *The Brussels I Regulation (EC) No. 44/2001* (München, 2008), p. 147.

the party who originally applied for a declaration of enforceability and the other party fails to appear, article 16 ESR applies [see art. 16], even if the defendant to the original application is domiciled in a country that is not a Member State. It follows that the court is therefore required to stay the proceedings until the claimant has demonstrated that the defendant was in a position to receive the document commencing the proceedings (or an equivalent document) in sufficient time to prepare his defence, or that all necessary requirements have been complied with to that end.[17]

[17] For comments on the similar provision under regulation no. 44/2001, see Kerameus, 'Article 43', p. 664 *et seq*.

Article 51

Procedure to Contest the Decision Given on Appeal

SALVATORE ZIINO

The decision given on the appeal may be contested only by the procedure communicated by the Member State concerned to the Commission in accordance with Article 78.

Article 52

Refusal or Revocation of a Declaration of Enforceability

The court with which an appeal is lodged under Article 50 or Article 51 shall refuse or revoke a declaration of enforceability only on one of the grounds specified in Article 40. It shall give its decision without delay.

Summary

I. REVIEW OF THE DECISION GIVEN ON APPEAL *page* 599

II. SCOPE OF THE REVIEW BY THE COURTS OF THE MEMBER STATE WHERE ENFORCEMENT IS SOUGHT 601

I. Review of the Decision Given on Appeal

1. In order to ensure the free circulation of decisions and to avoid decisions being opened up and re-examined as to their substance, articles 51 and 52 ESR establish that the decision on appeal can only be challenged in accordance with the procedures that each Member State is required to notify to the European Commission [see art. 77 and art. 79 no. 3], and the courts in the Member State requested are only able to refuse to grant or revoke the declaration of enforceability if one of the grounds set out in article 40 is met [see art. 40 and art. 41 no. 1 *et seq*].

Member States have therefore communicated details to the Commission of:

a) the court that is competent to hear an appeal against decisions on applications for a declaration of enforceability;
b) the court that is competent to hear a second appeal against the decision on an appeal pursuant to article 51 ESR, and
c) details of the procedure to contest the decision given on appeal in accordance with article 51.

On the basis of these communications, the parties can get a picture of the remedies afforded by the various pieces of national legislation;[1] the time limits and procedures to be followed in order to challenge the decision on appeal are governed by the domestic law in force in each individual Member State.

This provision corresponds with article 44 of regulation no. 44/2001[2] and article 37.2 of the Brussels Convention on jurisdiction and the enforcement of judgments in civil and commercial matters of 27 September 1968;[3] as is the case with these other provisions, it can be argued that its purpose is to 'avoid a plethora of appeals'.[4]

[1] The list of the authorities with competence to deal with appeals against decisions on applications in accordance with article 50(2) and that of the authorities to which the appeal for a procedure to contest the decision given on appeal in accordance with article 51 may be lodged, as well as details of the procedures to contest the decision given on appeal in accordance with article 51 itself, are available online through the e-justice portal: https://e-justice.europa.eu/content_successions-166-en.do (last accessed 5 July 2016).

[2] Council Regulation (EC) no. 44/2001 of 22 December 2000 on jurisdiction and the recognition and enforcement of judgments in civil and commercial matters, OJ no. L12, 16 January 2001, p. 1 (replaced as from 10 January 2015 by Regulation (EU) no. 1215/2012 of the European Parliament and of the Council of 12 December 2012 on jurisdiction and the recognition and enforcement of judgments in civil and commercial matters (recast), OJ no. L351, 20 December 2012, p. 1).

[3] The mechanism used by these three provisions differs, however: while the ESR refers to the communications by the Member States in accordance with article 78 ESR, article 37.2 of the Brussels Convention listed the appeals provided for in the different Member States and regulation no. 44/2001 referred to an annex that set out that list, in order to ease the task of adding to or amending its content. As we have seen in relation to article 50 ESR, recitals 34 and 59 ESR state that ESR rules on recognition and enforcement of decisions are similar to those of 'other Union instruments in the area of judicial cooperation in civil matters' [see art. 50 no. 1]; for the purposes of interpreting the provisions of the ESR, to the extent compatible with the specific matter of succession and obviously bearing in mind the differences that can be identified between the provisions of the different instruments, reference can therefore be made to rulings on interpretation by the ECJ regarding other instruments and, in particular, regarding regulation no. 44/2001 and its direct antecedent, the Brussels Convention of 1968.

[4] In relation to the Brussels Convention of 1968, see P. Jenard, 'Report on the Convention of 27 September 1968 on jurisdiction and the enforcement of judgments in civil and commercial matters', OJ 1979 no. C59, 5 March 1979, p. 51. For remarks on similar lines, see P. Schlosser, 'Report on the Convention of 9 October 1978 on the Accession of the Kingdom of Denmark, Ireland and the United Kingdom of Great Britain and Northern Ireland to that Convention and to the Protocol on its interpretation by the Court of Justice', OJ 1979 no. C59, pp. 133–134, who expresses the view that the provisions of the convention were designed to 'limit the number of appeals, in the interests of rapid enforcement, to a single appeal which may involve a full review of the facts and a second one limited to points of law'.

2. While the ESR does not expressly limit a second appeal to matters of law alone, the second appeal that can be launched in individual Member States is, however, usually limited to points of law, as in the case of an appeal to the *Corte di cassazione* in Italy, or the *pourvoi en cassation* under French law or the *Rechtsbeschwerde* in Germany.[5]

3. Only the parties themselves can launch a second appeal; other avenues that might potentially be pursued in order to challenge the decision on the application for a declaration of enforceability have to be treated as being precluded.[6]

4. In relation to the Brussels Convention of 1968, the ECJ has stated that a second appeal can only be made against decisions on the enforceability of a foreign decision. As a result, where the judge on appeal suspends the proceedings or orders that security be provided, these decisions cannot be the subject of a second appeal: these are orders made on an interim basis that do not qualify as a 'decision given on the appeal'.[7]

II. Scope of the Review by the Courts of the Member State Where Enforcement Is Sought

5. The powers of the courts of the Member State where a decision is to be enforced are limited to establishing whether the conditions necessary in order to grant or dismiss an application for enforceability pursuant to article 40 ESR are met. Pursuant to article 40, the only grounds on which a decision shall not be recognised are where recognition would be manifestly contrary to public policy, where the defendant was unintentionally absent (not having been served with the document instituting the proceedings or an equivalent document in sufficient time in order to

[5] On the appeal contemplated under article 44 of regulation no. 44/2001, see K. Kerameus, 'Article 44', in U. Magnus and P. Mankowski (eds), *Brussels I Regulation* (München, 2007), p. 664.

[6] ECJ, case C-172/91, *Volker Sonntag* v. *Hans Waidmann Elisabeth Waidmann and Stefan Waidmann* [1994] ECR I-01963; R. Geimer, 'Anerkennung und Vollstreckung', in R. Geimer and R. A. Schütze, *Europäisches Zivilverfahrensrecht*, 3rd ed. (München, 2010), p. 785; I. Pretelli, 'Article 51', in A. Bonomi and P. Wautelet, *Le droit européen des successions. Commentaire du Règlement n° 650/2012 du 4 juillet 2012* (Bruxelles, 2013), p. 636.

[7] ECJ, case C-432–93, *Société d'Informatique Service Réalisation Organisation* v. *Ampersand Software BV* [1995] ECR I-02269. See also M. De Cristofaro, 'Presupposti e rimedi per il provvedimento che «sospende» l'opposizione all'*exequatur* o il riconoscimento di sentenza comunitaria', *Riv dir int priv proc* (1998), p. 746 *et seq.*; in relation to the corresponding provision of regulation no. 44/2001, see Kerameus, 'Article 44', p. 665.

arrange for his defence), and where the decision is irreconcilable with a ruling previously given [see arts. 40–41].

6. Article 52 ESR does not expressly establish that the case having formed the subject of the foreign decision cannot be the subject of a new decision on the substance. Nevertheless, the prohibition on reviewing a decision as to its substance is set out in article 41 of the ESR in the form of a general rule that also applies to appeals against a decision on an application for a declaration of enforceability [see art. 40 and art. 41 no. 1].

Dealing with the interpretation of the corresponding provisions under regulation no. 44/2001, the ECJ has stated that the mutual trust in the administration of justice within the European Union implies that decisions issued in another Member State are recognised as of right and that the procedure in place for the purposes of granting the enforceability, in one particular Member State, of a decision handed down in another Member State must be quick and efficient. It follows that it is not open to the authorities in the Member State where the decision is potentially to be enforced to examine the dispute resolved by that decision in terms of the facts or the law involved. The checks carried out here are limited: they only deal with whether the grounds for a declaration of enforceability are in place and do not permit a review to be carried out of the actual content of the decision issued in the Member State of origin. It is for this reason that a declaration of enforceability cannot even be refused where the debtor claims that he has already complied with the judgment: such circumstances do not result in the decision no longer being an enforceable title, this being a specific feature of the judgment issued by the court in the Member State of origin. In such circumstances, the party against whom the declaration of enforceability has been issued may, if necessary, exercise his rights at the enforcement stage, making the appropriate application to the judge dealing with the enforcement proceedings.[8]

The ECJ has also provided clarification to the effect that regulation no. 44/2001 prevents the judge on appeal from refusing to grant a declaration of enforceability or revoking such a declaration for reasons other than those set out in articles 34 and 35 of that regulation, which contain an exhaustive list of the grounds for challenge.[9] It follows from this that, as judgments by the ECJ regarding interpretation of the previously-

[8] ECJ, case C-139/10, *Prism Investments BV* v. *J.A. van der Meer Ltd* [2011] ECR I-9511.

[9] ECJ, case C-157/12, *Salzgitter Mannesmann Handeln GmbH* v. *SC Laminorul SA* [2013] ECLI: EU: C: 2013: 597; ECJ, case C-139/10, *Prism Investments BV* v. *J.A. van der Meer Ltd* [2011] ECR I-9511.

mentioned rules of regulation no. 44/2001 must be treated as also being applicable, insofar as relevant, to article 52 ESR [see art. 50 no. 1], the competent court in the Member State where enforcement is sought can refuse to grant a declaration of enforceability or revoke such a declaration only where one of the grounds for non-recognition listed in article 40 ESR is in place, with the door firmly shut on any additional investigations being carried out.

7. The ESR does not specifically state whether it is open to the court seised in the Member State of enforcement to identify *ex officio* grounds on which to refuse a declaration of enforceability that have not been raised by the parties themselves.[10] In terms of the corresponding provisions of regulation no. 44/2001 and of the Brussels Convention, such a court is generally denied this power, which is one that would conflict with the prohibition on the courts in the Member State in which enforcement is sought, preventing them from detecting *ex officio* the existence of grounds for refusing a declaration of enforceability.[11]

8. Finally, article 52 ESR establishes that the court in the Member State where enforcement is sought 'shall give its decision without delay'. If an effective system of circulation of decisions within the European Union is to be established, it is essential that the relevant procedure is swift: the defendant should not be given the opportunity to act in bad faith and use delaying tactics in order to put off enforcement of the decision against him.[12]

[10] A. Davì and A. Zanobetti, 'Il nuovo diritto internazionale privato delle successioni nell'Unione Europea', *CdT* (2013), p. 129; A. Davì and A. Zanobetti, *Il nuovo diritto internazionale privato europeo delle successioni* (Torino, 2014), p. 224.

[11] In relation to the Brussels Convention of 1968, see Cour de cassation 17 November 1999, *Rev crit dr int priv* (2000), p. 52. For criticism of this point, see however F. Salerno, *Giurisdizione ed efficacia delle decisioni straniere nel regolamento (CE) 44/2001*, 3rd ed. (Padova, 2006), p. 365, and H. Gaudemet-Tallon, *Compétence et exécution des jugements en Europe*, 4th ed. (Paris, 2010), p. 475, who claim that, where an appeal is launched, the judge must be allowed as of right to detect a breach of public policy or of the right to a fair trial in the State of origin; with regard to the corresponding powers of the court seised of an application under article 36.2 regulation no. 1215/2012, F. Salerno, *Giurisdizione ed efficacia delle decisioni straniere nel regolamento (UE) n. 1215/2012 (rifusione)*, 4th ed. (Padova, 2015), p. 396 *et seq.*

[12] For an analysis of the average timescale for appeals pursuant to article 43 of regulation no. 44/2001 in certain European countries, see B. Hess, 'Free Movement of Judgments', in B. Hess, T. Pfeiffer and P. Schlosser (eds), *The Brussels I Regulation (EC) No. 44/2001* (München, 2008), p. 150.

Article 53

Staying of Proceedings

SALVATORE ZIINO

> The court with which an appeal is lodged under Article 50 or Article 51 shall, on the application of the party against whom enforcement is sought, stay the proceedings if the enforceability of the decision is suspended in the Member State of origin by reason of an appeal.

1. Reflecting the corresponding article 46.1 of regulation no. 44/2001,[1] article 53 ESR establishes that the proceedings on an appeal against the decision on the application for a declaration of enforceability of a decision given in another Member State, or on a second appeal against the decision on such an appeal, can be stayed where the enforceability of the decision whose enforcement is being sought has been suspended by a court in the Member State of origin because the decision itself has been appealed in that Member State. In line with the position established by article 46.1 of regulation no. 44/2001, there is no distinction to be made on the basis of whether the appeal concerns a decision that granted or refused a declaration of enforceability, with a stay being possible in either case.

A stay cannot be ordered by the court of its own motion: the party against whom enforcement is sought is required to lodge an application for that purpose.

[1] Council Regulation (EC) no. 44/2001 of 22 December 2000 on jurisdiction and the recognition and enforcement of judgments in civil and commercial matters, OJ no. L12, 16 January 2001, p. 1 (replaced as from 10 January 2015 by Regulation (EU) no. 1215/2012 of the European Parliament and of the Council of 12 December 2012 on jurisdiction and the recognition and enforcement of judgments in civil and commercial matters (recast), OJ no. L351, 20 December 2012, p. 1). As noted in relation to article 50 ESR, recitals 34 and 59 ESR state that the ESR rules on recognition and enforcement of decisions are similar to those of 'other Union instruments in the area of judicial cooperation in civil matters' [see art. 50 no. 1]. Accordingly, for the purposes of interpreting the provisions of the ESR, to the extent compatible with the peculiarities of succession matters and bearing in mind the differences that can be identified between the provisions of the different instruments, reference can therefore be made to rulings on the interpretation by the ECJ of other instruments, with particular regard to regulation no. 44/2001 and its direct antecedent, the Brussels Convention on jurisdiction and the enforcement of judgments in civil and commercial matters of 27 September 1968.

2. In contrast to a stay under article 46.1 of regulation no. 44/2001, a stay pursuant to article 53 ESR is not discretionary but *must* be ordered whenever the enforceability of the decision is suspended in the Member State of origin and the party against whom enforcement is sought applies for a stay. Article 53 ESR in fact states that the court 'shall' stay the proceedings, using wording that is quite different from that found under article 36 of regulation no. 44/2001, which states that the court 'may' stay the proceedings.

3. Article 53 applies whenever enforcement of the decision has been suspended in the Member State of origin on the basis that an appeal has been lodged;[2] there is no sign in this provision of the specification 'ordinary appeal', which can instead be found under article 42 ESR in respect of the recognition of decisions [see art. 42] as well as under article 46.1 of regulation 44/2001.[3]

4. On the basis of the mechanism introduced by article 53 ESR, the appeal must only be stayed where the enforceability of the decision has been suspended by a court in the Member State of origin. Accordingly, the ESR refers back to the provisions in place in the various Member States that govern the suspension of the enforceability of a decision by the courts in the event of an appeal, whether an ordinary or an extraordinary appeal. The terms in which article 53 has been drafted are, therefore, of particular significance on a practical level. If the foreign decision is enforceable in the Member State of origin, the court in the Member

[2] It follows that a stay of an appeal against a declaration of enforceability differs from a stay of proceedings on an application for recognition of a decision, where, pursuant to article 42 ESR, the court is able to exercise its discretion regarding the stay: see J. Foyer, 'Reconnaissance et exécution des jugements étrangers et des actes authentiques', in G. Khairallah and M. Revillard (eds), *Droit européen des successions internationales. Le règlement du 4 juillet 2012* (Paris, 2013), p. 160.

[3] The reference to an 'ordinary appeal' has given rise to considerable doubts over its interpretation and to problems with application: the difference between an ordinary and extraordinary appeal varies from Member State to Member State and in some countries is not to be found at all. On the difference between ordinary and extraordinary appeals, see ECJ case 43/77, *Industrial Diamond Supplies* v. *Luigi Riva* [1977] ECR 02175; R. Geimer, 'Anerkennung und Vollstreckung', in R. Geimer and R. A. Schütze, *Europäisches Zivilverfahrensrecht* (München, 2010), p. 796; and H. Gaudemet-Tallon, *Compétence et exécution des jugements en Europe*, 4th ed. (Paris, 2010), pp. 479–481. Reference to an 'ordinary' appeal has also been kept in place in article 51 of regulation no. 1215/2012, which governs a stay of the proceedings for refusal of enforcement or of the proceedings on an appeal against a decision given in such proceedings, and corresponds with article 46 of regulation no. 44/2001. Cf. F. Salerno, *Giurisdizione ed efficacia delle decisioni straniere nel regolamento (UE) n. 1215/2012 (rifusione)* (Padova, 2015), p. 407 *et seq.*

State where enforcement is sought must deliver a declaration of enforceability, or, in case of an appeal against such a declaration or against its denial as contemplated under the rule in question, must continue to hear the appeal, even if the decision has been appealed in the Member State of origin. In such circumstances, the court in the Member State requested does not even have the power to stay the proceedings on a discretionary basis.

Where, however, the appeal against the decision in the Member State of origin results in its enforceability being suspended, the court in the Member State where enforcement is sought cannot refuse nor withdraw a declaration of enforceability but, as contemplated by the rule under examination, is obliged – on the application of the party against whom enforcement is sought, as mentioned before – to stay the proceedings on the appeal against the decision on the application for such a declaration or on the second appeal against the decision given on the appeal, pending the outcome in the Member State of origin of the appeal against the decision whose enforcement is sought.

On the basis of this mechanism, where the court in the Member State of origin suspends enforceability of the decision, the party against whom a declaration of enforceability has been granted and who has appealed such a declaration cannot ask the court to withdraw the enforceability granted and is only able to secure a stay of the proceedings on the appeal. It can also be argued that, in such circumstances, the protective measures in place in the Member State where enforcement is sought continue to produce effects.[4]

Where the appeal in the Member State of origin is allowed, the decision forming the subject of the declaration of enforceability is obviously swept away, and, as a result, it cannot be considered enforceable in the Member State requested either. Where, however, the appeal in the Member State of origin is dismissed and the decision whose enforcement is sought is enforceable again in that Member State, the stay will no longer find its

[4] It should be noted that article 53 only provides for a stay of the proceedings on an appeal against the decision on the application for a declaration of enforceability, or on a second appeal against the decision on such an appeal, and not for a suspension of the effects of the declaration of enforceability as such. Nonetheless, given that the enforceability is inherent in the foreign judgment, the provision has to be interpreted as meaning that the effects of the declaration of enforceability are also suspended whenever the decision whose enforcement is sought is no longer enforceable in the Member State of origin as a consequence of its having been appealed there.

justification and proceedings on the appeal pursuant to article 50 or 51 ESR can be resumed.

5. Finally, whereas the last paragraph of article 46 of regulation no. 44/2001 establishes that the judge on appeal 'may also make enforcement conditional on the provision of such security as it shall determine', no such provision can be found in article 53 ESR. The result is that, in contrast to regulation no. 44/2001, the ESR does not empower the court in the Member State in which enforcement is sought to make enforcement dependent upon security being provided by the party that succeeded to obtain the declaration of enforceability [see art. 56 and art. 58 no. 6 *et seq.*].

Article 54

Provisional, Including Protective, Measures

SALVATORE ZIINO

1. When a decision must be recognised in accordance with this Chapter, nothing shall prevent the applicant from availing himself of provisional, including protective, measures in accordance with the law of the Member State of enforcement without a declaration of enforceability under Article 48 being required.
2. The declaration of enforceability shall carry with it by operation of law the power to proceed to any protective measures.
3. During the time specified for an appeal pursuant to Article 50(5) against the declaration of enforceability and until any such appeal has been determined, no measures of enforcement may be taken other than protective measures against the property of the party against whom enforcement is sought.

Summary

I. PROVISIONAL MEASURES BEFORE THE DECLARATION OF ENFORCEABILITY *page* 608
II. PROVISIONAL MEASURES AFTER THE DECLARATION OF ENFORCEABILITY 610
III. PROVISIONAL MEASURES PENDING APPEAL 610

I. Provisional Measures before the Declaration of Enforceability

1. Article 54 ESR sets out the exact wording of article 47 of regulation no. 44/2001, without introducing any changes whatsoever as compared to the wording of that provision.[1] It follows that here, too, when tackling the interpretation of this particular rule, reference can be made to the

[1] Council Regulation (EC) 44/2001 of 22 December 2000 on jurisdiction and the recognition and enforcement of judgments in civil and commercial matters, OJ no. L12, 16 January 2001, p. 1 (replaced as from 10 January 2015 by Regulation (EU) no. 1215/2012 of the European Parliament and of the Council of 12 December 2012 on jurisdiction and the recognition and enforcement of judgments in civil and commercial matters (recast), OJ no. L351, 20 December 2012, p. 1).

literature and to the case law emanating from the ECJ concerning the latter provision.[2]

2. Whilst the procedure followed to secure a declaration of enforceability is swift and does not involve in its first stage the participation of the party against whom enforcement is sought, the need may still arise for protective measures to be put in place before a decision is handed down on the application for enforceability.[3] Article 54 therefore provides that the parties that have obtained an enforceable decision in their favour in the Member State of origin before having secured (or in fact even applied for) a declaration of enforceability can ensure that the steps subsequently taken by way of enforcement of the decision do not become pointless. The grounds on which these measures are ordered are governed by domestic law in the individual Member States, and an application can be made for such measures to be adopted as are contemplated by the law of the Member State where enforcement is sought, before a decision is given on the application for a declaration of enforceability.[4] Enforcement of the protective measures granted under the rule is also governed by the law of the Member State where enforcement is sought.

3. The protective measures contemplated by article 54.1 only take effect in the Member State where they have been issued, as they are

[2] As stated in relation to article 50 ESR [see art. 50 no. 1], recitals 34 and 59 ESR state that the ESR rules on recognition and enforcement of decisions are similar to those of 'other Union instruments in the area of judicial cooperation in civil matters'; accordingly, for the purposes of interpreting the relevant provisions of the ESR, to the extent compatible with the peculiarities of succession matters and bearing in mind the differences that can be found between the provisions of the different instruments, reference can be made to judgments by the ECJ concerning the interpretation of other instruments, with particular regard to regulation no. 44/2001.

[3] P. Franzina and A. Leandro, 'Il nuovo diritto internazionale privato delle successioni per causa di morte in Europa', *N l civ comm* (2013), p. 333.

[4] A. Baumbach, W. Lauterbach, J. Albers and P. Hartman, *Zivilprozessordnung*, 71st ed. (München, 2013), p. 3055. These protective measures include, for example, seisure to protect the position of a creditor and seisure as part of court proceedings in Italy, or the *Vorpfändung*, the *Arrest*, the *einstweilige Verfügung* and the *Sicherungsvollstreckung* in Germany or the *mise sous séquestre*, the *consignation de sommes d'argent* and the *saisie conservatoire* in France. On the corresponding article 47.1 of regulation no. 44/2001 see F. Salerno, *Giurisdizione ed efficacia delle decisioni straniere nel regolamento (CE) n. 44/ 2001*, 3rd ed. (Padova, 2006), p. 371 *et seq.*; L. Pålsson, 'Article 47', in U. Magnus and P. Mankowski (eds), *Brussels I Regulation* (München, 2007), p. 677 *et seq.*; H. Gaudemet-Tallon, *Compétence et exécution des jugements en Europe*, 4th ed. (Paris, 2010), p. 481 *et seq.*; on the new rules contained in this respect under articles 40 and 44.1(a) regulation no. 1215/2012 (s. c. Brussels I-*bis*), cf. F. Salerno, *Giurisdizione ed efficacia delle decisioni straniere nel regolamento (UE) n. 1215/2012 (rifusione)*, 4th ed. (Padova, 2015), p. 397 *et seq.*

a means of securing the enforcement of the foreign decision in the same Member State, once declared enforceable there. They can only be granted where the court in the Member State where enforcement is sought has not yet ruled on the application for a declaration of enforceability. Where the court in that Member State has already handed down its decision declaring the foreign decision enforceable, article 54.2 ESR applies.

II. Provisional Measures after the Declaration of Enforceability

4. Article 54.2 ESR establishes that a declaration of enforceability adopted pursuant to article 48 ESR shall carry with it the entitlement for the party who applied for it to request protective measures. This is an automatic effect of the declaration of enforceability, with the result that there is no need for the court in the Member State in which enforcement is sought to specifically grant this entitlement.[5]

As enforceability, under article 48 ESR, is declared by an order issued without the other party being heard [see art. 46 and art. 49 no. 8], the possibility for protective measures to be immediately enforced implies that the creditor can take the party against whom enforcement is sought by surprise in order to protect his or her rights more effectively.[6]

III. Provisional Measures Pending Appeal

5. Pursuant to article 54.3 ESR, during the period of time allowed for an appeal against the declaration of enforceability and during the actual appeal proceedings, the party that obtained the declaration of

[5] In relation to the provisions of article 39 of the Brussels Convention, see ECJ case 119/84, *P. Capelloni and F. Aquilini* v. *J. Pelkmans* [1985] ECR 3147; Corte di cassazione 16 November 1987, n. 8380, *Riv dir int priv proc* (1989), p. 129; Appello Torino 22 April 1988, *Riv dir int priv proc* (1989), p. 399; Tribunal Bruxelles 29 July 1993, *Journal des Tribunaux*, 1994, p. 251; L. Salvadego, 'I provvedimenti conservativi in funzione dell'esecuzione di una sentenza straniera secondo il regolamento «Bruxelles I»', *N giur civ comm* (2012) p. 931; L. Sandrini, 'La tutela del creditore in pendenza del procedimento di 'exequatur' nel regolamento Bruxelles I', *Riv dir int priv proc* (2012), p. 595. As noted by B. Hess in 'Free Movement of Judgments', in B. Hess, T. Pfeiffer and P. Schlosser (eds), *The Brussels I Regulation 44/2001* (München, 2008), p. 153, the power to pursue protective measures without specific authorisation being required 'is derived from Belgian law', a country in which 'the creditor may seek all provisional measures of the Belgian procedural law on the simple presentation of an enforceable title'.

[6] In relation to the Brussels Convention of 1968, see Jenard, 'Report on the Convention of 27 September 1968 on jurisdiction and the enforcement of judgments in civil and commercial matters', OJ 1979 no. C59, 5 March 1979, pp. 50, 54.

enforceability cannot take steps to enforce the foreign decision and is limited to pursuing protective measures in relation to the assets belonging to the party against whom enforcement is sought. This provision is extremely important, as it limits the powers of the party that has obtained the declaration of enforceability. While the period of time for appealing or proceedings on an appeal are pending, the party that obtained the declaration of enforceability cannot undertake enforcement measures and can only apply for protective measures. Actual enforcement can only take place once the period of time for appealing against the declaration of enforceability has elapsed without an appeal being lodged, or an appeal against that declaration has been dismissed. In practice, the distinction between protective measures and enforcement measures will have to be established with regard to the law of the Member State where enforcement is sought.[7]

[7] The concept of protective measures, though having to be established pursuant to the domestic law of the Member State where such measures are sought, should, however, reflect the objectives and *ratio* of article 54 ESR; for arguments on similar lines regarding the corresponding provision under regulation no. 44/2001, see Pålsson, 'Article 47', p. 680. See also Gaudemet-Tallon, *Compétence et exécution*, p. 482, who, for the purposes of establishing what exactly comes under the umbrella of protective measures, prefers a solution based on a reference to an independent concept adopted by the European Union, on similar lines to the position established in relation to article 31 regulation no. 44/2001 [see art. 19].

Article 55

Partial Enforceability

SALVATORE ZIINO

1. Where a decision has been given in respect of several matters and the declaration of enforceability cannot be given for all of them, the court or competent authority shall give it for one or more of them.
2. An applicant may request a declaration of enforceability limited to parts of a decision.

1. Article 55 ESR sets out the exact wording of the corresponding article 48 of regulation no. 44/2001,[1] which in turn reproduced article 42 of the Brussels Convention of 1968.[2] It governs the situation in which the decision issued abroad deals with various aspects of a dispute and the declaration of enforceability can only be issued in relation to some of them (article 55.1), or where the applicant only requests a declaration of enforceability in relation to some of them (article 55.2).

2. In the first situation, the court in the Member State in which enforcement is to be carried out must declare enforceable those parts of the decision that meet the requirements for a declaration of enforceability

[1] Council Regulation (EC) 44/2001 of 22 December 2000 on jurisdiction and the recognition and enforcement of judgments in civil and commercial matters, OJ no. L12, 16 January 2001, p. 1 (replaced as from 10 January 2015 by Regulation (EU) no. 1215/2012 of the European Parliament and of the Council of 12 December 2012 on jurisdiction and the recognition and enforcement of judgments in civil and commercial matters (recast), OJ no. L351, 20 December 2012, p. 1).

[2] Convention on jurisdiction and the enforcement of judgments in civil and commercial matters, Brussels, 28 September 1968. As we have seen in relation to article 50 ESR [see art. 50], recitals 34 and 59 ESR state that the ESR rules on recognition and enforcement of decisions are similar to those of 'other Union instruments in the area of judicial cooperation in civil matters'; for the purposes of interpreting the provisions of the ESR, to the extent compatible with the specific matter of succession and obviously bearing in mind the differences that can be identified between the provisions of the different instruments, reference can therefore be made to rulings on interpretation by the ECJ regarding other instruments and, in particular, regarding regulation no. 44/2001 and its direct antecedent, the Brussels Convention of 1968.

[see arts. 40–41].[3] It cannot, however, make any changes whatsoever to the content of the foreign decision. If, for example, the application for a declaration of enforceability is dismissed in relation to one part of the judgment because the amount ordered payable is considered excessive or contrary to public policy, it is not open to the court in the Member State in which enforcement steps are to be taken to reduce that amount.[4]

3. Partial recognition may come for consideration where the judgment deals with matters that fall within the scope of application of the ESR as well as matters that fall beyond it. In such circumstances, and in a judgment that concerned the corresponding article 42 of the Brussels Convention of 27 September 1968, the ECJ had stated that recognition could extend simply to those parts of the decision that fell within the scope of application of the convention, even if they were dependent on the parts that could not benefit from the regime of free movement governed by the convention itself, the same applying under the corresponding provision of article 48 of regulation no. 44/2001.[5] It is of course possible that enforcement of those parts of the judgment that fall beyond the scope of application of the ESR is ordered either pursuant to national law, on the basis of other EU regulations, or pursuant to international conventions as may be applicable.

This possibility aside, a partial declaration of enforceability must concern independent parts of a decision that are distinct and separate from those parts that cannot be declared enforceable.

4. In the area of succession, the various parts of a decision are often linked to one another, with the consequence that one part of the decision might not be declared enforceable without having an impact on the remaining parts of that decision. Establishing a link between the various different parts of the decision can at times be a difficult task, particularly where the formation of the shares of the estate due to the heirs is based on their family *status*, and the decision on such *status* is in conflict with public policy in the Member State in which enforcement is to be carried out [see art. 35 and art. 40]. A careful analysis will be required in this respect in order to identify those parts of the decision that can be declared enforceable, despite the fact that parts of the decision are irreconcilable

[3] I. Pretelli, 'Article 55', in A. Bonomi and P. Wautelet, *Le droit européen des successions. Commentaire du Règlement n° 650/2012 du 4 juillet 2012* (Bruxelles, 2013), p. 592.

[4] See, in relation to article 48 of regulation no. 44/2001, H. Gaudemet-Tallon, *Compétence et exécution des jugements en Europe*, 4th ed. (Paris, 2010), p. 489.

[5] ECJ, Case C-220/95, *Antonius van den Boogaard* v. *Paula Laumen* [1997] ECR I-01147.

with public policy in the Member State where enforcement is being sought and cannot accordingly be enforced there.

5. The second paragraph of article 55 ESR establishes that the applicant may request a declaration of enforceability limited to parts of a decision. In such circumstances, the court in the Member State in which enforcement is to be carried out must comply with that request and is not at liberty to declare the entire decision enforceable.[6] One possible scenario in which an applicant may be interested in applying for partial enforceability is where the party against whom enforcement is sought has satisfied part of the judgment, and the applicant is now seeking to recover the residue.[7]

[6] Pretelli, 'Article 55', p. 593.

[7] L. Pålsson, 'Article 48', in U. Magnus and P. Mankowski (eds), *Brussels I Regulation* (München, 2007), p. 681.

Article 56

Legal Aid

SALVATORE ZIINO

An applicant who, in the Member State of origin, has benefited from complete or partial legal aid or exemption from costs or expenses shall be entitled, in any proceedings for a declaration of enforceability, to benefit from the most favourable legal aid or the most extensive exemption from costs or expenses provided for by the law of the Member State of enforcement.

Article 57

No Security, Bond or Deposit

No security, bond or deposit, however described, shall be required of a party who in one Member State applies for recognition, enforceability or enforcement of a decision given in another Member State on the ground that he is a foreign national or that he is not domiciled or resident in the Member State of enforcement.

Article 58

No Charge, Duty or Fee

In proceedings for the issue of a declaration of enforceability, no charge, duty or fee calculated by reference to the value of the matter at issue may be levied in the Member State of enforcement.

Summary

I. LEGAL AID *page* 617

II. EXCLUSION OF THE REQUIREMENT FOR A CAUTIO JUDICATUM SOLVI 620

III. EXCLUSION OF CHARGES CALCULATED BY REFERENCE TO THE VALUE OF THE MATTER IN ISSUE 622

I. Legal Aid

1. Article 56 ESR governs legal aid and exemption from costs or expenses in proceedings for a declaration of enforceability of a decision given in another Member State and reproduces to the letter article 50 of regulation no. 44/2001.[1]

The party intending to apply for a declaration of enforceability is eligible for legal aid and an exemption from costs in the Member State

[1] Council Regulation (EC) 44/2001 of 22 December 2000 on jurisdiction and the recognition and enforcement of judgments in civil and commercial matters, OJ no. L12, 16 January 2001, p. 1 (replaced as from 10 January 2015 by Regulation (EU) no. 1215/2012 of the European Parliament and of the Council of 12 December 2012 on jurisdiction and the recognition and enforcement of judgments in civil and commercial matters (recast), OJ no. L351, 20 December 2012, p. 1). As we have seen in relation to article 50 ESR [see art. 50], recitals 34 and 59 ESR state that the ESR rules on recognition and enforcement of decisions are similar to those of 'other Union instruments in the area of judicial cooperation in civil matters'; accordingly, for the purposes of interpreting the provisions of the ESR, to the extent compatible with the peculiarities of succession matters and bearing in mind the differences that can be found between the provisions of the different instruments, reference can be made to judgments by the ECJ on the interpretation of other instruments, with particular regard to regulation no. 44/2001 and its direct antecedent, the Brussels Convention on jurisdiction and the enforcement of judgments in civil and commercial matters of 27 September 1968.

of enforcement if he or she benefited from complete or partial legal aid or an exemption from costs or expenses in the proceedings that were heard in the Member State of origin. This entitlement is a consequence that flows automatically. The Member State where enforcement is sought is denied the opportunity to carry out checks of any type, and must guarantee that the party in question will be able to 'benefit from the most favourable legal aid or the most extensive exemption from costs or expenses provided for by the law of the Member State of enforcement'.

2. On 9 December 2014, the European Commission adopted Implementing regulation no. 1329/2014, setting out the forms to be used for the purposes of the application of various provisions in the ESR, including those concerning the enforcement of foreign decisions. Among these, form I is to be used for drawing up the attestation concerning a decision in matters of succession referred to in article 46.3(b) ESR.[2] Section 7 of the said form, which deals with '[c]osts or expenses', calls for a considerable amount of information to be provided about legal costs and asks whether any of the parties has benefited from legal aid or a costs exemption. On the basis of the information included in the attestation pursuant to the form, the party involved can automatically benefit from legal aid or an exemption from costs in the Member State of enforcement, and can therefore secure a declaration of enforceability fairly swiftly without having to wait for legal aid to be granted in the Member State of enforcement and is therefore in a position to take his or her opponent by surprise when enforcing protective measures against the relevant assets.[3]

3. The benefit of legal aid and an exemption from costs applies at all stages of the proceedings related to a declaration of enforceability, i.e. in the actual proceedings for a declaration themselves as well as in proceedings on any subsequent appeal.[4]

[2] Commission Implementing Regulation (EU) no. 1329/2014 of 9 December 2014 establishing the Forms referred to in Regulation (EU) no. 650/2012 of the European Parliament and of the Council on jurisdiction, applicable law, recognition and enforcement of decisions and acceptance and enforcement of authentic instruments in matters of succession and on the creation of a European Certificate of Succession, OJ 2014 no. L359, 16 December 2014, p. 32.

[3] On this point, and in relation to article 44 of the Brussels Convention of 1968, see P. Jenard, 'Report on the Convention of 27 September 1968 on jurisdiction and the enforcement of judgments in civil and commercial matters', OJ 1979 no. C59, 5 March 1979, p. 54.

[4] I. Pretelli, 'Article 56', in A. Bonomi and P. Wautelet, *Le droit européen des successions internationales. Commentaire du Règlement n° 650/2012 du 4 juillet 2012* (Bruxelles, 2014),

Article 56 ESR does not, however, concern the subsequent enforcement proceedings to be undertaken pursuant to the domestic law of the Member State of enforcement, nor the enforcement of protective measures. In these cases, the party in question is therefore required to make a specific application in the Member State of enforcement and to meet the conditions provided for under the law of that Member State in order to be granted legal aid or an exemption from costs.

4. Article 56 only governs legal aid and an exemption from costs in favour of an applicant who benefited from legal aid or an exemption from costs in the proceedings before the courts in the Member State of origin. Clearly, an applicant who was not in receipt of legal aid in that Member State may still be entitled to legal aid in the Member State of enforcement under the law of that Member State[5], with the party opposing the application for enforcement quite possibly being in the same position. Here, however, a specific application would have to be submitted to the relevant bodies in the Member State of enforcement.[6] The possibility of benefiting from legal aid is in fact considered by the ECJ and by the European Court of Human Rights as a necessary requirement in order for an effective right of access to justice to be guaranteed, with the European court in fact stating that the principle of effective judicial protection of rights as recognised under article 6 of the European Convention on Human Rights makes legal aid a specific requirement for a satisfactory standard of judicial protection.[7] This is now codified under article 47 of the Charter of Fundamental Rights of the European Union, which establishes that '[l]egal aid shall be made available to those who lack sufficient resources in so far as such aid is necessary to ensure effective access to justice'.[8]

5. On a European Union level, legal aid is governed by directive 2002/8/EC of 27 January 2003 to improve access to justice in cross-border

p. 594. Article 44 of the Brussels Convention of 1968 established that a party could only benefit from legal aid on an automatic basis in the initial phase of the proceedings for a declaration of enforceability of the foreign judgment.

5 In relation to the corresponding article 50 of regulation no. 44/2001, see L. Pålsson, 'Article 50', in U. Magnus and P. Mankowski (eds), *Brussels I Regulation* (München, 2007), p. 684.

6 In relation to regulation no. 44/2001, see R. Geimer, 'Anerkennung und Vollstreckung', in R. Geimer and R.A. Schütze, *Europäisches Zivilverfahrensrecht*, 3rd ed. (München, 2010), p. 816.

7 ECtHR, *Essaadi* v. *France*, Judgment of 26 February 2002, Application no. 49384/99, at 31; ECtHR, *Airey* v. *Ireland*, Judgment of 9 October 1979, Application no. 6289/73, at 26.

8 See also ECJ, Case C-156/12, *GREP GmbH* v. *Freistaat Bayern*, [2012] ECLI: EU: C: 2012: 342; ECJ, Case C-220/95, *A. van den Boogaard* v. *P. Laumen*, [1997] ECR I-1147.

disputes by establishing minimum common rules relating to legal aid for such disputes.[9] The directive applies to cross-border disputes and is intended 'to guarantee an adequate level of legal aid in cross-border disputes by laying down certain minimum common standards relating to legal aid' (article 1). Article 4 of the directive lays down the non-discrimination principle and establishes that 'Member States shall grant legal aid without discrimination to Union citizens and third-country nationals residing lawfully in a Member State'. Pursuant to this provision, parties resident in a Member State are eligible for legal aid in accordance with the provisions in place in the Member State of enforcement, regardless of their nationality. Legal aid legislation in the various Member States differs widely; information on the law in force in each Member State in this respect can be found through the European Judicial Network in Civil and Commercial Matters.[10]

II. Exclusion of the Requirement for a *cautio judicatum solvi*

6. Article 57 ESR reflects article 45 of the Brussels Convention of 1968[11] and article 51 of regulation no. 44/2001. The same provision can also be found in article 56 of regulation no. 1215/2012.[12]

Article 57 prohibits Member States from requiring the party applying for recognition, for a declaration of enforceability or for actual enforcement of a decision given in another Member State to provide security where such a requirement is based on the circumstance that such a party is a foreign national or his or her domicile or residence is not located in the Member State of enforcement.

This security, which is referred to as *cautio judicatum solvi*, is required pursuant to national legislation in place in certain Member States in order to protect the party against whom the declaration of enforceability

[9] OJ 2003 no. L 26, 31 January 2003, p. 41. See also A. De Luca, 'La Direttiva 2003/8/CE del Consiglio del 27 gennaio 2003, intesa a migliorare l'accesso alla giustizia nelle controversie transfrontaliere', in M. Taruffo and V. Varano (eds), *Manuale di diritto processuale europeo* (Torino, 2011), p. 365.

[10] See the dedicated page on the European Judicial Network in Civil and Commercial Matters' website: http://ec.europa.eu/civiljustice/legal_aid/legal_aid_gen_en.htm (last accessed 6 July 2016).

[11] The Convention on jurisdiction and the enforcement of judgments in civil and commercial matters, Brussels, 27 September 1968, being the direct antecedent of regulation no. 44/2001. Cf. recital 19 of that regulation, pointing to continuity between the two instruments.

[12] See footnote 1; cf. recital 34 of the recast regulation.

is sought. It operates to ensure that legal costs or damages for any losses incurred as a result of enforcement of the foreign decision or of orders for interim relief can be recovered in case the foreign decision is subsequently found not enforceable or is overturned in the Member State of origin. Clearly, however, it creates an additional obstacle for a party attempting to exercise their rights and can hamper the circulation of decisions in the European judicial area.

7. Article 57 does not impose an absolute prohibition on demanding that security be provided by the applicant seeking enforcement. It simply excludes requirements for security that are based on the discriminatory grounds of the applicant's foreign nationality or of his or her residence or domicile abroad.[13] It follows that where national legislation requires that security for costs or damages be provided, but such a requirement is not linked to the applicant's nationality or domicile, then such a requirement is legitimate and is not in conflict with article 57 ESR.

The provision makes no distinction between persons resident or domiciled in a different Member State and those resident or domiciled in a non-EU country. From this standpoint, it should be noted that article 57 ESR brings with itself a certain margin of risk: where the applicant resides or is domiciled in a non-EU country, significant difficulties might be encountered when attempting to recover costs or damages.[14]

8. Security may, in some cases, have an important role to play in ensuring that costs or damages can be recovered. In addition, the courts in a number of Member States can allow applications for security against a party enforcing protective measures or enforcing a judgment that can still be appealed, in circumstances other than those contemplated under article 57 ESR. In such circumstances, whilst the security itself might pass the legitimacy test, the amount involved must not result in the party required to provide security encountering excessive difficulties in exercising their rights, with the risk otherwise that the right to take action in court is prejudiced as to its substance.[15]

[13] I. Pretelli, 'Article 57', in Bonomi and Wautelet, *Le droit européen des successions. Commentaire du Règlement n° 650/2012 du 4 juillet 2012*, p. 596.

[14] On this point, and in relation to article 52 of regulation no. 44/2001, see Geimer, 'Anerkennung und Vollstreckung', p. 819.

[15] Security for costs might amount to a breach of the right to a fair trial if it jeopardises access to justice: French Cour de Cassation 16 March 1999, *Rev crit dr int priv* (2000), p. 223.

III. Exclusion of Charges Calculated by Reference to the Value of the Matter in Issue

9. Article 58 ESR restricts the power of Member States to establish the amount of the charges payable by the parties to proceedings for a declaration of enforceability of a decision given in another Member State. In particular, a Member State is prevented from levying tax on the basis of the value of the dispute.

Costs can be calculated solely as a fee in exchange for the service provided by the courts or other competent authorities in the Member State of enforcement. The charges therefore shall take the form of fixed amounts and must not be linked to the value of the dispute. The rationale for the rule clearly appears in this respect to iron out the various differences in the legislation in force in the individual Member States.

10. Article 58 ESR corresponds with article 52 of regulation no. 44/2001 and article III of the protocol to the Brussels Convention of 1968. The ECJ has in fact noted in respect of the latter that, as the intention pursued by the Brussels Convention is 'to secure the simplification of formalities governing the reciprocal recognition and enforcement of judgments of courts or tribunals', the Member States therefore ought to 'ensure that the costs of the procedure described in the convention are fixed so as to accord with that concern for simplification'.[16]

Provisions in force in the Member States to the effect that the amount of tax payable on a decision should be in proportion with the value of the dispute cannot, therefore, be applied to decisions given in other Member States that are being declared enforceable pursuant to the ESR.

11. Finally, it is worth recalling that, pursuant to article 56 ESR, a party that is exempt from costs or expenses in the Member State of origin is entitled to 'the most extensive exemption from costs or expenses provided for by the law of the Member State of enforcement'.

[16] ECJ, Case 42/76, *Jozef de Wolf* v. *Harry Cox BV* [1976] ECR 1759. The Member States generally have fixed costs on an extremely modest scale: see B. Hess, 'Free Movement of Judgments', in B. Hess, T. Pfeiffer and P. Schlosser (eds), *The Brussels I Regulation (EC) No. 44/2001* (München, 2008), p. 150, which sets out the court fees in various EU Member States.

CHAPTER V

Authentic Instruments and Court Settlements

Article 59

Acceptance of Authentic Instruments

HEINZ-PETER MANSEL

1. An authentic instrument established in a Member State shall have the same evidentiary effects in another Member State as it has in the Member State of origin, or the most comparable effects, provided that this is not manifestly contrary to public policy (*ordre public*) in the Member State concerned.

   A person wishing to use an authentic instrument in another Member State may ask the authority establishing the authentic instrument in the Member State of origin to fill in the form established in accordance with the advisory procedure referred to in Article 81(2) describing the evidentiary effects which the authentic instrument produces in the Member State of origin.
2. Any challenge relating to the authenticity of an authentic instrument shall be made before the courts of the Member State of origin and shall be decided upon under the law of that State. The authentic instrument challenged shall not produce any evidentiary effect in another Member State as long as the challenge is pending before the competent court.
3. Any challenge relating to the legal acts or legal relationships recorded in an authentic instrument shall be made before the courts having jurisdiction under this Regulation and shall be decided upon under the law applicable pursuant to Chapter III. The authentic instrument challenged shall not produce any evidentiary effect in a Member State other than the Member State of origin as regards the matter being challenged as long as the challenge is pending before the competent court.
4. If the outcome of proceedings in a court of a Member State depends on the determination of an incidental question relating to the legal acts or legal relationships recorded in an authentic instrument in matters of succession, that court shall have jurisdiction over that question.

Summary

I. INTRODUCTION *page* 626
- A. Purpose and Content of the Rule 626
- B. *Instrumentum* and *Negotium* of an Authentic Instrument 627
- C. The European Primary Law Background of Article 59 630

D. Secondary-Law Rules Related to Authentic Instruments 631
E. Legislative History 633
II. REQUIREMENTS FOR THE ACCEPTANCE OF AN AUTHENTIC INSTRUMENT: ARTICLE 59(1) 636
A. Authentic Instrument 636
B. Drawing up and Recording by the State of Origin and Member State of the ESR 637
C. Authentic Instrument in a Matter of Succession 639
D. *Ordre public* 643
E. Use of a Standard Formula within the Meaning of Article 59(1) Subparagraph 2 646
III. CONSEQUENCES OF AN ACCEPTANCE OF AN AUTHENTIC INSTRUMENT: ARTICLE 59(1) 647
A. Extension of the Evidentiary Effect in the Member State of Origin 647
B. Relationship to Articles 39, 69 648
C. Evidentiary Effect 649
1. Evidentiary Effect Referring to Factual Elements 649
2. Manner and Extent of Evidentiary Effect 650
3. Presumptions of Law 651
D. The Limitations on Evidentiary Effects 652
1. Register of Rights: Article 1(2)(l) 652
2. *Ordre public*: Article 59(1) Subparagraph 1 652
3. The Same or Most Comparable Effects: Article 59(1) Subparagraph 1 652
4. Formal Validity 654
IV. CHALLENGE RELATING THE AUTHENTICITY: ARTICLE 59(2) 655
A. Challenge of the *Instrumentum* (authenticity) 655
B. The State of Origin's Exclusive Power of Review 656
C. Legal Consequences 657
V. CHALLENGING SUBSTANTIVE LAW CONTENT: ARTICLE 59(3), (4) 659
A. Challenging the *Negotium*: Article 59(3) 659
B. Legal Consequences Regarding Evidentiary Effects: Article 59(3) 660
C. Incidental Question: Article 59(4) 660
VI. CONFLICT OF AUTHENTIC INSTRUMENTS AND DECISIONS 661
A. In General 661
B. Conflicting Instruments from Different ESR Member States 661
C. Conflict with a Decision from Another ESR Member State 662
VII. FREE MOVEMENT OF AUTHENTIC INSTRUMENTS AND NATIONAL LAW 663

I. Introduction

A. *Purpose and Content of the Rule*

1. Article 59 shall 'guarantee the acceptance and enforceability in all Member States of authentic instruments in matters of succession' (recital

60). In this manner, the free movement of authentic instruments (*acte authentique, authentieke akte, atto autentico, ato autêntico, documento público, öffentliche Urkunde*) within the Member States of the ESR (recital 22 sentence 3) is envisaged to be ensured.[1] This is because in succession matters authentic instruments are of special practical importance.[2] To this end, article 59 introduces the new concept of acceptance (*Aanvaarding*, acceptation, *accettazione, aceitação, aceptación, Annahme*) of authentic instruments. The term 'acceptance' is used only in the title of the article, not in the text of the provision itself. If the requirements of acceptance are fulfilled (on the requirements, see nos. 9 –14), the authentic instrument has the same evidentiary effect in another Member State (State of acceptance, secondary State) as it has in the Member State of origin (primary State, State of origin) (on the effects, see nos. 30 – 43). Article 59 therefore is a conflict of laws rule in procedural law[3] because it mandates that an instrument has the evidentiary effect in another Member State which it is afforded according to the law of the State of origin. Only in the case of a violation of the *ordre public* (public policy) shall the effect given in the primary State not be extended to the secondary State (on *ordre public*, see no 22 *et seq.*).

B. Instrumentum *and* Negotium *of an Authentic Instrument*

2. With regard to the effects of an instrument, a distinction must be drawn between its *negotium* and the *instrumentum*.[4] The *instrumentum*

[1] See P. Wautelet, 'Article 3', in A. Bonomi and P. Wautelet, *Le droit européen des successions. Commentaire du Règlement n° 650/2012 du 4 juillet 2012* (Bruxelles, 2013), p. 153.

[2] See Proposal for a Regulation of the European Parliament and of the Council on jurisdiction, applicable Law, recognition and enforcement of decisions and authentic instruments in matters of Succession and the creation of a European Certificate of Succession COM (2009) 154 final, explanatory memorandum 4.5.

[3] A. Dutta, 'Art. 59 EuErbVO', in J. von Hein (ed), *Münchener Kommentar zum BGB*, vol. X, 6th ed. (München, 2015), para. 1; A. Dutta, 'Das neue internationale Erbrecht der Europäischen Union – Eine erste Lektüre der Erbrechtsverordnung', *FamRZ* (2013), p. 13 *et seq.*; similarly P. Wautelet, 'Article 59', in A. Bonomi and P. Wautelet, *Le droit européen des successions – Commentaire du Règlement n° 650/2012 du 4 juillet 2012* (Bruxelles, 2013), p. 666; similarly J. Fitchen, '"Recognition", acceptance and enforcement of authentic instruments in the Succession Regulation', *JPIL* 8 (2012), pp. 323, 356; as a conflict of laws rule, see J. Foyer, 'Reconnaissance, acceptation et exécution des jugements étrangers, des actes authentiques et des transactions judiciaires', in G. Khairallah and M. Revillard (eds), *Droit européen des successions internationales: Le règlement du 4 juillet 2012* (Paris, 2013), p. 161.

[4] See Presidency of the Council of the European Union, Political guidelines for the future work (Brussels, 6 June 2011), document no. 11067/11, p. 12 para. 27; P. Pasqualis, *Le problème de la circulation des actes notariés dans l'espace juridique européen* (PE 425.656

is the instrument itself along with its evidentiary effect (see no. 30) for the factual elements recorded by the certifying authority.[5] These factual elements can be, for example, the making of a declaration using particular language at a particular point in time at a particular place in the presence of the certifying official and certain other persons (such as witnesses). Council document no. 1106/11 describes the content of the *instrumentum* as 'the form of the instrument and other officially recorded *facts*'.[6]

The *negotium* of an instrument is the entailed legal content. Article 59 (3) sentence 1 describes the *negotium* therefore as 'the legal acts or legal relationships recorded in an authentic instrument.' This means the substantive law content of the authentic instrument, i.e. the legal acts or legal relationships that were established by the authentic instrument or about which it is reporting. Recital 63 sentences 2 and 3 provide examples thereof and state:

> The legal acts recorded in an authentic instrument could be, for instance, the agreement between the parties on the sharing-out or the distribution of the estate, or a will or an agreement as to succession, or another declaration of intent. The legal relationships could be, for instance, the determination of the heirs and other beneficiaries as established under the law applicable to the succession, their respective shares and the existence of a reserved share, or any other element established under the law applicable to the succession.

To the extent, however, the authentic instrument also reflects testamentary dispositions, e.g. the designation of a testamentary heir, the fact that a declaration was made by a specific person and the language of the declaration fall within the scope of the *instrumentum*. Acceptance of the *instrumentum* is achieved in accordance with article 59(1) (see nos. 3, 8, 33, 52 *et seq.*). The *negotium* is not the subject matter of acceptance pursuant to article 59. It is judged solely according to the *lex causae*

FR) (Bruxelles, 2010), p. 16; the French original and the German translation (PE 425.656 DE) use and define the words *instrumentum* and *negotium*. The English translation 'The movement of notarial instruments in the European legal area' (PE 425.656 EN) (Brussels, 2010), p. 15, does not explicitly use the words *instrumentum* and *negotium*. The Italian wording of article 59 (3) uses the term '*negozi*' following the original Latin term '*negotium*'.

[5] See H.-P. Mansel, K. Thorn and R. Wagner, 'Europäisches Kollisionsrecht 2010: Verstärkte Zusammenarbeit als Motor der Vereinheitlichung?', *IPRax* (2011), pp. 1, 4; Wautelet, 'Article 59', p. 663.

[6] See Presidency of the Council, document no. 11067/11 (referred to in footnote 4), p. 12, para. 27 (emphasis added).

(see nos. 18, 52 *et seq.*).[7] The *lex causae* is determined by reference to the conflict of laws rules of the *lex fori.*[8] *Negotium* in succession law in the Member States of the ESR is thus subject solely to the succession rules pursuant to chapter III (article 59(3) sentence 1, see nos. 18, 52 *et seq.*).[9][10]

3. Article 59 only concerns the *instrumentum*, not the *negotium* of the instrument.[11] Therein lies the difference between acceptance of an authentic instrument pursuant to article 59 and the recognition of the decision (see article 3(1)(g)) pursuant to article 39.[12] A judgment influences the substantive law and its enforceability, respectively, in the State issuing the judgment by way of the effect of *res iudicata*. The effect of this judgment is extended to other States by article 39 [see art. 39 no. 1 *et seq.*]. Because the mandate of *res iudicata* of a judgment is the product of judicial, often contentious proceedings between the parties under the protection of civil procedural law, it is afforded stronger legitimacy than an authentic instrument which is typically drawn up in accordance with the will of the party.[13] Authentic instruments have no *res judicata* effects.[14] Additionally, the procedural rules which govern drafting an authentic instrument, e.g. recording requirements and notary-related regulations, are generally less strict due to their limited effects. These

[7] See A. Davì and A. Zanobetti, *Il nuovo diritto internazionale privato europeo delle successioni* (Torino, 2014), p. 227 *et seq.*

[8] Foyer, 'Reconnaissance, acceptation et exécution', p. 161.

[9] See Davì and Zanobetti, *Il nuovo diritto internazionale privato europeo*, p. 227 *et seq.*

[10] See Presidency of the Council, Document no. 11067/11 (referred to in footnote 4), p. 12, para. 27.

[11] Foyer, 'Reconnaissance, acceptation et exécution', pp. 149, 163; Wautelet, 'Article 3', p. 156.

[12] Foyer, 'Reconnaissance, acceptation et exécution', p. 143; Wautelet, 'Article 59', p. 662 *et seq.* On the difference in terminology of 'acceptance' and 'recognition' in the context of article 59 see Davì and Zanobetti, *Il nuovo diritto internazionale privato europeo*, p. 225 *et seq.* with further references, as well as J. Carrascosa González, *El Reglamento Sucesorio Europeo 650/2012 de 4 julio 2012 – Análisis crítico* (Granada, 2014), p. 314.

[13] For more on this argument generally, see J. Basedow, 'Das Prinzip der gegenseitigen Anerkennung im internationalen Wirtschaftsverkehr', in *Festschrift für Dieter Martiny zum 70. Geburtstag* (Tübingen, 2014), p. 248. However, this prevalence of a judgment over an authentic instrument only applies to those judgments that are eligible for recognition, see Davì and Zanobetti, *Il nuovo diritto internazionale privato europeo*, p. 229.

[14] B. Hess, C. Mariottini and C. Camara, 'Regulation (EC) Nr. 650/2012 of July 2012 on jurisdiction, applicable law, recognition and enforcement of authentic instruments in matters of sucession and on the creation of a European Certificate of Succession' (14. 12. 2012, PE 462.493), p. 21.

differences explain the stronger impact of a judgment as opposed to the mere evidentiary effect of an authentic instrument (see no. 30 *et seq.*).

C. *The European Primary Law Background of Article 59*

4. With regard to extending the evidentiary effects of an authentic instrument to the State of acceptance, article 59 is guided by the case law of the ECJ. According to ECJ case law, the public instruments of a Member State shall be observed by other Member States of the EU. In the *Dafeki* v. *Landesversicherungsanstalt Württemberg* case, the ECJ ruled that the administrative and judicial authorities of a Member State (that is, not only the Member States of the ESR)

> must accept certificates and analogous documents relative to personal status issued by the competent authorities of the other Member States, unless their accuracy is seriously undermined by concrete evidence relating to the individual case in question. . . . In those circumstances, a rule of national law which establishes a general and abstract presumption that, in the event of inconsistency between several documents of differing dates, it is the document closest in time to the event to be proved which prevails in the absence of other sufficient evidence, cannot justify refusal to take account of a rectification made by a court in another Member State.[15]

The court based the obligation of acceptance on the freedom of movement for workers (today: article 45 TFEU). This created a continuous line of case law that also applies to other fundamental rights in European Union law. Accordingly, the ECJ, in the *VALE* case, ruled that on the basis of the freedom of establishment of companies or firms (today: article 54, 49 TFEU),

> the authorities of the host [of a company in the context of cross-border company conversions] Member State are required, pursuant to the principle of effectiveness, to take due account, when examining a company's application for registration, of documents obtained from the authorities of the Member State of origin certifying that that company has indeed complied with the conditions laid down in that Member State, provided that those conditions are compatible with European Union law.[16]

The decision made clear, however, that the obligation to take due account does not mean the recognition of the *negotium* of the authentic

[15] ECJ, case C-336/94, *Eftalia Dafeki* v. *Landesversicherungsanstalt Württemberg* [1997] ECR I-06761, paras. 19 and 20.

[16] ECJ, case C-378/10, *VALE Építési kft* [2012] ECR I-0000, paras. 61 and 62.

instrument, but only the obligation to take the instruments into account.[17] The ECJ did not have to determine in the *VALE* decision the precise extent of this obligation to take due account. The court, however, can be interpreted as saying that the evidentiary effects of the document are indeed to be taken into account.

5. Since succession law, is protected at least by the free movement of capital,[18] the case law of the ECJ also covers succession-related instruments. It should be further emphasised that the concept of acceptance, in contrast to that of 'recognition' of an authentic instrument of article 59, can be traced back to the *Dafeki* decision. The ECJ pointed out that the general conditions for comprehensive recognition were not met.[19] The term 'acceptance of an authentic instrument' also derives from the *Dafeki* decision, for in this decision the ECJ held that a Member State 'must accept' an authentic instrument drawn up and recorded in another Member State. The term 'acceptance' is therefore neither 'sybillin',[20] nor any less serendipitous.[21] It follows from the *Dafeki* decision that this obligation to take due account only refers to the *instrumentum*, not to the *negotium* of the authentic instrument. However, the legal consequence goes beyond the *droit acquis* of European Law on taking into account the authentic instruments of Member States because article 59, as a conflict of laws rule in procedural law (ref: no. 1) commands a further extension of effect (ref: no. 37).

D. Secondary-Law Rules Related to Authentic Instruments

6. Article 59 provides for the acceptance of an authentic instrument occurring independently from enforceability. The enforceability of an authentic instrument is governed separately in article 60. Article 59 is

[17] See also H.-P. Mansel, K. Thorn and R. Wagner, 'Europäisches Kollisionsrecht 2012: Voranschreiten des Kodifikationsprozesses – Flickenteppich des Einheitsrechts', *IPRax* (2013), pp. 1, 5.

[18] A. Dutta, 'Art. 1 EuErbVO', in J. von Hein (ed), *Münchener Kommentar zum BGB*, vol. X, 6th ed. (München, 2015), para. 8, referring to the case law of the ECJ; for the most recent, see case C-132/10, *Olivier Halley, Julie Halley, Marie Halley* v. *Belgium* [2011] ECR I-8353.

[19] ECJ, case C-336/94, *Eftalia Dafeki* v. *Landesversicherungsanstalt Württemberg* [1997] ECR I-06761, paras. 14–18.

[20] But see S. Godechot-Patris, 'Le nouveau droit international privé des successions: entre satisfactions et craintes', *Dalloz* (2012), pp. 2462, 2468.

[21] But see P. Lagarde, 'Les principes de base du nouveau règlement européen sur les successions', *Rev crit dr int priv* (2012), pp. 691, 732.

now the model for article 58 Council Regulation (EU) no. 1103/2016 of 24 June 2016 implementing enhanced cooperation in the area of jurisdiction, applicable law and the recognition and enforcement of decisions in matters of matrimonial property regimes[22] and for article 58 Council Regulation (EU) 1104/ 2016 of 24 June 2016 implementing enhanced cooperation in the area of jurisdiction, applicable law and the recognition and enforcement of decisions in matters of the property consequences of registered partnerships.[23] Neither the European Treaties, nor the EU regulations knew before a rule comparable to article 59:[24]

Article 50 Brussels Convention of 27 September 1968[25] and the Lugano Convention of 16 September 1988[26] on jurisdiction and the enforcement of judgments in civil and commercial matters only deal with the enforcement of authentic instruments. The same can be said for article 57 Council Regulation (EC) no. 44/2001 of 22 December 2000 (Brussels I)[27], article 58 Council Regulation (EC) no. 1215/2012 of 12 December 2012 on jurisdiction and the recognition and enforcement of judgments in civil and commercial matters (Brussels I-*bis*)[28], article 57 Lugano Convention of 30 October 2007 on jurisdiction and the recognition and enforcement of judgments in civil and commercial matters (Lugano 2007),[29] and article 25(2) Regulation (EC) no. 805/2004 of 21 April 2004 creating a European Enforcement Order for uncontested claims.[30] Other regulations indeed govern recognition and enforcement of authentic instruments. These are article 46 Regulation (EC) no. 2201/2003 concerning jurisdiction and the recognition and enforcement of judgments in matrimonial matters and matters of parental responsibility (Brussels II-*bis*)[31] and article 48 Regulation (EC) no. 4/2009 on jurisdiction, applicable law, recognition and enforcement of decisions and cooperation in matters relating to

22 OJ 2016 no. L183, 8 July 2016, p. 1. 23 OJ 2016 no. L183, 8 July 2016, p. 30.

24 See also Fitchen, '"Recognition", acceptance and enforcement of authentic instruments', pp. 323, 336–343; for the deviating opinion to the effect that article 59 applies only the rules of the Brussels Convention from 1968 and of Brussels I from 2000, see, however, Foyer, 'Reconnaissance, acceptation et exécution', p. 141.

25 As amended by the Convention of 9 October 1978 on the accession of the kingdom of Denmark, Ireland and the United Kingdom of Great Britain and Northern Ireland, by the Convention of 25 October 1982 on the accession of the Hellenic Republic and by the Convention of 26 May 1989 on the accession of the kingdom of Spain and the Portuguese Republic, OJ 1972 no. L 299, 31 December 1972, p. 32; consolidated version in OJ 1998 no. C27, 26 January 1998, p. 1.

26 OJ 1988 no. L319, 25 November 1988, p. 9. 27 OJ 2001 no. L12, 16 January 2001, p. 1.

28 OJ 2012 no. L351, 20 December 2012, p. 1.

29 OJ 2007 no. L339, 21 December 2007, p. 3. 30 OJ 2004 no. L143, 30 April 2004, p. 15.

31 OJ 2003 no. L338, 23 December 2003, p. 1.

maintenance obligations (Maintenance regulation).[32] Both are different from article 59 in that they only govern the recognition of *enforceable* authentic instruments.[33] Moreover, recognition within the meaning of article 46 Brussels II and article 48 Maintenance regulation occurs pursuant to the rules on the recognition of judgments; this is an additional difference to article 59 (see no. 5).

7. The meaning of the term 'recognition' according to article 46 Brussels II and article 48 Maintenance regulation is disputed. Some are of the opinion that also the substantive law content of an authentic instrument is to be recognised by way of article 46 Brussels II[34] and article 48 Maintenance regulation[35] in the secondary State. Others[36] argue that both provisions refer only to procedural law effects. The recognition of the *negotium* of an instrument is not the subject matter of both provisions for this would mean a sweeping change in the normal demarcation of international private law and international procedural law. In any case, neither provision constitutes a model for article 59 since both only cover those authentic instruments that have enforceable content and which require recognition as a condition of enforcement.[37] This is different for article 59; this provision is applicable to all authentic instruments falling within the scope of application of the ESR. Above all, article 59 makes very clear that it does not govern any recognition of a substantive law legal status (*negotium*), but only the extension given to the evidentiary effect of the *instrumentum* [see art. 59 nos. 2, 3 and 8, 9, 33].

E. Legislative History

8. The legislative history confirms interpreting acceptance as an instrument pursuant to article 59 as in no way including the *negotium.*

[32] OJ 2009 no. L7, 10 January 2009, p. 1.

[33] F. Bauer, 'Art. 59 EuErbVO: Verfahrensrechtliche Kollisionsnorm zur Sicherung des freien Verkehrs öffentlicher Urkunden', in *Gedächtnisschrift für Hannes Unberath* (München, 2015), p. 19, footnote 1.

[34] See e.g. B. Ancel and H. Muir Watt, 'La désunion européenne : le règlement dit de Bruxelles II', *Rev crit dr int priv* (2001), p. 440 *et seq.*; S. Dornblüth, *Die europäische Regelung der Anerkennung und Vollstreckbarerklärung von Ehe- und Kindschaftsentscheidungen* (Tübingen, 2003), p. 63.

[35] M. Andrae, 'Art. 48 EG-UntVO', in T. Rauscher (ed), *Europäisches Zivilprozess- und Kollisionsrecht*, 4th ed. (München, 2015), para. 6.

[36] But see R. Geimer, *Internationales Zivilprozessrecht*, 7th ed. (Köln, 2015), para. 2865a.

[37] On this requirement in article 46 Brussels IIa, see T. Rauscher, 'Artikel 46 Brüssel IIa-VO' in T. Rauscher (ed), *Europäisches Zivilprozess- und Kollisionsrecht*, 4th ed. (München, 2015), paras. 1, 10.

The proposal by the Commission in 2009 still included recognising the instrument; however, non-executable instruments were not to be given recognition. The proposed legislation for article 34 ESR stated:

> Article 34. Recognition of authentic instruments
> Authentic instruments formally drawn up or registered in a Member State shall be recognised in the other Member States, except where the validity of these instruments is contested in accordance with the procedures provided for in the home Member State and provided that such recognition is not contrary to public policy in the Member State addressed.[38]

Recital 26 sentence 3 of the Commission's proposal further stated: 'The recognition of authentic instruments means that they enjoy the same evidentiary effect with regard to their contents and the same effects as in their country of origin, as well as a presumption of validity which can be eliminated if they are contested.'[39] According to this, the *negotium* was supposed to be afforded 'recognition'. That meant the recognition of an authentic instrument would have resulted in the recognition of legal situations or legal status. In such a case, however, the method of recognition and, in particular, the relationship between the 'recognition' of the authentic instrument and international private law with its conflict of laws rules was not defined clearly enough.[40] The proposed article 34 ESR therefore drew heavy criticism,[41] precisely because the method for

[38] 2009 Proposal referred to in footnote 2, p. 24.

[39] 2009 Proposal referred to in footnote 2, p. 12 *et seq.*

[40] P. Callé, 'La circulation des actes authentiques', in H. Bosse-Platière, N. Damas and Y. Dereu (eds), *L'avenir européen du droit des successions internationales* (Paris, 2011), p. 58 *et seq.*; for a critical view, see M. Buschbaum, 'Rechtslagenanerkennung aufgrund öffentlicher Urkunden? Bestandsaufnahme und Ausblick nach dem Inkrafttreten der EU-Erbrechtsverordnung', in *Festschrift für Dieter Martiny zum 70. Geburtstag* (Tübingen, 2014), pp. 259, 260 with further references.

[41] Foyer, 'Reconnaissance, acceptation et exécution', p. 161 *et seq.*; Mansel, Thorn and Wagner, 'Europäisches Kollisionsrecht 2010: Verstärkte Zusammenarbeit als Motor der Vereinheitlichung?', pp. 1, 4; with fundamental criticism and recommendation to discard the provision, Max Planck Institute for Comparative and International Private Law, 'Comments on the European Commission's Proposal for a Regulation of the European Parliament and of the Council on jurisdiction, applicable law, recognition and enforcement of decisions and authentic instruments in matters of succession and the creation of a European Certificate of Succession', *RabelsZ* (2010), pp. 522, 669 *et seq.*; against recognition of the authentic instrument with regard to the *negotium*, as well, and for the limited concept of acceptance with regard only to the *instrumentum*, see e.g. A. Bonomi, 'Il regolamento europeo sulle successioni', *Riv dir int priv proc* (2013), pp. 293, 319; S. Godechot-Patris, 'Le nouveau droit international privé des successions: entre satisfactions et craintes', *Dalloz* (2012), pp. 2462, 2468; M. Kohler and M. Buschbaum, 'Die „Anerkennung" öffentlicher Urkunden? – Kritische Gedanken über einen zweifelhaften

recognising legal situations or legal status was disputed from a doctrinal standpoint.[42] This led to the rejection of the concept of recognising authentic instruments, particularly the refusal to extend the effects of

Ansatz in der EU-Kollisionsrechtsvereinheitlichung', *IPRax* (2010), pp. 313, 314 *et seq.*; M. Kohler and M. Buschbaum, 'La "reconnaissance" des actes authentiques prévue pour les successions transfrontalières. Réflexions critiques sur une approche douteuse entamée dans l'harmonisation des règles de conflits de lois', *Rev crit dr int priv* (2010), p. 643 *et seq.*; for criticism of the deliberations surrounding the proposed regulation in the Commission and the European Council, see K. Lechner, 'Die Entwicklung der Erbrechtsverordnung - Eine Einführung zum Gesetzgebungsverfahren', in A. Dutta and S. Herrler (eds), *Die Europäische Erbrechtsverordnung* (München, 2014), p. 12 *et seq.*, paras. 31–33; Wautelet, 'Article 59', p. 678; B. Hess, E. Jayme and T. Pfeiffer, *Stellungnahme zum Vorschlag für eine Europäische Erbrechtsverordnung Version 2009/157 (COD) vom 16.1.2012 (PE 462.430 DE)* (Brussels, 2012), p. 44 *et seq.*; Buschbaum, 'Rechtslagenanerkennung aufgrund öffentlicher Urkunden?', pp. 259, 260 *et seq.*, with further references, p. 261 footnote 13, regarding how Belgian autonomous international private law also does not have authentic document recognition comparable to article 34 ESR proposal; likewise with a restrictive view, see Wautelet, 'Article 59', p. 679 *et seq.*, footnote 63. But for a more positive view with respect to the *negotium* being included, see e.g. C. Nourissat, P. Callé, P. Pasqualis and P. Wautelet, 'Pour la reconnaissance des actes authentiques au sein de l'espace de liberté, de securité et de justice', in *Petites affiches* (2012), no. 68, p. 6.

42 See the overview with respect to the relationship of international private law and the recognition of legal stituations (recognition of the legal situation) by P. Mayer, 'La reconnaissance: notions et méthodes', in P. Lagarde (ed), *La reconnaissance des situations en droit international privé* (Paris, 2013), p. 27; C.-F. Nordmeier, 'Stand, Perspektiven und Grenzen der Rechtslagenanerkennung im europäischen Rechtsraum anhand der Entscheidungen mitgliedstaatlicher Gerichte', *IPRax* (2012), p. 31; rejecting the recognition of the legal situation, E. Jayme and C. Kohler, 'Europäisches Kollisionsrecht 2001: Anerkennungsprinzip statt IPR?', *IPRax* (2001), p. 501 *et seq.*; H.-P. Mansel, 'Anerkennung als Grundprinzip des Europäischen Rechtsraums - Zur Herausbildung eines europäischen Anerkennungs-Kollisionsrechts: Anerkennung statt Verweisung als neues Strukturprinzip des Europäischen internationalen Privatrechts', *RabelsZ* (2006), pp. 654, 723 *et seq.*; H.-P. Mansel, D. Coester-Waltjen, D. Henrich and C. Kohler, 'Stellungnahme im Auftrag des Deutschen Rats für Internationales Privatrecht zum Grünbuch der Europäischen Kommission "Weniger Verwaltungsaufwand für EU-Bürger: Den freien Verkehr öffentlicher Urkunden und die Anerkennung der Rechtswirkungen von Personenstandsurkunden erleichtern" - KOM(2010) 747 endg', *IPRax* (2011), pp. 335, 338. H.-P. Mansel, 'Kritisches zur "Urkundsinhaltsanerkennung"', *IPRax* (2011), p. 342; R. Wagner, 'Anerkennung von Personenstandsurkunden - was heißt das? - Überlegungen vor dem Hintergrund des Grünbuchs der Europäischen Kommission vom 14. 12. 2010', *DNotZ - Deutsche Notar-Zeitschrift* (2011), p. 176; J. Basedow, 'La reconnaissance des situations juridiques en droit des affaires', in P. Lagarde (ed), *La reconnaissance des situations en droit international privé* (Paris, 2013), p. 221; M. Grünberger, 'Alles obsolet? - Anerkennungsprinzip vs. klassisches IPR', in S. Leible and H. Unberath (eds), *Brauchen wir eine Rom 0-Verordnung?* (München, 2013), p. 81; Buschbaum, 'Rechtslagenanerkennung aufgrund öffentlicher Urkunden?', p. 260 with further references; for a positive take on recognition of legal status, see e.g. P. Lagarde, 'Développements futurs du droit international privé dans une Europe en voie d'unification: quelques conjectures', *RabelsZ* (2004), pp. 225, 229 *et seq.*;

the *negotium* to the secondary State. The rule in article 59 restricted to the *instrumentum* took the place of the proposed article 34 ESR.

II. Requirements for the Acceptance of an Authentic Instrument: Article 59(1)

A. Authentic Instrument

9. Article 59 does not apply to every document, but only to the acceptance of authentic instruments. According to article 3.1(i)

> 'authentic instrument' means a document in a matter of succession which has been formally drawn up or registered as an authentic instrument in a Member State and the authenticity of which: (i) relates to the signature and the content of the authentic instrument; and (ii) has been established by a public authority or other authority that granted such authority for that purpose by the Member State of origin [for more details, see ref: art. 3 no. 16].

This definition follows the corresponding definition in article 2(c) Brussels I-*bis*, article 2.1 no. 3(a) Maintenance regulation and article 4 no. 3(a) regulation (EC) no. 805/2004 of 21 April 2004 creating a European Enforcement Order for uncontested claims.[43] In those legal orders influenced by the Latin notarial profession, the notary is also one such office authorized to draw up and record authentic instruments.[44]

10. The term 'authentic instrument' is subject to an autonomous interpretation of the regulation and not to one of national law.[45] The understanding of the term under national law (*lex fori*) is irrelevant. The case law of the ECJ on authentic instruments within the meaning of

S. Bollée, 'L'extension du domaine de la méthode de reconnaissance unilatérale', *Rev crit dr int priv* (2007), p. 307; P. Lagarde, 'La reconnaissance – mode d'emploi', in *Vers de nouveaux équilibres entre ordres juridiques. Liber Amicorum Hélène Gaudemet-Tallon* (Paris, 2008), p. 481; P. Lagarde, 'Introduction au thème de la reconnaissance des situations', in P. Lagarde (ed), *La reconnaissance des situations en droit international privé* (Paris, 2013), p. 19; C. Pamboukis, 'La renaissance-métamorphose de la méthode de reconnaissance', *Rev crit dr int priv* (2008), p. 513; G. P. Romano, 'La bilatéralité éclipsée par l'autorité', *Rev crit dr int priv* (2006), p. 457.

43 OJ 2004 no. L143, 30 April 2004, p. 15.

44 For the general view, see e.g. Wautelet, 'Article 59', pp. 153, 155 *et seq.*

45 See Wautelet, 'Article 3', p. 153. On the need of an autonomous interpretation of the terms of the regulation in order to achieve its uniform application see Carrascosa González, *El Reglamento Sucesorio Europeo*, p. 26 *et seq.*, and p. 315 on the term of 'authenticity' ('*autenticidad*').

article 2 Brussels I-*bis* and article 4 no. 3(a) European Enforcement Order regulation[46] has been drawn on to interpret article 3.1(i) and article 59. It must be noted here that an authentic instrument within the meaning of the ESR does not require substantive content which can be enforced (see no. 33). An authentic instrument only exists, according to the State of origin, if it has special evidentiary effects (article 59(1)) related to the authenticity of an authentic instrument (article 59(2)).

11. Whether an authentic instrument within the meaning of the ESR must be a written document[47] or whether an electronic document also is sufficient for an acceptance pursuant to article 59 is an open question.[48] Article 25(2) Brussels I-*bis* expressly provides that 'any communication by electronic means which provides a durable record of the agreement [of prorogation] be equivalent to "writing"'. Therefore in the regulatory law of the European Union, the equal status of the electronic and written forms is recognised. This is a further argument in favour of the view that the electronic form is sufficient under article 59.

B. Drawing up and Recording by the State of Origin and Member State of the ESR

12. An authentic instrument within the meaning of the ESR must have been drawn up and recorded by a public authority or an equivalent office [see art. 3 no. 15] (authority to draw up and record documents) of a Member State of the ESR. Drawing up and recording means the issuance or registration of a document by such an authority in a way that the document is given special evidentiary effect as an authentic instrument according to the law of the ESR Member State (see no. 30), which distinguishes it from documents without this type of official designation. The authority to draw up and record documents must derive from an ESR Member State. However, it is not necessary that the authentic instrument has any other relationship to the State of origin; in particular, none of the persons making a declaration in the instrument,

[46] ECJ, case C-260/97, *Unibank A/S* v. *Flemming G. Christensen* [1999] ECR I-3724, paras. 17 *et seq.*; accord. ECJ, case C-53/08, *European Commission* v. *Austria* [2011] I-4309; ECJ, case C-54/08, *European Commission* v. *Germany* [2011] I-4355.

[47] See D. Looschelders, 'Art. 3 EuErbVO', in R. Hüßtege and H.-P. Mansel (eds), *NomosKommentar, BGB, Rom-Verordnungen*, vol. VI, 2nd ed. (Baden-Baden, 2015), para. 27.

[48] See J. Schmidt, 'Art. 3 EuErbVO', in C. Budzikiewicz, M.-P. Weller and W. Wurmnest (eds), *Beck-Online Großkommentar, EuErbVO* (München, 2015), paras. 36 *et seq.*

nor the factual or legal issues documented in the authentic instrument, must have any relationship (e.g. domicile, residence, nationality, etc.) to the state in which the instrument is drawn up and recorded. Typically, the place where the instrument is drawn up and recorded will be located geographically in the State of origin. However, the State of origin is not defined by the place where the instrument is drawn up and recorded, but by looking to the state from which the public authority derives its competence. Consular authorities of an ESR Member State may therefore draw up and record such instruments overseas within its consular territory pursuant to international law.[49] All EU Member States besides three are also Member States of the ESR. Only the EU Member States Denmark, Ireland and the United Kingdom do not participate in the ESR. While the ESR does not expressly define the term Member State of the ESR, the idea of reciprocity is an underlying theme, particularly with regard to the recognition and enforcement of judicial decisions and the acceptance and enforcement of authentic instruments. Since the aforementioned three EU States have declided participation in the ESR, they are considered third countries [see art. 3 no. 9].[50]

13. Some EU States do not have the legal concept of the authentic instrument; these include Denmark, Ireland and the United Kingdom[51], which do not participate in the ESR (see no. 12). But also the EU Member States of Finland, Sweden and Cyprus, to which the ESR applies, do not have the authentic instrument.[52] As Member States of the ESR, however, they are required by article 59 to accept the authentic instruments of other ESR Member States.

14. Article 59 does not apply to succession documents that are not authentic instruments because they were not drawn up and recorded with the involvement of a public authority or equivalent office (so-called

[49] See also Geimer, *Internationales Zivilprozessrecht*, para. 2330e.

[50] See also Geimer, *Internationales Zivilprozessrecht*, para. 2330e; P. Lagarde, 'Introduction', in U. Bergquist, D. Damascelli, R. Frimston, P. Lagarde, F. Odersky and B. Reinhartz, *EU Regulation in Succession and Wills. Commentary* (Köln, 2015), para. 49; F. Odersky, 'Article 4', *ibid.*, para. 12; U. Bergquist, 'Article 39', *ibid.*, para. 3; for a contrary view (the three States are not seen as third countries), see R. Frimston, 'Article 3', *ibid.*, para. 44. Davì and Zanobetti, *Il nuovo diritto internazionale privato europeo*, p. 21 *et seq.*, retrace the background and timeline of the Irish and British decision not to opt-in.

[51] See Carrascosa González, *El Reglamento Sucesorio Europeo*, p. 313.

[52] Geimer, *Internationales Zivilprozessrecht*, para. 2330d; further information by D. Damascelli, 'Article 59', in U. Bergquist, D. Damascelli, R. Frimston, P. Lagarde, F. Odersky and B. Reinhartz, *EU Regulation in Succession and Wills. Commentary* (Köln, 2015), para. 6; Carrascosa González, *El Reglamento Sucesorio Europeo*, p. 313.

private instruments). With respect to the procedural effects, the respective *lex fori* applies; with respect to the substantive law effects, the rules of succession apply. As it relates to qualifying this substantive law presumption of proof, Anatol Dutta correctly refers to the general legal notion, as it also underlies article 18.1 Rome I regulation and article 22.1 Rome II regulation.[53] If a public official of a State of origin certifies an authentic instrument and fails to do so within the confines of his authority, e.g. because he is not geographically acting within his area of competence, then the law of the State of origin controls as to whether a valid authentic instrument has come into existance. If the State of origin answers this question in the negative, then it is considered a private instrument only.[54]

C. *Authentic Instrument in a Matter of Succession*

15. Authentic instruments within the meaning of article 59 (1) must have been drawn up and recorded 'in a matter of succession' (article 3(1)(a)). That means they must fall within the scope of the ESR set forth in article 1 [see art. 1 no. 1 *et seq.*] because only then is article 59 applicable in the first place. That means that the content of the authentic instrument (*negotium*) must fall into the scope of application of the ESR within the meaning of article 1.[55] Authentic instruments, for example, with respect to the status of natural persons, as well as family relationships, to the legal capacity of natural persons, to the disappearance, absence or presumed death of a natural person, relating to matrimonial property regimes, etc. (see article 1.2), may not be accepted, therefore, pursuant to article 59, even if their acceptance within the meaning of the ESR is an issue in a succession law proceeding. Therefore, birth, marriage and death certificates, for example, do not fall under article 59,[56] even when the issue of

[53] A. Dutta, 'Art. 3 EuErbVO', in J. von Hein (ed), *Münchener Kommentar zum BGB*, vol. X, 6th ed. (München, 2015), para. 13.

[54] See Bauer (referred to in footnote 33), p. 24, footnote 37, with an example from French law.

[55] See Geimer, *Internationales Zivilprozessrecht*, paras. 2330i–2330l.

[56] Bauer (referred to in footnote 33), pp. 25, 27; Dutta, 'Art. 59 EuErbVO', para. 6; Geimer, *Internationales Zivilprozessrecht*, para. 2330i; R. Geimer, '"Annahme" ausländischer öffentlicher Urkunden in Erbsachen gemäß Art. 59 EuErbVO', in A. Dutta and S. Herrler (eds), *Die Europäische Erbrechtsverordnung* (München, 2014), p. 143, para. 18; Kohler and Buschbaum, 'Die "Anerkennung" öffentlicher Urkunden?', pp. 313, 314 *et seq.*; Max Planck Institute for Comparative and International Private Law, 'Comments on the European Commission's Proposal for a Regulation of the European Parliament and of the Council on jurisdiction, applicable law, recognition and enforcement of decisions and authentic instruments in matters of succession and the creation of a European Certificate of Succession', p. 522, para. 256; M. Makowsky, 'Art. 59 EuErbVO', in R. Hüßtege and

acceptance of the authentic instrument with respect to the status of natural persons is raised in a succession proceeding within the meaning of article 2(2) ESR.[57]

16. Frank Bauer discusses whether article 59(1) also allows the acceptance of authentic instruments indicating *civil status* in succession proceedings pursuant to article 4 *et seq.* His view is that it does not.[58] This is correct. Article 59 is not supposed to guarantee the free movement of all authentic instruments generally, rather only the free movement of authentic instruments with succession law content. It also follows from article 59(3), that the legal content of an authentic instrument within the meaning of article 59 can only be such as falls under the conflict of laws rules of articles 20–37. Articles 20–37 govern the applicable succession law alone. The content of an authentic instrument, which is relevant in terms of article 59, must therefore relate to succession law. In light of this clear rule, a court of last instance would not have to submit the issue dealt with here to the ECJ under the preliminary ruling procedure pursuant to article 267 TFEU.[59]

17. If an authentic instrument embraces more than one legal question, of which some fall within the scope of the ESR while others do not, the effect of acceptance pursuant to article 59 is limited to those requirements covered by article 1 ESR.[60] As such, the effect extended is thus fragmented. The same applies to private instruments (see no. 14): With respect to the other requirements, an analysis must be undertaken according to the *lex fori* as to whether an extension of effect under procedural law is being commanded outside the ESR and, pursuant to the rules of succession, which are determined by reference to the international private law of the *lex fori,* the decision must be made whether substantive law presumptions of proof apply in such a case.

H.-P. Mansel (eds), *NomosKommentar, BGB, Rom-Verordnungen,* vol. VI, 2nd ed. (Baden-Baden, 2015), para. 5; Mansel, Thorn and Wagner, 'Europäisches Kollisionsrecht 2010: Verstärkte Zusammenarbeit als Motor der Vereinheitlichung?', pp. 1, 4; accord. J. Schmidt, 'Art. 59 EuErbVO', in C. Budzikiewicz, M.-P. Weller and W. Wurmnest (eds), *Beck-Online Großkommentar, EuErbVO* (München, 2015), para. 5.1.

[57] Dutta, 'Art. 59 EuErbVO', para. 6. [58] Bauer (referred to in footnote 33), p. 27 *et seq.*

[59] For a different view and one in support of the obligation to refer for a preliminary ruling: Bauer (referred to in footnote 33), p. 27 *et seq.*

[60] Similar Fitchen, '"Recognition", acceptance and enforcement of authentic instruments', pp. 323, 330 *et seq.*

18. The following are examples of authentic instruments within the meaning of article 59, if they fulfil the requirements of article 3(1)(i) (see no. 9 *et seq.*): a 'disposition of property upon death', i.e. a will, a joint will or an agreement as to succession (see article 3.1(d)), a declaration of the acceptance or waiver of the succession (see article 13). The only aspect covered by article 59, however, is the *instrumentum*, not the substantive law *negotium* (on this distinction see nos. 2, 3, 8, 33, 52 *et seq.*).

19. The treatment of national succession certificates is subject to dispute. According to one view[61] they do not fall under article 59 since article 59(3) speaks of 'legal acts or legal relationships recorded' and form II (see no. 28) allows entries for parties to the authentic instrument. This view is not convincing, however, because even a last will and testament does not have any parties and a national succession certificate includes a legal act if it provides information with regard to the testamentary succession. Thus, the widely held view should be followed[62] according to which a national succession certificate falls under article 59, provided the certificate fulfils the requirements of article 3(1)(i) (see no. 9 *et seq.*).

20. While pursuant to article 59 solely the 'formal evidentiary effect' of the national succession certificate is produced in the secondary State, the legal situation in terms of succession law documented in the national succession certificate is not (see no. 30 *et seq.*).[63] Article 59 is not applicable if the national succession certificates are a decision within the meaning of article 3(1)(g) and not an authentic instrument within the meaning of article 3(1)(i). [On the requirements of a decision, see art. 3 no. 11]. Burkhard Hess, Erik Jayme and Thomas Pfeiffer [64] hold the view that national succession certificates cannot be considered as decisions within the meaning of article 3(1)(g), if the effect of the national

[61] C. Dorsel and C. Schall, 'Die Umsetzung der ErbVO durch die Europäische Kommission – Ein erster Überblick unter besonderer Berücksichtigung des Europäischen Nachlasszeugnisses', *GPR – Zeitschrift für das Privatrecht der Europäischen Union* (2015), pp. 36, 37 *et seq.*; see also Buschbaum, 'Rechtslagenanerkennung aufgrund öffentlicher Urkunden?', pp. 259, 267 with further references in note 35.

[62] Dutta, 'Art. 59 EuErbVO', para. 1; Dutta, 'Das neue internationale Erbrecht der Europäischen Union', p. 14; A. Dutta, 'Die europäische Erbrechtsverordnung vor ihrem Anwendungsbeginn: Zehn ausgewählte Streitstandsminiaturen', *IPRax* (2015), pp. 32, 38; Kleinschmidt, 'Optionales Erbrecht', pp. 723, 737 *et seq.*; Makowsky, 'Art. 59 EuErbVO', para. 4; J. Schmidt, 'Art. 59 EuErbVO', paras. 12, 12.1; Wautelet, 'Article 59', p. 157.

[63] Makowsky, 'Art. 59 EuErbVO', para. 4.

[64] *Stellungnahme zum Vorschlag für eine Europäische Erbrechtsverordnung* (referred to in footnote 41), p. 47, note 168; approvingly Kleinschmidt, 'Optionales Erbrecht', pp. 723, 735 note 58.

succession certificates can be refuted – that is, the concept of *res iudicata* does not apply. One would have to agree with this view.

21. Because an Austrian *Einantwortungsbeschluss* acquires the force of law pursuant to sections 797 *et seq.* ABGB (Austrian civil code), it therefore qualifies as a decision[65] within the meaning of article 3(1)(g). Article 59 does not apply to it.[66] The *acte de notoriété* or *acte d'hérédité* governed under Belgian and French law are viewed as authentic instruments.[67] The German national succession certificate is called an *Erbschein* and is governed by sections 2352 *et seq.* BGB (German civil code), sections 352 *et seq.* FamFG (family procedure act). Because the *Erbschein* can be issued in a potentially adversarial judicial proceeding, it could qualify as a decision within the meaning of article 3(1)(g). It could then only be recognised according to article 39 and not accepted pursuant to article 59.[68] However, in the event that a certificate of inheritance within the meaning of section 2353 BGB, that has been issued, is incorrect the probate court must revoke it. The certificate of inheritance becomes invalid upon its revocation. Consequently, a German *Erbschein* does not have *res iudicata* effect.[69] Therefore it should not qualify as a decision within the meaning of article 3(1)(g). Consequently, the application of article 39 must be rejected. An *Erbschein* within the meaning of section 2353 BGB may therefore only be accepted pursuant to article 59. The Swedish *Steuerinventar*, on the other hand, is neither a decision nor an authentic instrument.[70] On the relationship between

[65] See Davì and Zanobetti, *Il nuovo diritto internazionale privato europeo*, p. 11.

[66] *Stellungnahme zum Vorschlag für eine Europäische Erbrechtsverordnung* (referred to in footnote 41), p. 47, note 168; approvingly, Kleinschmidt, 'Optionales Erbrecht', pp. 723, 735, note 58; for a different opinion to the effect that Art. 59 applies to the decision of devolution according to Austrian law, see Foyer, 'Reconnaissance, acceptation et exécution', p. 151.

[67] Wautelet, 'Article 3', p. 157 .

[68] Bauer (referred to in footnote 33), p. 32, note 69; Dutta, 'Art. 59 EuErbVO', para. 10; Dutta, 'Art. 13 EuErbVO', in J. van Hein (ed), *Münchener Kommentar zum BGB*, vol. X, 6th ed. (München, 2015), para. 13; Dutta, 'Die europäische Erbrechtsverordnung vor ihrem Anwendungsbeginn', pp. 32, 38; Makowsky, 'Art. 59 EuErbVO', para. 4. But see, for a contrary view (in favour of article 59): J. Schmidt, 'Art. 3 EuErbVO', para. 12.1; in the final analysis also dismissive, Hess, Jayme and Pfeiffer, *Stellungnahme zum Vorschlag für eine Europäische Erbrechtsverordnung* (referred to in footnote 41), p. 47, footnote 168; Kleinschmidt, 'Optionales Erbrecht', pp. 723, 735 footnote 58.

[69] On the practical importance of the German *Erbschein* in Spain, see Carrascosa González, *El Reglamento Sucesorio Europeo*, p. 218 *et seq.* and p. 319 for its influence on the creation of the European Certificate of Succession.

[70] M. Buschbaum, 'Europäisches Nachlasszeugnis und Annahme öffentlicher Urkunden – neue Mechanismen zur grenzüberschreitenden Nachlassabwicklung und ihr Verhältnis

the national succession certificates and the European Certificate of Succession see article 62 [see art. 62 no. 13].

D. Ordre public

22. Article 59(1) also requires for the acceptance of an authentic instrument that it is not 'manifestly contrary to public policy (*ordre public*) in the Member State concerned'. 'Member State concerned' means the State of acceptance (secondary State see no 1).[71] In the case of a violation of public policy, the effect given in the primary State (see no. 1) shall not be extended to the secondary State. The public policy exception of article 59(1) is to be interpreted in parallel to the *ordre public* clause of article 40(1) [see art. 40 nos. 6, 12] because both *ordre public* exceptions limit the effect of a decision within the meaning of article 3(1)(g) (case of article 40(1)) or of an authentic instrument (see no. 9 *et seq.*) (case of article 59(1)) has in the secondary State. [see art. 40 no. 6].

23. Acceptance can therefore not occur if acceptance is contrary to the national public policy of the State of acceptance.[72] That is only the case if the *effect* of the acceptance as an authentic instrument is contrary to the *ordre public* in the *specific individual case*. With article 59(1), only the formal evidentiary effect of the authentic instrument can be verified and limited. The national *ordre public* of the ESR has at least the same content as the European *ordre public*. Likewise, the European *ordre public* may place limitations upon the national *ordre public*.[73]

24. A contravention is only deemed to be relevant under article 59(1) if it is 'manifest'. This means that it must be particularly severe.[74] It is if the State of acceptance in the specific individual case had to accept a particularly significant deviation from the core values of its national legal order, which should not be imposed on it under any circumstances.[75] Thus, there must exist a glaring difference between the legal situation with and without acceptance. That will only be the

zum materiellen Sachenrecht', in J. Hager (ed), *Die neue europäische Erbrechtsverordnung* (Baden-Baden, 2013), p. 62, note 80; siehe auch Kleinschmidt, 'Optionales Erbrecht', pp. 723 and 735, footnote 58.

[71] See Wautelet, 'Article 59', p. 671 *et seq.* [72] See Wautelet, 'Article 59', p. 671 *et seq.*

[73] H.-P. Mansel, 'Vereinheitlichung des Internationalen Erbrechts in der Europäischen Gemeinschaft – Kompetenzfragen und Regelungsgrundsätze', in *Prof. Dr. Tuğrul Ansay'a Armağan* (Ankara, 2006), pp. 185, 215.

[74] See Wautelet, 'Article 59', p. 671.

[75] See generally E. Jayme, *Methoden der Konkretisierung des ordre public im internationalen Privatrecht* (Heidelberg, 1989), p. 33: 'a crass difference'.

case by way of exception. Hence, a public policy exception only exists 'in exceptional circumstances'.[76] Therefore, the *ordre public* exception under article 59(1) is to be interpreted narrowly. This generally corresponds to the case law of the ECJ with regard to the *ordre public* in EU regulations.[77] For that reason, the court of the State of acceptance that intends to refuse acceptance on the basis of a violation of the *ordre public* must state its reasons regarding the nature of the violation thoroughly.[78]

25. The legal consequence of an *ordre public* violation under article 59(1) is that an authentic instrument enjoys none of the formal evidentiary effects in the State of acceptance which are produced according to the law of the State of origin. However, partial acceptance is conceivable using the *argumentum a maiore a minus*. For example, an acceptance may generally occur but be limited, such as when rebuttal evidence is permitted even if the law of the State of origin itself does not allow such evidence (for an example of a knowingly untruthful authentic instrument, see no. 26).

26. In the literature, examples have been given where the *ordre public* exception of article 59 (1) applies:

- Where a signature under the authentic instrument was coerced through a threat or the application of force (see article 3(1)(i) and (ii)).[79] This likely constitutes a violation of the national *ordre public* in every State of acceptance.
- In the case of a discriminatory rule with respect to formal evidentiary effect in the State of origin. The literature gives the example of an unjustified unequal treatment of formal evidentiary effect given to an authentic instrument on the basis of sex, religion or race.[80] Only authentic instruments of ESR Member States are covered by article 59 (see nos. 12 *et seq.*). It is difficult to imagine the use of such discriminations in a Member State of the ESR. Also any unjustified unequal treatment based on 'colour, ethnic or social origin, genetic features, language, religion or

[76] See similarly recital 58 on the *ordre public* clause of article 35, pursuant to which the application of foreign substantive succession law can be rejected.

[77] See J. Schmidt, 'Art. 35 EuErbVO', in C. Budzikiewicz, M.-P. Weller and W. Wurmnest (eds), *Beck-Online Großkommentar, EuErbVO* (München, 2015), para. 12, with further references.

[78] See generally that the finding of a contravention of the *ordre public* also requires an accompanying justification, Jayme, *Methoden der Konkretisierung des ordre public im internationalen Privatrecht*, p. 12.

[79] J. Schmidt, 'Art. 59 EuErbVO', para. 26.3, with further references.

[80] J. Schmidt, 'Art. 59 EuErbVO', para. 26.1.

belief, political or any other opinion, membership of a national minority, property, birth, disability, age or sexual orientation' prohibited by article 21(1) EU Charter of Fundamental Rights may also not be used in similar fashion in the law of an ESR Member State for the formal evidentiary effectiveness of authentic instruments. Discrimination according to citizenship is prohibited under the requirements of article 21(2) EU Charter of Fundamental Rights. Thus, differing configurations of the formal evidentiary effect of authentic instruments by citizenship of affected persons would violate the *ordre public* for every State of acceptance within the meaning of article 59(1), provided that the formal evidentiary effect of the authentic instrument is governed by the law of the State of origin in breach of article 21(2) EU Charter of Fundamental Rights.

- In German doctrine it is disputed whether a violation of the *ordre public* within the meaning of article 59(1) can exist pursuant to the law of the secondary State if the law of the State of origin precludes the use of rebuttal evidence.[81]
- If an authentic instrument is drawn up and recorded by a public official which contains false content due to a bribe or another form of corruption,[82] a genuine authentic instrument is nevertheless created. If, for example, a public official of the State of origin certifies that a particular person made a particular testamentary disposition at a particular time although this is untrue, a genuine authentic instrument is created, the contents of which are untrue. To the extent that this cannot be resolved in a proceeding carried out in the State of origin, it stands to reason that in the secondary State acceptance could be refused due to a violation of the *ordre public* of the State of acceptance pursuant to article 59(1)[83] or that an acceptance occurs but in accordance with the law of the State of acceptance rebuttal evidence (of the false nature of the content) could be permitted even when the law of the State of origin does not permit this.[84]
- There is no violation of the *ordre public* as a result of the free movement of services under EU law in the event of an ESR Member State permitting its certifying officials, in particular notaries, to certify outside of the State of origin in another EU State.[85]

[81] In favour of a violation of the *ordre public* Dutta, 'Art. 59 EuErbVO', para. 14; Dutta, 'Das neue internationale Erbrecht der Europäischen Union', p. 14; Makowsky, 'Art. 59 EuErbVO', para. 13. More reluctantly J. Schmidt, 'Art. 59 EuErbVO', para. 26.2.

[82] For a report from everyday practice, see Bauer (referred to in footnote 33), p. 31.

[83] See Bauer (referred to in footnote 33), pp. 31, 34.

[84] See Bauer (referred to in footnote 33), p. 34.

[85] See Bauer (referred to in footnote 33), p. 26 *et seq.*

E. Use of a Standard Formula within the Meaning of Article 59(1) Subparagraph 2

27. Pursuant to the second subparagraph of article 59(1), a person wishing to use an authentic instrument in another Member State may ask the authority establishing the authentic instrument in the Member State of origin to fill in the form established in accordance with the advisory procedure referred to in article 81(2) describing the evidentiary effects which the authentic instrument produces in the Member State of origin. It is in this manner that in the State of acceptance information regarding the content and scope of an authentic instrument within the meaning of article 59(1) according to the law of the State of origin can be obtained simply and cost-effectively. Entries in the form are not legally constitutive. They only represent non-binding information.[86]

28. This form was published as annex 2 to the Commission Implementing Regulation (EU) no. 1329/2014 of 9 December 2014[87] (form II). Form II has boxes that have to be filled out by the issuing authority with respect to the following points: Member State of origin, authority having established the authentic instrument and issuing the attestation and/or registration and file number of the authentic instrument, information on the 'parties' involved; the form assumes as a default the participation of two persons. Presumably, this assumption will often likely be inaccurate. It does not take into account the possibility of a larger number of heirs or other affected persons. One must also indicate if the acceptance of the authentic instruments is being sought. If so, various options provided in the form regarding the extent of the formal evidentiary effect produced according to the law of the State of origin can be ticked. Further evidentiary effects can be added individually, depending on the relevant law. However, entries with regard to the evidentiary effects of the instrument are not legally constitutive. The law of the State of origin governs these effects (see no. 30 *et seq.*), not what was entered into the form. It is important to indicate the requirements according to which the authentic instrument loses its formal evidentiary effects

[86] See also Geimer, *Internationales Zivilprozessrecht*, para. 22330t; for a different view, see Dutta, 'Art. 59 EuErbVO', para. 15.

[87] Commission Implementing Regulation (EU) no. 1329/2014 of 9 December 2014 establishing the forms referred to in Regulation (EU) no. 650/2012 of the European Parliament and of the Council on jurisdiction, applicable law, recognition and enforcement of decisions and acceptance and enforcement of authentic instruments in matters of Succession and on the creation of a European Certificate of Succession, OJ no. L359, 16 December 2014, p. 30.

according to the law of the State of origin and which procedure is to be observed thereby. An entry must also be made with regard to whether the issuing authority is aware of any challenges that have been made to the authenticity of the document or to the certifying legal act or legal relationship. Additional entries are to be made regarding whether the authentic instrument should be enforced, what the enforcement requirements of the State of origin are and whether interest is to be enforced and how it is calculated according to the State of origin. Additional interest information is also requested.

29. Use of form II is not a requirement of acceptance of the authentic instrument. This follows from the fact that an acceptance may occur *ex lege* and without an application (see no. 30 *et seq.*). Furthermore, this understanding finds support in article 59(1) subparagraph 2. The provision only states that 'a person wishing to use an authentic instrument in another Member State *may ask* the authority establishing the authentic instrument in the Member State of origin to fill in the form.' Hence, the use of such a form by a person seeking acceptance is optional.[88] The position has been put forward that, based on the language 'may ask', one may also conclude that the State of acceptance is not obliged to provide such a form II and there is no right to receive a filled-out form.[89] This, however, is likely inaccurate. Form II already exists and is uniform in all ESR Member States. The language 'may ask' leaves it to the individual to request a filled-out form II but does not grant discretion to the authority of the State of origin as to whether it complies or not with the application. Such discretion does not arise from article 1 of the Commission Implementing regulation (EU) no. 1329/2014 of 9 December 2014.

III. Consequences of an Acceptance of an Authentic Instrument: Article 59(1)

A. *Extension of the Evidentiary Effect in the Member State of Origin*

30. The legal consequence of article 59(1) is that the authentic instrument has 'the same evidentiary effects in another Member State as it has in the Member State of origin, or the most comparable effects'. As for the

[88] Likewise: Wautelet, 'Article 59', p. 667; J. Schmidt, 'Art. 59 EuErbVO', para. 35; Davì and Zanobetti, *Il nuovo diritto internazionale privato europeo*, p. 227; Carrascosa González, *El Reglamento Sucesorio Europeo*, p. 314.

[89] J. Schmidt, 'Art. 59 EuErbVO', paras. 33, 34.1.

recognition of a decision pursuant to article 36 Brussels I Recast, there is no need for a special proceeding in order to accept an instrument according to article 59(1). There is also no need for an application. When the requirements for the acceptance of an authentic instrument (see nos. 9–26) are objectively met, the legal consequence of article 59(1) becomes effective immediately without the need for a court or authority of another ESR Member States to make a determination or take a decision. The effect of article 59(1) thus occurs *ex lege* and as an incident thereto. The courts or authorities of another ESR Member State must then take into consideration the evidentiary effects granted to the authentic instruments by the law of the State of origin.[90] According to recital 61 sentence 2 'reference should be made to the *nature* and the *scope* of the evidentiary effects of the authentic instrument in the Member State of origin.'

31. Article 59(1) mandates an extension of effect from the State of origin to the secondary State. The extension of the effect of an instrument is equivalent to the extension of the effect of a judgment pursuant to article 36 Brussels I Recast.[91]

B. *Relationship to Articles 39, 69*

32. Article 39 governs the recognition of judicial decisions. While decisions within the meaning of articles 3(1)(g), 39(1) generally also fulfil the criteria required of an authentic instrument within the meaning of articles 3(1)(i), 59(1), article 39(1). However, with regard to decisions, article 39(1), as *lex specialis*, supersedes article 59 (1)[92] (on the distinction between judicial decisions and authentic instruments see nos. 3, 21). Article 69 governs the extension of evidentiary effect with regard to a European Certificate of Succession.[93] According to article 69, the European Succession Certificate produces its effects in all Member States without the requirement of a special procedure.[94] Thus, article

[90] See Carrascosa González, *El Reglamento Sucesorio Europeo*, p. 314; Foyer, 'Reconnaissance, acceptation et exécution', p. 161.

[91] See Bauer (referred to in footnote 33), p. 32. On the extension of the effect of a judgment, see ECJ, case 145/86, *Horst Ludwig Martin Hoffmann* v. *Adelheid Krieg* [1988] ECR 00645.

[92] Dutta, 'Art. 59 EuErbVO', para. 5.

[93] The effects described in article 69 are exhaustive in nature, see Carrascosa González, *El Reglamento Sucesorio Europeo*, p. 317.

[94] On the discussion of a possible application of the *ordre public* exception as included in articles 59–69 see Davì and Zanobetti, *Il nuovo diritto internazionale privato europeo*, p. 245.

69 is also *lex specialis* vis-à-vis article 59(1).[95] Burkhard Hess, among others, suggests to apply article 69 by analogy when determining the legal effects of a foreign authentic instrument.[96] This view cannot be followed, however, since article 69 also covers substantive law effects that do not fall under article 59 (1) (see no. 33 *et seq.*).

C. Evidentiary Effect

1. Evidentiary Effect Referring to Factual Elements

33. Only the evidentiary effects (*force probante, efficacia probatoria, bewijskracht, força probatória, valor probatorio*), however, are extended. The German term *'formelle Beweiskraft'* and the distinction between *instrumentum* and *negotium* in article 59 (see nos. 2, 3, 8, 33) make it clear that no determinations made in the instrument are extended to any substantive law legal status (*negotium*); rather, the extension is given to the evidentiary effect of the *instrumentum.*[97] This evidentiary effect refers to the *factual* elements recorded by the certifying authority,[98] e.g. the making of a particular declaration (see nos. 2, 18). Such evidentiary effect could include, for example: the wording of a declaration; the personal details and identity of the declaring person,[99] the time and place where the declaration was made and/or where the instrument was drawn up and recorded,[100] information by the certifying authority regarding the manner in which the declaration was made.[101] Recital 62 sentence 2 gives an example for the possible content of evidentiary effects: 'the factual elements recorded in the authentic instrument by the authority concerned, such as the fact that the parties indicated appeared before that authority on the date indicated and that they made the declarations indicated.' The evidentiary

[95] Dutta, 'Art. 59 EuErbVO', para. 5.

[96] Hess, Mariottini and Camara, *Regulation (EC) Nr. 650/2012 of July 2012* (referred to in footnote 14), p. 22.

[97] But see Carrascosa González, *El Reglamento Sucesorio Europeo*, p. 314, who also refers to the term *negotium*.

[98] See Presidency of the Council, document no. 11067/11 (referred to in footnote 4), p. 12, para. 27: 'officially recorded *facts*.' Similarly Hess, Jayme and Pfeiffer, *Stellungnahme zum Vorschlag für eine Europäische Erbrechtsverordnung* (referred to in footnote 41), pp. 44, 58; Kleinschmidt, 'Optionales Erbrecht', pp. 723, 737 *et seq.*; Makowsky, 'Art. 59 EuErbVO', para. 9; Wautelet, 'Article 59', p. 663.

[99] Damascelli, 'Article 59', para. 5; J. Schmidt, 'Art. 59 EuErbVO', para. 19.

[100] See Wautelet, 'Article 59', p. 665.

[101] Damascelli, 'Article 59', para. 5.

effect of instruments that have been drawn up and recorded by German officials is determined in accordance with sections 415, 416a *et seq.* ZPO (German code of civil procedure).[102]

34. The courts and authorities of the State of acceptance are thus bound by the evidence of these facts. This mechanism restricts the principle of free judicial evaluation of evidence.[103] To this extent, the acceptance of an instrument pursuant to article 59 (1) directly interferes with the procedural law of the secondary Member State. The court or authority must therefore ascertain the scope of the evidentiary effect provided by the law of the State of origin.[104] The corresponding information with respect to the evidentiary effect of an instrument in form II (see no. 27) is not binding, but operates only *informandi causa* (see no. 28). The acceptance of an instrument involves the application of foreign law; as such, article 59(1) is a conflict of laws rule in procedural law (see no. 1). The required determination of foreign procedural law rules can therefore prolong the process.[105]

2. Manner and Extent of Evidentiary Effect

35. The issue of whether, in what manner (e.g. full proof to the contrary) and with what evidence the evidentiary effect of the instrument can be rebutted is determined according to the law of the State of origin (see no. 47).[106] For example, under German law authentic instruments establish 'full proof of the facts set out therein and evidence proving that the facts set out therein are wrong is admissible unless the laws . . . rule out or limit such evidence' (section 418(1), (2) German civil procedure).

The *ordre public* of the State of acceptance is to be taken into consideration if the manner in which, as well as the limitations of the evidentiary effects are determined in the State of acceptance (on *ordre public*, see no. 22 *et seq.* and no. 39); on the question of whether it amounts to a violation of the *ordre public* within the meaning of article 59(1) if the law of the State of origin precludes the use of rebuttal

[102] Makowsky, 'Art. 59 EuErbVO', para. 9; J. Schmidt, 'Art. 3 EuErbVO', para. 20.

[103] Dutta, 'Art. 59 EuErbVO', para. 10; Geimer, *Internationales Zivilprozessrecht*, para. 2330o.

[104] See Wautelet, 'Article 59', p. 665 *et seq.*

[105] Geimer, *Internationales Zivilprozessrecht*, para. 2330t.

[106] J. Schmidt, 'Art. 59 EuErbVO', para. 18; Dutta, 'Art. 59 EuErbVO', para. 17. For another view (according to which the restrictions on evidence are insignificant), see Geimer, *Internationales Zivilprozessrecht*, para. 2330; Lagarde, 'Introduction', para. 49.

evidence, (see no. 26). For more on the additional limitations of extending the effects, see no. 38 *et seq.*

3. Presumptions of Law

36. Authentic instruments may, however, also give rise under the national law of an ESR Member State to (rebuttable or non-rebuttable) presumptions of law.[107] This may include the presumption, for example, that a person designated in a particular document as an heir is also an heir entitled to a specific share of an estate (on the qualification and treatment of national succession certificates, see no. 19 *et seq.*). In the case of a presumption of law, the existence of a fact is not established by the authentic instrument, but rather the existence of a particular legal situation or legal status under substantive law. Such a presumption in the law changes the onus of presentation (German '*Darlegungslast*') and the substantive burden of proof.

37. Whether such presumptions of law have evidentiary effects within the meaning of article 59(1) still needs clarification. Since article 59 distinguishes between the *instrumentum* and the *negotium*, and the acceptance of an instrument covers only the effects of the *instrumentum*, but not the *negotium* (see nos. 2, 3 and 8 *et seq.*), a distinction seems necessary.[108] This will mean that such presumptions of law of the State of origin are not to be accepted via article 59(1) in the secondary State if they are related to the substantive legal transaction (the *negotium*). All other legal presumptions, however, can generally be extended to the secondary State pursuant to article 59(1). What is not accepted as an evidentiary effect within the meaning of article 59(1), is a legal presumption, according to which – comparable to the presumption of article 69(2) sentence 2 – it is presumed that the mentioned person in the authentic instrument as the legal or testamentary heir, legatee, executor of the will or administrator of the estate indeed has the status mentioned. This presumption of law is not an evidentiary effect within the meaning of article 59(1), because article 59 only governs the evidentiary effect of the *instrumentum*, not the legal status reflected in the authentic instrument.

[107] See Wautelet, 'Article 59', p. 678 *et seq.*

[108] Concluding similarly, see Buschbaum, 'Rechtslagenanerkennung aufgrund öffentlicher Urkunden?', pp. 259, 267 *et seq.*; Buschbaum, 'Europäisches Nachlasszeugnis und Annahme öffentlicher Urkunden', p. 58 *et seq.*; Makowsky, 'Art. 59 EuErbVO', para. 11; Wautelet, 'Article 59', p. 678 *et seq.* A similar observation can be found at Dutta, 'Art. 59 EuErbVO', para. 11.

D. *The Limitations on Evidentiary Effects*

1. Register of Rights: Article 1(2)(l)

38. It must be noted that under article 1(2)(l) 'any recording in a register of rights in immovable or movable property, including the legal requirements for such recording, and the effects of recording or failing to record such rights in a register' are excluded from the scope of the ESR. The acceptance of an instrument pursuant to article 59(1) thus has no effect on the register of rights in immovable or movable property. Here, the national law of the State that maintains the register determines whether an authentic instrument produces an effect in corresponding register proceedings.[109]

2. *Ordre public*: Article 59(1) Subparagraph 1

39. If the effect of the acceptance as an authentic instrument is contrary to the *ordre public* in the specific individual case under the law of the secondary State, there may be no acceptance of the authentic instrument to the extent of the *ordre public* contravention pursuant to article 59 (1) (on *ordre public*, see no. 22 *et seq.*).

3. The Same or Most Comparable Effects: Article 59(1) Subparagraph 1

40. Article 59(1) provides that an authentic instrument 'shall have the same evidentiary effects in another Member State as it has in the Member State of origin, or the most comparable effects.' Based on the reference to the 'most comparable effects' legal doctrine has concluded that in the secondary State the evidentiary effects as they are under the law of the State of origin may not go beyond the evidentiary effects stated by the State of acceptance. The law of the secondary State would therefore strictly limit the effect of accepting the instrument pursuant to article 59(1).[110] This has been referred to as the *'double limitation of the*

[109] On article 1 (2) (l) generally, see H.-P. Mansel, 'Art. 43 EGBGB', in D. Henrich (ed), Staudinger BGB – EGBGB/IPR, Artikel 43–46 EGBGB (Internationales Sachenrecht), 14th ed. (München, 2015), paras. 217 *et seq.*; for a deviating view, see Damascelli, 'Article 59', para. 7.

[110] For very forceful and well-reasoned arguments, see Geimer, *Internationales Zivilprozess-recht*, paras. 2330s–2330u with further references; further, Buschbaum, 'Europäisches Nachlasszeugnis und Annahme öffentlicher Urkunden', pp. 39, 43; U. Simon and M. Buschbaum, 'Die neue EU-Erbrechtsverordnung', *NJW* (2012), pp. 2393, 2397; B. Hess, 'Die internationale Zuständigkeit nach der Erbrechtsverordnung', in A. Dutta and S. Herrler (eds), *Die Europäische Erbrechtsverordnung* (München, 2014), p. 131 paras.

evidentiary effect pursuant to the law of the State of Origin and the target Member State'.[111] This view cannot be agreed with. The evidentiary effects recognised by the law of the secondary State do not, as such, impose limits on the evidentiary effects established in the State of origin.[112] The wording of article 59(1) indeed aims at extending precisely the *'same evidentiary effects'* of the State of origin to the secondary State. The argument, according to which the *ordre public* provision of article 59 (1) would otherwise lose significance, is less relevant see no. 42).[113] To the contrary, recital 61 sentence 3 unmistakably prescribes the provision's aim: *'reference should be made to the nature and the scope of the evidentiary effects of the authentic instrument in the Member State of origin. The evidentiary effects which a given authentic instrument should have in another Member State will therefore depend on the law of the Member State of origin.'*

41. If the impact of the evidentary effects under the law of the State of origin falls short of that of the law of the State of acceptance, the lesser effect prevails.[114] This is because the article mandates an extension of the effects, not a treatment equal to that of the law of the State of acceptance.

42. If the evidentiary effect of the instrument to be acccepted pursuant to the law of the State of origin, however, is unknown to the secondary State or indeed recognised but much more extensively, a situation will arise that requires an adaptation.[115] For such a case, article 59 (1) provides that in the State of acceptance *'the most comparable effects'* are to be applied. Under the law of the secondary State, therefore,

34 *et seq.*; Kleinschmidt, 'Optionales Erbrecht', pp. 723, 739, 743 with further references; Wautelet, 'Article 59', p. 668 *et seq.*

111 Simon and Buschbaum, 'Die neue EU-Erbrechtsverordnung', pp. 2393, 2397.

112 Bauer (referred to in footnote 33), p. 33; Dutta, 'Art. 59 EuErbVO', para. 11; Dutta, 'Die europäische Erbrechtsverordnung vor ihrem Anwendungsbeginn', pp. 32, 38; Dutta, 'Das neue internationale Erbrecht der Europäischen Union', p. 14 *et seq.*; Makowsky, 'Art. 59 EuErbVO', para. 12; J. Schmidt, 'Art. 59 EuErbVO', para. 21; Wautelet, 'Article 59', p. 670; Foyer, 'Reconnaissance, acceptation et exécution', p. 163.

113 This argument, however, is mainly brought forward by Dutta, 'Art. 59 EuErbVO', para. 11; Dutta, 'Die europäische Erbrechtsverordnung vor ihrem Anwendungsbeginn', pp. 32, 38; Dutta, 'Das neue internationale Erbrecht der Europäischen Union', p. 14 *et seq.*; see also Makowsky, 'Art. 59 EuErbVO', para. 12; J. Schmidt, 'Art. 59 EuErbVO', para. 21; Wautelet, 'Article 59', p. 670.

114 Kleinschmidt, 'Optionales Erbrecht', pp. 723, 742; Makowsky, 'Art. 59 EuErbVO', para. 12 with further references.

115 The European Commission also used the word adaption, see Council of the European Union, doc. 8448/11 (com. doc no. 14722/09 JUSTCIV 210 CODEC 1209) 11. 4. 2011, p. 7 para. 19.

the most functionally comparable effect possible must be produced.[116] This technique is known from article 31.[117] This provision coordinates the *lex successionis* and the applicable property law on tangible goods. If there exists a particular right *in rem* pursuant to the applicable *lex rei sitae*, but the succession law to be applied does not recognise such right *in rem*, the right *in rem* 'shall, if necessary and to the extent possible, be adapted to the closest equivalent right *in rem* under the law of [the applicable succession law], taking into account the aims and the interests pursued by the specific right in rem and the effects attached to it' (article 31). The situation at hand is comparable. If the rules of procedure of the secondary State do not recognise a particular evidentiary effect, a comparable effect should be produced without affecting the rules of procedure of the secondary State. The application of the evidentiary effects of the State of origin prevails, but the effects are adapted to a functionally equivalent legal institute of the secondary State. As such, article 59(1) does not provide an opportunity for adaptation only prior to the *ordre public* violation threshold,[118] but also in the event of a minor interference with the rules of procedure of the secondary State.[119]

4. Formal Validity

43. Article 59 does not govern with respect to the formal validity of a legal act consumated or given notice of in an authentic instrument. This is because the provision only deals with the issue of evidentiary effects. The substantive law issues of the *negotium* are not covered by article 59

116 Bauer (referred to in footnote 33), p. 33; Dutta, 'Art. 59 EuErbVO', para. 11; Dutta, 'Das neue internationale Erbrecht der Europäischen Union', p. 14; Fitchen, '"Recognition", acceptance and enforcement of authentic instruments', pp. 323, 356; Hess, Mariottini and Camara, *Regulation (EC) Nr. 650/2012 of July 2012* (referred to in footnote 14), p. 21 *et seq.*; Makowsky, 'Art. 59 EuErbVO', para. 12; J. Schmidt, 'Der Erbnachweis in Deutschland ab 2015: Erbschein vs. Europäisches Nachlasszeugnis', *Zeitschrift für Erbrecht und Vermögensnachfolge* (2014), pp. 389, 395; J. Schmidt, 'Art. 59 EuErbVO', para. 22, with further references; Wautelet, 'Article 59', p. 668 *et seq.*

117 On article 31 see also H.-P. Mansel, 'Art. 43 EGBGB', paras. 245 *et seq.*

118 For another view (adaptation only when there is a finding of a violation of the *ordre public*), see Makowsky, 'Art. 59 EuErbVO', para. 12.

119 See generally H.-P. Mansel, 'Anerkennung als Grundprinzip des Europäischen Rechtsraums – Zur Herausbildung eines europäischen Anerkennungs-Kollisionsrechts: Anerkennung statt Verweisung als neues Strukturprinzip des Europäischen internationalen Privatrechts', *RabelsZ* (2006), pp. 654, 723 *et seq.*; approvingly Hess, Mariottini and Camara, *Regulation (EC) Nr. 650/2012 of July 2012* (referred to in footnote 14), p. 21 *et seq.*; agreeing in the result, Bauer (referred to in footnote 33), p. 33.

(see nos. 2, 3, 8, 19, 33, 52 *et seq.*). The issue of whether a legal act consumated or given notice of in an authentic instrument is formally valid is a question of substantive law. It is to be evaluated in accordance with the rules on form as they are determined by international private law. Consequently, in the case of the formal validity of dispositions of property upon death, according to article 59(3), the rules on form set forth in articles 27 and 28 shall be applied. Hence, acceptance pursuant to article 59 has no effect on the issue of the form of the *negotium.*[120]

IV. Challenge Relating the Authenticity: Article 59(2)

A. *Challenge of the* Instrumentum *(Authenticity)*

44. Article 59(2) provides that any challenge relating to the authenticity of an 'authentic instrument' has to be made before the courts of the Member State of origin. The 'authenticity' of an instrument is an autonomous concept (recital 62 sentence 1). The term is therefore interpreted under national law in a manner that is autonomous of the regulation (on autonomous interpretation (see no. 10). The legislative meaning behind the ESR is delineated as follows:

> '[E]lements such as the genuineness of the instrument, . . . the powers of the authority drawing up the instrument and the procedure under which the instrument is drawn up . . . the factual elements recorded in the authentic instrument by the authority concerned, such as the fact that the parties indicated appeared before that authority on the date indicated and that they made the declarations indicated

and also the 'formal prerequisites of the instrument' (recital 62 sentence 1 and 2). This means the formal requirements of the *instrumentum* itself, not of the *negotium* (on the form of the *negotium* see no. 43). Therefore, authenticity of an authentic instrument means the factual basis[121] for the evidentiary effect of the authentic instrument and thus refers to errors in the *instrumentum.* Domenico Damascelli notes that authenticity is lacking, for example, if provisions related to the duties of a notary were violated, as when a notary acted outside of his local competence and this would invalidate his notarial activities according to the law of the State of origin.[122]

[120] Geimer, *Internationales Zivilprozessrecht*, para. 2330c; Makowsky, 'Art. 59 EuErbVO', para. 17.

[121] Makowsky, 'Art. 59 EuErbVO', para. 17.

[122] Damascelli, 'Article 59', para. 10.

B. *The State of Origin's Exclusive Power of Review*

45. The courts of the State of origin enjoy the exclusive powers of review and decision. Under article 59(2) they are competent to review the authenticity of an instrument when it is claimed, for example, the document actually was falsified or not issued by a public authority. This competence is exclusive.[123] Article 59(2) compels neither the courts of the State of origin, nor the courts of the secondary State to review the authenticity of an authentic instrument *ex officio*.[124] The respective autonomous *lex fori* decides with regard to the obligation to review even in the absence of an application for review.

46. To eliminate the authenticity of an authentic instrument in its entirety, the wording of article 59(2) requires a decision of a court in the State of origin[125] and the court shall decide under the law of that State. Article 59(2) makes reference to all provisions of the *lex fori* of the State of origin, which concern the authenticity of the instrument. Here, procedural and instrumental notarization as well as notarial law are of particular practical relevance. In some legal systems there are special review proceedings; other legal systems utilise general declaratory proceedings.[126] Under German law, section 46 of the international succession law procedure act of 29 June 2015[127] introduced a procedure to review the authenticity of a German public instrument.

47. There are two exceptions to exclusive power of review of the State of origin:

- If pursuant to the law of the State of origin, rebuttal evidence of a particular fact certified in the instrument is able to nullify the evidentiary effect of an authentic instrument as it concerns such facts, acceptance in the secondary State results in such evidence being permissible as well in proceedings before courts or authorities

[123] Dutta, 'Art. 59 EuErbVO', paras. 8, 16; Geimer, *Internationales Zivilprozessrecht*, paras. 2330w *et seq.*; Wautelet, 'Article 59', p. 675.

[124] Geimer, *Internationales Zivilprozessrecht*, para. 233i.

[125] For a more detailed discussion on individual related questions, see Geimer, *Internationales Zivilprozessrecht*, paras. 2330w *et seq.*

[126] See J. Fitchen, 'Authentic Instruments and European Private International Law in Civil and Commercial Matters: Is Now the Time to Break New Ground?', *JIPL* 7 (2011), pp. 33, 45 *et seq.*; Wautelet, 'Article 59', p. 674 *et seq.*; on special proceedings to contest notarial deeds, see Rat der Europäischen Union, doc. 8448/11 (com. doc no. 14722/09 JUSTCIV 210 CODEC 1209, (11. 4. 2011), p. 6, para. 17.

[127] *Bundesgesetzblatt* 2015 part I p. 1042; see M. Makowsky, '§ 46 Internationales Erbrechtsverfahrensgesetz', in R. Hüßtege and H.-P. Mansel (eds), *NomosKommentar, BGB, Rom-Verordnungen*, vol. VI, 2nd ed. (Baden-Baden, 2015), paras. 1 *et seq.*

of the secondary State in which the evidentiary effect of the authentic instrument is reviewed (see no. 35).[128] Only when the instrument as such should be discarded due to a lack of authenticity does the exclusive power of review of article 59(2) apply.

- If an authentic instrument is patently false, for example because the public authority that is purported to have drawn up and recorded the instrument does not exist, or it is obvious by other means that the document was falsified (e.g. a declaration of a person already deceased at the time of the declaration being certified, etc.), the document is not an authentic instrument. Article 59 is not applicable in that case.[129] In the rare cases where there is clear evidence of the instrument not being authentic, its authenticity will not be reviewed. Rather, the subject matter of a review will be whether the legal requirements of article 59(2) are fulfilled – that is, whether an authentic instrument exists at all.[130]

C. *Legal Consequences*

48. Pursuant to article 59(2), when such a review proceeding is pending before a competent court in the State of origin, the authentic instrument does not produce any evidentiary effect in the secondary State before the review proceeding is concluded. The suspension of evidentiary effect affects the *instrumentum* as a whole (this is different for article 59(3), see no. 55). The effects of the review proceedings in the State of origin are not governed by article 59; autonomous national law applies. The term pending before the court in article 59(2) is to be interpreted under national law and analogous to article 14.[131] An authentic instrument which has been declared invalid in the State of origin as a result of a challenge produces no evidentiary effects (recital 65 sentence 3).[132]

[128] Dutta, 'Art. 59 EuErbVO', paras. 8, 16; with well reasoned arguments with reference to article 81 TFEU, see Geimer, *Internationales Zivilprozessrecht*, para. 2331b.

[129] Similarly, Dutta, 'Art. 59 EuErbVO', paras. 8, 16; R. Fucik, 'Art. 59 EuErbVO', in W.H. Rechberger and B. Zöchling-Jud (eds), *Die EU-Erbrechtsverordnung in Österreich* (Vienna, 2015), para. 87.

[130] But see Geimer, *Internationales Zivilprozessrecht*, paras. 2331f–2331h.

[131] Dutta, 'Art. 59 EuErbVO', para. 19; different (contesting the authenticity of the instrument as a mandatory requirement) Geimer, *Internationales Zivilprozessrecht*, paras. 2331f–2331h.

[132] According to Fucik, 'Art. 59 EuErbVO', para. 91, the instrument ought to be usable, however, as a private instrument for evidentiary purposes. The practical importance of this suggestion remains unclear, however.

49. Article 59(2) does not expressly provide that proceedings in the secondary State in which the evidentiary effect of an authentic instrument is accepted must be suspended until the review proceedings within the meaning of article 59(2) are finally concluded in the State of origin. Nor do national laws always require suspension. This is the case, for example, with section 45 of the German international succession procedure act of 29 June 2015, which grants the court the discretion to suspend.

50. Article 59(2) must be interpreted, however, in light of the general principle of the *effet utile*. The exclusive power of review of the courts of the State of origin is only adequately given effect if the proceedings in the secondary State are not continued during the review proceedings if the evidentiary effect of the authentic instrument is dispositive for the decision to be taken in the secondary State. In such a case, article 59(2) must be read as requiring suspension in the courts of the secondary State. Otherwise, a proceeding, the results of which are based on the evidentiary effect of the challenged document, that is concluded in the secondary State during the review proceedings, would have to be reopened, even if the result attains *res iudicate* effect. This would result, in some cases,[133] in a disruption of the legal effect in the secondary State. This form of interference in the national law of the secondary State is more severe than suspending the proceedings in the secondary State.

51. Therefore, the milder measure of an obligation to suspend must be deduced from article 59(2), if (i) the final decision terminating the proceedings in the secondary State was based on the evidentiary effect of the challenged document, and (ii) there were no means permissible from a procedural law standpoint under national law to set aside the decision[134] in the event the review proceedings in the State of origin should confirm the authentic instrument's lack of authenticity once the proceeding in the secondary State has already been concluded.

[133] On various questions of detail, see Geimer, *Internationales Zivilprozessrecht*, paras. 2330z–2331a.

[134] Geimer, *Internationales Zivilprozessrecht*, para. 2331, points to the possible application by analogy of the provisions regarding the reopening of proceedings. Under German law, for example, this is governed by section 578 *et seq.* German code of civil procedure.

V. Challenging Substantive Law Content: Article 59(3), (4)

A. *Challenging the* Negotium: *Article 59(3)*

52. If the *negotium* qualifies as being a matter of succession within meaning of the ESR, article 59(3) applies. Article 59(3) makes clear that the acceptance of an authentic instrument pursuant to article 59 has no substantive law effects. The *negotium* may therefore not be 'accepted' pursuant to article 59(1) (see nos. 2, 3, 8, 33). Consequently, the provisions set forth in article 59(3) only make clear that article 59 does not mandate the recognition or acceptance of legal situations or legal status. This was the subject of controversial debates in the legislative history (see no. 8). If the *negotium* does not fall within the scope of the ESR, article 59 does not apply anyway; in that case, general rules outside of the ESR will be applicable.

53. Article 59(3) sentence 1 provides that any challenge relating to legal acts or legal relationships (*negotium*) (see nos. 2, 3, 8, 33) recorded in an authentic instrument shall be made before courts having jurisdiction under the ESR (chapter II, articles 4–19) and shall be decided under the law applicable pursuant to chapter III of the ESR (articles 20–37, see nos. 3, 18), provided the *negotium* falls within the scope of the ESR (on the scope thereof, see no. 15 *et seq.* and the commentary to article 1 [see art. 1 no. 1 *et seq.*]). If the issue of a challenge relating to legal acts or legal relationships recorded in an authentic instrument, however, arises in proceedings that do not fall within the scope of the ESR, article 59(4) applies, see no. 56). A 'challenge' as contemplated by article 59(3) exists when substantive objections are raised against the substantive law legal act or legal status recorded in the authentic instrument in a judicial or ministerial proceeding within the meaning of articles 4–19 (article 59(3) sentence 1: '*jurisdiction under this regulation*'). This may be a proceeding, which is only supposed to decide with respect to substantive law objections. This may, however, also be any other succession law proceeding in which a decision is taken with respect to substantive law objections,[135] such as a pending '*Erbschein*'-proceeding or probate proceedings, by other means. If, for example, there is no dispute about the fact, that the declaration in the authentic instrument was made by the testator, but it is disputed whether this declaration constitutes the appointment of an heir according to the *lex successionis*, this is a case contemplated by

[135] Dutta, 'Art. 59 EuErbVO', para. 21.

article 59(3); however, authenticity is not being challenged within the meaning of article 59(2).

B. *Legal Consequences Regarding Evidentiary Effects: Article 59(3)*

54. Article 59(3) sentence 2 provides that the authentic instrument that is being reviewed pursuant to article 59(3) sentence 1 with respect to its substantive law content by the competent[136] court produces no evidentiary effect (on this term of art, see no. 33 *et seq.*) in a Member State other than the Member State of origin, as long as the challenge is pending (on the term pending, see no. 48). The suspensory effect of article 59(3) includes (likewise for article 59(2), see no. 48 *et seq.*) only evidentiary effects (see the wording of article 53(2) and recital 65 sentence 1).

55. Article 59(3) mandates a very broad suspensory effect, for in a succession law proceeding in another ESR Member State as the State of origin where the existence, content or extent of the *negotium* is disputed in a succession law matter pursuant to the *lex successionis*, the evidentiary effect of the authentic instruments is suspended outside of the State of origin. Therefore, the extent of the suspensory effect is limited: If the challenge concerns only a specific matter relating to the legal acts or legal relationships recorded in the authentic instrument, the authentic instrument in question should not produce any evidentiary effects in a Member State other than in the Member State of origin with regard to the matter being challenged as long as the challenge is pending (recital 65 sentence 2). According to recital 65 sentence 3, the evidentiary effect is dispensed in its entirety when the '*authentic instrument . . . has been declared invalid as a result of a challenge.*' If, however, the authentic instrument was not declared invalid in such a proceeding and the proceeding concludes in this respect, evidentiary effects pursuant to article 59(1) can be produced again in the secondary State by means of acceptance. The question of an obligation to suspend is also not addressed in article 59(3) (on article 59 (2) see no. 49 *et seq.*).[137]

C. *Incidental Question: Article 59(4)*

56. An issue relating to legal acts or legal relationships recorded in an authentic instrument in matters of succession may also arise incidentally

[136] Jurisdiction per article 4 *et seq.* (see no. 52).

[137] See Geimer, *Internationales Zivilprozessrecht*, para. 2331l.

(*incidenter*) in a proceeding that does not fall within the scope of the ESR – that is, which does not qualify as a succession law matter. An example of this would be an action to recover payments brought against the heirs of the debtor. In such a case, a court of an ESR Member State may decide this question incidentally. This is provided for in article 59(4). Article 59(3) does not apply[138] since paragraph 3 requires a proceeding based on a competency set forth in articles 4–19 and to the subject matter of which the conflict of laws rules of articles 20–37 apply.

VI. Conflict of Authentic Instruments and Decisions

A. *In General*

57. If more than one authentic instrument from various ESR Member States exist, which completely or partially conflict with one another, or if there is a substantive conflict with a judicial decision, a decision must be taken about how such a conflict is to be resolved. Conflicts created by authentic instruments or decisions of the same ESR Member State are resolved according to the national law of the State in which the instrument is drawn up and recorded. Patrick Wautelet correctly notes that a conflict can extend especially to the *negotium* of both documents.[139] In this case there is no conflict of evidentiary effects. A conflict concerning the substantive content (*negotium*) of two or more authentic instruments is resolved pursuant to article 59(3) according to general rules. To this extent, the autonomous *lex fori* or the corresponding *lex causae*, respectively, of the authority or court assessing the conflict applies.

B. *Conflicting Instruments from Different ESR Member States*

58. If, however, the conflict relates to the *instrumentum* and there are differing evidentiary effects of the authentic instruments from more than one ESR Member State, the ESR contains no provision that addresses the resolution of the conflict. The ESR only mentions the problem in recital 66.[140] According to recital 66 sentence 1, when presented with two

[138] Dutta, 'Art. 59 EuErbVO', para. 23.

[139] Wautelet, 'Article 59', p. 673; approvingly, Bauer (referred to in footnote 33), p. 34.

[140] Recital 66 has been criticised and deemed not very helpful: Dutta, 'Art. 59 EuErbVO', para. 13; Lagarde, 'Les principes de base', pp. 691, 732; Geimer, '"Annahme" ausländischer öffentlicher Urkunden in Erbsachen gemäß Art. 59 EuErbVO', p. 158 *et seq.*; similarly Bauer (referred to in footnote 33), p. 34.

incompatible authentic instruments, an authority, taking into account the circumstances of the particular case, should assess which instrument should be given priority. Such assessment should not take into account the priority of establishing the authentic instruments.[141] There is also doubt as to whether the aspect of how demanding the procedure for drawing up and recording the respective instrument was may be decisive.[142] If priority of an instrument cannot be clearly determined by the authority concerned with such task, recital 66 sentence 2 provides that the question is judicially determined. However, the ESR also fails to provide criteria for determining such priority in a judicial decision. Insofar, the provision contains a gap.

59. Recital 66 is not a provision in the sense of article 1 *et seq.* Recitals indeed bind those applying the law. However, a regulation such as the ESR may only displace national law pursuant to article 288(2) TFEU provided the regulation contains unambigous legal norms. That is not the case here. Therefore, every authority dealing with the decision of this conflict must decide in accordance with its *lex fori* as to how it can be resolved. If one does not wish to follow this view and is looking for an autonomous solution within recital 66, the evidentiary effects of both authentic instruments should fail insofar as the conflict extends.[143] Thereby, there would be no conflict of effect in the absence of an effect to be accepted.

C. *Conflict with a Decision from Another ESR Member State*

60. Recital 66 sentence 3 provides that in the event of incompatibility between an authentic instrument and a decision from different ESR Member States, regard should be given to the grounds of non-recognition of decisions under the ESR. This instruction is unclear because the rules concerning recognition do not apply to authentic instruments. The formal evidentiary effect of the judicial decision must then be observed, not that of the instrument.[144] A decision will at any rate have compulsory priority over the evidentiary effects of an authentic instrument, provided that the decision is to be recognised and has resolved the question which triggered the conflict with *res iudicata* effect.[145]

[141] See Dutta, 'Art. 59 EuErbVO', para. 13.
[142] For another view, see Makowsky, 'Art. 59 EuErbVO', para. 15.
[143] Dutta, 'Art. 59 EuErbVO', para. 13.
[144] Wautelet, 'Article 59', p. 673 *et seq.*; consentaneous Dutta, 'Art. 59 EuErbVO', para. 13; Makowsky, 'Art. 59 EuErbVO', para. 16.
[145] See Makowsky, 'Art. 59 EuErbVO', para. 16.

VII. Free Movement of Authentic Instruments and National Law

61. Article 59 is meant to guarantee the free movement of authentic instruments in ESR Member States (see no. 1). Hence, the provision does not prevent giving evidentiary effects to an authentic instrument of the State of origin pursuant to the national law of the secondary State[146] These autonomous provisions remain cumulatively applicable besides article 59. The principle of favourability (German: *Günstigkeitsprinzip*) applies regarding the evidentiary effects of authentic instruments.[147] This is comparable to the well-known *favour recognitionis* in the recognition of judgments.

146 On the far ranging effects of foreign instruments under German national law, see C. Reithmann, 'Urkunden ausländischer Notare in inländischen Verfahren', *IPRax* (2012), p. 133.

147 Dutta, 'Art. 59 EuErbVO', para. 13.

Article 60

Enforceability of Authentic Instruments

HEINZ-PETER MANSEL

1. An authentic instrument which is enforceable in the Member State of origin shall be declared enforceable in another Member State on the application of any interested party in accordance with the procedure provided for in Articles 45 to 58.
2. For the purposes of point (b) of Article 46(3), the authority which established the authentic instrument shall, on the application of any interested party, issue an attestation using the form established in accordance with the advisory procedure referred to in Article 81(2).
3. The court with which an appeal is lodged under Article 50 or Article 51 shall refuse or revoke a declaration of enforceability only if enforcement of the authentic instrument is manifestly contrary to public policy (ordre public) in the Member State of enforcement.

Summary

I. PURPOSE AND CONTENT OF THE RULE *page* 664

II. INTERNATIONAL ENFORCEMENT ARISING FROM AN INSTRUMENT 665

I. Purpose and Content of the Rule

1. Article 60 supplements article 59 and makes possible the international enforcement of an authentic instrument in ESR Member States. Wautelet notes that in the area of authentic instruments involving succession law it will be rare to find enforceable instruments. An example that is mentioned is an instrument dividing up an estate.[1] Even a testamentary contract may provide for enforceable agreements.[2] Article 60 largely corresponds to

[1] P. Wautelet, 'Art. 60', in A. Bonomi and P. Wautelet, *Le droit européen des successions. Commentaire du Règlement n° 650/2012 du 4 juillet 2012* (Bruxelles, 2013), p. 682, with further reference.

[2] J. Schmidt, 'Art. 60 EuErbVO', in C. Budzikiewicz, M.-P. Weller and W. Wurmnest (eds.), *Beck-Online Großkommentar, EuErbVO* (München, 2015), para. 12.

article 58 Council Regulation (EC) no. 1215/2012 of 12 December 2012 on jurisdiction and the recognition and enforcement of judgments in civil and commercial matters (Brussels I-*bis*),[3] which itself is based on article 50 Brussels Convention of 27 September 1968[4] and article 57 Council Regulation (EC) no. 44/2001 of 22 December 2000 (Brussels I)[5]. For more on additional European enforcement norms of authentic instruments, which are the models for article 60, see article 59 [see art. 59 no. 6]. Article 60 is now the model for article 59 Council Regulation (EU) no. 1103/2016 of 24 June 2016 implementing enhanced cooperation in the area of jurisdiction, applicable law and the recognition and enforcement of decisions in matters of matrimonial property regimes[6] and for article 59 Council Regulation (EU) 1104/ 2016 of 24 June 2016 implementing enhanced cooperation in the area of jurisdiction, applicable law and the recognition and enforcement of decisions in matters of the property consequences of registered partnerships.[7] Both regulations will be applicable as of 29 January 2019 in the participating Member States.

II. International Enforcement Arising from an Instrument

2. If an authentic instrument within the meaning of article 3(1)(i) [see art. 3 nos. 15–17] is enforceable under the law of the ESR Member State of origin [see art. 3 no. 9], the authentic instrument can also be enforced in another ESR Member State [see art. 3 no. 10] in accordance with the requirements of article 60. Pursuant to article 60(1) an application by an interested party is required. This is frequently a judgment creditor.

3. Article 60(1) makes reference to articles 45–58 with regard to the procedure for declaring an authentic instrument enforceable. The commentary on these provisions therefore also applies accordingly to declaring authentic instruments enforceable. According to article 60(2) authority which established the authentic instrument, on the application of any interested party, shall issue an attestation of enforceability using the form established in accordance with the advisory procedure

[3] OJ 2012 no. L351, 20 December 2012, p. 1.

[4] As amended by the Convention of 9 October 1978 on the accession of the Kingdom of Denmark, Ireland and the United Kingdom of Great Britain and Northern Ireland, by the Convention of 25 October 1982 on the accession of the Hellenic Republic and by the Convention of 26 May 1989 on the accession of the Kingdom of Spain and the Portuguese Republic, OJ 1972 no. L 299, 31 December 1972, p. 32; consolidated version in OJ 1998 no. C27, 26 January 1998, p. 1.

[5] OJ 2001 no. L12, 16 January 2001, p. 1.

[6] OJ 2016 no. L183, 8 July 2016, p. 1.

[7] OJ 2016 no. L183, 8 July 2016, p. 30.

referred to in article 81(2). This form (form II) was published as annex 2 to the Commission Implementing Regulation (EU) no. 1329/2014 of 9 December 2014.[8] This attestation takes the place of the attestation required in article 46(3)(b).

4. According to article 60(3), a court, with which an appeal is lodged against the declaration of enforcement (under article 50 or article 51), may refuse or revoke a declaration of enforceability only if enforcement of the authentic instrument is manifestly contrary to public policy (*ordre public*) in the Member State of enforcement. Article 60(3) therefore supersedes here article 40(b)–(d). On a violation of the *ordre public* see article 59 [see art. 59 no. 22 *et seq.*].

[8] Commission Implementing Regulation (EU) no. 1329/2014 of 9 December 2014 establishing the forms referred to in Regulation (EU) no. 650/2012 of the European Parliament and of the Council on jurisdiction, applicable law, recognition and enforcement of decisions and Acceptance and Enforcement of authentic instruments in matters of succession and on the creation of a European Certificate of Succession, OJ no. L359, 16. December 2014, p. 30.

Article 61

Enforceability of Court Settlements

HEINZ-PETER MANSEL

1. Court settlements which are enforceable in the Member State of origin shall be declared enforceable in another Member State on the application of any interested party in accordance with the procedure provided for in Articles 45 to 58.
2. For the purposes of point (b) of Article 46(3), the court which approved the settlement or before which it was concluded shall, on the application of any interested party, issue an attestation using the form established in accordance with the advisory procedure referred to in Article 81(2).
3. The court with which an appeal is lodged under Article 50 or Article 51 shall refuse or revoke a declaration of enforceability only if enforcement of the court settlement is manifestly contrary to public policy *(ordre public)* in the Member State of enforcement.

Summary

I. PURPOSE AND CONTENT OF THE RULE *page* 667
II. INTERNATIONAL ENFORCEMENT ARISING FROM AN INSTRUMENT 668

I. Purpose and Content of the Rule

1. Article 60, as a supplement to article 59, makes possible the international enforcement of court settlements which have arisen in a proceeding in front of a court of an ESR Member State and which falls within the scope of the ESR. Article 61 is otherwise largely identical to article 60. Article 61 corresponds to a large extent with article 59 Council Regulation (EC) no. 1215/2012 of 12 December 2012 on jurisdiction and the recognition and enforcement of judgments in civil and commercial matters (Brussels I-*bis*),[1] which itself is based on article 51 Brussels Convention of 27

[1] OJ 2012 no. L351, 20 December 2012, p. 1.

September 1968[2] and article 58 Council regulation (EC) no. 44/2001 of 22 December 2000 (Brussels I).[3] There are additional European enforcement provision on court settlements, which served as models for article 61. These are article 46 regulation (EC) no. 2201/2003 concerning jurisdiction and the recognition and enforcement of judgments in matrimonial matters and matters of parental responsibility (Brussels II-*bis*)[4] and article 48 regulation (EC) no. 4/2009 on jurisdiction, applicable law, recognition and enforcement of decisions and cooperation in matters relating to maintenance obligations (Maintenance regulation).[5] Article 61 is now the model for article 60 Council Regulation (EU) no. 1103/2016 of 24 June 2016 implementing enhanced cooperation in the area of jurisdiction, applicable law and the recognition and enforcement of decisions in matters of matrimonial property regimes[6] and for article 60 Council Regulation (EU) 1104/2016 of 24 June 2016 implementing enhanced cooperation in the area of jurisdiction, applicable law and the recognition and enforcement of decisions in matters of the property consequences of registered partnerships.[7]

II. International Enforcement Arising from an Instrument

2. If a court settlement within the meaning of article 3(1)(h) [see art. 3 no. 14] is enforceable under the law of the ESR Member State of origin [see art. 3 no. 9], the court settlement can also be enforced in another ESR Member State [see art. 3 no. 10] in accordance with the requirements of article 61. Pursuant to article 61(1) an application by an interested party is required. This is frequently a judgment creditor.

3. Article 61(1) makes reference to articles 45–58 with regard to the procedure for declaring a court settlement enforceable. The commentary on these provisions therefore also applies accordingly to declaring court settlements enforceable. Pursuant to article 61(2) the court which approved the settlement or before which it was concluded may, on the application of any interested party, issue an attestation of enforceability using the form established in accordance with the advisory procedure

[2] As amended by the Convention of 9 October 1978 on the accession of the Kingdom of Denmark, Ireland and the United Kingdom of Great Britain and Northern Ireland, by the Convention of 25 October 1982 on the accession of the Hellenic Republic and by the Convention of 26 May 1989 on the accession of the Kingdom of Spain and the Portuguese republic, OJ 1972 no. L 299, 31 December 1972, p. 32; consolidated version in OJ 1998 no. C27, 26 January 1998, p. 1.

[3] OJ 2001 no. L12, 16 January 2001, p. 1.

[4] OJ 2003 no. L338, 23 December 2003, p. 1.

[5] OJ 2009 no. L7, 10 January 2009, p. 1.

[6] OJ 2016 no. L183, 8 July 2016, p. 1.

[7] OJ 2016 no. L183, 8 July 2016, p. 30.

referred to in article 81(2). This form (form III) was published as annex 3 to the Commission Implementing Regulation (EU) no. 1329/2014 of 9 December 2014.[8] This attestation takes the place of the attestation required in article 46(3)(b).

4. According to article 61(3), a court with which an appeal is lodged against the declaration of enforcement (under article 50 or article 51) may refuse or revoke a declaration of enforceability only if enforcement of the court settlement is manifestly contrary to public policy (*ordre public)* in the Member State of enforcement. Article 61(3) therefore supersedes here article 40(b)–(d). On a contravention of the *ordre public*, see the commentary – *mutatis mutandi* – on the parallel provision relating to the recognition of decisions article 40(a) in connection with article 52 [see art. 40 no. 6 *et seq*.].

[8] Commission Implementing Regulation (EU) no. 1329/2014 of 9 December 2014 establishing the forms referred to in Regulation (EU) no. 650/2012 of the European Parliament and of the Council on jurisdiction, applicable law, recognition and enforcement of decisions and acceptance and enforcement of authentic instruments in matters of succession and on the creation of a European Certificate of Succession, OJ no. L359, 16 December 2014, p. 30.

CHAPTER VI

European Certificate of Succession

Article 62

Creation of a European Certificate of Succession

BERNHARD KREßE

1. This Regulation creates a European Certificate of Succession (hereinafter referred to as 'the Certificate') which shall be issued for use in another Member State and shall produce the effects listed in Article 69.
2. The use of the Certificate shall not be mandatory.
3. The Certificate shall not take the place of internal documents used for similar purposes in the Member States. However, once issued for use in another Member State, the Certificate shall also produce the effects listed in Article 69 in the Member State whose authorities issued it in accordance with this Chapter.

Summary

I. GENERALITIES *page* 673
  A. EU Competence *page* 673
  B. Procedural Structure 675
II. NORMATIVE CONTENT 676
  A. Creation of a European Certificate of Succession 676
    1. Terminology 676
    2. Legal Nature 677
  B. Cross-Border Situation 678
  C. Effects of the ECS 679
  D. Optional Nature of the ECS 679
  E. Relation with National Documents 680
    1. Alternative Use of Documents 680
    2. Co-existence and Parallel Use of Documents 681
    3. Conflicting Documents 682

I. Generalities

A. EU Competence

1. According to recital 2 of the ESR, the competence of the EU for the whole regulation follows from article 81.2 TFEU. This is certainly true for most of its content, as it mainly, at least in its chapters III and IV, concerns measures aimed at ensuring the compatibility of the rules applicable in the Member States concerning conflict of laws and of jurisdiction. However, the creation of a European Certificate of Succession (ECS) does not fall easily under the scope of point (c) of article 81.2 TFEU, as the relevant provisions are mainly substantial law. Therefore, point (c) of article 81.2 TFEU is not suitable to justify an EU competence for chapter VI of the ESR introducing the ECS. EU competence cannot follow from point (a) of article 81.2 TFEU, either, as the ECS is not about mutual recognition and enforcement between Member States of judgments and of decisions in extrajudicial cases. Similarly, the ECS does not fall into the scope of points (d) and (f) of that provision.[1] In particular, the settlement of successions does not necessarily involve civil proceedings. Some authors therefore plead in favour of an annex competence of article 81 TFEU.[2] However, this is seen as critical with respect to the effects of the ECS in the Member State whose authorities have issued it; it is strongly doubted that the EU is competent for this specific matter.[3] It also has been objected that a mere annex competence would be unable to justify that those Member States that have not implemented certificates of succession in their legal order, should be obliged to create such instruments totally new to them.[4] In general, an extension of EU competences by means of the creation of annex

[1] Explicitly in favour of a competence according to points (a), (c) or (d) of article 81.2 TFEU: Max Planck Institute for Comparative and International Private Law, 'Comments on the European Commission's Proposal for a Regulation of the European Parliament and of the Council on jurisdiction, applicable law, recognition and enforcement of decisions and authentic instruments in matters of succession and the creation of a European Certificate of Succession', *RabelsZ* (2010), p. 530; K. W. Lange, 'Das geplante Europäische Nachlasszeugnis', *Deutsche Notar-Zeitschrift* (2012), p. 168; cf. A. Dutta, 'Art. 62 EuErbVO', in J. von Hein (ed), *Münchener Kommentar zum BGB*, vol. X, 6th ed. (München, 2015), para. 3.

[2] R. Wagner, 'Der Kommissionsvorschlag vom 14. 10. 2009 zum internationalen Erbrecht: Stand und Perspektiven des Gesetzgebungsverfahrens', *Deutsche Notar-Zeitschrift* (2010), p. 510 *et seq.*; S. Omlor, 'Gutglaubensschutz durch das Europäische Nachlasszeugnis', *GPR: Zeitschrift für das Privatrecht der Europäischen Union* (2014), p. 217; H.-P. Mansel, 'Vereinheitlichung des internationalen Erbrechts in der Europäischen Gemeinschaft – Kompetenzfragen und Regelungsgrundsätze', in *Prof. Dr. Tuğrul Ansay'a Armağan* (Ankara, 2006), p. 192 *et seq.*

[3] Mansel, 'Vereinheitlichung des internationalen Erbrechts', p. 193; C. F. Nordmeier, 'Art. 62 EuErbVO', in R. Hüßtege and H.-P. Mansel (eds), *NomosKommentar, BGB, Rom-Verordnungen*, vol. VI 2nd ed. (Baden-Baden, 2015), para. 12; M. Buschbaum and M. Kohler, 'Vereinheitlichung des Erbkollisionsrechts in Europa, Zweiter Teil', *GPR: Zeitschrift für Gemeinschaftsprivatrecht* (2010), pp. 162, 166; in favour of an annex competence concerning the effects of the ECS in the state of origin, however, e.g. Dutta, 'Art. 62 EuErbVO', para. 3.

[4] R. Süß, 'Das Europäische Nachlasszeugnis', *ZEuP* (2013), p. 730.

competences should be allowed only very carefully, due to the principle of conferral laid down in article 5.1 TEU and therefore the imperative of restrictive interpretation of provisions regarding EU competences.[5]

B. Procedural Structure

2. Chapter VI about the ECS is procedurally structured:[6] This means the provisions about the ECS are laid down in chronological order of the procedural steps and matters of interest in the context of the issuing of an ECS. The provisions about the creation and the purpose of the ECS (articles 62 and 63 ESR) as well as the competent authority (article 64 ESR) are followed by articles dealing with formalities relating to the application (article 65 ESR), its examination by the issuing authority (article 66 ESR), the issue of the ECS itself (article 67 ESR), its contents (article 68 ESR) and effects (article 69 ESR), questions relating to the issuing of certified copies of the ECS (article 70 ESR) and alterations concerning the ECS (article 71 ESR). The chapter then ends with provisions concerning the redress procedures (article 72 ESR) and the suspension of the effects of the ECS (article 73 ESR).

3. The procedural rules of the article 62 *et seq.* ESR have primacy of application over opposing provisions of national law. As far as the ESR does not contain provisions for procedure-related questions, the national courts or authorities have to apply their national procedural law (*lex fori*). Although the ESR lacks a provision similar to those in article 26 of the regulation creating a European order for payment procedure[7] and in article 19 of the regulation establishing a European Small Claims Procedure[8] that explicitly state that all procedural issues not specifically dealt with in these regulations shall be governed by national law, it contains some indication that national procedural law should be subsidiarily applicable: Examples are the third sentence of article 72.1 ESR, point (b) of article 64 ESR and the second sentence of recital 70 of the ESR.[9]

[5] Nordmeier, 'Art. 62 EuErbVO', para. 12. [6] Nordmeier, 'Art. 62 EuErbVO', para. 13.

[7] Regulation (EC) no. 1896/2006 of the European Parliament and of the Council of 12 December 2006 creating a European order for payment procedure, OJ 2006 no. L399, 30 December 2006, p. 1.

[8] Regulation (EC) no. 861/2007 of the European Parliament and of the Council of 11 July 2007 establishing a European Small Claims Procedure, OJ 2007 no. L199, 31 July 2007, p. 1.

[9] Cf. Dutta, 'Art. 62 EuErbVO ', para. 5.

II. Normative Content

A. *Creation of a European Certificate of Succession*

1. Terminology

4. Article 62.1 ESR begins with the simple notice that a European Certificate of Succession is created by the regulation. Indeed, most of the interested circles that have been consulted[10] by the European Commission after the presentation of its green paper 'Succession and Wills' on transnational successions[11] have appreciated the introduction of such certificate. It should be noted, however, that the green paper had used a different terminology, speaking only of a 'European Certificate of Inheritance'.[12] In the Commission's Proposal for an ESR, the terminology has then been changed to ECS.[13] The reason is that according to article 63 ESR, the ECS is not only for use for heirs, but also for legatees, executors of wills or administrators of the estate.[14] Beside this, the ECS has been modeled distinctly on the German certificate of inheritance.[15]

5. The ECS thus should enable the aforementioned persons involved in successions to assert their rights and powers as mentioned in article 63.1 ESR, and to give easy evidence of their status in another Member State without having to go through further formalities. Successions with cross-border implications should thus be settled 'speedily, smoothly and efficiently'[16] and this with a homogenous

[10] The contributions of the interested circles are available at http://ec.europa.eu/justice/newsroom/civil/opinion/050301_en.htm (last accessed 7 July 2016).

[11] COM(2005) 65 final. [12] Green paper 'Succession and Wills', p. 10.

[13] Commission's Proposal for a Regulation of the European Parliament and of the Council on jurisdiction, applicable law, recognition and enforcement of decisions and authentic instruments in matters of succession and the creation of a European Certificate of Succession, COM(2009) 154 final.

[14] See F. Sturm and G. Sturm, 'Das europäische Nachlasszeugnis – Zum Vorschlag der Kommission vom 14. Oktober 2009', *Zbornik Pravnog fakulteta u Zagrebu* (2012), p. 332 *et seq.*; Nordmeier, 'Art. 62 EuErbVO', para. 4.

[15] J. Schmidt, 'Art. 62 EuErbVO', in C. Budzikiewicz, M.-P. Weller and W. Wurmnest (eds), *Beck-Online Großkommentar, EuErbVO* (München, 2016), para. 6; J. Schmidt, 'Der Erbnachweis in Deutschland ab 2015: Erbschein vs. Europäisches Nachlasszeugnis', *ZEV* (2014), p. 389; T. Ballarino, 'Il nuovo regolamento europeo sulle successioni', *Riv dir int* (2013), p. 1144; J. Carrascosa González, 'Reglamento sucesorio europeo y actividad notarial', *CdT* (2014), p. 38. The German certificate of inheritance is codified in section 2353 *et seq.* BGB; cf. about the effects of the German certificate: P. Wautelet, 'Article 62', in A. Bonomi and P. Wautelet, *Le droit européen des successions. Commentaire du Règlement n° 650/2012 du 4 juillet 2012* (Bruxelles, 2013), pp. 703–704.

[16] Recital 67 of the ESR; green paper 'Succession and Wills', p. 10; cf. recital 27 of the Proposal for the ESR ('accelerated, manageable and efficient').

effect.[17] This may be necessary in particular if succession property is located in another Member State.[18]

2. Legal Nature

6. The legal nature of the ECS has not been specified in the ESR.[19] It would be conceivable to see it as an enforceable title allowing for the transcription or entry of the inherited acquisition in the public registers of the Member State in which the property is located. However, after for example the German and French versions of article 42.5 of the proposal for an ESR had used the term 'title', it has been made clear in article 69.5 ESR into which article 42.5 of the proposal has been transported that the ECS is not an enforceable title, as this provision merely speaks of a 'document'.[20]

7. The ECS is not an authentic instrument, either.[21] Article 2 of the proposal for an ESR distinguishes clearly between authentic instruments in its point (h) on one hand and European Certificates of Succession in its point (i) on the other hand. In article 3.1 of the ESR itself which contains the definitions of specific terms used in the ESR, the definition of the ECS has been eliminated, whereas authentic instruments are still defined explicitly in point (i) of article 3.1 ESR. However, the titles of chapter V (Authentic Instruments and Court Settlements) and chapter VI (European Certificate of Succession) of the ESR still make it clear that the ECS is not meant to be a mere subtype of authentic instruments. The ECS thus should be qualified as a type of EU instrument of its own kind.[22] The practical relevance of the

[17] R. Stürner, 'Arts. 62–73 EuErbVO', in O. Jauernig, *Bürgerliches Gesetzbuch: BGB*, 16th ed. (München, 2015), para. 1.

[18] Recital 67 of the ESR.

[19] A. Perscha, 'Art 62 EuErbVO', in A. Deixler-Hübner and M. Schauer (eds), *EuErbVO – Kommentar zur EU-Erbrechtsverordnung* (Wien, 2015), para. 29 *et seq.*; C. Dorsel, 'Europäische Erbrechtsverordnung und Europäisches Nachlasszeugnis', *Europäische Zeitschrift für die Steuer- und Erbrechtspraxis* (2014), p. 212.

[20] Cf. M. Buschbaum, 'Europäisches Nachlasszeugnis und Annahme öffentlicher Urkunden – neue Mechanismen zur grenzüberschreitenden Nachlassabwicklung und ihr Verhältnis zum materiellen Sachenrecht', in J. Hager (ed), *Die neue europäische Erbrechtsverordnung* (2013), p. 51 *et seq.*; see also Carrascosa González, 'Reglamento sucesorio europeo y actividad notarial', p. 37; S. Frodl, 'Einheit durch Aufgabe nationaler Rechtstraditionen? – EU-Erbrechtsverordnung kundgemacht', *Österreichische Juristen-Zeitung* (2012), p. 957 *et seq.*

[21] Cf. however Carrascosa González, 'Reglamento sucesorio europeo y actividad notarial', p. 39.

[22] Lange, 'Das geplante Europäische Nachlasszeugnis', p. 170; M. Buschbaum and U. Simon, 'EuErbVO: Das Europäische Nachlasszeugnis', *ZEV* (2012), p. 529; Dutta, 'Art. 62 EuErbVO', para. 1.

exact qualification is admittedly of subordinate relevance, as its EU-wide applicability is ensured in article 69 ESR, without any special procedure being required. There thus is no need to apply the article 59 *et seq.* ESR on ECS.

B. Cross-Border Situation

8. The ECS shall be issued for use in another Member State according to article 62.1 ESR. It is thus supposed to produce its effects in another Member State than where it has been issued. At first sight, the exact content of article 62 ESR seems to be inconsistent:[23] On one hand, the ECS shall be used in another Member State. This is picked up in article 63 ESR again, where it is laid down that the ECS is for use for certain kinds of persons who, 'in another Member State', need to demonstrate their specific involvement in the estate of the deceased. On the other hand, according to the second sentence of article 62.3 ESR, the ECS shall also produce its effects in the Member State of issuance.[24]

9. This apparent discrepancy correlates clearly, however, with the distinction between the requirements for the issuance of an ECS and its effect: Indeed, an ECS may not be issued in the absence of a cross-border situation. According to point (f) of article 65.3 ESR, the applicant for an ECS must demonstrate the transnational purpose of this document in accordance with article 63 ESR.[25] Most of the time, the cross-border situation is based on the fact that the assets of the succession are located in different Member States.[26] The mere residence of the applicant in another Member State is not sufficient to establish a transnational purpose.[27] The transnational purpose is a substantial requirement without the fulfillment of which the ECS must not be issued. Thus, if it is clear that there is only a need for the applicant to demonstrate his or her

[23] P. Lagarde, 'Les principes de base du nouveau règlement européen sur les successions', *Rev crit dr int priv* (2012), p. 727.

[24] Dutta, 'Art. 62 EuErbVO', para. 2; cf Wautelet, 'Article 62', p. 710.

[25] Wautelet, 'Article 62', p. 709; Schmidt, 'Art. 62 EuErbVO', para. 21; cf. Frodl, 'Einheit durch Aufgabe nationaler Rechtstraditionen?', p. 957.

[26] A. Bonomi, 'Il regolamento europeo sulle successioni', *Riv dir int priv proc* (2013), p. 320; cf. M. Fornasier, 'Art. 62 EuErbVO', in A. Dutta and J. Weber (eds), *Internationales Erbrecht – EuErbVO, Erbrechtliche Staatsverträge, EGBGB, IntErbRVG, IntErbStR, IntSchenkungsR* (München, 2016), para. 3.

[27] Perscha, 'Art 62 EuErbVO', para. 43; J. Kleinschmidt, 'Optionales Erbrecht – Das Europäische Nachlasszeugnis als Herausforderung an das Kollisionsrecht', *RabelsZ* (2013), p. 746.

position, rights or powers with respect to the succession within the Member State of application, the issuance of the ECS would be rejected. However, once the ECS has been issued, it produces its effects not only in the other Member States but also in the Member State whose authorities issued it. The applicant is not obliged to first make use of the ECS abroad.[28]

10. Article 62 (1), as well as article 63 (1) ESR, refers to the use of the ECS in 'another Member State' in the linguistic singular. Therefore, it would be conceivable to interpret this provision in the sense that there should be issued one ECS for every Member State in which the applicant needs to invoke her status, or to exercise his or her rights or powers, of course with the exception of the Member State whose authorities issues the ECS. However, according to article 69.1 ESR, the ECS produces its effect in all Member States. Also, the issuing authority's possibility to issue certified copies of the ECS, if necessary, shows that the ESR does not provide for the issuance of a multitude of ECS for one and the same succession.[29]

C. *Effects of the ECS*

11. According to article 62.1 ESR, the ECS shall produce the effects listed in article 69 ESR. Three different effects have thus to be distinguished: the presumption of substantial accuracy of the ECS, public faith in the ECS, and the validity for the recording of succession property in the relevant register of each Member State [see art. 69].[30]

D. *Optional Nature of the ECS*

12. Article 62.2 ESR states that the use of the ECS shall not be mandatory. This means that the kinds of persons mentioned in article 63.1 ESR who are entitled to apply for issuance of an ECS according to article 65.1 ESR, may demonstrate their status, rights or powers also by means of other instruments available under the regulation. Decisions, authentic instruments (article 59 *et seq.* ESR) and court settlements (article 61 ESR) can also be used by the persons entitled to apply for an ECS. Conversely, no authority or person presented with an ECS should be entitled to

[28] Cf. Dutta, 'Art. 62 EuErbVO', para. 3. [29] Nordmeier, 'Art. 62 EuErbVO', para. 12.

[30] Cf. Stürner, 'Arts. 62–73 EuErbVO', para. 6; C. Mariottini, 'Successione di cittadino straniero: questioni di diritto internazionale privato e processuale alla luce della proposta di regolamtento europeo sulle successioni internazionali', *Persona, famiglia e successioni* (2012), p. 123.

require the presentation of a decision, authentic instrument or court settlement instead.[31]

E. Relation with National Documents

1. Alternative Use of Documents

13. The optional nature of the ECS implies another important aspect laid down in article 62.3 ESR: The certificates of succession or inheritance as provided for by national laws shall not be affected according to the first sentence of this provision. Therefore, any person entitled to such a national certificate may apply for its issuance even if there is a cross-border situation.[32] The consequence of this is thus the possibility of an alternative use of the ECS and national documents of succession or inheritance: The applicant has the option to choose between both instruments. If he or she decides to apply for an ECS and is issued such a certificate, he or she usually should not need any national document of succession or inheritance in any Member State.[33]

14. The reasons why an applicant might nevertheless prefer to apply for a national certificate instead of an ECS are not necessarily due to the higher public recognition of the former, but can also emanate from differences in the substantial effects of both documents. For example, the public faith inherent in German certificates of inheritance is superseded only by positive cognition about its inaccuracy.[34] By contrast, according to article 69.3 ESR, a person who is merely unaware of the inaccuracy of an ECS due to gross negligence, may not invoke its public faith, either. Thus, the level of protection of those acting on the basis of the information certified in a German certificate of succession is higher than it is in case of the use of an ECS.[35]

[31] Recital 69 ESR; Dutta, 'Art. 62 EuErbVO', para. 4; Schmidt, 'Art. 62 EuErbVO', paras. 14 *et seq*; J. Kleinschmidt, 'Art. 62 EuErbVO', in M. Würdinger (ed), *Juris Praxiskommentar BGB, Internationales Privatrecht*, vol. VI, 7th ed. (Saarbrücken, 2014), para. 39.

[32] Wautelet, 'Article 62', p. 712; Buschbaum and Simon, 'EuErbVO', p. 528; Frodl, 'Einheit durch Aufgabe nationaler Rechtstraditionen?', p. 957; C. Azcárraga Monzonís, 'International Successions in Spain: The Impact of a New EU Regulation', *Spanish Yearbook of International Law* (2009), p. 57 *et seq.*; A. Köhler, 'Art. 62 EuErbVO', in L. Kroiß, C.-H. Horn and D. Solomon (eds), *Nachfolgerecht – Erbrechtliche Spezialgesetze, Zivilrecht/Strafrecht/Verwaltungsrecht/Steuerrecht/Verfahrensrecht/IPR* (Baden-Baden 2015), para. 3.

[33] Kleinschmidt, 'Optionales Erbrecht', p. 748 *et seq.* [34] Cf. section 2366 BGB.

[35] Wautelet, 'Article 62', p. 711 *et seq.*; Buschbaum and Simon, 'EuErbVO', p. 528; Dutta, 'Art. 62 EuErbVO', para. 7; cf. Köhler, 'Art. 62 EuErbVO', para. 4.

2. Co-existence and Parallel Use of Documents

15. It also may occur that a third party insists on the submission of a national certificate, although an ECS is presented to him.[36] This could however not be a public authority, given that it would violate the *effet utile* of the ECS if such authority was permitted to accept national certificates only.[37] The second sentence of recital 69 of the ESR seems to go even further than that, as its wording strongly suggests that private parties, too, are obliged to trust and accept an ECS and cannot insist on the submittal of a national certificate if presented with an ECS. However, in spite of the wording of recital 69, the ESR cannot be interpreted this way. First, the EU lacks competence for ordering private persons to always accept an ECS as sufficient evidence.[38] Second, the first sentence of article 62.3 ESR, stating clearly that the ECS does not take the place of internal certificates of succession or inheritance as provided for by national laws, does not only provide for the alternative use of the ECS and national documents, but also for the possibility of their parallel use. For if a private person was obliged to rely on the specifications recorded in the ECS only, this document would take indeed the place of internal certificates in the moment of its issuance. This, however, is explicitly dismissed in the first sentence of article 62.3 ESR and would also not be in accordance with the principle of subsidiarity.[39]

16. Another point of discussion is whether the issuance of an ECS bars the conferral of a national certificate.[40] To assume this would however mean an even stronger conflict with the first sentence of article 62.3 ESR, as not only the use, but already the issuance of national certificates would be averted by the ECS, so that the latter would indeed take the place of national certificates from the moment of its issuance.

[36] Buschbaum and Simon, 'EuErbVO', p. 528.

[37] Cf. C. Kohler and W. Pintens, 'Entwicklungen im europäischen Familien- und Erbrecht 2011–2012', *FamRZ* (2012), p. 1429; see also Carrascosa González, 'Reglamento sucesorio europeo y actividad notarial', p. 39, who holds that a private person could not insist on a national certificate, either; in the same sense Perscha, 'Art 62 EuErbVO', para. 47; *contra*: Buschbaum and Simon, 'EuErbVO', p. 528, footnote 26, who hold that authorities might also have good reasons to insist on national certificates; cf. also Wautelet, 'Article 62', p. 712.

[38] Buschbaum and Simon, 'EuErbVO', p. 528, footnote 26.

[39] In the same sense Nordmeier, 'Art. 62 EuErbVO', para. 32; Schmidt, 'Art. 62 EuErbVO', para. 17; cf. also recital 67 of the ESR and Ballarino, 'Il nuovo regolamento europeo sulle successioni', p. 1144.

[40] Cf. Kleinschmidt, 'Optionales Erbrecht', p. 749, who argues that the issuance of a national certificate should presuppose the cancellation of a prior ECS.

The question whether a national certificate can be issued regardless of the prior existence of an ECS can only be answered on the basis of national law.[41] Moreover, it is not convincing to allow a national certificate to be issued before the issuance of an ECS, but not thereafter, as also in the former case, a conflict between national certificates and – subsequent – ECS could not be prevented. To assume that a national certificate would be superseded by a posterior ECS[42] violates the first sentence of article 62.3 ESR.[43]

17. After all, the ESR provides for the possibility of co-existence and parallel use of national documents of succession or of inheritance and of the ECS. An ECS may be issued and used although a national document had been issued before. Vice versa, a national document may be issued and used although an ECS had been issued before. The existence of an ECS thus does not make the application for a national certificate inadmissible, except, of course, there is a national provision to this effect.[44]

3. Conflicting Documents

18. It is obvious that, due to the possibility of co-existence of national certificates and an ECS, there may arise substantial conflicts between the information certified in national certificates and in an ECS. Such conflicts may arise on two levels: First, according to article 69.2 ESR, the ECS is presumed to be accurate [see art. 69]. This means that in proceedings involving any question to which the ECS is supposed to give an answer according to its specific content, a party claiming that the ECS is incorrect and the question is to be answered differently would have to prove this. A similar presumption may, depending on national law, also exist with respect to the accuracy of the content of a national certificate.[45] If there is

41 Nordmeier, 'Art. 62 EuErbVO', para. 32; cf., however, Kleinschmidt, 'Art. 62 EuErbVO', para. 47, who holds that national certificates may only be issued by the authorities that have jurisdiction according to article 4 *et seq.* ESR.

42 Kleinschmidt, 'Optionales Erbrecht', p. 749; cf. Ballarino, 'Il nuovo regolamento europeo sulle successioni', p. 1144 *et seq.*

43 Wautelet, 'Article 62', p. 715; similar: H. Wilsch, 'EuErbVO: Die Verordnung in der deutschen Grundbuchpraxis', *ZEV* (2012), p. 532; *contra:* Lagarde, 'Les principes de base', p. 727. The Max Planck Institute for Comparative and International Private Law, 'Comments', p. 701, argues that a national certificate might be conferred priority in the state of its issuance, with a residual validity of the ECS in other Member States.

44 Buschbaum and Simon, 'EuErbVO', p. 528; Nordmeier, 'Art. 62 EuErbVO', para. 32; Dutta, 'Art. 62 EuErbVO', para. 9 *et seq.*; Schmidt, 'Art. 62 EuErbVO', para. 19; Stürner, 'Arts. 62–73 EuErbVO', para. 7; Fornasier, 'Art. 62 EuErbVO', para. 11; *contra:* Kleinschmidt, 'Optionales Erbrecht', p. 749.

45 See, e.g., section 2365 BGB.

a contradiction between the contents of an ECS and a national certificate, it is necessary to decide if any of the presumptions prevails over the other, and in the affirmative, which one prevails.

19. The ESR does not give an answer to this. In view of the first sentence of article 62.3 ESR, it is not possible to assume that the presumption of accuracy of the ECS rests on a stronger legal basis than the similar presumption concerning a national certificate, and should therefore prevail. For it results from the provision just mentioned that the ECS shall not have *per se* a higher rank than the corresponding national documents the effects of which continue to depend from national legislation.[46] Similarly, the presumption created by a national certificate cannot prevail over the presumption linked to the content of an ECS. Therefore, the conflict can only be dissolved by taking the presumptions of all certificates in question seriously in equal measure: Each presumption of accuracy thus refutes the presumptions of all contradicting certificates, no matter they are an ECS or national.[47] This holds at least true for those demonstrated elements which are in contradiction to each other (e.g. different persons are mentioned as the heir).[48] Insofar as the certificates correspond to each other there is no need to abrogate the presumption of accuracy.

20. Second, according to article 69(3) and (4) ESR, in addition to the presumption of accuracy, the ECS benefits of public faith [see art. 69]. This means that for certain transactions, the content of the ECS is regarded as accurate in favour of any person acting in good faith on the basis of the information certified. This is more than the mere simple presumption of article 69.2 ESR, as the public faith of the ECS allows irrevocable transactions to be made on the sole basis of the content of the ECS. The transaction can be carried out as if the information certified was true, even if it is not. It is irrelevant whether the ECS is shown to be

[46] Dutta, 'Art. 62 EuErbVO', para. 16; Wautelet, 'Article 62', p. 715; *contra* (in favour of prevalence of the ECS): Carrascosa González, 'Reglamento sucesorio europeo y actividad notarial', p. 39.

[47] Nordmeier, 'Art. 62 EuErbVO', para. 37; Dutta, 'Art. 62 EuErbVO', para. 16; Kleinschmidt, 'Art. 62 EuErbVO', para. 55; F. Wall, 'Richtet sich die international Zuständigkeit zur Erbscheinserteilung künftig ausschließlich nach Artt. 4ff. EuErbVO?', *Zeitschrift für die Steuer- und Erbrechtspraxis* (2015), p. 16; Dorsel, 'Europäische Erbrechtsverordnung und Europäisches Nachlasszeugnis', p. 222 *et seq.*; cf. Bonomi, 'Il regolamento europeo sulle successioni', p. 321.

[48] See C. Dorsel, 'Art. 62 EuErbVO', in R. Geimer and R. Schütze (eds), *Internationaler Rechtsverkehr in Zivil- und Handelssachen*, vol. III (München, 2015), para. 5 *et seq.*; Dutta, 'Art. 62 EuErbVO', para. 16.

inaccurate thereafter. Problems may arise if the contents of an ECS and a national certificate are conflicting, and the national law in question also knows the concept of public faith of certificates of succession or inheritance. In this case, each document should benefit of public faith, the ECS according to article 69.3 ESR, and the national certificate according to the relevant national provisions, if applicable.[49] The same applies in case of two conflicting ECS.[50]

21. The conflict is therefore usually resolved by the principle of priority: If, for example, succession property is transferred by a person who is (falsely) evidenced as heir by an ECS to a third bona fide party, this party will receive property of the asset on the basis of the public faith of the ECS. If subsequently, the property of the same asset is transferred by another person who is (falsely) evidenced as heir by a national certificate of succession which also enjoys the effect of public faith under national law, the acquirer of that person would not receive property of the asset just because of the public faith of the national certificate: With the first transaction, the asset has been withdrawn from the estate, and – depending, of course, on the national law in question: it is assumed here that it is similar to article 69.4 ESR in this respect, as is the case for example in German law[51] – the national certificate of succession may provide only public faith for the rights in the succession that are recorded in the document, but not for the contents of the estate itself.[52] A similar solution applies if succession property is first transferred by a person evidenced as heir by a national certificate providing public faith, and then by another person evidenced by an ECS. In this case, too, the first acquirer receives property and the second does not necessarily, as the public faith provided for in article 69.4 ESR also concerns only the content of the ECS, but not the substance of the estate.[53]

22. Another conflict between the public faith of an ECS and the public faith of a national certificate may arise if a person is acting on the basis of the information both certified in an ECS and in a national certificate, but is unaware of the inaccuracy of both certificates due to gross negligence. If the national law applicable to the effects of the

[49] Wautelet, 'Article 62', pp. 716–717; Dutta, 'Art. 62 EuErbVO', para. 16; Nordmeier, 'Art. 62 EuErbVO', para. 37; *contra:* Dorsel, 'Europäische Erbrechtsverordnung und Europäisches Nachlasszeugnis', p. 222; *id.*, 'Art. 62 EuErbVO', para. 15 *et seq.*; Fornasier, 'Art. 62 EuErbVO', para. 12.

[50] Cf. Lagarde, 'Les principes de base', p. 727 *et seq.*

[51] Section 2366 BGB.

[52] Dutta, 'Art. 62 EuErbVO', para. 16.

[53] Dutta, 'Art. 62 EuErbVO', para. 16.

national certificate also attaches public faith to the latter, but in contrast to article 69.4 ESR dismisses good faith only in case of positive knowledge of the inaccuracy of the certificate, but not in case of gross negligence,[54] the question is whether the national certificate is still regarded as accurate in favour of the acting person despite the relevance of gross negligence with respect to the ECS. The concepts of co-existence and parallel use of national succession documents and ECS require that the effect of each certificate be assessed according to the law governing it. Therefore, if according to one of the applicable provisions – article 69.4 ESR or the national public faith provision – the conditions of the assumption of accuracy of the document are fulfilled, this assumption has to be applied,[55] so there exists a principle of favourability.

[54] This is, for example, the case in German law, cf. section 2366 BGB.

[55] Dorsel, 'Europäische Erbrechtsverordnung und Europäisches Nachlasszeugnis', p. 222; cf. implicitly Dutta, 'Art. 62 EuErbVO', para. 16; Buschbaum and Simon, 'EuErbVO', p. 528.

Article 63

Purpose of the Certificate

BERNHARD KREẞE

1. The Certificate is for use by heirs, legatees having direct rights in the succession and executors of wills or administrators of the estate who, in another Member State, need to invoke their status or to exercise respectively their rights as heirs or legatees and/or their powers as executors of wills or administrators of the estate.
2. The Certificate may be used, in particular, to demonstrate one or more of the following:
   (a) the status and/or the rights of each heir or, as the case may be, each legatee mentioned in the Certificate and their respective shares of the estate;
   (b) the attribution of a specific asset or specific assets forming part of the estate to the heir(s) or, as the case may be, the legatee(s) mentioned in the Certificate;
   (c) the powers of the person mentioned in the Certificate to execute the will or administer the estate.

Summary

I. GENERALITIES *page* 686

II. LEGAL POSITIONS TO BE CERTIFIED 688

- A. Heirs 688
- B. Legatees Having Direct Rights in the Succession 690
- C. Executors of Wills 691
- D. Administrators of the Estate 692

III. OBJECTIVE REQUIREMENTS OF USE 694

- A. Need to Invoke the Status or to Exercise the Rights or Powers Relating to the Estate 694
- B. In another Member State 695
- C. Examples Mentioned in Article 63.2 696

I. Generalities

1. Article 63 ESR defines the abstract purpose of European Certificates of Succession (ECS). Outside the admissible purposes, an ECS must not be issued. Indirectly, the provision also outlines the range of persons who are entitled to apply for the issuance of an ECS, as article 65.1 explicitly refers to article 63.1.[1] This leads in turn to an indirect definition of the range of persons entitled to challenge decisions taken by the issuing authority, as the first paragraph of article 72.1 refers to article 65.1, as it states that any person entitled to apply for an ECS is qualified to initiate redress procedures. Furthermore, the effects an ECS can have according to article 69 ESR are limited to its admissible purposes as set out in article 63 ESR.[2] Thus, article 63 ESR is an essential provision in the context of ECS. The entirety of the articles 62 to 73 ESR has to be interpreted and understood in the light of the purpose of the ECS as defined in its article 63.[3]

2. It is clear from article 63.1 ESR that the ECS is only for use of the range of persons explicitly mentioned in this provision.[4] The ECS is an instrument destined to facilitate the demonstration of a specific legal position in the succession context by the legitimised person.[5] Its objective is not to enable third persons to demonstrate such legitimisation. In particular, the aim of the ECS is not to facilitate to creditors of the estate the implementation of their claims. Therefore, creditors of the estate do not belong to the group of persons who are entitled to apply for an ECS.[6]

3. The meaning of the terms describing the legal positions listed in article 63.1 ESR is to be established by an autonomous interpretation of

[1] P. Wautelet, 'Article 63', in A. Bonomi and P. Wautelet, *Le droit européen des successions. Commentaire du Règlement n° 650/2012 du 4 juillet 2012* (Bruxelles), p. 720.

[2] A. Dutta, 'Art. 63 EuErbVO', in J. von Hein (ed), *Münchener Kommentar zum BGB*, vol. X, 6th ed. (München, 2015), para. 1.

[3] Dutta, 'Art. 63 EuErbVO', para. 1. [4] Wautelet, 'Article 63', p. 721.

[5] J. Kleinschmidt, 'Art. 63 EuErbVO', in M. Würdinger (ed), *Juris Praxiskommentar BGB, Internationales Privatrecht*, vol. VI, 7th ed. (Saarbrücken, 2014), para. 24; H. L. Graf, in K. Firsching and H. L. Graf (eds), *Nachlassrecht – Erbfolge, Testament, Erbvertrag, Pflichtteilsrecht, Rechtspflege in Nachlasssachen, Nachlassinsolvenz, Nachlassverfahren sowie Erbschaftssteuer*, 10th ed. (München, 2014), para. 4.330; cf. green paper 'Succession and Wills', presented by the Commission, COM(2005) 65 final, p. 10; recital 27 of the Commission's Proposal for a Regulation of the European Parliament and of the Council on jurisdiction, applicable law, recognition and enforcement of decisions and authentic instruments in matters of succession and the creation of a European Certificate of Succession, COM(2009) 154 final.

[6] J. Schmidt, 'Art. 63 EuErbVO', in C. Budzikiewicz, M.-P. Weller and W. Wurmnest (eds), *Beck-Online Großkommentar, EuErbVO* (München, 2016), para. 6; Wautelet, 'Article 63', p. 721; K. W. Lange, 'Das Europäische Nachlasszeugnis', in A. Dutta and S. Herrler (eds), *Die Europäische Erbrechtsverordnung* (München, 2014), para. 7; M. Buschbaum and U. Simon, 'EuErbVO: Das Europäische Nachlasszeugnis', ZEV (2012), p. 525; C. Dorsel, 'Europäische Erbrechtsverordnung und Europäisches Nachlasszeugnis', *Europäische Zeitschrift für die Steuer- und Erbrechtspraxis* (2014), p. 213.

those terms, as legal acts of the European Union always need to be interpreted specifically according to the purpose of the specific provision of EU law.[7] The question whether the person in question holds such a legal position is in contrary to be answered according to the law applicable to succession pursuant to chapter III of the ESR.[8]

II. Legal Positions to Be Certified

A. Heirs

4. An ECS can be applied for and used in order to demonstrate the legal position as an heir. As indicated above, the exact patrimonial status of the relevant person with respect to the succession is determined by the law on succession according to point (b) of article 23.2 of the ESR [see art. 23 no. 7]. It is however a question of the interpretation of the ESR to know whether the status established in such a way can be subsumed under the notion of 'heir' in the sense of its article 63.1.[9] The ESR does not contain any explicit definition of this term. It has therefore been suggested to apprehend its meaning from an overview of the use of the term in the legal orders of all Member States.[10] It is then concluded that heirs are all persons who, by reason of death, are entitled to an entire estate and not only to certain assets. It does not matter whether intestate or voluntary succession applies, whether the entitlement refers only to a certain share, whether the succession of the person is limited in time, and whether the person is individually entitled or rather jointly with others.[11]

5. However, the starting point of the interpretation of legal texts of the European Union should be the consideration of the relevant text itself,[12] which *in concreto* leads to the same result as exposed in the precedent paragraph: Starting point for the definition of the concept of

[7] C. F. Nordmeier, 'Art. 63 EuErbVO', in R. Hüßtege and H.-P. Mansel (eds), *NomosKommentar, BGB, Rom-Verordnungen*, vol. VI, 2nd ed., (Baden-Baden, 2015), para. 2; Dutta, 'Art. 63 EuErbVO', para. 2; Dorsel, 'Europäische Erbrechtsverordnung', p. 213; cf. C. Baldus, 'Erbe und Vermächtnisnehmer nach der Erbrechtsverordnung', *GPR: Zeitschrift für Gemeinschaftsprivatrecht* (2012), p. 314.

[8] Dutta, 'Art. 63 EuErbVO', para. 2.

[9] Schmidt, 'Art. 63 EuErbVO', para. 7.

[10] Dutta, 'Art. 63 EuErbVO', paras. 5 and 7; cf. Schmidt, 'Art. 63 EuErbVO', para. 13.

[11] Dutta, 'Art. 63 EuErbVO', paras. 5 and 7; cf. Schmidt, 'Art. 63 EuErbVO', para. 13.

[12] B. Kreße, 'Die Auslegung mehrsprachiger Texte durch den EuGH', in I. Burr and G. Gréciano (eds), *Sprache und Recht – La construction européenne* (Baden-Baden, 2003), p. 157 *et seq.*; B. Kreße, 'Mehrsprachigkeit im Recht der Europäischen Union', *Zeitschrift für Rechtspolitik* (2014), p. 11 *et seq.*

'heir' is point (a) of article 3.1 which defines the succession [see art. 3 no. 2]. This term means succession to the estate of a deceased person, and it covers all forms of transfer of assets, rights and obligations by reason of death, irrespective of whether the transfer is accomplished through voluntary or intestate succession. Thus, an heir could be any person to whom assets, rights and obligation are transferred by reason of death. This potentially wide understanding of the notion has to be further restricted with regard to point (l) of article 68 ESR: The statement in this provision that an ECS shall contain 'the share for each heir', without necessarily requiring any specification of assets this would apply to – such specification should only be included in the ECS 'if applicable' – makes it clear that an heir is characterised by his or her entitlement to the entire estate, or a share thereof, e.g. of the succession as a whole.[13] This entitlement to the entire succession or an imaginary share of the entire estate is the element that distinguishes the heir of the legatee mentioned in point (m) of article 68 ESR: For the legatee, this provision requires that the ECS includes a list of specific assets and rights belonging to the estate, so that the legatee is only entitled to certain rights or assets of the estate, but not to a share of its entirety. Thus, heirs and legatees can be defined partly by distinguishing one from the other.[14]

6. It is disputed whether it is necessary to have direct rights in the succession in order to be an heir in the sense of the ESR,[15] or if a beneficiary of a succession may also be an heir if for example as in common law countries, he or she just has a personal claim upon a personal representative of estate,[16] and therefore merely indirect rights in the succession.[17] The second approach has the better arguments on its side: First, the restriction concerning the directness of rights is not unknown to the ESR, as it results from its article 63.1 that legatees may only make use of

[13] Nordmeier, 'Art. 63 EuErbVO', para. 3; Dutta, 'Art. 63 EuErbVO', para. 5.

[14] Cf. Baldus, 'Erbe und Vermächtnisnehmer', p. 314.

[15] Dutta, 'Art. 63 EuErbVO', para. 6; M. Fornasier, 'Art. 63 EuErbVO', in A. Dutta and J. Weber (eds), *Internationales Erbrecht – EuErbVO, Erbrechtliche Staatsverträge, EGBGB, IntErbRVG, IntErbStR, IntSchenkungsR* (München, 2016), para. 6.

[16] Cf. e.g. A.-L. Verbeke and Y-H. Leleu, 'Harmonization of the Law of Succession in Europe', in A. S. Hartkamp, M. W. Hesselink, E. H. Hondius, C. Mak and C. E. du Perron (eds), *Towards a European Civil Code*, 4th ed. (The Hague, 2010), p. 465; G. Kegel, 'Erbfolge und Vermächtnis: Heres ex re certa und Vindikationslegat', in *Liber amicorum Professor Ignaz Seidl-Hohenveldern in Honour of His 80th Birthday* (The Hague, 1998), p. 357; H. Dörner, C. Hertel, P. Lagarde and W. Riering, 'Auf dem Weg zu einem europäischen Internationalen Erb- und Erbverfahrensrecht', *IPRax* (2005), p. 7.

[17] Nordmeier, 'Art. 63 EuErbVO', para. 4.

an ECS if they have direct rights. This restriction is missing in the same provision with respect to heirs. It thus can be concluded that such restriction does not apply for heirs. Second, an heir having indirect rights only might still need to demonstrate his or her claim on the estate in another country if, for example, he or she would like to take out a loan and needs to provide a security.[18] It therefore cannot be argued that an indirect beneficiary of the entire estate would have no legal interest in the use of an ECS.[19]

B. Legatees Having Direct Rights in the Succession

7. Legatees are persons who have a right not in the entire estate, but only in certain rights or assets belonging to it. An ECS can only be issued to legatees having direct rights in the succession. Legatees having only indirect rights are excluded. Legatees under German law are thus, for example, not eligible to an ECS, as according to section 2174 BGB, they merely acquire a claim upon the heirs.[20] It could be argued, however, that claims under the law of obligations may also be understood as 'direct rights', as such claims can by asserted directly by the legatee against the heir and article 63.1 ESR does not explicitly define 'direct rights' as 'rights *in rem*' compared to rights under the law of obligations.[21] However, it results from the third sentence of recital 47 of the ESR that 'direct rights' are to be understood as direct shares in the estate, and that the mere claims against the heirs a legatee may acquire under certain national laws cannot be qualified as 'direct rights' in the sense of the ESR. Thus, only vindication legacies[22] as for example under French law[23] can be

[18] This example is taken from Nordmeier, 'Art. 63 EuErbVO', para. 4.

[19] Nordmeier, 'Art. 63 EuErbVO', para. 4.

[20] Nordmeier, 'Art. 63 EuErbVO', para. 5; Dutta, 'Art. 63 EuErbVO', para. 9.

[21] Cf. Wautelet, 'Article 63', p. 722, who states that the notion of 'direct rights' excludes in particular those persons who could assert rights only in a subsequent succession after the death of one heir in the actual succession, as in the case of grandchildren, for example; cf. also Lange, 'Das Europäische Nachlasszeugnis', para. 7.

[22] Cf. J. Kleinschmidt, 'Optionales Erbrecht – Das Europäische Nachlasszeugnis als Herausforderung an das Kollisionsrecht', *RabelsZ* (2013), p. 759; *id.*, 'Art. 63 EuErbVO', para. 10; K. W. Lange, 'Europäisches Nachlasszeugnis – Antragsverfahren und Verwendung im deutschen Grundbuchverkehr', *Deutsche Notar-Zeitschrift* (2016), p. 105; M. Buschbaum, 'Europäisches Nachlasszeugnis und Annahme öffentlicher Urkunden – neue Mechanismen zur grenzüberschreitenden Nachlassabwicklung und ihr Verhältnis zum materiellen Sachenrecht', in J. Hager (ed), *Die neue europäische Erbrechtsverordnung* (2013), p. 50 *et seq.*

[23] Cf. article 1014 of the French *code civil.*

subsumed under article 63.1. In contrast, a civil law legatee as under German law may not have certified his or her position by an ECS.[24] Article 37.1 of the Commission's Proposal for the ESR had, by the way, granted the entitlement to an ECS to any legatee, regardless of his or her 'direct' or only 'indirect' rights in the succession. The explicit limitation to vindication legatees has only been inserted in the course of the deliberations within the council.[25]

C. *Executors of Wills*

8. The third group of persons involved in a succession by whom the ECS is principally for use, are executors of wills. Neither in the ESR nor in other sources of EU law is there any explicit explanation of the EU concept of that term. The judgment of the ECJ of 6 December 2007[26] provides no clarification either, for the case merely dealt with the qualification under EU VAT provisions of an executor of will whose powers follow specifically from German law.[27] The starting point of the interpretation of the notion has therefore been its wording in the various official languages of the EU that are authentic and authoritative in equal measure.[28] Some examples for the denotation in other official languages of what is called executors of will in English are *exécuteurs testamentaires* in French, *Testamentsvollstrecker* in German, *esecutori testamentari* in Italian, *ejecutores testamentarios* in Spanish and *executeurs-testamentair* in Dutch.

9. All these denotations have in common that the part of the respective expression corresponding to the English 'executors' all imply the performance of an action related to a specific purpose. Thus, the notions of 'executors', 'exécuteurs', 'Vollstrecker' etc. contain two elements: one

[24] J. Schmidt, 'Der Erbnachweis in Deutschland ab 2015: Erbschein vs. Europäisches Nachlasszeugnis', *ZEV* (2014), p. 391; Schmidt, 'Art. 63 EuErbVO', para. 8; Nordmeier, 'Art. 63 EuErbVO', para. 5; Dutta, 'Art. 63 EuErbVO', para. 9; Fornasier, 'Art. 63 EuErbVO', para. 9 *et seq.*; cf. H. Wilsch, 'EuErbVO: Die Verordnung in der deutschen Grundbuchpraxis', *ZEV* (2012), p. 530; critical to this limitation A. Perscha, 'Art 63 EuErbVO', in A. Deixler-Hübner and M. Schauer (eds), *EuErbVO – Kommentar zur EU-Erbrechtsverordnung* (Wien, 2015), para. 24.

[25] Schmidt, 'Art. 63 EuErbVO', para. 8.

[26] ECJ, Case C-401/06, *Commission* v. *Germany* [2007] ECR I-10609.

[27] ECJ, Case C-401/06, *Commission* v. *Germany* [2007] ECR I-10609, para. 35 *et seq.*; Dutta, 'Art. 63 EuErbVO', para. 10, footnote 14.

[28] Cf. Kreße, 'Die Auslegung mehrsprachiger Texte durch den EuGH', p. 157 *et seq.*; Kreße, 'Mehrsprachigkeit im Recht der Europäischen Union', p. 11 *et seq.*; see also Schmidt, 'Art. 63 EuErbVO', para. 9.

element of action, and one reference point for this action; for example, the course of action supposedly performed by the executor stands not on its own, but needs to refer to *something* that is to be implemented, like e.g. a decision or a plan or a will.

10. Furthermore, the previously-mentioned language versions of the English term 'executors of will' have in common the point of reference of the respective persons' activities. The 'will' is the object that needs to be executed, or the 'testament' synonymous with 'will' in the context of the ESR. Therefore, an executor of will is a person that takes a course of action directed to implement the stipulations of a last will. A third element of the term 'executor of will' is the fact that the person invested with this function has to have certain 'powers', 'pouvoirs', 'Befugnisse', 'poteri', 'facultades' or 'bevoegdheden' in order to be an executor of will in the sense of the ESR. He or she thus must be entitled to exert at least some administrative rights on the estate in order to effectively implement the will of the *de cujus* as recorded in the testament.[29] That can be for example a personal representative or a trustee of a testamentary trust[30] according to the legal systems of common law[31], a German 'Testamentsvollstrecker' appointed by the *de cujus* in his or her testament according to section 2197 BGB, or a 'mandataire' in the sense of article 812 *et seq.* of the French civil code who can receive a simple warrant of attorney by the *de cujus* to administer the estate,[32] and thus exerts the administrative powers conferred by the mandate as far as these are not conflicting with the powers of an *exécuteur testamentaire* in the sense of article 1025 *et seq.* of the French civil code. It is not necessary that the executor be sole executor. Also co-executors are executors in the sense of article 63 ESR.[33]

D. *Administrators of the Estate*

11. The last type of persons on whose behalf an ECS may be issued are the administrators of the estate. The ESR does not contain any definition of this term, neither is the notion conceptualised in any other provision of EU law. The English version of the Commission's green paper 'Successions and Wills' does not give any definition of the administrator

[29] Cf. Dutta, 'Art. 63 EuErbVO', para. 10.

[30] In this sense explicitly the Commission's green paper 'Succession and Wills', p. 10.

[31] Cf. Verbeke and Leleu, 'Harmonization of the Law of Succession in Europe', p. 465; Kegel, 'Erbfolge und Vermächtnis', p. 357.

[32] Dutta, 'Art. 63 EuErbVO', para. 10.

[33] Dutta, 'Art. 63 EuErbVO', para. 10.

of the estate, either. Indeed, it does not even make use of the term 'administrator', but employs the term 'executor'. Other language versions of the green paper seem more helpful: The German version, for example, defines the 'Nachlassverwalter' (i.e. 'administrators of the estate' in the sense of the English language version of article 63 ESR that in its German version also employs the term 'Nachlassverwalter') as a third party charged with the administration or liquidation of the estate.[34] The Dutch version ('beheerders') correlates exactly. In the French, Italian and Spanish versions, the green paper uses the terms 'tiers administrateurs', 'terzi amministratori' or 'terceros administradores' (in English: 'third-party administrators of the estate'), respectively. This is exactly the terminology used in article 37 of the Commission's Proposal of the ESR corresponding thematically to article 63 ESR in its final version. However, the above-mentioned definitions of the 'Nachlassverwalter' and the 'beheerders' make it clear that also the German and Dutch versions of the green paper refer to third-party administrators only, thus excluding beneficiaries of the estate, as does article 37 of the Proposal of the ESR which – in its German version[35] – refers to 'Fremdverwalter'.

12. However, it results from article 29.1, subparagraph 2, ESR that administrators of the estate are not necessarily third-party administrators, but can also be beneficiaries of the estate [see art. 29 no. 16].[36] Apart from that, the definition of the administrator given by the German, French, Italian, Spanish and Dutch versions of the green paper can be used to define the notion.[37] Thus, an administrator of the estate is a party charged with the administration or liquidation of the estate. It results from article 29.2, subparagraph 2, ESR that the administrator of the estate should have powers to preserve the assets of the estate and to protect the rights of creditors and guarantors [see art. 29 nos. 17–18].[38]

13. The previously-mentioned definition also fits to executors of will. Therefore, the exact distinction between executors of will and administrators of the estate merits some remarks. A starting point of the discussion can be article 29 ESR which, according to its headline, deals with

[34] German version of the Commission's green paper 'Succession and Wills', p. 10: 'Die Bestellung eines Dritten zur Verwaltung oder Abwicklung des Nachlasses (im Folgenden "Nachlassverwalter") . . .'.

[35] The Dutch version of the proposal has not been published; available only are the English, French and German versions. Cf. http://ec.europa.eu/civiljustice/news/docs/succession_proposal_for_regulation_nl.pdf (last accessed 7 July 2016).

[36] Nordmeier, 'Art. 63 EuErbVO', para. 7.

[37] Cf. Nordmeier, 'Art. 63 EuErbVO', para. 7, with reference to the German version only.

[38] Cf. Nordmeier, 'Art. 63 EuErbVO', para. 7.

several aspects concerning administrators of the estate. Article 29.1, subparagraph 2, then disposes that the administrators shall be entitled to execute the will of the deceased and/or to administer the estate. This clearly shows that executors of will are supposed to be a subtype of administrators of the estate in the sense of the ESR, the more so as the ESR does not contain any provision similar to its article 29 dealing with executors of will only.[39] Point (f) of article 23 ESR is even more explicit, as it refers to 'the executors of the wills and other administrators of the estate' [see art. 23 no. 11].[40] The administrator of the estate thus is the superordinate concept, including executors of will as well as other administrators.[41] The fact that the different language versions of the green paper (cf. *supra* at no. 11) mention either the 'executor' (English version) or the 'administrator' (e.g. German, Italian, Spanish and Dutch versions), while obviously meaning the same group of people, supports this interpretation. The difference between executors of wills and other administrators of the estate is that the former have been authorised by the *de cujus* to administer the estate, whereas the latter have been authorised independently of any will of the *de cujus*, but rather by law or by appointment of the competent authority.[42]

III. Objective Requirements of Use

A. Need to Invoke the Status or to Exercise the Rights or Powers Relating to the Estate

14. Article 63.1 enounces the two alternative objective requirements[43] for the use of an ECS by the previously-mentioned status holders: The status holders must either need to invoke their status or they must need to exercise their rights as heirs or legatees or to exercise their powers as executors of wills or administrators of the estate. This gives reason to two remarks: First, one of the key words of the provision is the word 'need'. There must be a necessity for the status holders to invoke their status or to exercise their rights or powers.[44] 'Need' is

39 Schmidt, 'Art. 63 EuErbVO', para. 9; Nordmeier, 'Art. 63 EuErbVO', para. 7.

40 Cf. Schmidt, 'Art. 63 EuErbVO', para. 9.

41 Cf. Schmidt, 'Art. 63 EuErbVO', para. 9; Nordmeier, 'Art. 63 EuErbVO', para. 7.

42 Cf. Dutta, 'Art. 63 EuErbVO', para. 11; Fornasier, 'Art. 63 EuErbVO', para. 18.

43 Doubting that these are mandatory requirements that must be considered by the issuing authority: Lange, 'Das Europäische Nachlasszeugnis', para. 7.

44 P. Wautelet, 'Article 62', in Bonomi and Wautelet, *Le droit européen des successions. Commentaire du Règlement n° 650/2012 du 4 juillet 2012* (Bruxelles, 2013) p. 709.

however not to be understood as a legal obligation, but rather in a subjective sense, so that already the mere intention to invoke their status or to exercise their rights or powers is sufficient.[45] Furthermore, the status holders must have to have the intention to make use of the certificate in order to demonstrate their position,[46] and the demonstration of their position must be objectively necessary according to the contentions of the applicant. These contentions must be supported, however, by a minimum of evidence in order to make the allegation plausible;[47] elsewise there would be no 'need' for the ECS. It is not necessary to demonstrate that a dispute is coming up.[48]

15. Second, the relation between the alternative requirements just mentioned is not obvious. It is held that the invocation of the status is the superordinate concept with respect to the exercise of the rights or powers related to that status.[49] This is not convincing: A status holder will be led only to invoke that status if he or she wants to exercise the rights or powers related to it. Otherwise, i.e. without exercising those rights or powers, the invocation of the status and therefore the presentation of the ECS is not necessary, there is no need in the sense of article 63 ESR. Thus, in the meaning of article 63 ESR, both alternatives are synonymous; they are different ways to express the same thing.

B. In Another Member State

16. The status holder must have the intention to use the ECS in another Member State than the state of issuance.[50] The 'need' to invoke the status, understood in a subjective sense [see *supra* at no. 14], must therefore relate to a cross-border situation. If a cross-border situation is however objectively unconceivable in the concrete matter because it is evidently sufficient to implement the legal status of the persons mentioned in article 63 ESR only in the Member State that is competent to issue the ECS according to article 64 ESR, the ECS must not be issued [see art. 62 no. 8 *et seq.*].[51] The demands on the requirement of a cross-border

[45] Wautelet, 'Article 63', pp. 720–721; Schmidt, 'Art. 63 EuErbVO', para. 19; Nordmeier, Art. 63 EuErbVO', para. 9.
[46] Schmidt, 'Art. 63 EuErbVO', para. 19; Nordmeier, 'Art. 63 EuErbVO', para. 9.
[47] Wautelet, 'Article 63', pp. 720–721; *id.*, 'Article 62', p. 709.
[48] Wautelet, 'Article 63', pp. 720–721. [49] Nordmeier, 'Art. 63 EuErbVO', para. 9.
[50] Schmidt, 'Art. 63 EuErbVO', para. 20; Nordmeier, 'Art. 63 EuErbVO', para. 9.
[51] Schmidt, 'Art. 63 EuErbVO', para. 21; cf. Nordmeier, 'Art. 63 EuErbVO', para. 9; Dutta, 'Art. 63 EuErbVO', para. 3.

situation should not be too high.[52] Although most often, an ECS will be needed because part of the estate is situated in a Member State other than the state of issuance[53], this is not a prerequisite.[54] It is not sufficient, however, that the applicant has his or her habitual residence in another Member State if all of the estate is located in the state of issuance: In this case, a national certificate would fully serve the applicant's purposes.[55] This is different if the status holder demonstrates that he or she seeks to bring any assets of the estate into another Member State in order to alienate them there[56], or if he or she needs the ECS to establish whether there are any assets of the estate located abroad.[57]

17. The issuance of an ECS is not prevented by the intention of the applicant to use the ECS in the Member State of issuance, as long as there is also intention to use it in another Member State.[58] Likewise, the issuance of an ECS does not become inadmissible *a posteriori* if the status holder who had the intention to establish his or her position (also) in another Member State, makes use of the ECS only in the state of issuance.[59]

C. *Examples Mentioned in Article 63.2*

18. Article 63.2 ESR contains examples of a possible intended use of an ECS. The list is not exhaustive, as is shown by the wording 'in particular' in the beginning of the paragraph.[60] Point (a) provides for the utilisation in order to demonstrate the status of heir or legatee, including the respective share of the estate. The phrasing is somewhat unclear, as it suggests that a legatee's shares of the estate could also be demonstrated

[52] Dutta, 'Art. 63 EuErbVO', para. 20; Schmidt, 'Art. 63 EuErbVO', para. 21; Wautelet, 'Article 63', pp. 720–721; P. Lagarde, 'Les principes de base du nouveau règlement européen sur les successions', *Rev crit dr int priv* (2012), p. 726.

[53] Kleinschmidt, 'Optionales Erbrecht', p. 746.

[54] Wautelet, 'Article 63', pp. 720–721; R. Süß, 'Das Europäische Nachlasszeugnis', *ZEuP* (2013), p. 738.

[55] Kleinschmidt, 'Optionales Erbrecht', p. 746.

[56] Dutta, 'Art. 63 EuErbVO', para. 20; Lagarde, 'Les principes de base', p. 726; undecided Kleinschmidt, 'Optionales Erbrecht', p. 746, footnote 119.

[57] Süß, 'Das Europäische Nachlasszeugnis', p. 738; cf. for all of the preceeding in particular Dutta, 'Art. 63 EuErbVO', para. 20.

[58] Schmidt, 'Art. 63 EuErbVO', para. 22.

[59] Schmidt, 'Art. 63 EuErbVO', para. 22; cf. S. Frodl, 'Einheit durch Aufgabe nationaler Rechtstraditionen? – EU-Erbrechtsverordnung kundgemacht', *Österreichische Juristen-Zeitung* (2012), p. 957.

[60] Wautelet, 'Article 63', p. 723.

with an ECS. This is, however, not possible, as legatees do not have rights into the estate as a whole, and therefore no shares of the estate as such, but have only rights into certain rights or assets of the estate [see *supra* at no. 7).[61] But the ESR can demonstrate the mere fact that someone is a legatee with direct rights in the succession. A further syntactical ambiguity results from the fact that the phrase 'mentioned in the Certificate' refers immediately only to the word 'legatee' and not to the word 'heir'. It therefore could be concluded that those heirs that are not mentioned in the ECS could also demonstrate their status by means of the ECS. This is, however, not the case, as it is not conceivable to establish a fact by means of a document if this document is silent on that very fact.[62]

19. As the legal position of legatees is characterised by the fact that their rights in the succession refer to specific assets of the estate, it is obvious that the ECS should be able to be used to demonstrate the attribution of such assets to any vindication legatee mentioned in the ECS. Accordingly, this is part of the normative content of point (b) of article 63.2 ESR.[63] The other part of the provision indicates that the attribution of specific assets to heirs can also be demonstrated by means of an ECS. This also results from point (l) of article 68 ESR [see art. 68]. The attribution of assets to an heir, if he or she is not a legatee at the same time, can mainly result from provisions on how to separate the estate established in the last will.[64] For example, under German law, such instructions of the *de cujus* are provided for in section 2048 BGB. However, in order to be able to be certified in an ECS, such instructions have to have direct effect; thus, the heir to whom a specific asset has been given in the last will, must have been conferred a right *in rem* to this regard,[65] which is not the case concerning section 2048 BGB.[66] The fact that an asset belonged to the deceased and thus makes part of the estate cannot be certified in an ECS according to the third sentence of recital 71 of the ESR, as this question concerns an element which is not governed by the ESR.[67]

[61] Dutta, 'Art. 63 EuErbVO', para. 13; Nordmeier, 'Art. 63 EuErbVO', para. 10.

[62] Nordmeier, 'Art. 63 EuErbVO', para. 10. [63] Dutta, 'Art. 63 EuErbVO', para. 15.

[64] Dutta, 'Art. 63 EuErbVO', para. 16; Nordmeier, 'Art. 63 EuErbVO', para. 10, footnote 20.

[65] Dutta, 'Art. 63 EuErbVO', para. 16; U. Simon and M. Buschbaum, 'Die neue EU-Erbrechtsverordnung', NJW (2012), p. 2397; *contra:* M. Schauer, 'Europäisches Nachlasszeugnis', in M. Schauer and E. Scheuba (eds), *Europäische Erbrechtsverordnung* (Vienna, 2012), p. 83.

[66] Fornasier, 'Art. 63 EuErbVO', para. 37. [67] Dutta, 'Art. 63 EuErbVO', para. 18.

20. Point (c) of article 63.2 indicates that the powers of the person mentioned in the ECS to execute the will or administer the estate may also be demonstrated by means of an ECS. This refers, of course, on the one hand to the powers of the executors of will or administrators of the estate. Yet it also refers to the powers of the heirs if they are entitled themselves to administer the estate,[68] as the wording of article 37.1 of the Commission's Proposal for an ESR taking into account 'third-party' administrators only, has not been assumed in article 63.1 ESR [see *supra* at no. 11 *et seq.*].

[68] For example, in German law according to section 2038 BGB; Dutta, 'Art. 63 EuErbVO', para. 19; Nordmeier, 'Art. 63 EuErbVO', para. 10.

Article 64

Competence to Issue the Certificate

BERNHARD KREẞE

The Certificate shall be issued in the Member State whose courts have jurisdiction under Article 4, Article 7, Article 10 or Article 11. The issuing authority shall be:
(a) a court as defined in Article 3(2); or
(b) another authority which, under national law, has competence to deal with matters of succession.

Summary

I. PURPOSE OF THE PROVISION *page* 699
II. FIRST SENTENCE OF ARTICLE 64 ESR 700
A. Generalities 700
B. General and Subsidiary Competence 701
C. Competence in the Event of a Choice of Law 702
1. Article 7(a) ESR and Article 6 ESR 703
2. Article 7(b) ESR and Article 5 ESR 705
3. Article 7(c) ESR and Article 5 ESR 706
D. *Forum necessitatis* 707
E. Other Provisions Concerning International Competence 708
III. SECOND SENTENCE OF ARTICLE 64 ESR 709

I. Purpose of the Provision

1. Article 64 ESR governs the competence for the issuance of a European Certificate of Succession (ECS). The first sentence of the provision covers the issue of international competence. The reference made to the articles 4, 7, 10 and 11 ESR is intended to ensure synchronisation between international competence for the issuance of ECS and international jurisdiction in matters of succession,[1] as recital 70 ESR explicitly

[1] J. Schmidt, 'Art. 64 EuErbVO', in C. Budzikiewicz, M.-P. Weller and W. Wurmnest (eds), *Beck-Online Großkommentar, EuErbVO* (München, 2016), para. 3; *id.*, 'Der Erbnachweis in Deutschland ab 2015: Erbschein vs. Europäisches Nachlasszeugnis', *ZEV* (2014), p. 390;

clarifies, and thus a synchronisation between *forum* and *jus*.[2] The second sentence of article 64 ESR deals with the subordinate question of internal competence, e.g. which body within the competent Member State shall have local, substantial and functional competence to issue an ECS, once international competence has been established in the certain matter.

II. First Sentence of Article 64 ESR

A. Generalities

2. The first sentence of article 64 ESR starts with the self-evident clarification that only Member States can be internationally competent to issue an ECS. Which Member State is internationally competent is to be determined largely according to the provisions on international jurisdiction, as laid down in chapter II of the ESR. It must be noted, however, that article 64 ESR does not refer to chapter II as a whole. The provision rather lists only very specific rules of jurisdiction that shall be applied also to determine the international competence for the issuance of an ECS. As a result, provisions other than those mentioned explicitly in article 64 ESR must not be applied in that matter, unless they are referred to in turn by these, as is the case with articles 5 and 6 ESR.[3] A second general remark that should be made is that the relevant provisions of chapter II do not necessarily fit precisely to the procedure concerning the issuance of an ECS,[4] as the rules on jurisdiction are largely construed for the resolution of disputes involving two or more

C. F. Nordmeier, 'Art. 64 EuErbVO', in R. Hüßtege and H.-P. Mansel (eds), *NomosKommentar, BGB, Rom-Verordnungen*, vol. VI, 2nd ed. (Baden-Baden, 2015), para. 1; A. Dutta, 'Art. 64 EuErbVO', in J. von Hein (ed), *Münchener Kommentar zum Bürgerlichen Gesetzbuch*, vol. X, 6th ed. (München, 2015), para. 2; P. Wautelet, 'Article 64', in A. Bonomi and P. Wautelet, *Le droit européen des successions. Commentaire du Règlement n° 650/2012 du 4 juillet 2012* (Bruxelles, 2013), p. 727; J. Kleinschmidt, 'Optionales Erbrecht –Das Europäische Nachlasszeugnis als Herausforderung an das Kollisionsrecht', *RabelsZ* (2013), p. 768.

[2] Schmidt, 'Art. 64 EuErbVO', para. 3, 5; *id.*, 'Der Erbnachweis in Deutschland ab 2015', p. 390; M. Fornasier, 'Art. 64 EuErbVO', in A. Dutta and J. Weber (eds), *Internationales Erbrecht – EuErbVO, Erbrechtliche Staatsverträge, EGBGB, IntErbRVG, IntErbStR, IntSchenkungsR* (München, 2016), para. 3; F. Sturm and G. Sturm, 'Das europäische Nachlasszeugnis – Zum Vorschlag der Kommission vom 14. Oktober 2009', *Zbornik Pravnog fakulteta u Zagrebu* (2012), p. 335 *et seq.*

[3] Nordmeier, 'Art. 64 EuErbVO', para. 2; cf. C. Dorsel, 'Europäische Erbrechtsverordnung und Europäisches Nachlasszeugnis', *Europäische Zeitschrift für die Steuer- und Erbrechtspraxis* (2014), p. 213; *contra:* Dutta, 'Art. 64 EuErbVO', para. 8.

[4] Cf. Dutta, 'Art. 64 EuErbVO', para. 2.

persons, whereas the ECS is a document that can be applied for individually by any person having a legal interest as concretised in articles 65 and 63 ESR, without there being necessarily any additional person involved. This has to be taken into consideration when interpreting the rules on jurisdiction while applying article 64 ESR. Thus, the rules on international jurisdiction can only be applied *mutatis mutandis* in matters of issuance of an ECS.

B. *General and Subsidiary Competence*

3. The first sentence of article 64 ESR refers to the general and subsidiary jurisdiction of the courts of the Member States as laid down in articles 4 and 10 ESR. Thus, the competence of the Member States for the issuance of ECS also follows the prerequisites mentioned in these provisions. Article 4 ESR does not raise specific problems in relation to ECS.[5] An ECS concerning the whole estate – if necessary for the purpose demonstrated by the applicant in accordance with point (f) of article 65.3 ESR and with article 63 ESR – can be issued in the Member State where the *de cujus* had his or her habitual residence at the time of death [see art. 4 no. 4 *et seq.*].[6]

4. With respect to the application of article 10.1 ESR, specific problems in relation with ECS do not appear, either. Under the conditions specified in that provision, the articles 64 and 10.1 ESR confer competence to the courts or authorities of a Member State to issue an ECS, even in case the deceased had no habitual residence in any Member State at the time of death, but had his or her habitual residence in a third state. Article 10.1 ESR sets up three conditions, of which the first one has to be fulfilled imperatively: The ECS can be issued only in a Member State in which assets of the estate are located.[7] If the deceased had the nationality of one of these states at the time of death, the courts and authorities of this state have exclusive international competence in accordance with point (a) of article 10.1. If the deceased has the nationalities of several Member States in which assets of the estates are located, the ECS may be issued in any of these states [see art. 10 nos. 12–13].

[5] Wautelet, 'Article 64', p. 728.

[6] Cf. Wautelet, 'Article 64', p. 728; M. Buschbaum and U. Simon, 'EuErbVO: Das Europäische Nachlasszeugnis', *ZEV* (2012), p. 526; Dorsel, 'Europäische Erbrechtsverordnung', p. 213; Kleinschmidt, 'Optionales Erbrecht', p. 768; Nordmeier, 'Art. 64 EuErbVO', para. 3; Dutta, 'Art. 64 EuErbVO', para. 3; for details see R. Süß, 'Das Europäische Nachlasszeugnis', *ZEuP* (2013), p. 731 *et seq.*

[7] Nordmeier, 'Art. 64 EuErbVO', para. 4.

5. (Only) if no nationality of the deceased corresponds to a Member State in which assets of the estate are located, international competence of the courts or authorities of a Member State may result from point (b) of article 10.1 ESR. Thus, the ECS may be issued in the Member State in which assets of the estate are located and where the deceased had his or her previous habitual residence, provided that at the time of the application of the ECS (corresponding to the seisure of the court mentioned in the provision) a period of not more than five years has elapsed since that habitual residence changed and the applicant thus established his or her habitual residence in a third state.[8] In all the alternatives mentioned in article 10.1 ESR, the ECS can relate to the entire succession and not only to the assets located in the state of issuance, if necessary [see art. 10 nos. 14–16].[9]

6. If article 10.1 ESR does not lead to any Member State in which the ECS may be issued for the succession as a whole, article 10.2 ESR has to be applied. It is thus still possible to apply for and be issued an ECS. However, each Member State is then only entitled to issue an ECS related to the assets located in it [see art. 10 nos. 17–20].[10] This poses problems with respect to articles 62.1 and 63.1 ESR, as ECS may only be issued for use in another Member State [ref: art. 62 no. 8 *et seq.*; art. 63 no. 16 *et seq.*].[11] Nevertheless, this is conceivable if, for example, the applicant for an ECS has the intention to transfer assets of the estate into another Member State in order to alienate them there [see art. 63 no. 17],[12] or if a person who has acquired shares of a domestic partnership by succession needs to prove that acquisition in order to establish power of representation in a foreign trial.[13]

C. *Competence in the Event of a Choice of Law*

7. Article 64 ESR refers explicitly also to article 7 ESR which provides for an international jurisdiction – and therefore also for an international

[8] Nordmeier, 'Art. 64 EuErbVO', para. 4.

[9] Nordmeier, 'Art. 64 EuErbVO', para. 2; Wautelet, 'Article 64', p. 729.

[10] Wautelet, 'Article 64', p. 729; Nordmeier, 'Art. 64 EuErbVO', para. 4.

[11] Süß, 'Das Europäische Nachlasszeugnis', p. 735.

[12] A. Dutta, 'Art. 63 EuErbVO', in J. von Hein (ed), *Münchener Kommentar zum Bürgerlichen Gesetzbuch*, vol. X, 6th ed. (München, 2015), para. 20; P. Lagarde, 'Les principes de base du nouveau règlement européen sur les successions', *Rev crit dr int priv* (2012), p. 726; cf. Nordmeier, 'Art. 64 EuErbVO', para. 4, footnote 7; *contra:* Süß, 'Das Europäische Nachlasszeugnis', p. 735; undecided: Kleinschmidt, 'Optionales Erbrecht', p. 746, footnote 119.

[13] Dutta, 'Art. 64 EuErbVO', para. 3.

competence in matters of issuance of ECS – in the event of a choice of law by the *de cujus*.[14] The purpose of this provision is to synchronise the applicable law and the international jurisdiction or competence.[15] Thus, the courts or authorities of a Member State whose law had been chosen by the deceased pursuant to article 22 ESR, are competent to issue an ECS if one of the alternatives mentioned in points (a) to (c) of article 7 ESR is fulfilled.[16]

1. Article 7(a) ESR and Article 6 ESR

8. Article 7(a) ESR refers to article 6 ESR [see art. 7 nos 1–2 and 5–7]. Therefore, if the application of issuance of an ECS has been submitted to a court or authority according to the general and subsidiary rules of international competence laid down in the articles 4 and 10 ESR, the court or authority may decline its international competence in view of the choice of law of the deceased.[17] In this case, the ECS may be issued in the Member State whose law had been chosen by the deceased pursuant to article 64 and article 7(a) ESR. The question is, of course, which persons are to be regarded as 'parties to the proceedings' in the sense of article 6 ESR in matters of ECS, as the decline of jurisdiction and therefore competence is only possible upon request of one of the parties to the proceedings or in case of an 'agreement' of positive choice of jurisdiction according to article 5 ESR by the parties to the proceedings.

9. First of all, it is clear that the person applying for an ECS according to article 65.1 ESR is a party to the proceedings, as he or she has instituted them. Furthermore, it is at least conceivable that all beneficiaries of the application for an ECS can be regarded as parties, as article 66.4 ESR orders their information of the application, and as they also have to be informed of the issuance of the ECS according to article 67.2 ESR. Even further, the persons mentioned in article 72.1 ESR might be parties to the proceedings, i.e. all persons entitled to apply for an ECS, as they may challenge the decision of the issuing authority. It is clear that all these

[14] Cf. about legal aspects of choice of law: C. F. Nordmeier, 'Grundfragen der Rechtswahl in der neuen EU-Erbrechtsverordnung – eine Untersuchung des Art. 22 ErbRVO', *GPR: Zeitschrift für das Privatrecht der Europäischen Union* (2013), p. 148.

[15] Schmidt, 'Art. 64 EuErbVO', para. 3; *id.*, 'Der Erbnachweis in Deutschland ab 2015', p. 390; Sturm and Sturm, 'Das europäische Nachlasszeugnis', p. 335 *et seq.*; C. Dorsel, 'Art. 64 EuErbVO', in R. Geimer and R. Schütze (eds), *Internationaler Rechtsverkehr in Zivil- und Handelssachen*, vol. III (München, 2015), para. 1; cf. Wautelet, 'Article 64', p. 728.

[16] Wautelet, 'Article 64', p. 728.

[17] J. Kleinschmidt, 'Art. 64 EuErbVO', in M. Würdinger (ed), *Juris Praxiskommentar BGB, Internationales Privatrecht*, vol. VI, 7th ed. (Saarbrücken, 2014), para. 16.

persons must be entitled to present their observations and thus invoke their rights and prevent the issuance of an incorrect ECS. However, this mere entitlement cannot by itself qualify these persons to be 'parties to the proceedings', as this conceptually presupposes a formal participation or involvement in the proceedings. Hence, none of the persons mentioned in the articles 66.4, 67.2 or 72.1 ESR are already parties to the proceedings by the mere fact that they may have a substantial interest in the outcome of the procedure of application and issuance of an ECS. This procedure is by nature unilateral, unless joined by other persons.[18]

10. The counter-opinion that argues in favour of a wide concept of parties to the proceedings[19] disregards that this concept is not synonymous with the 'parties concerned' referred to in article 5 ESR.[20] The parties concerned in the sense of article 5 ESR may – in the scope of article 64 ESR – well comprehend all possible beneficiaries, persons involved and possible applicants that are mentioned in articles 66.4, 67.2 and 72.1 ESR.[21] The notion of the parties concerned must be, however, wider than that of the parties to the proceedings, as article 5 ESR does not presuppose that any proceedings have been instituted already. Therefore, in order to assume that a party is 'concerned' by the ECS, it is sufficient that that person is only potentially a party to later proceedings. Thus, for the application of article 6(a) ESR, it is of course not sufficient that any 'party concerned' requests a decline of jurisdiction or competence; the request must emanate precisely from a 'party to the proceedings', i.e. a party formally involved. Similarly, it is not sufficient for the application of point (b) of article 6 ESR that any parties concerned have concluded a choice-of-court agreement according to article 5 ESR; the agreement must have been concluded specifically by the parties to the proceedings.

11. Therefore, for the purposes of the issuance of an ECS and thus the application of article 64 ESR, the term 'parties to the proceedings' in the sense of article 6 ESR has to be understood as follows: Until none of

[18] Wautelet, 'Article 64', p. 729.

[19] Dutta, 'Art. 64 EuErbVO', para. 5; cf. A. Perscha, 'Art 64 EuErbVO', in A. Deixler-Hübner and M. Schauer (eds), *EuErbVO – Kommentar zur EU-Erbrechtsverordnung* (Vienna, 2015), para. 18.

[20] *Contra:* A. Dutta, 'Art. 5 EuErbVO', in J. von Hein (ed) *Münchener Kommentar zum Bürgerlichen Gesetzbuch*, vol. X, 6th ed. (München, 2015), para. 6.

[21] Cf. with respect to the wide the notion of 'parties concerned': M. Makowsky, 'Art. 5 EuErbVO', in R. Hüßtege and H.-P. Mansel (eds), *NomosKommentar, BGB, Rom-Verordnungen*, vol. VI, 2nd ed. (Baden-Baden, 2015), para. 17; J. Schmidt, 'Art. 5 EuErbVO', in C. Budzikiewicz, M.-P. Weller and W. Wurmnest (eds), *Beck-Online Großkommentar, EuErbVO* (München, 2016), para. 6; see also recital 28 of the ESR.

the beneficiaries or persons entitled to challenge the decision of the issuing authority have declared their intention to join the proceedings,[22] the applicant for the ECS is the only party in the proceedings. The intention to participate in the procedure does not necessarily have to be declared explicitly, as it can also result implicitly from the fact that the person in question submits observations opposing the issuance of the ECS with the requested content at least partly. From that moment, this person may, like the applicant, submit a request in accordance with article 64, article 7(a) and article 6(a) ESR that the authority dealing with the matter declines its competence. If he or she has concluded a choice-of-court agreement with the applicant, the authority would likewise decline its competence according to article 6(b) ESR, with the consequence that the issuing authorities of the Member State whose law had been chosen by the deceased shall be internationally competent pursuant to article 64 and article 7(a) ESR. This solution respects the right to be heard as laid down article 41.2 of the Charter of Fundamental Rights of the European Union[23] also with respect to the persons concerned by the decision about the issuance of an ECS.[24]

2. Article 7(b) ESR and Article 5 ESR

12. Article 7(b) ESR refers to article 5 ESR [see art. 7 nos. 3–4]. If the parties to the proceedings have agreed, in accordance with article 5 ESR, to confer jurisdiction on a court or the courts of the Member State whose law had been chosen by the deceased, the ECS shall be issued in that Member State. Two remarks are to be made in this context: First of all, it is not sufficient that the parties to the proceedings have concluded an isolated agreement just conferring international competence for the issuance of ECS to the authorities of the Member State whose law had been chosen by the *de cujus*. The wording of article 5 ESR makes it clear that there must be an agreement conferring exclusive jurisdiction to rule on any succession matter.[25]

13. Second, the question arises again what is meant by 'parties to the proceedings'. The solution is the same as has been discussed *supra* at

[22] Cf. Max Planck Institute for Comparative and International Private Law, 'Comments on the European Commission's Proposal for a Regulation of the European Parliament and of the Council on jurisdiction, applicable law, recognition and enforcement of decisions and authentic instruments in matters of succession and the creation of a European Certificate of Succession', *RabelsZ* (2010), p. 686.

[23] OJ 2012 no. C326, 26 October 2012, p. 391; cf. also article 47 of the Charter of Fundamental Rights.

[24] Cf. recital 81 ESR; see also Dutta, 'Art. 64 EuErbVO', para. 5.

[25] Nordmeier, 'Art. 64 EuErbVO', para. 6.

no. 8 *et seq.* with respect to article 7(a) ESR and article 6 ESR. Although article 7(b) ESR refers to article 5 ESR and article 5.1 ESR explicitly mentions the possibility of the conclusion of a choice-of-court agreement by the parties concerned, the notion of 'parties concerned' is wider than the concept of 'parties to the proceedings' mentioned in article 7(b) ESR. Only if the parties to the proceedings have concluded an agreement pursuant to article 5 ESR, the international competence of the issuing authorities of the Member State whose law had been chosen by the deceased may be founded on article 7(b) ESR. This means that as long as the applicant is the only party to the proceedings (cf. *supra* at no. 11), article 7(b) ESR cannot be applied, as agreements cannot be concluded by a single person. The applicant would however be able to induce the international competence of the issuing authority that has been seised by submitting an express acceptance according to article 7 (c) ESR.[26] Upon submittal of a declaration of intention to participate in the proceedings by any person mentioned in article 72.1 (cf. *supra* at no. 9 *et seq.*), international competence of the authority seised may result from article 7(b) ESR if the applicant and the new party to the proceedings have concluded a choice-of-court agreement,[27] or from article 7(c) ESR if the new party submits express acceptance. At any time of the proceedings, international competence of the authority seised may only be based on article 7(b) or (c) if the preconditions of these provisions are met by every party.[28] Therefore, an authority may lose its international competence in case another person joins the proceedings as a party without submitting express acceptance or concluding a choice-of-court agreement.

3. Article 7(c) ESR and Article 5 ESR

14. Article 7(c) ESR is sufficient in itself [see art. 7 nos. 8–9]. If the parties to the proceedings have expressly accepted the international competence of the issuing authority seised, this authority, provided it belongs to the Member State whose law had been chosen by the *de cujus*, is internationally competent. Thus, the applicant for an ECS can himself create at first the precondition for the international competence of the issuing authorities of that Member State.[29] Problems may arise upon participation of

[26] *Contra:* Dorsel, 'Art. 64 EuErbVO', para. 3.
[27] Cf. Fornasier, 'Art. 64 EuErbVO', para. 16 *et seq.; contra:* Dorsel, 'Art. 64 EuErbVO', para. 2.
[28] Fornasier, 'Art. 64 EuErbVO', para. 17.
[29] Cf. Wautelet, 'Article 64', p. 728; *contra:* Dorsel, 'Art. 64 EuErbVO', para. 3.

another person in the proceedings. In this case, the authority seised would usually decline international competence, unless the new participant also submits an express acceptance pursuant to article 7(c) ESR or the conditions of points (a) or (b) of article 7 ESR are fulfilled. Concerning the requirement that the acceptance be declared 'expressly' there are no particularities to be considered in matters of ECS, cf. therefore the comment of article 7 ESR; it is held that the simple application at the issuing authority of a specific Member State is sufficient to assume express acceptance of the applicant.[30] The comparison with points (b) of article 12.1 and (c) of article 12.3 of the Brussels II-*bis* regulation[31] which provide for the possibility to accept jurisdiction 'expressly or in another unequivocal manner' shows that 'another unequivocal manner' should not be sufficient for the purpose of article 7(c) ESR.[32] Hence, the acceptance has to be effected verbally, and the declaration of acceptance must not be subject to any interpretation.

D. *Forum necessitatis*

15. The last provision article 64 ESR refers to is article 11 ESR. The wording of article 11 ESR suggests that an ECS may always be issued in any Member State the matter is closely connected to. For it is in the very nature of an ECS as a specific certificate resulting from EU law that it cannot be issued in any third state. The issuance of an ECS in a third state is therefore always impossible, so that this precondition of article 11 ESR is always fulfilled.[33] Thus, if there is no international competence within the EU that can be established otherwise, it can always be relied on the *forum necessitatis*, provided that there is a close connection to any Member State. It is held that this result contradicts the intentions of the ESR, as recital 31 of the ESR shows a restrictive understanding of article 11 ESR, e.g. the case of a standstill of the administration of justice in reason of civil war, and that, therefore, article 11 ESR could only be

[30] Wautelet, 'Article 64', p. 728.

[31] Council Regulation (EC) no. 2201/2003 of 21 November 2003 concerning jurisdiction and the recognition and enforcement of judgments in matrimonial matters and the matters of parental responsibility, repealing Regulation (EC) no. 1347/2000, OJ 2003 no. L338, 23 December 2003, p. 1.

[32] Cf. A. Dutta, 'Art. 7 EuErbVO', in J. von Hein (ed) *Münchener Kommentar zum Bürgerlichen Gesetzbuch*, vol. X, 6th ed. (München, 2015), para. 7.

[33] Cf. Nordmeier, 'Art. 64 EuErbVO', para. 5.

applied if also other court proceedings could not be conducted in a third State closely connected to the matter [see art. 11].[34]

16. This, however, is not convincing. It is the intention of the ESR, *inter alia*, to provide for a speedy, smooth and efficient settlement of successions with cross-border implications within the EU. In order to ensure this purpose, the status holders mentioned in article 62 ESR have to be enabled to easily demonstrate their status or rights or powers in any Member State, if necessary. This is the reason for the creation of the ECS according of its recital 67. There is no reason whatsoever why the *forum necessitatis* of article 11 should not benefit to an applicant for the simple reason that there is no other internationally competent Member State according to article 64 ESR. An abuse of that provision should not be feared: The rules on international competence according to the articles 4, 7 and 10 ESR in conjunction with article 64 ESR remain paramount and exclude, in their scope of application, any recourse to the *forum necessitatis*. Furthermore, article 11 ESR presupposes a close connection of the 'case' – e.g. the envisaged ECS – to the Member State to whose authorities the application is submitted. It must also be taken into account that the applicant has to demonstrate the intended purpose of the ECS pursuant to article 65(f) ESR, and that if there is no necessity for the ECS according to article 63 ESR, the ECS will not be issued.

E. *Other Provisions Concerning International Competence*

17. The provisions of chapter II of the ESR other than those mentioned in article 64 ESR, are *e contrario* not applicable in procedures aimed at the issuance of an ECS. This means in concrete terms that in particular, the issuing authority may not limit its decision to certain assets pursuant to article 12 ESR [see art. 12],[35] although, of course, the applicant may achieve a similar result by limiting his or her application according to article 65(f) ESR.[36] Similarly, article 9 is not applicable;[37] in particular, article 47 of the Charter of Fundamental Rights of the European Union

[34] Nordmeier, 'Art. 64 EuErbVO', para. 5; cf. H. Dörner, 'EuErbVO: Die Verordnung zum Internationalen Erb- und Erbverfahrensrecht ist in Kraft!', *ZEV* (2012), p. 510.

[35] A. Dutta, 'Das neue internationale Erbrecht der Europäischen Union – Eine erste Lektüre der Erbrechtsverordnung', *FamRZ* (2013), p. 14; Dutta, 'Art. 64 EuErbVO', para. 7; Nordmeier, 'Art. 64 EuErbVO', para. 2; *contra:* Wautelet, 'Article 64', p. 729.

[36] Nordmeier, 'Art. 64 EuErbVO', para. 2; Wautelet, 'Article 64', p. 729.

[37] Wautelet, 'Article 64', p. 729; Fornasier, 'Art. 64 EuErbVO', para. 21; *contra:* Dutta, 'Art. 64 EuErbVO', para. 5.

does not call for its application.[38] Articles 13 and 19 ESR are also inapplicable in matters of ECS [see arts. 13 and 19].[39] There also exists no reason to apply the articles 17 and 18 ESR [see arts. 17 and 18].[40]

III. Second Sentence of Article 64 ESR

18. Recital 70 of the ESR states that it is 'for each Member State to determine in its internal legislation which authorities are to have competence to issue the ECS.' These may be courts as defined by article 3.2(a) ESR or any other authorities with competence in matters of succession. Thus, the internal substantive, geographical and functional competence is a matter of national legislation,[41] due to the principle of subsidiarity laid down in article 5 TEU.[42] The second sentence of article 64 ESR implements in the legislative text what has been formulated far more precisely in recital 70 of the ESR.[43] As both courts and other authorities are eligible to be established as issuing authorities by the Member States, the differentiation between the two kinds of issuing authorities is practically irrelevant for the purpose of article 64 ESR,[44] but may have relevance in the context of point (b) of the second sentence of article 67.1 ESR [see art. 67 no. 9].

19. For example, notaries could be courts according to the second sentence of recital 20 of the ESR[45] as well as other authorities according to the second sentence of recital 70 of the ESR[46]. This dispute, however,

[38] Cf. *supra* no. 11; *contra:* Dutta, 'Art. 64 EuErbVO', para. 5.

[39] Dutta, 'Art. 64 EuErbVO', para. 8. [40] *Contra:* Dutta, 'Art. 64 EuErbVO', para. 8.

[41] Kleinschmidt, 'Optionales Erbrecht', p. 768; U. Janzen, 'EU-Erbrechtsverordnung', *Deutsche Notar-Zeitschrift* (2012), p. 492; Lagarde, 'Les principes de base', p. 729; R. Wagner and P. Scholz, 'Der Referentenentwurf eines Gesetzes zur Durchführung der EU-Erbrechtsverordnung', *FamRZ* (2014), p. 718; R. Schaub, 'Die EU-Erbrechtsverordnung', in K. Muscheler (ed.), *Hereditare – Jahrbuch für Erbrecht und Schenkungsrecht*, vol. 3 (Tübingen, 2013), p. 125; K. W. Lange, 'Das Europäische Nachlasszeugnis', in A. Dutta and S. Herrler (eds), Die Europäische Erbrechtsverordnung (München, 2014), para. 9; Nordmeier, 'Art. 64 EuErbVO', para. 7; for German legislation cf. section 34 of the law on international successions ('Gesetz zum Internationalen Erbrecht und zur Änderung von Vorschriften zum Erbschein sowie zur Änderung sonstiger Vorschriften'), *Bundesgesetzblatt*, 2015, I-1042 of 3 July 2015.

[42] Schmidt, 'Art. 64 EuErbVO', para. 3. [43] Nordmeier, 'Art. 64 EuErbVO', para. 7.

[44] Nordmeier, 'Art. 64 EuErbVO', para. 8.

[45] Buschbaum and Simon, 'EuErbVO', p. 526; P. Lokin, 'De Erfrechtverordening', *NIPR* (2013), p. 336.

[46] Kleinschmidt, 'Optionales Erbrecht', p. 768 *et seq.*; T. Ballarino, 'Il nuovo regolamento europeo sulle successioni', *Riv dir int* (2013), p. 1145; Wautelet, 'Article 64', p. 726; Lagarde, 'Les principes de base', p. 782; J. Carrascosa González, 'Reglamento sucesorio

does not need to be resolved within the scope of this comment of article 64 ESR.[47] Even the apparent restriction concerning the appointment of 'other authorities' that must have competence to deal with matters of succession, as is stated in point (b) of the second sentence of article 64 ESR, is irrelevant. For in the moment a Member State confers the competence for the issuance of ECS to any authority, this authority acquires the requested competence by virtue of the appointment, regardless of whether it had had another competence to deal with matters of succession before.[48] Under article 78.1(c) ESR, the Member States are obliged to communicate to the EU Commission the relevant information regarding the authorities competent to issue the ECS pursuant to article 64 [see art. 77 and art. 79 no. 3].[49]

europeo y actividad notarial', *CdT* (2014), p. 43; cf. R. Crône, 'Le certificat successoral européen', in G. Khairallah and M. Revillard (eds), *Perspectives du droit des successions européennes et internationals – Etude de la proposition de règlement du 14 octobre 2009* (Paris, 2010), p. 165.

47 Nordmeier, 'Art. 64 EuErbVO', para. 8; cf. Lagarde, 'Les principes de base', p. 728.

48 Nordmeier, 'Art. 64 EuErbVO', para. 8.

49 Schmidt, 'Art. 64 EuErbVO', para. 1; Wautelet, 'Article 64', p. 727.

Article 65

Application for a Certificate

BERNHARD KREẞE

1. The Certificate shall be issued upon application by any person referred to in Article 63(1) (hereinafter referred to as 'the applicant').
2. For the purposes of submitting an application, the applicant may use the form established in accordance with the advisory procedure referred to in Article 81(2).
3. The application shall contain the information listed below, to the extent that such information is within the applicant's knowledge and is necessary in order to enable the issuing authority to certify the elements which the applicant wants certified, and shall be accompanied by all relevant documents either in the original or by way of copies which satisfy the conditions necessary to establish their authenticity, without prejudice to Article 66(2):
   (a) details concerning the deceased: surname (if applicable, surname at birth), given name(s), sex, date and place of birth, civil status, nationality, identification number (if applicable), address at the time of death, date and place of death;
   (b) details concerning the applicant: surname (if applicable, surname at birth), given name(s), sex, date and place of birth, civil status, nationality, identification number (if applicable), address and relationship to the deceased, if any;
   (c) details concerning the representative of the applicant, if any: surname (if applicable, surname at birth), given name(s), address and representative capacity;
   (d) details of the spouse or partner of the deceased and, if applicable, ex-spouse(s) or ex-partner(s): surname (if applicable, surname at birth), given name(s), sex, date and place of birth, civil status, nationality, identification number (if applicable) and address;
   (e) details of other possible beneficiaries under a disposition of property upon death and/or by operation of law: surname and given name(s) or organisation name, identification number (if applicable) and address;
   (f) the intended purpose of the Certificate in accordance with Article 63;
   (g) the contact details of the court or other competent authority which is dealing with or has dealt with the succession as such, if applicable;

(h) the elements on which the applicant founds, as appropriate, his claimed right to succession property as a beneficiary and/or his right to execute the will of the deceased and/or to administer the estate of the deceased;

(i) an indication of whether the deceased had made a disposition of property upon death; if neither the original nor a copy is appended, an indication regarding the location of the original;

(j) an indication of whether the deceased had entered into a marriage contract or into a contract regarding a relationship which may have comparable effects to marriage; if neither the original nor a copy of the contract is appended, an indication regarding the location of the original;

(k) an indication of whether any of the beneficiaries has made a declaration concerning acceptance or waiver of the succession;

(l) a declaration stating that, to the applicant's best knowledge, no dispute is pending relating to the elements to be certified;

(m) any other information which the applicant deems useful for the purposes of the issue of the Certificate.

Summary

I. GENERALITIES *page* 712
II. NORMATIVE CONTENT 713
A. Application Principle 713
B. Entitlement to File an Application 714
C. Possibility to Use a Standard form 717
D. Specifications Required 718
1. Generalities 718
2. Details Contained in Article 65.3 ESR 720

I. Generalities

1. This provision deals with the conditions and modalities of the application for an ECS: Article 65.1 ESR sets up an application requirement or principle, so that an issuance *ex officio* shall not take place.[1] The same provision defines the entitlement to file an application. Paragraphs 2 and 3 of article 65 ESR concern the formalities of the

[1] J. Schmidt, 'Art. 65 EuErbVO', in C. Budzikiewicz, M.-P. Weller and W. Wurmnest (eds), *Beck-Online Großkommentar, EuErbVO* (München, 2016), para. 4; C. F. Nordmeier, 'Art. 65 EuErbVO', in R. Hüßtege and H.-P. Mansel (eds), *NomosKommentar, BGB, Rom-Verordnungen*, vol. VI, 2nd ed. (Baden-Baden, 2015), para. 2.

application, while article 65.2 deals with the form *stricto sensu*, whereas article 65.3 sets up the specification the application must contain. This provision thus also contains a requirement to deliver a rationale for the application.[2] It thus contains procedural rules[3] that can be complemented with the national procedural rules concerning the issues that are not dealt with in the ESR.[4]

2. The person who intends to make use of an ECS in another Member State knows best which details the ECS should contain if it is to be of use for him or her. The person also usually disposes of the information that the issuing authority needs in order to examine whether or not an ECS shall be issued, and if so, with which content. Thus, the requirement of an application, as well as the specification of details to be provided in the application, serves the interests of both the applicant and the issuing authority.[5] The specifications required under article 65.3 ESR correspond largely to the details that the ECS should contain pursuant to article 68 ESR.[6] The possibility to use a standard form has been instituted in order to facilitate the filing of the application as well as its examination.[7]

II. Normative Content

A. *Application Principle*

3. The fact that an ECS can only be issued upon application implies that the issuing authority is bound to the content requested in the application. The issuing authority thus must not establish an ECS with a content that differs from the content requested by the applicant, as such an ECS would usually be an *aliud* to the ECS applied for.[8] If, for example, an heir applies for an ECS in order to prove his or her status, the issuing authority may not indicate any vindication legatees. In the same way, if the applicant

[2] A. Dutta, 'Art. 65 EuErbVO', in J. von Hein (ed), *Münchener Kommentar zum Bürgerlichen Gesetzbuch*, vol. X, 6th ed. (München, 2015), para. 1; cf. Nordmeier, 'Art. 65 EuErbVO', para. 1.

[3] P. Wautelet, 'Article 65', in A. Bonomi and P. Wautelet, *Le droit européen des successions – Commentaire du Règlement n° 650/2012 du 4 juillet 2012* (Bruxelles, 2013), p. 735; Dutta, 'Art. 65 EuErbVO', para. 1.

[4] Dutta, 'Art. 65 EuErbVO', para. 1; Nordmeier, 'Art. 65 EuErbVO', para. 1.

[5] Cf Schmidt, 'Art. 65 EuErbVO', para. 3. [6] Schmidt, 'Art. 65 EuErbVO', para. 3.

[7] Schmidt, 'Art. 65 EuErbVO', para. 3; cf. also recital 76 of the ESR.

[8] Dutta, 'Art. 65 EuErbVO', para. 2; *contra:* J. Kleinschmidt, 'Optionales Erbrecht: Das Europäische Nachlasszeugnis als Herausforderung an das Kollisionsrecht', *RabelsZ* (2013), p. 772, who opines that the ESR is silent with respect to this issue.

applies for certification of his or her position as sole heir, it would be inadmissible for the issuing authority to certify a 50 per cent share if it comes to the conclusion that there is another heir with equal share. Where necessary, as the issuing authority is not allowed to issue a false ECS, it would have to reject the application, although it may be possible according to national procedural law to give opportunity to the applicant to adjust his or her application.[9]

4. The application principle implies furthermore that the issuing authority has to refrain from issuing the ECS if the applicant withdraws his or her application. A withdrawal is possible in any stadium of the proceedings, until the issuance of the ECS. However, it cannot be withdrawn in the course of rectification, modification or redress procedures pursuant to the articles 71 or 72 ESR [see arts. 71 and 72].[10] The reason is that the ECS becomes fully effective at the moment of its issuance according to article 69.1 ESR. The mere withdrawal of the application cannot render the ECS ineffective. The issuing authority may indeed suspend the effects of an ECS in accordance with article 73.1 or withdraw the ECS pursuant to article 71.3 ESR. This is, however, only possible if the conditions of these provisions are fulfilled [see arts. 71 and 73].

B. *Entitlement to File an Application*

5. Any person referred to in article 63.1 ESR is entitled to apply for an ECS. Accordingly, the entitlement to file an application is to be verified by virtue of the three elements mentioned in article 63.1, the first one of them relating to the quality of the applicant, the two other of them relating to the purpose of the ECS requested. First, the applicant must be an heir, legatee, executor of wills or administrator of the estate [see art. 63 no. 4 *et seq.*]. Second, the applicant must need to invoke his or her status or to exercise his or her rights or powers relating to the estate [see art. 63 no. 14 *et seq.*]. Third, the applicant must have the intention to use the ECS in another Member State than the state of application [see art. 63 no. 16 *et seq.*]. If all the conditions established in article 63.1 ESR are thus fulfilled, the person applying for the issuance of an ECS is in principle eligible to be issued an ECS,[11] under reservation of the examination of the

[9] Dutta, 'Art. 65 EuErbVO', para. 2; Nordmeier, 'Art. 65 EuErbVO', para. 5; cf. A. Perscha, 'Art 67 EuErbVO', in A. Deixler-Hübner and M. Schauer (eds), *EuErbVO – Kommentar zur EU-Erbrechtsverordnung* (Wien, 2015), para. 31.

[10] *Contra*: Dutta, 'Art. 65 EuErbVO', para. 2.

[11] Dutta, 'Art. 65 EuErbVO', para. 3; Nordmeier, 'Art. 65 EuErbVO', para. 3.

application pursuant to article 66 ESR. The application may also be made by an authorised representative, as follows from article 65.3(c) ESR.[12]

6. The person filing an application for an ECS is defined as 'applicant' in article 65.1 ESR. The wording of the provision suggests, however, that a person can only be an applicant in the sense of articles 65 *et seq.* ESR if he or she fulfills the substantial requirements of article 63.1 ESR. This would however contradict the purely formal sense in which this term is used in article 66 ESR: According to article 66.1 ESR, the issuing authority shall verify the information and declarations and evidence provided by the 'applicant'. Evidently, the issuing authority has to examine in this context the fulfillment of the conditions of article 63.1 ESR, i.e. the entitlement of the person that has formally filed the application, in order to avoid that an ECS be issued for example in case of the absence of a cross-border situation in the sense of at least an intention to use the ECS in another Member State. Similarly, it would not be plausible to refuse to apply article 66.2 ESR on evidence concerning the legal status of the person filing the application, with the argument that this would be needed to establish his or her quality as applicant and that article 66.2 ESR would presuppose that quality.

7. In case of several possible applicants, every one of them may decide to apply for an ECS which shall certify his or her status or rights or powers only. It is, however, also possible that two or several entitled persons jointly apply for a single ECS which then would certify the status or rights or powers of all the applicants.[13] If the entitled persons apply each for an ECS on their own behalf only, the question is whether the issuing authority shall be entitled to join the proceedings in order to be able to issue a single ECS, or if it has to issue a separate ECS concerning each applicant. It should be noted here again that the ECS can only be issued with the exact content that has been requested by the applicant. The issuing authority is not entitled to unilaterally issue an ECS with a content that had not been requested, as such ECS would constitute a different ECS than the requested one [see *supra* no. 3].[14] This also applies if the alteration of the requested contents is due to the fact that the issuing authority has joined the application with another one. Such a procedure violates the application requirement laid down in

[12] Dutta, 'Art. 65 EuErbVO', para. 2; Schmidt, 'Art. 65 EuErbVO', para. 6.

[13] Wautelet, 'Article 65', p. 735; Dutta, 'Art. 65 EuErbVO', para. 4; doubting: K. W. Lange, 'Das Europäische Nachlasszeugnis', in A. Dutta and S. Herrler (eds), *Die Europäische Erbrechtsverordnung* (München, 2014), para. 7.

[14] Dutta, 'Art. 65 EuErbVO', para. 2; J. Kleinschmidt, 'Art. 65 EuErbVO', in M. Würdinger (ed), *Juris Praxiskommentar BGB, Internationales Privatrecht*, vol. VI, 7th ed. (Saarbrücken, 2014), para. 9.

article 65.1 ESR. However, it is no violation of the application requirement if the issuing authority contacts the applicants and encourages them to apply for a junction of the several applications. Still, the issuing authority may do so only if authorised by national law, as national law has to decide on the procedural issues that are not regulated by the ESR.[15]

8. Once an ECS has been issued, any person demonstrating a legitimate interest may request the issuance of certified copies of the ECS according to article 70.1 ESR. Thus, while the application of an ECS is limited to the persons mentioned in article 63.1 ESR, the delivery of certified copies is not. For example, creditors of the succession who are not entitled to apply for an ECS[16] [see art. 63 no. 2] may make use of an ECS applied for successfully by a status holder entitled to do so, by requesting certified copies.[17] As the content of a certified copy may not be altered with respect to the original certificate, the creditors or other persons demonstrating a legitimate interest cannot receive such copy with a content perhaps more useful for them.

9. An entitlement of creditors or other persons not mentioned in article 63 ESR to file an application cannot be introduced by national law, as this would violate article 65 ESR, regardless of the systematical embedding of such national provisions. If internal enforcement laws, as it is the case for example in Germany,[18] allow an enforcement creditor to apply for a certificate of inheritance instead of the debtor, or to apply for any other document the debtor would be entitled to, such provision is not applicable on ECS, as the limitation of article 65 ESR concerning possible applicants does not contain any exception.[19]

[15] Cf. Dutta, 'Art. 65 EuErbVO', para. 2; Nordmeier, 'Art. 65 EuErbVO', para. 3.

[16] J. Schmidt, 'Art. 63 EuErbVO', in C. Budzikiewicz, M.-P. Weller and W. Wurmnest (eds), *Beck-Online Großkommentar, EuErbVO* (München, 2016), para. 6; P. Wautelet, 'Article 63', in A. Bonomi and P. Wautelet, *Le droit européen des successions – Commentaire du Règlement n° 650/2012 du 4 juillet 2012* (Bruxelles, 2013), p. 736; Lange, 'Das Europäische Nachlasszeugnis', para. 7; M. Buschbaum and U. Simon, 'EuErbVO: Das Europäische Nachlasszeugnis', *ZEV* (2012), p. 525; C. Dorsel, 'Europäische Erbrechtsverordnung und Europäisches Nachlasszeugnis', *Europäische Zeitschrift für die Steuer- und Erbrechtspraxis* (2014), p. 213.

[17] Dutta, 'Art. 65 EuErbVO', para. 3; Nordmeier, 'Art. 65 EuErbVO', para. 4.

[18] Sections 792 and 896 of the German code of civil procedure (*Zivilprozessordnung*).

[19] R. Süß, 'Das Europäische Nachlasszeugnis', *ZEuP* (2013), p. 737; Wautelet, 'Article 63', p. 736; Nordmeier, 'Art. 65 EuErbVO', para. 4; R. Stürner, 'Arts. 62–73 EuErbVO', in O. Jauernig, *Bürgerliches Gesetzbuch: BGB*, 16th ed. (München, 2015), para. 3; *contra*: Dorsel, 'Europäische Erbrechtsverordnung', p. 213; Buschbaum and Simon, 'EuErbVO', p. 525; Kleinschmidt, Optionales Erbrecht, p. 770 *et seq.*; F. Sturm and G. Sturm, 'Das europäische Nachlasszeugnis: Zum Vorschlag der Kommission vom 14. Oktober 2009', *Zbornik Pravnog fakulteta u Zagrebu* (2012), p. 333; Dutta, 'Art. 65 EuErbVO', para. 7.

C. *Possibility to Use a Standard Form*

10. Article 65.2 ESR provides for the possibility to use a standard form established in accordance with the advisory procedure referred to in articles 81.2 ESR and 4 regulation no. 182/2011 [see arts. 80 and 82 no. 2].[20] The standard form is to be found in annex IV of the Commission Implementing regulation no. 1329/2014.[21] In spite of the wording of article 1.4 of the Commission Implementing regulation ('The form to be used . . .'), the use of the standard form is not mandatory, given the wording of the higher-ranking article 65.2 ESR ('the applicant may use . . .').[22] The applicant is however free to make use of it[23] in order to be sure to meet the formal requirement and to give all the necessary information. If the standard form is not used by the applicant, the issuing authority has to apply national procedural law, in order to establish, for example, whether the application needs to be filed in writing.[24] Even if the standard form is used, it still relies on national law to establish those details of the procedure that the ESR is silent on. This concerns for example the language to be used for the application with or without making use of the standard form,[25] or the quantity of copies of the application that need to be lodged.[26]

[20] Regulation (EU) no. 182/2011 of the European Parliament and of the Council of 16 February 2011 laying down the rules and general principles concerning mechanisms for Control by Member States of the Commission's exercise of implementing powers, OJ 2011 no. L55, 28 February 2011, p. 13.

[21] Commission Implementing Regulation no. 1329/2014 of 9 December 2014 establishing the Forms referred to in Regulation (EU) no. 650/2012 of the European Parliament and of the Council on jurisdiction, applicable law, recognition and enforcement of decisions and acceptance and enforcement of authentic instruments in matters of succession and on the creation of a European Certificate of Succession, OJ 2014 no. L359, 16 December 2014, p. 30.

[22] Nordmeier, 'Art. 65 EuErbVO', para. 6.

[23] Dutta, 'Art. 65 EuErbVO', para. 8; Nordmeier, 'Art. 65 EuErbVO', para. 6; Wautelet, 'Article 65', p. 735; P. Lokin, 'De Erfrechtverordening', *NIPR* (2013), p. 336.

[24] Dutta, 'Art. 65 EuErbVO', para. 8; for German legislation cf. section 35 of the law on international successions ('Gesetz zum Internationalen Erbrecht und zur Änderung von Vorschriften zum Erbschein sowie zur Änderung sonstiger Vorschriften'), *Bundesgesetzblatt*, 2015, I-1042, of 3 July 2015; the ESR itself does not prohibit an oral application, cf. Wautelet, 'Article 65', p. 735.

[25] Cf. for example section 35.2 of the German Law on International Successions; Dutta, 'Art. 65 EuErbVO', para. 8; *contra:* Nordmeier, 'Art. 65 EuErbVO', para. 10, who seemingly holds that the language issue is one concerning EU law.

[26] Wautelet, 'Article 65', pp. 736–737.

D. *Specifications Required*

1. Generalities

11. Article 65.3 ESR contains an exhaustive list of possible specifications that have to be made by the applicant. The issuing authority is not entitled to require further details than those laid down in points (a) to (l) of article 65.3 ESR.[27] The applicant may, however, provide further information on a voluntary basis, as is clarified in point (m) of article 65.3 ESR; this may be relevant particularly if the applicant wants to include information to solve an inheritance controversy.[28] The requirement of specification is placed under a double reserve by article 65.3 ESR:[29] The information must be within the applicant's knowledge, and it must be necessary in order to enable the issuing authority to certify the elements which the applicant wants certified. The first reserve means that the applicant has – in principle – no obligation of investigation.[30] However, pursuant to article 66.1 ESR, the issuing authority will engage only in further enquiries if such is provided for or authorised by its own law. This means that the issuing authority will not extend its own enquiries beyond the limits of its own national procedural law, but may instead invite the applicant to provide further evidence pursuant to the second sentence of article 66.1 ESR, if necessary [see art. 66 no. 2].[31] Even if the issuing authority is allowed or even obliged to institute enquiries according to its national law, it is entitled to invite the applicant to provide further evidence instead, as the legal impossibility for the issuing authority to make enquiries is not a precondition for such invitation according to the syntax structure of the second sentence of article 66.1 ESR, and the invitation to the applicant is one way of investigation.[32] Consequently, although the applicant does not have to provide information outside of his or her knowledge at the moment of application,[33] he or she may be required at a later stage to investigate into

[27] Cf. Schmidt, 'Art. 65 EuErbVO', para. 7; *contra:* Dutta, 'Art. 65 EuErbVO', para. 10.

[28] C. Azcárraga Monzonís, 'International Successions in Spain: The Impact of a New EU Regulation', *Spanish Yearbook of International Law* (2009), p. 58.

[29] Cf. Schmidt, 'Art. 65 EuErbVO', para. 8.

[30] Cf. Schmidt, 'Art. 65 EuErbVO', para. 10; Nordmeier, 'Art. 65 EuErbVO', para. 8; *contra:* Dorsel, 'Europäische Erbrechtsverordnung', p. 213.

[31] Nordmeier, 'Art. 65 EuErbVO', para. 8.

[32] C. Dorsel, 'Art. 65 EuErbVO', in R. Geimer and R. Schütze (eds), *Internationaler Rechtsverkehr in Zivil- und Handelssachen,* vol. III (München, 2015), para. 17; cf. P. Wautelet, 'Article 66', in A. Bonomi and P. Wautelet, *Le droit européen des successions. Commentaire du Règlement n° 650/2012 du 4 juillet 2012* (Bruxelles, 2013), p. 749.

[33] Nordmeier, 'Art. 65 EuErbVO', para. 8.

the relevant facts at the request of the issuing authority,[34] in order to enable the issuing authority to issue the ECS with the content envisaged by him.

12. The second reserve concerns the necessity of the information for the purpose of the ECS. The information listed in points (a) to (l) is only required to the extent that it is necessary in order to enable the issuing authority to certify the elements which the applicant wants certified.[35] Therefore, as the applicant decides on the concrete purpose of the ECS, he or she indirectly also decides which information must be necessarily provided in the application.[36]

13. The applicant is required, pursuant to article 65.3 ESR, to include 'all relevant documents'. The term 'relevant' refers to article 66.1 ESR, according to which the issuing authority shall verify the information provided by the applicant. Thus, 'relevant' documents are those that are suitable to support or to refute that information.[37] Examples are given in point 7 of the standard form established by annex 4 of the Commission Implementing regulation. The documents may be submitted in the original. Alternatively, they can be turned in as copies, which means photocopies[38] as well as other kinds of verbatim transcripts or duplications, as is in particular suggested by the German wording of article 65.3 ('Abschrift').[39] The copy must satisfy the conditions necessary to establish their authenticity. The conditions thereof are regulated by the internal law of the issuing authority. Under German law, for example, the authenticity of a copy can be established in general by a notary or by a municipal administration. It should be noted that the requirement of 'authenticity' of the copy merely refers to its conformity with the original, but not to the accuracy of its content.

14. The German wording of article 65.3 ESR is insofar somewhat ambiguous, as it refers to the fulfilment of the 'erforderlichen Voraussetzungen für ihre Beweiskraft', without clarifying which details should be covered exactly by the 'Beweiskraft' (probative force). Other

[34] Nordmeier, 'Art. 65 EuErbVO', para. 8; cf. Dorsel, 'Art. 65 EuErbVO', para. 9, who seems to hold that the applicant has to provide information on his or her own motion even if the applicant lacks knowledge, in case that information is necessary for the issuance of the ECS.

[35] Schmidt, 'Art. 65 EuErbVO', para. 11; Nordmeier, 'Art. 65 EuErbVO', para. 8; Wautelet, 'Article 65', p. 737; Dorsel, 'Europäische Erbrechtsverordnung', p. 215; cf. A. Bonomi, 'Il regolamento europeo sulle successioni', *Riv dir int priv proc* (2013), p. 321.

[36] Cf. Schmidt, 'Art. 65 EuErbVO', para. 12; Nordmeier, 'Art. 65 EuErbVO', para. 8; Dorsel, 'Europäische Erbrechtsverordnung', p. 215.

[37] Cf. Wautelet, 'Article 65', p. 736. [38] Nordmeier, 'Art. 65 EuErbVO', para. 27.

[39] Nordmeier, 'Art. 65 EuErbVO', para. 27; cf. Kleinschmidt, 'Art. 65 EuErbVO', para. 15.

language versions are however formulated more distinctly: In particular, the Dutch version refers to 'afschriften ... waarvan de echtheid ervan kan worden vastgesteld', which clearly relates to the conformity of the copy with the original document. The Italian version speaks of 'copia autentica'. The French, Spanish and Portuguese versions are formulated similarly to the English version and thus also refer to the mere authenticity of the copy in the sense of its conformity with the original, instead of requiring any additional probative force of the copy.[40] Only this interpretation also corresponds to the purpose of the relevant passage of the provision, as it aims at specifying the quality the copy of a document must have in order to take the place of the original.

2. Details Contained in Article 65.3 ESR

15. The details that the application shall contain according to points (a) to (m) of article 65.3 ESR find their equivalent in the standard form referred to by article 65.2 ESR that is established by annex 4 of the Commission Implementing regulation.[41] Some elements of the form may help to get further clarification concerning the meaning of details mentioned in article 65.3 ESR. Article 65.3(a) ESR, for example, stipulates that information concerning the deceased, in particular the 'identification number', should be given if applicable. However, it is not further defined what is meant by identification number. Point 5 of the standard form where the information concerning the deceased can be recorded, lists several possible identification numbers that are usually not changed during a lifetime under point 5.8, e.g. the national identity number or the social security number or the tax number. Thus, any of these numbers may be filled in.[42]

16. Details concerning the applicant must be given according to article 65.3(b) ESR. They can be filled in at point 3 of the standard form. The kind of information required corresponds largely to the information concerning the deceased,[43] but must contain also the relationship to the deceased, if any.[44] Points (d) and (e) of article 65.3 ESR concern details of other kinds of possible beneficiaries of the estate. It is

[40] Schmidt, 'Art. 65 EuErbVO', para. 51.

[41] Cf. for details concerning the standard form Nordmeier, 'Art. 65 EuErbVO', para. 12 *et seq.*

[42] Cf. Nordmeier, 'Art. 65 EuErbVO', para. 12; Schmidt, 'Art. 65 EuErbVO', para. 13.

[43] Wautelet, 'Article 65' p. 739; Nordmeier, 'Art. 65 EuErbVO', para. 13; cf. Schmidt, 'Art. 65 EuErbVO', para. 14.

[44] Wautelet, 'Article 65', p. 739.

important to note that the persons mentioned by the applicant do not actually really have to be beneficiaries of the estate. It is sufficient that there is such possibility because of familiar relationships ('by operation of law') or because of dispositions of the deceased.[45] It would not be useful to require the applicant to enter into legal analyses who is, in the end, to be regarded as beneficiary or not. Usually, heirs, legatees and persons entitled to a reserved share, are possible beneficiaries.[46] It does not matter for the qualification as beneficiary whether a legatee is a vindication legatee or civil-law legatee, as point (e) of article 65.3 ESR is not limited to 'direct' beneficiaries, in contrast to article 63.1 ESR [see art. 63 no. 7].

17. According to points (i) to (k) of article 65.3 ESR, the applicant should in addition provide complementary specifications of relevant dispositions (e.g. last wills or testamentary contracts[47]) and of marriage or similar – notably in the case of homosexual registered partnerships[48] – contracts of the deceased, and of declarations of beneficiaries concerning acceptance or waiver. The information on marriage or similar contracts is important in order to enable the issuing authority to examine whether the matrimonial property regime has any impact on the succession.[49] If the applicant cannot append the original or a copy any disposition of property upon death of the deceased, or of the marriage or similar contract of the deceased, an indication regarding the location of the respective original is sufficient, cf points (i) and (j) of article 65.3 ESR.[50] In case of several dispositions of property upon death, the applicant should mention all of them, as is clarified by point 6.4 of the standard form.[51]

18. Of utmost importance is the specification of the intended purpose of the ECS in accordance with articles 63 and 65.3(f) ESR, as the issuing authority needs this information in order to decide whether the

[45] M. Fornasier, 'Art. 65 EuErbVO', in A. Dutta and J. Weber (eds), *Internationales Erbrecht - EuErbVO, Erbrechtliche Staatsverträge, EGBGB, IntErbRVG, IntErbStR, IntSchenkungsR* (München, 2016), para. 12.

[46] Cf. the second sentence of recital 47 of the ESR; see also Dorsel, 'Art. 65 EuErbVO', para. 14.

[47] Cf. Nordmeier, 'Art. 65 EuErbVO', para. 20.

[48] Buschbaum and Simon, 'EuErbVO', p. 525; Schmidt, 'Art. 65 EuErbVO', para. 17; Nordmeier, 'Art. 65 EuErbVO', para. 22; Wautelet, 'Article 65', p. 743.

[49] Buschbaum and Simon, 'EuErbVO', p. 525; C. Dorsel, 'Art. 68 EuErbVO', in R. Geimer and R. Schütze (eds), *Internationaler Rechtsverkehr in Zivil- und Handelssachen*, vol. III (München, 2015), para. 13.

[50] Schmidt, 'Art. 65 EuErbVO', para. 34.

[51] Cf. Nordmeier, 'Art. 65 EuErbVO', para. 20; Schmidt, 'Art. 65 EuErbVO', para. 34.

issuance of the ECS with the requested content is justified [see art. 63 no. 14 *et seq.*].[52] Similarly, according to article 65.3(h) ESR, the applicant must specify the elements on which he or she bases the legal position in the sense of article 63.1 ESR that is to be certified on his or her behalf.[53]

19. Further information to be given, if applicable, is required by the points (c), (g) and (l) of article 65.3 ESR, and concern details about the representative of the applicant according to point (c),[54] and in particular about the existence of judicial or administrative proceedings with regard to the succession according to points (g) and (l).[55] The English wording of point (l) is not quite clear in this respect, as a 'dispute' does not presuppose formal proceedings, same as in the Italian ('controversie') and Dutch ('geschil') versions; however, the use of the words 'pending' or 'pendenti' in the English and Italian versions, as well as the wording of the German ('Rechtsstreit'), French ('litige'), Spanish ('litigio') or Portuguese ('litígio') versions provide clarity in the sense that only judicial proceedings can be meant.[56] Within point (l), the applicant is only required to inform about judicial proceedings that have not yet come to an end ('pending').[57] Concerning point (g), the contact details of the court or other competent authority dealing or having dealt with the succession comprise also the reference number of the case, as is clarified in point 6 of annex I to the standard form.

[52] Cf. Schmidt, 'Art. 65 EuErbVO', para. 24; Nordmeier, 'Art. 65 EuErbVO', para. 17.

[53] Cf. Wautelet, 'Article 65', p. 741; Schmidt, 'Art. 65 EuErbVO', para. 28 *et seq.*; Nordmeier, 'Art. 65 EuErbVO', para. 29.

[54] Cf. Nordmeier, 'Art. 65 EuErbVO', para. 14; Schmidt, 'Art. 65 EuErbVO', para. 15.

[55] Cf. Nordmeier, 'Art. 65 EuErbVO', paras. 18 and 24; Schmidt, 'Art. 65 EuErbVO', paras. 25 *et seq.*, 38 *et seq.*

[56] Cf. Nordmeier, 'Art. 65 EuErbVO', para. 24; Schmidt, 'Art. 65 EuErbVO', para. 40; concerning the interpretation of multilingual legal texts with different meanings of the linguistic versions, cf. B. Kreße, 'Die Auslegung mehrsprachiger Texte durch den EuGH', in I. Burr and G. Gréciano (eds), *Sprache und Recht – La construction européenne* (Baden-Baden, 2003), p. 157 *et seq.*; B. Kreße, 'Mehrsprachigkeit im Recht der Europäischen Union', *Zeitschrift für Rechtspolitik* (2014), p. 11 *et seq.*

[57] Schmidt, 'Art. 65 EuErbVO', para. 41.

Article 66

Examination of the Application

BERNHARD KREẞE

1. Upon receipt of the application the issuing authority shall verify the information and declarations and the documents and other evidence provided by the applicant. It shall carry out the enquiries necessary for that verification of its own motion where this is provided for or authorised by its own law, or shall invite the applicant to provide any further evidence which it deems necessary.
2. Where the applicant has been unable to produce copies of the relevant documents which satisfy the conditions necessary to establish their authenticity, the issuing authority may decide to accept other forms of evidence.
3. Where this is provided for by its own law and subject to the conditions laid down therein, the issuing authority may require that declarations be made on oath or by a statutory declaration in lieu of an oath.
4. The issuing authority shall take all necessary steps to inform the beneficiaries of the application for a Certificate. It shall, if necessary for the establishment of the elements to be certified, hear any person involved and any executor or administrator and make public announcements aimed at giving other possible beneficiaries the opportunity to invoke their rights.
5. For the purposes of this Article, the competent authority of a Member State shall, upon request, provide the issuing authority of another Member State with information held, in particular, in the land registers, the civil status registers and registers recording documents and facts of relevance for the succession or for the matrimonial property regime or an equivalent property regime of the deceased, where that competent authority would be authorised, under national law, to provide another national authority with such information.

Summary

I. GENERALITIES *page* 724

II. PRINCIPLE OF EX OFFICIO INVESTIGATION 724

III. FORMS OF EVIDENCE 726

IV. INFORMATION AND CONSULTATION 727

A. Information 728

B. Consultation 730

V. INTERNATIONAL ADMINISTRATIVE ASSISTANCE OF COMPETENT AUTHORITIES 732

I. Generalities

1. Article 66 ESR concerns the activity of the issuing authority between the deposition of the application and the decision about the issuance or not of the requested ECS. More precisely, the provision regulates the procedural steps to be taken by the issuing authority in order to examine whether the application is admissible and well founded.[1] In article 66.1 ESR, the principle of *ex officio* investigation with its relevant characteristics for the issuing authority is implemented.[2] The formulation 'upon receipt of the application' also implies a certain alacrity the application should be treated with by the issuing authority.[3] Paragraphs 2 and 3 of article 66 ESR then deal with the forms of evidence that are subject to be accepted by the issuing authority. Article 66.4 ESR determines some details concerning the information and consultation of persons involved that has to take place before the issuance of the ECS. Finally, article 66.5 ESR creates an obligation of national competent authorities to provide relevant information to the issuing authority upon requests and thus institutes an obligation of mutual international administrative assistance.[4]

II. Principle of *ex officio* Investigation

2. The issuing authority is not entitled to merely assume the correctness[5] and completeness[6] of the information given by the applicant without entering into investigations *in proprio motu*.[7] The investigations

[1] P. Wautelet, 'Article 66', in A. Bonomi and P. Wautelet, *Le droit européen des successions. Commentaire du Règlement n° 650/2012 du 4 juillet 2012* (Bruxelles, 2013), p. 747; A. Dutta, 'Art. 66 EuErbVO', in J. von Hein (ed), *Münchener Kommentar zum Bürgerlichen Gesetzbuch*, vol. X, 6th ed. (München, 2015), para. 1; C. F. Nordmeier, 'Art. 66 EuErbVO', in R. Hüßtege and H.-P. Mansel (eds), *NomosKommentar, BGB, Rom-Verordnungen*, vol. VI, 2nd ed. (Baden-Baden, 2015), para. 2.

[2] H. L. Graf, in K. Firsching and H. L. Graf, *Nachlassrecht – Erbfolge, Testament, Erbvertrag, Pflichtteilsrecht, Rechtspflege in Nachlasssachen, Nachlassinsolvenz, Nachlassverfahren sowie Erbschaftssteuer*, 10th ed. (München, 2014), para. 4.332.

[3] Wautelet, 'Article 66', p. 747.

[4] J. Kleinschmidt, 'Optionales Erbrecht – Das Europäische Nachlasszeugnis als Herausforderung an das Kollisionsrecht', *RabelsZ* (2013), p. 773, footnote 258.

[5] J. Schmidt, 'Art. 63 EuErbVO', in C. Budzikiewicz, M.-P. Weller and W. Wurmnest (eds), *Beck-Online Großkommentar, EuErbVO* (München, 2016), para. 6.

[6] Schmidt, 'Art. 66 EuErbVO', para. 5.

[7] Wautelet, 'Article 66', p. 746; A. Bonomi, 'Il regolamento europeo sulle successioni', *Riv dir int priv proc* (2013), p. 321; Buschbaum and Simon, 'EuErbVO', p. 525; Nordmeier, 'Art. 66 EuErbVO', para. 2; Dutta, 'Art. 66 EuErbVO', para. 2; A. Köhler, 'Art. 66 EuErbVO', in

concern all of the information and declarations, as well as the documents and other evidence provided by the applicant. The issuing authority thus has to perform an enquiry on the application *in toto*.[8] The extent to which the issuing authority may carry out the necessary enquiries depends however on its own national procedural law. Beyond the limits of the applicable national law, investigations *ex officio* are not possible.[9] The national law of the issuing authority also decides on how the enquiries can take place, i.e. the modalities of obtaining the evidence necessary to verify or falsify the content of the application.[10] However, the issuing authority may always invite the applicant to provide further evidence pursuant to the second sentence of article 66.1 ESR, if necessary.[11] This is possible even if the issuing authority is allowed or even obliged to institute enquiries according to its national law,[12] as the legal impossibility for the issuing authority to make enquiries is not a precondition for such invitation according to the syntax structure of the second sentence of article 66.1 ESR, and the invitation to the applicant is one way of investigation [see art. 65 no. 11].[13]

3. The issuing authority may only carry out enquiries or invite the applicant to provide further evidence as far as it 'deems' it to be necessary. In spite of this subjective formulation, the issuing authority is not entitled to order such enquiries or invitations in an arbitrary manner. In fact, the information resulting from the application or from the hearings of other persons involved according to article 66.4 ESR must give some objective reason to conduct further investigations.[14] The issuing authority thus has to apply its discretionary power in order to decide if and which further information is needed in order to come to a conclusion concerning the

L. Kroiß, C.-H. Horn and D. Solomon (eds), *Nachfolgerecht – Erbrechtliche Spezialgesetze, Zivilrecht/Strafrecht/Verwaltungsrecht/Steuerrecht/Verfahrensrecht/IPR* (Baden-Baden, 2015), para 1.

[8] Nordmeier, 'Art. 66 EuErbVO', para. 2; Wautelet, 'Article 66', p. 748.

[9] Schmidt, 'Art. 66 EuErbVO', para. 11; Wautelet, 'Article 66', p. 748; *contra:* Kleinschmidt, 'Art. 66 EuErbVO', para. 8.

[10] Buschbaum and Simon, 'EuErbVO', p. 525; Nordmeier, 'Art. 66 EuErbVO', para. 3; Schmidt, 'Art. 66 EuErbVO', para. 12.

[11] C. F. Nordmeier, 'Art. 65 EuErbVO', in R. Hüßtege and H.-P. Mansel (eds), *NomosKommentar, BGB, Rom-Verordnungen*, vol. VI, 2nd ed., (Baden-Baden, 2015), para. 8.

[12] *Contra:* Wautelet, 'Article 66', p. 749.

[13] Cf. P. Wautelet, 'Article 65', in Bonomi and Wautelet, *Le droit européen des successions. Commentaire du Règlement n° 650/2012 du 4 juillet 2012* (Bruxelles, 2013), pp. 738–739.

[14] Schmidt, 'Art. 66 EuErbVO', paras. 12 and 16.

issuance or not of the ECS. In principle, the issuing authority may carry out enquiries or invite the applicant to provide further information until the relevant facts have been determined or until no further relevant results can be expected.[15]

III. Forms of Evidence

4. Article 66 ESR contains in paragraphs 2 and 3 specifications concerning which forms of evidence may be accepted by the issuing authority. These provisions can be understood as complements to the national procedural law, although their impact should not be overestimated. Article 66.2 ESR contains an exception to the rule established in article 65.3 ESR that documents attached to the application shall be in principle submitted in the original or by way of copies which satisfy the conditions necessary to establish their authenticity [see art. 65 no. 13 *et seq.*]. The stipulation that the issuing authority 'may' decide to accept other forms of evidence is only relevant insofar as it makes clear that such acceptance does not violate article 65.3 ESR if the precondition of article 66.2 ESR is fulfilled. It does not, however, contain any obligation for the issuing authority to accept other forms of evidence.[16] Thus, in case the applicant has been unable to produce copies of the relevant documents which satisfy the conditions mentioned in article 65.3 ESR, the issuing authority may examine under its own law whether it accepts other forms of evidence or not[17] which may even include the application of a presumption.[18] If the national law strictly excludes the submittal of evidence in other ways than those provided by article 65.3 ESR, there is no possibility for the issuing authority to accept other forms of evidence according to article 66.3 ESR. If, however, the national law allows such acceptance, the issuing authority would have discretion to do so. Authentic instruments emanating from other Member States must always be accepted pursuant to article 59 ESR.[19]

5. It must be further noted that if the precondition of article 66.2 ESR is not fulfilled, i.e. the applicant has not been 'unable' to produce copies of the relevant documents satisfying the conditions necessary to establish their authenticity, the acceptance of other forms of evidence is barred by this provision. Such acceptance would then violate article 66.2 ESR, even

[15] Schmidt, 'Art. 66 EuErbVO', paras. 12 and 16.
[16] Cf. Schmidt, 'Art. 66 EuErbVO', para. 18.
[17] Nordmeier, 'Art. 66 EuErbVO', para. 9; cf. Dutta, 'Art. 66 EuErbVO', para. 4.
[18] Wautelet, 'Article 66', p. 751. [19] Dutta, 'Art. 66 EuErbVO', para. 4.

if it is admissible under national law. On the other hand, if the applicant is unable to turn in a qualified copy of a specific document, but would indeed be able to submit the original document as provided in article 65.3 ESR, the application of article 66.2 ESR is not barred by EU law. The reason for this is perhaps the consideration that it might be unreasonable for the applicant in certain cases to abandon possession of the original document for the duration of the procedure before the issuing authority. Yet perhaps article 66.2 ESR is just poorly drafted in this respect. 'Unability' to produce authentic copies can be assumed in particular if the delivery of such copies is generally not possible, if the applicant is not entitled to request such copies or if the effort to obtain such copies would imply an undue burden for the applicant, as in case of political persecution.[20] There is no unability if an authentic copy is in possession of a third person and the applicant has a claim for surrender against that person.[21]

6. Article 66.3 ESR allows the issuing authority to require the applicant to make declarations on oath or by a statutory declaration in lieu of an oath. The provision specifies, however, that such requirement is only possible where this is provided for by the national law of the issuing authority.[22] Moreover, declarations on oath and statutory declarations are subject to the conditions laid down in national law. As has been explained *supra* [ref: no. 2], however, the examination and verification procedure is subject to the internal law of the issuing authority, including the modalities of obtaining necessary evidence. Therefore, the issuing authority would be allowed to request declarations on oath or statutory declarations on the basis of national law even in absence of article 66.3 ESR. The precondition mentioned in article 66.2 ESR does not apply on such declarations, as article 66.3 ESR does not contain any similar requirement.[23] This provision is thus superfluous.

IV. Information and Consultation

7. The information and consultation of third parties provided in article 66.4 ESR is intended to satisfy two different purposes: First, it helps to

20 Schmidt, 'Art. 66 EuErbVO', para. 18; cf. Wautelet, 'Article 66', p. 750, who pleads for a generous interpretation of the concept of unability.

21 Dutta, 'Art. 66 EuErbVO', para. 4; Nordmeier, 'Art. 65 EuErbVO', para. 8.

22 Cf. Wautelet, 'Article 66', p. 752.

23 Nordmeier, 'Art. 66 EuErbVO', para. 3; *contra*: Buschbaum and Simon, 'EuErbVO', p. 526; Kleinschmidt, 'Optionales Erbrecht', p. 772; Wautelet, 'Article 66', p. 751.

avoid the issuance of incorrect ECS.[24] Second, it serves to ensure the right to be heard as laid down in article 41.2 of the Charter of Fundamental Rights of the European Union[25] with respect to persons concerned by the decision about the issuance of an ECS.[26]

A. *Information*

8. According to the first sentence of article 66.4 ESR, the issuing authority shall take all necessary steps to inform the beneficiaries of the application for an ECS. The term 'beneficiaries' relates to the beneficiaries of the succession and not of necessarily of the ECS[27] and is not synonymous with the status holders in the sense of article 63.1 ESR.[28] Beneficiaries are rather those who have whatever rights in the succession due to a disposition of property upon death or by operation of law,[29] and thus should have been mentioned in the application according to article 65.3(e) ESR [see art. 65 no. 16]. This corresponds to recital 47 of the ESR which refers in its first sentence to the law applicable to the succession in order to determine who is beneficiary or not and specifies in its second sentence that most laws would cover heirs, legatees and persons entitled to a reserved share. As article 65.3 ESR does not limit the required information to 'direct' beneficiaries, in contrast to article 63.1 ESR [see art. 65 no. 7], civil law legatees can also be covered by the term 'beneficiaries',[30] all the more so as persons entitled to a reserved share usually merely have a claim against the heirs, but no direct right *in rem* in the succession.[31] Executors and administrators of the estate are no beneficiaries although they are entitled to apply for an ECS under articles

[24] Kleinschmidt, 'Optionales Erbrecht', p. 773.

[25] OJ 2012 no. C326, 26 October 2012, p. 391; cf. also article 47(2) of the Charter of Fundamental Rights and recital 81 of the ESR; in this sense, also Kleinschmidt, 'Optionales Erbrecht', p. 773; Nordmeier, 'Art. 66 EuErbVO', para. 4.

[26] Cf. recital 81 of the ESR; see also A. Dutta, 'Art. 64 EuErbVO', in J. von Hein (ed), *Münchener Kommentar zum Bürgerlichen Gesetzbuch*, vol. X, 6th ed. (München, 2015), para. 5.

[27] Wautelet, 'Article 66', p. 753; cf. the first sentence of recital 47 ESR.

[28] *Contra:* Dutta, 'Art. 66 EuErbVO', para. 6.

[29] Cf. Nordmeier, 'Art. 66 EuErbVO', para. 5.

[30] Cf. the third sentence of recital 47 ESR; cf. in detail also J. Schmidt, 'Art. 23 EuErbVO', in C. Budzikiewicz, M.-P. Weller and W. Wurmnest (eds), *Beck-Online Großkommentar, EuErbVO* (München, 2015), para. 11 *et seq.*

[31] Cf. in German law section 2303(1) BGB; see also C. Baldus, 'Erbe und Vermächtnisnehmer nach der Erbrechtsverordnung', *GPR: Zeitschrift für Gemeinschaftsprivatrecht* (2012), p. 313.

65.1 and 63.1 ESR; they are specifically mentioned in the second sentence of article 66.4 ESR which shows that there is a distinction in terminology.

9. Moreover, beneficiaries are not necessarily only those whose rights in the succession are already established as certain. The mere (plausible) possibility that someone has rights in the succession must be sufficient, as otherwise the right to be heard of such persons would be violated. The right to be heard has to be ensured not only with respect to those who, in the opinion of the issuing authority, do enjoy rights into the succession, but also in favour of those who at least with some plausibility could entitled to rights in the succession. They, too, must be heard in order to be able to influence the decision in their favour.

10. It follows from all this that the issuing authority has first of all to take all necessary steps to inform the persons mentioned by the applicant in fulfillment of his or her obligation according to points (d) and (e) of article 65.3 ESR, regardless of whether they are effectively beneficiaries or not. Furthermore, it has to inform any possible beneficiaries resulting from the rest of the application and submitted documents. If the application or the documents contain any evidence that other beneficiaries might exist, yet their identity is not established, the issuing authority has to proceed pursuant to article 66.1 ESR, as this sort of investigation, too, is part of the 'necessary steps' in the sense of article 66.4 ESR.[32] The ESR does not contain any specification on how the information has to take place. This is therefore subject to the national laws. It would thus be conceivable to inform the beneficiaries by e-mail or by telephone.[33]

11. In order to give other possible beneficiaries the opportunity join the proceedings[34] and invoke their rights, the issuing authority has to make public announcements of the application for an ECS according to the second sentence of article 66.4 ESR. The text of this provision keeps silent on the modalities of such announcements, e.g. concerning in which Member States the announcements have to be made, in which language they shall be drafted and whether there exist any time periods that have to be fulfilled after the announcements are made before the ECS may be

[32] Schmidt, 'Art. 66 EuErbVO', para. 25.

[33] Schmidt, 'Art. 66 EuErbVO', para. 26; Nordmeier, 'Art. 66 EuErbVO', para. 7.

[34] Max Planck Institute for Comparative and International Private Law, 'Comments on the European Commission's Proposal for a Regulation of the European Parliament and of the Council on jurisdiction, applicable law, recognition and enforcement of decisions and authentic instruments in matters of succession and the creation of a European Certificate of Succession', *RabelsZ* (2010), p. 686.

issued.[35] The modalities of the required public announcements therefore have to comply with the national law of the issuing authority,[36] without prejudice, however, to the *effet utile* principle which needs to be respected[37] according to the second subparagraph of article 4.3 TEU. Thus, if it is for example clear from the outset that any possible beneficiaries are living in Asia, the issuing authority would have to grant them not just one day of time to invoke their rights before taking a decision,[38] and it would not be sufficient to make the public announcement in a daily local newspaper at the place of the issuing authority.[39] More generally, it should be said that the public announcement has in any case to take place, *inter alia*, on the internet, and that an English translation of the announcement must also be available on the internet. Only in very specific singular cases, a local public announcement in the official language of the issuing authority might be sufficient. If the issuing authority has any evidence that a possible beneficiary is living in a specific country, the public announcement should be made also in that country.[40]

B. Consultation

12. If necessary for the establishment of the elements to be certified by the ECS, the issuing authority has to hear any person involved and any executor or administrator. Executors and administrators are executors of will and administrators of the estate in the sense of article 63.1 ESR [see art. 63 no. 8 *et seq.*]. The meaning of the term 'person involved' is, however, quite unclear.[41] It should not be synonymous with 'beneficiaries', as this term is used immediately prior to the mentioning of the 'persons involved'. It is held that the notion of 'persons involved' is wider than the concept of 'beneficiaries' and means any person that is somehow concerned with the

35 C. Dorsel, 'Europäische Erbrechtsverordnung und Europäisches Nachlasszeugnis', *Europäische Zeitschrift für die Steuer- und Erbrechtspraxis* (2014), p. 214.

36 Dorsel, 'Europäische Erbrechtsverordnung', p. 214; C. Rudolf, 'Die Erbrechtsverordnung der Europäischen Union', *Österreichische Notariatszeitung* (2013), p. 239; Schmidt, 'Art. 66 EuErbVO', para. 32; Nordmeier, 'Art. 66 EuErbVO', para. 6; Dutta, 'Art. 66 EuErbVO', para. 7.

37 Schmidt, 'Art. 66 EuErbVO', para. 32.

38 Schmidt, 'Art. 66 EuErbVO', para. 32; cf. Dorsel, 'Europäische Erbrechtsverordnung', p. 214.

39 Schmidt, 'Art. 66 EuErbVO', para. 32.

40 Dorsel, 'Europäische Erbrechtsverordnung', p. 214.

41 A. Perscha, 'Art 66 EuErbVO', in A. Deixler-Hübner and M. Schauer (eds), *EuErbVO – Kommentar zur EU-Erbrechtsverordnung* (Wien, 2015), paras. 14 *et seq.*; Kleinschmidt, 'Optionales Erbrecht', p. 773.

succession or is interested in its handling.[42] The reason given is that several linguistic versions including the English version would be in this sense, in particular the French ('toute personne intéressée'), Italian ('interessati') and Portuguese ('pessoas interessadas') versions.[43] This is not convincing: The English version could also be understood as referring to the persons who are formally involved in the proceedings by joining them. The French, Italian and Portuguese versions do not exclude that the 'interest' mentioned in the legal texts is to be understood in a tangible and formal sense, and thus necessitates a formal involvement in the proceedings in order to establish that 'interest', the Latin word *interesse, intersum* meaning literally to 'take part in'. Finally, the German version ('Beteiligten') clearly is a denotation for a formal participation in the proceedings.[44]

14. The wording of the relevant phrase of article 66.4 ESR thus being unclear, its interpretation must be established on the basis of the purpose of the provision, exclusively.[45] Article 66.4 ESR is a specific expression of the right to be heard. Evidently, the beneficiaries in the succession enjoy such right. However, once they are informed of the application for an ECS in accordance with the first sentence of article 66.4 ESR, there is no need to consult them further, unless they react on the information given by invoking their rights or by indicating otherwise that they wish to take part in the proceedings. Apart from the beneficiaries, there is usually no reason to consult anyone who may have a perhaps only remote interest in the outcome of the proceedings. However, at the moment such a person asserts certain rights or whatever legal interest he or she may have concerning the succession within the proceedings carried out by the issuing authority, he or she implicitly or explicitly joins the proceedings as a party, and has to be heard as such. Therefore, it corresponds to the purpose of article 66.4 ESR to understand by 'person involved' anyone submitting observations to the issuing authority on behalf of his or her own rights or legal interests. The person thus becomes a party to the proceedings in a formal sense.[46] The national laws do not have discretion

[42] Nordmeier, 'Art. 66 EuErbVO', para. 7. [43] Nordmeier, 'Art. 66 EuErbVO', para. 7.

[44] Cf. C. Dorsel, 'Art. 66 EuErbVO', in R. Geimer and R. Schütze (eds), *Internationaler Rechtsverkehr in Zivil- und Handelssachen*, vol. III (München, 2015), para. 9.

[45] Concerning the interpretation of multilingual texts, cf. B. Kreße, 'Die Auslegung mehrsprachiger Texte durch den EuGH', in I. Burr and G. Gréciano (eds), *Sprache und Recht – La construction européenne* (Baden-Baden, 2003), p. 157 *et seq.*; B. Kreße, 'Mehrsprachigkeit im Recht der Europäischen Union', *Zeitschrift für Rechtspolitik* (2014), p. 11 *et seq.*

[46] Dutta, 'Art. 66 EuErbVO', para. 8; *contra:* M. Fornasier, 'Art. 66 EuErbVO', in A. Dutta and J. Weber (eds), *Internationales Erbrecht – EuErbVO, Erbrechtliche Staatsverträge, EGBGB, IntErbRVG, IntErbStR, IntSchenkungsR* (Munich, 2016), para. 7.

to restrict the notion of 'person involved'.[47] However, the details of the consultation are to be decided by the national laws.[48]

15. As article 66.4 ESR also aims at avoiding the issuance of incorrect ECS, the right to be heard enjoyed by the persons involved as well as by the executors and administrators that are also mentioned in the second sentence of article 66.4 ESR, has only to be ensured if this is necessary for the establishment of the elements to be certified. Otherwise, the consultation does not reduce the risk of the issuance of an incorrect ECS. This restriction to the consultation procedure does not affect the right to be heard of the persons in question. The right to be heard is no end in itself, but is supposed to ensure the possibility of the parties concerned to exert influence on the outcome of the specific proceedings only. If it is totally excluded according to the information available to the issuing authority that the observations of the person involved could possibly influence the decision of the issuing authority in their favour, a consultation is not required. Such would be the case, for example, if the applicant applies for an ECS certifying his or her legacy concerning certain property, and another person, even a beneficiary of the succession, notifies to the issuing authority that the applicant him- or herself has a legacy concerning a totally different property. This other person would not have to be heard under the second sentence of article 66.4 ESR.

V. International Administrative Assistance of Competent Authorities

16. Article 66.5 ESR is to be seen in the context of the issuing authority's obligation to verify *ex officio* the information, declarations and evidence provided by the applicant. The possibility to request necessary information from competent authorities of other Member States is one

[47] Schmidt, 'Art. 66 EuErbVO', para. 28; *contra:* R. Wagner and P. Scholz, 'Der Referentenentwurf eines Gesetzes zur Durchführung der EU-Erbrechtsverordnung', *FamRZ*, 2014, p. 719; J. Kleinschmidt, 'Art. 66 EuErbVO', in M. Würdinger (ed), *Juris Praxiskommentar BGB, Internationales Privatrecht*, vol. VI, 7th ed. (Saarbrücken, 2014), para. 19; cf. also section 37 of the German law on international successions ('Gesetz zum Internationalen Erbrecht und zur Änderung von Vorschriften zum Erbschein sowie zur Änderung sonstiger Vorschriften'), *Bundesgesetzblatt*, 2015, I-1042 of 3 July 2015, that clearly restricts the notion of persons involved; see also K. W. Lange, 'Europäisches Nachlasszeugnis – Antragsverfahren und Verwendung im deutschen Grundbuchverkehr', *Deutsche Notar-Zeitschrift* (2016) p. 107 *et seq.*, who states that the German legislator thus has used its 'power of discretion' ('Gestaltungsspielraum').

[48] Dutta, 'Art. 66 EuErbVO', para. 8.

helpful element of investigation.[49] Although article 66.5 ESR mentions explicitly only information held in certain registers, the international administrative assistance obligation may concern also other information, i.e. that is not held in the registers explicitly mentioned in the provision.[50] The competent authority is only obliged to provide the information where it would be authorised, under national law, to provide another national authority with such information. Thus, the issuing authority enjoys equal treatment with the authorities of any Member State, but is not in a better position than these.[51] However, it is sufficient to assume an obligation that the competent authority is authorised to provide the requested information to any national authority.[52] It is not required that the requested authority would be authorised to provide the information in particular to its national issuing authority.[53] There is no legal basis for such restriction in the text of article 66.5 ESR.

The information is provided only on request of the issuing authority. On the contrary, the competent judicial authorities for redress procedures according to article 72 ESR have no right to request such information. They are neither mentioned in the text of article 66.5 ESR nor would the intent and purpose of this provision require their entitlement.[54] It is rather up to the relevant national procedural law to enable the judicial authority to order the issuing authority to provide information, pursuant to which the issuing authority may submit a request in accordance with article 66.5 ESR, if necessary.

[49] Kleinschmidt, 'Optionales Erbrecht', p. 773, footnote 258; Wautelet, 'Article 66', p. 754.

[50] Nordmeier, 'Art. 66 EuErbVO', para. 11; *contra:* Dutta, 'Art. 66 EuErbVO', para. 10, who holds that only registration authorities are obliged under article 66.5 ESR.

[51] Schmidt, 'Art. 66 EuErbVO', para. 36. [52] Cf. Dutta, 'Art. 66 EuErbVO', para. 11.

[53] *Contra*, however: Nordmeier, 'Art. 66 EuErbVO', para. 13.

[54] *Contra:* Nordmeier, 'Art. 66 EuErbVO', para. 11.

Article 67

Issue of the Certificate

BERNHARD KREßE

1. The issuing authority shall issue the Certificate without delay in accordance with the procedure laid down in this Chapter when the elements to be certified have been established under the law applicable to the succession or under any other law applicable to specific elements. It shall use the form established in accordance with the advisory procedure referred to in Article 81(2).

   The issuing authority shall not issue the Certificate in particular if:

   (a) the elements to be certified are being challenged; or

   (b) the Certificate would not be in conformity with a decision covering the same elements.

2. The issuing authority shall take all necessary steps to inform the beneficiaries of the issue of the Certificate.

Summary

I. GENERALITIES *page* 734
II. NORMATIVE CONTENT 735
A. Preconditions for the issuance of an ECS 735
1. Substantive Requirements 735
2. Formal Requirements 737
3. Grounds for the Refusal of Issuance 738
B. Time Limit and Form 742
C. Information 743

I. Generalities

1. Article 67.1 ESR concerns the preconditions and the time limit for the issuance of an ECS, as well as the form of an ECS. The second subsection of this provision complements the substantive conditions by negative examples precluding the issuance of an ECS.[1] Article 67.2 ESR,

[1] J. Schmidt, 'Art. 67 EuErbVO', in C. Budzikiewicz, M.-P. Weller and W. Wurmnest (eds), *Beck-Online Großkommentar, EuErbVO* (München, 2016), para. 3; C. F. Nordmeier, 'Art.

similarly to the first sentence of article 66.4 ESR, establishes information requirements of the issuing authority with regard to the beneficiaries.[2] Article 67 ESR does not contain provisions on the procedural fees. This issue is therefore subject to national legislation which however, concerning the amount of fees, need to respect the *effet utile* principle according to the second subparagraph of article 4.3 TEU and thus may not charge prohibitive fees.[3]

II. Normative Content

A. *Preconditions for the Issuance of an ECS*

1. Substantive Requirements

2. The requested ECS may only be issued if the elements to be certified have been established. Thus, the examination carried by the issuing authority according to article 66 ESR must have led to the result that the applicant holds a legal status as described in article 63.1 ESR. More specifically, the legal status must correspond exactly to the status the applicant has requested to be certified pursuant to article 65.3(h) ESR.[4] The requirement that the elements to be certified have to be 'established' excludes the issuance of an ECS in case of mere probability of these elements.[5] The word 'elements' refers to elements of factual as well as legal nature,[6] which should not be problematic according to the English

67 EuErbVO', in R. Hüßtege and H.-P. Mansel (eds), *NomosKommentar, BGB, Rom-Verordnungen*, vol. VI, 2nd ed., (Baden-Baden, 2015), para. 1; A. Dutta, 'Art. 67 EuErbVO', in J. von Hein (ed), *Münchener Kommentar zum Bürgerlichen Gesetzbuch*, vol. X, 6th ed. (München, 2015), para. 2.

[2] Schmidt, 'Art. 67 EuErbVO', para. 3; Nordmeier, 'Art. 67 EuErbVO', para. 8; Dutta, 'Art. 67 EuErbVO', para. 1.

[3] Cf. Nordmeier, 'Art. 67 EuErbVO', para. 13; see also S. Stade, 'Die EU-Erbrechtsverordnung aus französischer Sicht', *Zeitschrift für die Steuer- und Erbrechtspraxis* (2015), p. 77, who holds that only small fees can be permitted.

[4] Dutta, 'Art. 67 EuErbVO', para. 9; cf. Nordmeier, 'Art. 67 EuErbVO', para. 5; S. Omlor, 'Gutglaubensschutz durch das Europäische Nachlasszeugnis', *European Union Private Law Review* (2014), p. 218.

[5] Schmidt, 'Art. 67 EuErbVO', para. 7.

[6] Cf. Nordmeier, 'Art. 67 EuErbVO', para. 2; J. Kleinschmidt, 'Art. 67 EuErbVO', in M. Würdinger (ed), *Juris Praxiskommentar BGB, Internationales Privatrecht*, vol. VI, 7th ed (Saarbrücken, 2014), para. 9; A. Perscha, 'Art 67 EuErbVO', in A. Deixler-Hübner and M. Schauer (eds), *EuErbVO – Kommentar zur EU-Erbrechtsverordnung* (Wien, 2015), para. 12; A. Köhler, 'Art. 67 EuErbVO', in L. Kroiß, C.-H. Horn and D. Solomon (eds), *Nachfolgerecht*, (Baden-Baden, 2015), para. 1; U. Janzen, 'Die EU-Erbrechtsverordnung', *Deutsche Notar-Zeitschrift*, 2012, p. 492.

wording. The German wording referring to the 'Sachverhalt' seems, however, to imply factual elements only. A comparison with the French ('elements'), Dutch ('gegevens'), Italian ('elementi'), Spanish ('extremos') and Portuguese ('elementos') wordings shows that the German linguistic version is an 'outlier' in this context and therefore should not be decisive for the interpretation of the relevant phrase.[7]

3. The establishment of the elements to be certified has to have been done under the law applicable to the succession or under any other law applicable to specific elements. The law applicable to the succession is the law to be applied according to chapter III of the ESR, i.e. the article 20 *et seq.* ESR. In case there are dispositions of property upon death of the deceased, in particular the hypothetical *lex successionis* as referred to in the articles 24 to 26 ESR [see art. 24 no. 6 *et seq.*; art. 25 no. 7 *et seq.*; art. 26 no. 3], and the law applicable to the form of dispositions of property upon death pursuant to article 27 ESR [see art. 27], have to be applied by the issuing authority.[8] The phrase 'any other law applicable to specific elements' refers notably to preliminary questions raised by the *lex successionis*. For example, intestate succession depends on the relevant family relationships with the deceased which therefore need to be established [see art. 1 no. 13 *et seq.*].[9] Moreover, another law than the *lex successionis* may be applicable to determine certain elements that have to be specified in the ECS: This is the case, for instance, with the information to be given according to article 68(h) ESR and which follows the applicable matrimonial property law.[10]

[7] Concerning the interpretation of multilingual legal texts with different meanings of the linguistic versions cf. B. Kreße, 'Die Auslegung mehrsprachiger Texte durch den EuGH', in I. Burr and G. Gréciano (eds), *Sprache und Recht – La construction européenne* (Baden-Baden, 2003), p. 157 *et seq.*; B. Kreße, 'Mehrsprachigkeit im Recht der Europäischen Union', *Zeitschrift für Rechtspolitik* (2014), p. 11 *et seq.*

[8] Nordmeier, 'Art. 67 EuErbVO', para. 4.

[9] Dutta, 'Art. 67 EuErbVO', para. 11; T. Ballarino, 'Il nuovo regolamento europeo sulle successioni', *Riv dir int* (2013), p. 1145; cf. Schmidt, 'Art. 67 EuErbVO', para. 6; J. Kleinschmidt, 'Optionales Erbrecht – Das Europäische Nachlasszeugnis als Herausforderung an das Kollisionsrecht', *RabelsZ* (2013), p. 754 *et seq.*; concerning the implications of preliminary questions in the context of the ESR cf. in detail C. F. Nordmeier, 'Art. 62 EuErbVO', in R. Hüßtege and H.-P. Mansel (eds), *NomosKommentar, BGB, Rom-Verordnungen*, vol. VI, 2nd ed. (Baden-Baden, 2015), para. 19 *et seq.*

[10] Kleinschmidt, 'Optionales Erbrecht', p. 755 *et seq.*; Nordmeier, 'Art. 67 EuErbVO', para. 4; cf. P. Lagarde, 'Les principes de base du nouveau règlement européen sur les successions', *Rev crit dr int priv* (2012), p. 729.

4. The fact that the first sentence of the first subparagraph of article 67.1 ESR explicitly refers only to the establishment of the 'elements to be certified', but not to the establishment of a purpose permitted by article 63.1 ESR, could lead to the conclusion that the ECS shall also be issued if the ECS is not 'needed' in the sense of article 63.1 ESR to invoke the relevant status or to exercise the rights or powers relating to the estate [see art. 63 no. 14 *et seq.*]. Also, the relevance of a cross-border situation could be doubted [see art. 63 no. 16 *et seq.*; art. 62 no. 8 *et seq.*].[11] Nevertheless, the mandatory requirement to indicate the purpose of the requested ECS in the application, pursuant to article 65.3(f) ESR, strongly suggests that the issuance of an ECS is to be denied if the need and the cross-border situation required in article 63.1 ESR cannot be established.[12] This interpretation can be brought into conformity with article 67.1 ESR by arguing that in case of a lack of permissible purpose in the sense of article 63.1 ESR, there are strictly no elements 'to be certified' in the sense of article 67.1 ESR because the application is inadmissible, so that the issuance of the ECS shall be rejected altogether. It could, to the same result, also be held that if the ECS does not serve any permissible purpose, its issuance would not be in conformity with the procedure laid down in chapter VI of the ESR, and would therefore violate article 67.1 ESR (cf. immediately *infra* no. 5).

2. Formal Requirements

5. The ECS has to be issued 'in accordance with the procedure laid down in this Chapter', according to the first sentence of the first subparagraph of article 67.1 ESR. Thus, the procedural rules of the article 62 *et seq.* must have been observed. The issuing authority must be internationally competent according to article 64.1 ESR and its substantive, geographical and functional competence must be established pursuant to the *lex fori*. There also must have been submitted an application meeting the requirements of article 65, and the applicant must be a person entitled to file an application according to articles 65.1 and 63.1. The existence of a purpose of the ECS as required by article 63.1 could also be seen as part the procedure laid down in the article 62 *et seq.* with the consequence that if such purpose is lacking, the ECS may not be

[11] Cf. K. W. Lange, 'Das Europäische Nachlasszeugnis', in A. Dutta and S. Herrler (eds), *Die Europäische Erbrechtsverordnung* (München, 2014), para. 7.

[12] Lange, 'Das Europäische Nachlasszeugnis', para. 7, footnote 8.

issued (cf. *supra* no. 4). Finally, the further procedural requirements of the *lex fori* must have been met.[13]

3. Grounds for the Refusal of Issuance

6. If the requirements of the first sentence of the first subparagraph of article 67.1 ESR are not met, the requested ECS, by reverse conclusion, must not be issued. Two specific grounds of refusal[14] are laid down in the second subparagraph of article 67.1 ESR. This provision is not exhaustive,[15] i.e. the issuance of an ECS may be refused also in other cases the requirements of the first subparagraph of article 67.1 ESR are not fulfilled. The issuing authority is not entitled automatically to certify other elements instead which might have been established in the course of the procedure:[16] An ECS may only be issued in accordance with the procedure laid down in chapter VI of the ESR, as is emphasised in the first subparagraph of article 67.1 ESR. The issuance of an ECS certifying different elements than those the certification of which had been requested in the application violates article 65.1 ESR and the application principle laid down in that provision [see for further details art. 65 no. 3 *et seq.*]. However, the issuing authority may issue a partial ECS, certifying only the elements requested in the application that have been established.[17]

7. According to point (a) of the second subparagraph of article 67.1 ESR, the ECS shall not be issued if the elements to be certified are being challenged. The exact meaning of 'being challenged' is unclear.[18] It could be required that the challenge has been made before a court in a judicial dispute.[19] On the contrary, it could be sufficient[20] or even necessary[21] that the challenge has been raised in the procedure concerning the issuance of the ECS before the issuing authority. First of all, it should

[13] Precisely in this sense, Nordmeier, 'Art. 67 EuErbVO', para. 3; Dutta, 'Art. 67 EuErbVO', para. 3.

[14] The term 'refuse' is used in the third sentence of recital 72 ESR.

[15] P. Wautelet, 'Article 67', in A. Bonomi and P. Wautelet, *Le droit européen des successions. Commentaire du Règlement n° 650/2012 du 4 juillet 2012* (Bruxelles, 2013), p. 758.

[16] *Contra*: Nordmeier, 'Art. 67 EuErbVO', paras. 5 and 9; cf. Wautelet, 'Article 67', p. 759.

[17] Wautelet, 'Article 67', p. 759.

[18] Lange, 'Das Europäische Nachlasszeugnis', para. 15; Nordmeier, 'Art. 67 EuErbVO', para. 11; Dutta, 'Art. 67 EuErbVO', para. 5.

[19] Schmidt, 'Art. 67 EuErbVO', para. 9; C. Dorsel, 'Art. 67 EuErbVO', in R. Geimer and R. Schütze (eds), *Internationaler Rechtsverkehr in Zivil- und Handelssachen*, vol. III (München, 2015), para. 6.

[20] Wautelet, 'Article 67', p. 759; Nordmeier, 'Art. 67 EuErbVO', para. 11.

[21] Dutta, 'Art. 67 EuErbVO', para. 5.

be noted that if a relevant challenge has been raised in the procedure before the issuing authority, the latter is required to either carry out the necessary enquiries or to invite the applicant to provide further evidence, in order to establish whether the challenge is justified or not. Only if in the end of the examination procedure, the elements to be certified have been positively established, the issuing authority is entitled and obliged to issue the ECS.[22] Else, it shall refuse the issuance. This shows that point (a) of the second subparagraph of article 67.1 ESR should be seen as a specification of the requirement that the elements to be certified need to be established properly.[23] Therefore, challenges in the sense of this provision are at any rate those that have been raised within the procedure before the issuing authority concerning the issuance of the ECS.

8. In order to establish whether the provision also means challenges that have been raised in judicial proceedings, it should be compared to article 59(2) and (3) ESR. These paragraphs of article 59 ESR both demonstrate that challenges in the sense of the ESR can also be made in judicial court proceedings.[24] This interpretation also corresponds to the purpose of article 65.3(l) ESR, according to which the applicant has to declare that no dispute is pending relating to the elements to be certified.[25] It has been shown [see art. 65 no. 19] that this provision relates to judicial disputes before the courts of any Member States. Point (a) of the second subparagraph of article 67.1 ESR is the necessary completion thereof,[26] as it sets forth that an ECS can only be issued if the declaration required by article 65.3(l) ESR has been truthfully submitted. This interpretation of the word 'challenges' corresponds furthermore to the systematic relation between the points (a) and (b) of the second subparagraph of article 67.1 ESR: Whereas point (b) gives precedence to a court decision that has been already delivered, point (a) extends that precedence to the earlier time span of the pending proceedings.[27] After all, 'challenges' in the sense of point (a) of

[22] S. Herzog, 'Die EU-Erbrechtsverordnung (EU-ErbVO)', *Zeitschrift für die gesamte erbrechtliche Praxis*, 2013, p. 14; Wautelet, 'Article 67', p. 759; *contra*: Dutta, 'Art. 67 EuErbVO', para. 6; M. Fornasier, 'Art. 67 EuErbVO', in A. Dutta and J. Weber (eds), *Internationales Erbrecht – EuErbVO, Erbrechtliche Staatsverträge, EGBGB, IntErbRVG, IntErbStR, IntSchenkungsR* (München, 2016), para. 5; who hold that the issuing authority is not entitled to take a decision on the justification of the challenge, but simply has to refuse the issuance of an ECS in case of a challenge.

[23] Nordmeier, 'Art. 67 EuErbVO', para. 11; Kleinschmidt, 'Art. 67 EuErbVO', para. 26.

[24] Nordmeier, 'Art. 67 EuErbVO', para. 11. [25] Cf. Wautelet, 'Article 67', pp.758–759.

[26] Schmidt, 'Art. 67 EuErbVO', para. 9.

[27] Precisely so, Nordmeier, 'Art. 67 EuErbVO', para. 11.

the second subparagraph of article 67.1 ESR are not only those raised in the procedure concerning the issuance of the ECS in question, but may also refer to any judicial proceedings before a court.

9. According to point (b) of the second subparagraph of article 67.1 ESR, the ECS shall not be issued if it would not be in conformity with a decision covering the same elements. The term 'decision' is legally defined in article 3(g) ESR and thus limited to decisions in matters of succession. The annulment of a marriage or a divorce decision could therefore not lead to a refusal pursuant to point (b) of the second subparagraph of article 67.1 ESR. Such a decision would, however, if applicable, lead to the conclusion that the elements to be certified are not established in the sense of the first subparagraph of article 67.1 ESR.[28]

10. The fact that decisions must by definition be given by a court of a Member State as defined in article 3.2 ESR, excludes *eo ipso* that an ECS that has been issued not by a court, but by another authority of a Member State according to article 64(b) ESR [see art. 64 no. 18] can preclude the issuance of a conflicting ECS under point (b) of the second subparagraph of article 67.1 ESR, although the issuance of an ECS by a court might be treated as 'decision' in the sense of article 3.1(g) ESR.[29] The potentially different treatment of decisions of courts and other authorities in connection with point (b) of the second subparagraph of article 67.1 ESR is justified, as every Member State may decide itself under article 64(b) ESR whether it entrusts the issuance of ECS to courts or to other authorities. The fact that the list of grounds of refusal mentioned in the second subparagraph of article 67 ESR is not exhaustive does not mean that other grounds of refusal may be freely extended: The legal limitations of the right to refuse the issuance of an ECS aside from the grounds of refusal stated in the second subparagraph of article 67.1 ESR, ensue from the first sentence of article 67.1 ESR: If the preconditions of this provision are fulfilled, the issuing authority must issue the ECS, unless there is a ground of refusal resulting from the second subparagraph of article 67.1 ESR. For the same reason, the issuance of an ECS may not be refused

[28] *Contra:* Wautelet, 'Article 67', p. 759.

[29] Cf. A. Dutta, 'Art. 3 EuErbVO', in J. von Hein (ed), *Münchener Kommentar zum Bürgerlichen Gesetzbuch*, vol. X, 6th ed. (München, 2015), para. 13, arguing in favour of the characterisation of at least German certificates of succession as decisions; in the same sense again Dutta, 'Die europäische Erbrechtsverordnung vor ihrem Anwendungsbeginn', *IPRax* (2015), p. 38, and Fornasier, 'Art. 67 EuErbVO', para. 11; however, J. Carrascosa González, 'Reglamento sucesorio europeo y actividad notarial', *CdT* (2014), p. 40, seems to see this differently with respect to the ECS ('no es una "resolución judicial"').

merely for the reason that there exists a conflicting decision of a court of a third State, as such decisions are no decisions in the sense of article 3.1 (g) ESR.[30]

11. Decisions other than the issuance of an ECS that takes effect automatically in all the Member States pursuant to article 69.1 ESR,[31] must be able to be recognised in order to have the effect mentioned in point (b) of the second subparagraph of article 67.1 ESR. Thus, there must be no grounds of non-recognition pursuant to article 40 ESR [see art. 40].[32] The decision precluding the issuance of an ECS must cover the same elements the certification of which is requested by the applicant.[33] The requirement that the ECS would not be in conformity with the precluding decision is to be interpreted in accordance with the principles applying to the interpretation of the term 'irreconcilable' in the sense of points (c) and (d) of article 40 ESR,[34] for which can be referred to the jurisprudence[35] concerning points (c) and (d) of article 45.1 of the Brussels I-*bis* regulation[36].[37] Therefore, the ECS would not be in conformity with a decision covering the same elements if the effects of the ECS would contradict the legal consequences of the decision,[38] or, in other words, if the legal consequences of the decision exclude the existence of the legal position to be certified in the ECS.[39] For example, if a certain person is the only heir according to a decision, an ECS certifying that another person is the only heir could not be issued.[40] However, an ECS certifying that another person is a vindication legatee would not be barred by that decision.[41]

[30] *Contra:* Nordmeier, 'Art. 67 EuErbVO', para. 12; Dutta, 'Art. 67 EuErbVO', para. 8.

[31] Cf. C. Azcárraga Monzonís, 'International Successions in Spain: The Impact of a New EU Regulation', *Spanish Yearbook of International Law* (2009), p. 59; T. Ballarino, 'Il nuovo regolamento europeo sulle successioni', *Riv dir int* (2013), p. 1145.

[32] Nordmeier, 'Art. 67 EuErbVO', para. 12.

[33] Cf. Dutta, 'Art. 67 EuErbVO', para. 7.

[34] Dutta, 'Art. 67 EuErbVO', para. 7; Schmidt, 'Art. 67 EuErbVO', para. 12.

[35] Cf., concerning yet the similar provisions of the Brussels I regulation: ECJ, Case 145/86, *Horst Ludwig Martin Hoffmann* v. *Adelheid Krieg* [1988] ECR 645, para. 22; ECJ, Case C-80/00, *Italian Leather SpA* v. *WECO Polstermöbel GmbH & Co.* [2002] ECR I-4995, para. 44.

[36] Regulation (EU) no. 1215/2012 of the European Parliament and of the Council of 12 December 2012 on jurisdiction and the recognition and enforcement of judgments in civil and commercial matters (recast), OJ 2012 no. L351, 20 December 2012, p. 1.

[37] Dutta, 'Art. 67 EuErbVO', para. 7; cf. Nordmeier, 'Art. 67 EuErbVO', para. 12.

[38] Schmidt, 'Art. 67 EuErbVO', para. 12.

[39] Nordmeier, 'Art. 67 EuErbVO', para. 12; Dutta, 'Art. 67 EuErbVO', para. 7.

[40] Schmidt, 'Art. 67 EuErbVO', para. 12.1.

[41] Schmidt, 'Art. 67 EuErbVO', para. 12.3.

B. *Time Limit and Form*

12. The ECS shall be issued 'without delay', according to the first sentence of the first subparagraph of article 67.1 ESR. This means that the issuing authority has to issue the ECS immediately after the preconditions of its issuance have been established.[42] Nevertheless, there may be a long period of time between the application and the issuance, in particular because of the public announcement required according to article 67.4 ESR,[43] but also with respect to the examination of the application pursuant to article 66 ESR, which may take time. Nevertheless, the issuing authority shall not delay the necessary enquiries and investigation measures, as this would also delay the issuance of the ECS. The ESR does not provide for any sanctions if the issuance of the ECS is delayed. These depend, therefore, on national law.[44] In case of constant decelerations concerning the issuance of ECS in a Member State, the Commission may institute infringement proceedings pursuant to article 258 TFEU for the reason of improper implementation of the ESR.[45]

13. It results from the second sentence of the first subparagraph of article 67.1 ESR that the issuing authority shall use a standard form established in accordance with the advisory procedure referred to in the articles 81.2 ESR and 4 of regulation no. 182/2011.[46] The standard form is to be found in annex V of the Commission Implementing regulation no. 1329/2014.[47] The use of the standard form is mandatory.[48] If the form is not used

[42] Dutta, 'Art. 67 EuErbVO', para. 13. [43] Dutta, 'Art. 67 EuErbVO', para. 13.

[44] Wautelet, 'Article 67', p. 758; Schmidt, 'Art. 67 EuErbVO', para. 18.

[45] Schmidt, 'Art. 67 EuErbVO', para. 18.

[46] Regulation (EU) no. 182/2011 of the European Parliament and of the Council of 16 February 2011 laying down the rules and general principles concerning mechanisms for Control by Member States of the Commission's exercise of implementing powers, OJ 2011 no. L55, 28 February 2011, p. 13.

[47] Commission Implementing Regulation no. 1329/2014 of 9 December 2014 establishing the Forms referred to in Regulation (EU) no. 650/2012 of the European Parliament and of the Council on jurisdiction, applicable law, recognition and enforcement of decisions and acceptance and enforcement of authentic instruments in matters of succession and on the creation of a European Certificate of Succession, OJ 2014 no. L359, 16 December 2014, p. 30.

[48] Wautelet, 'Article 67', p. 757; R. Schaub, 'Die EU-Erbrechtsverordnung', in K. Muscheler (ed), *Hereditare – Jahrbuch für Erbrecht und Schenkungsrecht*, vol 3 (Tübingen, 2013), p. 125; R. Süß, 'Das Europäische Nachlasszeugnis', *ZEuP* (2013), p. 738; Lange, 'Das Europäische Nachlasszeugnis', para. 16; M. Volmer, 'Die EU-Erbrechtsverordnung – erste Fragen an Dogmatik und Forensik', *Der Deutsche Rechtspfleger* (2013), p. 430; Janzen, 'Die EU-Erbrechtsverordnung', p. 492; C. Dorsel, 'Europäische Erbrechtsverordnung und Europäisches Nachlasszeugnis', *Europäische Zeitschrift für die Steuer- und Erbrechtspraxis* (2014), p. 215; H. Wilsch, 'EuErbVO: Die Verordnung

by the issuing authority, the ECS cannot not merely be challenged according to article 72 ESR,[49] but it is null and void.[50] On the one hand, only this strict legal consequence leads to a reliable use of the standard form by the issuing authorities. On the other hand, only the use of the form ensures that the ECS can be read appropriately by the authorities in the other Member States, as its largely does not need a translation in view of the identical structure of the standard form in all of the linguistic versions. The uniformity of design is one of the essential characteristics of the ECS.[51]

C. *Information*

14. Similarly to the information requirement of the first sentence of article 66.4 ESR, the issuing authority shall take all necessary steps to inform the beneficiaries of the issue of the ECS.[52] The terms 'beneficiaries' and 'necessary steps' are to be understood in the same way as in the context of article 66.4 ESR [see art. 66 no. 8 *et seq.*].[53] The information is, however, limited to those beneficiaries that are known to the issuing authority in the end of the proceedings, as article 67 ESR, contrary to article 66.4 ESR, does not provide for a public announcement. The rights of other potential beneficiaries are adequately preserved by the obligation to make public announcement of the submittal of the application.[54] The modalities of the information are set up by the *lex fori.*[55]

in der deutschen Grundbuchpraxis', ZEV (2012); p. 530; Dutta, 'Art. 67 EuErbVO', para. 14; Nordmeier, 'Art. 67 EuErbVO', para. 17; Schmidt, 'Art. 67 EuErbVO', para. 18; P. Lokin, 'De Erfrechtverordening', NIPR (2013), p. 336.

[49] In this sense, however, Dutta, 'Art. 67 EuErbVO', para. 14; Kleinschmidt, 'Art. 67 EuErbVO', para. 36.

[50] Wilsch, EuErbVO, p. 530; Volmer, Die EU-Erbrechtsverordnung, p. 430; *contra:* Süß, Das Europäische Nachlasszeugnis, p. 738 *et seq.*; Dutta, 'Art. 67 EuErbVO', para. 14; cf. also Carrascosa González, 'Reglamento sucesorio europeo y actividad notarial', p. 37, who speaks only of a '*modelo documental*'.

[51] Schmidt, 'Art. 67 EuErbVO', para. 13; Carrascosa González, 'Reglamento sucesorio europeo y actividad notarial', p. 39.

[52] Wautelet, 'Article 67', p. 760; Nordmeier, 'Art. 67 EuErbVO', para. 8; Schmidt, 'Art. 67 EuErbVO', para. 21.

[53] Dutta, 'Art. 67 EuErbVO', para. 15; cf. Schmidt, 'Art. 67 EuErbVO', para. 21; Wautelet, 'Article 67', p. 761.

[54] Nordmeier, 'Art. 67 EuErbVO', para. 8.

[55] Wautelet, 'Article 67', p. 761; Nordmeier, 'Art. 67 EuErbVO', para. 8; Dutta, 'Art. 67 EuErbVO', para. 15.

Article 68

Contents of the Certificate

CHRISTINE BUDZIKIEWICZ

The Certificate shall contain the following information, to the extent required for the purpose for which it is issued:

(a) the name and address of the issuing authority;
(b) the reference number of the file;
(c) the elements on the basis of which the issuing authority considers itself competent to issue the Certificate;
(d) the date of issue;
(e) details concerning the applicant: surname (if applicable, surname at birth), given name(s), sex, date and place of birth, civil status, nationality, identification number (if applicable), address and relationship to the deceased, if any;
(f) details concerning the deceased: surname (if applicable, surname at birth), given name(s), sex, date and place of birth, civil status, nationality, identification number (if applicable), address at the time of death, date and place of death;
(g) details concerning the beneficiaries: surname (if applicable, surname at birth), given name(s) and identification number (if applicable);
(h) information concerning a marriage contract entered into by the deceased or, if applicable, a contract entered into by the deceased in the context of a relationship deemed by the law applicable to such a relationship to have comparable effects to marriage, and information concerning the matrimonial property regime or equivalent property regime;
(i) the law applicable to the succession and the elements on the basis of which that law has been determined;
(j) information as to whether the succession is testate or intestate, including information concerning the elements giving rise to the rights and/or powers of the heirs, legatees, executors of wills or administrators of the estate;
(k) if applicable, information in respect of each beneficiary concerning the nature of the acceptance or waiver of the succession;
(l) the share for each heir and, if applicable, the list of rights and/or assets for any given heir;
(m) the list of rights and/or assets for any given legatee;

(n) the restrictions on the rights of the heir(s) and, as appropriate, legatee(s) under the law applicable to the succession and/or under the disposition of property upon death;

(o) the powers of the executor of the will and/or the administrator of the estate and the restrictions on those powers under the law applicable to the succession and/or under the disposition of property upon death.

Summary

I. INTRODUCTION *page* 745
- A. Exhaustive List of Information *page* 745
- B. Compulsory Use of a Standard Form 747

II. DETAILS ON THE CONTENTS OF THE CERTIFICATE 750
- A. Issuing Authority and Date of Issue 750
- B. Details Concerning the Applicant, the Deceased and the Beneficiaries 751
- C. Marriage Contract and Matrimonial Property Regime 753
- D. The Law Applicable to the Succession 755
- E. Testate and Intestate Succession 756
- F. Acceptance and Waiver of Succession 757
- G. Share for Each Heir and List of Rights and/or Assets 759
- H. List of Rights and/or Assets for Any Given Legatee 765
- I. Restriction of Rights of Heirs and Legatees 766
- J. Executor of the Will and Administrator of the Estate 767

I. Introduction

A. *Exhaustive List of Information*

1. Article 68 determines the relevant information that shall be included in the European Certificate of Succession (ECS). The positions listed in points (a) to (o) of article 68 are exclusive.[1] In this context, reference is made to the clear wording of the regulation ('The Certificate shall contain ...')[2] and the rationale of the provision.[3] Thus, no addition to

[1] J. Schmidt, 'Art. 68 EuErbVO', in C. Budzikiewicz, M.-P. Weller and W. Wurmnest (eds), *Beck-Online Großkommentar* (München, 2016), para. 4; C. Dorsel, 'Art. 68 EuErbVO', in R. Geimer and R. Schütze (eds), *Internationaler Rechtsverkehr in Zivil- und Handelssachen* (München, 2015), para. 11; K. Lange, 'Das Europäische Nachlasszeugnis', in A. Dutta and S. Herrler (eds), *Die Europäische Erbrechtsverordnung* (München, 2014), p. 166 para. 16.

[2] The same applies to other language versions, see, e.g., the French version ('Le certificat comporte ...') or the German version ('Das Zeugnis enthält ...').

[3] Schmidt, 'Art. 68 EuErbVO', para. 4.

the information provided by article 68 is permissible, all the more so in view of the effects attributed to the ECS by article 69. Any additional information beyond that provided by article 68 would render the ECS less intelligible and as a result diminish its usability.[4] It would also increase the risk of raising doubts about the effects the Certificate has according to article 69.[5]

If nonetheless the issuing authority includes information in the ECS that exceeds the scope of article 68, the question as to the consequences has to be raised. The ESR does not address this problem; articles 71.1 and 71.2 in particular do not cover this eventuality as it is neither a clerical error nor an inaccuracy of the Certificate. However, it seems obvious to treat inadmissible information no differently from incorrect information. This can be achieved through an analogous application of article 71.2: the issuing authority would be obliged to modify the ECS in accordance with the requirements of article 71.2 insofar as inadmissible information was present.

2. Article 68 provides a long catalogue of data to be included in the ECS. Even though various sources argued in favour of a limitation of the catalogue,[6] the regulator adhered to a detailed list.[7] This

[4] On the importance of simplifying the circulation of the ECS, see also the Proposal for a Regulation of the European Parliament and of the Council on jurisdiction, applicable law, recognition and enforcement of decisions and authentic instruments in matters of succession and the creation of a European Certificate of Succession, COM(2009)154 final, p. 8 (sub. 4.6.).

[5] Concerning the risk of confusion regarding the scope of the effects resulting from the Certificate in the case of increasing information density, cf. Max Planck Institute for Comparative and International Private Law, 'Comments on the European Commission's Proposal for a Regulation of the European Parliament and of the Council on jurisdiction, applicable law, recognition and enforcement of decisions and authentic instruments in matters of succession and the creation of a European Certificate of Succession', *RabelsZ* (2010), p. 691, para. 306. On the importance of the effects of the ECS referred to in article 69 for the understanding of article 68, see also A. Dutta, 'Art. 68 EuErbVO', in J. von Hein (ed), *Münchener Kommentar zum BGB,* vol. X, 6th ed. (München, 2015), para. 2.

[6] See, e.g., Max Planck Institute, 'Comments', *RabelsZ* (2010), p. 689 *et seq.*, paras. 302–306; K. Lange, 'Das geplante Europäische Nachlasszeugnis', *DNotZ – Deutsche Notar-Zeitschrift* (2012), p. 172 *et seq.*

[7] Critically: Lange, 'Das Europäische Nachlasszeugnis', p. 166 *et seq.* (paras. 17–19); M. Buschbaum, 'Europäisches Nachlasszeugnis und Annahme öffentlicher Urkunden – neue Mechanismen zur grenzüberschreitenden Nachlassabwicklung und ihr Verhältnis zum materiellen Sachenrecht', in Hager (ed),), p. 46; J. Kleinschmidt, 'Optionales Erbrecht: Das Europäische Nachlasszeugnis als Herausforderung an das Kollisionsrecht', *RabelsZ* (2013), p. 781 *et seq.*; A. Bonomi, 'Il regolamento europeo sulle successioni', *Riv dir int priv proc* (2013), p. 321.

ultimately expresses the endeavour to provide sufficient information for any (intended) use of the ECS (cf. article 63); the differing structures of succession laws of the Member States may have induced the regulator to provide for any eventuality.[8] Nonetheless, article 68 does not require that all information listed be included.[9] In any individual case, the ECS must only contain the information necessary for the purpose for which the Certificate is issued ('to the extent required for . . .'). The precise content of an ECS therefore depends on the purpose (as defined in article 63) which the applicant pursues as evidenced by his or her application (cf. point (f) of article 65.3 [see art. 65 no. 18].[10] For example, an executor of the will applies for an ECS to give proof of his or her powers and of the assets which are subject to his or her administration (cf. article 63.1 and point (c) of article 63.2), the Certificate will contain additional information about heirs and legatees only insofar as this is significant for the executor's powers.[11]

B. *Compulsory Use of a Standard Form*

3. To ensure a uniform implementation of the ECS, a form shall be used to issue the Certificate (see article 67.1 subsection 1 sentence 2). The standard form based on the requirements of article 68 is to be

[8] U. Janzen, 'Die EU-Erbrechtsverordnung', *DNotZ – Deutsche Notar-Zeitschrift* (2012), p. 492; Kleinschmidt, 'Optionales Erbrecht', p. 781; see also C. Dorsel and C. Schall, 'Die Umsetzung der ErbVO durch die Europäische Kommission – Ein erster Überblick unter besonderer Berücksichtigung des Europäischen Nachlasszeugnisses', *GPR – European Union Private Law Review* (2015), p. 45.

[9] Dutta, 'Art 68 EuErbVO', para. 2; W. Rechberger and F. Kieweler, in W. H. Rechberger and B. Zöchling-Jud (eds), *Die EU-Erbrechtsverordnung in Österreich* (Wien, 2015), p. 293, para. 45; M. Fornasier, 'Art. 68 EuErbVO', in A. Dutta and J. Weber (eds), *Internationales Erbrecht* (München, 2016), para. 2.

[10] C. F. Nordmeier, 'Art 68 EuErbVO', in R. Hüßtege and H.-P. Mansel (eds), *Nomos-Kommentar BGB, Rom-Verordnungen,* vol. VI, 2nd ed. (Baden-Baden, 2015), para. 2; Dutta, 'Art. 68 EuErbVO', para. 3; C. Dorsel, 'Europäische Erbrechtsverordnung und Europäisches Nachlasszeugnis', *ZErb – Zeitschrift für die Steuer- und Erbrechtspraxis* (2014), p. 215. See also J. Kleinschmidt, 'Art. 68 EuErbVO', in M. Herberger *et al.* (eds), *juris Praxiskommentar BGB*, vol. VI, 7th ed. (Saarbrücken, 2014, status: 15 September 2015), para. 5, who states that a deviation from the application is inadmissible.

[11] See also Dorsel, 'Europäische Erbrechtsverordnung und Europäisches Nachlasszeugnis', p. 216.

found as Form V in Annex 5 of the Implementing regulation (EU) no. 1329/2014.[12] The use of this form is mandatory; if it is not being used, no effective ECS can be issued [see art. 67 no. 13]. The form is available in all of the official languages of the EU.[13] The question as to which (official) language the ECS should be issued in is, however, not addressed by the provisions of the ESR. Therefore, national procedural law must be applied to fill the gap.[14] For example, a German court would issue the ECS in German;[15] a Dutch notary would, in principle, draw up the Certificate in Dutch but could also use a different (official) language if required by the applicant, provided he or she had the necessary language skills.[16] However, the applicant has no right deriving from the ESR to receive a certified copy[17] of the ECS in the language of the Member State in which it will most likely be used.[18]

4. Some of the positions listed in article 68 require information which is indispensable for the issuing of the ECS. As a result, such information must be considered as mandatory under the regulation. This unquestionably includes the information required in points (a), (b) and (d) of article 68 concerning the issuing authority, the file reference number and the date of issue.[19] Similarly, the details

[12] See article 1.5 of the Commission Implementing Regulation (EU) no. 1329/2014 of 9 December 2014 establishing the forms referred to in Regulation (EU) no. 650/2012 of the European Parliament and of the Council on jurisdiction, applicable law, recognition and enforcement of decisions and acceptance and enforcement of authentic instruments in matters of succession and on the creation of a European Certificate of Succession, OJ 2014 no. L 359/30, 16 December 2014.

[13] The form is available in all official languages of the Union on the e-justice Portal of the European Commission (https://e-justice.europa.eu, last access 15 July 2016).

[14] See also J. Kleinschmidt, 'Art. 67 EuErbVO', in M. Herberger *et al.* (eds), *juris Praxiskommentar BGB*, vol. VI, 7th ed. (Saarbrücken, 2014, status: 15 September 2015), para. 39. For a different view, see Nordmeier, 'Art 68 EuErbVO', para. 3: official language of the issuing authority.

[15] See section 35.1 of the (German) international succession law procedure act (*Gesetz zum Internationalen Erbrecht und zur Änderung von Vorschriften zum Erbschein sowie zur Änderung sonstiger Vorschriften – IntErbRVG*) and section 184 sentence 1 of the (German) courts constitution act (*Gerichtsverfassungsgesetz* – GVG).

[16] See article 42 of the (Dutch) notaries act (*Wet op het notarisambt*).

[17] According to article 70.1 ESR the original of the ECS remains in the possession of the issuing authority.

[18] On the language related problems, see also Max Planck Institute, 'Comments', p. 689 *et seq.* (para. 303).

[19] C. Hertel, 'European Certificate of Succession – Content, Issue and Effects', *ERA Forum* (2014), p. 402; Nordmeier, 'Art. 68 EuErbVO', para. 4; Schmidt, 'Art. 68 EuErbVO', paras. 5, 8; see also Dutta, 'Art. 68 EuErbVO', para. 4.

regarding the deceased listed under point (f) of article 68 must be included in every ECS.[20] Whether additional information about the competence of the issuing authority, the applicant, or the applicable law of succession (points (c), (e) and (i) of article 68) must always be included regardless of the purpose for which the Certificate is issued, or whether this is just useful information, has been debated.[21] The form that is relevant for issuing the ECS (see *supra* no. 3), however, identifies those details as 'mandatory information'. Similar comments can also be found in other parts of the standard form conceived by the Commission. By making these details mandatory, the Commission Implementing regulation no. 1329/2014 defines the criteria for particular purposes more concretely in relation to article 68. The resulting uniform application promotes legal certainty. However, it has rightly been pointed out that the Commission had to adhere to the material provisions of the ESR when creating the forms [see art. 65 no. 10].[22] This applies not only to the information to be included as such, but also to the mandatory nature of specific details: if the standard form requires information beyond that requested by the higher-ranking article 68, the corresponding fields need not be completed.[23]

With regard to the formal structure of the form, the Commission has a certain amount of discretion. This applies, for example, to the requirement that any annexes included in the Certificate be identified (page 1 of Form V), that the total number of sheets which have been added be indicated (page 7 of Form V) and that the points not filled in because they were not deemed relevant to the purpose for which the Certificate was issued be listed (page 7 of Form V). As these points provide no additional substantive information and simply give the Certificate's format a unified structure, the requested details are within the material scope of the ESR.

[20] Hertel, 'European Certificate of Succession', p. 402 (who states that 'civil status and nationality are useful, but not really necessary information'); Nordmeier, 'Art. 68 EuErbVO', para. 8; Schmidt, 'Art. 68 EuErbVO', paras. 5, 17; Bonomi, 'Il regolamento europeo sulle successioni', p. 321.

[21] See Hertel, 'European Certificate of Succession', p. 402 *et seq.*

[22] Dorsel and Schall, 'Die Umsetzung der ErbVO durch die Europäische Kommission', p. 43; C. Dorsel, 'Europäische Erbrechtsverordnung und Europäisches Nachlasszeugnis', *ZErb – Zeitschrift für die Steuer- und Erbrechtspraxis* (2014), p. 215.

[23] Dorsel and Schall, 'Die Umsetzung der ErbVO durch die Europäische Kommission', p. 43.

II. Details on the Contents of the Certificate

A. *Issuing Authority and Date of Issue*

5. In every ECS, the name and the address of the issuing authority must be mentioned as mandatory information, see point (a) of article 68. These details have to be entered under point 2 of Form V. The file reference number (see point (b) of article 68 and no. 3.1 of Form V) and the date of issue of the ECS (see point (d) of article 68 and no. 3.2 of Form V) are also obligatory.[24] Unlike certified copies (cf. article 70), the original ECS has no expiry date which has to be filled in on the document.[25] However, the date of issue may become relevant under national law if legal remedies (cf. article 72) can be filed only within a particular time frame.[26] Concerning the discussion on conflicting documents (and the question whether such conflict could be solved by the principle of priority) [see art. 62 no. 18 *et seq.*].[27]

6. Moreover, according to point (c) of article 68, the elements on the basis of which the issuing authority considers itself competent to issue the Certificate must be outlined (cf. article 64). The appropriate information has to be entered under no. 4 of Form V. Number 4.1 lists all articles specified in sentence 1 of article 64 that confer jurisdiction to the courts of the Member States; the issuing authority merely has to tick off the provision relevant for the case at hand. Number 4.2 of Form V allows additional elements to be entered in a blank space. The note to this point exemplarily asks for the last habitual residence of the deceased or a choice-of-court agreement. Additional reference to any factual or legal reasoning by the issuing authority is not required by the form. Whether it should nevertheless be included has met with different opinions. While some authors dispense with any further substantiation of the established international competence,[28] others demand at least an indication of the factual basis for the assessment of

[24] Kleinschmidt, 'Art. 68 EuErbVO', para. 8.

[25] P. Wautelet, 'Article 68', in A. Bonomi and P. Wautelet, *Le droit européen des successions – Commentaire du Règlement n° 650/2012 du 4 juillet 2012* (Bruxelles, 2013), p. 766, and *id.*, 'Article 70', *ibid.*, p. 811 *et seq.*

[26] This is pointed out by Wautelet, 'Article 68', p. 766; Kleinschmidt, 'Art. 68 EuErbVO', para. 8.

[27] See B. Reinhartz, 'Article 68', in U. Bergquist, D. Damascelli, R. Frimston, P. Lagarde, F. Odersky and B. Reinhartz, *Commentaire du Règlement européen sur les successions* (Paris, 2015), para. 9.

[28] Schmidt, 'Art. 68 EuErbVO', para. 15.

competence.[29] The broad term 'elements' in point (c) of article 68 rather seems to favour the latter alternative. Furthermore, the mere mention of, for example, the last habitual residence of the deceased would not provide any additional information supporting the conclusion that competence had been established in accordance with article 4. This could only be achieved by indicating the factual circumstances that had been relevant for determining the place of habitual residence.

But explanations to substantiate international competence are not all that is necessary. Likewise to be included are (national) provisions as well as factual circumstances on the basis of which the issuing authority establishes its geographical, substantive and functional competence.[30] This not only follows from the wording of point (c) of article 68, which does not differentiate between the four ('considers itself competent . . .'), but is also reflected in the comment in brackets on no. 4 of Form V, which refers explicitly to article 64 next to the title 'Competence of the Issuing Authority'. Article 64, however, covers the international competence to issue the ECS (see sentence 1 of article 64) as well as the question which authority of a Member State is competent as issuing authority (see sentence 2 of article 64); determining the latter is a matter of national procedural law [see art. 64 no. 18]. Space to enter the corresponding information is provided in the field under no. 4.2 of Form V.

B. Details Concerning the Applicant, the Deceased and the Beneficiaries

7. Details concerning the applicant are to be included in the ECS according to point (e) of article 68. The requested details are identical to those required in the application to issue the Certificate, see point (b) of article 65.3.[31] If the applicant is a natural person, this information must

[29] Dorsel and Schall, 'Die Umsetzung der ErbVO durch die Europäische Kommission', p. 43; Nordmeier, 'Art. 68 EuErbVO', para. 5.

[30] In the same sense probably Nordmeier, 'Art 68 EuErbVO', para. 5; see also Schmidt, 'Art. 68 EuErbVO', para. 14 *et seq.*, but only with respect to the national rules. For a different view, see Fornasier, 'Art. 68 EuErbVO', para. 3; Dorsel, 'Art. 68 EuErbVO', para. 12; Dorsel and Schall, 'Die Umsetzung der ErbVO durch die Europäische Kommission', p. 43: information on the internal substantive, geographical and functional competence of the issuing authority is not mandatory.

[31] On the need for verification of the correctness of the information given by the applicant see the comment of article 66 at no. 2 *et seq.* [see art. 66].

be entered under number 5 of Form V.[32] The content of the form is mostly self-explanatory. However, although point (e) of article 68 and no. 5 of Form V both just require 'nationality', all nationalities should be included in cases of multiple citizenship.[33] For a legal person, Annex I of Form V must be used. If the applicant has one or more representatives, Annex II of Form V is to be filled in. With regard to the information required by point (e), the form goes beyond the information requested by article 68. In contrast to point (c) of article 65.3, according to which details concerning any representatives of the applicant must also be included in the application, a corresponding point is missing in article 68. The fact that the note on no. 5 of Form V refers to Annex II may indicate that the Commission regards details concerning the representative to be details concerning the applicant.[34] However, the fact that the precise list of relevant details concerning the applicant in point (e) of article 68 does not include the representative speaks against the admissibility of such an extension. Furthermore, an extension of the details concerning the applicant to include details concerning the representative contradicts the clear distinction between these categories of individual that is made in points (b) and (c) of article 65.3. It must therefore be assumed that details concerning a representative are not required in the ECS. Accordingly, it would not be necessary to complete Annex II of Form V, even if the applicant has a representative (cf. *supra* no. 4).

8. Further, the mandatory information in every ECS includes the details concerning the deceased that are listed in point (f) of article 68.[35] This is the same information that is listed in point (a) of article 65.3. The necessary information must be entered under no. 6 of Form V. Once again, the content of the form is, in general, self-explanatory. However, as far as the nationality of the deceased is concerned (see no. 6.6 of Form V), all nationalities should be included in cases of

[32] See also Dorsel and Schall, 'Die Umsetzung der ErbVO durch die Europäische Kommission', p. 44, who consider that the civil status of the applicant is (although indicated differently in the standard form) not mandatory information. See also the critical comment by Hertel, 'European Certificate of Succession', p. 402.

[33] Schmidt, 'Art. 68 EuErbVO', para. 18.

[34] See also Nordmeier, 'Art. 68 EuErbVO', para. 7 (footnote 3).

[35] Cf. Bonomi, 'Il regolamento europeo sulle successioni', p. 321; Nordmeier, 'Art. 68 EuErbVO', para. 8; Schmidt, 'Art. 68 EuErbVO', para. 17; Kleinschmidt, 'Art. 68 EuErbVO', para. 14. See also Dorsel and Schall, 'Die Umsetzung der ErbVO durch die Europäische Kommission', p. 44, who consider that the sex of the deceased is not mandatory information.

multiple citizenship (cf. *supra* no. 7); if the deceased is stateless, this should be filled in as well.[36]

Whether the civil status of the deceased at the time of his or her death is a mandatory detail has been subject to discussion.[37] However, the status of the deceased becomes relevant in the context of the rights of surviving family members. In such a context, the question of the validity of the marriage or other partnership arises as a so-called preliminary question [see art. 1 no. 15]. Thus, the standard form marks the civil status of the deceased as mandatory information (see no. 6.5 of Form V). Regarding the question of which law has to be applied to determine the civil status, see the comment on article 1 at no. 14 *et seq*. [see art. 1 no. 14 *et seq*].

9. Finally, the details listed in point (g) of article 68 concerning the beneficiaries also have to be included in the ECS (surname, given name(s) and – if applicable – identification number[38]). In this respect, the issuing authority can resort to the information the applicant has provided in his or her application according to points (d) and (e) of article 65.3. However, only the actual beneficiaries should be mentioned in the ECS and not any further possible beneficiaries named by the applicant according to point (e) of article 65.3.[39] The form for issuing the ECS does not provide a separate field for this information. In case these details do not appear elsewhere in the ECS (e.g. under no. 5 or 7), the names and identification numbers (if applicable) of the beneficiaries should be recorded on an extra sheet.[40]

C. *Marriage Contract and Matrimonial Property Regime*

10. According to point (h) of article 68, information concerning the matrimonial property regime or 'equivalent property regime' of the deceased must be included in the ECS. The latter expression refers to the property regime applicable for different forms of partnerships[41], such as registered civil partnerships.[42] Likewise to be included is information

[36] Schmidt, 'Art. 68 EuErbVO', para. 19.

[37] Hertel, 'European Certificate of Succession', p. 402; Dorsel, 'Art. 68 EuErbVO', para. 13.

[38] See on this point Wautelet, 'Article 68', p. 766 footnote 4 (referring to Belgian law).

[39] Schmidt, 'Art. 68 EuErbVO', para. 21; Fornasier, 'Art. 68 EuErbVO', para. 6 ('nur tatsächlich erbberechtigte Personen').

[40] This is suggested by Nordmeier, 'Art. 68 EuErbVO', para. 9.

[41] Schmidt, 'Art. 68 EuErbVO', para. 25. See also Reinhartz, 'Article 68', para. 21 *et seq.*

[42] For example, the German *Eingetragene Lebenspartnerschaft* according to the (German) civil partnership act (*Lebenspartnerschaftsgesetz – LPartG*) or the Austrian *Eingetragene*

concerning any 'marriage contracts' (German: 'Ehevertrag'; French: 'contrat de mariage') that were entered into by the deceased. The seemingly complicated addition, 'or . . . a contract entered into by the deceased in the context of a relationship deemed by the law applicable to such a relationship to have comparable effects to marriage', extends the information to be included to contracts formed between partners other than spouses.[43] The concept of a 'relationship' which has comparable effects to marriage has the same meaning as in points (a) and (d) of article 1.2 [see art. 1 nos. 22 and 26]. The issuing authority can resort in this respect to the information the applicant has provided in his or her application according to point (j) of article 65.3.

11. The information requested in point (h) of article 68 must be entered in Annex III of Form V. According to some authors, these details are always mandatory, irrespective of whether or not the property regime influences the legal position to be certified according to article 63.1 or the size of the estate.[44] This assumption, however, contradicts the requirement to include in the ECS only information which is relevant to the purpose for which it is issued (cf. *supra* no. 2). No further information is required, even if the standard form designates it as mandatory (cf. *supra* no. 4). Nonetheless, the property regime under which the deceased and his or her partner lived may frequently influence the surviving family members' status as heirs and/or the size of the estate and must therefore be included.[45] In such cases, the information concerning the property regime that is required according to point (h) of article 68 includes not only the specification of the property regime (see no. 7 of Annex III of Form V), but also the law applicable to the property regime as determined by the issuing authority (see no. 6 of Annex III of Form V).[46] The relevance of the property regime for the

Partnerschaft according to the (Austrian) registered partnership act (*Eingetragene Partnerschaft-Gesetz* – EPG).

43 Schmidt, 'Art. 68 EuErbVO', para. 25; Lange, 'Das Europäische Nachlasszeugnis', para. 21; see also Reinhartz, 'Article 68', para. 21 *et seq.*

44 Nordmeier, 'Art. 68 EuErbVO', para. 10; Dutta, 'Art. 68 EuErbVO', para. 5. For a different view, see H. Dörner, 'Die Abgrenzung des Erbstatuts vom Güterstatut', in A. Dutta and S. Herrler (eds), *Die Europäische Erbrechtsverordnung* (München, 2014), p. 81 para. 21; see also Schmidt, 'Art. 68 EuErbVO', para. 5 ('Erforderlichkeitsklausel kann sich . . . nur auf die Angaben nach lit. g-o beziehen'). Unclear seems the position held by Reinhartz, 'Article 68', para. 21 *et seq.*

45 See Reinhartz, 'Article 68', para. 21 *et seq.*; Wautelet, 'Article 68', p. 776; Hertel, 'European Certificate of Succession', p. 402.

46 Dörner, 'Die Abgrenzung des Erbstatuts vom Güterstatut', p. 81 para. 21; Nordmeier, 'Art. 68 EuErbVO', para. 11.

legal position certified in the ESC can be determined only with this additional information.[47] Number 8 of Annex III of Form V further requests the designation of the property regime in its original language and the mention of all relevant legal provisions. The determination of the applicable law falls under the responsibility of the issuing authority. However, according to point (d) of article 1.2, questions relating to the matrimonial (or comparable) property regime are excluded from the scope of application of the ESR [see art. 1 no. 26 *et seq.*]. Therefore, the international matrimonial property law of the Member State in which the issuing authority is located must be applied.[48] Since no EU-wide uniform international matrimonial property law exists (yet),[49] the application of the conflict-of-law rules in the Member States may lead to varying results.[50]

D. *The Law Applicable to the Succession*

12. According to point (i) of article 68, both the law applicable to the succession and the circumstances used to determine the applicable law must be indicated. The appropriate information is always mandatory.[51] It must be entered under no. 8 of Form V. In addition to mentioning the *lex successionis* (see no. 8.1 of Form V), the legal and factual circumstances forming the basis for determining the law applicable to

[47] Dörner, 'Die Abgrenzung des Erbstatuts vom Güterstatut', p. 81, para. 21; referring to the *effet utile* of point (h) of article 68; see also Kleinschmidt, 'Die europäische Erbrechtsverordnung vor ihrem Anwendungsbeginn', p. 755 ('Angabe hilfreich'); Lange, 'Das Europäische Nachlasszeugnis', p. 167 para. 22 ('praktisch wichtiger Hinweis').

[48] Reinhartz, 'Article 68', para. 21; Wautelet, 'Article 68', p. 776; J. Müller-Lukoscheck, *Die neue EU-Erbrechtsverordnung*, 2nd ed. (Berlin, 2015), p. 160 para. 356; Dörner, 'Die Abgrenzung des Erbstatuts vom Güterstatut', p. 78 para. 14 and p. 81 para. 21.

[49] But see the Council Regulation (EU) 2016/1103 of 24 June 2016 implementing enhanced cooperation in the area of jurisdiction, applicable law and the recognition and enforcement of decisions in matters of matrimonial property regimes, OJ 2016 no. L 183/1, 8 July 2016, and the Council Regulation (EU) 2016/1104 of 24 June 2016 implementing enhanced cooperation in the area of jurisdiction, applicable law and the recognition and enforcement of decisions in matters of the property consequences of registered partnerships, OJ 2016 no. L 183/30, 8 July 2016. Both regulations will apply to the participating Member States as of 29 January 2019.

[50] See Dutta, 'Art. 68 EuErbVO', para. 5; Hertel, 'European Certificate of Succession', p. 402; A. Perscha, 'Art. 68 EuErbVO', in M. Schauer and A. Deixler-Hübner (eds), *EuErbVO - Kommentar zur EU-Erbrechtsverordnung* (Wien, 2015), para. 8.

[51] Dutta, 'Art. 68 EuErbVO', para. 6; Bonomi, 'Il regolamento europeo sulle successioni', p. 321; see also Nordmeier, 'Art 68 EuErbVO', para. 13; Kleinschmidt, 'Art. 68 EuErbVO', para. 19.

the succession must also be stated. Insofar as the issuing authority relied on the conflict-of-law rules of article 21.1 or 22.1,[52] the relevant option must be ticked off on the form (see no. 8.2 of Form V).[53] If the applicable law was determined with regard to the *renvoi* of any third State (cf. article 34.1), both the relevant conflict-of-law rules of the third State and the circumstances which formed the basis for their application (see no. 8.2.4 of Form V) must be detailed separately. Furthermore, if the applied law is based on a manifestly closer connection in accordance to article 21.2, the issuing authority has to state the reasons for this assumption (see no. 8.2.3). In cases where the regulation refers to the law of a State with more than one legal system in respect to succession (e.g. Spain) [see arts 36–38 no. 5], the 'applicable' rules of law must be named according to no. 8.3 of Form V. This applies to all internal conflict-of-law rules of the multi-unit State, cf. article 36.1 and sentence 1 of article 37 (territorial or inter-personal conflict of laws).[54] In the absence of such internal rules, the legal and factual circumstances on the basis of which the relevant legal subsystem was determined (cf. article 36.2 and sentence 2 of article 37) have to be specified. Finally, if special rules apply for specific assets as defined in article 30, those rules as well as the relevant assets must also be specified (see no. 8.4 of Form V). On the other hand, details about the determination of the *hypothetical* law of succession (cf. article 24 *et seq.*) are not required.[55]

E. Testate and Intestate Succession

13. According to point (j) of article 68, information must be provided regarding whether the succession to the estate of the deceased is testate or intestate. These details correspond to the information which has to be included in the application for the issue of the ECS according to point (i)

[52] On the choice of law according to article 22.1, see also Reinhartz, 'Article 68', para. 27: 'L'autorité émettrice doit établir si ce choix de loi est valable conformément au règlement, et ce doit être également mentionné dans le CSE . . .'.

[53] On the application of international conventions which concern matters covered by the ERS, see article 75. In particular on German law: M. Buschbaum and U. Simon, 'Beantragung und Erteilung eines Europäischen Nachlasszeugnisses sowie Verwendung eines ausländischen Europäischen Nachlasszeugnisses in Deutschland', *Rpfleger – Der Deutsche Rechtspfleger* (2015), p. 449.

[54] Nordmeier, 'Art. 68 EuErbVO', para. 13.

[55] Schmidt, 'Art. 68 EuErbVO', para. 28; Nordmeier, 'Art. 68 EuErbVO', para. 14.

of article 65.3. The respective entries must be made under no. 7 of Form V.[56] This information is mandatory.[57]

If the succession is testate (or partially testate), the issuing authority has to provide the information requested under no. 7.2 of Form V. Likewise to be included is information on 'other dispositions of property upon death made by the deceased, and which have been revoked or declared null and void' (see no. 7.3 of Form V). If the issuing authority should come to the conclusion that a disposition of property upon death is invalid (e.g. because of formal defects), this should be mentioned as well.[58] Number 7.4 of Form V provides space for such entries.

14. Details of the circumstances forming the basis for the rights of heirs and legatees and the powers of the executor of the will or the administrator of the estate are also necessary. For example, in the case of a disposition of property upon death, it must be stated which consequences result thereof for the parties concerned (e.g. rights of the heirs or competences of the administrator).[59] In the absence of a disposition of property upon death, information about the rules of intestate succession forming *in casu* the basis for the rights and competences of the concerned parties is necessary.[60] The pertinent information complements the provisions in points (l) to (o) of article 68, according to which the rights and powers as such must be stated.[61] The corresponding information has to be entered in Annexes IV–VI of Form V.

F. *Acceptance and Waiver of Succession*

15. As far as the purpose for which the ECS is issued requires relevant information,[62] it must be indicated whether the succession has been accepted or waived (see point (k) of article 68). This corresponds in principle with the applicant's obligation to state whether the beneficiary has made a declaration of acceptance or waiver of succession as specified

[56] Also see Buschbaum and Simon, 'Beantragung und Erteilung eines Europäischen Nachlasszeugnisses', p. 447, who point out that it is not necessary to attach to the ECS a copy of a disposition of property upon death.

[57] See Nordmeier, 'Art. 68 EuErbVO', para. 15; Reinhartz, 'Article 68', para. 29; for a different view, see Dutta, 'Art. 68 EuErbVO', para. 7.

[58] See also Buschbaum and Simon, 'Beantragung und Erteilung eines Europäischen Nachlasszeugnisses', p. 447: an invalid disposition of property upon death should be dealt with in the same way as those 'declared null and void'.

[59] Reinhartz, 'Article 68', paras. 29, 31.

[60] Reinhartz, 'Article 68', para. 30 *et seq.*

[61] Nordmeier, 'Art. 68 EuErbVO', para. 16; see also Reinhartz, 'Article 68', para. 32.

[62] See Dutta, 'Art. 68 EuErbVO', para. 8.

in point (k) of article 65.3.[63] In this context, the term 'succession' corresponds to the wide definition of the term in point (a) of article 3.1. However, in contrast to point (k) of article 65.3, point (k) of article 68 requires information about the 'nature' of the acceptance or waiver of succession (German: 'Art der Annahme oder der Ausschlagung der Erbschaft'). As a result, it is required not only to indicate whether a declaration of acceptance or waiver of succession was made, but also to specify any conditions (e.g. acceptance under the benefit of inventory[64] or acceptance of succession in competition of the net assets[65]).[66] The broad wording of the provision further suggests that information about the acceptance or waiver of succession must be provided not only in those cases in which the beneficiary has made an express declaration, but also when the applicable law of succession provides for an implied acceptance (*pro herede gestio*)[67] or for the fiction of acceptance.[68] The latter can be found in German law: the inheritance accordingly vests in the heir directly at the time of death of the deceased (acquisition *ipso iure*).[69] Regardless of this fact, the heir may still accept the succession – or waive his or her rights.[70] If the heir lets the period of time during which the waiver of succession is possible elapse, the inheritance will be considered to have been accepted upon expiry of the time limit; a waiver is then no longer possible.[71]

16. Information regarding the heir's acceptance or waiver of succession must be entered under no. 2 and nos. 4–6 of Annex IV of Form V. If the heir is entitled to more than one share of the estate and has accepted one and waived the other,[72] this should be recorded separately. Number 11 of Annex IV of Form V provides space for the appropriate entries. Information regarding the acceptance or waiver of a legacy can be made under nos. 2 and 3 of Annex V of Form V.

[63] Neither point (k) of article 65.3 nor point (k) of article 68 requires information about a contract (or any other declaration) concerning the renunciation of inheritance; see Dorsel, 'Art. 68 EuErbVO', para. 21. However, the information concerned could be relevant with regard to the information required according to point (j) of article 68; see Perscha, 'Art. 68 EuErbVO', para. 15.

[64] See, e.g., article 484 *et seq.* Italian civil code (*accettazione col beneficio d'inventario*).

[65] See, e.g., article 787 *et seq.* French civil code (*acceptation de la succession à concurrence de l'actif net*).

[66] Wautelet, 'Article 68', p. 771.

[67] See, e.g., article 782 French civil code.

[68] Wautelet, 'Article 68', p. 771; see also Nordmeier, 'Art. 68 EuErbVO', para. 17.

[69] See section 1922 BGB.

[70] See section 1942.1 BGB.

[71] See section 1943 BGB.

[72] See, e.g., section 1951 BGB.

G. *Share for Each Heir and List of Rights and/or Assets*

17. Information about the share for each heir must be included in the ECS according to point (l) of article 68 (see no. 8 of Annex IV of Form V). In contrast to some national documents, the ECS does not merely list the beneficiaries: it also substantiates the rights the heirs have in relation to the estate.[73] However, the *in casu* necessary information is based on the purpose for which the Certificate is issued (cf. *supra* no. 2). Therefore, the wording 'share for each heir' (French: 'part revenant à chaque héritier'; German: 'Erbteil jedes Erben') does not require mandatory statements for every share at all. With regard to the principle of relevance which determines the content of the ECS, it is possible to only state the individual share of one heir.[74] Thus, in the event that the deceased is succeeded by his or her spouse and his or her children and only the surviving spouse applies for the issue of the ECS in order to prove his or her share in the estate, the individual shares of the children need not be included if they do not influence the share of the spouse.[75] This can be of interest in those cases where the number of remaining children (or of grandchildren replacing their parents) is not known.[76]

18. However, the influence of the matrimonial property regime on the statement of the shares in the ECS remains an open issue.[77] This question arises when the surviving partner of the deceased is entitled to part of the estate not only according to succession law but also as a result of the matrimonial property regime. A well-known example is the generalised equalisation of accrued gains according to section 1371.1 German civil code. In the event of a death, the equalisation of accrued gains is realised by raising the share of the surviving spouse by one quarter. According to a controversial but convincing position, this provision belongs to the German law on matrimonial property regimes [see art. 1 no. 36]. Accordingly, it will only be applicable if the matrimonial property regime is governed by German law. The law

[73] See Wautelet, 'Article 68', p. 771 *et seq.*, referring to article 730–1 French civil code. On the term 'heir', see also A. Dutta, 'The European Certificate of Succession. A New European Instrument between Procedural and Substantive Law', *International Journal of Procedural Law* (2015), p. 44 ('doubtful whether heirs under English law can be characterised as 'heirs' under Article 65(1), 63(1) for purposes of the Certificate').

[74] Nordmeier, 'Art. 68 EuErbVO', para. 19. For a different view, see Buschbaum and Simon, 'Beantragung und Erteilung eines Europäischen Nachlasszeugnisses', p. 450.

[75] See, e.g., section 1931.1 BGB. [76] Cf. Reinhartz, 'Article 68', para. 35.

[77] See also Max Planck Institute, 'Comments on the Succession Proposal', *RabelsZ* (2010), p. 699 *et seq.*, para. 322 *et seq.*

applicable to the matrimonial property regime, however, is not determined by the conflict-of-law rules of the ESR: questions relating to the matrimonial (or comparable) property regime are expressly excluded from the scope of the regulation according to point (d) of article 1.2 (see *supra* no. 11). On the other hand, according to sentence 2 of recital 12, depending on the situation, the winding-up of the matrimonial property regime (or similar property regime) of the deceased should be taken into account when determining the estate of the deceased and the respective shares of the beneficiaries. Point (h) of article 68 accordingly determines that information concerning the matrimonial or equivalent property regime must be included in the ECS (cf. *supra* no. 10 *et seq.*). Hence it has been argued that although the effects of the matrimonial property regime on the participation in the estate must be stated in the ECS, this entry is merely for informational purposes.[78] These references will play no part in the effects of the ECS according to article 69.[79]

It is questionable whether this gives sufficient allowance for the needs of legal relations.[80] If, for example, a spouse who is entitled to inherit wants to dispose of his or her share,[81] the effects of article 69 would apply to his or her share according to succession law, but not to any additional share resulting from the matrimonial property regime.[82] As a result, the ECS would only be of limited use. Therefore, the ranks of those pleading to record shares with full recognition of the matrimonial property regime

[78] H. Dörner, 'EuErbVO: Die Verordnung zum Internationalen Erb- und Erbverfahrensrecht ist in Kraft!', *ZEV – Zeitschrift für Erbrecht und Vermögensnachfolge* (2012), p. 508; Nordmeier, 'Art. 68 EuErbVO', para. 20; P. Mankowski, 'Das erbrechtliche Viertel nach § 1371 Abs. 1 BGB im deutschen und europäischen Internationalen Privatrecht', *ZEV – Zeitschrift für Erbrecht und Vermögensnachfolge* (2014), p. 126.

[79] Dörner, 'Die Abgrenzung des Erbstatuts vom Güterstatut', p. 82 para. 24; Nordmeier, 'Art. 68 EuErbVO', para. 20; also see Wautelet, 'Article 68', p. 772; Reinhartz, 'Art. 69', para. 8; Mankowski, 'Das erbrechtliche Viertel nach § 1371 Abs. 1 BGB', p. 126, each with regard to article 69.2.

[80] See Fornasier, 'Art. 68 EuErbVO', para. 28; R. Süß, 'Das Europäische Nachlasszeugnis', *ZEuP* (2013), p. 742; R. Stürner, 'Art 62-73 EuErbVO', in R. Stürner (ed), *Jauernig – Bürgerliches Gesetzbuch* (München, 2015), para. 4; see also the critical comment by K. Schurig, 'Das internationale Erbrecht wird europäisch – Bemerkungen zur kommenden Europäischen Verordnung', *Festschrift für Ulrich Spellenberg* (München, 2010), p. 362. On the practical implications of the argument cited earlier, see further Dörner, 'Die Abgrenzung des Erbstatuts vom Güterstatut', p. 82 para. 24.

[81] See, e.g., section 2033.1 BGB.

[82] See Fornasier, 'Art. 63 EuErbVO', para. 27; Dörner, 'Die Abgrenzung des Erbstatuts vom Güterstatut', p. 82 para. 24.

are swelling.[83] Accordingly, a share increased by the matrimonial property regime will be fully subject to the effects of the ECS.[84] In this context sentence 2 of recital 12 in particular is being referred to.[85]

Additionally, it can be noted that the scope of the ESR also excludes the civil status and the family relationships of the deceased (cf. point (a) of article 1.2), but the effects of the ECS nonetheless extend to shares which depend on the preliminary question of a valid marriage or parentage by the deceased [see art. 1 no. 15 *et seq.*]. In this respect, the regulation differentiates between the (excluded) evidentiary effect of the Certificate regarding the civil status or family relationship as such (cf. sentence 3 of recital 71) and the share in the inheritance that is based upon this relationship (and regulated by the *lex successionis*).[86]

This differentiation can be transferred, *mutatis mutandis*, onto the matrimonial property regime. The ECS would then provide no evidence as to the matrimonial property regime the deceased lived in at the time of his or her death,[87] but it could very well be proof that the (additional) share based on the matrimonial property regime resulted from the applied law. This understanding would be in line with sentence 2 of recital 12. Moreover, it does not contradict the wording of article 69.2. The provision starts with sentence 1: 'The Certificate shall be presumed

[83] Stürner, 'Art 62-73 EuErbVO', para. 4; Süß, 'Das Europäische Nachlasszeugnis', p. 742 *et seq.*; Buschbaum and Simon, 'Beantragung und Erteilung eines Europäischen Nachlasszeugnisses', p. 451; Kleinschmidt, 'Art. 67 EuErbVO', para. 19; Fornasier, 'Art. 68 EuErbVO', paras. 7, 12.

[84] A. Köhler, 'Das Europäische Nachlasszeugnis', in W. Gierl, A. Köhler, L. Kroiß, H. Wilsch, *Internationales Erbrecht* (Baden-Baden, 2015), p. 200 *et seq.*, para. 14; J. Schmidt, 'Art. 69 EuErbVO', in C. Budzikiewicz, M.-P. Weller and W. Wurmnest, *Beck-Online Großkommentar* (München, 2016), para. 14; Kleinschmidt, 'Art. 67 EuErbVO', para. 19; see also A. Dutta, 'Die europäische Erbrechtsverordnung vor ihrem Anwendungsbeginn: Zehn ausgewählte Streitstandsminiaturen', *IPRax* (2015), p. 33.

[85] Dutta, 'Die europäische Erbrechtsverordnung vor ihrem Anwendungsbeginn', p. 33. Critical as regards the significance of recital 12: B. Walther, 'Die Qualifikation des § 1371 Abs. 1 BGB im Rahmen der europäischen Erb- und Güterrechtsverordnungen', *GPR – European Union Private Law Review* (2014), p. 327.

[86] See also Kleinschmidt, 'Optionales Erbrecht', p. 757.

[87] See recital 71 (sentence 3): 'The evidentiary effect of the Certificate should not extend to elements which are not governed by this Regulation, such as questions of affiliation . . .'. Questions relating to matrimonial property regimes belong to these elements, see point (d) of article 1.2. It follows from this that the Member State in which the Certificate is intended to be used, is not obliged to recognise a legal status (including the matrimonial property regime) established under the (not unified) law of the issuing State.

to accurately demonstrate *elements which have been established* under the law applicable to the succession or *under any other law applicable to specific elements*'.[88] The last clause is the same as sentence 1 of article 67.1 ('under any other law applicable to specific elements'). Therefore, one can suppose that the phrase 'specific elements' should be interpreted the same way. However, according to some sources, article 67.1 is frequently understood in the broader sense to include (preliminary) questions such as family relationships or the matrimonial property regime [see art. 67 no. 3]. A systematic interpretation of the regulation would suggest a commensurate understanding of article 69.2 [see art. 69 no. 6].[89] This means that the provision is also applicable in regard to matrimonial property law.

If this opinion is shared, the consequences for the reliability of the information provided by the Certificate must be discussed. According to article 69.2 (sentence 1), the Certificate shall be presumed to accurately demonstrate 'elements' which have been established under the law applicable to the succession or under any other law.[90] Many commentators share the (convincing) opinion that the phrase 'element' in this context refers to elements of a factual as well as a legal nature [see arts. 67 no. 2 and 69 no. 5], and to the legal consequences of the applied law in particular. Thus, if the issuing authority includes information regarding the shares according to matrimonial property law, it will be presumed that the relevant legal consequences have been correctly assessed. However, this does not mean that other Member States would be obliged to recognise a foreign legal status; rather, the Certificate merely provides evidence of the application of law by the issuing authority. This application is presumed to be accurate [see art. 69 no. 6].

However, this does not fully describe the effects of article 69.2. According to sentence 2 of article 69.2, it is further presumed that the person mentioned in the Certificate as heir actually has this status [see art. 69 no. 7]. This effect is rather problematic in the present context: it raises the question of whether a share according to matrimonial property law could participate in the evidentiary effect of the ECS. In principle, this question has to be answered in the negative. As long

[88] Emphasis added. [89] See also Kleinschmidt, 'Optionales Erbrecht', p. 756 *et seq.*

[90] This is even more clearly stated in the Dutch version: 'De erfrechtverklaring wordt geacht datgene nauwkeurig aan te tonen dat vaststaat . . . volgens enig ander recht van toepassing op specifieke gegevens.'

as the European conflict-of-law rules regarding the matrimonial property regime (and the property consequences of registered partnerships) are not applicable,[91] the presumption according to sentence 2 of article 69.2 must be limited: the evidentiary effect of the ECS can be extended only as far as it is presumed that the heir is entitled to his or her share according to matrimonial property law in the issuing Member State. Thus, in the issuing Member State, the Certificate will have full effect according to article 69 (including the share according to matrimonial property law).[92] For the other Member States, this will be the case only after the unified international matrimonial property law comes into force (and is applicable under the transitional provisions).[93] Until then, the consequences of the matrimonial property law for any participation in the inheritance should be stated in the ECS (including the share according to matrimonial property law),[94] but at present, they can have only the (limited) effects described above.

19. If applicable, the list of rights and/or assets for any given heir must also be included in the ECS. Form V, Annex IV (no. 9) provides space for such entries. The extent to which information must be included depends on the purpose for which the Certificate is issued (see *supra* no. 2).[95] As a result, regardless of the broad wording of 'for any given heir',[96] a list of the rights and assets must be compiled only insofar as it is necessary for the specific purpose. Thus, a list does not need to be compiled for each heir, nor does it need to contain all of the assets attributed to a given heir. The standard form takes this fact into account. According to no. 9 of Form V (Annex IV), only information about 'asset(s) ... for which certification was requested' is required.

[91] See on this point *supra* no. 11 (footnote 49).

[92] See also Stürner, 'Art. 62-73 EuErbVO', para. 4.

[93] The regulations (EU) 2016/1103 of 24 June 2016 and (EU) 2016/1104 of 24 June 2016 on the property regimes of international couples (see footnote 49) entered into force on 28 July 2016 (but will apply only as of 29 January 2019). However, they are only applicable in the participating Member States. For the non-participating Member States the current legal situation will remain.

[94] For a proposal for a possible formulation see Nordmeier, 'Art. 68 EuErbVO', para. 20.

[95] Reinhartz, 'Article 68', para. 37; Nordmeier, 'Art. 68 EuErbVO', para. 21.

[96] See in this context also the deviating French ('à un héritier déterminé') or German version ('einem bestimmten Erben'); closer to the English version is the Dutch version ('elke erfgenaam'). See also Nordmeier, 'Art. 68 EuErbVO', para. 21, who examines the difference in wording between the various language versions.

The issuing authority is thereby released from the obligation to assess the full extent of the estate in every case.[97]

According to point (l) of article 68, rights and/or assets attributed to the heir must be included in the ECS. As far as assets are concerned, and according to the comment on Form V, it must be specified if the heir acquired ownership of or other rights on the assets. The reason why the assets were attributed is therefore of no importance. The rights on the assets can result from a disposition of property upon death as well as through operation of the law.[98] If, for instance, the applicable law of succession provides for a separation of the estate that directly accomplishes the allocation of property (German: 'dingliche Teilungsanordnung'), this allocation can also be indicated in the ECS.[99]

The form does not provide a separate space for the 'list of rights' which, according to point (l) of article 68, are likewise to be included. The rights of the heir are merely mentioned in no. 10 of Form V (Annex IV). Under this point, conditions and restrictions relating to the rights of the heir are referred to (cf. point (n) of article 68).[100] The 'rights of the heir' must be understood in this context to be all of the rights which the heir has according to the applicable substantive law.[101] They can be entered, as far as necessary for the purpose of the Certificate, under no. 10 of Annex IV. However, it is not clear whether additional rights belonging to the estate (e.g. the deceased's claim of repayment of a loan) can be entered. The broad wording in point (l) of article 68 does not exclude such an interpretation. In view of the fact that several Member States compile a complete list of not only the tangible property, but also all of

[97] See also L. Leszay, in European Parliament, *Content and effects of the European Certificate of succession as proposed in the Proposal for a Regulation on Succession and Wills* (Brussels, 2010), available at www.europarl.europa.eu/studies (last access 1 July 2016), no. 2.4.6, who states that anyway 'the completeness of the list is impossible to guarantee'.

[98] See Schmidt, 'Art. 68 EuErbVO', para. 37.

[99] M. Buschbaum and U. Simon, 'EuErbVO: Das Europäische Nachlasszeugnis', *ZEV – Zeitschrift für Erbrecht und Vermögensnachfolge* (2012), p. 527 (with reference to French, Italian and Dutch law); Fornasier, 'Art. 68 EuErbVO', para. 12; Buschbaum and Simon, 'Beantragung und Erteilung eines Europäischen Nachlasszeugnisses', p. 451; Nordmeier, 'Art. 68 EuErbVO', para. 24; Dutta, 'Art. 68 EuErbVO', para. 9; Dorsel and Schall, 'Die Umsetzung der ErbVO durch die Europäische Kommission', p. 45.

[100] This corresponds to a suggestion by L. Leszay, *Content and effects*, referred to in footnote 97, 2.4.7.

[101] Cf. Nordmeier, 'Art. 68 EuErbVO', para. 22. See also the examples given by Wautelet, 'Article 68', p. 773 ('... de percevoir les fruits et de poser des actes d'administration à l'égard des biens successoraux'), and Perscha, 'Art. 68 EuErbVO', para. 18 ('Verwaltungs- und Vertretungsbefugnisse').

the inheritable rights and obligations of the deceased,[102] it seems obvious that information concerning all rights that form part of the estate should be included in the ECS.[103] Space for such an entry is provided under no. 11 of Annex IV of Form V.

H. *List of Rights and/or Assets for Any Given Legatee*

20. Point (m) of article 68 determines that the ECS must also include rights and assets of legatees. Despite the broad wording, this provision relates only to beneficiaries of a *legatum per vindicationem*.[104] The limitation follows from the purpose for the use of the ECS. The Certificate can only be used by legatees having direct rights in the succession (cf. article 63.1); in particular, it can serve as evidence for the attribution of a specific asset to the person mentioned in the Certificate as legatee (cf. point (b) of article 63.2). Therefore, the ECS is only intended to be used by vindication legatees [see art. 63 no. 7]. This limitation to purpose restricts the Certificate's content at the same time.[105] This mirrors the fact that the standard form to be used for the issue of the ECS requests only information about the 'status and rights of legatee(s) having direct rights in the succession' (see Annex V of Form V).

The rights and/or assets to which the legatee is entitled must be entered into the ECS. The term 'rights of the legatee' describes in this context all rights deriving from the status as legatee.[106] However, similarly to the

[102] See, e.g., section 166.1 of the (Austrian) Uncontested Matters Act (Außerstreitgesetz – AußStrG). For other examples, see L. Leszay, *Content and effects*, referred to in footnote 97, no. 2.4.6.

[103] In the same sense probably Reinhartz, 'Article 68', para. 35 *et seq.* For the comparative law method of interpretation, see K. Lenaerts and K. Gutman, 'The Comparative Law Method and the Court of Justice of the European Union: Interlocking Legal Orders Revisited', in Andenas and Fairgrieve (eds), *Courts and Comparative Law* (Oxford, 2015), p. 163 *et seq.*

[104] Schmidt, 'Art. 68 EuErbVO', para. 39; Kleinschmidt, 'Art. 68 EuErbVO', para. 27; Kleinschmidt, 'Optionales Erbrecht', p. 759; Dutta, 'The European Certificate of Succession', p. 44; J. P. Schmidt, 'Die kollisionsrechtliche Behandlung dinglich wirkender Vermächtnisse', *RabelsZ* (2013), p. 29 (footnote 154); Fornasier, 'Art. 68 EuErbVO', para. 13; see also Buschbaum, 'Europäisches Nachlasszeugnis und Annahme öffentlicher Urkunden', p. 53; Dutta, 'Art. 68 EuErbVO', para. 10; Dorsel, 'Art. 68 EuErbVO'para. 30. Unclear seems Nordmeier's position, 'Art. 68 EuErbVO', para. 25 ('Insbesondere ist anzugeben . . . ob es sich um ein Vindikations- oder Damnationslegat handelt.').

[105] Kleinschmidt, 'Die europäische Erbrechtsverordnung vor ihrem Anwendungsbeginn', p. 759.

[106] Nordmeier, 'Art. 68 EuErbVO', para. 25.

form to be used by heirs (see *supra* no. 19), Annex V of Form V does not provide a separate category for the list of 'rights'. As far as the rights of the legatee be subject to conditions and restrictions (cf. point (n) of article 68), they can be entered under no. 6 of Annex V. For those powers that have not been filled in under no. 6, no. 7 of Annex V provides space for additional information.[107]

I. Restrictions on the Rights of Heirs and Legatees

21. According to point (n) of article 68, the ECS must include also restrictions on the rights of heirs and, if applicable, of legatees. Similarly to point (m), point (n) also refers to vindication legatees only (cf. *supra* no. 20).[108] Regarding the restrictions to be included in the Certificate, the regulation refers to the applicable law of succession as well as to the disposition of property upon death. Legal practitioners have debated about the necessary entries: they hold the view that a detailed list of all restrictions, including those derived from statute, would overburden the issuing authority and thus limit the Certificate's suitability for practical purposes.[109] Therefore, it has been suggested that the regulation should be narrowly interpreted as requiring information about restrictions only insofar as they do not derive from statute.[110] Apart from that, it should refer to the applicable statutory provisions.[111] It must be acknowledged that this suggestion would significantly expedite the issue of the ECS. However, this approach would contradict the wording of the regulation. Point (n) of article 68 requires information about the restrictions

[107] For the powers of a vindication legatee, see the recommendation for a list of questions by J. P. Schmidt, 'Ausländische Vindikationslegate über im Inland belegene Immobilien – zur Bedeutung des Art. 1 Abs. 2 lit. l EuErbVO', *ZEV – Zeitschrift für Erbrecht und Vermögensnachfolge* (2014), p. 139.

[108] Schmidt, 'Art. 68 EuErbVO', para. 41.

[109] C. Dorsel, 'Europäische Erbrechtsverordnung und Europäisches Nachlasszeugnis', *ZErb – Zeitschrift für die Steuer- und Erbrechtspraxis* (2014), p. 215; Dorsel and Schall, 'Die Umsetzung der ErbVO durch die Europäische Kommission', p. 45; Buschbaum and Simon, 'Beantragung und Erteilung eines Europäischen Nachlasszeugnisses', p. 451; see also Lange, 'Das Europäische Nachlasszeugnis', p. 167 (para. 19).

[110] Dorsel, 'Europäische Erbrechtsverordnung und Europäisches Nachlasszeugnis', p. 215; Dorsel, 'Art. 68 EuErbVO', para. 31; see also Lange, 'Das Europäische Nachlasszeugnis', p. 167 (para. 19); M. Buschbaum, 'Die künftige Erbrechtsverordnung', in R. M. Beckmann, H.-P. Mansel and A. Matusche-Beckmann (eds), *Gedächtnisschrift für Ulrich Hübner* (Heidelberg, 2012), p. 600 *et seq.*

[111] Dorsel and Schall, 'Die Umsetzung der ErbVO durch die Europäische Kommission', p. 45; see also Dutta, 'Art. 68 EuErbVO', para. 11.

themselves, not merely about the provision from which they derive. The expression 'and/or' takes into account that restrictions can derive from either source, although it might not be possible to foresee this for all imaginable cases.[112] Therefore, one must include not only restrictions deriving from disposition of property upon death, but also those existing as a result of legal provisions. The relevant provisions must be indicated and the restrictions must thereby be described precisely enough for any user of the ECS to understand them without taking recourse to the provisions.[113]

However, only those restrictions that directly influence the rights of heirs and legatees and thus affect all and sundry are subject to the entry requirement (cf. *supra* nos. 19 and 20).[114] These include any restrictions on the heir's right to dispose of the property (e.g. provisional and reversionary succession or execution of will) in particular.[115] Likewise to be included are restrictions resulting from the status of a co-heir.[116] For example, under Dutch law, the surviving spouse and children succeed the deceased in equal shares.[117] However, the spouse (unless the deceased disposes otherwise) retains all items of property while the children are entitled only to a monetary claim against the surviving spouse in the amount of their share.[118] The resulting restrictions on the children's rights as heirs must be entered into the ECS.[119] However, liabilities of the heir or legatee which exist only in relation to certain persons (e.g. civil law legacies as under German law) are not included; such information is not required for the purpose of the ECS (cf. article 63.1).[120]

J. Executor of the Will and Administrator of the Estate

22. Finally, the powers of executors of the will or administrators of the estate as well as any restrictions on those powers must be entered in the

[112] Nordmeier, 'Art. 68 EuErbVO', para. 27.
[113] Nordmeier, 'Art. 68 EuErbVO', para. 31; see also Schmidt, 'Art. 68 EuERbVO', para. 42.
[114] See also Dutta, 'Art. 68 EuErbVO', para. 11; Fornasier, 'Art. 68 EuErbVO', para. 14; Kleinschmidt, 'Art. 68 EuErbVO', para. 28: restrictions in the internal relationship (e.g., a testamentary burden according to section 2192 *et seq.* German civil code) are no restrictions in the sense of point (n) of article 68.
[115] Dutta, 'Art. 68 EuErbVO', para. 11; Fornasier, 'Art. 68 EuErbVO', para. 14; Kleinschmidt, 'Art. 68 EuErbVO', para. 28; Perscha, 'Art. 68 EuErbVO', para. 23.
[116] See also Nordmeier, 'Art. 68 EuErbVO', para. 26; Perscha, 'Art. 68 EuErbVO', para. 23.
[117] See article 4:10 *et seq.* Dutch civil code. [118] See article 4:13 Dutch civil code.
[119] Reinhartz, 'Article 68', paras. 38, 42.
[120] Convincingly Dutta, 'Art. 68 EuErbVO', para. 11.

ECS, cf. point (o) of article 68. For the required entry, Annex VI of Form V is to be used. The powers of the executor of the will or the administrator of the estate can derive from the disposition of property upon death or from the law applicable to the succession. Included are competences exercised as residual powers in accordance with the second subparagraph of article 29.2 or the first subparagraph of article 29.3.[121] In order to specify those powers, no. 4 of Annex VI provides various predefined options to choose from. But the catalogue listed under no. 4 seems as a rule to cover only part of the possible powers;[122] therefore, the form provides space for additions and explanations. Regarding the restrictions, which must be entered as well, the provision correlates with the requirements made in point (n) of article 68. Also in the context of point (o), it therefore does not suffice to refer to the applicable law; instead, the powers must be adequately specified (see *supra* no. 21).[123]

[121] Schmidt, 'Art. 68 EuErbVO', para. 45.

[122] See also Nordmeier, 'Art. 68 EuErbVO', para. 28.

[123] See the examples given by Schmidt, 'Art. 68 EuErbVO', para. 47.1.

Article 69

Effects of the Certificate

CHRISTINE BUDZIKIEWICZ

(1) The Certificate shall produce its effects in all Member States, without any special procedure being required.

(2) The Certificate shall be presumed to accurately demonstrate elements which have been established under the law applicable to the succession or under any other law applicable to specific elements. The person mentioned in the Certificate as the heir, legatee, executor of the will or administrator of the estate shall be presumed to have the status mentioned in the Certificate and/or to hold the rights or the powers stated in the Certificate, with no conditions and/or restrictions being attached to those rights or powers other than those stated in the Certificate.

(3) Any person who, acting on the basis of the information certified in a Certificate, makes payments or passes on property to a person mentioned in the Certificate as authorised to accept payment or property shall be considered to have transacted with a person with authority to accept payment or property, unless he knows that the contents of the Certificate are not accurate or is unaware of such inaccuracy due to gross negligence.

(4) Where a person mentioned in the Certificate as authorised to dispose of succession property disposes of such property in favour of another person, that other person shall, if acting on the basis of the information certified in the Certificate, be considered to have transacted with a person with authority to dispose of the property concerned, unless he knows that the contents of the Certificate are not accurate or is unaware of such inaccuracy due to gross negligence.

(5) The Certificate shall constitute a valid document for the recording of succession property in the relevant register of a Member State, without prejudice to points (k) and (l) of Article 1(2).

Summary

I. INTRODUCTION *page* 770
II. EXTENSION OF EFFECTS IPSO IURE (ARTICLE 69.1) 771
III. EFFECT OF THE PRESUMPTION (ARTICLE 69.2) 775
IV. BONA FIDE EFFECT (PARAGRAPHS 3 AND 4 OF ARTICLE 69) 780
A. *Bona Fide* Protection within the Limits of Article 69.2 780
B. The Legal Transactions Covered by *Bona Fide* Protection 781
C. Authority according to the ECS 783
D. Inaccuracy of the Certificate with Regard to Content 784
E. No Knowledge or Unawareness Due to Gross Negligence 785
F. Legal Consequences 788
V. LEGITIMISING EFFECT (ARTICLE 69.5) 788

I. Introduction

1. The provision deals with the effects of the European Certificate of Succession (ECS). It is therefore the basis for achieving the objectives intended by the ECS (cf. article 63).[1] The declared purpose of the introduction of the ECS is to facilitate the demonstration of the legal status, rights and powers of heirs, legatees, executors of the will or administrators of the estate.[2] In order to achieve this aim, article 69.1 first of all stipulates that the Certificate shall produce its effects in all Member States without any special procedure being required. Recital 71 sentence 1 specifies that the same effects are produced by the Certificate in all Member States. This also includes the Member State of issuance (see article 62.3 sentence 2). However, the Certificate only serves as (declaratory) evidence of the rights and powers stated therein.[3] The applicable law still remains the basis for the conferral of the legal status indicated in

[1] See W. Rechberger and F. Kieweler, 'Das Europäische Nachlasszeugnis', in W. Rechberger and B. Zöchling-Jud (eds), *Die EU-Erbrechtsverordnung in Österreich* (Wien, 2015), p. 294 (para. 46); A. Dutta, 'Art. 69 EuErbVO', in J. von Hein (ed), *Münchener Kommentar zum BGB,* vol. X, 6th ed. (München, 2015), para. 1; M. Schauer, 'Europäisches Nachlasszeugnis', in M. Schauer and E. Scheuba (eds), *Europäische Erbrechtsverordnung* (Wien, 2012), p. 92.

[2] See also recital 67 sentence 1: 'In order for a succession with cross-border implications within the Union to be settled speedily, smoothly and efficiently, the heirs, legatees, executors of the will or administrators of the estate should be able to demonstrate easily their status and/or rights and powers in another Member State, for instance in a Member State in which succession property is located.'

[3] C. F. Nordmeier, 'Art. 69 EuErbVO', in R. Hüßtege and H.-P. Mansel (eds), *Nomos-Kommentar BGB, Rom-Verordnungen,* vol. VI, 2nd ed. (Baden-Baden, 2015), para. 2; K. Lange, 'Das Europäische Nachlasszeugnis', in A. Dutta and S. Herrler (eds), *Die Europäische Erbrechtsverordnung* (München, 2014), p. 168 (para. 23); C. Dorsel,

the Certificate. Specifically, the ECS is not an enforceable title in its own right (see recital 71 sentence 2).[4] However, the Certificate is provided with the effects stated in paragraphs 2–5 of article 69 that enable the beneficiary to establish his or her legal status. Accordingly, the ECS has an evidential function (article 69.2): it is presumed that the statements therein are accurate and comprehensive. In particular, it is presumed that the persons mentioned as heirs, legatees, executors of the will and administrators of the estate do have the legal status, rights and powers ascribed to them by the Certificate and that they have them to the extent indicated therein. This presumption is the basis for the further effects of the ECS.[5] Paragraphs 3 and 4 of article 69 accordingly stipulate *bona fide* rules for the benefit of third parties: in order to protect the legal transactions, even if the Certificate is inaccurate with regard to content, a *bona fide* third party shall be considered to have transacted with a person with authority either to accept performance or to dispose of succession property. Finally, and pursuant to article 69.5, the ECS constitutes a valid document for the recording of succession property in the relevant registers of the Member States; in this respect, the Certificate has a legitimising effect.

II. Extension of Effects *ipso iure* (Article 69.1)

2. The ECS produces its effects (cf. paragraphs 2–5 of article 69) in all Member States, without any special procedure being required (article 69.1). This includes the Member State in which the Certificate has been

'Europäische Erbrechtsverordnung und Europäisches Nachlasszeugnis', *ZErb – Zeitschrift für die Steuer- und Erbrechtspraxis* (2014), p. 216.

[4] M. Buschbaum, 'Europäisches Nachlasszeugnis und Annahme öffentlicher Urkunden – neue Mechanismen zur grenzüberschreitenden Nachlassabwicklung und ihr Verhältnis zum materiellen Sachenrecht', in J. Hager (ed), *Die neue europäische Erbrechtsverordnung* (Baden-Baden, 2013), p. 52; R. Schaub, 'Die EU-Erbrechtsverordnung', in K. Muscheler (ed), Hereditare – Jahrbuch für Erbrecht und Schenkungsrecht (Tübingen, 2013), p. 126; S. Frodl, 'Einheit durch Aufgabe nationaler Rechtstraditionen? – EU-Erbrechtsverordnung kundgemacht', *ÖJZ – Österreichische Juristenzeitung* (2012), p. 957; P. Lokin, 'De erfrechtverordening', *NiPR* (2013), p. 336; Nordmeier, 'Art. 69 EuErbVO', para. 2; see also K. Lechner, 'Die Entwicklung der Erbrechtsverordnung – Eine Einführung zum Gesetzgebungsverfahren', in A. Dutta and S. Herrler (eds), *Die Europäische Erbrechtsverordnung* (München, 2014), p. 12 (para. 27).

[5] Rechberger and Kieweler, 'Das Europäische Nachlasszeugnis', p. 297 (para. 51); Frodl, 'Einheit durch Aufgabe nationaler Rechtstraditionen?', p. 957; S. Omlor, 'Gutglaubensschutz durch das Europäische Nachlasszeugnis', *GPR - European Union Private Law Review* (2014), p. 219.

issued (see sentence 2 of article 62.3). The extension of the effects of the ECS beyond the State of issuance does not, however, encompass all of the Member States of the EU, regardless of the broad wording of article 69.1: Denmark, Ireland and the United Kingdom have not taken part in the adoption of the ESR and are neither bound by it nor obliged to apply it [see art. 3 no. 9]. Accordingly, they are not considered to be Member States within the meaning of the regulation; with respect to the effects of the ECS, they are to be treated like third States.[6]

The extension of the effects within the Member States takes place *ipso iure*. A formal recognition of the ECS or any other type of confirmation is not required.[7] Nor is there any possibility for the State where the ECS shall apply to prevent the ECS from producing its effects in any particular case; the possibility for the concerned Member State to raise the public policy exception is excluded in particular.[8] The extension of effects under article 69.1 differs in this respect from the rules on recognition and acceptance laid down in chapters IV and V.[9]

3. However, the ECS produces the effects mentioned in paragraphs 2–5 of article 69 only when it has been effectively issued.[10] Moreover, the ECS must not have undergone any modification or withdrawal at the time of its use (cf. article 71.2 and article 72.2 subparagraph 1) and its

6 See also Nordmeier, 'Art. 69 EuErbVO', para. 4; Dutta, 'Art. 69 EuErbVO', para. 3.

7 Nordmeier, 'Art. 69 EuErbVO', para. 4 (who states that in particular no legalisation or other formality [e.g. an apostille] is required); C. Hertel, 'European Certificate of Succession – content, issue and effects', *ERA Forum* (2014), p. 404; P. Wautelet, 'Article 69', in A. Bonomi and P. Wautelet, *Le droit européen des successions. Commentaire du Règlement n° 650/2012 du 4 juillet 2012* (Bruxelles, 2013), p. 780 *et seq.*; B. Reinhartz, 'Article 69', in U. Bergquist, D. Damascelli, R. Frimston, P. Lagarde, F. Odersky and B. Reinhartz, Commentaire du Règlement européen sur les successions (Paris, 2015), para. 4; Schauer, 'Europäisches Nachlasszeugnis', p. 92; J. Schmidt, 'Art. 69 EuErbVO', in C. Budzikiewicz, M.-P. Weller and W. Wurmnest (eds), *Beck-Online Großkommentar* (München, status: 1 February 2016), para. 4; Dutta, 'Art. 69 EuErbVO', para. 3.

8 Wautelet, 'Article 69', p. 782; Rechberger and Kieweler, 'Das Europäische Nachlasszeugnis', p. 294, para. 46; Dutta, 'Art. 69 EuErbVO', para. 3; Nordmeier, 'Art. 69 EuErbVO', para. 4. The European regulator has thus failed to comply with the legal policy request made in doctrine that the courts in the State where the ECS is utilised shall be entitled to raise the public policy general exception where they examine the effects of the ECS, see H.-P. Mansel, 'Vereinheitlichung des internationalen Erbrechts in der Europäischen Gemeinschaft – Kompetenzfragen und Regelungsgrundsätze', in *Prof. Dr. Tuğrul Ansay'a Armağan* (Ankara, 2006), p. 223; W. Rechberger, 'Das Europäische Nachlasszeugnis und seine Wirkungen', *ÖJZ – Österreichische Juristenzeitung* (2012), p. 17.

9 See also Dutta, 'Art. 69 EuErbVO', para. 3.

10 Dutta, 'Art. 69 EuErbVO', para. 2; Nordmeier, 'Art. 69 EuErbVO', para. 5; Rechberger and Kieweler, 'Das Europäische Nachlasszeugnis', p. 296 (para. 50).

effects must not have been suspended pursuant to article 73.1.[11] Procedural deficiencies do not, however, prevent the ECS from producing its effects as long as these deficiencies do not influence the legal effectiveness of the ECS itself [see art. 67 no. 13] on the consequences of not using the standard form). This also includes cases where the issuing authority has wrongfully assumed its international competence (cf. article 64).[12] The defective aspects of the ECS shall be corrected only by the issuing authority in accordance with the procedure laid down in article 71, or by the judicial authority in accordance with the procedure laid down in article 72.[13]

There are different opinions regarding whether, in addition to the effective issuance of the ECS, further conditions must be fulfilled in order for the Certificate to be able to produce its effects in accordance with paragraphs 2–5 of article 69. Some hold the view that at least one certified copy must have been issued (cf. article 70.1) and that this copy must still be valid at the decisive date (cf. article 70.3).[14] This view is upheld by referring to sentence 6 of recital 71: 'The protection should be ensured if certified copies which are still valid are presented.' This statement immediately follows sentences 4 and 5 of recital 71 which deal with the protection of *bona fide* third parties who either render a performance or acquire assets of the estate, relying on the accuracy of the information certified in the Certificate. The text of the regulation itself refers to the protection of *bona fide* third parties in paragraphs 3 and 4 of article 69. In view of the *bona fide* effects of the ECS laid down in these provisions, the statement of sentence 6 of recital 71 proves to be persuasive. Based on the fact that the original copy of the ECS always remains with the issuing authority (cf. article 70), the Certificate can ultimately only produce effects through its certified copies. The existence of a valid certified copy must therefore be a precondition for the *bona fide* effects under paragraphs 3 and 4 of article 69 to be able to take place.[15] The same considerations are valid for the legitimisation effect pursuant to article 69.5. Here, the relevant

[11] Dutta, 'Art. 69 EuErbVO', para. 2; Rechberger and Kieweler, 'Das Europäische Nachlasszeugnis', p. 297 (para. 50).

[12] See also Dutta, 'Art. 69 EuErbVO', paras. 2 and 3.

[13] Nordmeier, 'Art. 69 EuErbVO', para. 5.

[14] Dutta, 'Art. 69 EuErbVO', para. 2; Nordmeier, 'Art. 69 EuErbVO', para. 5; Rechberger and Kieweler, 'Das Europäische Nachlasszeugnis', p. 296 *et seq.* (para. 50); see also Lange, 'Das Europäische Nachlasszeugnis', p. 168 (para. 23).

[15] Nordmeier, 'Art. 69 EuErbVO', para. 6.

evidence can also only be produced by means of a certified copy. It follows that the effects laid down in article 69.5 must also depend on the existence of a certified copy that is still valid.[16] The situation is different, however, with respect to the evidential function according to article 69.2. The presumption of the accuracy and comprehensiveness of the information recorded in the Certificate is not bound to the validity of a certified copy;[17] rather, it is the ECS per se that produces the effects of the presumption. However, the submission of a valid certified copy is nevertheless necessary in proceedings where the evidential function of the ECS plays a decisive role.[18] Since the original copy remains with the issuing authority, as has been explained, the court cannot rely on the presumption that a certified copy still corresponds to the original; the latter may have been modified or withdrawn in the meantime. Consequently, the court may require the submission of a certified copy that is still valid at the time of its ruling.

According to article 70.3, certified copies of the ECS are only valid for a limited period of time. The effects provided for by article 69 paragraphs 3–5 can no longer be produced once the period of validity has expired. However, this does not answer the question of whether the circulating certified copies which have not yet expired can still produce effects pursuant to article 69 if the effects of the Certificate have been suspended (cf. article 73) or if the Certificate has been modified or withdrawn. According to the view held here, this question must be answered in the negative [see arts. 70 no. 10 and 73 no. 9].

The regulation also does not say what consequences of contradicting ECSs follow with regard to the effects under article 69. One can refer here to the comprehensive comment of article 62 [for more on the problem of conflicting documents in general, see art. 62 no. 18 *et seq.*; for more on the consequences of contradicting ECSs in particular, see art. 62 no. 20].

4. The extension of the effects pursuant to article 69.1 applies only to the Member States (see *supra* no. 2). The effects of the ECS in a third State are determined by the (autonomous or treaty-based) law of that

[16] Nordmeier, 'Art. 69 EuErbVO', para. 6; see also M. Buschbaum and U. Simon, 'EuErbVO: Das Europäische Nachlasszeugnis', *ZEV - Zeitschrift für Erbrecht und Vermögensnachfolge* (2012), p. 527.

[17] Nordmeier, 'Art. 69 EuErbVO', para. 6. For a different view, see Lange, 'Das Europäische Nachlasszeugnis', p. 168 (para. 23).

[18] For a different view, see Nordmeier, 'Art. 69 EuErbVO', para. 6.

State.[19] This applies particularly if the ECS is to be used before an authority in a third State[20] or if the legal situation is to be established by a court of a third State.[21] The situation is different, however, if a performance or a disposition have been rendered in a third State, but the consequences thereof are litigated before a court in a Member State. The courts of the Member State have to apply the ESR and therefore also article 69 paragraphs 3 and 4, irrespective of the national law under which the preconditions and consequences of that performance or disposition are otherwise regulated or where these preconditions and consequences take place.[22] If, however, the provision of article 69 is to be applied, the subsequent question can only be which requirements have to be fulfilled in order to ensure the protection of good faith. This question refers to the (autonomous) interpretation of article 69. According to the wording of the provision, only good faith is required from the third person. The provision does not indicate whether the person relying on the accuracy and comprehensiveness of the ECS has to be staying in a Member State at the time that he or she learns of the Certificate's content. Such a stay would in most cases be purely coincidental. The same applies to the place where a certified copy of an ECS is located at the time of performance or disposition; this same reasoning applies with even more force in the event that multiple valid copies are in existence: the question would then have to be raised as to which copy was the relevant one. Article 69 paragraphs 3 and 4 have the purpose of offering a *bona fide* third party the assurance that, in the case of a lawsuit before a court of a Member State, he or she shall be considered to have performed for or acquired from an authorised person. Limitations of this purpose in cases where circumstances relate to a third State are neither provided for by the regulation nor necessary.

III. Effect of the Presumption (Article 69.2)

5. It is presumed according to article 69.2 sentence 1 that the ECS accurately demonstrates the 'elements which have been established

[19] Dutta, 'Art. 69 EuErbVO' para. 4; Nordmeier, 'Art. 69 EuErbVO', para. 10; see also P. Wautelet, 'Article 62', in A. Bonomi and P. Wautelet, *Le droit européen des successions – Commentaire du Règlement n° 650/2012 du 4 juillet 2012* (Bruxelles, 2013), p. 718.

[20] Schauer, 'Europäisches Nachlasszeugnis', p. 94.

[21] Dutta, 'Art. 69 EuErbVO', para. 4.

[22] Dutta, 'Art. 69 EuErbVO', para. 4; see also Schauer, 'Europäisches Nachlasszeugnis', p. 94 *et seq.* For a different view, see Nordmeier, 'Art. 69 EuErbVO', para. 10; Rechberger and Kieweler, 'Das Europäische Nachlasszeugnis', p. 307 *et seq.* (para. 67).

under the law applicable to the succession or under any other law applicable to specific elements'. This wording is almost identical to that in article 67.1. It therefore seems obvious, on the basis of systematic interpretation, that the terminology used has the same meaning in both provisions. This is relevant for determining what is meant by the notion of 'elements' to which the presumption under sentence 1 of article 69.2 refers. Different conclusions are reached by different authors. Some hold that the effect of the presumption under sentence 1 of article 69.2 refers only to the legal situation attested by the ECS and not to the factual elements on which the legal situation is based.[23] Others take the view that sentence 1 of article 69.2 refers only to factual circumstances.[24] The predominant and more convincing position is, however, that an autonomous understanding of the broad notion of 'elements' also includes the factual circumstances specified in the Certificate as the legal situation established and recorded by the issuing authority.[25] This conclusion corresponds to the interpretation of the concept of 'element' in article 67.1, as it is supported in this publication [see art. 67 no. 2].

6. The effect of the presumption of article 69.2 relates first of all to the elements (cf. *supra* no. 5) that have been established in accordance with the law applicable on the succession *mortis causa* [see art. 67 no. 3], and second to those elements that have been established according to 'any other law applicable to specific elements'. The question is, however, what the term 'specific elements' is meant to refer to in this context. This question specifically arises with regard to the statement in sentence 3 of recital 71: 'The evidentiary effect of the Certificate should not extend to elements which are not governed by the regulation, such as questions of affiliation or the question whether or not a particular asset belonged to the deceased.' The view has been expressed that the term 'specific elements' in article 69.2 sentence 1 can only relate to issues that are directly linked to the succession to the estate of a deceased person, but are not governed by the law of succession. This would be the case, for example, where the validity of a disposition of property upon

[23] Dorsel, 'Europäische Erbrechtsverordnung und Europäisches Nachlasszeugnis', p. 216.

[24] W. Böhringer, 'Das Europäische Nachlasszeugnis im deutschen Grundbuchverfahren', *NotBZ – Zeitschrift für die notarielle Beratungs- und Beurkundungspraxis* (2015), p. 283.

[25] Schmidt, 'Art. 69 EuErbVO', para. 9; Dutta, 'Art. 69 EuErbVO', para. 7 *et seq.*; Nordmeier, 'Art. 69 EuErbVO', para. 11; Reinhartz, 'Article 69', para. 6; Rechberger and Kieweler, 'Das Europäische Nachlasszeugnis', p. 297 (para. 52); M. Fornasier, 'Art. 69 EuErbVO', in A. Dutta and J. Weber (eds), *Internationales Erbrecht* (München, 2016), para. 4.

death is concerned (cf. articles 24–27). Under this argument, the elements that are excluded from the regulation's scope of application are not covered by the effect of the presumption (cf. article 1.2).[26] This approach is, however, subject to discussion. Another line of reasoning is that the findings concerning the matrimonial property regime should always be subject to the effects stipulated in article 69.2 sentence 1.[27] This broad understanding of 'specific elements' corresponds to the seemingly predominant interpretation of this term in article 67.1, according to which (preliminary) questions such as family relationships or the matrimonial property regime shall also be included [see art. 67 no. 3]. A systematic interpretation of the regulation suggests a parallel understanding of the notion in both provisions. The aforementioned narrow interpretation of article 69.2 is neither prescribed by the provision's wording nor justified by the limits of the regulation's scope of application. Pursuant to sentence 1 of article 69.2, the presumption has been raised that the ECS accurately demonstrates the 'elements which have been established under ... any other law applicable to specific elements'. It is thus presumed that the issuing authority has drawn the correct legal conclusions on the factual basis that it has determined, and based on the law to be applied in the State of issuance. It by no means follows that the State where the ECS is used would be obliged to recognise a legal status that has been established under foreign family law (e.g. a child–parent relationship). With respect to the legal situation, the presumption of conformity of the ECS only goes so far as to presume that the authority has correctly determined and applied the applicable law. This can only lead to the following conclusion: as far as the applicable law has been determined in accordance with the unified conflict-of-law-rules within the EU (in particular based on the ESR), there is according to article 69.2 sentence 1 a (rebuttable) presumption that the established legal situation also exists in the other Member States. But if the issuing authority has instead acted on the basis of autonomous conflict-of-law provisions or on the basis of an international treaty (e.g. in order to determine the matrimonial property rules), it is merely presumed that the legal situation in question is (at least) accurate in the State of issuance.

7. It is also presumed that according to article 69.2 sentence 2 the person mentioned in the Certificate as the heir, legatee, executor of the will or administrator of the estate has the status mentioned in the

[26] Wautelet, 'Article 69', p. 789. [27] Schmidt, 'Art. 69 EuErbVO', para. 14.

Certificate and/or holds the rights or the powers stated in the Certificate, and that no conditions and/or restrictions are attached to those rights or powers other than those stated in the Certificate. Some view this provision as a specification of article 69.2 sentence 1,[28] while others consider it to be *lex specialis* to this provision.[29] But in point of fact, the effect of the presumption laid down in sentence 2 goes further than the effect laid down in sentence 1. According to article 69.2 sentence 2 it is presumed that the person mentioned in the ECS as the heir or legatee really holds this legal status. However, whether or not a person has the status of being an heir, what his or her share in a succession is, and whether he or she is the recipient of a legacy can all depend on preliminary questions whose criteria for determining the applicable law (e.g. marriage, matrimonial property regime, child-parent relationship, etc.) have not yet been unified.[30] If it is still presumed that an heir or a legatee mentioned in the ECS has the status and the rights and powers mentioned therein, this implies a legal result which does not necessarily correspond to the result that would have been found in the State where the ECS is to be used. The proposal that a dependent connection should be applied under the ESR changes nothing in this respect as long as this is not practised by all the Member States [see art. 1 no. 19]. Hence, the effect of the presumption laid down in article 69.2 sentence 2 goes further than the effect laid down in article 69.2 sentence 1. This situation is not without problems for the State in which the Certificate is used: there is always the risk of using a Certificate that is inaccurate from the perspective of the State's own law.[31]

In this context, the much-discussed question arises of whether the effect of the presumption of article 69.2 sentence 2 can also apply to a share of the succession that is conferred not by the *lex successionis*, but by matrimonial property provisions. A well-known example is the

[28] C. F. Nordmeier, 'Art. 69 EuErbVO', in R. Hüßtege and H.-P. Mansel (eds), *Nomos-Kommentar, BGB, Rom-Verordnungen*, para. 12; see also Rechberger and Kieweler, 'Das Europäische Nachlasszeugnis', p. 298 (para. 52): the regulation has no independent effect.

[29] Schmidt, 'Art. 69 EuErbVO', para. 15.

[30] But see, on the applicable law in matters of matrimonial property and in matters of the property consequences of registered partnerships, the Council Regulation (EU) 2016/1103 of 24 June 2016, OJ 2016 no. L 183/1, 8 July 2016, and the Council Regulation (EU) 2016/1104 of 24 June 2016, OJ 2016 no. L 183/30, 8 July 2016. Both regulations will apply to the participating Member States as of 29 January 2019.

[31] See also J. Kleinschmidt, 'Optionales Erbrecht: Das Europäische Nachlasszeugnis als Herausforderung an das Kollisionsrecht', *RabelsZ* (2013), p. 757; D. Lübcke, *Das neue europäische Internationale Nachlassverfahrensrecht* (Baden-Baden, 2013), p. 565 *et seq.*

equalisation of accrued gains according to section 1371.1 BGB. The problem has been discussed within the comment on point (l) of article 68 [see art. 68 no. 18].

8. Pursuant to article 69.2 sentence 2, it is not only presumed that the information given in the ECS is accurate; it is also presumed that no conditions and/or restrictions other than those stated in the Certificate are attached to the certified rights or powers. Thus, in addition to the presumption of accuracy, there is a presumption of comprehensiveness of the ECS.[32] For an example, if the Certificate contains no information concerning restrictions to the powers of an executor of the will or administrator of the estate, it is presumed that these powers are not subject to any restrictions; if certain restrictions are mentioned (cf. point (o) of article 68), it is presumed that these restrictions do indeed exist, but that there are no additional restrictions.[33]

9. The presumption under article 69.2 sentences 1–2 are rebuttable.[34] This is already indicated in sentence 2 of recital 71. Accordingly, the ECS shall not be an enforceable title but shall have an 'evidentiary effect'. This leads to the conclusion that the effect of the presumption of the ECS is only viable as long as its content has not been proven to be inaccurate. The Certificate does not give a legally-binding effect to the elements indicated therein, but rather serves as declaratory evidence of the rights and powers mentioned therein. Thus, the accuracy of the ECS is subject to contest. The party having doubts about the accuracy of the information has to provide proof of the inaccuracy of the ECS. But the regulation does not specify how such proof (e.g. admissible evidence) can be provided. Recourse shall accordingly be

[32] Schmidt, 'Art. 69 EuErbVO', para. 17 *et seq.*; Lange, 'Das Europäische Nachlasszeugnis', p. 168 (para. 24); Nordmeier, 'Art. 69 EuErbVO', para. 12; Kleinschmidt, 'Optionales Erbrecht', p. 775.

[33] See Nordmeier, 'Art. 69 EuErbVO', para. 12.

[34] A. Dutta, 'The European Certificate of Succession – A New European Instrument between Procedural and Substantive Law', *International Journal of Procedural Law* (2015), p. 48; Dutta, 'Art. 69 EuErbVO', para. 9; Nordmeier, 'Art. 69 EuErbVO', para. 13; Rechberger and Kieweler, 'Das Europäische Nachlasszeugnis', p. 298 *et seq.* (para. 53); A. Köhler, 'Art. 69 EuErbVO', in Kroiß *et al.* (eds), *Nachfolgerecht* (Baden-Baden, 2014), para. 3; C. Kohler and W. Pintens, 'Entwicklungen im europäischen Familien- und Erbrecht 2011–2012', *FamRZ* (2012), p. 1429; U. Janzen, 'Die EU-Erbrechtsverordnung', *DNotZ – Deutsche Notar-Zeitschrift* (2012), p. 493; Reinhartz, 'Article 69', para. 7; M. Schauer, 'Art. 69 EuErbVO', in A. Deixler-Hübner and M. Schauer (eds), *EuErbVO-Kommentar* (Wien, 2015), para. 12; see also Wautelet, 'Article 69', p. 791 *et seq.*

taken to national procedural law.[35] Rebuttal of the presumption does not require that the Certificate has previously been modified or withdrawn pursuant to article 71.2; proof of inaccuracy can be provided attached to the proceedings in which the effect of the presumption according to article 69.2 is relevant.[36]

IV. *Bona Fide* Effect (Paragraphs 3 and 4 of Article 69)

A. Bona Fide *Protection within the Limits of Article 69.2*

10. The ECS also produces *bona fide* effects (see paragraphs 3 and 4 of article 69). For the protection of the legal relations, a *bona fide* third party shall also be considered in the event of an inaccurate ECS to have rendered performance to an authorised person (article 69.3) or to have made an acquisition from an authorised person (article 69.4). *Bona fide* protection is likewise available for legal transactions with heirs, legatees, executors of the will and administrators of the estate.[37] However, it is only available within the limits of the presumption of accuracy and comprehensiveness according to article 69.2.

The provision can certainly help if the authorisation under succession law to accept a performance or to dispose of assets belonging to the estate is missing. If, however, an asset that does not belong to the estate (e.g. if the deceased had borrowed an object that is now falsely seen as his or her property) has been disposed of, article 69.4 cannot compensate for this deficiency.[38] Article 69.4 does not allow a *bona fide* acquisition of assets that do not belong to the estate. According to article 69.3, the same

[35] Nordmeier, 'Art. 69 EuErbVO', para. 13; Rechberger and Kieweler, 'Das Europäische Nachlasszeugnis', p. 299 (para. 53); Dutta, 'Art. 69 EuErbVO', para. 9.

[36] Nordmeier, 'Art. 69 EuErbVO', para. 13; Dutta, 'Art. 69 EuErbVO', para. 9.

[37] This applies regardless of the limiting statement in sentence 4 of recital 71: 'Any person who makes payments or passes on succession property to a person indicated in the Certificate as being entitled to accept such payment or property as an heir or legatee should be afforded appropriate protection if he acted in good faith relying on the accuracy of the information certified in the Certificate.' The explicit mention of heirs and legatees as persons that are entitled to accept performance should not be seen as an exhaustive enumeration. The provision of article 69.3 thus also applies when an executor of the will or administrator of the estate is mentioned as authorised person in the Certificate. In this respect, the wording of the provision 'to a person mentioned in the Certificate as authorised to accept payment or property' does not indicate any restriction; cf. convincingly Dutta, 'Art. 69 EuErbVO', para. 18.

[38] Dutta, 'Art. 69 EuErbVO', para. 17; Kleinschmidt, 'Optionales Erbrecht', p. 777; Nordmeier, 'Art. 69 EuErbVO', para. 20; Rechberger and Kieweler, 'Das Europäische Nachlasszeugnis', p. 300 (para. 54); Schauer, 'Art. 69 EuErbVO', para. 25.

applies to claims not belonging to the estate (cf. sentence 3 of recital 71).[39] In this respect, only (other) national bona fide provisions can be resorted to.[40] This applies even when specific rights or assets are (wrongly) attributed to the heir or legatee in accordance with points (l) and (m) of article 68.[41]

B. The Legal Transactions Covered by Bona Fide *Protection*

11. *Bona fide* protection is granted in cases of payment or transfer of property to a person mentioned in the Certificate as authorised to accept payment or property (see article 69.3). Such transactions can thus lead to the discharge of a debt owed to the estate. The term 'payment' here refers to monetary transactions. The form in which such a performance is made is irrelevant; it includes cash payments, bank transfers, payments by cheque or credit card, etc.[42]

As far as the fulfilment of claims for property other than money is concerned, there is only *bona fide* protection when a person 'passes on property to a person mentioned in the Certificate as authorised to accept property'.[43] The meaning of this stipulation is unclear. According to sentence 4 of recital 71, the following shall apply: 'Any person who ... passes on *succession property* to a person indicated in the Certificate as being entitled to accept such ... property as an heir or legatee should be afforded appropriate protection'.[44] Some conclude from this statement that the provision only concerns the restitution of assets of the estate (i.e. of objects that already belong to the estate) to the supposedly authorised person.[45] Such a narrow understanding of article 69.3 is, however, not necessarily suggested by the wording of the

[39] Recital 71 (sent. 3): 'The evidentiary effect of the Certificate should not extend to elements which are not governed by this Regulation, such as ... the question whether or not a particular asset belonged to the deceased.'

[40] Kleinschmidt, 'Optionales Erbrecht', p. 777; M. Buschbaum and U. Simon, 'EuErbVO: Das Europäische Nachlasszeugnis', *ZEV – Zeitschrift für Erbrecht und Vermögensnachfolge* (2012), p. 528; Dutta, 'Art. 69 EuErbVO', para. 25.

[41] Dutta, 'Art. 69 EuErbVO', para. 17; Nordmeier, 'Art. 69 EuErbVO', para. 20; M. Buschbaum and U. Simon, 'EuErbVO: Das Europäische Nachlasszeugnis', *ZEV – Zeitschrift für Erbrecht und Vermögensnachfolge* (2012), p. 528; Fornasier, 'Art. 69 EuErbVO', para. 19. For a different view, see Lange, 'Das Europäische Nachlasszeugnis', p. 170 (para. 29).

[42] Dutta, 'Art. 69 EuErbVO', para. 13; Nordmeier, 'Art. 69 EuErbVO', para. 17.

[43] The German version is misleading in this respect, as it requires that the assets have been 'handed over'.

[44] Emphasis added. [45] Kleinschmidt, 'Optionales Erbrecht', p. 778.

provision itself.[46] The provision merely requires that a person '[pass] on property' (Dutch: 'een goed overdraagt'; French: 'remet des biens'); this wording in no way excludes the transfer of assets external to the estate.[47] The decisive aspect is, however, that the third party's protection would be incomplete if only the transfer of succession property was included within the scope of application of the second alternative of article 69.3, while the transfer of other property was excluded. It is therefore preferable to apply the provision to all assets that are transmitted on the basis of a succession right, irrespective of the recitals. Due to the broad wording of the regulation ('passes on property'), it is therefore permissible to grant *bona fide* protection under article 69.3 both to the transfer of intellectual property rights and open claims and to the property transfer of movables and immovables.[48] But no protection is given when services are being rendered, as this does not imply the transfer of an asset.[49]

12. According to article 69.4, the ECS also produces a *bona fide* effect when the disposal of succession property in favour of another person is concerned. If, contrary to what is indicated in the Certificate, the disposing person has no authority to dispose of the property as an heir, legatee, executor of the will or administrator of the estate, this provision allows for a *bona fide* acquisition from that non-authorised person.[50] But article 69.4 only compensates the lack of authority of disposition as an heir, etc. When the object being disposed of does not belong to succession property, this deficiency cannot be overcome by means of the *bona fide* effect of the ECS. The regulation does not provide for a *bona fide* acquisition of assets not belonging to the estate (see *supra* no. 10).

The notion of 'succession property' indisputably means movables and immovables. But other rights (e.g. claims) should be included as well.[51] This arguably already follows from the English version of article

[46] In the same sense, see Dutta, 'Art. 69 EuErbVO', para. 14.

[47] See also Schmidt, 'Art. 69 EuErbVO', para. 23; Schauer, 'Art. 69 EuErbVO', para. 19.

[48] Schmidt, 'Art. 69 EuErbVO', para. 24 *et seq.*; Wautelet, 'Article 69', p. 794; see also Dutta, 'Art. 69 EuErbVO', para. 14 ('Abtretung nach §§ 398 ff., 413 BGB'); Fornasier, 'Art. 69 EuErbVO', para. 14; for a different opinion see Nordmeier, 'Art. 69 EuErbVO', para. 19: the transfer of rights is excluded from the scope of article 69.3.

[49] Dutta, 'Art. 69 EuErbVO', para. 14; Fornasier, 'Art. 69 EuErbVO', para. 14.

[50] On the notion 'person with authority to dispose' (cf. article 69.4), also see Omlor, 'Gutglaubensschutz durch das Europäische Nachlasszeugnis', p. 290.

[51] Dutta, 'Art. 69 EuErbVO', para. 16; Schmidt, 'Art. 69 EuErbVO', para. 41; Wautelet, 'Article 69', p. 794. For a different view, see Kleinschmidt, 'Optionales Erbrecht', p. 777 (footnote 283).

69, as choses in action are a sub-species of personal property. This conclusion is reinforced by the German wording ('Nachlassvermögen'), for example, which speaks of 'Vermögen' (i.e. 'patrimony', 'assets'). The term 'Vermögen' corresponds to the term 'assets of the estate' used in article 10.1 and has a broad interpretation in this context, including all other rights in addition to movables and immovables [see art. 10 no. 9].

The *bona fide* protection under article 69.4 can only take effect when an item of succession property has been 'disposed of'. However, the regulation does not define the notion of disposal; its meaning has therefore to be determined by means of (autonomous) interpretation of the regulation. Sentence 6 of recital 71 refers to the legal acts involved. *Bona fide* protection shall accordingly be granted to any person who, 'relying on the accuracy of the information certified in the Certificate, *buys or receives* succession property'.[52] The contractual transfer of succession property, at least, is covered by it.[53] However, the wording of article 69.4 is broader than in the corresponding recital ('to dispose of succession property'). This allows us to conclude that, in addition to property acquisition, all other legal transactions having a direct impact on the existence of a right *in rem* relating to a specific asset of the estate (e.g. charges *in rem*) are covered.[54] Whether the disposal has been carried out for payment or gratuitously is in this case irrelevant.[55] However, contracts strictly creating liabilities (e.g. the letting of an apartment belonging to the estate) are not included in the concept of disposal, as they do not have a direct impact on a right *in rem* relating to an asset of the estate.[56]

C. *Authority according to the ECS*

13. The authority held by the recipient of the performance (article 69.3) or by the disposing person (article 69.4) must follow from the ECS. This is the case when authority to accept the performance in question or to

[52] Emphasis added. [53] Schmidt, 'Art. 69 EuErbVO', para. 39.

[54] Omlor, 'Gutglaubensschutz durch das Europäische Nachlasszeugnis', p. 218; Nordmeier, 'Art. 69 EuErbVO', para. 20; Kleinschmidt, 'Optionales Erbrecht', p. 777; see also Dutta, 'Art. 69 EuErbVO', para. 16.

[55] Dutta, 'Art. 69 EuErbVO', para. 16; Omlor, 'Gutglaubensschutz durch das Europäische Nachlasszeugnis', p. 218; Schauer, 'Art. 69 EuErbVO', para. 24.

[56] Kleinschmidt, 'Optionales Erbrecht', p. 777; Omlor, 'Gutglaubensschutz durch das Europäische Nachlasszeugnis', p. 219; Dutta, 'Art. 69 EuErbVO', para. 16.

dispose of the relevant asset belonging to the estate is explicitly stated in the Certificate. If in this case the issuing authority has wrongly determined the applicable law or if the indicated legal position does not follow from the (correctly determined) succession law for factual or legal reasons, the good faith in the documented powers is nevertheless afforded protection. In order to prevent weakening the good faith in the ECS, such a discrepancy between the applicable law and the declared legal position has to be resolved at the expense of the truly authorised person and not at the expense of the *bona fide* third party.[57]

If, however, the ECS does not contain specific mention regarding the concrete powers of the recipient of the performance or of the disposing person and only makes a general statement about his or her position as an heir, legatee, executor of the will or administrator of the estate, the powers related to that position follow from the succession law that is referred to in the ECS (cf. point (i) of article 68).[58] If, for instance, a person is listed as the sole heir under German law, he or she can – provided that no execution of the will has been issued – freely dispose of succession property.[59] If it is later established that the person concerned is in fact only a co-heir and therefore does not have authority to dispose of succession property effectively,[60] the third party is afforded appropriate protection in view of his or her own good faith concerning the other person's authority to dispose.

D. *Inaccuracy of the Certificate with Regard to Content*

14. The protection of good faith according to paragraphs 3 and 4 of article 69 is only relevant when the ECS is inaccurate with regard to content. Otherwise, the recipient of the performance or the disposing person is acting with authority to do so. The inaccuracy of the Certificate may be based on incorrect factual assumptions or on wrong legal conclusions.[61] But if the issuing authority has, from its own point of view, assessed the relevant elements of law correctly, the Certificate still can be inaccurate in the eyes of the State whose authority or court has to decide on the effects of good faith pursuant to paragraphs 3 or 4 of article 69. This may be the case, for example, if preliminary questions are answered differently in the State of origin and in the State of destination

57 Dutta, 'Art. 69 EuErbVO', para. 17; Nordmeier, 'Art. 69 EuErbVO', para. 15.

58 Dutta, 'Art. 69 EuErbVO', para. 17; see also Schmidt, 'Art. 69 EuErbVO', para. 43.

59 See section 1922.1 BGB. 60 See section 2033 BGB.

61 Dutta, 'Art. 69 EuErbVO', para. 21.

(cf. *supra* no. 7), or if the State of destination is bound by international treaties as far as the determination of the succession law is concerned (cf. subparagraph 1 of article 75.1). If the inaccuracy of the ECS was assessed from the perspective of the issuing State, conflict-of-law provisions (concerning the determination of the law to be applied to the preliminary question) that have not been unified would also become the basis of the decision in other Member States.[62] Not only would this be an incentive for forum shopping,[63] but it would also go beyond the regulation's objectives. The same applies for the binding effect of international treaties according to article 75.1. Based on this, it only makes sense to always assess the inaccuracy of the ECS in accordance with the laws of the State whose authorities or courts must, in the event of a dispute, decide on the effect of good faith under article 69.[64]

E. No Knowledge or Unawareness Due to Gross Negligence

15. The *bona fide* effect under paragraphs 3 and 4 of article 69 requires the third party's good faith. The criterion of good faith is met when the third party was neither aware that the contents of the Certificate were inaccurate (cf. *supra* no. 14) nor ignorant of such inaccuracy due to gross negligence. The third party's good faith is refutably presumed; this follows from the phrase 'unless he knows'.[65] The person claiming bad faith therefore has to prove this allegation in the event of a dispute.[66]

According to paragraphs 3 and 4 of article 69, both positive knowledge of the inaccurate content and ignorance of it due to gross negligence are detrimental to the third party. The regulation thus goes beyond the Commission's proposal for the regulation, according to which only the third party's positive knowledge of the inaccuracy should be harmful.[67]

[62] This is pointed out by Dutta, 'Art. 69 EuErbVO', para. 21.

[63] See Dutta, 'Art. 69 EuErbVO', para. 21.

[64] Dutta, 'Art. 69 EuErbVO', para. 21; Nordmeier, 'Art. 69 EuErbVO', para. 22.

[65] Dutta, 'Art. 69 EuErbVO', para. 19; Omlor, 'Gutglaubensschutz durch das Europäische Nachlasszeugnis', p. 219.

[66] Schmidt, 'Art. 69 EuErbVO', paras. 34, 49; Nordmeier, 'Art. 69 EuErbVO', para. 25; Wautelet, 'Article 69', p. 799 *et seq.*; see also L. Kunz, 'Die neue Europäische Erbrechtsverordnung – ein Überblick (Teil II)', *GPR – European Community Private Law Review* (2012), p. 257.

[67] Cf. article 42 of the Proposal for a Regulation of the European Parliament and of the Council on jurisdiction, applicable law, recognition and enforcement of decisions and authentic instruments in matters of succession and the creation of a European Certificate of Succession, COM(2009)154 final, p. 30. Critical with regard to the introduction of the criterion of gross negligence are U. Simon and M. Buschbaum, 'Die neue EU-

Under what preconditions gross negligence (German: 'grobe Fahrlässigkeit'; French: 'négligence grave') can be assumed, is, however, left open by the regulation. Many rightly point out that the necessary requirements for gross negligence should not be set too low, in order to not substantially weaken acceptance of the ECS.[68] In fact, a particularly grave violation of due diligence requirements must take place.[69] The specific circumstances of the case always have to be taken into account.[70] Many hold the view that the third party's knowledge of pending proceedings concerning the modification or withdrawal of the ECS should not be sufficient (cf. articles. 71.2 and 72), as long as he or she is in good faith concerning the Certificate's accuracy with regard to content.[71] Where appropriate, the third party may be obliged to carry out investigations.[72] See *supra* no. 3 concerning the consequences of a modification or withdrawal of the ECS (cf. articles. 71.2 and 72) and of a suspension of its effects (cf. article 73.1).

Either knowledge or ignorance due to gross negligence must in each case relate to the elements that are relevant *in casu*. Bad faith regarding faults that are irrelevant for the specific legal transaction do not inhibit the effects of good faith under article 69.[73] The regulation leaves open, however, at what moment the person rendering performance or the acquirer must be in good faith. In the end, the moment of fulfilment of the acquisition of the right should be relevant. This is, in any case, what is suggested by the phrase 'have transacted'.[74] The time when the acquisition of the right is fulfilled has to be assessed in accordance with the law that is to be applied to the rendering of the performance or to the disposal.[75]

Erbrechtsverordnung', *NJW* (2012), p. 2397. On the background of the introduction of a stricter standard of good faith, also see Lechner, 'Die Entwicklung der Erbrechtsverordnung', p. 12 (para. 27).

68 Dutta, 'Art. 69 EuErbVO' para. 19.

69 Schmidt, 'Art. 69 EuErbVO', para. 33, referring to the opinion of Advocate General J. Kokott of 20 October 2007 in case C-308/06 *Intertanko* [2008] ECR I-04057, point 104.

70 Schmidt, 'Art. 69 EuErbVO', para. 33, referring to doc. 18096/10, p. 50 (footnote 2).

71 Dutta, 'Art. 69 EuErbVO', para. 19; Nordmeier, 'Art. 69 EuErbVO', para. 23.

72 Kleinschmidt, 'Optionales Erbrecht', p. 779; Omlor, 'Gutglaubensschutz durch das Europäische Nachlasszeugnis', p. 219; see also Nordmeier, 'Art. 69 EuErbVO', para. 24.

73 Nordmeier, 'Art. 69 EuErbVO', para. 24, who gives the following example: The third party gives payment to the heir indicated in the ECS, in order to discharge himself of a liability. He is *mala fide* concerning the legatee indicated in the Certificate, but not with respect to the heir who in reality does not have the certified legal position, either.

74 Omlor, 'Gutglaubensschutz durch das Europäische Nachlasszeugnis', p. 219; Nordmeier, 'Art. 69 EuErbVO', para. 25; see also Dutta, 'Art. 69 EuErbVO', para. 20 ('Vollendung des Leistungs- oder Verfügungstatbestands').

75 Omlor, 'Gutglaubensschutz durch das Europäische Nachlasszeugnis', p. 219; Nordmeier, 'Art. 69 EuErbVO', para. 25.

16. The *bona fide* protection under article 69 presupposes that at least one valid certified copy of the Certificate is circulating (see *supra* no. 3). It is, however, unclear whether beyond this requirement, the third party must be aware of the existence of the ECS[76] or whether a certified copy must even be presented to him or her[77] in order for him or her to benefit from the effects of paragraphs 3 and 4 of article 69. The wording of the provision requiring that a person be 'acting on the basis of the information certified in a Certificate' indicates that the third party must at least be aware of the content of the ECS. This assumption is supported by sentences 4 and 5 of recital 71 ('relying on the accuracy of the information certified in the Certificate'). Any requirement to present a valid copy does not, however, follow from this. Sentence 6 of recital 71 could suggest such an interpretation: '[t]he protection should be ensured if *certified copies which are still valid are presented*',[78] but the genesis of article 69 rather speaks against the assumption of any requirement of presentation.[79] The Commission's proposal, which expressly referred to 'the bearer of a certificate',[80] was deliberately changed to 'person mentioned . . . as authorised' and 'person with authority', following criticism from various sources.[81] This leads to the conclusion that the third party is indeed required to be aware of the content of the ECS, but

[76] Schmidt, 'Art. 69 EuErbVO', para. 29 *et seq.*; Dutta, 'Art. 69 EuErbVO', para. 22; Nordmeier, 'Art. 69 EuErbVO', para. 7; Omlor, 'Gutglaubensschutz durch das Europäische Nachlasszeugnis', p. 218 *et seq.*

[77] A. Köhler, 'Art. 69 EuErbVO', in Kroiß *et al.* (eds), *Nachfolgerecht*, para. 7; S. Herzog, 'Die EU-Erbrechtsverordnung (EU-ErbVO)', *ErbR – Zeitschrift für die gesamte erbrechtliche Praxis* (2013), p. 13; Lange, 'Das Europäische Nachlasszeugnis', p. 170 (para. 28); Schauer, 'Europäisches Nachlasszeugnis', p. 94; M. Volmer, 'Die EU-Erbrechtsverordnung – erste Fragen an Dogmatik und Forensik', *Rpfleger – Der Deutsche Rechtspfleger* (2013), p. 431; P. Vollmer, 'Die neue europäische Erbrechtsverordnung – ein Überblick', *Zerb – Zeitschrift für die Steuer- und Erbrechtspraxis* (2012), p. 233.

[78] Emphasis added.

[79] Schmidt, 'Art. 69 EuErbVO', para. 31; J. Schmidt, 'Der Erbnachweis in Deutschland ab 2015: Erbschein vs. Europäisches Nachlasszeugnis, *ZEV – Zeitschrift für Erbrecht und Vermögensnachfolge* (2014), p. 393.

[80] See article 42 of the proposal, COM(2009)154 final, p. 27.

[81] See Max Planck Institute for Comparative and International Private Law, 'Comments on the European Commission's Proposal for a Regulation of the European Parliament and of the Council on jurisdiction, applicable law, recognition and enforcement of decisions and authentic instruments in matters of succession and the creation of a European Certificate of Succession', *RabelsZ* (2010), p. 698, para. 320 ('a requirement to present the Certificate itself, which would limit the possibility of a disbursement or an acquisition in good faith'); M. Buschbaum and M. Kohler, 'Vereinheitlichung des Erbkollisionsrechts in Europa', *GPR- European Community Private Law Review* (2010), p. 168 ('Gutglaubenswirkungen erheblich eingeschränkt').

does not indicate that the presentation of a valid copy by either the recipient of the performance or the disposing person is necessary. The mere existence of an ECS at the time of fulfilment of the acquisition of the right (see *supra* no. 15) is not sufficient, however, for the *bona fide* protection pursuant to paragraph 3 or 4 of article 69 to be effective.[82]

F. Legal Consequences

17. If the preconditions for *bona fide* protection are met, the third party is treated as if the recipient of the performance has authority to receive that performance, or the disposing person has authority to dispose as indicated in the ECS. This does not, however, answer the question of whether all the further preconditions for the effectiveness of the legal transaction have been fulfilled. These questions have to be dealt with in accordance with the law that is to be applied on the claim to be satisfied or on the disposal.[83] Similarly, the question of whether the claim on which performance has been rendered or the object being disposed of was in fact part of the succession remains unaffected (see *supra* no. 10).

If the third party is released from his or her obligation through performance or if he or she acquires the right being disposed of, it remains to be decided whether the person with true authority may have claims for compensation (e.g. claims on the basis of unjust enrichment) against the person who only has apparent authority. Such claims are not barred by the regulation;[84] they underlay the relevant applicable national law (e.g. the law of unjust enrichment; cf. article 10 Rome II Regulation).[85]

V. Legitimising Effect (Article 69.5)

18. According to article 69.5, the ECS constitutes a valid document for the recording of succession property in the relevant registers of the Member States.[86] If the succession affects a right that must be recorded in a public register, the proof of legal position as an heir, legatee, executor of the will or administrator of the estate that is necessary for registration

[82] Nordmeier, 'Art. 69 EuErbVO', para. 7.
[83] Dutta, 'Art. 69 EuErbVO', para. 23; Schauer, 'Art. 69 EuErbVO', para. 26.
[84] Omlor, 'Gutglaubensschutz durch das Europäische Nachlasszeugnis', p. 221; Nordmeier, 'Art. 69 EuErbVO', para. 14.
[85] Omlor, 'Gutglaubensschutz durch das Europäische Nachlasszeugnis', p. 291.
[86] See also sentence 5 of recital 18.

can be provided by the ECS. The registration authority is obliged to accept the ECS as evidence of the legal position that it certifies. It is not entitled to request that a decision, authentic instrument or court settlement be presented instead of the Certificate (cf. sentence 2 of recital 69) [see art. 62 no. 12].[87] This does not, however, exclude the obligation to give proof of any *additional* requirements relating to the registration procedure (see *infra* no. 22). The Certificate can also only serve as evidence as far as a legal position that falls within the regulation's scope of application is concerned (see also *infra* no. 20).[88]

A controversial issue is whether the authority may deny the recording if it has reasonable doubts concerning the accuracy of the content of the ECS (cf. *supra* no. 14).[89] The discussion in this context particularly refers to those cases in which the State keeping the register is bound by international treaties concerning the determination of the law of succession (cf. subparagraph 1 of article 75.1), so that the registration of a transfer of rights on the basis of the ECS might constitute a violation of international obligations.[90] In any case, the regulation does not contain any obligation of the Member States to record entries in a register if the ECS is inaccurate from the point of view of their own law. Such an obligation would also be in conflict with the refutability of the presumption according to article 69.2 (see *supra* no. 9). Thus, it falls to the Member State to determine to what extent the register-keeping authority should be entitled to refuse the requested registration in cases of inaccuracy with regard to content.[91]

[87] Schmidt, 'Art. 69 EuErbVO', para. 56 *et seq.*; Schauer, 'Europäisches Nachlasszeugnis', p. 93; Rechberger and Kieweler, 'Das Europäische Nachlasszeugnis', p. 309 *et seq.* (para. 71).

[88] U. Janzen, 'Die EU-Erbrechtsverordnung', *DNotZ – Deutsche Notar-Zeitschrift* (2012), p. 493; Nordmeier, 'Art. 69 EuErbVO', para. 26.

[89] *Pro*: Schauer, 'Europäisches Nachlasszeugnis', p. 93; see also Dutta, 'Art. 69 EuErbVO', para. 26 (rebuttable presumption) and Nordmeier, 'Art. 69 EuErbVO', para. 28 (worth considering); *contra*: Rechberger and Kieweler, 'Das Europäische Nachlasszeugnis', p. 310 (para. 72); W. Böhringer, 'Das Europäische Nachlasszeugnis im deutschen Grundbuchverfahren', *NotBZ – Zeitschrift für die notarielle Beratungs- und Beurkundungspraxis* (2015), p. 283; see also M. Volmer, 'Definitive Entscheidung von Vorfragen aufgrund der Gerichtszuständigkeit nach der EuErbVO', *ZEV – Zeitschrift für Erbrecht und Vermögensnachfolge* (2014), p. 130.

[90] D. Lehmann, 'Der Referentenentwurf für ein Begleitgesetz zur EuErbVO', *ZEV – Zeitschrift für Erbrecht und Vermögensnachfolge* (2014), p. 234; Nordmeier, 'Art. 69 EuErbVO', para. 28; M. Buschbaum and U. Simon, 'Beantragung und Erteilung eines Europäischen Nachlasszeugnisses sowie Verwendung eines ausländischen Europäischen Nachlasszeugnisses in Deutschland', *Rpfleger – Der Deutsche Rechtspfleger* (2015), p. 453.

[91] See also Nordmeier, 'Art. 69 EuErbVO', para. 28.

19. The provision encompasses registerable rights of any kind.[92] It is not relevant only with respect to the recording of rights relating to immovable property (although this is particularly important, cf. recital 68); the legitimising effect also applies to movables,[93] claims and other rights requiring registration or at least being registerable.[94] Public registers of any kind in which rights can or must be recorded are likewise covered [see art. 1 no. 88] apart from the land register, one example is company registers, insofar as successions to company shares are reported in them.[95]

20. The legitimising effect of an ECS with regard to the relevant registers of the Member States is valid without prejudice to points (k) and (l) of article 1.2 (see the end of article 69.5). Both points deal with questions that are expressly excluded from the regulation's scope of application. The exact meaning of the reference to these provisions is currently a matter of lively discussion.

First of all, point (k) of article 1.2 rules that the nature of rights *in rem* is excluded from the regulation's scope of application. This provision ensures that the *numerus clausus* of the national rights *in rem* is not affected by the regulation (cf. recital 15).[96] The details of this derogation certainly raise questions [see art. 1 no. 74 *et seq.*]. There is at least consensus that the registering State is not obliged to record a right that is unknown in its own law (see also sentence 3 of recital 15);[97] however, in such a case, an adaptation according to article 31 should be taken into consideration. Yet if the law of the registering State knows the right documented in the ECS but assesses the modality of acquisition of such rights differently from the succession law, the question is, which law is

92 Schmidt, 'Art. 69 EuErbVO', para. 53.

93 Wautelet, 'Article 69', p. 801; Nordmeier, 'Art. 69 EuErbVO', para. 26; Rechberger and Kieweler, 'Das Europäische Nachlasszeugnis', p. 309 (para. 69).

94 Schmidt, 'Art. 69 EuErbVO', para. 53.

95 For details on German law (commercial register), see M. Buschbaum and U. Simon, 'EuErbVO: Das Europäische Nachlasszeugnis', *ZEV – Zeitschrift für Erbrecht und Vermögensnachfolge* (2012), p. 529; Nordmeier, 'Art. 69 EuErbVO', para. 31. On Austrian law (companies register), see Schauer, 'Europäisches Nachlasszeugnis', p. 93.

96 See H.-P. Mansel, 'Art. 43 EGBGB', in *Staudinger BGB – EGBGB/IPR, Artikel 43–46 EGBGB (Internationales Sachenrecht),* 14th ed. (Berlin, 2015), para. 229; K. Thorn, 'Art. 1 EuErbVO', in *Palandt*, 75th ed. (München, 2016), para. 15; M. Buschbaum and U. Simon, 'Beantragung und Erteilung eines Europäischen Nachlasszeugnisses sowie Verwendung eines ausländischen Europäischen Nachlasszeugnisses in Deutschland', *Rpfleger – Der Deutsche Rechtspfleger* (2015), p. 452.

97 Schmidt, 'Art. 69 EuErbVO', para. 59; Wautelet, 'Article 69', p. 801; Nordmeier, 'Art. 69 EuErbVO', para. 29.

relevant to decide on the change of allocation? Some scholars consider the exception under point (k) of article 1.2 to also cover the modalities of the acquisition of the right (i.e. the *modus*).[98] The decision regarding the change of allocation should then be made not according to the succession rules, but according to the applicable property law. The succession rules would merely determine which rights could *in principle* be accorded to the beneficiary.[99] This approach is used particularly as concerns vindication legacies having an effect *in rem*: if such vindication legacies are known under the applicable succession rules, the ECS can demonstrate the corresponding rights of the legatee. However, if the legatee's right has to be recorded in the register of a Member State whose laws only know civil law legacies which merely have an obligatory effect, the transfer of the right in accordance with the requirements of the applicable property law would have to be brought about before the right concerned could be recorded in the relevant register.[100] This approach is, however, not undisputed. According to another view, it is not the law of property but the succession rules that should decide how the transfer of the right is implemented [see art. 1 no. 75 *et seq.*].[101] This opinion is supported by the wording of point (k) of article 1.2, according to which only the 'nature' of rights *in rem* is excluded from the regulation's scope of application. This exclusion would accordingly only concern the *typus* from a property law perspective (in the case of a vindication legacy, the *typus* would be the property) and not the *modus* of acquisition (in the case of a vindication legacy, this would be the way in which property is

98 G. Hohloch, 'Art. 1 EuErbVO', in B. Grunewald *et al.* (eds), *Erman, BGB*, vol. II, 14th ed. (Köln, 2014), para. 13; H. Dörner, 'EuErbVO: Die Verordnung zum Internationalen Erb- und Erbverfahrensrecht ist in Kraft!', *ZEV – Zeitschrift für Erbrecht und Vermögensnachfolge* (2012), p. 509; Reinhartz, 'Article 69', para. 19.

99 H. Dörner, 'EuErbVO: Die Verordnung zum Internationalen Erb- und Erbverfahrensrecht ist in Kraft!', *ZEV – Zeitschrift für Erbrecht und Vermögensnachfolge* (2012), p. 509.

100 See U. Simon and M. Buschbaum, 'Die neue EU-Erbrechtsverordnung', *NJW* (2012), 2394; J. Müller-Lukoscheck, *Die neue EU-Erbrechtsverordnung*, 2nd ed. (Berlin, 2015), p. 161 (para. 361 *et seq.*); S. Herzog, 'Die EU-Erbrechtsverordnung (EU-ErbVO)', *ErbR – Zeitschrift für die gesamte erbrechtliche Praxis* (2013), p. 5.

101 Mansel, 'Art. 43 EGBGB', para. 234 *et seq.*; A. Dutta, 'Die europäische Erbrechtsverordnung vor ihrem Anwendungsbeginn: Zehn ausgewählte Streitstandsminiaturen', *IPRax* (2015), p. 34; C. Hertel, 'Die Abgrenzung des Erbstatuts vom Sachstatut und vom Gesellschaftsstatut', in A. Dutta and S. Herrler (eds), *Die Europäische Erbrechtsverordnung*, p. 98 (para. 40); M. Margonski, 'Ausländische Vindikationslegate nach der EU-Erbrechtsverordnung', *GPR – European Community Private Law Review* (2013), p. 109; J. P. Schmidt, 'Die kollisionsrechtliche Behandlung dinglich wirkender Vermächtnisse', *RabelsZ* (2013), p. 22.

transferred). The latter would have to be judged pursuant to the succession rules (singular succession, in the case of a vindication legacy).[102] This reasoning is convincing. It is also supported by point (e) of article 23.2, which explicitly states that the succession rules are to be applied to 'the transfer to the heirs and, as the case may be, to the legatees of the assets, rights and obligations forming part of the estate'.[103]

It should thus be kept in mind that referring to point (k) of article 1.2 does not preclude the immediate recording of a legal position acquired through universal or singular succession as long as the *numerus clausus* of the national laws is being respected. This also applies when the law of the registering State does not know the direct transfer of rights effected by the succession rules.

21. The legitimising effect of the ECS furthermore applies without prejudice to point (l) of article 1.2 (see the end of article 69.5). Like point (k) of article 1.2, point (l) also contains a sectoral exception: '[a]ny recording in a register of rights in immovable or movable property, including the legal requirements for such recording, and the effects of recording or failing to record such rights in a register' is accordingly excluded from the regulation's scope of application. The reference in article 69.5 to point (l) of article 1.2 is just as problematic as that same article's reference to point (k) of article 1.2 (see *supra* no. 20). In particular, the question this raises is what is meant by the exclusion of the 'legal requirements for such recording'? It has been repeatedly argued that the sectoral exception according to point (l) of article 1.2 would indicate that the register rules take priority over the succession rules concerning the transfer of the right.[104] This view is supported by the wording of the provision that explicitly covers the preconditions and the effects of a recording. In addition, some argue that the provision would

[102] Mansel, 'Art. 43 EGBGB', para. 234; see also Schmidt, 'Die kollisionsrechtliche Behandlung dinglich wirkender Vermächtnisse', p. 22.

[103] Mansel, 'Art. 43 EGBGB', para. 235, with further arguments.

[104] C. Döbereiner, 'Vindikationslegate unter Geltung der EU-Erbrechtsverordnung', *GPR – European Union Private Law Review* (2014), p. 43; U. Janzen, 'Die EU-Erbrechtsverordnung', *DNotZ – Deutsche Notar-Zeitschrift* (2012), p. 487 *et seq.*; Lange, 'Das Europäische Nachlasszeugnis', p. 172 (para. 36); Reinhartz, 'Article 69', para. 20; M. Buschbaum and U. Simon, 'Beantragung und Erteilung eines Europäischen Nachlasszeugnisses sowie Verwendung eines ausländischen Europäischen Nachlasszeugnisses in Deutschland', *Rpfleger – Der Deutsche Rechtspfleger* (2015), p. 452; see also Hertel, 'Die Abgrenzung des Erbstatuts vom Sachstatut und vom Gesellschaftsstatut', p. 99 *et seq.* (para. 41 *et seq.*): for immovable property the *lex rei sitae* takes precedence over the *lex successioni*; K. Lechner, 'Die EuErbVO im Spannungsfeld zwischen Erbstatut und Sachenrecht', *IPRax* (2013), p. 499.

be superfluous as regards priority of the succession rules, as succession rules do not contain any requirements for the recording; thus there would be no need for this exception.[105] The opinion previously outlined is particularly significant for vindication legacies with an effect *in rem*. If a vindication legacy concerns a land plot situated in a State whose law knows only civil law legacies, the preconditions for the acquisition of the land plot would be imposed by the property law rules (concretely, the *lex rei sitae*). For example, before a transition of rights could be recorded in the German land register, the conveyance from the heir to the legatee would be necessary.[106] French notaries use a similar line of argumentation as regards the need to present an 'attestation immobilière' in order to achieve the adjustment or transcription of the public land register.[107]

However, the more persuasive arguments are in favour of applying succession rules rather than the register rules to the substantive requirements of acquisition [see art. 1 no. 94 *et seq.*].[108] This position in particular is supported by the recitals. Neither recital 18 nor recital 19, which deal with the recording in national registers, excludes the modalities of the acquisition of a right from the scope of application of the succession rules. However, sentence 1 of recital 18 declares that the

[105] C. Döbereiner, 'Vindikationslegate unter Geltung der EU-Erbrechtsverordnung', *GPR – European Union Private Law Review* (2014), p. 43.

[106] Hertel, 'Die Abgrenzung des Erbstatuts vom Sachstatut und vom Gesellschaftsstatut', p. 100 (para. 46); F. Odersky, 'Die Europäische Erbrechtsverordnung in der Gestaltungspraxis', *notar* (2013), p. 4; U. Simon and M. Buschbaum, 'Die neue EU-Erbrechtsverordnung', *NJW* (2012), p. 2397; M. Buschbaum and U. Simon, 'Beantragung und Erteilung eines Europäischen Nachlasszeugnisses sowie Verwendung eines ausländischen Europäischen Nachlasszeugnisses in Deutschland', *Rpfleger – Der Deutsche Rechtspfleger* (2015), p. 452 *et seq.*; Böhringer, 'Das Europäische Nachlasszeugnis im deutschen Grundbuchverfahren', *NotBZ – Zeitschrift für die notarielle Beratungs- und Beurkundungspraxis* (2015), p. 287.

[107] See S. Stade, 'Die EU-Erbrechtsverordnung aus französischer Sicht', *ZErb – Zeitschrift für die Steuer- und Erbrechtspraxis* (2015), p. 77, with reference to P. Chassaing, 'La préparation des notaires et du notariat concernant la mise en application du règlement du 4 juillet 2012', in Khairallah and Revillard (eds), *Droit européen des successions internationales* (Paris, 2013), no. 94 *et seq.*

[108] Mansel, 'Art. 43 EGBGB', para. 238 *et seq.*; H.-P. Mansel, 'Gesamt- und Einzelstatut: Die Koordination von Erb- und Sachstatut nach der EuErbVO', *Festschrift für Dagmar Coester-Waltjen* (Bielefeld, 2015), p. 590 *et seq.*; K. Thorn, 'Art. 1 EuErbVO', in *Palandt*, 75th ed. (München, 2016), para. 16; A. Köhler, 'Art. 69 EuErbVO', in Kroiß *et al.* (eds), *Nachfolgerecht*, para. 22; Dutta, *IPRax* (2015), p. 34; Kleinschmidt, 'Optionales Erbrecht', p. 762 *et seq.*; Fornasier, 'Art. 69 EuErbVO', para. 40; J. P. Schmidt, 'Ausländische Vindikationslegate über im Inland belegene Immobilien – zur Bedeutung des Art. 1 Abs 2 lit. l EuErbVO', *ZEV – Zeitschrift für Erbrecht und Vermögensnachfolge* (2014), p. 135.

'requirements *for the recording* in a register of a right in immovable or movable property should be excluded from the scope of this Regulation'.[109] The register rules should determine 'under what legal conditions and how the recording must be carried out and which authorities, such as land registers or notaries, are in charge of checking that all requirements are met and that the documentation presented or established is sufficient or contains the necessary information'. This only raises formal issues of recording in the register.[110] Recital 19, too, only refers to the 'effects of the recording of a right in a register', which shall be excluded from the scope of application of the regulation. It continues: '[i]t should therefore be the law of the Member State in which the register is kept which determines whether the recording is, for instance, declaratory or constitutive in effect.' Some deduce from this that the property law rules are to be applied *in addition* to the succession rules, as far as the question whether the recording in the register is constitutive for the acquisition of the right is concerned [see art. 1 no. 96].[111] However, the modalities of acquisition (in the case of a vindication legacy: singular succession *ipso iure* at the moment of death of the *de cuius*) remain unaffected in such cases. It follows from this that the succession law decides upon the *modus* of the transition of the right; the property law rules are merely relevant insofar as they may contain complementary stipulations regarding which circumstances render a recording in the register constitutive for the transition of rights *mortis causa*.

22. The Member States are, however, free to lay down further procedural requirements for the recording (cf. sentences 5 and 6 of recital 18). The competent authorities may require additional information or the presentation of additional documents (e.g. tax documents) in particular. Yet no additional information or documents may be required that relate to the legal position certified in the ECS.[112]

[109] Emphasis added.

[110] Mansel, 'Art. 43 EGBGB', para. 239 *et seq.*; Mansel, 'Gesamt- und Einzelstatut', p. 590 *et seq.*; see also Schmidt, 'Ausländische Vindikationslegate', p. 135.

[111] Mansel, 'Art. 43 EGBGB', para. 241; Mansel, 'Gesamt- und Einzelstatut', p. 591 *et seq.*; see also Schmidt, 'Ausländische Vindikationslegate', p. 135.

[112] Schmidt, 'Art. 69 EuErbVO', para. 60; Dutta, 'Art. 69 EuErbVO', para. 27. See also S. Stade, 'Die EU-Erbrechtsverordnung aus französischer Sicht', *ZErb – Zeitschrift für die Steuer- und Erbrechtspraxis* (2015), p. 77 *et seq.* (concerning the French 'attestation immobilière').

Article 70

Certified Copies of the Certificate

CHRISTINE BUDZIKIEWICZ

1. The issuing authority shall keep the original of the Certificate and shall issue one or more certified copies to the applicant and to any person demonstrating a legitimate interest.
2. The issuing authority shall, for the purposes of Articles 71(3) and 73(2), keep a list of persons to whom certified copies have been issued pursuant to paragraph 1.
3. The certified copies issued shall be valid for a limited period of six months, to be indicated in the certified copy by way of an expiry date. In exceptional, duly justified cases, the issuing authority may, by way of derogation, decide that the period of validity is to be longer. Once this period has elapsed, any person in possession of a certified copy must, in order to be able to use the Certificate for the purposes indicated in Article 63, apply for an extension of the period of validity of the certified copy or request a new certified copy from the issuing authority.

Summary

I. OVERVIEW *page* 795
II. ISSUE OF CERTIFIED COPIES 796
III. LIST OF CERTIFIED COPIES 799
IV. PERIOD OF VALIDITY OF THE CERTIFIED COPIES 800

I. Overview

1. The applicant of a European Certificate of Succession (ECS) does not receive the original Certificate. Rather, according to article 70.1, it remains with the issuing authority. Nor does the applicant get an issue which could be used for preparing certified copies.[1] Instead, only certified copies

[1] M. Buschbaum and U. Simon, 'EuErbVO: Das Europäische Nachlasszeugnis', *ZEV – Zeitschrift für Erbrecht und Vermögensnachfolge* (2012), p. 526.

with a limited validity come into circulation. Specifying a limitation period shall ensure that the issuing authority remains in control over any copies of the ECS in circulation.[2] More specifically, any misuse of a Certificate containing incorrect statements shall be prevented:[3] as the original always remains with the issuing authority and certified copies will lose their validity within due time, legal transactions can only be endangered by outdated copies for a limited period of time.

2. Article 70 does not deal with the question to what extent persons unable to establish a legitimate interest as required in subsection 1 are permitted to view the original or obtain a simple copy thereof from the issuing authority. According to sentence 3 of recital 72, the Member States may make provisions regarding this matter.

II. Issue of Certified Copies

3. Article 70.1 rules that the original of the ECS shall remain with the issuing authority and that only certified copies shall be handed out. It is not expressly regulated but is implied by the nature of the provisions that the issuing authority has a monopoly on preparing certified copies.[4] Indeed, many consider that certified copies of a certified copy could be produced; however, those would not have the special effects of the ECS.[5]

4. Issuing a certified copy requires the existence of a valid ECS according to article 67.[6] The Certificate must not have been withdrawn

[2] A. Dutta, 'Art. 70 EuErbVO', in J. von Hein (ed), *Münchener Kommentar zum BGB*, vol. X, 6th ed. (München, 2015), para. 1.

[3] See R. Schaub, 'Die EU-Erbrechtsverordnung', *Heriditare – Jahrbuch für Erbrecht und Schenkungsrecht* (2013), p. 126; C. F. Nordmeier, 'Art. 70 EuErbVO', in R. Hüßtege and H.-P. Mansel (eds), *NomosKommentar, BGB, Rom-Verordnungen*, vol. VI, 2nd ed. (Baden-Baden, 2015), para. 1; Buschbaum and Simon, 'EuErbVO: Das Europäische Nachlasszeugnis', p. 526.

[4] M. Volmer, 'Die EU-Erbrechtsverordnung – erste Fragen an Dogmatik und Forensik', *Rpfleger – Der Deutsche Rechtspfleger* (2013), p. 431; Buschbaum and Simon, 'EuErbVO: Das Europäische Nachlasszeugnis', p. 526; W. Böhringer, 'Das Europäische Nachlasszeugnis im deutschen Grundbuchverfahren', *NotBZ - Zeitschrift für die notarielle Beratungs- und Beurkundungspraxis* (2015), p. 286; see also M. Fornasier, 'Art. 70 EuErbVO', in A. Dutta and J. Weber (eds), *Internationales Erbrecht* (München, 2016), para. 4 ('implizite Zuständigkeitsnorm').

[5] Volmer, 'Die EU-Erbrechtsverordnung', p. 431; Böhringer, 'Das Europäische Nachlasszeugnis, p. 286 *et seq.*; C. Dorsel, 'Art. 70 EuErbVO', in R. Geimer and R. Schütze (eds), *Internationaler Rechtsverkehr in Zivil- und Handelssachen*, vol. III (München, 2015), para. 3.

[6] Dutta, 'Art. 70 EuErbVO', para. 2; Nordmeier, 'Art. 70 EuErbVO', para. 3.

according to article 71.2 or article 72.2 subsection 1.[7] Likewise excluded is the issue of a certified copy if the effects of the ECS have been suspended according to article 73.1 (see article 73.2 subsection 2). This also implies that applying for the rectification or withdrawal of the ECS according to article 72.1 *without* applying for the suspension of its effects does not hinder the issue of further certified copies.[8] After the correction of a clerical error according to article 71.1 or a modification according to articles 71.2 or 72.2, only certified copies of the rectified or modified ECS may be issued.[9]

5. The certified copies will be issued for the benefit of the applicant (article 65) or of any other person demonstrating a legitimate interest. As a result, more than one certified copy may exist and be in the hands of different persons. Article 70.1 also makes clear that more than one copy may be issued per person.

6. Article 70.1 provides for the issue of a certified copy to the applicant. Demonstration of a special interest is not required. This is appropriate as one certified copy must be provided to the applicant for the simple fact that the original remains with the issuing authority. This copy has to be issued *ex officio;* a separate application is not necessary.[10] However, if the applicant requests further copies, he or she then needs to demonstrate a special interest. According to the wording of article 70.1, the requirement of a 'legitimate interest' indeed only applies to persons other than the applicant: this results from the fact that the applicant has a legitimate interest in the issue of *one* certified copy. An interest in the issue of further copies cannot be implied without further indications. The issuing authority cannot usually know how many copies the applicant may need. As a result, it seems appropriate to require the applicant to apply for the issue of any further copies.[11] The interest in obtaining more copies can result, for example, from the necessity to submit the ECS to various authorities.[12]

7. Apart from the applicant, any other person demonstrating a legitimate interest can request the issue of one or more certified copies. The regulation does not define the term 'legitimate interest', which is also

[7] Dutta, 'Art. 70 EuErbVO', para. 2; A. Perscha, 'Art. 70 EuErbVO', in A. Deixler-Hübner and M. Schauer (eds), *Kommentar zur EU-Erbrechtsverordnung* (Wien, 2015), para. 4.

[8] Nordmeier, 'Art. 70 EuErbVO', para. 3. [9] Nordmeier, 'Art. 70 EuErbVO', para. 3.

[10] Nordmeier, 'Art. 70 EuErbVO', para. 4.; see also J. Schmidt, 'Art. 70 EuErbVO', in C. Budzikiewicz, M.-P. Weller and W. Wurmnest (eds), *Beck-Online Großkommentar, EuErbVO* (München, 2016), para. 7.

[11] Nordmeier, 'Art. 70 EuErbVO', para. 4.

[12] Schmidt, 'Art. 70 EuErbVO', paras. 7 and 7.1.

used in articles 71–73. However, the persons mentioned in article 63.1 – namely, heirs, legatees having direct rights in the succession, executors of the will or administrators of the estate, as far as they are not already applicants themselves – at least must be recognised as having a legitimate interest.[13] But any third person who wants to have certainty concerning another person's legal position as a result of the succession should be considered to have a legitimate interest.[14] Conceivable examples are, with regard to article 69.4, transferees of any succession property,[15] creditors of the estate[16] or debtors of the estate; the latter have an interest in invoking the effects of the ECS according to article 69.3.[17] As far as a legitimate interest exists as defined by article 70.1, the issue of more than one copy may also be requested (cf. *supra* no. 6).

In contrast to the applicant, all other persons must give proof of their legitimate interest. The issuing authority is under no official duty to investigate in such cases.[18] By this token, the issue of a certified copy – other than for the applicant – requires an appropriate application.[19] In the absence of a legitimate interest, a right of access to the original or a simple copy may be granted under national law if applicable (cf. *supra* no. 2).

8. The regulation does not provide for any legal redress in the case that the issuing authority denies the issue of a certified copy. According to its wording, article 72 only concerns decisions made by the issuing authority pursuant to articles 67 and 71 or point (a) of article 73.1. Some suggest closing this *lacuna* by an analogous application of subsection 1 of article 72.1.[20] Sentence 4 of recital 72 can be used to substantiate this point of view; according to this sentence, the regulation should provide

[13] P. Wautelet, 'Article 70', in A. Bonomi and P. Wautelet, *Le droit européen des successions. Commentaire du Règlement n° 650/2012 du 4 juillet 2012* (Bruxelles, 2013), p. 809; Dutta, 'Art. 70 EuErbVO', para. 3; Perscha, 'Art. 70 EuErbVO', para. 3.

[14] Nordmeier, 'Art. 70 EuErbVO', para. 5; see also Fornasier, 'Art. 70 EuErbVO', para. 3. But see Wautelet, 'Article 70', p. 809 *et seq.*, who has doubts whether banking institutes or fiscal authorities are entitled to obtain certified copies.

[15] Schmidt, 'Art. 70 EuErbVO', para. 10.1; Fornasier, 'Art. 70 EuErbVO', para. 3.

[16] J. Kleinschmidt, 'Optionales Erbrecht: Das Europäische Nachlasszeugnis als Herausforderung an das Kollisionsrecht', *RabelsZ* (2013), p. 770; Nordmeier, 'Art. 70 EuErbVO', para. 5.

[17] Dutta, 'Art. 70 EuErbVO', para. 3; C. F. Nordmeier, 'Art. 68 EuErbVO', in R. Hüßtege and H.-P. Mansel (eds), *NomosKommentar, BGB, Rom-Verordnungen*, vol. VI, 2nd ed. (Baden-Baden, 2015), para. 5; Perscha, 'Art. 70 EuErbVO', para. 3; see also Schmidt, 'Art. 70 EuErbVO', para. 10, who states that also a mere academic interest should be sufficient.

[18] Nordmeier, 'Art. 70 EuErbVO', para. 5.

[19] See Nordmeier, 'Art. 70 EuErbVO', para. 4.

[20] Dutta, 'Art. 70 EuErbVO', para. 4; *id.*, 'Art. 72 EuErbVO', in J. von Hein (ed), *Münchener Kommentar zum BGB*, vol. X, 6th ed. (München, 2015), para. 3.

for redress against decisions made by the issuing authority, including decisions to refuse the issue of a Certificate. The opposing argument is that the decision of whether to issue a certified copy is not subject to legal redress.[21] The reference to recital 72 was not found to be convincing in this context, since the section in question ultimately only relates to the issue of the original and not to the issue of a certified copy.[22] In the event of a refusal to issue a certified copy, the applicant's remaining option would be to take recourse to national law.[23] In favour of the aforementioned opposing argument, it must be conceded that sentence 4 of recital 72 does not explicitly name the issue of certified copies. However, the recital establishes in a general way that '[t]his Regulation should provide for redress against decisions of the issuing authority'. The protection of the parties concerned would be incomplete if no legal redress was available against the refusal to issue a certified copy. This becomes very obvious when taking the applicant as an example: it would be of little help if he or she could take action against the refusal to issue the original according to article 72, but, once a verdict was granted in his or her favour, the issuing authority could nonetheless deny the issue of a certified copy. The applicant must therefore be in a position to enforce not only the issue of the original, but also the issue of a certified copy. This supports an analogous application of article 72.1. The same must hold for third-party applications.

III. List of Certified Copies

9. According to article 70.2, the issuing authority keeps a list of persons to whom a certified copy of the ECS has been issued. The list shall enable the issuing authority to fulfil its obligation to inform persons to whom a certified copy has been issued of any rectification, modification or withdrawal of the Certificate (cf. article 71.3), or of any suspension of the effects of the Certificate (cf. article 73.2).[24] An entry must include the

[21] C. F. Nordmeier, 'Art. 72 EuErbVO', in R. Hüßtege and H.-P. Mansel (eds), *NomosKommentar, BGB, Rom-Verordnungen,* vol. VI, 2nd ed. (Baden-Baden, 2015), para. 6.

[22] Nordmeier, 'Art. 70 EuErbVO', para. 7 (footnote 11).

[23] Nordmeier, 'Art. 70 EuErbVO', para. 7; see also J. Kleinschmidt, 'Art. 70 EuErbVO', in M. Herberger *et al.* (eds), *juris Praxiskommentar BGB*, vol. VI, 7th ed. (Saarbrücken, 2014, status: 15 September 2015), para. 18.

[24] See also sentence 5 of recital 72: 'Where the Certificate is rectified, modified or withdrawn, the issuing authority should inform the persons to whom certified copies have been issued so as to avoid wrongful use of such copies'.

name of the person concerned as well as his or her contact information.[25] Requirements as to the form of the register do not exist; it can therefore also be kept electronically.[26]

Legal academics have suggested establishing a central electronic register for European Certificates of Succession.[27] However, this reasonable idea has not yet been implemented.

IV. Period of Validity of the Certified Copies

10. In contrast to the original ECS,[28] the certified copies only have a limited period of validity, extending as a rule to six months (article 70.3 sentence 1).[29] The expiry date is of consequence for the effects resulting from the Certificate (cf. article 69).[30] However, article 70.3 only regulates the limitation period of the copies. It does not cover the question of whether the certified copies retain their validity until the expiry date independently of the original or, in particular, whether they remain effective if the original has been withdrawn or modified. Some suggest that a withdrawal of the ECS remains without consequences for the validity of the certified copies: the copies in circulation should thereby

25 Nordmeier, 'Art. 70 EuErbVO', para. 8. 26 Schmidt, 'Art. 70 EuErbVO', para. 14.

27 Max Planck Institute for Comparative and International Private Law, 'Comments on the European Commission's Proposal for a Regulation of the European Parliament and of the Council on jurisdiction, applicable law, recognition and enforcement of decisions and authentic instruments in matters of succession and the creation of a European Certificate of Succession', *RabelsZ* (2010), pp. 675 (para. 275), 706 *et seq.* (para. 338 *et seq.*); see also doc. 11870/11, 29 June 2011, p. 57 (footnote 3).

28 See P. Wautelet, 'Article 68', in A. Bonomi and P. Wautelet, *Le droit européen des successions. Commentaire du Règlement n° 650/2012 du 4 juillet 2012* (Bruxelles, 2013), p. 766, and *id.*, 'Article 70', p. 811 *et seq.*; Nordmeier, 'Art. 70 EuErbVO', para. 10.

29 The proposal of 2009 only provided for a period of validity of three months; see article 43.2 of the Proposal for a Regulation of the European parliament and of the council on jurisdiction, applicable law, recognition and enforcement of decisions and authentic instruments in matters of succession and the creation of a European Certificate of Succession, COM(2009) 154 final. The proposal has encountered criticism from many quarters, see in particular Max Planck Institute, 'Comments', p. 675, para. 274 *et seq.*; see also S. Frodl, 'Einheit durch Aufgabe nationaler Rechtstraditionen? – EU-Erbrechtsverordnung kundgemacht', *ÖJZ – Österreichische Juristenzeitung* (2012), p. 957.

30 This not least applies to the registry effects of the ECS (cf. article 69.5). For the consequences resulting from expiration before completion of the registry procedures, see (regarding German law) Böhringer, 'Das Europäische Nachlasszeugnis', p. 283 *et seq.*; K. Lange, 'Europäisches Nachlasszeugnis – Antragsverfahren und Verwendung im deutschen Grundbuchverkehr', *DNotZ -Deutsche Notar-Zeitschrift* (2016), p. 112 *et seq.*; (regarding Austrian law) Perscha, 'Art. 70 EuErbVO', para. 18.

be able to trigger the effects according to article 69 independently of the validity of the ECS until the expiry date is reached.[31] Reference is made in this context to the protection of legal transactions: it must be possible to rely upon the assumption that a certified copy has the intended effects until the period of validity expires.[32] This view is, however, not undisputed. According to an opposing argument, the withdrawal of an ECS annuls its effects independently of whether there are still circulating certified copies within their period of validity.[33] In support of this, special reference is made to the possibility of suspending the effects according to article 73.1. Measures of interim relief in accordance with article 73.1 would be defeated if the certified copies could continue to produce their effects even though the effects of the underlying ECS had been suspended.[34] This approach is convincing, in particular because of the wording of article 73: the 'effects of the Certificate' shall explicitly be suspended. These follow from article 69 and include the *bona fide* effects according to paragraphs 3 and 4 of article 69. The *bona fide* effects can, however, only be suspended if the certified copies also do not produce any effects for the duration of the suspension. Therefore, the suspension of the effects of the ECS provided for by article 73.1 must necessarily also include the certified copies.[35] Yet, if even the suspension of the effects of the ECS according to article 73.1 suspends the effects of the certified copies at the same time, the invalidity of all copies must *a fortiori* follow from the withdrawal of the ECS.[36] This is also supported by the consideration that the effects of a mere certified copy can hardly be held to be more extensive than those of the original.

[31] J. Schmidt, 'Art. 71 EuErbVO', in C. Budzikiewicz, M.-P. Weller and W. Wurmnest (eds), *Beck-Online Großkommentar, EuErbVO* (München, 2016), para. 36 *et seq*.; Perscha, 'Art. 70 EuErbVO', para. 12; see also Fornasier, 'Art. 70 EuErbVO', para. 7, who makes the following distinction: an ECS which has been modified, withdrawn or whose effect has been suspended, although losing its evidence effects according to articles 69.2 and 69.5, does not however lose its *bona fide* effects according to articles 69.3 and 69.4.

[32] Schmidt, 'Art. 71 EuErbVO', para. 37.

[33] A. Dutta, 'Art. 69 EuErbVO', in J. von Hein (ed), *Münchener Kommentar zum BGB*, vol. X, 6th ed. (München, 2015), para. 2; A. Köhler, 'Art. 71 EuErbVO', in Kroiß *et al.* (eds), *Nachfolgerecht* (Baden-Baden, 2014), para. 5; Volmer, 'Die EU-Erbrechtsverordnung', p. 432.

[34] Dutta, 'Art. 69 EuErbVO', para. 2.

[35] See Volmer, 'Die EU-Erbrechtsverordnung', p. 432; C. Dorsel, 'Europäische Erbrechtsverordnung und Europäisches Nachlasszeugnis', *ZErb – Zeitschrift für die Steuer- und Erbrechtspraxis* (2014), p. 223; Dorsel, 'Art. 70 EuErbVO', para. 6; W. Rechberger and F. Kieweler, in W. Rechberger and B. Zöchling-Jud (eds), *Die EU-Erbrechtsverordnung in Österreich* (Wien, 2015), p. 323 para. 100.

[36] Volmer, 'Die EU-Erbrechtsverordnung', p. 432.

As far as any modification or rectification of the ECS is concerned, it follows from the preceding that the certified copies can only produce effects insofar as they correspond with the altered version. A solution is thereby also found for the situation where conflicting certified copies are circulating after an alteration of the ECS:[37] as the outdated copies lose their effectiveness insofar as they contradict the altered ECS, a conflict is excluded from the outset.

11. The period of validity of the certified copies is in principle six months (see sentence 1 of article 70.3).[38] This period starts with the issuance of each copy.[39] If several certified copies have been issued, the copies in circulation may have different dates of expiry, depending on their dates of issuance.[40] The issuing authority shall indicate the date of expiry in the certified copy (see sentence 1 of article 70.3). The period of validity is strictly determined according to the relevant indication in the copy, even if the issuing authority has miscalculated the date of expiry.[41] If no date of expiry is indicated, the certified copy is nevertheless valid. In this case, the relevant period of validity shall be calculated from the date of issuance of the copy.[42] In accordance with recital 77, Regulation (EEC, Euratom) no. 1182/71 of the Council of 3 June 1971 determining the rules applicable to periods, dates and time limits[43] shall be applied for the calculation of the period of validity in the sense of article 70.3. The provisions of national law shall be complementarily applied.[44]

12. In accordance with sentence 2 of article 70.3, the issuing authority may, in 'exceptional, duly justified cases', decide that the period of validity is to last longer. The conditions of this exception, are, however,

[37] On this problem, see Nordmeier, 'Art. 70 EuErbVO', para. 14; R. Süß, 'Das Europäische Nachlasseugnis', *ZEuP* (2013), p. 747; Buschbaum and Simon, 'EuErbVO: Das Europäische Nachlasszeugnis', p. 528.

[38] The proposal of the regulation provided for a period of validity of three months, see article 43 of the Proposal for a Regulation of the European Parliament and of the Council on jurisdiction, applicable law, recognition and enforcement of decisions and authentic instruments in matters of succession and the creation of a European Certificate of Succession, COM(2009)154 final, p. 30. See also Lechner, 'Die Entwicklung der Erbrechtsverordnung – Eine Einführung zum Gesetzgebungsverfahren', in A. Dutta and S. Herrler (eds), *Die Europäische Erbrechtsverordnung* (München, 2014), p. 12 para. 27 *et seq.*

[39] Schmidt, 'Art. 70 EuErbVO', para. 18; Lange, 'Europäisches Nachlasszeugnis', p. 109.

[40] Nordmeier, 'Art. 70 EuErbVO', para. 12.

[41] Dutta, 'Art. 70 EuErbVO', para. 6; Nordmeier, 'Art. 70 EuErbVO', para. 10.

[42] Wautelet, 'Article 70', p. 812. [43] OJ 1971 no. L 124, 8 June 1971, p. 1.

[44] See, e.g., section 42 of the (German) international succession law procedure act (*Gesetz zum Internationalen Erbrecht und zur Änderung von Vorschriften zum Erbschein sowie zur Änderung sonstiger Vorschriften* – IntErbRVG).

not specified. The issuing authority will have to decide at its reasonable discretion.[45] In contrast, a reduction of the period of validity is not admissible in the absence of a corresponding provision.[46]

13. Once the period of validity has elapsed, an extension of the period of validity or a new certified copy may be requested from the issuing authority (see sentence 3 of article 70.3). Any person in possession of a certified copy may file such a request.[47] Whether further requirements exist is left open by the provision. In any case, a valid ECS must exist. This is the case not only for the issuance of a new certified copy, but also for the extension of the period of validity: if the effectiveness of a certified copy itself depends on the existence of a valid ECS (see *supra* no. 10), then the extension of the period of validity of a copy that no longer corresponds to the original is ruled out from the outset.[48]

It is also questionable whether a legitimate interest in the use of the ECS needs to be demonstrated again (cf. article 70.1).[49] The very wording of sentence 3 of article 70.3 speaks against such a requirement, as it does not refer to the demonstration of a legitimate interest, but simply to the possession of a certified copy. In addition, there is a systematic argument: the special rules of article 70.3 would be irrelevant if all the preconditions of article 70.1 had to be met. There would be no need for a special provision. Moreover, at least a reference to article 70.1 would have to be expected. Renouncing a further demonstration of a legitimate interest also corresponds to the rationale of the procedure of extension of validity. This procedure must be seen in connection with the limited validity of the certified copies, the purpose of which is to prevent a long-term circulation of outdated copies. The issuing authority should have the possibility to periodically examine whether the content of the certified copies is consistent with the original.[50] A further demonstration of

[45] Dutta, 'Art. 70 EuErbVO', para. 7; Schmidt, 'Art. 70 EuErbVO', para. 21; Nordmeier, 'Art. 70 EuErbVO', para 11; Böhringer, 'Das Europäische Nachlasszeugnis', p. 283; Lange, 'Europäisches Nachlasszeugnis', p. 110; Dorsel, 'Art. 70 EuErbVO', para. 4; see also Fornasier, 'Art. 70 EuErbVO', para. 8: one should weigh between the applicant's interest in a longer period of validity of the ECS and the risk that, in case of modification or withdrawal of the ECS, copies with a content contradictory to the original circulate for a longer period of time.

[46] Nordmeier, 'Art. 70 EuErbVO', para. 11.

[47] It is not the issuance of another ECS that is sought by such a request but rather the extension of the period of validity or the issuance of another certified copy; see Nordmeier, 'Art. 70 EuErbVO', para. 13.

[48] See also Schmidt, 'Art. 70 EuErbVO', para. 23.

[49] In this sense, see Schmidt, 'Art. 70 EuErbVO', para. 23.

[50] See also M. Schauer, 'Europäisches Nachlasszeugnis', in M. Schauer and E. Scheuba (eds), *Europäische Erbrechtsverordnung* (Wien, 2012), p. 92.

a legitimate interest is not necessary in this case. The holder of a certified copy can, however, request the extension of its period of validity if its content still corresponds to that of the original Certificate. Otherwise, he or she may only request a new copy of the (altered) ECS.

14. Finally, whether the extension of the period of validity can still be applied for if the original period of validity has already expired at the time of the application needs to be clarified.[51] On the one hand, a positive view is supported by the wording of the provision, according to which the extension of the period of validity may be applied for 'once this period has elapsed', and thus after completion of the original period of validity. On the other hand, the notion of 'extension' implies that the new period of validity should immediately follow the original period;[52] however, this is only possible if the application has already been filed before the date of expiry. Otherwise, the extended validity would have to have a retroactive effect. With regard to the effects pursuant to article 69, this would be by no means unproblematic. It seems therefore more convincing to merely offer the possibility to apply for the issuance of a new certified copy once the original period of validity of the applicant's copy has already expired.

15. The regulation does not contain any rules concerning the duration of the extended period of validity. The similarity of the effects of such an extension to the issuance of a new certified copy argues in favour of transferring the stipulations of sentences 1 and 2 of article 70.3.[53] The issuing authority would thus extend the period of validity of the certified copy for six months, unless a longer period of validity is exceptionally appropriate. The new period of validity begins on the very date the issuing authority has extended the period. Doing this is the only guarantee that the copy loses its effects after a maximum of six further months (see *supra* no. 13). As the application for an extension must be filed before the expiry date (see *supra* no. 14), the previous period of validity will usually not have been fully exhausted.

[51] In this sense, see Wautelet, 'Article 70', p. 813; *contra* Schmidt, 'Art. 70 EuErbVO', para. 23.

[52] See Schmidt, 'Art. 70 EuErbVO', para. 23.

[53] Nordmeier, 'Art. 70 EuErbVO ', para. 13.

Article 71

Rectification, Modification or Withdrawal of the Certificate

CHRISTINE BUDZIKIEWICZ

1. The issuing authority shall, at the request of any person demonstrating a legitimate interest or of its own motion, rectify the Certificate in the event of a clerical error.
2. The issuing authority shall, at the request of any person demonstrating a legitimate interest or, where this is possible under national law, of its own motion, modify or withdraw the Certificate where it has been established that the Certificate or individual elements thereof are not accurate.
3. The issuing authority shall without delay inform all persons to whom certified copies of the Certificate have been issued pursuant to Article 70(1) of any rectification, modification or withdrawal thereof.

Summary

I. OVERVIEW *page* 805
II. RECTIFICATION IN THE EVENT OF A CLERICAL ERROR 806
III. MODIFICATION AND WITHDRAWAL OF AN INACCURATE ECS 807
IV. INFORMATION 809

I. Overview

1. The provision deals with the rectification, modification or withdrawal of an inaccurate European Certificate of Succession (ECS) by the issuing authority. A distinction is made between the rectification of mere clerical errors (article 71.1) and the modification or withdrawal of an ECS whose content is not accurate (article 71.2). In any case, those persons to whom certified copies have been issued are to be informed (article 71.3). The redress procedures against decisions of the issuing authority pursuant to article 71 are specified in article 72.

II. Rectification in the Event of a Clerical Error

2. Article 71.1 allows for the rectification of a clerical error in the ECS by the issuing authority.[1] The Certificate then continues to exist in its rectified version. A clerical error exists if the text of the ECS contradicts the will of the issuing authority;[2] in contrast, no rectification pursuant to article 71.1 is possible when the very content of the ECS is not accurate; instead, only a modification or withdrawal pursuant to article 71.2 is possible. Examples of clerical errors are spelling mistakes[3] or the inaccurate transfer of data from the application.[4] A rectification is not possible, however, in the case of, for example, a miscalculation made by the issuing authority, as a miscalculation already concerns the formation of the will by the authority.[5]

3. The issuing authority rectifies clerical errors either of its own motion or upon request.[6] According to the wording of the provision, the person requesting rectification has to demonstrate a legitimate interest, but this requirement is of no practical relevance.[7] The issuing authority also has to take action of its own motion in accordance with article 71.1, and it has no discretionary power in this respect.[8] It is therefore obliged to rectify a clerical error even when it has been informed of such an error through the request of a person who has no legitimate interest

[1] 'Issuing authority' is the authority which has issued the certificate; see M. Fornasier, 'Art. 71 EuErbVO', in A. Dutta and J. Weber (eds), *Internationales Erbrecht* (München, 2016), para. 2.

[2] A. Dutta, 'Art. 71 EuErbVO', in J. von Hein (ed), *Münchener Kommentar zum BGB*, vol. X, 6th ed. (München, 2015), para. 2; C. F. Nordmeier, 'Art. 71 EuErbVO', in R. Hüßtege and H.-P. Mansel (eds), *NomosKommentar, BGB, Rom-Verordnungen*, vol. VI, 2nd ed. (Baden-Baden, 2015), para. 6; A. Köhler, 'Art. 71 EuErbVO', in Kroiß *et al.* (eds), *Nachfolgerecht* (Baden-Baden, 2014), para. 3.

[3] C. Dorsel, 'Art. 71 EuErbVO', in R. Geimer and R. Schütze (eds), *Internationaler Rechtsverkehr in Zivil- und Handelssachen*, vol. III (München, 2015), para. 3; J. Kleinschmidt, 'Art. 71 EuErbVO', in M. Herberger *et al.* (eds), *juris Praxiskommentar BGB*, vol. VI, 7th ed. (Saarbrücken, 2014, status: 15 September 2015), para. 4.

[4] Nordmeier, 'Art. 71 EuErbVO', para. 6; P. Wautelet, 'Article 71', in A. Bonomi and P. Wautelet, *Le droit européen des successions - Commentaire du Règlement n° 650/2012 du 4 juillet 2012* (Bruxelles, 2013), p. 817; B. Reinhartz, 'Article 71', in U. Bergquist, D. Damascelli, R. Frimston, P. Lagarde, F. Odersky and B. Reinhartz, *Commentaire du Règlement européen sur les successions* (Paris, 2015), para. 2.

[5] J. Schmidt, 'Art. 71 EuErbVO', in C. Budzikiewicz, M.-P. Weller and W. Wurmnest (eds), *Beck-Online Großkommentar, EuErbVO* (München, 2016), para. 7. For a different view, see W. Rechberger and F. Kieweler, in W. Rechberger and B. Zöchling-Jud (eds), *Die EU-Erbrechtsverordnung in Österreich* (Wien, 2015), p. 319, para. 92 (footnote 215).

[6] The regulation does not foresee a time limit for the rectification; see Dorsel, 'Art. 71 EuErbVO', para. 11.

[7] Dutta, 'Art. 71 EuErbVO', para. 7; Schmidt, 'Art. 71 EuErbVO', para. 10.

[8] Dutta, 'Art. 71 EuErbVO', para. 2.

him- or herself. The interpretation of the notion of legitimate interest is thus irrelevant within the scope of article 71.1. [9] However, it may become relevant within the scope of article 71.2 (see *infra* no. 6). Furthermore, according to article 72.1 subparagraph 2, only a person demonstrating a legitimate interest is entitled to challenge decisions taken by the issuing authority pursuant to article 71 [see art. 72 no. 5].

III. Modification and Withdrawal of an Inaccurate ECS

4. In the case that the ECS or individual elements thereof are not accurate, it can be modified or withdrawn in accordance with article 71.2. To start with, there is inaccuracy where the actual elements of law or fact differ from the specifications in the ECS.[10] The provision does not distinguish between initial or subsequent inaccuracy; therefore, it also has to be applied in the case when an heir has waived the inheritance.[11] For a modification or a withdrawal, article 71.2 does not require that the inaccuracy involve bona fide effects according to paragraphs 3 and 4 of article 69.[12]

5. It is unclear whether article 71.2 is also to be applied in cases of formal mistakes in the Certificate such as issuance by an incompetent authority. This could be questionable, particularly with respect to the French version ('que ledit certificat ou certains de ses éléments ne correspondent pas à la réalité') or the German version ('dass das Zeugnis oder einzelne Teile inhaltlich unrichtig sind'). Nevertheless, legal scholars rightly hold the view that the provision is also applicable in cases of formal mistakes.[13] Article 68 requires that the ECS provides, *inter alia,* information regarding the competence of the issuing authority

[9] See also Fornasier, 'Art. 71 EuErbVO', para. 2, who nevertheless assumes that the wording 'any person demonstrating a legitimate interest' comprises any person for which the Certificate is relevant.

[10] Dutta, 'Art. 71 EuErbVO', para. 2; Nordmeier, 'Art. 71 EuErbVO', para. 9; Kleinschmidt, 'Art. 71 EuErbVO', para. 7; see also Reinhartz, 'Article 71', para. 4; Fornasier, 'Art. 71 EuErbVO', para. 4, both with numerous examples.

[11] Nordmeier, 'Art. 71 EuErbVO', para. 9; also see Schmidt, 'Art. 71 EuErbVO', para. 20, who mentions the case that the revisionary heir has succeeded to the decedent's estate.

[12] Nordmeier, 'Art. 71 EuErbVO', para. 9; dissenting, Dutta, 'Art. 71 EuErbVO', para. 4; Fornasier, 'Art. 71 EuErbVO', para. 4.

[13] Schmidt, 'Art. 71 EuErbVO', para. 18; with respect to the particular case of colliding ECS, also see Nordmeier, 'Art. 71 EuErbVO', para. 17; dissenting, Fornasier, 'Art. 71 EuErbVO', para. 4.

(cf. point (c) of article 68). These aspects are thus part of the Certificate.[14] If they are violated, the Certificate is not accurate.

6. Modification or withdrawal takes place upon the request of any person demonstrating a legitimate interest or, when possible under national law, of the authority's own motion. Unlike with the rectification of clerical errors, here the issuing authority[15] may only take action on its own initiative when this is permitted by national law. If this is the case, the question whether the person requesting modification or withdrawal can demonstrate a legitimate interest has no practical relevance, as in article 71.1 (see *supra* no. 3): as the issuing authority has no power of discretion, it is obliged to modify or withdraw an ECS whenever it is informed of its inaccuracy, even if this occurs through an inadmissible request.[16] Only when national law does not permit the issuing authority to act on its own motion must a person requesting the modification or withdrawal of an ECS actually demonstrate a legitimate interest. Such interest can certainly be assumed in the case of persons who are entitled to apply for an ECS or a certified copy (cf. article 65.1).[17] Equally entitled to file a request is any person whose legal position has wrongly not yet been certified by the ECS.[18] A third person who is the owner of an object that has falsely been attributed to the succession in the ECS can also request modification or withdrawal.[19] Finally, some argue that persons against whom the ECS is being used can also have a legitimate interest as defined by article 71.2.[20] This conclusion is supported by the presumption laid down in article 69.2. For example, a debtor of the estate could have reason to fear that a presumptive heir legitimised by an ECS might take action against him or her. Although a debtor of the estate may be unable to perform by discharging the debt according to article 69.3 because he or she is aware of the inaccuracy of the ECS, the presumptive heir could nonetheless take action against him or her and invoke the presumption of article 69.2 in the proceedings. The debtor of the estate therefore has a legitimate interest in the modification or withdrawal of the ECS, so as not to be compelled to refute the presumptive effect of the

[14] Schmidt, 'Art. 71 EuErbVO', para. 18.

[15] 'Issuing authority' in terms of article 71.2 is the authority which has issued the Certificate (irrespective of the international competence according to article 64); see Fornasier, 'Art. 71 EuErbVO', para. 7.

[16] Dutta, 'Art. 71 EuErbVO', para. 5; Nordmeier, 'Art. 71 EuErbVO', para. 12.

[17] Schmidt, 'Art. 71 EuErbVO', para. 24; Wautelet, 'Article 71', p. 816 *et seq.*

[18] Dutta, 'Art. 71 EuErbVO', para. 5. [19] Nordmeier, 'Art. 71 EuErbVO', para. 12.

[20] Schmidt, 'Art. 71 EuErbVO', para. 9; also see Wautelet, 'Article 71', p. 817.

ECS in the proceedings.[21] The regulation does not foresee a time limit for the modification or withdrawal of an inaccurate ECS.[22]

7. The legal consequence mentioned in article 71.2 is the modification or withdrawal of the Certificate. The withdrawal annuls the effectiveness of the Certificate, while in the case of modification it continues to exist in its altered version.[23] The issuing authority has no power of discretion: if the ECS is inaccurate and if either the issuing authority acts of its own motion or an admissible request is made, the authority is obliged to modify or withdraw the ECS.[24] It is, however, unclear as to when it should be modified and when it should be withdrawn. Several criteria have been proposed. Some deem the seriousness of the mistake to be decisive.[25] For others, it depends on whether the mistake concerns the Certificate as a whole or only parts of it,[26] or whether the mistake can be corrected[27]. The latter criterion seems to deal with the problem adequately. A correction is thus not possible when an incompetent authority has acted (cf. *supra* no. 5) or when the applicant whose legal position is supposed to be certified by the ECS is in fact not a legitimate applicant. However, an alteration is possible in the case of specific incorrect details in the sense of article 68. The modification or withdrawal of the ECS has no retroactive effect; it has effect only *ex nunc*.[28]

IV. Information

8. The moment the ECS is withdrawn, the certified copies issued by the authority also become invalid. The regulation does not draw a distinction between whether the certified copies are valid independently of the original and whether they remain effective if the ECS is rectified, modified or withdrawn (cf. already article 70 paragraph 11). If the ECS is modified or rectified, the certified copies can only produce effects insofar as they conform to the altered version. Any further certified copies may only be issued based on the corrected version.

9. For reasons of protection of legal relations, article 71.3 rules that the issuing authorities shall without delay inform all persons to whom

[21] See also Kleinschmidt, 'Art. 71 EuErbVO', para. 8.
[22] Dorsel, 'Art. 71 EuErbVO', para. 11.
[23] Nordmeier, 'Art. 71 EuErbVO', para. 10; Schmidt, 'Art. 71 EuErbVO', para. 29 *et seq.*
[24] See Dutta, 'Art. 71 EuErbVO', para. 6. [25] Nordmeier, 'Art. 71 EuErbVO', para. 10.
[26] Schmidt, 'Art. 71 EuErbVO', para. 31.
[27] Dutta, 'Art. 71 EuErbVO', para. 6; Kleinschmidt, 'Art. 71 EuErbVO', para. 6.
[28] Dorsel, 'Art. 71 EuErbVO', para. 5.

certified copies have been issued about any rectification, modification or withdrawal. According to the fifth sentence of recital 72, this provision is supposed to prevent wrongful use of such copies. Many, however, consider this to be insufficient; a specific point of criticism has been that the regulator has not provided for the confiscation of the certified copies by the issuing authority.[29] Some go so far as to deduce such an obligation to surrender from the regulation by means of further developments of the law[30] or to apply national rules containing provisions ordering the surrender of certificates of succession in the event of annulments.[31] The exhaustive nature of article 71.3 does not, however, allow this.[32] The risk of wrongful use cannot indeed be denied as long as such copies circulate in legal relations. But this risk is not borne by the heirs, but by third persons to whom an outdated certified copy is presented:[33] as rectification, modification and withdrawal also render the certified copies ineffective, the *bona fide* effects of paragraphs 3 and 4 of article 69 cannot take place anymore.[34] In practice, legal relations can therefore only rely on the certified copies in a limited way. The risk of wrongful use of

[29] Dutta, 'Art. 71 EuErbVO', para. 7; Schmidt, 'Art. 71 EuErbVO', para. 42 *et seq.*; Dorsel, 'Art. 71 EuErbVO', para. 8; J. Kleinschmidt, 'Art. 70 EuErbVO', in M. Herberger *et al.* (eds), *juris Praxiskommentar BGB*, vol. VI, 7th ed. (Saarbrücken, 2014, status: 15 September 2015), para. 9; *id.*, 'Art. 71 EuErbVO', para. 13.

[30] Schmidt, 'Art. 71 EuErbVO', para. 42; *id.*, 'Der Erbnachweis in Deutschland ab 2015: Erbschein vs. Europäisches Nachlasszeugnis', *ZEV – Zeitschrift für Erbrecht und Vermögensnachfolge* (2014), p. 394.

[31] So with respect to German law, M. Buschbaum and U. Simon, 'EuErbVO: Das Europäische Nachlasszeugnis', *ZEV – Zeitschrift für Erbrecht und Vermögensnachfolge* (2012), p. 526, and S. Omlor, 'Gutglaubensschutz durch das Europäische Nachlasszeugnis', *GPR- European Union Private Law Review* (2014), p. 218; dissenting, Kleinschmidt, 'Art. 70 EuErbVO', para. 9.

[32] Dutta, 'Art. 71 EuErbVO', para. 7; Fornasier, 'Art. 71 EuErbVO', paras. 11, 13; also see Dorsel, 'Art. 71 EuErbVO', para. 2; Official Record of the German Bundestag (BT-Drucksache) 18/4201, p. 82 *et seq.*; also sceptical, W. Rechberger and F. Kieweler, in W. Rechberger and B. Zöchling-Jud (eds), *Die EU-Erbrechtsverordnung in Österreich*, p. 320 *et seq.*, para. 94. For a different view, see Schmidt, 'Art. 71 EuErbVO', para. 43; C. Dorsel, 'Art. 70 EuErbVO', in R. Geimer and R. Schütze (eds), *Internationaler Rechtsverkehr in Zivil- und Handelssachen*, vol. III (München, 2015), para. 13; *id.*, 'Art. 71 EuErbVO', para. 10, who assumes that the national legislators are free to enact provisions ordering the confiscation of the certified copies.

[33] Köhler, 'Art. 71 EuErbVO', para. 5; differing, M. Buschbaum and U. Simon, 'EuErbVO: Das Europäische Nachlasszeugnis', p. 526; K. W. Lange, 'Das Europäische Nachlasszeugnis', in A. Dutta and S. Herrler (eds), *Die Europäische Erbrechtsverordnung* (München, 2014), p. 174, para. 42.

[34] For a different view, see Fornasier, 'Art. 71 EuErbVO', para. 11; Dorsel, 'Art. 71 EuErbVO', para. 9.

ineffective copies is, however, reduced by the fact that the validity of certified copies is limited to six months after their issuance.[35]

10. The issuing authority has to inform the persons concerned without delay as required by article 71.3 [see art. 67 no. 12]. The requirement to inform also applies if modification or withdrawal is implemented by the judicial authority according to article 72.2.[36] In order to fulfil its obligation to inform in accordance with article 70.2, the issuing authority keeps a register of all persons to whom certified copies have been issued.[37]

[35] See also Nordmeier, 'Art. 71 EuErbVO', para. 13.

[36] Schmidt, 'Art. 71 EuErbVO', para. 46.

[37] See also Wautelet, 'Article 71', p. 819, who states that further details of the procedure (e.g. information by registered letter) have to be determined by the Member States.

Article 72

Redress Procedures

CHRISTINE BUDZIKIEWICZ

(1) Decisions taken by the issuing authority pursuant to Article 67 may be challenged by any person entitled to apply for a Certificate.

Decisions taken by the issuing authority pursuant to Article 71 and point (a) of Article 73(1) may be challenged by any person demonstrating a legitimate interest.

The challenge shall be lodged before a judicial authority in the Member State of the issuing authority in accordance with the law of that State.

(2) If, as a result of a challenge as referred to in paragraph 1, it is established that the Certificate issued is not accurate, the competent judicial authority shall rectify, modify or withdraw the Certificate or ensure that it is rectified, modified or withdrawn by the issuing authority.

If, as a result of a challenge as referred to in paragraph 1, it is established that the refusal to issue the Certificate was unjustified, the competent judicial authority shall issue the Certificate or ensure that the issuing authority re-assesses the case and makes a fresh decision.

Summary

I. OVERVIEW *page* 812
II. DECISIONS TO BE CHALLENGED 813
III. INDIVIDUAL RIGHT TO LODGE A CHALLENGE 814
IV. COMPETENCE AND PROCEDURE 816
V. SCOPE OF EXAMINATION AND DECISION 817

I. Overview

1. Article 72 deals with the legal remedies against the decisions of the issuing authorities in proceedings concerning the issuance, rectification, modification or withdrawal of a European Certificate of Succession (ECS). The redress procedures for these purposes are, however, only regulated in a rudimentary way.[1] Article 72.1(1) and article 72.1(2) deal with the

[1] Cf. K. Lange, 'Die internationale Zuständigkeit nach der Erbrechtsverordnung', in A. Dutta and S. Herrler (eds), *Die Europäische Erbrechtsverordnung* (München, 2014),

general admissibility of redress procedures and the individual right to lodge a challenge. Article 72.2 concerns the decision of the judicial redress authority and the further course of procedure. The challenge shall be lodged before a judicial authority in the Member State of the issuing authority (article 72.1(3)). However, the procedural details of the proceedings are left to the national legal order.[2] Article 72 is supplemented by point (b) of article 73.1, according to which the judicial authority may suspend the effects of the ECS upon request, pending a challenge.

The regulation provides no remedy for cases where the issuing authority refuses to issue a certified copy of the ECS (cf. article 70). In accordance with the view presented here, article 72.1 should be applied by way of an analogy [see art. 70 no. 8].

II. Decisions to Be Challenged

2. To begin with, the decisions taken by the issuing authority pursuant to article 67 may be challenged according to article 72.1(1). This primarily concerns the refusal to issue an ECS (cf. article 72.2(2)),[3] but the remedy provided for by article 72.1(1) is also generally admissible when the issuance of an ECS itself is challenged.[4] The wording of article 72.1(1) imposes no restrictions ('decisions taken . . . pursuant to Article 67'). Furthermore, the decisions taken pursuant to article 71 by the

p. 174 para. 44; C. F. Nordmeier, 'Art. 72 EuErbVO', in R. Hüßtege and H.-P. Mansel (eds), *NomosKommentar, BGB, Rom-Verordnungen*, vol. VI, 2nd ed. (Baden-Baden, 2015), para. 1; see also R. Schaub, 'Die EU-Erbrechtsverordnung', *Heriditare – Jahrbuch für Erbrecht und Schenkungsrecht* (2013), p. 126.

2 Also see P. Wautelet, 'Article 72', in A. Bonomi and P. Wautelet, *Le droit européen des successions – Commentaire du Règlement n° 650/2012 du 4 juillet 2012* (Bruxelles, 2013), p. 821 *et seq.*

3 Also see sentence 3 of recital 72: 'This Regulation should provide for redress against decisions of the issuing authority, including decisions to refuse the issue of a Certificate.'

4 Wautelet, 'Article 72', p. 823 *et seq.*; A. Dutta, 'Art. 72 EuErbVO', in J. von Hein (ed), *Münchener Kommentar zum BGB*, vol. X, 6th ed. (München, 2015), para. 2; Nordmeier, 'Art. 72 EuErbVO', para. 4; J. Schmidt, 'Art. 72 EuErbVO', in C. Budzikiewicz, M.-P. Weller and W. Wurmnest (eds), *Beck-Online Großkommentar*, EuErbVO (München, 2016), para. 4; M. Schauer, 'Europäisches Nachlasszeugnis', in M. Schauer and E. Scheuba (eds), *Europäische Erbrechtsverordnung* (Wien, 2012), p. 91; M. Fornasier, 'Art. 72 EuErbVO', in A. Dutta and J. Weber (eds), *Internationales Erbrecht* (München, 2016), para. 2. For a different view, see B. Reinhartz, 'Article 72', in U. Bergquist, D. Damascelli, R. Frimston, P. Lagarde, F. Odersky and B. Reinhartz, *Commentaire du Règlement européen sur les successions* (Paris, 2015), para. 1; W. Rechberger and F. Kieweler, 'Das Europäische Nachlasszeugnis', in W. Rechberger and B. Zöchling-Jud (eds), *Die EU-Erbrechtsverordnung in Österreich* (Wien, 2015), p. 321 *et seq.*, para. 96.

issuing authority may be challenged according to article 72.1(2). This includes the rectification of clerical errors (see article 71(1)), as well as the modification or withdrawal of the Certificate (see article 71.2). In this context, too, both a decision in favour of a rectification, modification or withdrawal of the ECS and a decision refusing such measures may be challenged.[5]

In the case that an ECS has been issued, a judicial review of its substantial accuracy can be obtained in two ways: the issuance of the Certificate can be challenged in accordance with article 72.1 subsection 1, or a request for modification or withdrawal pursuant to article 71.2 may be filed.[6] If the issuing authority refuses to modify or withdraw the ECS, this decision can then be challenged in accordance with article 72.1(2).[7] The persons entitled to apply for an ECS according to article 65.1 have both alternatives at their disposal.[8]

3. Decisions that the issuing authority has taken pursuant to point (a) of article 73.1 may also be challenged according to article 72.1(2). This includes decisions on the suspension of the effects of an ECS during a procedure concerning modification or withdrawal pursuant to article 71. In this case as well, both decisions granting the application and decisions repealing it can be subject to a redress procedure.[9] There is no legal remedy, however, against decisions made by the judicial redress authority concerning the suspension of the effects of the ECS (cf. point (b) of article 73.1).[10]

III. Individual Right to Lodge a Challenge

4. Decisions taken by the issuing authority pursuant to article 67 may be challenged by any person entitled to apply for a Certificate (see article 72.1(1)). It is thus not only the applicant, but also any person entitled to apply for the issuance of an ECS according to article

[5] Schmidt, 'Art. 72 EuErbVO', para. 9; Fornasier, 'Art. 72 EuErbVO', para. 3.

[6] Dutta, 'Art. 72 EuErbVO', para. 2; Wautelet, 'Article 72', p. 823.

[7] Wautelet, 'Article 72', p. 823. [8] Nordmeier, 'Art. 72 EuErbVO', para. 4.

[9] Nordmeier, 'Art. 72 EuErbVO', para. 5; Schmidt, 'Art. 72 EuErbVO', para. 9.

[10] P. Wautelet, 'Article 73', in A. Bonomi and P. Wautelet, *Le droit européen des successions – Commentaire du Règlement n° 650/2012 du 4 juillet 2012* (Bruxelles, 2013), p. 830 *et seq*; A. Dutta, 'Art. 73 EuErbVO', in J. von Hein (ed), *Münchener Kommentar zum BGB*, vol. X, 6th ed. (München, 2015), para. 7; Nordmeier, 'Art. 73 EuErbVO', in R. Hüßtege and H.-P. Mansel (eds), *NomosKommentar, BGB, Rom-Verordnungen*, vol. VI, 2nd ed. (Baden-Baden, 2015), para. 13.

65.1 who has the right to lodge a challenge [see art. 65 no. 5].[11] The provision does not contain any limitation of this right that is stricter than the requirement that the complainant be entitled to file an application according to article 65.1;[12] in particular, demonstration of a legitimate interest is not required, in contrast to article 72.1(2).[13] For the applicant, the redress procedure pursuant to article 72.1 offers the possibility to take action against the refusal to issue an ECS or against the issuance of an ECS whose content is other than that which was requested.[14]

However, persons who are not entitled to apply for an ECS are not entitled to challenge its issuance. They would first have to request the modification or withdrawal of the ECS from the issuing authority pursuant to article 71.2. If this application were rejected, the decision of refusal could then be challenged according to article 72.1(2) (see no. 5).[15]

5. Decisions that have been taken by the issuing authority pursuant to article 71 or to point (a) of article 73.1 can be challenged by any person who demonstrates a legitimate interest (see article 72.1(2)). The notion of 'legitimate interest' here corresponds to its meaning in article 71 paragraphs 1 and 2;[16] the corresponding explanations can be referred to [see art. 71 no. 6].

6. In accordance with the point of view presented here, as article 72.1 has to be applied by way of an analogy on decisions that the issuing authority has taken according to article 70 with respect to the issuance of a certified copy [see art. 70 no. 8], any person who previously applied for the issuance of an ECS is entitled to lodge a challenge pursuant to article 72.1(1) against a decision of refusal taken according to article 70.1.[17] For all other persons, a legitimate interest should be requested by way of an analogy to article 72.1(2). This conforms to the preconditions of an application as laid down in article 70.1 and mirrors the parallel structure found in article 72.1(2) and article 71 paragraphs 1 and 2.

[11] Wautelet, 'Article 72', p. 823 *et seq.*; Schmidt, 'Art. 72 EuErbVO', para. 5; Rechberger and Kieweler, 'Das Europäische Nachlasszeugnis', p. 321, para. 96; Schauer, 'Europäisches Nachlasszeugnis', p. 91.

[12] Wautelet, 'Article 72', p. 823 *et seq.*; A. Köhler, 'Art. 72 EuErbVO', in L. Kroiß et al. (eds), *Nachfolgerecht* (Baden-Baden, 2014), para. 1.

[13] But see M. Fornasier, 'Art. 72 EuErbVO', in A. Dutta and J. Weber (eds), *Internationales Erbrecht*, para. 2; Schmidt, 'Art. 72 EuErbVO', para. 5: the applicant needs to be affected by the decision in question.

[14] Nordmeier, 'Art. 72 EuErbVO', para. 6.

[15] Nordmeier, 'Art. 72 EuErbVO', para. 8.

[16] Schmidt, 'Art. 72 EuErbVO', para.11; Wautelet, 'Article 72', p. 824.

[17] Also see A. Dutta, 'Art. 70 EuErbVO', in J. von Hein (ed), *Münchener Kommentar zum BGB*, vol. X, 6th ed. (München, 2015), para. 4; *id.*, 'Art. 72 EuErbVO', para. 3.

IV. Competence and Procedure

7. Any challenge must be lodged before a judicial authority in the Member State of the issuing authority in accordance with the law of that State (see article 72.1(3)). The term 'judicial authority' corresponds to the one used in article 3.2 [see art. 3 no. 18]. Thus, neither 'other authorities' in the sense of article 3.2 nor 'another authority' in the sense of point (b) of the second sentence of article 64 are competent to decide on the challenge; this applies even if the issuing authority was 'another authority' within the meaning of article 64 (e.g. a notary[18]).[19] Article 72.1 (3) provides that the procedure has to take place in the Member State of the issuing authority; the provision contains a specific rule on international jurisdiction.[20] Apart from that, the procedural rules are left to the national laws of the Member States.[21] This is the case for the determination of geographical and substantial competence in particular.[22] It is uncertain whether national procedural law can set a time limit for the challenge.[23] The regulation leaves the specifications of the redress procedures to a large extent to the national laws. Nevertheless, it can be inferred from the fact that the regulation itself does not set any time limit for the lodging of the challenge that the challenge shall not be limited in time.[24] However, in German law, the national remedy of a complaint (German: 'Beschwerde'), for example, does have a time limit.[25]

[18] See, e.g., the legal situation in the Netherlands, where the notaries are the competent authority to issue the ECS but where the challenge according to article 72 has to be lodged before the 'kantonrechter' (article 9.1 *Uitvoeringswet Verordening erfrecht*); see on this point also J. G. Knot, 'Uitvoering van de Europese Erfrechtverordening in Nederland: wijziging van Boek 10 BW en inpassing van de Europese erfrechtverklaring', *TE – Tijdschrift Erfrecht* (2014), p. 41.

[19] See Wautelet, 'Article 72', p. 822; Fornasier, 'Art. 72 EuErbVO', para. 6; J. Kleinschmidt, 'Art. 72 EuErbVO', in M. Herberger *et al.* (eds), *juris Praxiskommentar BGB*, vol. VI, 7th ed. (Saarbrücken, 2014, status: 15 September 2015), para. 12.

[20] Schmidt, 'Art. 72 EuErbVO', para. 14.

[21] Wautelet, 'Article 72', pp. 822, 824; Nordmeier, 'Art. 72 EuErbVO', para. 9; Schauer, 'Europäisches Nachlasszeugnis', p. 91.

[22] Kleinschmidt, 'Art. 72 EuErbVO', para. 12; Schmidt, 'Art. 72 EuErbVO', para. 15.

[23] Also see Wautelet, 'Article 72', p. 824.

[24] See Dutta, 'Art. 72 EuErbVO', para. 5; see also C. Dorsel, 'Art. 72 EuErbVO', in R. Geimer and R. Schütze (eds), *Internationaler Rechtsverkehr in Zivil- und Handelssachen* (München, 2015), para. 11. For a different view, see Kleinschmidt, 'Art. 72 EuErbVO', para. 19.

[25] See section 43.3 of the (German) international succession law procedure act (*Gesetz zum Internationalen Erbrecht und zur Änderung von Vorschriften zum Erbschein sowie zur Änderung sonstiger Vorschriften* – IntErbRVG).

According to point (d) of article 78.1, the Member States were obliged to inform the Commission of the relevant redress procedure until 16 January 2014; the relevant details were published in the Official Journal of the European Union (cf. article 78.2).

V. Scope of Examination and Decision

8. If the competent judicial authority comes to the conclusion that the Certificate issued is not accurate, it shall rectify, modify or withdraw the Certificate or order the issuing authority to do so (article 72.2(1)). The question is, of course, which standard of judicial review is meant by the expression 'not accurate'. Uncertainties mainly result from the fact that some of the different linguistic versions deviate from each other (see, for example, the German version: 'nicht den Tatsachen entspricht', or the French version: 'ne correspond pas à la réalité'[26]). Given the fact that in the English version as well as in other (although not all) versions the corresponding expression ('not accurate'; 'ne correspondent pas à la réalité') is also used in article 71.2 concerning the scope of examination to be applied by the issuing authority,[27] it can be assumed that article 72.2 and article 71.2 prescribe the same scope of examination.[28] A prevalent view concludes that in both cases, only the substantive accuracy of the Certificate shall be examined; compliance with the correct procedure of issuance pursuant to article 64 *et seq.*, however, should not be subject to examination.[29] Yet, if one concurs with the view presented here that all information given in the ECS, including the entries concerning the original procedure, may be examined within the application of article 71.2 [see art. 71 no. 5], the same would have to apply for the judicial redress authority; i.e. the judicial redress authority could examine all information given in the Certificate. Hence, the standard of judicial review that has to be followed in the redress procedures also includes the competence of the issuing authority and the effectiveness of the application [for further details concerning the formal requirements of the issuance of an ECS see art. 67 no. 5].[30]

[26] The French version corresponds to the Italian version ('non corrisponde al vero') and the Dutch version ('niet met de werkelijkheid overeenstemt').

[27] Different is, however, the German version of article 71.2: 'inhaltlich unrichtig'.

[28] Nordmeier, 'Art. 72 EuErbVO', para. 11.

[29] Nordmeier, 'Art. 72 EuErbVO', para. 11 *et seq.*; Dutta, 'Art. 72 EuErbVO', para. 7; A. Perscha, 'Art. 72 EuErbVO', in M. Schauer and A. Deixler-Hübner (eds), *EuErbVO-Kommentar* (Wien, 2015), para. 12.

[30] See also Fornasier, 'Art. 72 EuErbVO', para. 8; Kleinschmidt, 'Art. 72 EuErbVO', para. 36.

According to the clear wording of article 72.2(1), it is irrelevant whether an initial or a subsequent inaccuracy is to be dealt with. The situation corresponds to what has been said about article 71 [see art. 71 no. 4]. If there are objections regarding the correctness of the certified elements (cf. point (a) of article 67.1(2)), then, – unlike in the original procedure [see art. 67 no. 8] – a decision (based if necessary on adversary proceedings) has to be taken about the legal position to be certified.[31]

9. If the judicial authority asserts that the ECS is inaccurate, it can rectify, modify or withdraw it itself or let the issuing authority do so (see article 72.2(1)). The detailed implementation of this provision is left to the national laws of the Member States.[32]

10. If the redress procedure leads to the conclusion that the refusal to issue the ECS was unjustified, the judicial authority shall either issue the Certificate with the content required by article 68 or ensure that the issuing authority re-assesses the case and makes a fresh decision.[33] The same applies when the issuance of a certified copy has been wrongly refused (see *supra* nos. 1 and 6).[34]

The regulation does not provide for further remedies against the decisions of the judicial redress authority. The Member States are free, however, to institute such remedies.[35]

11. There are no specifications in the regulation concerning the scope of the review or the redress decision for cases where a decision pursuant to point (a) of article 73.1 concerning the suspension of the effects of the ECS is challenged. As the issuing authority has a power of discretion in that regard [see art. 73 no. 4], the judicial authority can, in the end, only check for the proper exercise of that power of discretion.[36]

31 Dutta, 'Art. 72 EuErbVO', para. 7.

32 See Wautelet, 'Article 72', p. 825; Rechberger and Kieweler, 'Das Europäische Nachlasszeugnis', p. 323, para. 99.

33 See Wautelet, 'Article 72', p. 825: 'Le choix entre ces deux solutions sera en fonction de l'organisation concrète de la voie de recours dans le droit de l'État membre dont les autorités sont saisies'.

34 Dutta, 'Art. 72 EuErbVO', para. 8.

35 Wautelet, 'Article 72', p. 821 *et seq.*; Nordmeier, 'Art. 72 EuErbVO', para. 15; Köhler, 'Art. 72 EuErbVO', p. 206, para. 29.

36 Dutta, 'Art. 72 EuErbVO', para. 9; Nordmeier, 'Art. 72 EuErbVO', para. 16.

Article 73

Suspension of the Effects of the Certificate

CHRISTINE BUDZIKIEWICZ

1. The effects of the Certificate may be suspended by:
   (a) the issuing authority, at the request of any person demonstrating a legitimate interest, pending a modification or withdrawal of the Certificate pursuant to Article 71; or
   (b) the judicial authority, at the request of any person entitled to challenge a decision taken by the issuing authority pursuant to Article 72, pending such a challenge.
2. The issuing authority or, as the case may be, the judicial authority shall without delay inform all persons to whom certified copies of the Certificate have been issued pursuant to Article 70(1) of any suspension of the effects of the Certificate.
   During the suspension of the effects of the Certificate no further certified copies of the Certificate may be issued.

Summary

I. INTRODUCTION *page* 819
II. PREREQUISITES FOR A SUSPENSION 820
 A. Procedure before the Issuing Authority 820
 B. Suspension by the Judicial Authority 822
III. EFFECTS ON THE CERTIFIED COPIES 824
IV. REMEDIES 825

I. Introduction

1. A European Certificate of Succession (ECS) that is inaccurate as to content also triggers the effects laid down in article 69 as a rule. In particular, it is possible to issue certified copies of an inaccurate ECS which are in turn the basis for the *bona fide* effects according to subparagraphs 3 and 4 of article 69. This applies even while the issuing authority (cf. article 71.2) or the judicial redress authority (cf. article 72.1) is examining the possibility of a modification or withdrawal of the Certificate. Article 73 takes this situation into account. The provision allows for the suspension of the effects of the ECS upon application. It thus prevents the usage of a possibly inaccurate Certificate, as long as its accuracy is being reviewed.[1] The suspension of the effects of the ECS simultaneously suspends the effects of the certified copies [see art. 70 no. 10]. No further certified copies of the ECS may be issued during the period of suspension (see article 73.2 subparagraph 2).

II. Prerequisites for a Suspension

A. *Procedure before the Issuing Authority*

2. The issuing authority (cf. article 64) may, at the request of any person demonstrating a legitimate interest, suspend the effects of the ECS until its modification or withdrawal (see point (a) of article 73.1). The wording 'pending a modification or withdrawal of the Certificate' indicates that the suspension is only possible in a procedure pursuant to article 71.2. A procedure that is merely intended to rectify a clerical error (cf. article 71.1) cannot justify the suspension of the effects of the ECS.[2] Obviously, the European regulators did not see any need for interim relief measures. It is a further requirement that proceedings seeking the modification or withdrawal of the ECS already be pending.[3] This follows from the phrase 'pending a modification or withdrawal' (French: 'dans l'attente ...'; Dutch: 'in afwachting ...').[4] It is irrelevant in this context whether the proceedings have been initiated upon request or *ex officio*.[5] The application for the modification or withdrawal of the ECS under

[1] J. Schmidt, 'Art. 73 EuErbVO', in C. Budzikiewicz, M.-P. Weller and W. Wurmnest (eds), *Beck-Online Großkommentar* (München, 2016), para. 3.

[2] C. F. Nordmeier, 'Art. 73 EuErbVO', in R. Hüßtege and H.-P. Mansel (eds), *Nomos-Kommentar, BGB, Rom-Verordnungen*, vol. VI, 2nd ed. (Baden-Baden, 2015), para. 3; Schmidt, 'Art. 73 EuErbVO', para. 7.

[3] Nordmeier, 'Art. 73 EuErbVO', para. 3; J. Kleinschmidt, 'Art. 73 EuErbVO', in M. Herberger *et al.* (eds), *juris Praxiskommentar BGB*, vol. VI, 7th ed. (Saarbrücken, 2014, status: 15th September 2015), para. 1; for a different view, see P. Wautelet, 'Article 73', in A. Bonomi and P. Wautelet, *Le droit européen des successions. Commentaire du Règlement n° 650/2012 du 4 juillet 2012* (Bruxelles, 2013), p. 828, who argues that a request for the suspension of the effects of an ECS may already be lodged when an application for modification or withdrawal of the ECS is imminent, but has not yet been filed.

[4] The German version is, however, less obvious: 'bis zur Änderung oder zum Widerruf'.

[5] Nordmeier, 'Art. 73 EuErbVO', para. 6; but see Wautelet, 'Article 73', p. 828.

article 71.2 may also be joined with the request for suspension under point (a) of article 73.1.[6]

3. The suspension of the effects of the ECS pursuant to point (a) of article 73.1 requires a request for a suspension.[7] A suspension *ex officio* is not possible.[8] The request is not bound to a particular time limit; it can be lodged at any time until the issuing authority has come to a decision regarding the modification or withdrawal of the Certificate.[9] Any person demonstrating a legitimate interest is entitled to lodge such a request. Therefore, the request can be lodged not only by the person applying for modification or withdrawal under article 71.2, but also by any other person having a legitimate interest in the suspension of the effects of the ECS.[10] A legitimate interest exists for any person whose legal position may be affected by the actual Certificate.[11] This especially applies to persons who are entitled to apply for an ECS according to articles 65.1 and 63.1 if their legal position is not reflected correctly or at all in the ECS.[12]

4. The decision concerning the suspension of the effects of the ECS remains at the discretion of the issuing authority ('the Certificate may be suspended'). It is, however, not specified how the discretionary power is to be applied. First of all, the probability of a modification or withdrawal will have to be taken into account;[13] further criteria can be the extent of the possible inaccuracy[14] and the consequences of the (positive or negative)

[6] Nordmeier, 'Art. 73 EuErbVO', para. 3.

[7] M. Fornasier, 'Art. 73 EuErbVO', in A. Dutta and J. Weber (eds), *Internationales Erbrecht* (München, 2016), para. 3; Schmidt, 'Art. 73 EuErbVO', para. 6; W. Rechberger and F. Kieweler, 'Das Europäische Nachlasszeugnis', in W. H. Rechberger and B. Zöchling-Jud (eds), *Die EU-Erbrechtsverordnung in Österreich* (Wien, 2015), p. 323, para. 101.

[8] A. Köhler, 'Art. 73 EuErbVO', in Kroiß *et al.* (eds), *Nachfolgerecht* (Baden-Baden, 2014), para. 2; Nordmeier, 'Art. 73 EuErbVO', para. 5; A. Perscha, 'Art. 73 EuErbVO', in A. Deixler-Hübner and M. Schauer (eds), *EuErbVO - Kommentar zur EU-Erbrechtsverordnung* (Wien, 2015), para. 2.

[9] B. Reinhartz, 'Article 73', in U. Bergquist, D. Damascelli, R. Frimston, P. Lagarde, F. Odersky and B. Reinhartz, *Commentaire du Règlement européen sur les successions* (Paris, 2015), para. 2; Nordmeier, 'Art. 73 EuErbVO', para. 5.

[10] Nordmeier, 'Art. 73 EuErbVO', para. 6.

[11] A. Dutta, 'Art. 73 EuErbVO', in J. von Hein (ed), *Münchener Kommentar zum BGB*, vol. X, 6th ed. (München, 2015), para. 2; Nordmeier, 'Art. 73 EuErbVO', para. 6.

[12] Dutta, 'Art. 73 EuErbVO', para. 2; Nordmeier, 'Art. 73 EuErbVO', para. 6; see also Wautelet, 'Article 73', p. 828; Reinhartz, 'Article 73', para. 1.

[13] Dutta, 'Art. 73 EuErbVO', para. 4; Nordmeier, 'Art. 73 EuErbVO', para. 8; Fornasier, 'Art. 73 EuErbVO', para. 4; similarly Kleinschmidt, 'Art. 73 EuErbVO', para. 5 (prospects of success in the main proceedings).

[14] Nordmeier, 'Art. 73 EuErbVO', para. 8.

decision on suspension for those concerned.[15] If the issuing authority orders the suspension of the effects, this decision can be challenged pursuant to article 72.1 (2). The same applies for any decision rejecting the suspension [see art. 72 no. 3]. If the issuing authority has ordered the suspension but comes to the conclusion during the proceedings that a continuing suspension would no longer be justified, the question needs to be raised whether the authority is entitled to cancel the suspension.[16] As a rule, cancellation of the suspension will be considered only if it is established that a modification or withdrawal is to be rejected. The suspension of the effects of the ECS would in this case have to be cancelled anyway (see *infra* no. 5).

5. The consequence of the suspension is that the ECS temporarily does not produce the effects laid down in article 69.[17] It is important to note that the effects of the ECS can only be suspended as a whole; it is not possible to only suspend some of the effects laid down in article 69.[18] The decision of suspension takes effect only *ex nunc.*[19] It applies until a decision concerning the modification or withdrawal of the ECS has been taken;[20] this follows directly from the wording 'pending' (French: 'dans l'attente'; Dutch: 'in afwachting'). In the case that the issuing authority withdraws or modifies the ECS, the original Certificate irrevocably loses its effects.[21] If instead the issuing authority comes to the conclusion that the ECS shall not be subject to modification or cancellation, it must cancel the suspension of the effects of the ECS.[22]

B. *Suspension by the Judicial Authority*

6. The effects of the ECS may also be suspended by the judicial authority (see point (b) of article 73.1). As under point (a) of article 73.1, the

[15] Schmidt, 'Art. 73 EuErbVO', para. 17 *et seq.*

[16] In this sense, see Nordmeier, 'Art. 73 EuErbVO', para. 12.

[17] Schmidt, 'Art. 73 EuErbVO', para. 19; Nordmeier, 'Art. 73 EuErbVO', para. 9; Wautelet, 'Article 73', p. 829 *et seq.*; M. Volmer, 'Die EU-Erbrechtsverordnung – erste Fragen an Dogmatik und Forensik', *Rpfleger – Der Deutsche Rechtspfleger* (2013), p. 432.

[18] Rechberger and Kieweler, 'Das Europäische Nachlasszeugnis', p. 324, para. 101; Schmidt, 'Art. 73 EuErbVO', para. 19.

[19] Rechberger and Kieweler, 'Das Europäische Nachlasszeugnis', p. 324, para. 101.

[20] Schmidt, 'Art. 73 EuErbVO', para. 8; Rechberger and Kieweler, 'Das Europäische Nachlasszeugnis', p. 324, para. 101; see also Dutta, 'Art. 73 EuErbVO', para. 5.

[21] Schmidt, 'Art. 73 EuErbVO', para. 10; see also Dutta, 'Art. 73 EuErbVO', para. 5.

[22] Dutta, 'Art. 73 EuErbVO', para. 5; Schmidt, 'Art. 73 EuErbVO', para. 9; for a different view, see Kleinschmidt, 'Art. 73 EuErbVO', para. 9.

proceedings before the judicial authority must be already pending (see *supra* no. 2).[23] The decisive moment of the seising of the judicial authority will have to be determined in analogous application of article 14.[24] A suspension of the effects of the ECS can only come into consideration, however, when either the issuance of a Certificate by the issuing authority has been challenged [see art. 72 no. 2] or proceedings against a decision under article 71 that has not resulted in a withdrawal of the ECS are pending [see art. 72 no. 2]. If instead the challenge is directed against the refusal to issue an ECS or the withdrawal of a Certificate by the issuing authority (cf. article 71.2), there is no valid ECS whose effects could be suspended.[25] It is unclear whether the suspension by the judicial authority is also admissible if this authority is called to decide on the rectification of a clerical error (cf. article 71.1). The broad wording of point (b) of article 73.1 includes, in any case, all proceedings dealing with challenges of decisions made by the issuing authority under article 71.1. In this point, this provision goes further than point (a) of article 73.1, which only concerns proceedings aimed at modifying or withdrawing the Certificate pursuant to article 71.2 (see *supra* no. 2).

7. The suspension of the effects of the ECS can be requested by any person who is entitled to challenge a decision taken by the issuing authority pursuant to article 72 [for the entitlement to lodge a challenge pursuant to article 72, see art. 72 no. 4 *et seq.*].[26] A suspension *ex officio*, however, is not permitted for the judicial authority that wants to make a decision to that effect (see *supra* no. 3).[27] There is no time limit for the challenge (see *supra* no. 3).[28]

8. Like the issuing authority, the judicial authority also decides on the suspension of the effects of the ECS at its own discretion (see *supra* no. 4).[29] The decision to suspend takes effect *ex nunc* (see *supra* no. 5); the suspension lasts until the rectification, modification or withdrawal of the ECS has been decided upon.[30] If the judicial authority withdraws the Certificate (cf. article 72.2 (1)), it becomes irrevocably ineffective.

[23] Nordmeier, 'Art. 73 EuErbVO', para. 4.
[24] Schmidt, 'Art. 73 EuErbVO', para. 12.
[25] Schmidt, 'Art. 73 EuErbVO', para. 12.
[26] See also Reinhartz, 'Article 73', para. 1.
[27] Köhler, 'Art. 73 EuErbVO', para. 2; Nordmeier, 'Art. 73 EuErbVO', para. 5.
[28] Reinhartz, 'Article 73', para. 2; Nordmeier, 'Art. 73 EuErbVO', para. 5.
[29] Nordmeier, 'Art. 73 EuErbVO', para. 8; Schmidt, 'Art. 73 EuErbVO', para. 17; Dutta, 'Art. 73 EuErbVO', para. 4; Fornasier, 'Art. 73 EuErbVO', para. 4.
[30] Schmidt, 'Art. 73 EuErbVO', para. 14; Rechberger and Kieweler, 'Das Europäische Nachlasszeugnis', p. 324, para. 101.

When the judicial authority rectifies or modifies the Certificate, only the Certificate in its rectified or modified version shall have the effects provided for by article 69 from the moment the decision is taken. If the judicial authority assigns the rectification, modification or withdrawal to the issuing authority, the suspension of the effects of the ECS lasts until that decision has been implemented.[31] However, if the judicial authority comes to the conclusion that the Certificate shall continue to exist in its present form, the suspension of the effects must be cancelled (see *supra* no. 5).[32]

III. Effects on the Certified Copies

9. Once the effects of the ECS are suspended, the effects of the circulating certified copies (cf. article 70) are simultaneously suspended [see art. 70 no. 10].[33] Similarly to article 71.3, the regulation provides that the authority ordering the suspension – that is the issuing authority or the judicial authority – shall without delay (i.e. immediately) inform all persons to whom certified copies of the Certificate have been issued of any suspension of the effects of the Certificate (see article 73.2 (1)).[34] For this purpose, the list kept by the issuing authority under article 70.2 may be consulted [see art. 70 no. 9]. In addition, no further certified copies of the Certificate may be issued during the period of suspension (see article 71.2 (2)). This prohibition will also have to be applied to the extension of the period of validity of a certified copy (cf. sentence 3 of article 70.3).[35]

10. However, article 73 does not provide for the confiscation of the circulating certified copies. This has partly been met with strong criticism; the main point of criticism was that the measures laid down in

[31] But see Nordmeier, 'Art. 73 EuErbVO', para. 4, who argues that in case of remittal, the issuing authority may cancel the suspension of the effects of the ECS if its prerequisites are not fulfilled any more.

[32] Dutta, 'Art. 73 EuErbVO', para. 5.

[33] Dutta, 'Art. 69 EuErbVO', para. 2; Kleinschmidt, 'Art. 73 EuErbVO', para. 7; Rechberger and Kieweler, 'Das Europäische Nachlasszeugnis', p. 323, para. 100; Köhler, 'Art. 71 EuErbVO', para. 5; Volmer, 'Die EU-Erbrechtsverordnung', p. 432; C. Dorsel, 'Europäische Erbrechtsverordnung und Europäisches Nachlasszeugnis', *ZErb - Zeitschrift für die Steuer- und Erbrechtspraxis* (2014), p. 223. Disagreeing, see Schmidt, 'Art. 73 EuErbVO', para. 21; Nordmeier, 'Art. 73 EuErbVO', para. 9; S. Omlor, 'Gutglaubensschutz durch das Europäische Nachlasszeugnis', *GPR- European Union Private Law Review* (2014), p. 218.

[34] Wautelet, 'Article 73', p. 830 ('immédiatement après la décision de suspension').

[35] Nordmeier, 'Art. 73 EuErbVO', para. 11.

article 73.2 would not provide sufficient protection against improper use of the certified copies.[36] Some have deduced from the rationale of article 73 and the general *effet utile* principle that there is an obligation to confiscate the certified copies;[37] others consider a recourse to the rules of national law.[38] However, an obligation to confiscate the certified copies cannot be assumed either under article 73 or under article 71 [see art. 71 no. 9].[39] The regulation does not provide any legal basis in this respect.

IV. Remedies

11. The decision of the issuing authority pursuant to point (a) of article 73.1 may be challenged in accordance with article 72.1 (2) (see *supra* no. 4). However, the regulation does not provide for any redress procedures against the decision of the judicial authority pursuant to point (b) of article 73.1 [see art. 72].

[36] Schmidt, 'Art. 73 EuErbVO', para. 26; see also Nordmeier, 'Art. 73 EuErbVO', para. 15; Dutta, 'Art. 73 EuErbVO', para. 6.

[37] Schmidt, 'Art. 73 EuErbVO', para. 26.

[38] In this sense in case of German law (analogous application of section 2362.1 BGB) see Omlor, 'Gutglaubensschutz durch das Europäische Nachlasszeugnis', p. 218; see also Nordmeier, 'Art. 73 EuErbVO', para. 15. See also C. Dorsel, 'Art. 73 EuErbVO', in R. Geimer and R. Schütze (eds), *Internationaler Rechtsverkehr in Zivil- und Handelssachen* (München, 2015), para. 6, who considers that the national legislators are free to enable the issuing authority or the judicial authority to confiscate inaccurate certified copies.

[39] Wautelet, 'Article 73', p. 830; see also Kleinschmidt, 'Art. 73 EuErbVO', para. 11 (certified copies in circulation must not be confiscated).

CHAPTER VII

General and Final Provisions

Article 74

Legalisation and Other Similar Formalities

ALESSANDRA ZANOBETTI

No legalisation or other similar formality shall be required in respect of documents issued in a Member State in the context of this Regulation.

1. Article 74 ESR does not call for any particular comments to be made: it provides that documents issued in Member States who are bound by the ESR are exempt from legalisation or other similar formalities where they are to be used for the purposes contemplated by the ESR, unlike what is generally required for the purposes of the presentation of documents issued by an authority in a foreign country. The European legislator wants to remove any possible obstacles to the simple and swift operation of the regulation; the exemption from legalisation applies to any document connected with the working of the ESR, including appointments to act in court proceedings; the only condition imposed is that the document was issued in a Member State in which the ESR applies.[1]

The result is that there is no need to deal with legalisation by having the document authenticated by the consulate or diplomatic authorities, or to follow the procedure established by the Hague Convention of 5 October 1961 Abolishing the Requirement of Legalisation for Foreign Public Documents (Apostille Convention).[2]

2. The provisions of article 74 have in fact now become customary in all EU private international law regulations, and are called for because general rules on exemption from legalisation of documents in dealings between the Member States have yet to be adopted. Attempts were made in this direction in the form of the Convention Abolishing the Legalisation of Documents in the Member States of the European

[1] A. Bonomi, 'Article 74', in A. Bonomi and P. Wautelet, *Le droit européen des successions. Commentaire du Règlement n° 650/2012 du 4 juillet 2012* (Bruxelles, 2013), p. 833.

[2] Pursuant to the convention, which 108 countries, including all the EU Member States, are party to, the so-called apostille can be affixed to the document in order to simplify the task of verifying its authenticity.

Communities (Brussels, 25 May 1987), which has never come into force as it has not been ratified by all the States that were members of the European Community on the date on which it was signed, as required by its article 6.2. It is applied, however, on a provisional basis, but only in bilateral dealings between Belgium, Denmark, Estonia, France, Italy and Latvia.

Article 75

Relationship with Existing International Conventions

ALESSANDRA ZANOBETTI

1. This Regulation shall not affect the application of international conventions to which one or more Member States are party at the time of adoption of this Regulation and which concern matters covered by this Regulation. In particular, Member States which are Contracting Parties to the Hague Convention of 5 October 1961 on the Conflicts of Laws Relating to the Form of Testamentary Dispositions shall continue to apply the provisions of that Convention instead of Article 27 of this Regulation with regard to the formal validity of wills and joint wills.
2. Notwithstanding paragraph 1, this Regulation shall, as between Member States, take precedence over conventions concluded exclusively between two or more of them in so far as such conventions concern matters governed by this Regulation.
3. This Regulation shall not preclude the application of the Convention of 19 November 1934 between Denmark, Finland, Iceland, Norway and Sweden comprising private international law provisions on succession, wills and estate administration, as revised by the intergovernmental agreement between those States of 1 June 2012, by the Member States which are parties thereto, in so far as it provides for:
   (a) rules on the procedural aspects of estate administration as defined by the Convention and assistance in that regard by the authorities of the States Contracting Parties to the Convention; and
   (b) simplified and more expeditious procedures for the recognition and enforcement of decisions in matters of succession.

Summary

I. THE RELATIONSHIP BETWEEN THE ESR AND OTHER PRIVATE INTERNATIONAL LAW INSTRUMENTS REGARDING SUCCESSION: THE GENERAL RULE *page* 832
II. RELATIONSHIP WITH THE 1961 HAGUE CONVENTION ON THE FORM OF WILLS 832
III. RELATIONSHIP WITH TREATIES CONCLUDED EXCLUSIVELY BETWEEN MEMBER STATES 833
IV. RELATIONSHIP WITH THE NORDIC CONVENTION 834
V. OTHER CONVENTIONS REGARDING WILLS AND SUCCESSION AND FUTURE CONVENTIONS. 834

I. The Relationship between the ESR and Other Private International Law Instruments Regarding Succession: The General Rule

1. Article 75 governs the relationship between the ESR and other international instruments 'to which one or more Member States are party at the time of adoption of this Regulation and which concern matters covered by this Regulation'.

On similar lines to other EU private international law instruments, paragraph 1 of article 75 sets out a general rule that the regulation 'shall not affect' the application of conventions already in force at the time of its adoption. The occasions on which this provision will apply will, however, be extremely limited in number, given that other private international law instruments that deal with succession are very few in number.

II. Relationship with the 1961 Hague Convention on the Form of Wills

2. The second sentence of article 75 specifically sets out how the ESR relates to the Hague Convention of 5 October 1961 on the Conflicts of Laws Relating to the Form of Testamentary Dispositions. It establishes that the Member States who are party to the 1961 Hague Convention (which is in fact the only multilateral treaty that deals with private international law on succession to have been ratified by a significant number of countries) are to continue to apply that convention;[1] the European legislator was careful, however, to adopt a solution regarding

[1] The EU Member States who are signatories to the ESR and have ratified the 1961 Convention are Austria, Belgium, Croatia, Estonia, Finland, France, Germany, Greece, Luxembourg, Netherlands, Norway, Poland, Slovenia, Spain and Sweden. The other Member States will

form that paves the way for virtually perfect coordination between the two instruments [see art. 27 no. 1 *et seq.*].[2]

III. Relationship with Treaties Concluded Exclusively between Member States

3. On the basis of the provisions of article 75.2, the ESR instead prevails over bilateral or multilateral treaties concluded exclusively between the EU Member States bound by the ESR. This includes the Hague Convention of 2 October 1973 Concerning the International Administration of the Estates of Deceased Persons, which is in force in three States alone, all of whom participate to the ESR: Czech Republic, Portugal and Slovakia.[3]

Bilateral treaties entered into by Member States with third States will instead continue to apply. It should however be pointed out that many of the bilateral agreements that include succession within their sphere of application concern the mutual recognition and enforcement of decisions or establish forms of cooperation and judicial assistance; as the corresponding provisions of the regulation only apply *inter partes*, where bilateral agreements with third countries are concerned, here too, article 75 will apply on very few occasions.

always apply article 27 ESR. Denmark, Ireland and the UK have ratified the 1961 Convention but have not adopted the ESR.

2 A. Davì and A. Zanobetti, 'Il nuovo diritto internazionale privato delle successioni nell'Unione europea', *CdT* 5/2 (2013) p. 80; A. Davì and A. Zanobetti, *Il nuovo diritto internazionale privato europeo delle successioni* (Torino, 2014), p. 127.

3 See also A. Bonomi, 'Article 75', in A. Bonomi and P. Wautelet, *Le droit européen des successions. Commentaire du Règlement n° 650/2012 du 4 juillet 2012* (Bruxelles, 2013), p. 838. The possibility of other States signing up to the convention in the future cannot of course be ruled out; in such circumstances, Czech Republic, Portugal and Slovakia will apply the convention in dealings with other States who are party to it but are not bound by the ESR, whilst applying the regulation in dealings with the other participant Member States. This solution is basically in line with the wording of the convention where, at article 39.2, it states that it 'shall not affect the operation of other multilateral Conventions to which one or several Contracting States are or may in the future become Parties and which contain provisions relating to the same subject-matter'. Given that the Hague Convention sets out to 'facilitate the international administration of the estates of deceased persons', provisions such as those contained in the regulation, which have a much broader scope of application and are more incisive than those established by the convention, precisely because they are adopted against a backdrop that features a significant degree of integration, take precedence on the basis that they are better designed to reach the objectives of the convention itself.

IV. Relationship with the Nordic Convention

4. Article 75 contains a specific provision dealing with the convention on succession and wills adopted by the Nordic States in 1934.[4] In force between Denmark, Finland, Iceland, Norway and Sweden, this convention was revisited in 2012 precisely in order to cater for the effects on those countries that participate to the ESR, i.e. Finland and Sweden, of the ESR coming into force. These two countries will continue to apply the convention in dealings with contracting States that are not bound by the ESR, including Denmark of course. They will apply the ESR in all other cases, including in reciprocal dealings, although here the provisions of article 75.3 ESR dictate that the convention will continue to apply 'in so far as it provides for: (a) rules on the procedural aspects of estate administration as defined by the Convention and assistance in that regard by the authorities of the States Contracting Parties to the Convention; and (b) simplified and more expeditious procedures for the recognition and enforcement of decisions in matters of succession'.

V. Other Conventions Regarding Wills and Succession and Future Conventions

5. Two other multilateral instruments regarding succession have been ratified by Member States bound by the ESR: the Basel Convention of 16 May 1972 on the Establishment of a Scheme of Registration of Wills, adopted by the Council of Europe,[5] and the Washington Convention of 26 October 1973 Providing a Uniform Law on the Form of an International Will, the wording of which was drafted by Unidroit.[6] The first of these requires each contracting country to establish a national system for the registration of wills and envisages forms of cooperation between the national authorities in order to facilitate the location of wills upon the testator's death. The second places an obligation upon the contracting States to introduce

[4] Convention of 19 November 1934 among Denmark, Finland, Iceland, Norway and Sweden comprising private international law provisions on succession, wills and estate administration; on this convention see F. Korkisch, 'Der Anteil der nordischen Länder an den Fragen des internationalen Privatrechts', *RabelsZ* (1958), p. 599 *et seq.*

[5] The convention has been ratified by twelve countries, ten of which are EU Member States signatories to the ESR: Belgium, Cyprus, Estonia, France, Italy, Lithuania, Luxembourg, Netherlands, Portugal and Spain. The two other countries that have ratified the convention are Turkey and Ukraine.

[6] The contracting States are Belgium, Bosnia and Herzegovina, Canada (certain provinces only), Croatia, Cyprus, Ecuador, France, Italy, Libya, Niger, Portugal and Slovenia.

into their national law the format of an 'international will', which sits together with the various forms of wills currently in existence in each country without replacing them; dispositions by the testator in a document that meets the requirements established by this format are to be directly recognised as valid in all contracting countries.[7] Given their content, neither of these interferes with the rules established by the ESR, and it follows that they can both continue to apply.

6. Article 75 ESR only refers to conventions in force when the regulation is adopted. On the basis of the clarification provided by the Court of Justice of the European Union in opinion 1/03 of 7 February 2006,[8] which confirms its own previous case law, in adopting this regulation the European Union has acquired exclusive internal and external jurisdiction over the matters that the ESR governs.[9] It follows that any future bilateral or multilateral instrument that harmonises private international law on succession will have to be negotiated by the EU institutions directly.[10]

[7] It is obviously the case that in the other countries, a will drawn up in accordance with the requirements of the convention can be treated as valid or otherwise on the basis of the conflict-of-laws rules in each country in question, just like any other foreign will. The limited success of the convention can probably be explained by the fact that the requirements here include, in particular, that the testator signs the will or confirms his or her signature in the presence of two witnesses, a procedure based on the system in the United States; in many legal systems this is not an established legal requirement.

[8] ECJ, Opinion 1/03 [2006] ECR I-01145.

[9] The opinion, which was requested by the Council, deals with the powers of the Community to conclude the new convention amending the Lugano Convention of 16 September 1988 on jurisdiction and enforcement of judgments in civil and commercial matters. The Court stated that, whilst not expressly conferred by the treaties, the Community (as it was at the time) had exclusive competence where it is clear from 'a specific analysis of the relationship between the agreement envisaged and the Community law in force ... that the conclusion of such an agreement is capable of affecting the Community rules' (at 124).

[10] The Member States could, however, be authorised by the EU to directly take on international obligations in one of the areas covered by the regulation. See A. Zanobetti, 'Quelques réflexions sur les relations de l'Union européenne avec la Conférence de La Haye et Unidroit: ombres ou rayons de soleil?', in C. Flaesch-Mougin and L. S. Rossi (eds), *La dimension extérieure de l'espace de liberté, de sécurité et de justice après le Traité de Lisbonne* (Bruxelles, 2013), p. 269 *et seq.* A special procedure has been established by regulations no. 662/2009 and no. 664/2009 for the negotiation and conclusion of agreements between Member States and third countries (being bilateral or regional agreements that other States are excluded from signing up to) regarding matters dealt with respectively by the regulations concerning the law applicable to contractual and non-contractual obligations (regulations no. 593/2008 and no. 864/2007) and by the regulations concerning jurisdiction and the recognition and enforcement of judgments in matrimonial matters and matters of parental responsibility, and jurisdiction, applicable law, recognition and enforcement of decisions and cooperation in matters relating to maintenance obligations (regulations no. 2201/2003 and no. 4/2009).

Article 76

Relationship with Council Regulation (EC) 1346/2000

ALESSANDRA ZANOBETTI

> This Regulation shall not affect the application of Council Regulation (EC) No 1346/2000 of 29 May 2000 on insolvency proceedings.

1. Article 76 governs the interaction between the ESR and regulation no. 1346/2000 on insolvency.[1] Establishing that the Insolvency regulation remains untouched by the ESR, on a practical level it therefore affords precedence to application of the former over the latter.[2]

As from 26 June 2017, regulation no. 1346/2000 will be replaced by regulation no. 2015/848.[3] The reference in article 76 ESR will have to be treated as a reference also to the new regulation, whose article 91 (*Repeal*), after stating that 'Regulation (EC) No 1346/2000 is repealed', adds that '[r]eferences to the repealed Regulation shall be construed as references to this Regulation'.

A provision on the relationship between the ESR and the insolvency regulation did not feature in the proposal submitted by the EU Commission in 2009,[4] but was suggested in certain comments made when the proposal itself was put forward, and in the contribution submitted by the Max Planck Institute of Hamburg in particular.[5]

[1] Council Regulation (EC) no. 1346/2000 of 29 May 2000 on insolvency proceedings, JO L 160, 30 June 2000, p. 1.

[2] A. Bonomi, 'Article 76', in A. Bonomi and P. Wautelet, *Le droit européen des successions. Commentaire du Règlement n° 650/2012 du 4 juillet 2012* (Bruxelles, 2013), p. 844 *et seq.*

[3] Regulation (EU) no. 2015/848 of the European Parliament and of the Council of 20 May 2015 on insolvency proceedings (recast), JO L 141, 6 June 2015, p. 19.

[4] Proposal for a Regulation of the European Parliament and of the Council on jurisdiction, applicable law, recognition and enforcement of decisions and authentic instruments in matters of succession and the creation of a European Certificate of Succession, COM (2009)154 final.

[5] See Max Planck Institute for Comparative and International Private Law, 'Comments on the European Commission's Proposal for a Regulation of the European Parliament and of the Council on jurisdiction, applicable law, recognition and enforcement of decisions and authentic instruments in matters of succession and the creation of a European Certificate of Succession', *RabelsZ* (2010), p. 711 *et seq.*

In awarding priority to insolvency proceedings, the aim here is to ensure the protection of creditors, with this concept forming the basis on which the insolvency rules and regulations in all legal systems and in regulation no. 1346/2000 itself were designed.[6]

Article 76 only concerns insolvency proceedings that fall within the scope of application of regulation no. 1346/2000 (and, as from 26 June 2017, of regulation no. 2015/848) as defined by its articles 1 and 2, while coordination of application of the ESR with other insolvency procedures that the insolvency regulation does not apply to is dependent upon the limits on the scope of application of the respective provisions.

2. Interference between succession and insolvency proceedings can arise in a number of different ways. The situation can of course arise in which the liabilities of an estate exceed the assets; in systems in which the succession results in the deceased's assets being combined with those of the heirs, the beneficiaries can protect themselves against the risk of becoming liable for the debts of the deceased by waiving the succession or, where permitted by the succession law, accepting their inheritance hand in hand with a limitation on their liability. Pursuant to certain pieces of legislation, beneficiaries are afforded protection by means of a declaration that the estate is insolvent.[7] Insolvency proceedings launched after the opening of the succession at the behest of the creditors or the heirs themselves can, under certain laws, concern the estate as such, whilst in others they concern the deceased;[8] in circumstances such as these, the position of the heirs and the creditors needs to be established. Where, however, a person dies while proceedings that concern him or her are underway, it is necessary to establish whether the proceedings are to be stayed or are to continue, and to ascertain the role played by the heirs in those proceedings. In addition, interference between administration of the succession and the insolvency proceedings can also arise where the insolvency concerns an heir or legatee; this interference might, for example, involve the capacity of the insolvent beneficiary, or of the official receiver, to accept the inheritance.

In terms of this and other problems, article 76 does of course insist that the ESR be applied without affecting regulation no. 1346/2000; a limitation is therefore placed on the reciprocal scope of application of the two

6 Bonomi, 'Article 76', p. 845.

7 See, for example, § 130(3) of the Estonian law of succession act.

8 Article 11 of the Italian insolvency law act states that a deceased can be declared insolvent where the insolvency arose while he or she was still alive and where less than a year has passed since the date of death.

instruments, so that insolvency proceedings take priority over the procedure involving the administration of the succession.

In terms of the applicable law, the insolvency regulation adopts a jurisdictional approach on the basis of which 'the law applicable to insolvency proceedings and their effects shall be that of the Member State within the territory of which such proceedings are opened'; as parallel proceedings are possible, it is also possible that more than one law will apply. It follows that cases will arise that call for a limitation to be placed on the scope of application of the succession law in relation to the various laws governing the various insolvency proceedings. In the case of an insolvent heir, for example, the law referred to by the ESR will establish whether acceptance is necessary and the relevant procedure to be followed, whilst the task of establishing whether the insolvent person has the capacity to meet the relevant requirements or the matter of his or her representation, where necessary, by the receiver is left to the law governing the insolvency. The law established by the ESR will also dictate how any residue is to be distributed to the beneficiaries once the insolvency proceedings have concluded.

3. The Max Planck Institute had put forward a suggestion that the provisions catering for the relationship between the ESR and the insolvency regulation be supplemented with two further provisions. The first of these would have provided clarification to the effect that the 'centre of main interest' (referred to as the COMI) – which, where regulations no. 1346/2000 and no. 2015/848 are concerned, is the main ground on the basis of which competent jurisdiction and, as a result of the jurisdictional approach, the applicable law are identified – should in any event be ascertained by looking at the business carried on by the deceased and not by the heir.[9] This suggestion was rejected. First and foremost, the proposed rule was probably unnecessary: as the Max Planck Institute itself stated, this was not an issue that gave rise to any particular doubts;[10] in addition, arguably it would have been inappropriate to include rules governing the interpretation of the insolvency regulation in a different regulation which, in fact, applies to only some of the Member States that are subject to the former.[11]

The other suggestion tabled by the Max Planck Institute concerned a provision stating that where insolvency proceedings are commenced in

[9] Max Planck Institute, 'Comments', pp. 711, 714 *et seq.*

[10] Max Planck Institute, 'Comments', p. 714.

[11] Ireland and the United Kingdom, who are not bound by the ESR, have instead opted for participating to regulation no. 1346/2000 as well as to regulation no. 2015/848.

relation to a particular estate, any proceedings involving the administration of the succession that are already underway in another Member State should be stayed.[12] Given that the insolvency regulation takes precedence over the ESR, it is more than likely that this is what should in fact happen. This is, however, a decision to be made on a case-by-case basis and will not be an automatic consequence of the fact that the insolvency proceedings regarding that estate have been launched.[13] It may in fact not even prove necessary for the administration of the succession to be interrupted: the expression 'shall not affect' used by article 76 ESR leaves a room for discretion that insertion of the rule suggested by the Max Planck Institute would have closed the door on.

[12] Max Planck Institute, 'Comments', pp. 711, 714.

[13] Bonomi, 'Article 76', p. 848.

Article 77

Information Made Available to the Public

ALESSANDRA ZANOBETTI

The Member States shall, with a view to making the information available to the public within the framework of the European Judicial Network in civil and commercial matters, provide the Commission with a short summary of their national legislation and procedures relating to succession, including information on the type of authority which has competence in matters of succession and information on the type of authority competent to receive declarations of acceptance or waiver of the succession, of a legacy or of a reserved share.

The Member States shall also provide fact sheets listing all the documents and/or information usually required for the purposes of registration of immovable property located on their territory.

The Member States shall keep the information permanently updated.

Article 78

Information on Contact Details and Procedures

1. By 16 November 2014,[1] the Member States shall communicate to the Commission:
   (a) the names and contact details of the courts or authorities with competence to deal with applications for a declaration of enforceability in accordance with Article 45(1) and with appeals against decisions on such applications in accordance with Article 50(2);
   (b) the procedures to contest the decision given on appeal referred to in Article 51;
   (c) the relevant information regarding the authorities competent to issue the Certificate pursuant to Article 64; and
   (d) the redress procedures referred to in Article 72.

   The Member States shall apprise the Commission of any subsequent changes to that information.
2. The Commission shall publish the information communicated in accordance with paragraph 1 in the *Official Journal of the European Union*, with the exception of the addresses and other contact details of the courts and authorities referred to in point (a) of paragraph 1.
3. The Commission shall make all information communicated in accordance with paragraph 1 publicly available through any other appropriate means, in particular through the European Judicial Network in civil and commercial matters.

[1] See Corrigendum to Regulation (EU) no. 650/2012 of the European Parliament and of the Council of 4 July 2012 on jurisdiction, applicable law, recognition and enforcement of decisions and acceptance and enforcement of authentic instruments in matters of succession and on the creation of a European Certificate of Succession (OJ L 201, 27 July 2012). The original text read 16 January 2014, and was subsequently corrected.

Article 79

Establishment and Subsequent Amendment of the List Containing the Information Referred to in Article 3(2)

1. The Commission shall, on the basis of the notifications by the Member States, establish the list of the other authorities and legal professionals referred to in Article 3(2).
2. The Member States shall notify the Commission of any subsequent changes to the information contained in that list. The Commission shall amend the list accordingly.
3. The Commission shall publish the list and any subsequent amendments in the *Official Journal of the European Union.*
4. The Commission shall make all information notified in accordance with paragraphs 1 and 2 publicly available through any other appropriate means, in particular through the European Judicial Network in civil and commercial matters.

Summary

I. INFORMATION ABOUT NATIONAL LEGISLATION IN THE MEMBER STATES RELATING TO SUCCESSION AND THE REGISTRATION OF IMMOVABLE PROPERTY IN PUBLIC REGISTERS *page* 842

II. INFORMATION ABOUT THE AUTHORITIES COMPETENT TO DEAL WITH SUCCESSION AND CERTAIN PROCEDURES FOR APPEAL AND REDRESS 843

III. HOW THE INFORMATION IS PUBLISHED 845

I. Information about National Legislation in the Member States Relating to Succession and the Registration of Immovable Property in Public Registers

1. Articles 77, 78 and 79 ESR concern certain information that Member States are required to communicate to the EU Commission and which the Commission is required to publish as necessary.

2. The first category of information, which is dealt with in article 77, concerns the national law in the Member States on the matters covered by the ESR. Member States are required to provide the Commission with a brief description of the provisions governing succession and information about the authorities that deal with succession in each Member State, undertaking to keep this description and information up to date. In particular, article 77 mentions information about the authorities competent to receive declarations of acceptance or waiver of the succession, a legacy or a reserved share. Member States are also required to identify the documents required in order to register rights over immovable property located on their respective territories [see art. 62 no. 16].

An examination of the information sheets based on the details provided by each country and published on the Commission's website (in relation to succession as well as other matters already governed by EU regulations) reveals that this information is in somewhat summary form and at times lacks accurate references to sources. Though it offers a general idea of the law in a particular Member State, in terms of providing a basis for actual legal proceedings it falls short.[1] Whilst the information in question can of course be supplemented and made more helpful, it is probably of greater use in its current form to the public as a whole rather than those who specifically work in the area in question (judges, lawyers, notaries and administrative authorities) who at best might find that it points them in the right direction for the purposes of a more in-depth investigation into the law in force in the Member State concerned.

II. Information about the Authorities Competent to Deal with Succession and Certain Procedures for Appeal and Redress

3. The information in this second category is of a more technical nature and is indispensable in order for the ESR to function. As established by article 78, it was to be provided by the Member States by the deadline of 14 November 2014 and is accessible on the EU website.[2]

The information first of all comprises the names and contact details of the courts or authorities with competence to deal with applications for a declaration of enforceability in accordance with article 45.1 ESR [see arts. 44–45 nos. 2 and 3] and with appeals against decisions on such

[1] This information can be found on the EU website at the following address: https://e-justice.europa.eu/content_succession-166-en.do (retrieved 10 July 2016).

[2] https://e-justice.europa.eu/content_succession-166-en.do (retrieved on 10 July 2016)

applications in accordance with article 50.2 [see art. 50]; the Member States are also required to provide information about the procedure to follow in order to contest the decision given on appeal referred to in article 51, and must provide details of the authorities competent to issue the European Certificate of Succession pursuant to article 64 [see art. 64 no. 18 *et seq.*]. Finally, they are required to provide information about the redress procedures concerning the issue of that certificate as referred to in article 72 [see art. 72].

Despite the fact that, as previously noted, this information is essential for the purposes of the application of the ESR, the decision was taken not to insert it into the wording of the regulation itself. The reasons for this were twofold: (i) to avoid weighing the regulation down with lengthy lists; (ii) to avoid the need for updates and the addition of further information whenever an amendment is made to the national law in a Member State or a new Member State decides to sign up to the ESR.[3] The fact that this information has been kept out of the ESR itself does, however, prompt the need for an effective method of publishing it. This task was passed to the Commission, which has to publish the information that the Member States have provided it with by 16 November 2014 in the *Official Journal of the European Union*, and also has to circulate it using any means appropriate, in particular via the European Judicial Network in civil and commercial matters.

4. The same means of publication envisaged by article 78 are also established by article 79 in relation to the information regarding the list of authorities and legal professionals referred to in article 3.2 [see art. 3 no. 18] that the States are required to notify to the Commission, undertaking in addition to provide notification of any changes or additions to the list. This information is available via the EU website (see footnote 3).

[3] The system adopted here by the ESR is an evolved version of that followed by the European Union's (at the time, European Community) first private international law instruments. The Brussels Convention of 1968 on jurisdiction and enforcement of judgments in civil and commercial matters, for example, in fact contained all the necessary information in the text itself; whilst doubtless a much simpler solution when compared to that adopted by the ESR, it did, however, suffer from a serious defect: any change to the information provided prompted the need to amend the wording of the convention, and whenever another country signed up to the convention, additional information had to be added. Regulation no. 44/2001 instead adopted a system involving annexes; these could be amended by the Member States simply notifying the Commission, which then dealt with the changes or additions required.

III. How the Information Is Published

5. The official manner of publication of the information referred to in articles 78 and 79 is publication in the *Official Journal of the European Union*; pursuant to regulation no. 216/2013, with effect from 1 July 2013, the electronic edition of the *Official Journal* is the only edition that is authentic and produces legal effects.[4] The *Official Journal* can be accessed on eur-lex.europa.eu.

6. The other manner of publication referred to in articles 78 and 79 ESR is the European Judicial Network in civil and commercial matters. The Network was established in 2001 by a decision of the Council[5] and is made up of contact points nominated by each Member State (with the exception of Denmark, which is not a member of the Network) as well as other bodies and professionals.[6] Someone requiring information about the functioning of the ESR can refer to one of the contact points set up in the relevant Member State. Each contact point accepts responsibility for the information that it provides. It is also possible to access the information via the EU website (see footnote 3).

7. Turning now to the information about national law in the Member States regarding succession – and this includes the information regarding the authorities that are competent to receive declarations of acceptance and waiver or a succession or a legacy as well as the list of documents required in order to register immovable property in public registers as mentioned in article 77 – the manner of publication here is more informal and basically

[4] Council Regulation (EU) no. 216/2013 of 7 March 2013 on the electronic publication of the *Official Journal of the European Union*, OJ L 69, 13 March 2013, p. 1.

[5] Council Decision of 28 May 2001 establishing a European Judicial Network in civil and commercial matters, OJ L 174, 27 June 2001, p. 25. The decision was amended by Decision no. 568/2009/EC of the European Parliament and of the Council of 18 June 2009, OJ L 168, 30 June 2009, p. 35.

[6] There are 508 members of the Network, forming five different categories: the 103 contact points designated by Member States; bodies and central authorities specified in EU law, in international instruments whereby Member States are party, or in domestic law relating to judicial cooperation in civil and commercial matters; liaison magistrates with responsibilities for cooperation in civil and commercial matters; other judicial or administrative authorities responsible for judicial cooperation in civil and commercial matters whose membership is deemed to be useful by the pertinent Member State; professional associations representing legal practitioners directly involved in the application of EU law and international instruments in civil and commercial matters at a national level in the Member States.

involves inclusion on the Commission's website (see footnote 3). Recourse can, however, also be had to the European Judicial Network in civil and commercial matters and, in particular, to the contact points in the Member States, who can also be used as a source of this information.

Article 80

Establishment and Subsequent Amendment of the Attestations and Forms Referred to in Articles 46, 59, 60, 61, 65 and 67

ALESSANDRA ZANOBETTI

The Commission shall adopt implementing acts establishing and subsequently amending the attestations and forms referred to in Articles 46, 59, 60, 61, 65 and 67. Those implementing acts shall be adopted in accordance with the advisory procedure referred to in Article 81(2).

Article 81

Committee Procedure

1. The Commission shall be assisted by a committee. That committee shall be a committee within the meaning of Regulation (EU) No 182/2011.
2. Where reference is made to this paragraph, Article 4 of Regulation (EU) No 182/2011 shall apply.

Article 82

Review

By 18 August 2025 the Commission shall submit to the European Parliament, the Council and the European Economic and Social Committee a report on the application of this Regulation, including an evaluation of any practical problems encountered in relation to parallel out-of-court settlements of succession cases in different Member States or an out-of-court settlement in one Member State effected in parallel with a settlement before a court in another Member State. The report shall be accompanied, where appropriate, by proposals for amendments.

Summary

I. THE ADOPTION OF FORMS FOR THE IMPLEMENTATION OF THE ESR: IMPLEMENTING REGULATION 1329/2014 *page* 849

II. REPORT ON THE APPLICATION OF THE ESR 851

I. The Adoption of Forms for the Implementation of the ESR: Implementing Regulation no. 1329/2014

1. Articles 80, 81 and 82 allocate work to the Commission of an executive nature in order to facilitate the functioning of the ESR and monitor its application.

2. The first task involves the adoption of certain forms of certification: in terms of what is now established practice in all other EU regulations regarding private international law, the ESR follows suit and envisages standard forms being adopted for the purposes of issuing the attestations required in order for the ESR to operate as intended or in order to facilitate the completion of certain requirements. Article 80 ESR tasks the Commission with preparing these forms and dealing with any amendments to them that are required. The fact that this task definitely falls within the category of technical work for the purposes of implementation does not detract from its delicate nature, given that the forms that are drawn up must reflect the provisions of the ESR to the letter. As established by article 81 and in line with what is referred to as the comitology procedure, the Commission is assisted in its work here by a committee composed of representatives of the Member States (the so-called 'Succession Committee'), which acts in accordance with the advisory procedure set out in regulation no. 182/2011.[1]

On 9 December 2014, the Commission therefore adopted implementing regulation 1329/2014, to which the forms are annexed.[2]

3. The forms adopted by the Commission serve as a template for the following documents: the attestation issued by a court or competent authority of the Member State of origin that must accompany the application for enforceability of a decision in accordance with article 46 ESR (annex 1 as form I), or for enforceability of an authentic act in accordance with article 60 ESR (annex 2 as form II), or of a court settlement in accordance with article 61 ESR (annex 3 as form III); the attestation, the form of which is included in the same form set out for the enforceability of an authentic act (annex 2 as form II), which describes 'the evidentiary effects' produced by an authentic instrument in the Member State of origin and which anyone wishing to use that document in another Member State may, pursuant to article 59 ESR, ask to be delivered by the authority in the Member State of origin; the form to be used to submit an application for the issue of a European Certificate of Succession in accordance with article 65 ESR (annex 4 as form IV); the form to be used by the competent authority for the purposes of issuing the European Certificate of Succession pursuant to article 67 (annex 5 as form V).

These forms have of course been adopted in all of the EU languages, and this is an important advantage, because translation of documents to

[1] Regulation (EU) no. 182/2011 of the European Parliament and of the Council of 16 February 2011 laying down the rules and general principles concerning mechanisms for control by Member States of the Commission's exercise of implementing powers, JO L55, 28 February 2011, p. 13. According to article 4 of this regulation, when the advisory procedure applies the committee 'shall deliver its opinion, if necessary by taking a vote. If the committee takes a vote, the opinion shall be delivered by a simple majority of its component members', and the Commission shall adopt the implementing act 'taking the utmost account of the conclusions drawn from the discussions within the committee and of the opinion delivered'.

[2] Commission implementing Regulation (EU) no. 1329/2014 of 9 December 2014 establishing the Forms referred to in Regulation (EU) no. 650/2012 of the European Parliament and of the Council on jurisdiction, applicable law, recognition and enforcement of decisions and acceptance and enforcement of authentic instruments in matters of succession and on the creation of a European Certificate of Succession, JO L359, 16 December 2014, p. 30.

be produced in other Member States is at the same time simplified and made more uniform.

II. Report on the Application of the ESR

4. The Commission is required to present a report on the implementation of the ESR in the various Member States by 18 August 2025, i.e. ten years after it came into force. This report will be addressed to the European Parliament, the Council and the Economic and Social Committee. If the Commission sees fit, it is to include proposed amendments to provisions of the ESR that have given rise to problems or which might be improved upon, with a view to the ESR being amended to the extent necessary in light of how it has been found to operate in practice.

5. In this report, article 82 ESR specifically requires the Commission to address any problems that have arisen in relation to 'parallel out-of-court settlements of succession cases in different Member States' or in relation to 'an out-of-court settlement in one Member State effected in parallel with a settlement before a court in another Member State'. Cases such as these clearly do not fall within the scope of the *lis pendens* rule set out in article 17 ESR. Recital 36 ESR addresses the possible interference between out-of-court settlements and/or court settlements in different Member States, suggesting that where 'an amicable out-of-court settlement and court proceedings' or 'two amicable out-of-court settlements' regarding the same succession exist in parallel in different Member States, 'it should be for the parties involved . . . to agree among themselves how to proceed'. This does not prevent a party from asking the relevant competent authority to rule on the succession where agreement cannot be reached [see art. 18].

Article 83

Transitional Provisions

PIETRO FRANZINA

1. This Regulation shall apply to the succession of persons who die on or after 17 August 2015.
2. Where the deceased had chosen the law applicable to his succession prior to 17 August 2015, that choice shall be valid if it meets the conditions laid down in Chapter III or if it is valid in application of the rules of private international law which were in force, at the time the choice was made, in the State in which the deceased had his habitual residence or in any of the States whose nationality he possessed.
3. A disposition of property upon death made prior to 17 August 2015 shall be admissible and valid in substantive terms and as regards form if it meets the conditions laid down in Chapter III or if it is admissible and valid in substantive terms and as regards form in application of the rules of private international law which were in force, at the time the disposition was made, in the State in which the deceased had his habitual residence or in any of the States whose nationality he possessed or in the Member State of the authority dealing with the succession.
4. If a disposition of property upon death was made prior to 17 August 2015 in accordance with the law which the deceased could have chosen in accordance with this Regulation, that law shall be deemed to have been chosen as the law applicable to the succession.

Summary

I. THE TEMPORAL SCOPE OF APPLICATION OF THE ESR *page* 853

II. THE PRESERVATION OF PROFESSIONES JURIS MADE BEFORE 17 AUGUST 2015 856

III. THE PRESERVATION OF DISPOSITIONS OF PROPERTY MADE BEFORE 17 AUGUST 2015 859

IV. THE PRESUMPTIVE CHOICE OF THE LEX PATRIAE AS THE LAW GOVERNING THE SUCCESSION 861

I. The Temporal Scope of Application of the ESR

1. Article 83.1 is concerned with the temporal scope of application of the ESR. It determines whether a situation falling within the material scope of the regulation is in fact governed by its rules on account of the timing of the situation, or a particular element thereof. The decisive moment, for this purpose, is the death of the person whose succession is at issue; for the ESR to apply, the *de cujus* must have died 'on or after 17 August 2015'.[1]

This date is also the date of application of the ESR (article 84.2). While the two dates perform different functions, their coincidence is deliberate. Consistent with a general principle of EU law, the ESR is not meant to have retroactive effect and, accordingly, only applies to situations that occur after its provisions have become enforceable in their entirety.[2]

2. The successions of persons who died prior to 17 August 2015 remain unaffected by the ESR. They continue to be governed by the domestic rules of private international law of the forum (as supplemented by the relevant international conventions, if any), even if the issue is raised after that date.

3. Conversely, only the ESR applies to the succession of persons who died on or after 17 August 2015. Domestic rules, as will be seen,[3] may still have a role to play in respect of a succession arising after that date, but it is for the ESR to decide whether and how this should happen.

If the succession comes within the temporal scope of application of the ESR, the effects of its rules extend to acts and facts that have occurred prior to that date. Thus, for instance, the admissibility of an agreement as to succession made before 17 August 2015 must be assessed, in principle, against the law specified in article 25 (without prejudice to the effects attached to national rules of private international under article 83).[4]

[1] Pursuant to article 4.2 of regulation (EEC, Euratom) no. 1182/71 of the Council of 3 June 1971 determining the rules applicable to periods, dates and time limits (OJ 1971 L 124, 8 June 1971, p. 1), when the application of acts of secondary legislation is fixed at a given date, application 'shall occur at the beginning of the first hour of the day falling on that date'. To ensure uniformity in the application of the ESR, the relevant time zone, it is submitted, shall be the zone of the place where the *de cujus* has died.

[2] On non-retroactivity in EU law, see generally J. Raitio, 'The Principle of Legal Certainty as a General Principle of EU Law', in U. Bernitz, J. Nergelius and C. Cardner (eds), *General Principles of EC Law in a Process of Development* (Alphen aan den Rijn, 2008), p. 47 *et seq.*

[3] Paragraph 8 *et seq.*

[4] E. Fongaro, 'L'anticipation successorale à l'épreuve du "règlement successions"', *JDI* (2014), pp. 477–540 at 493 *et seq.*

4. This extension does not seem to be at odds with the principle of non-retroactivity. As a matter of fact, the ESR is exclusively concerned with the transfer of assets, rights and obligations by reason of death occurring on or after 17 August 2015. The only earlier occurrences that the ESR may come to regulate are acts and facts that the ESR addresses only insofar as relevant to a later transfer.

Far from jeopardizing the legitimate expectations of the interested persons, the extension expands, in a significant number of cases, the opportunities available to those wishing to plan their succession in advance. Relying on article 83.1, a person may have in fact decided to organise his or her succession in accordance with the law designated by the ESR, without waiting for the ESR to become applicable.[5] In particular, the *de cujus* may have made a *professio juris* in accordance with article 22, no matter whether a similar choice is allowed under the rules of private international law in force at the time of the choice.[6] Clearly, planning based on the ESR, made prior to 17 August 2015, run the risk of being frustrated by the death of the *de cujus* occurring before that date. Yet, a well-advised testator should normally be able to manage this variable since the implications of the possible scenarios should already be known at the moment of planning, based on article 83.

5. Referring to the death of the deceased for the purpose of determining the applicability *ratione temporis* of the ESR provides various advantages. To begin with, the death of the *de cujus* is a pure fact and may accordingly be established, in principle, without any legal assessment being required.[7] Indeed, the death of a person results in (and normally coincides with) the opening of that person's succession. The latter notion,

[5] P. de Vareilles-Sommières, 'Pour une meilleure consolidation européenne des dispositions de planification successorale prises avant le 17 août 2015 relativement à une succession internationale', *Dalloz* (2012), pp. 2321–2322, at 2321 *et seq*.

[6] J. Heinig, 'Rechtswahlen in Verfügungen von Todes wegen nach der EU-Erbrechts-Verordnung', *Rheinische Notar-Zeitschrift* (2014), pp. 197–229, at 213 *et seq*. In reality, as regards choice of law, the ESR is less liberal than the rules of private international law of certain (Member) States. For example, pursuant to article 79 of the Belgian code of private international law, the interested person may choose, in addition to the *lex patriae*, the law of the State of his or her habitual residence at the time of the choice. The expanded applicability of the ESR does not preclude the *de cujus* from taking advantage of such broader options, as long as a choice of law has been made in application of the national rules in question before 17 August 2015 and satisfies the requirements of article 83.2. See further, on the whole topic, C. Schoppe, 'Die Übergangsbestimmungen zur Rechtswahl im internationalen Erbrecht: Anwendungsprobleme und Gestaltungspotential', *IPRax* (2014), pp. 27–33, at 29 *et seq*.

[7] See, however, paragraph 6 for further developments.

however, a legal one, is not relevant to article 83.1. Incidentally, as the time of the opening of the succession is among the issues governed by the *lex successionis*, as stated in article 23.2(a), it would be problematic, and possibly a source of conflicting solutions, to assess the applicability of the ESR by reference to the law that the ESR would designate, if it were to apply.

Secondly, the date on which a person has passed away is generally recorded in a public document with formal evidentiary value: the certificate of death. Unless the accuracy or truthfulness of the certificate are contested, the certificate will normally be considered as *prima facie* evidence of the facts stated therein, including the moment of death. This holds true, in principle, for foreign vital records, provided that the requirements for their production in the Member State where the applicability of the ESR is at issue have been met.

6. Doubts may exist as to whether a person is still living at a given date. These cases involve the application of rules on disappearance, absence and presumed death. The ESR, pursuant to article 1.2(c), is not concerned with these institutions. It will thus be for the domestic rules of private international law of the forum to decide which law should determine the basis and effects of a similar declaration, and the conditions upon which a foreign declaration is entitled to recognition. In practice, it may happen that a declaration of disappearance, absence and presumed death is issued (or recognised) in the Member State where the applicability of the ESR is being discussed: if it creates a legal presumption that the person is dead, the day on which the presumption becomes effective will be the day on which the *de cujus* has died for the purposes of article 83.1 of the ESR.

This way of proceeding, based on a reference to domestic provisions of private international law, may give rise to difficulties. The authorities of two or more Member States, due to the diversity of their respective rules on conflicts of laws in this area, might come to different conclusions regarding the applicability of the ESR to the same succession. In this case, at least as a last resort, the authorities concerned should strive to overcome the divergence through dialogue, in conformity with the duty of sincere cooperation enshrined in article 4.3 of the TEU.

7. The obvious disadvantage of tying the application of the ESR to the death of the *de cujus* is the inherent unpredictability of the moment in which this event will occur. The benefits mentioned above may only be captured once the person concerned has passed away, but disappear if the succession is looked at from an *ex ante* perspective. As a matter of fact, if the *de cujus* survives 17 August 2015, the validity and enforceability of the acts of planning made prior to that date may have to be assessed against a law other than the law originally envisaged for this purpose, based on the contemplated applicability of domestic provisions of private international law.

As a means to mitigate uncertainty, the ESR lays down in article 83, paragraphs 2–4, a body of transitional provisions, the overall purpose of which is to preserve the effectiveness of acts made prior to the above date, once the succession comes to be governed by the ESR.[8] These provisions will be analysed in the following paragraphs.

II. The Preservation of *professiones juris* Made before 17 August 2015

8. Article 83.2 applies where the succession has been the object of a choice of law made prior to 17 August 2015, no matter whether it was made before or after 16 August 2012, i.e. the day on which the ESR entered into force (article 84.1).[9] As a rule, if the deceased died on or after 17 August 2015, the validity of the choice must be assessed against the ESR.[10] However, article 83.2 provides that, if the choice does not conform to the provisions in the ESR, it will nevertheless be upheld 'if it is valid in application of the rules of private international law which were in force, at the time the choice was made, in the State in which the deceased had his habitual residence or in any of the States whose nationality he possessed'.[11]

In practice, the validity of a *professio juris* may be asserted, alternatively, by reference to 'old' or 'new' standards. Conversely, the choice will

[8] The applicability of article 83 itself is restricted to the succession of persons who died on or after 17 August 2015; see H. Rosoux, 'Arrêt sur le régime transitoire du Règlement successions', *Revue de planification patrimoniale belge et international* (2014), pp. 157–166, at 158.

[9] Fongaro, 'L'anticipation successorale', p. 505.

[10] This is stated in article 83.2 in the form of a reference to chapter III of the ESR. In this part, article 83.2 is a mere restatement of what already prescribes article 83.1; thus, it merely serves a 'pedagogical' purpose, as opposed to the normative function performed by the remainder of the provision.

[11] By referring to the rules of private international law 'in force' in the specified States, the provision encompasses both domestic provisions on choice of law and provisions, if any, laid down in international conventions.

only be invalid if it fails to meet the requirements imposed both by the ESR and by all of the laws indicated above.

9. For the purposes of article 83.2, validity should be understood in broad terms as encompassing admissibility, formal validity, effectiveness and enforceability. If the rules of private international law of the relevant State make the enforceability of the choice contingent on a particular requirement, that requirement will also be relevant for the purposes of article 83.2. Thus, if a *de cujus* of Italian nationality has chosen the law of his or her residence, relying on article 46.2 of the Italian private international law act, the choice will be preserved under the ESR only if it is established that the deceased was still residing in that country at the moment of death, as required by the latter provision.

10. The same reasoning should be followed where the relevant national rules of private international law reduce the scope or the effectiveness of the *professio juris*. One such example is article 79 of the Belgian code of private international law. Under this rule, the enforceability of a choice of law by the deceased must be excluded to the extent to which the choice results in a reserved heir being deprived of the portion of the estate to which the latter would be entitled according to the law that would normally apply to the succession. If similar limitations affect the choice under the rules of private international law of the pertinent State, the choice will be preserved, under article 83.2 of the ESR, subject to the same limitations.[12] By the same token, if a German citizen, or a person habitually residing in Germany, has chosen the *lex rei sitae* to govern his or her succession in reliance on article 25.2 of the introductory law to the German civil code, the choice will only be preserved insofar as it relates to immoveable property located in Germany, consonant with the requirement in the latter provision.

In light of the goal pursued by article 83.2 of the ESR, i.e. safeguarding the expectations of the *de cujus* against the supervening application of the ESR, there is no reason why the ESR should grant an 'old' choice, made on the assumption that a given set of national rules would apply, broader effects than those entailed by such national rules.[13] As a matter of fact, the

[12] The contrary opinion is advocated, albeit in dubitative terms, by P. Wautelet, 'Article 83', in A. Bonomi and P. Wautelet, *Le droit européen des successions. Commentaire du Règlement n° 650/2012 du 4 juillet 2012* (Bruxelles, 2013), pp. 855–868 at 864.

[13] The concern for the authentic application of national conflict-of-law rules, however, should not go as far as allowing those rules to operate without restrictions whenever they infringe a provision of primary EU law (such as the prohibition of discrimination

ESR does nothing more than allow early choices of law to project their effects beyond the date of application of the uniform regime.

This implies that, if the conditions set out in article 83.2 are met, then the succession will be submitted to the law chosen by the deceased in precisely the same way as the private international law rules of the relevant State would require. Admittedly, this approach may prove cumbersome and lead to practical difficulties. Nonetheless, it should serve the interests of legal certainty better than any other approach.

11. Article 83.2 refers to the rules of private international law of several States, namely the State where the deceased was habitually resident or of any of the States of his or her nationality. Contrary to article 83.3, no relevance is given, here, to the private international law of the Member State 'of the authority dealing with the succession'. Given the similarity of the two provisions, the reasons for this difference are unclear.

If two or more of the said laws consider the choice to be valid, there is no need to determine which of them applies to the case at hand. Actually, the only issue at stake is whether the *professio* is valid or not, and once a law, among those specified previously, provides a positive answer to this question, there is no room for further inquiry.

If the choice is valid under two or more of those laws, but the scope of its effects varies from one law to another, reference should be made, under a teleological interpretation of article 83.2, to the most liberal of them, i.e. the law that ensures the widest respect for the intentions of the deceased.

12. It has been suggested that article 83.2, though referring to the States indicated previously without further qualifications, should be understood as referring only to the *Member* State of habitual residence and the *Member* State(s) of nationality of that person.[14] The purpose of article 83.2, so the argument goes, is to govern the transition from the rules of private international law in force in the Member States to the uniform regime set forth in the ESR; the conflict-of-law rules of third countries and their contemplated effects should thus lie outside its scope.

based on nationality) or are otherwise at odds with a fundamental policy of the EU legal order.

[14] Wautelet, 'Article 83', p. 863. The practical relevance of the issue, in reality, remains limited, as the possibility of a choice of law in matters of succession is known but to few third countries (see, e.g., article 49.1 of the Korean conflict of laws act of 2001).

This reading is not persuasive.[15] In the first place, the wording of article 83, far from leaving the issue open, seems to support the opposite interpretation. Article 83.3, the rationale of which resembles closely that of article 83.2, explicitly distinguishes 'the *State* in which the deceased had his habitual residence' and 'the *States* whose nationality he possessed' from 'the *Member State* of the authority dealing with the succession'.[16] This language denotes that the ESR did intend to address, in its transitional provisions, the fate of acts made in accordance with the rules of private international law of both Member and non-Member States.

Secondly, there is nothing in the ESR indicating that the task entrusted to article 83.2 consists solely in ensuring a smooth transition from 'old' to 'new' rules of private international law. The purpose of this rule, more generally, is to avert the risk that the introduction of the ESR may result in the expectations of the *de cujus* being irretrievably frustrated. One may be of the opinion that the provision is overly generous, but this does not allow the interpreter to hamper the realisation of this legislative policy.

III. The Preservation of Dispositions of Property Made before 17 August 2015

13. Article 83.3 purports to safeguard the effects of dispositions of property upon death – i.e. 'a will, a joint will or an agreement as to succession', according to the definition in article 3.1(d) – made prior to 17 August 2015. These must be regarded as admissible and valid, in substantive terms and as regards form, if they are admissible and valid either under the law(s) identified to this effect by the ESR or under the law designated by 'the rules of private international law which were in force, at the time the disposition was made, in the State in which the deceased had his habitual residence or in any of the States whose nationality he possessed or in the Member State of the authority dealing with the succession'.[17]

[15] See, along the same lines, Heinig, 'Rechtswahlen in Verfügungen von Todes wegen nach der EU-Erbrechts-Verordnung', p. 214.

[16] Emphasis added.

[17] For the reasons stated in paragraph 12, the reference in article 83.3 to the of habitual residence and the State(s) of nationality of the deceased should be understood as a reference to any such State(s), regardless of whether these are Member States of the EU, or not.

Similar to article 83.2, this provision aims to avert the danger that the intentions of the deceased could be neglected or prejudiced as a consequence of the supervening application of the ESR. To this end, article 83.3 provides for an alternative reference to the law designated by the ESR or the law(s) designated by the rules of private international law of the relevant State. The validity and admissibility of the dispositions of the deceased may be asserted either under the former law(s) or under the latter.

Contrary to article 83.2, which is concerned with the will expressed by the deceased as regards the law applicable to his or her succession, article 83.3 is meant to preserve the decisions made by the deceased as regards the substantive organisation of his or her estate. On a different note, while a *professio juris* made prior to 17 August 2015 may have a bearing, by virtue of article 83.2, on the succession as a whole, the preserving effects of article 83.3 affect a limited set of issues, i.e. the admissibility and the validity of the deceased's dispositions of property. In cases falling within the scope of the latter provision, it will thus remain necessary to determine, under the relevant rules of the ESR (including article 83, paragraphs 2 and 3, where appropriate), the law governing the succession as a whole.

14. As observed earlier, the list of possibly relevant States in article 83.3 includes the law of the Member State 'of the authority dealing with the succession'.[18] The authority in question may be either a 'court', within the meaning of article 3.2, or an official charged with functions relating to a succession, such as a notary.

15. Article 83.3 speaks, generally, of the 'dispositions of property' of the deceased. These, however, may in fact consist of several acts. If the dispositions of property of the deceased actually consist of two or more acts, nothing in article 83.3 seems to exclude the possibility of relying on two or more different laws, among those specified in the provision, for the purpose of preserving the effects of each of those acts.

16. Persons wishing to plan their succession in advance often bring together in one instrument a *professio juris* and a set of (substantive) dispositions of property upon death. An instrument of this kind, made prior to 17 August 2015, will trigger the application of both paragraphs 2 and 3 of article 83. The former will tell whether the choice of law may be deemed to be valid, while the latter will be used to assess the admissibility and the validity of the dispositions of property. As the two provisions

[18] The same expression is used in recitals 23, 25, 27 and 32 of the ESR.

address issues that are independent from each other, they may entail a reference to different laws.

IV. The Presumptive Choice of the *lex patriae* as the Law Governing the Succession

17. Under article 83.4, if a disposition of property upon death has been made prior to 17 August 2015 in accordance with the law that the deceased could have chosen in accordance with the ESR, 'that law shall be deemed to have been chosen as the law applicable to the succession'.

The reason for including this safeguard in the ESR may be explained as follows. Under the rules of private international law of several Member States – Austria, Germany, Greece, Italy, Romania, Spain and Sweden, among others – the nationality of the deceased has traditionally represented the main connecting factor in matters of successions. With the ESR now referring to the last habitual residence of the *de cujus* for the same purposes, a significant number of successions run the risk of being submitted to a law other than the law that the deceased and those interested in his or her succession would originally expect to apply.

Article 83.4 creates a presumption whereby the deceased is deemed to have chosen his or her *lex patriae* as the law governing the succession whenever it is established that his or her dispositions of property upon death have been made in conformity with that law. The presumption draws, in fact, on article 22.1, which allows the *de cujus* to 'choose as the law to govern his succession as a whole the law of the State whose nationality he possesses at the time of making the choice', and on article 25, which equally gives relevance to nationality for the purpose of determining the law applicable to an agreement as to succession [see arts. 22 and 25].

18. If the deceased possessed the nationality of two or more States at the time when his or her dispositions of property have been made, the presumption under article 83.4 may result, in principle, in the designation of the law of any of those States, in accordance with the first subparagraph of article 22.1 [see art. 22 no. 15]. Since the ESR does not allow for a choice of more than one law, the deceased will be presumed to have chosen, among the various *leges patriae*, the law that best serves the purpose of safeguarding the enforceability of his or her intentions.

19. For article 83.4 to apply, it must be established that the dispositions of property of the deceased meet the requirements of his or her *lex patriae*. If this condition is not met in the circumstances, or is met only partially – e.g. in respect of some clauses of the testament but not in respect of others – there is, in principle, no room for presuming a choice of law under the provision in question.

The latter assertion, it is submitted, may be departed from in two cases. On the one hand, a relatively flexible reading should be adopted whenever the application of the law presumptively chosen by the deceased would allow his or her dispositions of property to be preserved almost in their entirety, with only severable, accessory clauses being declared invalid under the *lex patriae*. An overly strict reading would in fact end up frustrating the expectations of the deceased, and ultimately contradict the purpose of article 83.4.

On the other hand, article 83.4 may, where appropriate, apply in combination with article 83.3. Based on a global assessment of the opportunities available for preserving the intentions of the deceased, the succession may be submitted to the law of the State of nationality of the *de cujus* pursuant to article 83.4. Simultaneously, a different law could be relied upon to assert the admissibility and the validity of one or more of his or her dispositions of property upon death, on the ground of article 83.3.

20. The presumption in article 83.4 is not meant to assist the competent authority in construing the existence and terms of an actual choice by the deceased. Actually, if it appears that the *de cujus* has actually made a choice of law, the provision should be deemed to be inapplicable altogether.[19] The principle of party autonomy, one of the key tenets of the ESR, implies that real choices, no matter whether they are based on article 22 or on the rules of private international law of one of the States referred to in article 83.2, should take precedence over presumed choices.

Rather, the purpose of article 83.4 is to create a legal fiction, i.e. to give the facts of the case the effects that would result from a choice of law, if such a choice had been made.[20] In practice, the presumption in article 83.4 is merely a device, operating at private international law level, whereby the ESR purports to preserve the substantive effects that the

[19] Heinig, 'Rechtswahlen in Verfügungen von Todes wegen nach der EU-Erbrechts-Verordnung', p. 205.

[20] Rosoux, 'Arrêt sur le régime transitoire', p. 163.

deceased had plausibly intended to bring about when planning his or her succession.

In applying article 83.4, there is accordingly no need to seek the indicia of an ambiguous or incomplete choice of law by the *de cujus*. The only relevant question is whether the dispositions of property made by the latter before 17 August 2015 are in conformity with the law of the State of his or her nationality, or not. In other words, the question is whether those dispositions would benefit, in terms of validity, effectiveness, and enforceability, if the *lex patriae* governed the succession.

21. Since the presumption in article 83.4 is fictional in nature, nothing excludes that a choice of law may be presumed under this provision even if the relevant dispositions of property predate the adoption of the ESR, i.e. if they were made at a time when an actual choice of law pursuant to the regulation was simply inconceivable.

22. On a different note, due the fictional character of the rule in article 83.4, the question as to whether the presumption is rebuttable, or not, appears to be misplaced.[21] The presumption in question is not meant to unveil the actual intentions of the *de cujus* as regards the law applicable to his or her succession. Rather, it is intended to restore the conditions for the substantive planning of the latter to be enforced. Thus, for the purposes of this provision, one cannot speak of a hypothetical state of mind whose reality might need to be confirmed through extra evidence, or could be denied through a rebuttal.

[21] The issue is raised, *inter alia*, by S. Godechot-Patris, 'Le nouveau droit international privé des successions entre satisfactions et craintes . . .', *Dalloz* (2012), pp. 2462–2469, at 2465.

Article 84

Entry into Force

PIETRO FRANZINA

This Regulation shall enter into force on the twentieth day following that of its publication in the *Official Journal of the European Union*.
It shall apply from 17 August 2015, except for Articles 77 and 78, which shall apply from 16 November 2014, and Articles 79, 80 and 81, which shall apply from 5 July 2012.

Summary

I. THE DATE OF ENTRY INTO FORCE OF THE ESR AND THE DATE OF APPLICATION OF ITS RULES *page* 864
II. PROVISIONS OF THE ESR THAT HAVE BECOME EFFECTIVE PRIOR TO THE DATE OF APPLICATION OF THE REGULATION IN ITS ENTIRETY 865

I. The Date of Entry into Force of the ESR and the Date of Application of Its Rules

1. Like other legislative measures in the field of judicial cooperation, the ESR separates the date for its entry into force from the date of application of its rules. The first of these dates is the date on which the regulation acquired binding force as a component of the EU legal order. Pursuant to the first paragraph of article 84, this occurred on the twentieth day following the day of the publication of the ESR in the *Official Journal*, i.e. on 16 August 2012.

The second date is the day beginning on which the authorities of the Member States bound by the ESR have been required to enforce the provisions therein (or, depending on the circumstances, the date on which specific measures of implementation were to be adopted). The ESR has been set to apply in its entirety from 17 August 2015, but particular provisions, as will be seen, have become effective at earlier dates.

2. Generally speaking, the main reason to delay the date of application of an act in relation to its entry into force is to enable the Member States or the EU institutions to perform, on the basis of that act, the prior obligations which are necessary to apply the act fully to all persons concerned.[1] This is certainly true for the ESR in light of the complex and innovative tasks it entrusted to the judicial and other authorities of Member States, in particular concerning the European Certificate of Succession.

3. Under appropriate circumstances, a delay in the date of application may also perform another function. While authorities and practitioners are afforded the time to study the new rules and prepare for their application, interested persons are put in a position to make decisions immediately that contemplate the effects of the newly enacted legislation, and to do so – for the sake of legal security – on the basis of rules that are already in force.

This concern, too, is relevant to the ESR. Those interested in planning their succession by making use of the opportunities offered by the ESR, have been given the possibility of proceeding this way without waiting for the regulation to apply. Pursuant to article 83(1), the ESR only applies to the succession of persons who died on or after 17 August 2015 [see art. 83]. However, interested individuals may have been willing to act before 17 August 2015 in contemplation of rules applicable from that date onwards. For some persons, namely those fearing an imminent loss of legal capacity, such an early move might have even represented the only available means to take advantage of the ESR. If these persons had no alternative but to wait for the date of application of the regulation, they would have in fact been precluded from benefiting from its rules.

II. Provisions of the ESR That Have become Effective Prior to the Date of Application of the Regulation in Its Entirety

4. Under article 84, two sets of rules of the ESR have become effective before 17 August 2015. On the one hand, articles 77 and 78, which determine the information that Member States are required to make available to the general public or provide to the EU Commission regarding their legislation in matters of successions and the measures adopted

[1] See in these terms, with reference to the Rome II regulation on the law applicable to non-contractual obligations, ECJ, case C-412/10, *Deo Antoine Homawoo* v. *GMF Assurances SA* [2011] ECLI:EU:C:2011:747, at 24.

for the implementation of the ESR, have become effective on 16 November 2014 [see arts. 77–79].[2] On the other hand, articles 79, 80, and 81, which identify the measures that the Commission must adopt in respect of the information supplied by Member States under the preceding rules and as regards the establishment (and subsequent amendment, where necessary) of the attestations and forms envisaged by the ESR, apply from 5 July 2012 [see arts. 77–79, 80–82].

[2] The text published in the *Official Journal* featured, in this respect, a reference to 16 January 2014. A corrigendum to article 84 changed it into 16 November 2014 (OJ 2012 L 344, 14 December 2012, p. 3). Article 78, which originally contained a reference to the same date, has later been corrected accordingly (OJ 2013 L 60, 2 March 2013, p. 140).

BIBLIOGRAPHY

Abadie L., 'La loi applicable au sein du règlement', *Droit de la famille*, 10 (2013), p. 12.

Akkermans B. and Ramaekers E., 'Article 345 TFEU (ex art. 295 EC), Its Meanings and Interpretation', *European Law Journal* (2010), p. 292.

Albrecht P., *Die steuerliche Behandlung deutsch-englischer Erbfälle* (Köln, Berlin, Bonn, München, 1992).

Althammer C., 'Art. 38', in T. Simons and R. Hausmann (eds), *Unalex Kommentar Brüssel I-Verordnung: Kommentar zur VO (EG) 44/2001 und zum Übereinkommen von Lugano* (München, 2012), p. 788.

Álvarez González S., 'Las legítimas en el Reglamento sobre sucesiones y testamentos', *An esp der int priv* 11 (2011), p. 369.

Álvarez Torné M., *La autoridad competente en materia de sucesiones internacionales: el nuevo reglamento de la UE* (Madrid, 2013).

Ancel B. and Muir-Watt H., 'Aliments sans frontières. Le règlement n° 4/2009 du 18 décembre 2008 relatif à la compétence, la loi applicable, la reconnaissance et l'exécution des décisions et la coopération en matière d'obligations alimentaires', *Rev crit dr int priv* (2010), p. 457.

Ancel B. and Muir-Watt H., 'La désunion européenne: le règlement dit de Bruxelles II', *Rev crit dr int priv* (2001), p. 440.

Andrae M., 'Art. 48 EG-UntVO', in T. Rauscher (ed), *Europäisches Zivilprozess- und Kollisionsrecht*, 4th ed. (München, 2015), vol. IV, p. 443.

Astolfi R., 'I beni vacanti e la legislazione caducaria', *Bullettino dell'istituto di diritto romano Vittorio Scialoja* 68 (1965), p. 323.

Attardi A., 'La nuova disciplina in tema di giurisdizione italiana e di riconoscimento delle sentenze straniere', *Riv dir proc* (1995), p. 727.

Audit B., *Droit international privé*, 3rd ed. (Paris, 2000).

Audit B. and Bermann G. A., 'The Application of Private International Norms to "Third Countries": The Jurisdiction and Judgments Example', in A. Nuyts and N. Watté (eds), *International Civil Litigation in Europe and Relations With Third States* (Bruxelles, 2005), p. 55.

Audit M., 'L'interprétation autonome du droit international privé communautaire', *JDI* (2004), p. 789.

Auteri P., 'Diritto d'autore', in P. Auteri, G. Floridia, V. Mangini, et al. (eds), *Diritto industriale. Proprietà e concorrenza*, 2nd ed. (Torino, 2005), p. 481.

Avasilencei C., 'La codification des conflits de lois dans le nouveau Code civil roumain: une nouvelle forme en attente d'un contentieux', *Rev crit dr int priv* (2012), p. 247.

Azavant M., 'L'ordre public successoral', *Droit de la famille* 10 (2013), p. 17.

Azcárraga Monzonís C., 'International Successions in Spain: The Impact of a New EU Regulation', *Spanish Yearbook of International Law* (2009), p. 39.

Bach I., 'Deine Rechtskraft? Meine Rechtskraft! Zur Entscheidung des EuGH, den unionsrechtlichen Rechtskraftbegriff auf zivilrechtliche Entscheidungen nationaler Gerichte anzuwenden', *EuZW* (2013) p. 56.

Baetge D., 'Auf dem Weg zu einem gemeinsamen europäischen Verständnis des gewöhnlichen Aufenthalts - Ein Beitrag zur Europäisierung des Internationalen Privat - und Verfahrensrechts', in *Die richtige Ordnung: Festschrift für Jan Kropholler zum 70. Geburtstag* (Tübingen, 2008), p. 77.

Baetge D., *Der gewöhnliche Aufenthalt im Internationalen Privatrecht* (Tübingen, 1994).

Bajons E.-M., 'Internationale Zuständigkeit und anwendbares Recht in Erbsachen', in M. Schauer and E. Scheuba (eds), *Europäische Erbrechtsverordnung (2012/650 EU vom 4. Juli 2012)* (Wien, 2012) p. 29.

Bajons E.-M., 'Internationale Zuständigkeit und anwendbares Recht in grenzüberschreitenden Erbrechtsfällen innerhalb des europäischen Justizraums', in *Festschrift für Andreas Heldrich zum 70. Geburtstag* (München, 2005), p. 495.

Baldus C., 'Erbe und Vermächtnisnehmer nach der Erbrechtsverordnung', *GPR-Zeitschrift für Gemeinschaftsprivatrecht* (2012), p. 312.

Baldus C., '¿Hacia un nuevo derecho sucesorio europeo?', *Anales de la Academia Matritense del Notariado* 49 (2009), p. 419.

Ballarino T., 'Il nuovo regolamento europeo sulle successioni', *Riv dir int* (2013), p. 1116.

Ballarino T., 'Le successioni nel diritto internazionale privato italiano', *Riv not* (1986), p. 1.

Balloriani M., De Rosa R. and Mezzanotte S., *Manuale breve. Diritto civile* (Milano, 2012).

Baratta R., 'The Process of Characterization in the EC Conflict of Laws: Suggesting a Flexible Approach', *YPIL* (2004), p. 155.

Barel B., 'La disciplina dei patti successori', in P. Franzina and A. Leandro (eds), *Il diritto internazionale privato europeo delle successioni mortis causa* (Milano, 2013), p. 105.

Bariatti S., 'Qualificazione e interpretazione del diritto internazionale privato comunitario: prime riflessioni', *Riv dir int priv proc* (2006), p. 361.

Barnett P. R., *Res judicata, Estoppel and Foreign Judgments: The Preclusive Effects of Foreign Judgments in Private International Law* (Oxford, 2001).

Bartin F., *De l'impossibilité d'arriver à la suppression définitive des conflits de lois* (Paris, 1897).

Basedow J., 'Das Prinzip der gegenseitigen Anerkennung im internationalen Wirtschaftsverkehr', in *Festschrift für Dieter Martiny zum 70. Geburtstag* (Tübingen, 2014), p. 248.

Basedow J., 'La reconnaissance des situations juridiques en droit des affaires', in P. Lagarde (ed), *La reconnaissance des situations en droit international privé* (Paris, 2013), p. 221.

Basedow J., 'Recherches sur la formation de l'ordre public européen dans la jurisprudence', in *Mélanges en l'honneur de Paul Lagarde* (Paris, 2005), p. 55.

Batiffol H., *Droit international privé*, vol. I (Paris, 1974).

Bauer F., 'Art. 59 EuErbVO: Verfahrensrechtliche Kollisionsnorm zur Sicherung des freien Verkehrs öffentlicher Urkunden', in *Gedächtnisschrift für Hannes Unberath* (München, 2015), p. 19.

Bauer F., 'Neues europäisches Kollisions- und Verfahrensrecht auf dem Weg: Stellungnahme des Deutschen Rates für IPR zum internationalen Erb- und Scheidungsrecht', *IPRax* (2006), p. 202.

Baumbach A., Lauterbach W., Albers J. and Hartman P., *Zivilprozessordnung*, 71st ed. (München, 2013).

Baur F., 'Der Begriff der Rechtsprechung und die freiwillige Gerichtsbarkeit', *DNotZ–Deutsche Notar-Zeitschrift* (1955), p. 507.

Béraudo J.-P., 'Convention de Bruxelles, Conventions de Lugano et règlement (CE) n° 44/2001 – Reconnaissance des décisions juridictionnelles', in *Juris Classeur Procédure civile*, fasc. 52–50 (Paris, 2010), p. 1.

Béraudo J.-P., 'Regards sur le nouveau règlement Bruxelles I sur la compétence juridictionnelle, la reconnaissance et l'exécution des décisions en matière civile et commerciale', *JDI* (2013), p. 741.

Bergquist U., Damascelli D., Frimston R., Lagarde P., Odersky F. and Reinhartz B., *Commentaire du Règlement européen sur les successions* (Paris, 2015).

Bergquist U., Damascelli D., Frimston R., Lagarde P., Odersky F. and Reinhartz B., *EU Regulation on Succession and Wills. Commentary* (Munich, 2015).

Biagioni G., 'Il nuovo regolamento comunitario sulla giurisdizione e sull'efficacia delle decisioni in materia matrimoniale e di responsabilità dei genitori', *Riv dir int* (2004), p. 991.

Biagioni G., 'Interferenze tra provvedimenti provvisori o cautelari e decisioni di merito nella Convenzione di Bruxelles', *Riv dir int* (2002), p. 713.

Biagioni G., 'L'ambito di applicazione del regolamento successioni', in P. Franzina and A. Leandro, *Il diritto internazionale privato europeo delle successioni mortis causa* (Milano, 2013), p. 25.

Biagioni G., 'L'art. 6 della Convenzione europea dei diritti dell'uomo e l'ordine pubblico processuale nel sistema della Convenzione di Bruxelles', *Riv dir int* (2001), p. 723.

Birk R., 'Art. 25', in *Münchener Kommentar zum Bürgerlichen Gesetzbuch*, vol. X, *Einführungsgesetz*, 3rd ed. (München, 1998), p. 1356.

Blackstone W., *Commentaries on the Law of England*, 15th ed. (London, 1809).

Blanco-Morales Limones P., 'Acciones declarativas negativas y forum delicti commissi. ¿Galgos o podencos? La litispendencia. Comentario a la Sentencia del Tribunal de Justicia (Sala Primera) de 25 de octubre de 2012. Folien Fischer AG y Fofitec AG contra Ritrama SpA', *CdT* 5/1 (2013), p. 240.

Blanco-Morales Limones P., 'Consideraciones sobre el ámbito de la Ley aplicable a las sucesiones en la propuesta de Reglamento del Parlamento Europeo y del Consejo relativo a la competencia, la Ley aplicable, el reconocimiento y la ejecución de las resoluciones y los actos auténticos en materia de sucesiones y a la creación de un certificado sucesorio europeo', in *Nuevas fronteras del Derecho de la Unión Europea. Liber amicorum José Luis Iglesias Buhígues* (Valencia, 2012), p. 413.

Blanco-Morales Limones P., 'El ámbito de la ley aplicable, incluida la administración de la sucesión', in *Cross-border Successions within the European Union*, Brussels, 15 August 2010, www.successions-europe.eu/event-downloads.

Blanco-Morales Limones P., 'Las sucesiones internacionales y su régimen jurídico', *Revista de Derecho de la Unión Europea* 22 (2012), p. 67.

Boele-Woelki K. and van Iterson D., 'The Dutch Private International Law Codification: Principles, Objectives and Opportunities', *Electronic Journal of Comparative Law*, 14/3 (2010).

Böhringer W., 'Das Europäische Nachlasszeugnis im deutschen Grundbuchverfahren', *NotBZ – Zeitschrift für die notarielle Beratungs- und Beurkundungspraxis* (2015), p. 281.

Bollée S., 'L'extension du domaine de la méthode de reconnaissance unilatérale', *Rev crit dr int priv* (2007), p. 307.

Bolas Alfonso J., 'Las sucesiones mortis causa transfronterizas en la Unión Europea', *Escritura Pública* 63 (mayo–junio 2010), p. 38.

Bonatti R., 'L'autonomia del diritto dell'Unione come cavallo di Troia per una nuova stagione di integrazione processuale: il caso della "nozione di parte"', *Int'Lis* 2 (2010), p. 69.

Bonilini G., 'Il negozio testamentario', in G. Bonilini (ed), *Trattato di diritto delle successioni e donazioni*, vol. II (Milano, 2009), p. 3.

Bonomi A., 'Il regolamento europeo sulle successioni', *Riv dir int priv proc* (2013), p. 293.

Bonomi A., 'Le choix de la loi applicable à la succession dans la proposition de règlement européen', in A. Bonomi and Ch. Schmid (eds), *Successions internationales. Réflexions autour du futur règlement européen et de son impact pour la Suisse* (Zürich, 2010), p. 23.

Bonomi A., 'Le choix de la loi applicable à la succession dans la proposition de règlement européen', in *Cursos de Derecho Internacional y Relaciones Internacionales de Vitoria-Gasteiz* (Bilbao, 2010), p. 241.

Bonomi A., 'Prime considerazioni sulla proposta di regolamento sulle successioni', *Riv dir int priv proc* (2010), p. 875.

Bonomi A., 'Successions internationales: conflits de lois et de juridictions', *Hague Recueil*, vol. 350 (2010) p. 71.

Bonomi A., 'Sull'opportunità e le possibili modalità di una regolamentazione comunitaria della competenza giurisdizionale applicabile erga omnes', *Riv dir int priv proc* (2007), p. 313.

Bonomi A., 'Testamentary freedom or forced heirship? Balancing party autonomy and the protection of family members', *NIPR* (2010), p. 605.

Bonomi A., 'The interaction among the future EU instruments on matrimonial property, registered partnerships and successions', *YPIL* (2011), p. 217.

Bonomi A. and Steiner M. (eds), *Les pactes successoraux en droit comparé et en droit international privé. Nouveautés en droit français, italien ainsi qu'espagnol et implications pratiques pour la Suisse. Actes de la Journée d'étude de Lausanne du 5 mars 2007* (Genève, 2008).

Bonomi A. and Wautelet P., *Le droit européen des successions. Commentaire du Règlement nº 650/2012 du 4 juillet 2012* (Brussels, 2013).

Borrás A., 'L'approche du renvoi dans un système d'unité de la succession', in *Mélanges en l'honneur de Mariel Revillard* (Paris, 2007), p. 23.

Boschiero N., 'Beni immateriali (diritto internazionale privato e processuale)', in *Enciclopedia del diritto, Annali*, vol. II.2 (Milano, 2008), p. 115.

Boschiero N., 'La nozione di mezzo ordinario di impugnazione ai sensi degli artt. 30 e 38 della Convenzione di Bruxelles del 1968', in T. Ballarino (ed), *La Convenzione di Bruxelles del 1968 e la riforma del processo civile italiano* (Milano, 1985), p. 97.

Boulanger F., 'Révolution juridique ou compromis en trompe l'oeil? – À propos du nouveau règlement européen sur les successions internationales', *La semaine juridique*, 15 (octobre 2012), p. 1120.

Boulanger F., *Droit international des successions* (Paris, 2004).

Braun A., 'Towards a Greater Autonomy for Testators and Heirs: Some Reflections on Recent Reforms in France, Belgium and Italy', *ZeuP* (2012), p. 461.

Bray J., *Unlocking land law*, 4th ed. (New York, 2014).

Bright S. and McFarlane B., 'Proprietary Estoppel and Property Rights', *CLJ* (2005), p. 449.

Bucher A., 'Art. 86', in A. Bucher (ed), *Commentaire romand. Loi sur le droit international privé. Convention de Lugano.* (Bâle, 2011), p. 791.

Bucher A. (ed), *Commentaire romand. Loi sur le droit international privé. Convention de Lugano* (Bâle, 2011).

Bucher A., *Droit international privé suisse, vol. I, 2, Partie générale - Droit applicable* (Bâle, Francfort-sur-le-Main, 1995); vol. II, *Personnes, Famille, Successions* (Bâle, Francfort-sur-le-Main, 1992).

Burandt W., 'Das europäische Erbrecht im Wandel (Teil 2)', *Familie und Recht* (2013), p. 377.

Burandt W., 'EuErbVO: Europäische Erbrechtsverordnung (VO Nr. (EU) Nr. 650/2012)', in W. Burandt and D. Rojahn (eds), *Erbrecht*, 2nd ed. (München, 2014), p. 1430.

Burandt W. and Rjahn D., *Erbrecht* (München, 2014).

Bureau D. and Muir Watt H., *Droit international privé, Tome 1. Partie générale*, 3rd ed. (Paris, 2014); Tome II (Paris, 2007).

Buschbaum M., 'Die künftige Erbrechtsverordnung - Wegbereiter für den acquis im europäischen Kollisionsrecht', in, *Weitsicht in Versicherung und Wirtschaft - Gedächtnisschrift für Ulrich Hübner* (Heidelberg, 2012), p. 589.

Buschbaum M., 'Europäisches Nachlasszeugnis und Annahme öffentlicher Urkunden - neue Mechanismen zur grenzüberschreitenden Nachlassabwicklung und ihr Verhältnis zum materiellen Sachenrecht', in J. Hager (ed), *Die neue europäische Erbrechtsverordnung* (Baden Baden, 2013), p. 39.

Buschbaum M. and Kohler M., 'Vereinheitlichung des Erbkollisionsrechts in Europa', *GPR Zeitschrift für Gemeinschaftsprivatrecht* (2010), pp. 106, 162.

Buschbaum M. and Simon U., 'Beantragung und Erteilung eines Europäischen Nachlasszeugnisses sowie Verwendung eines ausländischen Europäischen Nachlasszeugnisses in Deutschland', *Der Deutsche Rechtspfleger* (2015), p. 449.

Buschbaum M. and Simon U., 'EuErbVO: Das Europäische Nachlasszeugnis', *ZEV* (2012), p. 525.

Buschbaum M., 'Rechtslagenanerkennung aufgrund öffentlicher Urkunden? Bestandsaufnahme und Ausblick nach dem Inkrafttreten der EU-Erbrechtsverordnung', in *Festschrift für Dieter Martiny zum 70. Geburtstag* (Tübingen, 2014), p. 259.

Callé P., 'La circulation des actes authentiques', in H. Bosse-Platière, N. Damas and Y. Dereu (eds), *L'avenir européen du droit des successions internationales* (Paris, 2011), p. 58.

Calò E., 'El proyecto de Reglamento de la Unión Europea sobre la ley aplicable a las sucesiones: lo que no se ha dicho. Reflexiones desde el derecho italiano', *InDret* 3 (2010), p. 1.

Calò E., *Le successioni nel diritto internazionale privato* (Milanofiori Assago, 2007).

Calò E., 'L'etica dell'ordine pubblico internazionale e lo spirito della successione necessaria', *N giur civ comm* (1997), p. 167.

Calvo Caravaca A.-L., 'Artículo 9.8 del Código civil', in *Comentarios al Código Civil y compilaciones forales*, tome I, vol. II, 2nd ed. (Madrid, 1995), p. 350.

Calvo Caravaca A.-L., 'La sucesión hereditaria en el Derecho internacional privado español', *Revista General de Derecho* (1986), p. 3103.

Calvo Caravaca A.-L., 'Sucesión hereditaria', in J. D. González Campos et al. (eds), *Derecho internacional privado, parte especial* (Madrid, 1995), p. 393.

Calvo Caravaca A.-L. and Carrascosa González J., 'Capítulo 3. Los contratos internacionales. Ante el concurso de acreedores', in M. Yzquierdo Tolsada (ed), *Contratos, t. XVIII (Los contratos, ante el concurso de acreedores. Repercusiones tributarias del incumplimiento de los contratos)* (Pamplona, 2014), p. 569, p. 920.

Calvo Caravaca A.-L. and Carrascosa Gonzáles J., *Derecho internacional privado*, vol. I, 13th ed. (Granada, 2012); 15th ed. (Granada, 2014)

Calvo Caravaca A.-L. and Carrascosa González J., 'Persona física', in A. L. Calvo Caravaca and J. Carrascosa González (eds), *Derecho internacional privado*, 15th ed., vol. II (Granada, 2014), p. 15.

Calvo Vidal I. A., 'El Derecho de sucesiones en la Unión Europea. Ley aplicable y carácter universal de la nueva normativa en materia de sucesiones', *Noticias de la Unión Europea* (2012), p. 97.

Cámara Lapuente S., '¿Derecho europeo de sucesiones? Un apunte', in S. Cámara Lapuente (ed), *Derecho privado europeo* (Madrid, 2003), p. 1185.

Càmara Lapuente S., 'New Developments in the Spanish Law of Succession', *InDret* (2007), p. 1.

Campiglio C., 'Il diritto di famiglia islamico nella prassi italiana', *Riv dir int priv proc* (2008), p. 43.

Campiglio C., 'Il foro della residenza abituale del coniuge nel Regolamento (CE) N° 2201/2003: note a margine delle prime pronunce italiane', *CdT* 2/2 (2010), p. 242.

Carbone S. M., 'Il regime della litispendenza nelle convenzioni dell'Aja e di Bruxelles', in *L'efficacia delle sentenze straniere nelle convenzioni multilaterali dell'Aja e della C.E.E.* (Padova, 1969), p. 107.

Carbone S. M., *Lo spazio giudiziario europeo in materia civile e commerciale. Da Bruxelles I al regolamento CE n. 805/2004*, 6th ed. (Torino, 2009).

Carl I., *Einstweiliger Rechtsschutz bei Torpedoklagen* (Frankfurt am Main, Berlin, Bern, Wien, 2007).

Carrascosa González J., 'Reglamento sucesorio europeo y actividad notarial', *CdT* 1/6 (2014), p. 5.

Carrascosa González J., *El Reglamento Sucesorio Europeo 650/2012 de 4 de julio 2012: Análisis crítico* (Granada, 2014).

Carratta A., 'La sentenza civile straniera tra "riconoscimento" ed "estensione dell'efficacia"', *Riv dir proc* (2006), p. 1147.

Carrillo Salcedo J. A., 'La ley aplicable a la forma de las disposiciones testamentarias. Nota sobre el proyecto de Convenio adoptado por la Conferencia de La Haya de Derecho internacional privado', *Rev esp der int* (1961), p. 169.

Carter P. B., 'Domicile: The Case for Radical Reform in the United Kingdom', *ICLQ* 36 (1987), p. 713.

Castellaneta M. and Leandro A., 'Il regolamento CE n. 4/2009 relativo alle obbligazioni alimentari', *N l civ comm* (2009), p. 1051.

Castellanos Ruiz E., 'Sucesión hereditaria', in A.-L. Calvo Caravaca and J. Carrascosa González (eds), *Derecho internacional privado*, 14th ed, vol. II (Granada, 2013), p. 517.

Castellanos Ruiz E., 'Sucesión hereditaria. Reglamento 650/2012 sobre sucesión internacional', in A. L. Calvo Caravaca and J. Carrascosa González (eds), *Derecho internacional irivado. Parte especial*, 15th ed. (Granada, 2014), p. 529.

Castellanos Ruiz E., *Unidad versus pluralidad legal de la sucesión internacional* (Granada, 2001).

Catala P., 'Préparer sa succession', *La Semaine Juridique, Édition Générale* 1–2 (2011), p. 13.

Cavers D. F., '"Habitual Residence": A Useful Concept?', *The American University Law Review* 21 (1972), p. 475 (also in *id.*, *The Choice of Law, Selected Essays 1933–1983* [Durham, 1985], p. 244).

Chassaing P., 'La préparation des notaires et du notariat concernant la mise en application du règlement du 4 juillet 2012', in G. Khairallah and M. Revillard (eds), *Droit européen des successions internationales* (Paris, 2013), p. 37.

Chikoc Barreda N., 'Reflexiones sobre los regímenes especiales en derecho internacional privado sucesorio según el reglamento europeo 650/2012 de 4 Julio de 2012', *CdT* (2014), p. 132.

Cittadini M., 'L'orientamento della Corte di Giustizia in materia di residenza a fini fiscali', *Giur it* (2002), p. 869.

Clerici R., 'Articolo 50', in F. Pocar et al. (eds), *Commentario del nuovo diritto internazionale privato* (Padova, 1996), p. 246.

Coester-Waltjen D., 'Parteiautonomie in der internationalen Zuständigkeit', in *Festschrift für Andreas Heldrich zum 70. Geburtstag* (München, 2005), p. 549.

Coke E., *The First Institute of the Law of England*, 16th ed. (Dublin, 1809).

Collier J. B., *Conflict of Laws*, 2nd ed. (Cambridge, 1994).

Collins L. (ed), *Dicey & Morris on The Conflict of Laws*, 13th ed., vol. II (London, 2000).

Collins L. et al. (eds), *Dicey, Morris & Collins on The Conflict of Laws*, 15th ed. (London, 2012).

Conetti G., 'La successione del musulmano poligamo', *Studium Juris* (1997), p. 247.

Consolo C., 'Evoluzioni nel riconoscimento delle sentenze straniere', *Riv trim dir proc civ* (1997), p. 575.

Consolo C., 'La tutela sommaria e la convenzione di Bruxelles: la "circolazione" cautelare dei provvedimenti cautelari e dei decreti ingiuntivi', *Riv dir int priv proc* (1991), p. 593.

Consolo C., 'Profili della litispendenza internazionale', *Riv dir int* (1997), p. 5.

Consolo C., 'Van Uden e Mietz: un'evitabile Babele', *Int'l Lis* (2002), p. 30.

Consolo C. and Merlin E., 'Conflitto fra provvedimenti sommari-cautelari e diniego di riconoscimento: la Italian Leather segna una forzatura', *Int'l Lis* (2002), p. 110.

Contaldi G., *Il trust nel diritto internazionale privato italiano* (Milano, 2001).

Cook W. W., *The Logical and Legal Bases of the Conflict of Laws* (Cambridge, MA, 1942).

Corbion L., *Le déni de justice en droit international privé* (Aix - Marseille, 2004).

Coscia G., 'Contrasto fra decisioni e atti equiparati', *Foro it* (1996), IV, p. 463.

Courbe P., 'L'ordre public de proximité', in *Le droit international privé: esprit et méthodes. Mélanges en l'honneur de Paul Lagarde* (Paris, 2005), p. 227.

Cubbedu Wiedemann M. G. and Wiedemann A., 'Erbrecht in Italien', in R. Süß (ed), *Erbrecht in Europa*, 2nd ed. (Bonn, 2008), p. 827.

Cuniberti G., 'Debarment from Defending, Default Judgments and Public Policy', *Iprax* (2010), p. 148.

Cuniberti G., *Les mesures conservatoires portant sur des biens situés à l'étranger* (Paris, 2000).

D'Alessandro E., 'Exequatur secondo la Convenzione di Bruxelles', *Int'l Lis* (2008), I, p. 22.

D'Alessandro E., *Il riconoscimento delle sentenze straniere* (Torino, 2007).

D'Alessandro E., 'Pronunce declinatorie di giurisdizione: la Corte di giustizia impone limiti di efficacia europei', *Foro it* (2013), IV, p. 42.

D'Alessandro E., 'Provvedimento inglese di esclusione dal processo e diniego di riconoscimento per contrarietà all'ordine pubblico processuale. La Corte di giustizia si pronuncia sul caso "Gambazzi"', *Foro it* (2009), IV, p. 384.

Damascelli D., *Diritto internazionale privato delle successioni a causa di morte (dalla l. n. 218/1995 al reg. UE n. 650/2012)* (Milano, 2013).

Damascelli D., 'I criteri di collegamento impiegati dal regolamento n. 650/2012 per la designazione della legge regolatrice della successione a causa di morte', in P. Franzina and A. Leandro (eds.), *Il diritto internazionale privato europeo delle successioni mortis causa* (Milano, 2013), p. 87.

Damascelli D., 'La legge applicabile alla successione per causa di morte secondo il diritto internazionale privato italiano', *Riv dir int priv proc* (2003), p. 85.

Davì A., 'Ancora sulle finalità (e sui due diversi modelli) del rinvio nel diritto internazionale privato contemporaneo', *Riv dir int* (2014), p. 1032.

Davì A., *Comunità europee e sanzioni economiche internazionali* (Napoli, 1993).

Davì A., *L'adozione nel diritto internazionale privato italiano* (Milano, 1981).

Davì A., 'L'autonomie de la volonté en droit international privé des successions dans la perspective d'une future réglementation européenne', in *Les successions internationales dans l'UE: perspectives pour une armonisation* (Würzburg, 2004), p. 387 (also in *Riv dir int priv proc* (2004), p. 473).

Davì A., 'Le renvoi en droit international privé contemporain', *Hague Recueil*, vol. 352 (2010), p. 9.

Davì A., 'Riflessioni sul futuro diritto internazionale privato europeo delle successioni', *Riv dir int* (2005), p. 297.

Davì A. and Zanobetti A., 'Il nuovo diritto internazionale privato delle successioni nell'Unione Europea', *CdT* 5/2 (2013), p. 5.

Davì A. and Zanobetti A., *Il nuovo diritto internazionale privato europeo delle successioni* (Torino, 2014).

Davies M., Bell A. and Le Gay Brereton P., *Nygh's Conflict of Laws in Australia*, 8th ed. (Chatswood, NSW, 2010).

De Baere, 'Case C-420/07, Meletis Apostolides v. David Charles Orams, Linda Orams E., Judgment of the Court of Justice (Grand Chamber) of 28 April 2009, [2009] ECR I-3571', *CMLRev* (2010), p. 1123.

De Cesari P., *Autonomia della volontà e legge regolatrice delle successioni* (Padova, 2001).

De Cristofaro M., 'L'onere di impugnazione della sentenza quale limite al rilievo dei vizi nella fase introduttiva del giudizio chiuso da sentenza contumaciale: tra diritto di difesa e full faith and credit', *Int'l Lis* (2007), p. 7.

De Cristofaro M., 'Presupposti e rimedi per il provvedimento che «sospende» l'opposizione all'exequatur o il riconoscimento di una sentenza comunitaria', *Riv dir int priv proc* (1998), p. 745.

De Leval G., 'Une harmonisation des procédures d'exécution dans l'Union européenne est-elle concevable?', in G. de Leval (ed), *Seizure and Overindebtedness in the European Union* (The Hague, 1997), p. 595.

De Lima Pinheiro L., *Direito Internacional Privado. Direito de Conflitos. Parte especial*, 3rd ed. (Coimbra, 2009).

De Luca A., 'La Direttiva 2003/8/CE del Consiglio del 27 gennaio 2003, intesa a migliorare l'accesso alla giustizia nelle controversie transfrontaliere', in M. Taruffo and V. Varano (eds), *Manuale di diritto processuale europeo* (Torino, 2011), p. 365.

De Pablo Contreras P., 'Legítimas y mejora: su satisfacción en la sucesión testada', in M. A. Pérez Álvarez (ed), *Curso de Derecho Civil (V) Derecho de sucesiones* (Madrid, 2013), p. 295.

De Vareilles-Sommières P., 'Pour une meilleure consolidation européenne des dispositions de planification successorale prises avant le 17 août 2015 relativement à une succession internationale', *Dalloz* (2012), p. 2321.

De Vareilles-Sommières P., 'The Mandatory Nature of Article 2 of the Brussels Convention and Derogation from the Rule It Lays Down', in P. de Vareilles-Sommières (ed), *Forum Shopping in the European Judicial Area* (Oxford – Portland, OR, 2007), p. 101.

Dengel K., *Die europäische Vereinheitlichung des internationalen Ehegüterrechts und des internationalen Güterrechts für eingetragene Partnerschaften* (Tübingen, 2014).

Déprez J., 'Droit international privé et conflits de civilisations. Aspects méthodologiques. Les relations entre systèmes d'Europe occidentale et systèmes islamiques en matière de statut personnel', *Hague Recueil*, vol. 211 (1988), p. 9.

Derruppé J., 'Le renvoi dans les conventions internationales', *Juris-classeur de droit international* (1993), fasc. 532–3.

Deutsches Notarinstitut (ed), *Les successions internationales dans l'Union Européenne - Perspectives pour une harmonisation* (Würzburg, 2004).

Devaux A., 'The European Regulations on Succession of July 2012: A Path Towards the End of the Succession Conflicts of Law in Europe, or not?', *The International Lawyer* (2013), p. 229.

Di Blase A., *Connessione e litispendenza nella convenzione di Bruxelles* (Padova, 1993).

Dickinson A., 'Legal Certainty and the Brussels Convention - Too Much of a Good Thing?', in P. de Vareilles-Sommières (ed), *Forum Shopping in the European Judicial Area* (Oxford; Portland, OR, 2007), p. 115.

Dickinson A., *The Rome II Regulation* (Oxford, 2008).

Díez-Picazo L. and Gullón A., *Sistema de Derecho Civil, Vol. IV (Tomo 2) Derecho de sucesiones*, 11th ed. (Madrid, 2012).

Döbereiner C., 'Das internationale Erbrecht nach der EU-Erbrechtsverordnung', *MittBayNot* (2013), pp. 358, 437.

Döbereiner C., 'Vindikationslegate unter Geltung der EU-Erbrechtsverordnung', *Zeitschrift für das Privatrecht der Europäischen Union* (2014), p. 42.

Dölle H., 'Die Rechtswahl im internationalen Erbrecht', *RabelsZ* (1966), p. 205.

Domínguez Luelmo A., 'El testamento', in M. C. Gete-Alonso y Calera (ed), *Tratado de Derecho de Sucesiones*, vol. I (Cizur Menor, 2011), p. 375.

Donzallaz I., 'Le renouveau de l'ordre public dans la CB/CL au regard des ACJCE Krombach et Renault et de la révision de ces traités', *AJP* (2001), p. 160.

Dornblüth S., *Die europäische Regelung der Anerkennung und Vollstreckbarerklärung von Ehe- und Kindschaftsentscheidungen* (Tübingen, 2003).

Dörner H., 'Art. 25', in *J. von Staudingers Kommentar zum Bürgerlichen Gesetzbuch mit Einführungsgesetz und Nebengesetzen, Internationales Erbrecht* (Berlin, 2007), p. 278.

Dörner H., 'Das Grünbuch "Erb- und Testamentsrecht" der Europäischen Kommission', *ZEV* (2005), p. 137.

Dörner H., 'Der Entwurf einer europäischen Verordnung zum internationalen Erb- und Erbverfahrensrecht- Überblick und ausgewählte Probleme', *ZEV* (2010), p. 221.

Dörner H., 'Die Abgrenzung des Erbstatuts vom Güterstatut', in A. Dutta and S. Herrler (eds), *Die europäische Erbrechtsverordnung* (München, 2014), p. 73.

Dörner H., 'EuErbVO: Die Verordnung zum Internationalen Erb- und Erbverfahrensrecht ist in Kraft!', *ZEV* (2012), p. 505.

Dörner H., Hertel C., Lagarde P. and Riering W., 'Auf dem Weg zu einem europäischen Internationalen Erb- und Erbverfahrensrecht', *IPRax* (2005), p. 1.

Dorsel C., 'Art. 62-73 EuErbVO', in R. Geimer and R. Schütze (eds), *Internationaler Rechtsverkehr in Zivil- und Handelssachen*, vol. III (München, 2015), para. 1.

Dorsel C., 'Europäische Erbrechtsverordnung und Europäisches Nachlasszeugnis', *Europäische Zeitschrift für die Steuer- und Erbrechtspraxis* (2014), p. 212.

Dorsel C. and Schall C., 'Die Umsetzung der ErbVO durch die Europäische Kommission – Ein erster Überblick unter besonderer Berücksichtigung des Europäischen Nachlasszeugnisses', *GPR – Zeitschrift für das Privatrecht der Europäischen Union* (2015), p. 36.

Dreher K., *Die Rechtswahl im internationalen Erbrechter- Unter besonderer Berücksichtigung des italienischen IPR- Reformgesetzes N. 218 vom 31. Mai 1995* (Frankfurt, 1999).

Drobnig U., 'Verstößt das Staatsangehörigkeitsprinzip gegen das Diskriminierungsverbot des EWG-Vertrags?', *RabelsZ* (1970), p. 636.

Droz G., *Compétence judiciaire et effets des jugements dans le marché commun (Etude de la Convention de Bruxelles du 27 septembre 1968)* (Paris, 1972).

Droz G., 'L'activité notariale internationale', *Hague Recueil*, vol. 280 (1999), p. 9.

Dutoit B., *Commentaire de la loi fédérale du 18 décembre 1987*, 2nd ed. (Bâle, Francfort-sur-le-Main, 1997)

Dutoit B., *Droit international privé suisse. Commentaire de la loi fédérale du 18 Décembre 1987*, 4th ed. (Bâle, Geneva, Munich, 2005).

Dutta A., 'Das neue internationale Erbrecht der Europäischen Union – Eine erste Lektüre der Erbrechtsverordnung', *FamRZ* (2013), p. 4.

Dutta A., 'Die Abgrenzung von Gesellschaftsstatut und Erbstatut beim Tod des Gesellschafters', *RabelsZ* (2009), p. 740.

Dutta A., 'Die europäische Erbrechtsverordnung vor ihrem Anwendungsbeginn', *IPRax* (2015), p. 32.

Dutta A., 'Kommentierung der europäischen Erbrechtsverordnung', in J. von Hein (ed), *Münchener Kommentar BGB*, 6th ed., vol. X (München, 2015), p. 1427.

Dutta A., 'Succession and Wills in the Conflict of Laws on the Eve of Europeanisation', *RabelsZ* (2009), p. 547.

Dutta A., 'The European Certificate of Succession. A New European Instrument between Procedural and Substantive Law', *IJPL - International Journal of Procedural Law* (2015), p. 38.

Espinosa Calabuig R., *Custodia y visita de menores en el espacio judicial europeo* (Madrid, 2007).

Esplugues C. A., 'Legal Recognition of Polygamous Marriages', *The Comparative and International Law Journal of Southern Africa* (1984), p. 302.

Everts A., 'Neue Perspektiven zur Pflichtteilsdämpfung aufgrund der EuErbVO?', *ZEV* (2013), p. 124.

Fallon M. and Kruger Th., 'The Spatial Scope of the EU's Rules on Jurisdiction and Enforcement of Judgments: From Bilateral Modus to Unilateral Universality?', *YPIL* XIV (2012/2013), p. 1.

Fawcett J. J., 'The Impact of Article 6(1) of the ECHR on Private International Law', *ICLQ* (2007), p. 1.

Fawcett J. J., Carruthers J. M and North P. M., *Cheshire, North & Fawcett: Private International Law*, 14th ed. (Oxford, 2008).

Fentiman R., 'Access to Justice and Parallel Proceedings in Europe', *CLJ* (2005), p. 312.

Fentiman R., 'Domicile Revisited', *CLJ* (1991), p. 445.

Fentiman R., *International Commercial Litigation* (Oxford, 2010).

Fentiman R., 'National Law and the European Jurisdiction Regime', in A. Nuyts and N. Watté (eds), *International Civil Litigation in Europe and Relations with Third States* (Bruxelles, 2005), p. 83.

Fentiman R., 'Parallel Proceedings and Jurisdiction Agreements in Europe', in P. de Vareilles-Sommières (ed), *Forum Shopping in the European Judicial Area* (Oxford; Portland, OR, 2007), p. 27.

Feraci O., 'La nuova disciplina europea della competenza giurisdizionale in materia di successioni mortis causa', *CdT* 5/2 (2013), p. 291.

Feraci O., *L'ordine pubblico nel diritto dell'Unione europea* (Milano, 2012).

Ferid M., 'Le rattachement autonome de la transmission successorale en droit international privé', *Hague Recueil* vol. 142 (1974), p. 71.

Fernández Arroyo D. P., 'Compétence exclusive et compétence exorbitante dans les relations privées internationales', *Hague Recueil* vol. 323 (2006), p. 9.

Firsching K. and Graf H. L., *Nachlassrecht - Erbfolge, Testament, Erbvertrag, Pflichtteilsrecht, Rechtspflege in Nachlasssachen, Nachlassinsolvenz, Nachlassverfahren sowie Erbschaftssteuer*, 10th ed. (München, 2014).

Fitchen J., 'Authentic Instruments and European Private International Law in Civil and Commercial Matters: Is Now the Time to Break New Ground?', *JPIL* 7 (2011), p. 33.

Fitchen J., '"Recognition", acceptance and enforcement of authentic instruments in the Succession Regulation', *JPIL* 8 (2012), p. 323.

Föhlisch J., *Der gemeineuropäische ordre public* (Frankfurt am Main, 1997).

Fongaro E., 'L'anticipation successorale à l'épreuve du "règlement successions"', *JDI* (2014), p. 477.

Font i Segura A., 'La ley aplicable a los pactos sucesorios', *InDret* 2 (2009), p. 1.

Fontanellas Morell J. M., 'El nuevo Reglamento europeo en materia de sucesiones. Aspectos de Derecho internacional privado', *Rev esp der int* (2013), p. 284.

Fontanellas Morell J. M., 'La forma de la designación de Ley en la propuesta de Reglamento europeo en materia de sucesiones', *Rev esp der int* (2011), p. 123.

Fontanellas Morell J. M., *La professio iuris sucesoria* (Madrid, 2010).

Fornasier M., 'Art. 62–73 EuErbVO', in A. Dutta and J. Weber (eds), *Internationales Erbrecht - EuErbVO, Erbrechtliche Staatsverträge, EGBGB, IntErbRVG, IntErbStR, IntSchenkungsR* (München, 2016).

Foyer J., 'Reconnaissance, acceptation et exécution des jugements étrangers, des actes authentiques et des transaction judiciares', in G. Khairallah and M. Revillard (eds), *Droit européen des successions internationales* (Paris, 2013), p. 141.

Franzina P., 'Lis Pendens Involving a Third Country Under the Brussels I-bis Regulation: An Overview', *Riv dir int priv proc* (2014), p. 23.

Franzina P., 'Ragioni, valori e collocazione sistematica della disciplina internazionalprivatistica europea delle successioni *mortis causa*', in P. Franzina and A. Leandro (eds), *Il diritto internazionale privato europeo delle successioni mortis causa* (Milano, 2013), p. 1.

Franzina P., 'Sul forum necessitatis nello spazio giudiziario europeo', *Riv dir int* (2009), p. 1121.

Franzina P. and Leandro A. (eds), *Il diritto internazionale privato europeo delle successioni mortis causa* (Milano, 2013).

Franzina P. and Leandro A., 'Il nuovo diritto internazionale privato delle successioni per causa di morte in Europa', *N l civ comm* (2013), p. 333.

Frigo M. and Fumagalli L., *L'assistenza giudiziaria internazionale in materia civile* (Padova, 2003).

Frodl S., 'Einheit durch Aufgabe nationaler Rechtstraditionen? - EU-Erbrechtsverordnung kundgemacht', *Österreichische Juristen-Zeitung* (2012), p. 950.

Fucik R., 'Art. 59 EuErbVO', in W. H. Rechberger and B. Zöchling-Jud (eds), *Die EU-Erbrechtsverordnung in Österreich* (Wien, 2015), p. 263.

Fumagalli L., '*Lis Alibi Pendens*. The Rules on Parallel Proceedings in the Reform of the Brussels I Regulation', in F. Pocar, I. Viarengo, F. C. Villata (eds), *Recasting Brussels I* (Padova, 2012), p. 237.

Gallant E., *Responsabilité parentale et protection des enfants en droit international privé* (Paris, 2004).

Garb L., *International Succession* (The Hague, 2004).

Garb L. and Wood J., *International Succession*, 3rd ed. (Oxford, 2010).

García Rubio M.P. and Otero Crespo M., 'Capacidad, incapacidad e indignidad para suceder', in M. C. Gete-Alonso y Calera (dir.), *Tratado de Derecho de Sucesiones*, vol. I (Cizur Menor, 2011), p. 225.

Gaudemet-Tallon H., *Compétence et exécution des jugements en Europe*, 4th ed. (Paris, 2010).

Gaudemet-Tallon H., 'Le pluralisme en droit international privé: richesses et faiblesses', *Hague Recueil*, vol. 312 (2005), p. 271.

Gaudemet-Tallon H., 'Les règles de compétence judiciaire dans le règlement européen sur les successions', in G. Khairallah and M. Revillard (eds), *Droit européen des successions internationales. Le règlement du 4 juillet 2012* (Paris, 2013), p. 127.

Gaudemet-Tallon H., 'Quelques réflexions sur les propositions concernant la compétence judiciaire, la reconnaissance et l'exécution des décisions en matière successorale dans l'Union européenne', in Deutsches Notarinstitut (ed), *Les successions internationales dans l'Union Européenne – Perspectives pour une harmonisation* (Würzburg, 2004), p. 445.

Gaudemet-Tallon H. and Kessedjian C., 'La refonte du règlement Bruxelles I', *Revue trimestrielle de droit européen* (2013), p. 435.

Geimer R., '"Annahme" ausländischer öffentlicher Urkunden in Erbsachen gemäß Art. 59 EuErbVO', in A. Dutta and S. Herrler, *Die Europäische Erbrechtsverordnung* (München, 2014), p. 143.

Geimer R., 'Anmerkung zu KG 3.3.1987', *NJW* (1988), p. 651.

Geimer R., 'Art. 1 EuErbVO', in *Zöller, Kommentar ZPO*, (Köln, 2012), Annex II J.

Geimer R., 'Die europäische Erbrechtsverordnung im Überblick', in J. Hager (ed), *Die neue europäische Erbrechtsverordnung. Tagungsband* (Baden-Baden, 2013), p. 9.

Geimer R., *Internationales Zivilprozessrecht*, 5th ed. (Köln, 2005); 6th ed. (Köln, 2009).

Geimer R. and Schütze R. A., *Europäisches Zivilverfahrensrecht*, 3rd ed. (München, 2010).

Gewaltig R., *Von der nationalen zur europäischen Zuständigkeitsregelung im Familienrecht: die internationale Zuständigkeit nach den europäischen Verordnungen (EG) Nr. 1347/2000 und Nr. 2201/2003 (EuEheVO) in Deutschland und in den Niederlanden* (Frankfurt am Main, Berlin, Bern, Wien, 2008).

Gierl W., Köhler A., Kroiß L. and Wilsch H., *Internationales Erbrecht* (Baden-Baden, 2015).

Girerd P., 'Les principes d'équivalence et d'effectivité: encadrement ou désencadrement de l'autonomie procédurale des États membres', *Revue trimestrielle de droit européen* (2002), p. 75.

Giuliano M., *La giurisdizione civile italiana e lo straniero*, 2nd ed. (Milano, 1970).

Godechot S., *L'articulation du trust et du droit des successions* (Paris, 2004).

Godechot-Patris S., 'L'administration des successions', in G Khairallah and M. Revillard (eds), *Droit européen des successions internationales (Le Règlement du 4 juillet 2012)* (Paris, 2013), p. 87.

Godechot-Patris S., 'Le nouveau droit international privé des successions: entre satisfactions et craintes . . .', *Dalloz* (2012), p. 2462.

González González R., 'Límites a la construcción de un "orden público europeo" en materia de derechos fundamentales (A propósito de la sentencia del TJCE Krombach c. Bamberski, de 28 de marzo de 2000)', *Rev der com eur* (2000), p. 593.

Goré M., 'La professio juris', *Defrénois* 15–16 (2012), p. 762.

Goré M., *L'administration des successions en droit international privé français* (Paris, 2004).

Gothot P. and Holleaux D., *La convention de Bruxelles du 27 septembre 1968: Compétence judiciaire et effets des jugements dans la CEE* (Paris, 1985).

Gottwald P., 'Europäisches Zivilprozessrecht', in *Münchener Kommentar zur Zivilprozessordnung*, 4th ed., vol. 3 (München, 2013), p. 1738.

Gratton C., *Infinite Regress Arguments* (Dordrecht, 2010).

Greeske M., *Die Kollisionsnormen der neuen EU-Erbrechtsverordnung* (Frankfurt am Main, 2014).

Grimaldi M., 'Brèves réflexions sur l'ordre public et la réserve héréditaire', *Defrenois* (2012), p. 755.

Gröschl P., *Internationale Zuständigkeit im europäischen Eheverfahrensrecht* (Konstanz, 2007).

Grünberger M., 'Alles obsolet? – Anerkennungsprinzip vs. klassisches IPR', in S. Leible and H. Unberath (eds), *Brauchen wir eine Rom 0-Verordnung?* (München, 2013), p. 81.

Guillame F., 'O tempora! O mores!: l'effet du temps sur l'ordre public end droit international privé, in P. Zen-Ruffinen, *Le temps et le droit. Recueil de travaux offerts à la journée de la société suisse des juristes 2008* (Bâle, 2008) p. 101.

Gutzler H., 'Anmerkung zu LG Freiburg 4.11.1947 und LG Hamburg 10.10.1947', *NJW* (1949), p. 153.

Habscheid J. W., *Freiwillige Gerichtsbarkeit* (München, 1983).

Hajnczyk C., *Die Zuständigkeit für Entscheidungen in Ehesachen und in anderen Familiensachen aus Anlass von Ehesachen sowie deren Anerkennung und Vollstreckung in der EG und in der Schweiz* (Frankfurt am Main, 2003).

Hallstein W., 'Angleichung des Privat- und Prozessrechts in der Europäischen Wirtschaftsgemeinschaft', *RabelsZ* (1964), p. 211.

Hanisch H., 'Professio iuris, réserve légale und Pflichtteil', in *Mélanges Guy Flattet* (Lausanne, 1985), p. 473.

Haopei Li, 'Some Recent Developments in the Conflict of Laws of Succession', *Hague Recueil* vol. 224 (1990), p. 9.

Harris J., 'The Proposed EU Regulation on Succession and Wills: Prospects and Challenges', *Trust LI* (2008), p. 181.

Harris R. W., 'Federal estate consequences of common disasters or closely proximate deaths', *Tax Lawyer* (1993–1994), p. 763.

Hartley T. C., 'Choice-of-Court Agreements, lis pendens, Human Rights and the Realities of International Business: Reflections on the *Gasser* Case', in *Le droit international privé: esprit et méthodes, Mélanges en l'honneur de Paul Lagarde* (Paris, 2005), p. 383.

Hartley T. C., 'Interim Measures Under the Brussels Jurisdiction and Judgments Convention', *ELR* (1999), p. 674.

Hartley T. C., *International Commercial Litigation* (Cambridge, 2009).

Hartley T. C., 'Procedure for Enforcement: Effect of Appeal in Judgment-granting State', *ELRev* (1978), p. 160.

Hartley T. C., 'The "Italian Torpedo" and Choice-of-Court Agreements: Sunk At Last?', in P. Lindskoug et al. (eds), *Essays in Honour of Michael Bogdan* (Lund, 2013), p. 95.

Hauser W. G., 'Torpedoschutz im Fürstentum', in H. Schumacher and W. Zimmermann (eds), *90 Jahre Fürstlicher Oberster Gerichtshof* (Wien, 2013), p. 355.

Hausmann R., 'Article 4 EGBGB', in *J. von Staudingers Kommentar zum Bürgerlichen Gesetzbuch mit Einführungsgesetz und Nebengesetzen*, 15th ed. (Berlin, 2013), p. 154.

Hausmann R., *Internationales und europäisches Ehescheidungsrecht: mit Scheidungsfolgenrecht* (München, Basel, 2013).

Heini A., 'Art. 86–96', in D. Girsberger, A. Heini, M. Keller, J. Kren Kostkiewicz, K. Siehr, F. Vischer and P. Volken (eds), *Zürcher Kommentar zum IPRG*, 2nd ed. (Zürich, 2004), p. 1022.

Heini A., 'Der Grundsatz der Nachlasseinheit und das neue internationale Erbrecht der Schweiz', in *Festschriftt für Cyril Hegnauer zum 65. Geburtstag* (Bern, 1986), p. 187.

Heinig J., 'Rechtswahlen in Verfügungen von Todes wegen nach der EU-Erbrechts-Verordnung', *Rheinische Notar-Zeitschrift* (2014), p. 197.

Heldrich A., 'Die Interessen bei der Regelung der internationalen Zuständigkeit', in *Festschrift für Hans G. Ficker* (Frankfurt, Berlin, 1967), p. 205.

Heldrich A., *Internationale Zuständigkeit und anwendbares Recht* (Berlin, 1969).

Hellner M., 'El futuro reglamento de la UE sobre sucesiones. La relación con terceros estados', *An esp der int priv* 10 (2010), p. 379.

Henke A., 'Verso una nozione europea di res judicata: l'efficacia extraprocessuale della declinatoria di giurisdizione e il giudicato sui motivi', *Diritto del commercio internazionale* (2013), p. 1085.

Henrich D., 'Bericht zu OLG Hamm 13.3.1989', *IPRax* (1990), p. 58.

Henrich D., 'Der Domizilbegriff im englischen Internationalen Privatrecht', *RabelsZ* (1960), p. 456.

Hertel C., 'Die Abgrenzung des Erbstatuts vom Sachstatut und Gesellschaftsstatut', in A. Dutta and S. Herrler (eds), *Die europäische Erbrechtsverordnung* (München, 2014), p. 95.

Hertel C., 'European Certificate of Succession – Content, Issue and Effects', *ERA Forum* (2014), p. 402.

Hertel C., 'Zum Nachweis der Erbfolge im Grundbuchverfahren mittels im Ausland erstellten Erbscheinen', *DNotZ - Deutsche Notar-Zeitschrift* (2012), p. 688.

Herweg C., *Die Vereinheitlichung des Internationalen Erbrechts im Europäischen Binnenmarkt* (Baden-Baden, 2004).

Herzog S., 'Die EU-Erbrechtsverordnung (EU-ErbVO)', *ErbR – Zeitschrift für die gesamte erbrechtliche Praxis* (2013), p. 2.

Hess B., 'Die internationale Zuständigkeit nach der Erbrechtsverordnung', in A. Dutta and S. Herrler (eds), *Die Europäische Erbrechtsverordnung* (München, 2014), p. 131.

Hess B., 'Free Movement of Judgments', in B. Hess, T. Pfeiffer and P. Schlosser (eds), *The Brussels I – Regulation (EC) No. 44/2001* (München, 2008), p. 147.

Hess B., 'Konkurrierende Unterlassungsverfügungen im Europäischen Justizraum', *IPRax* (2005), p. 23.

Hess B., 'Urteilsfreizügigkeit und ordre public-Vorbehalt bei Verstößen gegen Verfahrensgrundrechte und Marktfreiheiten', *IPRax* (2001), p. 301.

Hohloch G., 'Kommentierung der EuErbRVO', in *Erman, BGB: Kommentar*, 14th ed. (Köln, 2014), p. 6693.

Hotz K. P., *Die Rechtswahl im Erbrecht im interkantonalen und internationalen Verhältnis* (Zürich, 1969).

Huebner R., *A History of Germanic Private Law*, Eng. trans. by S. F. Philbrick (New Jersey, 2000).

Huet A., 'Chronique de jurisprudence de la Cour de justice des Communautés européennes. Convention de Bruxelles du 27 septembre 1968', *JDI* (1989), p. 449.

Huet A., 'Chronique de jurisprudence du Tribunal et de la Cour de justice des Communautés européennes', *JDI* (1995), p. 466.

Hussain A., *The Islamic Law of Succession* (Riyadh, 2005).

Huzel E., Löber B. and Wollmann I., 'Erbrecht in Portugal', in R. Süß (ed), *Erbrecht in Europa*, 2nd ed. (Bonn, 2008), p. 1171.

Hye-Knudsen R., *Marken-, Patent- und Urheberrechtsverletzungen im europäischen Internationalen Zivilprozessrecht* (Tübingen, 2005), p. 170.

Idot L., 'Décisions contraires rendues dans un même État membre. L'article 34, point 4 du règlement (CE) n° 44/2001, qui prévoit la non reconnaissance d'une décision inconciliable ne s'applique pas à des décisions rendues dans le même État membre', *Europe* (2013/11), p. 52.

Idot L., 'Exécution d'un jugement rendu par défaut, ordre public et droits fondamentaux', *Europe* (2012/11), p. 50.

Impagnatiello G., *La provvisoria esecuzione e l'inibitoria nel processo civile* (Milano, 2010).

Ioratti Ferrari E., 'Draft Common Frame of Reference and Terminology', in L. Antoniolli and F. Fiorentini (eds), *A factual Assessment of the Draft Common Frame of Reference* (München, 2011), p. 313.

Jacobsen K., 'Die Rechtswahl im interlokalen Erbrecht Deutschlands', *Recht in Ost und West*, 3 (1983), p. 97.

Janzen U., 'Die EU-Erbrechtsverordnung', *DNotZ – Deutsche Notar-Zeitschrift* (2012), p. 492.

Jault-Seseke F., 'Conflit de juridictions. Les règles communautaires', *Dalloz* (2010), p. 1593.

Jayme E., *Methoden der Konkretisierung des ordre public im internationalen Privatrecht* (Heidelberg, 1989).

Jayme E., 'Party Autonomy in International Family and Succession Law: New Tendencies', *YPIL* (2009), p. 1.

Jayme E. and Kohler C., 'Europäisches Kollisionsrecht 2001: Anerkennungsprinzip statt IPR?', *IPRax* (2001), p. 501.

Jessel-Holst C., 'The Bulgarian International Law Code of 2005', *YPIL* (2007), p. 375.

Junghardt A., *Die Vereinheitlichung des Erb- und Testamentsrechts im Rahmen einer Europäischen Verordnung – Rom IV-VO* (Regensburg, 2009).

Kahn F., 'Die Lehre vom ordre public (Prohibitivgesetze)', in *Jherings Jahrbücher für die Dogmatik des bürgerlichen Rechts*, vol. 39 (Jena, 1898), pp. 1–112.

Kahn F., 'Gesetzeskollisionen. Ein Beitrag zur Lehre des IPR', in *Jherings Jahrbücher für Dogmatik*, vol. XXX (1891), p. 1

Kähr M., *Der Kampf um den Gerichtsstand – Forum Shopping im internationalen Verfahrensrecht der Schweiz* (Zürich, St. Gallen, 2010).

Kegel G., 'Erbfolge und Vermächtnis: Heres ex re certa und Vindikationslegat', in *Liber amicorum Professor Ignaz Seidl-Hohenveldern in honour of his 80th birthday* (The Hague, 1998), p. 339.

Keller M. and Kren Kostkiewicz J. 'Article 20', in *Zürcher Kommentar zum IPRG*, 2nd ed. (Zürich, 2004), p. 305.

Keller M. and Siehr K., *Allgemeine Lehren des internationalen Privatrechts* (Zürich, 1986).

Kerameus K., 'Article 38', in U. Magnus and P. Mankowski (eds), *Brussels I Regulation* (München, 2007), p. 641.

Kerridge R., 'Succession', in A. Burrows (ed), *English Private Law*, 3rd ed. (Oxford, 2013), p. 446

Khairallah G., 'La détermination de la loi applicable à la succession', in G. Khairallah and M. Revillard (eds), *Droit européen des successions internationales. Le règlement du 4 juillet 2012* (Paris, 2013), p. 47.

Kindler P., 'Der Aktionär im toskanischen Lebensabend – Zum Kollisionsrecht der Testamentsgestaltung bei Auslandsdomizil unter der neuen EU-Erbverordnung', in *Festschrift für Eberhard Stilz* (München, 2014), p. 345.

Kindler P., 'From Nationality to Habitual Residence: Some Brief Remarks on the Future EU Regulation on International Successions and Wills', in *Convergence and Divergence in Private International Law – Liber Amicorum Kurt Siehr* (The Hague, Zurich, 2010), p. 251.

Kindler P., 'La legge regolatrice delle successioni nella proposta di regolamento dell'Unione europea: qualche riflessione in tema di carattere universale, rinvio e professio juris', *Riv dir int* (2011), p. 422.

Kindler P., 'Vom Staatsangehörigkeits- zum Domizilprinzip: das künftige internationale Erbrecht der Europäischen Union', *IPRax* (2010), p. 44.

Kinsch P., 'Droits de l'homme, droits fondamentaux et droit international privé', *Hague Recueil* vol. 318 (2005), p. 9.

Kleinschmidt J., 'Art. 62-73 EuErbVO', in M. Würdinger (ed), *Juris Praxiskommentar BGB, Internationales Privatrecht,* vol. VI, 7th ed. (Saarbrücken, 2014).

Kleinschmidt J., 'Optionales Erbrecht: Das Europäische Nachlasszeugnis als Herausforderung an das Kollisionsrecht', *RabelsZ* (2013), p. 723.

Knot J. G., 'Uitvoering van de Europese Erfrechtverordening in Nederland: wijziging van Boek 10 BW en inpassing van de Europese erfrechtverklaring', *TE – Tijdschrift Erfrecht* (2014), p. 36.

Köhler A., '*Kommentierung der europäischen Erbrechtsverordnung*', in L. Kroiß, C.-H. Horn and D. Solomon (eds), *Nachfolgerecht,* Baden-Baden (2014).

Kohler C., 'L'autonomie de la volonté en droit international privé: un principe universel entre libéralisme et étatisme', *Hague Recueil,* vol. 359 (2013), p. 289.

Kohler M. and Buschbaum M., 'Die „Anerkennung" öffentlicher Urkunden? – Kritische Gedanken über einen zweifelhaften Ansatz in der EU-Kollisionsrechtsvereinheitlichung', *IPRax* (2010), p. 313.

Kohler M. and Buschbaum M., 'La "reconnaissance" des actes authentiques prévue pour les successions transfrontalières. Réflexions critiques sur une approche douteuse entamée dans l'harmonisation des règles de conflits de lois', *Rev crit dr int priv* (2010), p. 643.

Kohler C. and Pintens W., 'Ehe und Familien im europäischen Recht – Entwicklung und Tendenzen', *FamRZ* (2007), p. 1481.

Kohler C. and Pintens W., 'Entwicklungen im europäischen Familien- und Erbrecht 2011–2012', *FamRZ* (2012), p. 1425.

Korkisch F., 'Der Anteil der nordischen Länder an den Fragen des internationalen Privatrechts', *RabelsZ* (1958), p. 599.

Kreße B., 'Die Auslegung mehrsprachiger Texte durch den EuGH', in I. Burr and G. Gréciano (eds), *Sprache und Recht – La construction européenne* (Baden-Baden, 2003), p. 157.

Kreße B., 'Mehrsprachigkeit im Recht der Europäischen Union', *Zeitschrift für Rechtspolitik* (2014), p. 11.

Kropholler J., *Europäisches Zivilprozeßrecht,* 6th ed. (Heidelberg, 1998); 8th ed. (Frankfurt am Main, 2005).

Kropholler J., *Internationales Privatrecht einschließlich der Grundbegriffe des Internationalen Privatrechts,* 6th ed. (Tübingen, 2006).

Kropholler J. and von Hein J., *Europäisches Zivilprozessrecht,* 9th ed. (Frankfurt am Main, 2011).

Kruger Th., *Civil Jurisdiction Rules of the EU and Their Impact on Third States* (Oxford, 2008).

Kuhn H., *Der Renvoi im internationalen Erbrecht der Schweiz* (Zürich, 1998).

Kühne G., *Die Parteiautonomie im internationalen Erbrecht* (Bielefeld, 1973).

Kühne G., 'Testierfreiheit und Rechtswahl im internationalen Erbrecht. Die Parteiautonomie: eine "basic rule" des Kollisionsrechts?', *Juristen Zeitung* (1973), p. 403.

Kunz L., 'Die neue Europäische Erbrechtsverordnung – ein Überblick, Teil I', *GPR – Zeitschrift für das Privatrecht der Europäischen Union* (2012), p. 208.

Lafuente Sánchez R., 'Hacia un sistema unitario europeo en materia de ley aplicable a las sucesiones internacionales', *CdT* 5/2 (2013), p. 350.

Lagarde P., 'Développements futurs du droit international privé dans une Europe en voie d'unification: quelques conjectures', *RabelsZ* (2004), p. 225.

Lagarde P., 'La nouvelle Convention de La Haye sur la loi applicable aux successions', *Rev crit dr int priv* (1989), p. 249.

Lagarde P., 'La reconnaissance – mode d'emploi', in *Vers de nouveaux équilibres entre ordres juridiques. Liber Amicorum Hélène Gaudemet-Tallon* (Paris, 2008), p. 481.

Lagarde P., 'La théorie de l'ordre public international face à la polygamie et à la répudiation: l'expérience française', in *Nouveaux itinéraires en droit: hommage à François Rigaux* (Bruxelles, 1993), p. 263.

Lagarde P., 'Les principes de base du nouveau règlement européen sur les successions', *Rev crit dr int priv* (2012), p. 691.

Lagarde P., 'Observations sur l'articulation des questions de statut personnel et des questions alimentaires dans l'application des conventions de droit international privé', in A. E. von Overbeck (ed), *Conflits et harmonisation – Kollision und Vereinheitlichung – Conflicts and Harmonization* (Freiburg, 1990), p. 521.

Lagarde P., 'Présentation du règlement sur les successions', in G. Khairallah and M. Revillard (eds) *Droit européen des successions internationales (Le Règlement du 4 juillet 2012)* (Paris, 2013), p. 5.

Lagarde P., 'Successions', *Répertoire de droit international*, 2nd ed., vol. V, (Dalloz, 1998), par. 227.

Lagarde P., *Recherches sur l'ordre public en droit international privé* (Paris, 1959).

Lamont R., 'Case C-523/07, A, Judgment of the Court of Justice (Third Chamber) of 2 April 2009, not yet reported', *CMLRev* (2010), p. 235.

Lange H., 'Wohnsitz und Wohnung, einheitlicher und mehrfacher Wohnsitz bei Eltern und Kindern', in *Entwicklungstendenzen im Wirtschafts- und Unternehmensrecht: Festschrift für Horst Bartholomeyczik zum 70. Geburtstag* (Berlin, 1973), p. 241.

Lange K. W., 'Europäisches Nachlasszeugnis – Antragsverfahren und Verwendung im deutschen Grundbuchverkehr', *DNotZ – Deutsche Notar-Zeitschrift* (2016), p. 103.

Lange K. W., 'Das Europäische Nachlasszeugnis', in A. Dutta and S. Herrler (eds), *Die Europäische Erbrechtsverordnung* (München, 2014), p. 161.

Lange K. W., 'Das geplante Europäische Nachlasszeugnis', *Deutsche Notar-Zeitschrift* (2012), p. 168.

Laukemann B., 'Die lex rei sitae in der Europäischen Erbrechtsverordnung – Inhalt, Schranken und Funktion', in *Ars aequi et boni in mundo. Festschrift für Rolf A. Schütze zum 80. Geburtstag* (München, 2014), p. 325 (also available in Max Planck Institute Luxembourg for International, European and Regulatory Procedural Law, *Working Paper Series 2/2014*, at www.mpi.lu, last accessed 10 July 2016).

Laukemann B., in E. Jayme, B. Hess and T. Pfeiffer (eds), *Stellungnahme zum Vorschlag für eine europäische Erbrechtsverordnung Version 2009/157 (COD) vom 16.1.2012* (Brussels, 2012), p. 32.

Lauterbach W., 'Anmerkung zu RG 15.11.1941', *Deutsches Recht, Ausgabe A* (1942), p. 535.

Lawson F. H. and Rudden B., *The Law of Property*, 3rd ed. (Oxford, 2002).

Layton A. and Mercer H., *European Civil Practice*, 2nd ed., vol. I (London, 2004).

Le Guidec R. and Chabot G., 'Succession', in *Répertoire Droit Civil Dalloz* (Paris, 2013).

Leandro A., 'La giurisdizione nel regolamento dell'Unione europea sulle successioni mortis causa', in P. Franzina and A. Leandro (eds), *Il diritto internazionale privato europeo delle successioni mortis causa* (Milano, 2013), p. 59.

Leandro A., 'Prime osservazioni sul regolamento (UE) n. 1215/2012 ("Bruxelles I bis")', *Il giusto processo civile* (2013), p. 583.

Lechner K., 'Die Entwicklung der Erbrechtsverordnung – Eine Einführung zum Gesetzgebungsverfahren', in A. Dutta and S. Herrler (eds), *Die Europäische Erbrechtsverordnung* (München, 2014), p. 12.

Lechner K., 'Die EuErbVO im Spannungsfeld zwischen Erbstatut und Sachenrecht', *IPRax* (2013), p. 497.

Lechner K., 'Erbverträge und gemeinschaftliche Testamente in der neuen EU-Erbrechtsverordnung', *NJW* (2013), p. 26.

Lehmann D., 'Der Referentenentwurf für ein Begleitgesetz zur EuErbVO', *ZEV – Zeitschrift für Erbrecht und Vermögensnachfolge* (2014), p. 234.

Lehmann D., 'Die EU-Erbrechtsverordnung zur Abwicklung grenzüberschreitender Nachlässe', *DStR – Deutsches Steuerrecht* 41 (2012), p. 2085.

Lehmann D., *Die Reform des Internationalen Erb- und Erbprozessrechts im Rahmen der geplanten Brüssel-IV Verordnung* (Angelbachtal, 2006).

Leible S., 'Brussels I-VO', in T. Rauscher, *Europäisches Zivilprozess und Kollisionsrecht* (München, 2011), p. 743.

Leipold D., 'Ist unser Erbrecht noch zeitgemäß? Gedankensplitter zu einem großen Thema', *Juristenzeitung* (2010), p. 802.

Leitzen M., 'EuErbVO: Praxisfragen an der Schnittstelle zwischen Erb- und Gesellschaftsrecht', *ZEV* (2012), p. 520.

Leleu Y.-H., *La transmission de la succession en droit comparé* (Bruxelles, 1996).

Leleu Y.-H., 'Les pactes successoraux en droit comparé', in *Les relations contractuelles internationales. Le rôle du notaire* (Antwerpen-Apeldoorn, 1995), p. 546.

Lenaerts K. and Gutman K., 'The Comparative Law Method and the Court of Justice of the European Union: Interlocking Legal Orders Revisited', in M. Andenas and D. Fairgrieve (eds), *Courts and Comparative Law* (Oxford, 2015), p. 163.

Lequette Y., 'Le droit international privé de la famille à l'épreuve des conventions internationales', *Hague Recueil* vol. 246 (1994), p. 9.

Leroyer A. M., *Droit des successions*, 2nd ed. (Paris, 2011).

Linke H., 'Ungelöste Probleme des europäischen Zivilverfahrensrechts. Anderweitige Rechtshängigkeit - zusammenhängende Verfahren - unvereinbare Entscheidungen', *RIW* (1988), p. 822.

Lipstein K., 'Private International Law - Bona Vacantia and Ultimus Heres', *CLJ* (1954), p. 22.

Lisanti C., 'La professio iuris dans le Règlement successions du 4 juillet 2012', *Gaz Pal* 165–16 (2013) p. 1574.

Löber B. and Huzel E., 'Erbrecht in Spanien', in R. Süß (ed), *Erbrecht in Europa*, 2nd ed. (Bonn, 2008), p. 1409.

Lokin P., 'De Erfrechtverordening', *NIPR* (2013), p. 329.

Lopes Pegna O., *I procedimenti relativi all'efficacia delle decisioni straniere in materia civile* (Padova, 2009).

Lorenzen E. G., 'The Qualification, Classification, or Characterization problem in the Conflict of Laws', *Yale Law School Faculty Scholarship Series* (1941), paper 4584.

Lowenthal M. and Schwank F., 'Austria', in L. Garb and J. Wood (eds), *International Succession*, 3rd ed. (Oxford, 2010), p. 42.

Lübcke D., *Das neue europäische Internationale Nachlassverfahrensrecht* (Baden-Baden, 2013).

Lupoi M. A., *Conflitti transnazionali di giurisdizioni* (Milano, 2002).

Luzzatto R., 'Commorienza', in *Novissimo Digesto Italiano*, vol. III (Torino, 1959), p. 675.

Madriñán Vázquez M., *El Derecho de Representación en la Sucesión Testada* (Cizur Menor, 2009).

Magnus R., 'Gerichtsstandsvereinbarungen im Erbrecht?', *IPRax* (2013), p. 393.

Magnus U. and Mankowski P. (eds), *Brussels I Regulation* (München, 2007); 2nd ed. (München, 2011).

Majer C. F., 'Die Geltung der EU-Erbrechtsverordnung für reine Drittstaatensachverhalte', *ZEV* (2011), p. 445.

Makowsky M., 'Art. 39-61 EuErbVO', in R. Hüßtege and H.-P. Mansel (eds), *NomosKommentar, BGB, Rom-Verordnungen*, vol. VI, 2nd ed. (Baden-Baden, 2015).

Malaurie P., *Droit civil. Les successions, les libéralités*, 5th ed. (Paris, 2012).

Malaurie P., *Les successions. Les libéralités* (Paris, 2004).

Mankowski P., '§7. Der Allgemeine Teil des deutschen Internationalen Privatrechts', in C. von Bar and P. Mankowski, *Internationales Privatrecht*, 2nd ed., vol. I (München, 2003), p. 561.

Mankowski P., 'Das erbrechtliche Viertel nach § 1371 Abs. 1 BGB im deutschen und europäischen Internationalen Privatrecht', *ZEV* (2014), p. 121.

Mankowski P., 'Der gewöhnliche Aufenthalt eines verbrachten Kindes unter der Brüssel IIa-VO – Anmerkung zu EuGH, Urt. v. 22.12.2010 – Rs. C-497/10 PPU', *GPR – Zeitschrift für das Privatrecht der Europäischen Union* (2011), p. 209.

Mann F. A., 'Der "gewöhnliche Aufenthalt" im Internationalen Privatrecht', *Juristenzeitung* (1956), p. 466.

Mansel H.-P., 'Anerkennung als Grundprinzip des Europäischen Rechtsraums – Zur Herausbildung eines europäischen Anerkennungs-Kollisionsrechts: Anerkennung statt Verweisung als neues Strukturprinzip des Europäischen internationalen Privatrechts', *RabelsZ* (2006), p. 654.

Mansel H.-P., 'Art. 43 EGBGB', in *J. von Staudingers Kommentar zum Bürgerlichen Gesetzbuch mit Einführungsgesetz und Nebengesetzen – EGBGB/IPR Art 43–46 (Internationales Sachenrecht)* (Berlin, 2015).

Mansel H.-P., 'Das Staatsangehörigkeitsprinzip im deutschen und gemeinschaftlichen IPR: Schutz der kulturellen Identität oder Diskriminierung der Person?', in E. Jayme (ed), *Kulturelle Identität und internationales Privatrecht* (Heidelberg, 2003), p. 119.

Mansel H.-P., 'Kritisches zur "Urkundsinhaltsanerkennung"', *IPRax* (2011), p. 342.

Mansel H.-P., 'Vereinheitlichung des Internationalen Erbrechts in der Europäischen Gemeinschaft – Kompetenzfragen und Regelungsgrundsätze', in *Prof. Dr. Tuğrul Ansay'a armağan* (Ankara, 2006), p. 185.

Mansel H.-P., Coester-Waltjen D., Henrich D. and Kohler C., 'Stellungnahme im Auftrag des Deutschen Rats für Internationales Privatrecht zum Grünbuch der Europäischen Kommission "Weniger Verwaltungsaufwand für EU-Bürger: Den freien Verkehr öffentlicher Urkunden und die Anerkennung der Rechtswirkungen von Personenstandsurkunden erleichtern" – KOM(2010) 747 endg', *IPRax* (2011), p. 335.

Mansel H.-P., Thorn K. and Wagner R., 'Europäisches Kollisionsrecht 2010: Verstärkte Zusammenarbeit als Motor der Vereinheitlichung?', *IPRax* (2011), p. 1.

Mansel H.-P., Thorn K. and Wagner R., 'Europäisches Kollisionsrecht 2012: Voranschreiten des Kodifikationsprozesses – Flickenteppich des Einheitsrechts', *IPRax* (2013), p. 1.

Marchadier F., *Les objectives généraux du droit international privé à l'épreuve de la Convention européenne des droits de l'homme* (Bruxelles, 2007).

Margonski, M. 'Ausländische Vindikationslegate nach der EU-Erbrechtsverordnung', *GPR – Zeitschrift für Gemeinschaftsprivatrecht* (2013), p. 109.

Mari L., *Il diritto processuale civile della Convenzione di Bruxelles. (I) Il sistema della competenza* (Padova, 1999).

Marino S., 'La proposta di regolamento sulla cooperazione giudiziaria in materia di successioni', *Riv dir int* (2010), p. 463.

Mariottini C. M., 'The Proposed Recast of the Brussels I Regulation and Forum non conveniens in the European Union Judicial Area', in F. Pocar, I. Viarengo and F. C. Villata (eds), *Recasting Brussels I* (Padova, 2012), p. 285.

Mariottini C., 'Successione di cittadino straniero: questioni di diritto internazionale privato e processuale alla luce della proposta di regolamento europeo sulle successioni internazionali', *Persona, famiglia e successioni* (2012), p. 110.

Marmisse A. and Wilderspin M., 'Le régime jurisprudentiel des mesures provisoires à la lumière des arrêts *Van Uden et Mietz*', *Rev crit dr int priv* (1999), p. 669.

Marongiu Buonaiuti F., 'Emanazione di provvedimenti inibitori a sostegno della competenza arbitrale e reciproca fiducia tra i sistemi giurisdizionali degli Stati membri dell'Unione europea', *Rivista dell'arbitrato* (2009), p. 245.

Marongiu Buonaiuti F., 'La disciplina della litispendenza nei rapporti tra giudici di paesi membri e giudici di paesi terzi nella proposta di revisione del regolamento n. 44/2001', *Riv dir int* (2011), p. 496.

Marongiu Buonaiuti F., 'La tutela del diritto di accesso alla giustizia e della parità delle armi tra i litiganti nella proposta di revisione del regolamento n. 44/2001', in A. Di Stefano and R. Sapienza (eds), *La tutela dei diritti umani e il diritto internazionale* (Napoli 2012), p. 345.

Marongiu Buonaiuti F., *Le obbligazioni non contrattuali nel diritto internazionale privato* (Milano, 2013), p. 133.

Marongiu Buonaiuti F., 'Lis Alibi Pendens and Related Actions in the Relationships With the Courts of Third Countries in the Recast of the Brussels I Regulation', *YPIL* 15 (2013/2014), p. 87.

Marongiu Buonaiuti F., *Litispendenza e connessione internazionale. Strumenti di coordinamento tra giurisdizioni statali in materia civile* (Napoli, 2008).

Marongiu Buonaiuti F., 'Per una prima lettura del regolamento "Bruxelles I *bis*": il nuovo regime della litispendenza e della connessione privativa', www.aldricus.com (19 December 2012, n. 2).

Marongiu Buonaiuti F., 'Rinuncia all'immunità dello Stato estero dalle misure coercitive e tutela del diritto di accesso alla giustizia in alcune pronunce recenti della Cour de cassation francese', *Diritti umani e diritto internazionale* (2013), p. 615.

Martínez de Aguirre Aldaz C., 'Partición hereditaria: conceptos generales, operaciones particionales y tipos de partición', in M. A. Pérez Álvarez (ed), *Curso de Derecho Civil (V) Derecho de sucesiones* (Madrid, 2013), pp. 443–465.

Martiny D., *Handbuch des Internationalen Zivilverfahrensrechts*, vol. III (Tübingen, 1984).

Martiny D., 'Lex rei sitae as a connecting factor in EU Private International Law', *IPRax* (2012), p. 119.

Mäsch G., 'Keine Anwendbarkeit von Artikel 34 Nummer 4 auf unvereinbare Entscheidungen aus demselben Mitgliedstaat', *EuZW* (2013), p. 905.

Mayer P. and Heuzé V., *Droit international privé*, 11th ed. (Issy-les Moulineaux, 2014).

Mayer P., 'La reconnaissance: notions et méthodes', in P. Lagarde (ed), *La reconnaissance des situations en droit international privé* (Paris, 2013), p. 27.

Max Planck Institute for Comparative and International Private Law, 'Comments on the European Commission's Proposal for a Regulation of the European Parliament and of the Council on Jurisdiction, Applicable Law, Recognition and Enforcement of Decisions and Authentic Instruments in Matters of Succession and the Creation of a European Certificate of Succession', *RabelsZ* (2010), p. 522.

McEleavy P., 'Brussels II bis: Matrimonial Matters, Parental Responsibility, Child Abduction and Mutual Recognition', *ICLQ* (2004), p. 503.

Medainis H., 'The Brussels I Regulation and the Cyprus problem before the Court of Justice. Comment on Apostolides v Orams', *ELRev* (2009), p. 963.

Meeusen J., 'Le droit international privé et le principe de non-discrimination', *Hague Recueil* vol. 353 (2012), p. 137.

Merlin E., 'Le misure provvisorie e cautelari nello spazio giudiziario europeo: criteri di giurisdizione e limiti alla circolazione', in *Le discipline comunitarie relative al processo civile* (Milano, 2002), p. 222.

Merlin E., 'Riconoscimento ed esecutività della decisione straniera nel regolamento Bruxelles I', *Riv dir proc* (2001), p. 433.

Merrett L., 'The Enforcement of Jurisdiction Agreements within the Brussels Regime', *ICLQ* (2006), p. 315.

Meyer M., *Die Gerichtsstände der Erbrechtsverordnung unter besonderer Berücksichtigung des Forum Shopping* (Frankfurt am Main, 2013).

Michaels R., 'Die europäische IPR-Revolution – Regulierung, Europäisierung, Mediatisierung', in *Die richtige Ordnung: Festschrift für Jan Kropholler zum 70. Geburtstag* (Tübingen, 2008), p. 151.

Migliazza A., 'Successione – VII) Diritto internazionale privato e processuale', in *Enciclopedia Giuridica*, XXX, (Roma, 1993).

Moccia L., 'Basic Ways of Defining Property', in *Studi in memoria di Michele Giorgianni* (Napoli, 2007), p. 761.

Moccia L., 'Riflessioni sull'idea di proprietà', *Riv trim dir proc civ* (2008), p. 21.
Moissinac-Massénat V., *Les conflits de procédures et de décisions en droit international privé* (Paris, 2007).
Morelli G., *Diritto processuale civile internazionale*, 2nd ed. (Padova, 1954).
Moura Vicente D., *Direito Internacional Privado: Textos normativos e fundamentais* (Coimbra, 2012).
Moura Vicente D., 'La proprieté intellectuelle en droit international privé', *Hague Recueil*, vol. 335 (2008), p. 105.
Müller-Lukoschek J., *Die neue EU-Erbrechtsverordnung: Einführung in die neue Rechtslage* (Bonn, 2013).
Müller-Lukoschek J., *Die neue EU-Erbrechtsverordnung*, 2nd ed. (Berlin, 2015).
Nioche M., 'Reconnaissance d'une décision étrangère d'incompétence prise sur le fondement d'une clause attributive de juridiction', *Rev cr dr int priv* (2013), p. 686.
Nordmeier C. F., Artt. 62–73 EuErbVO, in R. Hüßtege and H.-P. Mansel (eds), *Nomos-Kommentar BGB*, vol. 6 (Rom-Verordnungen zum Internationalen Privatrecht), 2nd ed. (Baden-Baden, 2015), p. 1034.
Nordmeier C. F., 'Erbverträge und nachlassbezogene Rechtsgeschäfte in der EuErbVO – eine Begriffsklärung', *ZEV* (2013), p. 117.
Nordmeier C. F., 'Grundfragen der Rechtswahl in der neuen EU-Erbrechtsverordnung – eine Untersuchung des Art. 22 ErbRVO', *GPR - Zeitschrift für das Privatrecht der Europäischen Union* (2013), p. 148.
Nordmeier C. F., 'Stand, Perspektiven und Grenzen der Rechtslagenanerkennung im europäischen Rechtsraum anhand der Entscheidungen mitgliedstaatlicher Gerichte', *IPRax* (2012), p. 31.
Nourissat C., 'Le futur droit des successions internationales de l'Union européenne', *Defrénois* 13 (2010), p. 394.
Nourissat C., Callé P., Pasqualis P. and Wautelet P., 'Pour la reconnaissance des actes authentiques au sein de l'espace de liberté, de sécurité et de justice', *Petites affiches* (2012), p. 6.
Novelli G., *Compendio di diritto internazionale privato e processuale*, 7th ed. (Napoli, 2004).
Nuyts A., 'Article 11', in J. Erauw et al. (eds), *Het Wetboek internationaal Privaatrecht becommentarieerd – Le code de droit international privé commenté* (Oxford, Bruxelles, 2006), p. 64.
Nuyts A., 'La refonte du règlement Bruxelles I', *Rev crit dr int priv* (2013), p. 1.
Odersky F., 'Die Europäische Erbrechtsverordnung in der Gestaltungspraxis', *Notar* (2013), p. 4.
Omlor S., 'Gutglaubensschutz durch das Europäische Nachlasszeugnis', *European Union Private Law Review* (2014), p. 216.

Othenin-Girard S., 'Quelques observations sur le for de nécessité en droit international privé suisse', *RSuisseDIE* (1999), p. 251.

Pålsson L., 'Interim Relief under the Brussels and Lugano Conventions', in *Private Law in the International Arena - Liber amicorum Kurt Siehr* (The Hague, 2000), p. 621.

Pamboukis C., 'La renaissance-métamorphose de la méthode de reconnaissance', *Rev crit dr int priv* (2008), p. 513.

Pattar A. K., *Islamisch inspiriertes Erbrecht und deutscher Ordre public: Die Erbrechtsordnungen von Ägypten, Tunesien und Marokko und ihre Anwendbarkeit im Inland* (Berlin, 2007).

Persano F., 'Il rilievo della litispendenza internazionale nella convenzione di Bruxelles del 1968: la nozione di «stesse parti»', *Riv dir int priv proc* (2000), p. 713 *et seq.*

Perscha A., 'Art 62–68, 70–73 EuErbVO', in A. Deixler-Hübner and M. Schauer (eds), *EuErbVO - Kommentar zur EU-Erbrechtsverordnung* (Wien, 2015), p. 496.

Pertegás Sender M., 'Article 31', in U. Magnus and P. Mankowski (eds), *Brussels I Regulation* (München, 2007), p. 522.

Picheral C., *L'ordre public européen* (Paris, 2001).

Picone P., 'La legge applicabile alle successioni', in *La riforma del diritto internazionale privato e i suoi riflessi sull'attività notarile, Atti Convegno di studi in onore di Mario Marano* (Milano, 1991), p. 99.

Piekenbrock A., 'Kann der Ausschluß des ordre public in Art. 28 Abs. 3 EuGVÜ ausnahmslos gelten?' *IPRax* (2000), p. 364.

Pirrung J., 'Der gewöhnliche Aufenthalt des Kindes in internationalen Sorgerechtssachen - zum Urteil des EuGH vom 2. April 2009 in der Rechtssache A - C-523/07', in *Festschrift für Gunther Kühne zum 70. Geburtstag* (Frankfurt am Main, 2009), p. 843.

Pocar F., 'Faut-il remplacer le renvoi au droit national par des règles uniformes dans l'article 4 du règlement No. 44/2001?', in *Vers des nouveaux équilibres entre ordres juridiques. Liber amicorum Hélène Gaudemet-Tallon* (Paris, 2008), p. 573.

Pocar F., 'Révision de Bruxelles I et ordre juridique international: quelle approche uniforme?', *Riv dir int priv proc* (2011), p. 59.

Pocar F., *La Convenzione di Bruxelles sulla giurisdizione e l'esecuzione delle sentenze* (Milano, 1989).

Popa M. F., 'Brief Overview of the Rules Governing the Conflict of Laws in Succession Matters According to the New Romanian Civil Code', in *International Conference: CKS 2013 - Challenges of the Knowledge Society* (Bucharest, 2013), p. 366.

Popescu D. A., 'Some remarks on the applicable law to international succession in Romania', *YPIL* (2007), p. 277.

Quadri R., 'La successione dello Stato nel diritto internazionale privato', *Riv dir int* (1958), p. 51.

Queirolo I., 'Choice-of-Court Agreements in the New Brussels I-bis Regulation: A Critical Appraisal', *YPIL* 15 (2013/2014), p. 113.

Quinzá Redondo P. and Christandl G., 'Ordenamientos plurilegislativos en el Reglamento (UE) de Sucesiones con especial referencia al ordenamiento jurídico español', *InDret* 3 (2013), p. 1.

Rabel E., 'Das Problem der Qualifikation', *RabelsZ* (1931), p. 241.

Raitio J., 'The Principle of Legal Certainty as a General Principle of EU Law', in U. Bernitz, J. Nergelius and C. Cardner (eds), *General Principles of EC Law in a Process of Development* (Alphen aan den Rijn, 2008), p. 47.

Rauscher T. (ed.), *Europäisches Zivilprozessrecht / Europäisches Internationales Privatrecht* (Köln, 2015).

Rauscher T. (ed.), *Europäisches Zivilprozess und Kollisionsrecht* (München, 2011).

Rauscher T., 'Heimatlos in Europa? – Gedanken gegen eine Aufgabe des Staatsangehörigkeitsprinzips im IPR', in *Festschrift für Erik Jayme*, vol. I (München, 2004), pp. 719–745.

Ravidà F., 'Il regolamento n. 44/2001 sulla competenza giurisdizionale, il riconoscimento e l'esecuzione delle decisioni in materia civile e commerciale', in S. Scarafoni (ed), *Il processo civile e la normativa comunitaria* (Torino, 2012), p. 270.

Raynard J., 'De l'influence de la Convention européenne des droits de l'homme sur l'ordre public... international: de l'extra territorialité de la Convention européenne des droits de l'homme', *Rev trim dr civ* (2000), p. 944.

Rechberger W. H., 'Das Europäische Nachlasszeugnis und seine Wirkungen', *Österreichische Juristen-Zeitung* (2012), p. 14.

Rechberger W. H. and Kieweler F., 'Das Europäische Nachlasszeugnis', in W. H. Rechberger and B. Zöchling-Jud (eds), *Die EU-Erbrechtsverordnung in Österreich* (Wien, 2015), p. 269.

Reithmann C., 'Urkunden ausländischer Notare in inländischen Verfahren', *IPRax* (2012), p. 133.

Resch R., 'Wohnsitzerfordernis bei beitragsunabhängigen Sonderleistungen', *European Law Reporter* (1999), p. 188.

Rétornaz V. and Volders B., 'Le for de nécessité: tableau comparatif et évolutif', *Rev crit dr int priv* (2008), p. 225.

Revillard M., *Droit international privé et communautaire: pratique notariale*, 7th ed. (Paris, 2010).

Revillard M., 'Portée de la loi applicable', in G Khairallah and M. Revillard (eds), *Droit européen des successions internationales (Le Règlement du 4 juillet 2012)* (Paris, 2013), p. 67.

Revillard M., 'Successions internationales: le règlement du Parlement européen et du Conseil du 4 julliet 2012 en matière de successions', *Defrenois* (2012), p. 743.

Ricci C., 'Il foro della residenza abituale nel Regolamento n° 2201/2003 e nella proposta Roma III', in A.-L. Calvo Caravaca and E. Castellanos Ruíz (eds), *La Unión Europea ante el Derecho de la Globalización* (Madrid, 2008), p. 421.

Richez-Pons A., 'Commentaire CJCE, 4 avr. 2009, affaire C-523/07', *GPR – Zeitschrift für das Privatrecht der Europäischen Union* (2009), p. 247.

Richez-Pons A., 'La notion de résidence', in H. Fulchiron and C. Nourissat (eds), *Le nouveau droit communautaire du divorce et de la responsabilité parentale* (Paris, 2005), p. 149.

Richters P., 'Anwendungsprobleme der EuErbVO im deutsch-britischen Rechtsverkehr', *ZEV* (2012), p. 576.

Riezler E., *Internationales Zivilprozessrecht und prozessuales Fremdenrecht* (Berlin, 1949).

Rodríguez Benot A., 'La acreditación de la cualidad de administrador de una herencia internacional: el certificado Europeo de heredero', in R. Viñas and G. Garriga (cords.), *Perspectivas del Derecho sucesorio en Europa* (Barcelona, 2009), p. 175.

Rodríguez Rodrigo J., 'El centro de intereses principales, como foro de competencia internacional en el Reglamento 1346/2000, en el caso de un grupo de sociedades', *Anuario de Derecho concursal* 33 (2014), p. 501.

Rodríguez Sánchez S., *Una introducción al Reglamento de Sucesiones de la UE (desde la perspectiva de los derechos reales sobre bienes inmuebles y el Registro de la Propiedad en España)* (Madrid, 2013).

Rodríguez-Uría Suárez I., 'La ley aplicable a las sucesiones mortis causa en el Reglamento (UE) 650/2012', *InDret* 2 (2013), p. 1.

Rodríguez-Uría Suárez I., 'Nota a la STS de 11 de marzo 2010', *Rev esp der int* (2010), p. 251.

Rogerson P., *Collier's Conflict of Laws*, 4th ed. (Cambridge, 2013).

Rohe M., 'Staatsangehörigkeit oder Lebensmittelpunkt? – Anknüpfungsgerechtigkeit im Lichte neuerer Entwicklungen', in *Festschrift für Dietrich Rothoeft zum 65. Geburtstag* (München, 1994), p. 1.

Romano G. P., 'La bilatéralité éclipsée par l'autorité', *Rev crit dr int priv* (2006), p. 457.

Rosoux H., 'Arrêt sur le régime transitoire du Règlement successions', *Revue de planification patrimoniale belge et international* (2014), p. 157.

Rossolillo G., 'Forum necessitatis e flessibilità dei criteri di giurisdizione nel diritto internazionale privato nazionale e dell'Unione europea', *CdT* 2/1 (2010), p. 403.

Roth H., 'Der Einwand der Nichtzustellung des verfahrenseinleitenden Schriftstücks (Art. 34 Nr. 2, 54 EuGVVO) und die Anforderungen an Versäumnisurteile im Lichte des Art. 34 Nr. 1 EuGVVO', *IPRax* (2013), p. 402.

Roth H., 'Europäischer Rechtskraftbegriff im Zuständigkeitsrecht?' *IPRax* (2014) p. 136.

Roth W.-H., 'Der Einfluß des Europäischen Gemeinschaftsrechts auf das Internationale Privatrecht', *RabelsZ* (1991), p. 623.

Salerno F, *Giurisdizione ed efficacia delle decisioni straniere nel regolamento (CE) n. 44/2001 (La revisione della Convenzione di Bruxelles del 1968)*, 3rd ed. (Padova, 2006).

Salerno F., *Giurisdizione ed efficacia delle decisioni straniere nel Regolamento (UE) n. 1215/2012 (rifusione)*, 4th ed. (Padova, 2015).

Salerno F., 'Il diritto processuale civile internazionale comunitario e le garanzie processuali fondamentali', in P. Picone (ed), *Diritto internazionale privato e diritto comunitario* (Padova, 2004), p. 95.

Salerno F., 'La giurisdizione volontaria nella legge di riforma di diritto internazionale privato', *Riv dir int* (2005), p. 620.

Salten U. and Gräve K., *Gerichtliches Mahnverfahren und Zwangsvollstreckung* (Köln, 2007).

Salvadego L., 'I provvedimenti conservativi in funzione dell'esecuzione di una sentenza straniera secondo il regolamento "Bruxelles I"', *N giur civ comm* (2012) p. 931.

Sandrini L., 'La tutela del creditore in pendenza del procedimento di "exequatur" nel regolamento Bruxelles I', *Riv dir int priv proc* (2012), p. 595.

Sandrini L., *Tutela cautelare in funzione di giudizi esteri* (Padova, 2012).

Sanna T., 'Steuerbefreiung bei der vorübergehenden Einfuhr von Kraftfahrzeugen aufgrund gewöhnlichen Wohnsitzes im Ausland', *European Law Reporter* (2001), p. 369.

Sauer I., *Internationale Zuständigkeit für die Auflösung und Lockerung des Ehebandes nach deutschem, französischem und europäischem Recht* (Regensburg, 2003).

Sauvage F., 'L'option et la transmission du passif dans les successions internationales au regard du règlement européen', in G Khairallah and M. Revillard (eds), *Droit européen des successions internationales (Le Règlement du 4 juillet 2012)* (Paris, 2013), p. 105.

Schack H., *Internationales Zivilverfahrensrecht*, 6th ed. (München, 2014).

Schack H., 'Was bleibt vom Renvoi?', *IPRax* (2013), p. 315.

Schaub R., 'Die EU-Erbrechtsverordnung', in K. Muscheler (ed), *Hereditare – Jahrbuch für Erbrecht und Schenkungsrecht*, vol. 3 (Tübingen, 2013), p. 91.

Schauer M., 'Europäisches Nachlasszeugnis', in M. Schauer and E. Scheuba (eds), *Europäische Erbrechtsverordnung* (Vienna, 2012), p. 73.

Scheucher L., 'Das Haager Testamentsformabkommen', *ZfRV* (1965), p. 216 and (1966), p. 85.

Schilling K., *Binnenmarktkollisionsrecht* (Berlin, 2006).

Schilling Th., 'Internationale Rechtshängigkeit vs. Entscheidung binnen angemessener Frist. Zum Zusammenspiel von Art. 6 I EMRK, Art. 307 EGV und Art. 27 EuGVV', *IPRax* (2004), p. 294.

Schlosser P., *EU- Zivilprozessrecht*, 3rd ed. (München, 2009).

Schmehl C., *Parallelverfahren und Justizgewährung: zur Verfahrenskoordination nach europäischem und deutschem Zivilprozessrecht am Beispiel taktischer "Torpedoklagen"* (Tübingen, 2011).

Schmidt J., 'Art. 68-73 EuErbVO', in C. Budzikiewicz, M.-P. Weller and W. Wurmnest (eds), *Beck-Online Großkommentar, EuErbVO* (München, 2014, 2015, 2016).

Schmidt J., 'Der Erbnachweis in Deutschland ab 2015: Erbschein vs. Europäisches Nachlasszeugnis', *ZEV* (2014), p. 389.

Schmidt J. P., 'Ausländische Vindikationslegate über im Inland belegene Immobilien - zur Bedeutung des Art. 1 Abs. 2 lit. l EuErbVO', *ZEV* (2014), p. 133.

Schmidt J. P., 'Die kollisionsrechtliche Behandlung dinglich wirkender Vermächtnisse', *RabelsZ* (2013), p. 1.

Schoenblum J. A., *Multistate and Multinational Estate Planning*, vol. I (Chicago, 2009).

Schoppe C., 'Die Übergangsbestimmungen zur Rechtswahl im internationalen Erbrecht: Anwendungsprobleme und Gestaltungspotential', *IPRax* (2014), p. 27.

Schurig K., 'Das internationale Erbrecht wird europäisch - Bemerkungen zur kommenden Europäischen Verordnung', in *Festschrift für Ulrich Spellenberg zum 70. Geburtstag* (München, 2010), p. 343.

Schwimann M., 'Das neue internationale Eherecht Österreichs', *Juristische Blätter* (1979), p. 341.

Scoles E. F. and Hay P., *Conflict of laws*, 2nd ed. (St. Paul, 1992).

Scoles E. F., Hay P. and Symeonides S. C., *Conflict of Laws*, 4th ed. (St. Paul, 2004).

Seatzu F., 'The Meaning of "same parties" in Article 21 of the Brussels Jurisdiction and Judgments Convention', *ELRev* (1999), p. 540.

Siehr K., 'Connecting Factors, Party Autonomy and Renvoi', in A. Malatesta, S. Bariatti and F. Pocar (eds), *The External Dimension of EC Private International Law in Family and Succession Matters* (Padova, 2008), p. 251.

Siehr K., 'Das internationale Erbrecht nach dem Gesetz zur Neuregelung des IPR', *IPrax* (1987), p. 4.

Siehr K., 'General Problems of Private International Law in Modern Codifications - *De Lege Lata* and *De Lege Europea Ferenda*', *YPIL* (2005), p. 17.

Siehr K., 'Kindesentführung und EuEheVO - Vorfragen und gewöhnlicher Aufenthalt im Europäischen Kollisionsrecht', *IPRax* (2012), p. 316.

Simon U. and Buschbaum M., 'Die neue EU-Erbrechtsverordnung', *NJW* (2012), p. 2393.

Simons T. and Hausmann R. (eds), *Unalex Kommentar Brüssel I-Verordnung: Kommentar zur VO (EG) 44/2001 und zum Übereinkommen von Lugano* (München, 2012).

Solomon D., 'Die Renaissance des Renvoi im Europäischen Internationalen Privatrecht', in *Liber Amicorum Klaus Schurig* (München, 2012), p. 237.

Sonnenberger H. J., 'Grenzen der Verweisung durch europäisches internationales Privatrecht', *IPRax* (2011), p. 325.

Sonnentag M., 'Das Europäische Internationale Erbrecht im Spannungsfeld zwischen der Anknüpfung an die Staatsangehörigkeit und den gewöhnlichen Aufenthalt', *Europäisches Wirtschafts- und Steuerrecht* (2012), p. 457.

Sonnentag M., *Der Renvoi im internationalen Privatrecht* (Tübingen, 2001).

Spellenberg U., *Zeitschrift für Zivilprozess, Internationaler Teil* 12 (2007), p. 233.

Stade S., 'Die EU-Erbrechtsverordnung aus französischer Sicht', *ZErb – Zeitschrift für die Steuer- und Erbrechtspraxis* (2015), p. 77.

Stella M., 'Default judgments inglesi alla prova dell'ordine pubblico processuale europeo, tra aneliti deflattivi esasperati e superiori istanze di un'equa tutela del contumace', *Int'l Lis* (2012), p. 171.

Stoll H., 'Rezension zu "Der 'gewöhnliche Aufenthalt' im Internationalen Privatrecht", JZ 1956, 466–470, von F.A. Mann', *RabelsZ* (1957), p. 187.

Sturm F., 'Parteiautonomie als bestimmender Faktor im internationalen Familien und Erbrecht', in *Recht und Rechtserkenntnis. Festschrift für Ernst Wolf zum 70. Geburtstag* (Berlin, Bonn, München, 1985), p. 637.

Sturm F. and Sturm G., 'Das europäische Nachlasszeugnis: Zum Vorschlag der Kommission vom 14. Oktober 2009', *Zbornik Pravnog fakulteta u Zagrebu* (2012), p. 309.

Stürner M., 'Deutsch-italienische Erbfälle unter der kommenden Europäischen Erbrechtsverordnung', *Jahrbuch für italienisches Recht* 26 (2013), p. 59.

Stürner R., 'Arts. 62–73 EuErbVO', in O. Jauernig, *Bürgerliches Gesetzbuch*, 16th ed. (München, 2015).

Suderow J., 'Cuestiones de jurisdicción internacional en torno a la aplicación privada del Derecho antitrust: forum shopping y "demandas torpedo"', *CdT* 2/2 (2010), p. 315.

Suderow J., 'Nuevas normas de litispendencia y conexidad para Europa: ¿El ocaso del torpedo italiano? ¿Flexibilidad versus previsibilidad?', *CdT* 5/1 (2013), p. 184.

Sujecki B., 'Unverhältnismäßige Beeinträchtigung des Anspruchs auf rechtliches Gehör', *EuZW* (2009), p. 424.

Sujecki B., *Mahnverfahren: mit elektronischem und europäischen Mahnverfahren* (Heideberg-München-Landsberg-Berlin, 2008).

Süß R., 'Das Europäische Nachlasszeugnis', *ZEuP* (2013), p. 725.

Süß R., 'Der Vorschlag der EG-Kommission zu einer Erbrechtsverordnung (Rom IV-Verordnung) vom 14. Oktober 2009', *ZErb – Zeitschrift für die Steuer- und Erbrechtspraxis* (2009), p. 342.

Süß R., 'Die Vindikationslage im internationalen Privatrecht', *RabelsZ* (2001), p. 244.

Swadling W., 'Property: General Principles', in A. Burrows (ed), *English Private Law*, 3rd ed. (Oxford, 2013), para. 4.01.

Tarzia G., 'Les titres exécutoires et le recouvrement des créances dans l'Union Européenne', *Actualité du droit/Annales de droit de Liège* (1995), p. 381.

Teixeira de Sousa M., 'Die Bekàmpfung der Torpedoklagen durch einen europàischen Rechtskrafteinwand', in *Recht ohne Grenzen: Festschrift für Athanassios Kaissis zum 65. Geburtstag* (München, 2012), p. 1017.

Thorn K., 'EuErbVO', in *Palandt Bürgerliches Gesetzbuch*, 74th ed. (München, 2015), p. 270.

Tiedemann A., 'Die Rechtswahl im deutschen Internationalen Erbrecht', *RabelsZ* (1991), p. 27.

Troge T., *Europarecht und das Staatsangehörigkeitsprinzip im internationalen Privatrecht* (Baden-Baden, 2009).

Ubertazzi L. C. and Ammendola M., *Il diritto d'autore* (Torino, 1993).

Valente M. G., 'Recenti pronunciamenti in tema di residenza fiscale delle persone fisiche', *Diritto e pratica tributaria* (2001), p. 847.

Van Drooghenbroeck J. F., 'Les compétences internationale et territoriale du juge du provisoire (Les mesures provisoires et le litige européen)', in J. van Campernolle and G. Tarzia (eds), *Les mesures provisoires en droit belge, français et italien* (Bruxelles, 1998), p. 485.

Van Erp S., 'The new Succession Regulation: The lex rei sitae rule in need of reappraisal?', *European Property Law Journal* (2012), p. 187.

Vaquer Aloy A., 'Reflexiones sobre una eventual reforma de la legítima', *Indret*, 3 (2007), p. 1.

Verbeke A.-L. and Leleu Y-H., 'Harmonization of the Law of Succession in Europe', in A. S. Hartkamp, M. W. Hesselink, E. H. Hondius, C. Mak and C. E. du Perron (eds), *Towards a European Civil Code*, 4th ed. (The Hague, 2010), p. 459.

Verdera Izquierdo B. and Munar Bernat P.A., 'Interpretación del testamento' in M. C. Gete-Alonso y Calera (ed), *Tratado de Derecho de Sucesiones*, vol. I (Cizur Menor, 2011), p. 647 .

Virgós Soriano M. and Rodríguez Pineau E., 'Succession Law and Renvoi: the Spanish Solution', in *Festschrift für Erik Jayme* (München, 2004), vol. I, p. 977.

Vischer F., 'Das "Droit moral de l'auteur" aus rechtsvergleichender und kollisionrechtlicher Sicht', in R. Frank (ed), *Recht und Kunst. Symposium aus Anlass des 80. Geburstages von Wolfram Müller-Freienfels* (Heidelberg, 1996), p. 85.

Volken P., 'Art. 3', in D. Girsberger *et al.* (eds), *Zürcher Kommentar zum IPRG*, 2nd ed. (Zürich, 2004), p. 48.

Vollmer P., 'Die neue europäische Erbrechtsverordnung – ein Überblick', *ZErb – Zeitschrift für die Steuer- und Erbrechtspraxis* (2012), p. 233.

Volmer M., 'Definitive Entscheidung von Vorfragen aufgrund der Gerichtszuständigkeit nach der EuErbVO', *ZEV – Zeitschrift für Erbrecht und Vermögensnachfolge* (2014), p. 130.

Volmer M., 'Die EU-Erbrechtsverordnung – erste Fragen an Dogmatik und Forensik', *Der Deutsche Rechtspfleger* (2013), p. 421.

Von Hoffmann B. and Hau W., 'Deutscher Prozeßvergleich kein Anerkennungshindernis nach Art. 27 Nr. 3 EuGVÜ', *IPRax* (1995), p. 217.

Von Overbeck A. E., 'La Convention du premier août 1989 sur la loi applicable aux successions pour cause de mort', *Annuaire suisse de droit international* (1989), p. 150.

Von Overbeck A. E., 'La professio juris comme moyen de rapprocher les principes du domicile et de la nationalité en Droit international privé', *Liber amicorum B. L. Fredericq*, vol. II (Gent, 1965), pp. 1085–1112.

Von Overbeck A. E., 'Les règimes matrimoniaux et les successions dans le nouveau droit international privé suisse', in F. Dessemontet (ed), *Le nouveau droit international privé suisse* (Lausanne, 1989), p. 59.

Von Savigny F. C., *Private International Law. A Treatise on the Conflict of Laws* (Edinburgh, 1869).

Von Vangerow K. A., *Lehrbuch der Pandekten*, 7th ed. (Hamburg, 1867).

Wagner R., 'Änderungsbedarf im autonomen deutschen internationalen Privatrecht aufgrund der Rom II-Verordnung? Ein Überblick über den Regierungsentwurf eines Gesetzes zur Anpassung der Vorschriften des Internationalen Privatrechts an die Rom II-Verordnung', *IPRax* (2008), p. 314.

Wagner R., 'Anerkennung von Personenstandsurkunden – was heißt das? – Überlegungen vor dem Hintergrund des Grünbuchs der Europäischen Kommission vom 14. 12. 2010', *Deutsche Notar-Zeitschrift* (2011), p. 176.

Wagner R., 'Der Kommissionsvorschlag vom 14. 10. 2009 zum internationalen Erbrecht: Stand und Perspektiven des Gesetzgebungsverfahrens', *Deutsche Notar-Zeitschrift* (2010), p. 506.

Wall F., 'Richtet sich die internationale Zuständigkeit zur Erbscheinserteilung künftig ausschließlich nach Artt. 4 ff. EuErbVO?', *ZErb – Zeitschrift für die Steuer- und Erbrechtspraxis* (2015), p. 9.

Walther B., *Der Gleichlaufgrundsatz – Abkehr oder Rückkehr? Eine kritische Auseinandersetzung mit der Bestimmung der internationalen Zuständigkeit im Erbscheinsverfahren aus deutscher und europäischer Sicht* (Frankfurt am Main, 2013).

Walther B., 'Die Qualifikation des § 1371 Abs. 1 BGB im Rahmen der europäischen Erb- und Güterrechtsverordnung', *GPR – Zeitschrift für das Privatrecht der Europäischen Union* (2014), p. 325.

Wautelet P., 'Article 14. Litispendance internationale', in J. Erauw *et al.* (eds), *Het Wetboek Internationaal Privaatrecht becommentarieerd – Le Code de droit international privé commenté* (Antwerpen, Oxford, Brussels, 2006), p. 78.

Weber J., 'Universal Jurisdiction and Third States in the Reform of the Brussels I Regulation', *RabelsZ* (2011), p. 619.

Weber S. M., *Das Internationale Zivilprozessrecht erbrechtlicher Streitigkeiten* (Sipplingen, 2012).

Weber S., 'Von Torpedos, Tankern und deutsch-französischen Gefechten - Gerichte und Schiedsgerichte im Binnenmarkt -', in *Europäische Integration und Globalisierung: Festschrift zum 60-jährigen Bestehen des Europa-Instituts* (Baden-Baden, 2011), p. 607.

Weller M., 'Art. 1 Rome I Regulation', in G.-P. Calliess (ed), *Rome Regulations: Commentary on the European Rules of the Conflict of Laws* (Alphen aan den Rijn, 2015), para. 8.

Weller M., 'Europäisches Internationales Privatrecht, Allgemeiner Teil', in C. Teichmann and M. Gebauer (eds), *Enzyklopädie Europarecht - Europäisches Privat- und Unternehmensrecht* (Baden-Baden, forthcoming), section 8, para. 7282.

Weller M., 'Zur Abgrenzung von ehelichem Güterrecht und Unterhaltsrecht im EuGVÜ, zu EuGH 27. 2. 1997 - Van den Boogard / Laumen', *IPRax* (1999), p. 14.

Wendehorst C., 'Art. 43 EGBGB', in *Münchener Kommentar BGB*, 6th ed. (München, 2015), vol. XI.

Wilke F. M., 'Das internationale Erbrecht nach der neuen EU-Erbrechtsverordnung', *RIW* (2012), p. 601.

Williams T. C., 'The Terms Real and Personal in English Law', *LQR* (1888), p. 394.

Wilsch H., 'EuErbVO: Die Verordnung in der deutschen Grundbuchpraxis', *ZEV* (2012), p. 530.

Windscheid B., *Lehrbuch des Pandektenrechts*, 8th ed. (Frankfurt, 1901).

Wittwer A., 'EuGH-Debüt im europäischen Familienrecht', *European Law Reporter* (2008), p. 67.

Wolf C. and Lange S., 'Das Europäische System des einstweiligen Rechtschutzes - doch noch kein System?', *RIW* (2003), p. 55.

Wolff M., *Das internationale Privatrecht Deutschlands*, 3rd ed. (Berlin, Göttingen, Heidelberg, 1954).

Wysocka A., 'How can a valid *professio iuris* be made under the EU Succession Regulation?', *NIPR* (2012), p. 569.

Zabalo Escudero E., 'El testamento conjunto en Derecho internacional privado. Especial referencia al testamento mancomunado aragonés', *Revista General de Derecho* (1989), p. 6351.

Zambrano V., 'Ordine pubblico e matrimonio contratto all'estero secondo il rito mussulmano', *Famiglia e diritto* (1999), p. 327.

Zanobetti A., 'Quelques réflexions sur les relations de l'Union européenne avec la Conférence de La Haye et Unidroit: ombres ou rayons de soleil?', in C. Flaesch-Mougin and L. S. Rossi (eds), *La dimension extérieure de l'espace de liberté, de sécurité et de justice après le Traité de Lisbonne* (Bruxelles, 2013), p. 243.

Zitelmann E., *Internationales Privatrecht*, vol. I (Leipzig, 1897).

INDEX

acceptance of authentic instruments, *see*: authentic instruments
acceptance of jurisdiction
  based on appearance, 182–185
  express acceptance, 175–176, 184
acceptance or waiver of the succession
  and ECS, 757–758
  communication of declarations, 232–233
  competence to receive declarations, 222–223
  declarations of, 120, 536
  declarations *vs.* legal proceedings, 228–230, 536
  definition of 'court', 231
  formal validity, 231, 412–416
  law applicable to, 357–360
  legal capacity, 226–228
  habitual residence, 226–228
  tacit, 415
administration/administrators of estates, 418–421, 692–694, 732–733
  and ECS, 767–768, 691–694, 770–771, 777–779
  appointment, special rules, 418–421
  functional scission, 45–47
  in civil law jurisdictions, 419
  lex fori, competence in matters of, 41, 424
  persons eligible for appointment, 425–426
  powers of administrators, 426–427, 777–779
  succession law, competence in matters of, 426–427
  transfer to heirs, 357–360
admissibility
  of agreements as to succession, 389
  of dispositions of property upon death, 372–373
  of joint wills, 405–406
  of representation, 400
agreements as to succession, 392–393 (*see also*: hypothetical law)
  abdication agreements, 382
  admissibility and substantive validity of, 372–373, 389
  admissibility of, 387, 389
  choice of law by parties, 386–389
  classification, 382
  concerning succession of one person, 387–388
  concerning succession of several persons, 389–392
  defined, 117–118, 371–372, 381–382
  formal validity of, 4–7, 403–404, 405–408
  inheritance agreements, 382
  jurisdiction in matters of, 32, 134–135
  law applicable to, 117, 386–387
  mutual will as, 117–118, 341, 381, 392–393, 405–406, 448–450
  overview, 381–386
  public policy *(ordre public)*, 517–518
  renunciation agreements, 381–382
  reserved share and, 378, 388, 391
  revocability of, 392–393
  substantive validity, 387, 389, 390–391
  third party succession agreement (*pactum de hereditate tertii*), 382
agreement to settle amicably, 177–181
anticipated succession law, *see*: hypothetical succession law
appeal against declaration of enforceability, 544–545, 591–597

appeal against declaration (cont.)
  competent authorities, 843–844
  extraordinary, 605
  mutual recognition and, 594–596
  ordinary, 565–566, 605
  provisional measures pending, 610–611
applicable law (*see also*: agreements as to succession, exception clause, habitual residence, hypothetical succession law, *professio juris*, public policy (*ordre public*), *renvoi*, special rules of the *lex rei sitae*, succession law)
  admissibility and substantive validity of dispositions of property upon death, 370–377
  agreements as to succession, 58, 381–392
  matters governed by, 354–368
  modification/revocation of dispositions of property upon death, 378–379
  objective connecting factor, 299
  scope of, 35–38, 351–368
  universal application of, 291–292, 296
arbitration, 122–123
attestation, *see*: declaration of enforceability
authentic instruments
  acceptance of, 626–627
  and ECS, 680–685
  authenticity, 655–657
  conflict with other authentic instruments, 661–662
  conflict with ECS, 682–685
  conflict with a decision, 662
  defined, 121–122, 636–637
  drawing up/recording, 637–639
  enforceability of, 631, 664–666
  evidentiary effects, 649–654; *see also*: evidentiary effects of authentic instruments
  instrumentum and *negotium* in, 627–630, 649–650, 651, 659–661
  matters of succession, 639–643
  overview, 636–637
  public policy (*ordre public*), 643–645
  requirements for, 636–647
  review of, 656–660

Basel Convention of 1972 on the establishment of a scheme of registration of wills, 10, footnote 14, 834
beneficiaries (heirs, legatees) (*see also*: acceptance or waiver of the succession)
  co-heirs' shares, 39, 433, 767
  determination of, 355–356, 751–753
  ECS, list of rights/assets for heirs, 759–765
  ECS, list of rights/assets for legatee, 765–766
  ECS, restrictions on rights of heirs/legatees, 766–767
  forced heirship rights, 52–53; *see also*: reserved share of the estate
  liability for debts, 360–362
  powers of heirs, 360
  protection of heirs, 507–512
  State as final heir, 458–460; *see also*: estate without a claimant
  unworthy of inheriting, 356–357, 516–517
bona vacantia, *see*: estate without a claimant
Brussels Convention of 28 September 1968 on jurisdiction and the enforcement of judgments in civil and commercial matters, *see*: regulation (EU) no. 1215/2012
Brussels I and I-*bis* regulations, *see*: regulation (EU) no. 1215/2012
Brussels II-*bis* regulation, *see*: regulation (EC) no. 2201/2003

capacity
  to inherit, 356
  to make declarations of acceptance or waiver of the succession, 226–227
  to make a disposition of property upon death, 376, 379, 395–398

to make an agreement as to succession, 395–398
to make a *professio juris*, 338–339
capitulaciones matrimoniales (Spain), 383
cautio judicatum solvi, 620–621
certified copies, *see*: ECS, certified copies of
Charter of Fundamental Rights of the European Union, 206, 217, 246, 512, 545, 547, 549, 553, 594, 619, 645, 705, 708, 728
children, inheritance rights, 514, 515
choice-of-court agreements, 113, 149–161
and third parties, 182–184
choice of law and, 162–163, 171–172
formal validity, 157–158
parallelism of *forum* and *jus (Gleichlauf)* following a *professio juris*, 149–151, 154–155, 163
substantial validity, 158–160
choice of law by parties, *see*: agreements as to succession
choice of the law applicable to succession matters, *see*: agreements as to succession; *professio juris*
choice-of-law rules, *see*: conflict-of-laws rules
clawback, 15, 363, 365
closest connection as a connecting factor (*see also*: exception clause)
agreements as to succession, 389–391
determination of nationality in non-unified legal systems, 523, 526–527, 529
form of dispositions upon death in non unified legal systems, 528
co-heirs' shares, 433, 759–765
cohabitee succession, 435, 445–446, 513
collections of historic interest, 434–435
Commission Implementing Regulation (EU) no. 1329/2014 establishing the Forms referred to in Regulation (EU) no. 650/2012, 618, 646, 647, 666, 669, 717, 742, 748, 849–851
commorientes, 14, 45, 86, 112, 452–457
company law and succession matters, 98–101
concurrent jurisdiction, 193, 254–257 (*see also*: jurisdiction)
conflict-of-law rules (*see also*: closest connection; exception clause; habitual residence; *professio juris*; public policy (*ordre public*); *renvoi*; special rules of the *lex rei sitae*)
applicable law determination and ECS, 755–756
erga omnes character, 291–297
jurisdiction and, 35, 45–47
lex fori, 461, 662
non-unified legal systems, 522–525
presumptive choice of law, 349, 861–863
reciprocity and, 291
renvoi, 470, 475–479, 490–491, 497 (*see also*: *renvoi*)
universal character, 291–297
conflit mobile, 300, 317, 337, 407
consent and substantive validity, 338
contrat de mariage (France), 381, 384
contractual succession, *see*: agreements as to succession
Convention of 1934 among Denmark, Finland, Iceland, Norway and Sweden comprising private international law provisions on succession, wills and estate administration (revised in 2012) (Nordic Convention on succession and wills), 834
court settlement
enforceability, 667–669
defined, 121
courts (*see also*: jurisdiction; *lis pendens*; related actions)
allocation of jurisdiction, 254–255
choice-of-court agreements, 113, 149–161 (*see also*: choice-of-court agreements)
defined, 122–123, 231
determining competence, 128
determining jurisdiction, 128–133, 172–176, 182–185, 187–198, 200–208

courts (cont.)
  jurisdictional rules, scope, 234–236
  seising of, 234–239
creditor protection/payment, 361–362
Croatia, 14
cross-border situations, 25–27, 678–679

date of application of the ESR, 864–866
death order, laws governing, 354–355 (*see also*: *commorientes*)
debts under succession, 77, 360–362, 781, 808–809 (*see also*: acceptance and waiver of the succession)
decision, defined, 120
declaration of acceptance and waiver of the succession, *see*: acceptance and waiver of the succession
declaration of enforceability (*see also*: recognition of decisions)
  appeal against, 581–583, 591–597 (*see also*: appeal against declaration of enforceability)
  application, 586–587
  attestation, 581–583, 587
  authentic copy of the judgment, 587
  cautio judicatum solvi, exclusion, 620–621
  communication of the order granting or refusing, 588–589
  domicile of the person against whom enforcement is sought, 575–576
  inaudita altera parte stage, 581–590
  jurisdiction, 576–577
  jurisdiction of local courts, 22, 576–577
  legal aid, 617–620
  no charge, duty or fee, 622
  overview, 22, 581–586
  partial enforceability, 612–614
  lex fori, applicability to procedure, 586, 589
  provisional enforceability, 561–562, 563, 608–611
  provisional measures after, 610
  provisional measures before, 608–610
declaratory proceedings, *see*: recognition of decisions
definitions in the ESR
  agreement as to succession, 117–118
  authentic instrument, 120, 121–122
  court, 122–123
  court settlement, 121
  decision, 120
  disposition of property upon death, 119
  joint will, 118
  Member State of enforcement, 120
  Member State of origin, 119–120
  overview, 115–116
  register, 109
  succession, 116
déni de justice, 205; *see also*: *forum necessitatis*
denial of recognition, *see*: recognition
Denmark, position of, 14, 17–18
designation agreements, 382 (*see also*: agreements as to succession)
determination of beneficiaries, 355–356 (*see also*: succession law; ECS)
disclaimer of interest, 224 (*see also*: acceptance and waiver of the succession)
disinheritance/disqualification by conduct, 356–357
disposal of an asset of the estate, concept, 783
disposition of property upon death (*see also*: agreements as to succession; applicable law)
  admissibility, 372–373
  capacity in the making of, 395–398, 399–400
  consent and intention in the making of, 401
  defined, 119
  formal validity, *see*: formal validity of dispositions upon death
  interpretation of, 400–401
  modification/revocation of, 378–379, 409
  preservation of, 859–861
  substantive validity, 84, 372–373
document instituting proceedings, 249
domestic measures of implementation of the ESR, 864–866

domicile determination, 575–576
donation-partage (France), 117, 381, 384
double nationalities and subsidiary jurisdiction, 193–194
droit d'option (France), 225
droit réel, *see*: rights *in rem*

ECS, 7, 14, 18, 673–680
  application for issuance, 703–705, 712–722, 724–733
  authority of, 783–784
  bona fide effect, 780–788
  bona fide third parties, 773, 775, 784
  certified copies, 795–800, 801, 819
  certified copies, period of validity, 800–804
  competence for issuing, 699–709
  conflicting documents, 682–685
  creation by ESR of, 19, 35–37, 674, 676–677
  cross-border situations, 26, 678–679
  entitlement to file application, 714–716
  effects of, *see*: ECS, effects of
  inaccuracy, 784–785 (*see also*: ECS, redress procedure of an inaccurate ECS; ECS, rectification, modification or withdrawal)
  information and consultation, 727–732, 743
  legal nature, 677–678
  optional nature, 679–680
  rectification, modification or withdrawal, 805–811
  redress procedure, 812–818
  relation with national documents, 680–685
  use of standard forms, 747–749
ECS, contents, 745–768
  acceptance and waiver of succession, 757–758
  compulsory use of standard form, 747–749
  details concerning applicant, deceased and beneficiaries, 751–753
  exhaustive list of information, 745–747
  issuing authority and date, 750–751
  law applicable to succession, 755–756
  list of rights/assets for heirs, 759–765
  list of rights/assets for legatees, 765–766
  matrimonial regime, 753–755
  powers of executors/administrators, 767–768
  restrictions on rights of heirs/legatees, 766–767
  testate and intestate succession, 756–757
ECS, effects of, 28, 679, 770–794
  authority of, 783–784
  bona fide effect, 780–788
  evidentiary effects, 761, 776, 779
  extension of effects *ipso iure*, 771–775
  legal transactions covered, 781–783
  legitimising effect, 788–794
ECS, issue of, 734–735
  certified copies, 795–801, 819
  certified copies, period of validity, 800–804
  formal requirements, 737–738
  grounds for the refusal of issuance, 738–741
  preconditions, 724–733, 735–741
  substantive requirements, 735–737
  use of form, 742–743
ECS, suspension of the effects, 814–818, 819–824
  effects on certified copies, 824–825
  issuing authority and, 820–822
  prerequisites for suspension, 820–824
  remedies, 825
enforceability of authentic instruments, *see*: authentic instruments
enforceability of court settlements, 667–669
enforceability/enforcement of decisions, *see*: declaration of enforceability

entry into force of the ESR, 864–866
Erbschein (Germany), 642, 676, 680
erga-omnes application, *see*: ESR, universal application
escape clause, *see*: exception clause
ESR
  date of application, 864–866
  entry into force, 864–866
  key principles, 35–69
  object and scope, 22–35
  overview, 1–10
  process of drafting, 11–18
  ratione personae scope of application, 33
  scope of application, 74–77
  structure and features, 18–21
  temporal scope of application, 853–854
  universal application, 29, 291–297
ESR, matters excluded, 76–77, 79–80
  family relationships, status, 83–84
  formal validity of dispositions of property, 94–95
  law of companies, 98–101
  maintenance obligations, 93–94
  matrimonial property regimes, 86–93
  natural persons, status, 80–83
  nature of rights *in rem*, 104–108
  recording of rights in registers, 108–111
  transfers of property otherwise than by succession, 95–98
  trusts, creation/administration/ dissolution, 101–104
estate without a claimant, 458, 461–465, 469
  partially unclaimed estates, 465
  State as final heir, 458–460
EU Charter of Fundamental Rights, *see*: Charter of Fundamental rights of the European Union
European certificate of succession, *see*: ECS
European Convention of 1950 for the protection of human rights and fundamental freedoms (ECHR), 545, 549, 553, 594, 619
European Court of Human Rights (ECtHR), 207, 513, 515, 545, 619
European Court of Justice (ECJ), 55, 83, 139, 258, 424
European Insolvency regulation, *see*: Regulation (EU) 2015/848 on insolvency proceedings
European Judicial Network, 840, 845
European Succession regulation, *see*: ESR
European Union, legislative competence in matters of international succession, 4–5, 11–14, 293, 295–297, 673–675
evasion of the law, *see*: *fraude à la loi*
evidentiary effects of authentic instruments, 647–655
evidentiary effects of ECS, *see*: ECS, effects of
exception clause, 47–49, 55, 317–322, 396–397, 479–480
executors of wills, 358–359, 360–362, 418, 429, 449, 651, 677, 691–694, 747, 757, 767–768
exequatur procedure, 569–573, 581–586, 588–590 (*see also*: declaration of enforceability)
express choice of law, *see*: *professio juris*
extraordinary appeal, 605

family provisions, 2, 364, 512 footnote 23
family relationships, *see*: ESR, matters excluded
favor validitatis, 82, 95, 346, 348, 407 (*see also*: formal validity of dispositions upon death)
final decision, 561
forced heirship rights, *see*: reserved share of the estate
formal validity of declarations of acceptance and waiver of the succession, 231, 412–416
formal validity of dispositions of property upon death, 44, 50, 94–95, 403–411
formal validity of dispositions, made in writing, 405–408

Hague Convention of 1961 on the Conflicts of Laws Relating to the Form of Testamentary Dispositions, 403–405, 407–408, 484, 527–528, 832–833
holographic will, 316
modification/revocation, 409
permitted forms and personal conditions, 409–411
forum loci executionis, 282–284, 285
forum necessitatis, 199–207
absence of grounds of jurisdiction, 201–202
agreement to settle amicably, 177
close connection with third country, 202–203
creation of, 19
impossibility/unreasonableness of conducting proceedings, 203–207
jurisdiction and, 196–198, 506
operation of, 42–43
overview, 4, 19, 128, 131, 707–708
rationale for, 200–201
relevance of conflict of laws considerations, 218
sufficient connection requirement, 207–208
forum non conveniens, 267
forum patrimonii, 189 (*see also*: subsidiary jurisdiction)
forum shopping, 138, 143–146, 208, 294–295
fragmentation of succession, 163, 197, 352
fraude à la loi, 53, 143–145, 148, 315, 322, 328, 330
freedom of choice, 324, 375–377
of *forum*: *see*: choice-of-court agreements
of law: *see*: agreements as to succession; *professio juris*

general *forum*, *see*: jurisdiction, general *forum*
gifts, 96–97, 366

habitual residence, 38–39, 51–54, 137, 306, 317
and forum shopping, 138, 143–146
and matrimonial property law, 90, 91
and *professio juris*, 59, 328, 332–333, 342
as connecting factor, 298–299, 300, 301, 328, 391, 392, 861
as ground for jurisdiction, 128–133, 136–137, 255–256
concept, 138–139, 143, 418, 300–308, 318–319
determination of, 138, 140–143, 227, 303–312
exception (escape) clause, *see*: exception clause
lack of, 310–311
multiple habitual residences, 146–147, 304, 309
non-unified legal systems, 733–735
of persons making a declaration of acceptance or waiver of the succession, 226–228
Hague Conference on Private International Law, 6–10, 129, 301, 463
Hague Convention of 1961 on the Conflicts of Laws Relating to the Form of Testamentary Dispositions, 6, 9–10, 23, 44, 94–95, 129, 403, 404, 405–408, 484, 485, 528, 829–830, 832–833
Hague Convention of 1973 on the International Administration of the Estates of Deceased Persons, 7, 418, 833
Hague Convention of 1978 on the Law Applicable to Matrimonial Property Regimes, 87
Hague Convention of 1985 on the Law Applicable to Trusts and on their Recognition, 102, 445
Hague Convention of 1989 on the Law Applicable to Succession to the Estates of Deceased Persons, 8–9, 56, 95, 117, 129, 324–325, 353, 386, 419, 463–464
heirless assets, *see*: estate without a claimant
heirs, *see*: beneficiaries

holographic will, *see*: formal validity of dispositions of property upon death
hypothetical succession law
  admissibility and substantive validity of dispositions of property upon death, 9, 11, 19, 372–373
  agreements as to succession, 56–57, 387–388, 389–391
  and *renvoi*, 477, 480–481
  defined, 372–374
  determination of, 373, 375, 756
  limits of the reference, 59–61
  overview, 43, 50
  rationale of the adoption by ESR, 16, 19, 43, 50, 57–59

in rem rights, *see*: rights *in rem*
incidental questions, 80, 81–83
"incorporation by reference" clauses, 349–350
inheritance agreements, *see*: agreements as to succession
insolvency proceedings, 836–839 (*see also*: regulation (EU) no. 2015/848)
instrumentum, in authentic instruments, *see*: authentic instruments
intellectual property law, 107
inter-personal conflicts of laws, *see*: non-unified legal systems
inter vivos agreements, 365–366, 381, 383
internal conflicts of laws, 529 (*see also*: non-unified legal systems)
international character of succession, 25–27
international enforcement of authentic instruments, 666, 667–669
international jurisdiction, *see*: jurisdiction
Ireland, position of, 15, 16, 17–18
irreconcilability of decisions, 557–560 (*see also*: recognition)
Islamic law systems, 204, 366, 515–516, 549

joint wills, 118, 370–371, 405–406
joint and mutual wills, *see*: mutual wills, agreements as to succession
jurisdiction (*see also*: *forum necessitatis*; habitual residence; *lis pendens*; provisional (protective) measures; limitation of proceedings; related actions; subsidiary jurisdiction)
  agreements as to succession, 32, 134–135
  based on appearance, 182–185
  based on habitual residence, 140–143 (*see also*: habitual residence)
  choice-of-court agreements, *see*: choice-of-court agreements
  concurrent jurisdiction, 254–257
  for a declaration of enforceability, 576–577
  examination as to, 140, 174–175, 240–244, 273–275
  exceptions to, 31–33
  exercise, 276, 281–282
  express acceptance by parties, 175–176, 184
  general forum, 128–132, 133–136
  habitual residence as ground for, 38–39, 128–133, 136–137
  introduction, 127–128
  local jurisdiction for enforceability, 576–577
  matrimonial property law, 92
  objection to jurisdiction, 185
  parallelism between *forum* and *jus* (*Gleichlauf*), 42–49, 149–151, 163, 164, 170, 312–313, 320
  professio juris, effects on, 163–164, 171–172
  scope of, 30–31, 134–135
  sufficient connection, 131–132
  summary, 127–147, 162, 171

last habitual residence of the deceased, *see*: habitual residence
legal aid, 617–620
legal proceedings *vs.* declarations, *see*: acceptance and waiver of the succession

legalisation formalities, exemption, 829–830
legatees, 107, 690, 765–767 (*see also*: beneficiaries)
lex patriae, *see*: nationality as a connecting factor
lex rei sitae (*see also*: special rules of the *lex rei sitae*)
  and *renvoi*, 488
lex successionis, *see*: succession law
liability for debts, 360–362 (*see also*: acceptance and waiver of the succession)
limitation of proceedings
  conditions for, 212–219
  location of assets, 212–213
  rationale for the rule, 210–212
  relevance of considerations, 218–219
  right of parties to limit proceedings, 219–221
  summary, 209
lis pendens, 40, 146, 165, 173, 202, 216, 235, 251–267 (*see also*: related actions)
  decision to decline jurisdiction, 263–265
  effects from application of rule, 263–265
  identical cause of action, 258–259
  identical parties, 259–263
  in the relationship with non-member countries, 265–267
  relationship with related actions, 271–272
  requirements, 254–257
  temporal priority, 263
location of assets, 188–192, 212–213 (*see also*: limitations of proceedings; special rules of the *lex rei sitae*; subsidiary jurisdiction)
Lugano Convention of 1988 on Jurisdiction and the Enforcement of Judgments in Civil and Commercial Matters (revised: 2007), 263, 632
maintenance obligations, 79, 93–94, 364
mandatory provisions of the *lex rei sitae*, *see*: special rules of the *lex rei sitae*
matrimonial property regime, 333 (*see also*: regulation (EU) no. 2016/1103)
  agreements as to succession, 118, 383
  and ECS (European Certificate of Succession), 753–755, 759–763
  habitual residence, 313
matters excluded, *see*: ESR, matters excluded
Member State of enforcement, 120
Member State of origin, 119–120
Member State, notion, 17–18, 425, 470, 771–772
modification of dispositions of property upon death, *see*: dispositions of property upon death
Muslim law systems, *see*: Islamic law systems
mutual wills, 102, 117–118, 371, 381, 391–393, 405–406, 448–450 (*see also*: agreements as to succession; formal validity of dispositions of property upon death)

national documents, *see*: authentic instruments; ECS, conflicting documents
nationality, as a connecting factor, 50, 54–55, 316, 331–344, 861–863
  anticipated, introduction no. 20, 334–335
  choice as applicable law, *see*: *professio juris*
  determination, 337
  determination in non-unified legal systems, 523, 526
  effective, 333–334, 338
  plurality of nationalities, 193–194, 337–338, 375, 407–408, 752
negotium, in authentic instruments, *see*: authentic instruments

non-recognition, *see*: recognition of decisions; recognition of court settlements
non-unified legal systems, 521–528
  and *renvoi*, 482
  determination of nationality in, 523, 526
  territory-based, 522, 527
  person-based, 520, 528–529
  form of dispositions of property upon death in, 527–528
Nordic Convention on succession and wills, 834

objective connecting factor, 299, 312 (*see also*: habitual residence)
order of deaths, uncertainty over, 455 (*see also*: *commorientes*)
ordinary appeal, 565–566, 605
ordinary legislative procedure, 12–13
ordre public clause: *see* public policy (*ordre public*)
overriding mandatory provisions of the *lex rei sitae*, *see*: special rules of the *lex rei sitae*

pactum de hereditate tertii, 382 (*see also*: agreements as to succession)
parallel proceedings (*see also*: *lis pendens*; related actions)
pending before non-member country courts, absence of rule, 265–267
parallel use of documents, *see*: authentic instruments; ECS, conflicting documents
parallelism between *forum* and *jus*, *see*: jurisdiction
partial enforceability, *see*: declaration of enforceability
partial recognition, *see*: recognition of decisions
partial *renvoi*, 492 (*see also*: *renvoi*)
partially unclaimed estates, 465 (*see also*: estate without a claimant)
patto di famiglia (Italy), 381, 384, 392, 510 (*see also*: agreements as to succession)
pension plans, 97–98
perpetuatio jurisdictionis, 577
person-based non-unified legal systems, 528–529
personality rights *post mortem*, 85
persons eligible for appointment as administrators, 425–426
polygamous marriages, *see*: public policy (*ordre public*)
powers of administrators, 426–427, 777–779
powers of heirs, 360
prélèvement system (France), 509
presumptions of law, 349, 651, 775–780
principle of plurality and territoriality of successions, 46, 300
principle of unity and universality of successions, 37–38, 299
probate proceedings, 9, 97, 419, 421, 659
procedural public policy, 552–555 (*see also*: public policy (*ordre public*))
professio fori, *see*: choice-of-court agreements
professio juris
  advantages and disadvantages of, 326–331
  and evasion of law, 330
  and *renvoi*, 483
  and substantive autonomy, 349–350, 373–374
  choice consciousness, 345
  choice of conflict-of-laws rules not admitted, 336
  dispositions of property upon death, 55, 375
  effects on jurisdiction, 149–151, 163, 164, 170, 175
  express choice, 344–345
  formal validity, 404
  habitual residence, 61, 328, 332–333, 342
  "incorporation by reference" clauses, 349–350
  non-unified legal systems, 523–524
  overview, 27, 49
  preservation of, 856–859, 860
  presumptive choice of law, 349, 861–863

revocation, 339–344
substantive validity, 338
tacit choice, 340, 344, 345–349
proprietary estoppel doctrine, 450–451
protection of forced heirs, 507–512
provisional (protective) measures, 31, 280–288, 566, 570, 608–611
audi alteram partem principle, 284–285
ECJ case law, 286–288
forum loci executionis, 282–284
before or after a declaration of enforceability, 608, 610
public policy (*ordre public*), 505–518, 546–555, 643–645
agreements as to succession, 384–385, 517
authentic instruments, 643–645, 652, 666
consequences of recourse to, 518
court settlements, 669
discriminatory legislation, 512–516
heirs unworthy of inheriting, 516–517
same-sex couples, rights, 513–514

recognition of decisions (*see also*: declaration of enforceability)
as incidental issue, 540–541
automatic, 135, 537
concept of, 533–538, 633
decisions in default of appearance, 555–557
grounds for non-recognition, 543–546, 584
irreconcilability with previous decision, 557–560
negative declaratory relief, 539–540
no security, bond or deposit, 620–621
partial, 613
procedural public policy, 552–554
proceedings concerning recognition (declaratory proceedings), 538–540, 570
staying of recognition proceedings, 561–565
substantive public policy, 546–552
recognition of court settlements, *see*: enforceability of court settlements
recording in register of rights, 108–111, 789, 842–843
register, defined, 109
registered partnership (*see also*: regulation (EU) no. 2016/1104)
and ECS, 722, 753, 778
and ESR, 81, 356
public policy, 513–514
regulation (EC) no. 1346/2000 on insolvency proceedings, 191, 192, 836–839
regulation (EC) no. 44/2001 on jurisdiction and the recognition and enforcement of judgments in civil and commercial matters (Brussels I regulation): *see*: regulation (EU) no. 1215/2012
regulation (EC) no. 2201/2003 concerning jurisdiction and the recognition and enforcement of judgments in matrimonial matters and the matters of parental responsibility, 166, 168, 194, 242, 707
regulation (EC) no. 864/2007 on the law applicable to non-contractual obligations (Rome II regulation)
habitual residence, 140, 300
non-contractual obligations, 294
regulation (EC) no. 593/2008 on the law applicable to contractual obligations (Rome I regulation)
contractual obligations, 294, 366, 368
gifts, 96, 366
habitual residence, 140, 300
law of companies, 98
pension plans, 97
trust, 102
regulation (EC) no. 1259/2010 implementing enhanced cooperation in the area of the law applicable to divorce and legal separation (Rome III regulation), 157, 300
regulation (EU) no. 1215/2012 on jurisdiction and the recognition

and enforcement of judgments in civil and commercial matters (Brussels I *bis* regulation)
  domicile determination, 575–576
  foreign decision, 560
  lis pendens, 252, 259–260, 264–265, 266, 269, 271
  party autonomy under, 241
  provisional (protective) measures, 281, 283
regulation (EU) no. 2015/848 on insolvency proceedings, 191, 192, 836–839
regulation (EU) no. 2016/1103 implementing enhanced cooperation in the area of jurisdiction, applicable law and the recognition and enforcement of decisions in matters of matrimonial property regimes, 11, 20, 31, 54, 76, 313, 333, 755, 763, 778
regulation (EU) no. 2016/1104 implementing enhanced cooperation in the area of jurisdiction, applicable law and the recognition and enforcement of decisions in matters of the property consequences of registered partnerships, 11, 20, 31, 54, 76, 514, 755, 763, 778
related actions, 268–278 (*see also*: *lis pendens*)
  declining jurisdiction, 273–275
  defined, 271–272
  in the relationship with non-member countries courts, 277–278
  judicial/extra-judicial means of settlement, 278–279
  rationale for the rule, 269–271
  staying of proceedings, 273–274, 275–276
  temporal priority, 273
renunciation agreements, *see*: agreements as to succession
renunciation of inheritance/succession, *see*: acceptance and waiver of the succession
renvoi
  admission by the ESR of, 9, 19, 67, 470–473
  and non-unified legal systems, 470–473, 481
  cases in which it is not accepted by a third State's law, 499–502
  cases in which it is not admitted, 479–486, 499–502
  cases in which it may occur, 475–479, 487–491
  choice of law by the testator or parties, 482–483
  exception clause, 479–480
  foreign court theory, 491
  formal validity of acceptance and waiver, 486
  formal validity of dispositions of property upon death, 406–407
  indirect remission, 502
  international consistency, 67, 503–504
  mandatory provisions of *lex rei sitae*, 485–486
  partial and total *renvoi*, 491–495
  purpose of admission of, 470–473
  to national law 487–488
  to the law of a Member State, 497–499
  to the law of a non-Member State, 473–475, 499–502
  to the law of a third State (transmission), 473–475
  to the law of domicile or residence, 490–491
  to the law of the *forum*, 492–499, 502
  to the law of the *situs*, 488–490, 503–504
  transmission and remission, 503–504
  type adopted by the ESR, 491–499
Republic of Croatia, 14
res judicata (*see also*: final decision)
  effects of, 558–559, 563, 629, 658
  exequatur procedure, 581, 585
  judicial decisions, 65, 134, 541
  national succession certificates, 641–642

reserved share of the estate, 2–3, 52, 362–363, 441
acceptance or waiver of, 222, 230–231, 414
and agreements as to succession, 341
and *professio juris*, 329
and public policy (*ordre public*), 52 (footnote 109), 330–331, 507–512
determination of the amount, 214
law applicable to, 362–365, 378
revocation of dispositions of property upon death, 378–379
revocation of *professio iuris*, *see* *professio juris*
rights *in rem*, 104–108, 442, 444–447, 451, 570, 654, 790, 791
adaptation principle, 107–108, 441–442
field of application of art. 31 ESR, 444–447
nature of rights *in rem*, 104–108
numerus clausus, 106, 792
real *vs* personal rights, 442–444
unknown rights, 447–448
right of parties to limit proceedings, *see*: limitation of proceedings

same-sex couples, 513–514 (*see also*: registered partnerships)
scission
moveable/immoveable assets, 329
principle of, 39–41, 42
principle of plurality and territoriality of successions, 46, 300
renvoi, 488–490, 501
substantive and functional, 37–38, 45–47, 352
seising of court, 234–239 (*see also*: *lis pendens*)
settling out of court, *see*: agreement to settle amicably
sharing-out of the estate, 367–368
special rules of the *lex rei sitae*, 67, 430, 430–432, 432–438, 438–441
State as final heir, 458–460 (*see also*: estate without a claimant)
staying of proceedings, 561–565, 604–607
subsidiary jurisdiction, 32, 186, 187–188
absence of coordination, 244
concurrent jurisdiction, 193
double/multiple nationalities, 193–194
habitual residence, 194–196
location of assets, 188–192
substantive autonomy and *professio juris*, 349–350, 373–374
substantive validity (*see also*: hypothetical succession law)
agreements to succession, 387–389, 390–391
capacity as part of, 84, 410
consent and, 338
dispositions of property upon death, 84, 372–373
overview, 19, 24, 34, 50, 56–61, 65, 158–160
succession
defined, 76–77, 116
functional unity of, 37–38, 45–47
international character of, 25–26, 26–27, 112
special rules of the *lex rei sitae*, Art. 30
territorial unity of, 37–38, 39–41
succession law (*see also*: applicable law, exception clause, habitual residence, hypothetical succession law, *professio juris*, *renvoi*)
agreements as to successions, 371–372, 381–386
and matrimonial property regimes, 87–88
anticipated nationality, 334–335
applicable law, 351–369, 755
area of succession, 352–368
debts under the succession, 77, 223, 360–361, 412
habitual residence, 300, 328, 392
hypothetical law, 372–374, 388
mandatory provisions of, 35
powers that administrators may exercise, 426–427
property law on tangible goods, 654

succession law (cont.)
public policy (*ordre public*) and, 505–518
sharing-out of the estate, 367–368
unity of succession, 37–45
suspension of ECS (European certificate of succession), *see*: ECS, suspension of the effects

tacit choice of law, *see*: *professio juris*
temporal scope of ESR, 33–35, 853–856, 864–865
territory-based non-unified legal systems, 521–528
testamentary freedom, 57, 363–364
testamentary succession, 376, 379, 756–757
testamentary trust, 101–104
third country/State
court of, 213
exclusive jurisdiction of courts, 214–215
judgments delivered in, 213–214
lis pendens before courts of (*see*: *lis pendens*; parallel proceedings)
related actions pending before courts of (*see*: related actions; parallel proceedings)
renvoi, 473–475
third party succession agreements, 382 (*see also*: agreements as to succession)
total *renvoi*, 492, 493–495 (*see also*: *renvoi*)
transfers of assets otherwise than by succession, 95–98
transfers on death (TOD), 97
transitional provisions, 852–861
preservation of dispositions of property upon death, 859–861
preservation of *professiones juris*, 856–859
transmission of declarations of acceptance and waiver of succession, 232
trusts, creation/administration/ dissolution, 103, 101–104

ultra vires hereditatis liability, 361
United Kingdom (UK), position of, 15, 16, 17–18
unity of jurisdiction and applicable law, *see*: jurisdiction, parallelism between *forum* and *jus*
unity of succession, 37–45, 43–45, 47–49, 299–300, 324, 465, 489
and universality of, 299, 300, 336, 352, 488
exceptions to, 43, 430–432, 442–444, 454, 464–465
functional, 37–38, 45–47
territorial, 37–38, 39–41
unknown rights, *see*: rights *in rem*
usufruct rights, 90, 106, 447, 451, 511

waiver of the succession, *see*: acceptance and waiver of the succession
Washington Convention of 1973 Providing a Uniform Law on the Form of an International Will, 10 footnote 14, 834
wills
admissibility and substantive validity, *see*: dispositions of property upon death
conventions regarding, 834–835
formal validity, *see*: formal validity of dispositions of property upon death
interpretation of, 400–401
joint wills, 118, 370–371, 405–406
mutual wills, 118, 311, 381, 391–393, 405–406
preservation, 859–861
revocation by operation of law, 342–344

CPSIA information can be obtained
at www.ICGtesting.com
Printed in the USA
LVOW05*1731290817
546832LV00012B/157/P